AFRICA 68-69

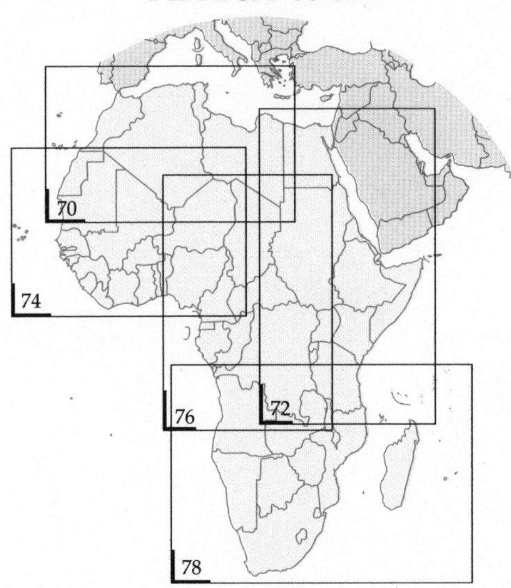
70
74
76
72
78

EUROPE 80-81

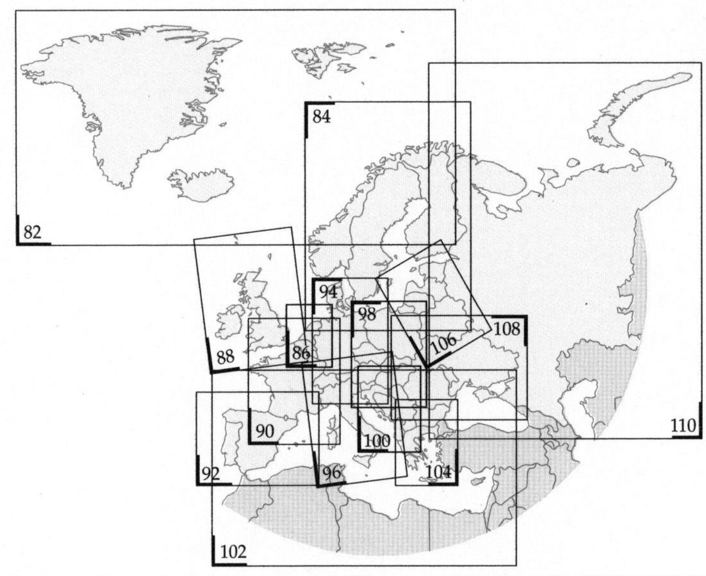
82
84
94
98
108
106
88
86
90
100
110
92
96
104
102

ESSENTIAL WORLD ATLAS

LONDON, NEW YORK, MUNICH,
MELBOURNE, DELHI

A DORLING KINDERSLEY PUBLISHING BOOK
www.dk.com

FOR THE THIRD EDITION

EDITOR-IN-CHIEF Andrew Heritage
SENIOR CARTOGRAPHIC MANAGER David Roberts
SENIOR CARTOGRAPHIC EDITOR Simon Mumford
PROJECT CARTOGRAPHERS Ed Merritt
SYSTEMS COORDINATOR Philip Rowles
PRODUCTION Melanie Dowland

DORLING KINDERSLEY CARTOGRAPHY

PROJECT CARTOGRAPHY AND DESIGN
Julia Lunn, Julie Turner

CARTOGRAPHERS
James Anderson, Roger Bullen, Martin Darlison,
Simon Mumford, John Plumer, Peter Winfield

DESIGN
Katy Wall

INDEX-GAZETTEER
Natalie Clarkson, Ruth Duxbury, Margaret Hynes, Margaret Stevenson

PRODUCTION
Hilary Stephens, David Proffit

EDITORIAL DIRECTION
Andrew Heritage

ART DIRECTION
Chez Picthall

First American edition 1997. Reprinted with revisions 1998. Second Edition 2001.
Reprinted with revisions 2003. Third Edition 2005
Previously published as the Concise World Atlas

Published in the United States by Dorling Kindersley Publishing, Inc., 375 Hudson Street,
New York, New York 10014

A Penguin Company

A CIP catalog record for this book is available from the Library of Congress

ISBN 0-7566-0964-X

Printed and bound in Singapore by Tien Wah Press

For the very latest information, visit:

www.dk.com and click on the Maps & Atlases icon

Key to Map Symbols

Physical Features

Elevation

4,000m/13,124ft
2,000m/6,562ft
1,000m/3,281ft
500m/1,640ft
250m/820ft
100m/328ft
0
Below sea level

Mountain
Depression
Volcano
Pass/tunnel
Sandy desert

Drainage Features

Major perennial river
Minor perennial river
Seasonal river
Canal
Waterfall
Perennial lake
Seasonal lake
Wetland

Ice Features

Permanent ice cap/ice shelf
Winter limit of pack ice
Summer limit of pack ice

Borders

Full international border
Disputed *de facto* border
Territorial claim border
Cease-fire line
Undefined boundary
Internal administrative boundary

Communications

Major road
Minor road
Rail
International airport

Settlements

Over 500,000
100,000 - 500,000
50,000 - 100,000
Less than 50,000
National capital
Internal administrative capital

Miscellaneous Features

Site of interest
Ancient wall

Graticule Features

Line of latitude/longitude/Equator
Tropic/Polar circle
25° Degrees of latitude/longitude

Names

Physical features

Andes *Sahara* *Ardennes*	Landscape features
Land's End	Headland
Mont Blanc 4,807m	Elevation/volcano/pass
Blue Nile	River/canal/waterfall
Ross Ice Shelf	Ice feature
PACIFIC OCEAN *Sulu Sea* *Palk Strait*	Sea features
Chile Rise	Undersea feature

Regions

FRANCE	Country
JERSEY (to UK)	Dependent territory
KANSAS	Administrative region
Dordogne	Cultural region

Settlements

PARIS	Capital city
SAN JUAN	Dependent territory capital city
Chicago Kettering Burke	Other settlements

Inset Map Symbols

Urban area
City
Park
Place of interest
Suburb/district

Contents

The World Today

Flags of the World 6-7
The Political World 8-9
The Physical World 10-11
Time Zones 12-13
Geology & Structure 14-15
World Climate 16-17
Ocean Currents 18-19
Life Zones 20-21
Population 22-23
Languages 24-25
Religion 26-27
The Global Economy 28-29
Global Conflict 30-31

The World's Regions

North & Central America

North & Central America 34-35
Western Canada & Alaska 36-37
Eastern Canada 38-39
USA: The Northeast 40-41
USA: The Southeast 42-43
Bermuda
USA: Central States 44-45
USA: The West 46-47
Los Angeles & Hawaii
USA: The Southwest 48-49
Mexico 50-51
Central America 52-53
The Caribbean 54-55
Jamaica, St. Lucia, & Barbados

South America

South America 56-57
Northern South America 58-59
Western South America 60-61
Galapagos Islands
Brazil 62-63
Southern South America 64-65
The Atlantic Ocean 66-67

Africa

Africa 68-69
Northwest Africa 70-71
Northeast Africa 72-73
West Africa 74-75
Central Africa 76-77
Sao Tome & Principe
Southern Africa 78-79

Europe

Europe .80-81
The North Atlantic 82-83
Scandinavia & Finland 84-85
The Low Countries 86-87
The British Isles 88-89
London

continued....

EUROPE *continued*

France, Andorra, & Monaco 90-91
Paris, Andorra, & Monaco
Spain & Portugal 92-93
Azores & Gibraltar
Germany & the Alpine States . . .94-95
Liechtenstein
Italy 96-97
San Marino & Vatican City
Central Europe 98-99
Southeast Europe 100-101
Bosnia & Herzegovina
The Mediterranean 102-103
Malta & Cyprus
Bulgaria & Greece 104-105
The Baltic States & Belarus 106-107
Ukraine, Moldova, & Romania 108-109
European Russia 110-111

NORTH & WEST ASIA

North & West Asia 112-113
Russia & Kazakhstan 114-115
Turkey & the Caucasus 116-117
The Near East 118-119
West Bank
The Middle East 120-121
Central Asia 122-123

SOUTH & EAST ASIA

South & East Asia 124-125
Western China & Mongolia . . .126-127
Eastern China & Korea 128-129
Hong Kong (Xianggang)
Japan 130-131
Tōkyō & Nansei-Shotō
South India & Sri Lanka 132-133
North India, Pakistan, & Bangladesh 134-135
Mainland Southeast Asia 136-137
Maritime Southeast Asia 138-139
Singapore
The Indian Ocean 140-141

AUSTRALASIA & OCEANIA

Australasia & Oceania 142-143
The Southwest Pacific 144-145
Western Australia 146-147
Eastern Australia 148-149
Sydney
New Zealand 150-151
The Pacific Ocean 152-153
Antarctica .154
The Arctic Ocean 155

INDEX – GAZETTEER

Overseas Territories & Dependencies 156-159
Glossary of Geographical Terms 160-161
Continental Factfiles 162-163
Geographical Comparisons . . .164-166
Index-Gazetteer of Places & Countries 167-256

FLAGS OF THE WORLD

NORTH & CENTRAL AMERICA

ANTIGUA & BARBUDA
PAGES 54-55

BAHAMAS
PAGES 54-55

BARBADOS
PAGES 54-55

BELIZE
PAGES 52-53

CANADA
PAGES 36-39

COSTA RICA
PAGES 52-53

CUBA
PAGES 54-55

DOMINICA
PAGES 54-55

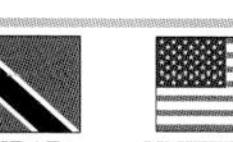

NICARAGUA
PAGES 52-53

PANAMA
PAGES 52-53

ST. KITTS & NEVIS
PAGES 54-55

ST. LUCIA
PAGES 54-55

ST.VINCENT & THE GRENADINES
PAGES 54-55

TRINIDAD & TOBAGO
PAGES 54-55

UNITED STATES OF AMERICA
PAGES 40-49

SOUTH AMERIC

ARGENTINA
PAGES 64-65

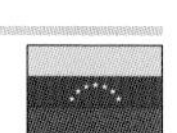

SURINAME
PAGES 58-59

URUGUAY
PAGES 64-65

VENEZUELA
PAGES 58-59

AFRICA

ALGERIA
PAGES 70-71

ANGOLA
PAGES 78-79

BENIN
PAGES 74-75

BOTSWANA
PAGES 78-79

BURKINA FASO
PAGES 74-75

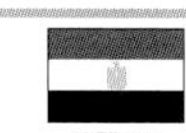

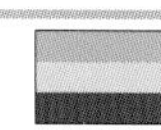

DEM. REP. CONGO
PAGES 76-77

DJIBOUTI
PAGES 72-73

EGYPT
PAGES 72-73

EQUATORIAL GUINEA
PAGES 76-77

ERITREA
PAGES 72-73

ETHIOPIA
PAGES 72-73

GABON
PAGES 76-77

GAMBIA
PAGES 74-75

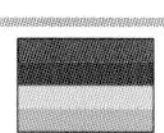

MALAWI
PAGES 78-79

MALI
PAGES 74-75

MAURITANIA
PAGES 74-75

MAURITIUS
PAGES 78-79

MOROCCO
PAGES 70-71

MOZAMBIQUE
PAGES 78-79

NAMIBIA
PAGES 78-79

NIGER
PAGES 74-75

SUDAN
PAGES 72-73

SWAZILAND
PAGES 78-79

TANZANIA
PAGES 72-73

TOGO
PAGES 74-75

TUNISIA
PAGES 70-71

UGANDA
PAGES 72-73

ZAMBIA
PAGES 78-79

ZIMBABWE
PAGES 78-79

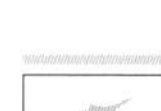

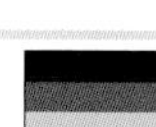
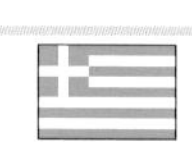

CYPRUS
PAGES 102-103

CZECH REPUBLIC
PAGES 98-99

DENMARK
PAGES 84-85

ESTONIA
PAGES 106-107

FINLAND
PAGES 84-85

FRANCE
PAGES 90-91

GERMANY
PAGES 94-95

GREECE
PAGES 104-105

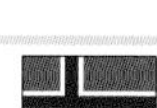

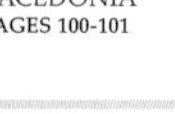

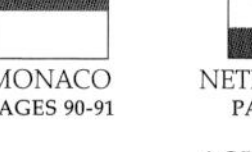

MACEDONIA
PAGES 100-101

MALTA
PAGES 96-97

MOLDOVA
PAGES 108-109

MONACO
PAGES 90-91

NETHERLANDS
PAGES 86-87

NORWAY
PAGES 84-85

POLAND
PAGES 98-99

PORTUGAL
PAGES 92-93

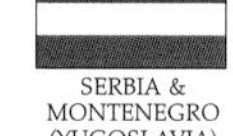

UKRAINE
PAGES 108-109

UNITED KINGDOM
PAGES 88-89

VATICAN CITY
PAGES 96-97

SERBIA & MONTENEGRO (YUGOSLAVIA)
PAGES 100-101

ASIA

AFGHANISTAN
PAGES 122-123

ARMENIA
PAGES 116-117

AZERBAIJAN
PAGES 116-117

BAHRAIN
PAGES 120-121

INDONESIA
PAGES 138-139

IRAN
PAGES 120-121

IRAQ
PAGES 120-121

ISRAEL
PAGES 118-119

JAPAN
PAGES 130-131

JORDAN
PAGES 118-119

KAZAKHSTAN
PAGES 114-115

KUWAIT
PAGES 120-121

OMAN
PAGES 120-121

PAKISTAN
PAGES 134-135

PHILIPPINES
PAGES 138-139

QATAR
PAGES 120-121

SAUDI ARABIA
PAGES 120-121

SINGAPORE
PAGES 138-139

SOUTH KOREA
PAGES 128-129

SRI LANKA
PAGES 132-133

VIETNAM
PAGES 136-137

YEMEN
PAGES 120-121

AUSTRALIA & OCEANIA

AUSTRALIA
PAGES 146-149

FIJI
PAGES 144-145

KIRIBATI
PAGES 144-145

MARSHALL ISLANDS
PAGES 144-145

MICRONESIA
PAGES 144-145

NAURU
PAGES 144-145

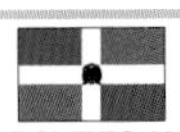

DOMINICAN REPUBLIC PAGES 54-55
EL SALVADOR PAGES 52-53
GRENADA PAGES 54-55
GUATEMALA PAGES 52-53
HAITI PAGES 54-55
HONDURAS PAGES 52-53
JAMAICA PAGES 54-55
MEXICO PAGES 50-51

BOLIVIA PAGES 60-61
BRAZIL PAGES 62-63
CHILE PAGES 64-65
COLOMBIA PAGES 58-59
ECUADOR PAGES 60-61
GUYANA PAGES 58-59
PARAGUAY PAGES 64-65
PERU PAGES 60-61

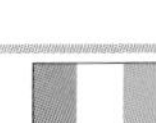

BURUNDI PAGES 72-73
CAMEROON PAGES 76-77
CAPE VERDE PAGES 74-75
CENTRAL AFRICAN REPUBLIC PAGES 76-77
CHAD PAGES 76-77
COMOROS PAGES 78-79
CONGO PAGES 76-77
CÔTE D'IVOIRE PAGES 74-75

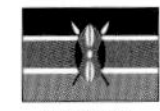

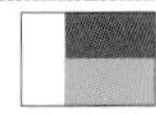

GHANA PAGES 74-75
GUINEA PAGES 74-75
GUINEA-BISSAU PAGES 74-75
KENYA PAGES 72-73
LESOTHO PAGES 78-79
LIBERIA PAGES 74-75
LIBYA PAGES 70-71
MADAGASCAR PAGES 78-79

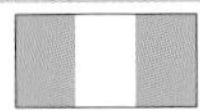

NIGERIA PAGES 74-75
RWANDA PAGES 72-73
SAO TOME & PRINCIPE PAGES 76-77
SENEGAL PAGES 74-75
SEYCHELLES PAGES 78-79
SIERRA LEONE PAGES 74-75
SOMALIA PAGES 72-73
SOUTH AFRICA PAGES 78-79

EUROPE

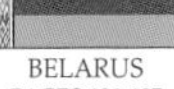

ALBANIA PAGES 100-101
ANDORRA PAGES 90-91
AUSTRIA PAGES 94-95
BELARUS PAGES 106-107
BELGIUM PAGES 86-87
BOSNIA & HERZEGOVINA PAGES 100-101
BULGARIA PAGES 104-105
CROATIA PAGES 100-101

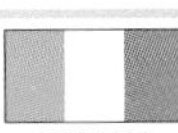

HUNGARY PAGES 98-99
ICELAND PAGES 82-83
IRELAND PAGES 88-89
ITALY PAGES 96-97
LATVIA PAGES 106-107
LIECHTENSTEIN PAGES 94-95
LITHUANIA PAGES 106-107
LUXEMBOURG PAGES 86-87

ROMANIA PAGES 108-109
RUSSIAN FEDERATION PAGES 110-111
SAN MARINO PAGES 96-97
SLOVAKIA PAGES 94-95
SLOVENIA PAGES 94-95
SPAIN PAGES 92-93
SWEDEN PAGES 84-85
SWITZERLAND PAGES 94-95

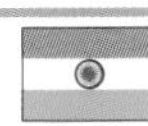

BANGLADESH PAGES 134-135
BHUTAN PAGES 134-135
BRUNEI PAGES 138-139
CAMBODIA PAGES 136-137
CHINA PAGES 126-129
EAST TIMOR PAGES 138-139
GEORGIA PAGES 116-117
INDIA PAGES 132-135

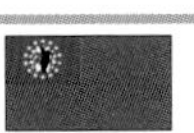

KYRGYZSTAN PAGES 122-123
LAOS PAGES 136-137
LEBANON PAGES 118-119
MALAYSIA PAGES 138-139
MALDIVES PAGES 132-133
MONGOLIA PAGES 126-127
MYANMAR (BURMA) PAGES 136-137
NEPAL PAGES 134-135
NORTH KOREA PAGES 128-129

SYRIA PAGES 118-119
TAIWAN PAGES 128-129
TAJIKISTAN PAGES 122-123
THAILAND PAGES 136-137
TURKEY PAGES 116-117
TURKMENISTAN PAGES 122-123
UNITED ARAB EMIRATES PAGES 120-121
UZBEKISTAN PAGES 122-123

NEW ZEALAND PAGES 150-151
PALAU PAGES 144-145
PAPUA NEW GUINEA PAGES 144-145
SAMOA PAGES 144-145
SOLOMON ISLANDS PAGES 144-145
TONGA PAGES 144-145
TUVALU PAGES 144-145
VANUATU PAGES 144-145

THE POLITICAL WORLD

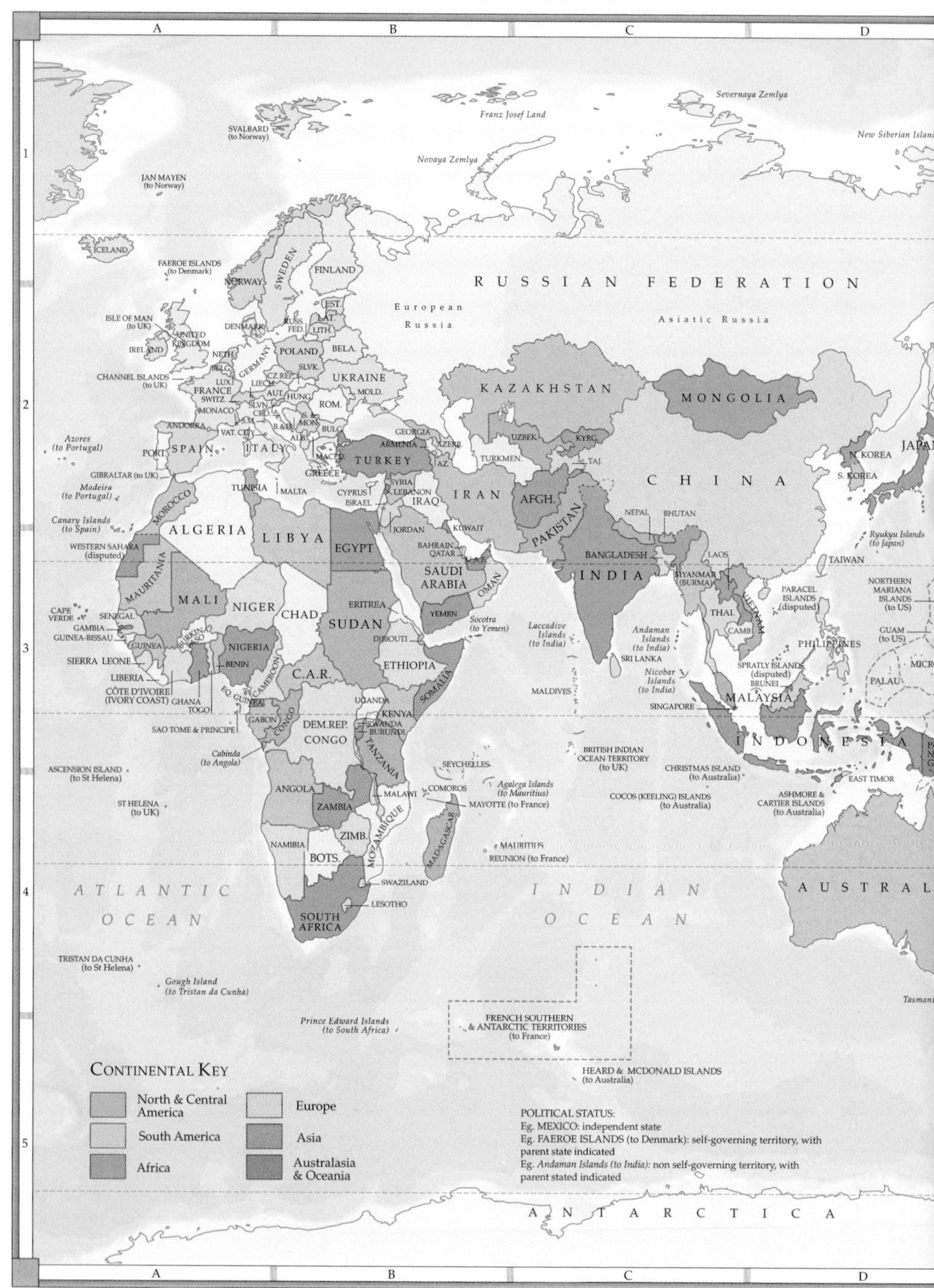

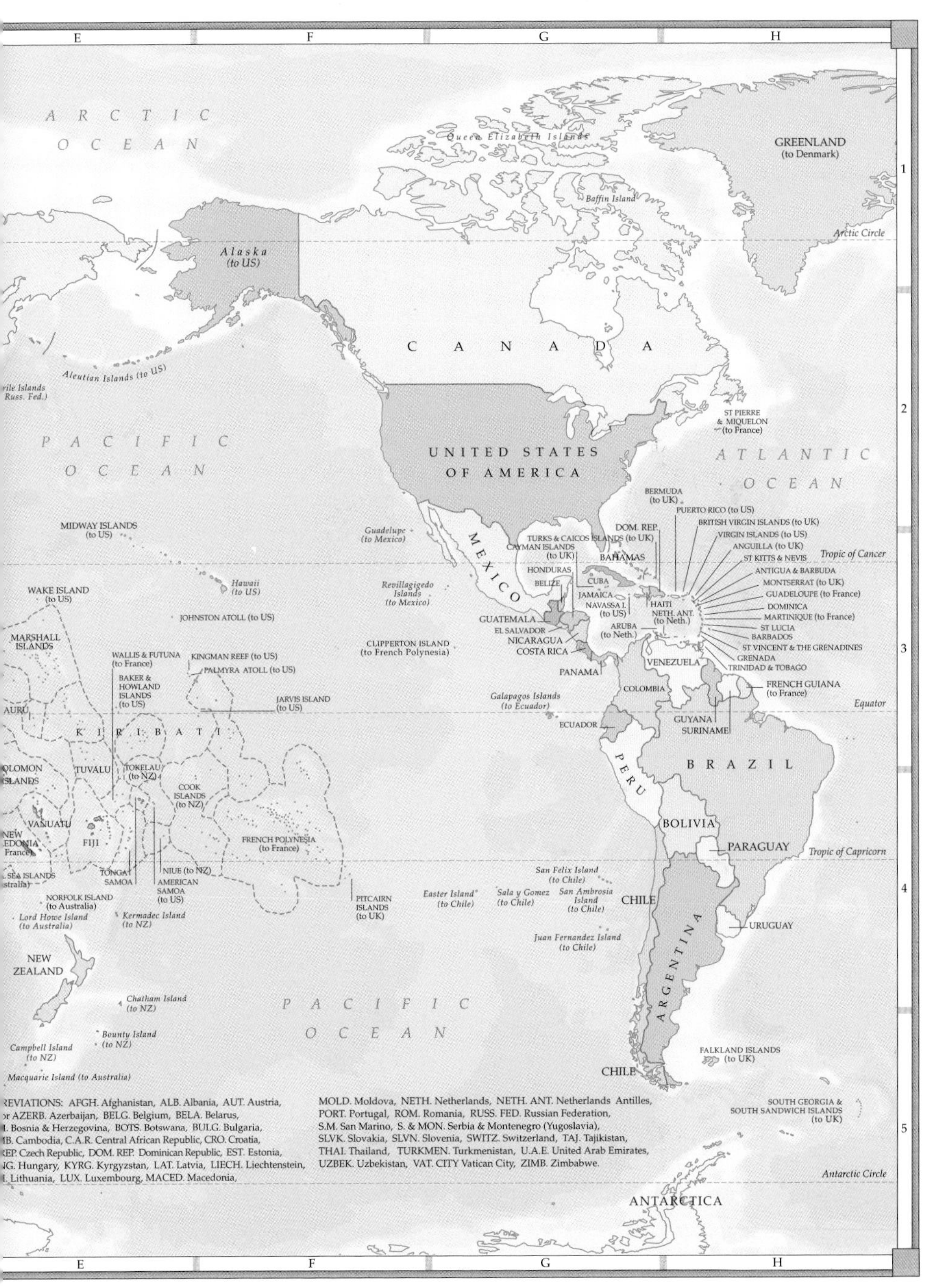
E
F
G
H
ARCTIC OCEAN
Queen Elizabeth Islands
GREENLAND (to Denmark)
Baffin Island
Arctic Circle
Alaska (to US)
CANADA
Aleutian Islands (to US)
rile Islands Russ. Fed.)
ST PIERRE & MIQUELON (to France)
PACIFIC OCEAN
UNITED STATES OF AMERICA
ATLANTIC OCEAN
BERMUDA (to UK)
PUERTO RICO (to US)
BRITISH VIRGIN ISLANDS (to UK)
VIRGIN ISLANDS (to US)
ANGUILLA (to UK)
ST KITTS & NEVIS
Tropic of Cancer
ANTIGUA & BARBUDA
MONTSERRAT (to UK)
GUADELOUPE (to France)
DOMINICA
MARTINIQUE (to France)
ST LUCIA
BARBADOS
ST VINCENT & THE GRENADINES
GRENADA
TRINIDAD & TOBAGO
MIDWAY ISLANDS (to US)
Guadelupe (to Mexico)
MEXICO
TURKS & CAICOS ISLANDS (to UK)
DOM. REP.
CAYMAN ISLANDS (to UK)
BAHAMAS
HONDURAS
BELIZE
CUBA
JAMAICA
NAVASSA I. (to US)
HAITI
NETH. ANT. (to Neth.)
ARUBA (to Neth.)
WAKE ISLAND (to US)
Hawaii (to US)
Revillagigedo Islands (to Mexico)
JOHNSTON ATOLL (to US)
GUATEMALA
EL SALVADOR
NICARAGUA
COSTA RICA
PANAMA
VENEZUELA
MARSHALL ISLANDS
CLIPPERTON ISLAND (to French Polynesia)
WALLIS & FUTUNA (to France)
KINGMAN REEF (to US)
PALMYRA ATOLL (to US)
BAKER & HOWLAND ISLANDS (to US)
JARVIS ISLAND (to US)
Galapagos Islands (to Ecuador)
COLOMBIA
FRENCH GUIANA (to France)
Equator
ECUADOR
GUYANA
SURINAME
AURU
KIRIBATI
OLOMON ISLANDS
TUVALU
TOKELAU (to NZ)
PERU
BRAZIL
COOK ISLANDS (to NZ)
VANUATU
BOLIVIA
NEW EDONIA France)
FIJI
FRENCH POLYNESIA (to France)
PARAGUAY
Tropic of Capricorn
SEA ISLANDS stralia)
TONGA
SAMOA
NIUE (to NZ)
AMERICAN SAMOA (to US)
San Felix Island (to Chile)
NORFOLK ISLAND (to Australia)
PITCAIRN ISLANDS (to UK)
Easter Island (to Chile)
Sala y Gomez (to Chile)
San Ambrosia Island (to Chile)
CHILE
Lord Howe Island (to Australia)
Kermadec Island (to NZ)
ARGENTINA
URUGUAY
Juan Fernandez Island (to Chile)
NEW ZEALAND
Chatham Island (to NZ)
PACIFIC OCEAN
Bounty Island (to NZ)
Campbell Island (to NZ)
FALKLAND ISLANDS (to UK)
Macquarie Island (to Australia)
CHILE
REVIATIONS: AFGH. Afghanistan, ALB. Albania, AUT. Austria, or AZERB. Azerbaijan, BELG. Belgium, BELA. Belarus, I. Bosnia & Herzegovina, BOTS. Botswana, BULG. Bulgaria, IB. Cambodia, C.A.R. Central African Republic, CRO. Croatia, REP. Czech Republic, DOM. REP. Dominican Republic, EST. Estonia, IG. Hungary, KYRG. Kyrgyzstan, LAT. Latvia, LIECH. Liechtenstein, I. Lithuania, LUX. Luxembourg, MACED. Macedonia,
MOLD. Moldova, NETH. Netherlands, NETH. ANT. Netherlands Antilles, PORT. Portugal, ROM. Romania, RUSS. FED. Russian Federation, S.M. San Marino, S. & MON. Serbia & Montenegro (Yugoslavia), SLVK. Slovakia, SLVN. Slovenia, SWITZ. Switzerland, TAJ. Tajikistan, THAI. Thailand, TURKMEN. Turkmenistan, U.A.E. United Arab Emirates, UZBEK. Uzbekistan, VAT. CITY Vatican City, ZIMB. Zimbabwe.
SOUTH GEORGIA & SOUTH SANDWICH ISLANDS (to UK)
Antarctic Circle
ANTARCTICA
1
2
3
4
5

THE PHYSICAL WORLD

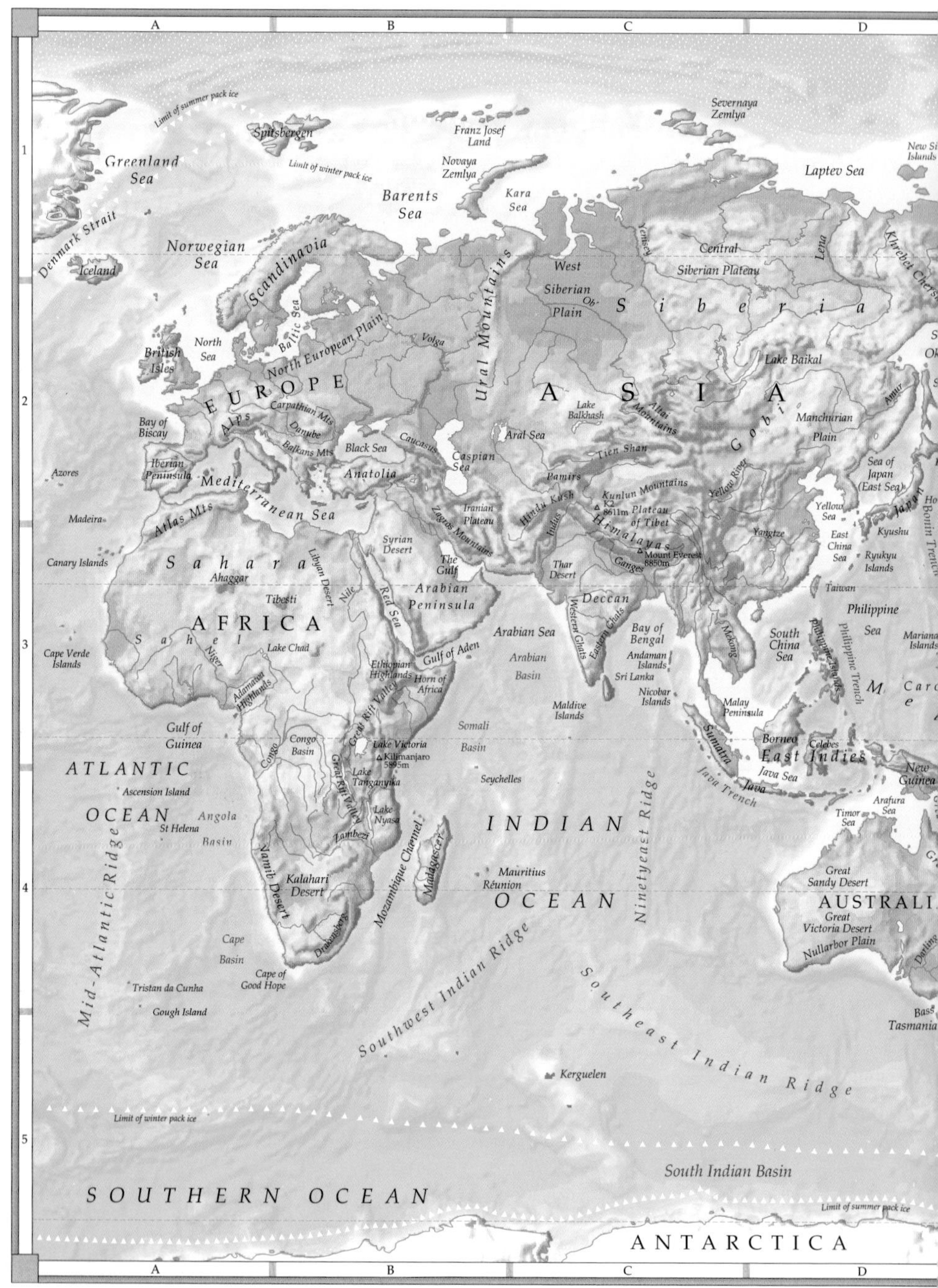

ARCTIC OCEAN
Queen Elizabeth Islands
Ellesmere Island
Greenland
Siberian Sea
Limit of summer pack ice
Beaufort Sea
Baffin Bay
Baffin Island
Chukchi Sea
Brooks Range
Bering Strait
Mackenzie
Great Bear Lake
Arctic Circle
Mount McKinley (Denali) 6194m
Great Slave Lake
Hudson Bay
Péninsula d'Ungava
Labrador Sea
Limit of winter pack ice
Bering Sea
Aleutian Basin
Aleutian Islands
Aleutian Trench
Gulf of Alaska
Coast Mountains
Rocky Mountains
Canadian Shield
Lake Winnipeg
Laurentian Mountains
NORTH AMERICA
Vancouver Island
Great Lakes
Grand Banks of Newfoundland
Emperor Seamounts
Coast Ranges
Great Plains
Appalachian Mts
Mendocino Fracture Zone
Mississippi
Mid-Atlantic Ridge
North American Basin
Murray Fracture Zone
Lower California
Sierra Madre Occidental
Sierra Madre Oriental
Gulf of Mexico
Tropic of Cancer
Hawaiian Islands
Hawaii
Yucatan Peninsula
Greater Antilles
West Indies
ATLANTIC OCEAN
Central Pacific Basin
Caribbean Sea
Lesser Antilles
Middle America Trench
Marshall Islands
PACIFIC OCEAN
Polynesia
Micronesia
Line Islands
Guiana Highlands
Equator
Galapagos Islands
Amazon
Phoenix Islands
Amazon Basin
SOUTH AMERICA
Andes
Marquesas Islands
Samoa
Brazilian Highlands
Brazil Basin
Peru - Chile Trench
Tuamotu Islands
Cook Islands
Peru Basin
Planalto de Mato Grosso
Fiji
Tonga
Vanuatu
New Caledonia
Tropic of Capricorn
East Pacific Rise
Easter Island
Gran Chaco
Paraná
Kermadec Trench
Cerro Aconcagua 6959m
Southwest Pacific Basin
Juan Fernandez Islands
Pampas
Tasman Sea
North Island
New Zealand
South Island
Argentine Basin
Patagonia
Campbell Plateau
Falkland Islands
Tierra del Fuego
South Georgia
Cape Horn
Drake Passage
South Sandwich Islands
SOUTHERN OCEAN
Limit of winter pack ice
Antarctic Peninsula
Antarctic Circle
E
F
G
H
1
2
3
4
5
ELEVATION
Below sea level
-4000m
-3000m
-2000m
-1000m
-500m
0
100m
250m
500m
1000m
2000m
4000m
-13 124ft
-9843ft
-6562ft
-3281ft
-1640ft
-820ft/-250m
0
328ft
820ft
1640ft
3281ft
6562ft
13 124ft

Time Zones

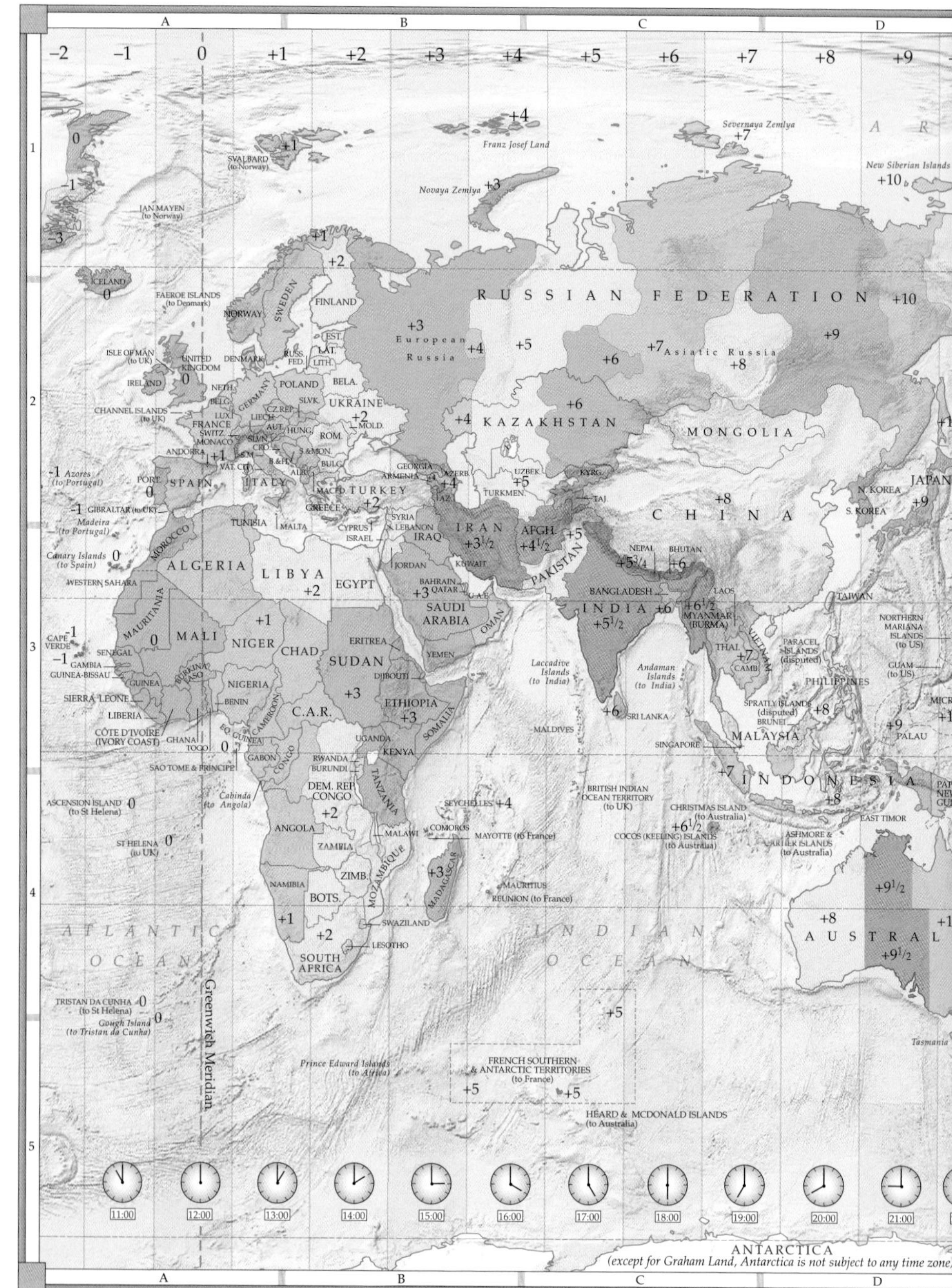

The numbers represented thus: +2/-2, indicate the number of hours each time zone is ahead or behind GMT (Greenwich Mean Time)

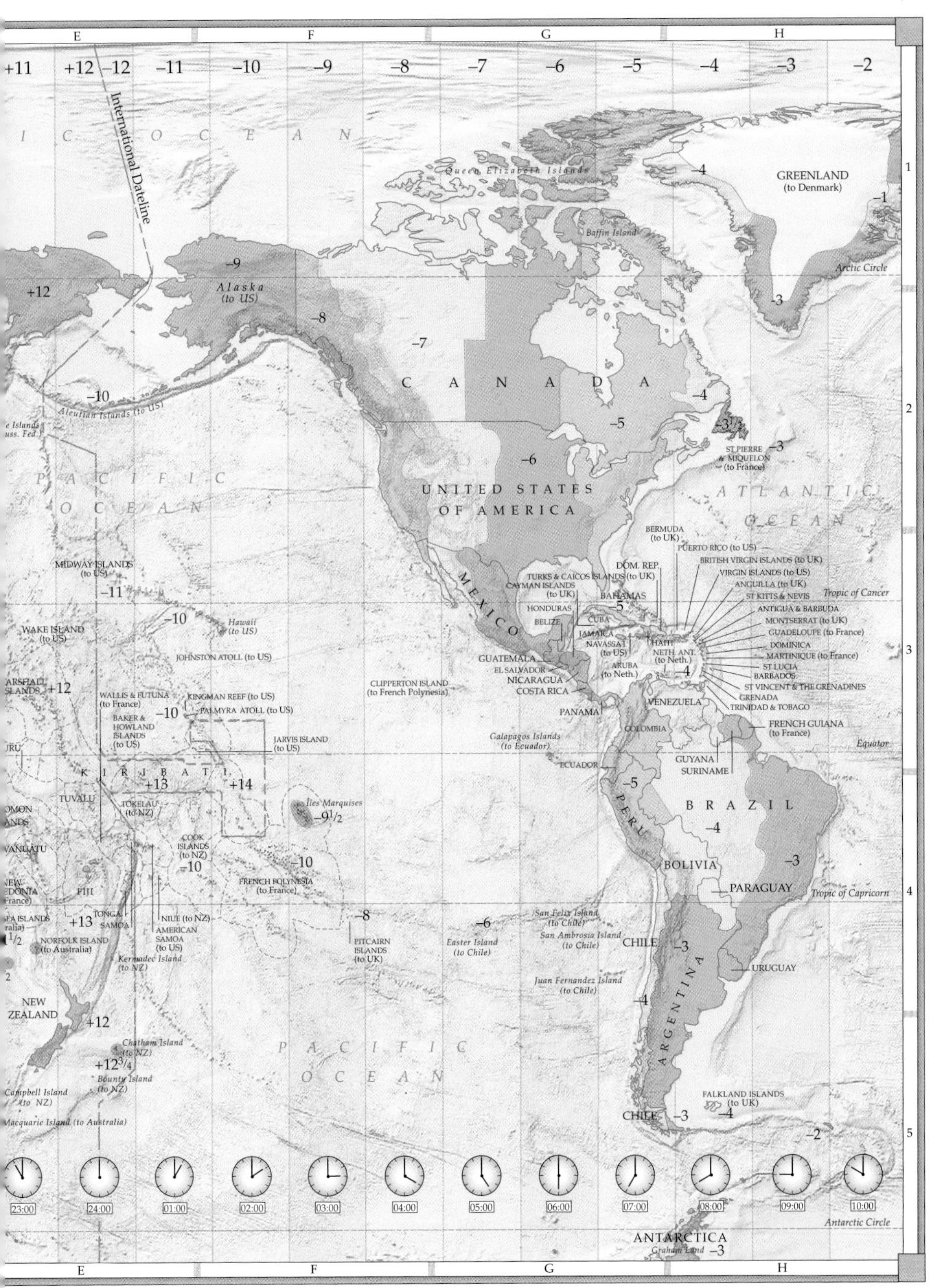

The clocks and 24-hour times given at the bottom of the map show the time in each time zone when it is 12.00 hours noon GMT

GEOLOGY & STRUCTURE

A B C D

1 2 3 4 5

Ural Mountains

EURASIAN PLATE

Alps

ANATOLIAN PLATE

IRANIAN PLATE

Himalayas

ARABIAN PLATE

PHILIPPINE PLATE

AFRICAN PLATE

INDO-AUSTRALIAN PLATE

ANTARCTIC PLATE

GEOLOGICAL REGIONS

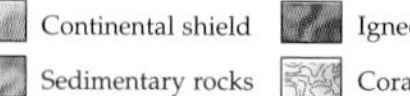

Continental shield

Sedimentary rocks

Igneous rock types

Coral formation

MOUNTAIN RANGES

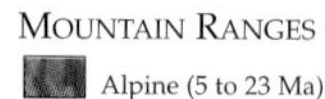

Alpine (5 to 23 Ma)

Hercynian (290 to 362 Ma)

Caledonian (386 to 439 Ma)

Ma= million years a

E
F
G
H
1
2
3
4
5
Arctic Circle
NORTH AMERICAN PLATE
Rocky Mountains
JUAN DE FUCA PLATE
Tropic of Cancer
CARIBBEAN PLATE
COCOS PLATE
ROLINE
ATE
PACIFIC PLATE
MARCK
ATE
SOLOMON PLATE
FIJI PLATE
Andes
Equator
SOUTH AMERICAN PLATE
NAZCA PLATE
Tropic of Capricorn
SCOTIA PLATE
ANTARCTIC PLATE
Antarctic Circle
Earthquake zone
Hot spot
Volcanic zone
Rift valley
Plate Boundaries
Sliding plates
Spreading plates
Colliding plates
Uncertain plate boundary

World Climate

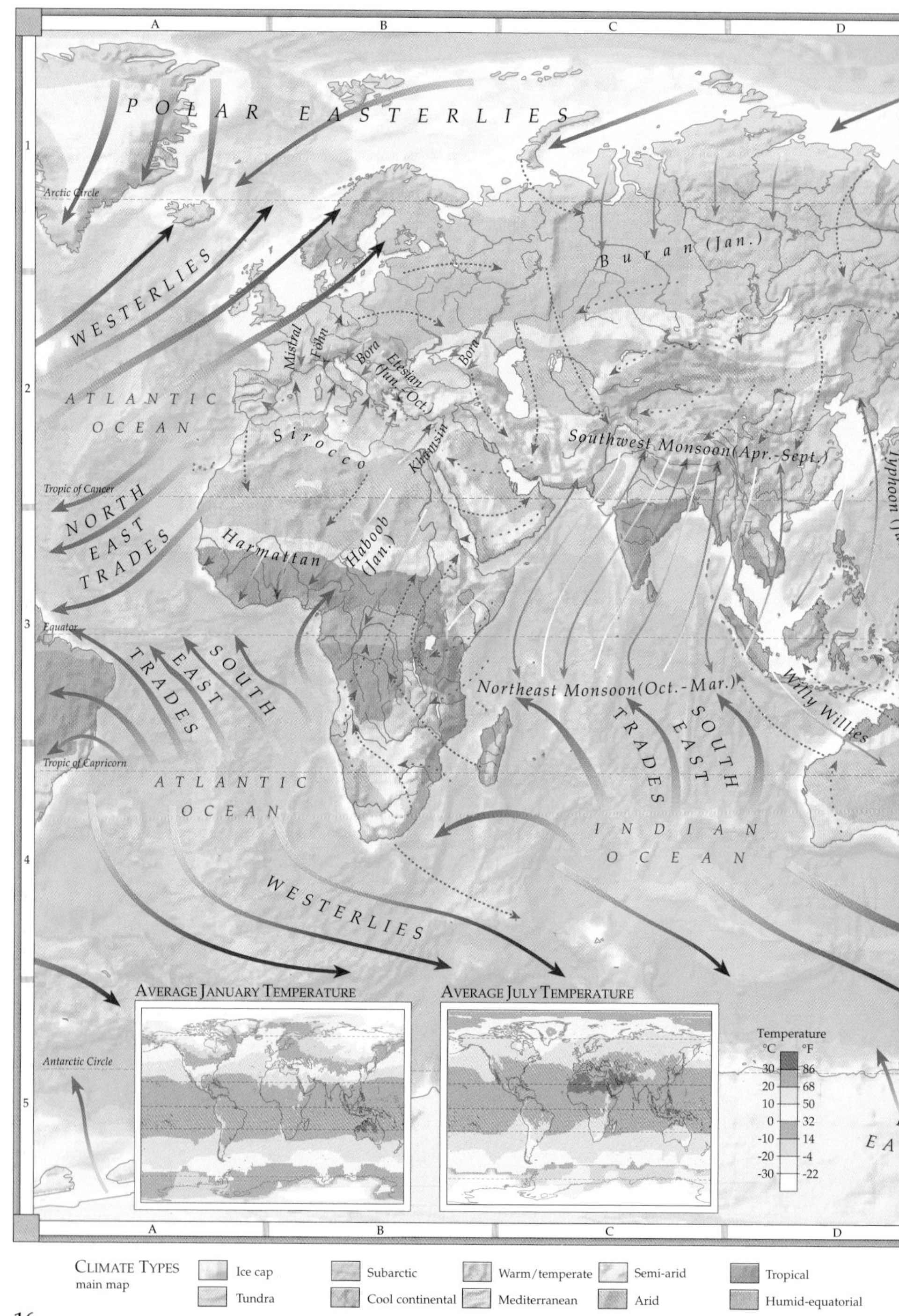

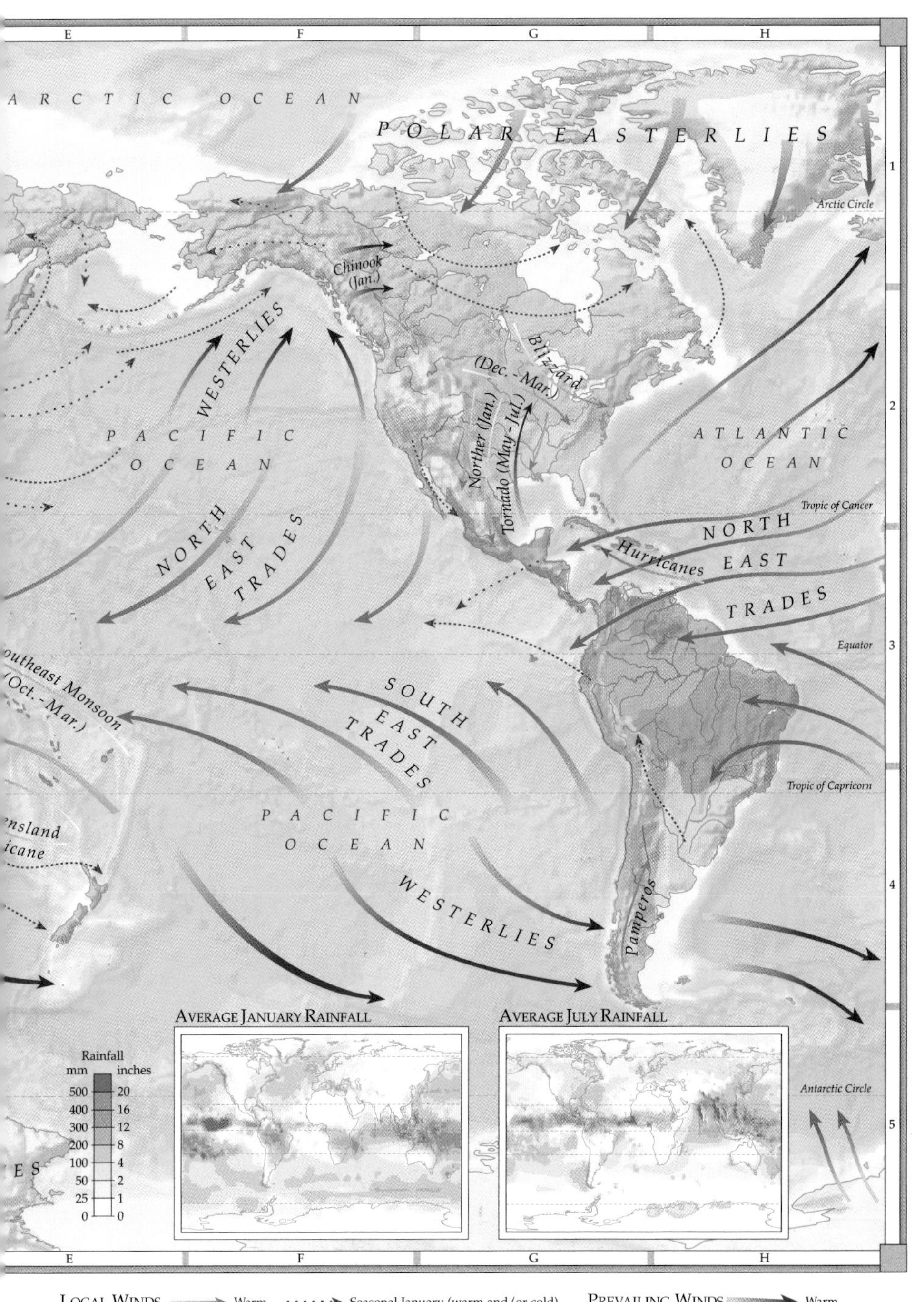
E
F
G
H
ARCTIC OCEAN
POLAR EASTERLIES
Arctic Circle
Chinook (Jan.)
Blizzard (Dec. - Mar.)
Norther (Jan.)
Tornado (May - Jul.)
WESTERLIES
PACIFIC OCEAN
ATLANTIC OCEAN
Tropic of Cancer
NORTH EAST TRADES
Hurricanes
Equator
outheast Monsoon (Oct. - Mar.)
SOUTH EAST TRADES
Tropic of Capricorn
nsland icane
PACIFIC OCEAN
WESTERLIES
Pamperos
Antarctic Circle
1
2
3
4
5
AVERAGE JANUARY RAINFALL
AVERAGE JULY RAINFALL
Rainfall
mm inches
500 20
400 16
300 12
200 8
100 4
50 2
25 1
0 0
ES
LOCAL WINDS
Warm
Cold
Seasonal January (warm and/or cold)
Seasonal July (warm and/or cold)
PREVAILING WINDS
Warm
Cold

OCEAN CURRENTS

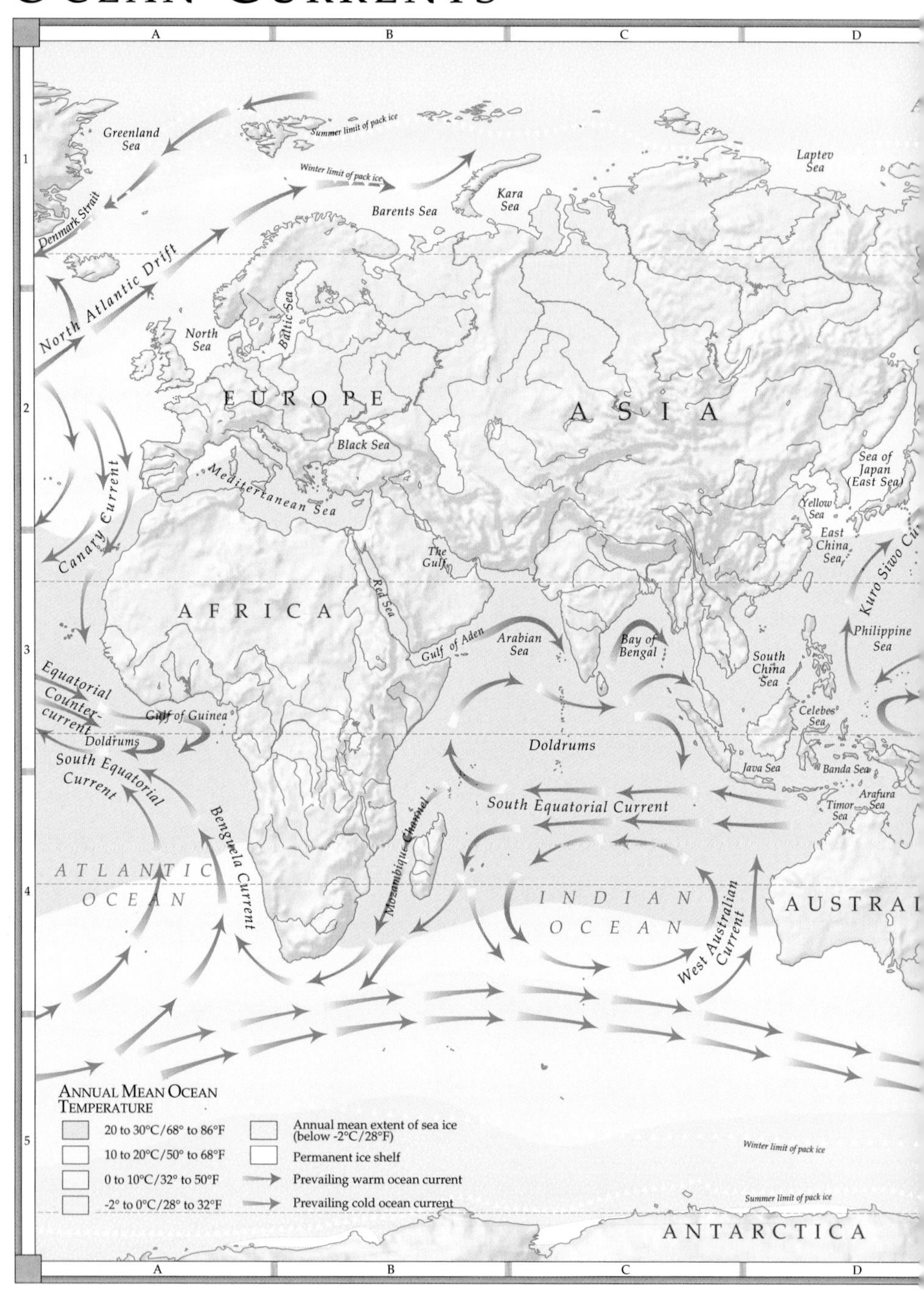

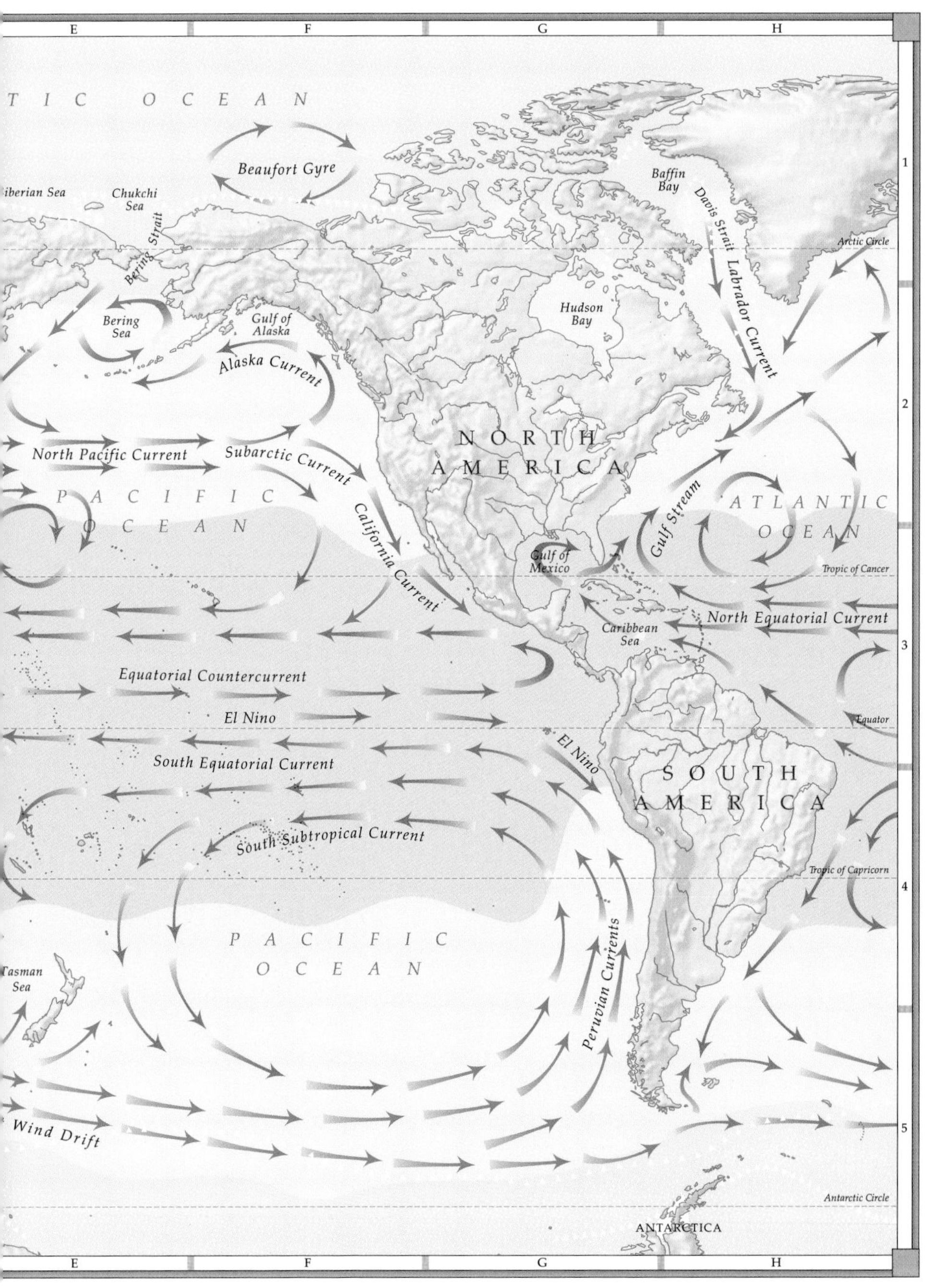
E
F
G
H
TIC OCEAN
Beaufort Gyre
iberian Sea
Chukchi Sea
Bering Strait
Baffin Bay
Davis Strait
Hudson Bay
Labrador Current
Arctic Circle
Bering Sea
Gulf of Alaska
Alaska Current
North Pacific Current
Subarctic Current
NORTH AMERICA
PACIFIC OCEAN
California Current
Gulf Stream
ATLANTIC OCEAN
Gulf of Mexico
Tropic of Cancer
Caribbean Sea
North Equatorial Current
Equatorial Countercurrent
El Nino
Equator
El Nino
South Equatorial Current
SOUTH AMERICA
South Subtropical Current
Tropic of Capricorn
PACIFIC OCEAN
Peruvian Currents
Tasman Sea
Wind Drift
Antarctic Circle
ANTARCTICA
1
2
3
4
5

LIFE ZONES

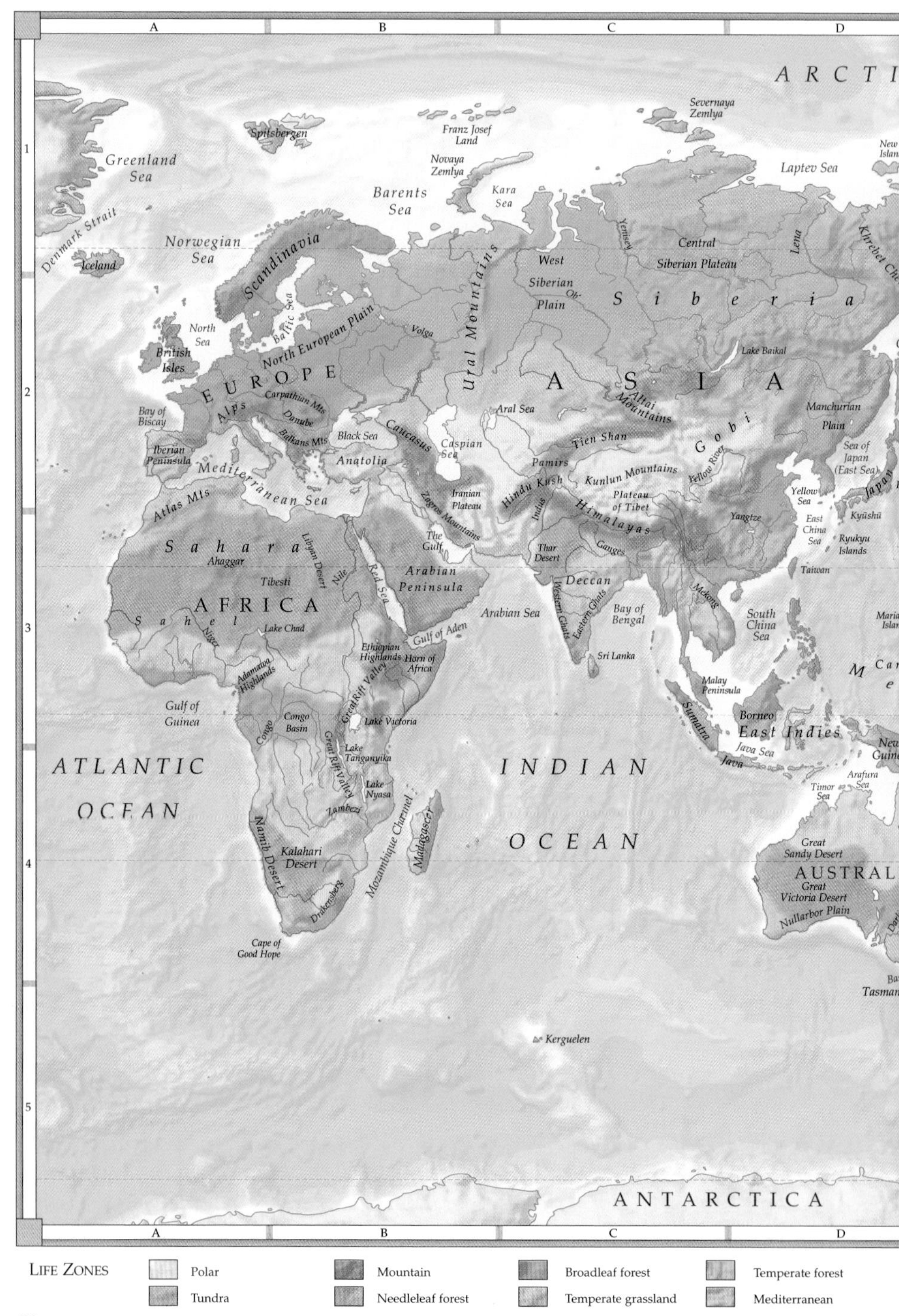

LIFE ZONES

Polar	Mountain	Broadleaf forest	Temperate forest
Tundra	Needleleaf forest	Temperate grassland	Mediterranean

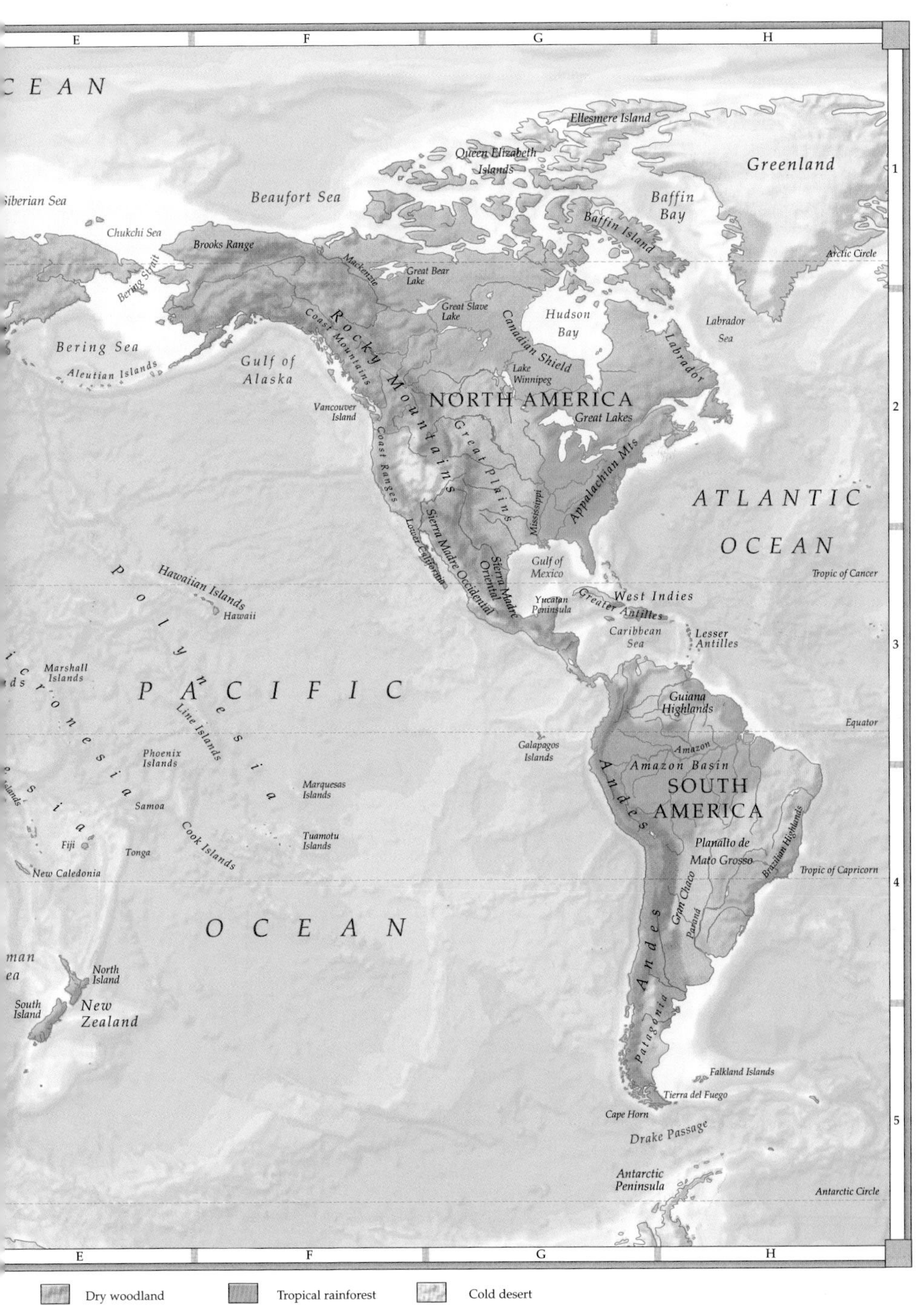
E
F
G
H
CEAN
Ellesmere Island
Queen Elizabeth Islands
Greenland
Siberian Sea
Beaufort Sea
Baffin Bay
Chukchi Sea
Baffin Island
Brooks Range
Arctic Circle
Bering Strait
Mackenzie
Great Bear Lake
Great Slave Lake
Hudson Bay
Labrador Sea
Bering Sea
Coast Mountains
Rocky Mountains
Canadian Shield
Labrador
Aleutian Islands
Gulf of Alaska
Lake Winnipeg
NORTH AMERICA
Vancouver Island
Great Lakes
Great Plains
Appalachian Mts
Coast Ranges
Mississippi
ATLANTIC OCEAN
Lower California
Sierra Madre Occidental
Sierra Madre Oriental
Gulf of Mexico
Tropic of Cancer
Hawaiian Islands
Hawaii
Polynesia
Yucatan Peninsula
Greater Antilles
West Indies
Caribbean Sea
Lesser Antilles
Marshall Islands
Micronesia
PACIFIC
Guiana Highlands
Line Islands
Equator
Galapagos Islands
Phoenix Islands
Amazon
Amazon Basin
Andes
SOUTH AMERICA
Marquesas Islands
Samoa
Brazilian Highlands
Planalto de Mato Grosso
Tuamotu Islands
Fiji
Tonga
Cook Islands
New Caledonia
Tropic of Capricorn
Gran Chaco
Paraná
OCEAN
North Island
South Island
New Zealand
Patagonia
Falkland Islands
Tierra del Fuego
Cape Horn
Drake Passage
Antarctic Peninsula
Antarctic Circle
1
2
3
4
5
Dry woodland
Tropical grassland
Tropical rainforest
Hot desert
Cold desert
Wetland

POPULATION

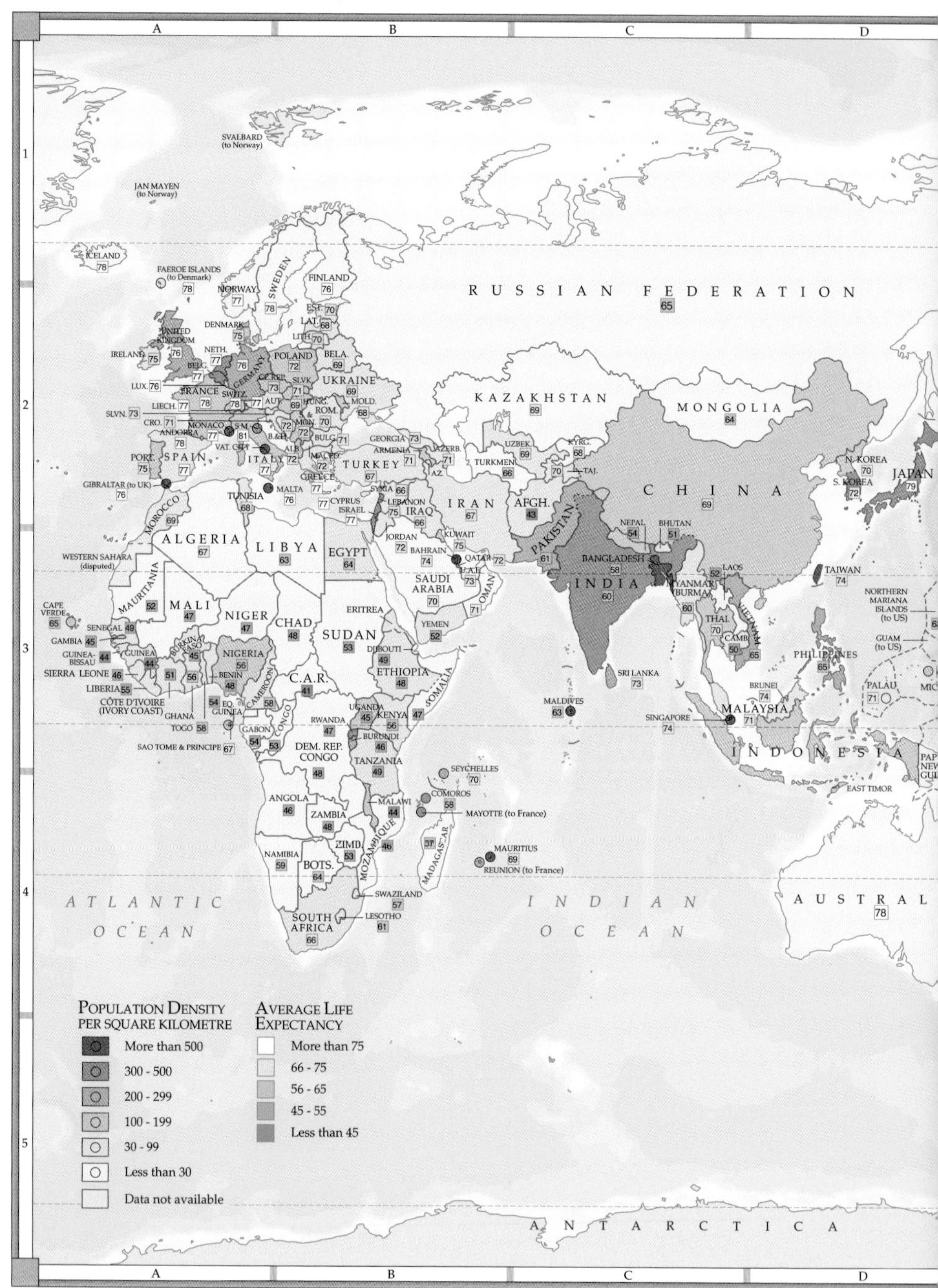
A
B
C
D
1
2
3
4
5
SVALBARD (to Norway)
JAN MAYEN (to Norway)
ICELAND 78
FAEROE ISLANDS (to Denmark) 78
NORWAY 77
SWEDEN 78
FINLAND 76
EST. 70
LAT. 68
LITH. 70
DENMARK 75
UNITED KINGDOM 76
IRELAND 75
NETH. 77
BELG. 77
GERMANY 76
POLAND 72
BELA. 69
UKRAINE 69
CZ. REP. 73
SLVK. 71
LUX. 76
FRANCE 78
SWITZ. 78
AUT. 77
HUNG. 69
ROM. 70
MOLD. 68
LIECH. 77
SLVN. 73
CRO. 71
MONACO 77
S.M. 81
B.&H. 72
Y. 72
MON. 72
BULG. 71
ANDORRA 78
VAT. CITY
ITALY 77
ALB. 72
MACED. 72
GREECE 77
PORT. 75
SPAIN 77
GIBRALTAR (to UK) 76
TURKEY 67
GEORGIA 73
ARMENIA 71
AZERB. 71
AZ.
MALTA 76
TUNISIA 68
CYPRUS 77
SYRIA 66
LEBANON 75
ISRAEL 77
IRAQ 66
JORDAN 72
KUWAIT 75
BAHRAIN 74
QATAR 72
U.A.E. 73
OMAN 71
SAUDI ARABIA 70
YEMEN 52
IRAN 67
AFGH. 43
PAKISTAN 61
INDIA 60
NEPAL 54
BHUTAN 51
BANGLADESH 58
SRI LANKA 73
MALDIVES 63
RUSSIAN FEDERATION 65
KAZAKHSTAN 69
UZBEK. 69
TURKMEN. 66
KYRG. 68
TAJ. 70
MONGOLIA 64
CHINA 69
N. KOREA 70
S. KOREA 72
JAPAN 79
TAIWAN 74
MYANMAR (BURMA) 60
LAOS 52
THAI. 70
CAMB. 50
VIETNAM 65
PHILIPPINES 65
BRUNEI 74
MALAYSIA 71
SINGAPORE 74
INDONESIA
EAST TIMOR
PALAU 71
NORTHERN MARIANA ISLANDS (to US)
GUAM (to US)
AUSTRALIA 78
MOROCCO 69
ALGERIA 67
LIBYA 63
EGYPT 64
WESTERN SAHARA (disputed)
MAURITANIA 52
MALI 47
NIGER 47
CHAD 48
SUDAN 53
ERITREA
DJIBOUTI 49
ETHIOPIA 48
SOMALIA 47
CAPE VERDE 65
SENEGAL 49
GAMBIA 45
GUINEA-BISSAU 44
GUINEA 44
BURKINA FASO 45
SIERRA LEONE 46
LIBERIA 55
CÔTE D'IVOIRE (IVORY COAST) 54
GHANA 56
TOGO 58
BENIN 48
NIGERIA 56
CAMEROON 58
EQ. GUINEA
C.A.R. 41
SAO TOME & PRINCIPE 67
GABON 54
CONGO 53
DEM. REP. CONGO 48
UGANDA 45
KENYA 56
RWANDA 47
BURUNDI 46
TANZANIA 49
SEYCHELLES 70
COMOROS 58
MAYOTTE (to France)
ANGOLA 46
ZAMBIA 48
MALAWI 44
MOZAMBIQUE 46
MADAGASCAR 57
ZIMB. 53
NAMIBIA 59
BOTS. 64
MAURITIUS 69
REUNION (to France)
SWAZILAND 57
LESOTHO 61
SOUTH AFRICA 66
ATLANTIC OCEAN
INDIAN OCEAN
ANTARCTICA
POPULATION DENSITY PER SQUARE KILOMETRE
More than 500
300 - 500
200 - 299
100 - 199
30 - 99
Less than 30
Data not available
AVERAGE LIFE EXPECTANCY
More than 75
66 - 75
56 - 65
45 - 55
Less than 45

E
F
G
H
1
2
3
4
5
ARCTIC OCEAN
GREENLAND (to Denmark) 67
Arctic Circle
Alaska (to US)
CANADA 78
PACIFIC OCEAN
UNITED STATES OF AMERICA 76
ATLANTIC OCEAN
75 BERMUDA (to UK)
PUERTO RICO (to US) 74
DOM. REP. 70
CAYMAN ISLANDS 77 (to UK)
BAHAMAS 73
66 ST KITTS & NEVIS
73 ANTIGUA & BARBUDA
75 GUADELOUPE (to France)
77 DOMINICA
76 MARTINIQUE (to France)
70 ST LUCIA
76 BARBADOS
72 ST VINCENT & THE GRENADINES
71 GRENADA
71 TRINIDAD & TOBAGO
75 FRENCH GUIANA (to France)
Tropic of Cancer
MEXICO 72
HONDURAS
CUBA 75
JAMAICA 74
BELIZE 74
68
57 HAITI
NETH. ANT. (to Neth.) 73
ARUBA (to Neth.) 76
GUATEMALA 65
EL SALVADOR 68
NICARAGUA 65
COSTA RICA 76
PANAMA 72
VENEZUELA 72
COLOMBIA 69
65 70
GUYANA
SURINAME
Equator
ECUADOR 69
PERU 66
BRAZIL 66
BOLIVIA 60
PARAGUAY 70
Tropic of Capricorn
CHILE 72
73 URUGUAY
ARGENTINA 71
CHILE
FALKLAND ISLANDS (to UK) 76
SOUTH GEORGIA & SOUTH SANDWICH ISLANDS (to UK)
Antarctic Circle
ANTARCTICA
Hawaii (to US)
MARSHALL ISLANDS 63
WALLIS & FUTUNA (to France)
67
KIRIBATI 58
71
TUVALU 63
TOKELAU (to NZ)
COOK ISLANDS (to NZ)
68
VANUATU 63
FIJI 63
68
FRENCH POLYNESIA (to France) 70
TONGA
SAMOA
NIUE (to NZ)
AMERICAN SAMOA (to US)
PITCAIRN ISLANDS (to UK)
NEW ZEALAND 76
PACIFIC OCEAN

LANGUAGES

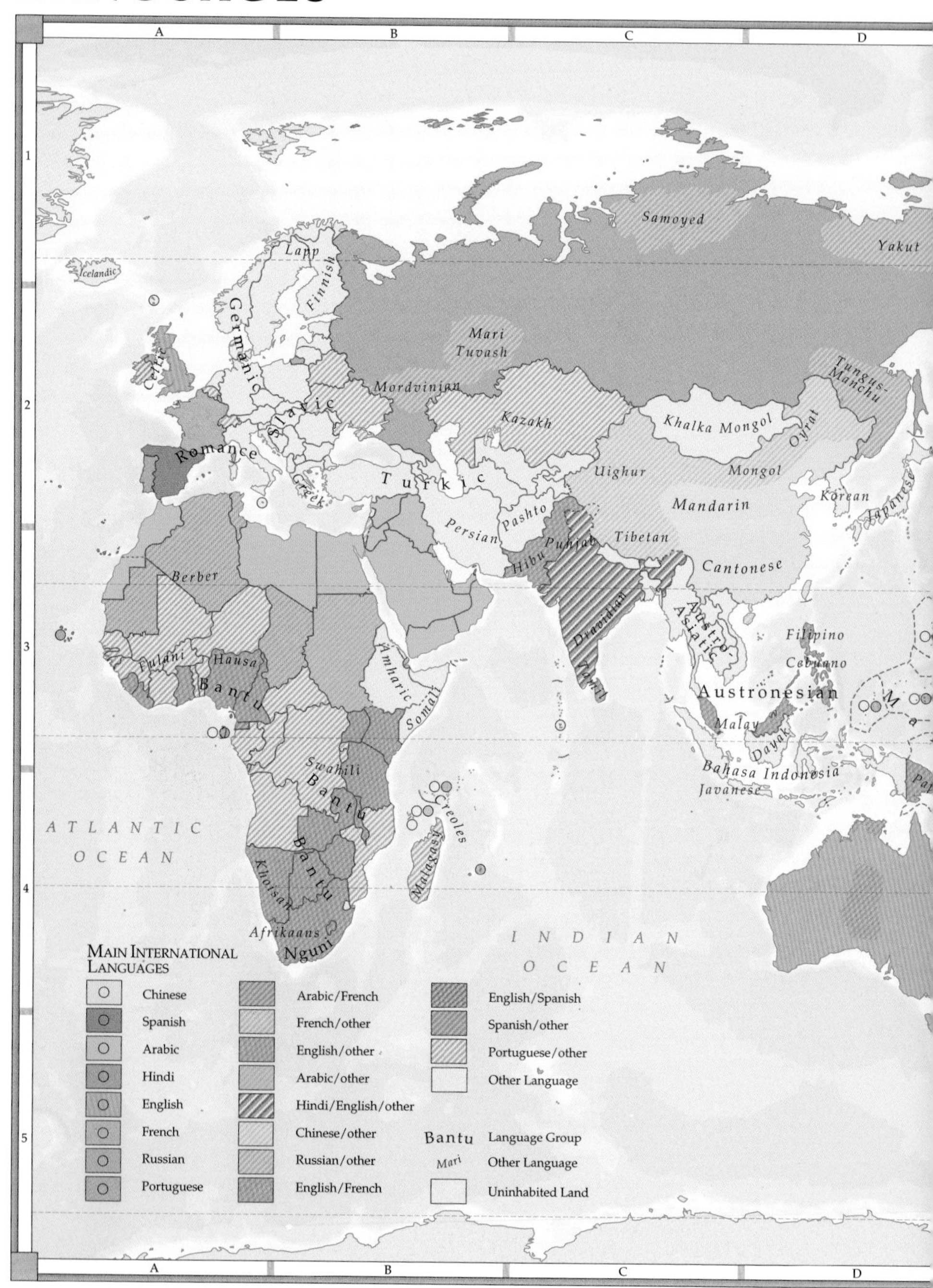

A
B
C
D
1
2
3
4
5
Icelandic
Lapp
Finnish
Germanic
Celtic
Slavic
Romance
Greek
Samoyed
Yakut
Mari
Tuvash
Mordvinian
Tungus-Manchu
Kazakh
Khalka Mongol
Oyrat
Turkic
Uighur
Mongol
Korean
Japanese
Mandarin
Persian
Pashto
Punjabi
Hibu
Tibetan
Cantonese
Berber
Austro-Asiatic
Dravidian
Tamil
Filipino
Cebuano
Fulani
Hausa
Bantu
Amharic
Somali
Austronesian
Malay
Dayak
Swahili
Bahasa Indonesia
Javanese
Creoles
ATLANTIC OCEAN
Malagasy
Khoisan
Afrikaans
Nguni
INDIAN OCEAN
MAIN INTERNATIONAL LANGUAGES
Chinese
Spanish
Arabic
Hindi
English
French
Russian
Portuguese
Arabic/French
French/other
English/other
Arabic/other
Hindi/English/other
Chinese/other
Russian/other
English/French
English/Spanish
Spanish/other
Portuguese/other
Other Language
Bantu Language Group
Mari Other Language
Uninhabited Land

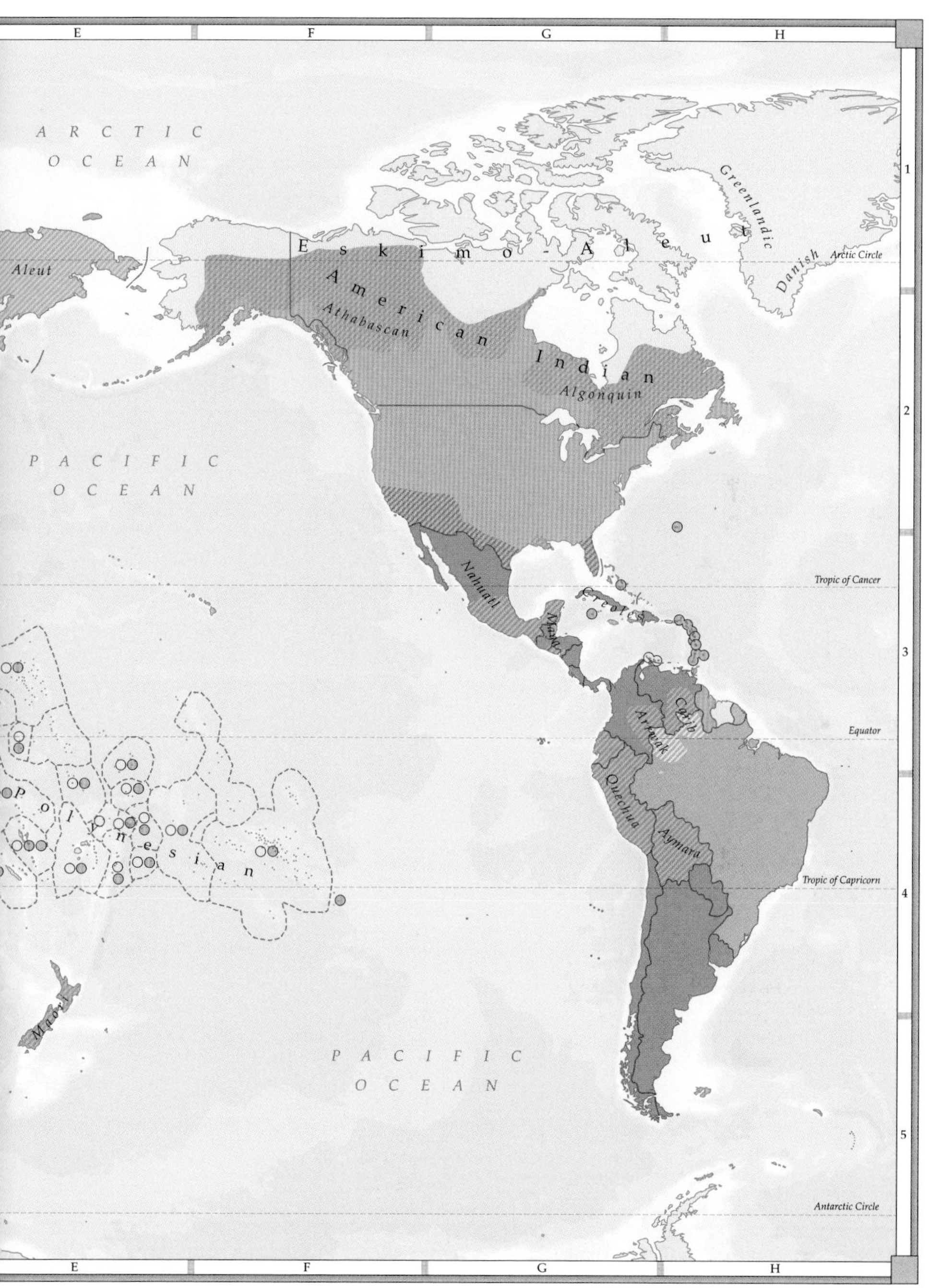
E
F
G
H
ARCTIC OCEAN
Greenlandic
Eskimo-Aleut
Aleut
Danish
Arctic Circle
American Indian
Athabascan
Algonquin
PACIFIC OCEAN
Nahuatl
Tropic of Cancer
Creoles
Maya
Carib
Arawak
Equator
Quechua
Aymara
Polynesian
Tropic of Capricorn
Maori
PACIFIC OCEAN
Antarctic Circle
1
2
3
4
5

Religion

A
B
C
D
1
2
3
4
5
SVALBARD (to Norway)
ICELAND
FAEROE ISLANDS (to Denmark)
NORWAY
SWEDEN
FINLAND
EST.
LAT.
LITH.
RUSS. FED.
DENMARK
UNITED KINGDOM
IRELAND
NETH.
BELG.
LUX.
GERMANY
POLAND
BELA.
CZ.REP.
SLVK.
UKRAINE
LIECH.
AUT.
HUNG.
MOLD.
FRANCE
SWITZ.
SLVN.
ROM.
MONACO
CRO.
ANDORRA
S.M.
B.&H.
MON.
BULG.
VAT. CITY
ALB.
MACED.
PORT.
SPAIN
ITALY
GREECE
TURKEY
GIBRALTAR (to UK)
MALTA
TUNISIA
CYPRUS
ISRAEL
SYRIA
LEBANON
IRAQ
JORDAN
KUWAIT
BAHRAIN
QATAR
U.A.E.
SAUDI ARABIA
OMAN
YEMEN
GEORGIA
ARMENIA
AZERB.
AZ.
R U S S I A N   F E D E R A T I O N
European Russia
Asiatic Russia
KAZAKHSTAN
MONGOLIA
UZBEK.
KYRG.
TURKMEN.
TAJ.
IRAN
AFGH.
PAKISTAN
N. KOREA
S. KOREA
JAPAN
CHINA
NEPAL
BHUTAN
BANGLADESH
INDIA
MYAN. BURMA
LAOS
THAI.
VIETNAM
CAMB.
TAIWAN
PARACEL ISLANDS (disputed)
PHILIPPINES
SPRATLY ISLANDS (disputed)
BRUNEI
MALAYSIA
SINGAPORE
INDONESIA
EAST TIMOR
SRI LANKA
MALDIVES
NORTHERN MARIANA ISLANDS (to US)
PALAU
MICRO
PA NE GU
AUSTRAL
MOROCCO
ALGERIA
LIBYA
EGYPT
WESTERN SAHARA (disputed)
MAURITANIA
MALI
NIGER
CHAD
SUDAN
ERITREA
DJIBOUTI
ETHIOPIA
SOMALIA
CAPE VERDE
SENEGAL
GAMBIA
GUINEA-BISSAU
GUINEA
BURKINA FASO
NIGERIA
BENIN
SIERRA LEONE
LIBERIA
CÔTE D'IVOIRE (IVORY COAST)
GHANA
TOGO
CAMEROON
EQ. GUINEA
SAO TOME & PRINCIPE
GABON
CONGO
C.A.R.
UGANDA
KENYA
RWANDA
BURUNDI
DEM. REP. CONGO
TANZANIA
SEYCHELLES
COMOROS
MAYOTTE (to France)
ANGOLA
ZAMBIA
MALAWI
MOZAMBIQUE
MADAGASCAR
ZIMB.
NAMIBIA
BOTS.
MAURITIUS
REUNION (to France)
SWAZILAND
LESOTHO
SOUTH AFRICA
ATLANTIC OCEAN
INDIAN OCEAN
ANTARCTICA (uninhabited)
MAJORITY RELIGIONS
Protestant Christianity
Catholic Christianity
Orthodox Christianity
Shi'a Islam
Sunni Islam
Hinduism
Judaism
Theravada Buddhism
Mahayana Buddhism
Tibetan Buddhism
Other
Marxism / Maoism
STATE POLICY
▲ Secular ideologies governing
● Communist states during 20th century
■ Non-pluralist states

ARCTIC OCEAN
GREENLAND (to Denmark)
Arctic Circle
Alaska (to US)
CANADA
PACIFIC OCEAN
UNITED STATES OF AMERICA
ATLANTIC OCEAN
BERMUDA (to UK)
PUERTO RICO (to US)
DOM. REP.
TURKS & CAICOS ISLANDS (to UK)
CAYMAN ISLANDS (to UK)
BAHAMAS
HONDURAS
BELIZE
CUBA
JAMAICA
HAITI
NETH. ANT. (to Neth.)
ARUBA (to Neth.)
BRITISH VIRGIN ISLANDS (to UK)
VIRGIN ISLANDS (to US)
ANGUILLA (to UK)
ST KITTS & NEVIS
ANTIGUA & BARBUDA
MONTSERRAT (to UK)
GUADELOUPE (to France)
DOMINICA
MARTINIQUE (to France)
ST LUCIA
BARBADOS
ST VINCENT & THE GRENADINES
GRENADA
TRINIDAD & TOBAGO
FRENCH GUIANA (to France)
Tropic of Cancer
MEXICO
Hawaii (to US)
GUATEMALA
EL SALVADOR
NICARAGUA
COSTA RICA
PANAMA
VENEZUELA
COLOMBIA
GUYANA
SURINAME
Equator
ECUADOR
MARSHALL ISLANDS
KIRIBATI
TUVALU
TOKELAU (to NZ)
COOK ISLANDS (to NZ)
FIJI
TONGA
SAMOA
AMERICAN SAMOA (to US)
FRENCH POLYNESIA (to France)
PITCAIRN ISLANDS (to UK)
PERU
BRAZIL
BOLIVIA
PARAGUAY
Tropic of Capricorn
CHILE
ARGENTINA
URUGUAY
NEW ZEALAND
PACIFIC OCEAN
FALKLAND ISLANDS (to UK)
Antarctic Circle
ANTARCTICA
E
F
G
H
1
2
3
4
5

The Global Economy

E
F
G
H
1
2
3
4
5
CEAN
GREENLAND
(to Denmark)
Arctic Circle
Alaska
(to US)
CANADA
PACIFIC
OCEAN
UNITED STATES
OF AMERICA
ATLANTIC
OCEAN
BERMUDA
(to UK)
PUERTO RICO
(to US)
DOM. REP.
TURKS & CAICOS ISLANDS (to UK)
CAYMAN ISLANDS
(to UK)
BAHAMAS
ST KITTS & NEVIS
ANTIGUA & BARBUDA
Tropic of Cancer
MEXICO
HONDURAS
CUBA
GUADELOUPE (to France)
BELIZE
JAMAICA
DOMINICA
MARTINIQUE (to France)
Hawaii
(to US)
HAITI
NETH. ANT.
(to Neth.)
ST LUCIA
GUATEMALA
EL SALVADOR
ARUBA
(to Neth.)
BARBADOS
MARSHALL
ISLANDS
NICARAGUA
ST VINCENT &
THE GRENADINES
COSTA RICA
GRENADA
PANAMA
VENEZUELA
TRINIDAD & TOBAGO
COLOMBIA
FRENCH GUIANA
(to France)
Equator
NAURU
KIRIBATI
ECUADOR
GUYANA
SURINAME
TUVALU
TOKELAU
(to NZ)
LOMON
LANDS
SAMOA
PERU
BRAZIL
VANUATU
TONGA
BOLIVIA
NEW
EDONIA
France)
FIJI
FRENCH POLYNESIA
(to France)
PARAGUAY
Tropic of Capricorn
PITCAIRN
ISLANDS
(to UK)
CHILE
URUGUAY
ARGENTINA
NEW
ZEALAND
PACIFIC
OCEAN
FALKLAND ISLANDS
(to UK)
CHILE
Antarctic Circle
ANTARCTICA

Global Conflict

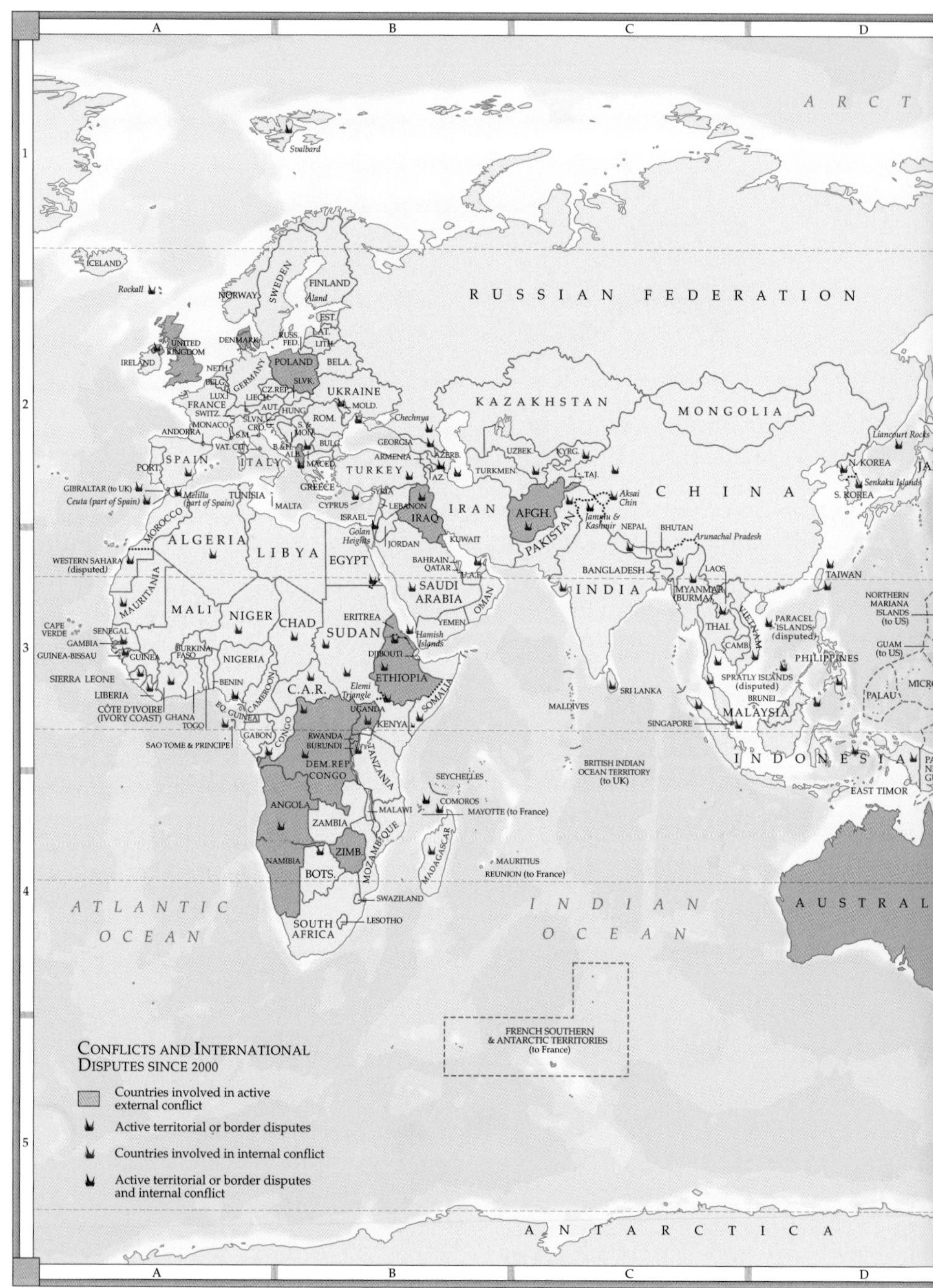

E
F
G
H
OCEAN
GREENLAND
(to Denmark)
Arctic Circle
Alaska
(to US)
CANADA
Kurile Islands
(part of Russ.Fed.)
ST PIERRE
& MIQUELON
(to France)
PACIFIC
OCEAN
UNITED STATES
OF AMERICA
ATLANTIC
OCEAN
BERMUDA
(to UK)
PUERTO RICO (to US)
DOM. REP.
BRITISH VIRGIN ISLANDS (to UK)
MEXICO
TURKS & CAICOS ISLANDS (to UK)
VIRGIN ISLANDS (to US)
ANGUILLA (to UK)
BAHAMAS
ST KITTS & NEVIS
Tropic of Cancer
GUANTANAMO BAY
(to US)
CUBA
ANTIGUA & BARBUDA
CAYMAN ISLANDS
(to UK)
MONTSERRAT (to UK)
Hawaii
(to US)
GUADELOUPE (to France)
BELIZE
JAMAICA
HAITI
DOMINICA
NAVASSA I.
(to US)
NETH. ANT.
(to Neth.)
MARTINIQUE (to France)
GUATEMALA
HONDURAS
ST LUCIA
ARUBA
(to Neth.)
BARBADOS
EL SALVADOR
ST VINCENT & THE GRENADINES
MARSHALL
ISLANDS
NICARAGUA
GRENADA
WALLIS & FUTUNA
(to France)
KINGMAN REEF (to US)
COSTA RICA
VENEZUELA
TRINIDAD & TOBAGO
PALMYRA ATOLL (to US)
PANAMA
FRENCH GUIANA
(to France)
BAKER &
HOWLAND
ISLANDS
(to US)
COLOMBIA
JARVIS ISLAND
(to US)
Equator
KIRIBATI
ECUADOR
GUYANA
SURINAME
TUVALU
TOKELAU
(to NZ)
COOK
ISLANDS
(to NZ)
BRAZIL
SOLOMON
ISLANDS
PERU
VANUATU
BOLIVIA
FIJI
FRENCH POLYNESIA
(to France)
PARAGUAY
Tropic of Capricorn
NEW
CALEDONIA
(to France)
TONGA
SAMOA
NIUE (to NZ)
AMERICAN
SAMOA
(to US)
PITCAIRN
ISLANDS
(to UK)
CHILE
URUGUAY
ARGENTINA
NEW
ZEALAND
PACIFIC
OCEAN
FALKLAND ISLANDS
(to UK)
CHILE
Antarctic Circle
ANTARCTICA
1
2
3
4
5

THE WORLD'S REGIONS

North & Central America

0 km 1000
0 miles 1000

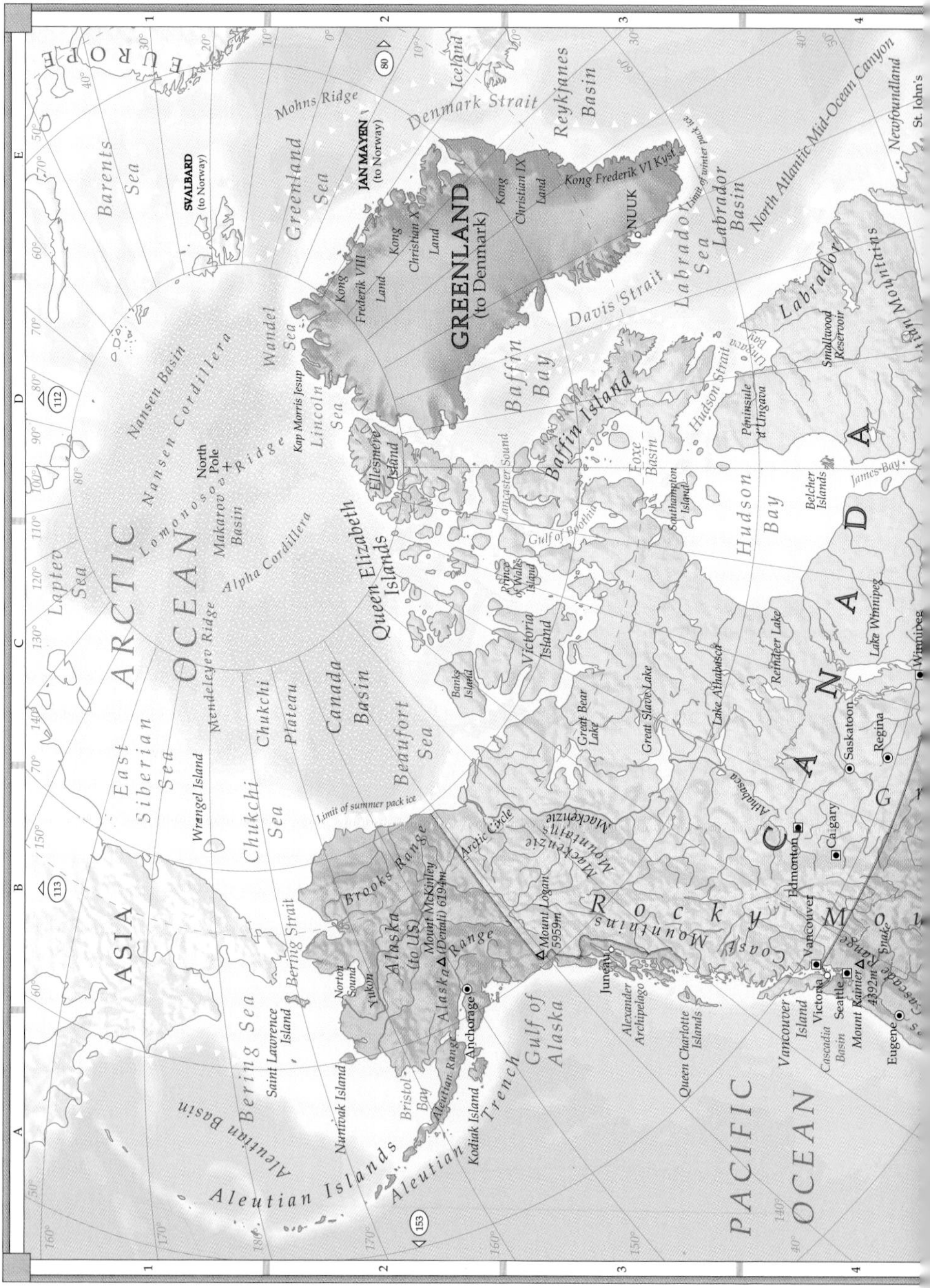

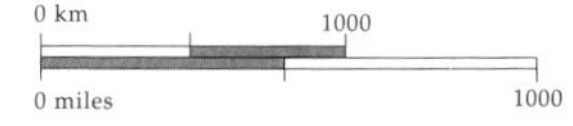

POPULATION
● National capital
○ Less than 50,000
○ 50,000 -100,000
◉ 100,000 - 500,000
▣ Over 500,000

UNITED STATES
OF AMERICA
MEXICO
ATLANTIC
OCEAN
PACIFIC
OCEAN
SOUTH
AMERICA
Gulf of Mexico
Caribbean Sea
Sargasso Sea
Gulf of California
Lower California
Mount Whitney 4418m
Death Valley -86m
Grand Canyon
Colorado
Los Angeles
San Diego
Phoenix
El Paso
Denver
Des Moines
Lincoln
Topeka
Missouri
Madison
Chicago
Milwaukee
Toronto
Lansing
Detroit
Lake Ontario
Niagara Falls
Lake Erie
Albany
Georges Bank
Boston
Cape Cod
Halifax
New York
Philadelphia
Baltimore
WASHINGTON D.C.
Richmond
Cleveland
Columbus
Indianapolis
Ohio
Springfield
Oklahoma City
Arkansas
Nashville
Appalachian Mountains
Raleigh
Little Rock
Memphis
Red River
Mississippi
Dallas
Atlanta
Columbia
Jackson
Montgomery
Austin
San Antonio
Houston
Baton Rouge
Jacksonville
Blake Plateau
New Orleans
Mississippi Delta
Tampa
Rio Grande
Sierra Madre Occidental
Sierra Madre Oriental
Monterrey
Guadalajara
MEXICO CITY
Volcán Pico de Orizaba 5700m
Acapulco
Middle America Trench
Revillagigedo Islands (to Mexico)
Clarion Fracture Zone
Fracture Zone
Tropic of Cancer
BERMUDA (to UK)
Bermuda Rise
Hatteras Plain
Nares Plain
Miami
Straits of Florida
BAHAMAS
NASSAU
HAVANA
CUBA
Greater Antilles
Yucatan Peninsula
Guantanamo Bay (to US)
PORT-AU-PRINCE
HAITI
DOMINICAN REPUBLIC
SANTO DOMINGO
PUERTO RICO (to US)
TURKS & CAICOS ISLANDS (to UK)
VIRGIN ISLANDS (to US)
BRITISH VIRGIN ISLANDS (to UK)
ANGUILLA (to UK)
ANTIGUA & BARBUDA
GUADELOUPE (to France)
DOMINICA
Lesser Antilles
ST KITTS & NEVIS
MONTSERRAT (to UK)
MARTINIQUE (to France)
ST LUCIA
BARBADOS
ST VINCENT & THE GRENADINES
GRENADA
PORT-OF-SPAIN
TRINIDAD & TOBAGO
ARUBA (to Neth.)
NETHERLANDS ANTILLES (to Neth.)
CAYMAN ISLANDS (to UK)
JAMAICA
KINGSTON
BELMOPAN
BELIZE
GUATEMALA
GUATEMALA CITY
HONDURAS
TEGUCIGALPA
SAN SALVADOR
EL SALVADOR
NICARAGUA
MANAGUA
Lake Nicaragua
COSTA RICA
SAN JOSÉ
PANAMA CITY
PANAMA
Colombian Basin
CLIPPERTON ISLAND (to French Polynesia)
Guatemala Basin
Colón Ridge
Cocos Ridge
Panama Basin
East Pacific Rise
Gallego Rise
Galapagos Islands (to Ecuador)
Andes
Equator
N

Western Canada & Alaska

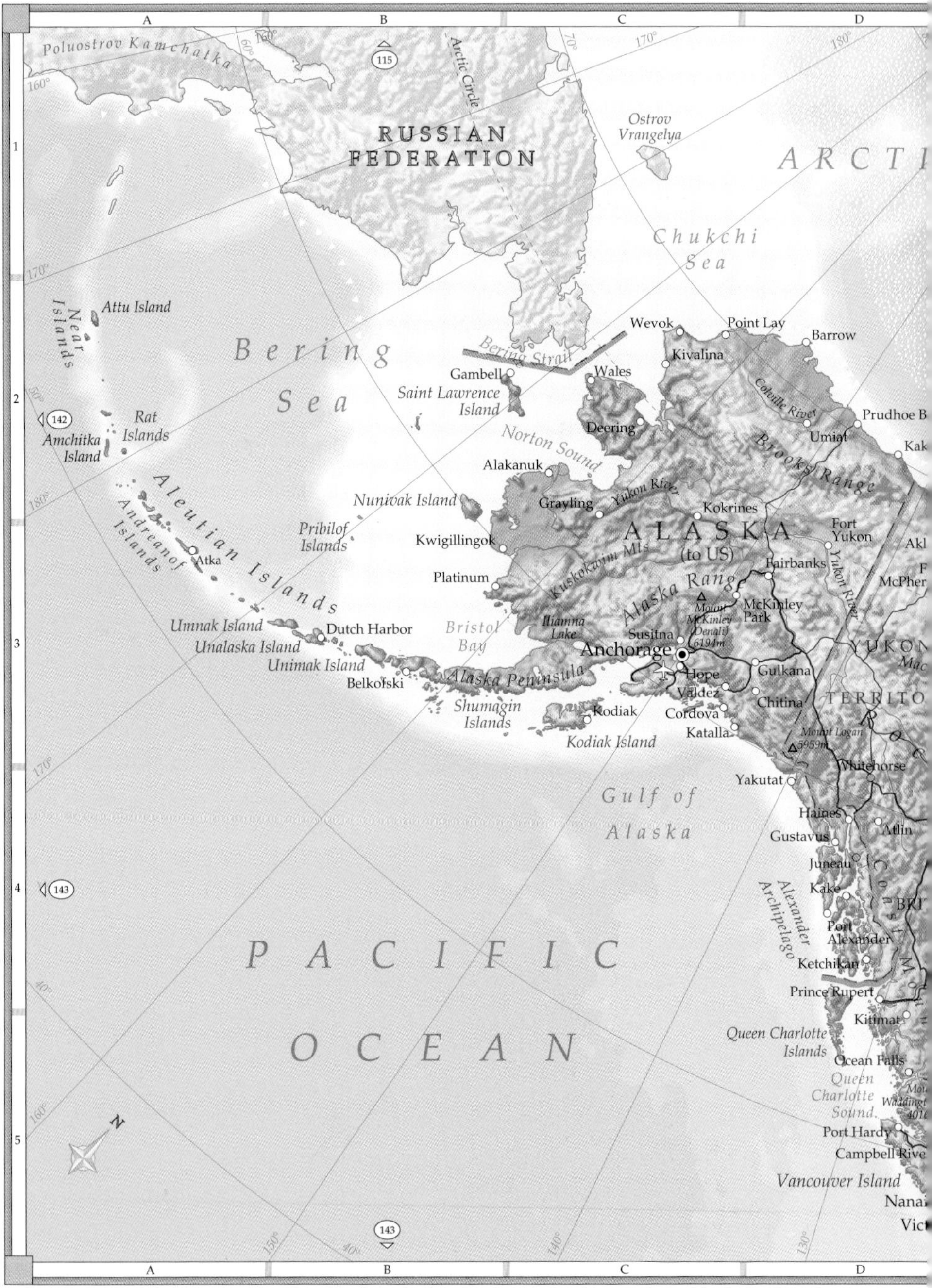

A B C D

1 2 3 4 5

Poluostrov Kamchatka
115
Arctic Circle
RUSSIAN FEDERATION
Ostrov Vrangelya
ARCTI
Chukchi Sea
Attu Island
Near Islands
Bering Sea
Bering Strait
Wevok
Point Lay
Barrow
Kivalina
Gambell
Wales
Saint Lawrence Island
Colville River
Prudhoe B
142
Rat Islands
Amchitka Island
Deering
Umiat
Norton Sound
Brooks Range
Kak
Alakanuk
Aleutian Islands
Andreanof Islands
Nunivak Island
Grayling
Yukon River
Kokrines
Pribilof Islands
Kwigillingok
ALASKA (to US)
Fort Yukon
Akl
Atka
Kuskokwim Mts
Fairbanks
Platinum
Alaska Range
Yukon River
McPher
Mount McKinley (Denali) 6194m
McKinley Park
Umnak Island
Dutch Harbor
Bristol Bay
Iliamna Lake
Susitna
Unalaska Island
Anchorage
YUKON
Unimak Island
Hope
Gulkana
Belkofski
Alaska Peninsula
Valdez
Chitina
TERRITO
Shumagin Islands
Kodiak
Cordova
Kodiak Island
Katalla
Mount Logan 5959m
Whitehorse
Yakutat
Gulf of Alaska
Haines
Atlin
Gustavus
Juneau
143
Kake
Alexander Archipelago
Port Alexander
PACIFIC OCEAN
Ketchikan
Prince Rupert
Kitimat
Queen Charlotte Islands
Ocean Falls
Queen Charlotte Sound
Mount Waddington 4016
Port Hardy
N
Campbell River
Vancouver Island
Nanai
Vict
143

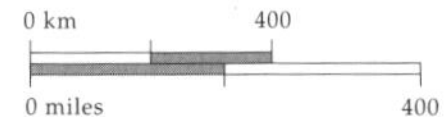

POPULATION

○ Less than 50,000 ○ 50,000 -100,000 ⊙ 100,000 - 500,000 ▣ Over 500,000

● Internal administrative capital

GREENLAND
(to Denmark)
Knud Rasmussen Land
Baffin Bay
Davis Strait
Baffin Island
Cumberland Sound
Iqaluit
Hudson Strait
Foxe Basin
Southampton Island
Coral Harbour
Hudson Bay
Péninsule d'Ungava
QUÉBEC
Belcher Islands
James Bay
ONTARIO
MANITOBA
SASKATCHEWAN
ALBERTA
NUNAVUT
NORTHWEST TERRITORIES
CANADA
UNITED STATES OF AMERICA
Queen Elizabeth Islands
Ellesmere Island
Axel Heiberg Island
Ellef Ringnes Island
Amund Ringnes Island
Prince Patrick Island
Melville Island
Bathurst Island
Cornwallis Island
Devon Island
Lancaster Sound
Banks Island
Victoria Island
Somerset Island
Prince of Wales Island
Boothia Peninsula
Gulf of Boothia
Melville Peninsula
King William Island
Alert
Isachsen
Mould Bay
Resolute
Holman
Cambridge Bay
Gjoa Haven
Pelly Bay
Igloolik
Repulse Bay
Kugluktuk
Baker Lake
Rankin Inlet
Whale Cove
Arviat
Churchill
Yellowknife
Fort Simpson
Hay River
Fort Smith
Lake Athabasca
Reindeer Lake
Wollaston Lake
Thompson
Flin Flon
The Pas
Lake Winnipeg
Edmonton
Saskatoon
Calgary
Regina
Winnipeg
Prince Albert
Red Deer
Leduc
Lethbridge
Medicine Hat
Brandon
Weyburn
Estevan
Melita
Kamloops
Kelowna
Cranbrook
Milk River
Lake of the Woods
Lake Superior
Lake Michigan
Lake Huron
Great Slave Lake
Great Bear Lake
Echo Bay
Fort McMurray
Fort St. John
Grande Prairie
Athabasca
Mount Robson 3954m
Fort Vermilion
Fort Nelson
Fort Liard
Fort Providence
Edzo
Reliance
Lutselk'e
Paulatuk
Amundsen Gulf
Viscount Melville Sound
McClintock Channel
Garry Lake
Fox Mine
Buffalo Narrows
Kindersley
Yorkton
Lake Manitoba
Southern Indian Lake
Coats Island
Mansel Island
Nettilling Lake
Amadjuak Lake
Arctic Circle
ELEVATION
Below sea level
0 100m 250m 500m 1000m 2000m 4000m
328ft 820ft 1640ft 3281ft 6562ft 13 124ft
-4000m -3000m -2000m -1000m -500m
-13 124ft -9843ft -6562ft -3281ft -1640ft -820ft/-250m 0

EASTERN CANADA

0 km 400
0 miles 400

POPULATION
● National capital
● Internal administrative capital
○ Less than 50,000
○ 50,000 -100,000
◉ 100,000 - 500,000
▣ Over 500,000

Baffin Island
Resolution Island
Button Islands
Akpatok Island
Ungava Bay
Labrador Sea
Nain
Hopedale
Makkovik
Cape Harrison
Cartwright
Labrador
NEWFOUNDLAND & LABRADOR
Schefferville
Smallwood Reservoir
Churchill
Lake Melville
St.Anthony
Strait of Belle Isle
Réservoir Manicouagan
Laurentian Mountains
Havre-St-Pierre
Sept-Îles
Île d'Anticosti
Corner Brook
Gander
Grand Falls
St.John's
Newfoundland
Cape Race
Channel-Port aux Basques
Baie-Comeau
Gaspé
Gulf of St. Lawrence
Péninsule de Gaspé
St.Lawrence
Matane
Îles de la Madeleine
Cabot Strait
ST PIERRE & MIQUELON
(to France)
Chicoutimi
Rimouski
Bathurst
PRINCE EDWARD ISLAND
Rivière-du-Loup
Edmundston
Glace Bay
Sydney
Charlottetown
NEW BRUNSWICK
Charlesbourg
Québec
Moncton
Amherst
Cape Breton Island
New Glasgow
Oromocto
Truro
St-Georges
Fredericton
NOVA SCOTIA
Drummondville
Saint John
MAINE
Bay of Fundy
Dartmouth
Halifax
Sable Island
Sherbrooke
Liverpool
Yarmouth
ATLANTIC OCEAN
NEW HAMPSHIRE
Cape Cod
RHODE ISLAND
ELEVATION
Below sea level
-4000m -3000m -2000m -1000m -500m 0
-13 124ft -9843ft -6562ft -3281ft -1640ft -820ft/-250m 0
100m 250m 500m 1000m 2000m 4000m
328ft 820ft 1640ft 3281ft 6562ft 13 124ft

USA: THE NORTHEAST

A B C D
1 2 3 4 5

95° 90° 85°

Upper Red Lake
Lower Red Lake
Namakan Lake
38
CANADA
ONTARIO
Isle Royale
Lake Superior
Keweenaw Peninsula
MINNESOTA
Apostle Islands
Superior
Houghton
Gogebic Range
Ashland
Ironwood
Marquette
MICHIGAN
Mille Lacs Lake
Saint Croix River
Sault Sainte Marie
Woodruff
Rice Lake
Iron Mountain
Rhinelander
Escanaba
Saint Ignace
North Channel
Georgian
45°
Ladysmith
Beaver Island
Cheboygan
WISCONSIN
Petoskey
Lake Huron
45
River Falls
Eau Claire
Wausau
Door Peninsula
Green Bay
Traverse City
Alpena
Mississippi River
Stevens Point
Lake Michigan
Wisconsin Rapids
Green Bay
Beulah
Roscommon
Appleton
Cadillac
Tomah
Oshkosh
Lake Winnebago
Saginaw Bay
La Crosse
Fond du Lac
Ludington
Sheboygan
Midland
Bay City
West Bend
Wisconsin River
Mount Pleasant
Saginaw
Madison
Milwaukee
Muskegon
Waukesha
Grand Rapids
Flint
Port Huron
Janesville
Racine
Wyoming
IOWA
Kenosha
Lansing
Pontiac
Lake Saint Clair
Rockford
Waukegan
Kalamazoo
Livonia
Warren
Detroit
Lake Erie
Elgin
Evanston
Ann Arbor
Sterling
Chicago
South Bend
Adrian
Aurora
Toledo
Rock Island
Joliet
Gary
Elkhart
Cleveland
Euclid
Ottawa
Valparaiso
Bowling Green
Sandusky
Galesburg
Kankakee
Fort Wayne
Findlay
Akron
Peoria
Wabash
Van Wert
Mansfield
Youngstown
Macomb
Bloomington
INDIANA
Marion
Canton
40°
Illinois River
Pekin
Lafayette
Kokomo
Aliquippa
Quincy
Champaign
Anderson
Muncie
OHIO
Sidney
Delaware
Wheeling
Springfield
Carmel
Springfield
Cambridge
45
Jacksonville
Decatur
Indianapolis
Columbus
Zanesville
ILLINOIS
Terre Haute
Dayton
Kettering
Wilmington
Ohio River
Effingham
Columbus
Chillicothe
Athens
Alton
Bloomington
Cincinnati
Clarksburg
Parkersburg
Lake of the Ozarks
Missouri River
East Saint Louis
Vincennes
Newport
Portsmouth
WEST VIRGINIA
Mount Vernon
Wabash River
Ohio River
Belleville
New Albany
Louisville
Huntington
Charleston
MISSOURI
Mississippi River
Evansville
Frankfort
Lexington
Saint Albans
Carbondale
Owensboro
Henderson
Elizabethtown
Richmond
Beckley
Ozark Plateau
Mississippi River
Paducah
KENTUCKY
Alton
Green River
Pikeville
Bluefield
Pulaski
Somerset
London
Hopkinsville
Bowling Green
Kentucky Lake
Middlesboro
Bristol
Appalachian
42
ARKANSAS
TENNESSEE
90°
85°

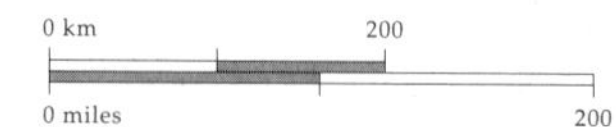

POPULATION
● National capital
● Internal administrative capital
○ Less than 50,000
○ 50,000 -100,000
◉ 100,000 - 500,000
■ Over 500,000

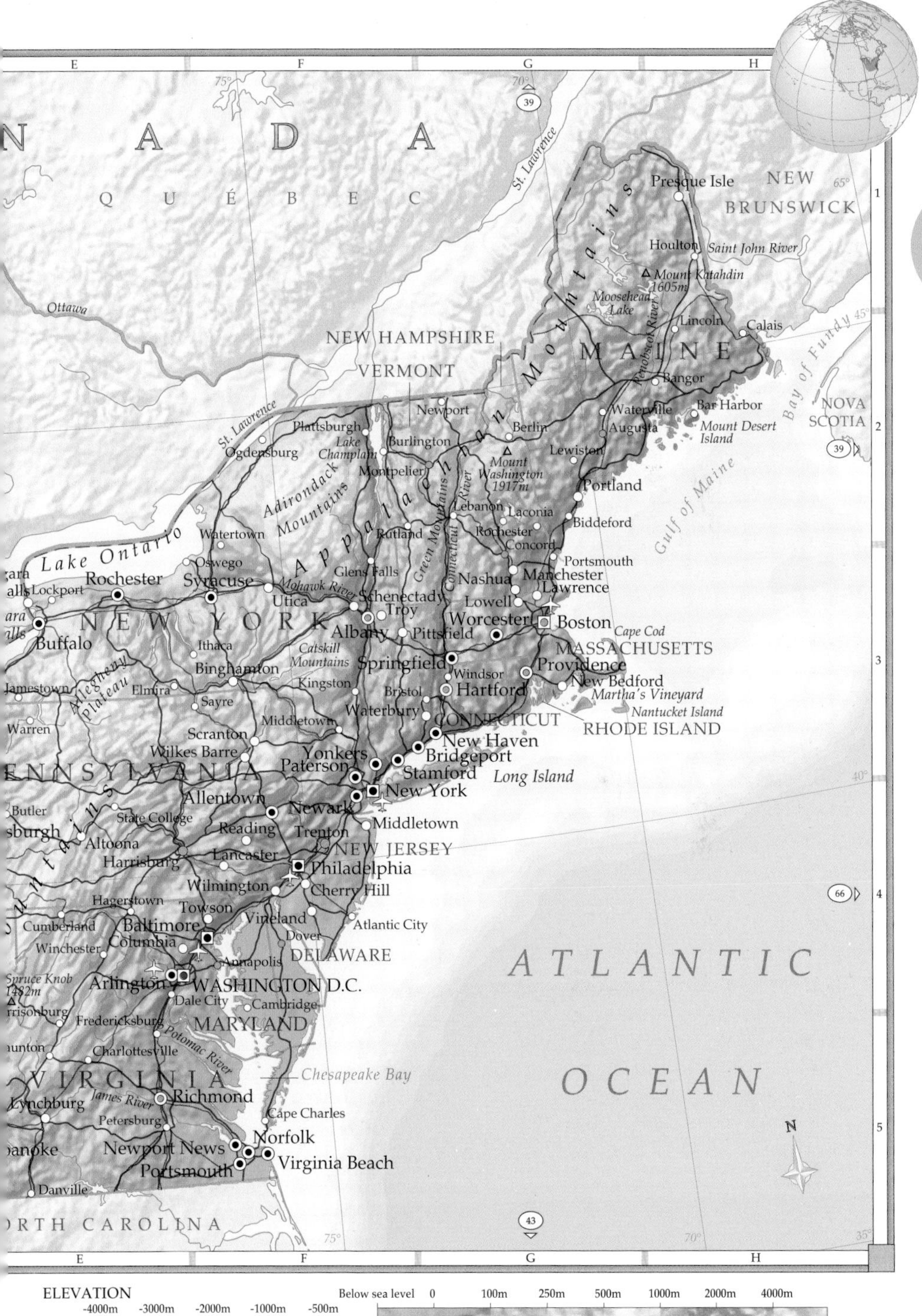

ELEVATION

Below sea level						0	100m	250m	500m	1000m	2000m	4000m
-4000m	-3000m	-2000m	-1000m	-500m								
-13 124ft	-9843ft	-6562ft	-3281ft	-1640ft	-820ft/-250m	0	328ft	820ft	1640ft	3281ft	6562ft	13 124ft

USA: THE SOUTHEAST

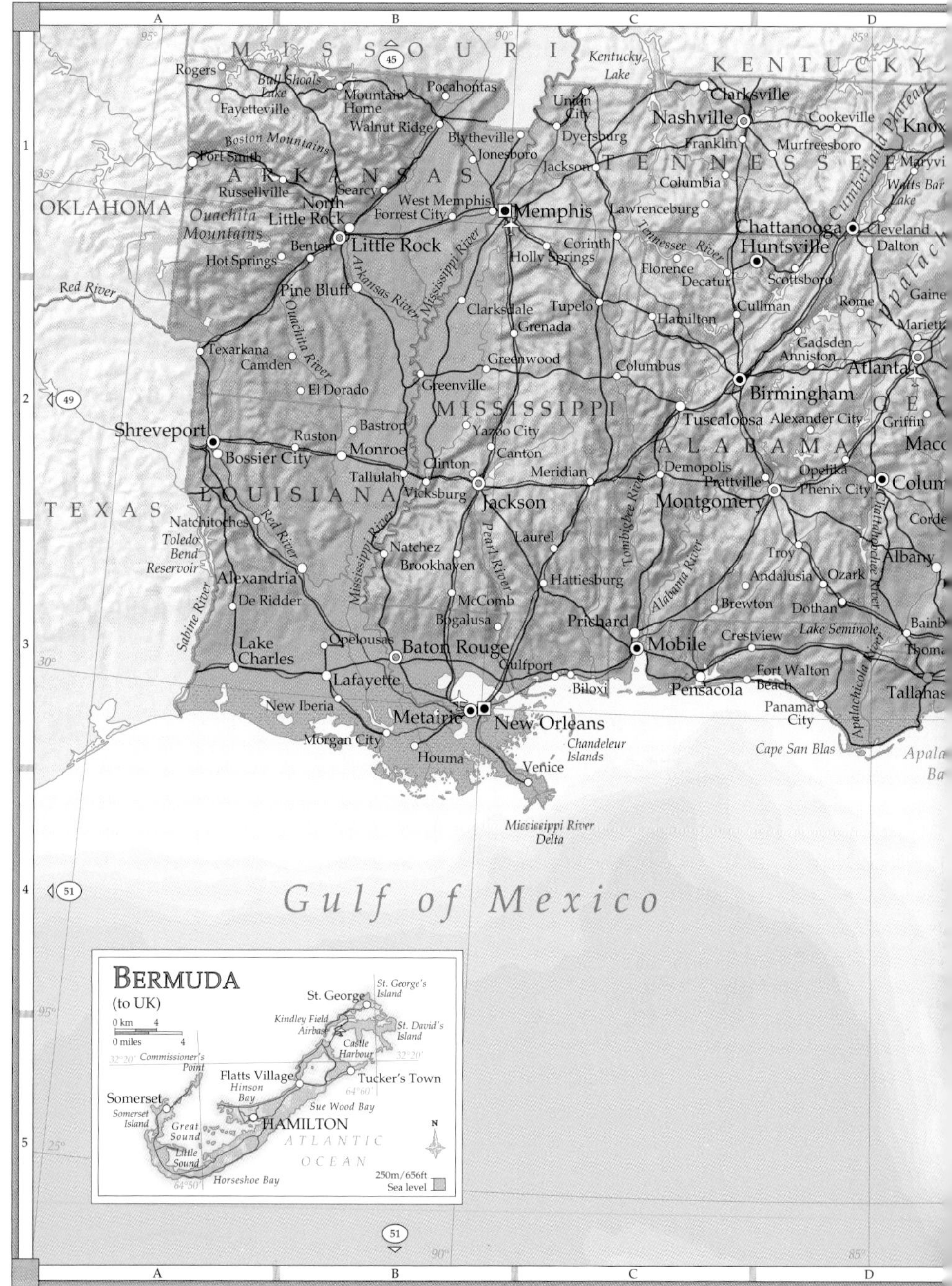

0 km 200

0 miles 200

POPULATION

○ Less than 50,000 ○ 50,000 -100,000 ◉ 100,000 - 500,000 ◼ Over 500,000

● Internal administrative capital

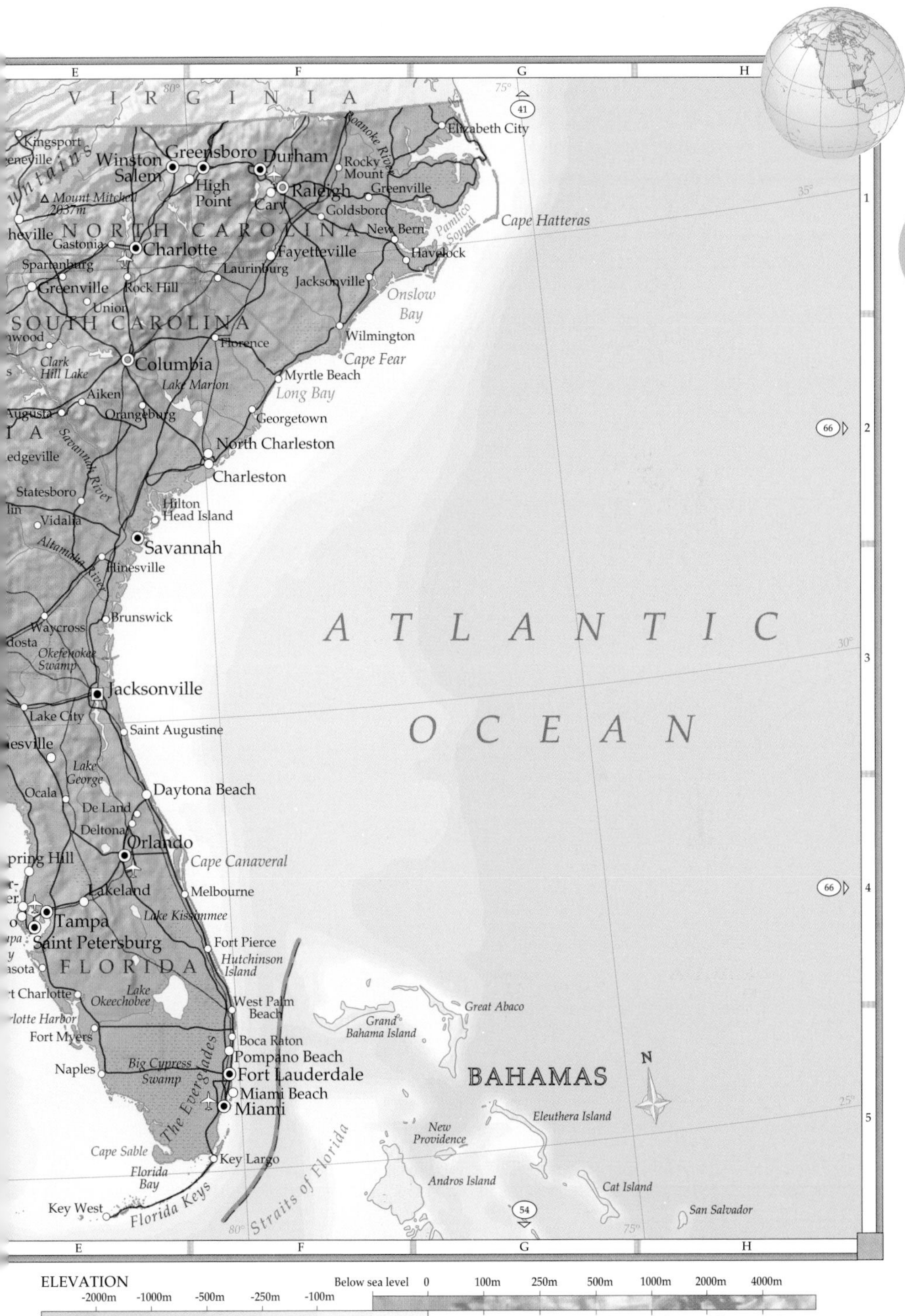

VIRGINIA
NORTH CAROLINA
SOUTH CAROLINA
FLORIDA
BAHAMAS
ATLANTIC OCEAN
Elizabeth City
Kingsport
Winston Salem
Greensboro
Durham
High Point
Rocky Mount
Raleigh
Cary
Greenville
Goldsboro
New Bern
Mount Mitchell 2037m
Gastonia
Charlotte
Havelock
Fayetteville
Spartanburg
Laurinburg
Jacksonville
Greenville
Rock Hill
Union
Onslow Bay
Pamlico Sound
Cape Hatteras
Roanoke River
Florence
Wilmington
Cape Fear
Columbia
Clark Hill Lake
Lake Marion
Myrtle Beach
Long Bay
Aiken
Augusta
Orangeburg
Georgetown
Savannah River
North Charleston
Charleston
Statesboro
Hilton Head Island
Vidalia
Savannah
Altamaha River
Hinesville
Brunswick
Waycross
Okefenokee Swamp
Jacksonville
Lake City
Saint Augustine
Lake George
Ocala
Daytona Beach
De Land
Deltona
Orlando
Cape Canaveral
Lakeland
Melbourne
Tampa
Lake Kissimmee
Saint Petersburg
Fort Pierce
Hutchinson Island
Lake Okeechobee
West Palm Beach
Fort Myers
Boca Raton
Pompano Beach
Naples
Big Cypress Swamp
Fort Lauderdale
Miami Beach
Miami
The Everglades
Cape Sable
Key Largo
Florida Bay
Key West
Florida Keys
Straits of Florida
Grand Bahama Island
Great Abaco
Eleuthera Island
New Providence
Andros Island
Cat Island
San Salvador
E
F
G
H
1
2
3
4
5
41
66
54
80°
75°
35°
30°
25°
N
ELEVATION
Below sea level
0
100m
250m
500m
1000m
2000m
4000m
328ft
820ft
1640ft
3281ft
6562ft
13 124ft
-2000m
-1000m
-500m
-250m
-100m
-6562ft
-3281ft
-1640ft
-820ft
-328ft
-164ft/-50m

USA: Central States

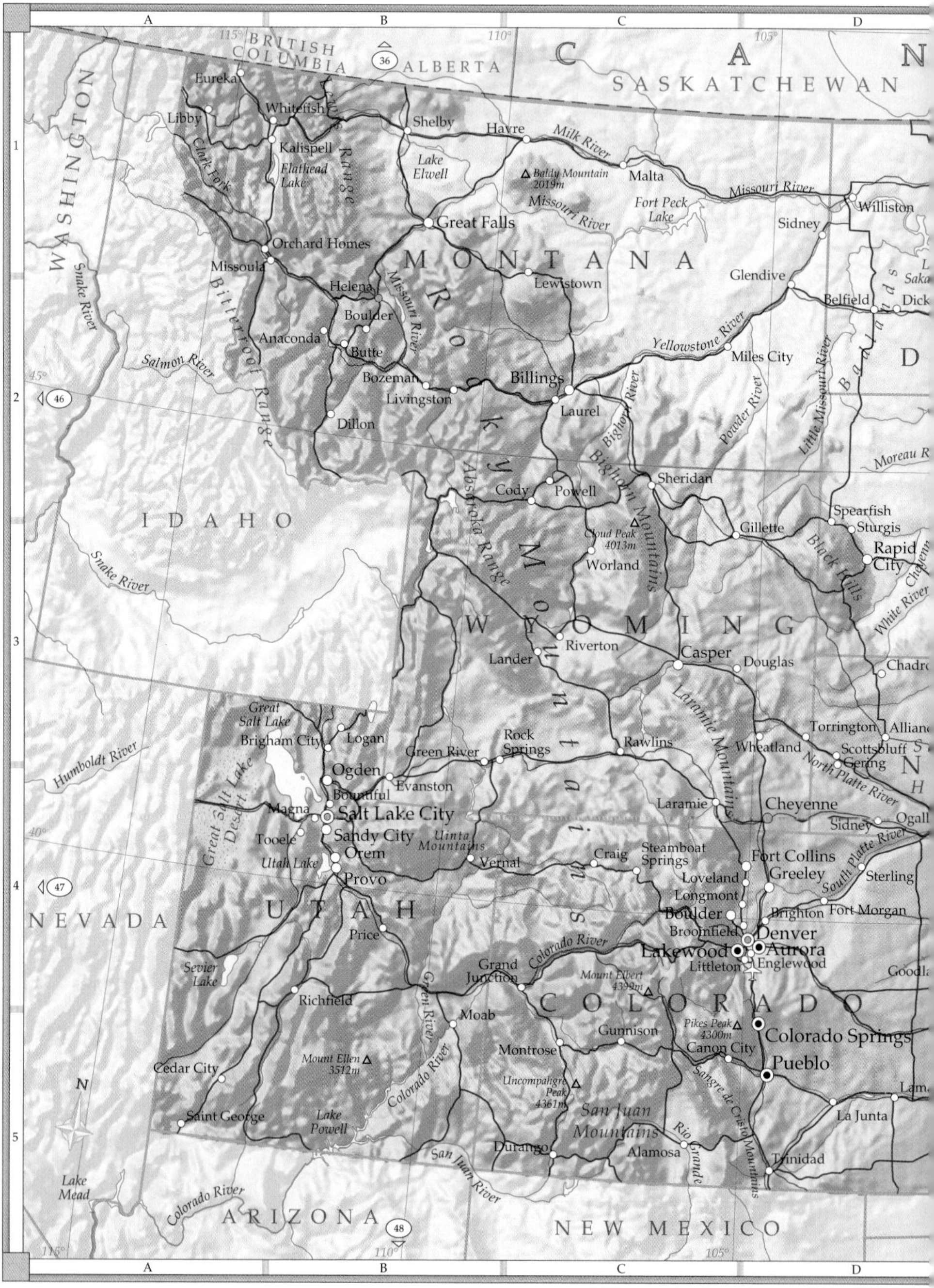

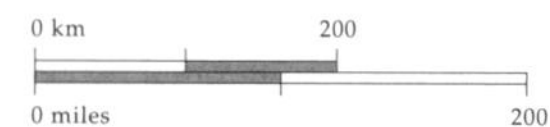

POPULATION

- ○ Less than 50,000
- ○ 50,000 -100,000
- ◉ 100,000 - 500,000
- ▣ Over 500,000
- ● Internal administrative capital

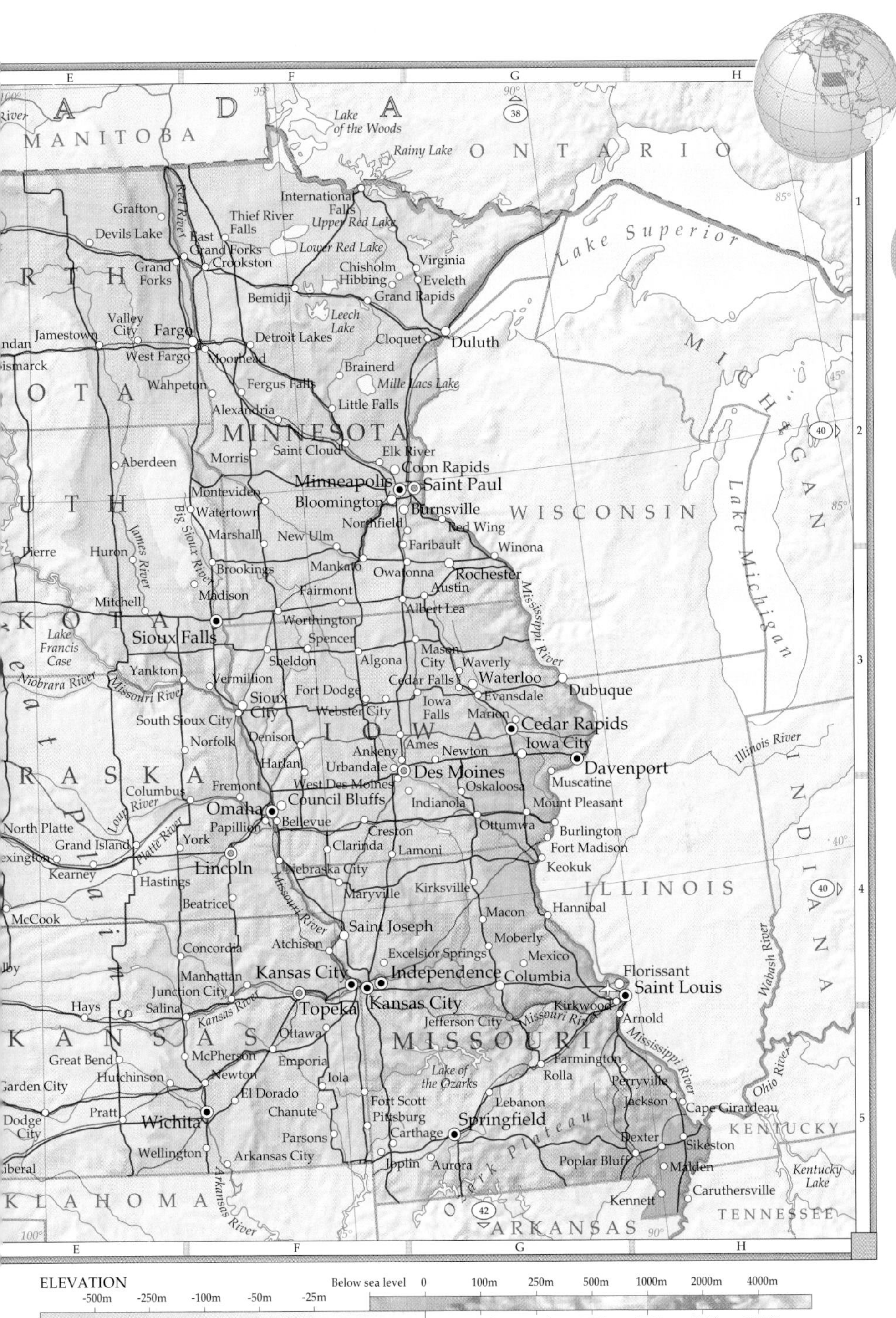
CANADA
MANITOBA
ONTARIO
Lake of the Woods
Rainy Lake
International Falls
Upper Red Lake
Lower Red Lake
Thief River Falls
Grafton
Devils Lake
East Grand Forks
Crookston
Grand Forks
NORTH DAKOTA
Chisholm
Hibbing
Virginia
Eveleth
Grand Rapids
Bemidji
Leech Lake
Lake Superior
Valley City
Jamestown
Fargo
Detroit Lakes
Cloquet
Duluth
West Fargo
Moorhead
Bismarck
Brainerd
Wahpeton
Fergus Falls
Mille Lacs Lake
Alexandria
Little Falls
MINNESOTA
Saint Cloud
Elk River
Morris
Aberdeen
Coon Rapids
Minneapolis
Saint Paul
Montevideo
Bloomington
Burnsville
Watertown
Big Sioux River
Northfield
Red Wing
WISCONSIN
MICHIGAN
Lake Michigan
SOUTH DAKOTA
James River
Marshall
New Ulm
Faribault
Winona
Pierre
Huron
Brookings
Mankato
Owatonna
Rochester
Austin
Fairmont
Madison
Mitchell
Albert Lea
Mississippi River
Lake Francis Case
Sioux Falls
Worthington
Spencer
Mason City
Sheldon
Algona
Waverly
Yankton
Niobrara River
Missouri River
Vermillion
Cedar Falls
Waterloo
Dubuque
Fort Dodge
Evansdale
Sioux City
Webster City
Iowa Falls
Marion
South Sioux City
Cedar Rapids
IOWA
Norfolk
Denison
Ames
Newton
Iowa City
Illinois River
Ankeny
Davenport
Harlan
Urbandale
Des Moines
NEBRASKA
Fremont
West Des Moines
Oskaloosa
Muscatine
Columbus
Loup River
Council Bluffs
Omaha
Indianola
Mount Pleasant
Bellevue
North Platte
Papillion
Ottumwa
Burlington
Platte River
York
Creston
Grand Island
Clarinda
Lamoni
Fort Madison
Lexington
Lincoln
Keokuk
Kearney
Nebraska City
Hastings
ILLINOIS
INDIANA
Maryville
Kirksville
Beatrice
Macon
Hannibal
McCook
Saint Joseph
Wabash River
Atchison
Moberly
Concordia
Excelsior Springs
Mexico
Florissant
Manhattan
Kansas City
Independence
Columbia
Saint Louis
Junction City
Hays
Salina
Topeka
Kirkwood
Kansas River
Jefferson City
Arnold
KANSAS
Ottawa
MISSOURI
McPherson
Great Bend
Emporia
Farmington
Hutchinson
Newton
Lake of the Ozarks
Rolla
Perryville
Iola
Garden City
El Dorado
Jackson
Ohio River
Fort Scott
Lebanon
Cape Girardeau
Chanute
Pratt
Pittsburg
Springfield
KENTUCKY
Dodge City
Wichita
Carthage
Ozark Plateau
Dexter
Parsons
Sikeston
Wellington
Arkansas City
Poplar Bluff
Joplin
Aurora
Malden
Kentucky Lake
Liberal
Caruthersville
OKLAHOMA
Kennett
Arkansas River
TENNESSEE
ARKANSAS
ELEVATION
Below sea level
-500m
-250m
-100m
-50m
-25m
0
100m
250m
500m
1000m
2000m
4000m
-1640ft
-820ft
-328ft
-164ft
-82ft
33ft/-10m
0
328ft
820ft
1640ft
3281ft
6562ft
13 124ft

USA: The West

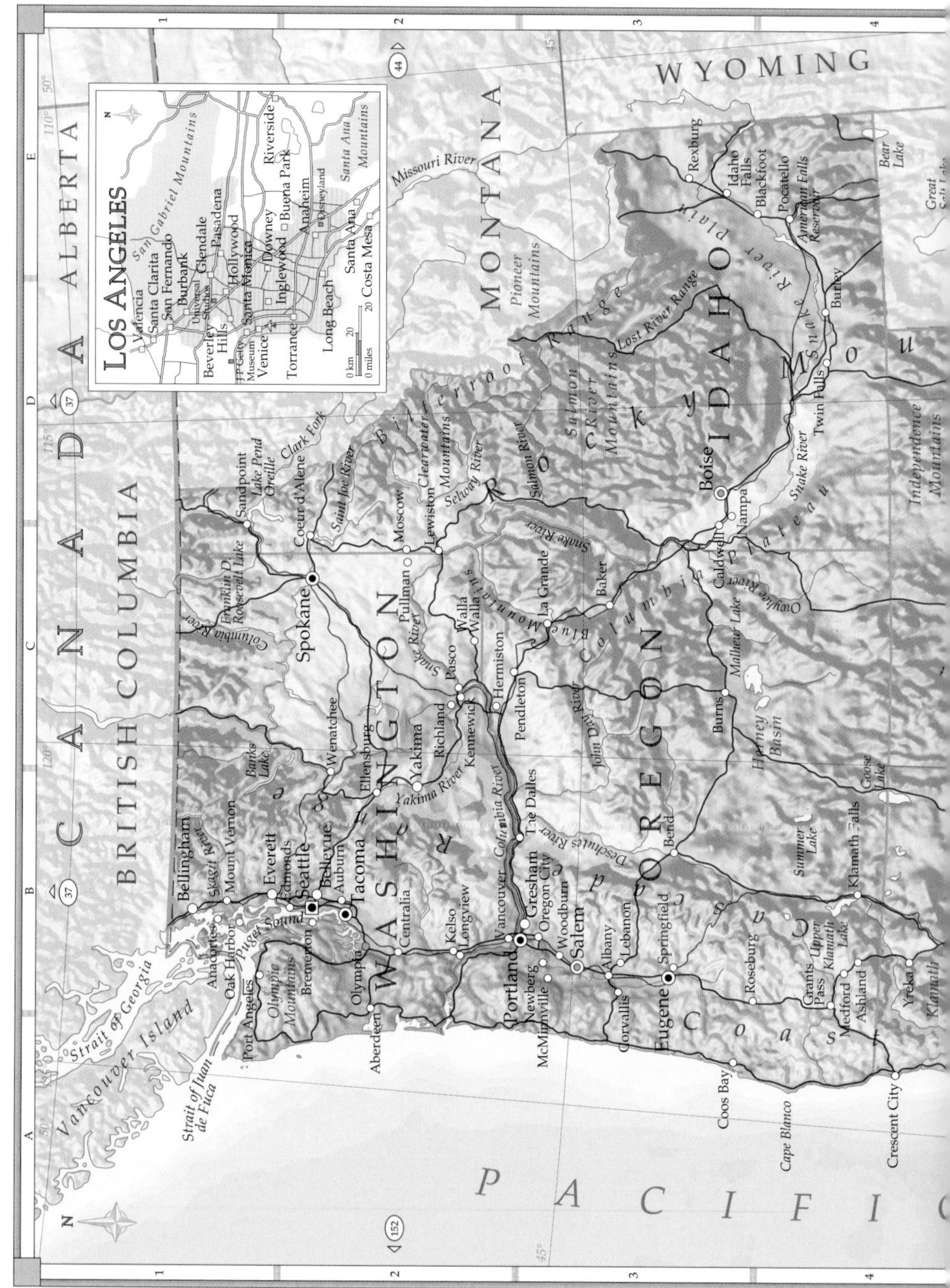

0 km 200
0 miles 200

POPULATION

○ Less than 50,000
○ 50,000 -100,000
◉ 100,000 - 500,000
▣ Over 500,000
● Internal administrative capital

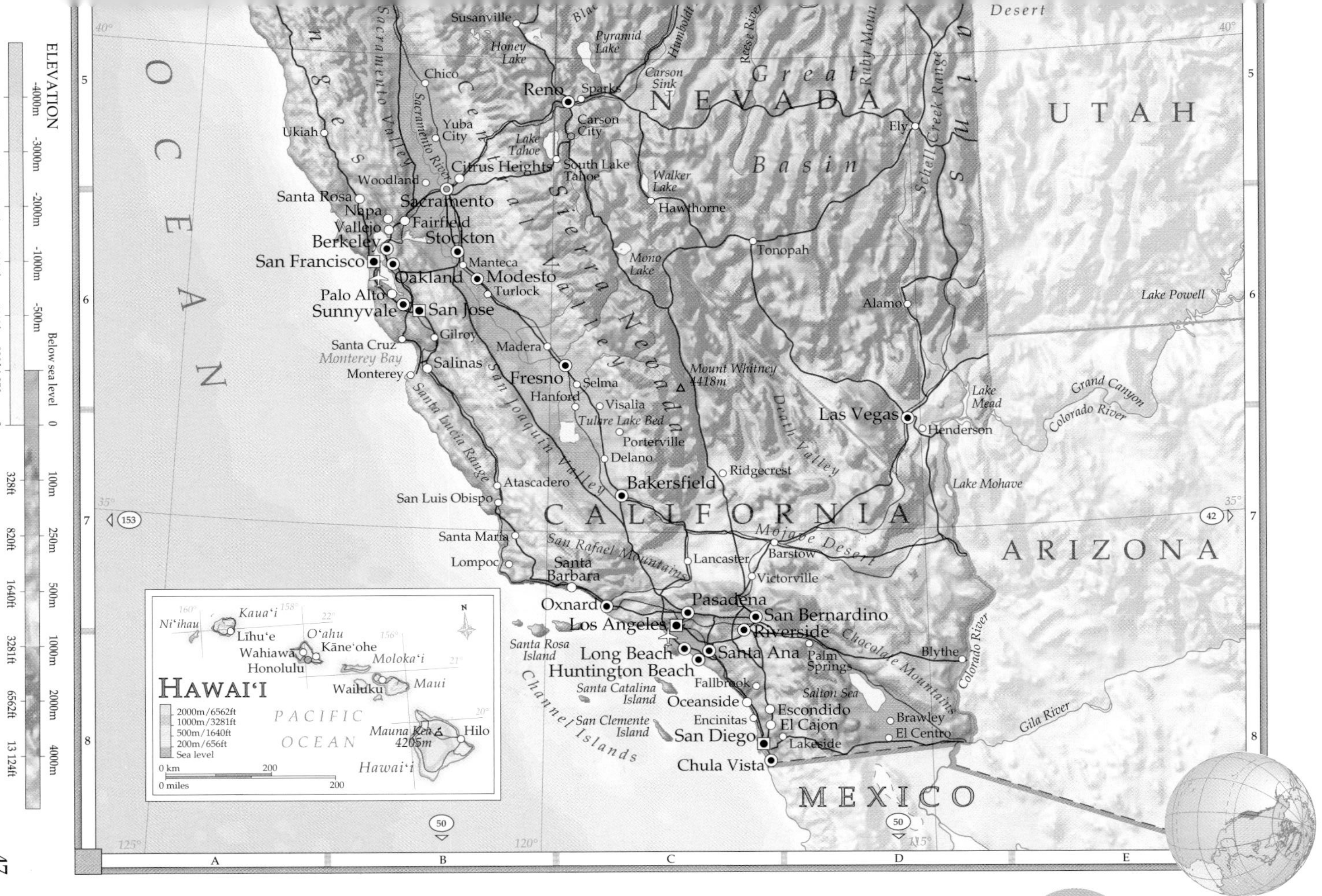
UTAH
NEVADA
ARIZONA
CALIFORNIA
MEXICO
OCEAN
Great Basin
Sierra Nevada
Central Valley
San Joaquin Valley
Sacramento Valley
Sacramento River
Death Valley
Mojave Desert
Mount Whitney 4418m
Lake Powell
Grand Canyon
Colorado River
Lake Mead
Lake Mohave
Gila River
Chocolate Mountains
Salton Sea
Channel Islands
Santa Rosa Island
Santa Catalina Island
San Clemente Island
Santa Lucia Range
San Rafael Mountains
Monterey Bay
Tulare Lake Bed
Mono Lake
Walker Lake
Carson Sink
Pyramid Lake
Honey Lake
Lake Tahoe
Schell Creek Range
Ruby Moun
Reese River
Humboldt
Desert
Reno
Sparks
Carson City
South Lake Tahoe
Susanville
Chico
Yuba City
Citrus Heights
Sacramento
Woodland
Fairfield
Stockton
Manteca
Modesto
Turlock
Napa
Vallejo
Santa Rosa
Ukiah
Berkeley
Oakland
San Francisco
Palo Alto
Sunnyvale
San Jose
Gilroy
Santa Cruz
Salinas
Monterey
Madera
Fresno
Selma
Hanford
Visalia
Porterville
Delano
Bakersfield
Atascadero
San Luis Obispo
Santa Maria
Lompoc
Santa Barbara
Oxnard
Los Angeles
Pasadena
Long Beach
Huntington Beach
Santa Ana
Riverside
San Bernardino
Lancaster
Victorville
Barstow
Ridgecrest
Palm Springs
Fallbrook
Oceanside
Encinitas
Escondido
El Cajon
Lakeside
San Diego
Chula Vista
Brawley
El Centro
Blythe
Las Vegas
Henderson
Alamo
Tonopah
Hawthorne
Ely
HAWAIʻI
Niʻihau
Kauaʻi
Līhuʻe
Oʻahu
Wahiawa
Kāneʻohe
Honolulu
Molokaʻi
Maui
Wailuku
Hawaiʻi
Mauna Kea 4205m
Hilo
PACIFIC OCEAN
2000m/6562ft
1000m/3281ft
500m/1640ft
200m/656ft
Sea level
0 km 200
0 miles 200
ELEVATION
Below sea level 0
-4000m -3000m -2000m -1000m -500m
100m 250m 500m 1000m 2000m 4000m
-13 124ft -9843ft -6562ft -3281ft -1640ft -820ft/-250m 0
328ft 820ft 1640ft 3281ft 6562ft 13 124ft

USA: THE SOUTHWEST

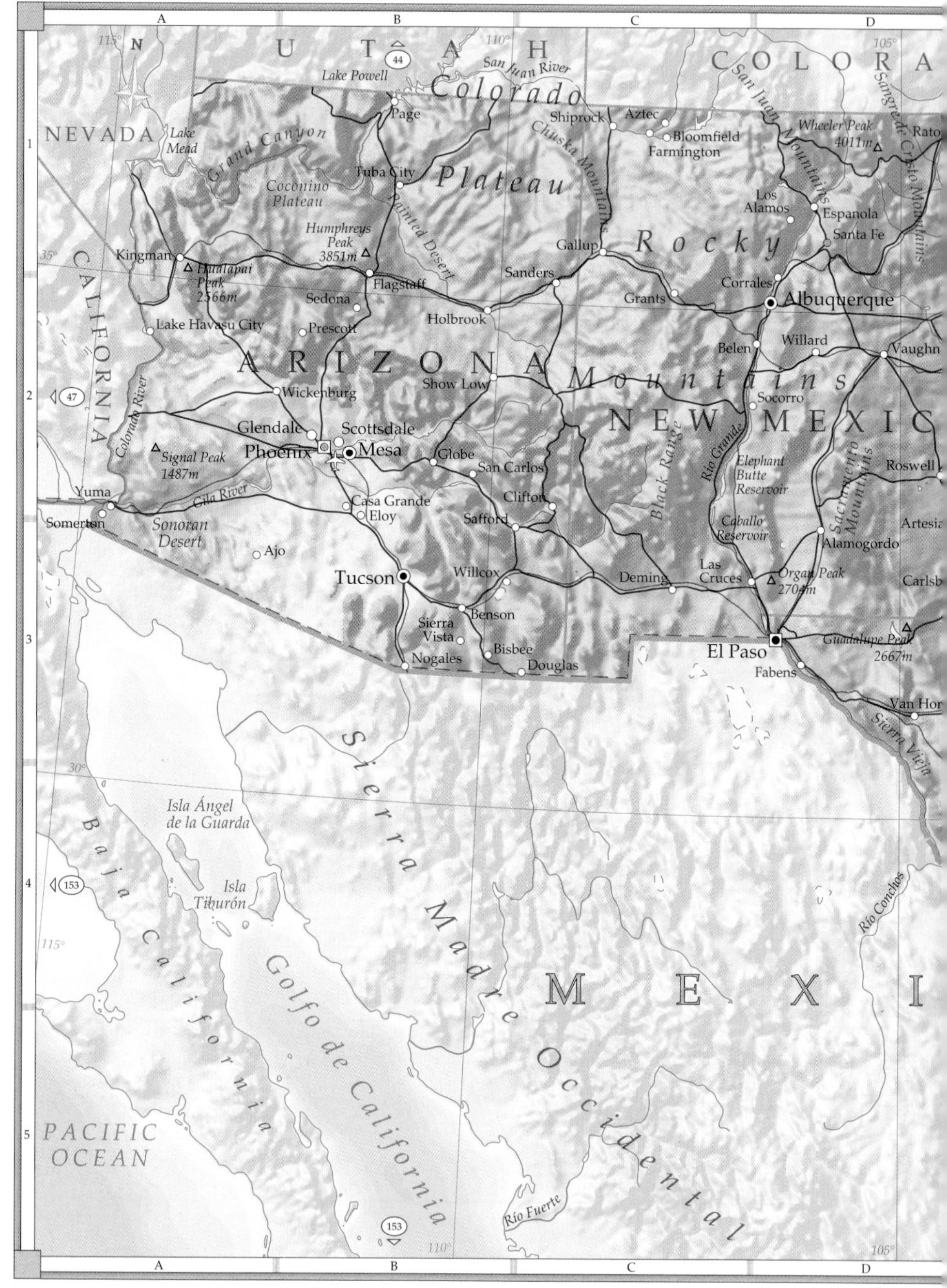

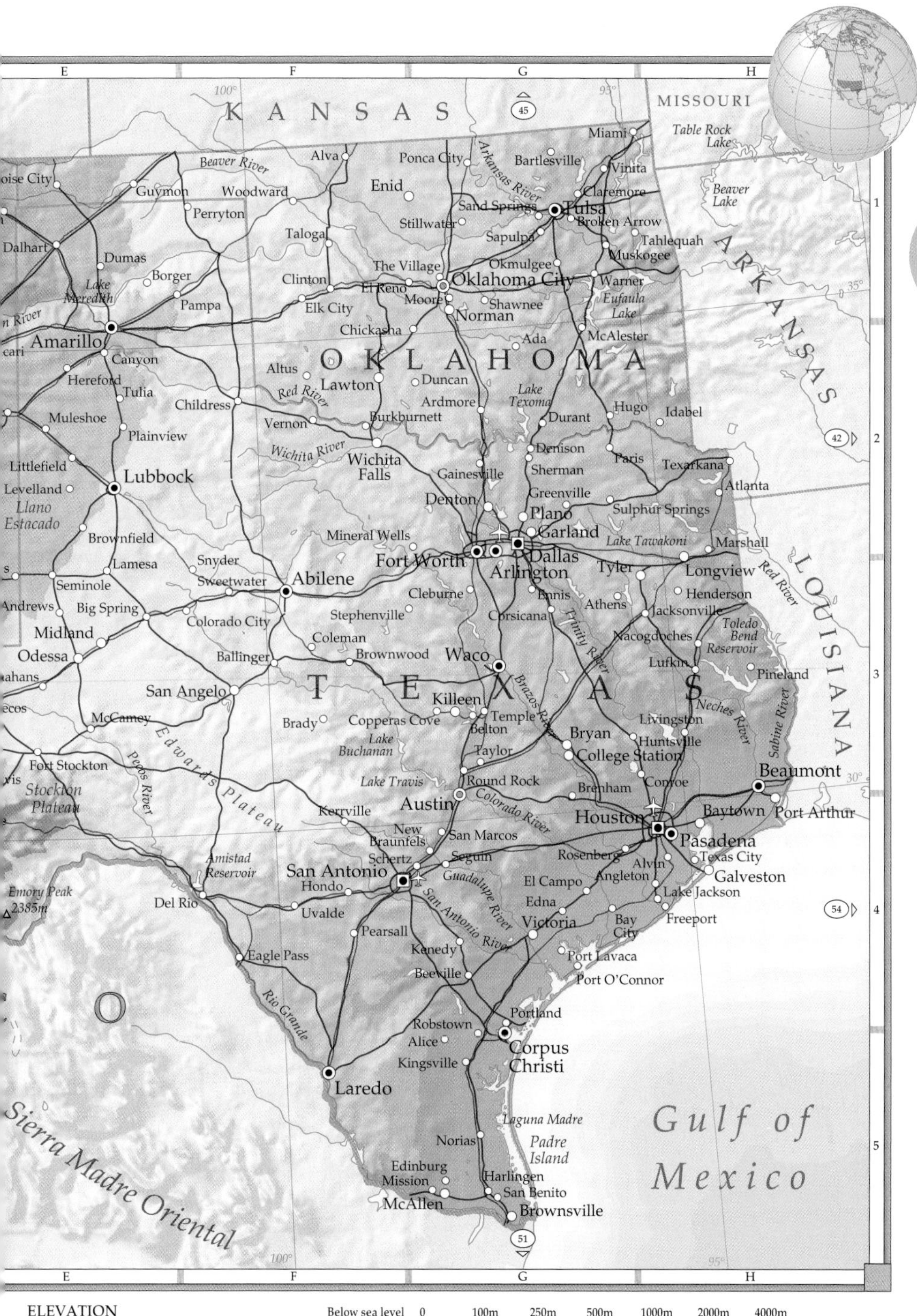

ELEVATION

Below sea level	-2000m	-1000m	-500m	-250m	-100m	0
	-6562ft	-3281ft	-1640ft	-820ft	-328ft	-164ft/-50m

0	100m	250m	500m	1000m	2000m	4000m
	328ft	820ft	1640ft	3281ft	6562ft	13 124ft

MEXICO

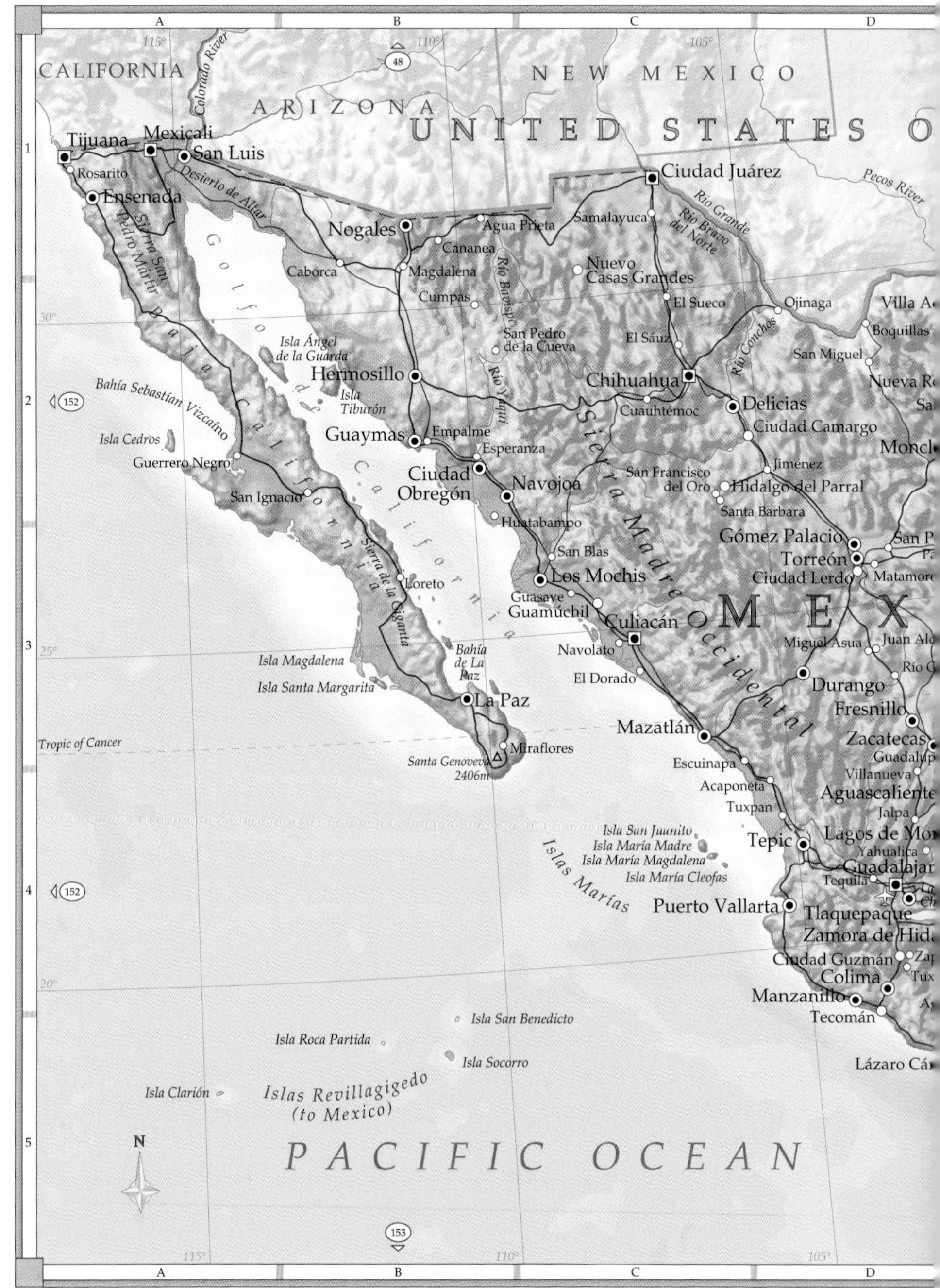

0 km 300

0 miles 300

POPULATION

● National capital

○ Less than 50,000 ○ 50,000 -100,000 ⊙ 100,000 - 500,000 ▣ Over 500,000

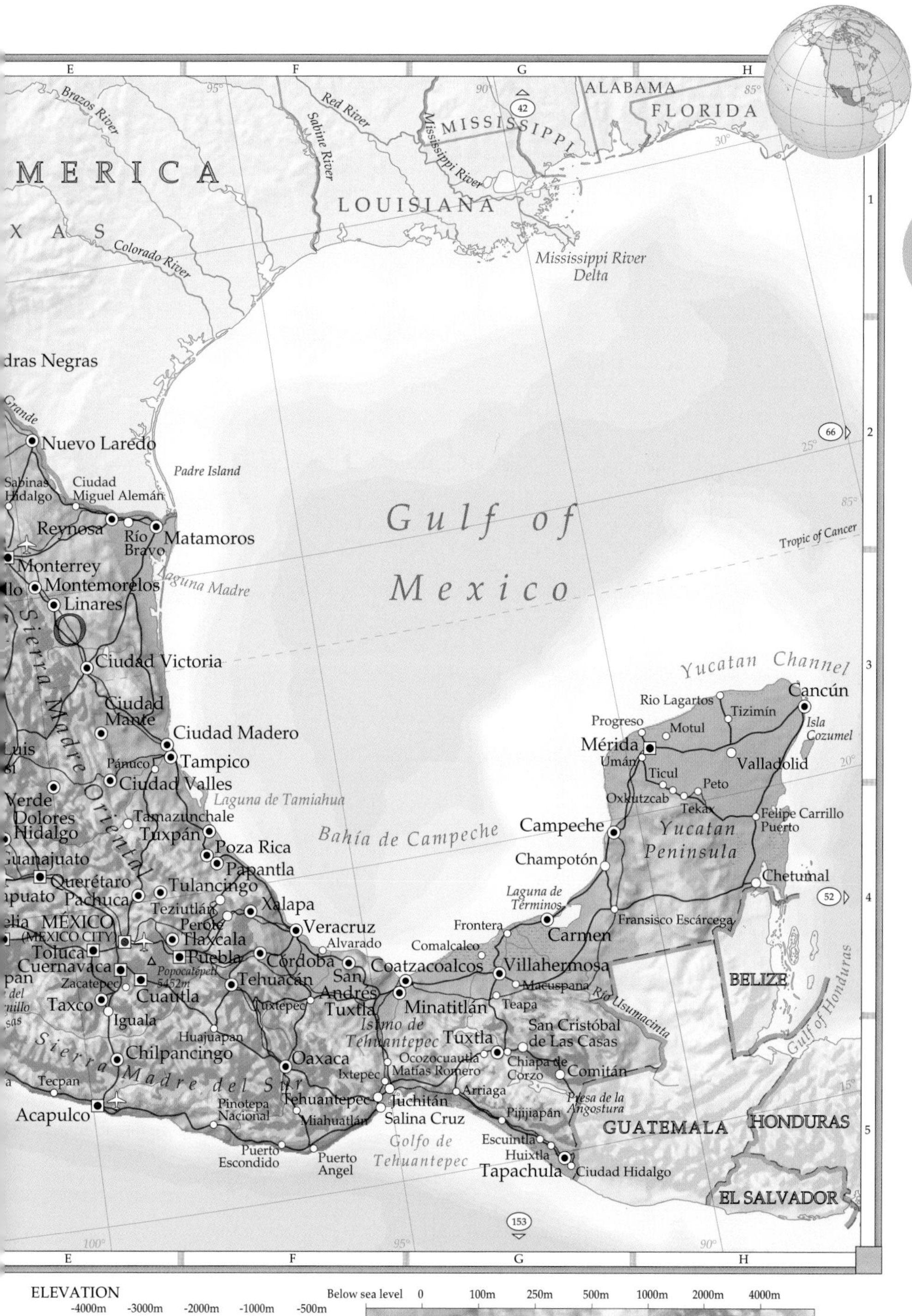

ELEVATION

-4000m	-3000m	-2000m	-1000m	-500m	Below sea level 0	100m	250m	500m	1000m	2000m	4000m
-13 124ft	-9843ft	-6562ft	-3281ft	-1640ft	-820ft/-250m 0	328ft	820ft	1640ft	3281ft	6562ft	13 124ft

Central America

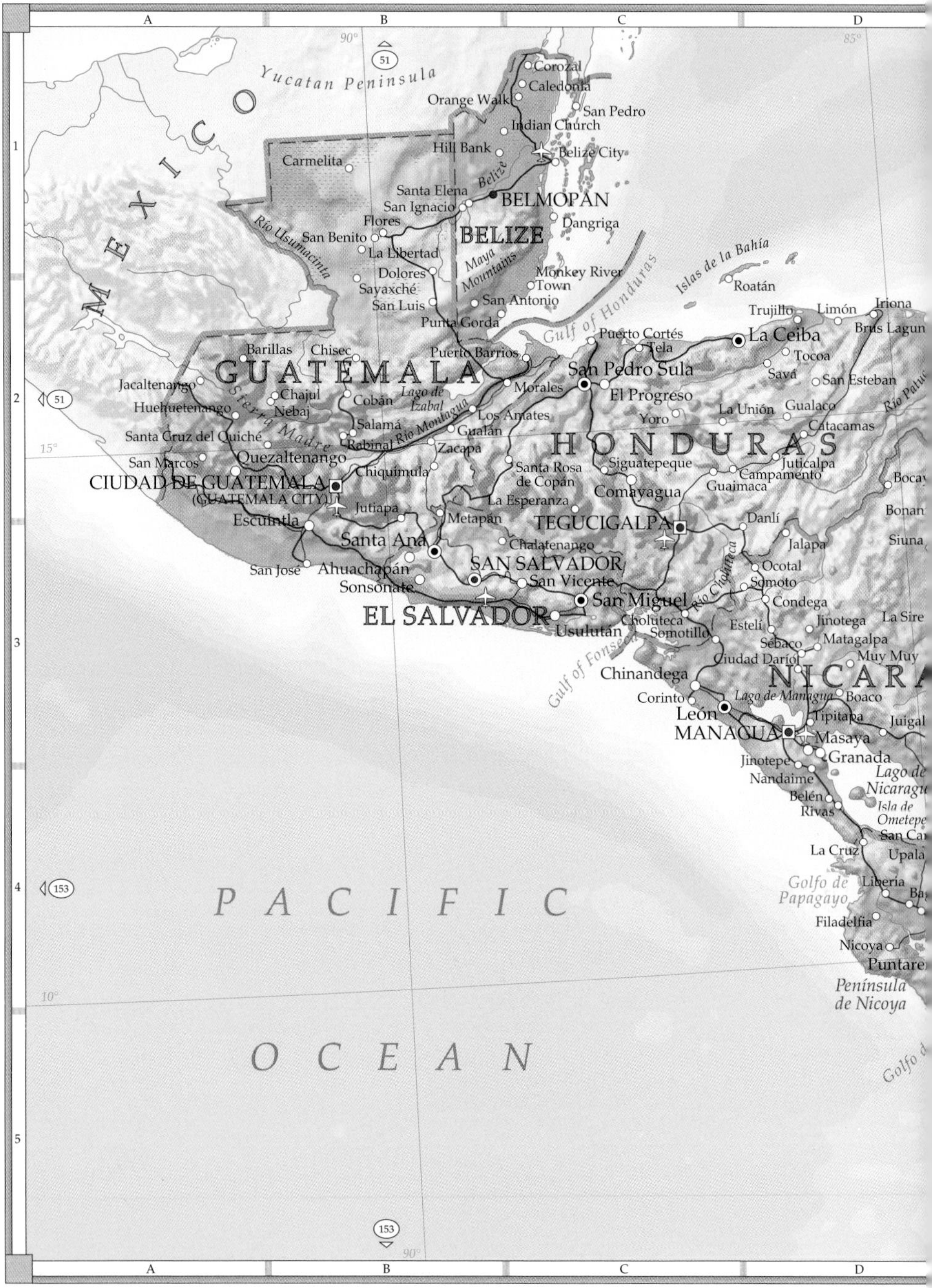

A B C D
90° 85°
51
Yucatan Peninsula
MEXICO
Corozal
Caledonia
Orange Walk
San Pedro
Indian Church
Hill Bank
Belize City
Carmelita
Belize
Santa Elena
BELMOPAN
San Ignacio
Flores
Dangriga
Río Usumacinta
San Benito
BELIZE
La Libertad
Maya Mountains
Islas de la Bahía
Dolores
Monkey River Town
Roatán
Sayaxché
San Luis
San Antonio
Gulf of Honduras
Trujillo
Limón
Iriona
Punta Gorda
Brus Lagun
Puerto Cortés
La Ceiba
Barillas
Chisec
Puerto Barrios
Tela
Tocoa
GUATEMALA
San Pedro Sula
Savá
San Esteban
Jacaltenango
Morales
El Progreso
Chajul
Cobán
Lago de Izabal
Río Patuca
Huehuetenango
Nebaj
Los Amates
La Unión
Gualaco
Sierra Madre
Yoro
Salamá
Río Motagua
Gualán
Catacamas
Santa Cruz del Quiché
Rabinal
HONDURAS
15°
Zacapa
San Marcos
Quezaltenango
Santa Rosa de Copán
Siguatepeque
Juticalpa
Campamento
CIUDAD DE GUATEMALA (GUATEMALA CITY)
Chiquimula
Guaimaca
Bocay
Comayagua
Jutiapa
La Esperanza
Escuintla
Metapán
TEGUCIGALPA
Danlí
Bonan
Santa Ana
Chalatenango
Jalapa
Siuna
SAN SALVADOR
Río Choluteca
San José
Ahuachapán
Ocotal
Sonsonate
San Vicente
Somoto
San Miguel
Condega
EL SALVADOR
Choluteca
Jinotega
La Sire
Usulután
Somotillo
Estelí
Sébaco
Matagalpa
Gulf of Fonseca
Ciudad Darío
Muy Muy
Chinandega
NICARA
Corinto
Lago de Managua
Boaco
León
Tipitapa
Juigal
MANAGUA
Masaya
Granada
Jinotepe
Lago de Nicaragu
Nandaime
Isla de Ometepe
Belén
Rivas
San Ca
La Cruz
Upala
Golfo de Papagayo
Liberia
Ba
Filadelfia
Nicoya
Puntare
Península de Nicoya
Golfo d
PACIFIC OCEAN
10°
153
90°
1 2 3 4 5

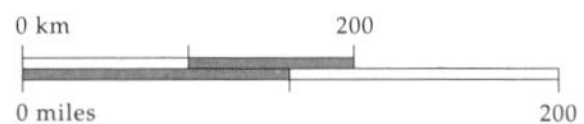

POPULATION
● National capital
○ Less than 50,000
○ 50,000 -100,000
⦿ 100,000 - 500,000
▣ Over 500,000

E
F
G
H
1
2
3
4
5
Santanilla
(Honduras)
Bajo Nuevo
(to Colombia)
Cayo de Serranilla
(to Colombia)
Puerto Lempira
Cayo de Serrana
(to Colombia)
Cayos Miskitos
Tuapi
Puerto Cabezas
Caribbean
Sea
Isla de Providencia
(to Colombia)
Mosquito Coast
Prinzapolka
Barra de Río Grande
Isla de San Andrés
(to Colombia)
Laguna de Perlas
Islas del Maíz
Bluefields
Punta Gorda
San Juan del Norte
COSTA RICA
Siquirres
Heredia
SAN JOSÉ
Limón
Cartago
Guabito
Almirante
Laguna de Chiriquí
Cordillera de Talamanca
Buenos Aires
Cortés
Palmar Sur
Bahía Coronado
La Concepción
Golfo Dulce
Volcán Barú 3475m
Boquete
Cordillera Central
David
Golfo de Chiriquí
Isla de Coiba
Golfo de los Mosquitos
Istmo de Panamá
El Porvenir
Portobelo
Colón
Cristóbal
Panama Canal
Lago Gatún
Balboa
San Miguelito
PANAMÁ
(PANAMA CITY)
Capira
Penonomé
Aguadulce
Santiago
Guarumal
Ocú
Chitré
Las Tablas
Península de Azuero
Isla Cébaco
PANAMA
Cordillera de San Blas
Lago Bayano
Chimán
Archipiélago de las Perlas
Isla del Rey
La Palma
Yaviza
Serranía del Darién
El Real
Garachiné
Jaqué
Golfo de Panamá
Gulf of Darien
Ailigandí
Puerto Obaldía
COLOMBIA
ELEVATION
Below sea level
0
100m
250m
500m
1000m
2000m
4000m
-4000m
-3000m
-2000m
-1000m
-500m
328ft
820ft
1640ft
3281ft
6562ft
13 124ft
-13 124ft
-9843ft
-6562ft
-3281ft
-1640ft
-820ft/-250m
0

THE CARIBBEAN

A B C D

85° 80° 75°

N

1 25°

Gulf of Mexico

The Everglades

43

UNITED STATES OF AMERICA

Florida Keys

Straits of Florida

Grand Bahama Island

Freeport

Marsh Harbour

Great Abaco

Bimini Islands

Berry Islands

Northeast Providence Channel

Nicholls Town

NASSAU

New Providence

Eleuthera Island

Rock Sound

Andros Town

Exuma Cays

Exuma Sound

Cat Island

Andros Island

BAHAMAS

San Salvador

Rum Cay

Tropic of Cancer

Cay Sal

LA HABANA (HAVANA)

Anguilla Cays

George Town

Great Exuma Island

Long Island

Guanabacoa

Artemisa

Cárdenas

Matanzas

Sagua la Grande

Pinar del Río

Consolación del Sur

La Fé

Santa Clara

Placetas

Cienfuegos

Archipiélago de Camagüey

Clarence Town

Crooked Island Passage

Crooked Island

Yucatan Channel

2 52

Nueva Gerona

Isla de la Juventud

Cayo Largo

Archipiélago de los Canarreos

Bahía de Cochinos

Sancti Spíritus

Morón

Ciego de Ávila

Ragged Island Range

Acklins Island

Mayaguana Passage

Mayaguana

Caicos Passage

CUBA

Nuevitas

Camagüey

Little Inagua

Lake Rosa

Matthew Town

Great Inagua

20°

Archipiélago de los Jardines de la Reina

Las Tunas

Holguín

Manzanillo

Bayamo

Palma Soriano

Guantánamo

Santiago de Cuba

Guantánamo Bay (to US)

Windward Passage

Haïti

Gonaïves

Little Cayman

Cayman Brac

GEORGE TOWN

Grand Cayman

3

CAYMAN ISLANDS (to UK)

Great

NAVASSA ISLAND (to US)

Île de la Gonâve

Jérémie

PORT-AU-PRINCE

Montego Bay

Spanish Town

Portmore

KINGSTON

Jamaica Channel

Cayes

JAMAICA

Pedro Cays

Caribbean Sea

HONDURAS

15°

4 52

NICARAGUA

5

COSTA RICA

10°

53

COLOMBIA

JAMAICA

Caribbean Sea

78° 77°

Montego Bay

Lucea

Falmouth

Runaway Bay

St Ann's Bay

Ocho Rios

The Cockpit Country

Cambridge

Annotto Bay

Buff Bay

Port Antonio

Savanna-La-Mar

Christiana

Ewarton

Blue Mountain Peak △2258m

Spanish Town

Mandeville

18°

Black River

KINGSTON

May Pen

Old Harbour

Portmore

Morant Bay

Portland Bight

N

0 km 20

0 miles 20

2000m/6562ft

1000m/3281ft

500m/1640ft

200m/656ft

Sea level

A B C D

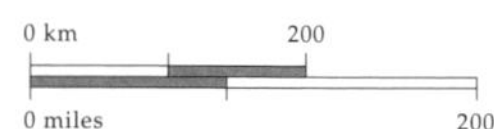

POPULATION

● National capital

○ Less than 50,000

○ 50,000 -100,000

◉ 100,000 - 500,000

▣ Over 500,000

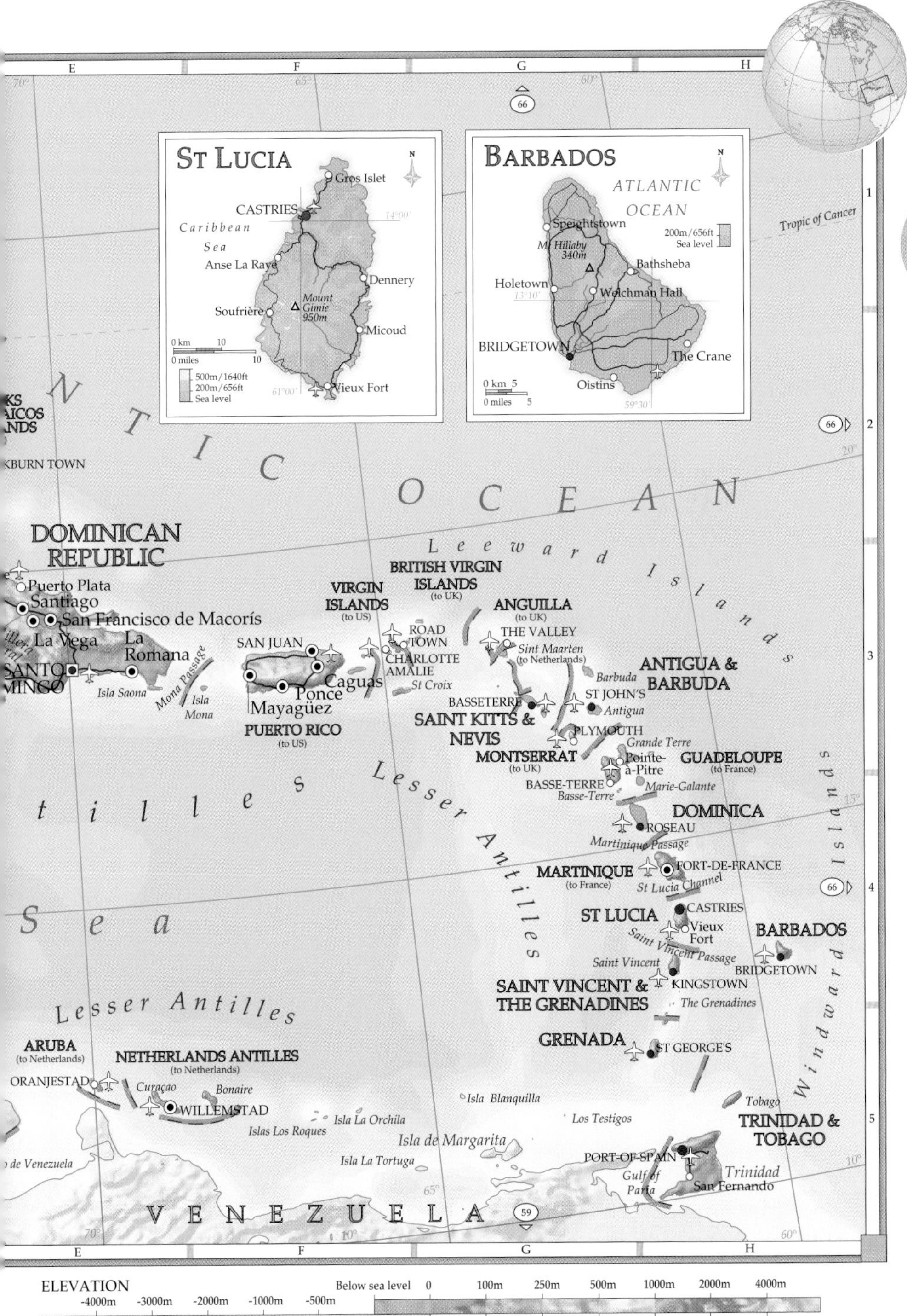
ST LUCIA
Gros Islet
CASTRIES
Caribbean Sea
Anse La Raye
Dennery
Mount Gimie 950m
Soufrière
Micoud
Vieux Fort
0 km 10
0 miles 10
500m/1640ft
200m/656ft
Sea level
BARBADOS
ATLANTIC OCEAN
Speightstown
Mt Hillaby 340m
Bathsheba
Holetown
Welchman Hall
BRIDGETOWN
The Crane
Oistins
0 km 5
0 miles 5
200m/656ft
Sea level
Tropic of Cancer
ATLANTIC OCEAN
DOMINICAN REPUBLIC
Puerto Plata
Santiago
San Francisco de Macorís
La Vega
La Romana
Mona Passage
Isla Saona
Isla Mona
SAN JUAN
Caguas
Ponce
Mayagüez
PUERTO RICO (to US)
VIRGIN ISLANDS (to US)
BRITISH VIRGIN ISLANDS (to UK)
ROAD TOWN
CHARLOTTE AMALIE
St Croix
ANGUILLA (to UK)
THE VALLEY
Sint Maarten (to Netherlands)
Leeward Islands
ANTIGUA & BARBUDA
Barbuda
ST JOHN'S
Antigua
BASSETERRE
SAINT KITTS & NEVIS
PLYMOUTH
MONTSERRAT (to UK)
Grande Terre
Pointe-à-Pitre
GUADELOUPE (to France)
BASSE-TERRE
Basse-Terre
Marie-Galante
DOMINICA
ROSEAU
Martinique Passage
FORT-DE-FRANCE
MARTINIQUE (to France)
St Lucia Channel
ST LUCIA
CASTRIES
Vieux Fort
BARBADOS
BRIDGETOWN
Saint Vincent Passage
Saint Vincent
KINGSTOWN
SAINT VINCENT & THE GRENADINES
The Grenadines
GRENADA
ST GEORGE'S
Windward Islands
Lesser Antilles
Antilles
Sea
ARUBA (to Netherlands)
ORANJESTAD
NETHERLANDS ANTILLES (to Netherlands)
Curaçao
Bonaire
WILLEMSTAD
Isla Blanquilla
Isla La Orchila
Islas Los Roques
Los Testigos
Isla de Margarita
Isla La Tortuga
Tobago
TRINIDAD & TOBAGO
PORT-OF-SPAIN
Gulf of Paria
Trinidad
San Fernando
VENEZUELA
de Venezuela
KBURN TOWN
ELEVATION
Below sea level 0 100m 250m 500m 1000m 2000m 4000m
-4000m -3000m -2000m -1000m -500m
328ft 820ft 1640ft 3281ft 6562ft 13 124ft
-13 124ft -9843ft -6562ft -3281ft -1640ft -820ft/-250m 0

SOUTH AMERICA

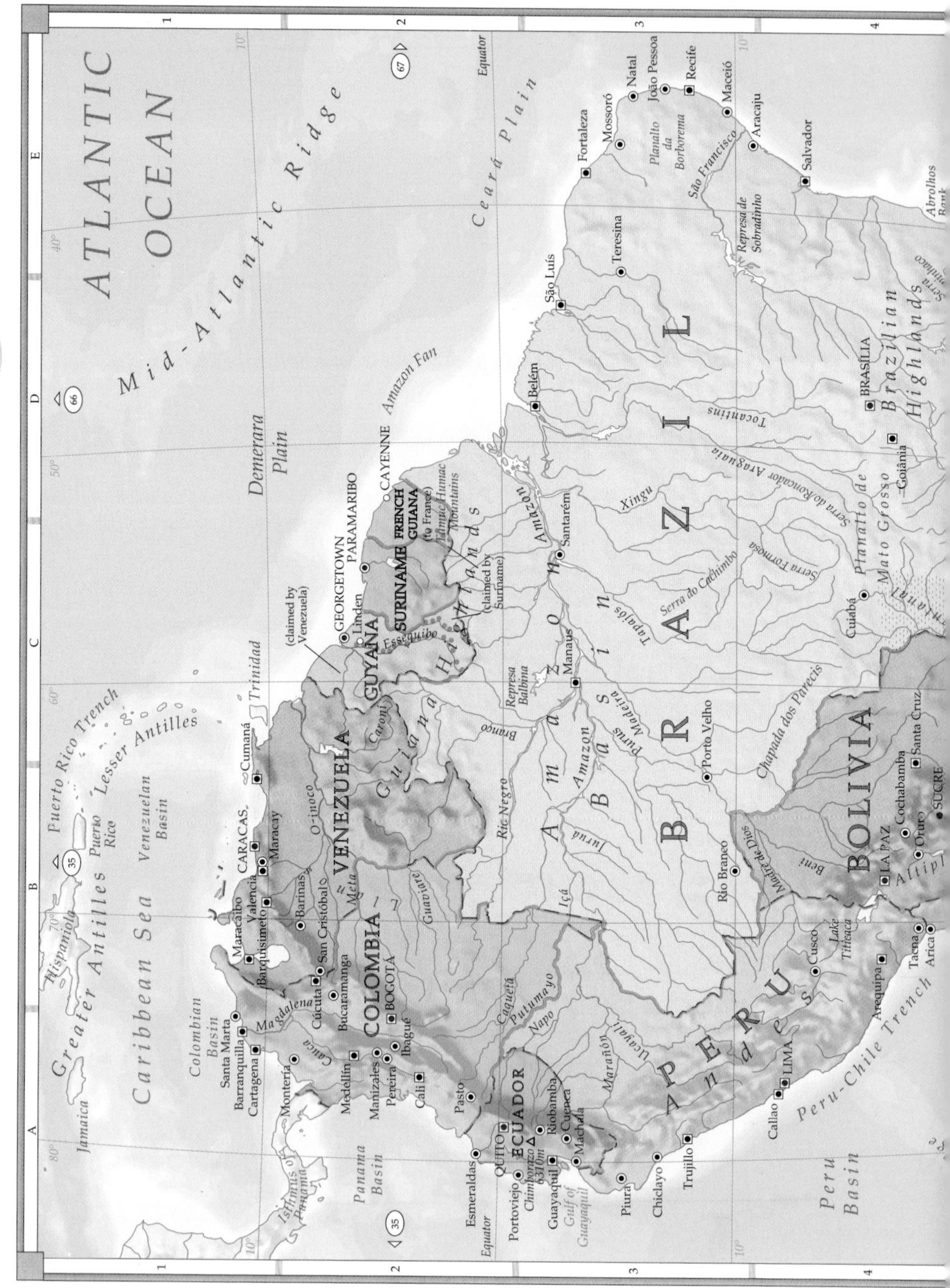

POPULATION ● National capital ○ Less than 50,000 ○ 50,000 -100,000 ⦿ 100,000 - 500,000 ▣ Over 500,000

0 km 500
0 miles 500

ATLANTIC OCEAN
PACIFIC OCEAN
Tropic of Capricorn
PARAGUAY
ASUNCIÓN
URUGUAY
MONTEVIDEO
BUENOS AIRES
SANTIAGO
FALKLAND ISLANDS
(to UK)
STANLEY
East Falkland
West Falkland
SOUTH GEORGIA
(to UK)
SOUTH SANDWICH ISLANDS
(to UK)
ANTARCTICA
Rio de Janeiro
São Paulo
Santos
Curitiba
Florianópolis
Porto Alegre
Lagoa dos Patos
Mirim Lagoon
Serra Geral
Santos Plateau
Rio Grande Rise
Argentine Basin
Falkland Plateau
Scotia Sea
South Sandwich Trench
South Orkney Islands
South Shetland Islands
Drake Passage
Winter limit of pack ice
Summer limit of pack ice
Cape Horn
Tierra del Fuego
Strait of Magellan
Bahía Grande
Punta Arenas
Gulf of San Jorge
Golfo San Matías
Península Valdés -40m
Rawson
Bahía Blanca
Mar del Plata
La Plata
Río de la Plata
Rosario
Santa Fe
Córdoba
Corrientes
Resistencia
Formosa
Posadas
Ciudad del Este
Santa Maria
Mesopotamia
Uruguay
Paraná
Negro
Pilcomayo
Gran Chaco
Pampas
Patagonia
Colorado
Río Negro
Chubut
Chico
Deseado
Neuquén
Mendoza
San Juan
Cerro Aconcagua 6959m
Cerro Ojos del Salado 6880m
La Rioja
Santiago del Estero
San Miguel de Tucumán
Salta
San Salvador de Jujuy
Atacama
Antofagasta
La Serena
Coquimbo
Viña del Mar
Valparaíso
Concepción
Temuco
Valdivia
Puerto Montt
Isla de Chiloé
Isla San Ambrosio (to Chile)
Isla San Félix (to Chile)
Islas Juan Fernández (to Chile)
Chile Basin
Chile Rise
N
A
B
C
D
E
5
6
7
8
153
154
67

NORTHERN SOUTH AMERICA

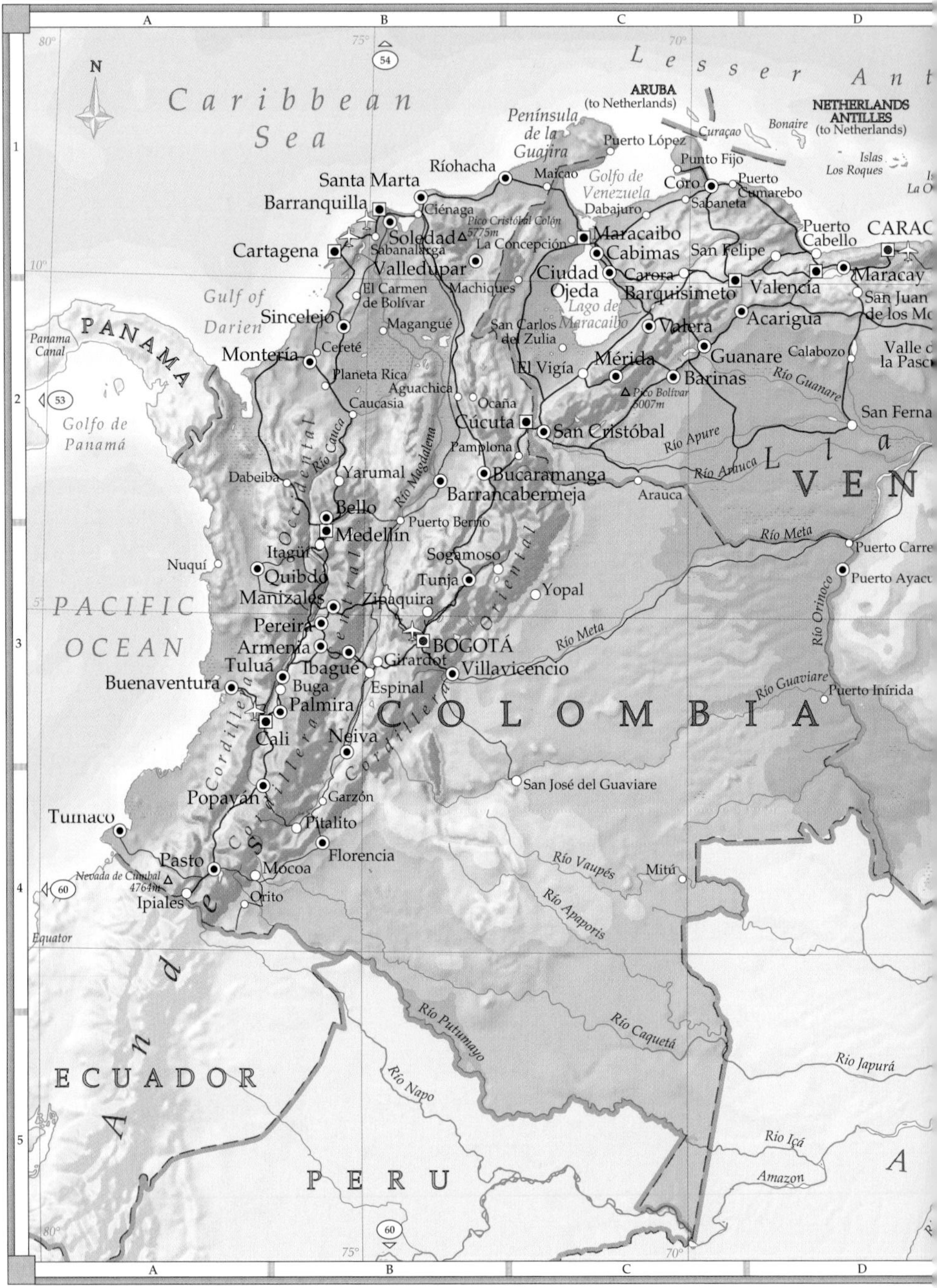

A
B
C
D
N
Caribbean Sea
Lesser Ant
ARUBA
(to Netherlands)
NETHERLANDS ANTILLES
(to Netherlands)
Curaçao
Bonaire
Islas Los Roques
Península de la Guajira
Puerto López
Punto Fijo
Ríohacha
Maicao
Golfo de Venezuela
Coro
Puerto Cumarebo
Santa Marta
Barranquilla
Ciénaga
Pico Cristóbal Colón 5775m
Dabajuro
Sabaneta
Soledad
Sabanalarga
Maracaibo
Cabimas
Cartagena
La Concepción
San Felipe
Puerto Cabello
CARAC
Valledupar
Ciudad Ojeda
Carora
Valencia
Maracay
Gulf of Darien
El Carmen de Bolívar
Machiques
Barquisimeto
Lago de Maracaibo
San Juan de los Mo
Sincelejo
Magangué
San Carlos del Zulia
Valera
Acarigua
PANAMA
Panama Canal
Cereté
Montería
Mérida
Guanare
Calabozo
Valle de la Pasc
Planeta Rica
El Vigía
Barinas
Aguachica
Pico Bolívar 5007m
Río Guanare
53
Caucasia
Ocaña
San Ferna
Golfo de Panamá
Cúcuta
San Cristóbal
Río Cauca
Pamplona
Río Apure
Llanos
Río Magdalena
Yarumal
Bucaramanga
Río Arauca
Dabeiba
Barrancabermeja
Arauca
VEN
Bello
Puerto Berrío
Medellín
Río Meta
Itagüí
Sogamoso
Puerto Carre
Nuquí
Quibdó
Tunja
Puerto Ayacu
Manizales
Zipaquira
Yopal
PACIFIC OCEAN
Pereira
Cordillera Oriental
Río Orinoco
Armenia
BOGOTÁ
Río Meta
Tuluá
Ibagué
Girardot
Villavicencio
Buenaventura
Buga
Espinal
Río Guaviare
Puerto Inírida
Palmira
COLOMBIA
Cali
Neiva
Cordillera Central
Cordillera Occidental
San José del Guaviare
Popayán
Garzón
Tumaco
Pitalito
Florencia
Pasto
Mocoa
Río Vaupés
Mitú
Nevada de Cumbal 4764m
Ipiales
Orito
Río Apaporis
60
Equator
Andes
Río Putumayo
Río Caquetá
Río Japurá
ECUADOR
Río Napo
Río Içá
Amazon
PERU
80°
75°
70°
10°
5°

0 km 200

0 miles 200

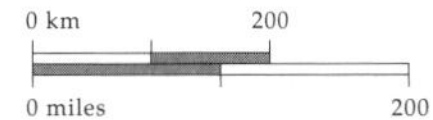

POPULATION

● National capital

○ Less than 50,000 ○ 50,000 -100,000 ◉ 100,000 - 500,000 ▣ Over 500,000

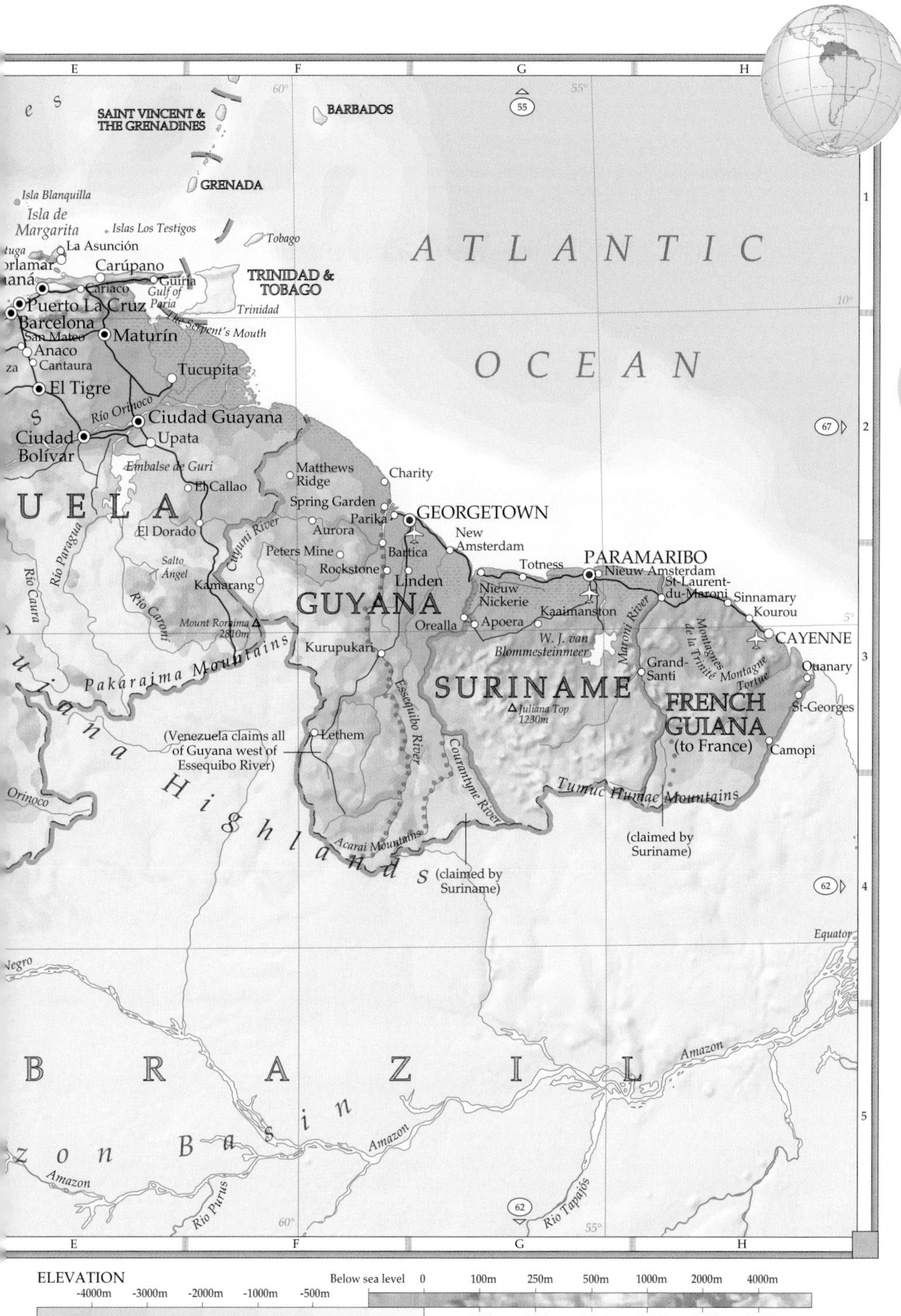

-4000m	-3000m	-2000m	-1000m	-500m	0	100m	250m	500m	1000m	2000m	4000m
-13 124ft	-9843ft	-6562ft	-3281ft	-1640ft	-820ft/-250m	0	328ft	820ft	1640ft	3281ft	6562ft	13 124ft

Western South America

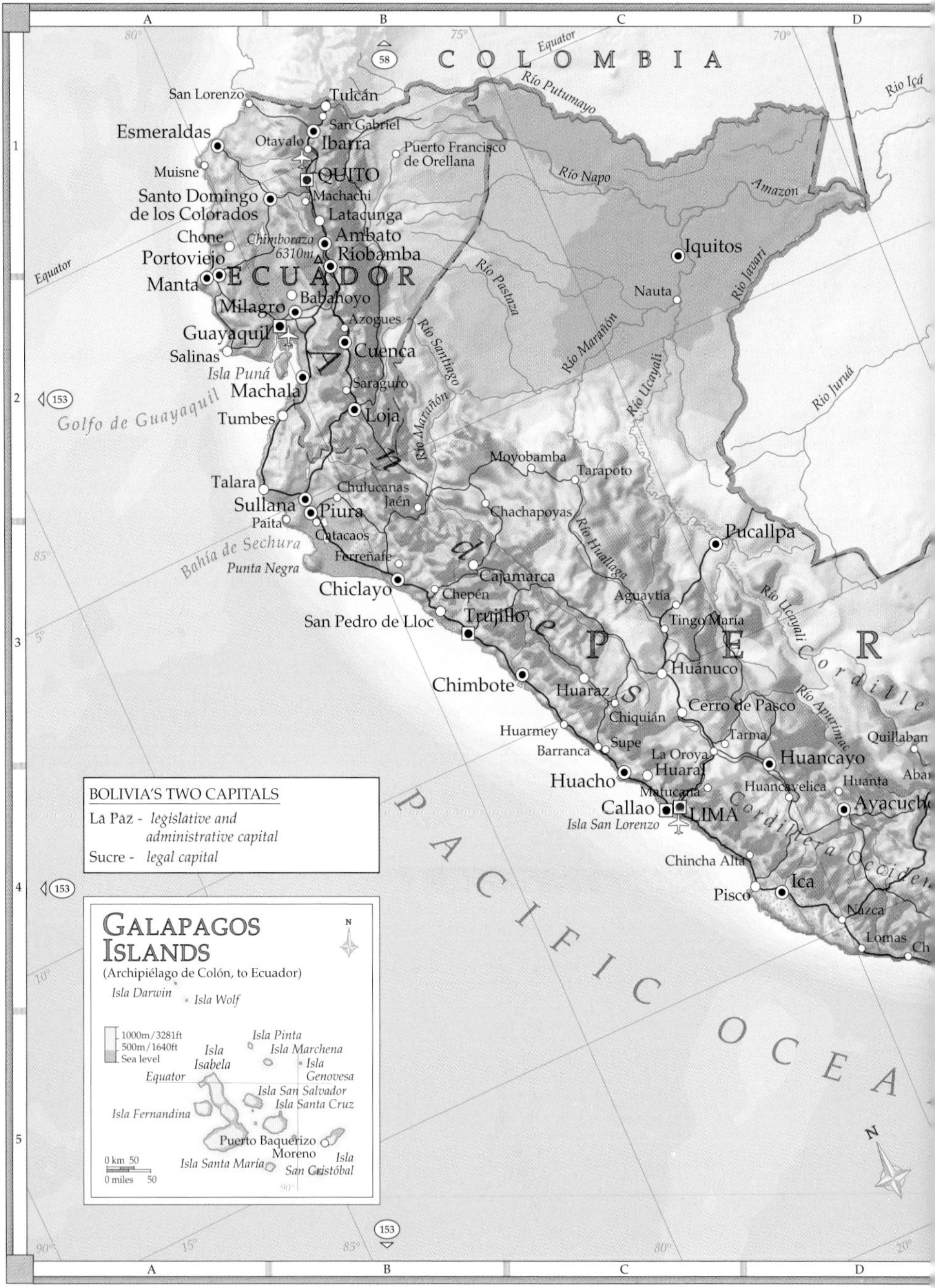

BOLIVIA'S TWO CAPITALS

La Paz - *legislative and administrative capital*

Sucre - *legal capital*

Galapagos Islands

(Archipiélago de Colón, to Ecuador)

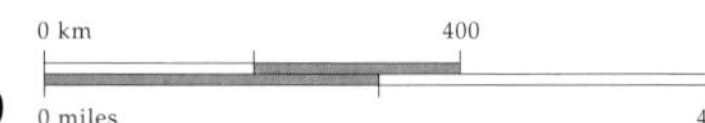

POPULATION

● National capital

○ Less than 50,000

○ 50,000 -100,000

◉ 100,000 - 500,000

▣ Over 500,000

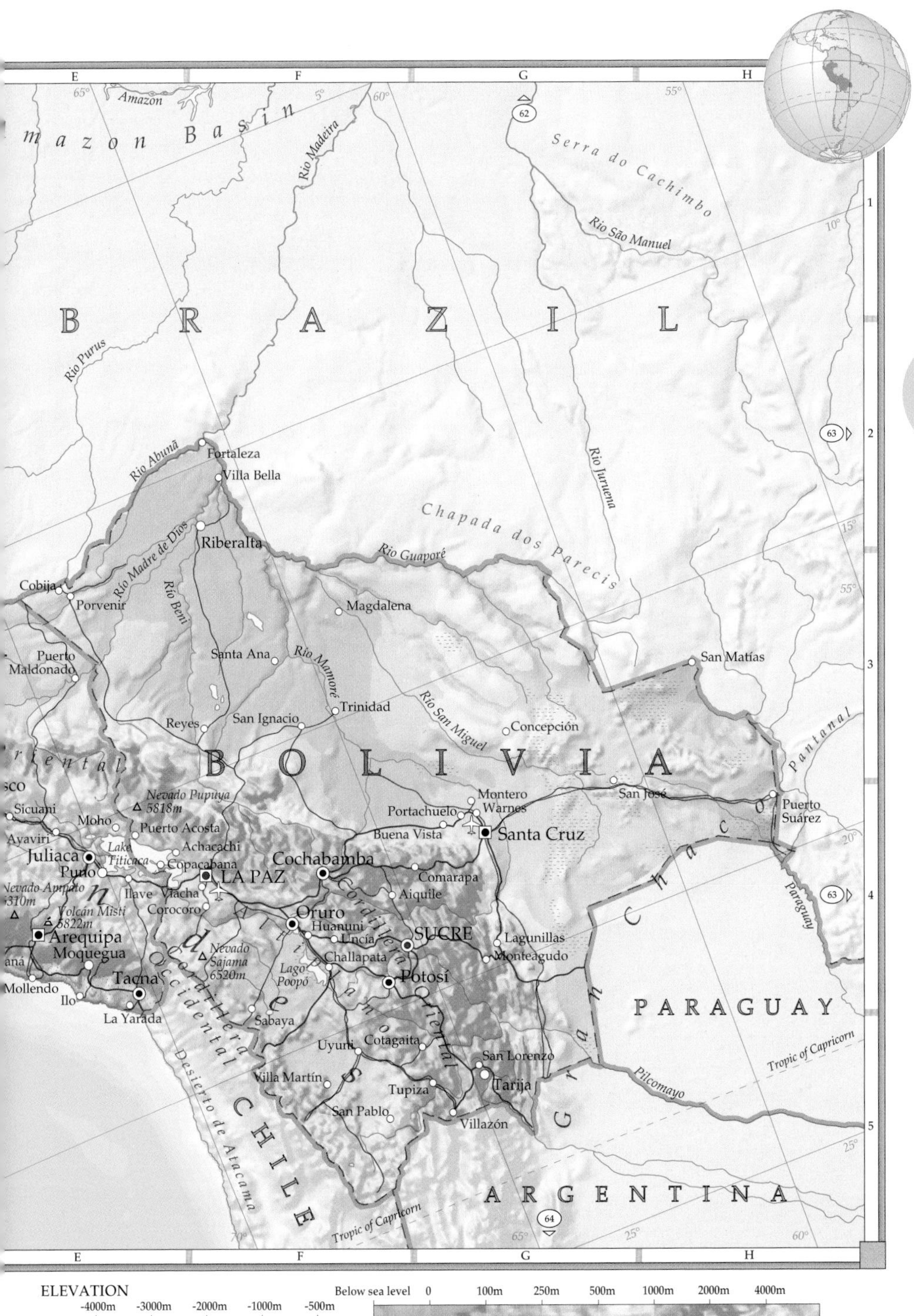
BRAZIL
BOLIVIA
PARAGUAY
ARGENTINA
CHILE
Amazon Basin
Serra do Cachimbo
Rio São Manuel
Rio Madeira
Rio Purus
Rio Abunã
Fortaleza
Villa Bella
Rio Juruena
Chapada dos Parecis
Rio Guaporé
Riberalta
Rio Madre de Dios
Cobija
Porvenir
Río Beni
Magdalena
Puerto Maldonado
Santa Ana
Río Mamoré
Trinidad
Río San Miguel
San Matías
Concepción
Reyes
San Ignacio
Pantanal
Nevado Pupuya 5818m
Montero
Warnes
San José
Puerto Suárez
Sicuani
Portachuelo
Moho
Puerto Acosta
Buena Vista
Santa Cruz
Ayaviri
Achacachi
Lake Titicaca
Juliaca
Puno
Copacabana
LA PAZ
Cochabamba
Comarapa
Ilave
Viacha
Aiquile
Corocoro
Oruro
Volcán Misti 5822m
Huanuni
SUCRE
Arequipa
Uncia
Lagunillas
Moquegua
Nevado Sajama 6520m
Challapata
Monteagudo
Lago Poopó
Potosí
Tacna
Mollendo
Ilo
La Yarada
Sabaya
Cordillera Occidental
Cordillera Oriental
Altiplano
Uyuni
Cotagaita
San Lorenzo
Villa Martín
Tarija
Tupiza
San Pablo
Villazón
Gran Chaco
Paraguay
Pilcomayo
Tropic of Capricorn
Desierto de Atacama
62
63
64
ELEVATION
Below sea level
0
100m
250m
500m
1000m
2000m
4000m
-4000m
-3000m
-2000m
-1000m
-500m
328ft
820ft
1640ft
3281ft
6562ft
13 124ft
-13 124ft
-9843ft
-6562ft
-3281ft
-1640ft
-820ft/-250m

BRAZIL

A B C D
1 2 3 4 5

VENEZUELA
COLOMBIA
ECUADOR
PERU
BOLIVIA
CHILE
ARGENTIN
PAR

PACIFIC OCEAN

Equator
Tropic of Capricorn
Galapagos Islands
(Archipiélago de Colón)
(to Ecuador)

Andes
Cordillera Occidental
Cordillera Oriental
Guiana Highlands
Roraima
Pico da Neblina
3014m
Amazon Basin
Acre
Rondônia
Chapada dos Parecis
Cordillera Oriental
Cordillera Occidental
Desierto de Atacama
Gran Chaco
Lake Titicaca
Lago Poopó
Represa Ba

Río Putumayo
Río Napo
Río Marañón
Río Ucayali
Rio Javari
Rio Japurá
Rio Içá
Rio Juruá
Rio Negro
Amazon
Rio Madeira
Rio Purus
Rio Abunã
Guaporé
Río Mamoré
Pilcomayo
Río Bermejo
Río Salado

Uraricoera
Boa Vista
Caracaraí
Manaus
Tefé
Coari
Humaitá
Porto Velho
Japiim
Feijó
Vi

58
153
153
153

80°
70°
60°
90°
10°
20°
30°

N

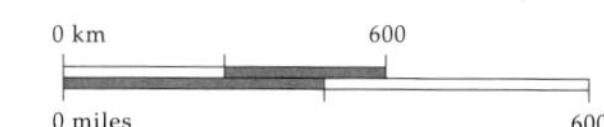

POPULATION ● National capital

○ Less than 50,000 ○ 50,000 -100,000 ◉ 100,000 - 500,000  Over 500,000

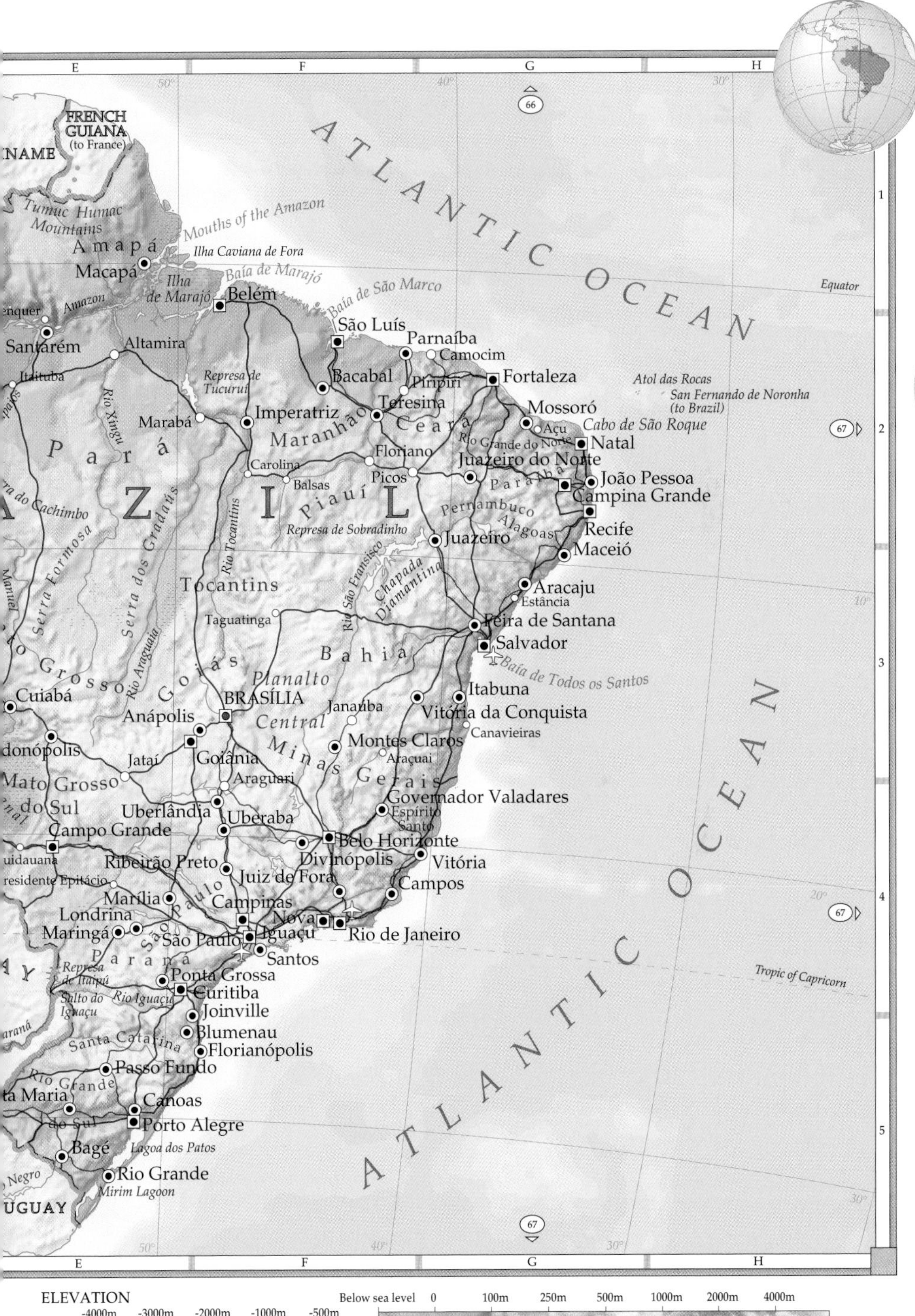
FRENCH GUIANA
(to France)
ATLANTIC OCEAN
Mouths of the Amazon
Tumuc Humac Mountains
Amapá
Macapá
Ilha Caviana de Fora
Baía de Marajó
Ilha de Marajó
Belém
Baía de São Marco
São Luís
Parnaíba
Camocim
Santarém
Altamira
Bacabal
Piripiri
Fortaleza
Atol das Rocas
San Fernando de Noronha
(to Brazil)
Represa de Tucuruí
Teresina
Imperatriz
Marabá
Mossoró
Açu
Cabo de São Roque
Maranhão
Ceará
Rio Grande do Norte
Natal
Floriano
Juazeiro do Norte
Carolina
Balsas
Picos
Paraíba
João Pessoa
Campina Grande
Piauí
Pernambuco
Recife
Alagoas
Represa de Sobradinho
Juazeiro
Maceió
Pará
Serra do Cachimbo
Serra Formosa
Serra dos Gradaús
Rio Xingu
Rio Tocantins
Tocantins
Rio São Francisco
Chapada Diamantina
Aracaju
Estância
Taguatinga
Feira de Santana
Salvador
Baía de Todos os Santos
Bahia
Mato Grosso
Goiás
Rio Araguaia
Planalto Central
Cuiabá
BRASÍLIA
Itabuna
Janaúba
Vitória da Conquista
Canavieiras
Anápolis
Montes Claros
Araçuai
Goiânia
Jataí
Minas Gerais
Araguari
Mato Grosso do Sul
Governador Valadares
Uberlândia
Uberaba
Espírito Santo
Campo Grande
Belo Horizonte
Vitória
Ribeirão Preto
Divinópolis
Presidente Epitácio
Juiz de Fora
Campos
Marília
Campinas
São Paulo
Londrina
Maringá
Nova Iguaçu
Rio de Janeiro
Santos
Paraná
Represa de Itaipú
Ponta Grossa
Salto do Iguaçu
Rio Iguaçu
Curitiba
Joinville
Blumenau
Santa Catarina
Florianópolis
Passo Fundo
Rio Grande do Sul
Canoas
Porto Alegre
Bagé
Lagoa dos Patos
Rio Grande
Mirim Lagoon
Rio Negro
URUGUAY
Equator
Tropic of Capricorn
66
67
ELEVATION
Below sea level
0
100m
250m
500m
1000m
2000m
4000m
-4000m
-3000m
-2000m
-1000m
-500m
328ft
820ft
1640ft
3281ft
6562ft
13 124ft
-13 124ft
-9843ft
-6562ft
-3281ft
-1640ft
-820ft/-250m

SOUTHERN SOUTH AMERICA

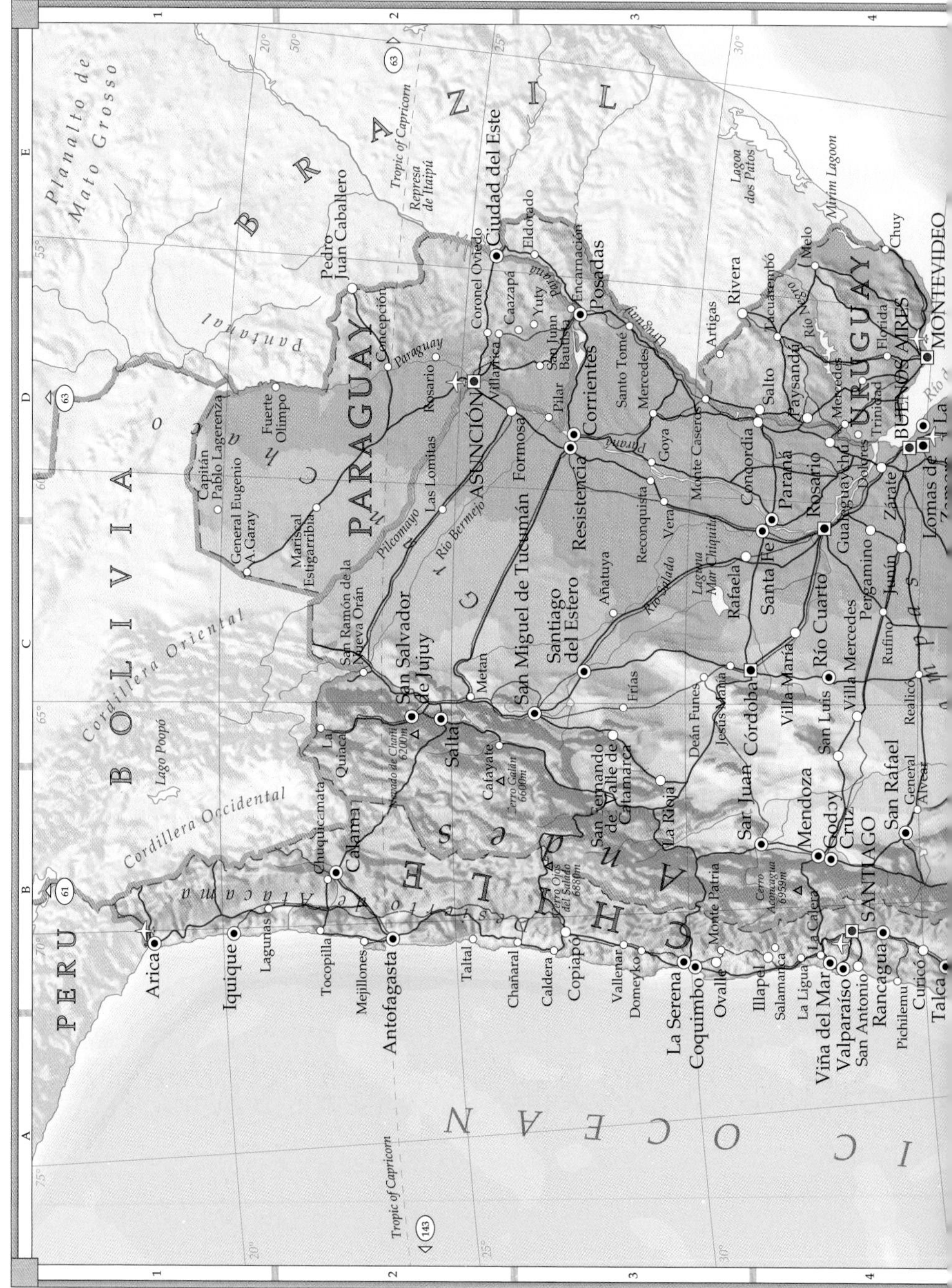

POPULATION ● National capital

○ Less than 50,000 ○ 50,000 -100,000 ◉ 100,000 - 500,000 ▣ Over 500,000

0 km 200

0 miles 200

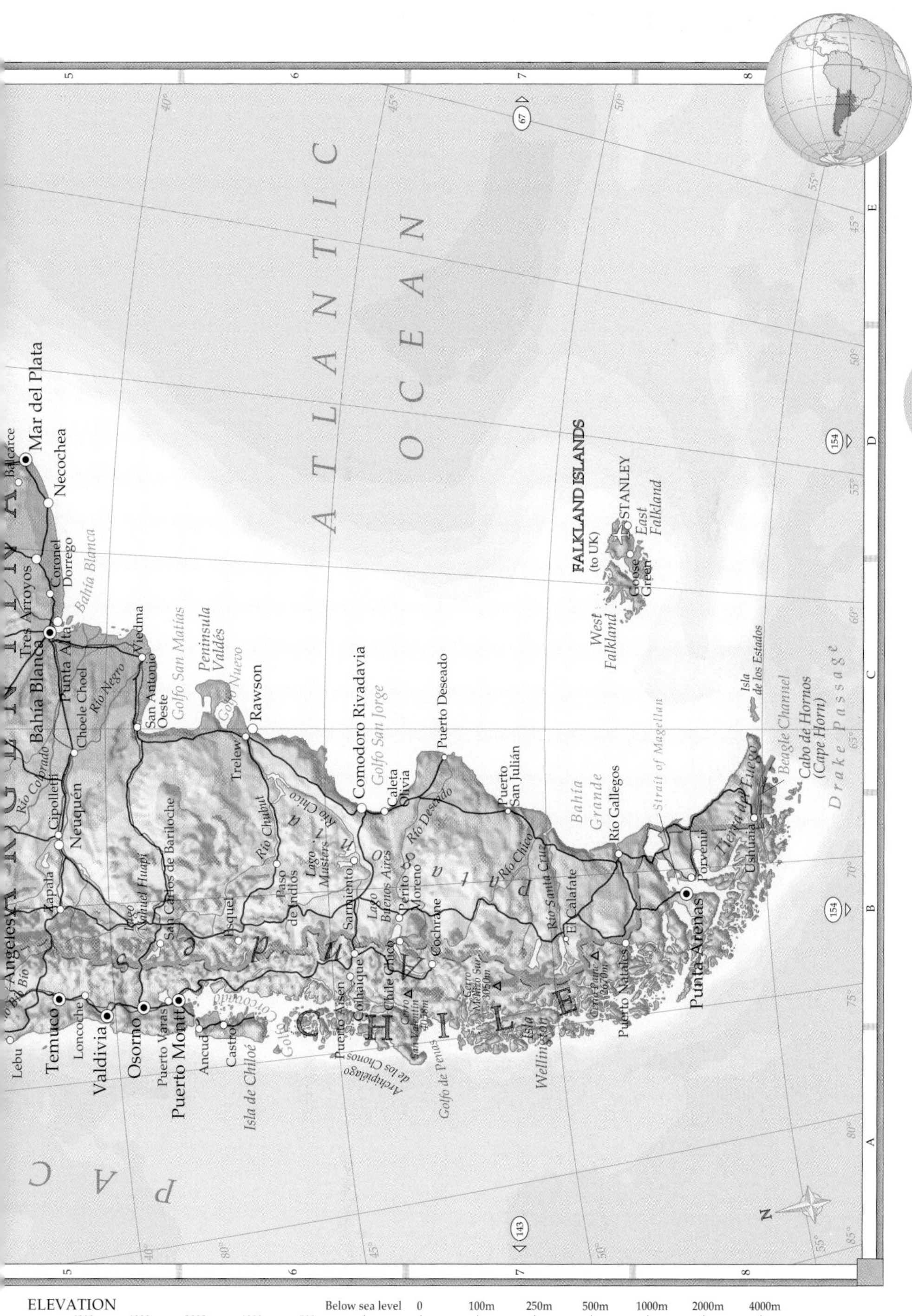

ELEVATION

	-6000m	-4000m	-2000m	-1000m	-500m	Below sea level 0	100m	250m	500m	1000m	2000m	4000m
	-19 686ft	-13 124ft	-6562ft	-3281ft	-1640ft	-820ft/-250m 0	328ft	820ft	1640ft	3281ft	6562ft	13 124ft

THE ATLANTIC OCEAN

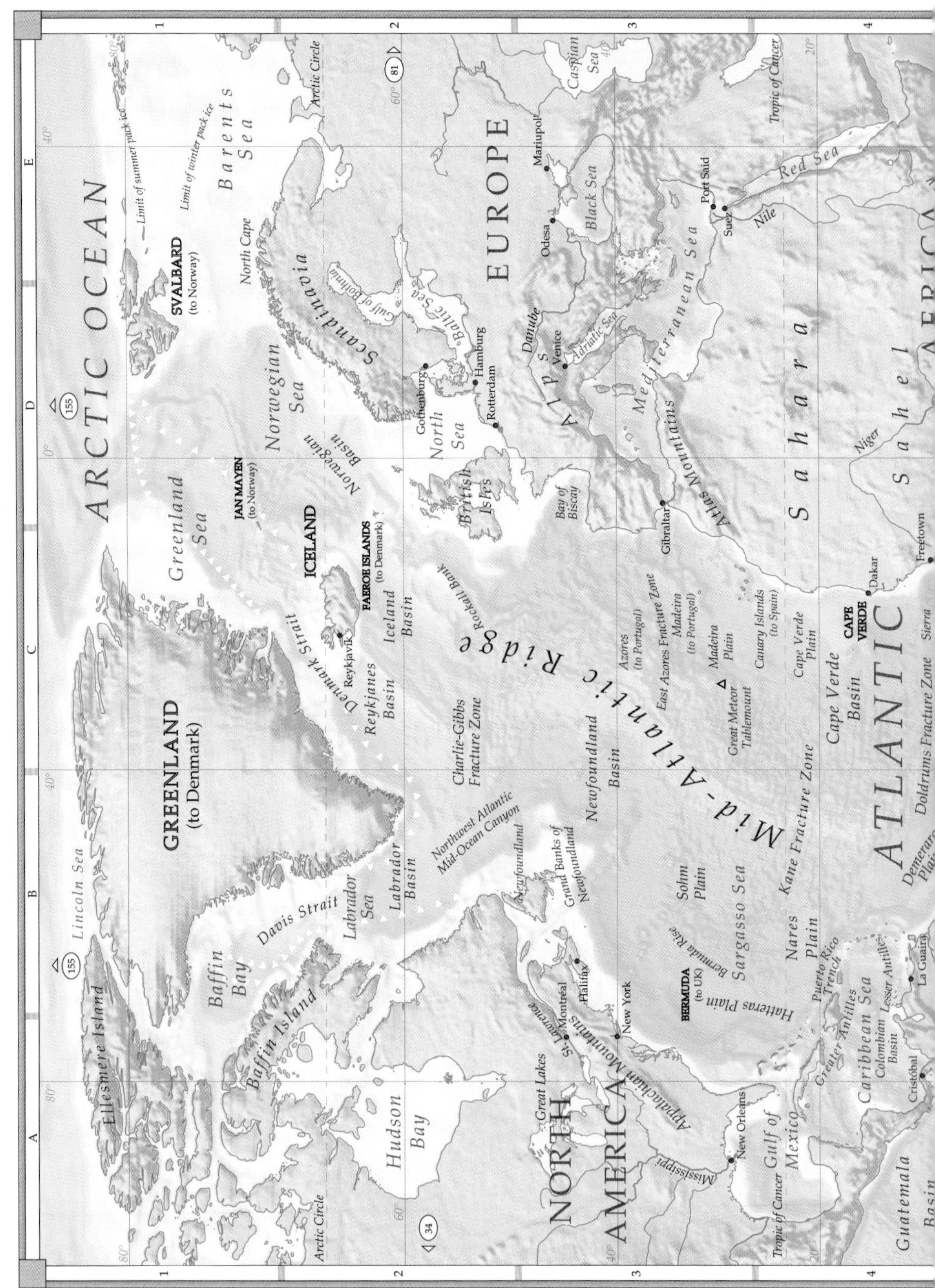

0 km 1000
0 miles 1000

• Major port

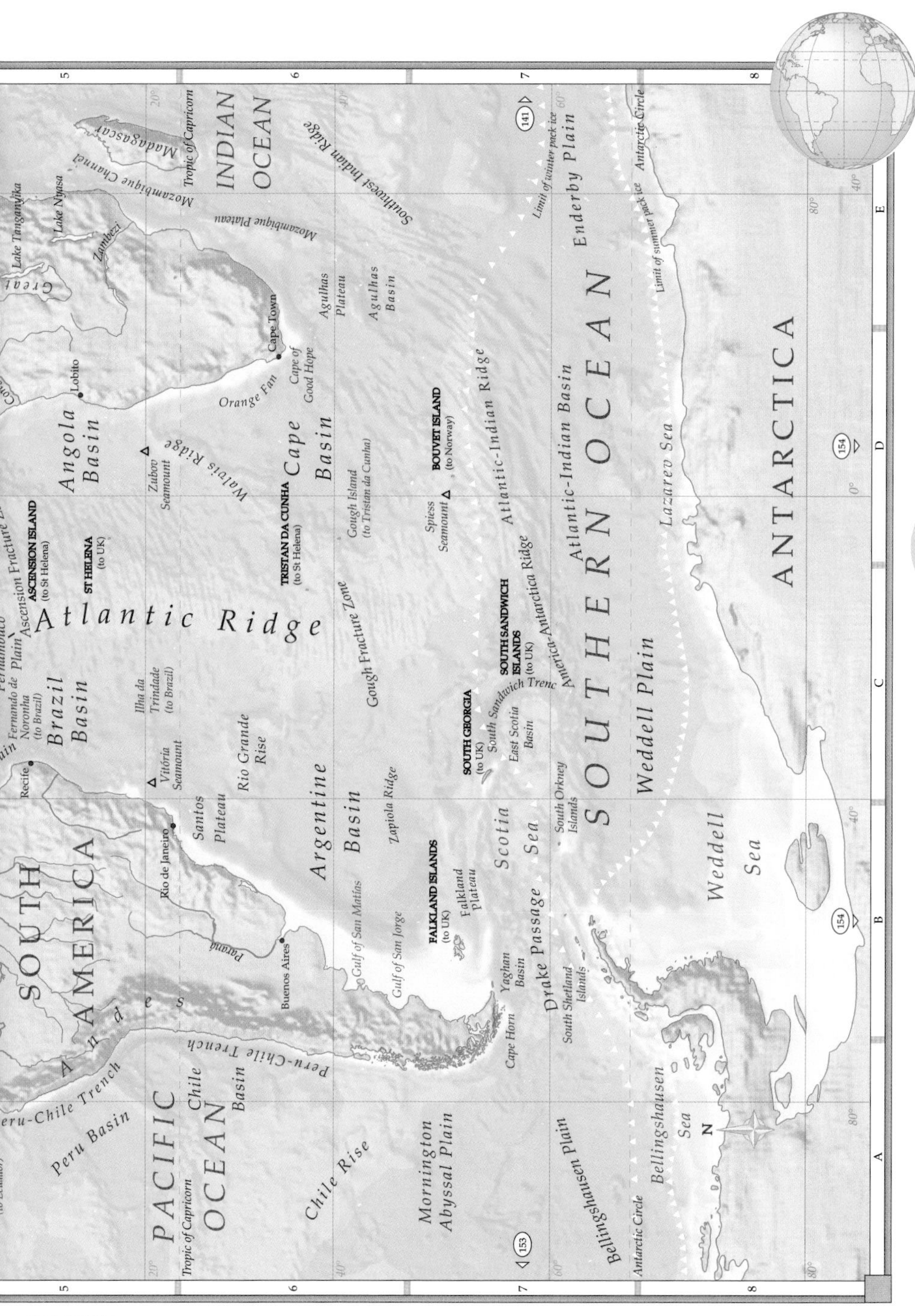

ELEVATION

-6000m	-4000m	-2000m	-1000m	-500m	-250m	0
-19 686ft	-13 124ft	-6562ft	-3281ft	-1640ft	-820ft	0

Africa

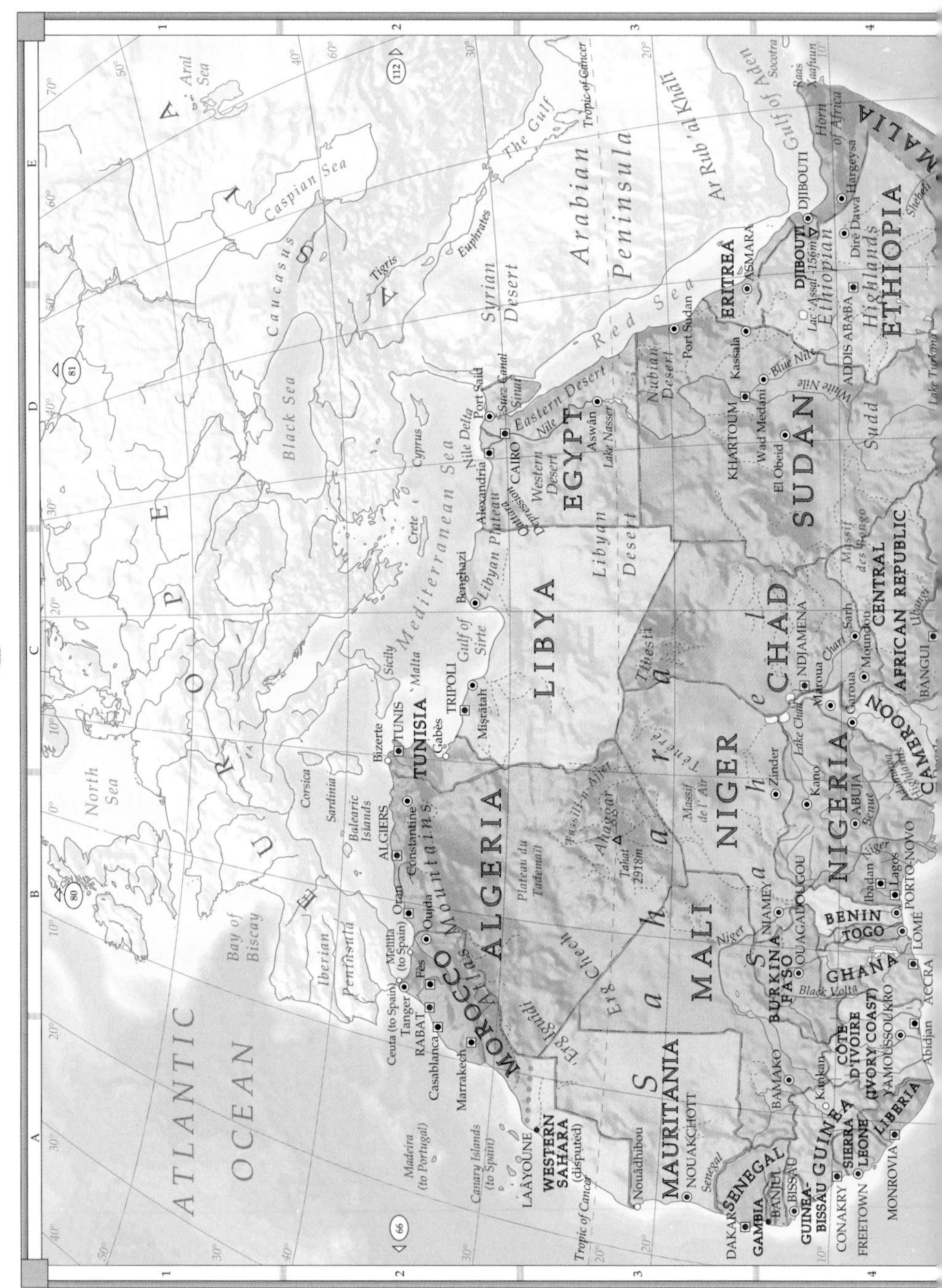

0 km 1000

0 miles 1000

POPULATION

● National capital

○ Less than 50,000 ○ 50,000 -100,000 ◉ 100,000 - 500,000 ▣ Over 500,000

ATLANTIC OCEAN
INDIAN OCEAN
DEM. REP. CONGO
CONGO
ANGOLA
NAMIBIA
BOTSWANA
ZAMBIA
ZIMBABWE
SOUTH AFRICA
LESOTHO
SWAZILAND
MOZAMBIQUE
MALAWI
TANZANIA
RWANDA
BURUNDI
MADAGASCAR
COMOROS
MAYOTTE (to France)
SAINT HELENA (to UK)
ASCENSION ISLAND (to Saint Helena)
TRISTAN DA CUNHA (to Saint Helena)
Gough Island (to Tristan da Cunha)
Prince Edward Islands (to South Africa)
Cabinda (to Angola)
Port-Gentil
BRAZZAVILLE
KINSHASA
Matadi
LUANDA
Huambo
Lubango
Namibe
Môco 2619m
Ilebo
Kananga
Kalemie
Bukavu
BUJUMBURA
DODOMA
Lubumbashi
Kitwe
Ndola
LUSAKA
HARARE
Bulawayo
Francistown
WINDHOEK
GABORONE
PRETORIA
Johannesburg
MAPUTO
MBABANE
MASERU
BLOEMFONTEIN
Durban
East London
Port Elizabeth
CAPE TOWN
Cape of Good Hope
LILONGWE
Blantyre
Beira
Nampula
Nacala
Mahajanga
MORONI
ANTANANARIVO
Fianarantsoa
Toliara
Mombasa
Tanga
Dar es Salaam
Zanzibar
Pemba
Kilimanjaro 5895m
Great Rift Valley
Lake Tanganyika
Lake Rukwa
Lake Nyasa
Lake Mweru
Lake Kariba
Victoria Falls
Okavango Delta
Etosha Pan
Kalahari Desert
Namib Desert
Great Karoo
Drakensberg
Bié Plateau
Masai Steppe
Congo
Kasai
Cuango
Cuanza
Lualaba
Luvua
Zambezi
Cuando
Cubango
Cunene
Orange River
Nossob
Vaal
Limpopo
Lúrio
Ruvuma
Mozambique Channel
Mozambique Plateau
Madagascar Basin
Madagascar Plateau
Somali Basin
Aldabra Group
Angola Basin
Cape Basin
Walvis Ridge
Orange Fan
Agulhas Plateau
Agulhas Basin
Crozet Plateau
Southwest Indian Ridge
Atlantic-Indian Ridge
Mid-Atlantic Ridge
Ascension Fracture Zone
Tropic of Capricorn
Winter limit of pack ice
141
154
67
A B C D E
5 6 7 8

Northwest Africa

A B C D

83

N

1

ATLANTIC

PORTUGAL

Tagus

SPAIN

Ebro

Islas Baleares (Balearic Islands)

35°

OCEAN

Strait of Gibraltar

GIBRALTAR (to UK)

Ceuta (to Spain)

ALGERIA

Chlef

Tanger

Melilla (to Spain)

Oran

Tetouan

Mostaganem

Ksar-el-Kebir

Chefchaouen

Madeira (to Portugal)

Salé

Kenitra

Sidi Bel Abbès

Oujda

Tlemcen

Madeira

Porto Santo

RABAT

Fès

2

66

Funchal

Casablanca

Jerada

Chott ech Chergui

Ilhas Desertas

El-Jadida

Mohammedia

Hauts Plateaux

Khouribga

Moyen Atlas

Atlas Mountains

Atlas Saharien

Safi

Beni-Mellal

Marrakech

Haut Atlas

30°

Essaouira

Figuig

Islas Canarias (Canary Islands) (to Spain)

Er-Rachidia

MOROCCO

Béchar

Ouarzazate

Agadir

Grand Erg Occidental

El Goléa

La Palma

Santa Cruz de Tenerife

Tiznit

Lanzarote

Gomera

Fuerteventura

Hierro

Las Palmas de Gran Canaria

Hamada du Dra

3

Tenerife

Tan-Tan

ALGERIA

Gran Canaria

LAÂYOUNE

Plateau du Tademaït

El Mahbas

Tindouf

Adrar

Boujdour

Smara

Bou Craa

Erg Iguîdi

I-n-Salah

25°

WESTERN SAHARA (disputed territory under Moroccan occupation)

Reggane

Galtat-Zemmour

Tropic of Cancer

Ad Dakhla

Erg Chech

4

66

Tanezrouft

Ouarâne

Sahara

Lagouira

20°

MAURITANIA

5

Azaouâd

Senegal

MALI

15°

Niger

SENEGAL

74

15° 10° 5° 0°

A B C D

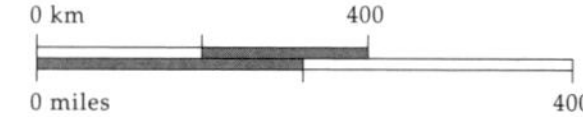

POPULATION

● National capital

○ Less than 50,000

○ 50,000 -100,000

◉ 100,000 - 500,000

▣ Over 500,000

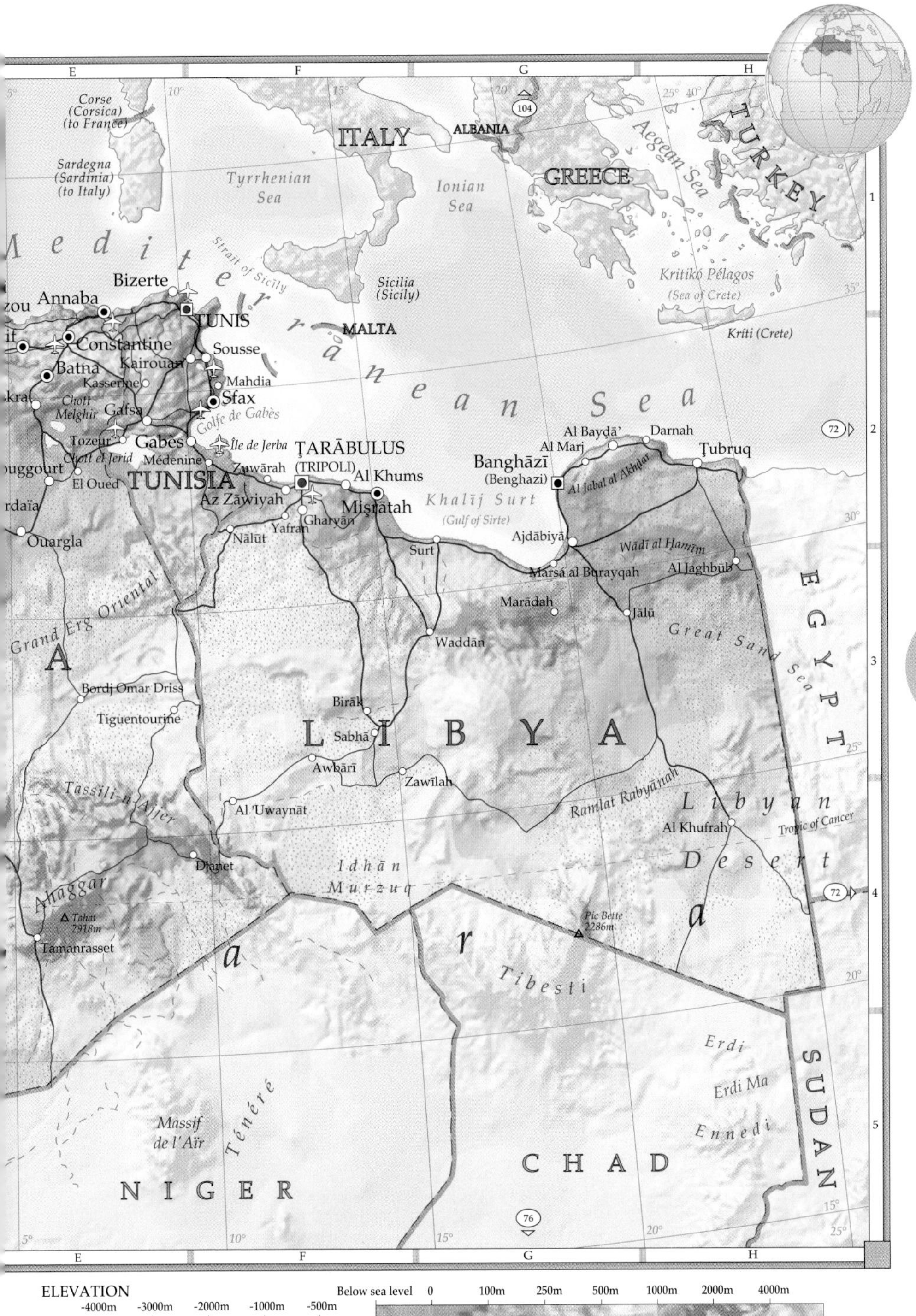

ITALY
ALBANIA
GREECE
TURKEY
Corse (Corsica) (to France)
Sardegna (Sardinia) (to Italy)
Tyrrhenian Sea
Ionian Sea
Aegean Sea
Strait of Sicily
Sicilia (Sicily)
MALTA
Kritikó Pélagos (Sea of Crete)
Kríti (Crete)
Mediterranean Sea
Bizerte
Annaba
TUNIS
Constantine
Sousse
Batna
Kairouan
Kasserine
Mahdia
Sfax
Chott Melghir
Gafsa
Golfe de Gabès
Tozeur
Gabès
Île de Jerba
Chott el Jerid
Médenine
Touggourt
El Oued
TUNISIA
Zuwārah
ṬARĀBULUS (TRIPOLI)
Al Khums
Az Zāwiyah
Miṣrātah
Gharyān
Yafran
Nālūt
Ouargla
Khalīj Surt (Gulf of Sirte)
Banghāzī (Benghazi)
Al Marj
Al Bayḍā'
Darnah
Ṭubruq
Al Jabal al Akhḍar
Ajdābiyā
Surt
Wādī al Ḥamīm
Marsá al Burayqah
Al Jaghbūb
Marādah
Jālū
Waddān
Grand Erg Oriental
Great Sand Sea
EGYPT
Bordj Omar Driss
Tiguentourine
Birāk
Sabhā
LIBYA
Awbārī
Zawīlah
Tassili-n-Ajjer
Al 'Uwaynāt
Ramlat Rabyānah
Libyan Desert
Al Khufrah
Tropic of Cancer
Djanet
Idhān Murzuq
Ahaggar
Tahat 2918m
Tamanrasset
Pic Bette 2286m
Tibesti
Erdi
Erdi Ma
Ennedi
SUDAN
Massif de l'Aïr
Ténéré
NIGER
CHAD
104
72
76
ELEVATION
Below sea level
-4000m -3000m -2000m -1000m -500m
-13 124ft -9843ft -6562ft -3281ft -1640ft -820ft/-250m 0
0 100m 250m 500m 1000m 2000m 4000m
328ft 820ft 1640ft 3281ft 6562ft 13 124ft

NORTHEAST AFRICA

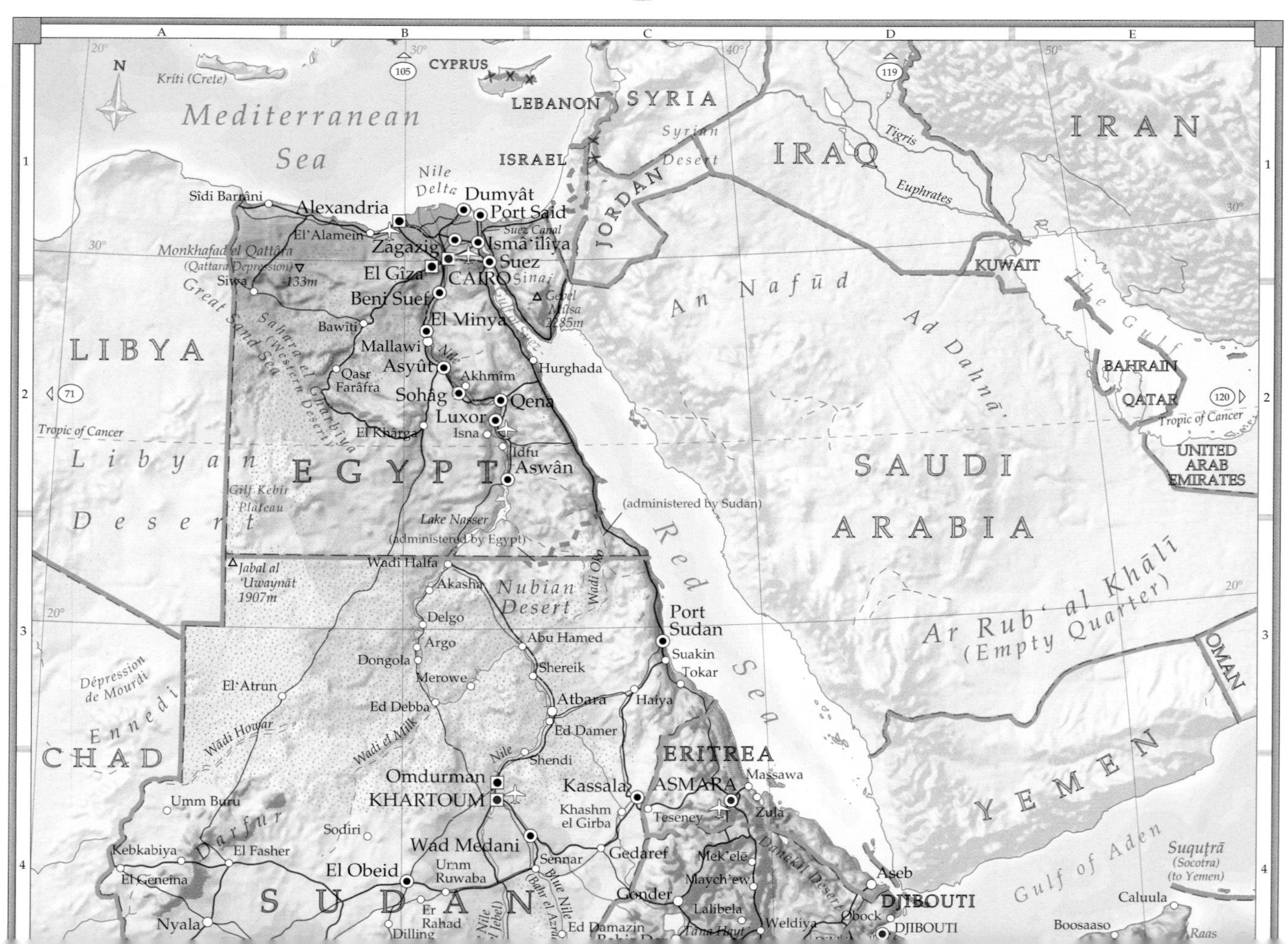

0 km 400

0 miles 400

POPULATION
● National capital
○ Less than 50,000
○ 50,000 -100,000
⦿ 100,000 - 500,000
▣ Over 500,000

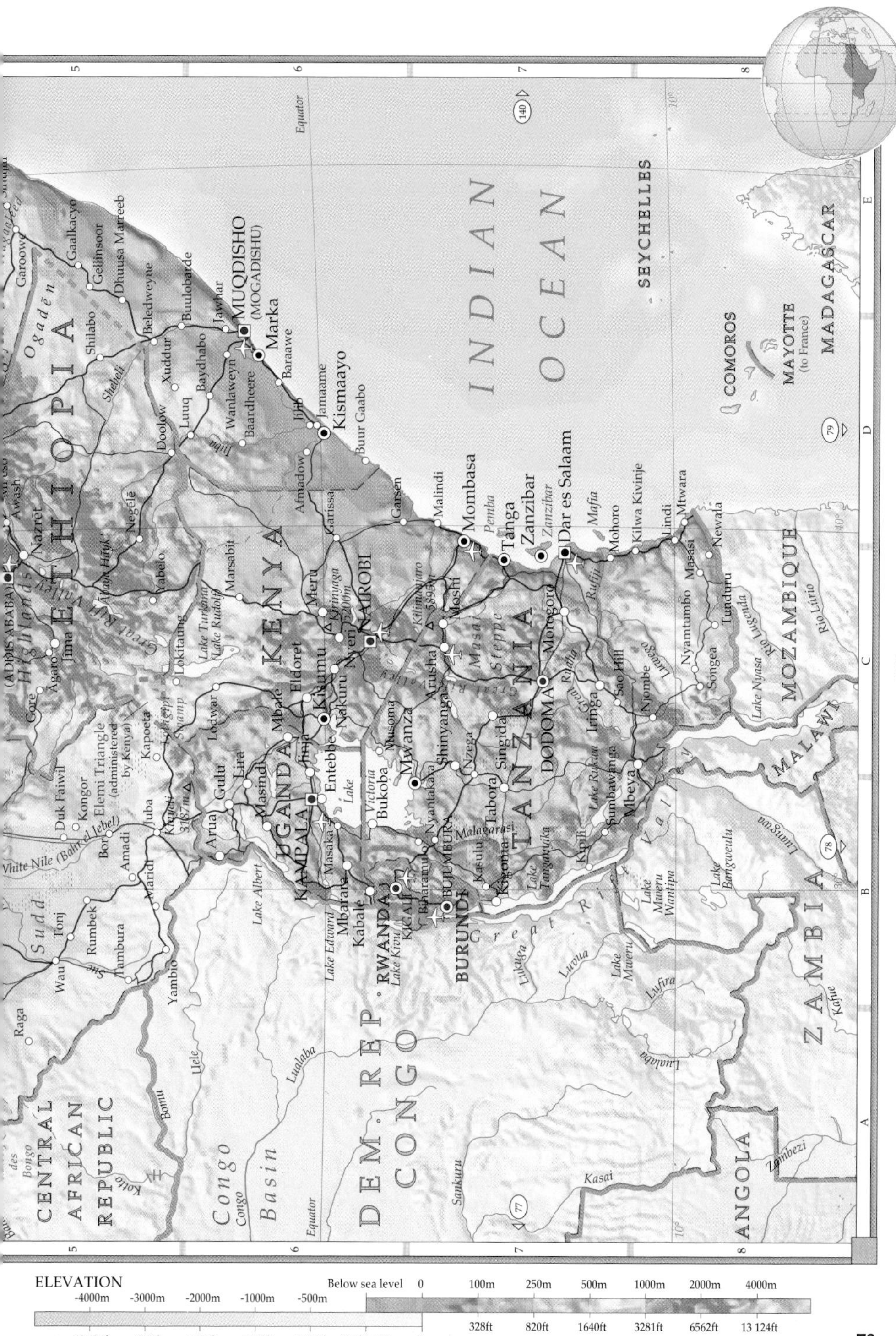
ETHIOPIA
KENYA
UGANDA
TANZANIA
RWANDA
BURUNDI
DEM. REP. CONGO
CENTRAL AFRICAN REPUBLIC
ZAMBIA
MALAWI
MOZAMBIQUE
ANGOLA
INDIAN OCEAN
SEYCHELLES
COMOROS
MAYOTTE (to France)
MADAGASCAR
(ADDIS ABABA)
MUQDISHO (MOGADISHU)
NAIROBI
KAMPALA
KIGALI
BUJUMBURA
DODOMA
Dar es Salaam
Mombasa
Kismaayo
Marka
Zanzibar
Tanga
Mwanza
Kisumu
Arusha
Tabora
Mbeya
Iringa
Morogoro
Nakuru
Eldoret
Jinja
Entebbe
Gulu
Lira
Arua
Juba
Wau
Lake Victoria
Lake Tanganyika
Lake Albert
Lake Edward
Lake Kivu
Lake Nyasa
Lake Turkana (Lake Rudolf)
Lake Mweru
Lake Bangweulu
Congo Basin
Great Rift Valley
Ogadēn
Equator
Ilemi Triangle (administered by Kenya)
Kilimanjaro 5895m
Kirinyaga 5200m
ELEVATION
Below sea level
0
100m
250m
500m
1000m
2000m
4000m
328ft
820ft
1640ft
3281ft
6562ft
13 124ft
-4000m
-3000m
-2000m
-1000m
-500m
-13 124ft
-9843ft
-6562ft
-3281ft
-1640ft
-820ft/-250m

West Africa

A B C D

N

WESTERN SAHARA
(disputed territory under Moroccan occupation)

Tropic of Cancer

ATLANTIC OCEAN

CAPE VERDE
Ilhas de Barlavento
Santo Antão
Mindelo
São Vicente
São Nicolau
Pedra Lume
Sal
Boa Vista
Santiago
Fogo
Maio
PRAIA
Ilhas de Sotavento

MAURITANIA
'Aïn Ben Tili
Bir Mogreïn
Erg Iguidi
Kâgheṭ
El Hank
Fdérik
Zouérat
Touâjîl
Ouarâne
Nouâdhibou
Choûm
Akchâr
Atâr
Chinguetti
Akjoujt
Oujeft
El Mreyyé
NOUAKCHOTT
Idîni
Tîchît
Tidjikja
Boutilimit
Magta' Lahjar
Boûmdeïd
Rkîz
Aoukâr
Oualâta
Tâmchekket
Aleg
Kiffa
'Ayoûn el 'Atroûs
Kaédi
Néma
Timbedgha
Amourj
Kobenni
Bassikounou
Sélibabi
Nioro

SENEGAL
Rosso
Dagana
Senegal
Richard Toll
Saint Louis
Louga
Matam
Mékhé
DAKAR
Thiès
Mbaké
Mbour
Diourbel
Kaolack
Sokone
Tambacounda
Kayes
Ziguinchor
Bignona
Kolda
Sédhiou

GAMBIA
BANJUL
Gambia

GUINEA-BISSAU
Bafatá
BISSAU

GUINEA
Gaoual
Boké
Labé
Pita
Dinguiraye
Niger
Siguiri
Mamou
Kindia
Kankan
Faranah
CONAKRY
Tokounou
Kissidougou
Beyla
Nzérékoré

SIERRA LEONE
FREETOWN
Makeni
Bo
Kenema

LIBERIA
Gbanga
Tubmanburg
Harbel
MONROVIA
Buchanan
Zwedru
Harper
Cavalla

Bafing
Toukoto
Kita
Kolokani
Ségou
Koulikoro
BAMAKO
Bagoé
Bougouni
Ténenkou
Odienné
Tengréla
Ferkessédougou
Boundiali
Korhogo

CÔTE D'IVOIRE (IVORY COAST)
Katiola
Danané
YAMOUSSOUKRO
Gagnoa
Sassandra
Divo
San-Pédro

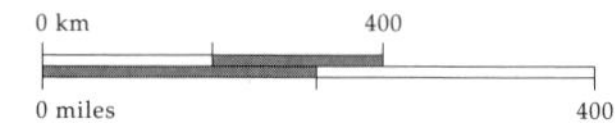

POPULATION
● National capital
○ Less than 50,000
○ 50,000 - 100,000
◉ 100,000 - 500,000
▣ Over 500,000

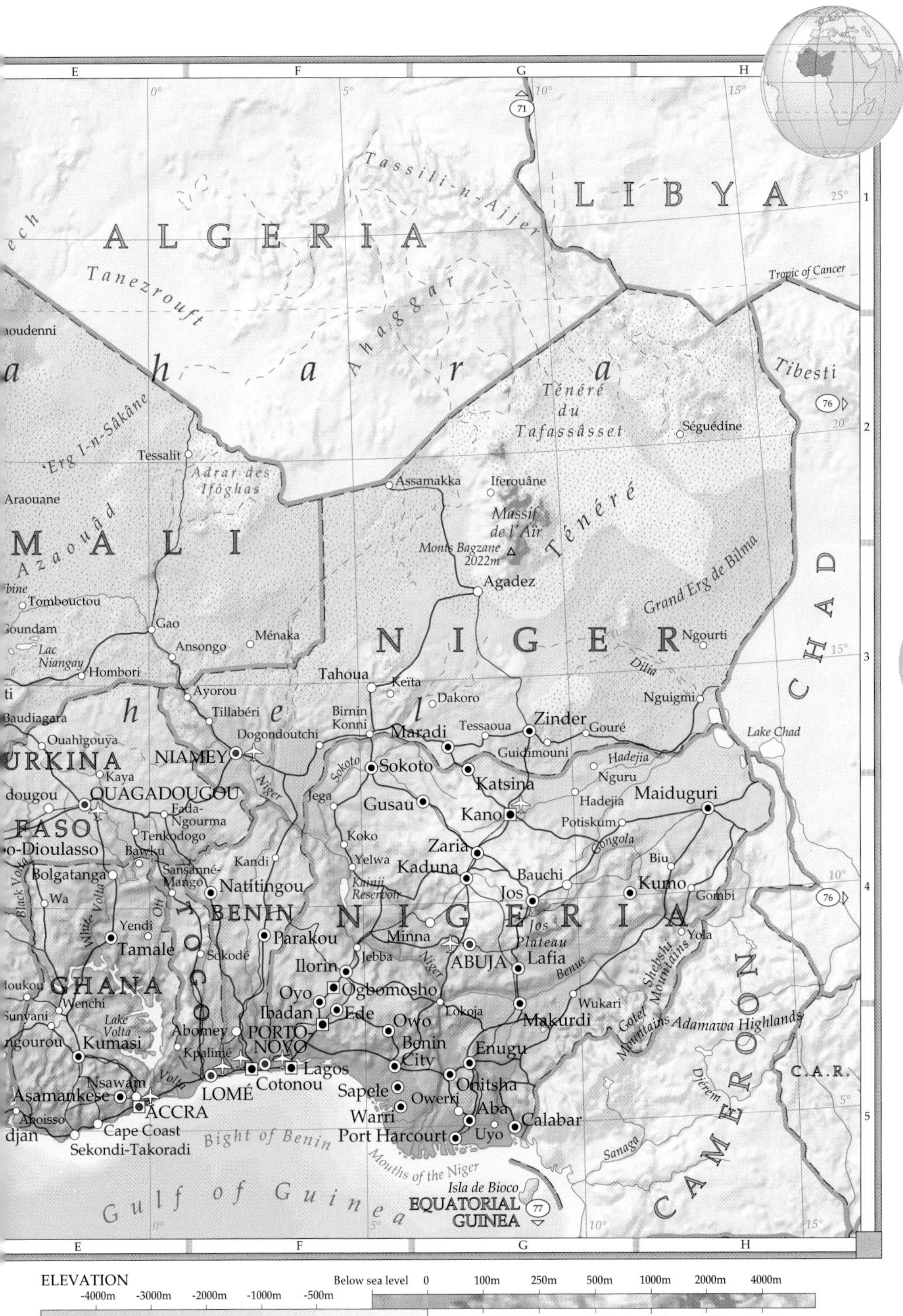
E
F
G
H
ALGERIA
LIBYA
Tassili-n-Ajjer
Tanezrouft
Ahaggar
Tropic of Cancer
Tibesti
Ténéré du Tafassâsset
Séguédine
Erg I-n-Sâkâne
Tessalit
Adrar des Ifôghas
Assamakka
Iferouâne
Massif de l'Aïr
Monts Bagzane 2022m
Ténéré
Grand Erg de Bilma
Araouane
MALI
Azaouâd
Tombouctou
Agadez
CHAD
Goundam
Gao
Ménaka
NIGER
Ngourti
Lac Niangay
Ansongo
Hombori
Tahoua
Keïta
Dilia
Ayorou
Dakoro
Nguigmi
Tillabéri
Birnin Konni
Maradi
Tessaoua
Zinder
Gouré
Lake Chad
Ouahigouya
Dogondoutchi
Guidimouni
Hadejia
NIAMEY
Sokoto
Katsina
Nguru
Kaya
Niger
Jega
Hadejia
Maiduguri
OUAGADOUGOU
Fada-Ngourma
Gusau
Kano
Potiskum
FASO
Tenkodogo
Koko
Zaria
Gongola
Bawku
Kandi
Yelwa
Kaduna
Biu
Bolgatanga
Sansanné-Mango
Natitingou
Kainji Reservoir
Bauchi
Kumo
Black Volta
Wa
White Volta
Oti
BENIN
NIGERIA
Jos
Gombi
Yendi
Parakou
Minna
Jos Plateau
Yola
Tamale
Sokodé
Jebba
ABUJA
Lafia
Benue
Shebshi Mountains
GHANA
Ilorin
Ogbomosho
TOGO
Oyo
Wukari
Wenchi
Ibadan
Ede
Lokoja
Makurdi
Lake Volta
Abomey
PORTO-NOVO
Owo
Goter Mountains
Adamawa Highlands
Kumasi
Kpalimé
Benin City
Enugu
Lagos
C.A.R.
Nsawam
Volta
Cotonou
Onitsha
Asamankese
LOMÉ
Sapele
Owerri
Djerem
ACCRA
Warri
Aba
Calabar
Aboisso
Cape Coast
Port Harcourt
Uyo
Sekondi-Takoradi
Bight of Benin
Sanaga
CAMEROON
Mouths of the Niger
Isla de Bioco
EQUATORIAL GUINEA
Gulf of Guinea
71
76
77
ELEVATION
Below sea level
0
100m
250m
500m
1000m
2000m
4000m
-4000m
-3000m
-2000m
-1000m
-500m
328ft
820ft
1640ft
3281ft
6562ft
13 124ft
-13 124ft
-9843ft
-6562ft
-3281ft
-1640ft
-820ft/-250m
0

Central Africa

0 km 400

0 miles 400

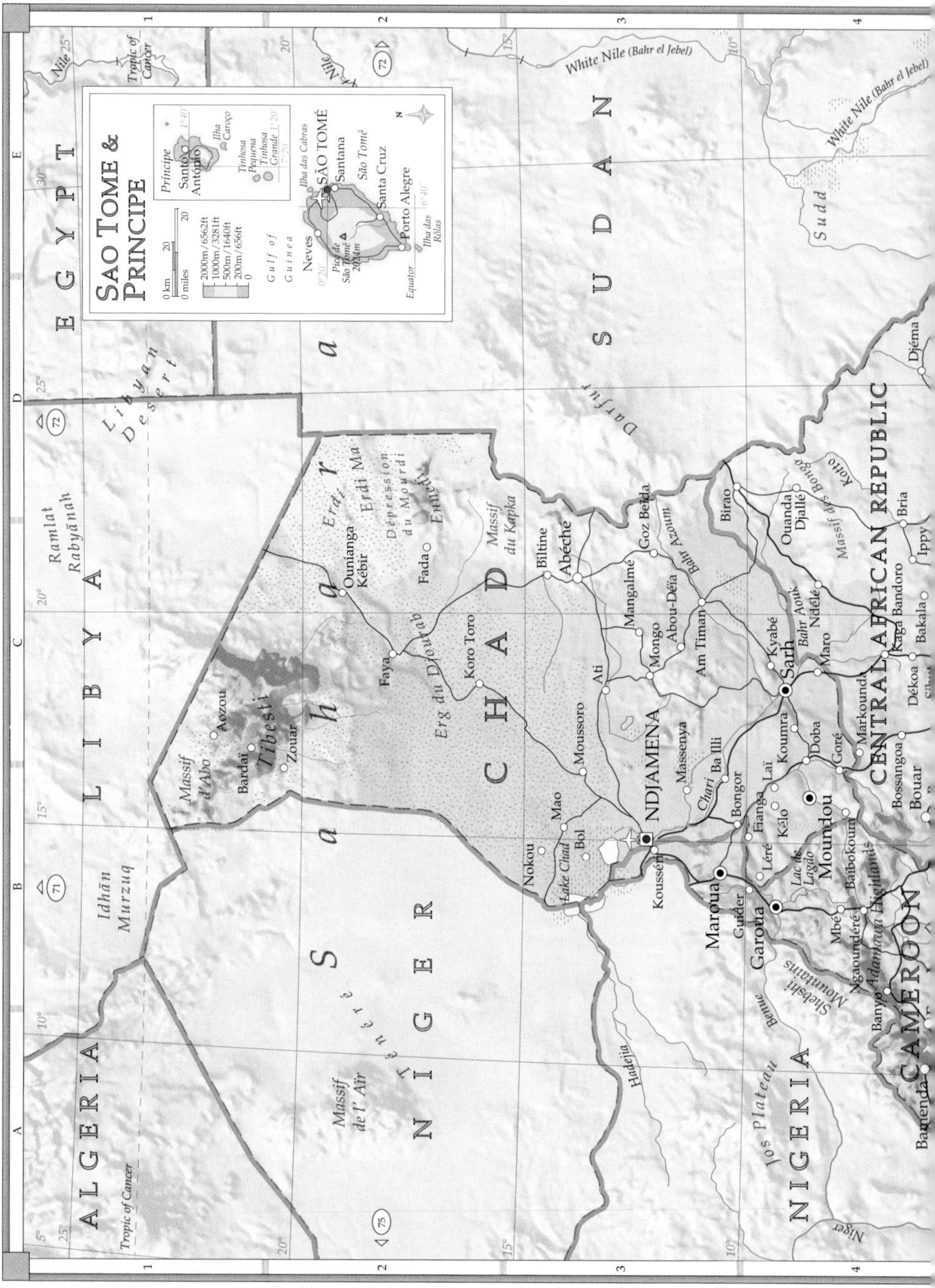

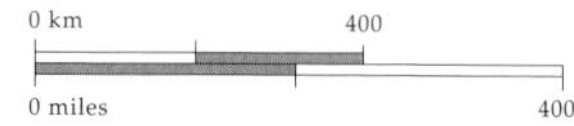

POPULATION ● National capital

○ Less than 50,000 ○ 50,000 -100,000 ⦿ 100,000 - 500,000 ▣ Over 500,000

ELEVATION

Below sea level						0	100m	250m	500m	1000m	2000m	4000m
-4000m	-3000m	-2000m	-1000m	-500m								
-13 124ft	-9843ft	-6562ft	-3281ft	-1640ft	-820ft/-250m	0	328ft	820ft	1640ft	3281ft	6562ft	13 124ft

SOUTHERN AFRICA

SOUTH AFRICA'S THREE CAPITALS

Pretoria -	*administrative capital*
Cape Town -	*legislative capital*
Bloemfontein -	*judicial capital*

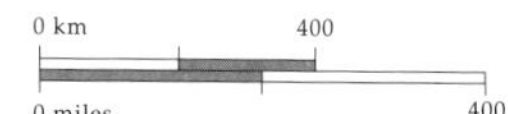

POPULATION
- ● National capital
- ○ Less than 50,000
- ○ 50,000 -100,000
- ◉ 100,000 - 500,000
- ▣ Over 500,000

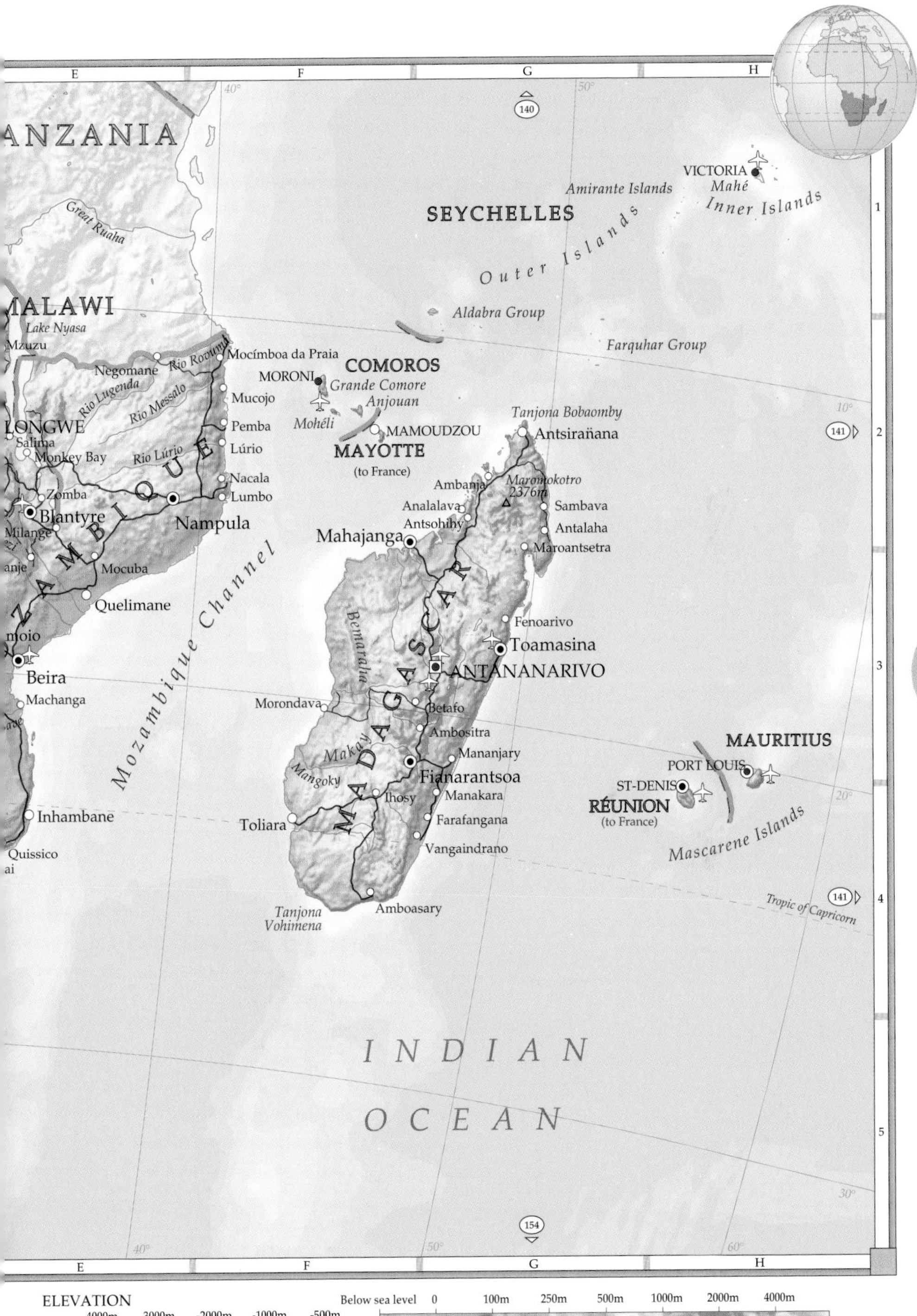

TANZANIA
Great Ruaha
MALAWI
Lake Nyasa
Mzuzu
LONGWE
Salima
Monkey Bay
Zomba
Blantyre
Milange
Negomane
Rio Rovuma
Rio Lugenda
Rio Messalo
Rio Lúrio
MOZAMBIQUE
Mocímboa da Praia
Mucojo
Pemba
Lúrio
Nacala
Lumbo
Nampula
Mocuba
Quelimane
Beira
Machanga
Inhambane
Quissico
Mozambique Channel
SEYCHELLES
VICTORIA
Mahé
Inner Islands
Amirante Islands
Outer Islands
Aldabra Group
Farquhar Group
COMOROS
MORONI
Grande Comore
Anjouan
Mohéli
MAMOUDZOU
MAYOTTE
(to France)
Tanjona Bobaomby
Antsirañana
Ambanja
Maromokotro 2376m
Analalava
Antsohihy
Sambava
Antalaha
Maroantsetra
Mahajanga
MADAGASCAR
Bemaraha
Fenoarivo
Toamasina
ANTANANARIVO
Morondava
Betafo
Ambositra
Makay
Mananjary
Mangoky
Fianarantsoa
Ihosy
Manakara
Farafangana
Toliara
Vangaindrano
Amboasary
Tanjona Vohimena
MAURITIUS
PORT LOUIS
ST-DENIS
RÉUNION
(to France)
Mascarene Islands
Tropic of Capricorn
INDIAN OCEAN
140
141
154
E
F
G
H
1
2
3
4
5
ELEVATION
Below sea level
-4000m -3000m -2000m -1000m -500m 0
100m 250m 500m 1000m 2000m 4000m
328ft 820ft 1640ft 3281ft 6562ft 13 124ft
-13 124ft -9843ft -6562ft -3281ft -1640ft -820ft/-250m 0

Europe

A B C D

1 2 3 4 5

Reykjanes Basin
155
Limit of winter pack ice
REYKJAVÍK
ICELAND
Vatnajökull
Arctic Circle
Norwegian Basin
Reykjanes Ridge
Charlie-Gibbs Fracture Zone
Faeroe-Iceland Ridge
Norwegian Sea
Iceland Basin
FAEROE ISLANDS (to Denmark)
Hatton Ridge
Faeroe-Shetland Trough
Trondheim
Mid-Atlantic Ridge
66
Shetland Islands
Rockall Bank
Outer Hebrides
Orkney Islands
Bergen
Rockall Trough
British Isles
Stavanger
OSLO
Glasgow
Edinburgh
North Sea
Ireland
Belfast
UNITED KINGDOM
Gothenburg
Aalborg
Jylland
IRELAND
ISLE OF MAN (to UK)
DUBLIN
Porcupine Plain
ATLANTIC OCEAN
Liverpool
Manchester
DENMARK
Odense
Britain
Celtic Sea
Birmingham
Cardiff
LONDON
NETHERLANDS
Hamburg
Celtic Shelf
THE HAGUE
AMSTERDAM
Rotterdam
Elbe
Hannover
English Channel
BELGIUM
BRUSSELS
BERLIN
Azores-Biscay Rise
Charcot Seamounts
Biscay Plain
CHANNEL IS. (to UK)
le Havre
Liège
Bonn
Seine
LUXEMBOURG
GERMANY
Rennes
PARIS
Frankfurt am Main
LUXEMBOURG
Iberian Plain
Nantes
Loire
Orléans
Rhine
Stuttgart
Strasbourg
A Coruña
Galicia Bank
Bay of Biscay
FRANCE
Munich
Zürich
LIECH.
BERN
Salzburg
Bordeaux
SWITZERLAND
Innsbruck
AUSTRIA
Cordillera Cantábrica
Bilbao
Lyon
Massif Central
Mont Blanc 4807m
Alps
66
Porto
Garonne
Rhône
Milan
Venice
SLOVENIA
PORTUGAL
Duero
Toulouse
Turin
Po
Trieste
Iberian
Zaragoza
Pyrenees
Nice
Bologna
Tagus Plain
Ebro
ANDORRA
Marseille
MONACO
SAN MARINO
LISBON
Tagus
MADRID
Pisa
Horseshoe Seamounts
SPAIN
Barcelona
Apennines
Peninsula
Corsica
Adriatic Sea
Madeira (to Portugal)
Seville
Guadalquivir
Valencia
VATICAN CITY
ROME
ITALY
Strait of Gibraltar
Palma
Sardinia
Málaga
Balearic Islands
Algerian Basin
Naples
Bari
GIBRALTAR (to UK)
Ceuta (to Spain)
Tyrrhenian Sea
Mediterranean Sea
Cagliari
Cosenza
Melilla (to Spain)
Palermo
Canary Islands (to Spain)
Sicily
Mount Etna 3340m
Catania
Atlas Mountains
AFRICA
68
MALTA
VALLETTA

A B C D

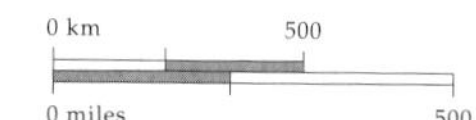

POPULATION
• National capital
○ Less than 50,000
○ 50,000 -100,000
◉ 100,000 - 500,000
▣ Over 500,000

Barents Sea
North Cape
Ostrov Kolguyev
Arctic Circle
Murmansk
Kola Peninsula
FINLAND
White Sea
Archangel
Northern Dvina
Ural Mountains
Ob'
Irtysh
RUSSIAN FEDERATION
Bothnia
Lake Onega
Perm'
Tampere
Turku
HELSINKI
Lake Ladoga
Saint Petersburg
Vologda
Ufa
TALLINN
ESTONIA
Yaroslavl'
Kazan'
Nizhniy Novgorod
European Plain
LATVIA
RIGA
Ul'yanovsk
Samara
Orenburg
Ural
MOSCOW
LITHUANIA
Vitsyebsk
Kaunas
VILNIUS
MINSK
Central Russian Upland
Volga Uplands
Volga
Syr Darya
Aral Sea
Babruysk
BELARUS
Homyel'
Voronezh
WARSAW
Brest
Pripet Marshes
Don
Bug
Dnieper Lowlands
Kharkiv
KIEV
Volgograd
Dnieper
Astrakhan'
Amu Darya
L'viv
UKRAINE
Dnipropetrovs'k
Donets'k
Volga Delta -28m
Carpathian Mountains
Dniester
Chernivtsi
Rostov-na-Donu
MOLDOVA
CHIŞINĂU
Caspian Sea
Cluj-Napoca
Sea of Azov
Stavropol'
ROMANIA
Odesa
Braşov
Crimea
Caucasus
El'brus 5642m
Simferopol'
BUCHAREST
Constanța
Black Sea
Danube
BULGARIA
Varna
Balkan Mountains
Burgas
SOFIA
SKOPJE
TURKEY
ASIA
Aegean Sea
Anatolia
GREECE
ATHENS
Piraeus
Peloponnese
Zāgros Mountains
Tigris
Euphrates
Cyprus
Iráklelo
Crete
E
F
G
H
1
2
3
4
5
155
112
118
20°
30°
40°
50°
60°
70°
80°

THE NORTH ATLANTIC

A B C D

1 2 3 4 5

37 38 39 66

Arctic Circle
Gulf of Boothia
Devon Island
Ellesmere Island
Nares Strait
NUNAVUT
Qaanaaq
Knud Rasmussen
Hudson Bay
Southampton Island
Innaanganeq
Savissivik
Foxe Basin
Qimusseriarsuaq
Baffin Bay
Kullorsuaq
CANADA
Baffin Island
Upernavik
Limit of summer pack ice
Péninsule d'Ungava
Hudson Strait
QUÉBEC
Uummannaq
Qeqertarsuaq
Qeqertarsuaq
Qeqertarsuup Tunua
Arnaud
Frobisher Bay
Cumberland Sound
Davis Strait
Qasigiannguit
Sisimiut
Kong Frederik IX Land
GREENLAND
(to Denmark)
Ungava Bay
Maniitsoq
NUUK
George
Kong Christian IX Land
Gunnbjø
Mont Forel 3360m
Paamiut
Ammassalik
Kong Frederik VI Kyst
Ivittuut
NEWFOUNDLAND & LABRADOR
Labrador Sea
Denm
Qaqortoq
Nanortalik
Limit of winter pack ice
Reykjanes Basin
Nunap Isua (Kap Farvel)
ATLANTIC OCEAN

90° 80° 70° 60° 50° 40° 30°

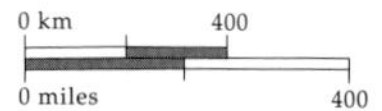

POPULATION
● National capital
○ Less than 50,000
○ 50,000 -100,000
◉ 100,000 - 500,000
▣ Over 500,000

ARCTIC OCEAN
Lincoln Sea
Kap Morris Jesup
Wandel Sea
Independence Fjord
Nord
SVALBARD
(to Norway)
Zemlya Frantsa-Iosifa
Kvitøya
Novaya Zemlya
Nordaustlandet
Kong Karls Land
Barentsøya
Spitsbergen
Edgeøya
LONGYEARBYEN
Barentsberg
Storfjorden
Barents Sea
Limit of winter pack ice
Kong Frederik VIII Land
Greenland Sea
Christian X Land
Limit of summer pack ice
Bjørnøya
(to Norway)
Nordkapp
(North Cape)
Daneborg
Petermann Bjerg
2940m
Mohns Ridge
FINLAND
Kong Oscar Fjord
Ittoqqortoormiit
Kangertittivaq
Kangikajik
JAN MAYEN
(to Norway)
Arctic Circle
Norwegian Sea
Vestfjorden
Norwegian Basin
ICELAND
SWEDEN
Siglufjördhur
Raufarhöfn
Húsavík
Akureyri
Stykkishólmur
Seydhisfjördhur
Neskaupstadhur
REYKJAVÍK
Selfoss
Vatnajökull
Djúpivogur
Hvannadalshnúkur
2119m
Vestmannaeyjar
Gulf of Bothnia
FAEROE ISLANDS
(to Denmark)
TÓRSHAVN
N
NORWAY
Shetland Islands
ELEVATION
Below sea level
-4000m -3000m -2000m -1000m -500m 0
-13 124ft -9843ft -6562ft -3281ft -1640ft -820ft/-250m 0
100m 250m 500m 1000m 2000m 4000m
328ft 820ft 1640ft 3281ft 6562ft 13 124ft

SCANDINAVIA & FINLAND

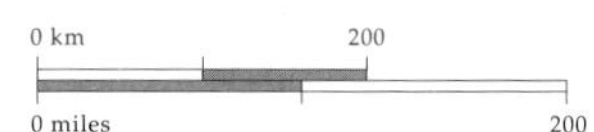

NORWAY
DENMARK
ESTONIA
LATVIA
LITHUANIA
RUSS. FED.
BELARUS
POLAND
GERMANY
KALININGRAD (to Russian Federation)
North Sea
Baltic Sea
Skagerrak
Kattegat
Gulf of Finland
Gulf of Riga
Gulf of Danzig
Ålands hav
Åland
Gotland
Öland
Bornholm
Saaremaa
Hiiumaa
Sjælland
Fyn
Lolland
Falster
Møn
Læsø
Rømø
Jylland
Lake Peipus
Ladozhskoye Ozero
Courland Lagoon
Hanöbukten
Storebælt
Western Dvina
Neman
Wisła
Oder
Elbe
Weser
Ems
Vänern
Vättern
Hjälmaren
Mälaren
Mjøsa
Glåma
Klarälven
Ljusnan
Setesdal
Hardangervidda
Jotunheimen
Glittertind 2472m
Sognefjorden
Hardangerfjorden
Boknafjorden
Ringkøbing Fjord
Yding Skovhøj 173m
HELSINKI
Espoo
Vantaa
Turku (Åbo)
Tampere
Lahti
Kotka
Porvoo
Lappeenranta
Jyväskylä
Pori
Rauma
Hanko (Hangö)
Salo
Hyvinkää
Riihimäki
Hämeenlinna
Nokia
Kouvola
Imatra
Varkaus
Seinäjoki
Närpes (Närpiö)
Kankaanpää
Keuruu
Joutseno
STOCKHOLM
Uppsala
Norrtälje
Täby
Sollentuna
Södertälje
Västerås
Örebro
Norrköping
Linköping
Nyköping
Jönköping
Göteborg (Gothenburg)
Mölndal
Kungsbacka
Borås
Varberg
Halmstad
Helsingborg
Malmö
Lund
Kristianstad
Karlskrona
Kalmar
Växjö
Visby
Gävle
Sundsvall
Härnösand
Hudiksvall
Söderhamn
Falun
Borlänge
Karlstad
Trollhättan
Uddevalla
Mora
Sala
Avesta
Oskarshamn
Borgholm
OSLO
Lillestrøm
Sandvika
Drammen
Bergen
Stavanger
Sandnes
Haugesund
Kristiansand
Arendal
Fredrikstad
Sarpsborg
Halden
Moss
Hamar
Lillehammer
Gjøvik
Hønefoss
Kongsberg
Porsgrunn
Horten
Ålesund
Røros
Dombås
KØBENHAVN (Copenhagen)
Århus
Aalborg
Odense
Esbjerg
Randers
Kolding
Hjørring
Viborg
Holstebro
Nykøbing
Slagelse
Rønne
ELEVATION
Below sea level
0
100m
250m
500m
1000m
2000m
4000m
328ft
820ft
1640ft
3281ft
6562ft
13 124ft
-2000m
-1000m
-500m
-250m
-100m
-6562ft
-3281ft
-1640ft
-820ft
-328ft
-164ft/-50m

THE LOW COUNTRIES

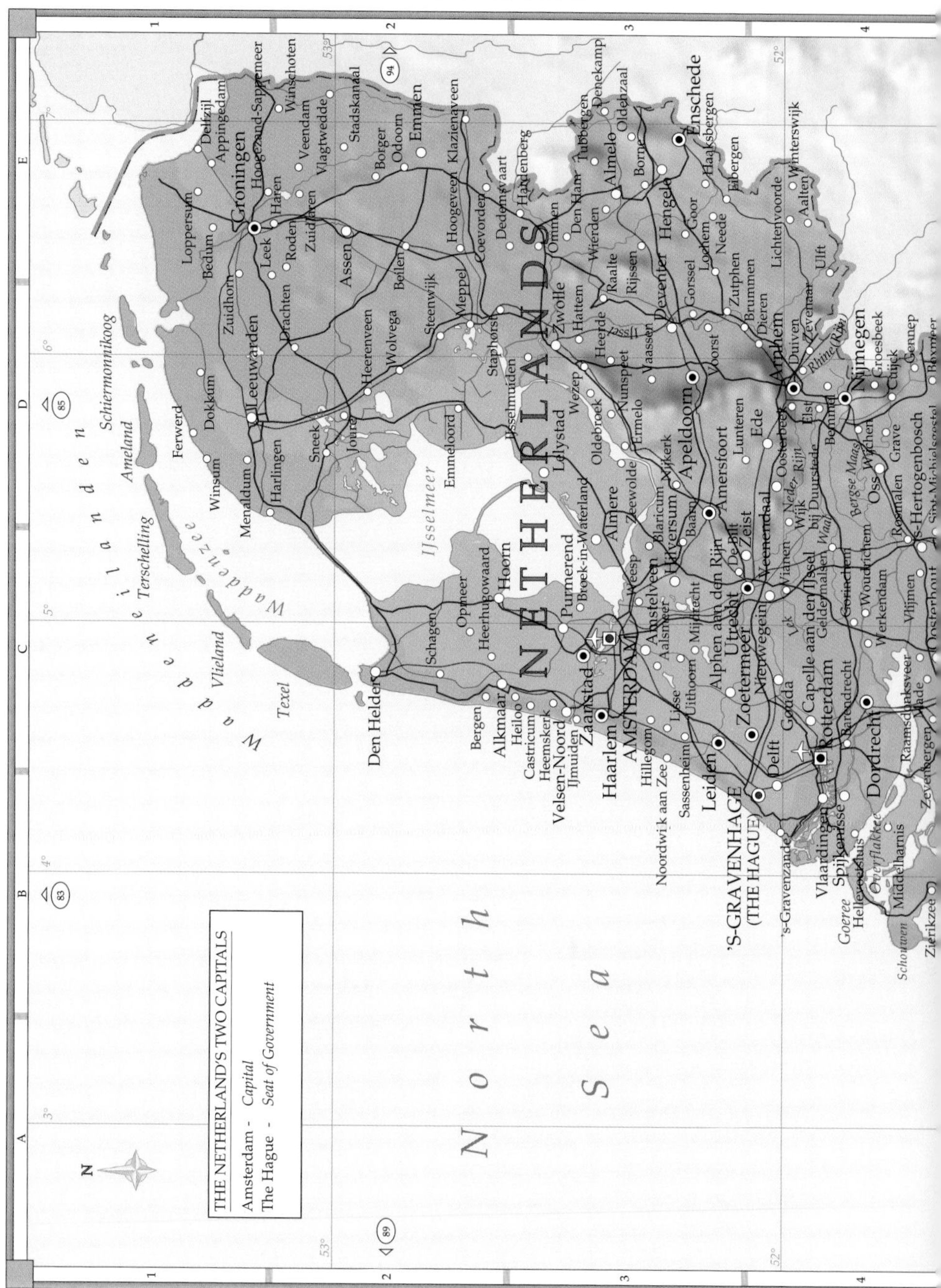

0 km 50

0 miles 50

POPULATION
● National capital
○ Less than 50,000
○ 50,000 -100,000
⦿ 100,000 - 500,000
▣ Over 500,000

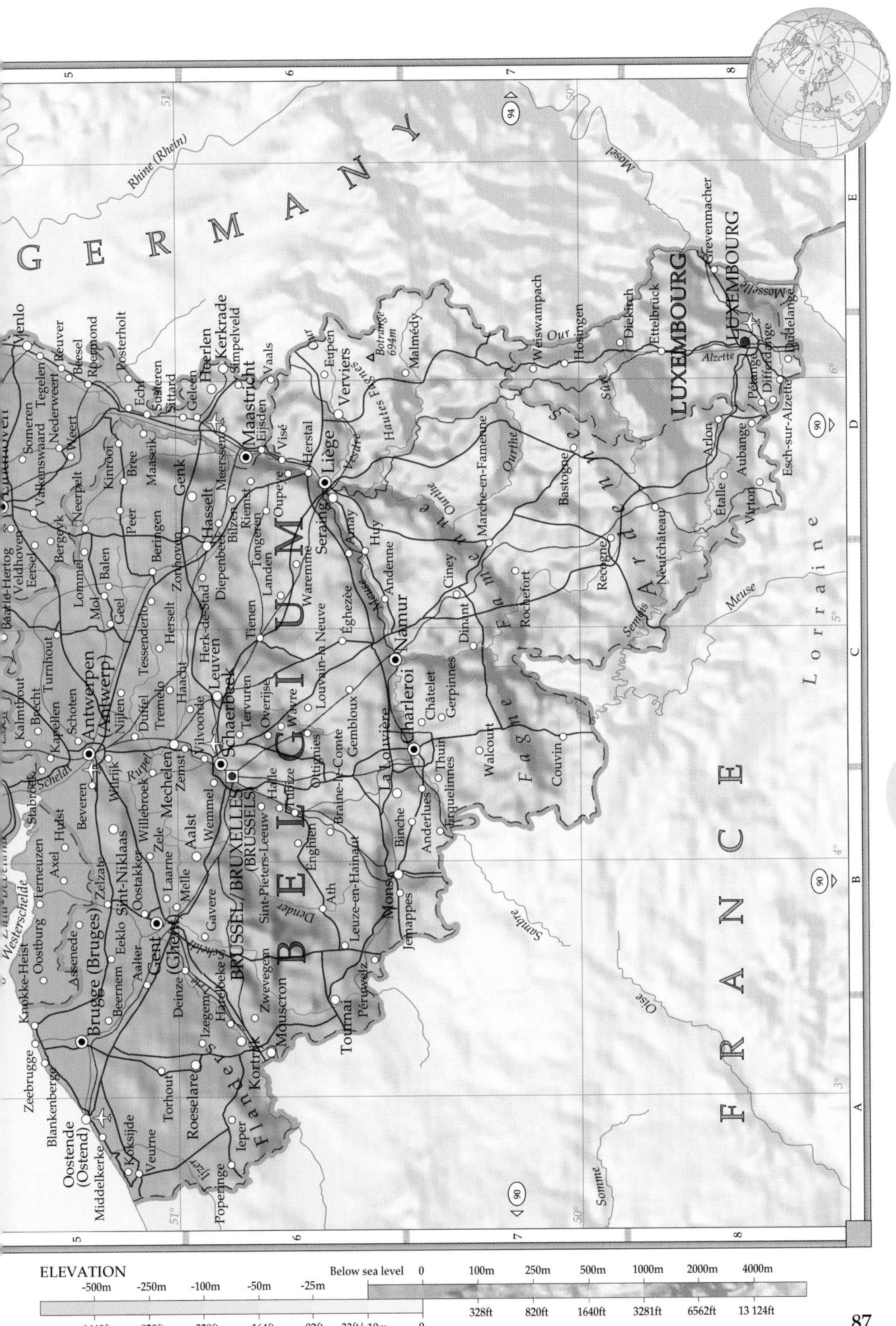
G E R M A N Y
B E L G I U M
F R A N C E
LUXEMBOURG
LUXEMBOURG
Flanders
Famenne
Fagne
Ardennes
Lorraine
Hautes Fagnes
BRUSSEL/BRUXELLES (BRUSSELS)
Antwerpen (Antwerp)
Gent (Ghent)
Brugge (Bruges)
Oostende (Ostend)
Liège
Namur
Charleroi
Maastricht
Mons
Leuven
Mechelen
Aalst
Kortrijk
Tournai
Mouscron
Roeselare
Ieper
Poperinge
Veurne
Koksijde
Middelkerke
Blankenberge
Zeebrugge
Knokke-Heist
Sint-Niklaas
Hasselt
Genk
Verviers
Eupen
Malmédy
Spa
Seraing
Herstal
Huy
Andenne
Dinant
Ciney
Rochefort
Marche-en-Famenne
Bastogne
Neufchâteau
Arlon
Virton
Couvin
Walcourt
Philippeville
Wavre
Nivelles
Halle
Vilvoorde
Tienen
Sint-Truiden
Tongeren
Turnhout
Geel
Mol
Lommel
Heerlen
Kerkrade
Sittard
Venlo
Roermond
Ettelbrück
Diekirch
Grevenmacher
Esch-sur-Alzette
Differdange
Dudelange
Rhine (Rhein)
Meuse
Sambre
Oise
Somme
Mosel
Moselle
Ourthe
Semois
Westerschelde
Botrange 694m
ELEVATION
Below sea level
0
100m
250m
500m
1000m
2000m
4000m
-500m
-250m
-100m
-50m
-25m
328ft
820ft
1640ft
3281ft
6562ft
13 124ft
-1640ft
-820ft
-328ft
-164ft
-82ft
33ft/-10m
0

THE BRITISH ISLES

North Sea

ATLANTIC OCEAN

Shetland Islands
Unst
Yell
Fetlar
Mainland
Lerwick
Fair Isle

Orkney Islands
Sanday
Kirkwall
Mainland
Hoy
John o'Groats
Thurso

Ben Hope 927m
Highlands
Ullapool
Inverness
Loch Ness
Aviemore
Elgin
Moray Firth
Spey
Fraserburgh
Peterhead
Aberdeen
Dee
Grampian Mountains
SCOTLAND
Ben Nevis 1343m
Fort William
Mallaig
Stromeferry
North West Highlands
Montrose
Arbroath
Dundee
St Andrews
Forfar
Tay
Perth
Firth of Forth
Edinburgh
Dunfermline
Stirling
Glasgow
Paisley
Greenock
East Kilbride
Hamilton
Clyde
Kilmarnock
Prestwick
Ayr
Isle of Arran
Kintyre
Loch Lomond
Berwick-upon-Tweed
Galashiels
Hawick
Cheviot Hills
Newcastle upon Tyne

The Minch
The Little Minch
Isle of Lewis
Stornoway
Harris
North Uist
South Uist
Barra
Outer Hebrides
St Kilda
Isle of Skye
Rhum
Eigg
Coll
Tiree
Isle of Mull
Oban
Firth of Lorn
Jura
Islay
Inner Hebrides

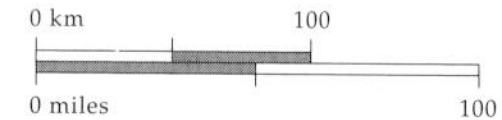

POPULATION
● National capital
● Internal administrative capital
○ Less than 50,000
○ 50,000 -100,000
◉ 100,000 - 500,000
▣ Over 500,000

ELEVATION

Below sea level	-2000m	-1000m	-500m	-250m	-100m	0	100m	250m	500m	1000m	2000m	4000m
	-6562ft	-3281ft	-1640ft	-820ft	-328ft	-164ft/-50m	0	328ft	820ft	1640ft	3281ft	6562ft	13 124ft

FRANCE, ANDORRA & MONACO

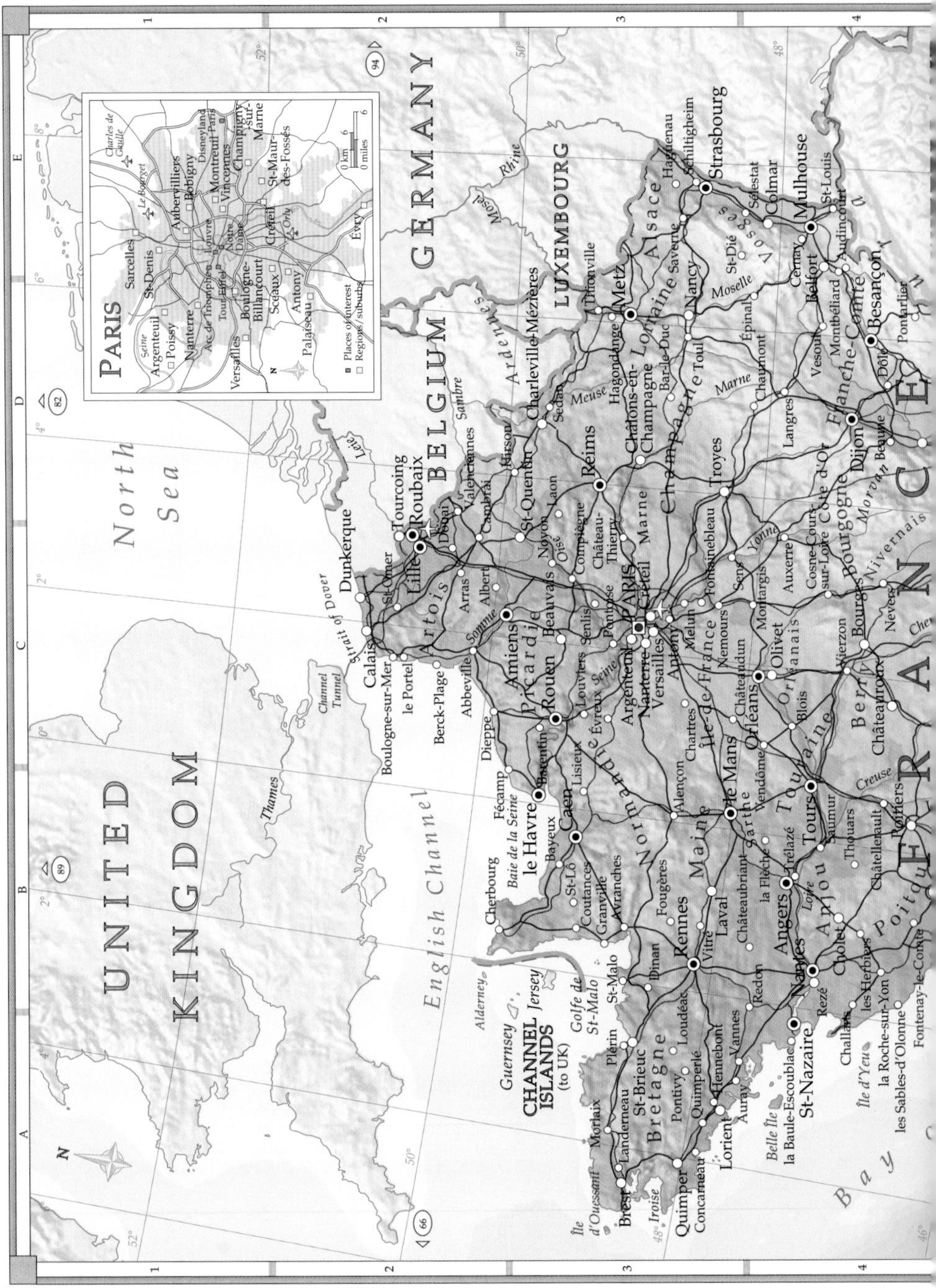

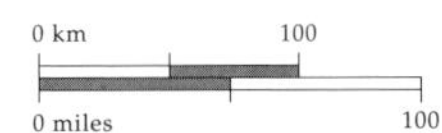

POPULATION

- ● National capital
- ○ Less than 50,000
- ○ 50,000 -100,000
- ◉ 100,000 - 500,000
- ▣ Over 500,000

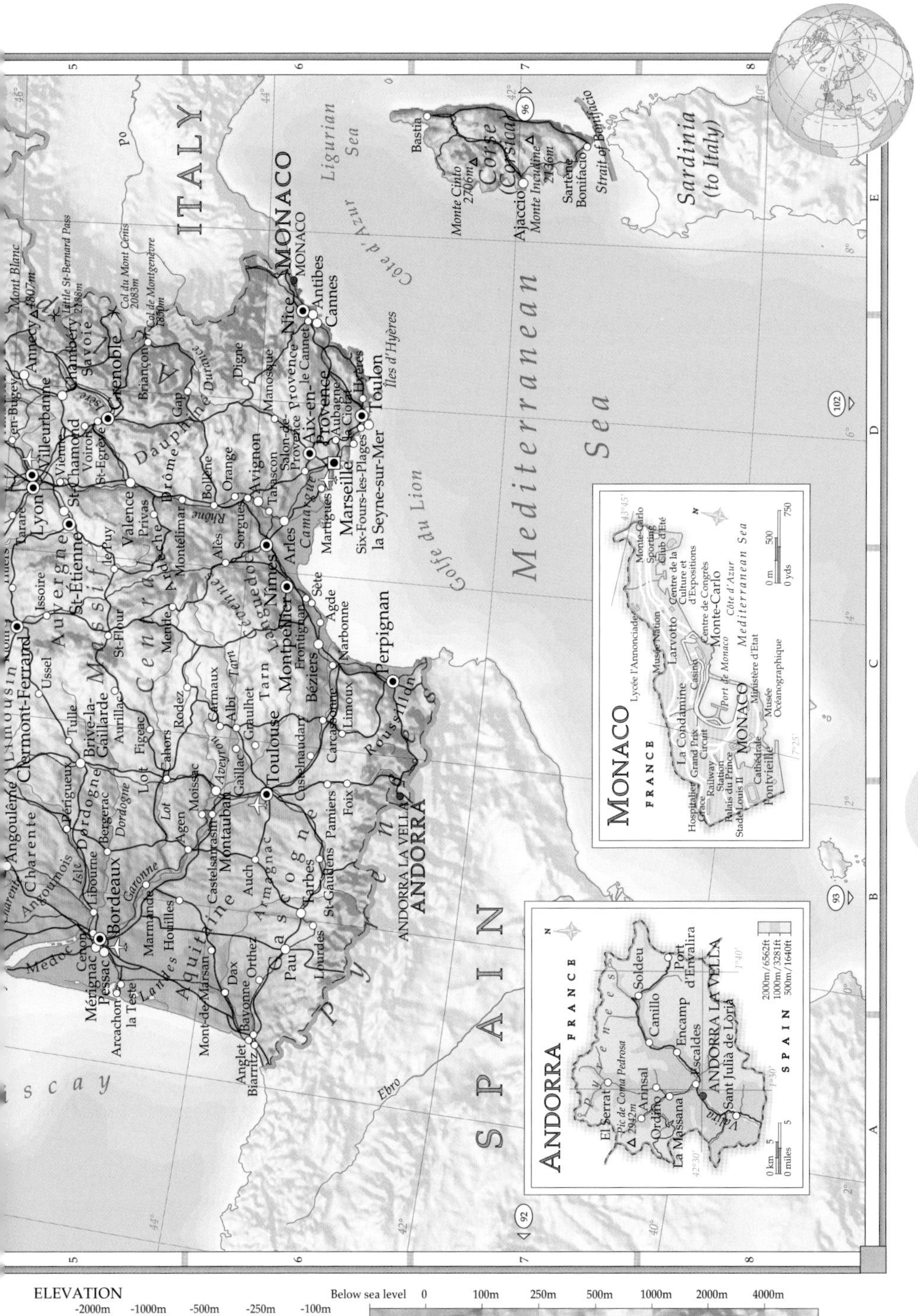

ELEVATION

-2000m	-1000m	-500m	-250m	-100m	Below sea level	0	100m	250m	500m	1000m	2000m	4000m
-6562ft	-3281ft	-1640ft	-820ft	-328ft	-164ft/-50m	0	328ft	820ft	1640ft	3281ft	6562ft	13 124ft

SPAIN & PORTUGAL

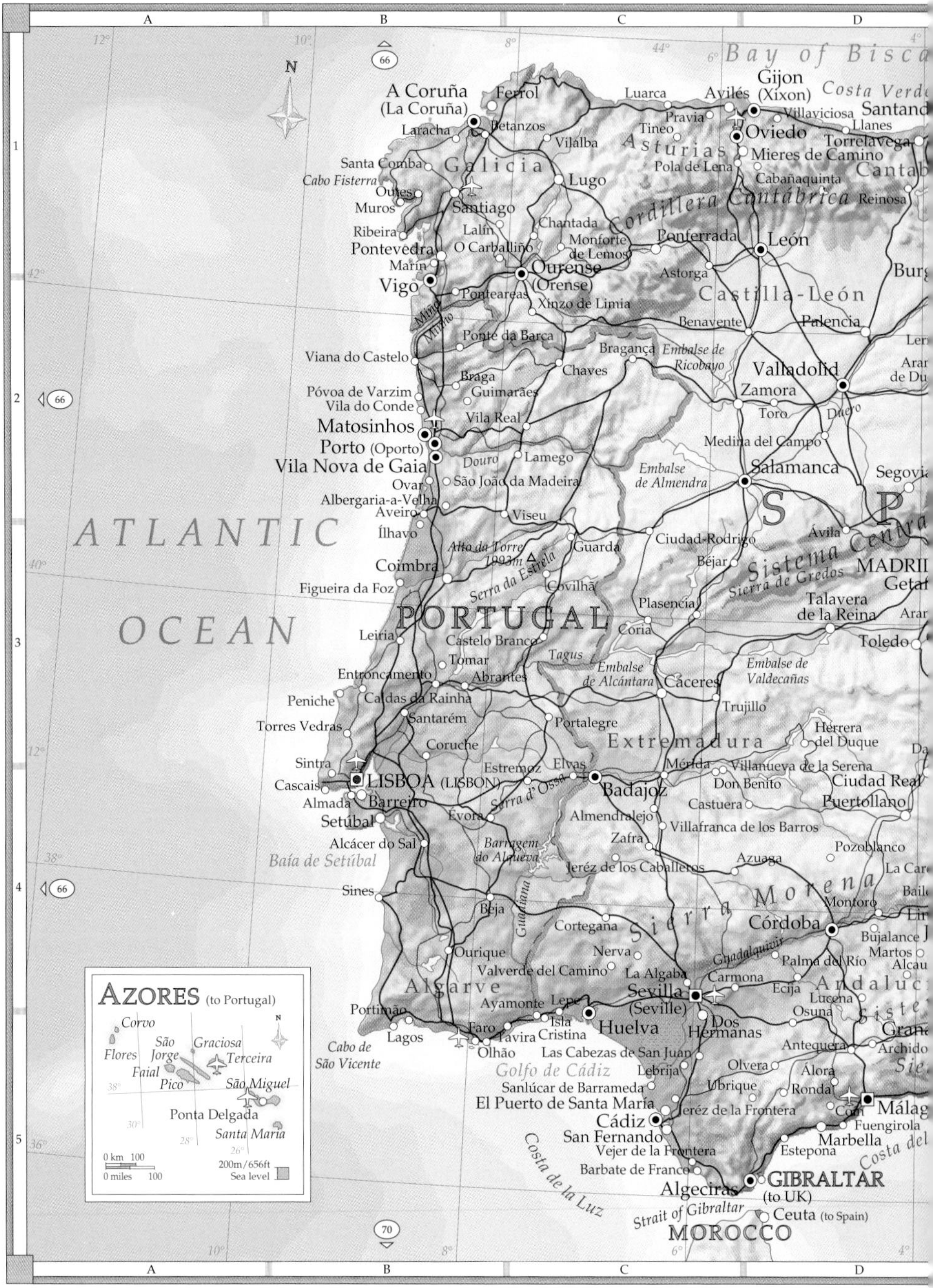

A B C D

Bay of Biscay

ATLANTIC OCEAN

A Coruña (La Coruña)
Ferrol
Laracha
Betanzos
Vilalba
Luarca
Avilés
Gijon (Xixon)
Costa Verde
Santander
Pravia
Tineo
Villaviciosa
Llanes
Oviedo
Torrelavega
Asturias
Mieres de Camino
Pola de Lena
Cabañaquinta
Cantabria
Reinosa
Santa Comba
Cabo Fisterra
Galicia
Lugo
Outes
Muros
Santiago
Cordillera Cantábrica
Chantada
Ribeira
Lalín
Monforte de Lemos
Ponferrada
León
Pontevedra
O Carballiño
Marín
Ourense (Orense)
Astorga
Burgos
Vigo
Ponteareas
Castilla-León
Xinzo de Limia
Miño
Minho
Benavente
Palencia
Ponte da Barca
Viana do Castelo
Bragança
Embalse de Ricobayo
Chaves
Valladolid
Braga
Guimarães
Zamora
Póvoa de Varzim
Vila do Conde
Toro
Duero
Vila Real
Matosinhos
Porto (Oporto)
Medina del Campo
Vila Nova de Gaia
Douro
Lamego
Embalse de Almendra
Salamanca
Segovia
Ovar
São João da Madeira
Albergaria-a-Velha
Aveiro
Viseu
SPAIN
Ílhavo
Guarda
Ciudad-Rodrigo
Ávila
Alto da Torre 1993m
Sistema Central
Coimbra
Serra da Estrela
Béjar
Sierra de Gredos
MADRID
Getafe
Figueira da Foz
Covilhã
Talavera de la Reina
PORTUGAL
Plasencia
Aranjuez
Leiria
Coria
Toledo
Castelo Branco
Tagus
Tomar
Embalse de Alcántara
Embalse de Valdecañas
Entroncamento
Abrantes
Cáceres
Peniche
Caldas da Rainha
Trujillo
Santarém
Torres Vedras
Portalegre
Herrera del Duque
Extremadura
Coruche
Sintra
Estremoz
Elvas
Mérida
Villanueva de la Serena
Cascais
LISBOA (LISBON)
Badajoz
Don Benito
Ciudad Real
Almada
Barreiro
Serra d'Ossa
Castuera
Puertollano
Setúbal
Évora
Almendralejo
Villafranca de los Barros
Alcácer do Sal
Barragem do Alqueva
Zafra
Pozoblanco
Baía de Setúbal
Jeréz de los Caballeros
Azuaga
Sines
Guadiana
Sierra Morena
Montoro
Beja
Córdoba
Cortegana
Bujalance
Ourique
Nerva
Guadalquivir
Palma del Río
Martos
Valverde del Camino
La Algaba
Carmona
Algarve
Sevilla (Seville)
Écija
Andalucía
Lucena
Portimão
Ayamonte
Lepe
Huelva
Dos Hermanas
Osuna
Lagos
Faro
Isla Cristina
Antequera
Cabo de São Vicente
Tavira
Olhão
Las Cabezas de San Juan
Golfo de Cádiz
Lebrija
Olvera
Álora
Sanlúcar de Barrameda
Ubrique
Ronda
El Puerto de Santa María
Jeréz de la Frontera
Coín
Málaga
Cádiz
Fuengirola
San Fernando
Marbella
Vejer de la Frontera
Estepona
Costa del Sol
Costa de la Luz
Barbate de Franco
Algeciras
GIBRALTAR (to UK)
Strait of Gibraltar
Ceuta (to Spain)
MOROCCO

AZORES (to Portugal)
Corvo
Flores
São Jorge
Graciosa
Terceira
Faial
Pico
São Miguel
Ponta Delgada
Santa Maria
0 km 100
0 miles 100
200m/656ft
Sea level

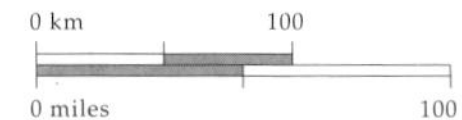

POPULATION
● National capital
○ Less than 50,000
○ 50,000 -100,000
◉ 100,000 - 500,000
▣ Over 500,000

E
F
G
H
1
2
3
4
5
2°
0°
44°
4°
42°
40°
38°
36°
90
96
97
71
FRANCE
Golfe du Lion
Bermeo
Zarautz
Donostia-San Sebastián
Irún
Eibar
Tolosa
Bergara
Pamplona
(Iruña)
Miranda
de Ebro
Estella
Navarra
Jaca
Pyrenees
Monte Perdido
3348m
ANDORRA
La Seu d'Urgell
Berga
Ripoll
Figueres
Girona
(Gerona)
Banyoles
Manlleu
Vic
Arnedo
Calahorra
Huesca
Ejea de
los Caballeros
Barbastro
Monzón
Balaguer
Cataluña
Palafrugell
Palamós
Costa Brava
Tudela
Tarazona
Soria
Ebro
Blanes
Arenys de Mar
Mataró
Cervera
Zaragoza
Lleida
(Lérida)
Tàrrega
Sabadell
Terrassa
Barcelona
L'Hospitalet de Llobregat
Fraga
Vilafranca del Penedès
Valls
Sitges
El Vendrell
Reus
Tarragona
Calatayud
Aragón
Medinaceli
Daroca
Alcañiz
Sistema Ibérico
SPAIN
Tortosa
Amposta
Sant Carles de la Ràpita
Vinaròs
Guadalajara
Teruel
Javalambre
2020m
Cuenca
País Valenciano
Onda
Castelló de la Plana
Burriana
Vall d' Uxó
Sagunto
Burjassot
Valencia
Torrent
Catarroja
Sueca
Cullera
Gandía
Oliva
Dénia
Costa del Azahar
Golfo de
Valencia
Tarancón
Castilla-La Mancha
Mota del Cuervo
Campo de Criptana
Socuéllamos
La Roda
Júcar
Algemesí
Xátiva
Tomelloso
Albacete
Almansa
Ontinyent
Alcoy
Villanueva de los Infantes
Villena
Hellín
Segura
Jumilla
Elda
Benidorm
Villajoyosa
San Juan de Alicante
Monovar
Beas de Segura
Moratalla
Cieza
Elche
(Elx)
Alicante (Alacant)
Callosa de Segura
Costa Blanca
Villacarrillo
Mula
Orihuela
Cazorla
Murcia
Totana
Huéscar
Lorca
La Unión
Cartagena
Baza
Aguilas
Guadix
Mojácar
Berja
Almería
Adra
Mediterranean Sea
Menorca
(Minorca)
Ciutadella de Menorca
Mahón
Pollença
Sa Pobla
Palma
Manacor
Llucmajor
Felanitx
Mallorca
(Majorca)
Cabrera
Eivissa
(Ibiza)
Eivissa
Formentera
Islas Baleares
(Balearic Islands)
ALGERIA
GIBRALTAR (to UK)
N
SPAIN
Gibraltar
Airport
North Mole
Gibraltar
Harbour
Catalan Bay
Catalan
Bay
The Rock
Bay of Gibraltar
Summit
426m
Sandy
Bay
Rosia
Rosia
Bay
Buena Vista
200m/656ft
Sea level
Little
Bay
0 km
1
0 mile
1
Europa Point
Strait of Gibraltar
ELEVATION
Below sea level
0
100m
250m
500m
1000m
2000m
4000m
-4000m
-3000m
-2000m
-1000m
-500m
328ft
820ft
1640ft
3281ft
6562ft
13 124ft
-13 124ft
-9843ft
-6562ft
-3281ft
-1640ft
-820ft/-250m
0

Germany & the Alpine States

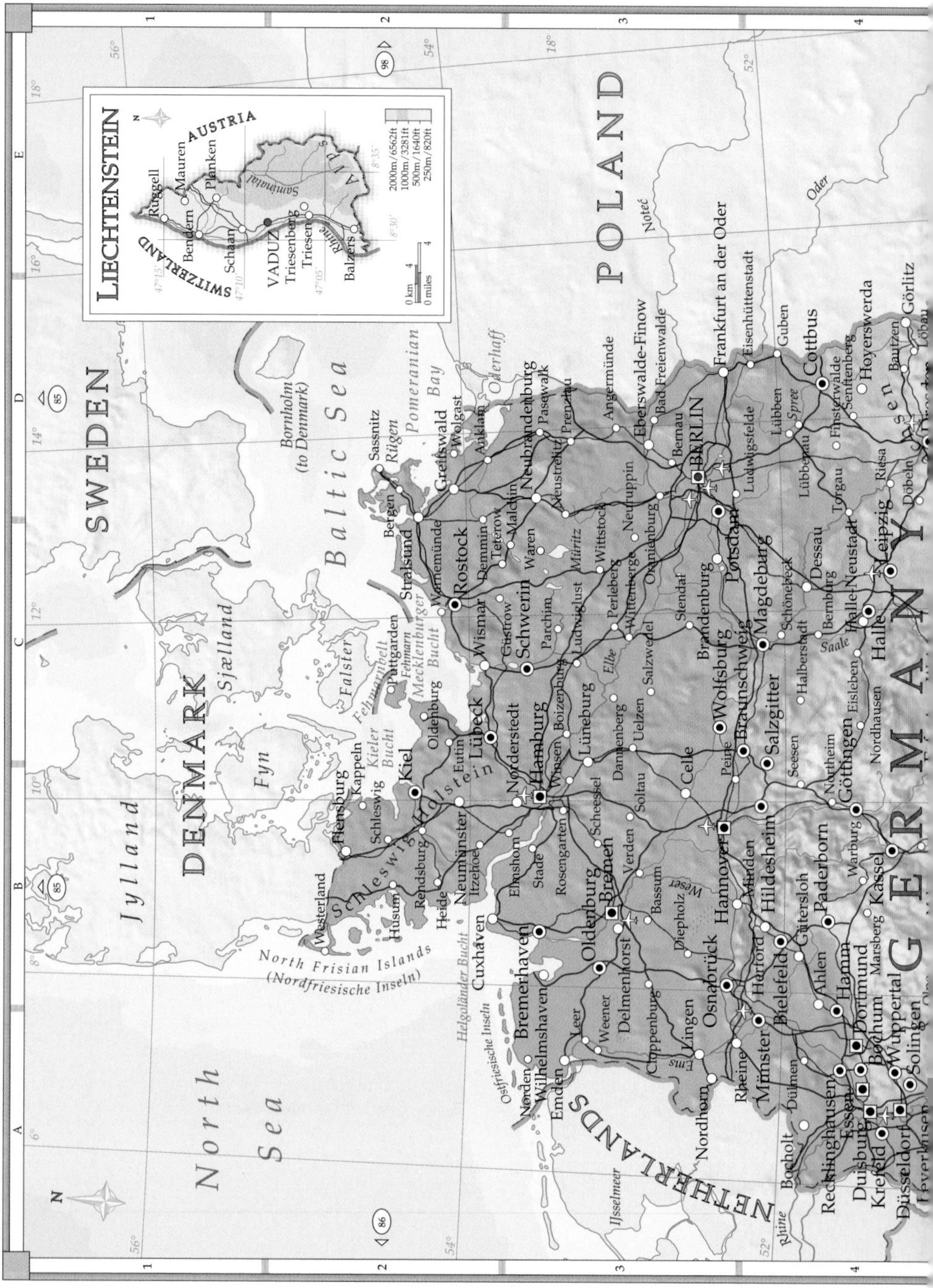

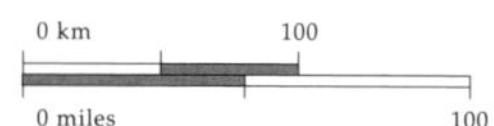

POPULATION ● National capital ○ Less than 50,000 ○ 50,000 -100,000 ⦿ 100,000 - 500,000 ▣ Over 500,000

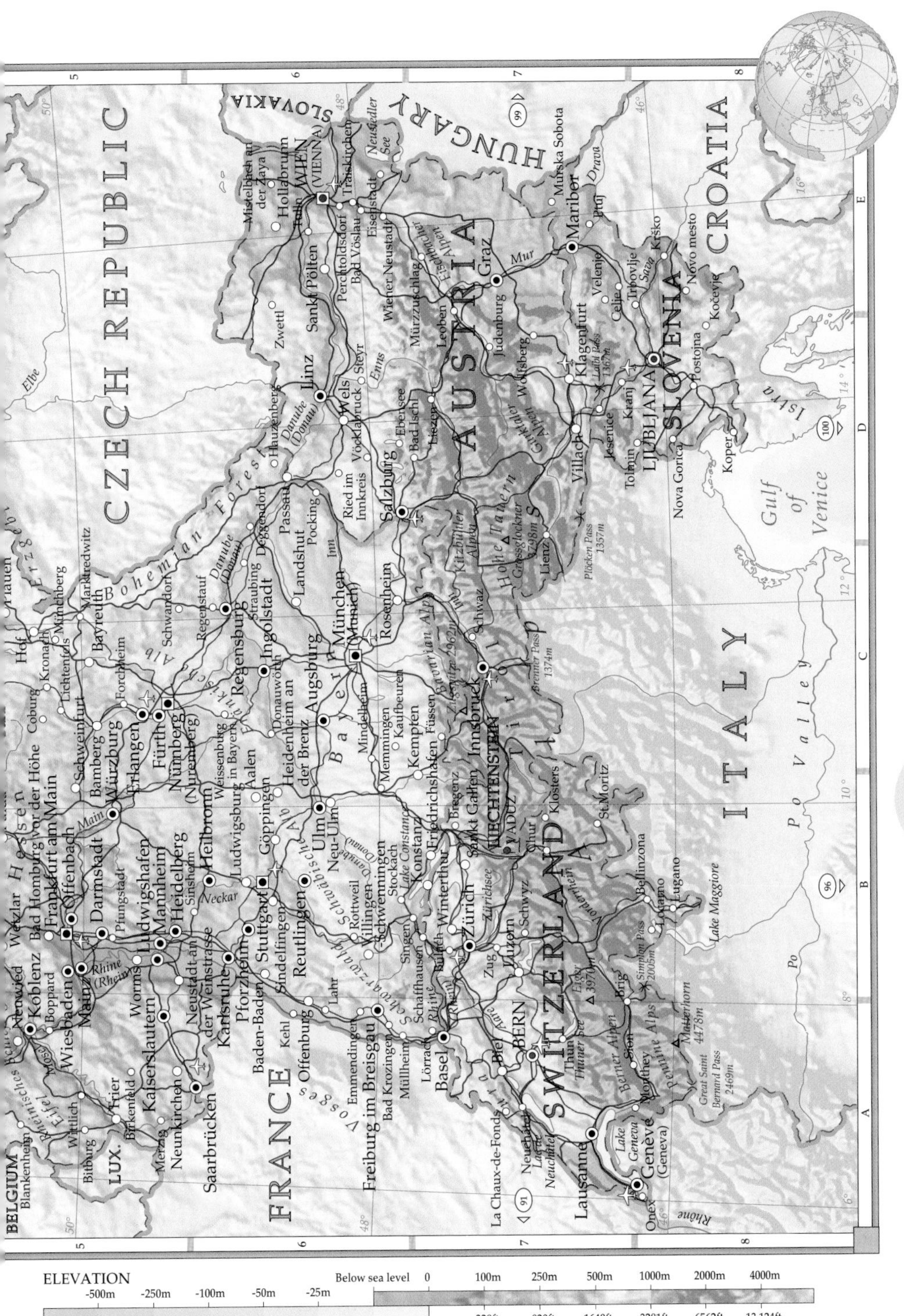
CZECH REPUBLIC
AUSTRIA
SWITZERLAND
FRANCE
ITALY
SLOVENIA
CROATIA
HUNGARY
SLOVAKIA
LIECHTENSTEIN
LUX.
BELGIUM
WIEN (VIENNA)
BERN
VADUZ
LJUBLJANA
München (Munich)
Nürnberg (Nuremberg)
Frankfurt am Main
Stuttgart
Zürich
Genève (Geneva)
Innsbruck
Salzburg
Graz
Linz
Bohemian Forest
Gulf of Venice
Po Valley
Lake Geneva
Lake Constance
Lake Maggiore
Danube (Donau)
Rhine (Rhein)
Hohe Tauern
Bernese Alpen
Pennine Alps
Grossglockner 3798m
Matterhorn 4478m
Zugspitze 2962m
Brenner Pass 1374m
Simplon Pass 2005m
Great Saint Bernard Pass 2469m
Plöcken Pass 1357m
ELEVATION
Below sea level
-500m -250m -100m -50m -25m 0
-1640ft -820ft -328ft -164ft -82ft 33ft/-10m 0
100m 250m 500m 1000m 2000m 4000m
328ft 820ft 1640ft 3281ft 6562ft 13 124ft

ITALY

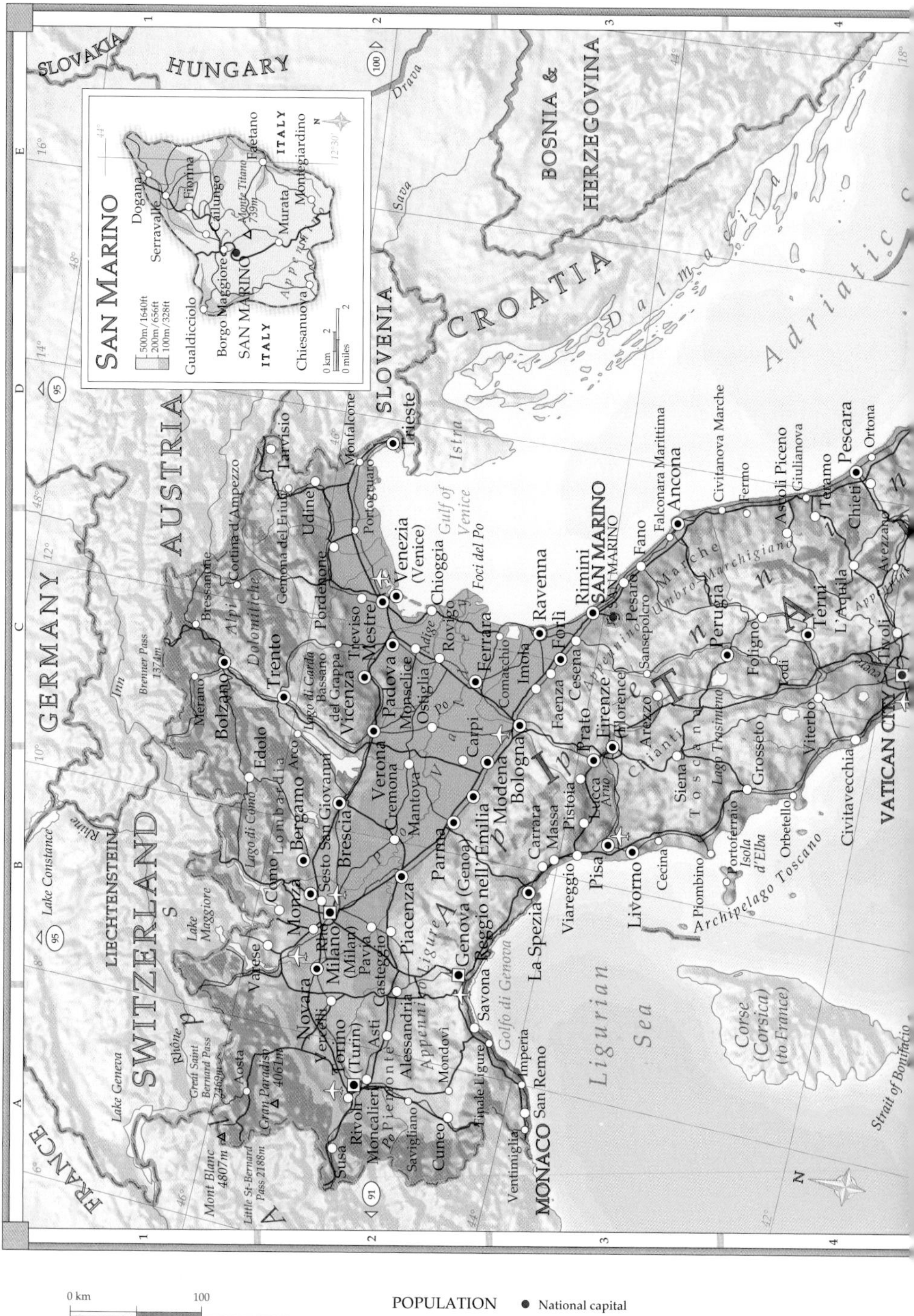

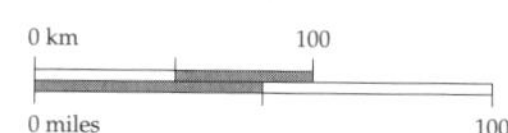

POPULATION

- ● National capital
- ○ Less than 50,000
- ○ 50,000 -100,000
- ⦿ 100,000 - 500,000
- ▣ Over 500,000

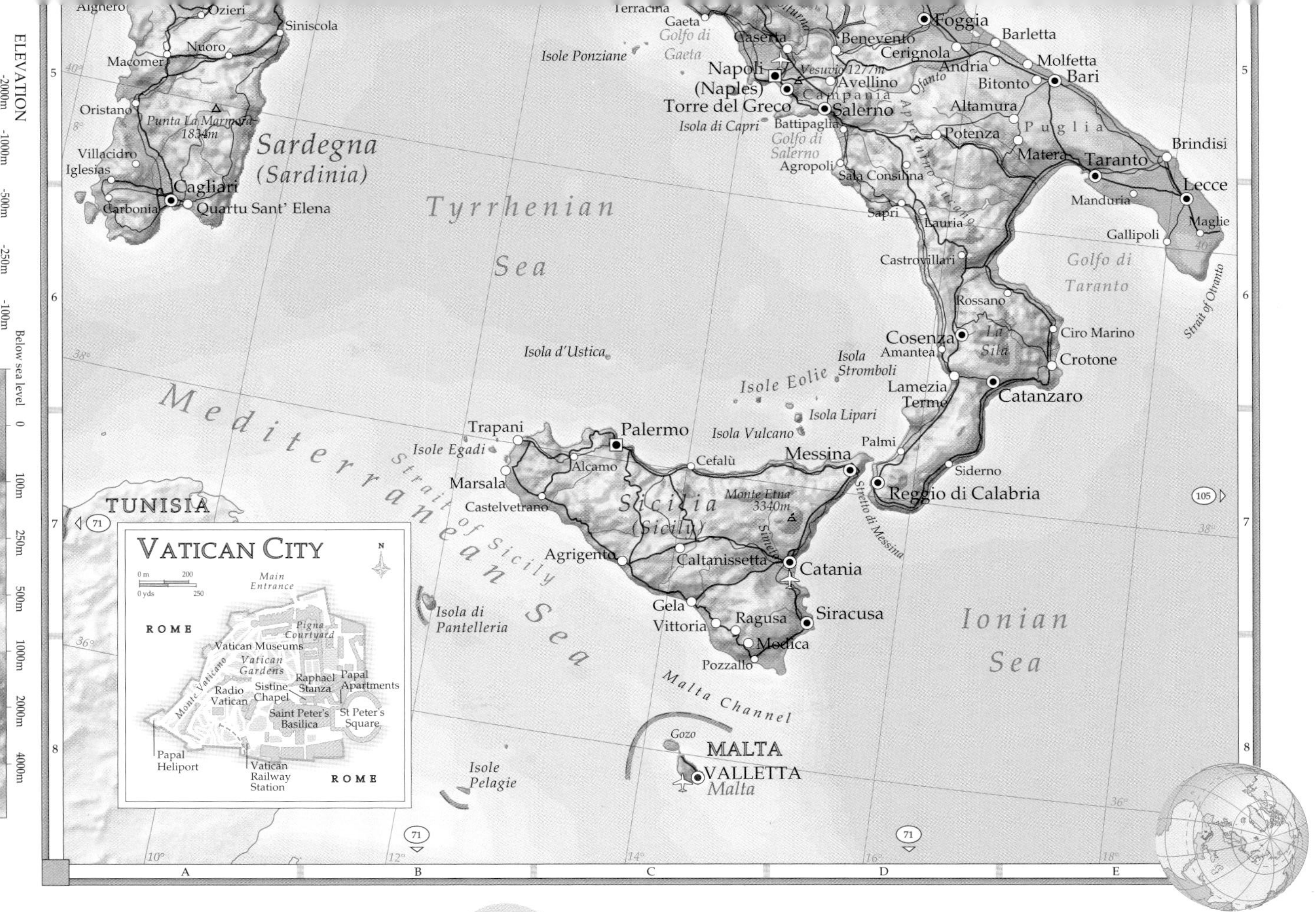

ELEVATION

Below sea level	-2000m	-1000m	-500m	-250m	-100m	0	100m	250m	500m	1000m	2000m	4000m
	-6562ft	-3281ft	-1640ft	-820ft	-328ft	-164ft/-50m 0	328ft	820ft	1640ft	3281ft	6562ft	13 124ft

CENTRAL EUROPE

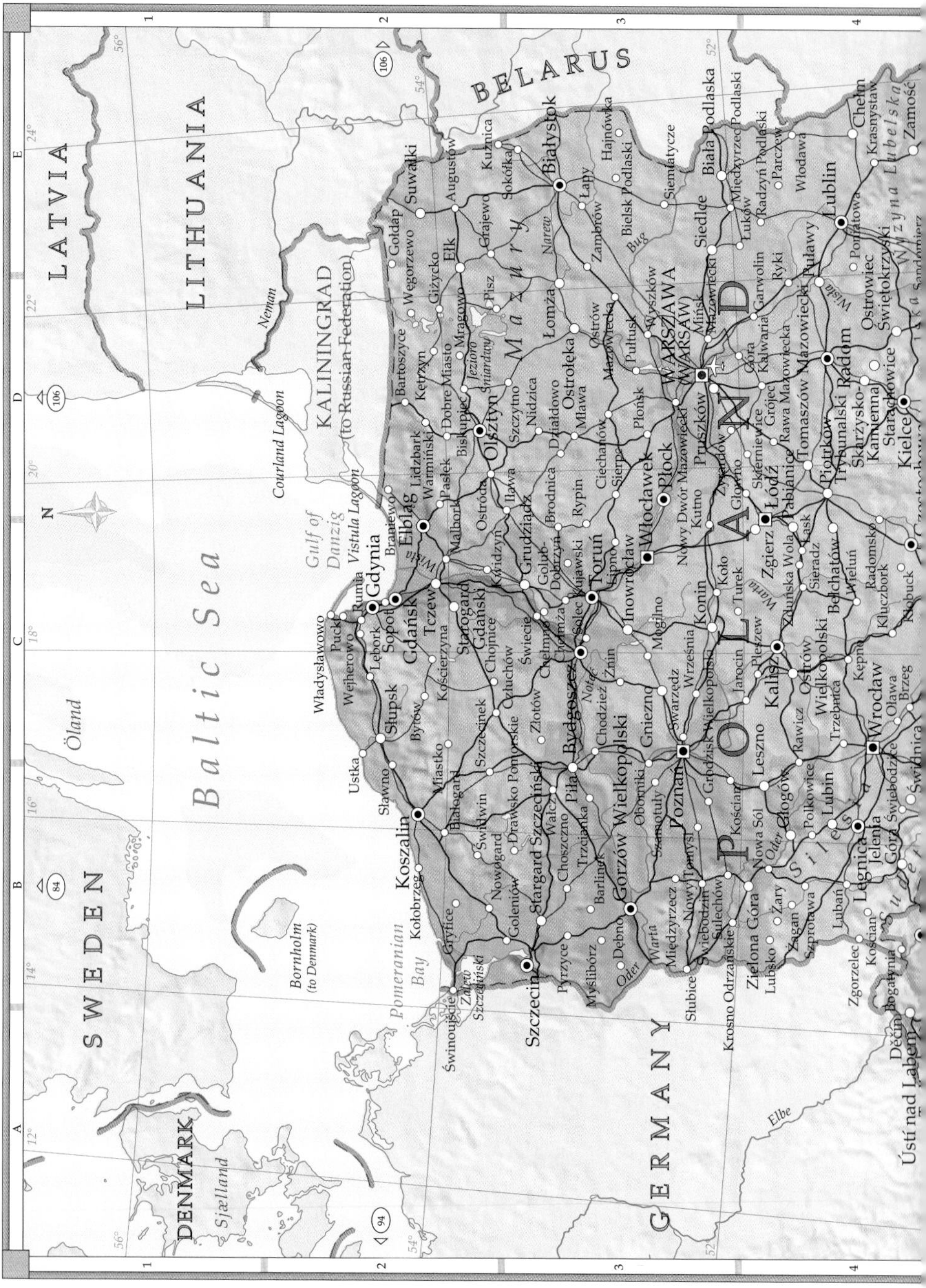

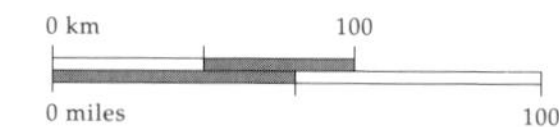

CZECH REPUBLIC
SLOVAKIA
HUNGARY
AUSTRIA
SLOVENIA
CROATIA
BOSNIA & HERZEGOVINA
SERBIA & MONTENEGRO (YUGOSLAVIA)
ROMANIA
UKRAINE
ITALY
PRAHA (PRAGUE)
BRATISLAVA
BUDAPEST
Adriatic Sea
Gulf of Venice
Bohemian Forest
Carpathian Mountains
Great Hungarian Plain
Little Alföld
Carpații Occidentali
Carpații Meridionali
Niedere Tauern
Alps
Danube
Tisza
Drava
ELEVATION
Below sea level
0
100m
250m
500m
1000m
2000m
4000m
-500m
-250m
-100m
-50m
-25m
328ft
820ft
1640ft
3281ft
6562ft
13 124ft
-1640ft
-820ft
-328ft
-164ft
-82ft
33ft/-10m
0

SOUTHEAST EUROPE

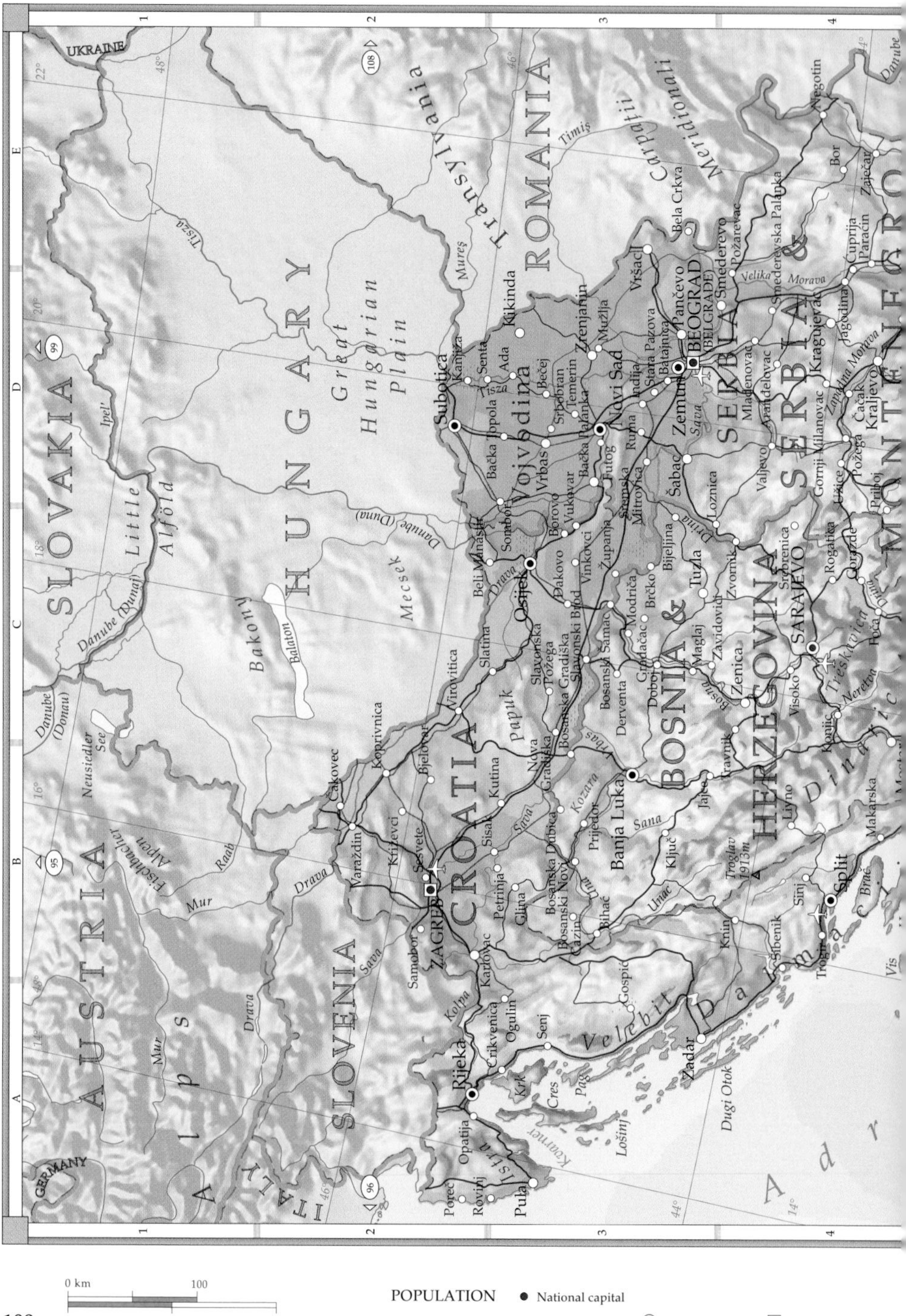

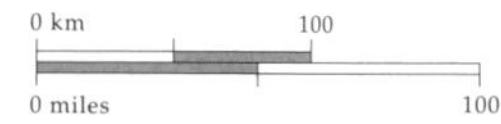

100,000 - 500,000 · Over 500,000

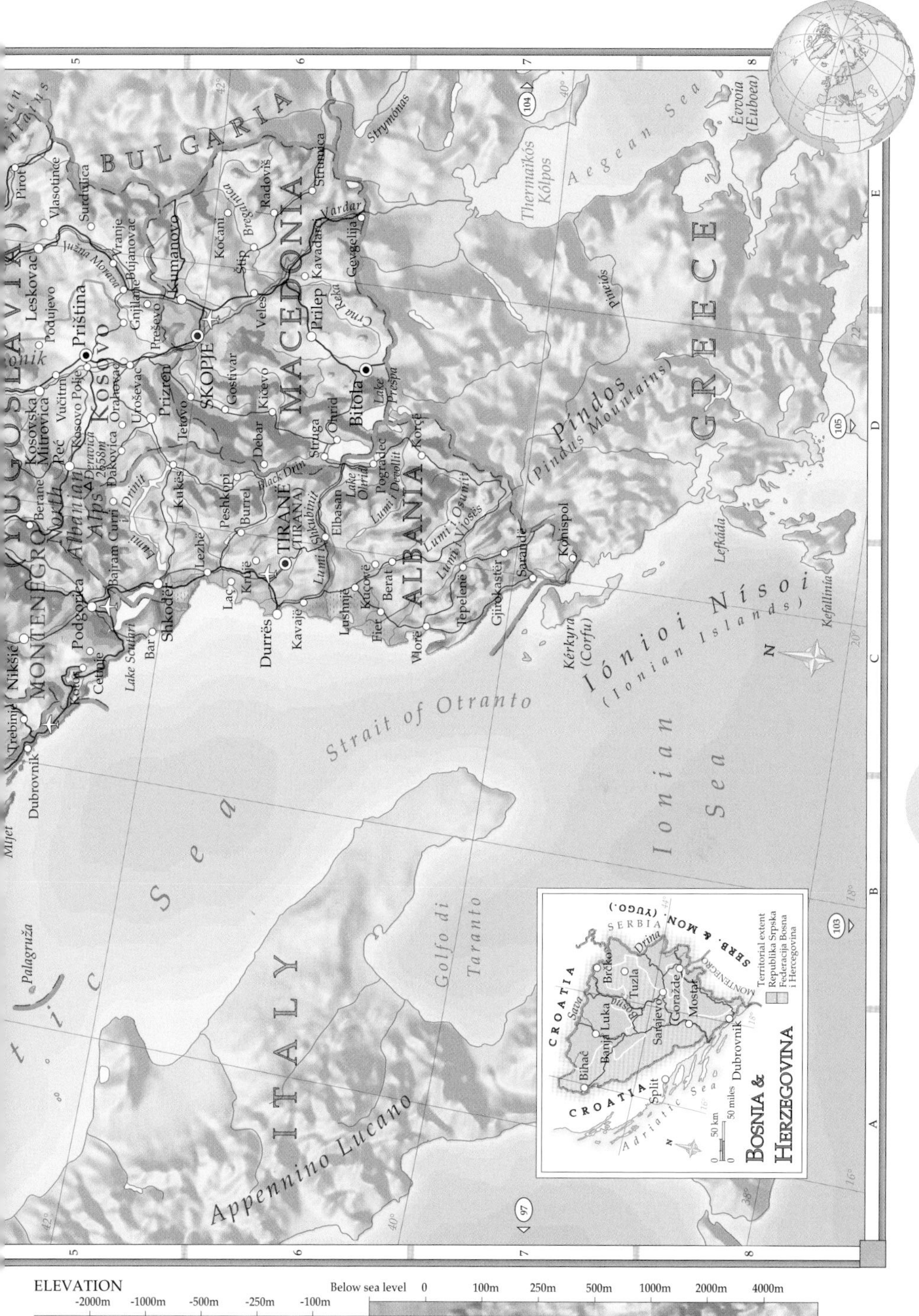

ELEVATION

Below sea level	-2000m	-1000m	-500m	-250m	-100m	0	100m	250m	500m	1000m	2000m	4000m
	-6562ft	-3281ft	-1640ft	-820ft	-328ft	-164ft/-50m	0	328ft	820ft	1640ft	3281ft	6562ft	13 124ft

THE MEDITERRANEAN

ATLANTIC OCEAN
Bay of Biscay
FRANCE
GERMANY
SWITZ.
LIECH.
VADUZ
BERN
MONACO
ANDORRA
SPAIN
PORTUGAL
MOROCCO
ALGERIA
TUNISIA
GIBRALTAR (to UK)
VATICAN CITY
ROMA (ROME)
LISBOA (LISBON)
MADRID
RABAT
ALGER (ALGIERS)
TUNIS
TARABULUS (TRIPOLI)

Quimper
St-Nazaire
Île d'Yeu
Nantes
Tours
Loire
Seine
Dijon
Zürich
München (Munich)
Innsbruck
Île de Ré
Île d'Oléron
Limoges
Lake Geneva
Mont Blanc 4807m
Lyon
Clermont-Ferrand
Massif Central
Dordogne
Garonne
Bordeaux
Rhône
Alps
Milano (Milan)
Alpi Dolomitiche
Venezia (Venice)
Torino (Turin)
Po
Genova (Genoa)
Bologna
Golfo di Genova
Ligurian Sea
Nîmes
Montpellier
Marseille
Nice
Côte d'Azur
Toulouse
Pyrenees
Golfe du Lion
Perpignan
Pisa
Appennini
Tevere
Corse (Corsica)
Isola d'Elba
Ajaccio
Isola Asinara
Sassari
Sardegna (Sardinia)
Cagliari
Tyrrhenian Sea

A Coruña
Santander
Bilbao
Cordillera Cantábrica
Ebro
Sistema Ibérico
Vigo
Duero
Valladolid
Zaragoza
Barcelona
Costa Brava
Tarragona
Porto
Sistema Central
Castelló de la Plana
Mallorca (Majorca)
Menorca (Minorca)
Palma
Tagus
Valencia
Golfo de Valencia
Eivissa (Ibiza)
Formentera
Islas Baleares (Balearic Islands)
Sierra Morena
Guadalquivir
Alicante
Costa Blanca
Sevilla (Seville)
Murcia
Sistemas Béticos
Cartagena
Golfo de Cádiz
Cádiz
Málaga
Costa del Sol
Almería
Strait of Gibraltar
Ceuta (to Spain)
Tangier
Tétouan
Melilla (to Spain)
Mediterranean Sea
Sicilia (Sicily)
Palermo
Golfe de Tunis
Cap Bon
Cap Bougaroun
Annaba
Tizi Ouzou
Oran
Mostaganem
Atlas Tellien
Sétif
Constantine
Massif de l'Aurès
Golfe de Hammamet
Sousse
Tlemcen
Oujda
Chott el Hodna
Chott ech Chergui
Fès
Îles de Kerkenah
Sfax
Golfe de Gabès
Chott el Jerid
Gabès
Île de Jerba
Casablanca
Haut Plateaux
Chott Melghir
Moyen Atlas
Haut Atlas
Atlas Mountains
Safi
Gharyan
Sahara

MALTA

Mediterranean Sea
Nadur
Victoria
Gozo
Comino (Kemmuna)
Mġarr
Mellieħa
St Julian's
Sliema
Mosta
VALLETTA
Hamrun
Paola
Malta
Rabat
Birżebbuġa
250m/820ft
100m/328ft
Sea Level
0 km 10
0 miles 10

CYPRUS

Mediterranean Sea
Agialoúsa (Yenierenköy)
TURKISH REPUBLIC OF NORTHERN CYPRUS (recognized only by Turkey)
Lápithos (Lapta)
Kerýneia (Girne)
Mórfou (Güzelyurt)
Kythréa (Değirmenlik)
Kólpos Ammóchostos (Gazimağusa Körfezi)
Pólis
NICOSIA
Ammóchostos (Gazimağusa) (Famagusta)
Troódos
Dekéleia
Sovereign Base Area (to UK)
Lárnaka
Páfos
Lemesós (Limassol)
Akrotírion
0 km 25
0 miles 25
1000m/3281ft
500m/1640ft
250m/820ft
Sea Level

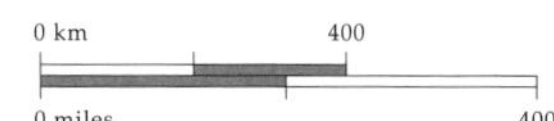

POPULATION
● National capital
○ Less than 50,000
○ 50,000 -100,000
◉ 100,000 - 500,000
▣ Over 500,000

SLOVAKIA
WIEN
(VIENNA)
BUDAPEST
HUNGARY
Great Hungarian Plain
ZAGREB
CROATIA
BOSNIA & HERZ.
SARAJEVO
BEOGRAD (BELGRADE)
SERBIA & MONTENEGRO (YUGOSLAVIA)
Priština
SKOPJE
MACED.
TIRANË (TIRANA)
ALBANIA
ROMANIA
Carpathian Mountains
Carpaţii Meridionali
Satu Mare
Târgu Mureş
Novi Sad
BUCUREŞTI (BUCHAREST)
Danube
Tisza
Sava
Galaţi
Constanţa
BULGARIA
Balkan Mountains
SOFIYA (SOFIA)
Varna
Burgas
Rhodope Mountains
MOLD.
CHIŞINĂU
Bălţi
UKRAINE
Kakhovs'ka Vodoskhovyshche
Dniester
Dnieper
Odesa
Berdyans'k
Sea of Azov
Kerch
Kryms'kyy Pivostrov
Sevastopol'
RUSS. FED.
Novorossiysk
Black Sea
Edirne
İstanbul
İstanbul Boğazi (Bosporus)
Marmara Denizi
Bursa
Zonguldak
Küre Dağlari
Samsun
Ordu
Kizil Irmak
ANKARA
Balikesir
TURKEY
İzmir
Tuz Gölü
Kayseri
Toros Dağlari
Antalya
Antalya Körfezi
Adana
Gaziantep
Euphrates
İskenderun Körfezi
Halab (Aleppo)
SYRIA
Thessaloníki (Salonica)
Límnos
Lárisa
Píndos (Pindus) Mts
GREECE
Aegean Sea
Chíos
Sámos
ATHÍNA (ATHENS)
Dodekánisos (Dodecanese)
Kykládes (Cyclades)
Mirtóo Pelagos
Kýthira
Kritikó Pélagos (Sea of Crete)
Ródos (Rhodes)
Kárpathos
Irákleio
Kríti (Crete)
Kérkyra (Corfu)
Kefallinía
Zákynthos
Ionian Sea
Strait of Otranto
Adriatic Sea
Dalmacija
Bari
Napoli (Naples)
Vesuvio 1277m
Lecce
Golfo di Taranto
Cosenza
Catanzaro
Monte Etna 3340m
Catania
Siracusa
VALLETTA
MALTA
Mediterranean Sea
NICOSIA
CYPRUS
Lárnaka
Lemesós (Limassol)
LEBANON
BEYROUTH (BEIRUT)
DIMASHQ (DAMASCUS)
Hefa
ISRAEL
Tel Aviv-Yafo
JERUSALEM
Gaza
'AMMĀN
Dead Sea
JORDAN
Elat
Al 'Aqabah
SAUDI ARABIA
Red Sea
Darnah
Banghāzī (Benghazi)
Misrātah
Khalīj Surt (Gulf of Sirte)
Surt
Tubruq
Ajdābiyā
Libyan Plateau
Great Sand Sea
Waddān
LIBYA
Libyan Desert
Alexandria
Nile Delta
Port Said
Suez Canal
Suez
CAIRO
El Gîza
Monkhafad al Qattâra (Qattara Depression)
Nile
Sahara el Sharqîya (Eastern Desert)
Gulf of Suez
Sinai
EGYPT
108
117
119
72
E
F
G
H
1
2
3
4
5
15°
20°
25°
30°
35°
40°
ELEVATION
Below sea level
0
100m
250m
500m
1000m
2000m
4000m
328ft
820ft
1640ft
3281ft
6562ft
13 124ft
-4000m
-3000m
-2000m
-1000m
-500m
-13 124ft
-9843ft
-6562ft
-3281ft
-1640ft
-820ft/-250m
0

BULGARIA & GREECE

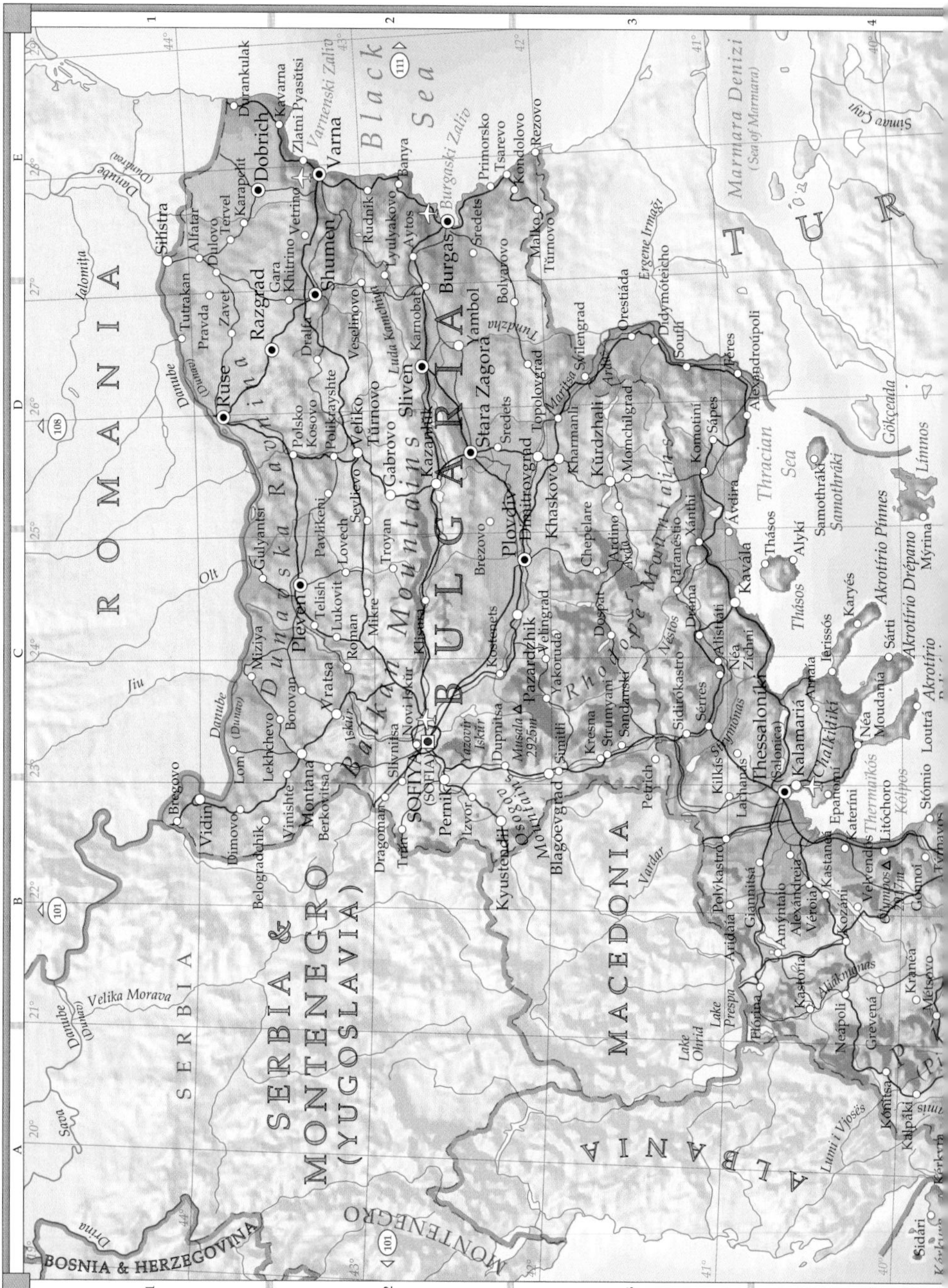

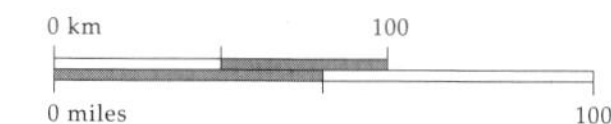

POPULATION

ELEVATION

Below sea level 0 | 100m 250m 500m 1000m 2000m 4000m

-2000m -1000m -500m -250m -100m

-6562ft -3281ft -1640ft -820ft -328ft -164ft/-50m 0

328ft 820ft 1640ft 3281ft 6562ft 13 124ft

THE BALTIC STATES & BELARUS

0 km 100
0 miles 100

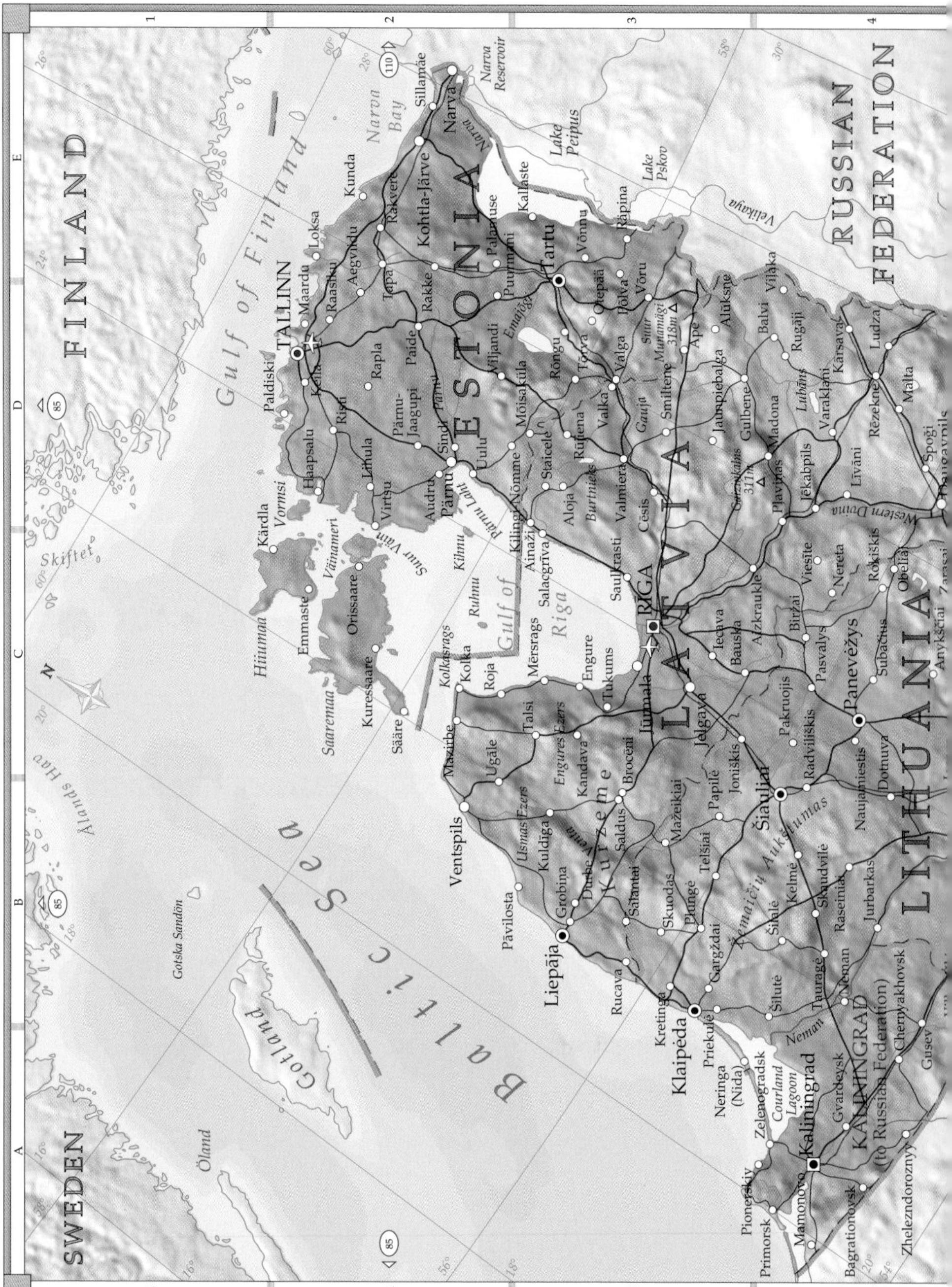

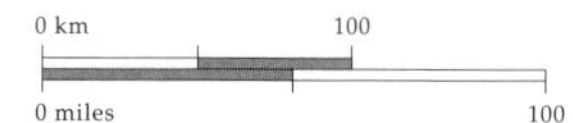

POPULATION
● National capital
○ Less than 50,000
○ 50,000 -100,000
⦿ 100,000 - 500,000
▣ Over 500,000

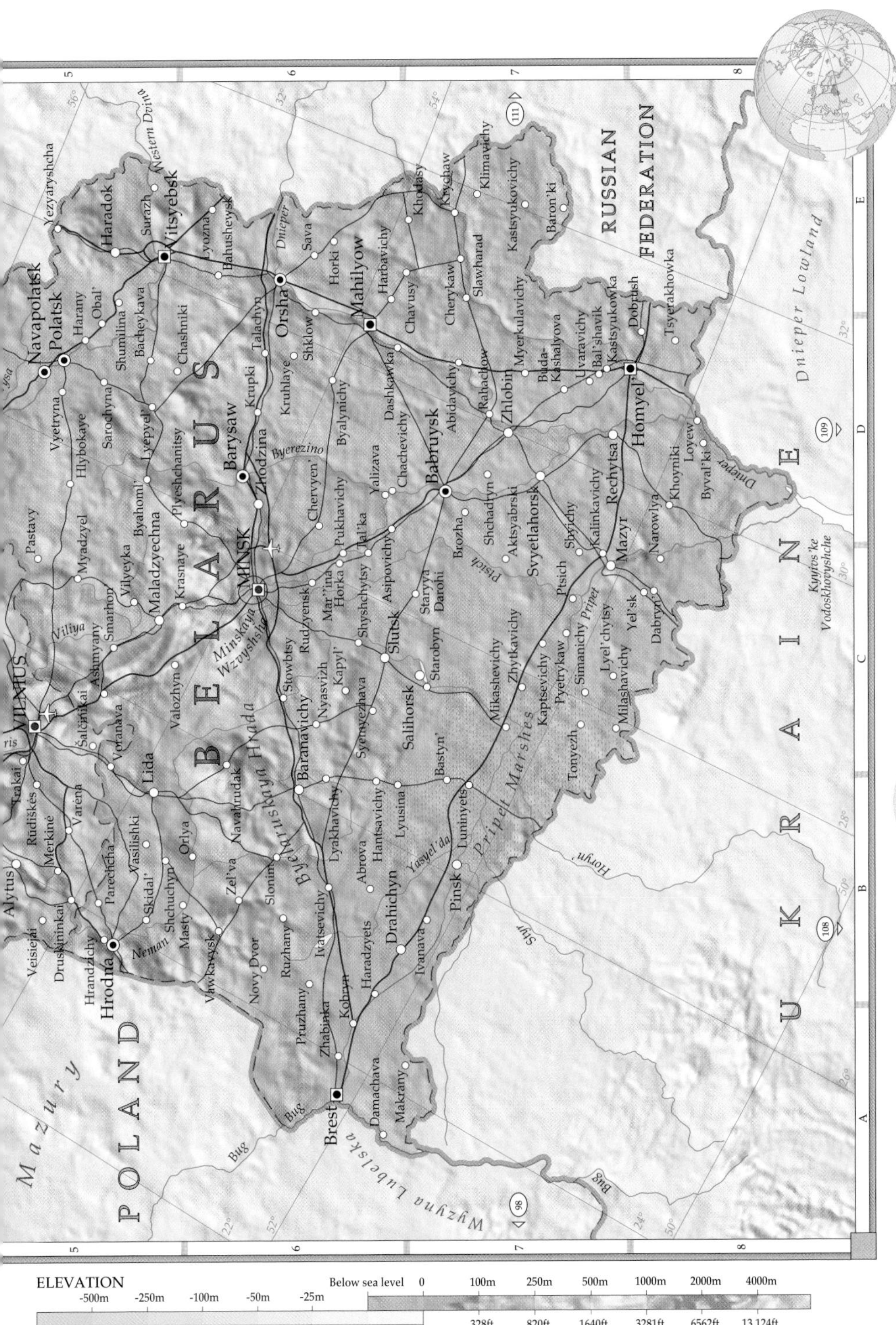

ELEVATION

Below sea level						0	100m	250m	500m	1000m	2000m	4000m
-500m	-250m	-100m	-50m	-25m								
-1640ft	-820ft	-328ft	-164ft	-82ft	33ft/-10m	0	328ft	820ft	1640ft	3281ft	6562ft	13 124ft

UKRAINE, MOLDOVA & ROMANIA

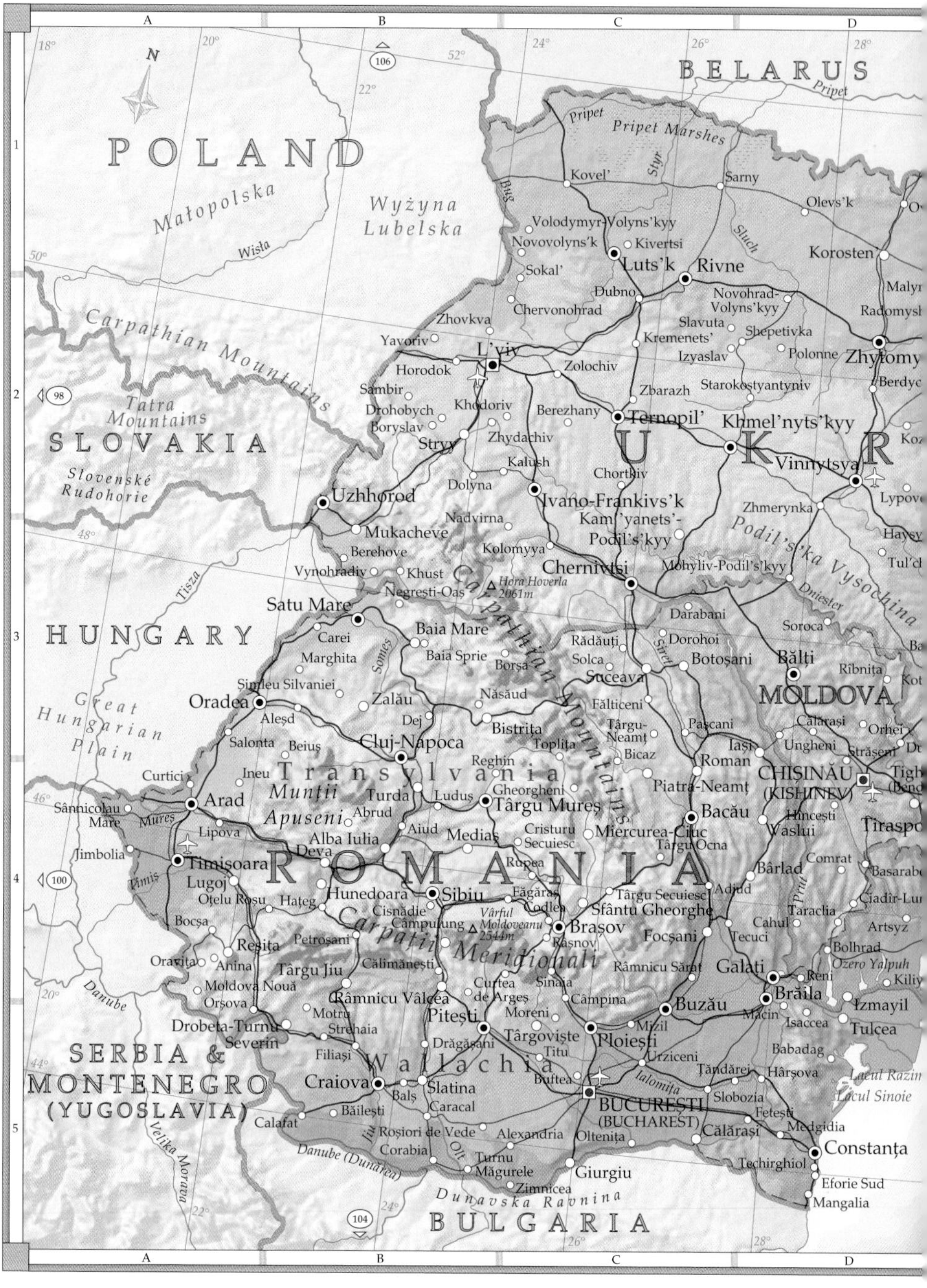

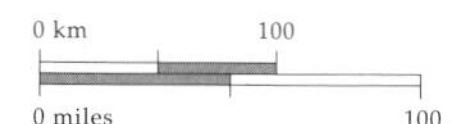

POPULATION

- ● National capital
- ○ Less than 50,000
- ○ 50,000 -100,000
- ◉ 100,000 - 500,000
- ◼ Over 500,000

RUSSIAN FEDERATION
Black Sea
Sea of Azov
Kerch Strait
Gulf of Taganrog
Chernihiv
Konotop
Sumy
Kharkiv
Poltava
Cherkasy
Kremenchuk
Dnipropetrovs'k
Zaporizhzhya
Kryvyy Rih
Kirovohrad
Mykolayiv
Kherson
Odesa
Melitopol'
Mariupol'
Berdyans'k
Donets'k
Luhans'k
Horlivka
Makiyivka
Kerch
Simferopol'
Sevastopol'
Yevpatoriya
Yalta
Feodosiya
Nikopol'
Pavlohrad
Kramators'k
Slov''yans'k
Syeverodonets'k
Lysychans'k
Krasnyy Luch
Stakhanov
Yenakiyeve
Kostyantynivka
Krymskyy Pivostriv
Kakhovs'ka Vodoskhovyshche
Kremenchuts'ke Vodoskhovyshche
Dniprodzerzhyns'ke Vodoskhovyshche
Dnieper Lowland
Black Sea Lowland
Srednerusskaya Vozvyshennost'
Dnieper (Dnipro)
Desna
Donets
Don
Kuban'
Yeya
Oskil
Psel
Pivdennyy Buh
Karkinits'ka Zatoka
Zatoka Syvash
Kryms'ki Hory
ELEVATION
Below sea level
-2000m -1000m -500m -250m -100m 0
-6562ft -3281ft -1640ft -820ft -328ft -164ft/-50m 0
100m 250m 500m 1000m 2000m 4000m
328ft 820ft 1640ft 3281ft 6562ft 13 124ft

EUROPEAN RUSSIA

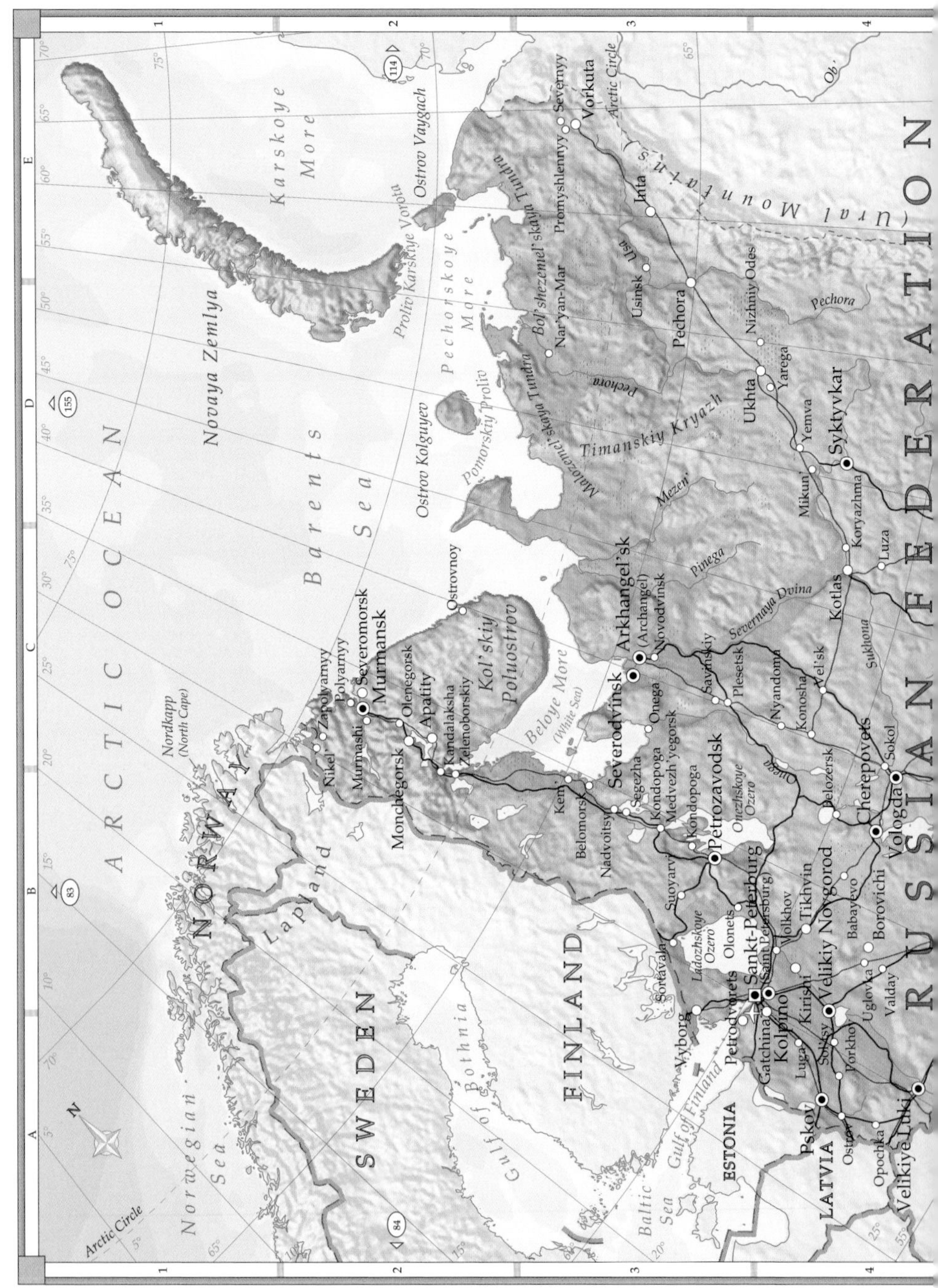

0 km 400
0 miles 400

POPULATION
- National capital
- Less than 50,000
- 50,000 - 100,000
- 100,000 - 500,000
- Over 500,000

KAZAKHSTAN
UZBEKISTAN
TURKMEN.
UKRAINE
GEORGIA
AZERB.
ARM.
TURKEY
Kirghiz Steppe
Kyzyl Kum
Ustyurt Plateau
Caspian Depression
Caspian Sea
Aral Sea
Black Sea
Sea of Azov
Ural'skiye Go
Syr Darya
Amu Darya
Ural
Volga
Don
Donets
Dnieper
Desna
Kuma
Euphrates
Doğu Karadeniz Dağlari
Kuybyshevskoye Vodokhranilishche
El'brus 5642m
Moskva (MOSCOW)
Vladimir
Dzerzhinsk
Nizhniy Novgorod
Yaransk
Nolinsk
Glazov
Krasnokamsk
Perm'
Chusovoy
Kungur
Izhevsk
Chaykovskiy
Neftekamsk
Birsk
Ufa
Beloretsk
Sibay
Baymak
Orsk
Novotroitsk
Saraktash
Kumertau
Salavat
Sterlitamak
Oktyabr'skiy
Al'met'yevsk
Naberezhnyye Chelny
Nizhnekamsk
Kazan'
Yoshkar-Ola
Novocheboksarsk
Cheboksary
Kanash
Murom
Sarov
Saransk
Ul'yanovsk
Dimitrovgrad
Tol'yatti
Samara
Buguruslan
Buzuluk
Orenburg
Sol'-Iletsk
Chapayevsk
Syzran'
Balakovo
Saratov
Vol'sk
Krasnyy Kut
Kamyshin
Kuznetsk
Penza
Tambov
Michurinsk
Sasovo
Ryazan'
Novomoskovsk
Kolomna
Serpukhov
Podol'sk
Tula
Aleksin
Shchëkino
Kaluga
Pochinok
Roslavl'
Bryansk
Klintsy
Zheleznogorsk
Orël
Yelets
Yefremov
Tovarkovskiy
Lipetsk
Gryazi
Voronezh
Liski
Staryy Oskol
Gubkin
Shebekino
Kursk
Belgorod
Rossosh'
Kantemirovka
Borisoglebsk
Balashov
Krasnoarmeysk
Mikhaylovka
Ilovlya
Volzhskiy
Volgograd
Akhtubinsk
Astrakhan'
Elista
Zimovniki
Volgodonsk
Millerovo
Kamensk-Shakhtinskiy
Novocherkassk
Novoshakhtinsk
Taganrog
Rostov-na-Donu
Starominskaya
Tikhoretsk
Sal'sk
Kropotkin
Krasnodar
Novorossiysk
Tuapse
Sochi
Maykop
Stavropol'
Svetlograd
Nevinnomyssk
Cherkessk
Kislovodsk
Pyatigorsk
Prokhladnyy
Nal'chik
Vladikavkaz
Groznyy
Khasavyurt
Buynaksk
Makhachkala
Kaspiysk
Derbent
Caucasus
109
114
117
122
ELEVATION
Below sea level
-2000m -1000m -500m -250m -100m
-6562ft -3281ft -1640ft -820ft -328ft -164ft/-50m 0
0 100m 250m 500m 1000m 2000m 4000m
328ft 820ft 1640ft 3281ft 6562ft 13 124ft

North & West Asia

A B C D

1 2 3 4 5

20° 40° 60° 80° 100° 10° 30° 50° 70° 80°

155 Franz Josef Land

ARCTI

Severnaya Ze

Ostrov Komsomolets

Ostrov Oktyabr'skoy Revolyutsii

Ostrov Bol'shevik

Summer limit of pack ice

Winter limit of pack ice

Novaya Zemlya

East Novaya Zemlya Trench

Kara Sea

Poluostrov Taymy

Norwegian Sea

North Cape

Barents Sea

Ostrov Kolguyev

Poluostrov Yamal

Gulf of Ob

North Siber

Kheta

Murmansk

Kola Peninsula

Noril'sk

Kureyka

Central Siberian Plateau

Arctic Circle

81

White Sea

Archangel

RUSSIAN F

Ural Mountains

West Siberian Plain

Ob'

Lower Tunguska

Yenisey

Gulf of Bothnia

Northern Dvina

Lake Onega

Stony Tunguska

Lake Ladoga

Saint Petersburg

Vologda

Baltic Sea

Perm'

Yekaterinburg

Irtysh

Ob

Angara

Yaroslavl'

Nizhniy Novgorod

Chulym

Volga

Irtysh

Tomsk

Krasnoyarsk

MOSCOW

Kazan'

Chelyabinsk

Novosibirsk

Kaliningrad

Central Russian Upland

Ufa

Ishim

Omsk

KALININGRAD (to Russ. Fed.)

Ul'yanovsk

Samara

Novokuznetsk

Voronezh

Saratov

Orenburg

Sayanskiy Khrebet

Volga

ASTANA

Ural'sk

Karaganda

Semipalatinsk

EUROPE

Kirghiz Steppe

Ural

Volgograd

Kazakh Uplands

Don

KAZAKHSTAN

Ozero Zaysan

Altai Mountains

Rostov-na-Donu

Aral'sk

Astrakhan'

Syr Darya

Lake Balkhash

Aral Sea

Stavropol'

Caspian Sea

Kyzylorda

Danube

Ustyurt Plateau

Ili

Aktau

Kyzyl Kum

Taraz

Almaty

Black Sea

El'brus 5642m

Caucasus

Shan

UZBEKISTAN

BISHKEK

Tien

Pik Pobedy 7443m

GEORGIA

Daşoguz

Istanbul

TBILISI

Amu Darya

TASHKENT

KYRGYZSTAN

Küre Dağları

ARMENIA

AZERB.

BAKU

TURKMENISTAN

ANKARA

YEREVAN

Garagum

DUSHANBE

Anatolia

Lake Van

TAJIKISTAN

TURKEY

Tabriz

AŞGABAT

Mediterranean Sea

Adana

Gaziantep

TEHRAN

Hindu Kush

Kunlun Mountains

Aleppo

Mosul

103

CYPRUS

SYRIA

IRAQ

Qom

IRAN

KABUL

Jalalabad

BEIRUT

DAMASCUS

Herat

LEBANON

BAGHDAD

Isfahan

Khyber Pass

Syrian Desert

Tigris

Iranian Plateau

AFGHANISTAN

ISRAEL

AMMAN

Euphrates

Zagros Mountains

Himalayas

JERUSALEM

JORDAN

Basra

Dead Sea -392m

An Nafud

KUWAIT

Shiraz

Zahedan

Thar Desert

KUWAIT

The Gulf

Bandar-e 'Abbas

MANAMA

BAHRAIN

Dubai

Ganges

RIYADH

DOHA

Gulf of Oman

QATAR

U.A.E.

MUSCAT

Tropic of Cancer

Indus Fan

SAUDI ARABIA

ABU DHABI

JEDDA

Sur

Nile

Red Sea

Arabian Peninsula

Murray Ridge

At Ta'if

OMAN

Ganges Fan

AFRICA

Ar Rub' al Khali

SANA

YEMEN

Arabian Sea

Bay of Bengal

Ta'izz

Socotra (to Yemen)

Aden

Gulf of Aden

69

S

G

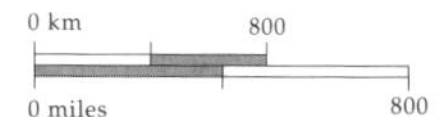

POPULATION

- ● National capital
- ○ Less than 50,000
- ○ 50,000 -100,000
- ◉ 100,000 - 500,000
- ▣ Over 500,000

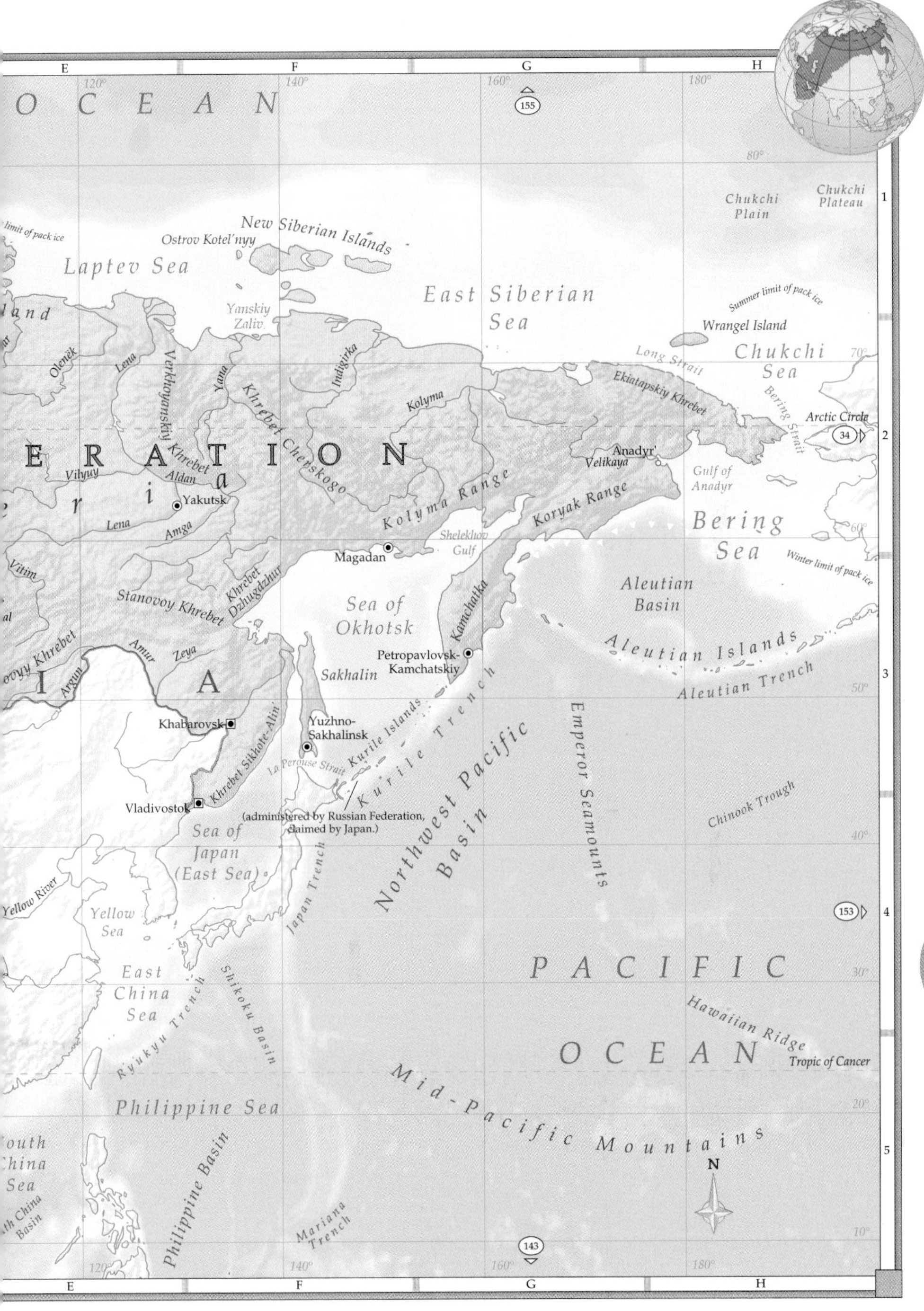
O C E A N
New Siberian Islands
Ostrov Kotel'nyy
Laptev Sea
East Siberian Sea
Chukchi Plain
Chukchi Plateau
Summer limit of pack ice
Wrangel Island
Chukchi Sea
Long Strait
Bering Strait
Arctic Circle
Yanskiy Zaliv
Olenëk
Lena
Verkhoyanskiy Khrebet
Yana
Indigirka
Khrebet Cherskogo
Kolyma
Ekiatapskiy Khrebet
E R A T I O N
Anadyr'
Velikaya
Gulf of Anadyr
Vilyuy
Aldan
Yakutsk
Kolyma Range
Koryak Range
Bering Sea
Lena
Amga
Magadan
Shelekhov Gulf
Winter limit of pack ice
Vitim
Khrebet Dzhugdzhur
Stanovoy Khrebet
Sea of Okhotsk
Kamchatka
Aleutian Basin
Aleutian Islands
Aleutian Trench
Amur
Zeya
Argun
Petropavlovsk-Kamchatskiy
Sakhalin
Khabarovsk
Yuzhno-Sakhalinsk
Kurile Islands
Kurile Trench
La Perouse Strait
Khrebet Sikhote-Alin'
Vladivostok
(administered by Russian Federation, claimed by Japan.)
Northwest Pacific Basin
Emperor Seamounts
Chinook Trough
Sea of Japan (East Sea)
Japan Trench
Yellow River
Yellow Sea
East China Sea
Shikoku Basin
Ryukyu Trench
P A C I F I C
O C E A N
Hawaiian Ridge
Tropic of Cancer
Mid-Pacific Mountains
Philippine Sea
Philippine Basin
South China Sea
Mariana Trench
N
155
34
153
143

RUSSIA & KAZAKHSTAN

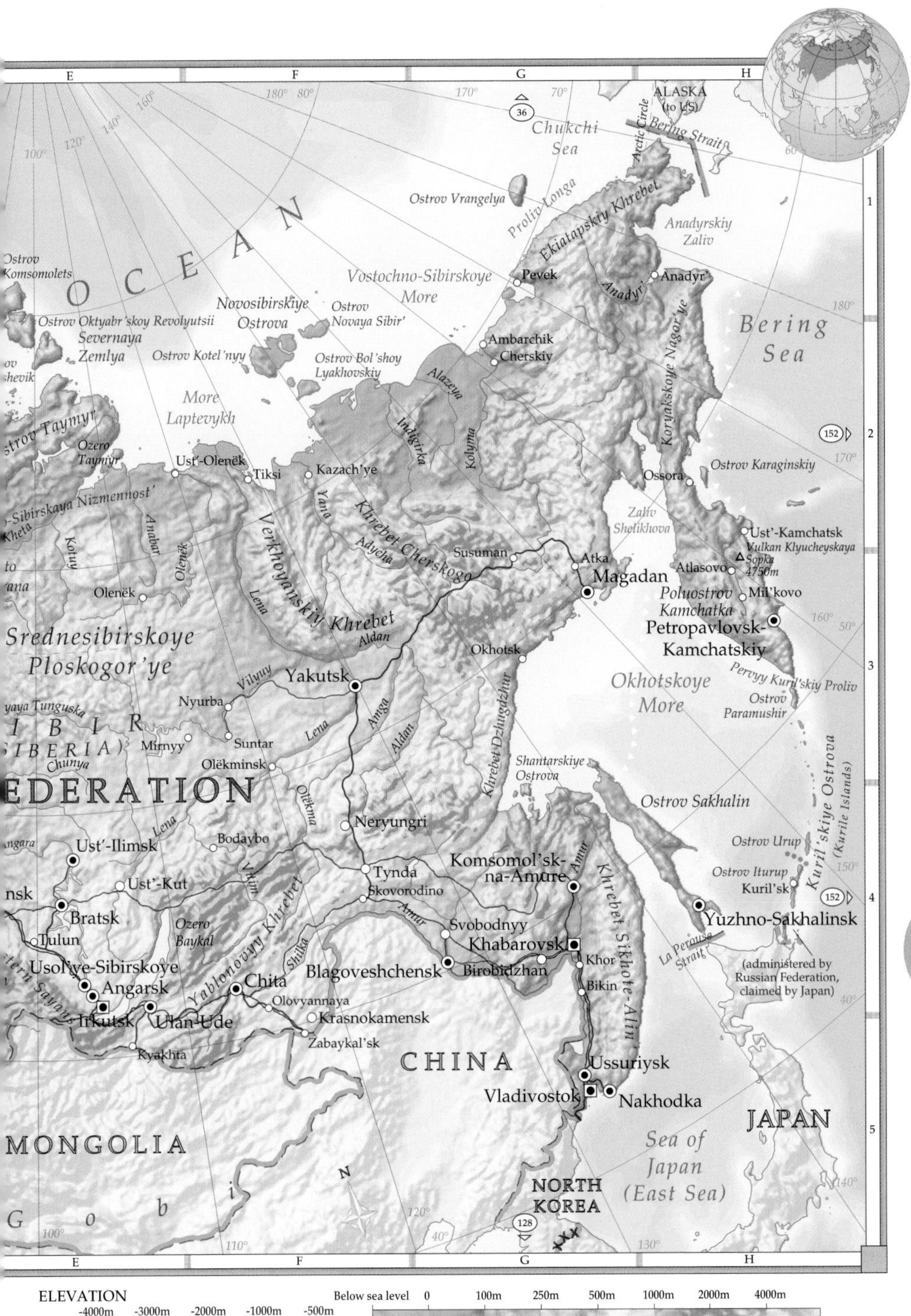
OCEAN
Chukchi Sea
ALASKA (to US)
Bering Strait
Arctic Circle
Ostrov Vrangelya
Proliv Longa
Ekiatapskiy Khrebet
Anadyrskiy Zaliv
Anadyr'
Pevek
Vostochno-Sibirskoye More
Novosibirskiye Ostrova
Ostrov Novaya Sibir'
Ostrov Komsomolets
Ostrov Oktyabr'skoy Revolyutsii
Severnaya Zemlya
Ostrov Kotel'nyy
Ostrov Bol'shoy Lyakhovskiy
Ambarchik
Cherskiy
Koryakskoye Nagor'ye
Bering Sea
More Laptevykh
Alazeya
Indigirka
Kolyma
Ozero Taymyr
Ust'-Olenëk
Tiksi
Kazach'ye
Ossora
Ostrov Karaginskiy
Yana
Khrebet Cherskogo
Zaliv Shelikhova
Ust'-Kamchatsk
Vulkan Klyucheyskaya Sopka 4750m
Anabar
Olenëk
Verkhoyanskiy Khrebet
Adycha
Susuman
Atka
Atlasovo
Magadan
Poluostrov Kamchatka
Mil'kovo
Lena
Petropavlovsk-Kamchatskiy
Srednesibirskoye Ploskogor'ye
Aldan
Okhotsk
Pervyy Kuril'skiy Proliv
Yakutsk
Vilyuy
Okhotskoye More
Ostrov Paramushir
Nyurba
Suntar
Mirnyy
Amga
Khrebet Dzhugdzhur
Kuril'skiye Ostrova (Kurile Islands)
Olëkminsk
Shantarskiye Ostrova
FEDERATION
Olëkma
Neryungri
Ostrov Sakhalin
Ust'-Ilimsk
Bodaybo
Ostrov Urup
Komsomol'sk-na-Amure
Amur
Tynda
Ostrov Iturup
Ust'-Kut
Vitim
Kuril'sk
Bratsk
Skovorodino
Khrebet Sikhote-Alin'
Yuzhno-Sakhalinsk
Ozero Baykal
Svobodnyy
Tulun
Khabarovsk
La Perouse Strait
Shilka
Khor
(administered by Russian Federation, claimed by Japan)
Usol'ye-Sibirskoye
Blagoveshchensk
Birobidzhan
Angarsk
Yablonovyy Khrebet
Chita
Bikin
Irkutsk
Olovyannaya
Ulan-Ude
Krasnokamensk
Zabaykal'sk
Kyakhta
CHINA
Ussuriysk
Vladivostok
Nakhodka
JAPAN
MONGOLIA
Sea of Japan (East Sea)
NORTH KOREA
G o b i
N
ELEVATION
Below sea level
-4000m -3000m -2000m -1000m -500m 0
100m 250m 500m 1000m 2000m 4000m
-13 124ft -9843ft -6562ft -3281ft -1640ft -820ft/-250m 0
328ft 820ft 1640ft 3281ft 6562ft 13 124ft

TURKEY & THE CAUCASUS

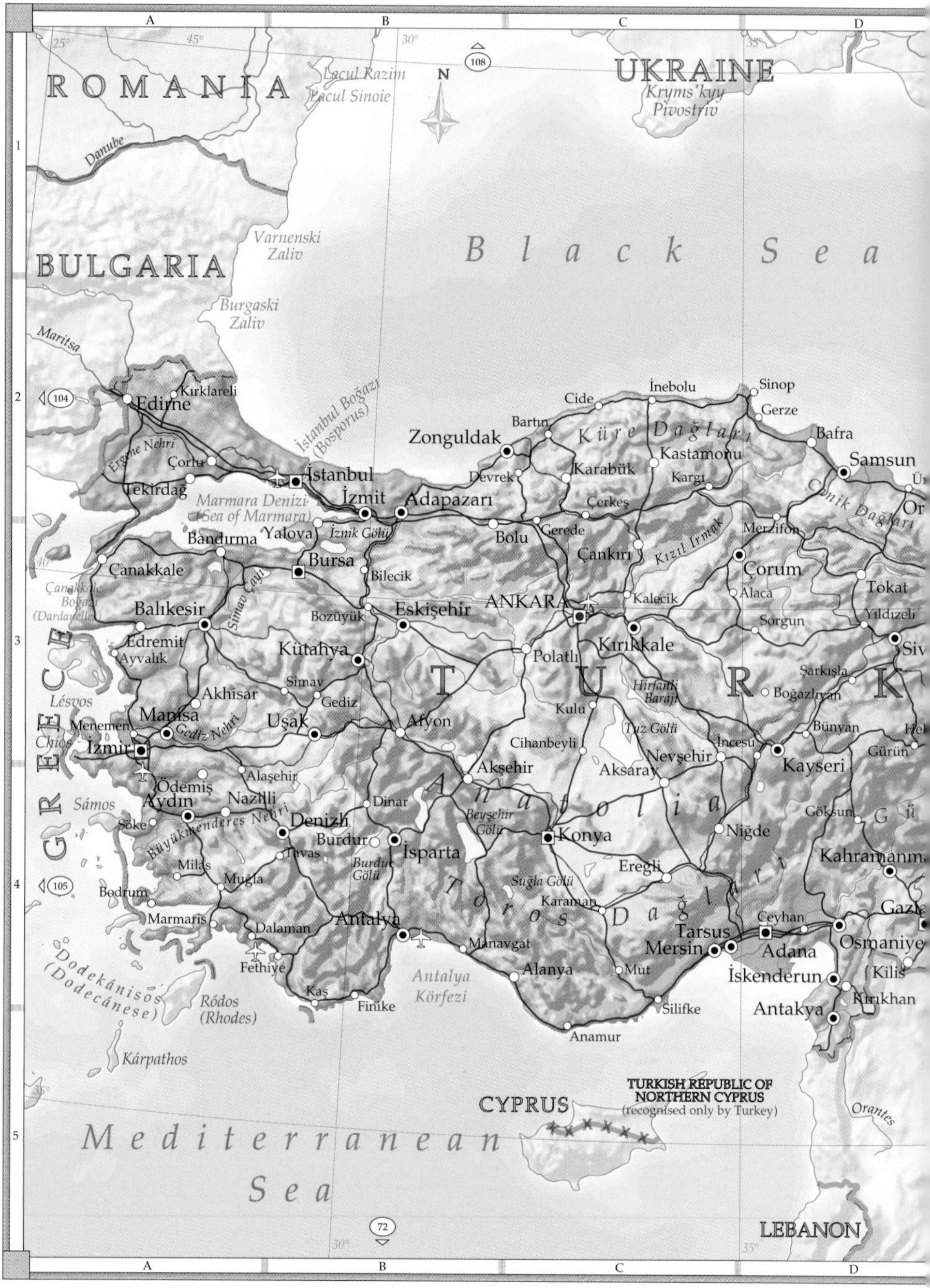

A B C D

1 2 3 4 5

ROMANIA
UKRAINE
Kryms'kyy Pivostriv
BULGARIA
GREECE
TURKEY
CYPRUS
TURKISH REPUBLIC OF NORTHERN CYPRUS (recognised only by Turkey)
LEBANON

Black Sea
Mediterranean Sea
Marmara Denizi (Sea of Marmara)
Antalya Körfezi
Lacul Razim
Lacul Sinoie
Varnenski Zaliv
Burgaski Zaliv
İstanbul Boğazı (Bosporus)
Çanakkale Boğazı (Dardanelles)
Danube
Maritsa
Ergene Nehri
Simav Çayı
Gediz Nehri
Büyükmenderes Nehri
Kızıl Irmak
Orantes
İznik Gölü
Hirfanlı Barajı
Tuz Gölü
Beyşehir Gölü
Burdur Gölü
Suğla Gölü
Küre Dağları
Canik Dağları
Anatolia
Toros Dağları
Lésvos
Chíos
Sámos
Dodekánisos (Dodecánese)
Ródos (Rhodes)
Kárpathos

Edirne
Kırklareli
Çorlu
Tekirdağ
İstanbul
İzmit
Adapazarı
Yalova
Bandırma
Bursa
Çanakkale
Bilecik
Bozüyük
Eskişehir
Balıkesir
Edremit
Ayvalık
Kütahya
Simav
Gediz
Akhisar
Manisa
Menemen
İzmir
Uşak
Afyon
Alaşehir
Ödemiş
Aydın
Nazilli
Söke
Denizli
Dinar
Burdur
Isparta
Tavas
Milas
Muğla
Bodrum
Marmaris
Dalaman
Fethiye
Kaş
Finike
Antalya
Manavgat
Alanya
Anamur
Zonguldak
Bartın
Devrek
Karabük
Cide
İnebolu
Kastamonu
Kargı
Çerkeş
Bolu
Gerede
Çankırı
ANKARA
Polatlı
Kalecik
Kırıkkale
Kulu
Cihanbeyli
Akşehir
Aksaray
Konya
Karaman
Ereğli
Nevşehir
İncesu
Niğde
Mut
Silifke
Sinop
Gerze
Bafra
Samsun
Merzifon
Çorum
Alaca
Sorgun
Tokat
Yıldızeli
Şarkışla
Boğazlıyan
Bünyan
Kayseri
Gürün
Göksun
Kahramanmaraş
Tarsus
Mersin
Adana
Ceyhan
Osmaniye
İskenderun
Kilis
Kırıkhan
Antakya

108
104
105
72

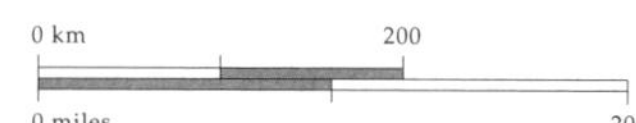

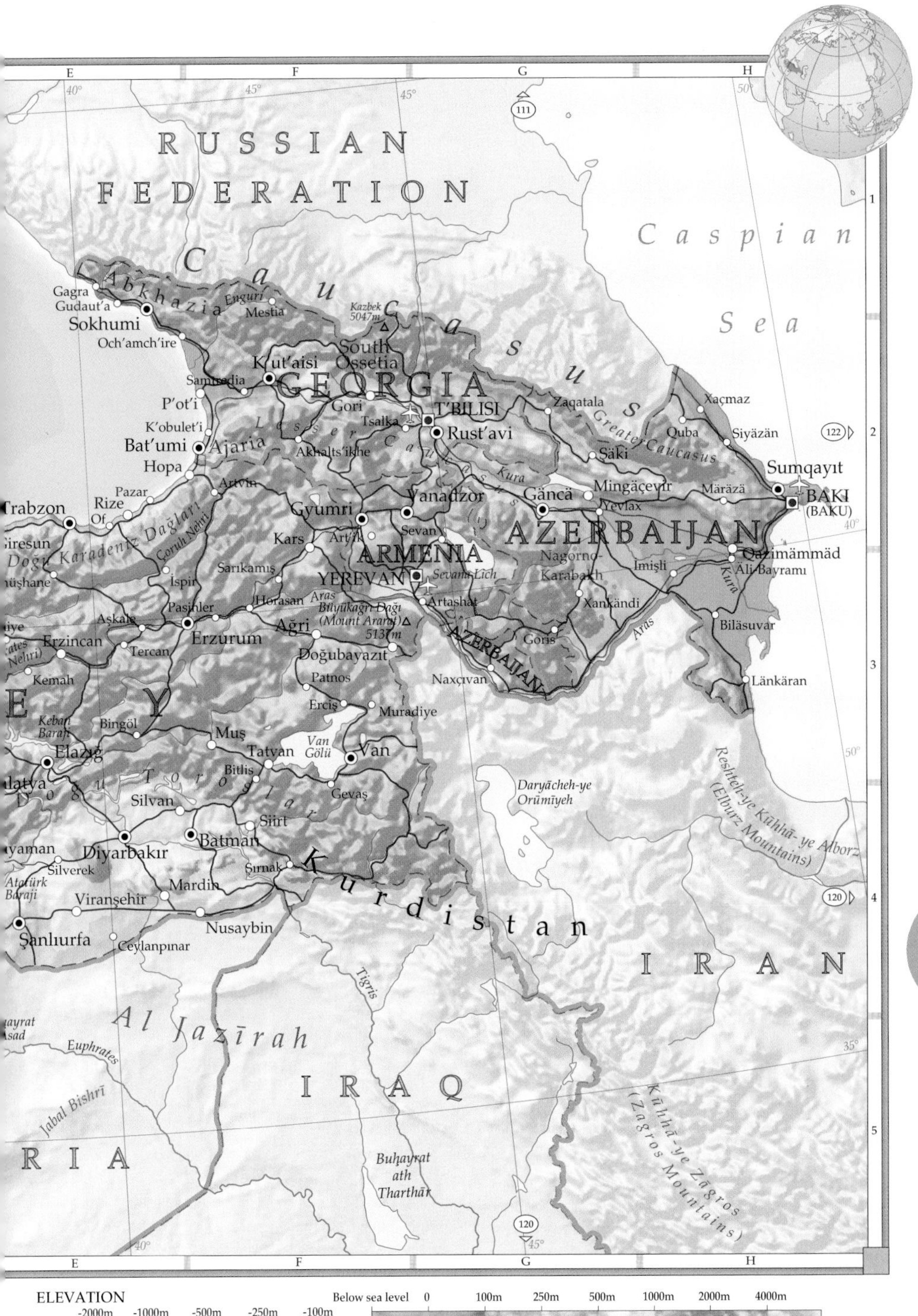
RUSSIAN FEDERATION
Caspian Sea
Caucasus
Abkhazia
Gagra
Gudaut'a
Sokhumi
Och'amch'ire
Enguri
Mestia
Kazbek 5047m
South Ossetia
K'ut'aisi
Samtredia
GEORGIA
P'ot'i
Gori
Tsalka
T'BILISI
Rust'avi
K'obulet'i
Bat'umi
Ajaria
Akhalts'ikhe
Lesser Caucasus
Hopa
Artvin
Pazar
Rize
Of
Trabzon
Giresun
Doğu Karadeniz Dağları
Çoruh Nehri
Gyumri
Vanadzor
Kars
Sevan
ARMENIA
YEREVAN
Sevana Lich
Artashat
Sarıkamış
İspir
Horasan
Aras
Büyükağrı Dağı (Mount Ararat) 5137m
Pasinler
Aşkale
Erzurum
Ağri
Erzincan
Tercan
Doğubayazıt
Kemah
Patnos
Erciş
Muradiye
Keban Barajı
Bingöl
Muş
Van Gölü
Van
Tatvan
Bitlis
Elazığ
Malatya
Toroslar
Silvan
Gevaş
Siirt
Batman
Diyarbakır
Silverek
Atatürk Barajı
Şırnak
Mardin
Viranşehir
Şanlıurfa
Ceylanpınar
Nusaybin
Kurdistan
Tigris
Al Jazīrah
Euphrates
Jabal Bishrī
IRAQ
Buḩayrat ath Tharthār
Zaqatala
Greater Caucasus
Xaçmaz
Quba
Siyäzän
Şäki
Kura
Mingäçevir
Gäncä
Yevlax
Märäzä
Sumqayıt
BAKI (BAKU)
AZERBAIJAN
Nagorno-Karabakh
İmişli
Qazimämmäd
Äli Bayramı
Xankändi
Goris
Naxçıvan
AZERBAIJAN
Biläsuvar
Länkäran
Daryācheh-ye Orūmīyeh
Reshteh-ye Kūhhā-ye Alborz (Elburz Mountains)
IRAN
Kūhhā-ye Zāgros (Zagros Mountains)
ELEVATION
Below sea level
0
100m
250m
500m
1000m
2000m
4000m
328ft
820ft
1640ft
3281ft
6562ft
13 124ft
-2000m
-1000m
-500m
-250m
-100m
-6562ft
-3281ft
-1640ft
-820ft
-328ft
-164ft/-50m

THE NEAR EAST

0 km 100
0 miles 100

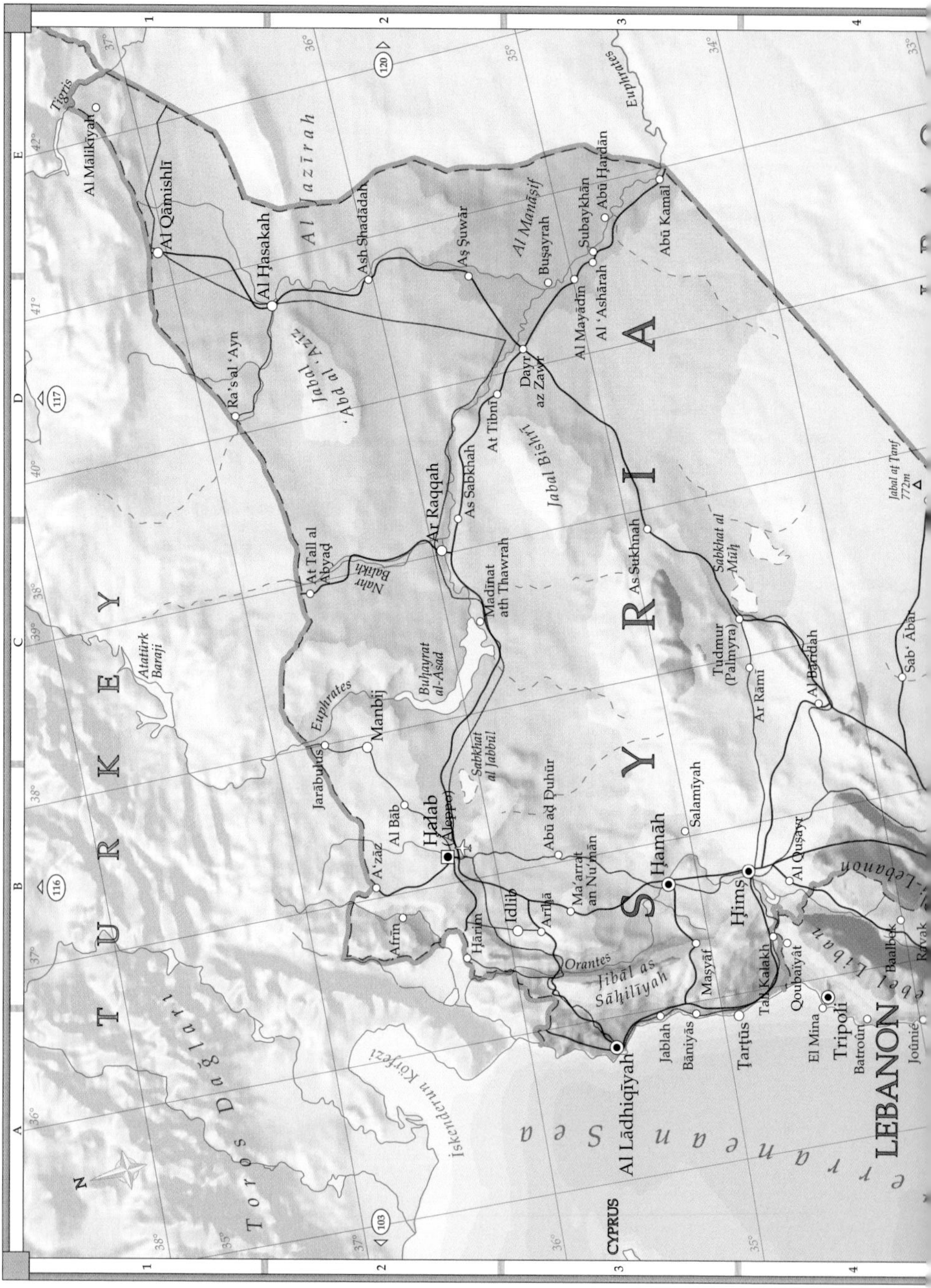

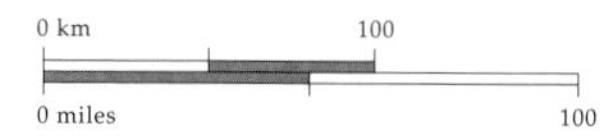

POPULATION
● National capital
○ Less than 50,000
○ 50,000 -100,000
◉ 100,000 - 500,000
▣ Over 500,000

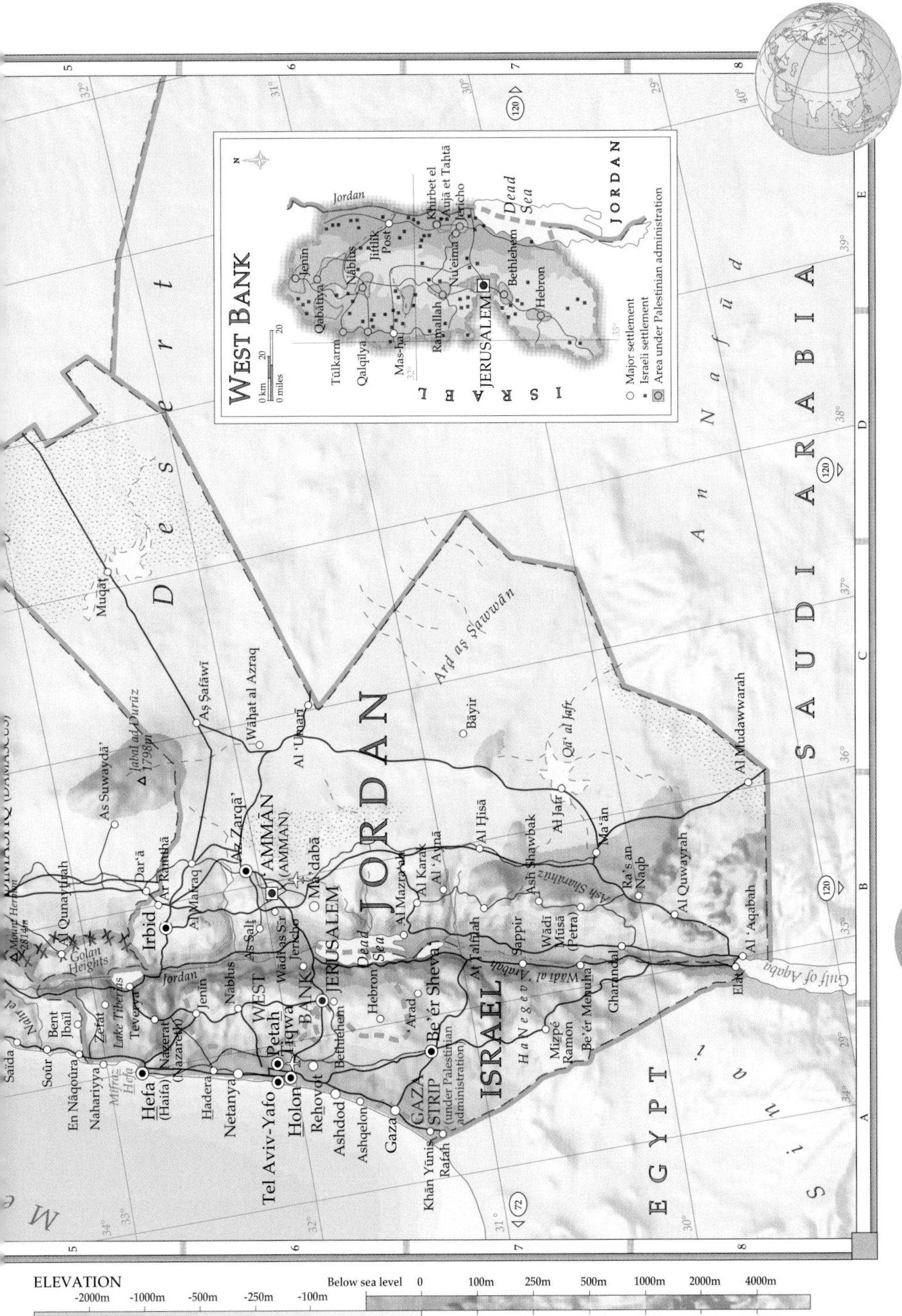

ELEVATION

-2000m	-1000m	-500m	-250m	-100m	Below sea level	0	100m	250m	500m	1000m	2000m	4000m
-6562ft	-3281ft	-1640ft	-820ft	-328ft	-164ft/-50m	0	328ft	820ft	1640ft	3281ft	6562ft	13 124ft

THE MIDDLE EAST

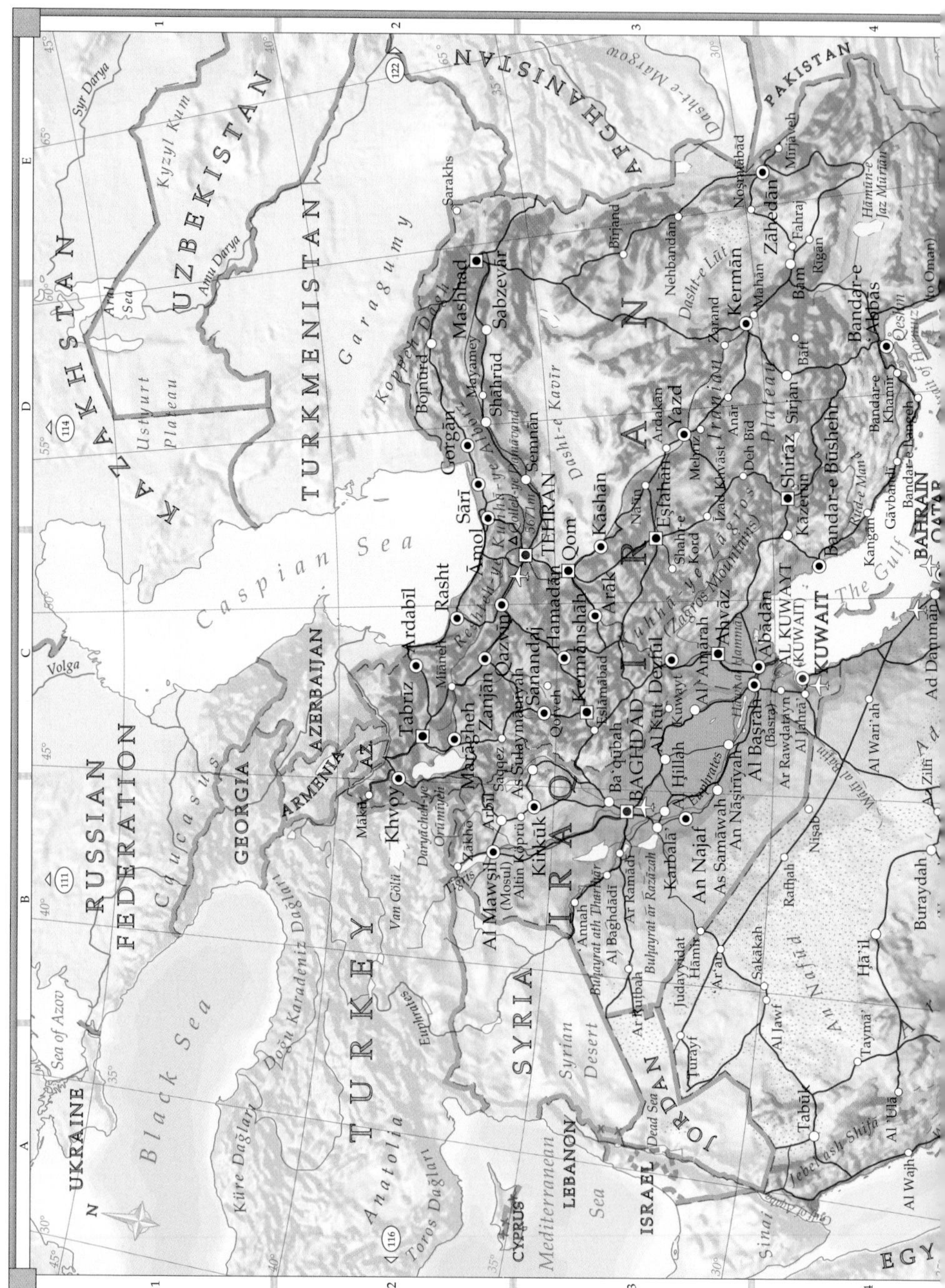

0 km 400
0 miles 400

POPULATION
● National capital
○ Less than 50,000
○ 50,000 -100,000
◉ 100,000 - 500,000
▣ Over 500,000

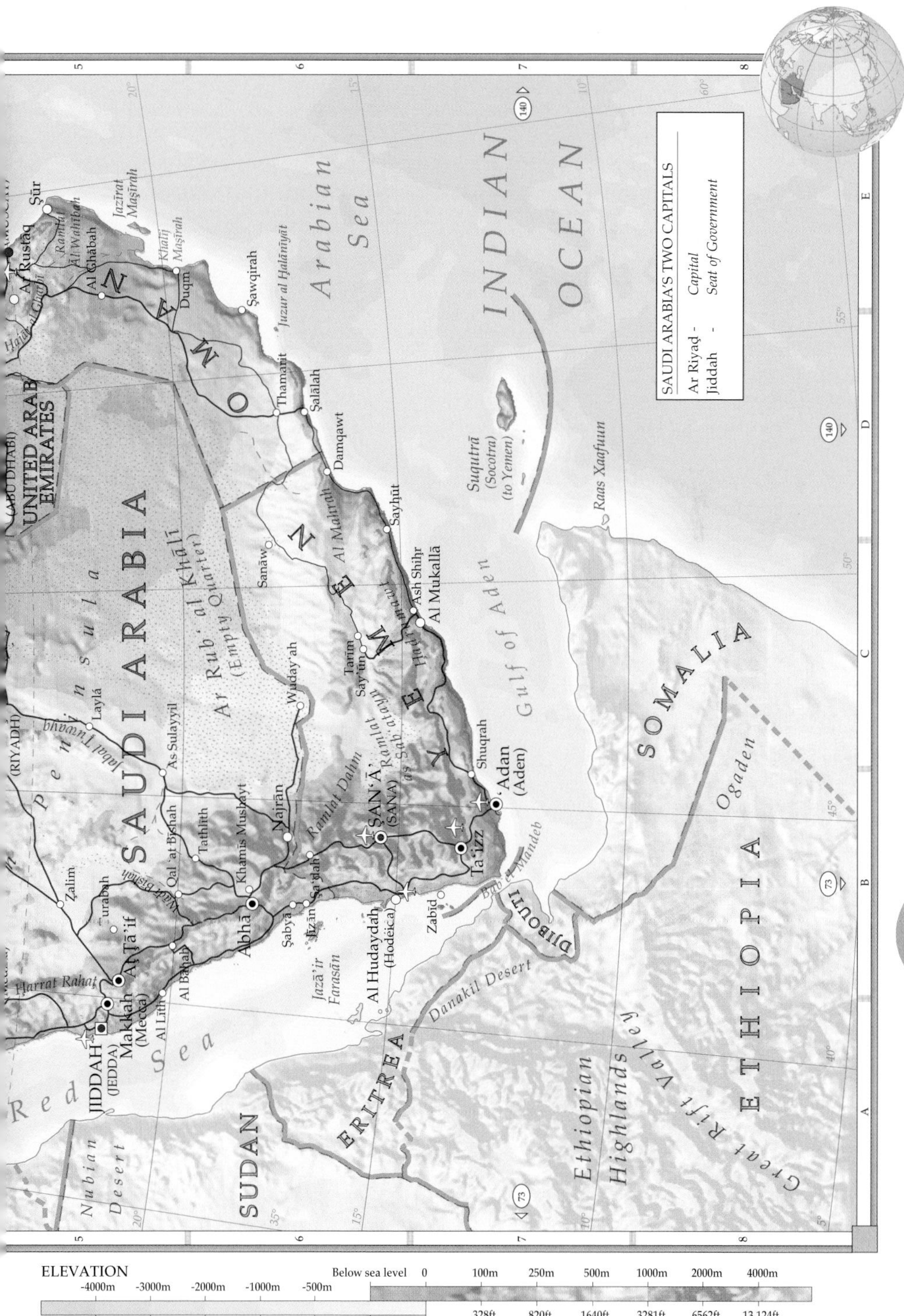
SAUDI ARABIA'S TWO CAPITALS
Ar Riyaḍ - Capital
Jiddah - Seat of Government
SAUDI ARABIA
UNITED ARAB EMIRATES
OMAN
YEMEN
ERITREA
DJIBOUTI
SOMALIA
ETHIOPIA
SUDAN
INDIAN OCEAN
Arabian Sea
Red Sea
Gulf of Aden
Bab el Mandeb
Ar Rub' al Khālī (Empty Quarter)
Ramlat as Sab'atayn
Ramlat Dahm
Nubian Desert
Danakil Desert
Ethiopian Highlands
Great Rift Valley
Ogaden
Ḥarrat Rahat
Jabal Ṭuwayq
Ḩaḑramawt
Al Mahrah
Suquṭrā (Socotra) (to Yemen)
Raas Xaafuun
Jazā'ir Farasān
Jazīrat Maşīrah
Khalīj Maşīrah
Juzur al Ḩalāniyāt
Ramlat Al Wahībah
JIDDAH (JEDDA)
Makkah (Mecca)
Aṭ Ṭā'if
Al Bāḩah
Al Līth
Abhā
Khamīs Mushayt
Najrān
Jīzān
Şabyā
Şa'dah
ŞAN'Ā' (SANA)
Al Hudaydah (Hodeida)
Zabīd
Ta'izz
'Adan (Aden)
Shuqrah
Al Mukallā
Ash Shiḩr
Tarīm
Say'ūn
Wuday'ah
Sanāw
Sayḩūt
Damqawt
Şalālah
Thamarīt
Şawqirah
Duqm
Al Ghābah
Şūr
Ar Rustāq
Laylā
As Sulayyil
Tathlīth
Qal'at Bīshah
Ẓalim
(RIYADH)
(ABU DHABI)
ELEVATION
Below sea level 0 100m 250m 500m 1000m 2000m 4000m
-4000m -3000m -2000m -1000m -500m
328ft 820ft 1640ft 3281ft 6562ft 13 124ft
-13 124ft -9843ft -6562ft -3281ft -1640ft -820ft/-250m 0

Central Asia

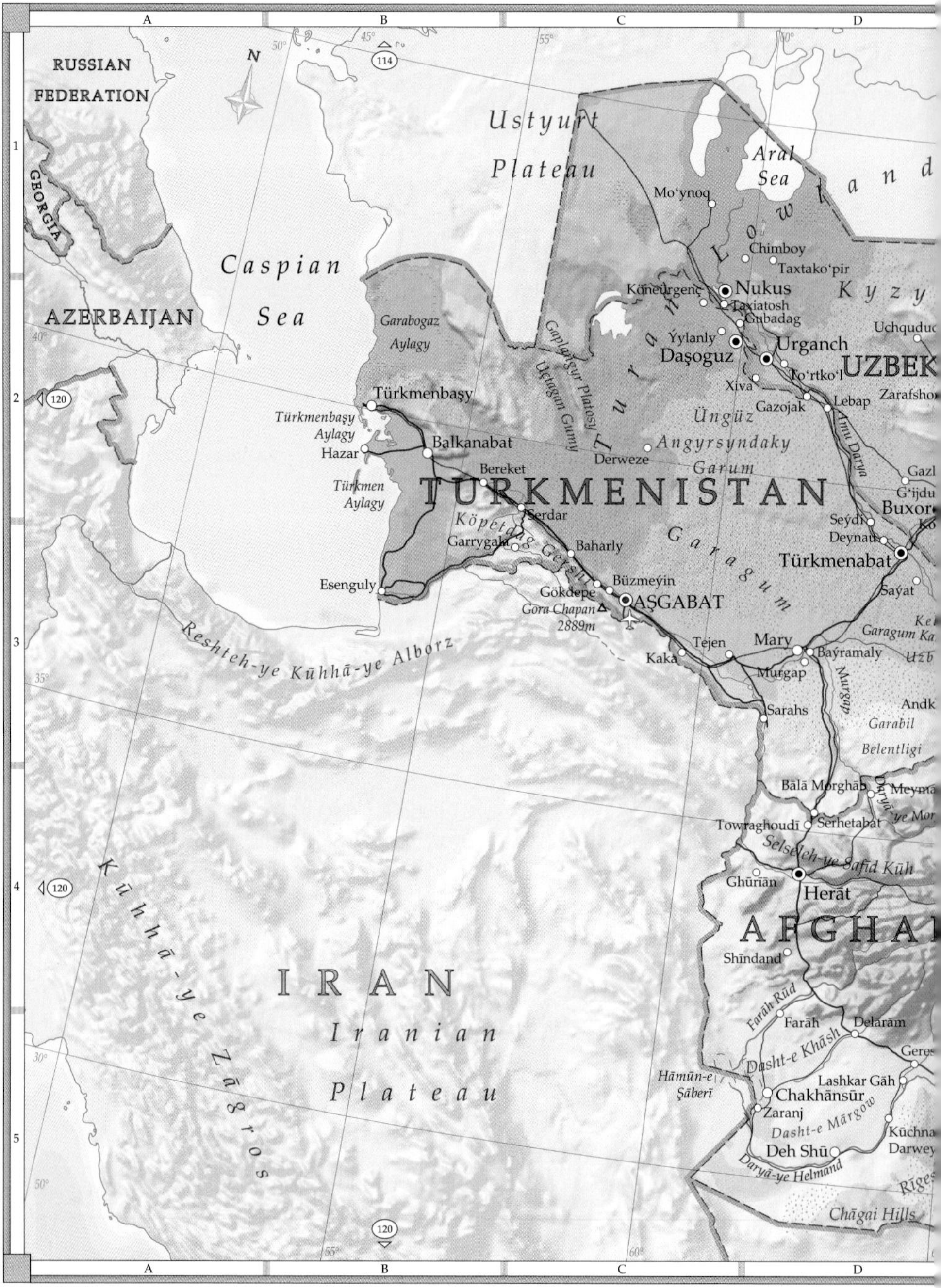

A B C D

RUSSIAN FEDERATION
N
114
Ustyurt Plateau
Aral Sea
Mo'ynoq
GEORGIA
Caspian Sea
AZERBAIJAN
Garabogaz Aylagy
Chimboy
Taxtako'pir
Köneürgenç
Nukus
Taxiatosh
Qubadag
Kyzy
Uchquduq
Ýylanly
Daşoguz
Urganch
To'rtko'l
UZBEK
Xiva
Turan Lowland
Gaplaňgyr Platosy
Uçtagan Gumy
Lebap
Zarafshon
Gazojak
Türkmenbaşy
Türkmenbaşy Aylagy
Hazar
Balkanabat
Üngüz
Angyrsyndaky Garum
Derweze
Amu Darya
Gazli
G'ijduvon
Bereket
Türkmen Aylagy
TURKMENISTAN
Buxoro
Serdar
Köpetdag Gershi
Seýdi
Deynau
Garrygala
Baharly
Garagum
Türkmenabat
Esenguly
Büzmeýin
Gökdepe
AŞGABAT
Sayat
Gora Chapan
2889m
Kaka
Tejen
Mary
Garagum Kanaly
Baýramaly
Murgap
Reshteh-ye Kūhhā-ye Alborz
Sarahs
Andkhvoy
Garabil
Belentligi
Bālā Morghāb
Meymaneh
Towraghoudī
Serhetabat
Daryā-ye Morghāb
Selseleh-ye Safīd Kūh
Ghūriān
Herāt
120
AFGHANISTAN
Shīndand
Kūhhā-ye Zāgros
IRAN
Iranian Plateau
Farāh Rūd
Farāh
Delārām
Dasht-e Khāsh
Gereshk
Hāmūn-e Şāberī
Lashkar Gāh
Chakhānsūr
Zaranj
Dasht-e Mārgow
Kūchnay Darweyshān
Deh Shū
Daryā-ye Helmand
Chāgai Hills

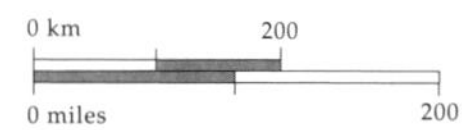

POPULATION
● National capital
○ Less than 50,000
○ 50,000 -100,000
⦿ 100,000 - 500,000
▣ Over 500,000

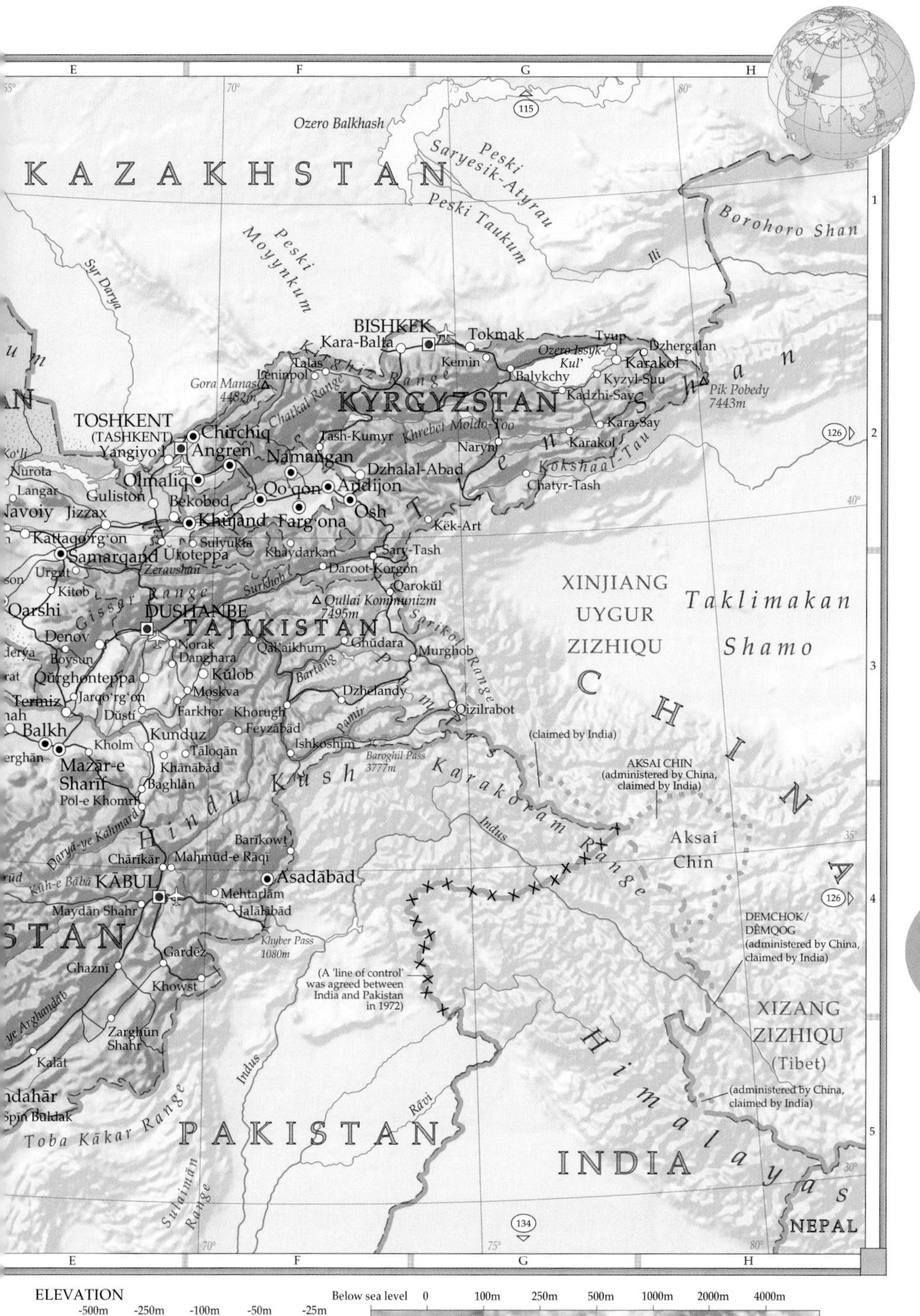
KAZAKHSTAN
Ozero Balkhash
Peski Saryesik-Atyrau
Peski Taukum
Peski Moyynkum
Borohoro Shan
Ili
Syr Darya
BISHKEK
Tokmak
Kara-Balta
Talas
Kirghiz Range
Leninpol
Gora Manas 4482m
Kemin
Balykchy
Tyup
Dzhergalan
Ozero Issyk-Kul'
Karakol
Kyzyl-Suu
Kadzhi-Say
Pik Pobedy 7443m
KYRGYZSTAN
Chatkal Range
Khrebet Moldo-Too
Kara-Say
TOSHKENT (TASHKENT)
Chirchiq
Yangiyo'l
Angren
Tash-Kumyr
Naryn
Karakol
Namangan
Dzhalal-Abad
Kokshaal-Tau
Chatyr-Tash
Olmaliq
Nurota
Langar
Guliston
Bekobod
Qo'qon
Andijon
Osh
Navoiy
Jizzax
Khujand
Farg'ona
Kěk-Art
Kattaqo'rg'on
Sulyukta
Samarqand
Ŭroteppa
Khaydarkan
Sary-Tash
Zeravshan
Urgut
Daroot-Korgon
Kitob
Qarokŭl
Qarshi
Gissar Range
Surkhob
Qullai Kommunizm 7495m
DUSHANBE
TAJIKISTAN
XINJIANG UYGUR ZIZHIQU
Taklimakan Shamo
Denov
Boysun
Norak
Danghara
Qal'aikhum
Ghŭdara
Murghob
Sarikol Range
Qŭrghonteppa
Kŭlob
Bartang
Moskva
Dzhelandy
Termiz
Jarqo'rg'on
Dŭstí
Farkhor
Khorugh
Pamir
Qizilrabot
Balkh
Kholm
Kunduz
Feyzābād
Ishkoshim
Tāloqān
Baroghil Pass 3777m
Mazār-e Sharīf
Khānābād
Baghlān
Pol-e Khomrī
Hindu Kush
Karakoram Range
(claimed by India)
AKSAI CHIN (administered by China, claimed by India)
CHINA
Aksai Chin
Indus
Barīkowt
Darya-ye Kahmard
Chārīkār
Maḥmūd-e Rāqi
KĀBUL
Asadābād
Kūh-e Bābā
Mehtarlām
Jalālābād
Maydān Shahr
Khyber Pass 1080m
DEMCHOK/ DÊMQOG (administered by China, claimed by India)
Gardēz
Ghaznī
Khowst
(A 'line of control' was agreed between India and Pakistan in 1972)
XIZANG ZIZHIQU (Tibet)
Zarghūn Shahr
Kalāt
Himalayas
(administered by China, claimed by India)
Spīn Buldak
Toba Kākar Range
Rāvi
PAKISTAN
INDIA
Sulaimān Range
NEPAL
115
126
134
ELEVATION
Below sea level
-500m -250m -100m -50m -25m 0
-1640ft -820ft -328ft -164ft -82ft 33ft/-10m 0
100m 250m 500m 1000m 2000m 4000m
328ft 820ft 1640ft 3281ft 6562ft 13 124ft

SOUTH & EAST ASIA

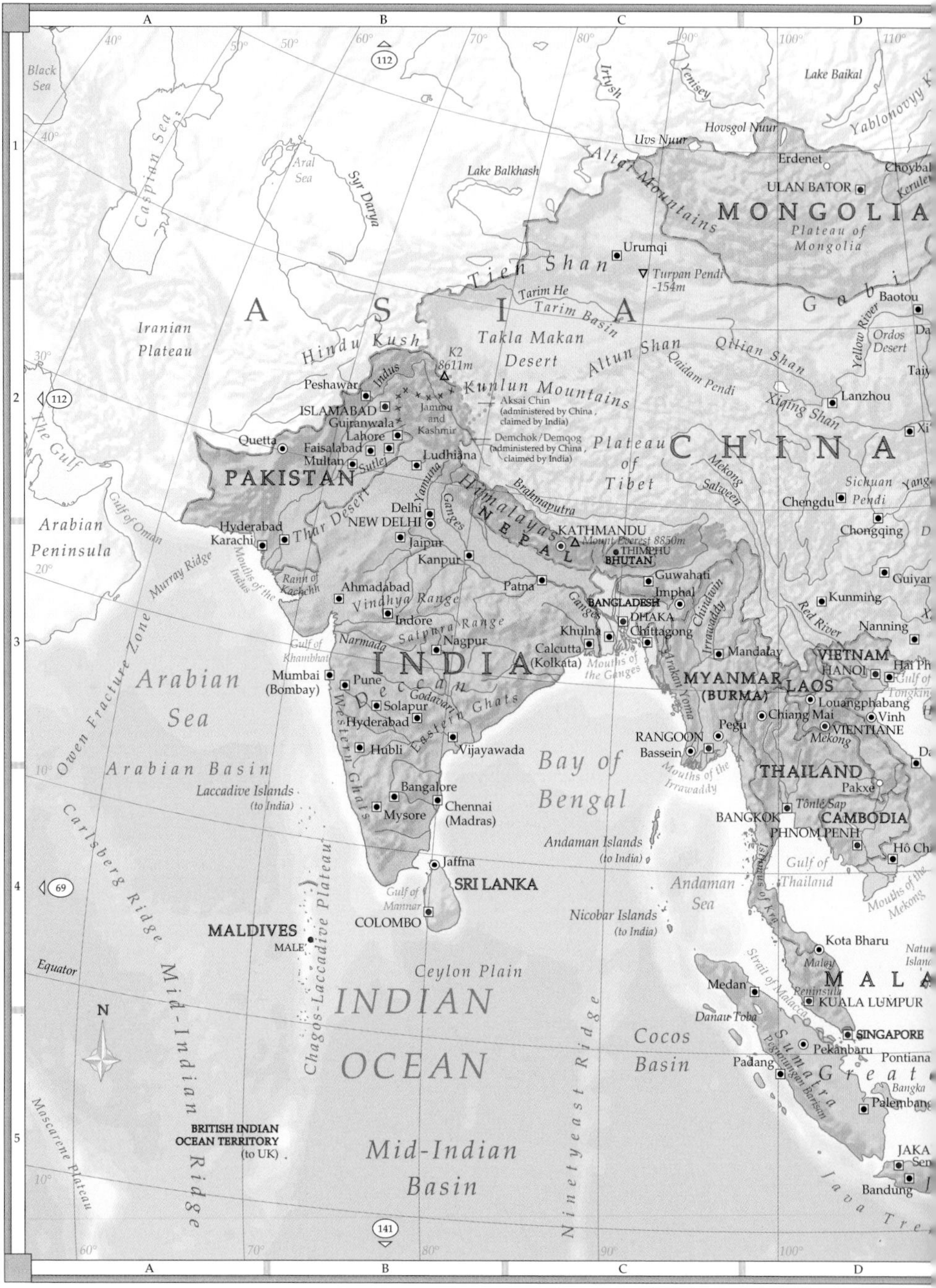

A B C D
1 2 3 4 5

ASIA
CHINA
MONGOLIA
PAKISTAN
INDIA
NEPAL
BHUTAN
BANGLADESH
MYANMAR (BURMA)
LAOS
VIETNAM
THAILAND
CAMBODIA
SRI LANKA
MALDIVES
BRITISH INDIAN OCEAN TERRITORY (to UK)

Black Sea
Caspian Sea
Aral Sea
Syr Darya
Lake Balkhash
Irtysh
Yenisey
Lake Baikal
Hovsgol Nuur
Uvs Nuur
Altai Mountains
Yablonovyy
Erdenet
ULAN BATOR
Plateau of Mongolia
Urumqi
Turpan Pendi -154m
Tien Shan
Tarim He
Tarim Basin
Gobi
Baotou
Ordos Desert
Yellow River
Iranian Plateau
Hindu Kush
Takla Makan Desert
Altun Shan
Qilian Shan
Qaidam Pendi
Xiqing Shan
Lanzhou
K2 8611m
Kunlun Mountains
Aksai Chin (administered by China, claimed by India)
Demchok/Demqog (administered by China, claimed by India)
Jammu and Kashmir
Peshawar
ISLAMABAD
Gujranwala
Lahore
Faisalabad
Multan
Quetta
Indus
Sutlej
Ludhiana
Plateau of Tibet
Mekong
Salween
Sichuan Pendi
Chengdu
Chongqing
Brahmaputra
Himalayas
Yamuna
Ganges
Delhi
NEW DELHI
Jaipur
Kanpur
KATHMANDU
Mount Everest 8850m
THIMPHU
Thar Desert
Hyderabad
Karachi
Mouths of the Indus
Rann of Kachchh
Murray Ridge
Gulf of Oman
The Gulf
Arabian Peninsula
Ahmadabad
Vindhya Range
Indore
Satpura Range
Narmada
Nagpur
Patna
Guwahati
Imphal
DHAKA
Khulna
Chittagong
Chindwin
Irrawaddy
Kunming
Red River
Nanning
Mandalay
Calcutta (Kolkata)
Mouths of the Ganges
Arakan Yoma
HANOI
Gulf of Tongking
Gulf of Khambhat
Mumbai (Bombay)
Pune
Deccan
Godavari
Solapur
Hyderabad
Western Ghats
Eastern Ghats
Hubli
Vijayawada
Louangphabang
Chiang Mai
Vinh
VIENTIANE
Mekong
Pegu
RANGOON
Bassein
Mouths of the Irrawaddy
Owen Fracture Zone
Arabian Sea
Arabian Basin
Laccadive Islands (to India)
Bangalore
Mysore
Chennai (Madras)
Bay of Bengal
Pakxe
BANGKOK
Tônlé Sap
PHNOM PENH
Andaman Islands (to India)
Carlsberg Ridge
Jaffna
Gulf of Mannar
COLOMBO
Andaman Sea
Isthmus of Kra
Gulf of Thailand
Mouths of the Mekong
Nicobar Islands (to India)
MALE
Chagos-Laccadive Plateau
Kota Bharu
Malay Peninsula
Strait of Malacca
Medan
KUALA LUMPUR
Danau Toba
SINGAPORE
Pekanbaru
Sumatra
Pegunungan Barisan
Padang
Pontianak
Palembang
Bangka
Ceylon Plain
INDIAN OCEAN
Mid-Indian Ridge
Ninetyeast Ridge
Cocos Basin
Mid-Indian Basin
Equator
Mascarene Plateau
Bandung
Java Trench

112
69
141

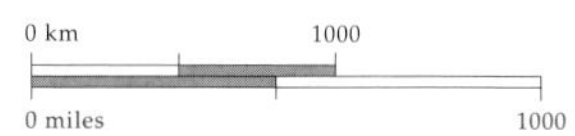

POPULATION
● National capital
○ Less than 50,000
○ 50,000 -100,000
⊙ 100,000 - 500,000
▣ Over 500,000

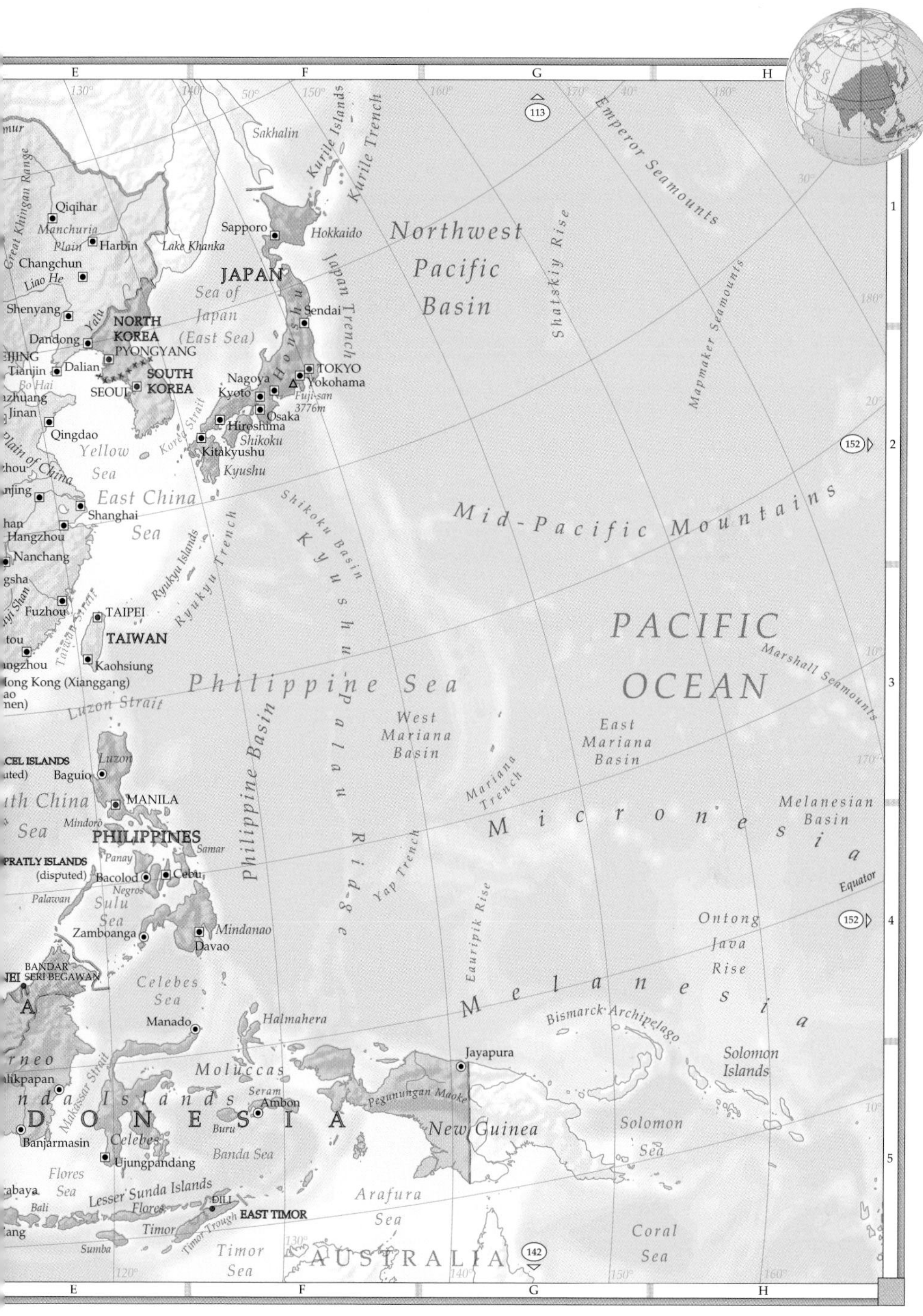

Sakhalin
Kurile Islands
Kurile Trench
Emperor Seamounts
Qiqihar
Manchurian Plain
Harbin
Lake Khanka
Sapporo
Hokkaido
Northwest Pacific Basin
Shatskiy Rise
Great Khingan Range
Changchun
Liao He
JAPAN
Sea of Japan (East Sea)
Japan Trench
Honshu
Sendai
Shenyang
Yalu
NORTH KOREA
PYONGYANG
Dandong
Dalian
Tianjin
Bo Hai
SOUTH KOREA
SEOUL
Nagoya
Kyoto
TOKYO
Yokohama
Fuji-san 3776m
Osaka
Hiroshima
Shikoku
Kitakyushu
Kyushu
Mapmaker Seamounts
Jinan
Qingdao
Yellow Sea
Korea Strait
East China Sea
Shanghai
Hangzhou
Nanchang
Fuzhou
Shikoku Basin
Kyushu Palau Ridge
Ryukyu Islands
Ryukyu Trench
Mid-Pacific Mountains
TAIPEI
TAIWAN
Taiwan Strait
Kaohsiung
Hong Kong (Xianggang)
Luzon Strait
Philippine Sea
PACIFIC OCEAN
Marshall Seamounts
West Mariana Basin
East Mariana Basin
Philippine Basin
Mariana Trench
Luzon
Baguio
MANILA
Mindoro
PHILIPPINES
Samar
Panay
PRATLY ISLANDS (disputed)
Bacolod
Cebu
Negros
Palawan
Sulu Sea
Zamboanga
Mindanao
Davao
Micronesia
Melanesian Basin
Yap Trench
Eauripik Rise
Equator
Ontong Java Rise
BANDAR SERI BEGAWAN
Celebes Sea
Manado
Halmahera
Melanesia
Bismarck Archipelago
Jayapura
Solomon Islands
Makassar Strait
Moluccas
Seram
Ambon
Pegunungan Maoke
New Guinea
Buru
Solomon Sea
Banjarmasin
Celebes
Ujungpandang
Banda Sea
Flores Sea
Lesser Sunda Islands
Bali
Flores
DILI
EAST TIMOR
Timor
Timor Trough
Sumba
Arafura Sea
Coral Sea
Timor Sea
AUSTRALIA
113
152
142

WESTERN CHINA & MONGOLIA

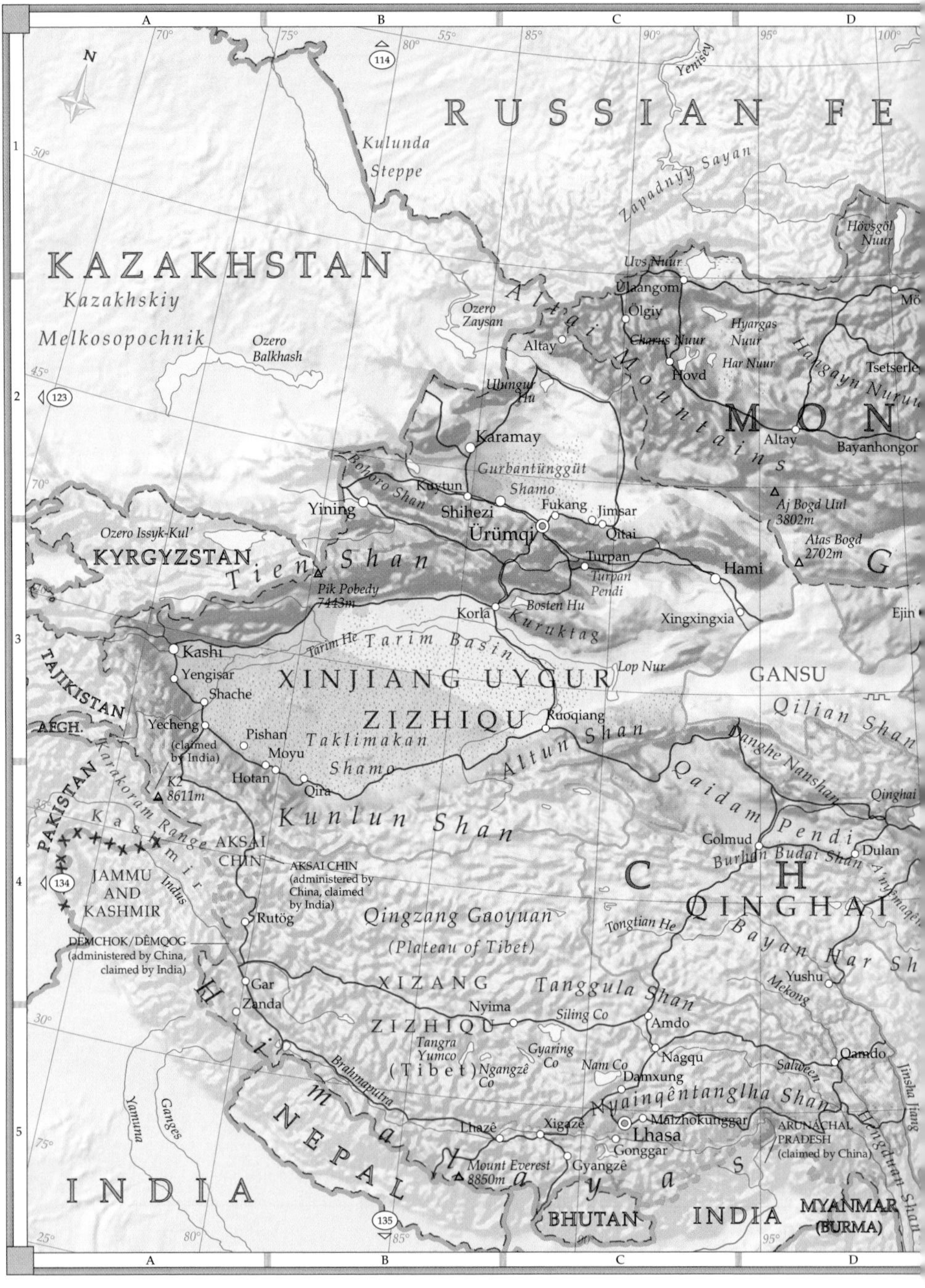

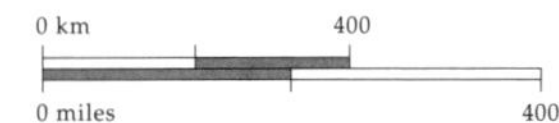

POPULATION
● National capital
● Internal administrative capital
○ Less than 50,000
○ 50,000 -100,000
⦿ 100,000 - 500,000
■ Over 500,000

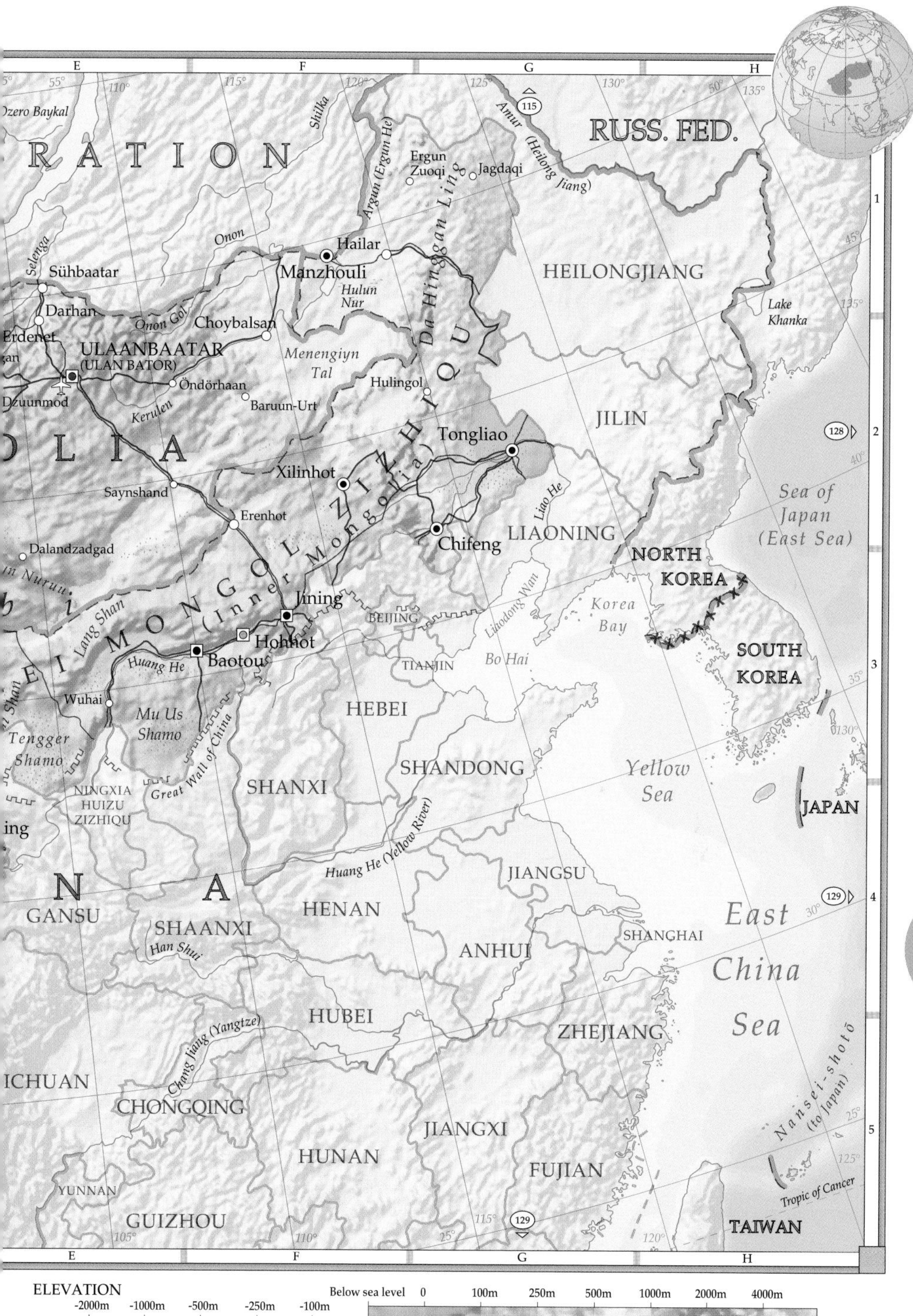

RUSS. FED.
HEILONGJIANG
JILIN
LIAONING
NORTH KOREA
SOUTH KOREA
JAPAN
TAIWAN
ULAANBAATAR (ULAN BATOR)
Sühbaatar
Darhan
Erdenet
Choybalsan
Öndörhaan
Baruun-Urt
Dzuunmod
Saynshand
Dalandzadgad
Erenhot
Manzhouli
Hailar
Ergun Zuoqi
Jagdaqi
Hulingol
Tongliao
Xilinhot
Chifeng
Jining
Hohhot
Baotou
Wuhai
BEIJING
TIANJIN
HEBEI
SHANXI
SHANDONG
HENAN
JIANGSU
SHANGHAI
ANHUI
HUBEI
ZHEJIANG
JIANGXI
FUJIAN
HUNAN
GUIZHOU
YUNNAN
CHONGQING
SICHUAN
SHAANXI
GANSU
NINGXIA HUIZU ZIZHIQU
NEI MONGOL ZIZHIQU (Inner Mongolia)
Ozero Baykal
Selenga
Onon
Onon Gol
Kerulen
Shilka
Argun (Ergun He)
Amur (Heilong Jiang)
Da Hinggan Ling
Hulun Nur
Menengiyn Tal
Lake Khanka
Liao He
Liaodong Wan
Korea Bay
Bo Hai
Sea of Japan (East Sea)
Yellow Sea
East China Sea
Nansei-shotō (to Japan)
Tropic of Cancer
Lang Shan
Huang He
Huang He (Yellow River)
Mu Us Shamo
Tengger Shamo
Great Wall of China
Han Shui
Chang Jiang (Yangtze)
115
128
129
ELEVATION
Below sea level
-2000m -1000m -500m -250m -100m
-6562ft -3281ft -1640ft -820ft -328ft -164ft/-50m 0
0 100m 250m 500m 1000m 2000m 4000m
328ft 820ft 1640ft 3281ft 6562ft 13 124ft

EASTERN CHINA & KOREA

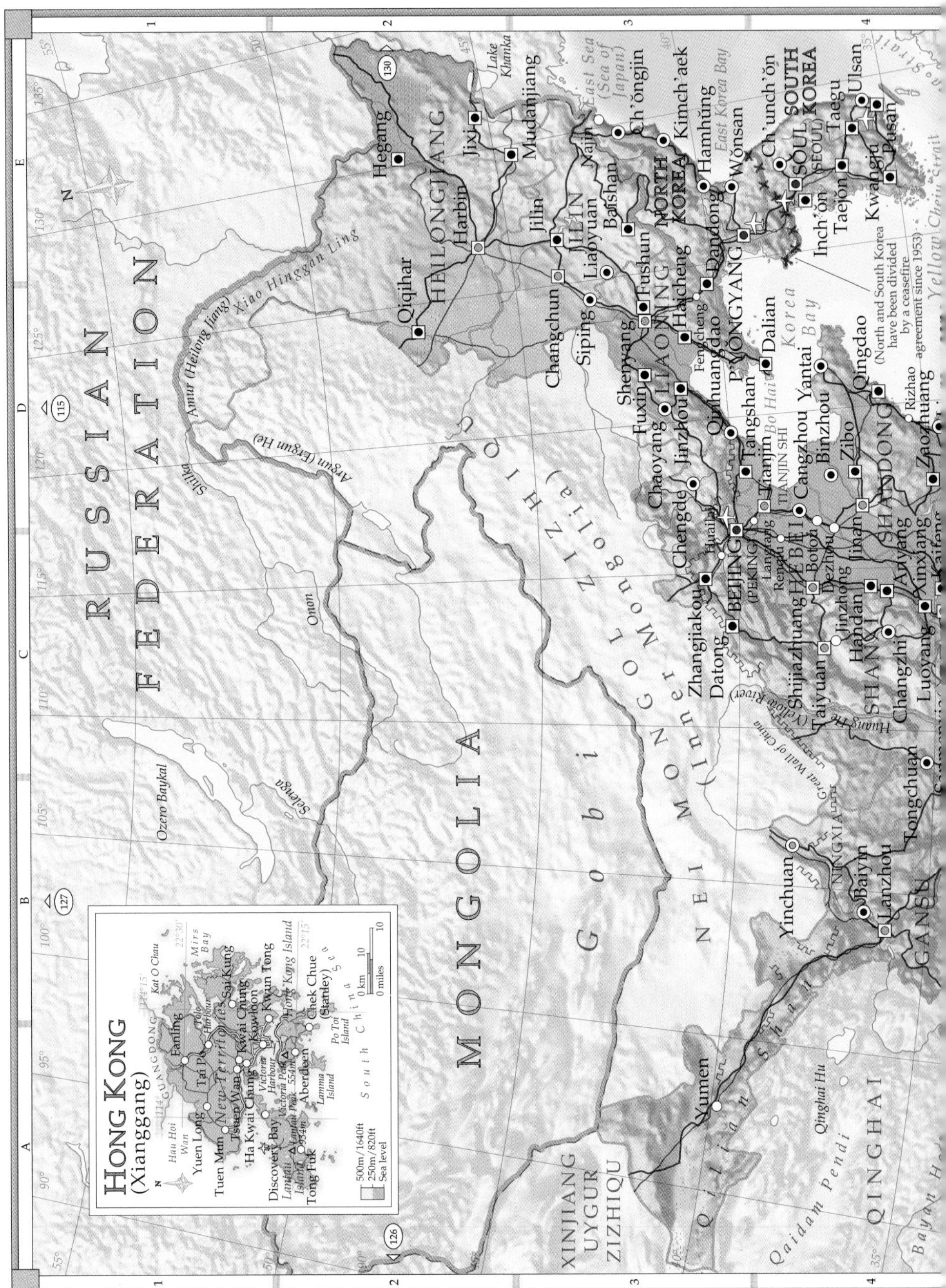

0 km 400
0 miles 400

POPULATION

- National capital
- Internal administrative capital
- Less than 50,000
- 50,000 -100,000
- 100,000 - 500,000
- Over 500,000

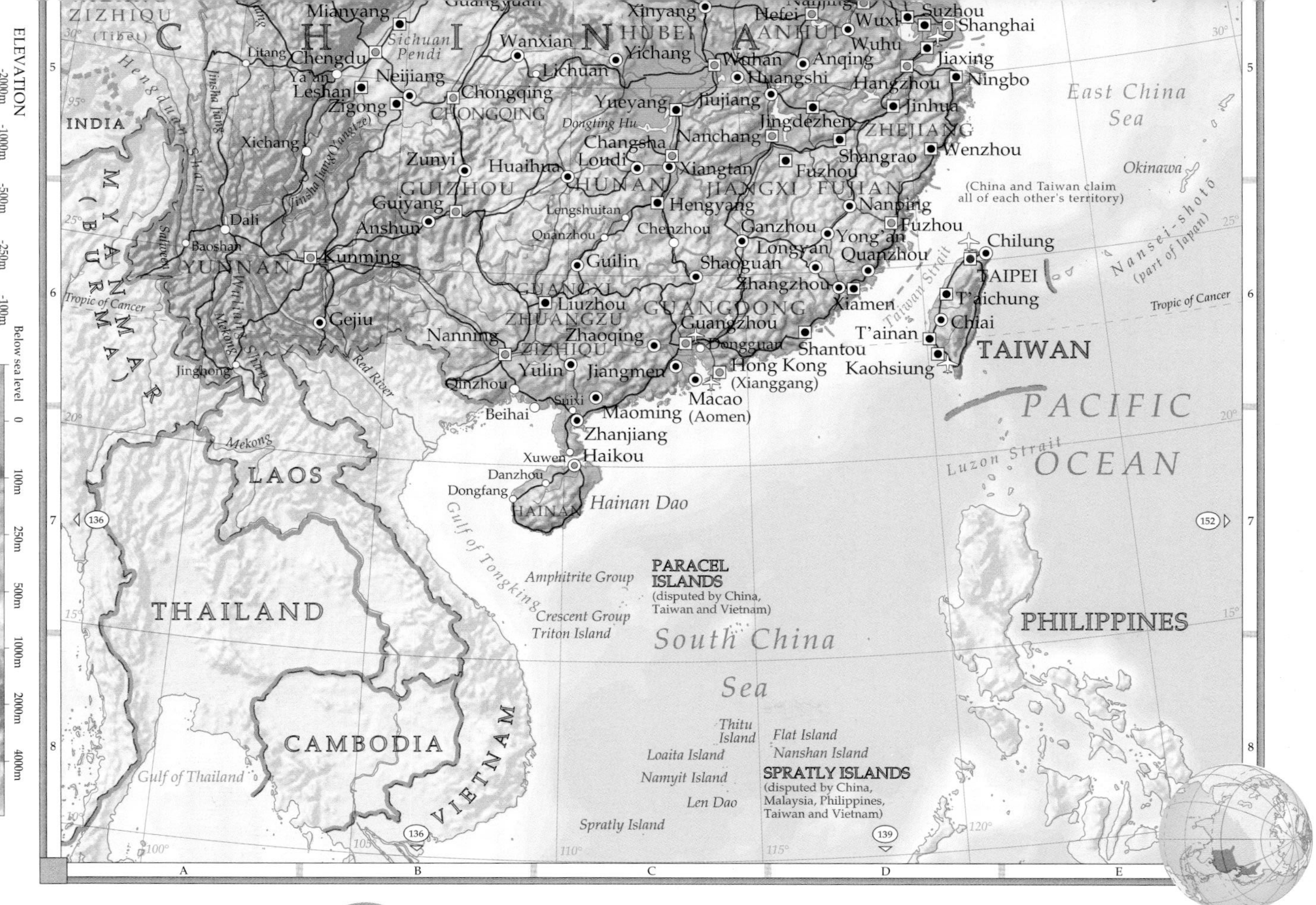

ELEVATION

Below sea level	0	100m	250m	500m	1000m	2000m	4000m
		328ft	820ft	1640ft	3281ft	6562ft	13 124ft

-2000m	-1000m	-500m	-250m	-100m		
-6562ft	-3281ft	-1640ft	-820ft	-328ft	-164ft/-50m	0

JAPAN

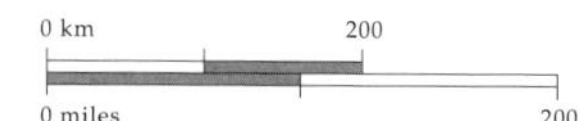
0 km
200
0 miles
200

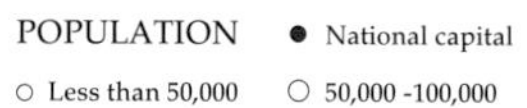
POPULATION
● National capital
○ Less than 50,000
○ 50,000 -100,000
◉ 100,000 - 500,000
▣ Over 500,000

ELEVATION

Below sea level 0 | 100m 250m 500m 1000m 2000m 4000m

-4000m -3000m -2000m -1000m -500m

-13 124ft -9843ft -6562ft -3281ft -1640ft -820ft/-250m 0 | 328ft 820ft 1640ft 3281ft 6562ft 13 124ft

SOUTHERN INDIA & SRI LANKA

A
B
C
D
1
2
3
4
5

N

Arabian Sea
Lakshadweep (Laccadive Islands) (to India)
Amīndīvi Islands
Kavaratti Island
Kalpeni Island
Nine Degree Channel
Minicoy Island
Eight Degree Channel
Malabar Coast
Coromandel Coast
Palk Strait
Gulf of Mannar
INDIAN
Equator

INDIA
Andhra Pradesh
Karnātaka
Tamil Nadu
Kerala
Deccan
Western Ghats
Eastern Ghats
Godāvari
Krishna
Tungabhadra Reservoir

Kalyān
Mumbai (Bombay)
Pune
Ahmadnagar
Bārāmati
Nānded
Nizāmābād
Karimnagar
Jagdalpur
Vizianagaram
Visākhapatnam
Rājahmundry
Kākinada
Solāpur
Sāngli
Gulbarga
Secunderābād
Hyderābād
Kolhāpur
Belgaum
Pānji
Gadag
Hubli
Rāichūr
Kurnool
Vijayawāda
Machilīpatnam
Chīrāla
Ongole
Kāvali
Nandyāl
Tādpatri
Anantapur
Cuddapah
Nellore
Dāvangere
Shimoga
Bhadrāvati
Udupi
Tumkūr
Chennai (Madras)
Mangalore
Bangalore
Vellore
Kānchīpuram
Kāsargod
Mandya
Krishnagiri
Tiruppattūr
Cannanore
Mysore
Salem
Pondicherry
Calicut
Erode
Neyveli
Coimbatore
Trichūr
Tiruchchirāppalli
Ernākulam
Dindigul
Madurai
Cochin
Jaffna
Alleppey
Rājapālaiyam
Quilon
Tuticorin
Trivandrum
Nāgercoil

SRI LANKA
Mannar
Vavuniya
Trincomalee
Puttalam
Anuradhapura
Batticaloa
Matale
Negombo
Kandy
COLOMBO
Sri Jayawardanapura
Kalutara
Ratnapura
Galle
Matara

MALDIVES
Ihavandippolhu Atoll
Faadhippolhu Atoll
Horsburgh Atoll
Male' Atoll
MALE'
Ari Atoll
Felidhu Atoll
Mulaku Atoll
Kolhumadulu Atoll
Hadhdhunmathi Atoll
North Huvadhu Atoll
South Huvadhu Atoll
Gan
Addu Atoll

70°
75°
80°
15°
10°
5°

134
121
73
140

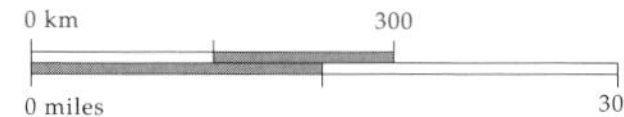

POPULATION
National capital
Less than 50,000
50,000 -100,000
100,000 - 500,000
Over 500,000

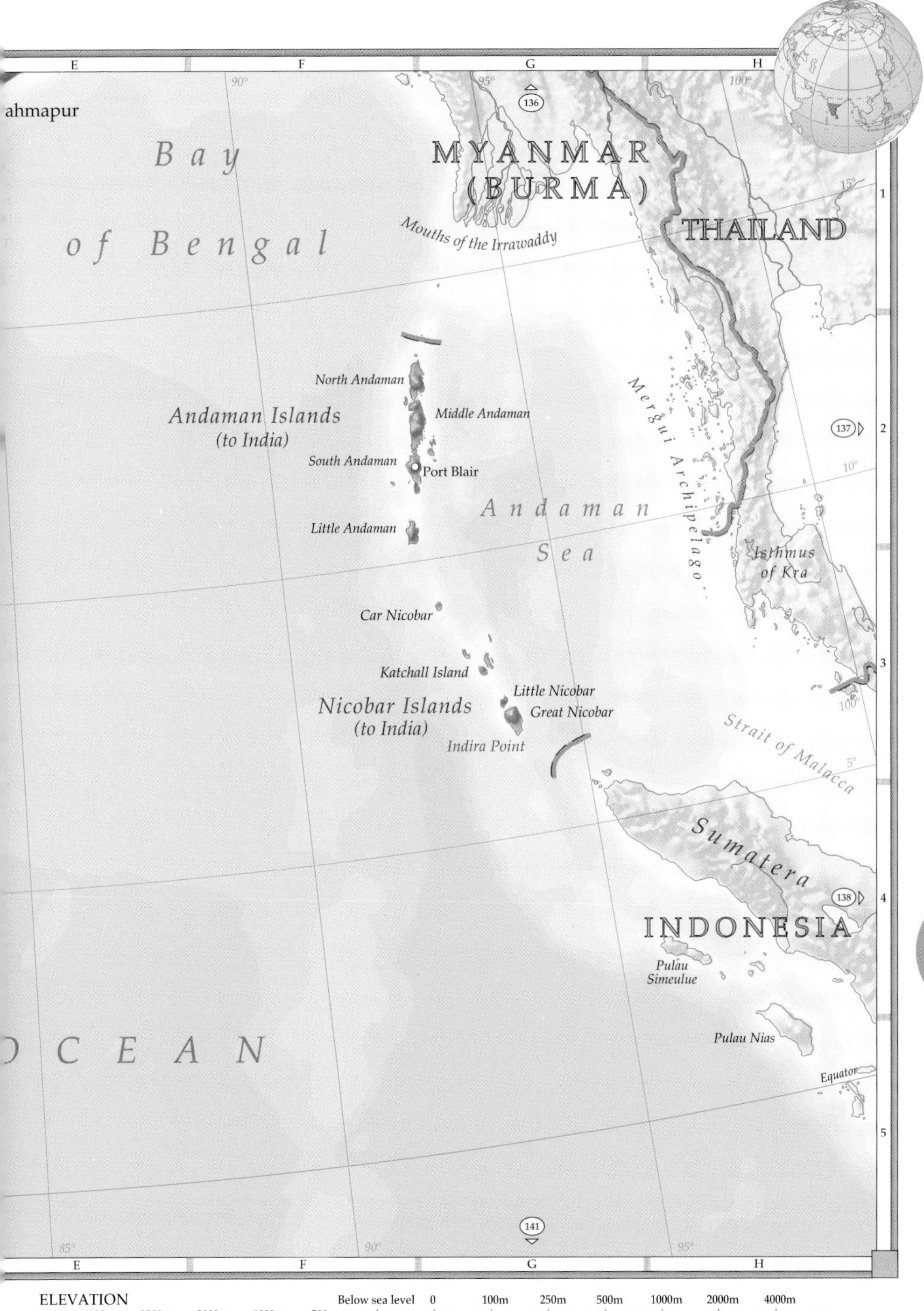

ELEVATION

Below sea level	-4000m	-3000m	-2000m	-1000m	-500m		0	100m	250m	500m	1000m	2000m	4000m
	-13 124ft	-9843ft	-6562ft	-3281ft	-1640ft	-820ft/-250m	0	328ft	820ft	1640ft	3281ft	6562ft	13 124ft

NORTHERN INDIA, PAKISTAN & BANGLADESH

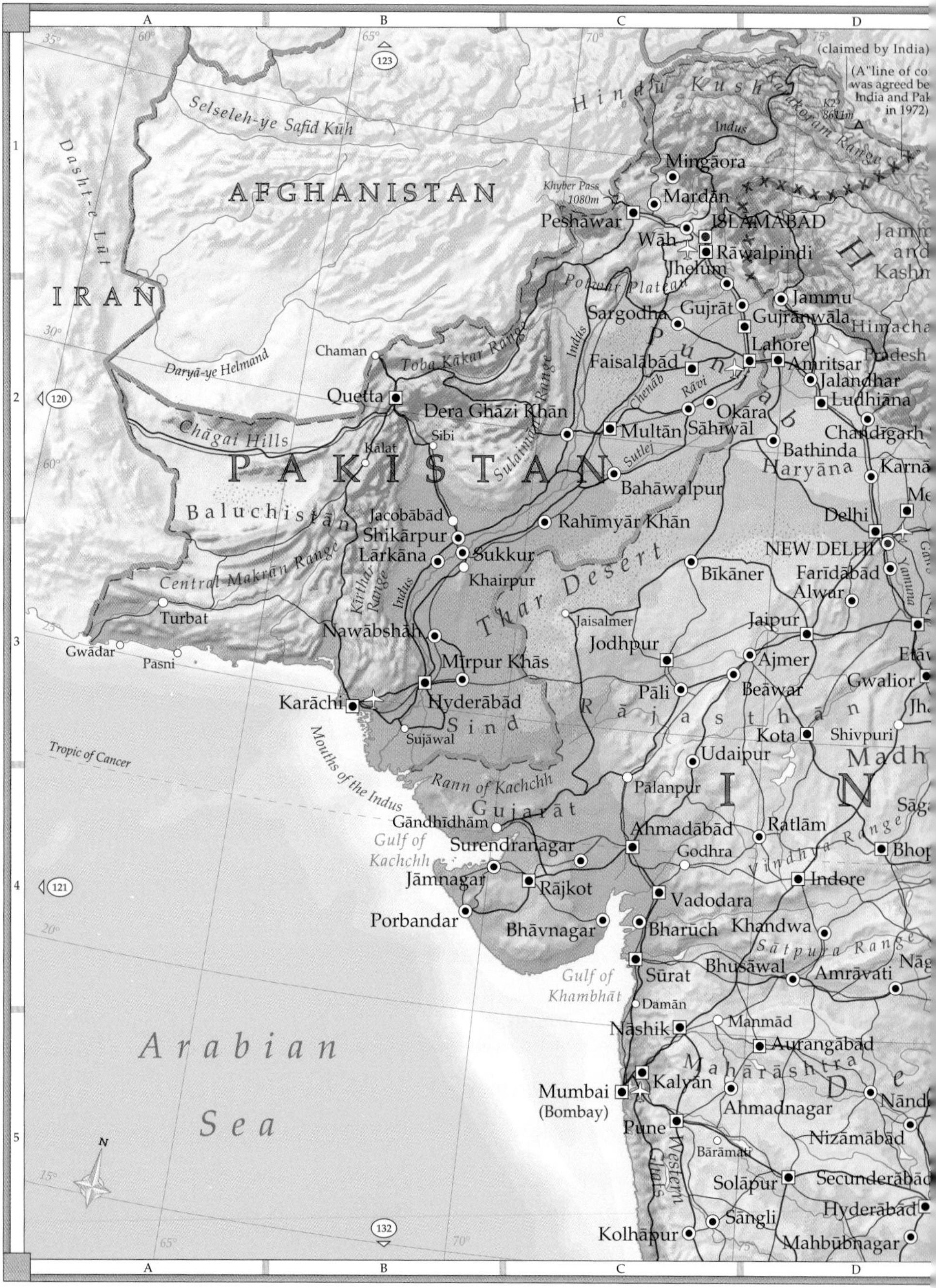

A B C D

35° 60° 65° 70° 75°

123 120 121 132

1 2 3 4 5

(claimed by India)
(A "line of co[ntrol] was agreed be[tween] India and Pak[istan] in 1972)
K2 8611m

Hindu Kush
Karakoram Range
Indus
Selseleh-ye Safid Kūh
Dasht-e Lūt
AFGHANISTAN
IRAN
PAKISTAN
Khyber Pass 1080m
Mingāora
Mardān
Peshāwar
ISLAMĀBĀD
Wāh
Rāwalpindi
Jhelum
Jammu and Kashmir
Potwar Plateau
Jammu
Gujrāt
Gujrānwāla
Himachal Pradesh
Sargodha
Punjab
Lahore
Amritsar
Faisalābād
Chaman
Toba Kākar Range
Indus
Sulaiman Range
Chenāb
Rāvi
Jalandhar
Ludhiāna
Daryā-ye Helmand
Quetta
Dera Ghāzi Khān
Multān
Okāra
Sāhīwāl
Chandīgarh
Chāgai Hills
Sibi
Kalat
Bathinda
Sutlej
Haryāna
Karnāl
Bahāwalpur
Baluchistān
Jacobābād
Shikārpur
Rahīmyār Khān
Delhi
Me[erut]
NEW DELHI
Lārkāna
Sukkur
Khairpur
Central Makrān Range
Kīrthar Range
Indus
Thar Desert
Bīkāner
Farīdābād
Alwar
Yamuna
Turbat
Jaisalmer
Jaipur
Gwādar
Pasni
Nawābshāh
Jodhpur
Ajmer
Mīrpur Khās
Beāwar
Gwalior
Pāli
Karāchi
Hyderābād
Sind
Rājasthān
Sujāwal
Kota
Shivpuri
Tropic of Cancer
Mouths of the Indus
Udaipur
Madh[ya Pradesh]
Rann of Kachchh
Pālanpur
INDIA
Gāndhīdhām
Gujarāt
Ratlām
Sāg[ar]
Gulf of Kachchh
Ahmadābād
Vindhya Range
Surendranagar
Godhra
Bhop[al]
Jāmnagar
Rājkot
Indore
Vadodara
Porbandar
Bhāvnagar
Bharūch
Khandwa
Sātpura Range
Sūrat
Bhusāwal
Amrāvati
Nāg[pur]
Gulf of Khambhāt
Damān
Nāshik
Manmād
Aurangābād
Arabian Sea
Mahārāshtra
Kalyān
Mumbai (Bombay)
Ahmadnagar
Deccan
Nānd[ed]
Pune
Western Ghats
Nizāmābād
Bārāmati
N
Solāpur
Secunderābād
Hyderābād
Sāngli
Kolhāpur
Mahbūbnagar
15° 20° 25° 30°

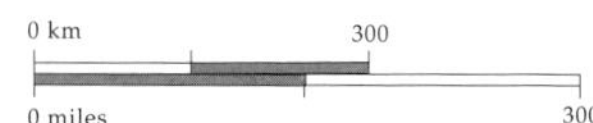

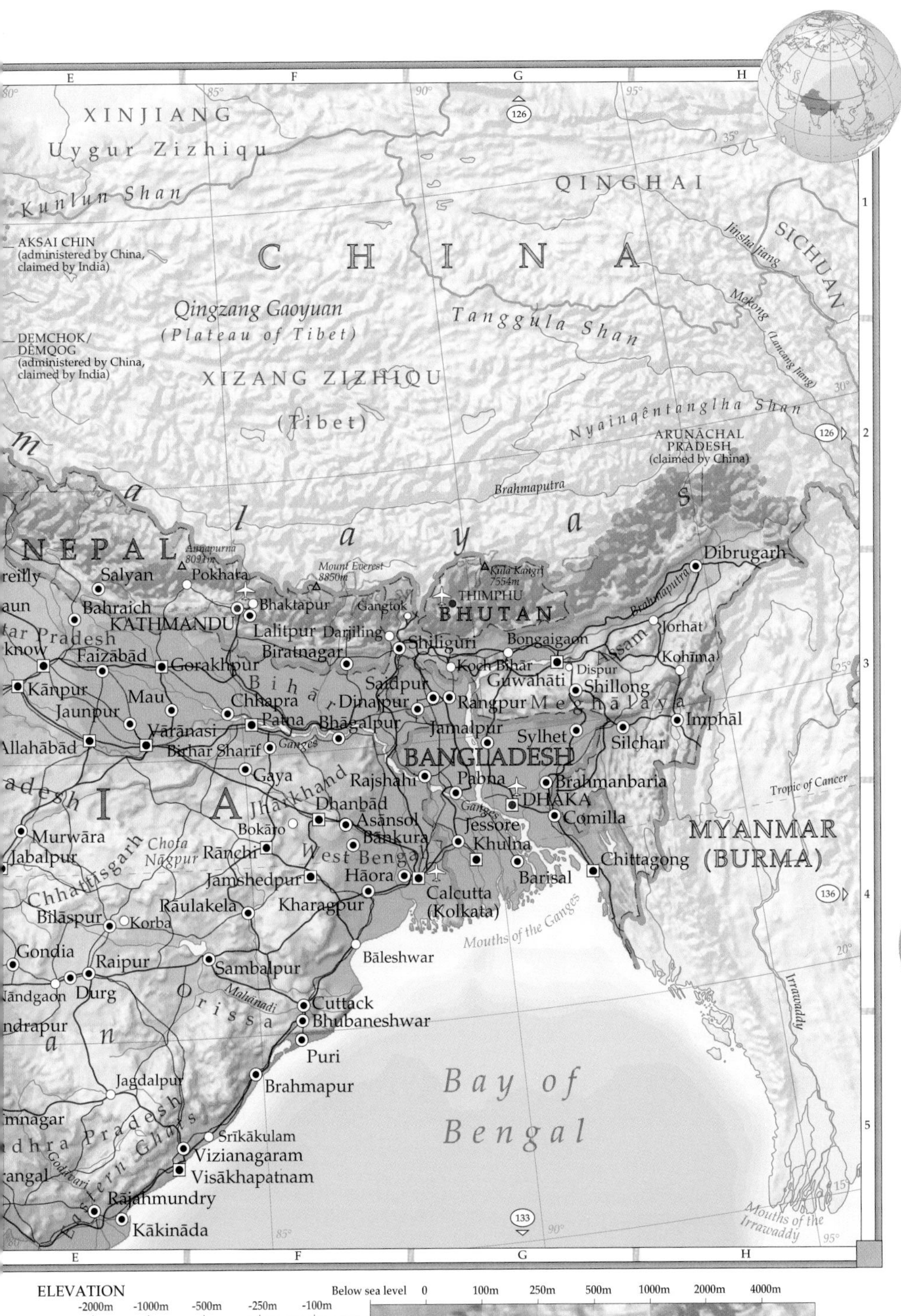

XINJIANG
Uygur Zizhiqu
Kunlun Shan
AKSAI CHIN (administered by China, claimed by India)
DEMCHOK/ DÊMQOG (administered by China, claimed by India)
CHINA
Qingzang Gaoyuan
(Plateau of Tibet)
XIZANG ZIZHIQU
(Tibet)
QINGHAI
SICHUAN
Jinsha Jiang
Mekong
(Lancang Jiang)
Tanggula Shan
Nyainqêntanglha Shan
ARUNĀCHAL PRADESH (claimed by China)
Brahmaputra
Himalayas
NEPAL
Annapurna 8091m
Mount Everest 8850m
Kula Kangri 7554m
THIMPHU
BHUTAN
Salyan
Pokhara
Bahraich
KATHMANDU
Bhaktapur
Lalitpur
Darjiling
Gangtok
Shiliguri
Bongaigaon
Biratnagar
Koch Bihār
Dispur
Guwāhāti
Shillong
Dibrugarh
Jorhāt
Kohīma
Assam
Imphāl
Meghālaya
Silchar
Sylhet
Faizābād
Gorakhpur
Kānpur
Mau
Jaunpur
Vārānasi
Allahābād
Chhapra
Patna
Bihār
Bihar Sharif
Gaya
Ganges
Bhāgalpur
Saidpur
Dinajpur
Rangpur
Jamalpur
BANGLADESH
Rajshahi
Pabna
Brahmanbaria
DHAKA
Comilla
Jessore
Khulna
Barisal
Chittagong
MYANMAR (BURMA)
Tropic of Cancer
INDIA
Jharkhand
Dhanbād
Bokāro
Āsānsol
Bānkura
West Bengal
Murwāra
Jabalpur
Chota Nāgpur
Rānchi
Jamshedpur
Hāora
Calcutta (Kolkata)
Chhattisgarh
Rāulakela
Kharagpur
Bilāspur
Korba
Mouths of the Ganges
Bāleshwar
Gondia
Raipur
Sambalpur
Durg
Nāndgaon
Mahānadi
Orissa
Cuttack
Bhubaneshwar
Puri
Brahmapur
Jagdalpur
Andhra Pradesh
Eastern Ghats
Godāvari
Srīkākulam
Vizianagaram
Visākhapatnam
Rājahmundry
Kākināda
Bay of Bengal
Irrawaddy
Mouths of the Irrawaddy
126
133
136
ELEVATION
Below sea level
-2000m -1000m -500m -250m -100m
-6562ft -3281ft -1640ft -820ft -328ft -164ft/-50m
0
100m 250m 500m 1000m 2000m 4000m
328ft 820ft 1640ft 3281ft 6562ft 13 124ft

Mainland Southeast Asia

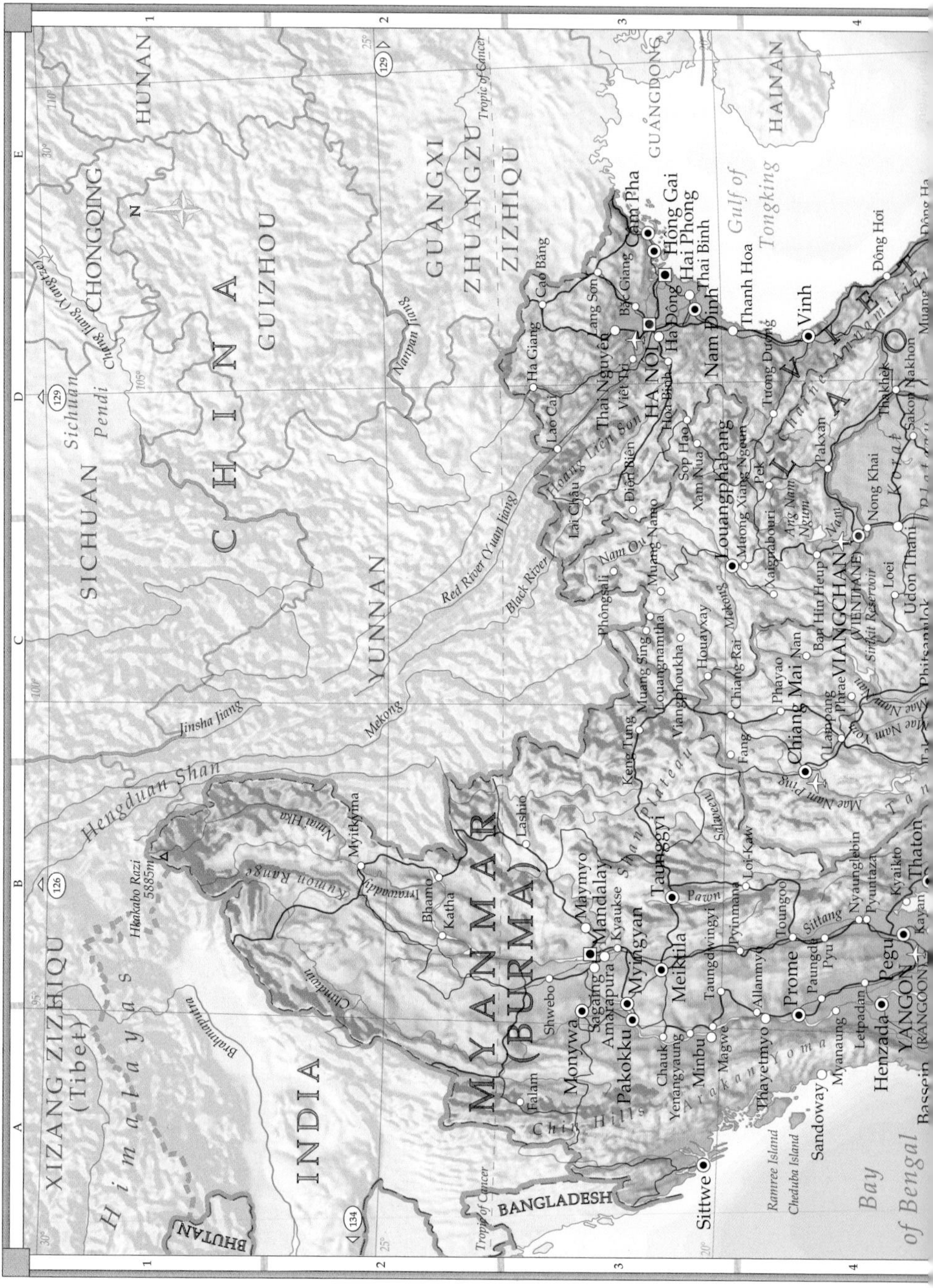

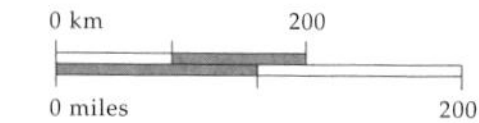

POPULATION ● National capital ○ Less than 50,000 ○ 50,000 -100,000 ⦿ 100,000 - 500,000 ▣ Over 500,000

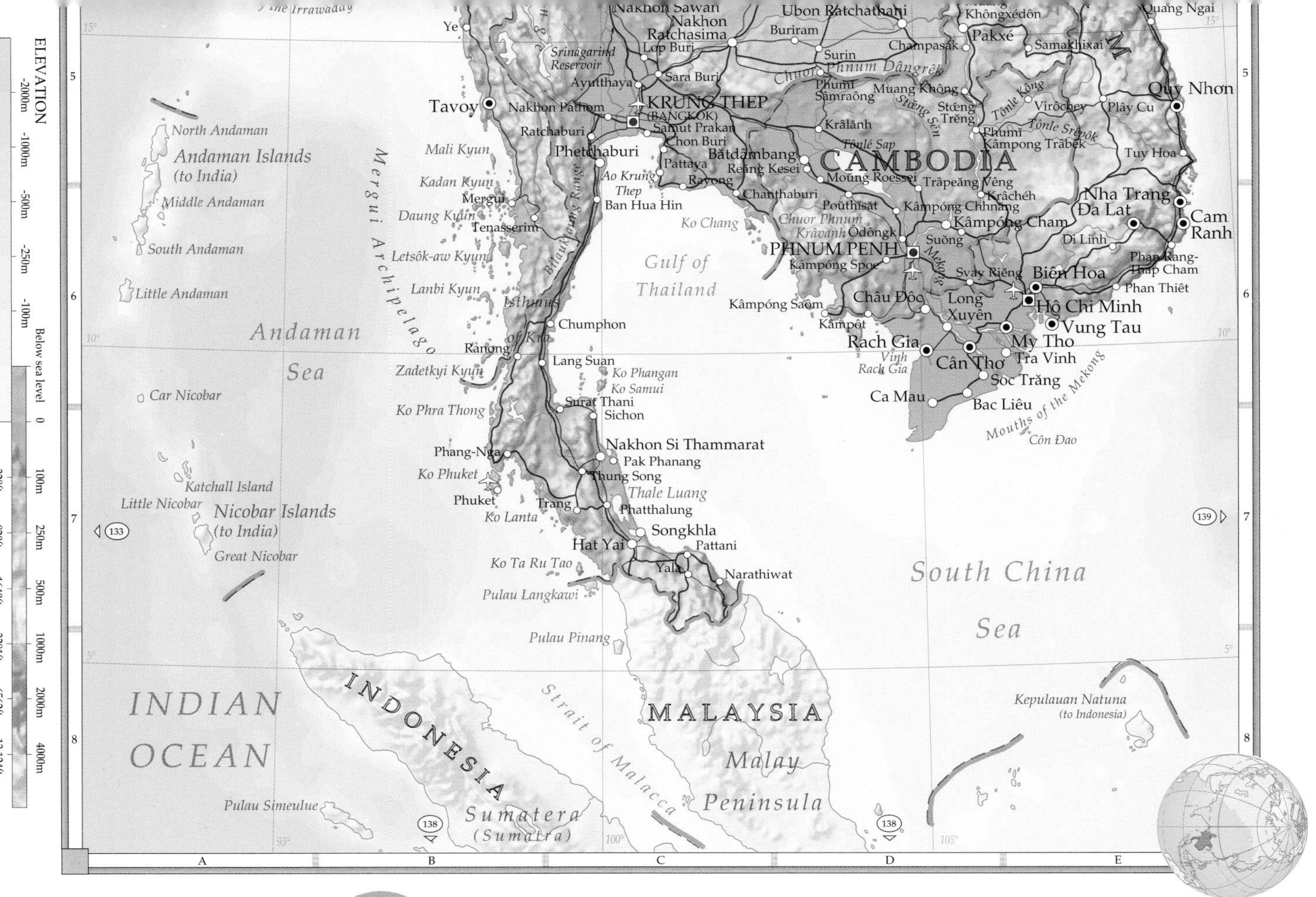

ELEVATION

Below sea level						0	100m	250m	500m	1000m	2000m	4000m
-2000m	-1000m	-500m	-250m	-100m								
-6562ft	-3281ft	-1640ft	-820ft	-328ft	-164ft/-50m	0	328ft	820ft	1640ft	3281ft	6562ft	13 124ft

Maritime Southeast Asia

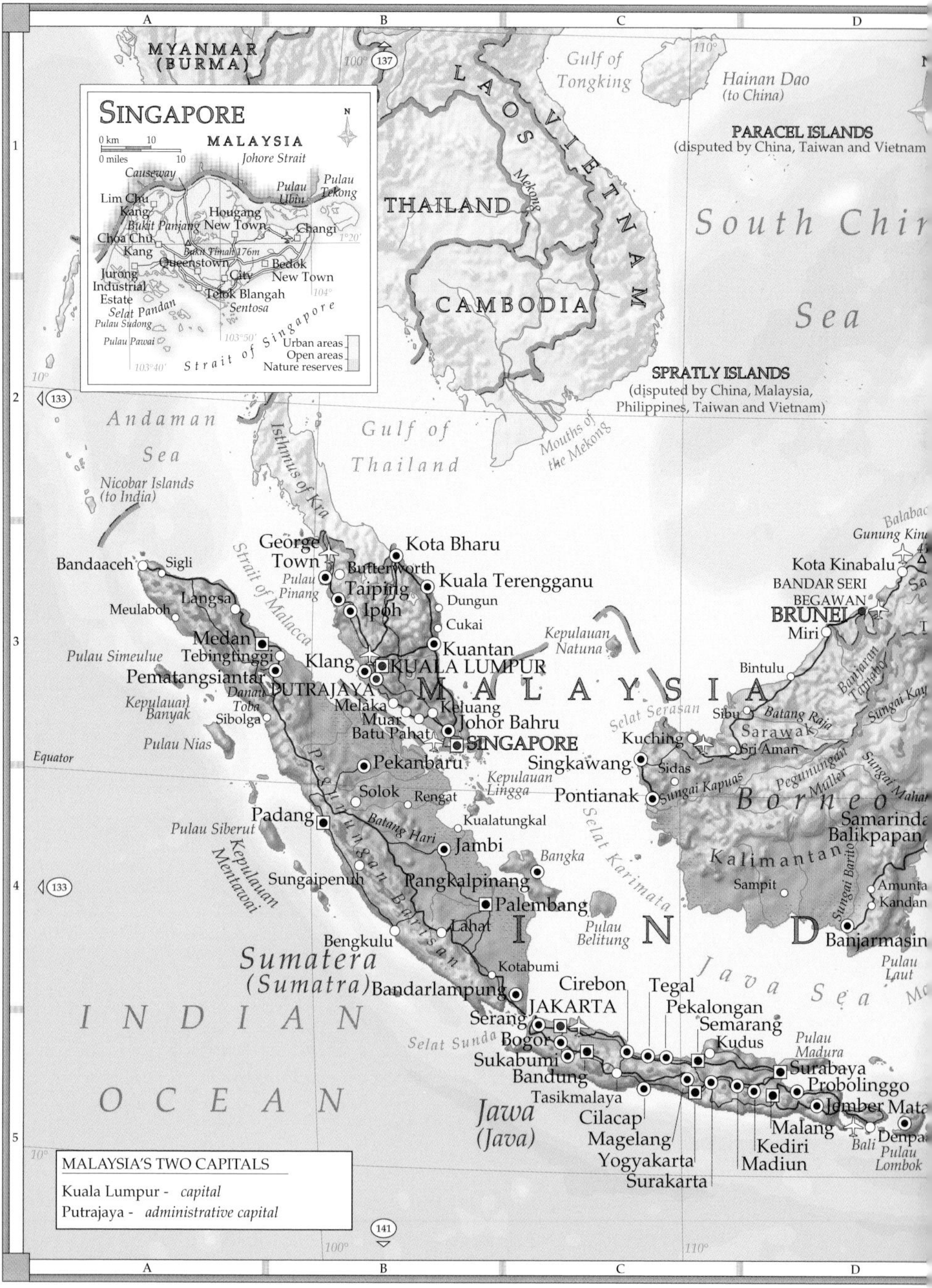

Singapore

MALAYSIA'S TWO CAPITALS

Kuala Lumpur - *capital*

Putrajaya - *administrative capital*

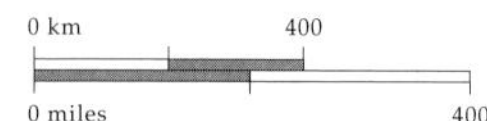

Luzon Strait
Babuyan Island
Babuyan Channel
Tuguegarao
Ilagan
Luzon
Dagupan
Cabanatuan
PHILIPPINES
Lucena
Naga
Legaspi
Mindoro
Sibuyan Sea
Calbayog
Samar
Roxas City
Cadiz
Tacloban
Panay Island
Leyte
Iloilo
Bacolod City
Cebu
Palawan
Negros
Bohol Sea
Butuan
Sulu Sea
Iligan
Cagayan de Oro
Bislig
Mindanao
Moro Gulf
Davao
Basilan
Lebak
General Santos
Davao Gulf
Sulu Archipelago
Philippine Sea
NORTHERN MARIANA ISLANDS (to US)
GUAM (to US)
Yap
MICRONESIA
PACIFIC
Babeldaob
PALAU
OCEAN
Kepulauan Talaud
Kepulauan Sangir
Celebes Sea
Pulau Morotai
Pulau Halmahera
Manado
Bitung
Molucca Sea
Gorontalo
Gulf of Tomini
Pulau Waigeo
Pulau Biak
Pulau Yapen
Halmahera Sea
Selat Dampier
Sorong
Jazirah Doberai
Teluk Cenderawasih
Equator
Jayapura
Sungai Mamberamo
Kepulauan Banggai
Sulawesi (Celebes)
Kepulauan Sula
Maluku (Moluccas)
Pulau Misool
Ceram Sea
Teluk Berau
Wahai
Danau Towuti
Waflia
Tifu
Ambon
Pulau Buru
Pulau Seram
INDONESIA
Puncak Jaya 5030m
Pegunungan Maoke
Papua (Irian Jaya)
PAPUA NEW GUINEA
New Guinea
Kendari
Kolaka
Pulau Buton
Teluk Bone
Watampone
Ujungpandang
Bulukumba
Kepulauan Kai
Kepulauan Aru
Sungai Digul
Banda Sea
Kepulauan Tanimbar
Pulau Yamdena
Tenggara
Pulau Wetar
Kepulauan Alor
Flores
DILI
Kepulauan Leti
EAST TIMOR
Sumba
Savu Sea
Timor
Nikiniki
Kupang
Arafura Sea
Torres Strait
Timor Sea
AUSTRALIA
ELEVATION
Below sea level
-4000m -3000m -2000m -1000m -500m 0
-13 124ft -9843ft -6562ft -3281ft -1640ft -820ft/-250m 0
100m 250m 500m 1000m 2000m 4000m
328ft 820ft 1640ft 3281ft 6562ft 13 124ft

THE INDIAN OCEAN

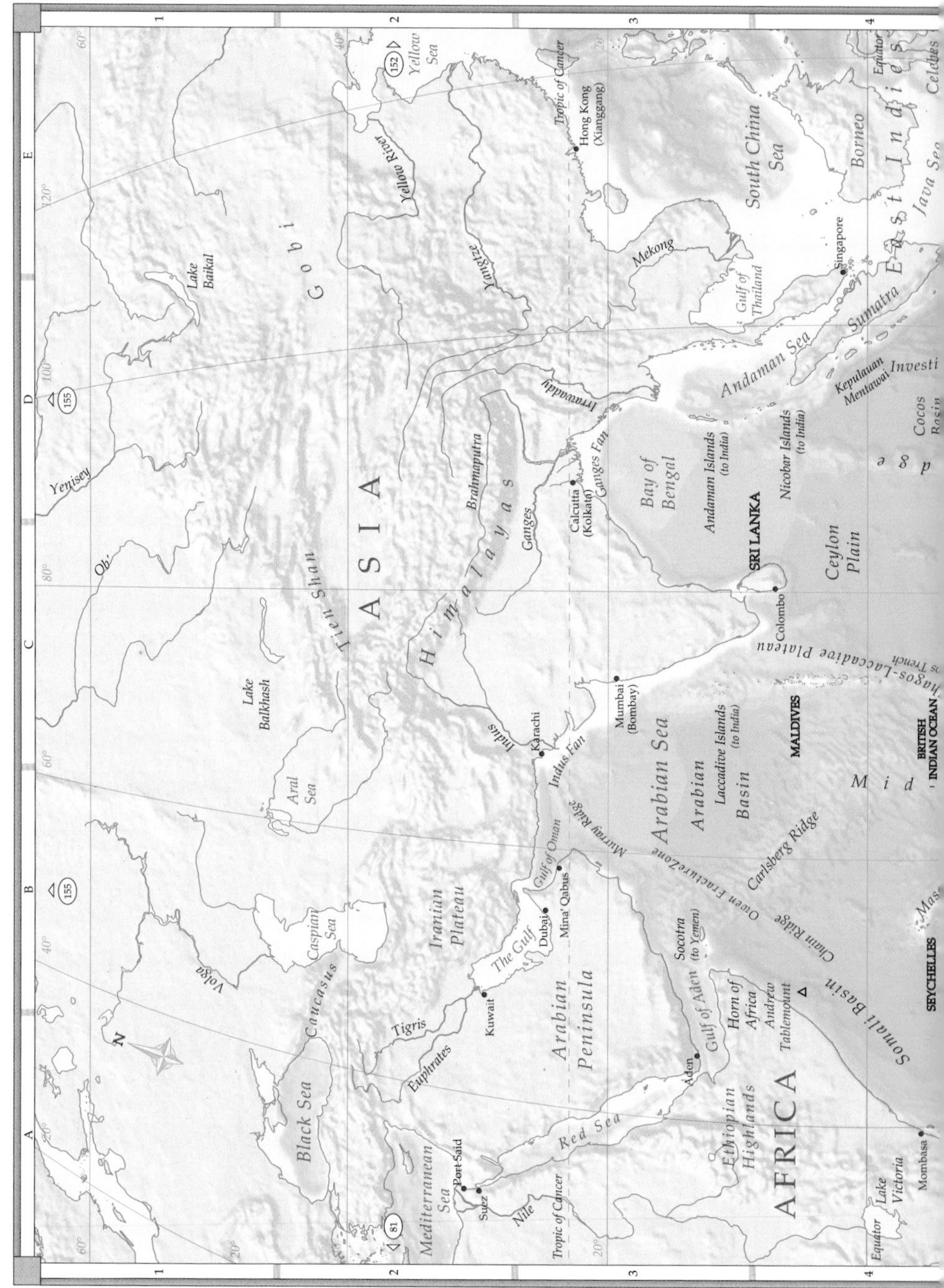

0 km 1500

0 miles 1500

• Major port

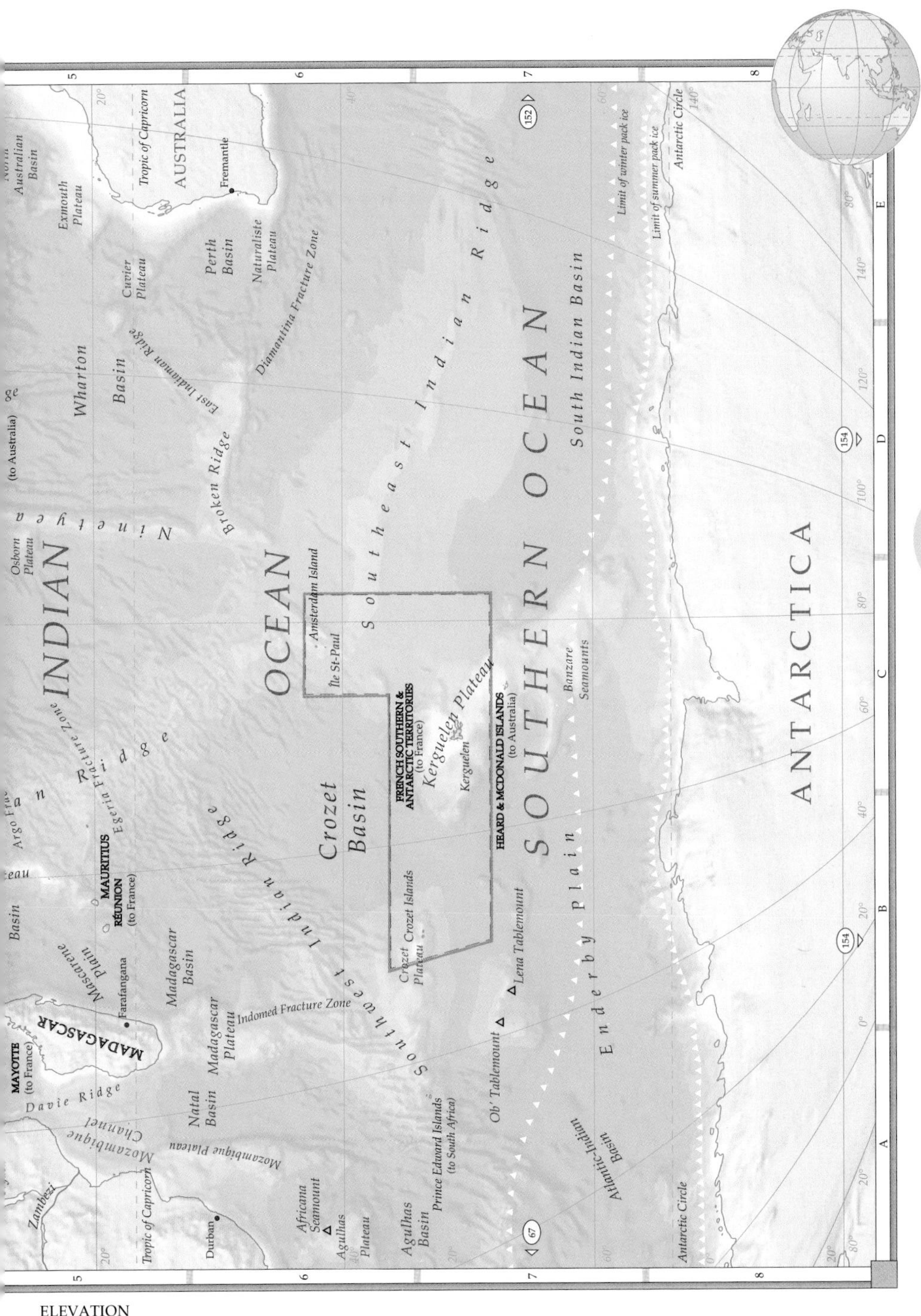

ELEVATION

-4000m	-3000m	-2000m	-1000m	-500m	-250m	0
-13 124ft	-9843ft	-6562ft	-3281ft	-1640ft	-820ft	0

AUSTRALASIA & OCEANIA

A B C D

1 2 3 4 5

NORTHERN MARIANA ISLANDS (to US)
Mid-Pacific Mountains
WAKE ISLAND (to US)
Philippine Sea
Philippine Basin
Kyushu-Palau Ridge
West Mariana Basin
Saipan
Mariana Trench
Micronesia
HAGÅTÑA
GUAM (to US)
East Mariana Basin
MARSHALL ISLANDS
Ratak Chain
Ralik Chain
MAJURO
Philippines
Philippine Trench
Yap
Yap Trench
Hall Islands
MICRONESIA
Chuuk Islands
PALIKIR
Pohnpei
Kosrae
Sulu Sea
Babeldaob
KOROR (OREOR)
Caroline Islands
PALAU
Eauripik Rise
Melanesian Basin
Tarawa
BAIRIKI
Tungaru
Celebes Sea
Melanesia
Nauru
NAURU
Banaba
Equator
Bismarck Archipelago
PAPUA NEW GUINEA
Bismarck Sea
New Britain
Mount Wilhelm 4509m
New Guinea
Solomon Islands
SOLOMON ISLANDS
TUVALU
FONGAFALE
Celebes
Banda Sea
Bougainville Island
Solomon Sea
HONIARA
Guadalcanal
PORT MORESBY
Santa Cruz Islands
Arafura Sea
Torres Strait
Timor
Flores
Coral Sea
North Fiji Basin
Espiritu Santo
Malekula
Vanua Levu
Viti Levu
Efate
PORT-VILA
SUVA
Darwin
Timor Sea
Arnhem Land
Gulf of Carpentaria
Cape York Peninsula
Cairns
Great Barrier Reef
CORAL SEA ISLANDS (to Australia)
ASHMORE & CARTIER ISLANDS (to Australia)
NEW CALEDONIA (to France)
VANUATU
FIJI
Townsville
New Caledonia
Îles Loyauté
NOUMÉA
Mackay
INDIAN OCEAN
Broome
AUSTRALIA
Rockhampton
Great Dividing Range
South Fiji Basin
Great Sandy Desert
Macdonnell Ranges
Alice Springs
Simpson Desert
New Caledonia Basin
Norfolk Ridge
NORFOLK ISLAND (to Australia)
Brisbane
Uluru (Ayers Rock)
Grey Range
Lord Howe Rise
Tropic of Capricorn
Gibson Desert
Lake Eyre North
-16m
Lord Howe Island (to Australia)
Great Victoria Desert
Lake Torrens
Flinders Range
Darling
Lake Gairdner
Newcastle
Sydney
Wollongong
North Cape
North Island
Auckland
Hamilton
Nullarbor Plain
CANBERRA
Murray
Mount Kosciuszko 2228m
NEW ZEALAND
Great Australian Bight
Adelaide
Kalgoorlie
Geraldton
Port Lincoln
Bendigo
Melbourne
Geelong
Kangaroo Island
WELLINGTON
Tasman Sea
Bass Strait
South Island
Perth
Esperance
South Australian Basin
Launceston
Aoraki (Mount Cook) 3744m
Christchurch
Cape Leeuwin
Albany
Hobart
Tasmania
Tasman Basin
Dunedin
Bounty Islands
Stewart Island
Antipodes Islands
Campbell Plateau
Tasman Plateau
Auckland Islands (to New Zealand)
Campbell Island (to New Zealand)

152
125
141
154

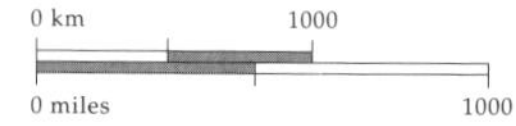

POPULATION
- ● National capital
- ○ Less than 50,000
- ○ 50,000 -100,000
- ◉ 100,000 - 500,000
- ▣ Over 500,000

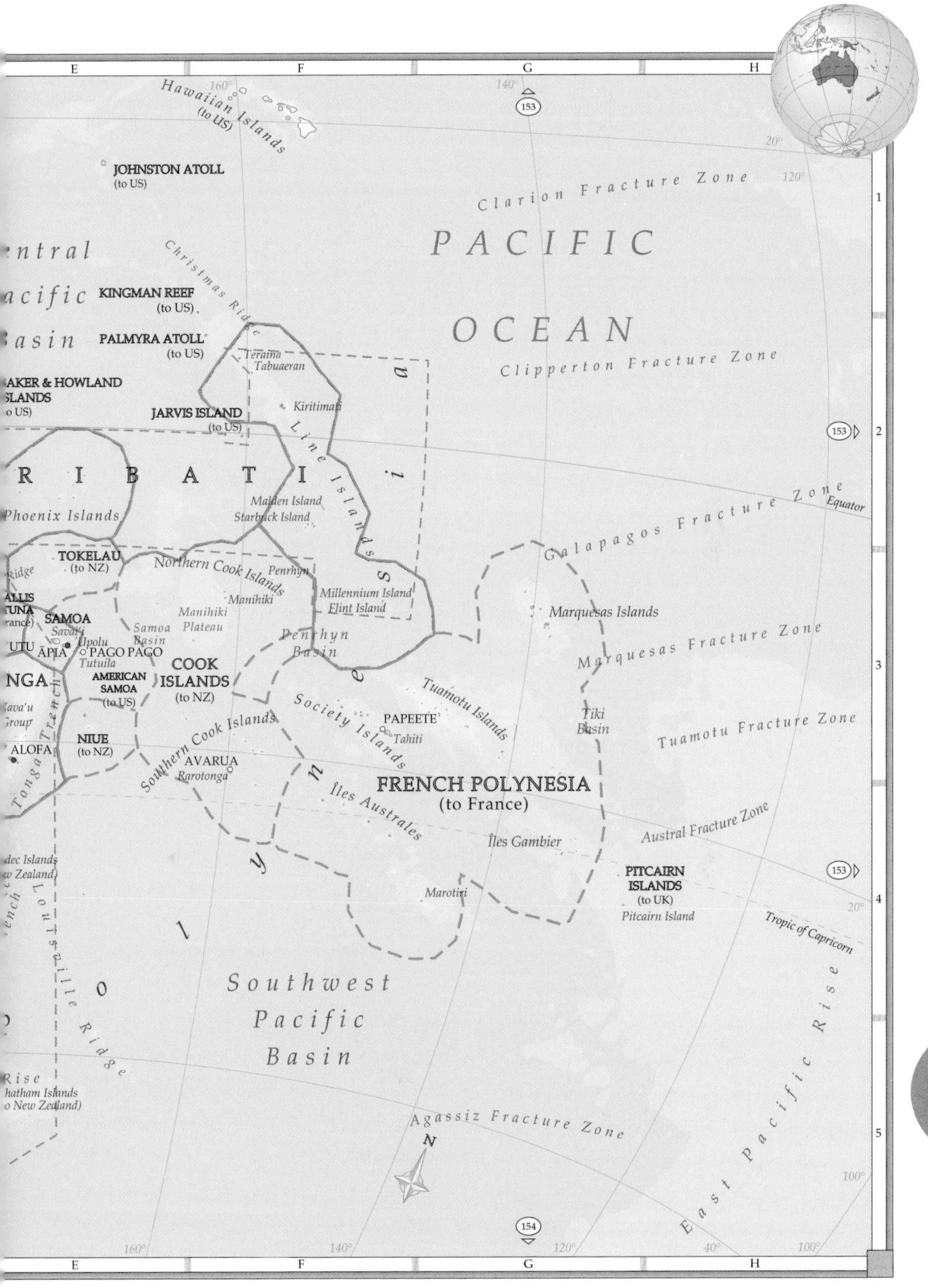

Hawaiian Islands (to US)
JOHNSTON ATOLL (to US)
Clarion Fracture Zone
PACIFIC OCEAN
Central Pacific Basin
Christmas Ridge
KINGMAN REEF (to US)
PALMYRA ATOLL (to US)
Teraina
Tabuaeran
Clipperton Fracture Zone
BAKER & HOWLAND ISLANDS (to US)
JARVIS ISLAND (to US)
Kiritimati
Line Islands
KIRIBATI
Malden Island
Starbuck Island
Phoenix Islands
Galapagos Fracture Zone
Equator
TOKELAU (to NZ)
Northern Cook Islands
Penrhyn
Millennium Island
Flint Island
Manihiki
Manihiki Plateau
Marquesas Islands
SAMOA
Savai'i
Upolu
APIA
PAGO PAGO
Tutuila
Samoa Basin
Penrhyn Basin
Marquesas Fracture Zone
COOK ISLANDS (to NZ)
AMERICAN SAMOA (to US)
TONGA
Tuamotu Islands
Society Islands
PAPEETE
Tahiti
Tiki Basin
Tuamotu Fracture Zone
Southern Cook Islands
NIUE (to NZ)
ALOFA
AVARUA
Rarotonga
Tonga Trench
FRENCH POLYNESIA (to France)
Îles Australes
Îles Gambier
Austral Fracture Zone
Polynesia
PITCAIRN ISLANDS (to UK)
Pitcairn Island
Marotiri
Tropic of Capricorn
Louisville Ridge
Southwest Pacific Basin
Agassiz Fracture Zone
East Pacific Rise
N
E
F
G
H
1
2
3
4
5
153
154
160°
140°
120°
100°
40°
20°

THE SOUTHWEST PACIFIC

0 km 750

0 miles 750

POPULATION
● National capital
○ Less than 50,000
○ 50,000 - 100,000
◉ 100,000 - 500,000
▣ Over 500,000

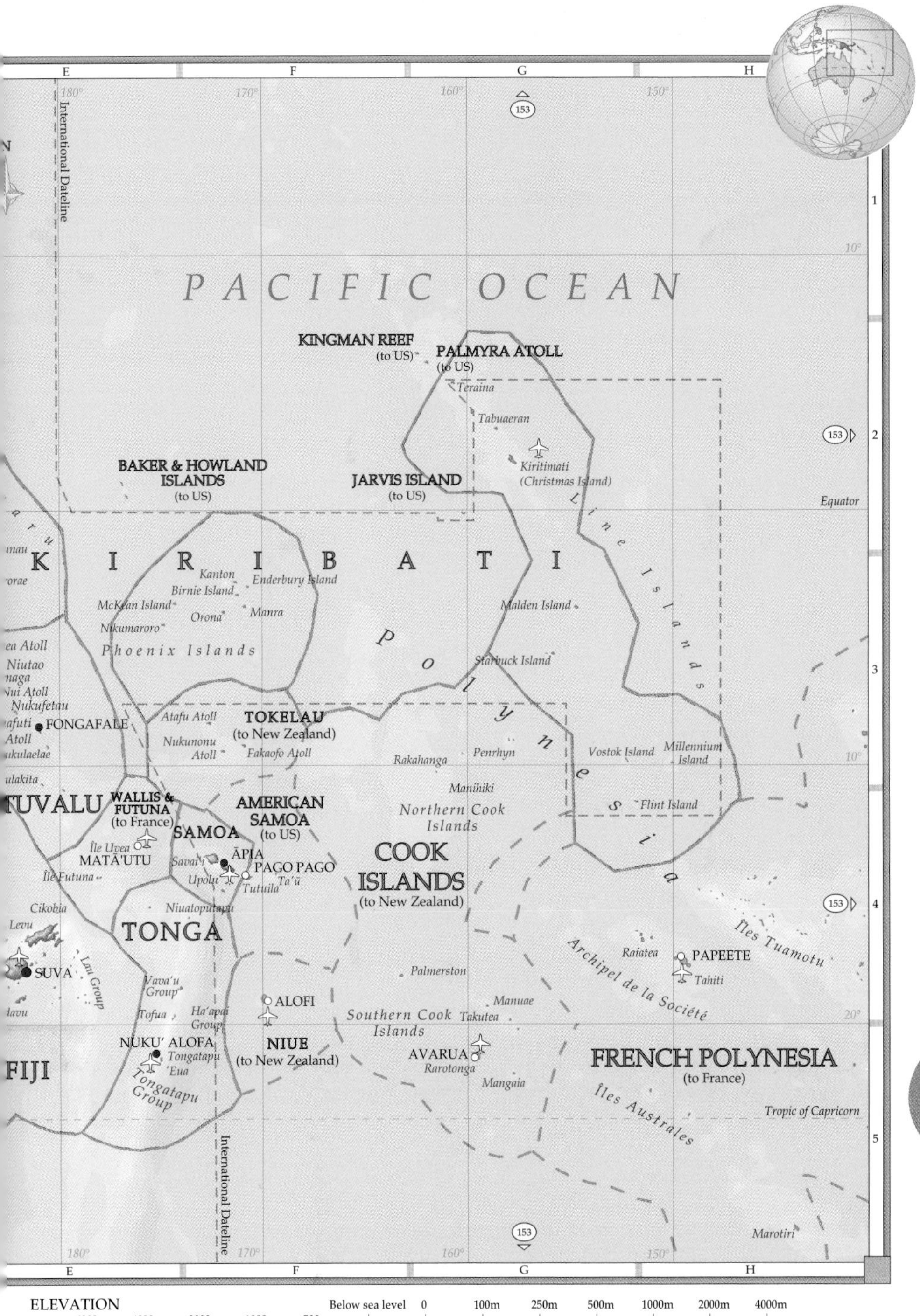
PACIFIC OCEAN
KINGMAN REEF (to US)
PALMYRA ATOLL (to US)
Teraina
Tabuaeran
Kiritimati (Christmas Island)
BAKER & HOWLAND ISLANDS (to US)
JARVIS ISLAND (to US)
Equator
KIRIBATI
Kanton
Enderbury Island
Birnie Island
McKean Island
Orona
Manra
Nikumaroro
Phoenix Islands
Line Islands
Malden Island
Starbuck Island
Polynesia
TOKELAU (to New Zealand)
Atafu Atoll
Nukunonu Atoll
Fakaofo Atoll
FONGAFALE
Nukufetau
TUVALU
WALLIS & FUTUNA (to France)
Île Uvea
MATĀ'UTU
Île Futuna
SAMOA
ĀPIA
Savai'i
Upolu
AMERICAN SAMOA (to US)
PAGO PAGO
Tutuila
Ta'ū
Rakahanga
Penrhyn
Manihiki
Northern Cook Islands
COOK ISLANDS (to New Zealand)
Vostok Island
Millennium Island
Flint Island
Niuatoputapu
TONGA
Cikobia
SUVA
Lau Group
FIJI
Vava'u Group
Tofua
Ha'apai Group
NUKU'ALOFA
Tongatapu
'Eua
Tongatapu Group
ALOFI
NIUE (to New Zealand)
Palmerston
Manuae
Southern Cook Islands
Takutea
AVARUA
Rarotonga
Mangaia
Raiatea
PAPEETE
Tahiti
Îles Tuamotu
Archipel de la Société
FRENCH POLYNESIA (to France)
Îles Australes
Tropic of Capricorn
Marotiri
International Dateline
153
ELEVATION
Below sea level 0 100m 250m 500m 1000m 2000m 4000m
328ft 820ft 1640ft 3281ft 6562ft 13 124ft
-6000m -4000m -2000m -1000m -500m
-19 686ft -13 124ft -6562ft -3281ft -1640ft -820ft/-250m 0

Western Australia

0 km 400

0 miles 400

POPULATION
● National capital
● Internal administrative capital
○ Less than 50,000
○ 50,000 -100,000
⦿ 100,000 - 500,000
▣ Over 500,000

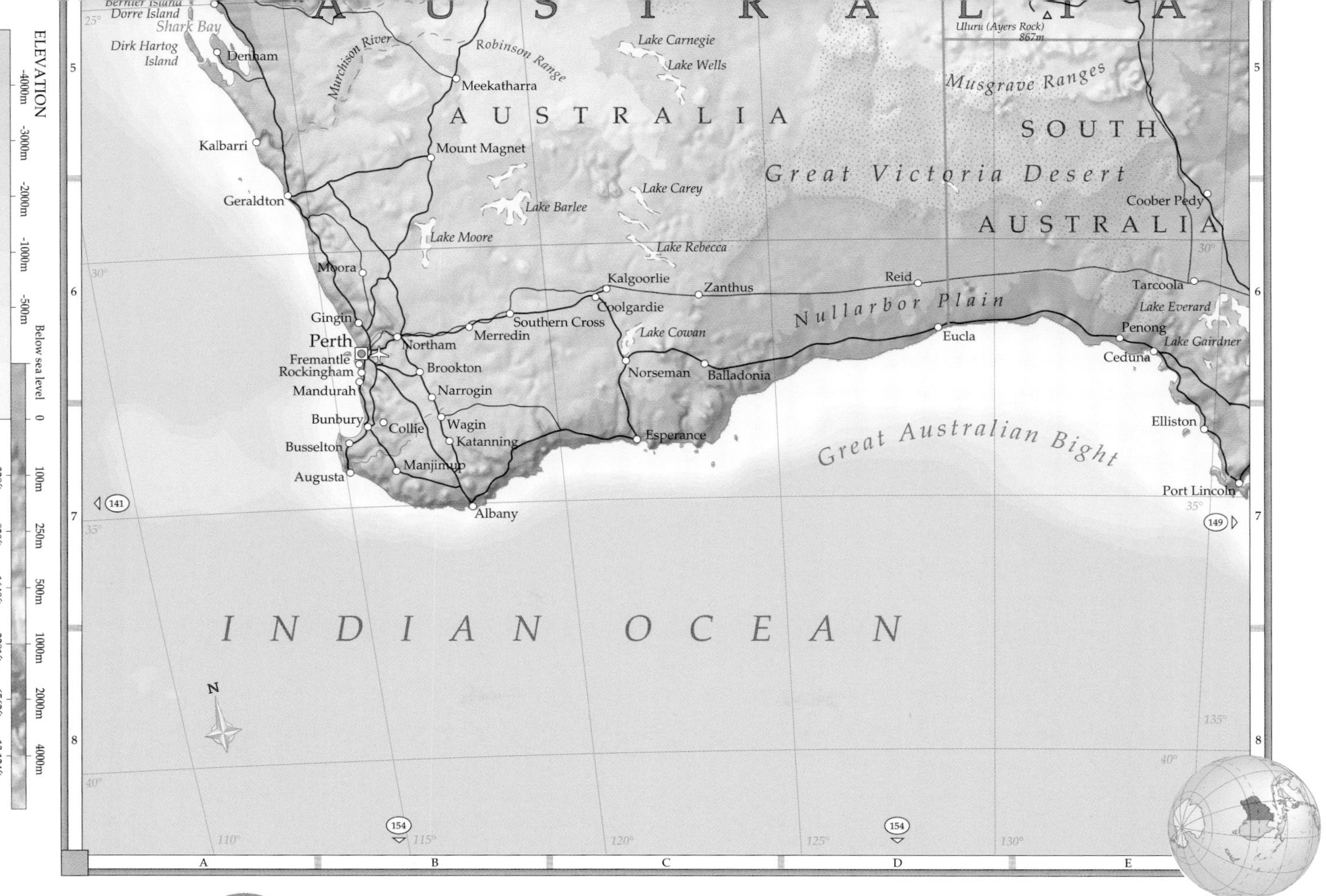

AUSTRALIA
SOUTH AUSTRALIA
INDIAN OCEAN
Great Australian Bight
Great Victoria Desert
Nullarbor Plain
Musgrave Ranges
Uluru (Ayers Rock) 867m
Robinson Range
Murchison River
Lake Carnegie
Lake Wells
Lake Carey
Lake Rebecca
Lake Barlee
Lake Moore
Lake Cowan
Lake Everard
Lake Gairdner
Shark Bay
Dirk Hartog Island
Dorre Island
Bernier Island
Denham
Meekatharra
Mount Magnet
Kalbarri
Geraldton
Moora
Gingin
Perth
Fremantle
Rockingham
Mandurah
Bunbury
Busselton
Augusta
Collie
Manjimup
Northam
Brookton
Narrogin
Wagin
Katanning
Albany
Merredin
Southern Cross
Kalgoorlie
Coolgardie
Zanthus
Norseman
Balladonia
Esperance
Reid
Eucla
Coober Pedy
Tarcoola
Penong
Ceduna
Elliston
Port Lincoln
N
ELEVATION
Below sea level
-4000m -3000m -2000m -1000m -500m
-13 124ft -9843ft -6562ft -3281ft -1640ft -820ft/-250m 0
0 100m 250m 500m 1000m 2000m 4000m
328ft 820ft 1640ft 3281ft 6562ft 13 124ft

EASTERN AUSTRALIA

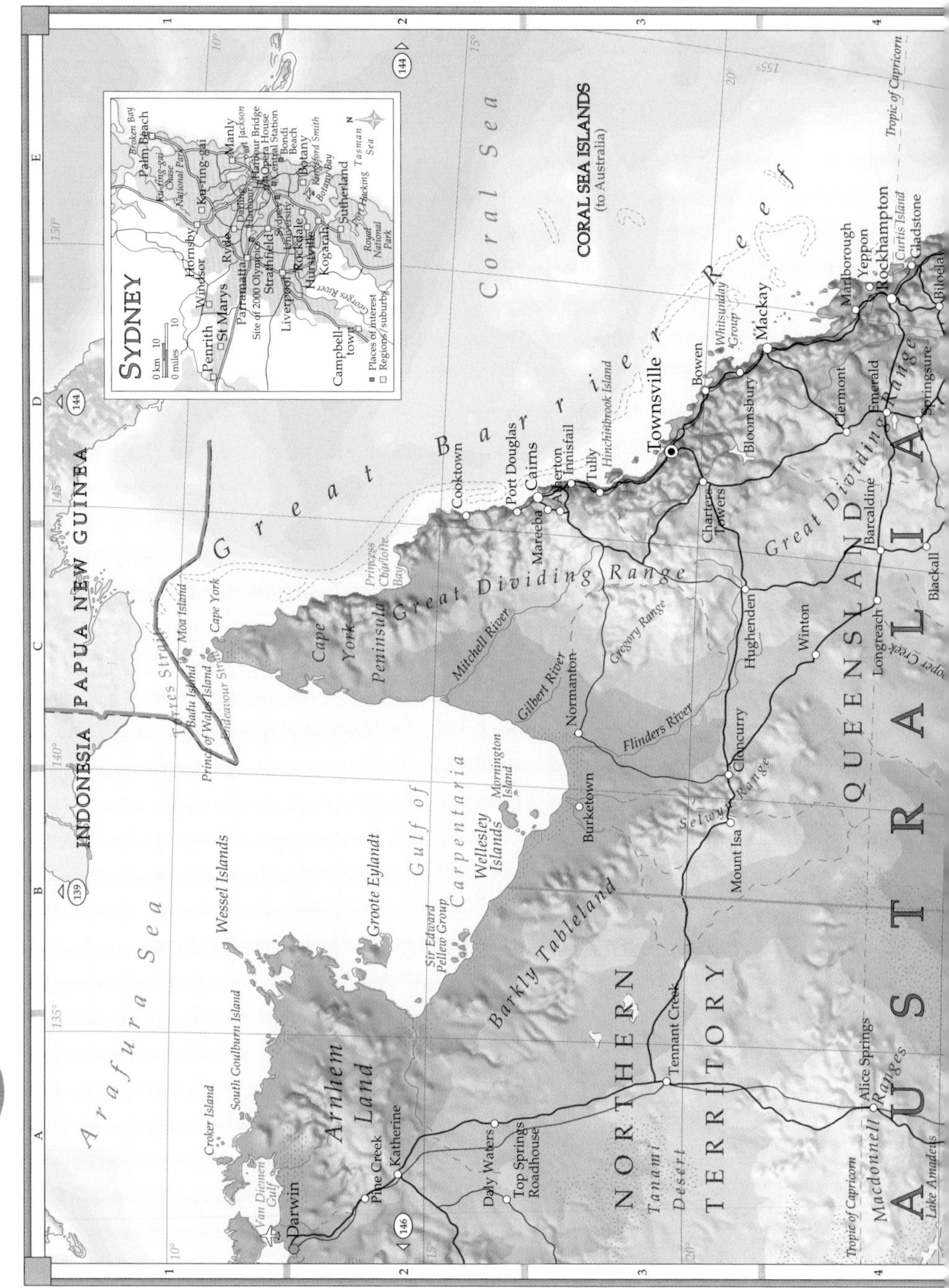

0 km 400
0 miles 400

POPULATION ● National capital ● Internal administrative capital
○ Less than 50,000 ○ 50,000 -100,000 ◉ 100,000 - 500,000 ▣ Over 500,000

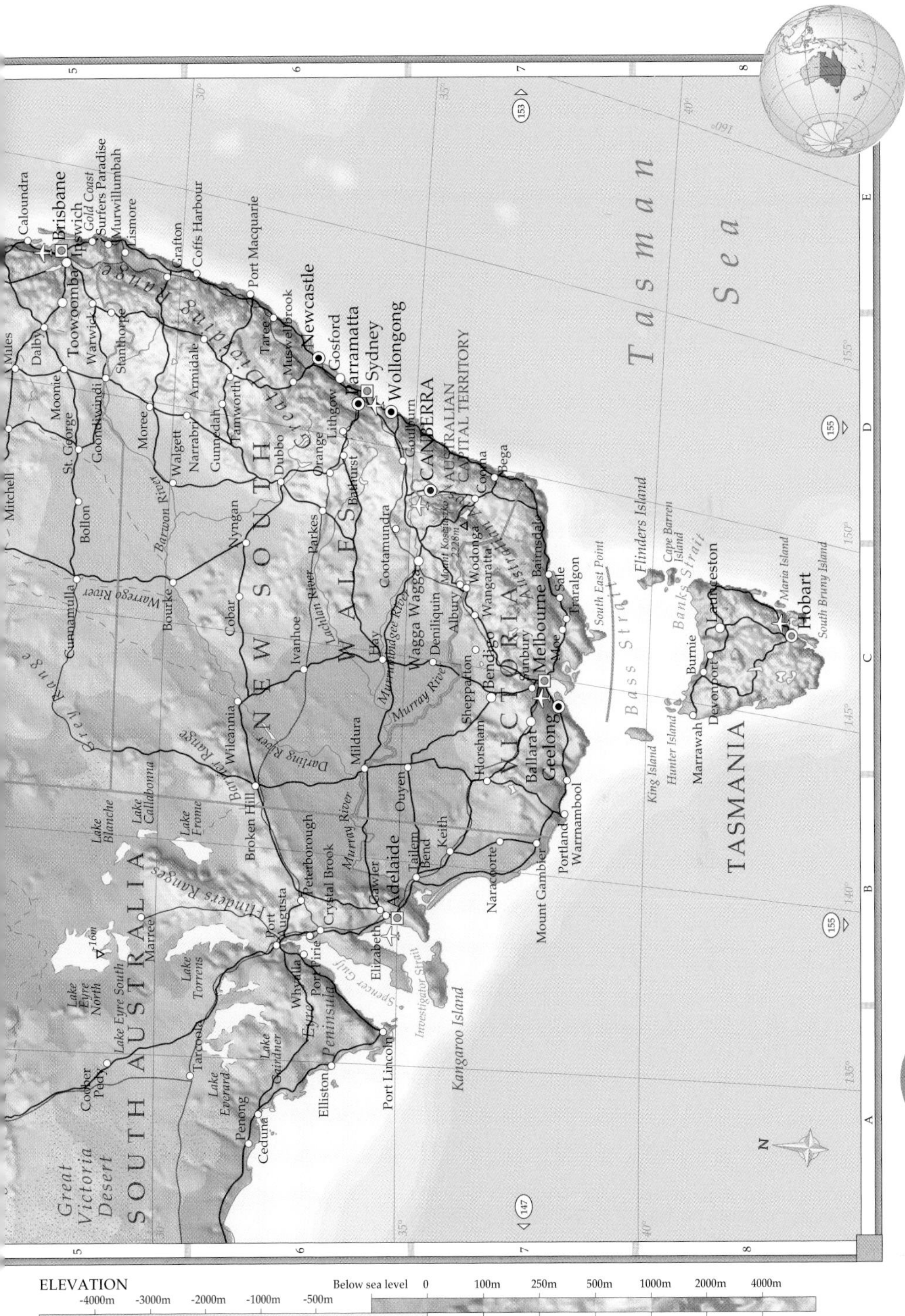

ELEVATION

Below sea level						0	100m	250m	500m	1000m	2000m	4000m
-4000m	-3000m	-2000m	-1000m	-500m			328ft	820ft	1640ft	3281ft	6562ft	13 124ft
-13 124ft	-9843ft	-6562ft	-3281ft	-1640ft	-820ft/-250m	0						

NEW ZEALAND

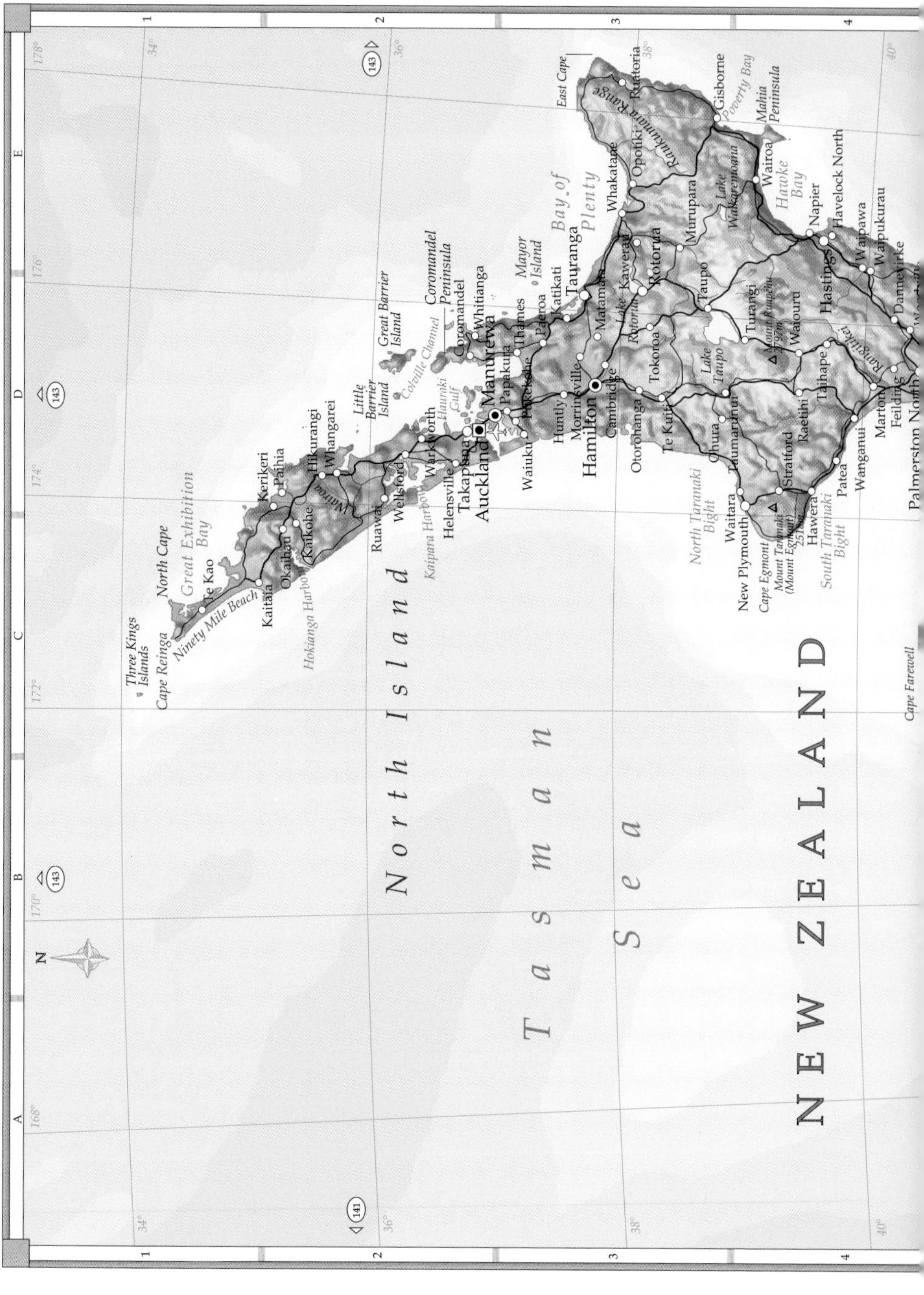

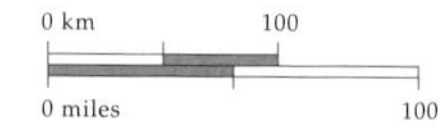

POPULATION ● National capital ○ Less than 50,000 ○ 50,000 -100,000 ⦿ 100,000 - 500,000 ▣ Over 500,000

South Island
Southern Alps
PACIFIC OCEAN
Canterbury Bight
Pegasus Bay
WELLINGTON
Lower Hutt
Cape Palliser
Cape Campbell
Cook
Seddon
Blenheim
Clarence
Kaikoura
Kaikoura Peninsula
Richmond
Richmond Range
Wairau
Mount Owen 1875m
Seddonville
Westport
Cape Foulwind
Reefton
Springs Junction
Hanmer Springs
Waipara
Rangiora
Kaiapoi
Christchurch
Lyttelton
Banks Peninsula
Lake Ellesmere
Oxford
Darfield
Canterbury Plains
Ashburton
Hinds
Geraldine
Temuka
Timaru
Studholme
Waimate
Oamaru
Hampden
Otago Peninsula
Dunedin
Mosgiel
Milton
Balclutha
Runanga
Greymouth
Lake Brunner
Hurunui
Hokitika
Ross
Otira
Arthur's Pass 920m
Rakaia
Mayfield
Fairlie
Aoraki (Mount Cook) 3744m
Mount Cook
Lake Pukaki
Waitaki
Abut Head
Whataroa
Fox Glacier
Haast
Jackson Head
Lake Hawea
Wanaka
Lake Wanaka
Lake Wakatipu
Queenstown
Cromwell
Alexandra
Clutha
Taieri
Lumsden
Mataura
Gore
Invercargill
Tokanui
Toetoes Bay
Ruapuke Island
Foveaux Strait
Stewart Island
South West Cape
Halfmoon Bay
Codfish Island
Muttonbird Islands
Riverton
Winton
Waiau
Lake Manapouri
Te Anau
Lake Te Anau
Milford Sound
Eyre Mts
Livingstone Mts
Fiordland
Lake Hauroko
Ta Waewae Bay
Resolution Island
West Cape
George Sound
Caswell Sound
ELEVATION
Below sea level
-4000m
-3000m
-2000m
-1000m
-500m
-13 124ft
-9843ft
-6562ft
-3281ft
-1640ft
-820ft/-250m
0
100m
250m
500m
1000m
2000m
4000m
328ft
820ft
1640ft
3281ft
6562ft
13 124ft

THE PACIFIC OCEAN

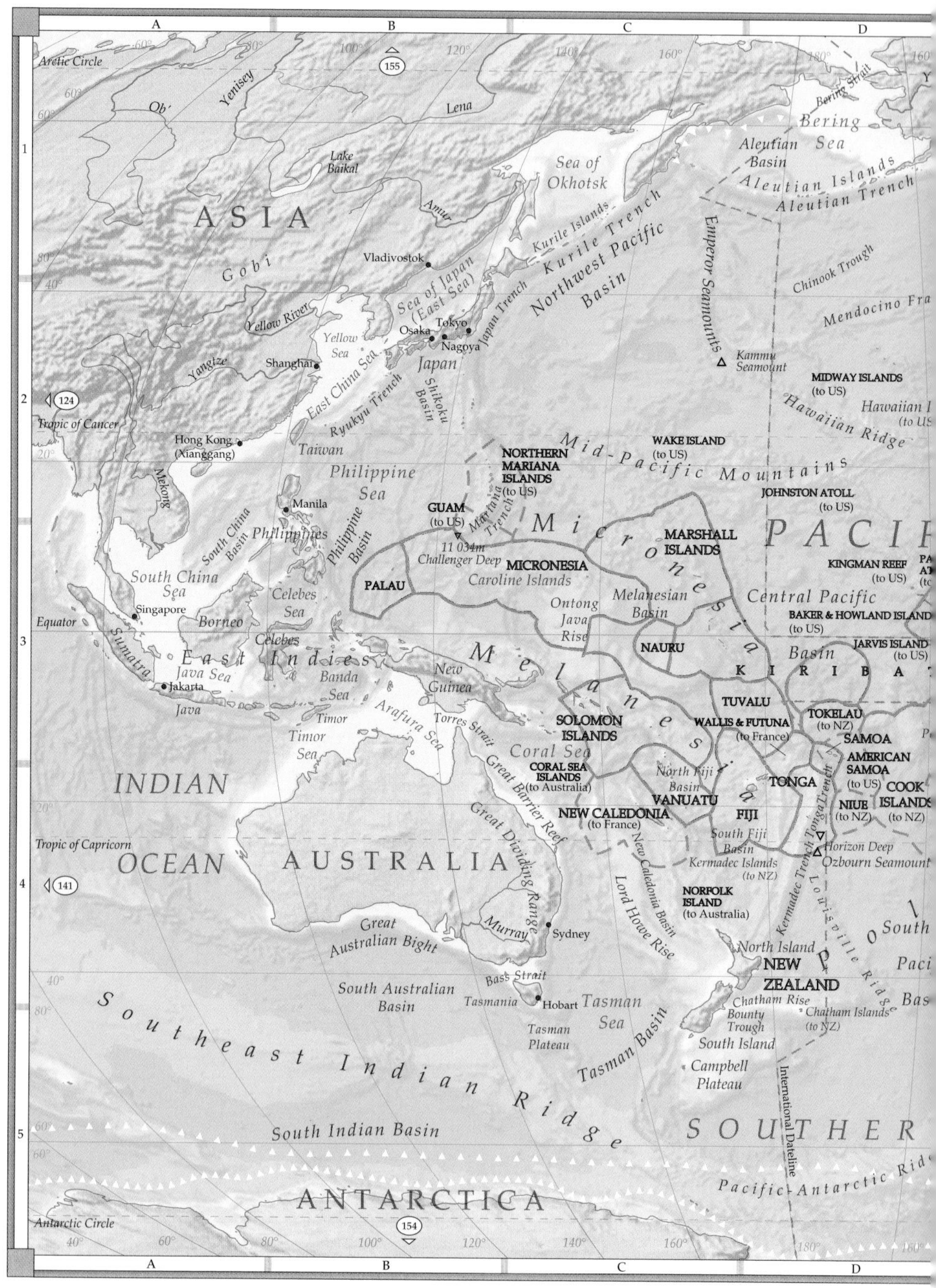

0 km 2000
0 miles 2000

• Major port

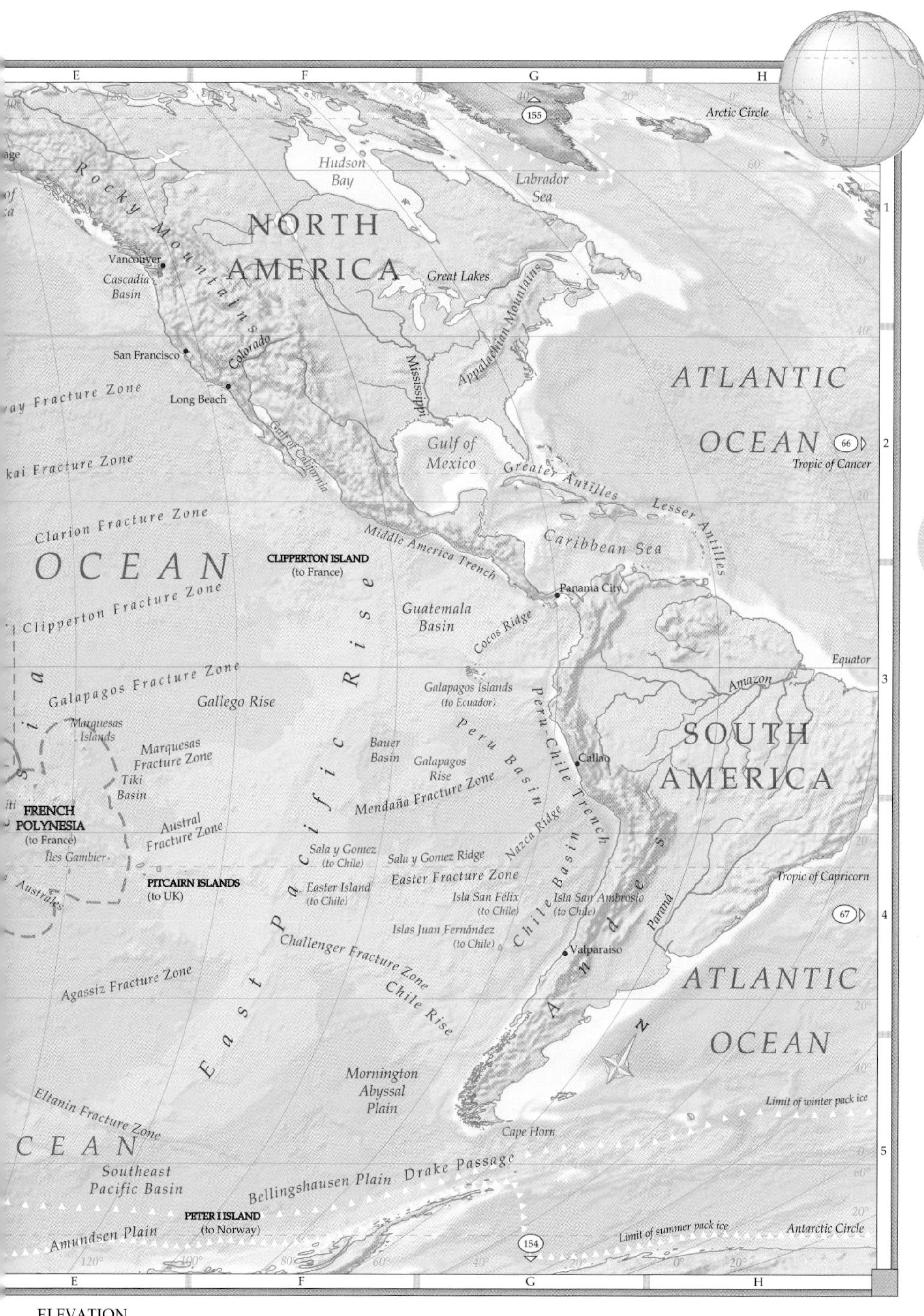

ELEVATION

-4000m	-3000m	-2000m	-1000m	-500m	-250m	0
-13 124ft	-9843ft	-6562ft	-3281ft	-1640ft	-820ft	0

ANTARCTICA

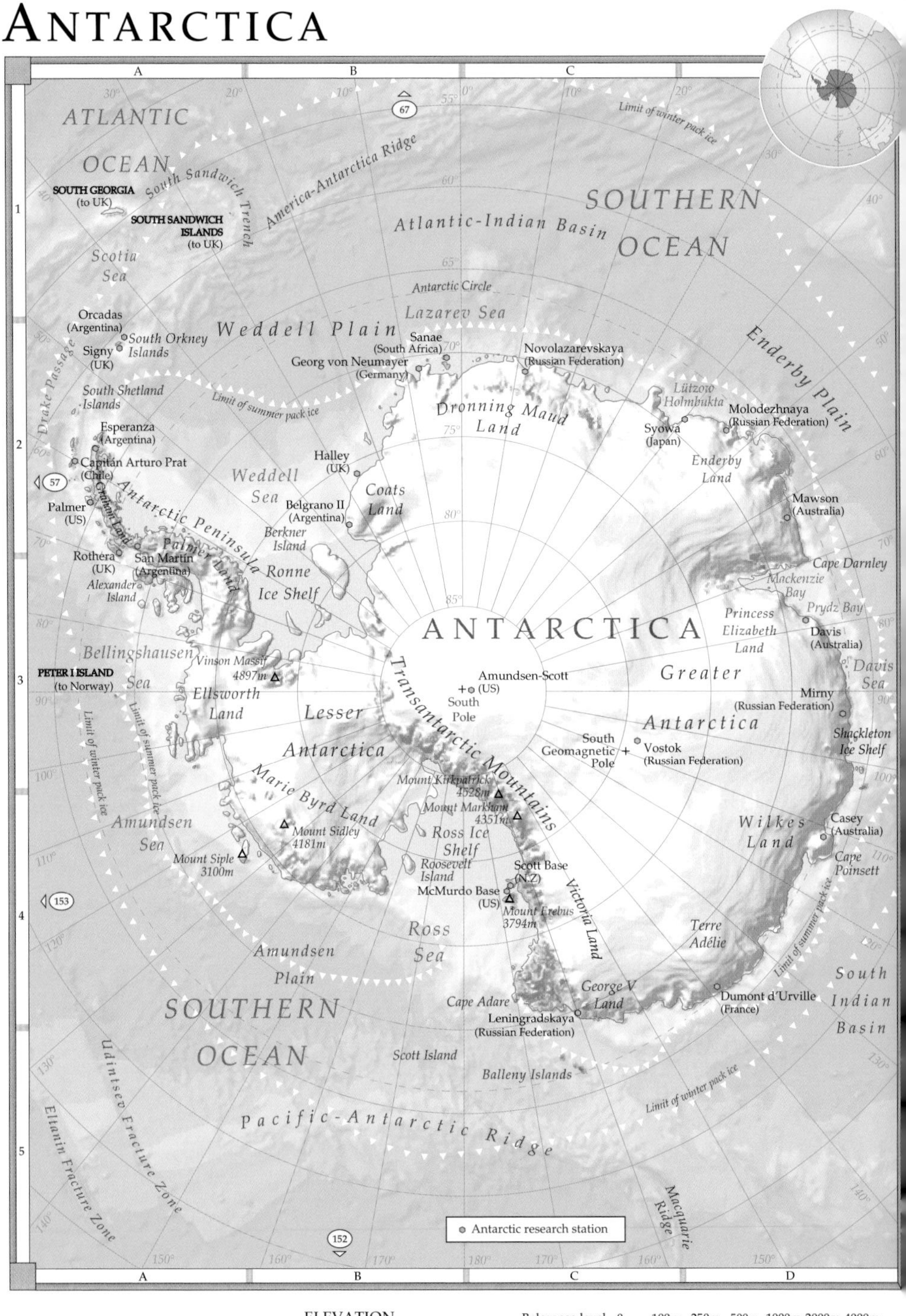

A B C D
1 2 3 4 5

ATLANTIC OCEAN
SOUTH GEORGIA (to UK)
SOUTH SANDWICH ISLANDS (to UK)
South Sandwich Trench
America-Antarctica Ridge
Scotia Sea
SOUTHERN OCEAN
Atlantic-Indian Basin
Limit of winter pack ice
Antarctic Circle
Lazarev Sea
Weddell Plain
Orcadas (Argentina)
South Orkney Islands
Signy (UK)
Drake Passage
South Shetland Islands
Limit of summer pack ice
Sanae (South Africa)
Georg von Neumayer (Germany)
Novolazarevskaya (Russian Federation)
Enderby Plain
Lützow Holmbukta
Molodezhnaya (Russian Federation)
Syowa (Japan)
Dronning Maud Land
Esperanza (Argentina)
Capitán Arturo Prat (Chile)
Halley (UK)
Enderby Land
Weddell Sea
Coats Land
Mawson (Australia)
Palmer (US)
Graham Land
Antarctic Peninsula
Belgrano II (Argentina)
Berkner Island
Rothera (UK)
San Martín (Argentina)
Palmer Land
Ronne Ice Shelf
Cape Darnley
Mackenzie Bay
Alexander Island
Prydz Bay
Princess Elizabeth Land
Davis (Australia)
ANTARCTICA
Bellingshausen Sea
Vinson Massif 4897m
PETER I ISLAND (to Norway)
Amundsen-Scott (US)
South Pole
Greater Antarctica
Davis Sea
Mirny (Russian Federation)
Ellsworth Land
Lesser Antarctica
Transantarctic Mountains
South Geomagnetic Pole
Vostok (Russian Federation)
Shackleton Ice Shelf
Marie Byrd Land
Mount Kirkpatrick 4528m
Mount Markham 4351m
Wilkes Land
Casey (Australia)
Amundsen Sea
Mount Sidley 4181m
Ross Ice Shelf
Mount Siple 3100m
Roosevelt Island
Scott Base (N.Z)
Cape Poinsett
McMurdo Base (US)
Mount Erebus 3794m
Victoria Land
Ross Sea
Terre Adélie
Amundsen Plain
South Indian Basin
George V Land
Dumont d'Urville (France)
Cape Adare
Leningradskaya (Russian Federation)
Udintsev Fracture Zone
Scott Island
Balleny Islands
Eltanin Fracture Zone
Pacific-Antarctic Ridge
Macquarie Ridge
Antarctic research station

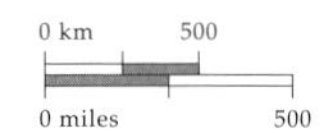

ELEVATION

Below sea level							0	100m	250m	500m	1000m	2000m	4000m
-4000m	-3000m	-2000m	-1000m	-500m									
-13 124ft	-9843ft	-6562ft	-3281ft	-1640ft	-820ft/-250m			328ft	820ft	1640ft	3281ft	6562ft	13 124ft

Arctic Ocean

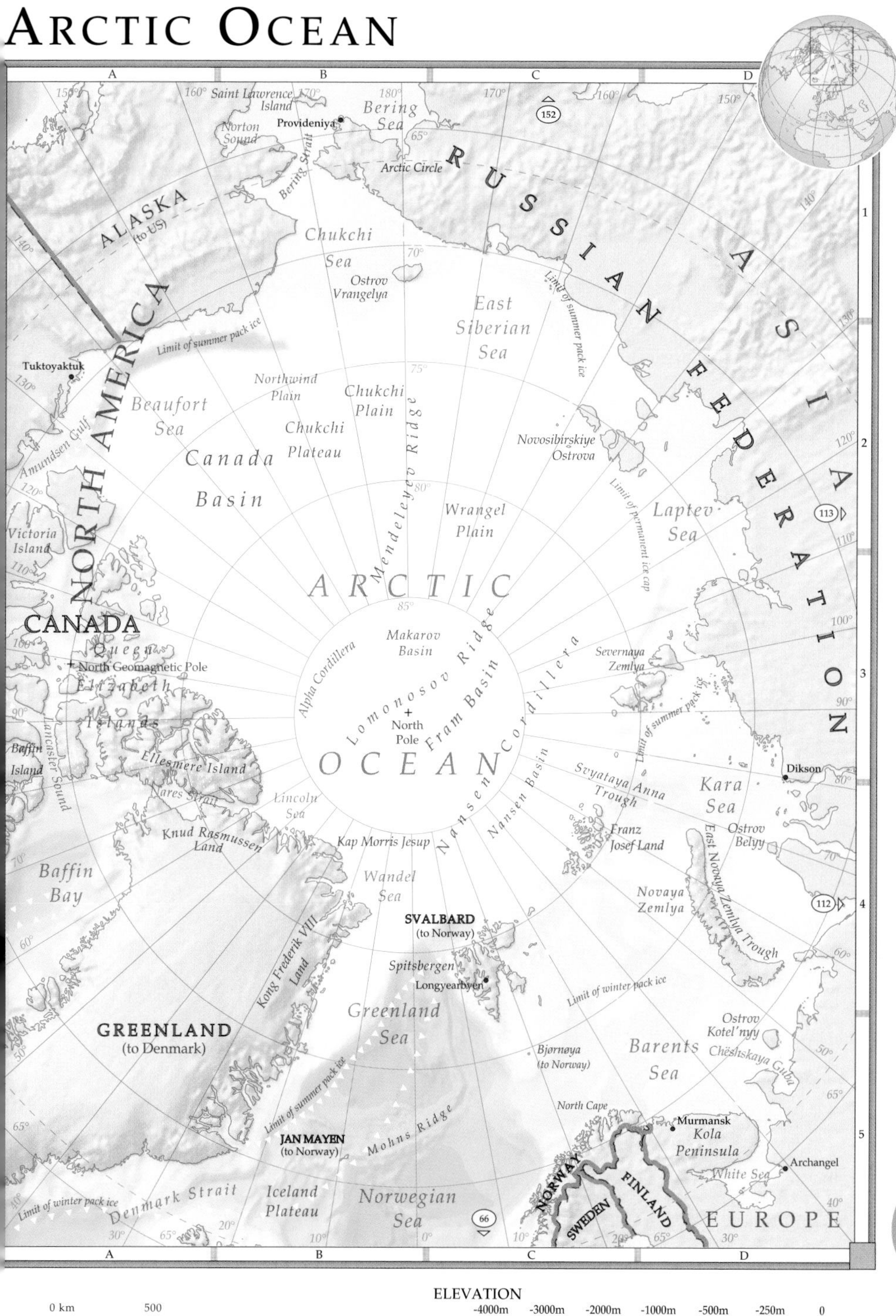

Overseas Territories & Dependencies

Despite the rapid process of global decolonization since the Second World War, around 10 million people in more than 50 territories around the world continue to live under the protection of France, Australia, the Netherlands, Denmark, Norway, New Zealand, the UK, or the USA. These remnants of former colonial empires may have persisted for economic, strategic or political reasons and are administered in a variety of ways.

AUSTRALIA

Australia's overseas territories have not been an issue since Papua New Guinea became independent in 1975. Consequently there is no overriding policy toward them. Norfolk Island is inhabited by descendants of the H.M.S Bounty mutineers and more recent Australian migrants.

Ashmore & Cartier Islands

Indian Ocean
Status: External territory
Claimed: 1931
Capital: Not applicable
Population: None
Area: 2 sq miles (5.2 sq km)

Christmas Island

Indian Ocean
Status: External territory
Claimed: 1958
Capital: The Settlement
Population: 433
Area: 52 sq miles (134.6 sq km)

Cocos Islands

Indian Ocean
Status: External territory
Claimed: 1955
Capital: No official capital
Population: 630
Area: 5.5 sq miles (14.24 sq km)

Coral Sea Islands

South Pacific
Status: External territory
Claimed: 1969
Capital: None
Population: 8 (meteorologists)
Area: Less than 1.16 sq miles (3 sq km)

Heard & McDonald Is.

Indian Ocean
Status: External territory
Claimed: 1947
Capital: Not applicable
Population: None
Area: 161 sq miles (417 sq km)

Norfolk Island

South Pacific
Status: External territory
Claimed: 1774
Capital: Kingston
Population: 1,853
Area: 13.3 sq miles (34.4 sq km)

DENMARK

The Faeroe Islands have been under Danish administration since Queen Margreth I of Denmark inherited Norway in 1380. The Home Rule Act of 1948 gave the Faeroese control over all their internal affairs. Greenland first came under Danish rule in 1380. Today, Denmark is responsible for the island's foreign affairs and defense.

Faeroe Islands

North Atlantic
Status: External territory
Claimed: 1380
Capital: Tórshavn
Population: 46,345
Area: 540 sq miles (1,399 sq km)

Greenland

North Atlantic
Status: External territory
Claimed: 1380
Capital: Nuuk
Population: 56,385
Area: 840,000 sq miles (2,175,516 sq km)

FRANCE

France has developed economic ties with its overseas territories, thereby stressing interdependence over independence. Overseas *départements,* officially part of France, have their own governments. Territorial *collectivités* and overseas *territoires* have varying degrees of autonomy.

Clipperton Island

East Pacific
Status: Dependency of French Polynesia
Claimed: 1935
Capital: Not applicable
Population: None
Area: 2.7 sq miles (7 sq km)

French Guiana

South America
Status: Overseas department
Claimed: 1817
Capital: Cayenne
Population: 186,917
Area: 35,135 sq miles (90,996 sq km)

French Polynesia

South Pacific
Status: Overseas territory
Claimed: 1843
Capital: Papeete
Population: 245,516
Area: 1,608 sq miles (4,165 sq km)

Guadeloupe

West Indies
Status: Overseas department
Claimed: 1635
Capital: Basse-Terre
Population: 440,000
Area: 687 sq miles (1,780 sq km)

MARTINIQUE
West Indies
STATUS: Overseas department
CLAIMED: 1635
CAPITAL: Fort-de-France
POPULATION: 393,000
AREA: 425 sq miles (1,100 sq km)

MAYOTTE
Indian Ocean
STATUS: Territorial collectivity
CLAIMED: 1843
CAPITAL: Not applicable
POPULATION: Not applicable
AREA: 144 sq miles (374 sq km)

NEW CALEDONIA
South Pacific
STATUS: Overseas territory
CLAIMED: 1853
CAPITAL: Nouméa
POPULATION: 228,000
AREA: 7,374 sq miles (19,103 sq km)

RÉUNION
Indian Ocean
STATUS: Overseas department
CLAIMED: 1638
CAPITAL: Saint-Denis
POPULATION: 756,000
AREA: 970 sq miles (2,512 sq km)

ST. PIERRE & MIQUELON
North America
STATUS: Territorial collectivity
CLAIMED: 1604
CAPITAL: Saint-Pierre
POPULATION: 6,976
AREA: 93.4 sq miles (242 sq km)

WALLIS & FUTUNA
South Pacific
STATUS: Overseas territory
CLAIMED: 1842
CAPITAL: Matā'Utu
POPULATION: 15,734
AREA: 106 sq miles (274 sq km)

NETHERLANDS

THE COUNTRY'S TWO REMAINING overseas territories were formerly part of the Dutch West Indies. Both are now self-governing, but the Netherlands remains responsible for their defense.

ARUBA
West Indies
STATUS: Autonomous part of the Netherlands
CLAIMED: 1643
CAPITAL: Oranjestad
POPULATION: 70,844
AREA: 75 sq miles (194 sq km)

NETHERLANDS ANTILLES
West Indies
STATUS: Autonomous part of the Netherlands
CLAIMED: 1816
CAPITAL: Willemstad
POPULATION: 221,000
AREA: 371 sq miles (960 sq km)

NEW ZEALAND

NEW ZEALAND'S GOVERNMENT has no desire to retain any overseas territories. However, the economic weakness of its dependent territory Tokelau and its freely associated states, Niue and the Cook Islands, has forced New Zealand to remain responsible for their foreign policy and defense.

COOK ISLANDS
South Pacific
STATUS: Associated territory
CLAIMED: 1901
CAPITAL: Avarua
POPULATION: 21,008
AREA: 91 sq miles (235 sq km)

NIUE
South Pacific
STATUS: Associated territory
CLAIMED: 1901
CAPITAL: Alofi
POPULATION: 2,145
AREA: 102 sq miles (264 sq km)

TOKELAU
South Pacific
STATUS: Dependent territory
CLAIMED: 1926
CAPITAL: Not applicable
POPULATION: 1,418
AREA: 4 sq miles (10.4 sq km)

NORWAY

IN 1920, 41 nations signed the Spitsbergen Treaty recognizing Norwegian sovereignty over Svalbard. There is a NATO base on Jan Mayen. Bouvet Island is a nature reserve.

BOUVET ISLAND
South Atlantic
STATUS: Dependency
CLAIMED: 1928
CAPITAL: Not applicable
POPULATION: None
AREA: 22 sq miles (58 sq km)

JAN MAYEN
North Atlantic
STATUS: Dependency
CLAIMED: 1929
CAPITAL: Not applicable
POPULATION: None
AREA: 147 sq miles (381 sq km)

PETER I. ISLAND
Southern Ocean
STATUS: Dependency
CLAIMED: 1931
CAPITAL: Not applicable
POPULATION: None
AREA: 69 sq miles (180 sq km)

SVALBARD
Arctic Ocean
STATUS: Dependency
CLAIMED: 1920
CAPITAL: Longyearbyen
POPULATION: 2,811
AREA: 24,289 sq miles (62,906 sq km)

Continued on p.158

UNITED KINGDOM

THE UK STILL has the largest number of overseas territories. These are locally-governed by a mixture of elected representatives and appointed officials, and they all enjoy a large measure of internal self-government, but certain powers, such as foreign affairs and defense, are reserved for Governors of the British Crown.

ANGUILLA
West Indies
STATUS: Dependent territory
CLAIMED: 1650
CAPITAL: The Valley
POPULATION: 12,738
AREA: 37 sq miles (96 sq km)

ASCENSION ISLAND
South Atlantic
STATUS: Dependency of St. Helena
CLAIMED: 1673
CAPITAL: Georgetown
POPULATION: 1,177
AREA: 34 sq miles (88 sq km)

BERMUDA
North Atlantic
STATUS: Crown colony
CLAIMED: 1612
CAPITAL: Hamilton
POPULATION: 64,482
AREA: 20.5 sq miles (53 sq km)

BRITISH INDIAN OCEAN TERRITORY
STATUS: Dependent territory
CLAIMED: 1814
CAPITAL: Diego Garcia
POPULATION: 3,000
AREA: 23 sq miles (60 sq km)

BRITISH VIRGIN ISLANDS
West Indies
STATUS: Dependent territory
CLAIMED: 1672
CAPITAL: Road Town
POPULATION: 21,730
AREA: 59 sq miles (153 sq km)

CAYMAN ISLANDS
West Indies
STATUS: Dependent territory
CLAIMED: 1670
CAPITAL: George Town
POPULATION: 41,934
AREA: 100 sq miles (259 sq km)

FALKLAND ISLANDS
South Atlantic
STATUS: Dependent territory
CLAIMED: 1832
CAPITAL: Stanley
POPULATION: 2,967
AREA: 4,699 sq miles (412,173 sq km)

GIBRALTAR
Southwest Europe
STATUS: Crown colony
CLAIMED: 1713
CAPITAL: Gibraltar
POPULATION: 27,776
AREA: 2.5 sq miles (6.5 sq km)

GUERNSEY
Channel Islands
STATUS: Crown dependency
CLAIMED: 1066
CAPITAL: St. Peter Port
POPULATION: 64,818
AREA: 25 sq miles (65 sq km)

ISLE OF MAN
British Isles
STATUS: Crown dependency
CLAIMED: 1765
CAPITAL: Douglas
POPULATION: 74,261
AREA: 221 sq miles (572 sq km)

JERSEY
Channel Islands
STATUS: Crown dependency
CLAIMED: 1066
CAPITAL: St. Helier
POPULATION: 90,156
AREA: 45 sq miles (116 sq km)

MONTSERRAT
West Indies
STATUS: Dependent territory
CLAIMED: 1632
CAPITAL: Plymouth (currently uninhabitable)
POPULATION: 8,995
AREA: 40 sq miles (102 sq km)

PITCAIRN ISLANDS
South Pacific
STATUS: Dependent territory
CLAIMED: 1887
CAPITAL: Adamstown
POPULATION: 47
AREA: 18 sq miles (47 sq km)

ST. HELENA
South Atlantic
STATUS: Dependent territory
CLAIMED: 1673
CAPITAL: Jamestown
POPULATION: 7,367
AREA: 47 sq miles (122 sq km)

SOUTH GEORGIA & THE SOUTH SANDWICH ISLANDS
South Atlantic
STATUS: Dependent territory
CLAIMED: 1775
CAPITAL: Not applicable
POPULATION: No permanent residents
AREA: 1,387 sq miles (3,592 sq km)

TRISTAN DA CUNHA
South Atlantic
STATUS: Dependency of St. Helena
CLAIMED: 1612
CAPITAL: Edinburgh
POPULATION: 313
AREA: 38 sq miles (98 sq km)

TURKS & CAICOS ISLANDS
West Indies
STATUS: Dependent territory
CLAIMED: 1766
CAPITAL: Cockburn Town
POPULATION: 19,350
AREA: 166 sq miles (430 sq km)

UNITED STATES OF AMERICA

AMERICA'S OVERSEAS TERRITORIES have been seen as strategically useful, if expensive, links with its "backyards." The US has, in most cases, given the local population a say in deciding their own status. A US Commonwealth territory, such as Puerto Rico, has a greater level of independence than that of a US unincorporated or external territory.

AMERICAN SAMOA
South Pacific
STATUS: Unincorporated territory
CLAIMED: 1900
CAPITAL: Pago Pago
POPULATION: 70,260
AREA: 75 sq miles (195 sq km)

BAKER & HOWLAND ISLANDS
South Pacific
STATUS: Unincorporated territory
CLAIMED: 1856
CAPITAL: Not applicable
POPULATION: None
AREA: 0.54 sq miles (1.4 sq km)

GUAM
West Pacific
STATUS: Unincorporated territory
CLAIMED: 1898
CAPITAL: Hagåtña
POPULATION: 163,000
AREA: 212 sq miles (549 sq km)

JARVIS ISLAND
South Pacific
STATUS: Unincorporated territory
CLAIMED: 1856
CAPITAL: Not applicable
POPULATION: None
AREA: 1.7 sq miles (4.5 sq km)

JOHNSTON ATOLL
Central Pacific
STATUS: Unincorporated territory
CLAIMED: 1858
CAPITAL: Not applicable
POPULATION: Not applicable
AREA: 1 sq mile (2.8 sq km)

KINGMAN REEF
Central Pacific
STATUS: Administered territory
CLAIMED: 1856
CAPITAL: Not applicable
POPULATION: None
AREA: 0.4 sq mile (1 sq km)

MIDWAY ISLANDS
Central Pacific
STATUS: Administered territory
CLAIMED: 1867
CAPITAL: Not applicable
POPULATION: 40
AREA: 2 sq miles (5.2 sq km)

NAVASSA ISLAND
West Indies
STATUS: Unincorporated territory
CLAIMED: 1856
CAPITAL: Not applicable
POPULATION: None
AREA: 2 sq miles (5.2 sq km)

NORTHERN MARIANA ISLANDS
West Pacific
STATUS: Commonwealth territory
CLAIMED: 1947
CAPITAL: Saipan
POPULATION: 80,006
AREA: 177 sq miles (457 sq km)

PALMYRA ATOLL
Central Pacific
STATUS: Unincorporated territory
CLAIMED: 1898
CAPITAL: Not applicable
POPULATION: None
AREA: 5 sq miles (12 sq km)

PUERTO RICO
West Indies
STATUS: Commonwealth territory
CLAIMED: 1898
CAPITAL: San Juan
POPULATION: 3.89 million
AREA: 3,515 sq miles (9,104 sq km)

VIRGIN ISLANDS
West Indies
STATUS: Unincorporated territory
CLAIMED: 1917
CAPITAL: Charlotte Amalie
POPULATION: 124,778
AREA: 137 sq miles (355 sq km)

WAKE ISLAND
Central Pacific
STATUS: Unincorporated territory
CLAIMED: 1898
CAPITAL: Not applicable
POPULATION: Not applicable
AREA: 2.5 sq miles (6.5 sq km)

Glossary of Geographical Terms

The following glossary lists all geographical terms occuring on the maps and in the main-entry names in the Index–Gazetteer. These terms may precede, follow or be run together with the proper elements of the name; where they precede it the term is reversed for indexing purposes – thus Poluostov Yamal is indexed as Yamal, Poluostrov.

A

Å *Danish, Norwegian,* River
Alpen *German,* Alps
Altiplanicie *Spanish,* Plateau
Älv(en) *Swedish,* River
Anse *French,* Bay
Archipiélago *Spanish,* Archipelago
Arcipelago *Italian,* Archipelago
Arquipélago *Portuguese,* Archipelago
Aukštuma *Lithuanian,* Upland

B

Bahía *Spanish,* Bay
Baía *Portuguese,* Bay
Baḩr *Arabic,* River
Baie *French,* Bay
Bandao *Chinese,* Peninsula
Banjaran *Malay,* Mountain range
Batang *Malay,* Stream
-berg *Afrikaans, Norwegian,* Mountain
Birket *Arabic ,* Lake
Boğazı *Turkish,* Strait
Bucht *German,* Bay
Bugten *Danish,* Bay
Buḩayrat *Arabic,* Lake, reservoir
Buḩeiret *Arabic,* Lake
Bukit *Malay,* Mountain
-bukta *Norwegian,* Bay
bukten *Swedish,* Bay
Burnu *Turkish,* Cape, point
Buuraha *Somali,* Mountains

C

Cabo *Portuguese,* Cape
Cap *French,* Cape
Cascada *Portuguese,* Waterfall
Cerro *Spanish,* Mountain
Chaîne *French,* Mountain range
Chau *Cantonese,* Island
Chāy *Turkish,* Stream
Chhâk *Cambodian,* Bay
Chhu *Tibetan,* River
-chôsuji *Korean,* Reservoir
Chott *Arabic,* Salt lake, depression
Ch'ün-tao *Chinese,* Island group
Cambodian, Mountains
Cordillera *Spanish,* Mountain range
Costa *Spanish,* Coast
Côte *French,* Coast
Cuchilla *Spanish,* Mountains

D

Dağı *Azerbaijani, Turkish,* Mountain
Dağları *Azerbaijani, Turkish,* Mountains
-dake *Japanese,* Peak
Danau *Indonesian,* Lake
Đao *Vietnamese,* Island
Daryā *Persian,* River
Daryācheh *Persian,* Lake
Dasht *Persian,* Plain, desert
Dawḩat *Arabic,* Bay
Dere *Turkish,* Stream
Dili *Azerbaijani,* Spit
-do *Korean,* Island
Dooxo *Somali,* Valley
Düzü *Azerbaijani,* Steppe
-dwīp *Bengali,* Island

E

Embalse *Spanish,* Reservoir
Erg *Arabic,* Dunes
Estany *Catalan,* Lake
Estrecho *Spanish,* Strait
-ey *Icelandic,* Island
Ezero *Bulgarian, Macedonian,* Lake

F

Fjord *Danish,* Fjord
-fjorden *Norwegian,* Fjord
-fjørdhur *Faeroese,* Fjord
Fleuve *French,* River
Fliegu *Maltese,* Channel
-fljór *Icelandic,* River

G

-gang *Korean,* River
Ganga *Nepali, Sinhala,* River
Gaoyuan *Chinese,* Plateau
-gawa *Japanese,* River
Gebel *Arabic,* Mountain
-gebirge *German,* Mountains
Ghubbat *Arabic,* Bay
Gjiri *Albanian,* Bay
Gol *Mongolian,* River
Golfe *French,* Gulf
Golfo *Italian, Spanish,* Gulf
Gora *Russian, Serbian,* Mountain
Gory *Russian,* Mountains
Guba *Russian,* Bay
Gunung *Malay,* Mountain

H

Ḩadd *Arabic,* Spit
-haehyŏp *Korean,* Strait
Haff *German,* Lagoon
Hai *Chinese,* Sea, bay
Ḩammādat *Arabic,* Plateau
Hāmūn *Persian,* Lake
Hawr *Arabic,* Lake
Hāyk' *Amharic,* Lake
He *Chinese,* River
Helodrano *Malagasy,* Bay
-hegység *Hungarian,* Mountain range
Hka *Burmese,* River
-ho *Korean,* Lake
Hô *Korean,* Reservoir
Ḩolot *Hebrew,* Dunes
Hora *Belorussian,* Mountain
Hrada *Belorussian,* Mountains, ridge
Hsi *Chinese,* River
Hu *Chinese,* Lake

I

Île(s) *French,* Island(s)
Ilha(s) *Portuguese,* Island(s)
Ilhéu(s) *Portuguese,* Islet(s)
Irmak *Turkish,* River
Isla(s) *Spanish,* Island(s)
Isola (Isole) *Italian,* Island(s)

J

Jabal *Arabic,* Mountain
Jāl *Arabic,* Ridge
-järvi *Finnish,* Lake
Jazīrat *Arabic,* Island
Jazīreh *Persian,* Island
Jebel *Arabic,* Mountain
Jezero *Serbian/Croatian,* Lake
Jiang *Chinese,* River
-joki *Finnish,* River
-jökull *Icelandic,* Glacier
Juzur *Arabic,* Islands

K

Kaikyō *Japanese,* Strait
-kaise *Lappish,* Mountain
Kali *Nepali,* River
Kalnas *Lithuanian,* Mountain
Kalns *Latvian,* Mountain
Kang *Chinese,* Harbor
Kangri *Tibetan,* Mountain(s)
Kaôh *Cambodian,* Island
Kapp *Norwegian,* Cape
Kavīr *Persian,* Desert
K'edi *Georgian,* Mountain range
Kediet *Arabic,* Mountain
Kepulauan *Indonesian, Malay,* Island group
Khalîg, Khalīj *Arabic,* Gulf
Khawr *Arabic,* Inlet
Khola *Nepali,* River
Khrebet *Russian,* Mountain range
Ko *Thai,* Island
Kolpos *Greek,* Bay
-kopf *German,* Peak
Körfäzi *Azerbaijani,* Bay
Körfezi *Turkish,* Bay
Kõrgustik *Estonian,* Upland
Koshi *Nepali,* River
Kowtal *Persian,* Pass
Kūh(hā) *Persian,* Mountain(s)
-kundo *Korean,* Island group
-kysten *Norwegian,* Coast
Kyun *Burmese,* Island

L

Laaq *Somali,* Watercourse
Lac *French,* Lake
Lacul *Romanian,* Lake
Lago *Italian, Portuguese, Spanish,* Lake
Laguna *Spanish,* Lagoon, Lake

Laht *Estonian,* Bay
Laut *Indonesian,* Sea
Lembalemba *Malagasy,* Plateau
Lerr *Armenian,* Mountain
Lerrnashght'a *Armenian,* Mountain range
Les *Czech,* Forest
Lich *Armenian,* Lake
Liqeni *Albanian,* Lake
Lumi *Albanian,* River
Lyman *Ukrainian,* Estuary

M

Mae Nam *Thai,* River
-mägi *Estonian,* Hill
Maja *Albanian,* Mountain
-man *Korean,* Bay
Marios *Lithuanian,* Lake
-meer *Dutch,* Lake
Melkosopochnik *Russian,* Plain
-meri *Estonian,* Sea
Mifraz *Hebrew,* Bay
Monkhafad *Arabic,* Depression
Mont(s) *French,* Mountain(s)
Monte *Italian, Portuguese,* Mountain
More *Russian,* Sea
Mörön *Mongolian,* River

N

Nagor'ye *Russian,* Upland
Nahal *Hebrew,* River
Nahr *Arabic,* River
Nam *Laotian,* River
Nehri *Turkish,* River
Nevado *Spanish,* Mountain (snow-capped)
Nisoi *Greek,* Islands
Nizmennost' *Russian,* Lowland, plain
Nosy *Malagasy,* Island
Nur *Mongolian,* Lake
Nuruu *Mongolian,* Mountains
Nuur *Mongolian,* Lake
Nyzovyna *Ukrainian,* Lowland, plain

O

Ostrov(a) *Russian,* Island(s)
Oued *Arabic,* Watercourse
-oy *Faeroese,* Island
-øy(a) *Norwegian,* Island
Oya *Sinhala,* River
Ozero *Russian, Ukrainian,* Lake

P

Passo *Italian,* Pass
Pegunungan *Indonesian, Malay,* Mountain range
Pelagos *Greek,* Sea
Penisola *Italian,* Peninsula
Peski *Russian,* Sands
Phanom *Thai,* Mountain
Phou *Laotian,* Mountain
Pic *Catalan,* Peak
Pico *Portuguese, Spanish,* Peak
Pik *Russian,* Peak
Planalto *Portuguese,* Plateau
Planina, Planini *Bulgarian, Macedonian, Serbian, Croatian,* Mountain range
Ploskogor'ye *Russian,* Upland
Poluostrov *Russian,* Peninsula
Potamos *Greek,* River
Proliv *Russian,* Strait
Pulau *Indonesian, Malay,* Island
Pulu *Malay,* Island
Punta *Portuguese, Spanish,* Point

Q

Qā' *Arabic,* Depression
Qolleh *Persian,* Mountain

R

Raas *Somali,* Cape
-rags *Latvian,* Cape
Ramlat *Arabic,* Sands
Ra's *Arabic,* Cape, point, headland
Ravnina *Bulgarian, Russian,* Plain
Récif *French,* Reef
Represa (Rep.) *Spanish, Portuguese,* Reservoir
-rettō *Japanese,* Island chain
Riacho *Spanish,* Stream
Riban' *Malagasy,* Mountains
Rio *Portuguese,* River
Río *Spanish,* River
Riu *Catalan,* River
Rivier *Dutch,* River
Rivière *French,* River
Rowd *Pashtu,* River
Rūd *Persian,* River
Rudohorie *Slovak,* Mountains
Ruisseau *French,* Stream

S

Sabkhat *Arabic,* Salt marsh
Şaḩrā' *Arabic,* Desert
Samudra *Sinhala,* Reservoir
-san *Japanese, Korean,* Mountain
-sanchi *Japanese,* Mountains
-sanmaek *Korean,* Mountains
Sarīr *Arabic,* Desert
Sebkha, Sebkhet *Arabic,* Salt marsh, depression
See *German,* Lake
Selat *Indonesian,* Strait
-selkä *Finnish,* Ridge
Selseleh *Persian,* Mountain range
Serra *Portuguese,* Mountain
Serranía *Spanish,* Mountain
Sha'īb *Arabic,* Watercourse
Shamo *Chinese,* Desert
Shan *Chinese,* Mountain(s)
Shan-mo *Chinese,* Mountain range
Shaţţ *Arabic,* Distributary
-shima *Japanese,* Island
Shui-tao *Chinese,* Channel
Sierra *Spanish,* Mountains
Sơn *Vietnamese,* Mountain
Sông *Vietnamese,* River
-spitze *German,* Peak
Štít *Slovak,* Peak
Stoeng *Cambodian,* River
Stretto *Italian,* Strait
Su Anbarı *Azerbaijani,* Reservoir
Sungai *Indonesian, Malay,* River
Suu *Turkish,* River

T

Tal *Mongolian,* Plain
Tandavan' *Malagasy,* Mountain range
Tangorombohitr' *Malagasy,* Mountain massif
Tao *Chinese,* Island
Tassili *Berber,* Plateau, mountain
Tau *Russian,* Mountain(s)
Taungdan *Burmese,* Mountain range
Teluk *Indonesian, Malay,* Bay
Terara *Amharic,* Mountain
Tog *Somali,* Valley
Tônlé *Cambodian,* Lake
Top *Dutch,* Peak
-tunturi *Finnish,* Mountain
Tur'at *Arabic,* Channel

V

Väin *Estonian,* Strait
-vatn *Icelandic,* Lake
-vesi *Finnish,* Lake
Vinh *Vietnamese,* Bay
Vodokhranilishche (Vdkhr.) *Russian,* Reservoir
Vodoskhovyshche (Vdskh.) *Ukrainian,* Reservoir
Volcán *Spanish,* Volcano
Vozvyshennost' *Russian,* Upland, plateau
Vrh *Macedonian,* Peak
Vysochyna *Ukrainian,* Upland
Vysočina *Czech,* Upland

W

Waadi *Somali,* Watercourse
Wādī *Arabic,* Watercourse
Wāḩat, Wâhat *Arabic,* Oasis
Wald *German,* Forest
Wan *Chinese,* Bay
Wyżyna *Polish,* Upland

X

Xé *Laotian,* River

Y

Yarımadası *Azerbaijani,* Peninsula
Yazovir *Bulgarian,* Reservoir
Yoma *Burmese,* Mountains
Yü *Chinese,* Island

Z

Zaliv *Bulgarian, Russian,* Bay
Zatoka *Ukrainian,* Bay
Zemlya *Russian,* Land

Continental Factfiles

NORTH & CENTRAL AMERICA

Political Features

Total area: 9,400,000 sq miles (24,346,000 sq km)

Total number of countries: 23

Total population: 501 million

Largest city with population: Mexico City, Mexico 22.2 million

Country with highest population density: Barbados 1,627 people per sq mile (628 people per sq km)

Largest country: Canada 3,851,788 sq miles (9,984,670 sq km)

Smallest country: St. Kitts & Nevis 101 sq miles (261 sq km)

Physical Features

Largest lake: Lake Superior, Canada/ USA 32,151 sq miles (83,270 sq km)

Longest river: Mississippi-Missouri, USA 3,710 miles (5,969 km)

Highest point: Mt. McKinley (Denali), Alaska, USA 20,322 ft (6,194 m)

Lowest point: Death Valley, California, USA 282 ft (86 m) below sea level

SOUTH AMERICA

Political Features

Total area: 6,880,000 sq miles (17,819,000 sq km)

Total number of countries: 12

Total population: 362 million

Largest city with population: São Paulo, Brazil 19.9 million

Country with highest population density: Ecuador 122 people per sq mile (47 people per sq km)

Largest country: Brazil 3,286,470 sq miles (8,511,965 sq km)

Smallest country: Suriname 63,039 sq miles (163,270 sq km)

Physical Features

Largest lake: Lake Titicaca, Bolivia/Peru 3,220 sq miles (8,340 sq km)

Longest river: Amazon, Brazil 4,049 miles (6,516 km)

Highest point: Cerro Aconcagua, Argentina 22,831 ft (6,959 m)

Lowest point: Peninsula Valdés,Argentina 131 ft (40 m) below sea level

AFRICA

Political Features

Total area: 11,677,250 sq miles (30,244,050 sq km)

Total number of countries: 53

Total population: 849 million

Largest city with population: Cairo, Egypt 15.1 million

Country with highest population density: Mauritius 1,671 people per sq mile (645 people per sq km)

Largest country: Sudan 967,493 sq miles (2,505,810 sq km)

Smallest country: Seychelles 176 sq miles (455 sq km)

Physical Features

Largest lake: Lake Victoria, Uganda, Kenya, Tanzania, 26,828 sq miles (69,484 sq km)

Longest river: Nile, Uganda/Sudan/Egypt 4,160 miles (6,695 km)

Highest point: Kilimanjaro, Tanzania 19,340 ft (5,895 m)

Lowest point: Lac', Assal, Djibouti 512 ft (156 m) below sea level

EUROPE

Political Features

Total area: 4,809,200 sq miles (12,456,000 sq km)

Total number of countries: 43

Total population: 707 million

Largest city with population: Moscow, Euro. Russia 15.5 million

Country with highest population density: Monaco 42,840 people per sq mile (16,477 people per sq km)

Largest country: European Russia 1,527,341 sq miles (3,955,818 sq km)

Smallest country: Vatican City, Italy 0.17 sq miles (0.44 sq km)

Physical Features

Largest lake: Ladoga, European Russia 7,100 sq miles (18,390 sq km)

Longest river: Volga, European Russia 2,290 miles (3,688 km)

Highest point: El' brus, Caucasus Mts, European Russia 18,510 ft (5,642 m)

Lowest point: Volga Delta, Caspian Sea, European Russia 92 ft (28 m) below sea level

NORTH & WEST ASIA

POLITICAL FEATURES

TOTAL AREA: 9,585,550 sq miles (24,826,600 sq km)

TOTAL NUMBER OF COUNTRIES: 24

TOTAL POPULATION: 370 million

LARGEST CITY WITH POPULATION: Tehran, Iran 11.6 million

COUNTRY WITH HIGHEST POPULATION DENSITY: Bahrain 2,652 people per sq mile (1,025 people per sq km)

LARGEST COUNTRY: Asiatic Russia 5,065,471 square miles (13,119,582 sq km)

SMALLEST COUNTRY: Bahrain 239 sq miles (620 sq km)

PHYSICAL FEATURES

LARGEST LAKE: Caspian Sea 142,243 sq miles (371,000 sq km)

LONGEST RIVER: Ob'-Irtysh, Asiatic Russia 3,461 miles (5,570 km)

HIGHEST POINT: Pik Pobedy, Kyrgyzstan/China 24,408 ft (7,439 m)

LOWEST POINT: Dead Sea, Israel/Jordan 1,286 ft (392 m) below sea level

SOUTH & EAST ASIA

POLITICAL FEATURES

TOTAL AREA: 7,936,200 sq miles (20,554,700 sq km)

TOTAL NUMBER OF COUNTRIES: 24

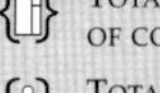
TOTAL POPULATION: 3,483 million

LARGEST CITY WITH POPULATION: Tokyo, Japan 33.9 million

COUNTRY WITH HIGHEST POPULATION DENSITY: Singapore 18,200 people per sq mile (7,049 people per sq km)

LARGEST COUNTRY: China 3,705,386 sq miles (9,596,960 sq km)

SMALLEST COUNTRY: Maldives 116 sq miles (300 sq km)

PHYSICAL FEATURES

LARGEST LAKE: Tônlé Sap, Cambodia 1,000 sq miles (2,850 sq km)

LONGEST RIVER: Chang Jiang (Yangtze), China 3,965 miles (6,380 km)

HIGHEST POINT: Mount Everest, Nepal 29,035 ft (8,850 m)

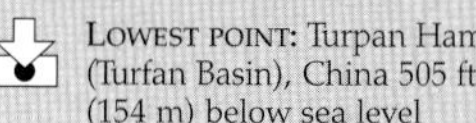
LOWEST POINT: Turpan Hami (Turfan Basin), China 505 ft (154 m) below sea level

AUSTRALASIA & OCEANIA

POLITICAL FEATURES

TOTAL AREA: 3,376,700 sq miles (8,745,750 sq km)

TOTAL NUMBER OF COUNTRIES: 14

TOTAL POPULATION: 31.4 million

LARGEST CITY WITH POPULATION: Sydney, Australia 4.25 million

COUNTRY WITH HIGHEST POPULATION DENSITY: Nauru 1,522 people per sq mile (599 people per sq km)

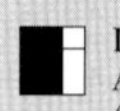
LARGEST COUNTRY: Australia 2,967,892 sq miles (7,686,850 sq km)

SMALLEST COUNTRY: Nauru 8 sq miles (21 sq km)

PHYSICAL FEATURES

LARGEST LAKE: Lake Eyre, Australia 3,700 sq miles (9,583 sq km)

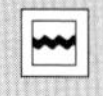
LONGEST RIVER: Murray-Darling, Australia 2,330 miles (3,750 km)

HIGHEST POINT: Mt. Wilhelm Papua New Guinea 14,794 ft (4,509 m)

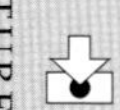
LOWEST POINT: Lake Eyre, Australia 52 ft (16 m) below sea level

ANTARCTICA

POLITICAL FEATURES

TOTAL AREA: 5,405,500 sq miles (14,000,000 sq km) of which approx. 324,300 sq miles (840,000 sq km) is ice-free

TOTAL NUMBER OF COUNTRIES: The Antarctic Treaty has 30 participating nations and 14 with observer status. Claims by Australia, France, New Zealand, Norway, Argentina, Chile and the UK are not recognized by other member states.

TOTAL POPULATION: No indigenous population. 74 research stations, (42 are staffed all year-round). Population varies between about 1,000 (winter) and 4,000 (summer).

PHYSICAL FEATURES

TOTAL VOLUME OF ICE: 7,200,000 cu miles (30,000,000 cu km): contains 90% of the Earth's fresh water

SEA ICE: 1,158,300 sq miles (3,000,000 sq km) in February. 7,722,000 sq miles (20,000,000 sq km) in October

LOWEST TEMPERATURE: Vostok Station -89.5°C (-129°F)

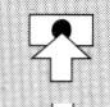
HIGHEST POINT: Vinson Massif 16,072 ft (4,897 m)

LOWEST POINT: Coastline 0ft/m

Geographical Comparisons

Largest Countries

Country	Area (sq miles)	Area (sq km)
Russ. Fed.	6,592,735 sq miles	(17,075,200 sq km)
Canada	3,855,171 sq miles	(9,984,670 sq km)
USA	3,717,792 sq miles	(9,629,091 sq km)
China	3,705,386 sq miles	(9,596,960 sq km)
Brazil	3,286,470 sq miles	(8,511,965 sq km)
Australia	2,967,893 sq miles	(7,686,893 sq km)
India	1,269,339 sq miles	(3,287,590 sq km)
Argentina	1,068,296 sq miles	(2,766,890 sq km)
Kazakhstan	1,049,150 sq miles	(2,717,300 sq km)
Sudan	967,493 sq miles	(2,505,810 sq km)

Smallest Countries

Country	Area (sq miles)	Area (sq km)
Vatican City	0.17 sq miles	(0.44 sq km)
Monaco	0.75 sq miles	(1.95 sq km)
Nauru	8 sq miles	(21 sq km)
Tuvalu	10 sq miles	(26 sq km)
San Marino	24 sq miles	(61 sq km)
Liechtenstein	62 sq miles	(160 sq km)
Marshall Islands	70 sq miles	(181 sq km)
St. Kitts & Nevis	101 sq miles	(261 sq km)
Maldives	116 sq miles	(300 sq km)
Malta	122 sq miles	(316 sq km)

Largest Islands

(to the nearest 1,000 - or 100,000 for the largest)

Island	Area (sq miles)	Area (sq km)
Greenland	849,400 sq miles	(2,200,000 sq km)
New Guinea	312,000 sq miles	(808,000 sq km)
Borneo	292,222 sq miles	(757,050 sq km)
Madagascar	229,300 sq miles	(594,000 sq km)
Sumatra	202,300 sq miles	(524,000 sq km)
Baffin Island	183,800 sq miles	(476,000 sq km)
Honshu	88,800 sq miles	(230,000 sq km)
Britain	88,700 sq miles	(229,800 sq km)
Victoria Island	81,900 sq miles	(212,000 sq km)
Ellesmere Island	75,700 sq miles	(196,000 sq km)

Richest Countries

(GNP per capita, in US$)

Country	GNP per capita
Liechtenstein	50,000
Luxembourg	39,470
Norway	38,730
Switzerland	36,170
USA	35,400
Japan	34,010
Denmark	30,260
Iceland	27,960
Monaco	27,500
Sweden	25,970

Poorest Countries

(GNP per capita, in US$)

Country	GNP per capita
Congo, Dem. Rep.	100
Burundi	100
Ethiopia	100
Somalia	120
Guinea-Bissau	130
Sierra Leone	140
Liberia	140
Malawi	160
Tajikistan	180
Niger	180

Most Populous Countries

China	1,304,200,000
India	1,065,500,000
USA	294,000,000
Indonesia	219,900,000
Brazil	178,500,000
Pakistan	153,600,000
Bangladesh	146,700,000
Russian Federation	143,200,000
Japan	127,700,000
Nigeria	124,000,000

Least Populous Countries

Vatican City	921
Tuvalu	11,305
Nauru	12,570
Palau	19,717
San Marino	28,119
Monaco	32,130
Liechtenstein	33,145
St. Kitts & Nevis	38,763
Marshall Islands	56,429
Antigua & Barbuda	67,897

Most Densely Populated Countries

Monaco	42,840 people per sq mile	(16,477 per sq km)
Singapore	18,220 people per sq mile	(7,049 per sq km)
Vatican City	5,359 people per sq mile	(2,070 per sq km)
Malta	3,177 people per sq mile	(1,231 per sq km)
Bangladesh	2,837 people per sq mile	(1,096 per sq km)
Maldives	2,741 people per sq mile	(1,060 per sq km)
Bahrain	2,652 people per sq mile	(1,025 per sq km)
Taiwan	1,815 people per sq mile	(701 per sq km)
Mauritius	1,671 people per sq mile	(645 per sq km)
Barbados	1,627 people per sq mile	(628 per sq km)

Most Sparsely Populated Countries

Mongolia	4 people per sq mile	(2 per sq km)
Namibia	6 people per sq mile	(2 per sq km)
Suriname	7 people per sq mile	(3 per sq km)
Mauritania	7 people per sq mile	(3 per sq km)
Iceland	7 people per sq mile	(3 per sq km)
Australia	7 people per sq mile	(3 per sq km)
Libya	8 people per sq mile	(3 per sq km)
Botswana	8 people per sq mile	(3 per sq km)
Canada	9 people per sq mile	(3 per sq km)
Guyana	10 people per sq mile	(4 per sq km)

Most Widely Spoken Languages

1. Chinese (Mandarin)
2. English
3. Hindi
4. Spanish
5. Russian
6. Arabic
7. Bengali
8. Portuguese
9. Malay-Indonesian
10. French

Countries With The Most Land Borders

14: China *(Afghanistan, Bhutan, Myanmar, India, Kazakhstan, Kyrgyzstan, Laos, Mongolia, Nepal, North Korea, Pakistan, Russian Federation, Tajikistan, Vietnam)*

14: Russian Federation *(Azerbaijan, Belarus, China, Estonia, Finland, Georgia, Kazakhstan, Latvia, Lithuania, Mongolia, North Korea, Norway, Poland, Ukraine)*

10: Brazil *(Argentina, Bolivia, Colombia, French Guiana, Guyana, Paraguay, Peru, Suriname, Uruguay, Venezuela)*

9: Congo, Dem. Rep. *(Angola, Burundi, Central African Republic, Congo, Rwanda, Sudan, Tanzania, Uganda, Zambia)*

9: Germany *(Austria, Belgium, Czech Republic, Denmark, France, Luxembourg, Netherlands, Poland, Switzerland)*

9: Sudan *(Central African Republic, Chad, Congo, Dem. Rep., Egypt, Eritrea, Ethiopia, Kenya, Libya, Uganda)*

8: Austria *(Czech Republic, Germany, Hungary, Italy, Liechtenstein, Slovakia, Slovenia, Switzerland)*

8: France *(Andorra, Belgium, Germany, Italy, Luxembourg, Monaco, Spain, Switzerland)*

8: Tanzania *(Burundi, Congo, Dem. Rep., Kenya, Malawi, Mozambique, Rwanda, Uganda, Zambia)*

8: Turkey *(Armenia, Azerbaijan, Bulgaria, Georgia, Greece, Iran, Iraq, Syria)*

8: Zambia *(Angola, Botswana, Congo, Dem. Rep., Malawi, Mozambique, Namibia, Tanzania, Zimbabwe)*

Longest Rivers

Nile (NE Africa)	4,160 miles	(6,695 km)
Amazon (South America)	4,049 miles	(6,516 km)
Yangtze (China)	3,915 miles	(6,299 km)
Mississippi/Missouri (US)	3,710 miles	(5,969 km)
Ob'-Irtysh (Russ. Fed.)	3,461 miles	(5,570 km)
Yellow River (China)	3,395 miles	(5,464 km)
Congo (Central Africa)	2,900 miles	(4,667 km)
Mekong (Southeast Asia)	2,749 miles	(4,425 km)
Lena (Russian Federation)	2,734 miles	(4,400 km)
Mackenzie (Canada)	2,640 miles	(4,250 km)
Yenisey (Russ. Federation)	2,541 miles	(4,090 km)

Highest Mountains

(HEIGHT ABOVE SEA LEVEL)

Everest	29,035 ft	(8,850 m)
K2	28,253 ft	(8,611 m)
Kanchenjunga I	28,210 ft	(8,598 m)
Makalu I	27,767 ft	(8,463 m)
Cho Oyu	26,907 ft	(8,201 m)
Dhaulagiri I	26,796 ft	(8,167 m)
Manaslu I	26,783 ft	(8,163 m)
Nanga Parbat I	26,661 ft	(8,126 m)
Annapurna I	26,547 ft	(8,091 m)
Gasherbrum I	26,471 ft	(8,068 m)

Largest Bodies of Inland Water

(WITH AREA AND DEPTH)

Caspian Sea	143,243 sq miles (371,000 sq km)	3,215 ft (980 m)
Lake Superior	32,151 sq miles (83,270 sq km)	1,289 ft (393 m)
Lake Victoria	26,560 sq miles (68,880 sq km)	328 ft (100 m)
Lake Huron	23,436 sq miles (60,700 sq km)	751 ft (229 m)
Lake Michigan	22,402 sq miles (58,020 sq km)	922 ft (281 m)
Lake Tanganyika	12,703 sq miles (32,900 sq km)	4,700 ft (1,435 m)
Great Bear Lake	12,274 sq miles (31,790 sq km)	1,047 ft (319 m)
Lake Baikal	11,776 sq miles (30,500 sq km)	5,712 ft (1,741 m)
Great Slave Lake	10,981 sq miles (28,440 sq km)	459 ft (140 m)
Lake Erie	9,915 sq miles (25,680 sq km)	197 ft (60 m)

......continued on p.166

Deepest Ocean Features

Feature	Depth (ft)	Depth (m)
Challenger Deep, Marianas Trench (Pacific)	36,201 ft	(11,034 m)
Vityaz III Depth, Tonga Trench (Pacific)	35,704 ft	(10,882 m)
Vityaz Depth, Kurile-Kamchatka Trench (Pacific)	34,588 ft	(10,542 m)
Cape Johnson Deep, Philippine Trench (Pacific)	34,441 ft	(10,497 m)
Kermadec Trench (Pacific)	32,964 ft	(10,047 m)
Ramapo Deep, Japan Trench (Pacific)	32,758 ft	(9,984 m)
Milwaukee Deep, Puerto Rico Trench (Atlantic)	30,185 ft	(9,200 m)
Argo Deep, Torres Trench (Pacific)	30,070 ft	(9,165 m)
Meteor Depth, South Sandwich Trench (Atlantic)	30,000 ft	(9,144 m)
Planet Deep, New Britain Trench (Pacific)	29,988 ft	(9,140 m)

Greatest Waterfalls

(Mean flow of water)

Waterfall	Flow (cu. ft/sec)	Flow (cu.m/sec)
Boyoma (Congo)	600,400 cu. ft/sec	(17,000 cu.m/sec)
Khône (Laos/Cambodia)	410,000 cu. ft/sec	(11,600 cu.m/sec)
Niagara (USA/Canada)	195,000 cu. ft/sec	(5,500 cu.m/sec)
Grande (Uruguay)	160,000 cu. ft/sec	(4,500 cu.m/sec)
Paulo Afonso (Brazil)	100,000 cu. ft/sec	(2,800 cu.m/sec)
Urubupunga (Brazil)	97,000 cu. ft/sec	(2,750 cu.m/sec)
Iguaçu (Argentina/Brazil)	62,000 cu. ft/sec	(1,700 cu.m/sec)
Maribondo (Brazil)	53,000 cu. ft/sec	(1,500 cu.m/sec)
Victoria (Zimbabwe)	39,000 cu. ft/sec	(1,100 cu.m/sec)
Kabalega (Uganda)	42,000 cu. ft/sec	(1,200 cu.m/sec)
Churchill (Canada)	35,000 cu. ft/sec	(1,000 cu.m/sec)
Cauvery (India)	33,000 cu. ft/sec	(900 cu.m/sec)

Highest Waterfalls

Waterfall	Height (ft)	Height (m)
Angel (Venezuela)	3,212 ft	(979 m)
Tugela (South Africa)	3,110 ft	(948 m)
Utigard (Norway)	2,625 ft	(800 m)
Mongefossen (Norway)	2,539 ft	(774 m)
Mtarazi (Zimbabwe)	2,500 ft	(762 m)
Yosemite (USA)	2,425 ft	(739 m)
Ostre Mardola Foss (Norway)	2,156 ft	(657 m)
Tyssestrengane (Norway)	2,119 ft	(646 m)
***Cuquenan** (Venezuela)	2,001 ft	(610 m)
Sutherland (New Zealand)	1,903 ft	(580 m)
***Kjellfossen** (Norway)	1,841 ft	(561 m)

** indicates that the total height is a single leap*

Largest Deserts

Desert	Area (sq miles)	Area (sq km)
Sahara	3,450,000 sq miles	(9,065,000 sq km)
Gobi	500,000 sq miles	(1,295,000 sq km)
Ar Rub al Khali	289,600 sq miles	(750,000 sq km)
Great Victorian	249,800 sq miles	(647,000 sq km)
Sonoran	120,000 sq miles	(311,000 sq km)
Kalahari	120,000 sq miles	(310,800 sq km)
Kara Kum	115,800 sq miles	(300,000 sq km)
Takla Makan	100,400 sq miles	(260,000 sq km)
Namib	52,100 sq miles	(135,000 sq km)
Thar	33,670 sq miles	(130,000 sq km)

NB – Most of Antarctica is a polar desert, with only 50 mm of precipitation annually

Hottest Inhabited Places

Djibouti (Djibouti)	86° F	(30 °C)
Timbouctou (Mali)	84.7° F	(29.3 °C)
Tirunelveli (India)	84.7° F	(29.3 °C)
Tuticorin (India)	84.7° F	(29.3 °C)
Nellore (India)	84.5° F	(29.2 °C)
Santa Marta (Colombia)	84.5° F	(29.2 °C)
Aden (Yemen)	84° F	(29 °C)
Madurai (India)	84° F	(29 °C)
Niamey (Niger)	84° F	(29 °C)
Hodeida (Yemen)	83.8° F	(28.8 °C)
Ouagadougou (Burkina Faso)	83.8° F	(28.8 °C)
Thanjavur (India)	83.8° F	(28.8 °C)
Tirunelveli (India)	83.8° F	(28.8 °C)

Driest Inhabited Places

Aswân (Egypt)	0.02 in	(0.5 mm)
Luxor (Egypt)	0.03 in	(0.7 mm)
Arica (Chile)	0.04 in	(1.1 mm)
Ica (Peru)	0.1 in	(2.3 mm)
Antofagasta (Chile)	0.2 in	(4.9 mm)
El Minya (Egypt)	0.2 in	(5.1 mm)
Asyût (Egypt)	0.2 in	(5.2 mm)
Callao (Peru)	0.5 in	(12.0 mm)
Trujillo (Peru)	0.55 in	(14.0 mm)
El Faiyûm (Egypt)	0.8 in	(19.0 mm)

Wettest Inhabited Places

Buenaventura (Colombia)	265 in	(6,743 mm)
Monrovia (Liberia)	202 in	(5,131 mm)
Pago Pago (American Samoa)	196 in	(4,990 mm)
Moulmein (Myanmar)	191 in	(4,852 mm)
Lae (Papua New Guinea)	183 in	(4,645 mm)
Baguio (Luzon Island, Philippines)	180 in	(4,573 mm)
Sylhet (Bangladesh)	176 in	(4,457 mm)
Padang (Sumatra, Indonesia)	166 in	(4,225 mm)
Bogor (Java, Indonesia)	166 in	(4,225 mm)
Conakry (Guinea)	171 in	(4,341 mm)

Glossary of Abbreviations

This Glossary provides a comprehensive guide to the abbreviations used in this Atlas, and in the Index.

A
abbrev. abbreviated
Afr. Afrikaans
Alb. Albanian
Amh. Amharic
anc. ancient
Ar. Arabic
Arm. Armenian
Az. Azerbaijani

B
Basq. Basque
Bel. Belorussian
Ben. Bengali
Bibl. Biblical
Bret. Breton
Bul. Bulgarian
Bur. Burmese

C
Cam. Cambodian
Cant. Cantonese
Cast. Castilian
Cat. Catalan
Chin. Chinese
Cro. Croat
Cz. Czech

D
Dan. Danish
Dut. Dutch

E
Eng. English
Est. Estonian
est. estimated

F
Faer. Faeroese
Fij. Fijian
Fin. Finnish
Flem. Flemish
Fr. French
Fris. Frisian

G
Geor. Georgian
Ger. German
Gk. Greek
Guj. Gujarati

H
Haw. Hawaiian
Heb. Hebrew
Hind. Hindi
hist. historical
Hung. Hungarian

I
Icel. Icelandic
Ind. Indonesian
In. Inuit
Ir. Irish
It. Italian

J
Jap. Japanese

K
Kaz. Kazakh
Kir. Kirghiz
Kor. Korean
Kurd. Kurdish

L
Lao. Laotian
Lapp. Lappish
Lat. Latin
Latv. Latvian
Lith. Lithanian
Lus. Lusatian

M
Mac. Macedonian
Mal. Malay
Malg. Malagasy
Malt. Maltese
Mong. Mongolian

N
Nepali. Nepali
Nor. Norwegian

O
off. officially

P
Pash. Pashtu
Per. Persian
Pol. Polish
Port. Portuguese
prev. previously

R
Rmsch. Romansch
Roman. Romanian
Rus. Russian

S
SCr. Serbo - Croatian
Serb. Serbian
Slvk. Slovak
Slvn. Slovene
Som. Somali
Sp. Spanish
Swa. Swahili
Swe. Swedish

T
Taj. Tajik
Th. Thai
Tib. Tibetan
Turk. Turkish
Turkm. Turkmenistan

U
Uigh. Uighur
Ukr. Ukrainian
Uzb. Uzbek

V
var. variant
Vtn. Vietnamese

W
Wel. Welsh

X
Xh. Xhosa

Y
Yugo. Yugoslavia

Key to country factboxes within the Index:

Formation
Date of independence

Population
Total population / population density - based on total *land* area .

Calorie consumption
Average number of calories consumed daily per person.

A

Aachen *94 A4 Dut.* Aken, *Fr.* Aix-la-Chapelle; *anc.* Aquae Grani, Aquisgranum. Nordrhein-Westfalen, W Germany
Aaiún *see* Laâyoune
Aalborg *80 D3 var.* Ålborg, Ålborg-Nørresundby; *anc.* Alburgum. Nordjylland, N Denmark
Aalen *95 B6* Baden-Württemberg, S Germany
Aalsmeer *86 C3* Noord-Holland, C Netherlands
Aalst *87 B6 Fr.* Alost. Oost-Vlaanderen, C Belgium
Aalten *86 E4* Gelderland, E Netherlands
Aalter *87 B5* Oost-Vlaanderen, NW Belgium
Äänekoski *85 D5* Länsi-Suomi, W Finland
Aar *see* Aare
Aare *95 A7 var.* Aar. *River* W Switzerland
Aarhus *see* Århus
Aat *see* Ath
Aba *75 G5* Abia, S Nigeria
Aba *77 E5* Orientale, NE Dem. Rep. Congo
Abā as Su'ūd *see* Najrān
Abaco Island *see* Great Abaco
Ābādān *120 C4* Khūzestān, SW Iran
Abai *see* Blue Nile
Abakan *114 D4* Respublika Khakasiya, S Russian Federation
Abancay *60 D4* Apurímac, SE Peru
Abariringa *see* Kanton
Abashiri *130 D2 var.* Abasiri. Hokkaidō, NE Japan
Abasiri *see* Abashiri
Ābaya Hāyk' *73 C5 Eng.* Lake Margherita, *It.* Abbaia. *Lake* SW Ethiopia
Ābay Wenz *see* Blue Nile
Abbeville *90 C2 anc.* Abbatis Villa. Somme, N France
'Abd al 'Azīz, Jabal *118 D2 mountain range* NE Syria
Abéché *76 C3 var.* Abécher, Abeshr. Ouaddaï, SE Chad
Abécher *see* Abéché
Abela *see* Ávila
Abemama *144 D2 var.* Apamama; *prev.* Roger Simpson Island. *Atoll* Tungaru, W Kiribati
Abengourou *75 E5* E Côte d'Ivoire
Aberdeen *88 D3 anc.* Devana. NE Scotland, UK
Aberdeen *45 E2* South Dakota, N USA
Aberdeen *46 B2* Washington, NW USA
Abergwaun *see* Fishguard
Abertawe *see* Swansea
Aberystwyth *89 C6* W Wales, UK
Abeshr *see* Abéché
Abhā *121 B6* 'Asīr, SW Saudi Arabia
Abidavichy *107 D7 Rus.* Obidovichi. Mahilyowskaya Voblasts', E Belarus
Abidjan *75 E5* S Côte d'Ivoire
Abilene *49 F3* Texas, SW USA
Abingdon *see* Pinta, Isla
Abkhazia *117 E1 autonomous republic* NW Georgia
Åbo *85 D6* Länsi-Suomi, W Finland
Aboisso *75 E5* SE Côte d'Ivoire
Abo, Massif d' *76 B1 mountain range* NW Chad
Abomey *75 F5* S Benin
Abou-Déïa *76 C3* Salamat, SE Chad
Abrantes *92 B3 var.* Abrántes. Santarém, C Portugal
Abrolhos Bank *56 E4 undersea feature* W Atlantic Ocean
Abrova *107 B6 Rus.* Obrovo. Brestskaya Voblasts', SW Belarus
Abrud *108 B4 Ger.* Gross-Schlatten, *Hung.* Abrudbánya. Alba, SW Romania
Abruzzese, Appennino *96 C4 mountain range* C Italy
Absaroka Range *44 B2 mountain range* Montana/Wyoming, NW USA
Abū aḑ Ḑuhūr *118 B3 Fr.* Aboudouhour. Idlib, NW Syria
Abu Dhabi *see* Abū Z̧aby
Abu Hamed *72 C3* River Nile, N Sudan
Abū Ḩardān *118 E3 var.* Hajîne. Dayr az Zawr, E Syria
Abuja *75 G4 country capital* (Nigeria) Federal Capital District, C Nigeria
Abū Kamāl *118 E3 Fr.* Abou Kémal. Dayr az Zawr, E Syria
Abula *see* Ávila
Abunã, Rio *62 C2 var.* Río Abuná. *River* Bolivia/Brazil
Abut Head *151 B6 headland* South Island, NZ
Ābuyē Mēda *72 D4 mountain* C Ethiopia
Abū Z̧abī *see* Abū Z̧aby
Abū Z̧aby *121 C5 var.* Abū Z̧abī, *Eng.* Abu Dhabi. *Country capital* (UAE) Abū Z̧aby, C UAE
Abyla *see* Ávila
Acalayong *77 A5* SW Equatorial Guinea
Acaponeta *50 D4* Nayarit, C Mexico
Acapulco *51 E5 var.* Acapulco de Juárez. Guerrero, S Mexico
Acapulco de Juárez *see* Acapulco
Acarai Mountains *59 F4 Sp.* Serra Acaraí. *Mountain range* Brazil/Guyana
Acarigua *58 D2* Portuguesa, N Venezuela
Accra *75 E5 country capital* (Ghana) SE Ghana
Achacachi *61 E4* La Paz, W Bolivia
Acklins Island *54 C2 island* SE Bahamas
Aconcagua, Cerro *64 B4 mountain* W Argentina
Açores *see* Azores
A Coruña *92 B1 Cast.* La Coruña, *Eng.* Corunna; *anc.* Caronium. Galicia, NW Spain
Acre *62 C2 off.* Estado do Acre. *State* W Brazil
Açu *63 G2 var.* Assu. Rio Grande do Norte, E Brazil
Ada *49 G2* Oklahoma, C USA
Ada *100 D3* Serbia, N Serbia and Montenegro (Yugo.)
Adalia, Gulf of *see* Antalya Körfezi
Adama *see* Nazrēt
Adamawa Highlands *76 B4 plateau* NW Cameroon
'Adan *121 B7 Eng.* Aden. SW Yemen
Adana *116 D4 var.* Seyhan. Adana, S Turkey
Adapazarı *116 B2 prev.* Ada Bazar. Sakarya, NW Turkey
Adare, Cape *154 B4 headland* Antarctica
Ad Dahnā' *120 C4 desert* E Saudi Arabia
Ad Dakhla *70 A4 var.* Dakhla. SW Western Sahara
Ad Dalanj *see* Dilling
Ad Damar *see* Ed Damer
Ad Damazīn *see* Ed Damazin
Ad Dāmir *see* Ed Damer
Ad Dammān *120 C4 var.* Dammām. Ash Sharqīyah, NE Saudi Arabia
Ad Dāmūr *see* Damoûr
Ad Dawḩah *120 C4 Eng.* Doha. *Country capital* (Qatar) C Qatar
Aḑ Ḑiffah *see* Libyan Plateau
Addis Ababa *see* Ādīs Ābeba
Addu Atoll *132 A5 atoll* S Maldives
Adelaide *149 B6 state capital* South Australia

Aden *see* 'Adan
Aden, Gulf of *121 C7 gulf* SW Arabian Sea
Adige *96 C2 Ger.* Etsch. *River* N Italy
Adirondack Mountains *41 F2 mountain range* New York, NE USA
Ādīs Ābeba *73 C5 Eng.* Addis Ababa. *Country capital* (Ethiopia) C Ethiopia
Adıyaman *117 E4* Adıyaman, SE Turkey
Adjud *108 C4* Vrancea, E Romania
Admiralty Islands *144 B3 island group* N PNG
Adra *93 E5* Andalucía, S Spain
Adrar *70 D3* C Algeria
Adrar des Iforas *see* Ifôghas, Adrar des
Adrian *40 C3* Michigan, N USA
Adriatic Sea *103 E2 Alb.* Deti Adriatik, *It.* Mare Adriatico, *SCr.* Jadransko More, *Slvn.* Jadransko Morje. *Sea* N Mediterranean Sea
Adycha *115 F2 river* NE Russian Federation
Aegean Sea *105 C5 Gk.* Aigaíon Pélagos, Aigaío Pélagos, *Turk.* Ege Denizi. *Sea* NE Mediterranean Sea
Aegviidu *106 D2 Ger.* Charlottenhof. Harjumaa, NW Estonia
Aelana *see* Al 'Aqabah
Aelok *see* Ailuk Atoll
Aelōnlaplap *see* Ailinglaplap Atoll
Aeolian Islands *see* Eolie, Isole
Afar Depression *see* Danakil Desert
Afghanistan *122 C4 Per.* Dowlat-e Eslāmī-ye Afghānestān; *prev.* Republic of Afghanistan. *Country* C Asia

Afghanistan 122

Official name Islamic State of Afghanistan
Formation 1919
Capital Kabul
Population 23.9 million / 95 people per sq mile (37 people per sq km)
Total area 250,000 sq. miles (647,500 sq. km)
Languages Pashtu, Tajik, Dari, Farsi, Uzbek, Turkmen
Religions Sunni Muslim 84%, Shi'a Muslim 15%, other 1%
Ethnic mix Pashtun 38%, Tajik 25%, Hazara 19%, Uzbek and Turkmen 15%, other 3%
Government Transitional regime
Currency New afghani = 100 puls
Literacy rate 36%
Calorie consumption 1539 calories

Afmadow *73 D6* Jubbada Hoose, S Somalia
Africa *68 continent*
Africa, Horn of *68 E4 physical region* Ethiopia/Somalia
Africana Seamount *141 A6 undersea feature* SW Indian Ocean
'Afrīn *118 B2* Ḩalab, N Syria
Afyon *116 B3 prev.* Afyonkarahisar. Afyon, W Turkey
Agadez *75 G3 prev.* Agadès. Agadez, C Niger
Agadir *70 B3* SW Morocco
Agana/Agaña *see* Hagåtña
Āgaro *73 C5* C Ethiopia
Agassiz Fracture Zone *143 G5 tectonic feature* S Pacific Ocean
Agathónisi *105 D6 island* Dodekánisos, Greece, Aegean Sea
Agde *91 C6 anc.* Agatha. Hérault, S France
Agedabia *see* Ajdābiyā
Agen *91 B5 anc.* Aginnum. Lot-et-Garonne, SW France
Aghri Dagh *see* Büyükağrı Dağı
Agiá *104 B4 var.* Ayiá. Thessalía, C Greece
Agialoúsa *102 D4 var.* Yenierenköy. NE Cyprus
Agía Marína *105 E6* Léros, Dodekánisos, Greece, Aegean Sea
Ágios Nikólaos *105 D8 var.* Áyios Nikólaos. Kríti, Greece, E Mediterranean Sea
Āgra *134 D3* Uttar Pradesh, N India
Agram *see* Zagreb
Ağrı *117 F3 var.* Karaköse; *prev.* Karakılısse. Ağrı, NE Turkey
Agri Dagi *see* Büyükağrı Dağı
Agrigento *97 C7 Gk.* Akragas; *prev.* Girgenti. Sicilia, Italy, C Mediterranean Sea
Agriovótano *105 C5* Évvoia, C Greece
Agropoli *97 D5* Campania, S Italy
Aguachica *58 B2* Cesar, N Colombia
Aguadulce *53 F5* Coclé, S Panama
Agua Prieta *50 B1* Sonora, NW Mexico
Aguascalientes *50 D4* Aguascalientes, C Mexico
Aguaytía *60 C3* Ucayali, C Peru
Aguilas *93 E4* Murcia, SE Spain
Aguililla *50 D4* Michoacán de Ocampo, SW Mexico
Agulhas Basin *69 D8 undersea feature* SW Indian Ocean
Agulhas Plateau *67 D6 undersea feature* SW Indian Ocean
Ahaggar *75 F2 high plateau region* SE Algeria
Ahlen *94 B4* Nordrhein-Westfalen, W Germany
Ahmadābād *134 C4 var.* Ahmedabad. Gujarāt, W India
Ahmadnagar *134 C5 var.* Ahmednagar. Mahārāshtra, W India
Ahmedabad *see* Ahmadābād
Ahmednagar *see* Ahmadnagar
Ahuachapán *52 B3* Ahuachapán, W El Salvador
Ahvāz *120 C3 var.* Ahwāz; *prev.* Nāsiri. Khūzestān, SW Iran
Ahvenanmaa *see* Åland
Ahwāz *see* Ahvāz
Aïdin *see* Aydın
Aígina *105 C6 var.* Aíyina, Egina. Aígina, C Greece
Aígio *105 B5 var.* Egio; *prev.* Aíyion. Dytikí Ellás, S Greece
Aiken *43 E2* South Carolina, SE USA
Ailigandí *53 G4* San Blas, NE Panama
Ailinglaplap Atoll *144 D2 var.* Aelōnlaplap. *Atoll* Ralik Chain, S Marshall Islands
Ailuk Atoll *144 D1 var.* Aelok. *Atoll* Ratak Chain, NE Marshall Islands
Ainaži *106 D3 Est.* Heinaste, *Ger.* Hainasch. Limbaži, N Latvia
'Aïn Ben Tili *74 D1* Tiris Zemmour, N Mauritania
Aintab *see* Gaziantep
Aïoun el Atrous *see* 'Ayoûn el 'Atroûs
Aïoun el Atroûss *see* 'Ayoûn el 'Atroûs
Aiquile *61 F4* Cochabamba, C Bolivia
Aïr *see* Aïr, Massif de l'
Air du Azbine *see* Aïr, Massif de l'
Aïr, Massif de l' *75 G2 var.* Aïr, Air du Azbine, Asben. *Mountain range* NC Niger
Aiud *108 B4 Ger.* Strassburg, *Hung.* Nagyenyed; *prev.* Engeten. Alba, SW Romania
Aix *see* Aix-en-Provence
Aix-en-Provence *91 D6 var.* Aix; *anc.* Aquae Sextiae. Bouches-du-Rhône, SE France
Aíyina *see* Aígina
Aíyion *see* Aígio
Aizkraukle *106 C4* Aizkraukle, S Latvia
Ajaccio *91 E7* Corse, France, C Mediterranean Sea
Ajaria *117 F2 autonomous republic* SW Georgia
Aj Bogd Uul *126 D2 mountain* SW Mongolia
Ajdābiyā *71 G2 var.* Agedabia, Ajdābiyah. NE Libya
Ajdābiyah *see* Ajdābiyā
Ajjinena *see* El Geneina
Ajmer *134 D3 var.* Ajmere. Rājasthān, N India
Ajmere *see* Ajmer
Ajo *48 A3* Arizona, SW USA
Akaba *see* Al 'Aqabah
Akamagaseki *see* Shimonoseki
Akasha *72 B3* Northern, N Sudan
Akchâr *74 C2 desert* W Mauritania
Akhalts'ikhe *117 F2* SW Georgia
Akhisar *116 A3* Manisa, W Turkey
Akhmîm *72 B2 anc.* Panopolis. C Egypt
Akhtubinsk *111 C7* Astrakhanskaya Oblast', SW Russian Federation
Akimiski Island *38 C3 island* Northwest Territories, C Canada
Akinovka *109 F4* Zaporiz'ka Oblast', S Ukraine
Akita *130 D4* Akita, Honshū, C Japan
Akjoujt *74 C2 prev.* Fort-Repoux. Inchiri, W Mauritania
Akkeshi *130 E2* Hokkaidō, NE Japan
Aklavik *36 D3* Northwest Territories, NW Canada
Akmola *see* Astana
Akpatok Island *39 E1 island* Northwest Territories, E Canada
Akra Dhrepanon *see* Drépano, Akrotírio
Akra Kanestron *see* Palioúri, Akrotírio
Akron *40 D4* Ohio, N USA
Akrotiri *see* Akrotírion
Akrotírion *102 C5 var.* Akrotiri. *UK air base* S Cyprus
Aksai Chin *124 B2 Chin.* Aksayqin. *Disputed region* China/India
Aksaray *116 C4* Aksaray, C Turkey
Akşehir *116 B4* Konya, W Turkey
Aktau *114 A4 Kaz.* Aqtaū; *prev.* Shevchenko. Mangistau, W Kazakhstan
Aktobe *114 B4 Kaz.* Aqtöbe. *prev.* Aktyubinsk. Aktyubinsk, NW Kazakhstan
Aktsyabrski *107 C7 Rus.* Oktyabr'skiy; *prev.* Karpilovka. Homyel'skaya Voblasts', SE Belarus
Aktyubinsk *see* Aktobe
Akula *77 C5* Equateur, NW Dem. Rep. Congo
Akureyri *83 E4* Nordhurland Eystra, N Iceland
Akyab *see* Sittwe
Alabama *51 G1 off.* State of Alabama; also known as Camellia State, Heart of Dixie, The Cotton State, Yellowhammer State. *State* S USA
Alabama River *42 C3 river* Alabama, S USA
Alaca *116 C3* Çorum, N Turkey
Alacant *see* Alicante
Alagoas *63 G2 off.* Estado de Alagoas. *State* E Brazil
Alajuela *53 E4* Alajuela, C Costa Rica
Alakanuk *36 C2* Alaska, USA
Al 'Alamayn *see* El 'Alamein
Al 'Amārah *120 C3 var.* Amara. E Iraq
Alamo *47 D6* Nevada, W USA
Alamogordo *48 D3* New Mexico, SW USA
Alamosa *44 C5* Colorado, C USA
Åland *85 C6 var.* Aland Islands, *Fin.* Ahvenanmaa. *Island group* SW Finland
Aland Islands *see* Åland
Aland Sea *see* Ålands Hav
Ålands Hav *85 C6 var.* Aland Sea. *Strait* Baltic Sea/Gulf of Bothnia
Alanya *116 C4* Antalya, S Turkey
Alappuzha *see* Alleppey
Al 'Aqabah *119 B8 var.* Akaba, Aqaba, 'Aqaba; *anc.* Aelana, Elath. Ma'ān, SW Jordan
Alasca, Golfo de *see* Alaska, Gulf of
Alaşehir *116 A4* Manisa, W Turkey
Al 'Ashārah *118 E3 var.* Ashara. Dayr az Zawr, E Syria
Alaska *36 C3 off.* State of Alaska; also known as Land of the Midnight Sun, The Last Frontier, Seward's Folly; *prev.* Russian America. *State* NW USA
Alaska, Gulf of *36 C4 var.* Golfo de Alasca. *Gulf* Canada/USA
Alaska Peninsula *36 C3 peninsula* Alaska, USA
Alaska Range *34 B2 mountain range* Alaska, USA
Al-Asnam *see* Chlef
Al Awaynāt *see* Al 'Uwaynāt
Al 'Aynā *119 B7* Al Karak, W Jordan
Alazeya *115 G2 river* NE Russian Federation
Al Bāb *118 B2* Ḩalab, N Syria
Albacete *93 E3* Castilla-La Mancha, C Spain
Al Baghdādī *120 B3 var.* Khān al Baghdādī. SW Iraq
Al Bāha *see* Al Bāḩah
Al Bāḩah *121 B5 var.* Al Bāha. Al Bāḩah, SW Saudi Arabia
Al Baḩr al Mayyit *see* Dead Sea
Alba Iulia *108 B4 Ger.* Weissenburg, *Hung.* Gyulafehérvár; *prev.* Bălgrad, Karlsburg, Károly-Fehérvár. Alba, W Romania
Albania *101 C7 Alb.* Republika e Shqipërisë, Shqipëria; *prev.* People's Socialist Republic of Albania. *Country* SE Europe

Albania 101

Official name Republic of Albania
Formation 1912
Capital Tirana
Population 3.2 million / 302 people per sq mile (117 people per sq km)
Total area 11,100 sq. miles (28,748 sq. km)
Languages Albanian, Greek
Religions Sunni Muslim 70%, Orthodox Christian 20%, Roman Catholic 10%
Ethnic mix Albanian 86%, Greek 12%, other 2%
Government Parliamentary system
Currency Lek = 100 qindarka (qintars)
Literacy rate 99%
Calorie consumption 2900 calories

Albany *38 C3 river* Ontario, S Canada
Albany *41 F3 state capital* New York, NE USA
Albany *42 D3* Georgia, SE USA
Albany *46 B3* Oregon, NW USA
Albany *147 B7* Western Australia
Al Bāridah *118 C4 var.* Bāridah. Ḩimş, C Syria
Al Başrah *120 C3 Eng.* Basra; *hist.* Busra, Bussora. SE Iraq
Al Batrūn *see* Batroûn
Al Bayḑā' *71 G2 var.* Beida. NE Libya
Albemarle Island *see* Isabela, Isla
Albemarle Sound *43 G1 inlet* W Atlantic Ocean
Albergaria-a-Velha *92 B2* Aveiro, N Portugal
Albert *90 C3* Somme, N France
Alberta *37 E4 province* SW Canada
Albert Edward Nyanza *see* Edward, Lake
Albert, Lake *73 B6 var.* Albert Nyanza, Lac Mobutu Sese Seko. *Lake* Uganda/Dem. Rep. Congo
Albert Lea *45 F3* Minnesota, N USA
Albert Nyanza *see* Albert, Lake
Albi *91 C6 anc.* Albiga. Tarn, S France
Ålborg *see* Aalborg
Ålborg-Nørresundby *see* Aalborg
Alborz, Reshteh-ye Kūhhā-ye *120 C2 Eng.* Elburz Mountains. *Mountain range* N Iran
Albuquerque *48 D2* New Mexico, SW USA
Al Burayqah *see* Marsá al Burayqah
Alburgum *see* Aalborg
Albury *149 C7* New South Wales, SE Australia
Alcácer do Sal *92 B4* Setúbal, W Portugal
Alcalá de Henares *93 E3 Ar.* Alkal'a; *anc.* Complutum. Madrid, C Spain

Alcamo *97 C7* Sicilia, Italy, C Mediterranean Sea
Alcañiz *93 F2* Aragón, NE Spain
Alcántara, Embalse de *92 C3 reservoir* W Spain
Alcaudete *92 D4* Andalucía, S Spain
Alcázar *see* Ksar-el-Kebir
Alcoi *see* Alcoy
Alcoy *93 F4 var.* Alcoi. País Valenciano, E Spain
Aldabra Group *79 G2 island group* SW Seychelles
Aldan *115 F3 river* NE Russian Federation
al Dar al Baida *see* Rabat
Alderney *90 A2 island* Channel Islands
Aleg *74 C3* Brakna, SW Mauritania
Aleksandropol' *see* Gyumri
Aleksin *111 B5* Tul'skaya Oblast', W Russian Federation
Aleksinac *100 E4* Serbia, SE Serbia and Montenegro (Yugo.)
Alençon *90 B3* Orne, N France
Alenquer *63 E2* Pará, NE Brazil
Aleppo *see* Ḩalab
Alert *37 F1* Ellesmere Island, Nunavut, N Canada
Alès *91 C6 prev.* Alais. Gard, S France
Aleşd *108 B3 Hung.* Élesd. Bihor, SW Romania
Alessandria *96 B2 Fr.* Alexandrie. Piemonte, N Italy
Ålesund *85 A5* Møre og Romsdal, S Norway
Aleutian Basin *113 G3 undersea feature* Bering Sea
Aleutian Islands *36 A3 island group* Alaska, USA
Aleutian Range *34 A2 mountain range* Alaska, USA
Aleutian Trench *113 H3 undersea feature* S Bering Sea
Alexander Archipelago *36 D4 island group* Alaska, USA
Alexander City *42 D2* Alabama, S USA
Alexander Island *154 A3 island* Antarctica
Alexandra *151 B7* Otago, South Island, NZ
Alexándreia *104 B4 var.* Alexándria. Kentrikí Makedonía, N Greece
Alexandria *72 B1 Ar.* Al Iskandarīyah. N Egypt
Alexándria *see* Alexándreia
Alexandria *42 B3* Louisiana, S USA
Alexandria *45 F2* Minnesota, N USA
Alexandria *108 C5* Teleorman, S Romania
Alexandroúpoli *104 D3 var.* Alexandroúpolis, *Turk.* Dedeagaç, Dedeagach. Anatolikí Makedonía kai Thráki, NE Greece
Alexandroúpolis *see* Alexandroúpoli
Al Fāshir *see* El Fasher
Alfatar *104 E1* Silistra, NE Bulgaria
Alfeiós *105 B6 prev.* Alfiós, *anc.* Alpheius, Alpheus. *River* S Greece
Alföld *see* Great Hungarian Plain
Alga *114 B4 Kaz.* Algha. Aktyubinsk, NW Kazakhstan
Algarve *92 B4 cultural region* S Portugal
Algeciras *92 C5* Andalucía, SW Spain
Algemesí *93 F3* País Valenciano, E Spain
Al-Genain *see* El Geneina
Alger *71 E1 var.* Algiers, El Djazaïr, Al Jazair. *Country capital* (Algeria) N Algeria
Algeria *70 C3 Country* N Africa

Algeria 70

Official name People's Democratic Republic of Algeria
Formation 1962
Capital Algiers
Population 31.8 million / 35 people per sq mile (13 people per sq km)

Algeria (continued)

Total area 919,590 sq. miles (2,381,740 sq. km)
Languages Arabic, Tamazight (Kabyle, Shawia, Tamashek), French
Religions Sunni Muslim 99%, Christian and Jewish 1%
Ethnic mix Arab 75%, Berber 24%, European and Jewish 1%
Government Presidential system
Currency Algerian dinar = 100 centimes
Literacy rate 69%
Calorie consumption 2987 calories

Algerian Basin *80 C5 var.* Balearic Plain *undersea feature* W Mediterranean Sea
Al Ghābah *121 E5 var.* Ghaba. C Oman
Alghero *97 A5* Sardegna, Italy, C Mediterranean Sea
Al Ghurdaqah *see* Hurghada
Algiers *see* Alger
Al Golea *see* El Goléa
Algona *45 F3* Iowa, C USA
Al Ḩajār al Gharbī *121 D5 mountain range* N Oman
Al Ḩasakah *118 D2 var.* Al Hasijah, El Haseke, *Fr.* Hassetché. Al Ḩasakah, NE Syria
Al Hasijah *see* Al Ḩasakah
Al Ḩillah *120 B3 var.* Hilla. C Iraq
Al Ḩisā *119 B7* Aţ Ţafīlah, W Jordan
Al Ḩudaydah *121 B6 Eng.* Hodeida. W Yemen
Al Hufūf *120 C4 var.* Hofuf. Ash Sharqīyah, NE Saudi Arabia
Aliákmonas *104 B4 prev.* Aliákmon, *anc.* Haliacmon. *River* N Greece
Alíartos *105 C5* Stereá Ellás, C Greece
Alicante *93 F4 Cat.* Alacant;. País Valenciano, SE Spain
Alice *49 G5* Texas, SW USA
Alice Springs *148 A4* Northern Territory, C Australia
Aliki *see* Alykí
Alima *77 B6 river* C Congo
Alindao *76 C4* Basse-Kotto, S Central African Republic
Aliquippa *40 D4* Pennsylvania, NE USA
Alistráti *104 C3* Kentrikí Makedonía, NE Greece
Alivéri *105 C5 var.* Alivérion. Évvoia, C Greece
Alivérion *see* Alivéri
Al Jabal al Akhḑar *71 G2 mountain range* NE Libya
Al Jabal ash Sharqī *see* Anti-Lebanon
Al Jafr *119 B7* Ma'ān, S Jordan
Al Jaghbūb *71 H3* NE Libya
Al Jahrā' *120 C4 var.* Al Jahrah, Jahra. C Kuwait
Al Jahrah *see* Al Jahrā'
Al Jawf *120 B4 var.* Jauf. Al Jawf, NW Saudi Arabia
Al Jazair *see* Alger
Al Jazīrah *118 E2 physical region* Iraq/Syria
Al Jīzah *see* El Gîza
Al Junaynah *see* El Geneina
Al Karak *119 B7 var.* El Kerak, Karak, Kerak; *anc.* Kir Moab, Kir of Moab. Al Karak, W Jordan
Al-Kasr al-Kebir *see* Ksar-el-Kebir
Al Khalīl *see* Hebron
Al Khārijah *see* El Khârga
Al Khufrah *71 H4* SE Libya
Al Khums *71 F2 var.* Homs, Khoms, Khums. NW Libya
Alkmaar *86 C2* Noord-Holland, NW Netherlands
Al Kūt *120 C3 var.* Kūt al 'Amārah, Kut al Imara. E Iraq
Al-Kuwait *see* Al Kuwayt
Al Kuwayt *120 C4 var.* Al-Kuwait, *Eng.* Kuwait, Kuwait City; *prev.* Qurein. *Country capital* (Kuwait) E Kuwait
Al Lādhiqīyah *118 A3 Eng.* Latakia, *Fr.* Lattaquié; *anc.* Laodicea, Laodicea ad Mare. Al Lādhiqīyah, W Syria
Allahābād *135 E3* Uttar Pradesh, N India
Allanmyo *136 B4* Magwe, C Myanmar
Allegheny Plateau *41 E3 mountain range* New York/Pennsylvania, NE USA
Allentown *41 F4* Pennsylvania, NE USA
Alleppey *132 C3 var.* Alappuzha; *prev.* Alleppi. Kerala, SW India
Alleppi *see* Alleppey
Alliance *44 D3* Nebraska, C USA
Al Līth *121 B5* Makkah, SW Saudi Arabia
Alma-Ata *see* Almaty
Almada *92 B4* Setúbal, W Portugal
Al Madīnah *121 A5 Eng.* Medina. Al Madīnah, W Saudi Arabia
Al Mafraq *119 B6 var.* Mafraq. Al Mafraq, N Jordan
Al Mahdīyah *see* Mahdia
Al Mahrah *121 C6 mountain range* E Yemen
Al Majma'ah *120 B4* Ar Riyāḑ, C Saudi Arabia
Al Mālikīyah *118 E1* Al Ḩasakah, NE Syria
Al Manāmah *120 C4 Eng.* Manama. *Country capital* (Bahrain) N Bahrain
Al Manāşif *118 E3 mountain range* E Syria
Almansa *93 F4* Castilla-La Mancha, C Spain
Al Marj *71 G2 var.* Barka, *It.* Barce. NE Libya
Almaty *114 C5 var.* Alma-Ata. Almaty, SE Kazakhstan
Al Mawşil *120 B2 Eng.* Mosul. N Iraq
Al Mayādīn *118 D3 var.* Mayadin, *Fr.* Meyadine. Dayr az Zawr, E Syria
Al Mazra' *see* Al Mazra'ah
Al Mazra'ah *119 B6 var.* Al Mazra', Mazra'a. Al Karak, W Jordan
Almelo *86 E3* Overijssel, E Netherlands
Almendra, Embalse de *92 C2 reservoir* Castilla-León, NW Spain
Almendralejo *92 C4* Extremadura, W Spain
Almere *86 C3 var.* Almere-stad. Flevoland, C Netherlands
Almere-stad *see* Almere
Almería *93 E5 Ar.* Al-Mariyya; *anc.* Unci, *Lat.* Portus Magnus. Andalucía, S Spain
Al'met'yevsk *111 D5* Respublika Tatarstan, W Russian Federation
Al Mīnā' *see* El Mina
Al Minyā *see* El Minya
Almirante *53 E4* Bocas del Toro, NW Panama
Al Mudawwarah *119 B8* Ma'ān, SW Jordan
Al Mukallā *121 C6 var.* Mukalla. SE Yemen
Al Obayyid *see* El Obeid
Alofi *145 F4 dependent territory capital* (Niue) W Niue
Aloja *106 D3* Limbaži, N Latvia
Alónnisos *105 C5 island* Vóreioi Sporádes, Greece, Aegean Sea
Álora *92 D5* Andalucía, S Spain
Alor, Kepulauan *139 E5 island group* E Indonesia
Al Oued *see* El Oued
Alpen *see* Alps
Alpena *40 D2* Michigan, N USA
Alpes *see* Alps
Alpha Cordillera *155 B3 var.* Alpha Ridge. *Undersea feature* Arctic Ocean
Alpha Ridge *see* Alpha Cordillera
Alphen *see* Alphen aan den Rijn
Alphen aan den Rijn *86 C3 var.* Alphen. Zuid-Holland, C Netherlands
Alpi *see* Alps
Alpine *49 E4* Texas, SW USA
Alpi Transilvaniei *see* Carpaţii Meridionali
Alps *102 C1 Fr.* Alpes, *Ger.* Alpen, *It.* Alpi. *Mountain range* C Europe
Al Qaḑārif *see* Gedaref
Al Qāmishlī *118 E1 var.* Kamishli, Qamishly. Al Ḩasakah, NE Syria
Al Qaşrayn *see* Kasserine
Al Qayrawān *see* Kairouan
Al-Qsar *see* Ksar-el-Kebir
Al Qubayyāt *see* Qoubaïyât
Alqueva, Barragem do *92 C4 reservoir* S Portugal
Al Qunayţirah *119 B5 var.* El Kuneitra, El Quneitra, Kuneitra, Qunaytra. Al Qunayţirah, SW Syria
Al Quşayr *118 B4 var.* El Quseir, Quşayr, *Fr.* Kousseir. Ḩimş, W Syria
Al Quwayrah *119 B8 var.* El Quweira. Ma'ān, SW Jordan
Alsace *90 E3 cultural region* NE France
Alsdorf *94 A4* Nordrhein-Westfalen, W Germany
Alt *see* Olt
Alta *84 D2 Fin.* Alattio. Finnmark, N Norway
Altai *see* Altai Mountains
Altai Mountains *126 C2 var.* Altai, *Chin.* Altay Shan, *Rus.* Altay. *Mountain range* Asia/Europe
Altamaha River *43 E3 river* Georgia, SE USA
Altamira *63 E2* Pará, NE Brazil
Altamura *97 E5 anc.* Lupatia. Puglia, SE Italy
Altar, Desierto de *50 A1 var.* Sonoran Desert. *Desert* Mexico/USA *see also* Sonoran Desert
Altay *126 C2 Chin.* A-le-t'ai, *Mong.* Sharasume; *prev.* Ch'eng-hua, Chenghwa. Xinjiang Uygur Zizhiqu, NW China
Altay *see* Altai Mountains
Altay *126 D2* Govĭ-Altay, W Mongolia
Altay Shan *see* Altai Mountains
Altin Köprü *120 B3 var.* Altun Kupri. N Iraq
Altiplano *61 F4 physical region* W South America
Alton *40 B5* Illinois, N USA
Alton *40 B4* Missouri, C USA
Altoona *41 E4* Pennsylvania, NE USA
Alto Paraná *see* Paraná
Altun Kupri *see* Altin Köprü
Altun Shan *126 C3 var.* Altyn Tagh. *Mountain range* NW China
Altus *49 F2* Oklahoma, C USA
Altyn Tagh *see* Altun Shan
Al Ubayyiḑ *see* El Obeid
Alūksne *106 D3 Ger.* Marienburg. Alūksne, NE Latvia
Al 'Ulā *120 A4* Al Madīnah, NW Saudi Arabia
Al 'Umarī *119 C6* 'Ammān, E Jordan
Alupka *109 F5* Respublika Krym, S Ukraine
Alushta *109 F5* Respublika Krym, S Ukraine
Al 'Uwaynāt *71 F4 var.* Al Awaynāt. SW Libya
Alva *49 F1* Oklahoma, C USA
Alvarado *51 F4* Veracruz-Llave, E Mexico
Alvin *49 H4* Texas, SW USA
Al Wajh *120 A4* Tabūk, NW Saudi Arabia
Alwar *134 D3* Rājasthān, N India
Al Wari'ah *120 C4* Ash Sharqīyah, N Saudi Arabia
Alykí *104 C4 var.* Aliki. Thásos, N Greece
Alytus *107 B5 Pol.* Olita. Alytus, S Lithuania
Alzette *87 D8 river* S Luxembourg
Amadeus, Lake *147 D5 seasonal lake* Northern Territory, C Australia
Amadi *73 B5* Western Equatoria, SW Sudan
Amadjuak Lake *37 G3 lake* Baffin Island, Nunavut, N Canada
Amakusa-nada *131 A7 gulf* Kyūshū, SW Japan
Åmål *85 B6* Västra Götaland, S Sweden

Amami-guntō 130 *A3 island group* SW Japan
Amami-ō-shima 130 *A3 island* S Japan
Amantea 97 *D6* Calabria, SW Italy
Amapá 63 *E1* Amapá, NE Brazil
Amara *see* Al 'Amārah
Amarapura 136 *B3* Mandalay, C Myanmar
Amarillo 49 *E2* Texas, SW USA
Amay 87 *C6* Liège, E Belgium
Amazon 63 *E1 Sp.* Amazonas. *River* Brazil/Peru
Amazon Basin 62 *D2 basin* N South America
Amazon, Mouths of the 63 *F1 delta* NE Brazil
Ambam 77 *B5* Sud, S Cameroon
Ambanja 79 *G2* Antsirañana, N Madagascar
Ambarchik 115 *G2* Respublika Sakha (Yakutiya), NE Russian Federation
Ambato 60 *B1* Tungurahua, C Ecuador
Ambérieu-en-Bugey 91 *D5* Ain, E France
Amboasary 79 *F4* Toliara, S Madagascar
Ambon 139 *F4 prev.* Amboina, Amboyna. Pulau Ambon, E Indonesia
Ambositra 79 *G3* Fianarantsoa, SE Madagascar
Ambrim *see* Ambrym
Ambriz 78 *A1* Bengo, NW Angola
Ambrym 144 *D4 var.* Ambrim. *Island* C Vanuatu
Amchitka Island 36 *A2 island* Aleutian Islands, Alaska, USA
Amdo 126 *C5* Xizang Zizhiqu, W China
Ameland 86 *D1 Fris.* It Amelân. *Island* Waddeneilanden, N Netherlands
America-Antarctica Ridge 67 *C7 undersea feature* S Atlantic Ocean
American Falls Reservoir 46 *E4 reservoir* Idaho, NW USA
American Samoa 145 *E4 US unincorporated territory* W Polynesia
Amersfoort 86 *D3* Utrecht, C Netherlands
Ames 45 *F3* Iowa, C USA
Amfilochía 105 *A5 var.* Amfilokhía. Dytikí Ellás, C Greece
Amfilokhía *see* Amfilochía
Amga 115 *F3 river* NE Russian Federation
Amherst 39 *F4* Nova Scotia, SE Canada
Amida *see* Diyarbakır
Amiens 90 *C3 anc.* Ambianum, Samarobriva. Somme, N France
Amíndaion *see* Amýntaio
Amindeo *see* Amýntaio
Amīndīvi Islands 132 *A2 island group* Lakshadweep, India, N Indian Ocean
Amirante Islands 79 *G1 var.* Amirantes Group. *Island group* C Seychelles
Amirantes Group *see* Amirante Islands
Amistad Reservoir 49 *F4 var.* Presa de la Amistad. *Reservoir* Mexico/USA
'Ammān 119 *B6 var.* Amman; *anc.* Philadelphia, *Bibl.* Rabbah Ammon, Rabbath Ammon. *Country capital* (Jordan) 'Ammān, NW Jordan
Amman *see* 'Ammān
Ammassalik 82 *D4 var.* Angmagssalik. S Greenland
Ammóchostos 102 *D5 var.* Famagusta, Gazimağusa. E Cyprus
Āmol 120 *D2 var.* Amul. Māzandarān, N Iran
Amorgós 105 *D6 island* Kykládes, Greece, Aegean Sea
Amorgós 105 *D6* Amorgós, Kykládes, Greece, Aegean Sea
Amos 38 *D4* Québec, SE Canada
Amourj 74 *D3* Hodh ech Chargui, SE Mauritania
Amoy *see* Xiamen
Ampato, Nevado 61 *E4 mountain* S Peru
Amposta 93 *F2* Cataluña, NE Spain
Amrāvati 134 *D4 prev.* Amraoti. Mahārāshtra, C India
Amritsar 134 *D2* Punjab, N India
Amstelveen 86 *C3* Noord-Holland, C Netherlands
Amsterdam 86 *C3 country capital* (Netherlands) Noord-Holland, C Netherlands
Amsterdam Island 141 *C6 island* NE French Southern and Antarctic Territories
Am Timan 76 *C3* Salamat, SE Chad
Amu Darya 122 *D2 Rus.* Amudar'ya, *Taj.* Dar"yoi Amu, *Turkm.* Amyderya, *Uzb.* Amudaryo; *anc.* Oxus. *River* C Asia
Amu-Dar'ya *see* Āmyderýa
Amul *see* Āmol
Amund Ringnes Island 37 *F2 island* Nunavut, N Canada
Amundsen Basin *see* Fram Basin
Amundsen Gulf 37 *E2 gulf* Northwest Territories, N Canada
Amundsen Plain 154 *A4 undersea feature* S Pacific Ocean
Amundsen-Scott 154 *B3 US research station* Antarctica
Amundsen Sea 154 *A4 sea* S Pacific Ocean
Amuntai 138 *D4 prev.* Amoentai. Borneo, C Indonesia
Amur 115 *G4 Chin.* Heilong Jiang. *River* China/Russian Federation
Amvrosiyivka 109 *H3 Rus.* Amvrosiyevka. Donets'ka Oblast', SE Ukraine
Amyderýa 123 *E3 Rus.* Amu-Dar'ya. Lebapskiy Velayat, NE Turkmenistan
Amýntaio 104 *B4 var.* Amindeo; *prev.* Amíndaion. Dytikí Makedonía, N Greece
Anabar 115 *E2 river* NE Russian Federation
An Abhainn Mhór *see* Blackwater
Anaco 59 *E2* Anzoátegui, NE Venezuela
Anaconda 44 *B2* Montana, NW USA
Anacortes 46 *B1* Washington, NW USA
Anadolu Dağları *see* Doğu Karadeniz Dağları
Anadyr' 115 *G1 river* NE Russian Federation
Anadyr' 115 *H1* Chukotskiy Avtonomnyy Okrug, NE Russian Federation
Anadyr, Gulf of *see* Anadyrskiy Zaliv
Anadyrskiy Zaliv 115 *H1 Eng.* Gulf of Anadyr. *Gulf* NE Russian Federation
Anáfi 105 *D7 anc.* Anaphe. *Island* Kykládes, Greece, Aegean Sea
'Ānah *see* 'Annah
Anaheim 46 *E2* California, W USA
Anaiza *see* 'Unayzah
Analalava 79 *G2* Mahajanga, NW Madagascar
Anamur 116 *C5* İçel, S Turkey
Anantapur 132 *C2* Andhra Pradesh, S India
Anápolis 63 *F3* Goiás, C Brazil
Anār 120 *D3* Kermān, C Iran
Anatolia 116 *C4 plateau* C Turkey
Anatom *see* Aneityum
Añatuya 64 *C3* Santiago del Estero, N Argentina
An Bhearú *see* Barrow
Anchorage 36 *C3* Alaska, USA
Ancona 96 *C3* Marche, C Italy
Ancud 65 *B6 prev.* San Carlos de Ancud. Los Lagos, S Chile
Åndalsnes 85 *A5* Møre og Romsdal, S Norway
Andalucía 92 *D4 cultural region* S Spain
Andalusia 42 *C3* Alabama, S USA
Andaman Islands 124 *B4 island group* India, NE Indian Ocean
Andaman Sea 124 *C4 sea* NE Indian Ocean
Andenne 87 *C6* Namur, SE Belgium
Anderlues 87 *B7* Hainaut, S Belgium
Anderson 40 *C4* Indiana, N USA
Andes 64 *B3 mountain range* W South America
Andhra Pradesh 135 *E5 state* E India
Andijon 123 *F2 Rus.* Andizhan. Andijon Wiloyati, E Uzbekistan
Andikíthira *see* Antikýthira
Andipaxi *see* Antípaxoi
Andípsara *see* Antípsara
Ándissa *see* Ántissa
Andkhvoy 122 *D3* Fāryāb, N Afghanistan
Andorra 91 *A7 Cat.* Valls d'Andorra, *Fr.* Vallée d'Andorre. *Country* SW Europe

Andorra 91

Official name Principality of Andorra
Formation 1278
Capital Andorra la Vella
Population 69,150 / 384 people per sq mile (149 people per sq km)
Total area 181 sq. miles (468 sq. km)
Languages Spanish, Catalan, French, Portuguese
Religions Roman Catholic 94%, other 6%
Ethnic mix Spanish 46%, Andorran 28%, other 18%, French 8%
Government Parliamentary system
Currency Euro = 100 cents
Literacy rate 99%
Calorie consumption Not available

Andorra *see* Andorra la Vella
Andorra la Vella 91 *A8 var.* Andorra, *Fr.* Andorre la Vielle, *Sp.* Andorra la Vieja. *Country capital* (Andorra) C Andorra
Andorra la Vieja *see* Andorra la Vella
Andorre la Vielle *see* Andorra la Vella
Andover 89 *D7* S England, UK
Andøya 84 *C2 island* C Norway
Andreanof Islands 36 *A3 island group* Aleutian Islands, Alaska, USA
Andrews 49 *E3* Texas, SW USA
Andrew Tablemount 140 *A4 var.* Gora Andryu. *Undersea feature* W Indian Ocean
Andria 97 *D5* Puglia, SE Italy
An Droichead Nua *see* Newbridge
Ándros 105 *C6 island* Kykládes, Greece, Aegean Sea
Ándros 105 *D6* Ándros, Kykládes, Greece, Aegean Sea
Andros Island 54 *B2 island* NW Bahamas
Andros Town 54 *C1* Andros Island, NW Bahamas
Aneityum 144 *D5 var.* Anatom; *prev.* Kéamu. *Island* S Vanuatu
Ānewetak *see* Enewetak Atoll
Angara 115 *E4 river* C Russian Federation
Angarsk 115 *E4* Irkutskaya Oblast', S Russian Federation
Ånge 85 *C5* Västernorrland, C Sweden
Ángel de la Guarda, Isla 50 *B2 island* NW Mexico
Angeles 139 *E1 off.* Angeles City. Luzon, N Philippines
Angel Falls *see* Ángel, Salto
Ángel, Salto 59 *E3 Eng.* Angel Falls. *Waterfall* E Venezuela
Ångermanälven 84 *C4 river* N Sweden
Angermünde 94 *D3* Brandenburg, NE Germany
Angers 90 *B4 anc.* Juliomagus. Maine-et-Loire, NW France
Anglesey 89 *C5 island* NW Wales, UK
Anglet 91 *A6* Pyrénées-Atlantiques, SW France
Angleton 49 *H4* Texas, SW USA
Angmagssalik *see* Ammassalik
Ang Nam Ngum 136 *C4 lake* C Laos
Angola 78 *B2 prev.* People's Republic of Angola, Portuguese West Africa. *Country* SW Africa

Angola 78

Official name Republic of Angola
Formation 1975
Capital Luanda
Population 13.6 million / 28 people per sq mile (11 people per sq km)
Total area 481,351 sq. miles (1,246,700 sq. km)
Languages Portuguese, Umbundu, Kimbundu, Kikongo
Religions Roman Catholic 50%, other 30%, Protestant 20%
Ethnic mix Ovimbundu 37%, other 25%, Kimbundu 25%, Bakongo 13%
Government Presidential system
Currency Readjusted kwanza = 100 lwei
Literacy rate 40%
Calorie consumption 1953

Angola Basin 69 *B5 undersea feature* E Atlantic Ocean
Angostura, Presa de la 51 *G5 reservoir* SE Mexico
Angoulême 91 *B5 anc.* Iculisma. Charente, W France
Angoumois 91 *B5 cultural region* W France
Angren 123 *F2* Toshkent Wiloyati, E Uzbekistan
Anguilla 55 *G3 UK dependent territory* E West Indies
Anguilla Cays 54 *B2 islets* SW Bahamas
Anhui 128 *C5 var.* Anhui Sheng, Anhwei, Wan. Admin. region *province* E China
Anhui Sheng *see* Anhui
Anhwei *see* Anhui
Anina 108 *A4 Ger.* Steierdorf, *Hung.* Stájerlakanina; *prev.* Ştaierdorf-Anina, Steierdorf-Anina, Steyerlak-Anina. Caraş-Severin, SW Romania
Anjou 90 *B4 cultural region* NW France
Anjouan 79 *F2 var.* Nzwani, Johanna Island. *Island* SE Comoros
Ankara 116 *C3 prev.* Angora, *anc.* Ancyra. *Country capital* (Turkey) Ankara, C Turkey
Ankeny 45 *F3* Iowa, C USA
Anklam 94 *D2* Mecklenburg-Vorpommern, NE Germany
Anykščiai 106 *C4* Anykščiai, E Lithuania
An Longfort *see* Longford
An Mhuir Cheilteach *see* Celtic Sea
Annaba 71 *E1 prev.* Bône. NE Algeria
An Nafūd 120 *B4 desert* NW Saudi Arabia
'Annah 120 *B3 var.* 'Ānah. NW Iraq
An Najaf 120 *B3 var.* Najaf. S Iraq
Annamitique, Chaîne 136 *D4 mountain range* C Laos
Annapolis 41 *F4 state capital* Maryland, NE USA
Annapurna 135 *E3 mountain* C Nepal
An Nāqūrah *see* En Nâqoûra
Ann Arbor 40 *C3* Michigan, N USA
An Nāşirīyah 120 *C3 var.* Nasiriya. SE Iraq
Annecy 91 *D5 anc.* Anneciacum. Haute-Savoie, E France
An Nīl al Azraq *see* Blue Nile
Anniston 42 *D2* Alabama, S USA
Annotto Bay 54 *B4* C Jamaica
An Ómaigh *see* Omagh
Anqing 128 *D5* Anhui, E China
Anse La Raye 55 *F1* NW Saint Lucia
Anshun 128 *B6* Guizhou, S China
Ansongo 75 *E3* Gao, E Mali
An Srath Bán *see* Strabane

Antakya *116 D4 anc.* Antioch, Antiochia. Hatay, S Turkey
Antalaha *79 G2* Antsirañana, NE Madagascar
Antalya *116 B4 prev.* Adalia, *anc.* Attaleia, *Bibl.* Attalia. Antalya, SW Turkey
Antalya, Gulf of *see* Antalya Körfezi
Antalya Körfezi *116 B4 var.* Gulf of Adalia, *Eng.* Gulf of Antalya. *Gulf* SW Turkey
Antananarivo *79 G3 prev.* Tananarive. *Country capital* (Madagascar) Antananarivo, C Madagascar
Antarctica *154 B3 continent*
Antarctic Peninsula *154 A2 peninsula* Antarctica
Antep *see* Gaziantep
Antequera *92 D5 anc.* Anticaria, Antiquaria. Andalucía, S Spain
Antequera *see* Oaxaca
Antibes *91 D6 anc.* Antipolis. Alpes-Maritimes, SE France
Anticosti, Île d' *39 F3 Eng.* Anticosti Island. *Island* Québec, E Canada
Antigua *55 G3 island* S Antigua and Barbuda, Leeward Islands
Antigua and Barbuda *55 G3 country* E West Indies

Antigua and Barbuda 55

Official name Antigua and Barbuda
Formation 1981
Capital St. John's
Population 67,897 / 399 people per sq mile (154 people per sq km)
Total area 170 sq. miles (442 sq. km)
Languages English, English patois
Religions Anglican 45%, Other Protestant 42%, Roman Catholic 10%, Rastafarian 1%, other 2%
Ethnic mix Black African 95%, other 5%
Government Parliamentary system
Currency Eastern Caribbean dollar = 100 cents
Literacy rate 87%
Calorie consumption 2381 calories

Antikýthira *105 B7 var.* Andikíthira. *Island* S Greece
Anti-Lebanon *118 B4 var.* Jebel esh Sharqi, *Ar.* Al Jabal ash Sharqī, *Fr.* Anti-Liban. *Mountain range* Lebanon/Syria
Anti-Liban *see* Anti-Lebanon
Antípaxoi *105 A5 var.* Andipaxi. *Island* Iónioi Nísoi, Greece, C Mediterranean Sea
Antipodes Islands *142 D5 island group,* S NZ
Antípsara *105 D5 var.* Andípsara. *Island* E Greece
Ántissa *105 D5 var.* Ándissa. Lésvos, E Greece
An tIúr *see* Newry
Antofagasta *64 B2* Antofagasta, N Chile
Antony *90 E2* Hauts-de-Seine, N France
Antserana *see* Antsirañana
An tSionainn *see* Shannon
Antsirañana *79 G2 var.* Antserana; *prev.* Antsirane, Diégo-Suarez. Antsirañana, N Madagascar
Antsirane *see* Antsirañana
Antsohihy *79 G2* Mahajanga, NW Madagascar
An-tung *see* Dandong
Antwerp *see* Antwerpen
Antwerpen *87 C5 Eng.* Antwerp, *Fr.* Anvers. Antwerpen, N Belgium
Anuradhapura *132 D3* North Central Province, C Sri Lanka
Anyang *128 C4* Henan, C China
A'nyêmaqên Shan *126 D4 mountain range* C China
Anzio *97 C5* Lazio, C Italy
Aomen *see* Macao
Aomori *130 D3* Aomori, Honshū, C Japan
Aóos *see* Vjosës, Lumi i
Aoraki *151 B6 prev.* Aorangi, Mount Cook. *Mountain* South Island, NZ
Aorangi *see* Aoraki
Aosta *96 A1 anc.* Augusta Praetoria. Valle d'Aosta, NW Italy
Ao Thai *see* Thailand, Gulf of
Aoukâr *74 D3 var.* Aouker. *Plateau* C Mauritania
Aouk, Bahr *76 C4 river* Central African Republic/Chad
Aouker *see* Aoukâr
Aozou *76 C1* Borkou-Ennedi-Tibesti, N Chad
Apalachee Bay *42 D3 bay* Florida, SE USA
Apalachicola River *42 D3 river* Florida, SE USA
Apamama *see* Abemama
Apaporis, Río *58 C4 river* Brazil/Colombia
Apatity *110 C2* Murmanskaya Oblast', NW Russian Federation
Ape *106 D3* Alūksne, NE Latvia
Apeldoorn *86 D3* Gelderland, E Netherlands
Apennines *see* Appennino
Āpia *145 F4 country capital* (Samoa) Upolu, SE Samoa
Apoera *59 G3* Sipaliwini, NW Suriname
Apostle Islands *40 B1 island group* Wisconsin, N USA
Appalachian Mountains *35 D5 mountain range* E USA
Appennino *96 E2 Eng.* Apennines. *Mountain range* Italy/San Marino
Appingedam *86 E1* Groningen, NE Netherlands
Appleton *40 B2* Wisconsin, N USA
Apure, Río *58 C2 river* W Venezuela
Apurímac, Río *60 D3 river* S Peru
Apuseni, Munţii *108 A4 mountain range* W Romania
'Aqaba *see* Al 'Aqabah
Aqaba, Gulf of *120 A4 var.* Gulf of Elat, *Ar.* Khalīj al 'Aqabah; *anc.* Sinus Aelaniticus. *Gulf* NE Red Sea
Āqchah *123 E3 var.* Āqcheh. Jowzjān, N Afghanistan
Āqcheh *see* Āqchah
Aquae Augustae *see* Dax
Aquae Sextiae *see* Aix-en-Provence
Aquae Tarbelicae *see* Dax
Aquidauana *63 E4* Mato Grosso do Sul, S Brazil
Aquila *see* L'Aquila
Aquila degli Abruzzo *see* L'Aquila
Aquitaine *91 B6 cultural region* SW France
'Arabah, Wādī al *135 B7 Heb.* Ha'Arava. *Dry watercourse* Israel/Jordan
Arabian Basin *124 A4 undersea feature* N Arabian Sea
Arabian Desert *see* Eastern Desert
Arabian Peninsula *121 B5 peninsula* SW Asia
Arabian Sea *124 A3 sea* NW Indian Ocean
Aracaju *63 G3 state capital* Sergipe, E Brazil
Araçuai *63 F3* Minas Gerais, SE Brazil
Arad *108 A4* Arad, W Romania
'Arad *119 B7* Southern, S Israel
Arafura Sea *142 A3 Ind.* Laut Arafuru. *Sea* W Pacific Ocean
Aragón *93 E2 cultural region* E Spain
Araguaia, Río *63 E3 var.* Araguaya. *River* C Brazil
Araguari *63 F3* Minas Gerais, SE Brazil
Araguaya *see* Araguaia, Río
Arāk *120 C3 prev.* Sultānābād. Markazī, W Iran
Arakan Yoma *136 A3 mountain range* W Myanmar
Aral Sea *122 C1 Kaz.* Aral Tengizi, *Rus.* Aral'skoye More, *Uzb.* Orol Dengizi. *Inland sea* Kazakhstan/Uzbekistan
Aral'sk *114 B4 Kaz.* Aral. Kyzylorda, SW Kazakhstan
Aranda de Duero *92 D2* Castilla-León, N Spain
Arandelovac *100 D4 prev.* Arandjelovac. Serbia, C Serbia and Montenegro (Yugo.)
Aranjuez *92 D3 anc.* Ara Jovis. Madrid, C Spain
Araouane *75 E2* Tombouctou, N Mali
'Ar'ar *120 B3* Al Ḥudūd ash Shamālīyah, NW Saudi Arabia
Aras *117 G3 Arm.* Arak's, *Az.* Araz Nehri, *Per.* Rūd-e Aras, *Rus.* Araks; *prev.* Araxes. *River* SW Asia
Arauca *58 C2* Arauca, NE Colombia
Arauca, Río *58 C2 river* Colombia/Venezuela
Arbela *see* Arbīl
Arbīl *120 B2 var.* Erbil, Irbīl, *Kurd.* Hawlēr; *anc.* Arbela. N Iraq
Arbroath *88 D3 anc.* Aberbrothock. E Scotland, UK
Arbyzynka *109 E3 Rus.* Arbuzinka. Mykolayivs'ka Oblast', S Ukraine
Arcachon *91 B5* Gironde, SW France
Arcata *46 A4* California, W USA
Archangel *see* Arkhangel'sk
Archangel Bay *see* Chëshskaya Guba
Archidona *92 D5* Andalucía, S Spain
Archipel des Australes *see* Australes, Îles
Archipel des Tuamotu *see* Tuamotu, Îles
Archipel de Tahiti *see* Société, Archipel de la
Arco *96 C2* Trentino-Alto Adige, N Italy
Arctic-Mid Oceanic Ridge *see* Nansen Cordillera
Arctic Ocean *172 B3 ocean*
Arda *104 C3 var.* Ardhas, *Gk.* Ardas. *River* Bulgaria/Greece *see also* Ardas
Arda *see* Ardas
Ardabīl *120 C2 var.* Ardebil. Ardabīl, NW Iran
Ardakān *120 D3* Yazd, C Iran
Ardas *104 D3 var.* Ardhas, *Bul.* Arda. *River* Bulgaria/Greece *see also* Arda
Ardas *see* Arda
Arḑ aş Şawwān *119 C7 var.* Ardh es Suwwān. *Plain* S Jordan
Ardebil *see* Ardabīl
Ardèche *91 C5 cultural region* E France
Ardennes *87 C8 plateau* W Europe
Ardhas *see* Ardas
Ardh es Suwwān *see* Arḑ aş Şawwān
Ardino *104 D3* Kŭrdzhali, S Bulgaria
Ard Mhacha *see* Armagh
Ardmore *49 G2* Oklahoma, C USA
Arelas *see* Arles
Arelate *see* Arles
Arendal *85 A6* Aust-Agder, S Norway
Arenys de Mar *93 G2* Cataluña, NE Spain
Areópoli *105 B7 prev.* Areópolis. Pelopónnisos, S Greece
Arequipa *61 E4* Arequipa, SE Peru
Arezzo *96 C3 anc.* Arretium. Toscana, C Italy
Argalastí *105 C5* Thessalía, C Greece
Argenteuil *90 D1* Val-d'Oise, N France
Argentina *65 B5 Country* S South America

Argentina 65

Official name Republic of Argentina
Formation 1816
Capital Buenos Aires
Population 38.4 million / 36 people per sq mile (14 people per sq km)
Total area 1,068,296 sq. miles (2,766,890 sq. km)
Languages Spanish, Italian, Amerindian languages

Argentina (continued)

Religions Roman Catholic 90%, other 6%, Protestant 2%, Jewish 2%
Ethnic mix Indo-European 83%, Mestizo 14%, Jewish 2%, Amerindian 1%
Government Presidential system
Currency Argentine peso = 100 centavos
Literacy rate 97%
Calorie consumption 3171 calories

Argentina Basin *see* Argentine Basin
Argentine Basin *57 C7 var.* Argentina Basin. *Undersea feature* SW Atlantic Ocean
Argentine Rise *see* Falkland Plateau
Arghandāb, Daryā-ye *123 E5 river* SE Afghanistan
Argirocastro *see* Gjirokastër
Argo *72 B3* Northern, N Sudan
Argo Fracture Zone *141 C5 tectonic feature* C Indian Ocean
Árgos *105 B6* Pelopónnisos, S Greece
Argostóli *105 A5 var.* Argostólion. Kefallinía, Iónioi Nísoi, Greece, C Mediterranean Sea
Argostólion *see* Argostóli
Argun *125 E1 Chin.* Ergun He, *Rus.* Argun'. *River* China/Russian Federation
Argyrokastron *see* Gjirokastër
Århus *85 B7 var.* Aarhus. Århus, C Denmark
Aria *see* Herāt
Ari Atoll *132 A4 atoll* C Maldives
Arica *64 B1 hist.* San Marcos de Arica. Tarapacá, N Chile
Aridaía *104 B3 var.* Aridea, Aridhaía. Dytikí Makedonía, N Greece
Aridea *see* Aridaía
Aridhaía *see* Aridaía
Arīḩā *118 B3 var.* Arīhā. Idlib, W Syria
Arīḩā *see* Jericho
Arinsal *91 A7* NW Andorra
Arizona *48 A2 off.* State of Arizona; also known as Copper State, Grand Canyon State. Admin. region *state* SW USA
Arkansas *42 A1 off.* State of Arkansas; also known as The Land of Opportunity. *State* S USA
Arkansas City *45 F5* Kansas, C USA
Arkansas River *49 G1 river* C USA
Arkhangel'sk *114 B2 Eng.* Archangel. Arkhangel'skaya Oblast', NW Russian Federation
Arkoí *105 E6 island* Dodekánisos, Greece, Aegean Sea
Arles *91 D6 var.* Arles-sur-Rhône; *anc.* Arelas, Arelate. Bouches-du-Rhône, SE France
Arles-sur-Rhône *see* Arles
Arlington *49 G2* Texas, SW USA
Arlington *41 E4* Virginia, NE USA
Arlon *87 D8 Dut.* Aarlen, *Ger.* Arel; *Lat.* Orolaunum. Luxembourg, SE Belgium
Armagh *89 B5 Ir.* Ard Mhacha. S Northern Ireland, UK
Armagnac *91 B6 cultural region* S France
Armenia *117 F3 var.* Ajastan, *Arm.* Hayastani Hanrapetut'yun; *prev.* Armenian Soviet Socialist Republic. *Country* SW Asia

Armenia 117

Official name Republic of Armenia
Formation 1991
Capital Yerevan
Population 3.1 million / 269 people per sq mile (104 people per sq km)
Total area 11,506 sq. miles (29,800 sq. km)
Languages Armenian, Azeri, Russian

Armenia (continued)

Religions Armenian Apostolic Church (Orthodox) 94%, other 6%
Ethnic mix Armenian 93%, Azeri 3%, other 2%, Russian 2%
Government Presidential system
Currency Dram = 100 luma
Literacy rate 99%
Calorie consumption 1991 calories

Armenia *58 B3* Quindío, W Colombia
Armidale *149 D6* New South Wales, SE Australia
Armstrong *38 B3* Ontario, S Canada
Armyans'k *109 F4 Rus.* Armyansk. Respublika Krym, S Ukraine
Arnaía *104 C4 var.* Arnea. Kentrikí Makedonía, N Greece
Arnaud *82 A3 river* Quebec, E Canada
Arnea *see* Arnaía
Arnedo *93 E2* La Rioja, N Spain
Arnhem *86 D4* Gelderland, SE Netherlands
Arnhem Land *148 A2 physical region* Northern Territory, N Australia
Arno *96 B3 river* C Italy
Arnold *45 G4* Missouri, C USA
Arorae *145 E3 atoll* Tungaru, W Kiribati
Arquipélago da Madeira *see* Madeira
Arquipélago dos Açores *see* Azores
Ar Rahad *see* Er Rahad
Ar Ramādī *120 B3 var.* Ramadi, Rumadiya. SW Iraq
Ar Rāmī *118 C4* Ḩimş, C Syria
Ar Ramthā *119 B5 var.* Ramtha. Irbid, N Jordan
Arran, Isle of *88 C4 island* SW Scotland, UK
Ar Raqqah *118 C2 var.* Rakka; *anc.* Nicephorium. Ar Raqqah, N Syria
Arras *90 C2 anc.* Nemetocenna. Pas-de-Calais, N France
Ar Rawḑatayn *120 C4 var.* Raudhatain. N Kuwait
Arriaga *51 G5* Chiapas, SE Mexico
Ar Riyāḑ *121 C5 Eng.* Riyadh. *Country capital* (Saudi Arabia) Ar Riyāḑ, C Saudi Arabia
Ar Rub 'al Khālī *121 C6 Eng.* Empty Quarter, Great Sandy Desert. *Desert* SW Asia
Ar Rustāq *121 E5 var.* Rostak, Rustaq. N Oman
Ar Ruţbah *120 B3 var.* Rutba. SW Iraq
Árta *105 A5 anc.* Ambracia. Ípeiros, W Greece
Artashat *117 F3* S Armenia
Artemisa *54 B2* La Habana, W Cuba
Artesia *48 D3* New Mexico, SW USA
Arthur's Pass *151 C6 pass* South Island, NZ
Artigas *64 D3 prev.* San Eugenio, San Eugenio del Cuareim. Artigas, N Uruguay
Art'ik *117 F2* W Armenia
Artois *90 C2 cultural region* N France
Artsyz *108 D4 Rus.* Artsiz. Odes'ka Oblast', SW Ukraine
Artvin *117 F2* Artvin, NE Turkey
Arua *73 B6* NW Uganda
Aruângua *see* Luangwa
Aruba *58 C1 var.* Oruba. *Dutch autonomous region* S West Indies
Aru, Kepulauan *139 G4 Eng.* Aru Islands; *prev.* Aroe Islands. *Island group* E Indonesia
Arunāchal Pradesh *135 G3 cultural region* NE India
Arusha *73 C7* Arusha, N Tanzania
Arviat *37 G4 prev.* Eskimo Point. Nunavut, C Canada
Arvidsjaur *84 C4* Norrbotten, N Sweden
Arys' *114 B5 Kaz.* Arys. Yuzhnyy Kazakhstan, S Kazakhstan
Asadābād *123 F4 var.* Asadābād; *prev.* Chaghasarāy. Kunar, E Afghanistan
Asad, Buḩayrat al- *134 C2 Eng.* Lake Assad. *Lake* N Syria
Asahi-dake *130 D2 mountain* Hokkaidō, N Japan
Asahikawa *130 D2* Hokkaidō, N Japan
Asamankese *75 E5* SE Ghana
Āsānsol *135 F4* West Bengal, NE India
Asben *see* Aïr, Massif de l'
Ascension Fracture Zone *69 A5 tectonic feature* C Atlantic Ocean
Ascension Island *85 A5 dependency of St. Helena* C Atlantic Ocean
Ascoli Piceno *96 C4 anc.* Asculum Picenum. Marche, C Italy
Aseb *72 D4 var.* Assab, *Amh.* Āseb. SE Eritrea
Aşgabat *122 C3 Rus.* Ashgabat; *prev.* Ashkhabad, Poltoratsk. *Country capital* (Turkmenistan) Akhalskiy Velayat, C Turkmenistan
Ashara *see* Al 'Ashārah
Ashburton *151 C6* Canterbury, South Island, NZ
Ashburton River *146 A4 river* Western Australia
Ashdod *119 A6 anc.* Azotos, *Lat.* Azotus. Central, W Israel
Asheville *43 E1* North Carolina, SE USA
Ashgabat *see* Aşgabat
Ashkelon *see* Ashqelon
Ashland *46 B4* Oregon, NW USA
Ashland *40 B1* Wisconsin, N USA
Ashmore and Cartier Islands *142 A3 Australian external territory* E Indian Ocean
Ashmyany *107 C5 Rus.* Oshmyany. Hrodzyenskaya Voblasts', W Belarus
Ashqelon *119 A6 var.* Ashkelon. Southern, C Israel
Ash Shadādah *118 D2 var.* Ash Shaddādah, Jisr ash Shadadi, Shaddādī, Shedadi, Tell Shedadi. Al Ḩasakah, NE Syria
Ash Shaddādah *see* Ash Shadādah
Ash Shām *see* Dimashq
Ash Sharāh *119 B7 var.* Esh Sharā. *Mountain range* W Jordan
Ash Shāriqah *120 D4 Eng.* Sharjah. Ash Shāriqah, NE UAE
Ash Shawbak *119 B7* Ma'ān, W Jordan
Ash Shiḩr *121 C6* SE Yemen
Asia *25 C2 continent*
Asinara, Isola *96 A4 island* W Italy
Asipovichy *107 D6 Rus.* Osipovichi. Mahilyowskaya Voblasts', C Belarus
Aşkale *117 E3* Erzurum, NE Turkey
Askersund *85 C6* Örebro, C Sweden
Asmara *72 C4 Amh.* Āsmera. *Country capital* (Eritrea) C Eritrea
Assab *see* Aseb
As Sabkhah *118 D2 var.* Sabkha. Ar Raqqah, NE Syria
Assad, Lake *see* Asad, Buḩayrat al-
Aş Şafāwī *119 C6* Al Mafraq, N Jordan
Aş Şaḩrā' al Gharbīyah *see* Sahara el Gharbîya
Aş Şaḩrā' al Lībīyah *see* Libyan Desert
Aş Şaḩrā' ash Sharqīyah *see* Eastern Desert
As Salamīyah *see* Salamīyah
'Assal, Lac *68 E4 lake* W Djibouti
As Salţ *119 B6 var.* Salt. Al Balqā', NW Jordan
Assamaka *see* Assamakka
Assamakka *75 F2 var.* Assamaka. Agadez, NW Niger
As Samāwah *120 B3 var.* Samawa. S Iraq
Assen *86 E2* Drenthe, NE Netherlands
Assenede *87 B5* Oost-Vlaanderen, NW Belgium
Assiout *see* Asyût
Assiut *see* Asyût
Assouan *see* Aswân
Assu *see* Açu
Assuan *see* Aswân
As Sukhnah *118 C3 var.* Sukhne, *Fr.* Soukhné. Ḩimş, C Syria
As Sulaymānīyah *120 C3 var.* Sulaimaniya, *Kurd.* Slēmānī. NE Iraq
As Sulayyil *121 B5* Ar Riyāḑ, S Saudi Arabia
Aş Şuwār *118 D2 var.* Şuwār. Dayr az Zawr, E Syria
As Suwaydā' *119 B5 var.* El Suweida, Es Suweida, Suweida, *Fr.* Soueida. As Suwaydā', SW Syria
Astacus *see* İzmit
Astana *114 C4 prev.* Akmola, Akmolinsk, Tselinograd, Kaz. Aqmola. *country capital* (Kazakhstan) Akmola, N Kazakhstan
Astarabad *see* Gorgān
Asterābād *see* Gorgān
Asti *96 A2 anc.* Asta Colonia, Asta Pompeia, Hasta Colonia, Hasta Pompeia. Piemonte, NW Italy
Astipálaia *see* Astypálaia
Astorga *92 C1 anc.* Asturica Augusta. Castilla-León, N Spain
Astrabad *see* Gorgān
Astrakhan' *111 C7* Astrakhanskaya Oblast', SW Russian Federation
Asturias *92 C1 cultural region* NW Spain
Astypálaia *105 D7 var.* Astipálaia, *It.* Stampalia. *Island* Kykládes, Greece, Aegean Sea
Asunción *64 D2 country capital* (Paraguay) Central, S Paraguay
Aswân *72 B2 var.* Assouan, Assuan; *anc.* Syene. SE Egypt
Asyût *72 B2 var.* Assiout, Assiut, Siut; *anc.* Lycopolis. C Egypt
Atacama Desert *see* Atacama, Desierto de
Atacama, Desierto de *64 B2 Eng.* Atacama Desert. *Desert* N Chile
Atafu Atoll *145 E3 island* NW Tokelau
Atamyrat *122 D3 prev.* Kerki. Lebapskiy Velayat, E Turkmenistan
Aţâr *74 C2* Adrar, W Mauritania
Atas Bogd *126 D3 mountain* SW Mongolia
Atascadero *47 B7* California, W USA
Atatürk Barajı *117 E4 reservoir* S Turkey
Atbara *72 C3 var.* 'Aţbārah. River Nile, NE Sudan
'Aţbārah *see* Atbara
Atbasar *114 C4* Akmola, N Kazakhstan
Atchison *45 F4* Kansas, C USA
Ath *87 B6 var.* Aat. Hainaut, SW Belgium
Athabasca *37 E5 var.* Athabaska. *River* Alberta, SW Canada
Athabasca *37 E5* Alberta, SW Canada
Athabasca, Lake *37 F4 lake* Alberta/Saskatchewan, SW Canada
Athabaska *see* Athabasca
Athens *see* Athína
Athens *43 E2* Georgia, SE USA
Athens *40 D4* Ohio, N USA
Athens *49 G3* Texas, SW USA
Atherton *148 D3* Queensland, NE Australia
Athína *105 C6 Eng.* Athens; *prev.* Athínai, *anc.* Athenae. *Country capital* (Greece) Attikí, C Greece
Athlone *89 B5 Ir.* Baile Átha Luain. C Ireland
Ath Thawrah *see* Madīnat ath Thawrah
Ati *76 C3* Batha, C Chad
Atikokan *38 B4* Ontario, S Canada
Atka *36 A3* Atka Island, Alaska, USA
Atka *115 G3* Magadanskaya Oblast', E Russian Federation
Atlanta *42 D2 state capital* Georgia, SE USA
Atlanta *49 H2* Texas, SW USA
Atlantic City *41 F4* New Jersey, NE USA
Atlantic-Indian Basin *67 D7 undersea feature* SW Indian Ocean
Atlantic-Indian Ridge *69 B8 undersea feature* SW Indian Ocean
Atlantic Ocean *66 B4 ocean*
Atlas Mountains *70 C2 mountain range* NW Africa
Atlasovo *115 H3* Kamchatskaya Oblast', E Russian Federation
Atlas Saharien *70 D2 var.* Saharan Atlas. *Mountain range* Algeria/Morocco
Atlas Tellien *102 C3 Eng.* Tell Atlas. *Mountain range* N Algeria
Atlin *36 D4* British Columbia, W Canada
Aţ Ţafīlah *119 B7 var.* Et Tafila, Tafila. Aţ Ţafīlah, W Jordan
Aţ Ţā'if *121 B5* Makkah, W Saudi Arabia
At Tall al Abyaḑ *118 C2 var.* Tall al Abyaḑ, Tell Abyad, *Fr.* Tell Abiad. Ar Raqqah, N Syria
Aţ Ţanf *118 D4* Ḩimş, S Syria
Attapu *see* Samakhixai
Attawapiskat *38 C3 river* Ontario, S Canada
Attawapiskat *38 C3* Ontario, C Canada
At Tibnī *118 D2 var.* Tibnī. Dayr az Zawr, NE Syria
Attopeu *see* Samakhixai
Attu Island *36 A2 island* Aleutian Islands, Alaska, USA
Atyrau *114 B4 prev.* Gur'yev. Atyrau, W Kazakhstan
Aubagne *91 D6 anc.* Albania. Bouches-du-Rhône, SE France
Aubange *87 D8* Luxembourg, SE Belgium
Aubervilliers *90 E1* Seine-St-Denis, N France
Auburn *46 B2* Washington, NW USA
Auch *91 B6 Lat.* Augusta Auscorum, Elimberrum. Gers, S France
Auckland *150 D2* Auckland, North Island, NZ
Auckland Islands *142 C5 island group* S NZ
Audincourt *90 E4* Doubs, E France
Audru *106 D2 Ger.* Audern. Pärnumaa, SW Estonia
Augathella *149 D5* Queensland, E Australia
Augsburg *95 C6 Fr.* Augsbourg; *anc.* Augusta Vindelicorum. Bayern, S Germany
Augusta *41 G2 state capital* Maine, NE USA
Augusta *43 E2* Georgia, SE USA
Augusta *147 A7* Western Australia
Augustów *98 E2 Rus.* Avgustov. Podlaskie, NE Poland
'Aujā et Tahtā *see.* Khirbet el 'Aujā et Tahtā
Aulie Ata/Auliye-Ata *see* Taraz
Auob *78 B4 var.* Oup. *River* Namibia/South Africa
Aurangābād *134 D5* Mahārāshtra, C India
Auray *90 A3* Morbihan, NW France
Aurès, Massif de l' *102 C4 mountain range* NE Algeria
Aurillac *91 C5* Cantal, C France
Aurora *44 D4* Colorado, C USA
Aurora *40 B3* Illinois, N USA
Aurora *45 G5* Missouri, C USA
Aurora *59 F2* NW Guyana
Aus *78 B4* Karas, SW Namibia
Ausa *see* Vic
Austin *49 G3 state capital* Texas, S USA
Austin *45 G3* Minnesota, N USA
Australes, Îles *143 F4 var.* Archipel des Australes, Îles Tubuai, Tubuai Islands, *Eng.* Austral Islands. *Island group* SW French Polynesia
Austral Fracture Zone *143 H4 tectonic feature* S Pacific Ocean
Australia *142 A4 Country*

Australia 142

Official name Commonwealth of Australia
Formation 1901
Capital Canberra

Australia (continued)

Population 19.7 million / 7 people per sq mile (3 people per sq km)
Total area 2,967,893 sq. miles (7,686,850 sq. km)
Languages English, Italian, Cantonese, Greek, Arabic, Vietnamese, Aboriginal languages
Religions Christian 64%, other 34%
Ethnic mix European 92%, Asian 5%, Aboriginal and other 3%
Government Parliamentary system
Currency Australian dollar = 100 cents
Literacy rate 99%
Calorie consumption 3126 calories

Australian Alps *149 C7 mountain range* SE Australia
Australian Capital Territory *149 D7 prev.* Federal Capital Territory. *Territory* SE Australia
Austral Islands *see* Australes, Îles
Austria *95 D7 Ger.* Österreich. *Country* C Europe

Austria 95

Official name Republic of Austria
Formation 1918
Capital Vienna
Population 8.1 million / 254 people per sq mile (98 people per sq km)
Total area 32,378 sq. miles (83,858 sq. km)
Languages German, Croatian, Slovenian, Hungarian (Magyar)
Religions Roman Catholic 78%, Nonreligious 9%, Protestant 5%, Other (including Jewish and Muslim) 8%
Ethnic mix Austrian 93%, Croat, Slovene, and Hungarian 6%, other 1%
Government Parliamentary system
Currency Euro = 100 cents
Literacy rate 99%
Calorie consumption 3799 calories

Auvergne *91 C5 cultural region* C France
Auxerre *90 C4 anc.* Autesiodorum, Autissiodorum. Yonne, C France
Avarua *145 G5 dependent territory capital* (Cook Islands) Rarotonga, S Cook Islands
Ávdira *104 C3* Anatolikí Makedonía kai Thráki, NE Greece
Aveiro *92 B2 anc.* Talabriga. Aveiro, W Portugal
Avela *see* Ávila
Avellino *97 D5 anc.* Abellinum. Campania, S Italy
Avesta *85 C6* Kopparberg, C Sweden
Aveyron *91 C6 river* S France
Avezzano *96 C4* Abruzzo, C Italy
Aviemore *88 C3* N Scotland, UK
Avignon *91 D6 anc.* Avenio. Vaucluse, SE France
Avila *see* Ávila
Ávila *92 D3 var.* Avila; *anc.* Abela, Abula, Abyla, Avela. Castilla-León, C Spain
Avilés *92 C1* Asturias, NW Spain
Avranches *90 B3* Manche, N France
Awaji-shima *131 C6 island* SW Japan
Āwash *73 D5 var.* Hawash. *River* C Ethiopia
Awbārī *71 F3* SW Libya
Ax *see* Dax
Axel *87 B5* Zeeland, SW Netherlands
Axel Heiberg Island *37 E1 var.* Axel Heiburg. *Island* Nunavut, N Canada
Axel Heiburg *see* Axel Heiberg Island
Ayacucho *60 D4* Ayacucho, S Peru
Ayagoz *130 C5 var.* Ayaguz, *Kaz.* Ayaköz; *prev.* Sergiopol. Vostochnyy Kazakhstan, E Kazakhstan
Ayaguz *see* Ayagoz
Ayaköz *see* Ayagoz
Ayamonte *92 C4* Andalucía, S Spain
Ayaviri *61 E4* Puno, S Peru
Aydarko'l Ko'li *123 E2 var.* Aydarkŭl, *Rus.* Ozero Aydarkul'. *Lake* C Uzbekistan
Aydarkŭl *see* Aydarko'l Ko'li
Aydın *116 A4 var.* Aïdin; *anc.* Tralles. Aydın, SW Turkey
Ayers Rock *see* Uluru
Ayeyarwady *see* Irrawaddy
Ayiá *see* Agiá
Ayios Evstratios *see* Efstrátios, Ágios
Áyios Nikólaos *see* Ágios Nikólaos
Ayorou *75 E3* Tillabéri, W Niger
'Ayoûn el 'Atroûs *74 D3 var.* Aïoun el Atrous, Aïoun el Atroûss. Hodh el Gharbi, SE Mauritania
Ayr *88 C4* W Scotland, UK
Ayteke Bi *130 B4 . Kaz.* Zhangaqazaly, *prev.* Novokazalinsk Kyzylorda, SW Kazakhstan
Aytos *104 E2* Burgas, E Bulgaria
Ayutthaya *137 C5 var.* Phra Nakhon Si Ayutthaya. Phra Nakhon Si Ayutthaya, C Thailand
Ayvalık *116 A3* Balıkesir, W Turkey
Azahar, Costa del *93 F3 coastal region* E Spain
Azaouâd *75 E3 desert* C Mali
A'zāz *118 B2* Ḩalab, NW Syria
Azerbaijan *117 G2 Az.* Azärbaycan, Azärbaycan Respublikası; *prev.* Azerbaijan SSR. *Country* SE Asia

Azerbaijan 117

Official name Republic of Azerbaijan
Formation 1991
Capital Baku
Population 8.4 million / 251 people per sq mile (97 people per sq km)
Total area 33,436 sq. miles (86,600 sq. km)
Languages Azeri, Russian
Religions Shi'a Muslim 68%, Sunni Muslim 26%, Russian Orthodox 3%, Armenian Apostolic Church (Orthodox) 2%, other 1%
Ethnic mix Azeri 90%, Dagestani 3%, Russian 3%, Armenian 2%, other 2%
Government Presidential system
Currency Manat = 100 gopik
Literacy rate 97%
Calorie consumption 2474 calories

Azimabad *see* Patna
Azogues *60 B2* Cañar, S Ecuador
Azores *92 A4 var.* Açores, Ilhas dos Açores, *Port.* Arquipélago dos Açores. *Island group* Portugal, NE Atlantic Ocean
Azores-Biscay Rise *80 A3 undersea feature* E Atlantic Ocean
Azoum, Bahr *76 C3 seasonal river* SE Chad
Azov, Sea of *103 H1 Rus.* Azovskoye More, *Ukr.* Azovs'ke More. *Sea* NE Black Sea
Azraq, Wāḩat al *135 C6 oasis* N Jordan
Aztec *48 C1* New Mexico, SW USA
Azuaga *92 C4* Extremadura, W Spain
Azuero, Península de *53 F5 peninsula* S Panama
Azul *65 D5* Buenos Aires, E Argentina
Azur, Côte d' *107 E6 Coastal region* SE France
Az Zaqāzīq *see* Zagazig
Az Zarqā' *119 B6 var.* Zarqa. Az Zarqā', NW Jordan
Az Zāwiyah *71 F2 var.* Zawia. NW Libya
Az Zilfī *120 B4* Ar Riyāḑ, N Saudi Arabia
Æsernia *see* Isernia

B

Ba *100 D3 prev.* Mba. Viti Levu, W Fiji
Baalbek *118 B4 var.* Ba'labakk; *anc.* Heliopolis. E Lebanon
Bá an Daingin *see* Dingle Bay
Baardheere *73 D6 var.* Bardere, *It.* Bardera. Gedo, SW Somalia
Baarle-Hertog *87 C5* Antwerpen, N Belgium
Baarn *86 C3* Utrecht, C Netherlands
Babadag *108 D5* Tulcea, SE Romania
Babahoyo *60 B2 prev.* Bodegas. Los Ríos, C Ecuador
Bābā, Kūh-e *123 E4 mountain range* C Afghanistan
Babayevo *110 B4* Vologodskaya Oblast', NW Russian Federation
Babeldaob *144 A1 var.* Babeldaop, Babelthuap. *Island* N Palau
Babeldaop *see* Babeldaob
Bab el Mandeb *121 B7 strait* Gulf of Aden/Red Sea
Babelthuap *see* Babeldaob
Bá Bheanntraí *see* Bantry Bay
Babruysk *107 D7 Rus.* Bobruysk. Mahilyowskaya Voblasts', E Belarus
Babuyan Channel *139 E1 channel* N Philippines
Babuyan Island *139 E1 island* N Philippines
Bacabal *63 F2* Maranhão, E Brazil
Bacău *108 C4 Hung.* Bákó. Bacău, NE Romania
Bắc Giang *136 D3* Ha Bắc, N Vietnam
Bacheykava *107 D5 Rus.* Bocheykovo. Vitsyebskaya Voblasts', N Belarus
Back *37 F3 river* Nunavut, N Canada
Bačka Palanka *100 D3 prev.* Palanka. Serbia, NW Serbia and Montenegro (Yugo.)
Bačka Topola *100 D3 Hung.* Topolya; prev. *Hung.* Bácstopolya. Serbia, N Serbia and Montenegro (Yugo.)
Bac Liêu *137 D6 var.* Vinh Loi. Minh Hai, S Vietnam
Bacolod *125 E4 off.* Bacolod City. Negros, C Philippines
Bacolod City *see* Bacolod
Bácsszenttamás *see* Srbobran
Badajoz *92 C4 anc.* Pax Augusta. Extremadura, W Spain
Baden-Baden *95 B6 anc.* Aurelia Aquensis. Baden-Württemberg, SW Germany
Bad Freienwalde *94 D3* Brandenburg, NE Germany
Bad Hersfeld *94 B4* Hessen, C Germany
Bad Homburg *see* Bad Homburg vor der Höhe
Bad Homburg vor der Höhe *95 B5 var.* Bad Homburg. Hessen, W Germany
Bá Dhún na nGall *see* Donegal Bay
Bad Ischl *95 D7* Oberösterreich, N Austria
Bad Krozingen *95 A6* Baden-Württemberg, SW Germany
Badlands *44 D2 physical region* North Dakota, N USA
Badu Island *148 C1 island* Queensland, NE Australia
Bad Vöslau *95 E6* Niederösterreich, NE Austria
Baetic Cordillera *see* Béticos, Sistemas
Baetic Mountains *see* Béticos, Sistemas
Bafatá *74 C4* C Guinea-Bissau
Baffin Bay *37 G2 bay* Canada/Greenland
Baffin Island *37 G2 island* Nunavut, NE Canada
Bafing *74 C3 river* W Africa
Bafoussam *76 A4* Ouest, W Cameroon
Bafra *116 D2* Samsun, N Turkey
Bāft *120 D4* Kermān, S Iran
Bagaces *52 D4* Guanacaste, NW Costa Rica
Bagdad *see* Baghdād
Bagé *63 E5* Rio Grande do Sul, S Brazil
Baghdād *120 B3 var.* Bagdad, *Eng.* Baghdad. *Country capital* (Iraq) C Iraq
Baghlān *123 E3* Baghlān, NE Afghanistan
Bago *see* Pegu
Bagoé *74 D4 river* Côte d'Ivoire/Mali
Bagrationovsk *106 A4 Ger.* Preussisch Eylau. Kaliningradskaya Oblast', W Russian Federation
Bagrax Hu *see* Bosten Hu
Baguio *139 E1 off.* Baguio City. Luzon, N Philippines
Bagzane, Monts *75 F3 mountain* N Niger
Bahama Islands *see* Bahamas
Bahamas *54 C2 Country* N West Indies

Bahamas 54

Official name Commonwealth of the Bahamas
Formation 1973
Capital Nassau
Population 314,000 / 81 people per sq mile (31 people per sq km)
Total area 5382 sq. miles (13,940 sq. km)
Languages English, English Creole, French Creole
Religions Baptist 32%, Anglican 20%, Roman Catholic 19%, Methodist 6%, Church of God 6%, other 17%
Ethnic mix Black African 85%, other 15%
Government Parliamentary system
Currency Bahamian dollar = 100 cents
Literacy rate 96%
Calorie consumption 2777 calories

Bahamas *35 D6 var.* Bahama Islands. *Island group* N West Indies
Baharly *122 C3 var.* Bäherden, *Rus.* Bakharden; *prev.* Bakherden. Akhalskiy Velayat, C Turkmenistan
Bahāwalpur *134 C2* Punjab, E Pakistan
Bäherden *see* Baharly
Bahía *63 F3 off.* Estado da Bahia. *State* E Brazil
Bahía Blanca *65 C5* Buenos Aires, E Argentina
Bahía, Islas de la *52 C1 Eng.* Bay Islands. *Island group* N Honduras
Bahir Dar *72 C4 var.* Bahr Dar, Bahrdar Giyorgis. NW Ethiopia
Bahraich *135 E3* Uttar Pradesh, N India
Bahrain *120 C4 Ar.* Al Baḩrayn; *prev.* Bahrein, *anc.* Tylos or Tyros. *Country* SW Asia

Bahrain 120

Official name Kingdom of Bahrain
Formation 1971
Capital Manama
Population 724,000 / 2652 people per sq mile (1025 people per sq km)
Total area 239 sq. miles (620 sq. km)
Languages Arabic
Religions Muslim (mainly Shi'a) 99%, other 1%
Ethnic mix Bahraini 70%, Iranian, Indian, and Pakistani 24%, Other Arab 4%, European 2%
Government Monarchy
Currency Bahraini dinar = 1000 fils
Literacy rate 89%
Calorie consumption Not available

Baḩr al Milḩ *see* Razāzah, Buḩayrat ar
Baḩrat Lūt *see* Dead Sea
Bahrat Tabariya *see* Tiberias, Lake
Bahr Dar *see* Bahir Dar
Bahrdar Giyorgis *see* Bahir Dar
Bahr el Azraq *see* Blue Nile
Bahr el Jebel *see* White Nile

Bahret Lut *see* Dead Sea
Bahr Tabariya, Sea of *see* Tiberias, Lake
Bahushewsk *107 E6 Rus.* Bogushëvsk. Vitsyebskaya Voblasts', NE Belarus
Baia Mare *108 B3 Ger.* Frauenbach, *Hung.* Nagybánya; *prev.* Neustadt. Maramureş, NW Romania
Baia Sprie *108 B3 Ger.* Mittelstadt, *Hung.* Felsőbánya. Maramureş, NW Romania
Baïbokoum *76 B4* Logone-Oriental, SW Chad
Baidoa *see* Baydhabo
Baie-Comeau *39 E3* Québec, SE Canada
Baikal, Lake *see* Baykal, Ozero
Baile Átha Luain *see* Athlone
Bailén *92 D4* Andalucía, S Spain
Baile na Mainistreach *see* Newtownabbey
Băileşti *108 B5* Dolj, SW Romania
Ba Illi *76 B3* Chari-Baguirmi, SW Chad
Bainbridge *42 D3* Georgia, SE USA
Bā'ir *see* Bāyir
Baireuth *see* Bayreuth
Bairiki *144 D2 country capital* (Kiribati) Tarawa, NW Kiribati
Bairnsdale *149 C7* Victoria, SE Australia
Baishan *129 E3 prev.* Hunjiang. Jilin, NE China
Baiyin *128 B4* Gansu, C China
Baja *99 C7* Bács-Kiskun, S Hungary
Baja California *48 A4 Eng.* Lower California. *Peninsula* NW Mexico
Baja California *50 B2 state* NW Mexico
Bajo Boquete *see* Boquete
Bajram Curri *101 D5* Kukës, N Albania
Bakala *76 C4* Ouaka, C Central African Republic
Bakan *see* Shimonoseki
Baker *46 C3* Oregon, NW USA
Baker and Howland Islands *145 E2 US unincorporated territory* W Polynesia
Baker Lake *37 F3* Nunavut, N Canada
Bakersfield *47 C7* California, W USA
Bakharden *see* Baharly
Bakhchysaray *109 F5 Rus.* Bakhchisaray. Respublika Krym, S Ukraine
Bakhmach *109 F1* Chernihivs'ka Oblast', N Ukraine
Bākhtarān *see* Kermānshāh
Bakı *117 H2 Eng.* Baku. *Country capital* (Azerbaijan) E Azerbaijan
Bakony *99 C7 Eng.* Bakony Mountains, *Ger.* Bakonywald. *Mountain range* W Hungary
Baku *see* Bakı
Balabac Island *129 C8 island* W Philippines
Balabac Strait *138 D2 var.* Selat Balabac. *Strait* Malaysia/Philippines
Ba'labakk *see* Baalbek
Balaguer *93 F2* Cataluña, NE Spain
Balakovo *111 C6* Saratovskaya Oblast', W Russian Federation
Bālā Morghāb *122 D4* Laghmān, NW Afghanistan
Balashov *111 B6* Saratovskaya Oblast', W Russian Federation
Balaton *C7 var.* Lake Balaton, *Ger.* Plattensee. *Lake* W Hungary
Balaton, Lake *see* Balaton
Balbina, Represa *62 D1 reservoir* NW Brazil
Balboa *53 G4* Panamá, C Panama
Balcarce *65 D5* Buenos Aires, E Argentina
Balclutha *151 B7* Otago, South Island, NZ
Baldy Mountain *44 C1 mountain* Montana, NW USA
Bâle *see* Basel
Baleares, Islas *93 G3 Eng.* Balearic Islands. *Island group* Spain, W Mediterranean Sea
Balearic Islands *see* Baleares, Islas
Balearic Plain *see* Algerian Basin
Baleine, Rivière à la *39 E2 river* Québec, E Canada
Balen *87 C5* Antwerpen, N Belgium
Bāleshwar *135 F4 prev.* Balasore. Orissa, E India
Bali *138 D5 island* C Indonesia
Balıkesir *116 A3* Balıkesir, W Turkey
Balīkh, Nahr *118 C2 river* N Syria
Balikpapan *138 D4* Borneo, C Indonesia
Balkanabat *122 B2 var.* Nebitdag. Balkanskiy Velayat, W Turkmenistan
Balkan Mountains *104 C2 Bul./SCr.* Stara Planina. *Mountain range* Bulgaria/Serbia and Montenegro (Yugo.)
Balkh *123 E3 anc.* Bactra. Balkh, N Afghanistan
Balkhash *114 C5 Kaz.* Balqash. Karaganda, SE Kazakhstan
Balkhash, Lake *see* Balkhash, Ozero
Balkhash, Ozero *114 C5 Eng.* Lake Balkhash, *Kaz.* Balqash. *Lake* SE Kazakhstan
Balladonia *147 C6* Western Australia
Ballarat *149 C7* Victoria, SE Australia
Balleny Islands *154 B5 island group* Antarctica
Ballinger *49 F3* Texas, SW USA
Balochistān *see* Baluchistān
Balş *108 B5* Olt, S Romania
Balsas *63 F2* Maranhão, E Brazil
Balsas, Río *51 E5 var.* Río Mexcala. *River* S Mexico
Bal'shavik *107 D7 Rus.* Bol'shevik. Homyel'skaya Voblasts', SE Belarus
Balta *108 D3* Odes'ka Oblast', SW Ukraine
Bălţi *108 D3 Rus.* Bel'tsy. N Moldova
Baltic Sea *85 C7 Ger.* Ostee, *Rus.* Baltiskoye More. *Sea* N Europe
Baltimore *41 F4* Maryland, NE USA
Baltkrievija *see* Belarus
Baluchistān *134 B3 var.* Balochistān, Beluchistan. Admin. region *province* SW Pakistan
Balvi *106 D4* Balvi, NE Latvia
Balykchy *123 G2 Kir.* Ysyk-Köl; *prev.* Issyk-Kul', Rybach'ye. Issyk-Kul'skaya Oblast', NE Kyrgyzstan
Balzers *94 E2* S Liechtenstein
Bam *120 E4* Kermān, SE Iran
Bamako *74 D4 country capital* (Mali) Capital District, SW Mali
Bambari *76 C4* Ouaka, C Central African Republic
Bamberg *95 C5* Bayern, SE Germany
Bamenda *76 A4* Nord-Ouest, W Cameroon
Banaba *144 D2 var.* Ocean Island. *Island* Tungaru, W Kiribati
Bandaaceh *138 A3 var.* Banda Atjeh; *prev.* Koetaradja, Kutaradja, Kutaraja. Sumatera, W Indonesia
Banda Atjeh *see* Bandaaceh
Bandama *74 D5 var.* Bandama Fleuve. *River* S Côte d'Ivoire
Bandama Fleuve *see* Bandama
Bandar 'Abbās *see* Bandar-e 'Abbās
Bandarbeyla *73 E5 var.* Bender Beila, Bender Beyla. Bari, NE Somalia
Bandar-e 'Abbās *120 D4 var.* Bandar 'Abbās; *prev.* Gombroon. Hormozgān, S Iran
Bandar-e Būshehr *120 C4 var.* Būshehr, *Eng.* Bushire. Būshehr, S Iran
Bandar-e Khamīr *120 D4* Hormozgān, S Iran
Bandar-e Langeh *120 D4 var.* Bandar-e Lengeh, Lingeh. Hormozgān, S Iran
Bandar-e Lengeh *see* Bandar-e Langeh
Bandar Kassim *see* Boosaaso
Bandarlampung *138 C4 prev.* Tanjungkarang, Teloekbetoeng, Telukbetung. Sumatera, W Indonesia
Bandar Maharani *see* Muar
Bandar Masulipatnam *see* Machilīpatnam
Bandar Seri Begawan *138 D3 prev.* Brunei Town. *Country capital* (Brunei) N Brunei
Bandar Sri Aman *see* Sri Aman
Banda Sea *139 F5 var.* Laut Banda. *Sea* E Indonesia
Bandiagara *75 E3* Mopti, C Mali
Bandırma *116 A3 var.* Penderma. Balıkesir, NW Turkey
Bandundu *77 C6 prev.* Banningville. Bandundu, W Dem. Rep. Congo
Bandung *138 C5 prev.* Bandoeng. Jawa, C Indonesia
Bangalore *132 C2* Karnātaka, S India
Bangassou *76 D4* Mbomou, SE Central African Republic
Banggai, Kepulauan *139 E4 island group* C Indonesia
Banghāzī *71 G2 Eng.* Bengazi, Benghazi, *It.* Bengasi. NE Libya
Bangka, Pulau *138 C4 island* W Indonesia
Bangkok *see* Krung Thep
Bangkok, Bight of *see* Krung Thep, Ao
Bangladesh *135 G3 prev.* East Pakistan. *Country* S Asia

Bangladesh 135

Official name People's Republic of Bangladesh
Formation 1971
Capital Dhaka
Population 147 million / 2837 people per sq mile (1096 people per sq km)
Total area 55,598 sq. miles (144,000 sq. km)
Languages Bengali, Urdu, Chakma, Marma (Magh), Garo, Khasi, Santhali, Tripuri, Mro
Religions Muslim (mainly Sunni) 87%, Hindu 12%, other 1%
Ethnic mix Bengali 98%, other 2%
Government Parliamentary system
Currency Taka = 100 poisha
Literacy rate 41%
Calorie consumption 2187 calories

Bangor *89 B5 Ir.* Beannchar. E Northern Ireland, UK
Bangor *41 G2* Maine, NE USA
Bangor *89 C6* NW Wales, UK
Bangui *77 B5 country capital* (Central African Republic) Ombella-Mpoko, SW Central African Republic
Bangweulu, Lake *73 B8 var.* Lake Bengweulu. *Lake* N Zambia
Ban Hat Yai *see* Hat Yai
Ban Hin Heup *136 C4* Viangchan, C Laos
Ban Houayxay *see* Houayxay
Ban Houei Sai *see* Houayxay
Ban Hua Hin *137 C6 var.* Hua Hin. Prachuap Khiri Khan, SW Thailand
Bani *74 D3 river* S Mali
Banias *see* Bāniyās
Banī Suwayf *see* Beni Suef
Bāniyās *118 B3 var.* Banias, Baniyas, Paneas. Tarṭūs, W Syria
Baniyas *see* Bāniyās
Banja Luka *100 B3* Republika Srpska, NW Bosnia and Herzegovina
Banjarmasin *138 D4 prev.* Bandjarmasin. Borneo, C Indonesia
Banjul *74 B3 prev.* Bathurst. *Country capital* (Gambia) W Gambia
Banks Island *37 E2 island* Banks Island, Northwest Territories, NW Canada
Banks Islands *144 D4 Fr.* Îles Banks. *Island group* N Vanuatu
Banks Lake *46 B1 reservoir* Washington, NW USA
Banks Peninsula *151 C6 peninsula* South Island, NZ
Banks Strait *149 C8 strait* SW Tasman Sea
Bānkura *135 F4* West Bengal, NE India
Ban Mak Khaeng *see* Udon Thani
Banmo *see* Bhamo
Bañolas *see* Banyoles
Ban Pak Phanang *see* Pak Phanang
Ban Sichon *see* Sichon
Banská Bystrica *99 C6 Ger.* Neusohl, *Hung.* Besztercebánya. Banskobystrický Kraj, C Slovakia
Bantry Bay *89 A7 Ir.* Bá Bheanntraí. *Bay* SW Ireland
Banya *104 E2* Burgas, E Bulgaria
Banyak, Kepulauan *138 A3 prev.* Kepulauan Banjak. *Island group* NW Indonesia
Banyo *76 B4* Adamaoua, NW Cameroon
Banyoles *93 G2 var.* Bañolas. Cataluña, NE Spain
Banzare Seamounts *141 C7 undersea feature* S Indian Ocean
Baoji *128 B4 var.* Pao-chi, Paoki. Shaanxi, C China
Baoro *76 B4* Nana-Mambéré, W Central African Republic
Baoshan *128 A6 var.* Pao-shan. Yunnan, SW China
Baotou *127 F3 var.* Pao-t'ou, Paotow. Nei Mongol Zizhiqu, N China
Ba'qūbah *120 B3 var.* Qubba. C Iraq
Baquerizo Moreno *see* Puerto Baquerizo Moreno
Bar *101 C5 It.* Antivari. Montenegro, SW Serbia and Montenegro (Yugo.)
Baraawe *73 D6 It.* Brava. Shabeellaha Hoose, S Somalia
Baraji, Hirfanli *116 C3 lake* C Turkey
Bārāmati *134 C5* Mahārāshtra, W India
Baranavichy *107 B6 Pol.* Baranowicze, *Rus.* Baranovichi. Brestskaya Voblasts', SW Belarus
Barbados *55 G1 country* SE West Indies

Barbados 55

Official name Barbados
Formation 1966
Capital Bridgetown
Population 270,000 / 1627 people per sq mile (628 people per sq km)
Total area 166 sq. miles (430 sq. km)
Languages English, Bajan (Barbadian English)
Religions Anglican 40%, other 24%, Nonreligious 17%, Pentecostal 8%, Methodist 7%, Roman Catholic 4%
Ethnic mix Black African 90%, other 10%
Government Parliamentary system
Currency Barbados dollar = 100 cents
Literacy rate 99%
Calorie consumption 2992 calories

Barbastro *93 F2* Aragón, NE Spain
Barbate de Franco *92 C5* Andalucía, S Spain
Barbuda *55 G3 island* N Antigua and Barbuda
Barcaldine *148 C4* Queensland, E Australia
Barce *see* Al Marj
Barcelona *93 G2 anc.* Barcino, Barcinona. Cataluña, E Spain
Barcelona *59 E2* Anzoátegui, NE Venezuela
Barcoo *see* Cooper Creek
Barcs *99 C7* Somogy, SW Hungary
Bardaï *76 C1* Borkou-Ennedi-Tibesti, N Chad
Bardejov *99 D5 Ger.* Bartfeld, *Hung.* Bártfa. Prešovský Kraj, E Slovakia
Bardera *see* Baardheere
Bardere *see* Baardheere
Bareilly *135 E3 var.* Bareli. Uttar Pradesh, N India

Bareli *see* Bareilly
Barendrecht *86 C4* Zuid-Holland, SW Netherlands
Barentin *90 C3* Seine-Maritime, N France
Barentsberg *83 G2* Spitsbergen, W Svalbard
Barentsøya *83 G2 island* E Svalbard
Barents Sea *110 C2 Nor.* Barents Havet, *Rus.* Barentsevo More. *Sea* Arctic Ocean
Barents Trough *81 E1 undersea feature* SW Barents Sea
Bar Harbor *41 H2* Mount Desert Island, Maine, NE USA
Bari *97 E5 var.* Bari delle Puglie; *anc.* Barium. Puglia, SE Italy
Bāridah *see* Al Bāridah
Bari delle Puglie *see* Bari
Barikot *see* Barīkowṯ
Barīkowṯ *123 F4 var.* Barikot. Kunar, NE Afghanistan
Barillas *52 A2 var.* Santa Cruz Barillas. Huehuetenango, NW Guatemala
Barinas *58 C2* Barinas, W Venezuela
Barisal *135 G4* Khulna, S Bangladesh
Barisan, Pegunungan *138 B4 mountain range* Sumatera, W Indonesia
Barito, Sungai *138 D4 river* Borneo, C Indonesia
Barium *see* Bari
Barka *see* Al Marj
Barkly Tableland *148 B3 plateau* Northern Territory/Queensland, N Australia
Bârlad *108 D4 prev.* Bîrlad. Vaslui, E Romania
Barlavento, Ilhas de *74 A2 var.* Windward Islands. *Island group* N Cape Verde
Bar-le-Duc *90 D3 var.* Bar-sur-Ornain. Meuse, NE France
Barlee, Lake *147 B6 lake* Western Australia
Barlee Range *146 A4 mountain range* Western Australia
Barletta *97 D5 anc.* Barduli. Puglia, SE Italy
Barlinek *98 B3 Ger.* Berlinchen. Zachodniopomorskie, NW Poland
Barmouth *89 C6* NW Wales, UK
Barnaul *114 D4* Altayskiy Kray, C Russian Federation
Barnet *89 A7* SE England, UK
Barnstaple *89 C7* SW England, UK
Baroghil Pass *123 F3 var.* Kowtal-e Barowghīl. *Pass* Afghanistan/Pakistan
Baron'ki *107 E7 Rus.* Boron'ki. Mahilyowskaya Voblasts', E Belarus
Barquisimeto *58 C2* Lara, NW Venezuela
Barra *88 B3 island* NW Scotland, UK
Barra de Río Grande *53 E3* Región Autónoma Atlántico Sur, E Nicaragua
Barragem de Sobradinho *see* Sobradinho, Represa de
Barranca *60 C3* Lima, W Peru
Barrancabermeja *58 B2* Santander, N Colombia
Barranquilla *58 B1* Atlántico, N Colombia
Barreiro *92 B4* Setúbal, W Portugal
Barrier Range *149 C6 hill range* New South Wales, SE Australia
Barrow *89 B6 Ir.* An Bhearú. *River* SE Ireland
Barrow *36 D2* Alaska, USA
Barrow-in-Furness *89 C5* NW England, UK
Barrow Island *146 A4 island* Western Australia
Barstow *47 C7* California, W USA
Bar-sur-Ornain *see* Bar-le-Duc
Bartang *123 F3 river* SE Tajikistan
Bartica *59 F3* N Guyana
Bartın *116 C2* Bartın NW Turkey
Bartlesville *49 G1* Oklahoma, C USA
Bartoszyce *98 D2 Ger.* Bartenstein. Warmińsko-Mazurskie, NE Poland
Baruun-Urt *127 F2* Sühbaatar, E Mongolia
Barú, Volcán *53 E5 var.* Volcán de Chiriquí. *Volcano* W Panama
Barwon River *149 D5 river* New South Wales, SE Australia
Barysaw *107 D6 Rus.* Borisov. Minskaya Voblasts', NE Belarus
Basarabeasca *108 D4 Rus.* Bessarabka. SE Moldova
Basel *95 A7 Eng.* Basle, *Fr.* Bâle. Basel-Stadt, NW Switzerland
Basilan *139 E3 island* SW Philippines
Basle *see* Basel
Basra *see* Al Başrah
Bassano del Grappa *96 C2* Veneto, NE Italy
Bassein *136 A4 var.* Pathein. Irrawaddy, SW Myanmar
Basse-Terre *55 G4 dependent territory capital* (Guadeloupe) Basse Terre, SW Guadeloupe
Basse Terre *55 G4 island* W Guadeloupe
Basseterre *55 G3 country capital* (Saint Kitts and Nevis) Saint Kitts, Saint Kitts and Nevis
Bassikounou *74 D3* Hodh ech Chargui, SE Mauritania
Bass Strait *149 C7 strait* SE Australia
Bassum *94 B3* Niedersachsen, NW Germany
Bastia *91 E7* Corse, France, C Mediterranean Sea
Bastogne *87 D7* Luxembourg, SE Belgium
Bastrop *42 B2* Louisiana, S USA
Bastyn' *107 B7 Rus.* Bostyn'. Brestskaya Voblasts', SW Belarus
Basuo *see* Dongfang
Bata *77 A5* NW Equatorial Guinea
Batabanó, Golfo de *54 A2 gulf* W Cuba
Batajnica *100 D3* Serbia, N Serbia and Montenegro (Yugo.)
Batangas *139 E2 off.* Batangas City. Luzon, N Philippines
Bătdâmbâng *137 C5 prev.* Battambang. Bătdâmbâng, NW Cambodia
Batéké, Plateaux *77 B6 plateau* S Congo
Bath *89 D7 hist.* Akermanceaster, *anc.* Aquae Calidae, Aquae Solis. SW England, UK
Bathinda *134 D2* Punjab, NW India
Bathsheba *55 G1* E Barbados
Bathurst *39 F4* New Brunswick, SE Canada
Bathurst *149 D6* New South Wales, SE Australia
Bathurst Island *146 D2 island* Northern Territory, N Australia
Bathurst Island *37 F2 island* Parry Islands, Nunavut, N Canada
Bāṯin, Wādī al *136 C4 dry watercourse* SW Asia
Batman *117 E4 var.* İluh. Batman, SE Turkey
Batna *71 E2* NE Algeria
Baton Rouge *42 B3 state capital* Louisiana, S USA
Batroûn *118 A4 var.* Al Batrūn. N Lebanon
Batticaloa *132 D3* Eastern Province, E Sri Lanka
Battipaglia *97 D5* Campania, S Italy
Bat'umi *117 F2* W Georgia
Batu Pahat *138 B3 prev.* Bandar Penggaram. Johor, Peninsular Malaysia
Bauchi *75 G4* Bauchi, NE Nigeria
Bauer Basin *153 F3 undersea feature* E Pacific Ocean
Bauska *106 C3 Ger.* Bauske. Bauska, S Latvia
Bautzen *94 D4 Lus.* Budyšin. Sachsen, E Germany
Bavarian Alps *95 C7 Ger.* Bayrische Alpen. *Mountain range* Austria/Germany
Bavispe, Río *50 C2 river* NW Mexico
Bawīṭi *72 B2* N Egypt
Bawku *75 E4* N Ghana
Bayamo *54 C3* Granma, E Cuba
Bayan Har Shan *126 D4 var.* Bayan Khar. *Mountain range* C China
Bayanhongor *126 D2* Bayanhongor, C Mongolia
Bayan Khar *see* Bayan Har Shan
Bayano, Lago *53 G4 lake* E Panama
Bay City *40 C3* Michigan, N USA
Bay City *49 G4* Texas, SW USA
Baydhabo *73 D6 var.* Baydhowa, Isha Baydhabo, *It.* Baidoa. Bay, SW Somalia
Baydhowa *see* Baydhabo
Bayern *95 C6 cultural region* SE Germany
Bayeux *90 B3 anc.* Augustodurum. Calvados, N France
Bāyir *119 C7 var.* Bā'ir. Ma'ān, S Jordan
Baykal, Ozero *115 E4 Eng.* Lake Baikal. *Lake* S Russian Federation
Baymak *111 D6* Respublika Bashkortostan, W Russian Federation
Bayonne *91 A6 anc.* Lapurdum. Pyrénées-Atlantiques, SW France
Baýramaly *122 D3 var.* Bayramaly; *prev.* Bayram-Ali. Maryyskiy Velayat, S Turkmenistan
Bayreuth *95 C5 var.* Baireuth. Bayern, SE Germany
Bayrūt *see* Beyrouth
Baytown *49 H4* Texas, SW USA
Baza *93 E4* Andalucía, S Spain
Beagle Channel *65 C8 channel* Argentina/Chile
Béal Feirste *see* Belfast
Beannchar *see* Bangor
Bear Lake *46 E4 lake* Idaho/Utah, NW USA
Beas de Segura *93 E4* Andalucía, S Spain
Beata, Isla *55 E3 island* SW Dominican Republic
Beatrice *45 F4* Nebraska, C USA
Beaufort Sea *36 D2 sea* Arctic Ocean
Beaufort West *78 C5 Afr.* Beaufort-Wes. Western Cape, SW South Africa
Beaumont *49 H3* Texas, SW USA
Beaune *90 D4* Côte d'Or, C France
Beauvais *90 C3 anc.* Bellovacum, Caesaromagus. Oise, N France
Beaver Island *40 C2 island* Michigan, N USA
Beaver Lake *49 H1 reservoir* Arkansas, C USA
Beaver River *49 F1 river* Oklahoma, C USA
Beāwar *134 C3* Rājasthān, N India
Bečej *100 D3 Ger.* Altbetsche, *Hung.* Óbecse, Rácz-Becse; *prev.* Magyar-Becse, Stari Bečej. Serbia, N Serbia and Montenegro (Yugo.)
Béchar *70 D2 prev.* Colomb-Béchar. W Algeria
Beckley *40 D5* West Virginia, NE USA
Bedford *89 D6* E England, UK
Bedum *86 E1* Groningen, NE Netherlands
Be'ér Menuẖa *119 B7 var* Be'er Menukha. Southern, S Israel
Be'er Menukha *see* Be'ér Menuẖa
Beernem *87 A5* West-Vlaanderen, NW Belgium
Beersheba *see* Be'ér Sheva'
Be'ér Sheva' *119 A7 var.* Beersheba, *Ar.* Bir es Saba. Southern, S Israel
Beesel *87 D5* Limburg, SE Netherlands
Beeville *49 G4* Texas, SW USA
Bega *149 D7* New South Wales, SE Australia
Beida *see* Al Bayḍā'
Beihai *128 B6* Guangxi Zhuangzu Zizhiqu, S China
Beijing *128 C3 var.* Pei-ching, *Eng.* Peking; *prev.* Pei-p'ing. *Country/municipality capital* (China) Beijing Shi, E China
Beilen *86 E2* Drenthe, NE Netherlands
Beira *79 E3* Sofala, C Mozambique
Beirut *see* Beyrouth
Beit Leḥm *see* Bethlehem
Beiuş *108 B3 Hung.* Belényes. Bihor, NW Romania
Beja *92 B4 anc.* Pax Julia. Beja, SE Portugal
Béjar *92 C3* Castilla-León, N Spain
Bejraburi *see* Phetchaburi
Békéscsaba *99 D7 Rom.* Bichiş-Ciaba. Békés, SE Hungary
Bekobod *123 E2 Rus.* Bekabad; *prev.* Begovat. Toshkent Wiloyati, E Uzbekistan
Bela Crkva *100 E3 Ger.* Weisskirchen, *Hung.* Fehértemplom. Serbia, W Serbia and Montenegro (Yugo.)
Belarus *107 B6 var.* Belorussia, *Latv.* Baltkrievija; *prev.* Belorussian SSR, *Rus.* Belorusskaya SSR. *Country* E Europe

Belarus 107

Official name Republic of Belarus
Formation 1991
Capital Minsk
Population 9.9 million / 124 people per sq mile (48 people per sq km)
Total area 80,154 sq. miles (207,600 sq. km)
Languages Belarussian, Russian
Religions Orthodox Christian 60%, other 32%, Roman Catholic 8%
Ethnic mix Belarussian 78%, Russian 13%, Polish 4%, Ukrainian 3%, other 2%
Government Presidential system
Currency Belarussian rouble = 100 kopeks
Literacy rate 99%
Calorie consumption 2925 calories

Belau *see* Palau
Belchatow *see* Bełchatów
Bełchatów *98 C4 var.* Belchatow. Łódzkie, C Poland
Belcher Islands *38 C2 Fr.* Îles Belcher. *Island group* Northwest Territories, SE Canada
Beledweyne *73 D5 var.* Belet Huen, *It.* Belet Uen. Hiiraan, C Somalia
Belém *63 F1 var.* Pará. *State capital* Pará, N Brazil
Belen *48 D2* New Mexico, SW USA
Belén *52 D4* Rivas, SW Nicaragua
Belet Huen *see* Beledweyne
Belet Uen *see* Beledweyne
Belfast *89 B5 Ir.* Béal Feirste. *Admin capital* E Northern Ireland, UK
Belfield *44 D2* North Dakota, N USA
Belfort *90 E4* Territoire-de-Belfort, E France
Belgaum *132 B1* Karnātaka, W India
Belgium *87 B6 Dut.* België, *Fr.* Belgique. *Country* NW Europe

Belgium 87

Official name Kingdom of Belgium
Formation 1830
Capital Brussels
Population 10.3 million / 813 people per sq mile (314 people per sq km)
Total area 11,780 sq. miles (30,510 sq. km)
Languages Dutch, French, German
Religions Roman Catholic 88%, Muslim 2%, other 10%
Ethnic mix Fleming 58%, Walloon 33%, Italian 2%, Moroccan 1%, other 6%
Government Parliamentary system
Currency Euro = 100 cents
Literacy rate 99%
Calorie consumption 3682 calories

Belgorod *111 A6* Belgorodskaya Oblast', W Russian Federation
Belgrade *see* Beograd
Belgrano II *154 A2 Argentinian research station* Antarctica
Belice *see* Belize City
Beligrad *see* Berat
Beli Manastir *100 C3 Hung.* Pélmonostor; *prev.* Monostor. Osijek-Baranja, NE Croatia

Bélinga *77 B5* Ogooué-Ivindo, NE Gabon
Belitung, Pulau *138 C4 island* W Indonesia
Belize *52 B1 Sp.* Belice; *prev.* British Honduras, Colony of Belize. *Country* Central America

Belize 52

Official name Belize
Formation 1981
Capital Belmopan
Population 256,000 / 29 people per sq mile (11 people per sq km)
Total area 8867 sq. miles (22,966 sq. km)
Languages English Creole, Spanish, English, Mayan, Garifuna (Carib)
Religions Roman Catholic 62%, other 13%, Anglican 12%, Methodist 6%, Mennonite 4%, Seventh-day Adventist 3%
Ethnic mix Mestizo 44%, Creole 30%, Maya 11%, Garifuna 7%, other 4%, Asian Indian 4%
Government Parliamentary system
Currency Belizean dollar = 100 cents
Literacy rate 77%
Calorie consumption 2886 calories

Belize *52 B1 river* Belize/Guatemala
Belize *see* Belize City
Belize City *52 C1 var.* Belize, *Sp.* Belice. Belize, NE Belize
Belkofski *36 B3* Alaska, USA
Belle Île *90 A4 island* NW France
Belle Isle, Strait of *39 G3 strait* Newfoundland and Labrador, E Canada
Belleville *40 B4* Illinois, N USA
Bellevue *45 F4* Iowa, C USA
Bellevue *46 B2* Washington, NW USA
Bellingham *46 B1* Washington, NW USA
Belling Hausen Mulde *see* Southeast Pacific Basin
Bellingshausen Abyssal Plain *see* Bellingshausen Plain
Bellingshausen Plain *153 F5 var.* Bellingshausen Abyssal Plain. *Undersea feature* SE Pacific Ocean
Bellingshausen Sea *154 A3 sea* Antarctica
Bellinzona *95 B8 Ger.* Bellenz. Ticino, S Switzerland
Bello *58 B2* Antioquia, W Colombia
Bellville *78 B5* Western Cape, SW South Africa
Belmopan *52 C1 country capital* (Belize) Cayo, C Belize
Belogradchik *104 B1* Vidin, NW Bulgaria
Belo Horizonte *63 F4 prev.* Bello Horizonte. *State capital* Minas Gerais, SE Brazil
Belomorsk *110 B3* Respublika Kareliya, NW Russian Federation
Beloretsk *111 D6* Respublika Bashkortostan, W Russian Federation
Belorussia/Belorussian SSR *see* Belarus
Belorusskaya SSR *see* Belarus
Beloye More *110 C3 Eng.* White Sea. *Sea* NW Russian Federation
Belozersk *110 B4* Vologodskaya Oblast', NW Russian Federation
Belton *49 G3* Texas, SW USA
Beluchistan *see* Baluchistān
Belukha, Gora *114 D5 mountain* Kazakhstan/Russian Federation
Belyy, Ostrov *114 D2 island* N Russian Federation
Bemaraha *79 F3 var.* Plateau du Bemaraha. *Mountain range* W Madagascar
Bemidji *45 F1* Minnesota, N USA
Bemmel *86 D4* Gelderland, SE Netherlands
Benaco *see* Garda, Lago di
Benavente *92 D2* Castilla-León, N Spain
Bend *46 B3* Oregon, NW USA
Bender Beila *see* Bandarbeyla
Bender Beyla *see* Bandarbeyla
Bender Cassim *see* Boosaaso
Bendern *94 E1* NW Liechtenstein
Bender Qaasim *see* Boosaaso
Bendery *see* Tighina
Bendigo *149 C7* Victoria, SE Australia
Benešov *99 B5 Ger.* Beneschau. Středočesky Kraj, W Czech Republic
Benevento *97 D5 anc.* Beneventum, Malventum. Campania, S Italy
Bengal, Bay of *124 C4 bay* N Indian Ocean
Bengbu *128 D5 var.* Peng-pu. Anhui, E China
Benghazi *see* Banghāzī
Bengkulu *138 B4 prev.* Bengkoeloe, Benkoelen, Benkulen. Sumatera, W Indonesia
Benguela *78 A2 var.* Benguella. Benguela, W Angola
Benguella *see* Benguela
Bengweulu, Lake *see* Bangweulu, Lake
Ben Hope *88 B2 mountain* N Scotland, UK
Beni *56 B4 var.* El Beni. Admin. region *department* N Bolivia
Beni *77 E5* Nord Kivu, NE Dem. Rep. Congo
Benidorm *93 F4* País Valenciano, SE Spain
Beni-Mellal *70 C2* C Morocco
Benin *75 F4 prev.* Dahomey. *Country* W Africa

Benin 75

Official name Republic of Benin
Formation 1960
Capital Porto-Novo
Population 6.7 million / 157 people per sq mile (61 people per sq km)
Total area 43,483 sq. miles (112,620 sq. km)
Languages Fon, Bariba, Yoruba, Adja, Houeda, Somba, French
Religions Voodoo 50%, Muslim 30%, Christian 20%
Ethnic mix Fon 47%, other 31%, Adja 12%, Bariba 10%
Government Presidential system
Currency CFA franc = 100 centimes
Literacy rate 40%
Calorie consumption 2455 calories

Benin, Bight of *75 F5 gulf* W Africa
Benin City *75 F5* Edo, SW Nigeria
Beni, Río *61 E3 river* N Bolivia
Beni Suef *72 B2 var.* Banī Suwayf. N Egypt
Ben Nevis *88 C3 mountain* N Scotland, UK
Benson *48 B3* Arizona, SW USA
Bent Jbaïl *119 A5 var.* Bint Jubayl. S Lebanon
Benton *42 B1* Arkansas, C USA
Benue *76 B4 Fr.* Bénoué. *River* Cameroon/Nigeria
Benue *75 G4 state* SE Nigeria
Beograd *100 D3 Eng.* Belgrade, *Ger.* Belgrad; *anc.* Singidunum. *Country capital.* Serbia, N Serbia and Montenegro (Yugo.)
Berane *101 D5 prev.* Ivangrad. Montenegro, SW Serbia and Montenegro (Yugo.)
Berat *101 C6 var.* Berati, *SCr.* Beligrad. Berat, C Albania
Berati *see* Berat
Berau, Teluk *139 G4 var.* MacCluer Gulf. *Bay* Papua, E Indonesia
Berbera *72 D4* Woqooyi Galbeed, NW Somalia
Berbérati *77 B5* Mambéré-Kadéï, SW Central African Republic
Berck-Plage *90 C2* Pas-de-Calais, N France
Berdyans'k *109 G4 Rus.* Berdyansk; *prev.* Osipenko. Zaporiz'ka Oblast', SE Ukraine
Berdychiv *108 D2 Rus.* Berdichev. Zhytomyrs'ka Oblast', N Ukraine
Bereket *122 B2 prev.* Gazandzhyk, Kazandzhik, *Turkm.* Gazanjyk. Balkanskiy Velayat, W Turkmenistan
Berehove *108 B3 Cz.* Berehovo, *Hung.* Beregszász, *Rus.* Beregovo. Zakarpats'ka Oblast', W Ukraine
Berettyó *99 D7 Rom.* Barcău; *prev.* Berătău, Beretău. *River* Hungary/Romania
Berettyóújfalu *99 D6* Hajdú-Bihar, E Hungary
Berezhany *108 C2 Pol.* Brzeżany. Ternopil's'ka Oblast', W Ukraine
Berezniki *111 D5* Permskaya Oblast', NW Russian Federation
Berga *93 G2* Cataluña, NE Spain
Bergamo *96 B2 anc.* Bergomum. Lombardia, N Italy
Bergara *93 E1* País Vasco, N Spain
Bergen *85 A5* Hordaland, S Norway
Bergen *94 D2* Mecklenburg-Vorpommern, NE Germany
Bergen *86 C2* Noord-Holland, NW Netherlands
Bergerac *91 B5* Dordogne, SW France
Bergeyk *87 C5* Noord-Brabant, S Netherlands
Bergse Maas *86 D4 river* S Netherlands
Beringen *87 C5* Limburg, NE Belgium
Bering Sea *36 A2 sea* N Pacific Ocean
Bering Strait *36 C2 Rus.* Beringov Proliv. *Strait* Bering Sea/Chukchi Sea
Berja *93 E5* Andalucía, S Spain
Berkeley *47 B6* California, W USA
Berkner Island *154 A2 island* Antarctica
Berkovitsa *104 C2* Montana, NW Bulgaria
Berlin *94 D3 country capital* (Germany) Berlin, NE Germany
Berlin *41 G2* New Hampshire, NE USA
Bermejo, Río *64 C2 river* N Argentina
Bermeo *93 E1* País Vasco, N Spain
Bermuda *35 D6 var.* Bermuda Islands, Bermudas; *prev.* Somers Islands. *UK crown colony* NW Atlantic Ocean
Bermuda Islands *see* Bermuda
Bermuda Rise *35 E6 undersea feature* C Sargasso Sea
Bermudas *see* Bermuda
Bern *95 A7 Fr.* Berne. *Country capital* (Switzerland) Bern, W Switzerland
Bernau *94 D3* Brandenburg, NE Germany
Bernburg *94 C4* Sachsen-Anhalt, C Germany
Berne *see* Bern
Berner Alpen *95 A7 var.* Berner Oberland, *Eng.* Bernese Oberland. *Mountain range* SW Switzerland
Berner Oberland *see* Berner Alpen
Bernese Oberland *see* Berner Alpen
Bernier Island *147 A5 island* Western Australia
Berry *90 C4 cultural region* C France
Berry Islands *54 C1 island group* N Bahamas
Bertoua *77 B5* Est, E Cameroon
Beru *145 E2 var.* Peru. *Atoll* Tungaru, W Kiribati
Berwick-upon-Tweed *88 D4* N England, UK
Berytus *see* Beyrouth
Besançon *90 D4 anc.* Besontium, Vesontio. Doubs, E France
Beskra *see* Biskra
Betafo *79 G3* Antananarivo, C Madagascar
Betanzos *92 B1* Galicia, NW Spain
Bethlehem *119 B6 Ar.* Beit Laḥm, *Heb.* Bet Lehem. C West Bank
Bethlehem *78 D4* Free State, C South Africa
Béticos, Sistemas *92 D4 var.* Sistema Penibético, *Eng.* Baetic Cordillera, Baetic Mountains. *Mountain range* S Spain
Bet Lehem *see* Bethlehem
Bétou *77 C5* La Likouala, N Congo
Bette, Picco *see* Bette, Pic
Bette, Pic *71 G4 var.* Bīkkū Bīttī, *It.* Picco Bette. *Mountain* S Libya
Bette, Picco *see* Bette, Pic
Beulah *40 C2* Michigan, N USA
Beuthen *see* Bytom
Beveren *87 B5* Oost-Vlaanderen, N Belgium
Beverley *89 D5* E England, UK
Bexley *89 B8* SE England, UK
Beyla *74 D4* Guinée-Forestière, SE Guinea
Beyrouth *118 A4 var.* Bayrūt, *Eng.* Beirut; *anc.* Berytus. *Country capital* (Lebanon) W Lebanon
Beyşehir *116 B4* Konya, SW Turkey
Beyşehir Gölü *116 B4 lake* C Turkey
Béziers *91 C6 anc.* Baeterrae, Baeterrae Septimanorum, Julia Beterrae. Hérault, S France
Bhadrāvati *132 C2* Karnātaka, SW India
Bhāgalpur *135 F3* Bihār, NE India
Bhaktapur *135 F3* Central, C Nepal
Bhamo *136 B2 var.* Banmo. Kachin State, N Myanmar
Bharūch *134 C4* Gujarāt, W India
Bhāvnagar *134 C4 prev.* Bhaunagar. Gujarāt, W India
Bhopāl *134 D4* Madhya Pradesh, C India
Bhubaneshwar *135 F5 prev.* Bhubaneswar, Bhuvaneshwar. Orissa, E India
Bhuket *see* Phuket
Bhusāwal *134 D4 prev.* Bhusaval. Mahārāshtra, C India
Bhutan *135 G3 var.* Druk-yul. *Country* S Asia

Bhutan 135

Official name Kingdom of Bhutan
Formation 1656
Capital Thimphu
Population 2.3 million / 127 people per sq mile (49 people per sq km)
Total area 18,147 sq. miles (47,000 sq. km)
Languages Dzongkha, Nepali, Assamese
Religions Mahayana Buddhist 70%, Hindu 24%, other 6%
Ethnic mix Bhute 50%, other 25%, Nepalese 25%
Government Monarchy
Currency Ngultrum = 100 chetrum
Literacy rate 47%
Calorie consumption Not available

Biak, Pulau *139 G4 island* E Indonesia
Biała Podlaska *98 E3* Lubelskie, E Poland
Białogard *98 B2 Ger.* Belgard. Zachodniopomorskie, NW Poland
Białystok *98 E3 Rus.* Belostok, Bielostok. Podlaskie, NE Poland
Biarritz *91 A6* Pyrénées-Atlantiques, SW France
Bicaz *108 C3 Hung.* Békás. Neamț, NE Romania
Biddeford *41 G2* Maine, NE USA
Bideford *89 C7* SW England, UK
Biel *95 A7 Fr.* Bienne. Bern, W Switzerland
Bielefeld *94 B4* Nordrhein-Westfalen, NW Germany
Bielsko-Biała *99 C5 Ger.* Bielitz, Bielitz-Biala. Śląskie, S Poland
Bielsk Podlaski *98 E3* Podlaskie, NE Poland
Bien Bien *see* Điện Biên
Biên Hoa *137 E6* Đồng Nai, S Vietnam
Bienville, Lac *38 D2 lake* Québec, C Canada
Bié, Planalto do *78 B2 var.* Bié Plateau. *Plateau* C Angola
Bié Plateau *see* Bié, Planalto do

Big Cypress Swamp *43 E5 wetland* Florida, SE USA
Bigge Island *146 C2 island* Western Australia
Bighorn Mountains *44 C2 mountain range* Wyoming, C USA
Bighorn River *44 C2 river* Montana/Wyoming, NW USA
Bignona *74 B3* SW Senegal
Big Sioux River *45 E2 river* Iowa/South Dakota, N USA
Big Spring *49 E3* Texas, SW USA
Bihać *100 B3* Federacija Bosna I Hercegovina, NW Bosnia and Herzegovina
Bihār *135 F3prev.* Behar. Admin. region *state* N India
Biharamulo *73 B7* Kagera, NW Tanzania
Bihosava *107 D5 Rus.* Bigosovo. Vitsyebskaya Voblasts', NW Belarus
Bijeljina *100 C3* Republika Srpska, NE Bosnia and Herzegovina
Bijelo Polje *101 D5* Montenegro, SW Serbia and Montenegro (Yugo.)
Bīkāner *134 C3* Rājasthān, NW India
Bikin *115 G4* Khabarovskiy Kray, SE Russian Federation
Bikini Atoll *144 C1 var.* Pikinni. *Atoll* Ralik Chain, NW Marshall Islands
Bīkkū Bīttī *see* Bette, Pic
Bilāspur *135 E4* Madhya Pradesh, C India
Biläsuvar *117 H3 Rus.* Bilyasuvar; *prev.* Pushkino. SE Azerbaijan
Bila Tserkva *109 E2 Rus.* Belaya Tserkov'. Kyyivs'ka Oblast', N Ukraine
Bilauktaung Range *137 C6 var.* Thanintari Taungdan. *Mountain range* Myanmar/Thailand
Bilbao *93 E1 Basq.* Bilbo. País Vasco, N Spain
Bilecik *116 B3* Bilecik, NW Turkey
Billings *44 C2* Montana, NW USA
Bilma, Grand Erg de *75 H3 desert* NE Niger
Biloela *148 D4* Queensland, E Australia
Biloxi *42 C3* Mississippi, S USA
Biltine *76 C3* Biltine, E Chad
Bilwi *see* Puerto Cabezas
Bilzen *87 D6* Limburg, NE Belgium
Bimini Islands *54 C1 island group* W Bahamas
Binche *87 B7* Hainaut, S Belgium
Bindloe Island *see* Marchena, Isla
Binghamton *41 F3* New York, NE USA
Bingöl *117 E3* Bingöl, E Turkey
Bint Jubayl *see* Bent Jbaïl
Bintulu *138 D3* Sarawak, East Malaysia
Binzhou *128 D4* Shandong, E China
Bío Bío, Río *65 B5 river* C Chile
Bioco, Isla de *77 A5 var.* Bioko, *Eng.* Fernando Po, *Sp.* Fernando Póo; *prev.* Macías Nguema Biyogo. *Island* NW Equatorial Guinea
Bioko *see* Bioco, Isla de
Birāk *71 F3 var.* Brak. C Libya
Birao *76 D3* Vakaga, NE Central African Republic
Biratnagar *135 F3* Eastern, SE Nepal
Bir es Saba *see* Be'ér Sheva'
Birhār Sharīf *135 F3* Bihar, N India
Bīrjand *120 E3* Khorāsān, E Iran
Birkenfeld *95 A5* Rheinland-Pfalz, SW Germany
Birkenhead *89 C5* NW England, UK
Birmingham *42 C2* Alabama, S USA
Birmingham *89 C6* C England, UK
Bir Moghrein *see* Bîr Mogreïn
Bîr Mogreïn *74 C1 var.* Bir Moghrein; *prev.* Fort-Trinquet. Tiris Zemmour, N Mauritania
Birnie Island *145 E3 atoll* Phoenix Islands, C Kiribati
Birni-Nkonni *see* Birnin Konni
Birnin Konni *75 F3 var.* Birni-Nkonni. Tahoua, SW Niger
Birobidzhan *115 G4* Yevreyskaya Avtonomnaya Oblast', SE Russian Federation
Birsk *111 D5* Respublika Bashkortostan, W Russian Federation
Biržai *106 C4 Ger.* Birsen. Biržai, NE Lithuania
Birżebbuġa *102 B5* SE Malta
Bisbee *48 B3* Arizona, SW USA
Biscay, Bay of *80 B4 Sp.* Golfo de Vizcaya, *Port.* Baía de Biscaia. *Bay* France/Spain
Biscay Plain *80 B3 undersea feature* SE Bay of Biscay
Bīshah, Wādī *121 B5 dry watercourse* C Saudi Arabia
Bishkek *123 G2 var.* Pishpek; *prev.* Frunze. *Country capital* (Kyrgyzstan) Chuyskaya Oblast', N Kyrgyzstan
Bishop's Lynn *see* King's Lynn
Bishrī, Jabal *118 D3 mountain range* E Syria
Biskara *see* Biskra
Biskra *71 E2 var.* Beskra, Biskara. NE Algeria
Biskupiec *98 D2 Ger.* Bischofsburg. Warmińsko-Mazurskie, NE Poland
Bislig *139 F2* Mindanao, S Philippines
Bismarck *45 E2 state capital* North Dakota, N USA
Bismarck Archipelago *144 B3 island group* NE PNG
Bismarck Sea *144 B3 sea* W Pacific Ocean
Bisnulok *see* Phitsanulok
Bissau *74 B4 country capital* (Guinea-Bissau) W Guinea-Bissau
Bistrița *108 B3 Ger.* Bistritz, *Hung.* Beszterce; *prev.* Nösen. Bistrița-Năsăud, N Romania
Bitam *77 B5* Woleu-Ntem, N Gabon
Bitburg *95 A5* Rheinland-Pfalz, SW Germany
Bitlis *117 F3* Bitlis, SE Turkey
Bitola *101 D6 Turk.* Monastir; *prev.* Bitolj. S FYR Macedonia
Bitonto *97 D5 anc.* Butuntum. Puglia, SE Italy
Bitterroot Range *46 D2 mountain range* Idaho/Montana, NW USA
Bitung *139 F3 prev.* Bitoeng. Sulawesi, C Indonesia
Biu *75 H4* Borno, E Nigeria
Biwa-ko *131 C6 lake* Honshū, SW Japan
Bizerte *71 E1 Ar.* Banzart, *Eng.* Bizerta. N Tunisia
Bjelovar *100 B2 Hung.* Belovár. Bjelovar-Bilogora, N Croatia
Bjørnøya *83 F3 Eng.* Bear Island. *Island* N Norway
Blackall *148 C4* Queensland, E Australia
Black Drin *101 D6 Alb.* Lumi i Drinit të Zi, *SCr.* Crni Drim. *River* Albania/FYR Macedonia
Blackfoot *46 E4* Idaho, NW USA
Black Forest *see* Schwarzwald
Black Hills *44 D3 mountain range* South Dakota/Wyoming, N USA
Blackpool *89 C5* NW England, UK
Black Range *48 C2 mountain range* New Mexico, SW USA
Black River *136 C3 Chin.* Babian Jiang, Lixian Jiang, *Fr.* Rivière Noire, *Vtn.* Sông Đa. *River* China/Vietnam
Black River *54 A5* W Jamaica
Black Rock Desert *47 C5 desert* Nevada, W USA
Black Sand Desert *see* Garagum
Black Sea *116 B1 var.* Euxine Sea, *Bul.* Cherno More, *Rom.* Marea Neagră, *Rus.* Chernoye More, *Turk.* Karadeniz, *Ukr.* Chorne More. *Sea* Asia/Europe
Black Sea Lowland *109 E4 Ukr.* Prychornomors'ka Nyzovyna. *Depression* SE Europe
Black Volta *75 E4 var.* Borongo, Mouhoun, Moun Hou, *Fr.* Volta Noire. *River* W Africa
Blackwater *89 A6 Ir.* An Abhainn Mhór. *River* S Ireland
Blagoevgrad *104 C3 prev.* Gorna Dzhumaya. Blagoevgrad, SW Bulgaria
Blagoveshchensk *115 G4* Amurskaya Oblast', SE Russian Federation
Blake Plateau *35 D6 var.* Blake Terrace. *Undersea feature* W Atlantic Ocean
Blake Terrace *see* Blake Plateau
Blanca, Bahía *65 C5 bay* E Argentina
Blanca, Costa *93 F4 physical region* SE Spain
Blanche, Lake *149 B5 lake* South Australia
Blanc, Mont *91 D5 It.* Monte Bianco. *Mountain* France/Italy
Blanco, Cape *46 A4 headland* Oregon, NW USA
Blanes *93 G2* Cataluña, NE Spain
Blankenberge *87 A5* West-Vlaanderen, NW Belgium
Blankenheim *95 A5* Nordrhein-Westfalen, W Germany
Blanquilla, Isla *59 E1 var.* La Blanquilla. *Island* N Venezuela
Blantyre *79 E2 var.* Blantyre-Limbe. Southern, S Malawi
Blantyre-Limbe *see* Blantyre
Blaricum *86 C3* Noord-Holland, C Netherlands
Blenheim *151 C5* Marlborough, South Island, NZ
Blida *70 D2 var.* El Boulaida, El Boulaïda. N Algeria
Bloemfontein *78 C4 var.* Mangaung. *Country capital* (South Africa-judicial capital) Free State, C South Africa
Blois *90 C4 anc.* Blesae. Loir-et-Cher, C France
Bloomfield *48 C1* New Mexico, SW USA
Bloomington *40 B4* Illinois, N USA
Bloomington *40 C4* Indiana, N USA
Bloomington *45 F2* Minnesota, N USA
Bloomsbury *148 D3* Queensland, NE Australia
Bluefield *40 D5* West Virginia, NE USA
Bluefields *53 E3* Región Autónoma Atlántico Sur, SE Nicaragua
Blue Mountain Peak *54 B5 mountain* E Jamaica
Blue Mountains *46 C3 mountain range* Oregon/Washington, NW USA
Blue Nile *68 D4 var.* Abai, Bahr el Azraq, *Amh.* Ābay Wenz, *Ar.* An Nīl al Azraq. *River* Ethiopia/Sudan
Blue Nile *72 C4 state* E Sudan
Blumenau *63 E5* Santa Catarina, S Brazil
Blythe *47 D8* California, W USA
Blytheville *42 C1* Arkansas, C USA
Bo *74 C4* S Sierra Leone
Boaco *52 D3* Boaco, S Nicaragua
Boa Vista *74 A3 island* Ilhas de Barlavento, E Cape Verde
Boa Vista *62 D1 state capital* Roraima, NW Brazil
Bobaomby, Tanjona *79 G2 Fr.* Cap d'Ambre. *Headland* N Madagascar
Bobigny *90 E1* Seine-St-Denis, N France
Bobo-Dioulasso *74 D4* SW Burkina faso
Bobrynets' *109 E3 Rus.* Bobrinets. Kirovohrads'ka Oblast', C Ukraine
Boca Raton *43 F5* Florida, SE USA
Bocay *52 D2* Jinotega, N Nicaragua
Bocche del Po *see* Po, Foci del
Bocholt *94 A4* Nordrhein-Westfalen, W Germany
Bochum *94 A4* Nordrhein-Westfalen, W Germany
Bocșa *108 A4 Ger.* Bokschen, *Hung.* Boksánbánya. Caraș-Severin, SW Romania
Bodaybo *115 F4* Irkutskaya Oblast', E Russian Federation
Boden *84 D4* Norrbotten, N Sweden
Bodmin *89 C7* SW England, UK
Bodø *84 C3* Nordland, C Norway
Bodrum *116 A4* Muğla, SW Turkey
Boende *77 C5* Equateur, C Dem. Rep. Congo
Boetoeng *see* Buton, Pulau
Bogale *136 B4* Irrawaddy, SW Myanmar
Bogalusa *42 B3* Louisiana, S USA
Bogatynia *98 B4 Ger.* Reichenau. Dolnośląskie, SW Poland
Boğazlıyan *116 D3* Yozgat, C Turkey
Bogor *138 C5 Dut.* Buitenzorg. Jawa, C Indonesia
Bogotá *58 B3 prev.* Santa Fe, Santa Fe de Bogotá. *Country capital* (Colombia) Cundinamarca, C Colombia
Bo Hai *128 D4 var.* Gulf of Chihli. *Gulf* NE China
Bohemia *99 A5 Cz.* Čechy, *Ger.* Böhmen. *Cultural and historical region* W Czech Republic
Bohemian Forest *95 C5 Cz.* Český Les, Šumava, *Ger.* Böhmerwald. *Mountain range* C Europe
Böhmisch-Krumau *see* Český Krumlov
Bohol Sea *139 E2 var.* Mindanao Sea. *Sea* S Philippines
Bohoro Shan *126 B2 mountain range* NW China
Bohuslav *109 E2 Rus.* Boguslav. Kyyivs'ka Oblast', N Ukraine
Boise *46 D3 var.* Boise City. *State capital* Idaho, NW USA
Boise City *see* Boise
Boise City *49 E1* Oklahoma, C USA
Boizenburg *94 C3* Mecklenburg-Vorpommern, N Germany
Bojador *see* Boujdour
Bojnūrd *120 D2 var.* Bujnurd. Khorāsān, N Iran
Bokāro *135 F4* Bihār, N India
Boké *74 C4* Guinée-Maritime, W Guinea
Bokhara *see* Buxoro
Boknafjorden *85 A6 fjord* S Norway
Bol *76 B3* Lac, W Chad
Bolgatanga *75 E4* N Ghana
Bolhrad *108 D4 Rus.* Bolgrad. Odes'ka Oblast', SW Ukraine
Bolívar, Pico *58 C2 mountain* W Venezuela
Bolivia *61 F3 Country* W South America

Bolivia 61

Official name Republic of Bolivia
Formation 1825
Capital La Paz (administrative); Sucre (judicial)
Population 8.8 million / 21 people per sq mile (8 people per sq km)
Total area 424,162 sq. miles (1,098,580 sq. km)
Languages Aymara, Quechua, Spanish
Religions Roman Catholic 93%, other 7%
Ethnic mix Quechua 37%, Aymara 32%, Mixed race 13%, European 10%, other 8%
Government Presidential system
Currency Boliviano = 100 centavos
Literacy rate 87%
Calorie consumption 2267 calories

Bollène *91 D6* Vaucluse, SE France
Bollnäs *85 C5* Gävleborg, C Sweden
Bollon *149 D5* Queensland, C Australia
Bologna *96 C3* Emilia-Romagna, N Italy
Bol'shevik, Ostrov *115 E2 island* Severnaya Zemlya, N Russian Federation
Bol'shezemel'skaya Tundra *110 E3 physical region* NW Russian Federation
Bol'shoy Lyakhovskiy, Ostrov *115 F2 island* NE Russian Federation
Bolton *89 D5 prev.* Bolton-le-Moors. NW England, UK

Bosnia and Herzegovina 100

Official name Bosnia and Herzegovina
Formation 1992
Capital Sarajevo
Population 4.2 million / 213 people per sq mile (82 people per sq km)
Total area 19,741 sq. miles (51,129 sq. km)
Languages Serbo-Croat
Religions Muslim (mainly Sunni) 40%, Orthodox Christian 31%, Roman Catholic 15%, other 10%, Protestant 4%
Ethnic mix Bosniak 48%, Serb 38%, Croat 14%
Government Parliamentary system
Currency Marka = 100 pfeninga
Literacy rate 95%
Calorie consumption 2845 calories

Botswana 78

Official name Republic of Botswana
Formation 1966
Capital Gaborone
Population 1.8 million / 8 people per sq mile (3 people per sq km)
Total area 231,803 sq. miles (600,370 sq. km)
Languages Setswana, English, Shona, San, Khoikhoi, isiNdebele
Religions Traditional beliefs 50%, Christian (mainly Protestant) 30%, Other (including Muslim) 20%
Ethnic mix Tswana 98%, other 2%
Government Presidential system
Currency Pula = 100 thebe
Literacy rate 79%
Calorie consumption 2292 calories

Brazil 62

Official name Federative Republic of Brazil
Formation 1822
Capital Brasília
Population 179 million / 55 people per sq mile (21 people per sq km)
Total area 3,286,470 sq. miles (8,511,965 sq. km)
Languages Portuguese, German, Italian, Spanish, Polish, Japanese, Amerindian languages
Religions Roman Catholic 74%, Protestant 15%, Atheist 7%, Afro-American Spiritist 1%, other 3%
Ethnic mix Black 53%, Mixed race 40%, White 6%, other 1%
Government Presidential system
Currency Real = 100 centavos
Literacy rate 86%
Calorie consumption 3002 calories

Brazos River *49 G3 river* Texas, SW USA
Brazza *see* Brač
Brazzaville *77 B6 country capital* (Congo) Capital District, S Congo
Brecht *87 C5* Antwerpen, N Belgium
Brecon Beacons *89 C6 mountain range* S Wales, UK
Breda *86 C4* Noord-Brabant, S Netherlands
Bree *87 D5* Limburg, NE Belgium
Bregalnica *101 E6 river* E FYR Macedonia
Bregenze *57 B7 anc.* Brigantium. Vorarlberg, W Austria
Bregovo *104 B1* Vidin, NW Bulgaria
Brčko *100 C3* Republika Srpska, NE Bosnia and Herzegovina
Bremen *94 B3 Fr.* Brême. Bremen, NW Germany
Bremerhaven *94 B3* Bremen, NW Germany
Bremerton *46 B2* Washington, NW USA
Brenham *49 G3* Texas, SW USA
Brenner Pass *96 C1 var.* BrennerSattel, *Fr.* Col du Brenner, *Ger.* Brennerpass, *It.* Passo del Brennero. *Pass* Austria/Italy
Brennerpass *see* Brenner Pass
Brenner Sattel *see* Brenner Pass
Brescia *96 B2 anc.* Brixia. Lombardia, N Italy
Bressanone *96 C1 Ger.* Brixen. Trentino-Alto Adige, N Italy
Brest *107 A6 Pol.* Brześć nad Bugiem, *Rus.* Brest-Litovsk; *prev.* Brześć Litewski. Brestskaya Voblasts', SW Belarus
Brest *90 A3* Finistère, NW France
Bretagne *90 A3 Eng.* Brittany; *Lat.* Britannia Minor. *Cultural region* NW France
Brewton *42 C3* Alabama, S USA
Brezovo *104 D2 prev.* Abrashlare. Plovdiv, C Bulgaria
Bria *76 D4* Haute-Kotto, C Central African Republic
Briançon *91 D5 anc.* Brigantio. Hautes-Alpes, SE France
Bridgeport *41 F3* Connecticut, NE USA
Bridgetown *55 G2 country capital* (Barbados) SW Barbados
Bridlington *89 D5* E England, UK
Bridport *89 D7* S England, UK
Brig *95 A7 Fr.* Brigue, *It.* Briga. Valais, SW Switzerland
Brigham City *44 B3* Utah, W USA
Brighton *44 D4* Colorado, C USA
Brighton *89 E7* SE England, UK
Brindisi *97 E5 anc.* Brundisium, Brundusium. Puglia, SE Italy
Brisbane *149 E5 state capital* Queensland, E Australia
Bristol *89 D7 anc.* Bricgstow. SW England, UK
Bristol *41 F3* Connecticut, NE USA
Bristol *40 D5* Virginia, NE USA
Bristol Bay *36 B3 bay* Alaska, USA
Bristol Channel *89 C7 inlet* England/Wales, UK
Britain *80 C3 var.* Great Britain. *Island* UK
British Columbia *36 D4 Fr.* Colombie-Britannique. *Province* SW Canada
British Indian Ocean Territory *141 B5 UK dependent territory* C Indian Ocean
British Isles *89 island group* NW Europe
British Virgin Islands *55 F3 var.* Virgin Islands. *UK dependent territory* E West Indies
Brive-la-Gaillarde *91 C5 prev.* Brive, *anc.* Briva Curretia. Corrèze, C France
Brno *99 B5 Ger.* Brünn. Brněnský Kraj, SE Czech Republic
Brocēni *106 B3* Saldus, SW Latvia
Brodeur Peninsula *37 F2 peninsula* Baffin Island, Nunavut, NE Canada
Brodnica *98 C3 Ger.* Buddenbrock. Kujawski-pomorskie, C Poland
Broek-in-Waterland *86 C3* Noord-Holland, C Netherlands
Broken Arrow *49 G1* Oklahoma, C USA
Broken Bay *148 E1 bay* New South Wales, SE Australia
Broken Hill *149 B6* New South Wales, SE Australia
Broken Ridge *141 D6 undersea feature* S Indian Ocean
Bromley *89 B8* SE England, UK
Brookhaven *42 B3* Mississippi, S USA
Brookings *45 F3* South Dakota, N USA
Brooks Range *36 D2 mountain range* Alaska, USA
Brookton *147 B6* Western Australia
Broome *146 B3* Western Australia
Broomfield *44 D4* Colorado, C USA
Broucsella *see* Brussel
Brovary *109 E2* Kyyivs'ka Oblast', N Ukraine
Brownfield *49 E2* Texas, SW USA
Brownville *49 G5* Texas, SW USA
Brownwood *49 F3* Texas, SW USA
Brozha *107 D7* Mahilyowskaya Voblasts', E Belarus
Brugge *87 A5 Fr.* Bruges. West-Vlaanderen, NW Belgium
Brummen *86 D3* Gelderland, E Netherlands
Brunei *138 D3Mal.* Negara Brunei Darussalam. *Country* SE Asia

Brunei 138

Official name Sultanate of Brunei
Formation 1984
Capital Bandar Seri Begawan
Population 358,000 / 176 people per sq mile (68 people per sq km)
Total area 2228 sq. miles (5770 sq. km)
Languages Malay, English, Chinese
Religions Muslim (mainly Sunni) 66%, Buddhist 14%, other 10%, Christian 10%
Ethnic mix Malay 67%, Chinese 16%, other 11%, Indigenous 6%
Government Monarchy
Currency Brunei dollar = 100 cents
Literacy rate 94%
Calorie consumption 2814 calories

Brunner, Lake *151 C5 lake* South Island, NZ
Brunswick *43 E3* Georgia, SE USA
Brusa *see* Bursa
Brus Laguna *52 D2* Gracias a Dios, E Honduras
Brussa *see* Bursa
Brussel *var.* Brussels, *Fr.* Bruxelles, *Ger.* Brüssel; *anc.* Broucsella. *Country capital* (Belgium) Brussels, C Belgium *see also* Bruxelles
Brüssel *see* Brussel
Brussels *see* Brussel
Bruxelles *see* Brussels
Bryan *49 G3* Texas, SW USA
Bryansk *111 A5* Bryanskaya Oblast', W Russian Federation
Brzeg *98 C4 Ger.* Brieg; *anc.* Civitas Altae Ripae. Opolskie, S Poland
Bucaramanga *58 B2* Santander, N Colombia
Buchanan *74 C5 prev.* Grand Bassa. SW Liberia
Buchanan, Lake *49 F3 reservoir* Texas, SW USA
Bucharest *see* București
Bu Craa *see* Bou Craa
București *108 C5 Eng.* Bucharest, *Ger.* Bukarest; *prev.* Altenburg, *anc.* Cetatea Damboviţei. *Country capital* (Romania) București, S Romania
Buda-Kashalyova *107 D7 Rus.* Buda-Koshelëvo. Homyel'skaya Voblasts', SE Belarus
Budapest *99 C6 off.* Budapest Főváros, *SCr.* Budimpešta. *Country capital* (Hungary) Pest, N Hungary
Budaun *134 D3* Uttar Pradesh, N India
Buena Park *46 E2* California, W USA
Buenaventura *58 A3* Valle del Cauca, W Colombia
Buena Vista *93 H5* S Gibraltar
Buena Vista *61 G4* Santa Cruz, C Bolivia
Buenos Aires *64 D4 hist.* Santa Maria del Buen Aire. *Country capital* (Argentina) Buenos Aires, E Argentina
Buenos Aires *53 E5* Puntarenas, SE Costa Rica
Buenos Aires, Lago *65 B6 var.* Lago General Carrera. *Lake* Argentina/Chile
Buffalo *41 E3* New York, NE USA
Buffalo Narrows *37 F4* Saskatchewan, C Canada
Buff Bay *54 B5* E Jamaica
Buftea *108 C5* București, S Romania
Bug *81 E3 Bel.* Zakhodni Buh, *Eng.* Western Bug, *Rus.* Zapadnyy Bug, *Ukr.* Zakhidnyy Buh. *River* E Europe
Buga *58 B3* Valle del Cauca, W Colombia
Bughotu *see* Santa Isabel
Buguruslan *111 D6* Orenburgskaya Oblast', W Russian Federation
Buḥayrat Nāṣir *see* Nasser, Lake
Buḥeiret Nâṣir *see* Nasser, Lake
Bujalance *92 D4* Andalucía, S Spain
Bujanovac *101 E5* Serbia, SE Serbia and Montenegro (Yugo.)
Bujnurd *see* Bojnūrd
Bujumbura *73 B7 prev.* Usumbura. *Country capital* (Burundi) W Burundi
Bukavu *77 E6 prev.* Costermansville. Sud Kivu, E Dem. Rep. Congo
Bukhara *see* Buxoro
Bukhoro *see* Buxoro
Bukoba *73 B6* Kagera, NW Tanzania
Bülach *95 B7* Zürich, NW Switzerland
Bulawayo *78 D3 var.* Buluwayo. Matabeleland North, SW Zimbabwe
Buldur *see* Burdur
Bulgan *127 E2* Bulgan, N Mongolia
Bulgaria *104 C2 Bul.* Bŭlgariya; *prev.* People's Republic of Bulgaria. *Country* SE Europe

Bulgaria 104

Official name Republic of Bulgaria
Formation 1908
Capital Sofia
Population 7.9 million / 185 people per sq mile (71 people per sq km)
Total area 42,822 sq. miles (110,910 sq. km)
Languages Bulgarian, Turkish, Romani
Religions Orthodox Christian 83%, Muslim 12%, other 4%, Roman Catholic 1%
Ethnic mix Bulgarian 84%, Turkish 9%, Roma 5%, other 2%
Government Parliamentary system
Currency Lev = 100 stotinki
Literacy rate 99%
Calorie consumption 2626 calories

Bull Shoals Lake *42 B1 reservoir* Arkansas/Missouri, C USA
Bulukumba *139 E4 prev.* Boeloekoemba. Sulawesi, C Indonesia
Buluwayo *see* Bulawayo
Bumba *77 D5* Equateur, N Dem. Rep. Congo
Bunbury *147 A7* Western Australia
Bundaberg *148 E4* Queensland, E Australia
Bungo-suidō *131 B7 strait* SW Japan
Bunia *77 E5* Orientale, NE Dem. Rep. Congo
Bünyan *116 D3* Kayseri, C Turkey
Buraida *see* Buraydah
Buraydah *120 B4 var.* Buraida. Al Qaşīm, N Saudi Arabia
Burdur *116 B4 var.* Buldur. Burdur, SW Turkey
Burdur Gölü *116 B4 salt lake* SW Turkey
Burē *72 C4* C Ethiopia
Burgas *104 E2 var.* Bourgas. Burgas, E Bulgaria
Burgaski Zaliv *104 E2 gulf* E Bulgaria
Burgos *92 D2* Castilla-León, N Spain
Burhan Budai Shan *126 D4 mountain range* C China
Buri Ram *see* Buriram
Buriram *137 D5 var.* Buri Ram, Puriramya. Buri Ram, E Thailand
Burjassot *93 F3* País Valenciano, E Spain
Burkburnett *49 F2* Texas, SW USA
Burketown *148 B3* Queensland, NE Australia
Burkina *see* Burkina Faso
Burkina Faso *75 E4* var. Burkina; *prev.* Upper Volta. *Country* W Africa

Burkina Faso 75

Official name Burkina Faso
Formation 1960
Capital Ouagadougou
Population 13 million / 123 people per sq mile (47 people per sq km)
Total area 105,869 sq. miles (274,200 sq. km)
Languages Mossi, Fulani, French, Tuareg, Dyula, Songhai
Religions Muslim 55%, Traditional beliefs 35%, Roman Catholic 9%, Other Christian 1%
Ethnic mix Other 50%, Mossi 50%
Government Presidential system
Currency CFA franc = 100 centimes
Literacy rate 25%
Calorie consumption 2485 calories

Burley *46 D4* Idaho, NW USA
Burlington *45 G4* Iowa, C USA
Burlington *41 F2* Vermont, NE USA
Burma *see* Myanmar
Burnie *149 C8* Tasmania, SE Australia
Burns *46 C3* Oregon, NW USA
Burnside *37 F3 river* Nunavut, NW Canada
Burnsville *45 F2* Minnesota, N USA
Burrel *101 D6 var.* Burreli. Dibër, C Albania
Burreli *see* Burrel
Burriana *93 F3* País Valenciano, E Spain
Bursa *116 B3 var.* Brussa; *prev.* Brusa, *anc.* Prusa. Bursa, NW Turkey
Burtnieks *106 C3 var.* Burtnieku Ezers. *Lake* N Latvia
Burtnieku Ezers *see* Burtnieks
Burundi *73 B7 prev.* Kingdom of Burundi, Urundi. *Country* C Africa

Burundi 73

Official name Republic of Burundi
Formation 1962
Capital Bujumbura
Population 6.8 million / 687 people per sq mile (265 people per sq km)
Total area 10,745 sq. miles (27,830 sq. km)
Languages Kirundi, French, Kiswahili

Burundi (continued)

Religions Christian 60%, Traditional beliefs 39%, Muslim 1%
Ethnic mix Hutu 85%, Tutsi 14%, Twa 1%
Government Transitional regime
Currency Burundi franc = 100 centimes
Literacy rate 50%
Calorie consumption 1612 calories

Buru, Pulau *139 F4 prev.* Boeroe. *Island* E Indonesia
Buşayrah *118 D3* Dayr az Zawr, E Syria
Būshehr *see* Bandar-e Būshehr
Bushire *see* Bandar-e Būshehr
Busselton *147 A7* Western Australia
Buta *77 D5* Orientale, N Dem. Rep. Congo
Butembo *77 E5* Nord Kivu, NE Dem. Rep. Congo
Butler *41 E4* Pennsylvania, NE USA
Buton, Pulau *139 E4 var.* Pulau Butung; *prev.* Boetoeng. *Island* C Indonesia
Butte *44 B2* Montana, NW USA
Butterworth *138 B3* Pinang, Peninsular Malaysia
Button Islands *39 E1 island group* Northwest Territories, NE Canada
Butuan *139 F2 off.* Butuan City. Mindanao, S Philippines
Buulobarde *73 D5 var.* Buulo Berde. Hiiraan, C Somalia Africa
Buulo Berde *see* Buulobarde
Buur Gaabo *73 D6* Jubbada Hoose, S Somalia
Buxoro *122 D2 var.* Bokhara, Bukhoro, *Rus.* Bukhara. Bukhoro Wiloyati, C Uzbekistan
Buynaksk *111 B8* Respublika Dagestan, SW Russian Federation
Büyükağrı Dağı *117 F3 var.* Aghri Dagh, Agri Dagi, Koh I Noh, Masis, *Eng.* Great Ararat, Mount Ararat. *Mountain* E Turkey
Büyükmenderes Nehri *116 A4 river* SW Turkey
Buzău *108 C4* Buzău, SE Romania
Büzmeýin *122 C3 Rus.* Byuzmeyin; *prev.* Bezmein. Akhalskiy Velayat, C Turkmenistan
Buzuluk *111 D6* Akmola, C Kazakhstan
Byahoml' *107 D5 Rus.* Begoml'. Vitsyebskaya Voblasts', N Belarus
Byalynichy *107 D6 Rus.* Belynichi. Mahilyowskaya Voblasts', E Belarus
Bydgoszcz *98 C3 Ger.* Bromberg. Kujawskie-pomorskie, C Poland
Byelaruskaya Hrada *107 B6 Rus.* Belorusskaya Gryada. *Ridge* N Belarus
Byerezino *107 D6 Rus.* Berezina. *River* C Belarus
Byron Island *see* Nikunau
Bytom *99 C5 Ger.* Beuthen. Śląskie, S Poland
Bytča *99 C5* Žilinský Kraj, N Slovakia
Bytów *98 C2 Ger.* Bütow. Pomorskie, N Poland
Byuzmeyin *see* Büzmeýin
Byval'ki *107 D8* Homyel'skaya Voblasts', SE Belarus
Byzantium *see* İstanbul

C

Caála *78 B2 var.* Kaala, Robert Williams, *Port.* Vila Robert Williams. Huambo, C Angola
Caazapá *64 D3* Caazapá, S Paraguay
Caballo Reservoir *48 C3 reservoir* New Mexico, SW USA
Cabañaquinta *92 D1* Asturias, N Spain
Cabanatuan *139 E1 off.* Cabanatuan City. Luzon, N Philippines
Cabimas *58 C1* Zulia, NW Venezuela
Cabinda *78 A1 var.* Kabinda. Cabinda, NW Angola
Cabinda *78 A1 var.* Kabinda. Admin. region *province* NW Angola
Cabora Bassa, Lake *see* Cahora Bassa, Albufeira de
Caborca *50 B1* Sonora, NW Mexico
Cabot Strait *39 G4 strait* E Canada
Cabras, Ilha das *76 E2 island* S Sao Tome and Principe
Cabrera *93 G3 anc.* Capraria. *Island* Islas Baleares, Spain, W Mediterranean Sea
Cáceres *92 C3 Ar.* Qazris. Extremadura, W Spain
Cachimbo, Serra do *63 E2 mountain range* C Brazil
Caconda *78 B2* Huíla, C Angola
Čadca *99 C5 Hung.* Csaca. Žilinský Kraj, N Slovakia
Cadillac *40 C2* Michigan, N USA
Cadiz *139 E2 off.* Cadiz City. Negros, C Philippines
Cádiz *92 C5 anc.* Gades, Gadier, Gadir, Gadire. Andalucía, SW Spain
Cádiz, Golfo de *92 B5 Eng.* Gulf of Cadiz. *Gulf* Portugal/Spain
Cadiz, Gulf of *see* Cádiz, Golfo de
Caen *90 B3* Calvados, N France
Caene *see* Qena
Caenepolis *see* Qena
Caerdydd *see* Cardiff
Caer Gybi *see* Holyhead
Caesarea Mazaca *see* Kayseri
Cafayate *64 C2* Salta, N Argentina
Cagayan de Oro *139 E2 off.* Cagayan de Oro City. Mindanao, S Philippines
Cagliari *97 A6 anc.* Caralis. Sardegna, Italy, C Mediterranean Sea
Caguas *55 F3* E Puerto Rico
Cahora Bassa, Albufeira de *78 D2 var.* Lake Cabora Bassa. *Reservoir* NW Mozambique
Cahors *91 C5 anc.* Cadurcum. Lot, S France
Cahul *108 D4 Rus.* Kagul. S Moldova
Caicos Passage *54 D2 strait* Bahamas/Turks and Caicos Islands
Caiffa *see* Hefa
Cailungo *96 E1* N San Marino
Caiphas *see* Hefa
Cairns *148 D3* Queensland, NE Australia
Cairo *72 B2 Ar.* Al Qāhirah, *var.* El Qâhira. *Country capital* (Egypt) N Egypt
Caisleán an Bharraigh *see* Castlebar
Cajamarca *60 B3 prev.* Caxamarca. Cajamarca, NW Peru
Čakovec *100 B2 Ger.* Csakathurn, *Hung.* Csáktornya; *prev. Ger.* Tschakathurn. Međimurje, N Croatia
Calabar *75 G5* Cross River, S Nigeria
Calabozo *58 D2* Guárico, C Venezuela
Calafat *108 B5* Dolj, SW Romania
Calafate *see* El Calafate
Calahorra *93 E2* La Rioja, N Spain
Calais *41 H2* Maine, NE USA
Calais *90 C2* Pas-de-Calais, N France
Calama *64 B2* Antofagasta, N Chile
Calamianes *see* Calamian Group
Calamian Group *129 C7 var.* Calamianes. *Island group* W Philippines
Călăras *see* Călărași
Călărași *108 D3 var.* Călăras, *Rus.* Kalarash. C Moldova
Călărași *108 C5* Călărași, SE Romania
Calatayud *93 E2* Aragón, NE Spain
Calbayog *139 E2 off.* Calbayog City. Samar, C Philippines
Calcutta *135 G4 var.* Kolkata. West Bengal, NE India
Caldas da Rainha *92 B3* Leiria, W Portugal
Caldera *64 B3* Atacama, N Chile
Caldwell *46 C3* Idaho, NW USA
Caledonia *52 C1* Corozal, N Belize
Caleta *see* Catalan Bay
Caleta Olivia *65 B6* Santa Cruz, SE Argentina
Calgary *37 E5* Alberta, SW Canada
Cali *58 B3* Valle del Cauca, W Colombia
Calicut *132 C2 var.* Kozhikode. Kerala, SW India
California *47 B7 off.* State of California; also known as El Dorado, The Golden State. *State* W USA
California, Golfo de *50 B2 Eng.* Gulf of California; *prev.* Sea of Cortez. *Gulf* W Mexico
California, Gulf of *see* California, Golfo de
Călimănești *108 B4* Vâlcea, SW Romania
Callabonna, Lake *149 B5 lake* South Australia
Callao *60 C4* Callao, W Peru
Callosa de Segura *93 F4* País Valenciano, E Spain
Calmar *see* Kalmar
Caloundra *149 E5* Queensland, E Australia
Caltanissetta *97 C7* Sicilia, Italy, C Mediterranean Sea
Caluula *72 E4* Bari, NE Somalia
Camabatela *78 B1* Cuanza Norte, NW Angola
Camacupa *78 B2 var.* General Machado, *Port.* Vila General Machado. Bié, C Angola
Camagüey *54 C2 prev.* Puerto Príncipe. Camagüey, C Cuba
Camagüey, Archipiélago de *54 C2 island group* C Cuba
Camaná *61 E4* Arequipa, SW Peru
Camargue *91 D6 physical region* SE France
Ca Mau *137 D6 prev.* Quan Long. Minh Hai, S Vietnam
Cambodia *137 D5 var.* Democratic Kampuchea, Roat Kampuchea, *Cam.* Kampuchea; *prev.* People's Democratic Republic of Kampuchea. *Country* SE Asia

Cambodia 137

Official name Kingdom of Cambodia
Formation 1953
Capital Phnom Penh
Population 14.1 million / 207 people per sq mile (80 people per sq km)
Total area 69,900 sq. miles (181,040 sq. km)
Languages Khmer, French, Chinese, Vietnamese, Cham
Religions Buddhist 93%, Muslim 6%, Christian 1%
Ethnic mix Khmer 90%, other 5%, Vietnamese 4%, Chinese 1%
Government Parliamentary system
Currency Riel = 100 sen
Literacy rate 69%
Calorie consumption 1967 calories

Cambrai *90 C2 Flem.* Kambryk; *prev.* Cambray, *anc.* Cameracum. Nord, N France
Cambrian Mountains *89 C6 mountain range* C Wales, UK
Cambridge *89 E6 Lat.* Cantabrigia. E England, UK
Cambridge *41 F4* Maryland, NE USA
Cambridge *40 D4* Ohio, NE USA
Cambridge *54 A4* W Jamaica
Cambridge *150 D3* Waikato, North Island, NZ
Cambridge Bay *37 F3 district capital* Victoria Island, Nunavut, NW Canada
Camden *42 B2* Arkansas, C USA
Cameroon *76 A4 Fr.* Cameroun. *Country* W Africa

Cameroon

Official name Republic of Cameroon
Formation 1960
Capital Yaoundé
Population 16 million / 89 people per sq mile (34 people per sq km)
Total area 183,567 sq. miles (475,400 sq. km)
Languages Bamileke, Fang, Fulani, French, English
Religions Roman Catholic 35%, Traditional beliefs 25%, Muslim 22%, Protestant 18%
Ethnic mix Cameroon highlanders 31%, other 21%, Equatorial Bantu 19%, Kirdi 11%, Fulani 10%, Northwestern Bantu 8%
Government Presidential system
Currency CFA franc = 100 centimes
Literacy rate 68%
Calorie consumption 2242 calories

Camocim *63 F2* Ceará, E Brazil
Camopi *59 H3* E French Guiana
Campamento *52 C2* Olancho, C Honduras
Campania *97 D5 cultural region* SE Italy
Campbell, Cape *151 D5 headland* South Island, NZ
Campbell Island *142 D5 island* S NZ
Campbell Plateau *142 D5 undersea feature* SW Pacific Ocean
Campbell River *36 D5* Vancouver Island, British Columbia, SW Canada
Campeche *51 G4* Campeche, SE Mexico
Campeche, Bahía de *51 F4 Eng.* Bay of Campeche. *Bay* E Mexico
Câm Pha *136 E3* Quang Ninh, N Vietnam
Câmpina *108 C4 prev.* Cîmpina. Prahova, SE Romania
Campina Grande *63 G2* Paraíba, E Brazil
Campinas *63 F4* São Paulo, S Brazil
Campobasso *97 D5* Molise, C Italy
Campo Criptana *see* Campo de Criptana
Campo de Criptana *93 E3 var.* Campo Criptana. Castilla-La Mancha, C Spain
Campo dos Goitacazes *see* Campos
Campo Grande *63 E4 state capital* Mato Grosso do Sul, SW Brazil
Campos *63 F4 var.* Campo dos Goitacazes. Rio de Janeiro, SE Brazil
Câmpulung *108 B4 prev.* Câmpulung-Mușcel, Cîmpulung. Argeș, S Romania
Campus Stellae *see* Santiago
Cam Ranh *137 E6* Khanh Hoa, S Vietnam
Canada *34 B4 country* N North America

Canada 34

Official name Canada
Formation 1867
Capital Ottawa
Population 31.5 million / 9 people per sq mile (3 people per sq km)
Total area 3,855,171 sq. miles (9,984,670 sq. km)
Languages English, French, Chinese, Italian, German, Ukrainian, Portuguese, Inuktitut, Cree
Religions Roman Catholic 44%, Protestant 29%, Other and nonreligious 27%
Ethnic mix British origin 44%, French origin 25%, Other European 20%, other 11%
Government Parliamentary system
Currency Canadian dollar = 100 cents
Literacy rate 99%
Calorie consumption 3176 calories

Canada Basin *34 C2 undersea feature* Arctic Ocean

Canadian River *49 E2 river* SW USA
Çanakkale *116 A3 var.* Dardanelli; *prev.* Chanak, Kale Sultanie. Çanakkale, W Turkey
Çanakkale Boğazı *116 A2 Eng.* Dardanelles. *Strait* NW Turkey
Cananea *50 B1* Sonora, NW Mexico
Canarias, Islas *70 A2 Eng.* Canary Islands. *Island group* Spain, NE Atlantic Ocean
Canarreos, Archipiélago de los *54 B2 island group* W Cuba
Canary Islands *see* Canarias, Islas
Cañas *52 D4* Guanacaste, NW Costa Rica
Canaveral, Cape *43 E4 headland* Florida, SE USA
Canavieiras *63 G3* Bahia, E Brazil
Canberra *142 C4 country capital* (Australia) Australian Capital Territory, SE Australia
Cancún *51 H3* Quintana Roo, SE Mexico
Candia *see* Irákleio
Canea *see* Chaniá
Cangzhou *128 D4* Hebei, E China
Caniapiscau *39 E2 river* Québec, E Canada
Caniapiscau, Réservoir de *38 D3 reservoir* Québec, C Canada
Canik Dağları *116 D2 mountain range* N Turkey
Canillo *91 A7* C Andorra
Çankırı *116 C3 var.* Chankiri; *anc.* Gangra, Germanicopolis. Çankın, N Turkey
Cannanore *132 B2 var.* Kananur, Kannur. Kerala, SW India
Cannes *91 D6* Alpes-Maritimes, SE France
Canoas *63 E5* Rio Grande do Sul, S Brazil
Canon City *44 C5* Colorado, C USA
Cantabria *92 D1 cultural region* N Spain
Cantábrica, Cordillera *92 C1 mountain range* N Spain
Cantaura *59 E2* Anzoátegui, NE Venezuela
Canterbury *89 E7 hist.* Cantwaraburh, *anc.* Durovernum, *Lat.* Cantuaria. SE England, UK
Canterbury Bight *151 C6 bight* South Island, NZ
Canterbury Plains *151 C6 plain* South Island, NZ
Cân Thơ *137 E6* Cân Thơ, S Vietnam
Canton *see* Guangzhou
Canton *42 B2* Mississippi, S USA
Canton *40 D4* Ohio, N USA
Canton Island *see* Kanton
Canyon *49 E2* Texas, SW USA
Cao Băng *136 D3 var.* Caobang. Cao Băng, N Vietnam
Caobang *see* Cao Băng
Cape Barren Island *149 C8 island* Furneaux Group, Tasmania, SE Australia
Cape Basin *69 B7 undersea feature* S Atlantic Ocean
Cape Breton Island *39 G4 Fr.* Île du Cap-Breton. *Island* Nova Scotia, SE Canada
Cape Charles *41 F5* Virginia, NE USA
Cape Coast *75 E5 prev.* Cape Coast Castle. S Ghana
Cape Farewell *see* Uummannarsuaq
Cape Girardeau *45 H5* Missouri, C USA
Cape Horn *see* Hornos, Cabo de
Capelle aan den IJssel *86 C4* Zuid-Holland, SW Netherlands
Cape Palmas *see* Harper
Cape Town *78 B5 var.* Ekapa, *Afr.* Kaapstad, Kapstad. *Country capital* (South Africa-legislative capital) Western Cape, SW South Africa
Cape Verde *74 A2 Port.* Cabo Verde, Ilhas do Cabo Verde. *Country* E Atlantic Ocean

Cape Verde 74

Official name Republic of Cape Verde
Formation 1975
Capital Praia
Population 463,000 / 298 people per sq mile (115 people per sq km)
Total area 1557 sq. miles (4033 sq. km)
Languages Portuguese Creole, Portuguese
Religions Roman Catholic 97%, other 2%, Protestant (Church of the Nazarene) 1%
Ethnic mix Mestiço 60%, African 30%, other 10%
Government Mixed presidential–parliamentary system
Currency Cape Verde escudo = 100 centavos
Literacy rate 76%
Calorie consumption 3308 calories

Cape Verde Basin *66 C4 undersea feature* E Atlantic Ocean
Cape Verde Plain *66 C4 undersea feature* E Atlantic Ocean
Cape York Peninsula *148 C2 peninsula* Queensland, N Australia
Cap-Haïtien *54 D3 var.* Le Cap. N Haiti
Capira *53 G5* Panamá, C Panama
Capitán Arturo Prat *154 A2 Chilean research station* South Shetland Islands, Antarctica
Capitán Pablo Lagerenza *64 D1 var.* Mayor Pablo Lagerenza. Chaco, N Paraguay
Capri, Isola di *97 C5 island* S Italy
Caprivi Strip *78 C3 Ger.* Caprivizipfel; *prev.* Caprivi Concession. *Cultural region* NE Namibia
Caquetá *56 B3 off.* Departamanto del Caquetá. *Province* S Colombia
Caquetá, Río *58 C5 var.* Rio Japurá, Yapurá. *River* Brazil/Colombia *see also* Japurá, Rio
CAR *see* Central African Republic
Caracal *108 B5* Olt, S Romania
Caracaraí *62 D1* Rondônia, W Brazil
Caracas *58 D1 country capital* (Venezuela) Distrito Federal, N Venezuela
Caratasca, Laguna de *53 E2 lagoon* NE Honduras
Carballiño *see* O Carballiño
Carbondale *40 B5* Illinois, N USA
Carbonia *97 A6 var.* Carbonia Centro. Sardegna, Italy, C Mediterranean Sea
Carbonia Centro *see* Carbonia
Carcassonne *91 C6 anc.* Carcaso. Aude, S France
Cárdenas *54 B2* Matanzas, W Cuba
Cardiff *89 C7 Wel.* Caerdydd. *Admin capital* S Wales, UK
Cardigan Bay *89 C6 bay* W Wales, UK
Carei *108 B3 Ger.* Gross-Karol, Karol, *Hung.* Nagykároly; *prev.* Careii-Mari. Satu Mare, NW Romania
Carey, Lake *147 B6 lake* Western Australia
Cariaco *59 E1* Sucre, NE Venezuela
Caribbean Sea *54 C4 sea* W Atlantic Ocean
Carlisle *88 C4 anc.* Caer Luel, Luguvallium, Luguvallum. NW England, UK
Carlow *89 B6 Ir.* Ceatharlach. SE Ireland
Carlsbad *48 D3* New Mexico, SW USA
Carlsberg Ridge *140 B4 undersea feature* S Arabian Sea
Carlsruhe *see* Karlsruhe
Carmana *see* Kermān
Carmarthen *89 C6* SW Wales, UK
Carmaux *91 C6* Tarn, S France
Carmel *40 C4* Indiana, N USA
Carmelita *52 B1* Petén, N Guatemala
Carmen *51 G4 var.* Ciudad del Carmen. Campeche, SE Mexico
Carmona *92 C4* Andalucía, S Spain
Carnaro *see* Kvarner
Carnarvon *147 A5* Western Australia
Carnegie, Lake *147 B5 salt lake* Western Australia
Car Nicobar *133 F3 island* Nicobar Islands, India, NE Indian Ocean
Caroço, Ilha *76 E1 island* N Sao Tome and Principe
Carolina *63 F2* Maranhão, E Brazil
Caroline Island *see* Millennium Island
Caroline Islands *106 C2 island group* C Micronesia
Caroní, Río *59 E3 river* E Venezuela
Caronium *see* A Coruña
Carora *58 C1* Lara, N Venezuela
Carpathian Mountains *81 E4 var.* Carpathians, *Cz./Pol.* Karpaty, *Ger.* Karpaten. *Mountain range* E Europe
Carpathians *see* Carpathian Mountains
Carpații Meridionali *108 B4 var.* Alpi Transilvaniei, Carpații Sudici, *Eng.* South Carpathians, Transylvanian Alps, *Ger.* Südkarpaten, Transsylvanische Alpen, *Hung.* Déli-Kárpátok, Erdélyi-Havasok. *Mountain range* C Romania
Carpații Occidentali *99 E7 Eng.* Western Carpathians. *Mountain range* W Romania
Carpații Sudici *see* Carpații Meridionali
Carpentaria, Gulf of *148 B2 gulf* N Australia
Carpi *96 C2* Emilia-Romagna, N Italy
Carrara *96 B3* Toscana, C Italy
Carson City *47 C5 state capital* Nevada, W USA
Carson Sink *47 C5 salt flat* Nevada, W USA
Cartagena *93 F4 anc.* Carthago Nova. Murcia, SE Spain
Cartagena *58 B1 var.* Cartagena de los Indes. Bolívar, NW Colombia
Cartagena de los Indes *see* Cartagena
Cartago *53 E4* Cartago, C Costa Rica
Carthage *45 F5* Missouri, C USA
Cartwright *39 F2* Newfoundland and Labrador, E Canada
Carúpano *59 E1* Sucre, NE Venezuela
Caruthersville *45 H5* Missouri, C USA
Cary *43 F1* North Carolina, SE USA
Casablanca *70 C2 Ar.* Dar-el-Beida. NW Morocco
Casa Grande *48 B2* Arizona, SW USA
Cascade Range *46 B3 mountain range* Oregon/Washington, NW USA
Cascadia Basin *34 A4 undersea feature* NE Pacific Ocean
Cascais *92 B4* Lisboa, C Portugal
Caserta *97 D5* Campania, S Italy
Casey *154 D4 Australian research station* Antarctica
Casino *91 C8* New South Wales, SE Australia
Čáslav *99 B5 Ger.* Tschaslau. Středočesky Kraj, C Czech Republic
Casper *44 C3* Wyoming, C USA
Caspian Depression *111 B7 Kaz.* Kaspīy Mangy Oypaty, *Rus.* Prikaspiyskaya Nizmennost'. *Depression* Kazakhstan/Russian Federation
Caspian Sea *114 A4 Az.* Xäzär Dänizi, *Kaz.* Kaspiy Tengizi, *Per.* Baḩr-e Khazar, Daryā-ye Khazar, *Rus.* Kaspiyskoye More. *Inland sea* Asia/Europe
Cassai *see* Kasai
Castamoni *see* Kastamonu
Casteggio *96 B2* Lombardia, N Italy
Castelló de la Plana *93 F3 var.* Castellón. País Valenciano, E Spain
Castellón *see* Castelló de la Plana
Castelnaudary *91 C6* Aude, S France
Castelo Branco *92 C3* Castelo Branco, C Portugal
Castelsarrasin *91 B6* Tarn-et-Garonne, S France
Castelvetrano *97 C7* Sicilia, Italy, C Mediterranean Sea
Castilla-La Mancha *93 E3 cultural region* NE Spain
Castilla-León *92 C2 cultural region* NW Spain
Castlebar *89 A5 Ir.* Caisleán an Bharraigh. W Ireland
Castleford *89 D5* N England, UK
Castle Harbour *42 B5 inlet* Bermuda, NW Atlantic Ocean
Castricum *86 C3* Noord-Holland, W Netherlands
Castries *55 F1 country capital* (Saint Lucia) N Saint Lucia
Castro *65 B6* Los Lagos, W Chile
Castrovillari *97 D6* Calabria, SW Italy
Castuera *92 D4* Extremadura, W Spain
Caswell Sound *151 A7 sound* South Island, NZ
Catacamas *52 D2* Olancho, C Honduras
Catacaos *60 B3* Piura, NW Peru
Catalan Bay *93 H4 var.* Caleta. *Bay* E Gibraltar
Cataluña *93 G2 cultural region* N Spain
Catamarca *see* San Fernando del Valle de Catamarca
Catania *97 D7* Sicilia, Italy, C Mediterranean Sea
Catanzaro *97 D6* Calabria, SW Italy
Catarroja *93 F3* País Valenciano, E Spain
Cat Island *54 C1 island* C Bahamas
Catskill Mountains *41 F3 mountain range* New York, NE USA
Cauca, Río *58 B2 river* N Colombia
Caucasia *58 B2* Antioquia, NW Colombia
Caucasus *81 G4 Rus.* Kavkaz. *Mountain range* Georgia/Russian Federation
Caura, Río *59 E3 river* C Venezuela
Cavalla *74 D5 var.* Cavally, Cavally Fleuve. *River* Côte d'Ivoire/Liberia
Cavally *see* Cavalla
Cavally Fleuve *see* Cavalla
Caviana de Fora, Ilha *63 E1 var.* Ilha Caviana. *Island* N Brazil
Caxito *78 B1* Bengo, NW Angola
Cayenne *59 H3 de6pendent territory capital* (French Guiana) NE French Guiana
Cayes *54 D3 var.* Les Cayes. SW Haiti
Cayman Brac *54 B3 island* E Cayman Islands
Cayman Islands *54 B3 UK dependent territory* W West Indies
Cay Sal *54 B2 islet* SW Bahamas
Cazin *100 B3* Federacija Bosna I Hercegovina, NW Bosnia and Herzegovina
Cazorla *93 E4* Andalucía, S Spain
Ceadâr-Lunga *see* Ciadîr-Lunga
Ceará *63 F2 off.* Estado do Ceará. *State* C Brazil
Ceara Abyssal Plain *see* Ceará Plain
Ceará Plain *56 E3 var.* Ceara Abyssal Plain. *Undersea feature* W Atlantic Ocean
Ceatharlach *see* Carlow
Cébaco, Isla *53 F5 island* SW Panama
Cebu *139 E2 off.* Cebu City. Cebu, C Philippines
Cecina *96 B3* Toscana, C Italy
Cedar City *44 A5* Utah, W USA
Cedar Falls *45 G3* Iowa, C USA
Cedar Lake *38 A2 lake* Manitoba, C Canada

Cedar Rapids *45 G3* Iowa, C USA
Cedros, Isla *50 A2 island* W Mexico
Ceduna *149 A6* South Australia
Cefalu *97 C7 anc.* Cephaloedium. Sicilia, Italy, C Mediterranean Sea
Celebes *see* Sulawesi
Celebes Sea *139 E3 Ind.* Laut Sulawesi. *Sea* Indonesia/Philippines
Celje *95 E7 Ger.* Cilli. C Slovenia
Celldömölk *99 C6* Vas, W Hungary
Celle *94 B3 var.* Zelle. Niedersachsen, N Germany
Celtic Sea *89 B7 Ir.* An Mhuir Cheilteach. *Sea* SW British Isles
Celtic Shelf *80 B3 undersea feature* E Atlantic Ocean
Cenderawasih, Teluk *139 G4 var.* Teluk Irian, Teluk Sarera. *Bay* W Pacific Ocean
Cenon *91 B5* Gironde, SW France
Central African Republic *76 C4 var.* République Centrafricaine, *abbrev.* CAR; *prev.* Ubangi-Shari, Oubangui-Chari, Territoire de l'Oubangui-Chari. *Country* C Africa

Central African Republic 76

Official name Central African Republic
Formation 1960
Capital Bangui
Population 3.9 million / 16 people per sq mile (6 people per sq km)
Total area 240,534 sq. miles (622,984 sq. km)
Languages Sango, Banda, Gbaya, French
Religions Traditional beliefs 60%, Christian 35%, Muslim 5%
Ethnic mix Baya 34%, Banda 27%, Mandjia 21%, Sara 10%, other 8%
Government Transitional regime
Currency CFA franc = 100 centimes
Literacy rate 49%
Calorie consumption 1949 calories

Central, Cordillera *55 E3 mountain range* C Dominican Republic
Central, Cordillera *53 F5 mountain range* C Panama
Central, Cordillera *139 E1 mountain range* Luzon, N Philippines
Central, Cordillera *58 B3 mountain range* W Colombia
Central Group *see* Inner Islands
Centralia *46 B2* Washington, NW USA
Central Indian Ridge *see* Mid-Indian Ridge
Central Makrān Range *134 A3 mountain range* W Pakistan
Central Pacific Basin *142 D1 undersea feature* C Pacific Ocean
Central, Planalto *63 F3 var.* Brazilian Highlands. *Mountain range* E Brazil
Central Range *144 B3 mountain range* NW PNG
Central Russian Upland *see* Srednerusskaya Vozvyshennost'
Central Siberian Plateau *see* Srednesibirskoye Ploskogor'ye
Central Siberian Uplands *see* Srednesibirskoye Ploskogor'ye
Central, Sistema *92 D3 mountain range* C Spain
Central Valley *47 B6 valley* California, W USA
Cephaloedium *see* Cefalu
Ceram *see* Seram, Pulau
Ceram Sea *139 F4 Ind.* Laut Seram. *Sea* E Indonesia
Cerasus *see* Giresun
Cereté *58 B2* Córdoba, NW Colombia
Cerignola *97 D5* Puglia, SE Italy
Cerigo *see* Kýthira
Çerkeş *116 C2* Çankın, N Turkey
Cernay *90 E4* Haut-Rhin, NE France
Cerro Chirripó *see* Chirripó Grande, Cerro
Cerro de Mulhacén *see* Mulhacén
Cerro de Pasco *60 C3* Pasco, C Peru
Cervera *93 F2* Cataluña, NE Spain
Cesena *96 C3 anc.* Caesena. Emilia-Romagna, N Italy
Cēsis *106 D3 Ger.* Wenden. Cēsis, C Latvia
České Budějovice *99 B5 Ger.* Budweis. Budějovický Kraj, S Czech Republic
Český Krumlov *99 A5 var.* Böhmisch-Krumau, *Ger.* Krummau. Budějovický Kraj, S Czech Republic
Cetinje *101 C5 It.* Cettigne. Montenegro, SW Serbia and Montenegro (Yugo.)
Ceuta *70 C2 enclave* Spain, N Africa
Cévennes *91 C6 mountain range* S France
Ceyhan *116 D4* Adana, S Turkey
Ceylanpınar *117 E4* Şanlıurfa, SE Turkey
Ceylon Plain *124 B4 undersea feature* N Indian Ocean
Ceyre to the Caribs *see* Marie-Galante
Chachapoyas *60 B2* Amazonas, NW Peru
Chachevichy *107 D6 Rus.* Chechevichi. Mahilyowskaya Voblasts', E Belarus
Chaco *see* Gran Chaco
Chad *76 C3 Fr.* Tchad. *Country* C Africa

Chad 76

Official name Republic of Chad
Formation 1960
Capital N'Djamena
Population 8.6 million / 18 people per sq mile (7 people per sq km)
Total area 495,752 sq. miles (1,284,000 sq. km)
Languages French, Sara, Arabic, Maba
Religions Muslim 55%, Traditional beliefs 35%, Christian 10%
Ethnic mix Nomads (Tuareg and Toubou) 38%, Sara 30%, other 17%, Arab 15%
Government Presidential system
Currency CFA franc = 100 centimes
Literacy rate 46%
Calorie consumption 2245 calories

Chad, Lake *76 B3 Fr.* Lac Tchad. *Lake* C Africa
Chadron *44 D3* Nebraska, C USA
Chadyr-Lunga *see* Ciadîr-Lunga
Chāgai Hills *134 A2 var.* Chāh Gay. *Mountain range* Afghanistan/Pakistan
Chaghasarāy *see* Asadābād
Chagos-Laccadive Plateau *124 B4 undersea feature* N Indian Ocean
Chagos Trench *141 C5 undersea feature* N Indian Ocean
Chāh Gay *see* Chāgai Hills
Chaillu, Massif du *77 B6 mountain range* C Gabon
Chaîne des Dangrek *see* Dângrêk, Chuŏr Phnum
Chaîne des Mitumba *see* Mitumba, Monts
Chaîne des Mongos *see* Bongo, Massif des
Chain Ridge *140 B4 undersea feature* W Indian Ocean
Chajul *52 B2* Quiché, W Guatemala
Chakhānsūr *122 D5* Nīmrūz, SW Afghanistan
Chala *60 D4* Arequipa, SW Peru
Chalatenango *52 C3* Chalatenango, N El Salvador
Chalcidice *see* Chalkidikí
Chalcis *see* Chalkída
Chálki *105 E7 island* Dodekánisos, Greece, Aegean Sea
Chalkída *105 C5 var.* Halkida; *prev.* Khalkís, *anc.* Chalcis. Evvoia, E Greece
Chalkidikí *104 C4 var.* Khalkidhikí; *anc.* Chalcidice. *Peninsula* NE Greece
Challans *90 B4* Vendée, NW France
Challapata *61 F4* Oruro, SW Bolivia
Challenger Deep *152 B3 undersea feature* W Pacific Ocean
Challenger Fracture Zone *153 F4 tectonic feature* SE Pacific Ocean
Châlons-en-Champagne *90 D3 prev.* Châlons-sur-Marne, *hist.* Arcae Remorum, *anc.* Carolopois. Marne, NE France
Chalon-sur-Saône *90 D4 anc.* Cabillonum. Saône-et-Loire, C France
Cha Mai *see* Thung Song
Chaman *134 B2* Baluchistān, SW Pakistan
Chambéry *91 D5 anc.* Camberia. Savoie, E France
Champagne *90 D3* Yukon Territory, W Canada
Champaign *40 B4* Illinois, N USA
Champasak *137 D5* Champasak, S Laos
Champlain, Lake *41 F2 lake* Canada/USA
Champotón *51 G4* Campeche, SE Mexico
Chanak *see* Çanakkale
Chañaral *64 B3* Atacama, N Chile
Chanchiang *see* Zhanjiang
Chandeleur Islands *42 C3 island group* Louisiana, S USA
Chandīgarh *134 D2* Punjab, N India
Chandrapur *135 E5* Mahārāshtra, C India
Changan *see* Xi'an
Changane *79 E3 river* S Mozambique
Changchun *128 D3 var.* Ch'angch'un, Ch'ang-ch'un; *prev.* Hsinking. Jilin, NE China
Ch'angch'un *see* Changchun
Chang Jiang *128 B5 var.* Yangtze Kiang, *Eng.* Yangtze. *River* C China
Changkiakow *see* Zhangjiakou
Chang, Ko *137 C6 island* S Thailand
Changsha *128 C5 var.* Ch'angsha, Ch'ang-sha. Hunan, S China
Ch'angsha *see* Changsha
Changzhi *128 C4* Shanxi, C China
Chaniá *105 C7 var.* Hania, Khaniá, *Eng.* Canea; *anc.* Cydonia. Kríti, Greece, E Mediterranean Sea
Chañi, Nevado de *64 B2 mountain* NW Argentina
Chankiri *see* Çankırı
Channel Islands *89 C8 Fr.* Îles Normandes. *Island group* S English Channel
Channel Islands *47 B8 island group* California, W USA
Channel-Port aux Basques *39 G4* Newfoundland, Newfoundland and Labrador, SE Canada
Channel, The *see* English Channel
Channel Tunnel *90 C2 tunnel* France/UK
Chantabun *see* Chanthaburi
Chantaburi *see* Chanthaburi
Chantada *92 C1* Galicia, NW Spain
Chanthaburi *137 C6 var.* Chantabun, Chantaburi. Chantaburi, S Thailand
Chanute *45 F5* Kansas, C USA
Chaouèn *see* Chefchaouen
Chaoyang *128 D3* Liaoning, NE China
Chapala, Lago de *50 D4 lake* C Mexico
Chapan, Gora *122 B3 mountain* C Turkmenistan
Chapayevsk *111 C6* Samarskaya Oblast', W Russian Federation
Chaplynka *109 F4* Khersons'ka Oblast', S Ukraine
Charcot Seamounts *80 B3 undersea feature* E Atlantic Ocean
Charente *91 B5 cultural region* W France
Charente *91 B5 river* W France
Chari *76 B3 var.* Shari. *River* Central African Republic/Chad
Chārīkār *123 E4* Parwān, NE Afghanistan
Charity *59 F2* NW Guyana
Charkhlik *see* Ruoqiang
Charkhliq *see* Ruoqiang
Charleroi *87 C7* Hainaut, S Belgium
Charlesbourg *39 E4* Québec, SE Canada
Charles de Gaulle *90 E1 international airport* (Paris) Seine-et-Marne, N France
Charles Island *38 D1 island* Northwest Territories, NE Canada
Charles Island *see* Santa María, Isla
Charleston *40 D5 state capital* West Virginia, NE USA
Charleston *43 F2* South Carolina, SE USA
Charleville *149 D5* Queensland, E Australia
Charleville-Mézières *90 D3* Ardennes, N France
Charlie-Gibbs Fracture Zone *66 C2 tectonic feature* N Atlantic Ocean
Charlotte *43 E1* North Carolina, SE USA
Charlotte Amalie *55 F3 prev.* Saint Thomas. *Dependent territory capital* (Virgin Islands (US)) Saint Thomas, N Virgin Islands (US)
Charlotte Harbor *43 E5 inlet* Florida, SE USA
Charlottesville *41 E5* Virginia, NE USA
Charlottetown *39 F4* Prince Edward Island, Prince Edward Island, SE Canada
Charsk *see* Shar
Charters Towers *148 D3* Queensland, NE Australia
Chartres *90 C3 anc.* Autricum, Civitas Carnutum. Eure-et-Loir, C France
Charus Nuur *126 C2 lake* NW Mongolia
Chashniki *107 D5 Rus.* Chashniki. Vitsyebskaya Voblasts', N Belarus
Châteaubriant *90 B4* Loire-Atlantique, NW France
Châteaudun *90 C3* Eure-et-Loir, C France
Châteauroux *90 C4 prev.* Indreville. Indre, C France
Château-Thierry *90 C3* Aisne, N France
Châtelet *87 C7* Hainaut, S Belgium
Châtelherault *see* Châtellerault
Châtellerault *90 B4 var.* Châtelherault. Vienne, W France
Chatham Island *see* San Cristóbal, Isla
Chatham Island Rise *see* Chatham Rise
Chatham Islands *143 E5 island group* NZ, SW Pacific Ocean
Chatham Rise *142 D5 var.* Chatham Island Rise. *Undersea feature* S Pacific Ocean
Chatkal Range *123 F2 Rus.* Chatkal'skiy Khrebet. *Mountain range* Kyrgyzstan/Uzbekistan
Chattahoochee River *42 D3 river* SE USA
Chattanooga *42 D1* Tennessee, S USA
Chatyr-Tash *123 G2* Narynskaya Oblast', C Kyrgyzstan
Châu Đốc *137 D6 var.* Chauphu, Chau Phu. An Giang, S Vietnam
Chauk *136 A3* Magwe, W Myanmar
Chaumont *90 D4 prev.* Chaumont-en-Bassigny. Haute-Marne, N France
Chau Phu *see* Châu Đốc
Chaves *92 C2 anc.* Aquae Flaviae. Vila Real, N Portugal
Chávez, Isla *see* Santa Cruz, Isla
Chavusy *107 E6 Rus.* Chausy. Mahilyowskaya Voblasts', E Belarus
Chaykovskiy *111 D5* Permskaya Oblast', NW Russian Federation
Cheb *99 A5 Ger.* Eger. Karlovarský Kraj, W Czech Republic

Cheboksary *111 C5* Chuvashskaya Respublika, W Russian Federation
Cheboygan *40 C2* Michigan, N USA
Chechaouèn *see* Chefchaouen
Chech, Erg *74 D1 desert* Algeria/Mali
Che-chiang *see* Zhejiang
Cheduba Island *136 A4 island* W Myanmar
Chefchaouen *70 C2 var.* Chaouèn, Chechaouèn, *Sp.* Xauen. N Morocco
Chefoo *see* Yantai
Cheju-do *129 E4 Jap.* Saishū; *prev.* Quelpart. *Island* S South Korea
Cheju Strait *129 E4 strait* S South Korea
Chekiang *see* Zhejiang
Hazar *122 B2 prev.* Cheleken. Balkanskiy Velayat, W Turkmenistan
Chelkar *see* Shalkar
Chełm *98 E4 Rus.* Kholm. Lubelskie, E Poland
Chełmno *98 C3 Ger.* Culm, Kulm. Kujawski-pomorskie, C Poland
Chełmża *98 C3 Ger.* Culmsee, Kulmsee. Kujawski-pomorskie, C Poland
Cheltenham *89 D6* C England, UK
Chelyabinsk *114 C3* Chelyabinskaya Oblast', C Russian Federation
Chemnitz *94 D4 prev.* Karl-Marx-Stadt. Sachsen, E Germany
Chenāb *134 C2 river* India/Pakistan
Chengchiatun *see* Liaoyuan
Ch'eng-chou *see* Zhengzhou
Chengchow *see* Zhengzhou
Chengde *128 D3 var.* Jehol. Hebei, E China
Chengdu *128 B5 var.* Chengtu, Ch'eng-tu. Sichuan, C China
Chenghsien *see* Zhengzhou
Ch'eng-tu *see* Chengdu
Chennai *132 D2 prev* Madras. Tamil Nādu, S India
Chenxian *see* Chenzhou
Chen Xian *see* Chenzhou
Chen Xiang *see* Chenzhou
Chenzhou *128 C6 var.* Chenxian, Chen Xian, Chen Xiang. Hunan, S China
Chepelare *104 C3* Smolyan, S Bulgaria
Chepén *60 B3* La Libertad, C Peru
Cher *90 C4 river* C France
Cherbourg *90 B3 anc.* Carusbur. Manche, N France
Cherepovets *110 B4* Vologodskaya Oblast', NW Russian Federation
Chergui, Chott ech *70 D2 salt lake* NW Algeria
Cherkasy *109 E2 Rus.* Cherkassy. Cherkas'ka Oblast', C Ukraine
Cherkessk *111 B7* Karachayevo-Cherkesskaya Respublika, SW Russian Federation
Chernihiv *109 E1 Rus.* Chernigov. Chernihivs'ka Oblast', NE Ukraine
Chernivtsi *108 C3 Ger.* Czernowitz, *Rom.* Cernăuţi, *Rus.* Chernovtsy. Chernivets'ka Oblast', W Ukraine
Cherno More *see* Black Sea
Chernoye More *see* Black Sea
Chernyakhovsk *106 A4 Ger.* Insterburg. Kaliningradskaya Oblast', W Russian Federation
Cherry Hill *41 F4* New Jersey, NE USA
Cherski Range *see* Cherskogo, Khrebet
Cherskiy *115 G2* Respublika Sakha (Yakutiya), NE Russian Federation
Cherskogo, Khrebet *115 F2 var.* Cherski Range. *Mountain range* NE Russian Federation
Chervonohrad *108 C2 Rus.* Chervonograd. L'vivs'ka Oblast', NW Ukraine
Chervyen' *107 D6 Rus.* Cherven'. Minskaya Voblasts', C Belarus
Cherykaw *107 E7 Rus.* Cherikov. Mahilyowskaya Voblasts', E Belarus
Chesapeake Bay *41 F5 inlet* NE USA
Chesha Bay *see* Chëshskaya Guba
Chëshskaya Guba *172 D5 var.* Archangel Bay, Chesha Bay, Dvina Bay. *Bay* NW Russian Federation
Chester *89 C6 Wel.* Caerleon; *hist.* Legaceaster, *Lat.* Deva, Devana Castra. C England, UK
Chetumal *51 H4 var.* Payo Obispo. Quintana Roo, SE Mexico
Cheviot Hills *88 D4 hill range* England/Scotland, UK
Cheyenne *44 D4 state capital* Wyoming, C USA
Cheyenne River *44 D3 river* South Dakota/Wyoming, N USA
Chhapra *135 F3 prev.* Chapra. Bihār, N India
Chhattīsgarh *135 E4* Admin. region *state* N India
Chiai *128 D6 var.* Chia-i, Chiayi, Kiayi, Jiayi, *Jap.* Kagi. C Taiwan
Chia-i *see* Chiai
Chiang-hsi *see* Jiangxi
Chiang Mai *136 B4 var.* Chiangmai, Chiengmai, Kiangmai. Chiang Mai, NW Thailand
Chiangmai *see* Chiang Mai
Chiang Rai *136 C3 var.* Chianpai, Chienrai, Muang Chiang Rai. Chiang Rai, NW Thailand
Chiang-su *see* Jiangsu
Chian-ning *see* Nanjing
Chianpai *see* Chiang Rai
Chianti *96 C3 cultural region* C Italy
Chiapa *see* Chiapa de Corzo
Chiapa de Corzo *51 G5 var.* Chiapa. Chiapas, SE Mexico
Chiayi *see* Chiai
Chiba *130 B1 var.* Tiba. Chiba, Honshū, S Japan
Chibougamau *38 D3* Québec, SE Canada
Chicago *40 B3* Illinois, N USA
Ch'i-ch'i-ha-erh *see* Qiqihar
Chickasha *49 G2* Oklahoma, C USA
Chiclayo *60 B3* Lambayeque, NW Peru
Chico *47 B5* California, W USA
Chico, Río *65 B6 river* S Argentina
Chico, Río *65 B7 river* SE Argentina
Chicoutimi *39 E4* Québec, SE Canada
Chiengmai *see* Chiang Mai
Chienrai *see* Chiang Rai
Chiesanuova *96 D2* SW San Marino
Chieti *96 D4 var.* Teate. Abruzzo, C Italy
Chifeng *127 G2 var.* Ulanhad. Nei Mongol Zizhiqu, N China
Chih-fu *see* Yantai
Chihli *see* Hebei
Chihli, Gulf of *see* Bo Hai
Chihuahua *50 C2* Chihuahua, NW Mexico
Childress *49 F2* Texas, SW USA
Chile *64 B3 Country* SW South America

Chile 64

Official name Republic of Chile
Formation 1818
Capital Santiago
Population 15.8 million / 55 people per sq mile (21 people per sq km)
Total area 292,258 sq. miles (756,950 sq. km)
Languages Spanish, Amerindian languages
Religions Roman Catholic 80%, Other and nonreligious 20%
Ethnic mix Mixed race and European 90%, Amerindian 10%
Government Presidential system
Currency Chilean peso = 100 centavos
Literacy rate 96%
Calorie consumption 2868 calories

Chile Basin *57 A5 undersea feature* E Pacific Ocean
Chile Chico *65 B6* Aisén, W Chile
Chile Rise *57 A7 undersea feature* SE Pacific Ocean
Chililabombwe *78 D2* Copperbelt, C Zambia
Chi-lin *see* Jilin
Chillán *65 B5* Bío Bío, C Chile
Chillicothe *40 D4* Ohio, N USA
Chiloé, Isla de *65 A6 var.* Isla Grande de Chiloé. *Island* W Chile
Chilpancingo *51 E5 var.* Chilpancingo de los Bravos. Guerrero, S Mexico
Chilpancingo de los Bravos *see* Chilpancingo
Chilung *128 D6 var.* Keelung, *Jap.* Kirun, Kirun'; *prev. Sp. Santissima Trinidad.* N Taiwan
Chimán *53 G5* Panamá, E Panama
Chimborazo *60 A1 volcano* C Ecuador
Chimbote *60 C3* Ancash, W Peru
Chimboy *122 D1 Rus.* Chimbay. Qoraqalpoghiston Respublikasi, NW Uzbekistan
Chimoio *79 E3* Manica, C Mozambique
China *124 C2 Chin.* Chung-hua Jen-min Kung-ho-kuo, Zhonghua Renmin Gongheguo; *prev.* Chinese Empire. *Country* E Asia

China 124

Official name People's Republic of China
Formation 960
Capital Beijing
Population 1.3 billion / 362 people per sq mile (140 people per sq km)
Total area 3,705,386 sq. miles (9,596,960 sq. km)
Languages Mandarin, Wu, Cantonese, Hsiang, Min, Hakka, Kan
Religions Nonreligious 59%, Traditional beliefs 20%, other 13%, Buddhist 6%, Muslim 2%
Ethnic mix Han 92%, other 7%
Government One-party state
Currency Renminbi (known as yuan) = 10 jiao = 100 fen
Literacy rate 91%
Calorie consumption 2963 calories

Chi-nan *see* Jinan
Chinandega *52 C3* Chinandega, NW Nicaragua
Chincha Alta *60 D4* Ica, SW Peru
Chin-chiang *see* Quanzhou
Chin-chou *see* Jinzhou
Chinchow *see* Jinzhou
Chindwin *136 B2 river* N Myanmar
Ch'ing Hai *see* Qinghai Hu
Chingola *78 D2* Copperbelt, C Zambia
Ching-Tao *see* Qingdao
Chinguețți *74 C2 var.* Chinguetti. Adrar, C Mauritania
Chin Hills *136 A3 mountain range* W Myanmar
Chinhsien *see* Jinzhou
Chinnereth *see* Tiberias, Lake
Chinook Trough *113 H4 undersea feature* N Pacific Ocean
Chioggia *96 C2 anc.* Fossa Claudia. Veneto, NE Italy
Chíos *105 D5 var.* Hios, Khíos, *It.* Scio, *Turk.* Sakiz-Adasi. Chíos, E Greece
Chíos *105 D5 var.* Khíos. *Island* E Greece
Chipata *78 D2 prev.* Fort Jameson. Eastern, E Zambia
Chiquián *60 C3* Ancash, W Peru
Chiquimula *52 B2* Chiquimula, SE Guatemala
Chīrāla *132 D1* Andhra Pradesh, E India
Chirchiq *123 E2 Rus.* Chirchik. Toshkent Wiloyati, E Uzbekistan
Chiriquí, Golfo de *53 E5 Eng.* Chiriqui Gulf. *Gulf* SW Panama
Chiriquí, Laguna de *53 E5 lagoon* NW Panama
Chirripó Grande, Cerro *52 D4 var.* Cerro Chirripó. *Mountain* SE Costa Rica
Chisec *52 B2* Alta Verapaz, C Guatemala
Chisholm *45 F1* Minnesota, N USA
Chisimaio *see* Kismaayo
Chisimayu *see* Kismaayo
Chişinău *108 D4 Rus.* Kishinev. *Country capital* (Moldova) C Moldova
Chita *115 F4* Chitinskaya Oblast', S Russian Federation
Chitato *78 C1* Lunda Norte, NE Angola
Chitina *36 D3* Alaska, USA
Chitose *130 D2 var.* Titose. Hokkaidō, NE Japan
Chitré *53 F5* Herrera, S Panama
Chittagong *135 G4 Ben.* Chāttagām. Chittagong, SE Bangladesh
Chitungwiza *78 D3 prev.* Chitangwiza. Mashonaland East, NE Zimbabwe
Chlef *70 D2 var.* Ech Cheliff, Ech Chleff; *prev.* Al-Asnam, El Asnam, Orléansville. NW Algeria
Chocolate Mountains *47 D8 mountain range* California, W USA
Chodzież *98 C3* Wielkopolskie, C Poland
Choele Choel *65 C5* Río Negro, C Argentina
Choiseul *144 C3 var.* Lauru. *Island* NW Solomon Islands
Chojnice *98 C2 Ger.* Knoitz. Pomorskie, N Poland
Ch'ok'ē *72 C4 var.* Choke Mountains. *Mountain range* NW Ethiopia
Choke Mountains *see* Ch'ok'ē
Cholet *90 B4* Maine-et-Loire, NW France
Choluteca *52 C3* Choluteca, S Honduras
Choluteca, Río *52 C3 river* SW Honduras
Choma *78 D2* Southern, S Zambia
Chomutov *98 A4 Ger.* Komotau. Ústecký Kraj, NW Czech Republic
Chona *113 E2 river* C Russian Federation
Chon Buri *137 C5 prev.* Bang Pla Soi. Chon Buri, S Thailand
Chone *60 A1* Manabí, W Ecuador
Ch'ŏngjin *129 E3* NE North Korea
Chongqing *128 B5 var.* Ch'ung-ching, Ch'ung-ch'ing, Chungking, Pahsien, Tchongking, Yuzhou. Chongqing, C China
Chongqing *128 B5* Admin. region *province* C China
Chonos, Archipiélago de los *65 A6 island group* S Chile
Chorne More *see* Black Sea
Chornomors'ke *109 E4 Rus.* Chernomorskoye. Respublika Krym, S Ukraine
Chortkiv *108 C2 Rus.* Chortkov. Ternopil's'ka Oblast', W Ukraine
Chorum *see* Çorum
Chorzów *99 C5 Ger.* Königshütte; *prev.* Królewska Huta. Śląskie, S Poland
Chōshi *131 D5 var.* Tyôsi. Chiba, Honshū, S Japan
Choszczno *98 B3 Ger.* Arnswalde. Zachodniopomorskie, NW Poland
Chota Nāgpur *135 E4 plateau* N India
Chott el-Hodna *see* Hodna, Chott El
Chott Melrhir *see* Melghir, Chott
Choûm *74 C2* Adrar, C Mauritania
Choybalsan *127 F2* Dornod, E Mongolia
Christchurch *151 C6* Canterbury, South Island, NZ
Christiana *54 B5* C Jamaica
Christiansand *see* Kristiansand
Christianshåb *see* Qasigiannguit
Christiansund *see* Kristiansund

Christmas Island 141 D5 *Australian external territory* E Indian Ocean
Christmas Ridge 143 E1 *undersea feature* C Pacific Ocean
Chuan *see* Sichuan
Ch'uan-chou *see* Quanzhou
Chubut 57 B7 *off.* Provincia de Chubut. Admin. region *province* S Argentina
Chubut, Río 65 B6 *river* SE Argentina
Ch'u-chiang *see* Shaoguan
Chūgoku-sanchi 131 B6 *mountain range* Honshū, SW Japan
Chuí *see* Chuy
Chukai *see* Cukai
Chukchi Plain 155 B2 *undersea feature* Arctic Ocean
Chukchi Plateau 34 C2 *undersea feature* Arctic Ocean
Chukchi Sea 34 B2 *Rus.* Chukotskoye More. *Sea* Arctic Ocean
Chula Vista 47 C8 California, W USA
Chulucanas 60 B2 Piura, NW Peru
Chulym 114 D4 *river* C Russian Federation
Chumphon 137 C6 *var.* Jumporn. Chumphon, SW Thailand
Ch'unch'ŏn 129 E4 *Jap.* Shunsen. N South Korea
Ch'ung-ching *see* Chongqing
Chungking *see* Chongqing
Chunya 115 E3 *river* C Russian Federation
Chuquicamata 64 B2 Antofagasta, N Chile
Chur 95 B7 *Fr.* Coire, *It.* Coira, *Rmsch.* Cuera, Quera; *anc.* Curia Rhaetorum. Graubünden, E Switzerland
Churchill 38 B2 *river* Manitoba/Saskatchewan, C Canada
Churchill 39 F2 *river* Newfoundland and Labrador, E Canada
Churchill 37 G4 Manitoba, C Canada
Chuska Mountains 48 C1 *mountain range* Arizona/New Mexico, SW USA
Chusovoy 111 D5 Permskaya Oblast', NW Russian Federation
Chuuk Islands 144 B2 *var.* Hogoley Islands; *prev.* Truk Islands. *Island group* Caroline Islands, C Micronesia
Chuy 64 E4 *var.* Chuí. Rocha, E Uruguay
Chyhyryn 109 E2 *Rus.* Chigirin. Cherkas'ka Oblast', N Ukraine
Ciadîr-Lunga 108 D4 *var.* Ceadâr-Lunga, *Rus.* Chadyr-Lunga. S Moldova
Cide 116 C2 Kastamonu, N Turkey
Ciechanów 98 D3 *prev.* Zichenau. Mazowieckie, C Poland
Ciego de Ávila 54 C2 Ciego de Ávila, C Cuba
Ciénaga 58 B1 Magdalena, N Colombia
Cienfuegos 54 B2 Cienfuegos, C Cuba
Cieza 93 E4 Murcia, SE Spain
Cihanbeyli 116 C3 Konya, C Turkey
Cikobia 145 E4 *prev.* Thikombia. *Island* N Fiji
Cilacap 138 C5 *prev.* Tjilatjap. Jawa, C Indonesia
Cill Airne *see* Killarney
Cill Chainnigh *see* Kilkenny
Cill Mhantáin *see* Wicklow
Cincinnati 40 C4 Ohio, N USA
Ciney 87 C7 Namur, SE Belgium
Cinto, Monte 91 E7 *mountain* Corse, France, C Mediterranean Sea
Cipolletti 65 B5 Río Negro, C Argentina
Cirebon 138 C4 *prev.* Tjirebon. Jawa, S Indonesia
Ciro Marino 97 E6 Calabria, S Italy
Cisnădie 108 B4 *Ger.* Heltau, *Hung.* Nagydisznód. Sibiu, SW Romania
Citlaltépetl *see* Orizaba, Volcán Pico de
Citrus Heights 47 B5 California, W USA
Ciudad Bolívar 59 E2 *prev.* Angostura. Bolívar, E Venezuela
Ciudad Acuña *see* Villa Acuña
Cuidad Camargo 50 D2 Chihuahua, N Mexico
Ciudad Cortés *see* Cortés
Ciudad Darío 52 D3 *var.* Dario. Matagalpa, W Nicaragua
Ciudad de Dolores Hidalgo *see* Dolores Hidalgo
Ciudad de Guatemala 52 B2 *var.* Gautemala City *Eng.* Guatemala City; *prev.* Santiago de los Caballeros. *Country capital* (Guatemala) Guatemala, C Guatemala
Ciudad del Carmen *see* Carmen
Ciudad del Este 64 E2 *prev.* Cuidad Presidente Stroessner, Presidente Stroessner, Puerto Presidente Stroessner. Alto Paraná, SE Paraguay
Ciudad Delicias *see* Delicias
Ciudad de México *see* México
Ciudad de Panamá *see* Panamá
Ciudad Guayana 59 E2 *prev.* San Tomé de Guayana, Santo Tomé de Guayana. Bolívar, NE Venezuela
Ciudad Guzmán 50 D4 Jalisco, SW Mexico
Ciudad Hidalgo 51 G5 Chiapas, SE Mexico
Ciudad Juárez 50 C1 Chihuahua, N Mexico
Ciudad Lerdo 50 D3 Durango, C Mexico
Ciudad Madero 51 E3 *var.* Villa Cecilia. Tamaulipas, C Mexico
Ciudad Mante 51 E3 Tamaulipas, C Mexico
Ciudad Miguel Alemán 51 E2 Tamaulipas, C Mexico
Ciudad Obregón 50 B2 Sonora, NW Mexico
Ciudad Ojeda 58 C1 Zulia, NW Venezuela
Ciudad Porfirio Díaz *see* Piedras Negras
Ciudad Quesada *see* Quesada
Ciudad Real 92 D3 Castilla-La Mancha, C Spain
Ciudad-Rodrigo 92 C3 Castilla-León, N Spain
Ciudad Valles 51 E3 San Luis Potosí, C Mexico
Ciudad Victoria 51 E3 Tamaulipas, C Mexico
Ciutadella *see* Ciutadella de Menorca
Ciutadella de Menorca 93 H3 *var.* Ciutadella. Menorca, Spain, W Mediterranean Sea
Civitanova Marche 96 D3 Marche, C Italy
Civitavecchia 96 C4 *anc.* Centum Cellae, Trajani Portus. Lazio, C Italy
Claremore 49 G1 Oklahoma, C USA
Clarence 151 C5 *river* South Island, NZ
Clarence 151 C5 Canterbury, South Island, NZ
Clarence Town 54 D2 Long Island, C Bahamas
Clarinda 45 F4 Iowa, C USA
Clarion Fracture Zone 153 E2 *tectonic feature* NE Pacific Ocean
Clarión, Isla 50 A5 *island* W Mexico
Clark Fork 44 A1 *river* Idaho/Montana, NW USA
Clark Hill Lake 43 E2 *var.* J.Storm Thurmond Reservoir. *Reservoir* Georgia/South Carolina, SE USA
Clarksburg 40 D4 West Virginia, NE USA
Clarksdale 42 B2 Mississippi, S USA
Clarksville 42 C1 Tennessee, S USA
Clayton 49 E1 New Mexico, SW USA
Clearwater 43 E4 Florida, SE USA
Clearwater Mountains 46 D2 *mountain range* Idaho, NW USA
Cleburne 49 G3 Texas, SW USA
Clermont 148 D4 Queensland, E Australia
Clermont-Ferrand 91 C5 Puy-de-Dôme, C France
Cleveland 40 D3 Ohio, N USA
Cleveland 42 D1 Tennessee, S USA
Clifton 48 C2 Arizona, SW USA
Clinton 42 B2 Mississippi, S USA
Clinton 49 F1 Oklahoma, C USA
Clipperton Fracture Zone 153 E3 *tectonic feature* E Pacific Ocean
Clipperton Island 35 A7 *French dependency of French Polynesia* E Pacific Ocean
Cloncurry 148 B3 Queensland, C Australia
Clonmel 89 B6 *Ir.* Cluain Meala. S Ireland
Cloppenburg 94 B3 Niedersachsen, NW Germany
Cloquet 45 G2 Minnesota, N USA
Cloud Peak 44 C3 *mountain* Wyoming, C USA
Clovis 49 E2 New Mexico, SW USA
Cluain Meala *see* Clonmel
Cluj-Napoca 108 B3 *Ger.* Klausenburg, *Hung.* Kolozsvár; *prev.* Cluj. Cluj, NW Romania
Clutha 151 B7 *river* South Island, NZ
Clyde 88 C4 *river* W Scotland, UK
Coari 62 D2 Amazonas, N Brazil
Coast Mountains 36 D4 *Fr.* Chaîne Côtière. *Mountain range* Canada/USA
Coast Ranges 46 A4 *mountain range* W USA
Coats Island 37 G3 *island* Nunavut, NE Canada
Coats Land 154 B2 *physical region* Antarctica
Coatzacoalcos 51 G4 *var.* Quetzalcoalco; *prev.* Puerto México. Veracruz-Llave, E Mexico
Cobán 52 B2 Alta Verapaz, C Guatemala
Cobar 149 C6 New South Wales, SE Australia
Cobija 61 E3 Pando, NW Bolivia
Coburg 95 C5 Bayern, SE Germany
Coca *see* Puerto Francisco de Orellana
Cochabamba 61 F4 *hist.* Oropeza. Cochabamba, C Bolivia
Cochin 132 C3 *var.* Kochi. Kerala, SW India
Cochinos, Bahía de 54 B2 *Eng.* Bay of Pigs. *Bay* SE Cuba
Cochrane 65 B7 Aisén, S Chile
Cochrane 38 C4 Ontario, S Canada
Cocibolca *see* Nicaragua, Lago de
Cockburn Town 55 E2 *var.* Grand *Turk. dependent territory capital* (Turks and Caicos Islands) Grand Turk Island, SE Turks and Caicos Islands
Cockpit Country, The 54 A4 *physical region* W Jamaica
Cocobeach 77 A5 Estuaire, NW Gabon
Coconino Plateau 48 B1 *plain* Arizona, SW USA
Coco, Río 53 E2 *var.* Río Wanki, Segoviao Wangkí. *River* Honduras/Nicaragua
Cocos Basin 124 C5 *undersea feature* E Indian Ocean
Cocos Island Ridge *see* Cocos Ridge
Cocos Islands 141 D5 *island group* E Indian Ocean
Cocos Ridge 35 C8 *var.* Cocos Island Ridge. *Undersea feature* E Pacific Ocean
Cod, Cape 41 G3 *headland* Massachusetts, NE USA
Codfish Island 151 A8 *island* SW NZ
Codlea 108 C4 *Ger.* Zeiden, *Hung.* Feketehalom. Braşov, C Romania
Cody 44 C2 Wyoming, C USA
Coeur d'Alene 46 C2 Idaho, NW USA
Coevorden 86 E2 Drenthe, NE Netherlands
Coffs Harbour 149 E6 New South Wales, SE Australia
Cognac 91 B5 *anc.* Compniacum. Charente, W France
Coiba, Isla de 53 E5 *island* SW Panama
Coihaique 65 B6 *var.* Coyhaique. Aisén, S Chile
Coimbatore 132 C3 Tamil Nādu, S India
Coimbra 92 B3 *anc.* Conimbria, Conimbriga. Coimbra, W Portugal
Coín 92 D5 Andalucía, S Spain
Coirib, Loch *see* Corrib, Lough
Colby 45 E4 Kansas, C USA
Colchester 89 E6 *hist.* Colneceaste, *anc.* Camulodunum. E England, UK
Col du Brenner *see* Brenner Pass
Coleman 49 F3 Texas, SW USA
Coleraine 88 B4 *Ir.* Cúil Raithin. N Northern Ireland, UK
Colesberg 78 C5 Northern Cape, C South Africa
Colima 50 D4 Colima, S Mexico
Coll 88 B3 *island* W Scotland, UK
College Station 49 G3 Texas, SW USA
Collie 147 A7 Western Australia
Colmar 90 E4 *Ger.* Kolmar. Haut-Rhin, NE France
Cöln *see* Köln
Cologne *see* Köln
Colombia 58 B3 *Country* N South America

Colombia 58

Official name Republic of Colombia
Formation 1819
Capital Bogotá
Population 44.2 million / 110 people per sq mile (43 people per sq km)
Total area 439,733 sq. miles (1,138,910 sq. km)
Languages Spanish, Wayuu, Páez, and other Amerindian languages
Religions Roman Catholic 95%, other 5%
Ethnic mix Mestizo 58%, White 20%, European–African 14%, African 4%, African–Amerindian 3%, Amerindian 1%
Government Presidential system
Currency Colombian peso = 100 centavos
Literacy rate 92%
Calorie consumption 2580 calories

Colombian Basin 56 A1 *undersea feature* SW Caribbean Sea
Colombo 132 C4 *country capital* (Sri Lanka) Western Province, W Sri Lanka
Colón 53 G4 *prev.* Aspinwall. Colón, C Panama
Colonia Agrippina *see* Köln
Colón Ridge 35 B8 *undersea feature* E Pacific Ocean
Colorado 44 C4 *off.* State of Colorado; also known as Centennial State, Silver State. *State* C USA
Colorado City 49 F3 Texas, SW USA
Colorado Plateau 48 B1 *plateau* W USA
Colorado, Río 65 C5 *river* E Argentina
Colorado, Río *see* Colorado River
Colorado River 35 B5 *var.* Río Colorado. *River* Mexico/USA
Colorado River 49 G4 *river* Texas, SW USA
Colorado Springs 44 D5 Colorado, C USA
Columbia 46 B3 *river* Canada/USA

Columbia *43 E2 state capital* South Carolina, SE USA
Columbia *41 E4* Maryland, NE USA
Columbia *45 G4* Missouri, C USA
Columbia *42 C1* Tennessee, S USA
Columbia Plateau *46 C3 plateau* Idaho/Oregon, NW USA
Columbus *40 D4 state capital* Ohio, N USA
Columbus *42 D2* Georgia, SE USA
Columbus *40 C4* Indiana, N USA
Columbus *42 C2* Mississippi, S USA
Columbus *45 F4* Nebraska, C USA
Colville Channel *150 D2 channel* North Island, NZ
Colville River *36 D2 river* Alaska, USA
Comacchio *96 C3 var.* Commachio; *anc.* Comactium. Emilia-Romagna, N Italy
Comactium *see* Comacchio
Comalcalco *51 G4* Tabasco, SE Mexico
Coma Pedrosa, Pic de *91 A7 mountain* NW Andorra
Comarapa *61 F4* Santa Cruz, C Bolivia
Comayagua *52 C2* Comayagua, W Honduras
Comer See *see* Como, Lago di
Comilla *135 G4 Ben.* Kumillā. Chittagong, E Bangladesh
Comino *102 A5 Malt.* Kemmuna. *Island* C Malta
Comitán *51 G5 var.* Comitán de Domínguez. Chiapas, SE Mexico
Comitán de Domínguez *see* Comitán
Commachio *see* Comacchio
Commissioner's Point *42 A5 headland* W Bermuda
Communism Peak *see* Kommunizm, Qullai
Como *96 B2 anc.* Comum. Lombardia, N Italy
Comodoro Rivadavia *65 B6* Chubut, SE Argentina
Como, Lago di *B2 var.* Lario, *Eng.* Lake Como, *Ger.* Comer See. *Lake* N Italy
Como, Lake *see* Como, Lago di
Comoros *79 F2 Fr.* République Fédérale Islamique des Comores. *Country* W Indian Ocean

Comoros 79

Official name Union of the Comoros
Formation 1975
Capital Moroni
Population 768,000 / 892 people per sq mile (344 people per sq km)
Total area 838 sq. miles (2170 sq. km)
Languages Arabic, Comoran, French
Religions Muslim (mainly Sunni) 98%, other 1%, Roman Catholic 1%
Ethnic mix Comoran 97%, other 3%
Government Presidential system
Currency Comoros franc = 100 centimes
Literacy rate 56%
Calorie consumption 1735 calories

Compiègne *90 C3* Oise, N France
Compostella *see* Santiago
Comrat *108 D4 Rus.* Komrat. S Moldova
Conakry *74 C4 country capital* (Guinea) Conakry, SW Guinea
Concarneau *90 A3* Finistère, NW France
Concepción *64 D2 var.* Villa Concepción. Concepción, C Paraguay
Concepción *see* La Concepción
Concepción *65 B5* Bío Bío, C Chile
Concepción *61 G3* Santa Cruz, E Bolivia
Concepción de la Vega *see* La Vega
Conchos, Río *50 D2 river* C Mexico
Conchos, Río *48 D4 river* NW Mexico
Concord *41 G3 state capital* New Hampshire, NE USA
Concordia *64 D4* Entre Ríos, E Argentina
Concordia *45 E4* Kansas, C USA
Côn Đao *137 E7 var.* Con Son. *Island* S Vietnam
Condate *see* Cosne-Cours-sur-Loire
Condega *52 D3* Estelí, NW Nicaragua
Congo *77 D5 Fr.* Moyen-Congo; *prev.* Middle Congo. *Country* C Africa

Congo 77

Official name Republic of the Congo
Formation 1960
Capital Brazzaville
Population 3.7 million / 28 people per sq mile (11 people per sq km)
Total area 132,046 sq. miles (342,000 sq. km)
Languages Kongo, Teke, Lingala, French
Religions Traditional beliefs 50%, Roman Catholic 25%, Protestant 23%, Muslim 2%
Ethnic mix Bakongo 48%, Sangha 20%, Teke 17%, Mbochi 12%, other 3%
Government Presidential system
Currency CFA franc = 100 centimes
Literacy rate 83%
Calorie consumption 2221 calories

Congo, Dem. Rep. *77 C6 prev.* Zaire, Belgian Congo, Congo (Kinshasa). *Country* C Africa

Congo, Dem. Rep. 77

Official name Democratic Republic of the Congo
Formation 1960
Capital Kinshasa
Population 52.8 million / 60 people per sq mile (23 people per sq km)
Total area 905,563 sq. miles (2,345,410 sq. km)
Languages Kiswahili, Tshiluba, Kikongo, Lingala, French
Religions Roman Catholic 50%, Protestant 20%, Traditional beliefs and other 10%, Muslim 10%, Kimbanguist 10%
Ethnic mix Other 55%, Bantu and Hamitic 45%
Government Transitional regime
Currency Congolese franc = 100 centimes
Literacy rate 63%
Calorie consumption 1535 calories

Congo *77 C6 var.* Kongo, *Fr.* Zaire. *River* C Africa
Congo Basin *77 C6 drainage basin* W Dem. Rep. Congo
Connacht *see* Connaught
Connaught *89 A5 var.* Connacht, *Ir.* Chonnacht, Cúige. *Cultural region* W Ireland
Connecticut *41 F3 off.* State of Connecticut; also known as Blue Law State, Constitution State, Land of Steady Habits, Nutmeg State. *State* NE USA
Connecticut *41 G3 river* Canada/USA
Conroe *49 G3* Texas, SW USA
Consolación del Sur *54 A2* Pinar del Río, W Cuba
Con Son *see* Côn Đao
Constance *see* Konstanz
Constance, Lake *B7 Ger.* Bodensee. *Lake* C Europe
Constanța *108 D5 var.* Küstendje, *Eng.* Constanza, *Ger.* Konstanza, *Turk.* Küstence. Constanța, SE Romania
Constantia *see* Konstanz
Constantine *71 E2 var.* Qacentina, *Ar.* Qoussantîna. NE Algeria
Constantinople *see* İstanbul
Constanz *see* Konstanz
Constanza *see* Constanța
Coober Pedy *149 A5* South Australia
Cookeville *42 D1* Tennessee, S USA
Cook Islands *145 F4 territory in free association with NZ* S Pacific Ocean
Cook, Mount *see* Aoraki
Cook Strait *151 D5 var.* Raukawa. *Strait* NZ
Cooktown *148 D2* Queensland, NE Australia
Coolgardie *147 B6* Western Australia
Cooma *149 D7* New South Wales, SE Australia
Coon Rapids *45 F2* Minnesota, N USA
Cooper Creek *148 C4 var.* Barcoo, Cooper's Creek. *Seasonal river* Queensland/South Australia
Cooper's Creek *see* Cooper Creek
Coos Bay *46 A3* Oregon, NW USA
Cootamundra *149 D6* New South Wales, SE Australia
Copacabana *61 E4* La Paz, W Bolivia
Copenhagen *see* København
Copiapó *64 B3* Atacama, N Chile
Copperas Cove *49 G3* Texas, SW USA
Coppermine *see* Kugluktuk
Coquimbo *64 B3* Coquimbo, N Chile
Corabia *108 B5* Olt, S Romania
Coral Harbour *37 G3* Southampton Island, Nunavut, NE Canada
Coral Sea *142 B3 sea* SW Pacific Ocean
Coral Sea Islands *144 B4 Australian external territory* SW Pacific Ocean
Corantijn Rivier *see* Courantyne River
Corcaigh *see* Cork
Corcovado, Golfo *65 B6 gulf* S Chile
Cordele *42 D3* Georgia, SE USA
Cordillera Ibérica *see* Ibérico, Sistema
Cordoba *see* Córdoba
Córdoba *92 D4 var.* Cordoba, *Eng.* Cordova; *anc.* Corduba. Andalucía, SW Spain
Córdoba *64 C3* Córdoba, C Argentina
Córdoba *51 F4* Veracruz-Llave, E Mexico
Cordova *see* Córdoba
Cordova *36 C3* Alaska, USA
Corduba *see* Córdoba
Corentyne River *see* Courantyne River
Corfu *see* Kérkyra
Coria *92 C3* Extremadura, W Spain
Corinth *see* Kórinthos
Corinth *42 C1* Mississippi, S USA
Corinth, Gulf of *see* Korinthiakós Kólpos
Corinthiacus Sinus *see* Korinthiakós Kólpos
Corinto *52 C3* Chinandega, NW Nicaragua
Cork *89 A6 Ir.* Corcaigh. S Ireland
Çorlu *116 A2* Tekirdağ, NW Turkey
Corner Brook *39 G3* Newfoundland, Newfoundland and Labrador, E Canada
Corn Islands *see* Maíz, Islas del
Cornwallis Island *37 F2 island* Nunavut, N Canada
Coro *58 C1 prev.* Santa Ana de Coro. Falcón, NW Venezuela
Corocoro *61 F4* La Paz, W Bolivia
Coromandel *150 D2* Waikato, North Island, NZ
Coromandel Coast *132 D2 coast* E India
Coromandel Peninsula *150 D2 peninsula* North Island, NZ
Coronado, Bahía de *52 D5 bay* S Costa Rica
Coronel Dorrego *65 C5* Buenos Aires, E Argentina
Coronel Oviedo *64 D2* Caaguazú, SE Paraguay
Corozal *52 C1* Corozal, N Belize
Corpus Christi *49 G4* Texas, SW USA
Corrales *48 D2* New Mexico, SW USA
Corrib, Lough *89 A5 Ir.* Loch Coirib. *Lake* W Ireland
Corrientes *64 D3* Corrientes, NE Argentina
Corriza *see* Korçë
Corse *91 E7 Eng.* Corsica. *Island* France, C Mediterranean Sea
Corsica *see* Corse
Corsicana *49 G3* Texas, SW USA
Cortegana *92 C4* Andalucía, S Spain
Cortés *53 E5 var.* Ciudad Cortés. Puntarenas, SE Costa Rica
Cortina d'Ampezzo *96 C1* Veneto, NE Italy
Coruche *92 B3* Santarém, C Portugal
Çoruh Nehri *117 E3 Geor.* Chorokhi, *Rus.* Chorokh. *River* Georgia/Turkey
Çorum *116 D3 var.* Chorum. Çorum, N Turkey
Corunna *see* A Coruña
Corvallis *46 B3* Oregon, NW USA
Corvo *92 A5 var.* Ilha do Corvo. *Island* Azores, Portugal, NE Atlantic Ocean
Cosenza *97 D6 anc.* Consentia. Calabria, SW Italy
Cosne-Cours-sur-Loire *90 C4 var.* Cosne-sur-Loire; *anc.* Condate. Nièvre, C France
Cosne-sur-Loire *see* Cosne-Cours-sur-Loire
Costa Mesa *46 D2* California, W USA
Costa Rica *53 E4 Country* Central America

Costa Rica 53

Official name Republic of Costa Rica
Formation 1838
Capital San José
Population 4.2 million / 213 people per sq mile (82 people per sq km)
Total area 19,730 sq. miles (51,100 sq. km)
Languages Spanish, English Creole, Bribri, Cabecar
Religions Roman Catholic 76%, Other (including Protestant) 24%
Ethnic mix Mestizo and European 96%, Black 2%, Chinese 1%, Amerindian 1%
Government Presidential system
Currency Costa Rican colón = 100 centimos
Literacy rate 96%
Calorie consumption 2761 calories

Cotagaita *61 F5* Potosí, S Bolivia
Côte d'Ivoire *74 D4 Eng.* Ivory Coast, Republic of the Ivory Coast. *Country* W Africa

Côte d'Ivoire 74

Official name Republic of Côte d'Ivoire
Formation 1960
Capital Yamoussoukro
Population 16.6 million / 135 people per sq mile (52 people per sq km)
Total area 124,502 sq. miles (322,460 sq. km)
Languages Akan, French, Kru, Voltaic
Religions Muslim 38%, Traditional beliefs 25%, Roman Catholic 25%, other 6%, Protestant 6%
Ethnic mix Baoulé 23%, other 19%, Bété 18%, Senufo 15%, Agni-Ashanti 14%, Mandinka 11%
Government Presidential system
Currency CFA franc = 100 centime

Côte d'Ivoire (continued)

Literacy rate 50%
Calorie consumption 2594 calories

Côte d'Or *90 D4 cultural region* C France
Cotonou *75 F5 var.* Kotonu. S Benin
Cotrone *see* Crotone
Cotswold Hills *89 D6 var.* Cotswolds. *Hill range* S England, UK
Cotswolds *see* Cotswold Hills
Cottbus *94 D4 prev.* Kottbus. Brandenburg, E Germany
Council Bluffs *45 F4* Iowa, C USA
Courantyne River *59 G4 var.* Corantijn Rivier, Corentyne River. *River* Guyana/Suriname
Courland Lagoon *106 A4 Ger.* Kurisches Haff, *Rus.* Kurskiy Zaliv. *Lagoon* Lithuania/Russian Federation
Coutances *90 B3 anc.* Constantia. Manche, N France
Couvin *87 C7* Namur, S Belgium
Coventry *89 D6 anc.* Couentrey. C England, UK
Covilhã *92 C3* Castelo Branco, E Portugal
Cowan, Lake *147 B6 lake* Western Australia
Coxen Hole *see* Roatán
Coxin Hole *see* Roatán
Coyhaique *see* Coihaique
Cozumel, Isla *51 H3 island* SE Mexico
Cradock *78 C5* Eastern Cape, S South Africa
Craig *44 C4* Colorado, C USA
Craiova *108 B5* Dolj, SW Romania
Cranbrook *37 E5* British Columbia, SW Canada
Crane *see* The Crane
Crawley *89 E7* SE England, UK
Cremona *96 B2* Lombardia, N Italy
Cres *100 A3 It.* Cherso; *anc.* Crexa. *Island* W Croatia
Crescent City *46 A4* California, W USA
Crescent Group *128 C7 island group* C Paracel Islands
Creston *45 F4* Iowa, C USA
Crestview *42 D3* Florida, SE USA
Crete *see* Kríti
Créteil *90 E2* Val-de-Marne, N France
Crete, Sea of *see* Kritikó Pélagos
Creuse *90 B4 river* C France
Crewe *89 D6* C England, UK
Crikvenica *100 A3 It.* Cirquenizza; *prev.* Cirkvenica, Crjkvenica. Primorje-Gorski Kotar, NW Croatia
Crimea *81 F4 var.* Krym, *Eng.* Crimea, Crimean Oblast; *prev.* Rus. Krymskaya ASSR, Krymskaya Oblast'. Admin. region *province* SE Ukraine
Crimean Oblast *see* Crimea
Cristóbal *53 G4* Colón, C Panama
Cristóbal Colón, Pico *58 B1 mountain* N Colombia
Cristuru Secuiesc *108 C4 prev.* Cristur, Cristuru Săcuiesc, Sitaș Cristuru, *Ger.* Kreutz, *Hung.* Székelykeresztúr, Szitás-Keresztúr. Harghita, C Romania
Crna Reka *101 D6 river* S FYR Macedonia
Croatia *100 B3 Ger.* Kroatien, *SCr.* Hrvatska. *Country* SE Europe

Croatia 100

Official name Republic of Croatia
Formation 1991
Capital Zagreb
Population 4.4 million / 202 people per sq mile (78 people per sq km)
Total area 21,831 sq. miles (56,542 sq. km)
Languages Croatian

Croatia 100 (continued)

Religions Roman Catholic 88%, other 7%, Orthodox Christian 4%, Muslim 1%
Ethnic mix Croat 90%, other 5%, Serb 4%, Bosniak 1%
Government Parliamentary system
Currency Kuna = 100 lipas
Literacy rate 98%
Calorie consumption 2678 calories

Crocodile *see* Limpopo
Croia *see* Krujë
Croker Island *146 E2 island* Northern Territory, N Australia
Cromwell *151 B7* Otago, South Island, NZ
Crooked Island *54 D2 island* SE Bahamas
Crooked Island Passage *54 D2 channel* SE Bahamas
Crookston *45 F1* Minnesota, N USA
Croton *see* Crotone
Crotona *see* Crotone
Crotone *97 E6 var.* Cotrone; *anc.* Croton, Crotona. Calabria, SW Italy
Croydon *89 A8* SE England, UK
Crozet Basin *141 B6 undersea feature* S Indian Ocean
Crozet Islands *141 B7 island group* French Southern and Antarctic Territories
Crozet Plateau *141 B7 var.* Crozet Plateaus. *Undersea feature* SW Indian Ocean
Crozet Plateaus *see* Crozet Plateau
Crystal Brook *149 B6* South Australia
Csorna *99 C6* Győr-Moson-Sopron, NW Hungary
Csurgó *99 C7* Somogy, SW Hungary
Cuando *78 C2 var.* Kwando. *River* S Africa
Cuango *78 B1 var.* Kwango. *River* Angola/Dem. Rep. Congo *see also* Kwango
Cuan na Gaillimhe *see* Galway Bay
Cuanza *78 B1 var.* Kwanza. *River* C Angola
Cuauhtémoc *50 C2* Chihuahua, N Mexico
Cuautla *51 E4* Morelos, S Mexico
Cuba *54 B2 Country* W West Indies

Cuba 54

Official name Republic of Cuba
Formation 1902
Capital Havana
Population 11.3 million / 264 people per sq mile (102 people per sq km)
Total area 42,803 sq. miles (110,860 sq. km)
Languages Spanish
Religions Nonreligious 49%, Roman Catholic 40%, Atheist 6%, other 4%, Protestant 1%
Ethnic mix White 66%, European–African 22%, Black 12%
Government One-party state
Currency Cuban peso = 100 centavos
Literacy rate 97%
Calorie consumption 2643 calories

Cubal *78 B2* Benguela, W Angola
Cubango *78 B2 var.* Kavango, Kavengo, Kubango, Okavango, Okavanggo. *River* S Africa *see also* Okavango
Cubango *78 B2 var.* Kuvango, *Port.* Vila Artur de Paiva, Vila da Ponte. Huíla, SW Angola
Cúcuta *58 C2 var.* San José de Cúcuta. Norte de Santander, N Colombia
Cuddapah *132 C2* Andhra Pradesh, S India
Cuenca *93 E3 anc.* Conca. Castilla-La Mancha, C Spain
Cuenca *60 B2* Azuay, S Ecuador
Cuernavaca *51 E4* Morelos, S Mexico
Cuiabá *63 E3 prev.* Cuyabá. *State capital* Mato Grosso, SW Brazil
Cúige *see* Connaught
Cúige Laighean *see* Leinster
Cúige Mumhan *see* Munster
Cuijck *86 D4* Noord-Brabant, SE Netherlands
Cúil Raithin *see* Coleraine
Cuito *78 B2 var.* Kwito. *River* SE Angola
Cukai *138 B3 var.* Chukai, Kemaman. Terengganu, Peninsular Malaysia
Culiacán *50 C3 var.* Culiacán Rosales, Culiacán-Rosales. Sinaloa, C Mexico
Culiacán-Rosales *see* Culiacán
Cullera *93 F3* País Valenciano, E Spain
Cullman *42 C2* Alabama, S USA
Culmsee *see* Chełmża
Culpepper Island *see* Darwin, Isla
Cumaná *59 E1* Sucre, NE Venezuela
Cumbal, Nevada de *58 A4 mountain* SW Colombia
Cumberland *41 E4* Maryland, NE USA
Cumberland Plateau *42 D1 plateau* E USA
Cumberland Sound *37 H3 inlet* Baffin Island, Nunavut, NE Canada
Cumpas *50 B2* Sonora, NW Mexico
Cunene *69 C6 var.* Kunene. *River* Angola/Namibia *see also* Kunene
Cunene *78 A3 province* S Angola
Cuneo *96 A2 Fr.* Coni. Piemonte, NW Italy
Cunnamulla *149 C5* Queensland, E Australia
Ćuprija *100 E4* Serbia, E Serbia and Montenegro (Yugo.)
Curaçao *55 E5 island* Netherlands Antilles
Curicó *64 B4* Maule, C Chile
Curitiba *63 E4 prev.* Curytiba. *State capital* Paraná, S Brazil
Curtea de Argeș *108 C4 var.* Curtea-de-Arges. Argeș, S Romania
Curtea-de-Arges *see* Curtea de Argeș
Curtici *108 A4 Ger.* Kurtitsch, *Hung.* Kürtös. Arad, W Romania
Curtis Island *148 E4 island* Queensland, SE Australia
Cusco *61 E4 var.* Cuzco. Cusco, C Peru
Cusset *91 C5* Allier, C France
Cutch, Gulf of *see* Kachchh, Gulf of
Cuttack *135 F4* Orissa, E India
Cuvier Plateau *141 E6 undersea feature* E Indian Ocean
Cuxhaven *94 B2* Niedersachsen, NW Germany
Cuyuni, Río *see* Cuyuni River
Cuyuni River *59 F3 var.* Río Cuyuni. *River* Guyana/Venezuela
Cuzco *see* Cusco
Cyclades *see* Kykládes
Cydonia *see* Chaniá
Cymru *see* Wales
Cyprus *102 C4 Gk.* Kypros, *Turk.* Kıbrıs, Kıbrıs Cumhuriyeti. *Country* E Mediterranean Sea

Cyprus 102

Official name Republic of Cyprus
Formation 1960
Capital Nicosia
Population 802,000 / 225 people per sq mile (87 people per sq km)
Total area 3571 sq. miles (9250 sq. km)
Languages Greek, Turkish
Religions Orthodox Christian 78%, Muslim 18%, other 4%
Ethnic mix Greek 85%, Turkish 12%, other 3%

Cyprus (continued)

Government Presidential system
Currency Cyprus pound (Turkish lira in TRNC) = 100 cents (Cyprus pound); 100 kurus (Turkish lira)
Literacy rate 97%
Calorie consumption 3302 calories

Cythera *see* Kýthira
Cythnos *see* Kýthnos
Czech Republic *99 A5 Cz.* Česká Republika. *Country* C Europe

Czech Republic 99

Official name Czech Republic
Formation 1993
Capital Prague
Population 10.2 million / 335 people per sq mile (129 people per sq km)
Total area 30,450 sq. miles (78,866 sq. km)
Languages Czech, Slovak, Hungarian (Magyar)
Religions Roman Catholic 39%, Atheist 38%, other 18%, Protestant 3%, Hussite 2%
Ethnic mix Czech 81%, Moravian 13%, Slovak 6%
Government Parliamentary system
Currency Czech koruna = 100 haleru
Literacy rate 99%
Calorie consumption 3097 calories

Częstochowa *98 C4 Ger.* Czenstochau, Tschenstochau, *Rus.* Chenstokhov. Śląskie, S Poland
Człuchów *98 C3 Ger.* Schlochau. Pomorskie, N Poland

D

Dabajuro *58 C1* Falcón, NW Venezuela
Dabeiba *58 B2* Antioquia, NW Colombia
Dąbrowa Tarnowska *99 D5* Małopolskie, S Poland
Dabryn' *107 C8 Rus.* Dobryn'. Homyel'skaya Voblasts', SE Belarus
Dagana *74 B3* N Senegal
Dagda *106 D4* Krāslava, SE Latvia
Dagenham *89 B8* SE England, UK
Dağliq Qarabağ *see* Nagorno-Karabakh
Dagupan *139 E1 off.* Dagupan City. Luzon, N Philippines
Da Hinggan Ling *127 G1 Eng.* Great Khingan Range. *Mountain range* NE China
Dahm, Ramlat *121 B6 desert* NW Yemen
Daimiel *92 D3* Castilla-La Mancha, C Spain
Daimoniá *105 B7* Pelopónnisos, S Greece
Dairen *see* Dalian
Dakar *74 B3 country capital* (Senegal) W Senegal
Dakhla *see* Ad Dakhla
Dakoro *75 G3* Maradi, S Niger
Đakovica *101 D5 var.* Djakovica, *Alb.* Gjakovë. Serbia, S Serbia and Montenegro (Yugo.)
Đakovo *100 C3 var.* Djakovo, *Hung.* Diakovár. Osijek-Baranja, E Croatia
Dalai *see* Hulun Nur
Dalain Hob *see* Ejin Qi
Dalaman *116 A4* Muğla, SW Turkey
Dalandzadgad *127 E3* Ömnögovĭ, S Mongolia
Đa Lat *137 E6* Lâm Đông, S Vietnam
Dalby *149 D5* Queensland, E Australia
Dale City *41 E4* Virginia, NE USA
Dalhart *49 E1* Texas, SW USA
Dali *128 A6 var.* Xiaguan. Yunnan, SW China

Dalian 128 D4 var. Dairen, Dalien, Lüda, Ta-lien, Rus. Dalny. Liaoning, NE China
Dalien see Dalian
Dallas 49 G2 Texas, SW USA
Dalmacija 100 B4 Eng. Dalmatia, Ger. Dalmatien, It. Dalmazia. Cultural region S Croatia
Dalny see Dalian
Dalton 42 D1 Georgia, SE USA
Daly Waters 148 A2 Northern Territory, N Australia
Damachava 107 A6 var. Damachova, Pol. Domaczewo, Rus. Domachëvo. Brestskaya Voblasts', SW Belarus
Damachova see Damachava
Damān 134 C4 Damān and Diu, W India
Damara 76 C4 Ombella-Mpoko, S Central African Republic
Damas see Dimashq
Damasco see Dimashq
Damascus see Dimashq
Damāvand, Qolleh-ye 120 D3 mountain N Iran
Dammām see Ad Dammān
Damoûr 119 A5 var. Ad Dāmūr. W Lebanon
Dampier 146 A4 Western Australia
Dampier, Selat 139 F4 strait Papua, E Indonesia
Damqawt 121 D6 var. Damqut. E Yemen
Damqut see Damqawt
Damxung 126 C5 Xizang Zizhiqu, W China
Danakil Desert 72 D4 var. Afar Depression, Danakil Plain. Desert E Africa
Danakil Plain see Danakil Desert
Danané 74 D5 W Côte d'Ivoire
Đa Năng 137 E5 prev. Tourane. Quang Nam-Đa Năng, C Vietnam
Danborg see Daneborg
Dandong 128 D3 var. Tan-tung; prev. An-tung. Liaoning, NE China
Daneborg 83 E3 var. Danborg. N Greenland
Dänew see Deynau
Dangerous Archipelago see Tuamotu, Îles
Danghara 123 E3 Rus. Dangara. SW Tajikistan
Danghe Nanshan 126 D3 mountain range W China
Dangla see Tanggula Shan
Dângrêk, Chuŏr Phnum 137 D5 var. Phanom Dang Raek, Phanom Dong Rak, Fr. Chaîne des Dangrek. Mountain range Cambodia/Thailand
Dangriga 52 C1 prev. Stann Creek. Stann Creek, E Belize
Danish West Indies see Virgin Islands (US)
Danlí 52 D2 El Paraíso, S Honduras
Danmarksstraedet see Denmark Strait
Dannenberg 94 C3 Niedersachsen, N Germany
Dannevirke 150 D4 Manawatu-Wanganui, North Island, NZ
Danube 81 E4 Bul. Dunav, Cz. Dunaj, Ger. Donau, Hung. Duna, Rom. Dunărea. River C Europe
Danville 41 E5 Virginia, NE USA
Dan Xian see Danzhou
Danxian/Dan Xian see Danzhou
Danzhou 128 C7 prev. Dan Xian, Danxian, Nada. Hainan, S China
Danziger Bucht see Danzig, Gulf of
Danzig, Gulf of 98 C2 var. Gulf of Pomorskie, Ger. Danziger Bucht, Pol. Zakota Pomorskiea, Rus. Gdan'skaya Bukhta. Gulf N Poland
Daqm see Duqm
Dar'ā 119 B5 var. Der'a, Fr. Déraa. Dar'ā, SW Syria
Darabani 108 C3 Botoșani, NW Romania
Daraut-Kurgan see Daroot-Korgon
Dardanelli see Çanakkale
Dar es Salaam 73 C7 Dar es Salaam, E Tanzania
Darfield 151 C6 Canterbury, South Island, NZ
Darfur 72 A4 var. Darfur Massif. Cultural region W Sudan
Darfur Massif see Darfur
Darhan 127 E2 Selenge, N Mongolia
Darien, Gulf of 58 A2 Sp. Golfo del Darién. Gulf S Caribbean Sea
Darién, Serranía del 53 H5 mountain range Colombia/Panama
Dario see Ciudad Darío
Darjeeling see Darjiling
Darjiling 135 F3 prev. Darjeeling. West Bengal, NE India
Darling River 149 C6 river New South Wales, SE Australia
Darlington 89 D5 N England, UK
Darmstadt 95 B5 Hessen, SW Germany
Darnah 71 G2 var. Dérna. NE Libya
Darnley, Cape 154 D2 headland Antarctica
Daroca 93 E2 Aragón, NE Spain
Daroot-Korgon 123 F3 var. Daraut-Kurgan. Oshskaya Oblast', SW Kyrgyzstan
Dartford 89 B8 SE England, UK
Dartmoor 89 C7 moorland SW England, UK
Dartmouth 39 F4 Nova Scotia, SE Canada
Darvaza see Derweze
Darwaza see Derweze
Darwin 146 D2 prev. Palmerston, Port Darwin. Territory capital Northern Territory, N Australia
Darwin, Isla 60 A4 var. Culpepper Island. Island W Ecuador
Daryācheh-ye Hāmūn see Şāberī, Hāmūn-e
Daryācheh-ye Sīstān see Şāberī, Hāmūn-e
Daryā-ye Morghāb see Murgab
Daryā-ye Pāmīr see Pamir
Daryoi Pomir see Pamir
Dashhowuz see Daşoguz
Dashkawka 107 D6 Rus. Dashkovka. Mahilyowskaya Voblasts', E Belarus
Dashkhovuz see Daşoguz
Daşoguz 122 C2 var. Dashhowuz, Dashkhovuz; prev. Tashauz. Dashkhovuzskiy Velayat, N Turkmenistan
Datong 128 C3 var. Tatung, Ta-t'ung. Shanxi, C China
Daugavpils 106 D4 Ger. Dünaburg; prev. Rus. Dvinsk. Municipality Daugvapils, SE Latvia
Daung Kyun 137 B6 island S Myanmar
Dauphiné 91 D5 cultural region E France
Dāvangere 132 C2 Karnātaka, W India
Davao 139 F3 off. Davao City. Mindanao, S Philippines
Davao Gulf 139 F3 gulf Mindanao, S Philippines
Davenport 45 G3 Iowa, C USA
David 53 E5 Chiriquí, W Panama
Davie Ridge 141 A5 undersea feature W Indian Ocean
Davis 154 D3 Australian research station Antarctica
Davis Sea 154 D3 sea Antarctica
Davis Strait 82 B3 strait Baffin Bay/Labrador Sea
Dawei see Tavoy
Dax 91 B6 var. Ax; anc. Aquae Augustae, Aquae Tarbelicae. Landes, SW France
Dayr az Zawr 118 D3 var. Deir ez Zor. Dayr az Zawr, E Syria
Dayton 40 C4 Ohio, N USA
Daytona Beach 43 E4 Florida, SE USA
De Aar 78 C5 Northern Cape, C South Africa
Dead Sea 119 B6 var. Bahret Lut, Lacus Asphaltites, Ar. Al Baḩr al Mayyit, Baḩrat Lūt, Heb. Yam HaMelaḥ. Salt lake Israel/Jordan
Deán Funes 64 C3 Córdoba, C Argentina
Death Valley 47 C7 valley California, W USA
Deatnu 84 D2 Fin. Tenojoki, Nor. Tana. River Finland/Norway see also Tenojoki
Debar 101 D6 Ger. Dibra, Turk. Debre. W FYR Macedonia
Debica 99 D5 Podkarpackie, SE Poland
De Bildt see De Bilt
De Bilt 86 C3 var. De Bildt. Utrecht, C Netherlands
Dębno 98 B3 Zachodniopomorskie, NW Poland
Debrecen 99 D6 Ger. Debreczin, Rom. Debreţin; prev. Debreczen. Hajdú-Bihar, E Hungary
Decatur 42 C1 Alabama, S USA
Decatur 40 B4 Illinois, N USA
Deccan 134 D5 Hind. Dakshin. Plateau C India
Děčín 98 B4 Ger. Tetschen. Ústecký Kraj, NW Czech Republic
Dedeagaç see Alexandroúpoli
Dedeagach see Alexandroúpoli
Dedemsvaart 86 E3 Overijssel, E Netherlands
Dee 88 C3 river NE Scotland, UK
Deering 36 C2 Alaska, USA
Deggendorf 95 D6 Bayern, SE Germany
Değirmenlik 102 C5 N Cyprus
Deh Bīd 120 D3 Fārs, C Iran
Dehli see Delhi
Deh Shū 122 D5 var. Deshu. Helmand, S Afghanistan
Deinze 87 B5 Oost-Vlaanderen, NW Belgium
Deir ez Zor see Dayr az Zawr
Deirgeirt, Loch see Derg, Lough
Dej 108 B3 Hung. Dés; prev. Deés. Cluj, NW Romania
Dékoa 76 C4 Kémo, 188C Central African Republic
De Land 43 E4 Florida, SE USA
Delano 47 C7 California, W USA
Delārām 122 D5 Farāh, SW Afghanistan
Delaware 41 F4 off. State of Delaware; also known as Blue Hen State, Diamond State, First State. State NE USA
Delaware 40 D4 Ohio, N USA
Delft 86 B4 Zuid-Holland, W Netherlands
Delfzijl 86 E1 Groningen, NE Netherlands
Delgo 72 B3 Northern, N Sudan
Delhi 134 D3 var. Dehli, Hind. Dilli; hist. Shahjahanabad. Delhi, N India
Delicias 50 D2 var. Ciudad Delicias. Chihuahua, N Mexico
Déli-Kárpátok see Carpaţii Meridionali
Delmenhorst 94 B3 Niedersachsen, NW Germany
Del Rio 49 F4 Texas, SW USA
Deltona 43 E4 Florida, SE USA
Demba 77 D6 Kasai Occidental, C Dem. Rep. Congo
Dembia 76 D4 Mbomou, SE Central African Republic
Demchok var. Dêmqog. Disputed region China/India see also Dêmqog
Demchok 126 A4 var. Dêmqog. China/India see also Dêmqog
Demerara Plain 56 C2 undersea feature W Atlantic Ocean
Deming 48 C3 New Mexico, SW USA
Demmin 94 C2 Mecklenburg-Vorpommern, NE Germany
Demopolis 42 C2 Alabama, S USA
Dêmqog var. Demchok. Disputed region China/India see also Demchok
Denali see McKinley, Mount
Denau see Denov
Dender 87 B6 Fr. Dendre. River W Belgium
Denekamp 86 E3 Overijssel, E Netherlands
Den Haag see 's-Gravenhage
Den Ham 86 E3 Overijssel, E Netherlands
Denham 147 A5 Western Australia
Den Helder 86 C2 Noord-Holland, NW Netherlands
Dénia 93 F4 País Valenciano, E Spain
Deniliquin 149 C7 New South Wales, SE Australia
Denison 45 F3 Iowa, C USA
Denison 49 G2 Texas, SW USA
Denizli 116 B4 Denizli, SW Turkey
Denmark 85 A7 Dan. Danmark; anc. Hafnia. Country N Europe

Denmark 85

Official name Kingdom of Denmark
Formation 950
Capital Copenhagen
Population 5.4 million / 330 people per sq mile (127 people per sq km)
Total area 16,639 sq. miles (43,094 sq. km)
Languages Danish
Religions Evangelical Lutheran 89%, other 10%, Roman Catholic 1%
Ethnic mix Danish 96%, Other (including Scandinavian and Turkish) 3%, Faeroese and Inuit 1%
Government Parliamentary system
Currency Danish krone = 100 øre
Literacy rate 99%
Calorie consumption 3454 calories

Denmark Strait 82 D4 var. Danmarksstraedet. Strait Greenland/Iceland
Dennery 55 F1 E Saint Lucia
Denov 123 E3 var. Denow, Rus. Denau. Surkhondaryo Wiloyati, S Uzbekistan
Denow see Denov
Denpasar 138 D5 prev. Paloe. Bali, C Indonesia
Denton 49 G2 Texas, SW USA
D'Entrecasteaux Islands 144 B3 island group SE PNG
Denver 44 D4 state capital Colorado, C USA
Der'a see Dar'ā
Déraa see Dar'ā
Dera Ghāzi Khān 134 C2 var. Dera Ghāzikhān. Punjab, C Pakistan
Dera Ghāzikhān see Dera Ghāzi Khān
Đeravica 101 D5 mountain S Serbia and Montenegro (Yugo.)
Derbent 111 B8 Respublika Dagestan, SW Russian Federation
Derby 89 D6 C England, UK
Derelí see Gónnoi
Derg, Lough 89 A6 Ir. Loch Deirgeirt. Lake W Ireland
Derhachi 109 G2 Rus. Dergachi. Kharkivs'ka Oblast', E Ukraine
De Ridder 42 A3 Louisiana, S USA
Dérna see Darnah
Derry see Londonderry
Derventa 100 B3 Republika Srpska, N Bosnia and Herzegovina
Derweze 122 C2 var. Darvaza, Darwaza. Akhalskiy Velayat, C Turkmenistan'
Deschutes River 46 B3 river Oregon, NW USA
Desē 72 C4 var. Desse, It. Dessie. N Ethiopia
Deseado, Río 65 B7 river S Argentina
Desertas, Ilhas 70 A2 island group Madeira, Portugal, NE Atlantic Ocean
Deshu see Deh Shū
Desierto de Altar see Sonoran Desert
Des Moines 45 F3 state capital Iowa, C USA
Desna 109 E2 river Russian Federation/Ukraine
Dessau 94 C4 Sachsen-Anhalt, E Germany
Desse see Desē
Dessie see Desē
Detroit 40 D3 Michigan, N USA
Detroit Lakes 45 F2 Minnesota, N USA

Deurne *87 D5* Noord-Brabant, SE Netherlands
Deva *108 B4 Ger.* Diemrich, *Hung.* Déva. Hunedoara, W Romania
Đevđelija *see* Gevgelija
Deventer *86 D3* Overijssel, E Netherlands
Devils Lake *45 E1* North Dakota, N USA
Devoll *see* Devollit, Lumi i
Devollit, Lumi i *101 D6 var.* Devoll. *River* SE Albania
Devon Island *37 F2 prev.* North Devon Island. *Island* Parry Islands, Nunavut, NE Canada
Devonport *149 C8* Tasmania, SE Australia
Devrek *116 C2* Zonguldak, N Turkey
Dexter *45 H5* Missouri, C USA
Deynau *122 D3 var.* Dyanev, *Turkm.* Dänew. Lebapskiy Velayat, NE Turkmenistan
Dezfūl *120 C3 var.* Dizful. Khūzestān, SW Iran
Dezhou *128 D4* Shandong, E China
Dhaka *135 G4 prev.* Dacca. *Country capital* (Bangladesh) Dhaka, C Bangladesh
Dhanbād *135 F4* Bihār, NE India
Dhekélia *102 C5 Eng.* Dhekelia. *Gk.* Dekéleia. *UK air base* SE Cyprus
Dhidhimótikhon *see* Didymóteicho
Dhíkti Ori *see* Díkti
Dhodhekánisos *see* Dodekánisos
Dhomokós *see* Domokós
Dhráma *see* Dráma
Dhrepanon, Akrotírio *see* Drépano Akrotírio
Dhuusa Marreeb *73 E5 var.* Dusa Marreb, *It.* Dusa Mareb. Galguduud, C Somalia
Diakovár *see* Đakovo
Diamantina, Chapada *63 F3 mountain range* E Brazil
Diamantina Fracture Zone *141 E6 tectonic feature* E Indian Ocean
Diarbekr *see* Diyarbakır
Dibrugarh *135 H3* Assam, NE India
Dickinson *44 D2* North Dakota, N USA
Didimotiho *see* Didymóteicho
Didymóteicho *104 D3 var.* Dhidhimótikhon, Didimotiho. Anatolikí Makedonía kai Thráki, NE Greece
Diégo-Suarez *see* Antsirañana
Diekirch *87 D7* Diekirch, C Luxembourg
Điên Biên *136 D3 var.* Bien Bien, Dien Bien Phu. Lai Châu, N Vietnam
Dien Bien Phu *see* Điên Biên
Diepenbeek *87 D6* Limburg, NE Belgium
Diepholz *94 B3* Niedersachsen, NW Germany
Dieppe *90 C2* Seine-Maritime, N France
Dieren *86 D4* Gelderland, E Netherlands
Differdange *87 D8* Luxembourg, SW Luxembourg
Digne *91 D6 var.* Digne-les-Bains. Alpes-de-Haute-Provence, SE France
Digne-les-Bains *see* Digne
Digoin *90 C4* Saône-et-Loire, C France
Digul, Sungai *139 H5 prev.* Digoel. *River* Papua, E Indonesia
Dihang *see* Brahmaputra
Dijon *90 D4 anc.* Dibio. Côte d'Or, C France
Dikhil *72 D4* SW Djibouti
Dikson *114 D2* Taymyrskiy (Dolgano-Nenetskiy) Avtonomnyy Okrug, N Russian Federation
Díkti *105 D8 var.* Dhíkti Ori. *Mountain range* Kríti, Greece, E Mediterranean Sea
Dili *139 F5 var.* Dilli, Dilly. *Country capital* (East Timor), N East Timor
Dilia *75 G3 var.* Dillia. *River* SE Niger
Di Linh *137 E6* Lâm Đông, S Vietnam
Dilli *see* Delhi
Dilli *see* Dili
Dillia *see* Dilia
Dilling *72 B4 var.* Ad Dalanj. Southern Kordofan, C Sudan
Dillon *44 B2* Montana, NW USA
Dilly *see* Dili
Dilolo *77 D7* Ngounié, S Gabon
Dimashq *119 B5 var.* Ash Shām, Esh Sham, *Eng.* Damascus, *Fr.* Damas, *It.* Damasco. *Country capital* (Syria) Dimashq, SW Syria
Dimitrovgrad *104 D3* Khaskovo, S Bulgaria
Dimitrovgrad *111 C6* Ul'yanovskaya Oblast', W Russian Federation
Dimovo *104 B1* Vidin, NW Bulgaria
Dinajpur *135 F3* Rajshahi, NW Bangladesh
Dinan *90 B3* Côtes d'Armor, NW France
Dinant *87 C7* Namur, S Belgium
Dinar *116 B4* Afyon, SW Turkey
Dinara *see* Dinaric Alps
Dinaric Alps *100 C4 var.* Dinara. *Mountain range* Bosnia and Herzegovina/Croatia
Dindigul *132 C3* Tamil Nādu, SE India
Dingle Bay *89 A6 Ir.* Bá an Daingin. *Bay* SW Ireland
Dinguiraye *74 C4* Haute-Guinée, N Guinea
Diourbel *74 B3* W Senegal
Dirē Dawa *73 D5* E Ethiopia
Dirk Hartog Island *147 A5 island* Western Australia
Disappointment, Lake *146 C4 salt lake* Western Australia
Dispur *135 G3* Assam, NE India
Divinópolis *63 F4* Minas Gerais, SE Brazil
Divo *74 D5* S Côte d'Ivoire
Diyarbakır *117 E4 var.* Diarbekr; *anc.* Amida. Dıyarbakır, SE Turkey
Dizful *see* Dezfūl
Djajapura *see* Jayapura
Djakovica *see* Đakovica
Djakovo *see* Đakovo
Djambala *77 B6* Plateaux, C Congo
Djambi *see* Jambi
Djanet *71 E4 prev.* Fort Charlet. SE Algeria
Djéblé *see* Jablah
Djelfa *70 D2 var.* El Djelfa. N Algeria
Djéma *76 D4* Haut-Mbomou, E Central African Republic
Djérablous *see* Jarābulus
Djerba *see* Jerba, Île de
Djérem *76 B4 river* C Cameroon
Djevdjelija *see* Gevgelija
Djibouti *72 D4 var.* Jibuti; *prev.* French Somaliland, French Territory of the Afars and Issas, *Fr.* Côte Française des Somalis, Territoire Français des Afars et des Issas. *Country* E Africa

Djibouti 72

Official name Republic of Djibouti
Formation 1977
Capital Djibouti
Population 703,000 / 79 people per sq mile (30 people per sq km)
Total area 8494 sq. miles (22,000 sq. km)
Languages Somali, Afar, French, Arabic
Religions Muslim (mainly Sunni) 94%, Christian 6%
Ethnic mix Issa 60%, Afar 35%, other 5%
Government Presidential system
Currency Djibouti franc = 100 centimes
Literacy rate 66%
Calorie consumption 2218 calories

Djibouti *72 D4 var.* Jibuti. *Country capital* (Djibouti) E Djibouti
Djourab, Erg du *76 C2 dunes* N Chad
Djúpivogur *83 E5* Austurland, SE Iceland
Dnieper *81 F4 Bel.* Dnyapro, *Rus.* Dnepr, *Ukr.* Dnipro. *River* E Europe
Dnieper Lowland *109 E2 Bel.* Prydnyaprowskaya Nizina, *Ukr.* Prydniprovs'ka Nyzovyna. *Lowlands* Belarus/Ukraine
Dniester *81 E4 Rom.* Nistru, *Rus.* Dnestr, *Ukr.* Dnister; *anc.* Tyras. *River* Moldova/Ukraine
Dnipro *see* Dnieper
Dniprodzerzhyns'k *109 F3 Rus.* Dneprodzerzhinsk; *prev.* Kamenskoye. Dnipropetrovs'ka Oblast', E Ukraine
Dniprodzerzhyns'ke Vodoskhovyshche *109 F3 Rus.* Dneprodzerzhinskoye Vodokhranilishche. *Reservoir* C Ukraine
Dnipropetrovs'k *109 F3 Rus.* Dnepropetrovsk; *prev.* Yekaterinoslav. Dnipropetrovs'ka Oblast', E Ukraine
Dniprorudne *109 F3 Rus.* Dneprorudnoye. Zaporiz'ka Oblast', SE Ukraine
Doba *76 C4* Logone-Oriental, S Chad
Döbeln *94 D4* Sachsen, E Germany
Doberai, Jazirah *139 G4 Dut.* Vogelkop. *Peninsula* Papua, E Indonesia
Doboj *100 C3* Republika Srpska, N Bosnia and Herzegovina
Dobre Miasto *98 D2 Ger.* Guttstadt. Warmińsko-Mazurskie, NE Poland
Dobrich *104 E1 Rom.* Bazargic; *prev.* Tolbukhin. Dobrich, NE Bulgaria
Dobrush *107 D7* Homyel'skaya Voblasts', SE Belarus
Dodecánese *see* Dodekánisos
Dodekánisos *105 D6 var.* Nóties Sporádes, *Eng.* Dodecanese; *prev.* Dhodhekánisos. *Island group* SE Greece
Dodge City *45 E5* Kansas, C USA
Dodoma *69 D5 country capital* (Tanzania) Dodoma, C Tanzania
Dodoma *73 C7 region* C Tanzania
Dogana *96 E1* NE San Marino
Dōgo *131 B6 island* Oki-shotō, SW Japan
Dogondoutchi *75 F3* Dosso, SW Niger
Doğubayazıt *117 F3* Ağrı, E Turkey
Doğu Karadeniz Dağları *117 E3 var.* Anadolu Dağları. *Mountain range* NE Turkey
Doha *see* Ad Dawḩah
Doire *see* Londonderry
Dokkum *86 D1* Friesland, N Netherlands
Dokuchayevs'k *109 G3 var.* Dokuchayevsk. Donets'ka Oblast', SE Ukraine
Dokuchayevsk *see* Dokuchayevs'k
Doldrums Fracture Zone *66 C4 tectonic feature* W Atlantic Ocean
Dôle *90 D4* Jura, E France
Dolisie *77 B6 prev.* Loubomo. Le Niari, S Congo
Dolomites *see* Dolomitiche, Alpi
Dolomiti *see* Dolomitiche, Alpi
Dolomitiche, Alpi *96 C1 var.* Dolomiti, *Eng.* Dolomites. *Mountain range* NE Italy
Dolores *64 D4* Buenos Aires, E Argentina
Dolores *52 B1* Petén, N Guatemala
Dolores *64 D4* Soriano, SW Uruguay
Dolores Hidalgo *51 E4 var.* Ciudad de Dolores Hidalgo. Guanajuato, C Mexico
Dolyna *108 B2 Rus.* Dolina. Ivano-Frankivs'ka Oblast', W Ukraine
Dolyns'ka *109 F3 Rus.* Dolinskaya. Kirovohrads'ka Oblast', S Ukraine
Domachëvo *see* Damachava
Domaczewo *see* Damachava
Dombås *85 B5* Oppland, S Norway
Domel Island *see* Letsôk-aw Kyun
Domeyko *64 B3* Atacama, N Chile
Dominica *55 H4 Country* E West Indies

Dominica 55

Official name Commonwealth of Dominica
Formation 1978
Capital Roseau
Population 69,655 / 240 people per sq mile (93 people per sq km)
Total area 291 sq. miles (754 sq. km)
Languages French Creole, English
Religions Roman Catholic 77%, Protestant 15%, other 8%
Ethnic mix Black 91%, Mixed race 6%, Carib 2%, other 1%
Government Parliamentary system
Currency Eastern Caribbean dollar = 100 cents
Literacy rate 76%
Calorie consumption 2995 calories

Dominica Channel *see* Martinique Passage
Dominican Republic *55 E2 country* C West Indies

Dominican Republic 55

Official name Dominican Republic
Formation 1865
Capital Santo Domingo
Population 8.7 million / 466 people per sq mile (180 people per sq km)
Total area 18,679 sq. miles (48,380 sq. km)
Languages Spanish, French Creole
Religions Roman Catholic 92%, Other and nonreligious 8%
Ethnic mix Mixed race 75%, White 15%, Black 10%
Government Presidential system
Currency Dominican Republic peso = 100 centavos
Literacy rate 84%
Calorie consumption 2333 calories

Domokós *105 B5 var.* Dhomokós. Stereá Ellás, C Greece
Don *111 B6 var.* Duna, Tanais. *River* SW Russian Federation
Donau *see* Danube
Donauwörth *95 C6* Bayern, S Germany
Don Benito *92 C3* Extremadura, W Spain
Doncaster *89 D5 anc.* Danum. N England, UK
Dondo *78 B1* Cuanza Norte, NW Angola
Donegal *89 B5 Ir.* Dún na nGall. NW Ireland
Donegal Bay *89 A5 Ir.* Bá Dhún na nGall. *Bay* NW Ireland
Donets *109 G2 var. Sivers'kyy Donets', Rus.* Severskiy Donets. Serra Acaraí. *river* Russian Federation/Ukraine
Donets'k *109 G3 Rus.* Donetsk; *prev.* Stalino. Donets'ka Oblast', E Ukraine
Dongfang *128 B7 var.* Basuo. Hainan, S China
Dongguan *128 C6* Guangdong, S China
Đông Ha *136 E4* Quang Tri, C Vietnam
Đông Hơi *136 D4* Quang Binh, C Vietnam
Dongliao *see* Liaoyuan
Dongola *72 B3 var.* Donqola, Dunqulah. Northern, N Sudan
Dongou *77 C5* La Likouala, NE Congo
Dongting Hu *128 C5 var.* Tung-t'ing Hu. *Lake* S China
Donji Vakuf *var.* Srbobran, Federacija Bosna I Hercegovina, N Serbia and Montenegro (Yugo.)
Donostia-San Sebastián *93 E1* País Vasco, N Spain

Donqola *see* Dongola
Doolow *73 D5* E Ethiopia
Doornik *see* Tournai
Door Peninsula *40 C2 peninsula* Wisconsin, N USA
Dooxo Nugaaleed *73 E5 var.* Nogal Valley. *Valley* E Somalia
Dordogne *91 B5 cultural region* SW France
Dordogne *91 B5 river* W France
Dordrecht *86 C4 var.* Dordt, Dort. Zuid-Holland, SW Netherlands
Dordt *see* Dordrecht
Dorohoi *108 C3* Botoşani, NE Romania
Dorotea *84 C4* Västerbotten, N Sweden
Dorre Island *147 A5 island* Western Australia
Dort *see* Dordrecht
Dortmund *94 A4* Nordrhein-Westfalen, W Germany
Dos Hermanas *92 C4* Andalucía, S Spain
Dospad Dagh *see* Rhodope Mountains
Dospat *104 C3* Smolyan, S Bulgaria
Dothan *42 D3* Alabama, S USA
Dotnuva *106 B4* Kėdainiai, C Lithuania
Douai *90 C2 prev.* Douay, *anc.* Duacum. Nord, N France
Douala *77 A5 var.* Duala. Littoral, W Cameroon
Douglas *89 C5 dependent territory capital* (Isle of Man) E Isle of Man
Douglas *48 C3* Arizona, SW USA
Douglas *44 D3* Wyoming, C USA
Douro *92 B2 Sp.* Duero. *River* Portugal/Spain *see also* Duero
Dover *89 E7 Fr.* Douvres; *Lat.* Dubris Portus. SE England, UK
Dover *41 F4 state capital* Delaware, NE USA
Dover, Strait of *90 C2 var.* Straits of Dover, *Fr.* Pas de Calais. *Strait* England, UK/France
Dover, Straits of *see* Dover, Strait of
Dovrefjell *85 B5 plateau* S Norway
Downpatrick *89 B5 Ir.* Dún Pádraig. SE Northern Ireland, UK
Dōzen *131 B6 island* Oki-shotō, SW Japan
Drač *see* Durrës
Drachten *86 D2* Friesland, N Netherlands
Drăgăşani *108 B5* Vâlcea, SW Romania
Dragoman *104 B2* Sofiya, W Bulgaria
Dra, Hamada du *70 C3 var.* Hammada du Drâa, Haut Plateau du Dra. *Plateau* W Algeria
Drahichyn *107 B6 Pol.* Drohiczyn Poleski, *Rus.* Drogichin. Brestskaya Voblasts', SW Belarus
Drakensberg *78 D5 mountain range* Lesotho/South Africa
Drake Passage *57 B8 passage* Atlantic Ocean/Pacific Ocean
Dralfa *104 D2* Tŭrgovishte, N Bulgaria
Dráma *104 C3 var.* Dhráma. Anatolikí Makedonía kai Thráki, NE Greece
Drammen *85 B6* Buskerud, S Norway
Drau *see* Drava
Drava *100 C3 var.* Drau, *Eng.* Drave, *Hung.* Dráva. *River* C Europe *see also* Drau
Dráva *see* Drava
Drave *see* Drava
Drawsko Pomorskie *98 B3 Ger.* Dramburg. Zachodniopomorskie, NW Poland
Drépano, Akrotírio *104 C4 var.* Akra Dhrepanon. *Headland* N Greece
Dresden *94 D4* Sachsen, E Germany
Drin *see* Drinit, Lumi i
Drina *100 C3 river* Bosnia and Herzegovina/Serbia and Montenegro (Yugo.)
Drinit, Lumi i *101 D5 var.* Drin. *River* NW Albania
Drobeta-Turnu Severin *108 B5 prev.* Turnu Severin. Mehedinţi, SW Romania
Drogheda *89 B5 Ir.* Droichead Átha. NE Ireland
Drohobych *108 B2 Pol.* Drohobycz, *Rus.* Drogobych. L'vivs'ka Oblast', NW Ukraine
Droichead Átha *see* Drogheda
Drôme *91 D5 cultural region* SE France
Dronning Maud Land *154 B2 physical region* Antarctica
Drummondville *39 E4* Québec, SE Canada
Druskininkai *107 B5 Pol.* Druskienniki. Druskininkai, S Lithuania
Dryden *38 B3* Ontario, C Canada
Drysa *107 D5 Rus.* Drissa. *River* N Belarus
Duala *see* Douala
Dubai *see* Dubayy
Dubăsari *108 D3 Rus.* Dubossary. NE Moldova
Dubawnt *37 F4 river* Northwest Territories/Nunavut, NW Canada
Dubayy *120 D4 Eng.* Dubai. Dubayy, NE UAE
Dubbo *149 D6* New South Wales, SE Australia
Dublin *89 B5 Ir.* Baile Átha Cliath; *anc.* Eblana. *Country capital* (Ireland), E Ireland
Dublin *43 E2* Georgia, SE USA
Dubno *108 C2* Rivnens'ka Oblast', NW Ukraine
Dubrovnik *101 B5 It.* Ragusa. Dubrovnik-Neretva, SE Croatia
Dubuque *45 G3* Iowa, C USA
Dudelange *87 D8 var.* Forge du Sud, *Ger.* Dudelingen. Luxembourg, S Luxembourg
Dudelingen *see* Dudelange
Duero *92 D2 Port.* Douro. *River* Portugal/Spain *see also* Douro
Duesseldorf *see* Düsseldorf
Duffel *87 C5* Antwerpen, C Belgium
Dugi Otok *100 A4 var.* Isola Grossa, *It.* Isola Lunga. *Island* W Croatia
Duisburg *94 A4 prev.* Duisburg-Hamborn. Nordrhein-Westfalen, W Germany
Duiven *86 D4* Gelderland, E Netherlands
Duk Faiwil *73 B5* Jonglei, SE Sudan
Dulan *126 D4 var.* Qagan Us. Qinghai, C China
Dulce, Golfo *53 E5 gulf* S Costa Rica
Dülmen *94 A4* Nordrhein-Westfalen, W Germany
Dulovo *104 E1* Silistra, NE Bulgaria
Duluth *45 G2* Minnesota, N USA
Dūmā *119 B5 Fr.* Douma. Dimashq, SW Syria
Dumas *49 E1* Texas, SW USA
Dumfries *88 C4* S Scotland, UK
Dumont d'Urville *154 C4 French research station* Antarctica
Dumyât *72 B1 Eng.* Damietta. N Egypt
Duna *see* Danube
Duna *see* Don
Dunaj *see* Danube
Dunaújváros *99 C7 prev.* Dunapentele, Sztálinváros. Fejér, C Hungary
Dunav *see* Danube
Dunavska Ravnina *104 C2 Eng.* Danubian Plain. *Plain* N Bulgaria
Duncan *49 G2* Oklahoma, C USA
Dundalk *89 B5 Ir.* Dún Dealgan. NE Ireland
Dún Dealgan *see* Dundalk
Dundee *88 C4* E Scotland, UK
Dundee *78 D4* KwaZulu/Natal, E South Africa
Dunedin *151 B7* Otago, South Island, NZ
Dunfermline *88 C4* C Scotland, UK
Dungu *77 E5* Orientale, NE Dem. Rep. Congo
Dungun *138 B3 var.* Kuala Dungun. Terengganu, Peninsular Malaysia
Dunkerque *90 C2 Eng.* Dunkirk, *Flem.* Duinekerke; *prev.* Dunquerque. Nord, N France
Dún Laoghaire *89 B6 Eng.* Dunleary; *prev.* Kingstown. E Ireland
Dún na nGall *see* Donegal
Dún Pádraig *see* Downpatrick
Dunqulah *see* Dongola
Dunărea *see* Danube
Dupnitsa *104 C2 prev.* Marek, Stanke Dimitrov. Kyustendil, W Bulgaria
Duqm *121 E5 var.* Daqm. E Oman
Durance *91 D6 river* SE France
Durango *50 D3 var.* Victoria de Durango. Durango, W Mexico
Durango *44 C5* Colorado, C USA
Durankulak *104 E1 Rom.* Răcari; *prev.* Blatnitsa, Duranulac. Dobrich, NE Bulgaria
Durant *49 G2* Oklahoma, C USA
Durazzo *see* Durrës
Durban *78 D4 var.* Port Natal. KwaZulu/Natal, E South Africa
Durbe *106 B3 Ger.* Durben. Liepāja, W Latvia
Durg *135 E4 prev.* Drug. Madhya Pradesh, C India
Durham *89 D5 hist.* Dunholme. N England, UK
Durham *43 F1* North Carolina, SE USA
Durostorum *see* Silistra
Durrës *101 C6 var.* Durrësi, Dursi, *It.* Durazzo, *SCr.* Drač, *Turk.* Draç. Durrës, W Albania
Durrësi *see* Durrës
Dursi *see* Durrës
Durūz, Jabal ad *119 C5 mountain* SW Syria
D'Urville Island *150 C4 island* C NZ
Dusa Mareb *see* Dhuusa Marreeb
Dusa Marreb *see* Dhuusa Marreeb
Dushanbe *123 E3 var.* Dyushambe; *prev.* Stalinabad, *Taj.* Stalinobod. *Country capital* (Tajikistan) W Tajikistan
Düsseldorf *94 A4 var.* Duesseldorf. Nordrhein-Westfalen, W Germany
Dŭstí *123 E3 Rus.* Dusti. SW Tajikistan
Dutch Harbor *36 B3* Unalaska Island, Alaska, USA
Dutch New Guinea *see* Papua
Duzdab *see* Zāhedān
Dvina *see* Severnaya Dvina
Dvina Bay *see* Chëshskaya Guba
Dyanev *see* Deynau
Dyersburg *42 C1* Tennessee, S USA
Dyushambe *see* Dushanbe
Dza Chu *see* Mekong
Dzerzhinsk *111 C5* Nizhegorodskaya Oblast', W Russian Federation
Dzhalal-Abad *123 F2 Kir.* Jalal-Abad. Dzhalal-Abadskaya Oblast', W Kyrgyzstan
Dzhambul *see* Taraz
Dzhankoy *109 F4* Respublika Krym, S Ukraine
Dzhelandy *123 F3* SE Tajikistan
Dzhergalan *123 G2 Kir.* Jyrgalan. Issyk-Kul'skaya Oblast', NE Kyrgyzstan
Dzhugdzhur, Khrebet *115 G3 mountain range* E Russian Federation
Dzhusaly *114 B4 Kaz.* Zholsaly. Kyzylorda, SW Kazakhstan
Działdowo *98 D3* Warmińsko-Mazurskie, NE Poland
Dzuunmod *127 E2* Töv, C Mongolia

E

Eagle Pass *49 F4* Texas, SW USA
East Açores Fracture Zone *see* East Azores Fracture Zone
East Antarctica *see* Greater Antarctica
East Australian Basin *see* Tasman Basin
East Azores Fracture Zone *66 C3 var.* East Açores Fracture Zone. *Tectonic feature* E Atlantic Ocean
Eastbourne *89 E7* SE England, UK
East Cape *150 E3 headland* North Island, NZ
East China Sea *125 E2 Chin.* Dong Hai. *Sea* W Pacific Ocean
Easter Fracture Zone *153 G4 tectonic feature* E Pacific Ocean
Easter Island *153 F4 var.* Rapa Nui, *island* E Pacific Ocean
Eastern Desert *68 D3 var.* Aş Şaḩrā' ash Sharqīyah, *Eng.* Arabian Desert, Eastern Desert. *Desert* E Egypt
Eastern Ghats *124 B3 mountain range* SE India
Eastern Sayans *115 E4 Mong.* Dzüün Soyonï Nuruu, *Rus.* Vostochnyy Sayan. *Mountain range* Mongolia/Russian Federation
East Falkland *65 D8 var.* Isla Soledad. *Island* E Falkland Islands
East Grand Forks *45 E1* Minnesota, N USA
East Indiaman Ridge *141 D6 undersea feature* E Indian Ocean
East Indies *152 A3 island group* SE Asia
East Kilbride *88 C4* S Scotland, UK
East Korea Bay *129 E3 bay* E North Korea
Eastleigh *89 D7* S England, UK
East London *78 D5 Afr.* Oos-Londen; *prev.* Emonti, Port Rex. Eastern Cape, S South Africa
Eastmain *38 D3 river* Québec, C Canada
East Mariana Basin *142 B1 undersea feature* W Pacific Ocean
East Novaya Zemlya Trench *112 C1 var.* Novaya Zemlya Trench. *Undersea feature* W Kara Sea
East Pacific Rise *153 F4 undersea feature* E Pacific Ocean
East Saint Louis *40 B4* Illinois, N USA
East Scotia Basin *67 C7 undersea feature* SE Scotia Sea
East Sea *130 A4 var.* Sea of Japan *Rus.* Yapanskoye More. *Sea* NW Pacific Ocean *see also* Japan, Sea of
East Siberian Sea *see* Vostochno-Sibirskoye More
East Timor *139 F5 var.* Loro Sae *prev.* Portuguese Timor, Timor Timur. Country, SE Asia

East Timor 139

Official name Democratic Republic of Timor-Leste
Formation 2002
Capital Dili
Population 778,000 / 138 people per sq mile (53 people per sq km)
Total area 5756 sq. miles (14,874 sq. km)
Languages Tetum (Portuguese/Austronesian), Bahasa Indonesia, and Portuguese
Religions Roman Catholic 95%, Other (including Muslim and Protestant) 5%
Ethnic mix Papuan groups approx 85%, Indonesian approx 13%, Chinese 2%
Government Parliamentary system
Currency US dollar = 100 cents
Literacy rate 59%
Calorie consumption Not available

Eau Claire *40 A2* Wisconsin, N USA
Eauripik Rise *142 B2 undersea feature* W Pacific Ocean
Ebensee *95 D6* Oberösterreich, N Austria
Eberswalde-Finow *94 D3* Brandenburg, E Germany
Ebetsu *130 D2 var.* Ebetu. Hokkaidō, NE Japan

Ebetu *see* Ebetsu
Ebolowa *77 A5* Sud, S Cameroon
Ebon Atoll *144 D2 var.* Epoon. *Atoll* Ralik Chain, S Marshall Islands
Ebro *93 E2 river* NE Spain
Ebusus *see* Eivissa
Ech Cheliff *see* Chlef
Ech Chleff *see* Chlef
Echo Bay *37 E3* Northwest Territories, NW Canada
Echt *87 D5* Limburg, SE Netherlands
Ecija *92 D4 anc.* Astigi. Andalucía, SW Spain
Ecuador *60 B1 Country* NW South America

Ecuador 60

Official name Republic of Ecuador
Formation 1830
Capital Quito
Population 13 million / 122 people per sq mile (47 people per sq km)
Total area 109,483 sq. miles (283,560 sq. km)
Languages Spanish, Quechua, other Amerindian languages
Religions Roman Catholic 93%, Protestant, Jewish, and other 7%
Ethnic mix Mestizo 55%, Amerindian 25%, White 10%, Black 10%
Government Presidential system
Currency US dollar = 100 cents
Literacy rate 91%
Calorie consumption 2792 calories

Ed Da'ein *72 A4* Southern Darfur, W Sudan
Ed Damazin *72 C4 var.* Ad Damazīn. Blue Nile, E Sudan
Ed Damer *72 C3 var.* Ad Damar, Ad Dāmir. River Nile, NE Sudan
Ed Debba *72 B3* Northern, N Sudan
Ede *86 D4* Gelderland, C Netherlands
Ede *75 F5* Osun, SW Nigeria
Edéa *77 A5* Littoral, SW Cameroon
Edeyin Murzuq *see* Murzuq, Idhān
Edfu *see* Idfu
Edgeøya *83 G2 island* S Svalbard
Edgware *89 A7* SE England, UK
Edinburg *49 G5* Texas, SW USA
Edinburgh *88 C4 admin capital* S Scotland, UK
Edirne *116 A2 Eng.* Adrianople; *anc.* Adrianopolis, Hadrianopolis. Edirne, NW Turkey
Edmonds *46 B2* Washington, NW USA
Edmonton *37 E5* Alberta, SW Canada
Edmundston *39 E4* New Brunswick, SE Canada
Edna *49 G4* Texas, SW USA
Edolo *96 B1* Lombardia, N Italy
Edremit *116 A3* Balıkesir, NW Turkey
Edward, Lake *77 E5 var.* Albert Edward Nyanza, Edward Nyanza, Lac Idi Amin, Lake Rutanzige. *Lake* Uganda/Zaire
Edward Nyanza *see* Edward, Lake
Edwards Plateau *49 F3 plain* Texas, SW USA
Eeklo *87 B5 var.* Eekloo. Oost-Vlaanderen, NW Belgium
Edzo *53 E4 prev.* Rae-Edzo. Northwest Territories, NW Canada
Eekloo *see* Eeklo
Eersel *87 C5* Noord-Brabant, S Netherlands
Efate *144 D4 var.* Éfaté *Fr.* Vaté; *prev.* Sandwich Island. *Island* C Vanuatu
Effingham *40 B4* Illinois, N USA
Eforie Sud *108 D5* Constanța, E Romania
Efstrátios, Ágios *104 D4 var.* Ayios Evstratios. *Island* E Greece
Egadi, Isole *97 B7 island group* S Italy
Eger *99 D6 Ger.* Erlau. Heves, NE Hungary
Egeria Fracture Zone *141 C5 tectonic feature* W Indian Ocean
Éghezèe *87 C6* Namur, C Belgium
Egina *see* Aígina
Egio *see* Aígio
Egmont, Mount *see* Taranaki, Mount
Egmont, Cape *150 C4 headland* North Island, NZ
Egoli *see* Johannesburg
Egypt *72 B2 Ar.* Jumhūrīyah Mişr al 'Arabīyah; *prev.* United Arab Republic, *anc.* Aegyptus. *Country* NE Africa

Egypt 72

Official name Arab Republic of Egypt
Formation 1936
Capital Cairo
Population 71.9 million / 187 people per sq mile (72 people per sq km)
Total area 386,660 sq. miles (1,001,450 sq. km)
Languages Arabic, French, English, Berber
Religions Muslim (mainly Sunni) 94%, Coptic Christian and other 6%
Ethnic mix Eastern Hamitic 90%, Nubian, Armenian, and Greek 10%
Government Presidential system
Currency Egyptian pound = 100 piastres
Literacy rate 56%
Calorie consumption 3385 calories

Eibar *93 E1* País Vasco, N Spain
Eibergen *86 E3* Gelderland, E Netherlands
Eidfjord *85 A5* Hordaland, S Norway
Eier-Berg *see* Suur Munamägi
Eifel *95 A5 plateau* W Germany
Eiger *95 B7 mountain* C Switzerland
Eigg *88 B3 island* W Scotland, UK
Eight Degree Channel *132 B3 channel* India/Maldives
Eighty Mile Beach *146 B4 beach* Western Australia
Eijsden *87 D6* Limburg, SE Netherlands
Eilat *see* Elat
Eindhoven *87 D5* Noord-Brabant, S Netherlands
Eipel *see* Ipel'
Eipel *see* Ipoly
Eisenhüttenstadt *94 D4* Brandenburg, E Germany
Eisenstadt *95 E6* Burgenland, E Austria
Eisleben *94 C4* Sachsen-Anhalt, C Germany
Eivissa *93 G3 var.* Iviza, *Cast.* Ibiza; *anc.* Ebusus. *Island* Islas Baleares, Spain, W Mediterranean Sea
Eivissa *93 G3 var.* Iviza, *Cast.* Ibiza; *anc.* Ebusus. Eivissa, Spain, W Mediterranean Sea
Ejea de los Caballeros *93 E2* Aragón, NE Spain
Ejin Qi *126 D3 var.* Dalain Hob. Nei Mongol Zizhiqu, N China
Ekapa *see* Cape Town
Ekiatapskiy Khrebet *115 G1 mountain range* NE Russian Federation
El 'Alamein *72 B1 var.* Al 'Alamayn. N Egypt
El Asnam *see* Chlef
Elat *119 B8 var.* Eilat, Elath. Southern, S Israel
Elat, Gulf of *see* Aqaba, Gulf of
Elath *see* Al 'Aqabah
Elath *see* Elat
El'Atrun *72 B3* Northern Darfur, NW Sudan
Elazığ *117 E3 var.* Elâzıǧ, Elâziz. Elâzıǧ, E Turkey
Elâziz *see* Elazığ
Elba, Isola d' *96 B4 island* Archipelago Toscano, C Italy
Elbasan *101 D6 var.* Elbasani. Elbasan, C Albania
Elbasani *see* Elbasan
Elbe *80 D3 Cz.* Labe. *River* Czech Republic/Germany
El Beni *see* Beni
Elbert, Mount *44 C4 mountain* Colorado, C USA
Elbing *see* Elbląg
Elbląg *98 C2 var.* Elblag, *Ger.* Elbing. Warmińsko-Mazurskie, NE Poland
El Boulaida *see* Blida
El'brus *111 A8 var.* Gora El'brus. *Mountain* SW Russian Federation
El Burgo de Osma *93 E2* Castilla-León, C Spain
El Cajon *47 C8* California, W USA
El Calafate *65 B7 var.* Calafate. Santa Cruz, S Argentina
El Callao *59 E2* Bolívar, E Venezuela
El Campo *49 G4* Texas, SW USA
El Carmen de Bolívar *58 B2* Bolívar, NW Colombia
El Centro *47 D8* California, W USA
Elche *93 F4 var.* Elx; *anc.* Ilici, *Lat.* Illicis. País Valenciano, E Spain
Elda *93 F4* País Valenciano, E Spain
El Djazaïr *see* Alger
El Djelfa *see* Djelfa
El Dorado *42 B2* Arkansas, C USA
El Dorado *59 F2* Bolívar, E Venezuela
El Dorado *45 F5* Kansas, C USA
El Dorado *50 C3* Sinaloa, C Mexico
Eldorado *64 E3* Misiones, NE Argentina
Eldoret *73 C6* Rift Valley, W Kenya
Elektrostal' *111 B5* Moskovskaya Oblast', W Russian Federation
Elemi Triangle *73 B5 disputed region* Kenya/Sudan
Elephant Butte Reservoir *48 C2 reservoir* New Mexico, SW USA
Eleuthera Island *54 C1 island* N Bahamas
El Fasher *72 A4 var.* Al Fāshir. Northern Darfur, W Sudan
El Ferrol *see* Ferrol
El Ferrol del Caudillo *see* Ferrol
El Gedaref *see* Gedaref
El Geneina *72 A4 var.* Ajjinena, Al-Genain, Al Junaynah. Western Darfur, W Sudan
Elgin *40 B3* Illinois, N USA
Elgin *88 C3* NE Scotland, UK
El Gîza *72 B1 var.* Al Jīzah, Gîza, Gizeh. N Egypt
El Goléa *70 D3 var.* Al Golea. C Algeria
El Ḩank *74 D1 cliff* N Mauritania
El Haseke *see* Al Ḩasakah
Elista *111 B7* Respublika Kalmykiya, SW Russian Federation
Elizabeth *149 B6* South Australia
Elizabeth City *43 G1* North Carolina, SE USA
Elizabethtown *40 C5* Kentucky, S USA
El-Jadida *70 C2 prev.* Mazagan. W Morocco
Ełk *98 E2 Ger.* Lyck. Warmińsko-Mazurskie, NE Poland
Elk City *49 F1* Oklahoma, C USA
El Kerak *see* Al Karak
El Khalīl *see* Hebron
El Khârga *72 B2 var.* Al Khārijah. C Egypt
Elkhart *40 C3* Indiana, N USA
El Khartûm *see* Khartoum
Elk River *45 F2* Minnesota, N USA
El Kuneitra *see* Al Qunayţirah
Ellef Ringnes Island *37 E1 island* Nunavut, N Canada
Ellen, Mount *44 B5 mountain* Utah, W USA
Ellensburg *46 B2* Washington, NW USA
Ellesmere Island *37 F1 island* Queen Elizabeth Islands, Nunavut, N Canada
Ellesmere, Lake *151 C6 lake* South Island, NZ
Elliston *149 A6* South Australia
Ellsworth Land *154 A3 physical region* Antarctica
El Mahbas *70 B3 var.* Mahbés. SW Western Sahara
El Mina *118 B4 var.* Al Mīnā'. N Lebanon
El Minya *72 B2 var.* Al Minyā, Minya. C Egypt
Elmira *41 E3* New York, NE USA
El Mreyyé *74 D2 desert* E Mauritania
Elmshorn *94 B3* Schleswig-Holstein, N Germany
El Muglad *72 B4* Western Kordofan, C Sudan
El Obeid *72 B4 var.* Al Obayyid, Al Ubayyiḑ. Northern Kordofan, C Sudan
El Ouâdi *see* El Oued
El Oued *71 E2 var.* Al Oued, El Ouâdi, El Wad. NE Algeria
Eloy *48 B2* Arizona, SW USA
El Paso *48 D3* Texas, SW USA
El Porvenir *53 G4* San Blas, N Panama
El Progreso *52 C2* Yoro, NW Honduras
El Puerto de Santa María *92 C5* Andalucía, S Spain
El Quds *see* Jerusalem
El Quneitra *see* Al Qunayţirah
El Quseir *see* Al Quşayr
El Quweira *see* Al Quwayrah
El Rama *53 E3* Región Autónoma Atlántico Sur, SE Nicaragua
El Real *53 H5 var.* El Real de Santa María. Darién, SE Panama
El Real de Santa María *see* El Real
El Reno *49 F1* Oklahoma, C USA
El Salvador *52 B3 Country* Central America

El Salvador 52

Official name Republic of El Salvador
Formation 1841
Capital San Salvador
Population 6.5 million / 812 people per sq mile (314 people per sq km)
Total area 8124 sq. miles (21,040 sq. km)
Languages Spanish
Religions Roman Catholic 80%, Evangelical 18%, other 2%
Ethnic mix Mestizo 94%, Amerindian 5%, White 1%
Government Presidential system
Currency Salvadorean colón & US dollar = 100 centavos (colón); 100 cents (US dollar)
Literacy rate 80%
Calorie consumption 2512 calories

El Sáuz *50 C2* Chihuahua, N Mexico
El Serrat *91 A7* N Andorra
Elst *86 D4* Gelderland, E Netherlands
El Sueco *50 C2* Chihuahua, N Mexico
El Suweida *see* As Suwaydā'
Eltanin Fracture Zone *153 E5 tectonic feature* SE Pacific Ocean
El Tigre *59 E2* Anzoátegui, NE Venezuela
Elvas *92 C4* Portalegre, C Portugal
El Vendrell *93 G2* Cataluña, NE Spain
El Vigía *58 C2* Mérida, NW Venezuela
El Wad *see* El Oued
Elwell, Lake *44 B1 reservoir* Montana, NW USA
Elx *see* Elche
Ely *47 D5* Nevada, W USA
El Yopal *see* Yopal
Emajõgi *106 D3 Ger.* Embach. *River* SE Estonia
Emba *114 B4 Kaz.* Embi. Aktyubinsk, W Kazakhstan
Emden *94 A3* Niedersachsen, NW Germany
Emerald *148 D4* Queensland, E Australia
Emerald Isle *see* Montserrat
Emesa *see* Ḩimş

Emmaste *106 C2* Hiiumaa, W Estonia
Emmeloord *86 D2* Flevoland, N Netherlands
Emmen *86 E2* Drenthe, NE Netherlands
Emmendingen *95 A6* Baden-Württemberg, SW Germany
Emory Peak *49 E4 mountain* Texas, SW USA
Empalme *50 B2* Sonora, NW Mexico
Emperor Seamounts *113 G3 undersea feature* NW Pacific Ocean
Emporia *45 F5* Kansas, C USA
Empty Quarter *see* Ar Rub 'al Khālī
Ems *94 A3 Dut.* Eems. *River* NW Germany
Encamp *91 A8* C Andorra
Encarnación *64 D3* Itapúa, S Paraguay
Encinitas *47 C8* California, W USA
Encs *99 D6* Borsod-Abaúj-Zemplén, NE Hungary
Endeavour Strait *148 C1 strait* Queensland, NE Australia
Enderbury Island *145 F3 atoll* Phoenix Islands, C Kiribati
Enderby Land *154 C2 physical region* Antarctica
Enderby Plain *154 D2 undersea feature* S Indian Ocean
Enewetak Atoll *144 C1 var.* Ānewetak, Eniwetok. *Atoll* Ralik Chain, W Marshall Islands
Enfield *89 A7* SE England, UK
Engannim *see* Jenīn
Enghien *87 B6 Dut.* Edingen. Hainaut, SW Belgium
England *89 D5 Lat.* Anglia. *National region* UK
Englewood *44 D4* Colorado, C USA
English Channel *89 D8 var.* The Channel, *Fr.* la Manche. *Channel* NW Europe
Engure *106 C3* Tukums, W Latvia
Engures Ezers *106 B3 lake* NW Latvia
Enguri *117 F1 Rus.* Inguri. *River* NW Georgia
Enid *49 F1* Oklahoma, C USA
Enikale Strait *see* Kerch Strait
Eniwetok *see* Enewetak Atoll
En Nâqoûra *119 A5 var.* An Nāqūrah. SW Lebanon
Ennedi *76 D2 plateau* E Chad
Ennis *89 A6 Ir.* Inis. W Ireland
Ennis *49 G3* Texas, SW USA
Enniskillen *89 B5 var.* Inniskilling, *Ir.* Inis Ceithleann. SW Northern Ireland, UK
Enns *95 D6 river* C Austria
Enschede *86 E3* Overijssel, E Netherlands
Ensenada *50 A1* Baja California, NW Mexico
Entebbe *73 B6* S Uganda
Entroncamento *92 B3* Santarém, C Portugal
Enugu *75 G5* Enugu, S Nigeria
Eolie, Isole *97 C6 var.* Isole Lipari, *Eng.* Aeolian Islands, Lipari Islands. *Island group* S Italy
Epanomí *104 B4* Kentrikí Makedonía, N Greece
Epéna *77 B5* La Likouala, NE Congo
Eperies *see* Prešov
Eperjes *see* Prešov
Epi *144 D4 var.* Épi. *Island* C Vanuatu
Épi *see* Epi
Épinal *90 D4* Vosges, NE France
Epiphania *see* Ḩamāh
Epitoli *see* Pretoria
Epoon *see* Ebon Atoll
Epsom *89 A8* SE England, UK
Equatorial Guinea *77 A5 Country* C Africa

Equatorial Guinea 77

Official name Republic of Equatorial Guinea
Formation 1968
Capital Malabo

Equatorial Guinea (continued)

Population 494,000 / 46 people per sq mile (18 people per sq km)
Total area 10,830 sq. miles (28,051 sq. km)
Languages Spanish, Fang, Bubi
Religions Roman Catholic 90%, other 10%
Ethnic mix Fang 85%, other 11%, Bubi 4%
Government Presidential system
Currency CFA franc = 100 centimes
Literacy rate 84%
Calorie consumption Not available

Erautini *see* Johannesburg
Erbil *see* Arbīl
Erciş *117 F3* Van, E Turkey
Erdélyi-Havasok *see* Carpaţii Meridionali
Erdenet *127 E2* Bulgan, N Mongolia
Erdi *76 C2 plateau* NE Chad
Erdi Ma *76 D2 desert* NE Chad
Erebus, Mount *154 B4 mountain* Ross Island, Antarctica
Ereğli *116 C4* Konya, S Turkey
Erenhot *127 F2 var.* Erlian. Nei Mongol Zizhiqu, NE China
Erevan *see* Yerevan
Erfurt *94 C4* Thüringen, C Germany
Ergene Irmağı *116 A2 var.* Ergene Irmağı. *River* NW Turkey
Erg Iguid *see* Iguîdi, 'Erg
Ergun He *see* Argun
Ergun Zuoqi *127 F1* Nei Mongol Zizhiqu, N China
Erie *40 D3* Pennsylvania, NE USA
Erie, Lake *40 D3 Fr.* Lac Érié. *Lake* Canada/USA
Eritrea *72 C4 Tig.* Ērtra. *Country* E Africa

Eritrea 72

Official name State of Eritrea
Formation 1993
Capital Asmara
Population 4.1 million / 90 people per sq mile (35 people per sq km)
Total area 46,842 sq. miles (121,320 sq. km)
Languages Tigrinya, English, Tigre, Afar, Arabic, Bilen, Kunama, Nara, Saho, Hadareb
Religions Christian 45%, Muslim 45%, other 10%
Ethnic mix Tigray 50%, Tigray and Kunama 40%, Afar 4%, other 3%, Saho 3%
Government Transitional regime
Currency Nakfa = 100 cents
Literacy rate 57%
Calorie consumption 1690 calories

Erivan *see* Yerevan
Erlangen *95 C5* Bayern, S Germany
Erlian *see* Erenhot
Ermelo *86 D3* Gelderland, C Netherlands
Ermióni *105 C6* Pelopónnisos, S Greece
Ermoúpoli *105 D6 var.* Hermoupolis; *prev.* Ermoúpolis. Sýros, Kykládes, Greece, Aegean Sea
Ermoúpolis *see* Ermoúpoli
Ernākulam *132 C3* Kerala, SW India
Erode *132 C2* Tamil Nādu, SE India
Erquelinnes *87 B7* Hainaut, S Belgium
Er-Rachidia *70 C2 var.* Ksar al Soule. E Morocco
Er Rahad *72 B4 var.* Ar Rahad. Northern Kordofan, C Sudan
Erromango *144 D4 island* S Vanuatu
Ertis *see* Irtysh
Erzgebirge *95 C5 Cz.* Krušné Hory, *Eng.* Ore Mountains. *Mountain range* Czech Republic/Germany *see also* Krušné Hory
Erzincan *117 E3 var.* Erzinjan. Erzincan, E Turkey
Erzinjan *see* Erzincan
Erzurum *117 E3 prev.* Erzerum. Erzurum, NE Turkey
Esbjerg *85 A7* Ribe, W Denmark
Escaldes *91 A8* C Andorra
Escanaba *40 C2* Michigan, N USA
Esch-sur-Alzette *87 D8* Luxembourg, S Luxembourg
Escondido *47 C8* California, W USA
Escuinapa *50 D3 var.* Escuinapa de Hidalgo. Sinaloa, C Mexico
Escuinapa de Hidalgo *see* Escuinapa
Escuintla *51 G5* Chiapas, SE Mexico
Escuintla *52 B2* Escuintla, S Guatemala
Esenguly *122 B3 var.* Gasan-Kuli. Balkanskiy Velayat, W Turkmenistan
Eşfahān *120 C3 Eng.* Isfahan; *anc.* Aspadana. Eşfahān, C Iran
Esh Sham *see* Dimashq
Esh Sharā *see* Ash Sharāh
Eskişehir *116 B3 var.* Eskishehr. Eskişehir, W Turkey
Eskishehr *see* Eskişehir
Eslāmābād *120 C3 var.* Eslāmābād-e Gharb; *prev.* Harunabad, Shāhābād. Kermānshāhān, W Iran
Eslāmābād-e Gharb *see* Eslāmābād
Esmeraldas *60 A1* Esmeraldas, N Ecuador
Esna *see* Isna
Espanola *48 D1* New Mexico, SW USA
Esperance *147 B7* Western Australia
Esperanza *154 A2 Argentinian research station* Antarctica
Esperanza *50 B2* Sonora, NW Mexico
Espinal *58 B3* Tolima, C Colombia
Espinhaço, Serra do *56 D4 mountain range* SE Brazil
Espírito Santo *63 F4 off.* Estado do Espírito Santo. *State* E Brazil
Espiritu Santo *144 C4 var.* Santo. *Island* W Vanuatu
Espoo *85 D6 Swe.* Esbo. Etelä-Suomi, S Finland
Esquel *65 B6* Chubut, SW Argentina
Essaouira *70 B2 prev.* Mogador. W Morocco
Es Semara *see* Smara
Essen *94 A4 var.* Essen an der Ruhr. Nordrhein-Westfalen, W Germany
Essen *87 C5* Antwerpen, N Belgium
Essen an der Ruhr *see* Essen
Essequibo River *59 F3 river* C Guyana
Es Suweida *see* As Suwaydā'
Estacado, Llano *49 E2 plain* New Mexico/Texas, SW USA
Estados, Isla de los *65 C8 prev. Eng.* Staten Island. *Island* S Argentina
Estância *63 G3* Sergipe, E Brazil
Estelí *52 D3* Estelí, NW Nicaragua
Estella *93 E1 Bas.* Lizarra. Navarra, N Spain
Estepona *92 D5* Andalucía, S Spain
Estevan *37 F5* Saskatchewan, S Canada
Estonia *106 D2Est.* Eesti Vabariik, *Ger.* Estland, *Latv.* Igaunija; *prev.* Estonian SSR, *Rus.* Estonskaya SSR. *Country* NE Europe

Estonia 106

Official name Republic of Estonia
Formation 1991
Capital Tallinn
Population 1.3 million / 75 people per sq mile (29 people per sq km)
Total area 17,462 sq. miles (45,226 sq. km)
Languages Estonian, Russian
Religions Evangelical Lutheran 56%, Orthodox Christian 25%, other 19%
Ethnic mix Estonian 62%, Russian 30%, other 8%
Government Parliamentary system
Currency Kroon = 100 senti
Literacy rate 99%
Calorie consumption 3048 calories

Estrela, Serra da *92 C3 mountain range* C Portugal
Estremoz *92 C4* Évora, S Portugal
Esztergom *99 C6 Ger.* Gran; *anc.* Strigonium. Komárom-Esztergom, N Hungary
Étalle *87 D8* Luxembourg, SE Belgium
Etāwah *134 D3* Uttar Pradesh, N India
Ethiopia *73 C5 prev.* Abyssinia, People's Democratic Republic of Ethiopia. *Country* E Africa

Ethiopia 73

Official name Federal Democratic Republic of Ethiopia
Formation 1896
Capital Addis Ababa
Population 70.7 million / 165 people per sq mile (64 people per sq km)
Total area 435,184 sq. miles (1,127,127 sq. km)
Languages Amharic, Tigrinya, Galla, Sidamo, Somali, English, Arabic
Religions Orthodox Christian 40%, Muslim 40%, Traditional beliefs 15%, other 5%
Ethnic mix Oromo 40%, Amhara 25%, Sidamo 9%, Berta 6%, Somali 6%, other 14%
Government Parliamentary system
Currency Ethiopian birr = 100 cents
Literacy rate 42%
Calorie consumption 2037 calories

Ethiopian Highlands *73 C5 var.* Ethiopian Plateau. *Plateau* N Ethiopia
Ethiopian Plateau *see* Ethiopian Highlands
Etna, Monte *97 C7 Eng.* Mount Etna. *Volcano* Sicilia, Italy, C Mediterranean Sea
Etna, Mount *see* Etna, Monte
Etosha Pan *78 B3 salt lake* N Namibia
Etoumbi *77 B5* Cuvette, NW Congo
Et Tafila *see* Aţ Ţafīlah
Ettelbrück *87 D8* Diekirch, C Luxembourg
'Eua *145 E5 prev.* Middleburg Island. *Island* Tongatapu Group, SE Tonga
Euboea *see* Évvoia
Eucla *147 D6* Western Australia
Euclid *40 D3* Ohio, N USA
Eufaula Lake *49 G1 var.* Eufaula Reservoir. *Reservoir* Oklahoma, C USA
Eufaula Reservoir *see* Eufaula Lake
Eugene *46 B3* Oregon, NW USA
Eupen *87 D6* Liège, E Belgium
Euphrates *112 B4 Ar.* Al Furāt, *Turk.* Firat Nehri. *River* SW Asia
Eureka *47 A5* California, W USA
Eureka *44 A1* Montana, NW USA
Europa Point *93 H5 headland* S Gibraltar
Europe *34 E1 continent*
Eutin *94 C2* Schleswig-Holstein, N Germany
Euxine Sea *see* Black Sea
Evansdale *45 G3* Iowa, C USA
Evanston *40 B3* Illinois, N USA
Evanston *44 B4* Wyoming, C USA
Evansville *40 B5* Indiana, N USA
Eveleth *45 G1* Minnesota, N USA
Everard, Lake *149 A6 salt lake* South Australia
Everest, Mount *126 B5 Chin.* Qomolangma Feng, *Nep.* Sagarmatha. *Mountain* China/Nepal
Everett *46 B2* Washington, NW USA
Everglades, The *43 F5 wetland* Florida, SE USA
Evje *85 A6* Aust-Agder, S Norway
Évora *92 B4 anc.* Ebora, *Lat.* Liberalitas Julia.Évora, C Portugal
Évreux *90 C3 anc.* Civitas Eburovicum. Eure, N France
Évros *see* Maritsa

Évry *90 E2* Essonne, N France
Évvoia *101 E8 Lat.* Euboea. *Island* C Greece
Ewarton *54 B5* C Jamaica
Excelsior Springs *45 F4* Missouri, C USA
Exe *89 C7 river* SW England, UK
Exeter *89 C7 anc.* Isca Damnoniorum. SW England, UK
Exmoor *89 C7 moorland* SW England, UK
Exmouth *89 C7* SW England, UK
Exmouth *146 A4* Western Australia
Exmouth Gulf *146 A4 gulf* Western Australia
Exmouth Plateau *141 E5 undersea feature* E Indian Ocean
Extremadura *92 C3 cultural region* W Spain
Exuma Cays *54 C1 islets* C Bahamas
Exuma Sound *54 C1 sound* C Bahamas
Eyre Mountains *151 A7 mountain range* South Island, NZ
Eyre North, Lake *149 A5 salt lake* South Australia
Eyre Peninsula *149 A6 peninsula* South Australia
Eyre South, Lake *149 A5 salt lake* South Australia

F

Faadhippolhu Atoll *132 B4 var.* Fadiffolu, Lhaviyani Atoll. *Atoll* N Maldives
Fabens *48 D3* Texas, SW USA
Fada *76 C2* Borkou-Ennedi-Tibesti, E Chad
Fada-Ngourma *75 E4* E Burkina faso
Fadiffolu *see* Faadhippolhu Atoll
Faenza *96 C3 anc.* Faventia. Emilia-Romagna, N Italy
Faeroe-Iceland Ridge *80 C1 undersea feature* NW Norwegian Sea
Faeroe-Shetland Trough *80 C2 undersea feature* NE Atlantic Ocean
Faeroes Islands *83 E5 Dan.* Færøerne, *Faer.* Føroyar. *Danish external territory* N Atlantic Ocean
Faetano *96 E2* E San Marino
Făgăraş *108 C4 Ger.* Fogarasch, *Hung.* Fogaras. Braşov, C Romania
Fagibina, Lake *see* Faguibine, Lac
Fagne *87 C7 hill range* S Belgium
Faguibine, Lac *75 E3 var.* Lake Fagibina. *Lake* NW Mali
Fahlun *see* Falun
Fahraj *120 E4* Kermān, SE Iran
Faial *92 A5 var.* Ilha do Faial. *Island* Azores, Portugal, NE Atlantic Ocean
Fairbanks *36 D3* Alaska, USA
Fairfield *47 B6* California, W USA
Fair Isle *88 D2 island* NE Scotland, UK
Fairlie *151 B6* Canterbury, South Island, NZ
Fairmont *45 F3* Minnesota, N USA
Faisalābād *134 C2 prev.* Lyallpur. Punjab, NE Pakistan
Faizābād *see* Feyzābād
Faizābād *135 E3* Uttar Pradesh, N India
Fakaofo Atoll *145 F3 island* SE Tokelau
Falam *136 A3* Chin State, W Myanmar
Falconara Marittima *96 C3* Marche, C Italy
Falkland Islands *65 D7 var.* Falklands, Islas Malvinas. *UK dependent territory* SW Atlantic Ocean
Falkland Plateau *57 D7 var.* Argentine Rise. *Undersea feature* SW Atlantic Ocean
Falklands *see* Falkland Islands
Fallbrook *47 C8* California, W USA
Falmouth *89 C7* SW England, UK
Falmouth *54 A4* W Jamaica
Falster *85 B8 island* SE Denmark
Fălticeni *108 C3 Hung.* Falticsén. Suceava, NE Romania
Falun *85 C6 var.* Fahlun. Kopparberg, C Sweden
Famagusta *see* Ammóchostos
Famagusta Bay *see* Kólpos Ammóchostos
Famenne *87 C7 physical region* SE Belgium
Fang *136 C3* Chiang Mai, NW Thailand
Fano *96 C3 anc.* Colonia Julia Fanestris, Fanum Fortunae. Marche, C Italy
Farafangana *79 G4* Fianarantsoa, SE Madagascar
Farāh *122 D4 var.* Farah, Fararud. Farāh, W Afghanistan
Farāh Rūd *122 D4 river* W Afghanistan
Faranah *74 C4* Haute-Guinée, S Guinea
Fararud *see* Farāh
Farasān, Jazā'ir *121 A6 island group* SW Saudi Arabia
Farewell, Cape *150 C4 headland* South Island, NZ
Farewell, Cape *see* Nunap Isua
Farghona *see* Farg'ona
Fargo *45 F2* North Dakota, N USA
Farg'ona *123 F2 var.* Farghona, *Rus.* Fergana; *prev.* Novyy Margilan. Farghona Wiloyati, E Uzbekistan
Faribault *45 F2* Minnesota, N USA
Farīdabād *134 D3* Haryāna, N India
Farkhor *123 E3 Rus.* Parkhar. SW Tajikistan
Farmington *45 G5* Missouri, C USA
Farmington *48 C1* New Mexico, SW USA
Faro *92 B5* Faro, S Portugal
Farquhar Group *79 G2 island group* S Seychelles
Farvel, Kap *see* Nunap Isua
Fastiv *109 E2 Rus.* Fastov. Kyyivs'ka Oblast', NW Ukraine
Fauske *84 C3* Nordland, C Norway
Faxaflói *82 D5 Eng.* Faxa Bay. *Bay* W Iceland
Faya *76 C2 prev.* Faya-Largeau, Largeau. Borkou-Ennedi-Tibesti, N Chad
Fayetteville *42 A1* Arkansas, C USA
Fayetteville *43 F1* North Carolina, SE USA
Fdérick *see* Fdérik
Fdérik *74 C2 var.* Fdérick, *Fr.* Fort Gouraud. Tiris Zemmour, NW Mauritania
Fear, Cape *43 F2 headland* Bald Head Island, North Carolina, SE USA
Fécamp *90 B3* Seine-Maritime, N France
Federation of the separate territories of *see* Malaysia
Fehérgyarmat *99 E6* Szabolcs-Szatmár-Bereg, E Hungary
Fehmarn *94 C2 island* N Germany
Fehmarnbelt *94 C2 var* Fehmarn Belt, *Dan.* Fehmern Bælt. *Strait* Denmark/Germany
Fehmern Bælt *see* Fehmarnbelt
Feijó *62 C2* Acre, W Brazil
Feilding *150 D4* Manawatu-Wanganui, North Island, NZ
Feira *see* Feira de Santana
Feira de Santana *63 G3 var.* Feira. Bahia, E Brazil
Felanitx *93 G3 anc.* Canati, Felaniche. Mallorca, Spain, W Mediterranean Sea
Felidhu Atoll *132 B4 atoll* C Maldives
Felipe Carrillo Puerto *51 H4* Quintana Roo, SE Mexico
Felixstowe *89 E6* E England, UK
Femunden *85 B5 lake* S Norway
Fengcheng *128 D3 var.* Feng-cheng, Fenghwangcheng. Liaoning, NE China
Feng-cheng *see* Fengcheng
Fenghwangcheng *see* Fengcheng
Fengtien *see* Liaoning
Fenoarivo *79 G3* Toamasina, E Madagascar
Fens, The *89 E6 wetland* E England, UK
Feodosiya *109 F5 var.* Kefe, *It.* Kaffa; *anc.* Theodosia. Respublika Krym, S Ukraine
Féres *104 D3* Anatolikí Makedonía kai Thráki, NE Greece
Fergus Falls *45 F2* Minnesota, N USA
Ferkessédougou *74 D4* N Côte d'Ivoire
Ferghana *see* Farg'ona
Fermo *96 C4 anc.* Firmum Picenum. Marche, C Italy
Fernandina, Isla *60 A5 var.* Narborough Island. *Island* Galapagos Islands, Ecuador, E Pacific Ocean
Fernando de Noronha *63 H2 island* E Brazil
Fernando Po *see* Bioco, Isla de
Fernando Póo *see* Bioco, Isla de
Ferrara *96 C2 anc.* Forum Alieni. Emilia-Romagna, N Italy
Ferreñafe *60 B3* Lambayeque, W Peru
Ferro *see* Hierro
Ferrol *92 B1 var.* El Ferrol; *prev.* El Ferrol del Caudillo. Galicia, NW Spain
Ferwerd *86 D1 Fris.* Ferwert. Friesland, N Netherlands
Fès *70 C2 Eng.* Fez. N Morocco
Feteşti *108 D5* Ialomiţa, SE Romania
Fethiye *116 B4* Muğla, SW Turkey
Fetlar *88 D1 island* NE Scotland, UK
Feyzābād *123 F3 var.* Faizabad, Faizābād, Feyzābād, Fyzabad. Badakhshān, NE Afghanistan
Fianarantsoa *79 F3* Fianarantsoa, C Madagascar
Fianga *76 B4* Mayo-Kébbi, SW Chad
Fier *101 C6 var.* Fieri. Fier, SW Albania
Fieri *see* Fier
Figeac *91 C5* Lot, S France
Figig *see* Figuig
Figueira da Foz *92 B3* Coimbra, W Portugal
Figueres *93 G2* Cataluña, E Spain
Figuig *70 D2 var.* Figig. E Morocco
Fiji *145 E5 Fij.* Viti. *Country* SW Pacific Ocean

Fiji 145

Official name Republic of the Fiji Islands
Formation 1970
Capital Suva
Population 839,000 / 119 people per sq mile (46 people per sq km)
Total area 7054 sq. miles (18,270 sq. km)
Languages Fijian, English, Hindi, Urdu, Tamil, Telugu
Religions Hindu 38%, Methodist 37%, Roman Catholic 9%, other 8%, Muslim 8%
Ethnic mix Melanesian 48%, Indian 46%, other 6%
Government Parliamentary system
Currency Fiji dollar = 100 cents
Literacy rate 93%
Calorie consumption 2789 calories

Filadelfia *52 D4* Guanacaste, W Costa Rica
Filiaşi *108 B5* Dolj, SW Romania
Filipstad *85 B6* Värmland, C Sweden
Finale Ligure *96 A3* Liguria, NW Italy
Finchley *89 A7* SE England, UK
Findlay *40 C4* Ohio, N USA
Finike *116 B4* Antalya, SW Turkey
Finland *84 D4 Fin.* Suomen Tasavalta, Suomi. *Country* N Europe

Finland 84

Official name Republic of Finland
Formation 1917

Finland (continued)

Capital Helsinki
Population 5.2 million / 44 people per sq mile (17 people per sq km)
Total area 130,127 sq. miles (337,030 sq. km)
Languages Finnish, Swedish, Sámi
Religions Evangelical Lutheran 89%, other 9%, Orthodox Christian 1%, Roman Catholic 1%
Ethnic mix Finnish 93%, Other (including Sámi) 7%
Government Parliamentary system
Currency Euro = 100 cents
Literacy rate 99%
Calorie consumption 3202 calories

Finland, Gulf of *85 D6 Est.* Soome Laht, *Fin.* Suomenlahti, *Ger.* Finnischer Meerbusen, *Rus.* Finskiy Zaliv, *Swe.* Finska Viken. *Gulf* E Baltic Sea
Finnmarksvidda *84 D2 physical region* N Norway
Finsterwalde *94 D4* Brandenburg, E Germany
Fiordland *151 A7 physical region* South Island, NZ
Fiorina *96 E1* NE San Marino
Firenze *96 C3 Eng.* Florence; *anc.* Florentia. Toscana, C Italy
Fischbacher Alpen *95 E7 mountain range* E Austria
Fish *78 B4 var.* Vis. *River* S Namibia
Fishguard *89 C6 Wel.* Abergwaun. SW Wales, UK
Fisterra, Cabo *92 B1 headland* NW Spain
Fitzroy Crossing *146 C3* Western Australia
Fitzroy River *146 C3 river* Western Australia
Flagstaff *48 B2* Arizona, SW USA
Flanders *87 A6 Dut.* Vlaanderen, *Fr.* Flandre. *Cultural region* Belgium/France
Flathead Lake *44 B1 lake* Montana, NW USA
Flat Island *128 C8 island* NE Spratly Islands
Flatts Village *42 B5 var.* The Flatts Village. C Bermuda
Flensburg *94 B2* Schleswig-Holstein, N Germany
Flinders Island *149 C8 island* Furneaux Group, Tasmania, SE Australia
Flinders Ranges *149 B6 mountain range* South Australia
Flinders River *148 C3 river* Queensland, NE Australia
Flin Flon *37 F5* Manitoba, C Canada
Flint *40 C3* Michigan, N USA
Flint Island *145 G4 island* Line Islands, E Kiribati
Floreana, Isla *see* Santa María, Isla
Florence *see* Firenze
Florence *42 C1* Alabama, S USA
Florence *43 F2* South Carolina, SE USA
Florencia *58 B4* Caquetá, S Colombia
Florentia *see* Firenze
Flores *92 A5 island* Azores, Portugal, NE Atlantic Ocean
Flores *139 E5 island* Nusa Tenggara, C Indonesia
Flores *52 B1* Petén, N Guatemala
Flores Sea *138 D5 Ind.* Laut Flores. *Sea* C Indonesia
Floriano *63 F2* Piauí, E Brazil
Florianópolis *63 F5 prev.* Destêrro. *State capital* Santa Catarina, S Brazil
Florida *43 E4 off.* State of Florida; also known as Peninsular State, Sunshine State. *State* SE USA
Florida *64 D4* Florida, S Uruguay
Florida Bay *43 E5 bay* Florida, SE USA
Florida Keys *43 E5 island group* Florida, SE USA
Florida, Straits of *54 B1 strait* Atlantic Ocean/Gulf of Mexico

Flórina *104 B4 var.* Phlórina. Dytikí Makedonía, N Greece
Florissant *45 G4* Missouri, C USA
Floúda, Akrotírio *105 D7 headland* Astypálaia, Kykládes, Greece, Aegean Sea
Foča *100 C4 var.* Srbinje, Republika Srpska, SE Bosnia and Herzegovina
Focşani *108 C4* Vrancea, E Romania
Foggia *97 D5* Puglia, SE Italy
Fogo *74 A3 island* Ilhas de Sotavento, SW Cape Verde
Foix *91 B6* Ariège, S France
Folégandros *105 C7 island* Kykládes, Greece, Aegean Sea
Foleyet *38 C4* Ontario, S Canada
Foligno *96 C4* Umbria, C Italy
Folkestone *89 E7* SE England, UK
Fond du Lac *40 B2* Wisconsin, N USA
Fongafale *145 E3 var.* Funafuti. *Country capital* (Tuvalu) Funafuti Atoll, SE Tuvalu
Fonseca, Gulf of *52 C3 Sp.* Golfo de Fonseca. *Gulf* Central America
Fontainebleau *90 C3* Seine-et-Marne, N France
Fontenay-le-Comte *90 B4* Vendée, NW France
Fontvieille *91 B8* SW Monaco
Fonyód *99 C7* Somogy, W Hungary
Foochow *see* Fuzhou
Forchheim *95 C5* Bayern, SE Germany
Forel, Mont *82 D4 mountain* SE Greenland
Forfar *88 C3* E Scotland, UK
Forge du Sud *see* Dudelange
Forlì *96 C3 anc.* Forum Livii. Emilia-Romagna, N Italy
Formentera *93 G4 anc.* Ophiusa, *Lat.* Frumentum. *Island* Islas Baleares, Spain, W Mediterranean Sea
Formosa *64 D2* Formosa, NE Argentina
Formosa, Serra *63 E3 mountain range* C Brazil
Formosa Strait *see* Taiwan Strait
Forrest City *42 B1* Arkansas, C USA
Fort Albany *38 C3* Ontario, C Canada
Fortaleza *63 G2 prev.* Ceará. *State capital* Ceará, NE Brazil
Fortaleza *61 F2* Pando, N Bolivia
Fort-Bayard *see* Zhanjiang
Fort-Cappolani *see* Tidjikja
Fort Collins *44 D4* Colorado, C USA
Fort Davis *49 E3* Texas, SW USA
Fort-de-France *55 H4 prev.* Fort-Royal. *Dependent territory capital* (Martinique) W Martinique
Fort Dodge *45 F3* Iowa, C USA
Fortescue River *146 A4 river* Western Australia
Fort Frances *38 B4* Ontario, S Canada
Fort Good Hope *37 E3 var.* Good Hope. Northwest Territories, NW Canada
Fort Gouraud *see* Fdérik
Forth *88 C4 river* C Scotland, UK
Forth, Firth of *88 C4 estuary* E Scotland, UK
Fort-Lamy *see* Ndjamena
Fort Lauderdale *43 F5* Florida, SE USA
Fort Liard *37 E4 var.* Liard. Northwest Territories, W Canada
Fort Madison *45 G4* Iowa, C USA
Fort McMurray *37 E4* Alberta, C Canada
Fort McPherson *36 D3 var.* McPherson. Northwest Territories, NW Canada
Fort Morgan *44 D4* Colorado, C USA
Fort Myers *43 E5* Florida, SE USA
Fort Nelson *37 E4* British Columbia, W Canada
Fort Peck Lake *44 C1 reservoir* Montana, NW USA
Fort Pierce *43 F4* Florida, SE USA
Fort Providence *37 E4 var.* Providence. Northwest Territories, W Canada
Fort St.John *37 E4* British Columbia, W Canada
Fort Scott *45 F5* Kansas, C USA
Fort Severn *38 C2* Ontario, C Canada
Fort-Shevchenko *114 A4* Mangistau, W Kazakhstan
Fort Simpson *37 E4 var.* Simpson. Northwest Territories, W Canada
Fort Smith *37 E4 district capital* Northwest Territories, W Canada
Fort Smith *42 B1* Arkansas, C USA
Fort Stockton *49 E3* Texas, SW USA
Fort-Trinquet *see* Bîr Mogreïn
Fort Vermilion *37 E4* Alberta, W Canada
Fort Walton Beach *42 C3* Florida, SE USA
Fort Wayne *40 C4* Indiana, N USA
Fort William *88 C3* N Scotland, UK
Fort Worth *49 G2* Texas, SW USA
Fort Yukon *36 D3* Alaska, USA
Fougamou *77 A6* Ngounié, C Gabon
Fougères *90 B3* Ille-et-Vilaine, NW France
Fou-hsin *see* Fuxin
Foulwind, Cape *151 B5 headland* South Island, NZ
Foumban *76 A4* Ouest, NW Cameroon
Fou-shan *see* Fushun
Foveaux Strait *151 A8 strait* S NZ
Foxe Basin *37 G3 sea* Nunavut, N Canada
Fox Glacier *151 B6* West Coast, South Island, NZ
Fox Mine *37 F4* Manitoba, C Canada
Fraga *93 F2* Aragón, NE Spain
Fram Basin *155 C3 var.* Amundsen Basin. *Undersea feature* Arctic Ocean
France *90 B4 It./Sp.* Francia; *prev.* Gaul, Gaule, *Lat.* Gallia. *Country* W Europe

France 90

Official name French Republic
Formation 987
Capital Paris
Population 60.1 million / 283 people per sq mile (109 people per sq km)
Total area 211,208 sq. miles (547,030 sq. km)
Languages French, Provençal, German, Breton, Catalan, Basque
Religions Roman Catholic 88%, Muslim 8%, Protestant 2%, Jewish 1%, Buddhist 1%
Ethnic mix French 90%, North African 6%, German (Alsace) 2%, Breton 1%, Other 1%
Government Mixed presidential–parliamentary system
Currency Euro = 100 cents
Literacy rate 99%
Calorie consumption 3629 calories

Franceville *77 B6 var.* Massoukou, Masuku. Haut-Ogooué, E Gabon
Francfort prev *see* Frankfurt am Main
Franche-Comté *90 D4 cultural region* E France
Francis Case, Lake *45 E3 reservoir* South Dakota, N USA
Francisco Escárcega *51 G4* Campeche, SE Mexico
Francistown *78 D3* North East, NE Botswana
Franconian Jura *see* Fränkische Alb
Frankenalb *see* Fränkische Alb
Frankenstein *see* Ząbkowice Śląskie
Frankenstein in Schlesien *see* Ząbkowice Śląskie
Frankfort *40 C5 state capital* Kentucky, S USA
Frankfort on the Main *see* Frankfurt am Main
Frankfurt *see* Frankfurt am Main
Frankfurt am Main *95 B5 var.* Frankfurt, *Fr.* Francfort; prev. *Eng.* Frankfort on the Main. Hessen, SW Germany
Frankfurt an der Oder *94 D3* Brandenburg, E Germany
Fränkische Alb *95 C6 var.* Frankenalb, *Eng.* Franconian Jura. *Mountain range* S Germany
Franklin *42 C1* Tennessee, S USA
Franklin D.Roosevelt Lake *46 C1 reservoir* Washington, NW USA
Frantsa-Iosifa, Zemlya *114 D1 Eng.* Franz Josef Land. *Island group* N Russian Federation
Franz Josef Land *see* Frantsa-Iosifa, Zemlya
Fraserburgh *88 D3* NE Scotland, UK
Fraser Island *148 E4 var.* Great Sandy Island. *Island* Queensland, E Australia
Fredericksburg *41 E5* Virginia, NE USA
Fredericton *39 F4* New Brunswick, SE Canada
Frederikshåb *see* Paamiut
Fredrikstad *85 B6* Østfold, S Norway
Freeport *54 C1* Grand Bahama Island, N Bahamas
Freeport *49 H4* Texas, SW USA
Freetown *74 C4 country capital* (Sierra Leone) W Sierra Leone
Freiburg *see* Freiburg im Breisgau
Freiburg im Breisgau *95 A6 var.* Freiburg, *Fr.* Fribourg-en-Brisgau. Baden-Württemberg, SW Germany
Fremantle *147 A6* Western Australia
Fremont *45 F4* Nebraska, C USA
French Guiana *59 H3 var.* Guiana, Guyane. *French overseas department* N South America
French Polynesia *143 F4 French overseas territory* C Polynesia
French Southern and Antarctic Territories *141 B7 Fr.* Terres Australes et Antarctiques Françaises. *French overseas territory* S Indian Ocean
Fresnillo *50 D3 var.* Fresnillo de González Echeverría. Zacatecas, C Mexico
Fresnillo de González Echeverría *see* Fresnillo
Fresno *47 C6* California, W USA
Frías *64 C3* Catamarca, N Argentina
Fribourg-en-Brisgau *see* Freiburg im Breisgau
Friedrichshafen *95 B7* Baden-Württemberg, S Germany
Frobisher Bay *82 B3 inlet* Baffin Island, Northwest Territories, NE Canada
Frohavet *84 B4 sound* C Norway
Frome, Lake *149 B6 salt lake* South Australia
Frontera *51 G4* Tabasco, SE Mexico
Frontignan *91 C6* Hérault, S France
Frostviken *see* Kvarnbergsvattnet
Frøya *84 A4 island* W Norway
Frunze *see* Bishkek
Frýdek-Místek *99 C5 Ger.* Friedek-Mistek. Ostravský Kraj, E Czech Republic
Fu-chien *see* Fujian
Fu-chou *see* Fuzhou
Fuengirola *92 D5* Andalucía, S Spain
Fuerte Olimpo *64 D2 var.* Olimpo. Alto Paraguay, NE Paraguay
Fuerte, Río *48 C5 river* C Mexico
Fuerteventura *70 B3 island* Islas Canarias, Spain, NE Atlantic Ocean
Fuhkien *see* Fujian
Fu-hsin *see* Fuxin
Fuji *131 D6 var.* Huzi. Shizuoka, Honshū, S Japan
Fujian *128 D6 var.* Fu-chien, Fuhkien, Fujian Sheng, Fukien, Min. Admin. region *province* SE China
Fujian Sheng *see* Fujian
Fuji-san *131 C6 var.* Fujiyama, *Eng.* Mount Fuji. *Mountain* Honshū, SE Japan
Fujiyama *see* Fuji-san
Fukang *126 C2* Xinjiang Uygur Zizhiqu, W China
Fukien *see* Fujian
Fukui *131 C6 var.* Hukui. Fukui, Honshū, SW Japan
Fukuoka *131 A7 var.* Hukuoka; *hist.* Najima. Fukuoka, Kyūshū, SW Japan
Fukushima *130 D4 var.* Hukusima. Fukushima, Honshū, C Japan
Fulda *95 B5* Hessen, C Germany
Funafuti *see* Fongafale
Funafuti Atoll *145 E3 atoll* C Tuvalu
Funchal *70 A2* Madeira, Portugal, NE Atlantic Ocean
Fundy, Bay of *39 F5 bay* Canada/USA
Furnes *see* Veurne
Fürth *95 C5* Bayern, S Germany
Furukawa *130 D4 var.* Hurukawa. Miyagi, Honshū, C Japan
Fushun *128 D3 var.* Fou-shan, Fu-shun. Liaoning, NE China
Fu-shun *see* Fushun
Fusin *see* Fuxin
Füssen *95 C7* Bayern, S Germany
Futog *100 D3* Serbia, NW Serbia and Montenegro (Yugo.)
Futuna, Île *145 E4 island* S Wallis and Futuna
Fuxin *128 D3 var.* Fou-hsin, Fu-hsin, Fusin. Liaoning, NE China
Fuzhou *128 D6 var.* Foochow, Fu-chou. Fujian, SE China
Fuzhou *128 D5 prev.* Linchuan. Jiangxi, S China
Fyn *85 B8 Ger.* Fünen. *Island* C Denmark
Fyzabad *see* Feyẕābād

Gaafu Alifu Atoll *see* North Huvadhu Atoll
Gaafu Dhaalu Atoll *see* South Huvadhu Atoll
Gaalkacyo *73 E5 var.* Galka'yo, *It.* Galcaio. Mudug, C Somalia
Gabela *78 B2* Cuanza Sul, W Angola
Gabès *71 E2 var.* Qābis. E Tunisia
Gabès, Golfe de *71 F2 Ar.* Khalīj Qābis. *Gulf* E Tunisia
Gabon *77 B6 Country* C Africa

Gabon 77

Official name Gabonese Republic
Formation 1960
Capital Libreville
Population 1.3 million / 13 people per sq mile (5 people per sq km)
Total area 103,346 sq. miles (267,667 sq. km)
Languages Fang, French, Punu, Sira, Nzebi, Mpongwe
Religions Christian (mainly Roman Catholic) 55%, Traditional beliefs 40%, other 4%, Muslim 1%
Ethnic mix Fang 35%, Other Bantu 29%, Eshira 25%, European and other African 9%, French 2%
Government Presidential system
Currency CFA franc = 100 centimes
Literacy rate 71%
Calorie consumption 2602 calories

Gaborone *78 C4 prev.* Gaberones. *Country capital* (Botswana) South East, SE Botswana
Gabrovo *104 D2* Gabrovo, N Bulgaria
Gadag *132 C1* Karnātaka, W India
Gadsden *42 D2* Alabama, S USA
Gaeta *97 C5* Lazio, C Italy
Gaeta, Golfo di *97 C5 var.* Gulf of Gaeta. *Gulf* C Italy
Gaeta, Gulf of *see* Gaeta, Golfo di
Gäfle *see* Gävle
Gafsa *71 E2 var.* Qafşah. W Tunisia
Gagnoa *74 D5* C Côte d'Ivoire
Gagra *117 E1* NW Georgia
Gaillac *91 C6 var.* Gaillac-sur-Tarn. Tarn, S France
Gaillac-sur-Tarn *see* Gaillac
Gaillimh *see* Galway
Gainesville *43 E3* Florida, SE USA
Gainesville *42 D2* Georgia, SE USA

Gainesville *49 G2* Texas, SW USA
Gairdner, Lake *149 A6 salt lake* South Australia
Gaiziņkalns *106 C3 var.* Gaizina Kalns. *Mountain* E Latvia
Gaizina Kalns *see* Gaiziņkalns
Galán, Cerro *64 B3 mountain* NW Argentina
Galanta *99 C6 Hung.* Galánta. Trnavský Kraj, W Slovakia
Galapagos Fracture Zone *153 E3 tectonic feature* E Pacific Ocean
Galapagos Islands *153 F3 var.* Islas de los Galápagos, *Tortoise Islands. Island group* Ecuador, E Pacific Ocean
Galapagos Rise *153 F3 undersea feature* E Pacific Ocean
Galashiels *88 C4* SE Scotland, UK
Galați *108 D4 Ger.* Galatz. Galați, E Romania
Galcaio *see* Gaalkacyo
Galesburg *40 B3* Illinois, N USA
Galicia *92 B1 cultural region* NW Spain
Galicia Bank *80 B4 undersea feature* E Atlantic Ocean
Galilee, Sea of *see* Tiberias, Lake
Galka'yo *see* Gaalkacyo
Galle *132 D4 prev.* Point de Galle. Southern Province, SW Sri Lanka
Gallego Rise *153 F3 undersea feature* E Pacific Ocean
Gallegos *see* Río Gallegos
Gallipoli *97 E6* Puglia, SE Italy
Gällivare *84 C3* Norrbotten, N Sweden
Gallup *48 C1* New Mexico, SW USA
Galtat-Zemmour *70 B3* C Western Sahara
Galveston *49 H4* Texas, SW USA
Galway *89 A5 Ir.* Gaillimh. W Ireland
Galway Bay *89 A6 Ir.* Cuan na Gaillimhe. *Bay* W Ireland
Gambell *36 C2* Saint Lawrence Island, Alaska, USA
Gambia *74 C3 Fr.* Gambie. *River* W Africa

Gambia 74

Official name Republic of the Gambia
Formation 1965
Capital Banjul
Population 1.4 million / 363 people per sq mile (140 people per sq km)
Total area 4363 sq. miles (11,300 sq. km)
Languages Mandinka, Fulani, Wolof, Jola, Soninke, English
Religions Sunni Muslim 90%, Christian 9%, Traditional beliefs 1%
Ethnic mix Mandinka 42%, Fulani 18%, Wolof 16%, Jola 10%, Serahuli 9%, other 5%
Government Presidential system
Currency Dalasi = 100 butut
Literacy rate 38%
Calorie consumption 2300 calories

Gambia *74 B3 Country* W Africa
Gambier, Îles *143 G4 island group* E French Polynesia
Gamboma *77 B6* Plateaux, E Congo
Gan *see* Gansu
Gan *see* Jiangxi
Gan *132 B5* Addu Atoll, C Maldives
Gäncä *117 G2 Rus.* Gyandzha; *prev.* Kirovabad, Yelisavetpol. W Azerbaijan
Gandajika *77 D7* Kasai Oriental, S Dem. Rep. Congo
Gander *39 G3* Newfoundland, Newfoundland and Labrador, SE Canada
Gāndhīdhām *134 C4* Gujarāt, W India
Gandía *93 F3* País Valenciano, E Spain
Ganges *135 F3 Ben.* Padma. *River* Bangladesh/India *see also* Padma
Ganges Cone *see* Ganges Fan
Ganges Fan *140 D3 var.* Ganges Cone. *Undersea feature* N Bay of Bengal
Ganges, Mouths of the *135 G4 delta* Bangladesh/India
Gangra *see* Çankiri
Gangtok *135 F3* Sikkim, N India
Gansu *128 B4 var.* Gan, Gansu Sheng, Kansu. Admin. region *province* N China
Gansu Sheng *see* Gansu
Ganzhou *128 D6* Jiangxi, S China
Gao *75 E3* Gao, E Mali
Gaoual *74 C4* Moyenne-Guinée, N Guinea
Gaoxiong *see* Kaohsiung
Gap *91 D5 anc.* Vapincum. Hautes-Alpes, SE France
Gaplaňgyr Platosy *122 C2 Rus.* Kaplangky, Plato. *Ridge* Turkmenistan/Uzbekistan
Gar *126 A4 var.* Gar Xincun. Xizang Zizhiqu, W China
Garabil Belentligi *122 D3 Rus.* Karabil', Vozvyshennost'. *Mountain range* S Turkmenistan
Garabogaz Aylagy *122 B2 Rus.* Zaliv Kara-Bogaz-Gol. *Bay* Balkanskiy Velayat, W Turkmenistan
Garachiné *53 G5* Darién, SE Panama
Garagum *122 C3 var.* Garagumy, Qara Qum, *Eng.* Black Sand Desert, Kara Kum; *prev.* Peski Karakumy. *Desert* C Turkmenistan
Garagum Kanaly *122 D3 var.* Kara Kum Canal, Karakumskiy Kanal, *Turkm.* Garagumskiy Kanaly. *Canal* C Turkmenistan
Garagumskiy Kanal *see* Garagum Kanaly
Garagumy *see* Garagum
Gara Khitrino *104 D2* Shumen, NE Bulgaria
Garda, Lago di *C2 var.* Benaco, *Eng.* Lake Garda, *Ger.* Gardasee. *Lake* NE Italy
Garda, Lake *see* Garda, Lago di
Gardasee *see* Garda, Lago di
Garden City *45 E5* Kansas, C USA
Gardeyz *see* Gardēz
Gardēz *123 E4 var.* Gardeyz, Gordiaz. Paktīā, E Afghanistan
Gargždai *106 B3* Gargždai, W Lithuania
Garissa *73 D6* Coast, E Kenya
Garland *49 G2* Texas, SW USA
Garman, Loch *see* Wexford
Garoe *see* Garoowe
Garonne *91 B5 anc.* Garumna. *River* S France
Garoowe *73 E5 var.* Garoe. Nugaal, N Somalia
Garoua *76 B4 var.* Garua. Nord, N Cameroon
Garrygala *122 C3 Rus.* Kara-Kala. Balkanskiy Velayat, W Turkmenistan
Garry Lake *37 F3 lake* Nunavut, N Canada
Garsen *73 D6* Coast, S Kenya
Garua *see* Garoua
Garwolin *98 D4* Mazowieckie, C Poland
Gar Xincun *see* Gar
Gary *40 B3* Indiana, N USA
Garzón *58 B4* Huila, S Colombia
Gasan-Kuli *see* Esenguly
Gascogne *91 B6 Eng.* Gascony. *Cultural region* S France
Gascoyne River *147 A5 river* Western Australia
Gaspé *39 F3* Québec, SE Canada
Gaspé, Péninsule de *39 E4 var.* Péninsule de la Gaspésie. *Peninsula* Québec, SE Canada
Gastonia *43 E1* North Carolina, SE USA
Gastoúni *105 B6* Dytikí Ellás, S Greece
Gatchina *110 B4* Leningradskaya Oblast', NW Russian Federation
Gatineau *38 D4* Québec, SE Canada
Gatún, Lago *53 F4 reservoir* C Panama
Gauja *106 D3 Ger.* Aa. *River* Estonia/Latvia
Gauteng *see* Johannesburg
Gāvbandī *120 D4* Hormozgān, S Iran
Gávdos *105 C8 island* SE Greece
Gavere *87 B6* Oost-Vlaanderen, NW Belgium
Gävle *85 C6 var.* Gäfle; *prev.* Gefle. Gävleborg, C Sweden
Gawler *149 B6* South Australia
Gaya *135 F3* Bihār, N India
Gayndah *149 E5* Queensland, E Australia
Gaza *119 A6 Ar.* Ghazzah, *Heb.* 'Azza. NE Gaza Strip
Gaz-Achak *see* Gazojak
Gaza Strip *119 A7 Ar.* Qiṭā' Ghazzah. *Disputed region* SW Asia
Gazi Antep *see* Gaziantep
Gaziantep *116 D4 var.* Gazi Antep; *prev.* Aintab, Antep. Gaziantep, S Turkey
Gazimağusa *see* Ammóchostos
Gazimağusa Körfezi *see* Kólpos Ammóchostos
Gazli *122 D2* Bukhoro Wiloyati, C Uzbekistan
Gazojak *122 D2 var.* Gaz-Achak. Lebapskiy Velayat, NE Turkmenistan
Gbanga *74 D5 var.* Gbarnga. N Liberia
Gbarnga *see* Gbanga
Gdansk *98 C2 Fr.* Dantzig, *Ger.* Danzig. Pomorskie, N Poland
Gdan'skaya Bukhta *see* Danzig, Gulf of
Pomorskie, Gulf of *see* Danzig, Gulf of
Gdynia *98 C2 Ger.* Gdingen. Pomorskie, N Poland
Gedaref *72 C4 var.* Al Qaḍārif, El Gedaref. Gedaref, E Sudan
Gediz *116 B3* Kütahya, W Turkey
Gediz Nehri *116 A3 river* W Turkey
Geel *87 C5 var.* Gheel. Antwerpen, N Belgium
Geelong *149 C7* Victoria, SE Australia
Ge'e'mu *see* Golmud
Gefle *see* Gävle
Geilo *85 A5* Buskerud, S Norway
Gejiu *128 B6 var.* Kochiu. Yunnan, S China
Gëkdepe *see* Gökdepe
Gela *97 C7 prev.* Terranova di Sicilia. Sicilia, Italy, C Mediterranean Sea
Geldermalsen *86 C4* Gelderland, C Netherlands
Geleen *87 D6* Limburg, SE Netherlands
Gelinsoor *see* Gellinsoor
Gellinsoor *73 E5 var.* Gelinsoor. Mudug, NE Somalia
Gembloux *87 C6* Namur, Belgium
Gemena *77 C5* Equateur, NW Dem. Rep. Congo
Gemona del Friuli *96 D2* Friuli-Venezia Giulia, NE Italy
Genck *see* Genk
General Alvear *64 B4* Mendoza, W Argentina
General Eugenio A.Garay *64 C1* Guairá, S Paraguay
General Machado *see* Camacupa
General Santos *139 F3 off.* General Santos City. Mindanao, S Philippines
Geneva *see* Genève
Geneva, Lake *A7 Fr.* Lac de Genève, Lac Léman, le Léman, *Ger.* Genfer See. *Lake* France/Switzerland
Genève *95 A7 Eng.* Geneva, *Ger.* Genf, *It.* Ginevra. Genève, SW Switzerland
Genf *see* Genève
Genk *87 D6 var.* Genck. Limburg, NE Belgium
Gennep *86 D4* Limburg, SE Netherlands
Genoa *see* Genova
Genova *102 D1 Eng.* Genoa, *Fr.* Gênes; *anc.* Genua. Liguria, NW Italy
Genova, Golfo di *96 A3 Eng.* Gulf of Genoa. *Gulf* NW Italy
Genovesa, Isla *60 B5 var.* Tower Island. *Island* Galapagos Islands, Ecuador, E Pacific Ocean
Gent *87 B5 Eng.* Ghent, *Fr.* Gand. Oost-Vlaanderen, NW Belgium
Geok-Tepe *see* Gökdepe
George *82 A4 river* Newfoundland and Labrador/Quebec, E Canada
George *78 C5* Western Cape, S South Africa
George, Lake *43 E3 lake* Florida, SE USA
Georges Bank *35 D5 undersea feature* W Atlantic Ocean
George Sound *151 A7 sound* South Island, NZ
Georges River *148 D2 river* New South Wales, SE Australia
George Town *54 B3 var.* Georgetown. *Dependent territory capital* (Cayman Islands) Grand Cayman, SW Cayman Islands
George Town *138 B3 var.* Penang, Pinang. Pinang, Peninsular Malaysia
George Town *54 C2* Great Exuma Island, C Bahamas
Georgetown *59 F2 country capital* (Guyana) N Guyana
Georgetown *43 F2* South Carolina, SE USA
George V Land *154 C4 physical region* Antarctica
Georgia *117 F2 Geor.* Sak'art'velo, *Rus.* Gruzinskaya SSR, Gruziya; *prev.* Georgian SSR. *Country* SW Asia

Georgia 117

Official name Georgia
Formation 1991
Capital Tbilisi
Population 5.1 million / 190 people per sq mile (73 people per sq km)
Total area 26,911 sq. miles (69,700 sq. km)
Languages Georgian, Russian, Azeri, Armenian, Mingrelian, Ossetian, Abkhazian
Religions Georgian Orthodox 65%, Muslim 11%, Russian Orthodox 10%, Armenian Apostolic Church (Orthodox) 8%, other 6%
Ethnic mix Georgian 70%, Armenian 8%, other 7%, Russian 6%, Azeri 6%, Ossetian 3%
Government Presidential system
Currency Lari = 100 tetri
Literacy rate 99%
Calorie consumption 2247 calories

Georgia *42 D2 off.* State of Georgia; also known as Empire State of the South, Peach State. *State* SE USA
Georgian Bay *40 D2 lake bay* Ontario, S Canada
Georgia, Strait of *46 A1 strait* British Columbia, W Canada
Georg von Neumayer *154 A2 German research station* Antarctica
Gera *94 C4* Thüringen, E Germany
Geráki *105 B6* Pelopónnisos, S Greece
Geraldine *151 B6* Canterbury, South Island, NZ
Geraldton *147 A6* Western Australia
Geral, Serra *57 D5 mountain range* S Brazil
Gerede *116 C2* Bolu, N Turkey
Gereshk *122 D5* Helmand, SW Afghanistan
Gering *44 D3* Nebraska, C USA
Germanicopolis *see* Çankiri
Germany *94 B4 Ger.* Bundesrepublik Deutschland, Deutschland. *Country* N Europe

Germany 94

Official name Federal Republic of Germany
Formation 1871
Capital Berlin
Population 82.5 million / 611 people per sq mile (236 people per sq km)

Germany (continued)

Total area 137,846 sq. miles (357,021 sq. km)
Languages German, Turkish
Religions Protestant 34%, Roman Catholic 33%, other 30%, Muslim 3%
Ethnic mix German 92%, other 3%, Other European 3%, Turkish 2%
Government Parliamentary system
Currency Euro = 100 cents
Literacy rate 99%
Calorie consumption 3567 calories

Geroliménas *105 B7* Pelopónnisos, S Greece
Gerona *see* Girona
Gerpinnes *87 C7* Hainaut, S Belgium
Gerunda *see* Girona
Gerze *116 D2* Sinop, N Turkey
Gesoriacum *see* Boulogne-sur-Mer
Gessoriacum *see* Boulogne-sur-Mer
Getafe *92 D3* Madrid, C Spain
Gevaş *117 F3* Van, SE Turkey
Gevgeli *see* Gevgelija
Gevgelija *101 E6 var.* Đevđelija, Djevdjelija, *Turk.* Gevgeli. SE FYR Macedonia
Ghaba *see* Al Ghābah
Ghana *75 E5 Country* W Africa

Ghana 75

Official name Republic of Ghana
Formation 1957
Capital Accra
Population 20.9 million / 235 people per sq mile (91 people per sq km)
Total area 92,100 sq. miles (238,540 sq. km)
Languages Twi, Ewe, Ga, Adangbe, Fanti, Gurma, Dagomba (Dagbani)
Religions Christian 69%, Muslim 16%, Traditional beliefs 9%, other 6%
Ethnic mix Ashanti and Fanti 52%, Moshi-Dagomba 16%, Ewe 12%, Ga and Ga-adanbe 8%, Yoruba 1%, other 11%
Government Presidential system
Currency Cedi = 100 psewas
Literacy rate 74%
Calorie consumption 2670 calories

Ghanzi *78 C3 var.* Khanzi. Ghanzi, W Botswana
Gharandal *119 B7* Ma'ān, SW Jordan
Ghardaïa *70 D2* N Algeria
Gharvān *see* Gharyān
Gharyān *71 F2 var.* Gharvān. NW Libya
Ghaznī *123 E4 var.* Ghazni. Ghaznī, E Afghanistan
Ghazni *see* Ghaznī
Gheel *see* Geel
Gheorgheni *108 C4 prev.* Gheorghieni, Sînt-Miclăuş, *Ger.* Niklasmarkt, *Hung.* Gyergyószentmiklós. Harghita, C Romania
Ghijduwon *see* G'ijduvon
Ghŭdara *123 F3 var.* Gudara, *Rus.* Kudara. SE Tajikistan
Ghurdaqah *see* Hurghada
Ghūrīān *122 D4* Herāt, W Afghanistan
Giannitsá *104 B4 var.* Yiannitsá. Kentrikí Makedonía, N Greece
Gibraltar *93 G4 UK dependent territory* SW Europe
Gibraltar, Bay of *93 G5 bay* Gibraltar/Spain
Gibraltar, Strait of *92 C5 Fr.* Détroit de Gibraltar, *Sp.* Estrecho de Gibraltar. *Strait* Atlantic Ocean Mediterranean Sea
Gibson Desert *147 B5 desert* Western Australia
Giedraičiai *107 C5* Molėtai, E Lithuania
Giessen *95 B5* Hessen, W Germany
Gifu *131 C6 var.* Gihu. Gifu, Honshū, SW Japan
Giganta, Sierra de la *50 B3 mountain range* W Mexico
Gihu *see* Gifu
G'ijduvon *122 D2 var.* Ghijduwon, *Rus.* Gizhduvan. Bukhoro Wiloyati, C Uzbekistan
Gijón *92 D1 var.* Xixón. Asturias, NW Spain
Gilani *see* Gnjilane
Gila River *48 A2 river* Arizona, SW USA
Gilbert River *148 C3 river* Queensland, NE Australia
Gilf Kebir Plateau *72 A2 Ar.* Haḍabat al Jilf al Kabīr. *Plateau* SW Egypt
Gillette *44 D3* Wyoming, C USA
Gilroy *47 B6* California, W USA
Gimie, Mount *55 F1 mountain* C Saint Lucia
Gimma *see* Jīma
Ginevra *see* Genève
Gingin *147 A6* Western Australia
Giohar *see* Jawhar
Girardot *58 B3* Cundinamarca, C Colombia
Giresun *117 E2 var.* Kerasunt; *anc.* Cerasus, Pharnacia. Giresun, NE Turkey
Girin *see* Jilin
Girne *see* Kerýneia
Girona *93 G2 var.* Gerona; *anc.* Gerunda. Cataluña, NE Spain
Gisborne *150 E3* Gisborne, North Island, NZ
Gissar Range *123 E3 Rus.* Gissarskiy Khrebet. *Mountain range* Tajikistan/Uzbekistan
Githio *see* Gýtheio
Giulianova *96 D4* Abruzzo, C Italy
Giumri *see* Gyumri
Giurgiu *108 C5* Giurgiu, S Romania
Gîza *see* El Gîza
Gizeh *see* El Gîza
Gizhduvan *see* G'ijduvon
Giżyeko *98 D2* Warmiúsko-Mazurskie, NE Poland
Gjakovë *see* Đakovica
Gjilan *see* Gnjilane
Gjinokastër *see* Gjirokastër
Gjirokastër *101 C7 var.* Gjirokastra; *prev.* Gjinokastër, *Gk.* Argyrokastron, *It.* Argirocastro. Gjirokastër, S Albania
Gjirokastra *see* Gjirokastër
Gjoa Haven *37 F3* King William Island, Nunavut, NW Canada
Gjøvik *85 B5* Oppland, S Norway
Glace Bay *39 G4* Cape Breton Island, Nova Scotia, SE Canada
Gladstone *148 E4* Queensland, E Australia
Glåma *85 B5 river* SE Norway
Glasgow *88 C4* S Scotland, UK
Glavn'a Morava *see* Velika Morava
Glazov *111 D5* Udmurtskaya Respublika, NW Russian Federation
Glendale *48 B2* Arizona, SW USA
Glendive *44 D2* Montana, NW USA
Glens Falls *41 F3* New York, NE USA
Glina *100 B3* Sisak-Moslavina, NE Croatia
Glittertind *85 A5 mountain* S Norway
Gliwice *99 C5 Ger.* Gleiwitz. Śląskie, S Poland
Globe *48 B2* Arizona, SW USA
Głogów *98 B4 Ger.* Glogau, Glogow. Dolnośląskie
Gloucester *89 D6 hist.* Caer Glou, *Lat.* Glevum. C England, UK
Głowno *98 D4* Łódź, C Poland
Gniezno *98 C3 Ger.* Gnesen. Wielkopolskie, C Poland
Gnjilane *101 D5 var.* Gilani, *Alb.* Gjilan. Serbia, S Serbia and Montenegro (Yugo.)
Goa *see* Panaji
Gobabis *78 B3* Omaheke, E Namibia
Gobi *126 D3 desert* China/Mongolia
Gobō *131 C6* Wakayama, Honshū, SW Japan
Godāvari *124 B3 var.* Godavari. *River* C India
Godhavn *see* Qeqertarsuaq
Godhra *134 C4* Gujarāt, W India
Godoy Cruz *64 B4* Mendoza, W Argentina
Godthaab *see* Nuuk
Godthåb *see* Nuuk
Goeree *86 B4 island* SW Netherlands
Goes *87 B5* Zeeland, SW Netherlands
Goettingen *see* Göttingen
Gogebic Range *40 B1 hill range* Michigan/Wisconsin, N USA
Goiânia *63 E3 prev.* Goyania. *State capital* Goiás, C Brazil
Goiás *63 E3* Goiás, C Brazil
Gojōme *130 D4* Akita, Honshū, NW Japan
Gökçeada *104 D4 var.* Imroz Adası, *Gk.* Imbros. *Island* NW Turkey
Gökdepe *122 C3 var.* Gëkdepe, Geok-Tepe. Akhalskiy Velayat, C Turkmenistan
Göksun *116 D4* Kahramanmaraş, C Turkey
Gol *85 A5* Buskerud, S Norway
Golan Heights *119 B5 Ar.* Al Jawlān, *Heb.* HaGolan. *Mountain range* SW Syria
Gołdap *98 E2 Ger.* Goldap. Warmińsko-Mazurskie, NE Poland
Gold Coast *149 E5 cultural region* Queensland, E Australia
Golden Bay *150 C4 bay* South Island, NZ
Goldsboro *43 F1* North Carolina, SE USA
Goleniów *98 B3 Ger.* Gollnow. Zachodniopomorskie, NW Poland
Golmo *see* Golmud
Golub-Dobrzyń *98 C3* Kujawski-pomorskie, C Poland
Golmud *126 D4 var.* Ge'e'mu, Golmo, *Chin.* Ko-erh-mu. Qinghai, C China
Goma *77 E6* Nord Kivu, NE Dem. Rep. Congo
Gombi *75 H4* Adamawa, E Nigeria
Gombroon *see* Bandar-e 'Abbās
Gomera *70 A3 island* Islas Canarias, Spain, NE Atlantic Ocean
Gómez Palacio *50 D3* Durango, C Mexico
Gonaïves *54 D3 var.* Les Gonaïves. N Haiti
Gonâve, Île de la *54 D3 island* C Haiti
Gondar *see* Gonder
Gonder *72 C4 var.* Gondar. N Ethiopia
Gondia *135 E4* Mahārāshtra, C India
Gonggar *126 C5* Xizang Zizhiqu, W China
Gongola *75 G4 river* E Nigeria
Gonni *see* Gónnoi
Gónnoi *104 B4 var.* Gonni, Gónnos; *prev.* Derelí. Thessalía, C Greece
Gónnos *see* Gónnoi
Good Hope *see* Fort Good Hope
Good Hope, Cape of *78 B5 Afr.* Kaap de Goede Hoop, Kaap die Goeie Hoop. *Headland* SW South Africa
Goodland *44 D4* Kansas, C USA
Goondiwindi *149 D5* Queensland, E Australia
Goor *86 E3* Overijssel, E Netherlands
Goose Green *65 D7 var.* Prado del Ganso. East Falkland, Falkland Islands
Goose Lake *46 B4 var.* Lago dos Gansos. *Lake* California/Oregon, W USA
Göppingen *95 B6* Baden-Württemberg, SW Germany
Gora Andryu *see* Andrew Tablemount
Gora El'brus *see* El'brus
Góra Kalwaria *114 D4* Mazowieckie, C Poland
Gorakhpur *135 E3* Uttar Pradesh, N India
Goražde *100 C4* Federacija Bosna I Hercegovina, SE Bosnia and Herzegovina
Gordiaz *see* Gardēz
Gore *151 B7* Southland, South Island, NZ
Gorē *73 C5* C Ethiopia
Goré *76 C4* Logone-Oriental, S Chad
Gorgān *120 D2 var.* Astarabad, Astrabad, Gurgan; *prev.* Asterābād, *anc.* Hyrcania. Golestān, N Iran
Gori *117 F2* C Georgia
Gorinchem *86 C4 var.* Gorkum. Zuid-Holland, C Netherlands
Goris *117 G3* SE Armenia
Gorkum *see* Gorinchem
Görlitz *94 D4* Sachsen, E Germany
Gornji Milanovac *100 C4* Serbia, C Serbia and Montenegro (Yugo.)
Gorontalo *139 E4* Sulawesi, C Indonesia
Gorontalo, Teluk *see* Tomini, Gulf of
Gorssel *86 D3* Gelderland, E Netherlands
Gory Putorana *see* Putorana, Plato
Gorzów Wielkopolski *98 B3 Ger.* Landsberg, Landsberg an der Warthe. Lubuskie, W Poland
Gosford *149 D6* New South Wales, SE Australia
Goshogawara *130 D3 var.* Gosyogawara. Aomori, Honshū, C Japan
Gospić *100 A3* Lika-Senj, C Croatia
Gostivar *101 D6* W FYR Macedonia
Gosyogawara *see* Goshogawara
Göteborg *85 B7 Eng.* Gothenburg. Västra Götaland, S Sweden
Gotel Mountains *75 G5 mountain range* E Nigeria
Gotha *94 C4* Thüringen, C Germany
Gothenburg *see* Göteborg
Gothenburg *80 D3* Nebraska, C USA
Gotland *85 C7 island* SE Sweden
Gotō-rettō *131 A7 island group* SW Japan
Gotska Sandön *106 B1 island* SE Sweden
Gōtsu *131 B6 var.* Gôtu. Shimane, Honshū, SW Japan
Göttingen *94 B4 var.* Goettingen. Niedersachsen, C Germany
Gôtu *see* Gōtsu
Gouda *86 C4* Zuid-Holland, C Netherlands
Gough Fracture Zone *67 C6 tectonic feature* S Atlantic Ocean
Gough Island *69 B8 island* Tristan da Cunha, S Atlantic Ocean
Gouin, Réservoir *38 D4 reservoir* Québec, SE Canada
Goulburn *149 D6* New South Wales, SE Australia
Goundam *75 E3* Tombouctou, NW Mali
Gouré *75 G3* Zinder, SE Niger
Governador Valadares *63 F4* Minas Gerais, SE Brazil
Govĭ Altayn Nuruu *127 E3 mountain range* S Mongolia
Goya *64 D3* Corrientes, NE Argentina
Goz Beïda *76 C3* Ouaddaï, SE Chad
Gozo *97 C8 Malt.* Ghawdex. *Island* N Malta
Graciosa *92 A5 var.* Ilha Graciosa. *Island* Azores, Portugal, NE Atlantic Ocean
Gradačac *100 C3* Federacija Bosna I Hercegovina, N Bosnia and Herzegovina
Gradaús, Serra dos *63 E3 mountain range* C Brazil
Gradiška *see* Bosanska Gradiška
Grafton *149 E5* New South Wales, SE Australia
Grafton *45 E1* North Dakota, N USA
Graham Land *154 A2 physical region* Antarctica
Grajewo *98 E3* Podlaskie, NE Poland

Grampian Mountains *88 C3 mountain range* C Scotland, UK
Granada *92 D5* Andalucía, S Spain
Granada *52 D3* Granada, SW Nicaragua
Gran Canaria *70 A3 var.* Grand Canary. *Island* Islas Canarias, Spain, NE Atlantic Ocean
Gran Chaco *64 D2 var.* Chaco. *Lowland plain* South America
Grand *see* Cockburn Town
Grand Bahama Island *54 B1 island* N Bahamas
Grand Banks of Newfoundland *34 E4 undersea feature* NW Atlantic Ocean
Grand Canary *see* Gran Canaria
Grand Canyon *48 A1 canyon* Arizona, SW USA
Grand Cayman *54 B3 island* SW Cayman Islands
Grande, Bahía *65 B7 bay* S Argentina
Grande Comore *79 F2 var.* Njazidja, Great Comoro. *Island* NW Comoros
Grande de Chiloé, Isla *see* Chiloé, Isla de
Grande Prairie *37 E4* Alberta, W Canada
Grand Erg Occidental *70 D3 desert* W Algeria
Grand Erg Oriental *71 E3 desert* Algeria/Tunisia
Grande, Rio *35 B6 var.* Río Bravo, *Sp.* Río Bravo del Norte, Bravo del Norte. *River* Mexico/USA
Grande, Rio *49 F4 river* Texas, SW USA
Grande, Rio *see* Bravo, Río
Grande, Río *51 E2 river* S Mexico
Grande Terre *55 G3 island* E West Indies
Grand Falls *39 G3* Newfoundland, Newfoundland and Labrador, SE Canada
Grand Forks *45 E1* North Dakota, N USA
Grand Island *45 E4* Nebraska, C USA
Grand Junction *44 C4* Colorado, C USA
Grand Rapids *40 C3* Michigan, N USA
Grand Rapids *45 F1* Minnesota, N USA
Grand-Santi *59 G3* W French Guiana
Gran Lago *see* Nicaragua, Lago de
Gran Malvina, Isla *see* West Falkland
Gran Paradiso *96 A2 Fr.* Grand Paradis. *Mountain* NW Italy
Gran Santiago *see* Santiago
Grants *48 C2* New Mexico, SW USA
Grants Pass *46 B4* Oregon, NW USA
Granville *90 B3* Manche, N France
Graulhet *91 C6* Tarn, S France
Grave *86 D4* Noord-Brabant, SE Netherlands
Grayling *36 C2* Alaska, USA
Graz *95 E7 prev.* Gratz. Steiermark, SE Austria
Great Abaco *54 C1 var.* Abaco Island. *Island* N Bahamas
Great Alfold *see* Great Hungarian Plain
Great Ararat *see* Büyükağrı Dağı
Great Australian Bight *147 D7 bight* S Australia
Great Barrier Island *150 D2 island* N NZ
Great Barrier Reef *148 D2 reef* Queensland, NE Australia
Great Basin *47 C5 basin* W USA
Great Bear Lake *37 E3 Fr.* Grand Lac de l'Ours. *Lake* Northwest Territories, NW Canada
Great Belt *see* Storebælt
Great Bend *45 E5* Kansas, C USA
Great Bermuda *see* Bermuda
Great Britain *see* Britain
Great Comoro *see* Grande Comore
Great Dividing Range *148 D4 mountain range* NE Australia
Greater Antarctica *154 C3 var.* East Antarctica. *Physical region* Antarctica
Greater Antilles *54 D3 island group* West Indies
Greater Caucasus *117 G2 Az.* Bas Qafqaz Silsiläsi, *Geor.* Kavkasioni, *Rus.* Bol'shoy Kavkaz. *Mountain range* Asia/Europe
Greater Sunda Islands *124 D5 var.* Sunda Islands. *Island group* Indonesia
Great Exhibition Bay *150 C1 inlet* North Island, NZ
Great Exuma Island *54 C2 island* C Bahamas
Great Falls *44 B1* Montana, NW USA
Great Hungarian Plain *99 C7 var.* Great Alfold, Plain of Hungary, *Hung.* Alföld. *Plain* SE Europe
Great Inagua *54 D2 var.* Inagua Islands. *Island* S Bahamas
Great Indian Desert *see* Thar Desert
Great Karoo *see* Great Karoo
Great Lakes *35 C5 lakes* Ontario, Canada/USA
Great Meteor Seamount *see* Great Meteor Tablemount
Great Meteor Tablemount *66 B3 var.* Great Meteor Seamount. *Undersea feature* E Atlantic Ocean
Great Nicobar *133 G3 island* Nicobar Islands, India, NE Indian Ocean
Great Plain of China *125 E2 plain* E China
Great Plains *45 E3 var.* High Plains. *Plains* Canada/USA
Great Rift Valley *73 C5 var.* Rift Valley. *Depression* Asia/Africa
Great Ruaha *73 C7 river* S Tanzania
Great Saint Bernard Pass *96 A1 Fr.* Col du Grand-Saint-Bernard, *It.* Passo di Gran San Bernardo. *Pass* Italy/Switzerland
Great Salt Desert *see* Kavīr, Dasht-e
Great Salt Lake *44 A3 salt lake* Utah, W USA
Great Salt Lake Desert *44 A4 plain* Utah, W USA
Great Sand Sea *71 H3 desert* Egypt/Libya
Great Sandy Desert *146 C4 desert* Western Australia
Great Sandy Island *see* Fraser Island
Great Slave Lake *37 E4 Fr.* Grand Lac des Esclaves. *Lake* Northwest Territories, NW Canada
Great Sound *42 A5 bay* Bermuda, NW Atlantic Ocean
Great Victoria Desert *147 C5 desert* South Australia/Western Australia
Great Wall of China *128 C4 ancient monument* N China
Great Yarmouth *89 E6 var.* Yarmouth. E England, UK
Gredos, Sierra de *92 D3 mountain range* W Spain
Greece *105 A5 Gk.* Ellás; *anc.* Hellas. *Country* SE Europe

Greece 105

Official name Hellenic Republic
Formation 1829
Capital Athens
Population 11 million / 218 people per sq mile (84 people per sq km)
Total area 50,942 sq. miles (131,940 sq. km)
Languages Greek, Turkish, Macedonian, Albanian
Religions Orthodox Christian 98%, other 1%, Muslim 1%
Ethnic mix Greek 98%, other 2%
Government Parliamentary system
Currency Euro = 100 cents
Literacy rate 97%
Calorie consumption 3754 calories

Greece *81 E5* New York, NE USA
Greeley *44 D4* Colorado, C USA
Green Bay *40 B2 lake bay* Michigan/Wisconsin, N USA
Green Bay *40 B2* Wisconsin, N USA
Greeneville *43 E1* Tennessee, S USA
Greenland *82 D3 Dan.* Grønland, *Inuit* Kalaallit Nunaat. *Danish external territory* NE North America
Greenland Sea *83 F2 sea* Arctic Ocean
Green Mountains *41 G2 mountain range* Vermont, NE USA
Greenock *88 C4* W Scotland, UK
Green River *40 C5 river* Kentucky, C USA
Green River *44 B4 river* Utah, W USA
Green River *44 B3* Wyoming, C USA
Greensboro *43 F1* North Carolina, SE USA
Greenville *42 B2* Mississippi, S USA
Greenville *43 F1* North Carolina, SE USA
Greenville *43 E1* South Carolina, SE USA
Greenville *49 G2* Texas, SW USA
Greenwich *89 B8* SE England, UK
Greenwood *42 B2* Mississippi, S USA
Greenwood *43 E2* South Carolina, SE USA
Gregory Range *148 C3 mountain range* Queensland, E Australia
Greifswald *94 D2* Mecklenburg-Vorpommern, NE Germany
Grenada *55 G5 country* SE West Indies

Grenada 55

Official name Grenada
Formation 1974
Capital St. George's
Population 89,258 / 681 people per sq mile (263 people per sq km)
Total area 131 sq. miles (340 sq. km)
Languages English, English Creole
Religions Roman Catholic 68%, Anglican 17%, other 15%
Ethnic mix Black African 82%, Mulatto (mixed race) 13%, East Indian 3%, other 2%
Government Parliamentary system
Currency Eastern Caribbean dollar = 100 cents
Literacy rate 94%
Calorie consumption 2749 calories

Grenada *42 C2* Mississippi, S USA
Grenadines, The *55 H4 island group* Grenada/St Vincent and the Grenadines
Grenoble *91 D5 anc.* Cularo, Gratianopolis. Isère, E France
Gresham *46 B3* Oregon, NW USA
Grevená *104 B4* Dytikí Makedonía, N Greece
Grevenmacher *87 E8* Grevenmacher, E Luxembourg
Greymouth *151 B5* West Coast, South Island, NZ
Grey Range *149 C5 mountain range* New South Wales/Queensland, E Australia
Greytown *see* San Juan del Norte
Griffin *42 D2* Georgia, SE USA
Grimari *76 C4* Ouaka, C Central African Republic
Grimsby *89 E5 prev.* Great Grimsby. E England, UK
Grobiņa *106 B3 Ger.* Grobin. Liepāja, W Latvia
Grodzisk Wielkopolski *98 B3* Wielkolpolskie, C Poland
Groesbeek *86 D4* Gelderland, SE Netherlands
Grójec *98 D4* Mazowieckie, C Poland
Groningen *86 E1* Groningen, NE Netherlands
Groote Eylandt *148 B2 island* Northern Territory, N Australia
Grootfontein *78 B3* Otjozondjupa, N Namibia
Groot Karasberge *78 B4 mountain range* S Namibia
Groot Karoo *see* Great Karoo
Gros Islet *55 F1* N Saint Lucia
Grosse Morava *see* Velika Morava
Grosseto *96 B4* Toscana, C Italy
Grossglockner *95 C7 mountain* W Austria
Groznyy *111 B8* Chechenskaya Respublika, SW Russian Federation
Grudziądz *98 C3 Ger.* Graudenz. Kujawski-pomorskie, C Poland
Grums *85 B6* Värmland, C Sweden
Gryazi *111 B6* Lipetskaya Oblast', W Russian Federation
Gryfice *98 B2 Ger.* Greifenberg, Greifenberg in Pommern. Zachodniopomorskie, NW Poland
Guabito *53 E4* Bocas del Toro, NW Panama
Guadalajara *93 E3 Ar.* Wad Al-Hajarah; *anc.* Arriaca. Castilla-La Mancha, C Spain
Guadalajara *50 D4* Jalisco, C Mexico
Guadalcanal *144 C3 island* C Solomon Islands
Guadalquivir *92 D4 river* W Spain
Guadalupe *50 D3* Zacatecas, C Mexico
Guadalupe Peak *48 D3 mountain* Texas, SW USA
Guadalupe River *49 G4 river* SW USA
Guadarrama, Sierra de *93 E2 mountain range* C Spain
Guadeloupe *55 H3 French overseas department* E West Indies
Guadiana *92 C4 river* Portugal/Spain
Guadix *93 E4* Andalucía, S Spain
Guaimaca *52 C2* Francisco Morazán, C Honduras
Guajira, Península de la *58 B1 peninsula* N Colombia
Gualaco *52 D2* Olancho, C Honduras
Gualán *52 B2* Zacapa, C Guatemala
Gualdicciolo *96 D1* NW San Marino
Gualeguaychú *64 D4* Entre Ríos, E Argentina
Guam *144 B1 US unincorporated territory* W Pacific Ocean
Guamúchil *50 C3* Sinaloa, C Mexico
Guanabacoa *54 B2* La Habana, W Cuba
Guanajuato *51 E4* Guanajuato, C Mexico
Guanare *58 C2* Portuguesa, N Venezuela
Guanare, Río *58 D2 river* W Venezuela
Guangdong *128 C6 var.* Guangdong Sheng, Kuang-tung, Kwangtung, Yue. Admin. region *province* S China
Guangdong Sheng *see* Guangdong
Guangxi *see* Guangxi Zhuangzu Zizhiqu
Guangxi Zhuangzu Zizhiqu *128 C6 var.* Guangxi, Gui, Kuang-hsi, Kwangsi, *Eng.* Kwangsi Chuang Autonomous Region. Admin. region *autonomous region* S China
Guangyuan *128 B5 var.* Kuang-yuan, Kwangyuan. Sichuan, C China
Guangzhou *128 C6 var.* Kuang-chou, Kwangchow, *Eng.* Canton. Guangdong, S China
Guantánamo *54 D3* Guantánamo, SE Cuba
Guantánamo Bay *54 D3 US military installation*, SE Cuba
Guaporé, Rio *62 D3 var.* Río Iténez. *River* Bolivia/Brazil *see also* Iténez, Río
Guarda *92 C3* Guarda, N Portugal
Guarumal *53 F5* Veraguas, S Panama

Guasave *50 C3* Sinaloa, C Mexico
Guatemala *52 A2 Country* Central America

Guatemala 52

Official name Republic of Guatemala
Formation 1838
Capital Guatemala City
Population 12.3 million / 294 people per sq mile (113 people per sq km)
Total area 42,042 sq. miles (108,890 sq. km)
Languages Quiché, Mam, Cakchiquel, Kekchí, Spanish
Religions Roman Catholic 65%, Protestant 33%, Other and nonreligious 2%
Ethnic mix Amerindian 60%, Mestizo 30%, other 10%
Government Presidential system
Currency Quetzal = 100 centavos
Literacy rate 70%
Calorie consumption 2203 calories

Guatemala Basin *35 B7 undersea feature* E Pacific Ocean
Guatemala City *see* Ciudad de Guatemala
Guaviare *56 B2 off.* Comisaría Guaviare. *Province* S Colombia
Guaviare, Río *58 D3 river* E Colombia
Guayaquil *60 A2 var.* Santiago de Guayaquil. Guayas, SW Ecuador
Guayaquil, Golfo de *60 A2 var.* Gulf of Guayaquil. *Gulf* SW Ecuador
Guayaquil, Gulf of *see* Guayaquil, Golfo de
Guaymas *50 B2* Sonora, NW Mexico
Gubadag *122 C2 Turkm.* Tel'man; *prev.* Tel'mansk. Dashkhovuzskiy Velayat, N Turkmenistan
Guben *94 D4 var.* Wilhelm-Pieck-Stadt. Brandenburg, E Germany
Gudara *see* Ghŭdara
Gudaut'a *117 E1* NW Georgia
Guéret *90 C4* Creuse, C France
Guernsey *89 D8 UK dependent territory* NW Europe
Guerrero Negro *50 A2* Baja California Sur, NW Mexico
Gui *see* Guangxi Zhuangzu Zizhiqu
Guiana *see* French Guiana
Guiana Highlands *62 D1 var.* Macizo de las Guayanas. *Mountain range* N South America
Guidder *see* Guider
Guider *76 B4 var.* Guidder. Nord, N Cameroon
Guidimouni *75 G3* Zinder, S Niger
Guildford *89 D7* SE England, UK
Guilin *128 C6 var.* Kuei-lin, Kweilin. Guangxi Zhuangzu Zizhiqu, S China
Guimarães *92 B2 var.* Guimaráes. Braga, N Portugal
Guinea *74 C4 var.* Guinée; *prev.* French Guinea, People's Revolutionary Republic of Guinea. *Country* W Africa

Guinea 74

Official name Republic of Guinea
Formation 1958
Capital Conakry
Population 8.5 million / 90 people per sq mile (35 people per sq km)
Total area 94,925 sq. miles (245,857 sq. km)
Languages Fulani, Malinke, Soussou, French
Religions Muslim 65%, Traditional beliefs 33%, Christian 2%
Ethnic mix Fulani 30%, Malinke 30%, Soussou 15%, Kissi 10%, Other tribes 10%, other 5%
Government Presidential system
Currency Guinea franc = 100 centimes
Literacy rate 41%
Calorie consumption 2362 calories

Guinea Basin *69 A5 undersea feature* E Atlantic Ocean
Guinea-Bissau *74 B4 Fr.* Guinée-Bissau, *Port.* Guiné-Bissau; *prev.* Portuguese Guinea. *Country* W Africa

Guinea-Bissau 74

Official name Republic of Guinea-Bissau
Formation 1974
Capital Bissau
Population 1.5 million / 138 people per sq mile (53 people per sq km)
Total area 13,946 sq. miles (36,120 sq. km)
Languages Portuguese Creole, Balante, Fulani, Malinke, Portuguese
Religions Traditional beliefs 52%, Muslim 40%, Christian 8%
Ethnic mix Other tribes 31%, Balante 25%, Fula 20%, Mandinka 12%, Mandyako 11%, other 1%
Government Transitional regime
Currency CFA franc = 100 centimes
Literacy rate 40%
Calorie consumption 2481 calories

Guinea, Gulf of *68 B4 Fr.* Golfe de Guinée. *Gulf* E Atlantic Ocean
Güiria *59 E1* Sucre, NE Venezuela
Guiyang *128 B6 var.* Kuei-Yang, Kuei-yang, Kueyang, Kweiyang; *prev.* Kweichu. Guizhou, S China
Guizhou *128 B6 var.* Guizhou Sheng, Kuei-chou, Kweichow, Qian. Admin. region *province* S China
Guizhou Sheng *see* Guizhou
Gujarāt *134 C4 var.* Gujerat. Admin. region *state* W India
Gujerat *see* Gujarāt
Gujrānwāla *134 D2* Punjab, NE Pakistan
Gujrāt *134 D2* Punjab, E Pakistan
Gulbarga *132 C1* Karnātaka, C India
Gulbene *106 D3 Ger.* Alt-Schwanenburg. Gulbene, NE Latvia
Gulfport *42 C3* Mississippi, S USA
Gulf, The *120 C4 var.* Persian Gulf, *Ar.* Khalīj al 'Arabī, *Per.* Khalīj-e Fars. *Gulf* SE Asia
Guliston *123 E2 Rus.* Gulistan. Sirdaryo Wiloyati, E Uzbekistan
Gulja *see* Yining
Gulkana *36 D3* Alaska, USA
Gulu *73 B6* N Uganda
Gulyantsi *104 C1* Pleven, N Bulgaria
Guma *see* Pishan
Gümülcine *see* Komotiní
Gümüljina *see* Komotiní
Gümüşane *see* Gümüşhane
Gümüşhane *117 E3 var.* Gümüşane, Gumushkhane. Gümüşhane, NE Turkey
Gumushkhane *see* Gümüşhane
Güney Doğu Toroslar *117 E4 mountain range* SE Turkey
Gunnbjørn Fjeld *82 D4 var.* Gunnbjörns Bjerge. *Mountain* C Greenland
Gunnbjörns Bjerge *see* Gunnbjørn Fjeld
Gunnedah *149 D6* New South Wales, SE Australia
Gunnison *44 C5* Colorado, C USA
Gurbantünggüt Shamo *126 B2 desert* W China
Gurgan *see* Gorgān
Guri, Embalse de *59 E2 reservoir* E Venezuela
Gurktaler Alpen *95 D7 mountain range* S Austria
Gürün *116 D3* Sivas, C Turkey
Gusau *75 G4* Zamfara, NW Nigeria
Gusev *106 B4 Ger.* Gumbinnen. Kaliningradskaya Oblast', W Russian Federation
Gustavus *36 D4* Alaska, USA
Güstrow *94 C3* Mecklenburg-Vorpommern, NE Germany
Gütersloh *94 B4* Nordrhein-Westfalen, W Germany
Guwāhāti *135 G3 prev.* Gauhāti. Assam, NE India
Guyana *59 F3 prev.* British Guiana. *Country* N South America

Guyana 59

Official name Cooperative Republic of Guyana
Formation 1966
Capital Georgetown
Population 765,000 / 10 people per sq mile (4 people per sq km)
Total area 83,000 sq. miles (214,970 sq. km)
Languages English Creole, Hindi, Tamil, Amerindian languages, English
Religions Christian 57%, Hindu 33%, Muslim 9%, other 1%
Ethnic mix East Indian 52%, Black African 38%, other 4%, Amerindian 4%, European and Chinese 2%
Government Presidential system
Currency Guyana dollar = 100 cents
Literacy rate 97%
Calorie consumption 2515 calories

Guyane *see* French Guiana
Guymon *49 E1* Oklahoma, C USA
Güzelyurt *see* Mórfou
Gvardeysk *106 A4 Ger.* Tapaiu. Kaliningradskaya Oblast', W Russian Federation
Gwādar *134 A3 var.* Gwadur. Baluchistān, SW Pakistan
Gwadur *see* Gwādar
Gwalior *134 D3* Madhya Pradesh, C India
Gwanda *78 D3* Matabeleland South, SW Zimbabwe
Gwy *see* Wye
Gyangzê *126 C5* Xizang Zizhiqu, W China
Gyaring Co *126 C5 lake* W China
Gympie *149 E5* Queensland, E Australia
Gyomaendrőd *99 D7* Békés, SE Hungary
Gyöngyös *99 D6* Heves, NE Hungary
Győr *99 C6 Ger.* Raab; *Lat.* Arrabona. Győr-Moson-Sopron, NW Hungary
Gýtheio *105 B6 var.* Githio; *prev.* Yíthion. Pelopónnisos, S Greece
Gyumri *117 F2 var.* Giumri, *Rus.* Kumayri; *prev.* Aleksandropol', Leninakan. W Armenia

H

Haabai *see* Ha'apai Group
Haacht *87 C6* Vlaams Brabant, C Belgium
Haaksbergen *86 E3* Overijssel, E Netherlands
Ha'apai Group *145 F4 var.* Haabai. *Island group* C Tonga
Haapsalu *106 D2 Ger.* Hapsal. Läänemaa, W Estonia
Haarlem *86 C3 prev.* Harlem. Noord-Holland, W Netherlands
Haast *151 B6* West Coast, South Island, NZ
Hachijō-jima *131 D6 var.* Hatizyô Zima. *Island* Izu-shotō, SE Japan
Hachinohe *130 D3* Aomori, Honshū, C Japan
Hadama *see* Nazrēt
Haddummati Atoll *see* Hadhdhunmathi Atoll
Hadejia *75 G3 river* N Nigeria
Hadejia *75 G4* Jigawa, N Nigeria
Hadera *119 A6 var.* Khadera. Haifa, C Israel
Hadhdhunmathi Atoll *132 A5 var.* Haddummati Atoll, Laamu Atoll. *Atoll* S Maldives
Ha Đông *136 D3 var.* Hadong. Ha Tây, N Vietnam
Hadong *see* Ha Đông
Ḩaḑramawt *121 C6 Eng.* Hadhramaut. *Mountain range* S Yemen
Haerbin *see* Harbin
Haerhpin *see* Harbin
Hafren *see* Severn
Hagåtña *160 B1 var.* Agana/Agaña. *Dependent territory capital* (Guam), NW Guam
Hagerstown *41 E4* Maryland, NE USA
Ha Giang *136 D3* Ha Giang, N Vietnam
Hagondange *90 D3* Moselle, NE France
Haguenau *90 E3* Bas-Rhin, NE France
Haicheng *128 D3* Liaoning, NE China
Haidarabad *see* Hyderābād
Haifa *see* Hefa
Haifong *see* Hai Phong
Haikou *128 C7 var.* Hai-k'ou, Hoihow, *Fr.* Hoï-Hao. Hainan, S China
Hai-k'ou *see* Haikou
Ḩā'il *120 B4 off.* Minţaqah Ḩā'il. *Province* N Saudi Arabia
Hai-la-erh *see* Hailar
Hailar *127 F1 var.* Hai-la-erh; *prev.* Hulun. Nei Mongol Zizhiqu, N China
Hailuoto *84 D4 Swe.* Karlö. *Island* W Finland
Hainan *128 B7 var.* Hainan Sheng, Qiong. Admin. region *province* S China
Hainan Dao *128 C7 island* S China
Hainan Sheng *see* Hainan
Haines *36 D4* Alaska, USA
Hainichen *94 D4* Sachsen, E Germany
Hai Phong *136 D3 var.* Haifong, Haiphong. N Vietnam
Haiphong *see* Hai Phong
Haiti *54 D3* C West Indies

Haiti 54

Official name Republic of Haiti
Formation 1804
Capital Port-au-Prince
Population 8.3 million / 780 people per sq mile (301 people per sq km)
Total area 10,714 sq. miles (27,750 sq. km)
Languages French Creole, French
Religions Roman Catholic 80%, Protestant 16%, Other (including Voodoo) 3%, Nonreligious 1%
Ethnic mix Black African 95%, Mulatto (mixed race) and European 5%
Government Transitional regime
Currency Gourde = 100 centimes
Literacy rate 52%
Calorie consumption 2045 calories

Haiya *72 C3* Red Sea, NE Sudan
Hajdúhadház *99 D6* Hajdú-Bihar, E Hungary
Hajîne *see* Abū Ḩardān
Hajnówka *98 E3 Ger.* Hermhausen. Podlaskie, NE Poland
Hakodate *130 D3* Hokkaidō, NE Japan
Ḩalab *118 B2 Eng.* Aleppo, *Fr.* Alep; *anc.* Beroea. Ḩalab, NW Syria
Ḩalāniyāt, Juzur al 137 D6 var. Jazā'ir Bin Ghalfān, *Eng.* Kuria Muria Islands. *Island group* S Oman
Halberstadt *94 C4* Sachsen-Anhalt, C Germany
Halden *85 B6 prev.* Fredrikshald. Østfold, S Norway
Halfmoon Bay *151 A8 var.* Oban. Stewart Island, Southland, NZ
Halifax *39 F4* Nova Scotia, SE Canada
Halkida *see* Chalkída
Halle *87 B6 Fr.* Hal. Vlaams Brabant, C Belgium
Halle *94 C4 var.* Halle an der Saale. Sachsen-Anhalt, C Germany
Halle an der Saale *see* Halle
Halle-Neustadt *94 C4* Sachsen-Anhalt, C Germany
Halley *154 B2 UK research station* Antarctica

Hall Islands *142 B2 island group* C Micronesia
Halls Creek *146 C3* Western Australia
Halmahera, Pulau *139 F3 prev.* Djailolo, Gilolo, Jailolo. *Island* E Indonesia
Halmahera Sea *139 F4 Ind.* Laut Halmahera. *Sea* E Indonesia
Halmstad *85 B7* Halland, S Sweden
Hama *see* Ḩamāh
Hamada *131 B6* Shimane, Honshū, SW Japan
Hamadān *120 C3 anc.* Ecbatana. Hamadān, W Iran
Ḩamāh *118 B3 var.* Hama; *anc.* Epiphania, *Bibl.* Hamath. Ḩamāh, W Syria
Hamamatsu *131 D6 var.* Hamamatu. Shizuoka, Honshū, S Japan
Hamamatu *see* Hamamatsu
Hamar *85 B5 prev.* Storhammer. Hedmark, S Norway
Hamath *see* Ḩamāh
Hamburg *94 B3* Hamburg, N Germany
Ḩamḑ, Wādī al 136 A4 dry watercourse W Saudi Arabia
Hämeenlinna *85 D5 Swe.* Tavastehus. Etelä-Suomi, S Finland
Hamersley Range *146 A4 mountain range* Western Australia
Hamhŭng *129 E3* C North Korea
Hami *126 C3 var.* Ha-mi, *Uigh.* Kumul, Qomul. Xinjiang Uygur Zizhiqu, NW China
Ha-mi *see* Hami
Hamilton *42 C2* Alabama, S USA
Hamilton *38 D5* Ontario, S Canada
Hamilton *88 C4* S Scotland, UK
Hamilton *150 D3* Waikato, North Island, NZ
Ḩamīm, Wād¯ı al 87 G2 river NE Libya
Hamīs Musait *see* Khamīs Mushayt
Hamiton *42 A5 dependent territory capital* (Bermuda) C Bermuda
Hamm *94 B4 var.* Hamm in Westfalen. Nordrhein-Westfalen, W Germany
Hammada du Drâa *see* Dra, Hamada du
Hammamet, Golfe de *102 D3 Ar.* Khalīj al Ḩammāmāt. *Gulf* NE Tunisia
Ḩammār, Hawr al 136 C3 lake SE Iraq
Hamm in Westfalen *see* Hamm
Hampden *151 B7* Otago, South Island, NZ
Hampstead *89 A7* SE England, UK
Hamrun *102 B5* C Malta
Hânceşti *see* Hînceşti
Handan *128 C4 var.* Han-tan. Hebei, E China
Haneda *130 A2 international airport* (Tōkyō) Tōkyō, Honshū, S Japan
HaNegev *119 A7 Eng.* Negev. *Desert* S Israel
Hanford *47 C6* California, W USA
Hangayn Nuruu *126 D2 mountain range* C Mongolia
Hang-chou *see* Hangzhou
Hangchow *see* Hangzhou
Hangö *see* Hanko
Hangzhou *128 D5 var.* Hang-chou, Hangchow. Zhejiang, SE China
Hania *see* Chaniá
Hanka, Lake *see* Khanka, Lake
Hanko *85 D6 Swe.* Hangö. Etelä-Suomi, SW Finland
Han-k'ou *see* Wuhan
Hankow *see* Wuhan
Hanmer Springs *151 C5* Canterbury, South Island, NZ
Hannibal *45 G4* Missouri, C USA
Hannover *94 B3 Eng.* Hanover. Niedersachsen, NW Germany
Hanöbukten *85 B7 bay* S Sweden
Ha Nôi *136 D3 Eng.* Hanoi, *Fr.* Ha noï. *Country capital* (Vietnam) N Vietnam
Hanoi *see* Ha Nôi
Han Shui *127 E4 river* C China
Han-tan *see* Handan
Hantsavichy *107 B6 Pol.* Hancewicze, *Rus.* Gantsevichi. Brestskaya Voblasts', SW Belarus
Hanyang *see* Wuhan
Hanzhong *128 B5* Shaanxi, C China
Hāora *135 F4 prev.* Howrah. West Bengal, NE India
Haparanda *84 D4* Norrbotten, N Sweden
Haradok *107 E5 Rus.* Gorodok. Vitsyebskaya Voblasts', N Belarus
Haradzyets *107 B6 Rus.* Gorodets. Brestskaya Voblasts', SW Belarus
Haramachi *130 D4* Fukushima, Honshū, E Japan
Harany *107 D5 Rus.* Gorany. Vitsyebskaya Voblasts', N Belarus
Harare *78 D3 prev.* Salisbury. *Country capital* (Zimbabwe) Mashonaland East, NE Zimbabwe
Harbavichy *107 E6 Rus.* Gorbovichi. Mahilyowskaya Voblasts', E Belarus
Harbel *74 C5* W Liberia
Harbin *129 E2 var.* Haerbin, Ha-erh-pin, Kharbin; *prev.* Haerhpin, Pingkiang, Pinkiang. Heilongjiang, NE China
Hardangerfjorden *85 A6 fjord* S Norway
Hardangervidda *85 A6 plateau* S Norway
Hardenberg *86 E3* Overijssel, E Netherlands
Harelbeke *87 A6 var.* Harlebeke. West-Vlaanderen, W Belgium
Harem *see* Ḩārim
Haren *86 E2* Groningen, NE Netherlands
Hārer *73 D5* E Ethiopia
Hargeisa *see* Hargeysa
Hargeysa *73 D5 var.* Hargeisa. Woqooyi Galbeed, NW Somalia
Hariana *see* Haryāna
Hari, Batang *138 B4 prev.* Djambi. *River* Sumatera, W Indonesia
Ḩārim *118 B2 var.* Harem. Idlib, W Syria
Harima-nada *131 B6 sea* S Japan
Harīrūd *var.* Tedzhen, *Turkm.* Tejen. *River* Afghanistan/Iran *see also* Tedzhen
Harlan *45 F3* Iowa, C USA
Harlebeke *see* Harelbeke
Harlingen *86 D2 Fris.* Harns. Friesland, N Netherlands
Harlingen *49 G5* Texas, SW USA
Harlow *89 E6* E England, UK
Harney Basin *46 B4 basin* Oregon, NW USA
Härnösand *85 C5 var.* Hernösand. Västernorrland, C Sweden
Har Nuur *126 C2 lake* NW Mongolia
Harper *74 D5 var.* Cape Palmas. NE Liberia
Harricana *38 D3 river* Québec, SE Canada
Harris *88 B3 physical region* NW Scotland, UK
Harrisburg *41 E4 state capital* Pennsylvania, NE USA
Harrisonburg *41 E4* Virginia, NE USA
Harrison, Cape *39 F2 headland* Newfoundland and Labrador, E Canada
Harris Ridge *see* Lomonosov Ridge
Harrogate *89 D5* N England, UK
Hârşova *108 D5 prev.* Hîrşova. Constanța, SE Romania
Harstad *84 C2* Troms, N Norway
Hartford *41 G3 state capital* Connecticut, NE USA
Hartlepool *89 D5* N England, UK
Harunabad *see* Eslāmābād
Harwich *89 E6* E England, UK
Haryāna *134 D2 var.* Hariana. Admin. region *state* N India
Hasselt *87 C6* Limburg, NE Belgium
Hassetché *see* Al Ḩasakah
Hastings *150 E4* Hawke's Bay, North Island, NZ
Hastings *45 E4* Nebraska, C USA
Hastings *89 E7* SE England, UK
Hațeg *108 B4 Ger.* Wallenthal, *Hung.* Hátszeg; *prev.* Hatzeg, Hötzing. Hunedoara, SW Romania
Hatizyô Zima *see* Hachijō-jima
Hattem *86 D3* Gelderland, E Netherlands
Hatteras, Cape *43 G1 headland* North Carolina, SE USA
Hatteras Plain *35 D6 undersea feature* W Atlantic Ocean
Hattiesburg *42 C3* Mississippi, S USA
Hatton Bank *see* Hatton Ridge
Hatton Ridge *80 B2 var.* Hatton Bank. *Undersea feature* N Atlantic Ocean
Hat Yai *137 C7 var.* Ban Hat Yai. Songkhla, SW Thailand
Haugesund *85 A6* Rogaland, S Norway
Haukeligrend *85 A6* Telemark, S Norway
Haukivesi *85 E5 lake* SE Finland
Hauraki Gulf *150 D2 gulf* North Island, NZ
Hauroko, Lake *151 A7 lake* South Island, NZ
Haut Atlas *70 C2 Eng.* High Atlas. *Mountain range* C Morocco
Hautes Fagnes *87 D6 Ger.* Hohes Venn. *Mountain range* E Belgium
Haut Plateau du Dra *see* Dra, Hamada du
Hauts Plateaux *70 D2 plateau* Algeria/Morocco
Hauzenberg *95 D6* Bayern, SE Germany
Havana *see* La Habana
Havana *35 D6* Illinois, N USA
Havant *89 D7* S England, UK
Havelock *43 F1* North Carolina, SE USA
Havelock North *150 E4* Hawke's Bay, North Island, NZ
Haverfordwest *89 C6* SW Wales, UK
Havířov *99 C5* Ostravský Kraj, E Czech Republic
Havre *44 C1* Montana, NW USA
Havre-St-Pierre *39 F3* Québec, E Canada
Hawai'i *47 B8 var.* Hawaii. *Island* Hawaiian Islands, USA, C Pacific Ocean
Hawai'i *47 A8 off.* State of Hawaii; also known as Aloha State, Paradise of the Pacific, *var.* Hawaii. *State* USA, C Pacific Ocean
Hawaiian Islands *152 D2 prev.* Sandwich Islands. *Island group* Hawaii, USA, C Pacific Ocean
Hawaiian Ridge *113 H4 undersea feature* N Pacific Ocean
Hawash *see* Āwash
Hawea, Lake *151 B6 lake* South Island, NZ
Hawera *150 D4* Taranaki, North Island, NZ
Hawick *88 C4* SE Scotland, UK
Hawke Bay *150 E4 bay* North Island, NZ
Hawlēr *see* Arbīl
Hawthorne *47 C6* Nevada, W USA
Hay *149 C6* New South Wales, SE Australia
Hayes *38 B2 river* Manitoba, C Canada
Hay River *37 E4* Northwest Territories, W Canada
Hays *45 E5* Kansas, C USA
Haysyn *108 D3 Rus.* Gaysin. Vinnyts'ka Oblast', C Ukraine
Hazar *122 B2 prev.* Cheleken. Balkanskiy Velayat, W Turkmenistan
Heard and McDonald Islands *141 B7 Australian external territory* S Indian Ocean
Hearst *38 C4* Ontario, S Canada
Heathrow *89 A8 international airport* (London)SE England, UK
Hebei *128 C4 var.* Hebei Sheng, Hopeh, Hopei, Ji; *prev.* Chihli. Admin. region *province* E China
Hebei Sheng *see* Hebei
Hebron *119 A6 var.* Al Khalīl, El Khalil, *Heb.* Ḫevron; *anc.* Kiriath-Arba. S West Bank
Hebrus *see* Maritsa
Heemskerk *86 C3* Noord-Holland, W Netherlands
Heerde *86 D3* Gelderland, E Netherlands
Heerenveen *86 D2 Fris.* It Hearrenfean. Friesland, N Netherlands
Heerhugowaard *86 C2* Noord-Holland, NW Netherlands
Heerlen *87 D6* Limburg, SE Netherlands
Heerwegen *see* Polkowice
Ḫefa *119 A5 var.* Haifa; *hist.* Caiffa, Caiphas, *anc.* Sycaminum. Haifa, N Israel
Ḫefa, Mifraẕ *119 A5 Eng.* Bay of Haifa. *Bay* N Israel
Hefei *128 D5 var.* Hofei; *hist.* Luchow. Anhui, E China
Hegang *129 E2* Heilongjiang, NE China
Hei *see* Heilongjiang
Heide *94 B2* Schleswig-Holstein, N Germany
Heidelberg *95 B5* Baden-Württemberg, SW Germany
Heidenheim *see* Heidenheim an der Brenz
Heidenheim an der Brenz *95 B6 var.* Heidenheim. Baden-Württemberg, S Germany
Heilbronn *95 B6* Baden-Württemberg, SW Germany
Heilongjiang *128 D2 var.* Hei, Heilongjiang Sheng, Hei-lung-chiang, Heilungkiang. Admin. region *province* NE China
Heilongjiang Sheng *see* Heilongjiang
Heiloo *86 C3* Noord-Holland, NW Netherlands
Hei-lung-chiang *see* Heilongjiang
Heilungkiang *see* Heilongjiang
Heimdal *85 B5* Sør-Trøndelag, S Norway
Hekimhan *116 D3* Malatya, C Turkey
Helena *44 B2 state capital* Montana, NW USA
Helensville *150 D2* Auckland, North Island, NZ
Helgoland Bay *see* Helgoländer Bucht
Helgoländer Bucht *94 A2 var.* Helgoland Bay, Heligoland Bight. *Bay* NW Germany
Heligoland Bight *see* Helgoländer Bucht
Heliopolis *see* Baalbek
Hellevoetsluis *86 B4* Zuid-Holland, SW Netherlands
Hellín *93 E4* Castilla-La Mancha, C Spain
Helmand, Daryā-ye *var.* Rūd-e Hīrmand. *River* Afghanistan/Iran *see also* Hīrmand, Rūd-e
Helmond *87 D5* Noord-Brabant, S Netherlands
Helsingborg *85 B7 prev.* Hälsingborg. Skåne, S Sweden
Helsinki *85 D6 Swe.* Helsingfors. *Country capital* (Finland) Etelä-Suomi, S Finland
Henan *128 C5 var.* Henan Sheng, Honan, Yu. Admin. region *province* C China
Henan Sheng *see* Henan
Henderson *40 B5* Kentucky, S USA
Henderson *47 D7* Nevada, W USA
Henderson *49 H3* Texas, SW USA
Hengchow *see* Hengyang
Hengduan Shan *128 A5 mountain range* SW China
Hengelo *86 E3* Overijssel, E Netherlands
Hengnan *see* Hengyang
Hengyang *128 C6 var.* Hengnan, Heng-yang; *prev.* Hengchow. Hunan, S China
Heng-yang *see* Hengyang
Heniches'k *109 F4 Rus.* Genichesk. Khersons'ka Oblast', S Ukraine
Hennebont *90 A3* Morbihan, NW France
Henzada *136 B4* Irrawaddy, SW Myanmar
Herakleion *see* Irákleio
Herāt *122 D4 var.* Herat; *anc.* Aria. Herāt, W Afghanistan

Herat *see* Herāt
Heredia *53 E4* Heredia, C Costa Rica
Hereford *49 E2* Texas, SW USA
Herford *94 B4* Nordrhein-Westfalen, NW Germany
Herk-de-Stad *87 C6* Limburg, NE Belgium
Hermansverk *85 A5* Sogn Og Fjordane, S Norway
Hermhausen *see* Hajnówka
Hermiston *46 C2* Oregon, NW USA
Hermon, Mount *119 B5 Ar.* Jabal ash Shaykh. *Mountain* S Syria
Hermosillo *50 B2* Sonora, NW Mexico
Hermoupolis *see* Ermoúpoli
Hernösand *see* Härnösand
Herrera del Duque *92 D3* Extremadura, W Spain
Herselt *87 C5* Antwerpen, C Belgium
Herstal *87 D6 Fr.* Héristal. Liège, E Belgium
Hessen *95 B5 cultural region* C Germany
Hevron *see* Hebron
Heydebrech *see* Kędzierzyn-Kole
Heywood Islands *146 C3 island group* Western Australia
Hibbing *45 F1* Minnesota, N USA
Hidalgo del Parral *50 C2 var.* Parral. Chihuahua, N Mexico
Hida-sanmyaku *131 C5 mountain range* Honshū, S Japan
Hierro *70 A3 var.* Ferro. *Island* Islas Canarias, Spain, NE Atlantic Ocean
High Plains *see* Great Plains
High Point *43 E1* North Carolina, SE USA
High Veld *see* Great Karoo
Hiiumaa *106 C2 Ger.* Dagden, *Swe.* Dagö. *Island* W Estonia
Hikurangi *150 D2* Northland, North Island, NZ
Hildesheim *94 B4* Niedersachsen, N Germany
Hilla *see* Al Ḥillah
Hillaby, Mount *55 G1 mountain* N Barbados
Hill Bank *52 C1* Orange Walk, N Belize
Hillegom *86 C3* Zuid-Holland, W Netherlands
Hilo *47 B8* Hawai'i, USA, C Pacific Ocean
Hilton Head Island *43 E2* South Carolina, SE USA
Hilversum *86 C3* Noord-Holland, C Netherlands
Himalaya *see* Himalayas
Himalayas *135 E2 var.* Himalaya, *Chin.* Himalaya Shan. *Mountain range* S Asia
Himalaya Shan *see* Himalayas
Himeji *131 C6 var.* Himezi. Hyōgo, Honshū, SW Japan
Himezi *see* Himeji
Ḥimş *118 B4 var.* Homs; *anc.* Emesa. Ḥimş, C Syria
Hînceşti *108 D4 var.* Hânceşti; *prev.* Kotovsk. C Moldova
Hinchinbrook Island *148 D3 island* Queensland, NE Australia
Hinds *151 C6* Canterbury, South Island, NZ
Hindu Kush *123 F4 Per.* Hendū Kosh. *Mountain range* Afghanistan/Pakistan
Hinesville *43 E3* Georgia, SE USA
Hinnøya *84 C3 island* C Norway
Hinson Bay *42 A5 bay* W Bermuda
Hios *see* Chíos
Hirosaki *130 D3* Aomori, Honshū, C Japan
Hiroshima *131 B6 var.* Hirosima. Hiroshima, Honshū, SW Japan
Hirosima *see* Hiroshima
Hirson *90 D3* Aisne, N France
Hispaniola *56 B1 island* Dominion Republic/Haiti
Hitachi *131 D5 var.* Hitati. Ibaraki, Honshū, S Japan
Hitati *see* Hitachi
Hitra *84 A4 prev.* Hitteren. *Island* S Norway
Hjälmaren *85 C6 Eng.* Lake Hjalmar. *Lake* C Sweden
Hjørring *85 B7* Nordjylland, N Denmark
Hkakabo Razi *136 B1 mountain* Myanmar/China
Hlobyne *109 F2 Rus.* Globino. Poltavs'ka Oblast', NE Ukraine
Hlukhiv *109 F1 Rus.* Glukhov. Sums'ka Oblast', NE Ukraine
Hlybokaye *107 D5 Rus.* Glubokoye. Vitsyebskaya Voblasts', N Belarus
Hoa Binh *136 D3* Hoa Binh, N Vietnam
Hoang Liên Sơn *136 D3 mountain range* N Vietnam
Hobart *149 C8 prev.* Hobarton, Hobart Town. *State capital* Tasmania, SE Australia
Hobbs *49 E3* New Mexico, SW USA
Hobro *85 A7* Nordjylland, N Denmark
Hô Chi Minh *137 E6 var.* Ho Chi Minh City; *prev.* Saigon. S Vietnam
Ho Chi Minh City *see* Hô Chi Minh
Hódmezővásárhely *99 D7* Csongrád, SE Hungary
Hodna, Chott El 118 C4 var. Chott el-Hodna, *Ar.* Shatt al-Hodna. *Salt lake* N Algeria
Hodonín *99 C5 Ger.* Göding. Brněnský Kraj, SE Czech Republic
Hoë Karoo *see* Great Karoo
Hof *95 C5* Bayern, SE Germany
Hofei *see* Hefei
Hōfu *131 B7* Yamaguchi, Honshū, SW Japan
Hofuf *see* Al Hufūf
Hogoley Islands *see* Chuuk Islands
Hohe Tauern *95 C7 mountain range* W Austria
Hohhot *127 F3 var.* Huhehot, Huhuohaote, *Mong.* Kukukhoto; *prev.* Kweisui, Kwesui. Nei Mongol Zizhiqu, N China
Hôi An *137 E5 prev.* Faifo. Quang Nam-Đa Năng, C Vietnam
Hoï-Hao *see* Haikou
Hoihow *see* Haikou
Hokianga Harbour *150 C2 inlet* SE Tasman Sea
Hokitika *151 B5* West Coast, South Island, NZ
Hokkaidō *130 C2 prev.* Ezo, Yeso, Yezo. *Island* NE Japan
Hola Prystan' *109 E4 Rus.* Golaya Pristan. Khersons'ka Oblast', S Ukraine
Holbrook *48 B2* Arizona, SW USA
Holetown *55 G1 prev.* Jamestown. W Barbados
Holguín *54 C2* Holguín, SE Cuba
Hollabrunn *95 E6* Niederösterreich, NE Austria
Hollandia *see* Jayapura
Holly Springs *42 C1* Mississippi, S USA
Holman *37 E3* Victoria Island, Northwest Territories, N Canada
Holmsund *84 D4* Västerbotten, N Sweden
Holon *119 A6 var.* Kholon. Tel Aviv, C Israel
Holovanivs'k *109 E3 Rus.* Golovanevsk. Kirovohrads'ka Oblast', C Ukraine
Holstebro *85 A7* Ringkøbing, W Denmark
Holsteinborg *see* Sisimiut
Holsteinsborg *see* Sisimiut
Holstenborg *see* Sisimiut
Holstensborg *see* Sisimiut
Holyhead *89 C5 Wel.* Caer Gybi. NW Wales, UK
Hombori *75 E3* Mopti, S Mali
Homs *see* Al Khums
Homs *see* Ḥimş
Homyel' *107 D7 Rus.* Gomel'. Homyel'skaya Voblasts', SE Belarus
Honan *see* Henan
Honan *see* Luoyang
Hondo *see* Honshū
Hondo *49 F4* Texas, SW USA
Honduras *52 C2 Country* Central America

Honduras 52

Official name Republic of Honduras
Formation 1838
Capital Tegucigalpa
Population 6.9 million / 160 people per sq mile (62 people per sq km)
Total area 43,278 sq. miles (112,090 sq. km)
Languages Spanish, Garífuna (Carib), English Creole
Religions Roman Catholic 97%, Protestant 3%
Ethnic mix Mestizo 90%, Black African 5%, Amerindian 4%, White 1%
Government Presidential system
Currency Lempira = 100 centavos
Literacy rate 80%
Calorie consumption 2406 calories

Honduras, Gulf of *52 C2 Sp.* Golfo de Honduras. *Gulf* W Caribbean Sea
Hønefoss *85 B6* Buskerud, S Norway
Honey Lake *47 B5 lake* California, W USA
Hon Gai *see* Hông Gai
Hongay *see* Hông Gai
Hông Gai *136 E3 var.* Hon Gai, Hongay. Quang Ninh, N Vietnam
Hong Kong *128 A1 Chin.* Xianggang. S China
Hong Kong Island *128 B2 Chin.* Xianggang. *Island* S China
Honiara *144 C3 country capital* (Solomon Islands) Guadalcanal, C Solomon Islands
Honjō *130 D4 var.* Honzyô. Akita, Honshū, C Japan
Honolulu *47 A8 admin capital* O'ahu, Hawai'i, USA, C Pacific Ocean
Honshū *131 E5 var.* Hondo, Honsyû. *Island* SW Japan
Honsyû *see* Honshū
Honzyô *see* Honjō
Hoogeveen *86 E2* Drenthe, NE Netherlands
Hoogezand-Sappemeer *86 E2* Groningen, NE Netherlands
Hoorn *86 C2* Noord-Holland, NW Netherlands
Hopa *117 E2* Artvin, NE Turkey
Hope *36 C3* British Columbia, SW Canada
Hopedale *39 F2* Newfoundland and Labrador, NE Canada
Hopeh *see* Hebei
Hopei *see* Hebei
Hopkinsville *40 B5* Kentucky, S USA
Horasan *117 F3* Erzurum, NE Turkey
Horizon Deep *152 D4 undersea feature* W Pacific Ocean
Horki *107 E6 Rus.* Gorki. Mahilyowskaya Voblasts', E Belarus
Horlivka *109 G3 Rom.* Adâncata, *Rus.* Gorlovka. Donets'ka Oblast', E Ukraine
Hormuz, Strait of *120 D4 var.* Strait of Ormuz, *Per.* Tangeh-ye Hormoz. *Strait* Iran/Oman
Hornos, Cabo de *65 C8 Eng.* Cape Horn. *Headland* S Chile
Hornsby *148 E1* New South Wales, SE Australia
Horodnya *109 E1 Rus.* Gorodnya. Chernihivs'ka Oblast', NE Ukraine
Horodyshche *109 E2 Rus.* Gorodishche. Cherkas'ka Oblast', C Ukraine
Horokok *108 B2 Pol.* Gródek Jagielloński, *Rus.* Gorodok, Gorodok Yagellonski. L'vivs'ka Oblast', NW Ukraine
Horoshiri-dake *130 D2 var.* Horosiri Dake. *Mountain* Hokkaidō, N Japan
Horosiri Dake *see* Horoshiri-dake
Horsburgh Atoll *132 A4 atoll* N Maldives
Horseshoe Bay *42 A5 bay* W Bermuda
Horseshoe Seamounts *80 A4 undersea feature* E Atlantic Ocean
Horsham *149 B7* Victoria, SE Australia
Horst *87 D5* Limburg, SE Netherlands
Horten *85 B6* Vestfold, S Norway
Horyn' *107 B7 Rus.* Goryn. *River* NW Ukraine
Hosingen *87 D7* Diekirch, NE Luxembourg
Hospitalet *see* L'Hospitalet de Llobregat
Hotan *126 B4 var.* Khotan, *Chin.* Ho-t'ien. Xinjiang Uygur Zizhiqu, NW China
Ho-t'ien *see* Hotan
Hoting *84 C4* Jämtland, C Sweden
Hot Springs *42 B1* Arkansas, C USA
Houayxay *136 C3 var.* Ban Houayxay, Ban Houei Sai. Bokèo, N Laos
Houghton *40 B1* Michigan, N USA
Houilles *91 B5* Yvelines, N France
Houlton *41 H1* Maine, NE USA
Houma *42 B3* Louisiana, S USA
Houston *49 H4* Texas, SW USA
Hovd *126 C2 var.* Khovd. Hovd, W Mongolia
Hove *89 E7* SE England, UK
Hoverla, Hora *108 C3 Rus.* Gora Goverla. *Mountain* W Ukraine
Hovsgol, Lake *see* Hövsgöl Nuur
Hövsgöl Nuur *126 D1 var.* Lake Hovsgol. *Lake* N Mongolia
Howar, Wādi *72 A3 var.* Ouadi Howa. *River* Chad/Sudan *see also* Howa, Ouadi
Hoy *88 C2 island* N Scotland, UK
Hoyerswerda *94 D4* Sachsen, E Germany
Hradec Králové *99 B5 Ger.* Königgrätz. Hradecký Kraj, N Czech Republic
Hrandzichy *107 B5 Rus.* Grandichi. Hrodzyenskaya Voblasts', W Belarus
Hranice *99 C5 Ger.* Mährisch-Weisskirchen. Olomoucký Kraj, E Czech Republic
Hrebinka *109 E2 Rus.* Grebenka. Poltavs'ka Oblast', NE Ukraine
Hrodna *107 B5 Pol.* Grodno. Hrodzyenskaya Voblasts', W Belarus
Hsia-men *see* Xiamen
Hsiang-t'an *see* Xiangtan
Hsi Chiang *see* Xi Jiang
Hsing-k'ai Hu *see* Khanka, Lake
Hsining *see* Xining
Hsinking *see* Changchun
Hsin-yang *see* Xinyang
Hsu-chou *see* Xuzhou
Huacho *60 C4* Lima, W Peru
Hua Hin *see* Ban Hua Hin
Huaihua *128 C5* Hunan, S China
Huailai *128 C3 prev.* Shacheng. Hebei, E China
Huainan *128 D5 var.* Huai-nan, Hwainan. Anhui, E China
Huai-nan *see* Huainan
Huajuapan *51 F5 var.* Huajuapan de León. Oaxaca, SE Mexico
Huajuapan de León *see* Huajuapan
Hualapai Peak *48 A2 mountain* Arizona, SW USA
Huallaga, Río *60 C3 river* N Peru
Huambo *78 B2 Port.* Nova Lisboa. Huambo, C Angola
Huancavelica *60 D4* Huancavelica, SW Peru
Huancayo *60 D3* Junín, C Peru
Huang He *128 C4 var.* Yellow River. *River* C China
Huangshi *128 C5 var.* Huang-shih, Hwangshih. Hubei, C China
Huang-shih *see* Huangshi
Huanta *60 D4* Ayacucho, C Peru
Huánuco *60 C3* Huánuco, C Peru
Huanuni *61 F4* Oruro, W Bolivia
Huaral *60 C4* Lima, W Peru
Huarás *see* Huaraz
Huaraz *60 C3 var.* Huarás. Ancash, W Peru

Huarmey *60 C3* Ancash, W Peru
Huatabampo *50 C2* Sonora, NW Mexico
Hubli *124 B3* Karnātaka, SW India
Huddersfield *89 D5* N England, UK
Hudiksvall *85 C5* Gävleborg, C Sweden
Hudson Bay *37 G4 bay* NE Canada
Hudson Strait *37 H3 Fr.* Détroit d'Hudson. *Strait* Nunavut/Québec, NE Canada
Hudur *see* Xuddur
Huê *136 E4* Thưa Thiên-Huê, C Vietnam
Huehuetenango *52 A2* Huehuetenango, W Guatemala
Huelva *92 C4 anc.* Onuba. Andalucía, SW Spain
Huesca *93 F2 anc.* Osca. Aragón, NE Spain
Huéscar *93 E4* Andalucía, S Spain
Hughenden *148 C3* Queensland, NE Australia
Hugo *49 G2* Oklahoma, C USA
Huhehot *see* Hohhot
Huhuohaote *see* Hohhot
Huíla Plateau *78 B2 plateau* S Angola
Huixtla *51 G5* Chiapas, SE Mexico
Hukui *see* Fukui
Hukuoka *see* Fukuoka
Hukusima *see* Fukushima
Hulingol *127 G2 prev.* Huolin Gol. Nei Mongol Zizhiqu, N China
Hull *see* Kingston upon Hull
Hull *38 D4* Québec, SE Canada
Hulst *87 B5* Zeeland, SW Netherlands
Hulun *see* Hailar
Hu-lun Ch'ih *see* Hulun Nur
Hulun Nur *127 F1 var.* Hu-lun Ch'ih; *prev.* Dalai *Nor. lake* NE China
Humaitá *62 D2* Amazonas, N Brazil
Humboldt River *47 C5 river* Nevada, W USA
Humphreys Peak *48 B1 mountain* Arizona, SW USA
Humpolec *99 B5 Ger.* Gumpolds, Humpoletz. Jihlavský Kraj, C Czech Republic
Hunan *128 C6 var.* Hunan Sheng, Xiang. Admin. region *province* S China
Hunan ShEng *see* Xiang
Hunedoara *108 B4 Ger.* Eisenmarkt, *Hung.* Vajdahunyad. Hunedoara, SW Romania
Hünfeld *95 B5* Hessen, C Germany
Hungary *99 C6 Ger.* Ungarn, *Hung.* Magyarország, *Rom.* Ungaria, *SCr.* Mađarska, *Ukr.* Uhorshchyna; *prev.* Hungarian People's Republic. *Country* C Europe

Hungary 99

Official name Republic of Hungary
Formation 1918
Capital Budapest
Population 9.9 million / 278 people per sq mile (107 people per sq km)
Total area 35,919 sq. miles (93,030 sq. km)
Languages Hungarian (Magyar)
Religions Roman Catholic 52%, Calvinist 16%, other 15%, Nonreligious 14%, Lutheran 3%
Ethnic mix Magyar 90%, other 7%, Roma 2%, German 1%
Government Parliamentary system
Currency Forint = 100 fillér
Literacy rate 99%
Calorie consumption 3520 calories

Hungary, Plain of *see* Great Hungarian Plain
Hunter Island *149 B8 island* Tasmania, SE Australia
Huntington *40 D4* West Virginia, NE USA
Huntington Beach *47 B8* California, W USA
Huntly *150 D3* Waikato, North Island, NZ
Huntsville *42 D1* Alabama, S USA
Huntsville *49 G3* Texas, SW USA
Hurghada *72 C2 var.* Al Ghurdaqah, Ghurdaqah. E Egypt
Huron *45 E3* South Dakota, N USA
Huron, Lake *40 D2 lake* Canada/USA
Hurukawa *see* Furukawa
Hurunui *151 C5 river* South Island, NZ
Húsavík *83 E4* Nordhurland Eystra, NE Iceland
Husum *94 B2* Schleswig-Holstein, N Germany
Hutchinson *45 E5* Kansas, C USA
Hutchinson Island *43 F4 island* Florida, SE USA
Huy *87 C6 Dut.* Hoei, Hoey. Liège, E Belgium
Huzi *see* Fuji
Hvannadalshnúkur *83 E5 mountain* S Iceland
Hvar *100 B4 It.* Lesina; *anc.* Pharus. *Island* S Croatia
Hwainan *see* Huainan
Hwange *78 D3 prev.* Wankie. Matabeleland North, W Zimbabwe
Hwangshih *see* Huangshi
Hyargas Nuur *126 C2 lake* NW Mongolia
Hyderābād *134 D5 var.* Haidarabad. Andhra Pradesh, C India
Hyderābād *134 B3 var.* Haidarabad. Sind, SE Pakistan
Hyères *91 D6* Var, SE France
Hyères, Îles d' *91 D6 island group* S France
Hypanis *see* Kuban'
Hyrcania *see* Gorgān
Hyvinkää *85 D5 Swe.* Hyvinge. Etelä-Suomi, S Finland

I

Ialomiţa *108 C5 river* SE Romania
Iaşi *108 D3 Ger.* Jassy. Iaşi, NE Romania
Ibadan *75 F5* Oyo, SW Nigeria
Ibagué *58 B3* Tolima, C Colombia
Ibar *100 D4 Alb.* Ibër. *River* C Serbia and Montenegro (Yugo.)
Ibarra *60 B1 var.* San Miguel de Ibarra. Imbabura, N Ecuador
Iberian Mountains *see* Ibérico, Sistema
Iberian Peninsula *80 B4 physical region* Portugal/Spain
Iberian Plain *80 B4 undersea feature* E Atlantic Ocean
Ibérico, Sistema *93 E2 var.* Cordillera Ibérica, *Eng.* Iberian Mountains. *Mountain range* NE Spain
Ibiza *see* Eivissa
Ibo *see* Sassandra
Ica *60 D4* Ica, SW Peru
Içá *see* Putumayo, Río
Icaria *see* Ikaría
Içá, Rio *62 C2 var.* Río Putumayo. *River* NW South America *see also* Putumayo, Río
Iceland *83 E4 Dan.* Island, *Icel.* Ísland. *Country* N Atlantic Ocean

Iceland 83

Official name Republic of Iceland
Formation 1944
Capital Reykjavík
Population 290,000 / 7 people per sq mile (3 people per sq km)
Total area 39,768 sq. miles (103,000 sq. km)
Languages Icelandic
Religions Evangelical Lutheran 93%, Nonreligious 6%, Other (mostly Christian) 1%

Iceland (continued)

Ethnic mix Icelandic 94%, other 5%, Danish 1%
Government Parliamentary system
Currency Icelandic króna = 100 aurar
Literacy rate 99%
Calorie consumption 3231 calories

Iceland Basin *80 B1 undersea feature* N Atlantic Ocean
Icelandic Plateau *see* Iceland Plateau
Iceland Plateau *172 B5 var.* Icelandic Plateau. *Undersea feature* S Greenland Sea
Iconium *see* Konya
Idabel *49 H2* Oklahoma, C USA
Idaho *46 D3 off.* State of Idaho; also known as Gem of the Mountains, Gem State. *State* NW USA
Idaho Falls *46 E3* Idaho, NW USA
Idensalmi *see* Iisalmi
Idfu *72 B2 var.* Edfu. SE Egypt
Ídhra *see* Ýdra
Idi Amin, Lac *see* Edward, Lake
Idîni *74 B2* Trarza, W Mauritania
Idlib *118 B3* Idlib, NW Syria
Idre *85 B5* Kopparberg, C Sweden
Iecava *106 C3* Bauska, S Latvia
Ieper *87 A6 Fr.* Ypres. West-Vlaanderen, W Belgium
Ierápetra *105 D8* Kríti, Greece, E Mediterranean Sea
Ierisós *see* Ierissós
Ierissós *104 C4 var.* Ierisós. Kentrikí Makedonía, N Greece
Iferouâne *75 G2* Agadez, N Niger
Ifôghas, Adrar des *75 E2 var.* Adrar des Iforas. *Mountain range* NE Mali
Igarka *114 D3* Krasnoyarskiy Kray, N Russian Federation
Iglesias *97 A5* Sardegna, Italy, C Mediterranean Sea
Igloolik *37 G2* Nunavut, N Canada
Igoumenítsa *104 A4* Ípeiros, W Greece
Iguaçu, Rio *63 E4 Sp.* Río Iguazú. *River* Argentina/Brazil *see also* Iguazú, Río
Iguaçu, Salto do *63 E4 Sp.* Cataratas del Iguazú; *prev.* Victoria Falls. *Waterfall* Argentina/Brazil *see also* Iguazú, Cataratas del
Iguala *51 E4 var.* Iguala de la Independencia. Guerrero, S Mexico
Iguala de la Independencia *see* Iguala
Iguîdi, 'Erg *70 C3 var.* Erg Iguid. *Desert* Algeria/Mauritania
Ihavandiffulu Atoll *see* Ihavandippolhu Atoll
Ihavandippolhu Atoll *132 A3 var.* Ihavandiffulu Atoll. *Atoll* N Maldives
Ihosy *79 F4* Fianarantsoa, S Madagascar
Ijmuiden *86 C3* Noord-Holland, W Netherlands
Iisalmi *84 E4 var.* Idensalmi. Itä-Suomi, C Finland
IJssel *86 D3 var.* Yssel. *River* Netherlands/Germany
IJsselmeer *86 C2 prev.* Zuider Zee. *Lake* N Netherlands
IJsselmuiden *86 D3* Overijssel, E Netherlands
Ijzer *87 A6 river* W Belgium
Ikaría *105 D6 var.* Kariot, Nicaria, Nikaria; *anc.* Icaria. *Island* Dodekánisos, Greece, Aegean Sea
Ikela *77 D6* Equateur, C Dem. Rep. Congo
Iki *131 A7 island* SW Japan
Ilagan *139 E1* Luzon, N Philippines
Ilave *61 E4* Puno, S Peru
Iława *98 D3 Ger.* Deutsch-Eylau. Warmińsko-Mazurskie, NE Poland
Ilebo *77 C6 prev.* Port-Francqui. Kasai Occidental, W Dem. Rep. Congo
Île-de-France *90 C3 cultural region* N France
Îles de la Société *see* Société, Archipel de la
Îles Tubuai *see* Australes, Îles
Ilfracombe *89 C7* SW England, UK
Ilha Caviana *see* Caviana de Fora, Ilha
Ilha de Madeira *see* Madeira
Ilha do Corvo *see* Corvo
Ilha do Faial *see* Faial
Ilha do Pico *see* Pico
Ilha do Porto Santo *see* Porto Santo
Ilha Graciosa *see* Graciosa
Ilhas dos Açores *see* Azores
Ilha Terceira *see* Terceira
Ílhavo *92 B2* Aveiro, N Portugal
Ili *112 C3 Kaz.* Ile, *Rus.* Reka Ili. *River* China/Kazakhstan
Iliamna Lake *36 C3 lake* Alaska, USA
Ilici *see* Elche
Iligan *139 E2 off.* Iligan City. Mindanao, S Philippines
Illapel *64 B4* Coquimbo, C Chile
Illichivs'k *109 E4 Rus.* Il'ichevsk. Odes'ka Oblast', SW Ukraine
Illicis *see* Elche
Illinois *40 A4 off.* State of Illinois; also known as Prairie State, Sucker State. *State* C USA
Illinois River *40 B4 river* Illinois, N USA
Ilo *61 E4* Moquegua, SW Peru
Iloilo *139 E2 off.* Iloilo City. Panay Island, C Philippines
Ilorin *75 F4* Kwara, W Nigeria
Îlots de Bass *see* Marotiri
Ilovlya *111 B6* Volgogradskaya Oblast', SW Russian Federation
İluh *see* Batman
Il'yaly *see* Ýylanly
Imatra *85 E5* Etelä-Suomi, S Finland
Imbros *see* Gökçeada
İmişli *117 H3 Rus.* Imishli. C Azerbaijan
Imola *96 C3* Emilia-Romagna, N Italy
Imperatriz *63 F2* Maranhão, NE Brazil
Imperia *96 A3* Liguria, NW Italy
Impfondo *77 C5* La Likouala, NE Congo
Imphāl *135 H3* Manipur, NE India
Imroz Adası *see* Gökçeada
Inagua Islands *see* Great Inagua
Inagua Islands *see* Little Inagua
Inarijärvi *84 D2 Lapp.* Aanaarjävri, *Swe.* Enareträsk. *Lake* N Finland
Inawashiro-ko *131 D5 var.* Inawasiro Ko. *Lake* Honshu, C Japan
Inawasiro Ko *see* Inawashiro-ko
İncesu *116 D3* Kayseri, C Turkey
Inch'ŏn *129 E4 off.* Inch'ŏn-gwangyŏksi, *Jap.* Jinsen; *prev.* Chemulpo. NW South Korea
Incudine, Monte *91 E7 mountain* Corse, France, C Mediterranean Sea
Indefatigable Island *see* Santa Cruz, Isla
Independence *45 F4* Missouri, C USA
Independence Fjord *83 E1 fjord* N Greenland
Independence Mountains *46 C4 mountain range* Nevada, W USA
India *124 B3 var.* Indian Union, Union of India, *Hind.* Bhārat. *Country* S Asia

India 124

Official name Republic of India
Formation 1947
Capital New Delhi
Population 1.07 billion / 928 people per sq mile (358 people per sq km)
Total area 1,269,338 sq. miles (3,287,590 sq. km)
Languages Hindi, English, and 16 regional languages

India (continued)

Religions Hindu 83%, Muslim 11%, Christian 2%, Sikh 2%, Buddhist 1%, other 1%
Ethnic mix Indo-Aryan 72%, Dravidian 25%, Mongoloid and other 3%
Government Parliamentary system
Currency Indian rupee = 100 paise
Literacy rate 61%
Calorie consumption 2487 calories

Indiana *40 B4 off.* State of Indiana; also known as The Hoosier State. *State* N USA
Indianapolis *40 C4 state capital* Indiana, N USA
Indian Church *52 C1* Orange Walk, N Belize
Indian Desert *see* Thar Desert
Indianola *45 F4* Iowa, C USA
Indigirka *115 F2 river* NE Russian Federation
Inđija *100 D3 Hung.* India; *prev.* Indjija. Serbia, N Serbia and Montenegro (Yugo.)
Indira Point *132 G3 headland* Andaman and Nicobar Islands, India, NE Indian Ocean
Indomed Fracture Zone *141 B6 tectonic feature* SW Indian Ocean
Indonesia *138 B4 Ind.* Republik Indonesia; *prev.* Dutch East Indies, Netherlands East Indies, United States of Indonesia. *Country* SE Asia

Indonesia 138

Official name Republic of Indonesia
Formation 1949
Capital Jakarta
Population 220 million / 317 people per sq mile (122 people per sq km)
Total area 741,096 sq. miles (1,919,440 sq. km)
Languages Javanese, Sundanese, Madurese, Bahasa Indonesia, Dutch
Religions Sunni Muslim 87%, Protestant 6%, Roman Catholic 3%, Hindu 2%, Buddhist 1%, other 1%
Ethnic mix Javanese 45%, other 25%, Sundanese 14%, Coastal Malays 8%, Madurese 8%
Government Presidential system
Currency Rupiah = 100 sen
Literacy rate 88%
Calorie consumption 2904 calories

Indore *134 D4* Madhya Pradesh, C India
Indus *134 C2 Chin.* Yindu He; *prev.* Yin-tu Ho. *River* S Asia
Indus Cone *see* Indus Fan
Indus Fan *112 C5 var.* Indus Cone. *Undersea feature* N Arabian Sea
Indus, Mouths of the *134 B4 delta* S Pakistan
İnebolu *116 C2* Kastamonu, N Turkey
Ineu *108 A4 Hung.* Borosjenő; *prev.* Inău. Arad, W Romania
Infiernillo, Presa del *51 E4 reservoir* S Mexico
Inglewood *46 D2* California, W USA
Ingolstadt *95 C6* Bayern, S Germany
Inhambane *79 E4* Inhambane, SE Mozambique
Inhulets' *109 F3 Rus.* Ingulets. Dnipropetrovs'ka Oblast', E Ukraine
I-ning *see* Yining
Inis *see* Ennis
Inis Ceithleann *see* Enniskillen
Inn *95 C6 river* C Europe
Innaanganeq *82 C1 var.* Kap York. *Headland* NW Greenland
Inner Hebrides *88 B4 island group* W Scotland, UK
Inner Islands *79 H1 var.* Central Group. *Island group* NE Seychelles
Inner Mongolia *127 F3 var.* Nei Mongol, *Eng.* Inner Mongolia, Inner Mongolian Autonomous Region; *prev.* Nei Monggol Zizhiqu. Admin. region *autonomous region* N China
Inner Mongolian Autonomous Region *see* Inner Mongolia
Innisfail *148 D3* Queensland, NE Australia
Inniskilling *see* Enniskillen
Innsbruch *see* Innsbruck
Innsbruck *95 C7 var.* Innsbruch. Tirol, W Austria
Inoucdjouac *see* Inukjuak
Inowrocław *98 C3 Ger.* Hohensalza; *prev.* Inowrazlaw. Kujawski-pomorskie, C Poland
I-n-Salah *70 D3 var.* In Salah. C Algeria
In Salah *see* I-n-Salah
Insula *see* Lille
Inta *110 E3* Respublika Komi, NW Russian Federation
International Falls *45 F1* Minnesota, N USA
Inukjuak *38 D2 var.* Inoucdjouac; *prev.* Port Harrison. Québec, NE Canada
Inuuvik *see* Inuvik
Inuvik *36 D3 var.* Inuuvik. *District capital* Northwest Territories, NW Canada
Invercargill *151 A7* Southland, South Island, NZ
Inverness *88 C3* N Scotland, UK
Investigator Ridge *141 D5 undersea feature* E Indian Ocean
Investigator Strait *149 B7 strait* South Australia
Inyangani *78 D3 mountain* NE Zimbabwe
Ioánnina *104 A4 var.* Janina, Yannina. Ípeiros, W Greece
Iola *45 F5* Kansas, C USA
Ionia Basin *see* Ionian Basin
Ionian Basin *80 D5 var.* Ionia Basin. *Undersea feature* Ionian Sea, C Mediterranean Sea
Ionian Islands *see* Iónioi Nísoi
Ionian Sea *103 E3 Gk.* Iónio Pélagos, *It.* Mar Ionio. *Sea* C Mediterranean Sea
Iónioi Nísoi *105 A5 Eng.* Ionian Islands. *Island group* W Greece
Íos *105 D6 var.* Nio. *Island* Kykládes, Greece, Aegean Sea
Íos *105 D6* Íos, Kykládes, Greece, Aegean Sea
Iowa *45 F3 off.* State of Iowa; also known as The Hawkeye State. *State* C USA
Iowa City *45 G3* Iowa, C USA
Iowa Falls *45 G3* Iowa, C USA
Ipel' *99 C6 var.* Ipoly, *Ger.* Eipel. *River* Hungary/Slovakia
Ipiales *58 A4* Nariño, SW Colombia
Ipoh *138 B3* Perak, Peninsular Malaysia
Ipoly *99 C6 var.* Ipel', *Ger.* Eipel. *River* Hungary/Slovakia
Ippy *76 C4* Ouaka, C Central African Republic
Ipswich *89 E6 hist.* Gipeswic. E England, UK
Ipswich *149 E5* Queensland, E Australia
Iqaluit *37 H3 prev.* Frobisher Bay. Baffin Island, Nunavut, NE Canada
Iquique *64 B1* Tarapacá, N Chile
Iquitos *60 C1* Loreto, N Peru
Irákleio *105 D7 var.* Herakleion, *Eng.* Candia; *prev.* Iráklion. Kríti, Greece, E Mediterranean Sea
Iráklion *see* Irákleio
Iran *120 C3 prev.* Persia. *Country* SW Asia

Iran 120

Official name Islamic Republic of Iran
Formation 1502
Capital Tehran
Population 68.9 million / 109 people per sq mile (42 people per sq km)
Total area 636,293 sq. miles (1,648,000 sq. km)
Languages Farsi, Azeri, Luri, Gilaki, Mazanderani, Kurdish, Turkmen, Arabic, Baluchi
Religions Shi'a Muslim 93%, Sunni Muslim 6%, other 1%
Ethnic mix Persian 50%, Azari 24%, other 10%, Kurdish 8%, Lur and Bakhtiari 8%
Government Islamic theocracy
Currency Iranian rial = 100 dinars
Literacy rate 77%
Calorie consumption 2931 calories

Iranian Plateau *120 D3 var.* Plateau of Iran. *plateau* N Iran
Iran, Plateau of *see* Iranian Plateau
Irapuato *51 E4* Guanajuato, C Mexico
Iraq *120 B3 Ar.* 'Irāq. *Country* SW Asia

Iraq 120

Official name Republic of Iraq
Formation 1932
Capital Baghdad
Population 25.2 million / 149 people per sq mile (58 people per sq km)
Total area 168,753 sq. miles (437,072 sq. km)
Languages Arabic, Kurdish, Turkic languages, Armenian, Assyrian
Religions Shi'a Muslim 62%, Sunni Muslim 33%, Other (including Christian) 5%
Ethnic mix Arab 79%, Kurdish 16%, Persian 3%, Turkmen 2%
Government Transitional regime
Currency New Iraqi dinar = 1000 fils
Literacy rate 40%
Calorie consumption 2197 calories

Irbid *119 B5* Irbid, N Jordan
Irbīl *see* Arbīl
Ireland *80 C3 Lat.* Hibernia. *Island* Ireland/UK
Ireland *89 A5 var.* Republic of Ireland, *Ir.* Éire. *Country* NW Europe

Ireland 89

Official name Ireland
Formation 1922
Capital Dublin
Population 4 million / 150 people per sq mile (58 people per sq km)
Total area 27,135 sq. miles (70,280 sq. km)
Languages English, Irish Gaelic
Religions Roman Catholic 88%, Other and nonreligious 9%, Anglican 3%
Ethnic mix Irish 93%, other 4%, British 3%
Government Parliamentary system
Currency Euro = 100 cents
Literacy rate 99%
Calorie consumption 3666 calories

Irian Barat *see* Papua
Irian Jaya *see* Papua
Irian, Teluk *see* Cenderawasih, Teluk
Iringa *73 C7* Iringa, C Tanzania
Iriomote-jima *130 A4 island* Sakishima-shotō, SW Japan
Iriona *52 D2* Colón, NE Honduras
Irish Sea *89 C5 Ir.* Muir Éireann. *Sea* C British Isles
Irkutsk *115 E4* Irkutskaya Oblast', S Russian Federation
Irminger Basin *see* Reykjanes Basin
Iroise *90 A3 sea* NW France
Iron Mountain *40 B2* Michigan, N USA
Ironwood *40 B1* Michigan, N USA
Irrawaddy *136 B2 var.* Ayeyarwady. *River* W Myanmar
Irrawaddy, Mouths of the *137 A5 delta* SW Myanmar
Irtish *see* Irtysh
Irtysh *114 C4 var.* Irtish, *Kaz.* Ertis. *River* C Asia
Irún *93 E1* País Vasco, N Spain
Iruña *see* Pamplona
Isabela, Isla *60 A5 var.* Albemarle Island. *Island* Galapagos Islands, Ecuador, E Pacific Ocean
Isaccea *108 D4* Tulcea, E Romania
Isachsen *37 F1* Ellef Ringnes Island, Nunavut, N Canada
Ísafjördhur *83 E4* Vestfirdhir, NW Iceland
Isbarta *see* Isparta
Ise *131 C6* Mie, Honshū, SW Japan
Isère *91 D5 river* E France
Isernia *97 D5 var.* Æsernia. Molise, C Italy
Ise-wan *131 C6 bay* S Japan
Isha Baydhabo *see* Baydhabo
Ishigaki-jima *130 A4 var.* Isigaki Zima. *Island* Sakishima-shotō, SW Japan
Ishikari-wan *130 C2 bay* Hokkaidō, NE Japan
Ishim *114 C4 Kaz.* Esil. *River* Kazakhstan/Russian Federation
Ishim *114 C4* Tyumenskaya Oblast', C Russian Federation
Ishinomaki *130 D4 var.* Isinomaki. Miyagi, Honshū, C Japan
Ishkoshim *123 F3 Rus.* Ishkashim. S Tajikistan
Isigaki Zima *see* Ishigaki-jima
Isinomaki *see* Ishinomaki
Isiro *77 E5* Orientale, NE Dem. Rep. Congo
Iskăr *see* Iskŭr
İskenderun *116 D4 Eng.* Alexandretta. Hatay, S Turkey
İskenderun Körfezi *118 A2 Eng.* Gulf of Alexandretta. *Gulf* S Turkey
Iskŭr *104 C2 var.* Iskăr. *River* NW Bulgaria
Iskŭr, Yazovir *104 B2 prev.* Yazovir Stalin. *Reservoir* W Bulgaria
Isla Cristina *92 C4* Andalucía, S Spain
Isla Gran Malvina *see* West Falkalnd
Islāmābād *134 C1 country capital* (Pakistan) Federal Capital Territory Islāmābād, NE Pakistan
I-n-Sâkâne, 'Erg *75 E2 desert* N Mali
Islas de los Galápagos *see* Galapagos Islands
Islas Malvinas *see* Falkland Islands
Islay *88 B4 island* SW Scotland, UK
Isle *91 B5 river* W France
Isle of Man *89 B5 UK crown dependency* NW Europe
Ismailia *see* Ismâ'ilîya
Ismâ'ilîya *72 B1 var.* Ismailia. N Egypt
Ismid *see* İzmit
Isna *72 B2 var.* Esna. SE Egypt
Isoka *78 D1* Northern, NE Zambia
Isola Grossa *see* Dugi Otok
Isola Lunga *see* Dugi Otok
Isole Lipari *see* Eolie, Isole
Isparta *116 B4 var.* Isbarta. Isparta, SW Turkey
İspir *117 E3* Erzurum, NE Turkey
Israel *119 A7 var.* Medinat Israel, *Heb.* Yisrael, Yisra'el. *Country* SW Asia

Israel 119

Official name State of Israel
Formation 1948
Capital Jerusalem

Israel (continued)

Population 6.4 million / 815 people per sq mile (315 people per sq km)
Total area 8019 sq. miles (20,770 sq. km)
Languages Hebrew, Arabic, Yiddish, German, Russian, Polish, Romanian, Persian
Religions Jewish 80%, Muslim (mainly Sunni) 16%, Druze and other 2%, Christian 2%
Ethnic mix Jewish 80%, Other (mostly Arab) 20%
Government Parliamentary system
Currency Shekel = 100 agorot
Literacy rate 95%
Calorie consumption 3512 calories

Issiq Köl *see* Issyk-Kul', Ozero
Issoire *91 C5* Puy-de-Dôme, C France
Issyk-Kul', Ozero *123 G2 var.* Issiq Köl, *Kir.* Ysyk-Köl. *Lake* E Kyrgyzstan
İstanbul *116 B2 Bul.* Tsarigrad, *Eng.* Istanbul; *prev.* Constantinople, *anc.* Byzantium. İstanbul, NW Turkey
İstanbul Boğazı *116 B2 var.* Bosporus Thracius, *Eng.* Bosphorus, Bosporus, *Turk.* Karadeniz Boğazı. *Strait* NW Turkey
Istra *100 A3 Eng.* Istria, *Ger.* Istrien. *Cultural region* NW Croatia
Istra *96 D2 Eng.* Istria. *Peninsula* NW Croatia
Itabuna *63 G3* Bahia, E Brazil
Itagüí *58 B3* Antioquia, W Colombia
Itaipú, Represa de *63 E4 reservoir* Brazil/Paraguay
Itaituba *63 E2* Pará, NE Brazil**Italy** *96 C3 It.* Italia, Republica Italiana. *Country* S Europe
Italy *96 C3 It.* Italia, Republica Italiana. *Country* S Europe

Italy 96

Official name Italian Republic
Formation 1861
Capital Rome
Population 57.4 million / 506 people per sq mile (195 people per sq km)
Total area 116,305 sq. miles (301,230 sq. km)
Languages Italian, German, French, Rhaeto-Romanic, Sardinian
Religions Roman Catholic 85%, Other and nonreligious 13%, Muslim 2%
Ethnic mix Italian 94%, other 4%, Sardinian 2%
Government Parliamentary system
Currency Euro = 100 cents
Literacy rate 99%
Calorie consumption 3680 calories

Italy *80 D4* Texas, SW USA
Iténez, Río *see* Guaporé, Rio
Ithaca *41 E3* New York, NE USA
Itoigawa *131 C5* Niigata, Honshū, C Japan
Itseqqortoormiit *see* Ittoqqortoormiit
Ittoqqortoormiit *83 E3 var.* Itseqqortoormiit, *Dan.* Scoresbysund, *Eng.* Scoresby Sound. C Greenland
Iturup, Ostrov *130 E1 island* Kuril'skiye Ostrova, SE Russian Federation
Itzehoe *94 B2* Schleswig-Holstein, N Germany
Ivalo *84 D2 Lapp.* Avveel, Avvil. Lappi, N Finland
Ivanava *107 B7 Pol.* Janów, Janów Poleski, *Rus.* Ivanovo. Brestskaya Voblasts', SW Belarus
Ivanhoe *149 C6* New South Wales, SE Australia
Ivano-Frankivs'k *108 C2 Ger.* Stanislau, *Pol.* Stanisławów, *Rus.* Ivano-Frankovsk; *prev.* Stanislav. Ivano-Frankivs'ka Oblast', W Ukraine
Ivanovo *111 B5* Ivanovskaya Oblast', W Russian Federation
Ivatsevichy *107 B6 Pol.* Iwacewicze, *Rus.* Ivantsevichi, Ivatsevichi. Brestskaya Voblasts', SW Belarus
Ivigtut *see* Ivittuut
Ivittuut *82 B4 var.* Ivigtut. S Greenland
Iviza *see* Eivissa
Ivory Coast *see* Côte d'Ivoire
Ivujivik *38 D1* Québec, NE Canada
Iwaki *131 D5* Fukushima, Honshū, N Japan
Iwakuni *131 B7* Yamaguchi, Honshū, SW Japan
Iwanai *130 C2* Hokkaidō, NE Japan
Iwate *130 D3* Iwate, Honshū, N Japan
Ixtapa *51 E5* Guerrero, S Mexico
Ixtepec *51 F5* Oaxaca, SE Mexico
Iyo-nada *131 B7 sea* S Japan
Izabal, Lago de *52 B2 prev.* Golfo Dulce. *Lake* E Guatemala
Īzad Khvāst *120 D3* Fārs, C Iran
Izegem *87 A6 prev.* Iseghem. West-Vlaanderen, W Belgium
Izhevsk *111 D5 prev.* Ustinov. Udmurtskaya Respublika, NW Russian Federation
Izmayil *108 D4 Rus.* Izmail. Odes'ka Oblast', SW Ukraine
İzmir *116 A3 prev.* Smyrna. İzmir, W Turkey
İzmit *116 B2 var.* Ismid; *anc.* Astacus. Kocaeli, NW Turkey
İznik Gölü *116 B3 lake* NW Turkey
Izu-hantō *131 D6 peninsula* Honshū, S Japan
Izu Shichito *see* Izu-shotō
Izu-shotō *131 D6 var.* Izu Shichito. *Island group* S Japan
Izvor *104 B2* Pernik, W Bulgaria
Izyaslav *108 C2* Khmel'nyts'ka Oblast', W Ukraine
Izyum *109 G2* Kharkivs'ka Oblast', E Ukraine

J

Jabal ash Shifā *120 A4 desert* NW Saudi Arabia
Jabalpur *135 E4 prev.* Jubbulpore. Madhya Pradesh, C India
Jabbūl, Sabkhat al 134 B2 salt flat NW Syria
Jablah *118 A3 var.* Jeble, *Fr.* Djéblé. Al Lādhiqīyah, W Syria
Jaca *93 F1* Aragón, NE Spain
Jacaltenango *52 A2* Huehuetenango, W Guatemala
Jackson *42 B2 state capital* Mississippi, S USA
Jackson *45 H5* Missouri, C USA
Jackson *42 C1* Tennessee, S USA
Jackson Head *151 A6 headland* South Island, NZ
Jacksonville *43 E3* Florida, SE USA
Jacksonville *40 B4* Illinois, N USA
Jacksonville *43 F1* North Carolina, SE USA
Jacksonville *49 G3* Texas, SW USA
Jacmel *54 D3 var.* Jaquemel. S Haiti
Jacobābād *134 B3* Sind, SE Pakistan
Jaén *92 D4* Andalucía, SW Spain
Jaén *60 B2* Cajamarca, N Peru
Jaffna *132 D3* Northern Province, N Sri Lanka
Jagannath *see* Puri
Jagdalpur *135 E5* Madhya Pradesh, C India
Jagdaqi *127 G1* Nei Mongol Zizhiqu, N China
Jagodina *100 D4 prev.* Svetozarevo. Serbia, C Serbia and Montenegro (Yugo.)
Jahra *see* Al Jahrā'
Jaipur *134 D3 prev.* Jeypore. Rājasthān, N India
Jaisalmer *134 C3* Rājasthān, NW India
Jajce *100 B3* Federacija Bosna I Hercegovina, W Bosnia and Herzegovina
Jakarta *138 C5 prev.* Djakarta, *Dut.* Batavia. *Country capital* (Indonesia) Jawa, C Indonesia
Jakobstad *84 D4 Fin.* Pietarsaari. Länsi-Suomi, W Finland
Jalālābād *123 F4 var.* Jalalabad, Jelalabad. Nangarhār, E Afghanistan
Jalandhar *134 D2 prev.* Jullundur. Punjab, N India
Jalapa *see* Xalapa
Jalapa *52 D3* Nueva Segovia, NW Nicaragua
Jalapa Enríquez *see* Xalapa
Jalpa *50 D4* Zacatecas, C Mexico
Jālū *71 G3 var.* Jūlā. NE Libya
Jaluit Atoll *144 D2 var.* Jālwōj. *Atoll* Ralik Chain, S Marshall Islands
Jālwōj *see* Jaluit Atoll
Jamaame *73 D6 It.* Giamame; *prev.* Margherita. Jubbada Hoose, S Somalia
Jamaica *54 A4 country* W West Indies

Jamaica 54

Official name Jamaica
Formation 1962
Capital Kingston
Population 2.7 million / 646 people per sq mile (249 people per sq km)
Total area 4243 sq. miles (10,990 sq. km)
Languages English Creole, English
Religions Other Protestant 20%, Church of God 18%, Baptist 10%, Other and nonreligious 45%, Anglican 7%
Ethnic mix Black African 75%, Mulatto (mixed race) 13%, European and Chinese 11%, East Indian 1%
Government Parliamentary system
Currency Jamaican dollar = 100 cents
Literacy rate 88%
Calorie consumption 2705 calories

Jamaica *56 A1 island* W West Indies
Jamaica Channel *54 D3 channel* Haiti/Jamaica
Jamālpur *135 F3* Bihār, NE India
Jambi *138 B4 var.* Telanaipura; *prev.* Djambi. Sumatera, W Indonesia
James Bay *38 C3 bay* Ontario/Québec, E Canada
James River *45 E2 river* North Dakota/South Dakota, N USA
James River *41 E5 river* Virginia, NE USA
Jamestown *41 E3* New York, NE USA
Jamestown *45 E2* North Dakota, N USA
Jammu *134 D2 prev.* Jummoo. Jammu and Kashmir, NW India
Jammu and Kashmīr *134 D1 disputed region* India/Pakistan
Jāmnagar *134 C4 prev.* Navanagar. Gujarāt, W India
Jamshedpur *135 F4* Bihār, NE India
Jamuna *see* Brahmaputra
Janaúba *63 F3* Minas Gerais, SE Brazil
Janesville *40 B3* Wisconsin, N USA
Janīn *see* Jenīn
Janina *see* Ioánnina
Jan Mayen *83 F4 Norwegian dependency* N Atlantic Ocean
Jánoshalma *99 C7 SCr.* Jankovac. Bács-Kiskun, S Hungary
Japan *130 C4 var.* Nippon, *Jap.* Nihon. *Country* E Asia

Japan 130

Official name Japan
Formation 1590
Capital Tokyo
Population 128 million / 878 people per sq mile (339 people per sq km)

Japan (continued)

Total area 145,882 sq. miles (377,835 sq. km)
Languages Japanese, Korean, Chinese
Religions Shinto and Buddhist 76%, Buddhist 16%, Other (including Christian) 8%
Ethnic mix Japanese 99%, Other (mainly Korean) 1%
Government Parliamentary system
Currency Yen = 100 sen
Literacy rate 99%
Calorie consumption 2746 calories

Japan, Sea of *130 A4 var.* East Sea, *Rus.* Yapanskoye More. *Sea* NW Pacific Ocean *see also* East Sea
Japan Trench *125 F1 undersea feature* NW Pacific Ocean
Japiim *62 C2 var.* Máncio Lima. Acre, W Brazil
Japurá, Rio *62 C2 var.* Río Caquetá, Yapurá. *River* Brazil/Colombia *see also* Caquetá, Río
Jaqué *53 G5* Darién, SE Panama
Jaquemel *see* Jacmel
Jarablos *see* Jarābulus
Jarābulus *118 C2 var.* Jarablos, Jerablus, *Fr.* Djérablous. Ḥalab, N Syria
Jardines de la Reina, Archipiélago de los *54 B2 island group* C Cuba
Jarocin *98 C4* Wielkopolskie, C Poland
Jarosław *99 E5 Ger.* Jaroslau, *Rus.* Yaroslav. Podkarpackie, SE Poland
Jarqo'rg'on *123 E3 var.* Jarqŭrghon, *Rus.* Dzharkurgan. Surkhondaryo Wiloyati, S Uzbekistan
Jarqŭrghon *see* Jarqo'rg'on
Jarvis Island *145 G2 US unincorporated territory* C Pacific Ocean
Jasło *99 D5* Podkarpackie, SE Poland
Jastrzębie-Zdrój *99 C5* Śląskie, S Poland
Jataí *63 E3* Goiás, C Brazil
Jativa *see* Xátiva
Jauf *see* Al Jawf
Jaunpiebalga *106 D3* Gulbene, NE Latvia
Jaunpur *135 E3* Uttar Pradesh, N India
Java *152 A3 prev.* Djawa. *Island* C Indonesia
Javalambre *93 E3 mountain* E Spain
Javari, Rio *62 C2 var.* Yavarí. *River* Brazil/Peru
Java Sea *138 D4 Ind.* Laut Jawa. *Sea* W Indonesia
Java Trench *124 D5 var.* Sunda Trench. *Undersea feature* E Indian Ocean
Jawhar *73 D6 var.* Jowhar, *It.* Giohar. Shabeellaha Dhexe, S Somalia
Jaya, Puncak *139 G4 prev.* Puntjak Carstensz, Puntjak Sukarno. *Mountain* Papua, E Indonesia
Jayapura *139 H4 var.* Djajapura, *Dut.* Hollandia; *prev.* Kotabaru, Sukarnapura. Papua, E Indonesia
Jazā'ir Bin Ghalfān *see* Ḥalāniyāt, Juzur al
Jazīrat Jarbah *see* Jerba, Île de
Jazīreh-ye Qeshm *see* Qeshm
Jaz Mūrīān, Hāmūn-e *120 E4 lake* SE Iran
Jebba *75 F4* Kwara, W Nigeria
Jebel esh Sharqi *see* Anti-Lebanon
Jebel Uweinat *see* 'Uwaynāt, Jabal al
Jeble *see* Jablah
Jedda *see* Jiddah
Jędrzejów *98 D4 Ger.* Endersdorf. Świętokrzyskie, C Poland
Jefferson City *45 G5 state capital* Missouri, C USA

Jega *75 F4* Kebbi, NW Nigeria
Jehol *see* Chengde
Jēkabpils *106 D4 Ger.* Jakobstadt. Jēkabpils, S Latvia
Jelalabad *see* Jalālābād
Jelenia Góra *98 B4 Ger.* Hirschberg, Hirschberg im Riesengebirge, Hirschberg in Riesengebirge, Hirschberg in Schlesien. Dolnośląskie, SW Poland
Jelgava *106 C3 Ger.* Mitau. Jelgava, C Latvia
Jemappes *87 B6* Hainaut, S Belgium
Jember *138 D5 prev.* Djember. Jawa, C Indonesia
Jena *94 C4* Thüringen, C Germany
Jenīn *119 A6 var.* Janīn, Jinīn; *anc.* Engannim. N West Bank
Jerablus *see* Jarābulus
Jerada *70 D2* NE Morocco
Jerba, Île de *71 F2 var.* Djerba, Jazīrat Jarbah. *Island* E Tunisia
Jérémie *54 D3* SW Haiti
Jerez *see* Jeréz de la Frontera
Jeréz de la Frontera *92 C5 var.* Jerez; *prev.* Xeres. Andalucía, SW Spain
Jeréz de los Caballeros *92 C4* Extremadura, W Spain
Jericho *119 B6 Ar.* Arīḩā, *Heb.* Yeriḥo. E West Bank
Jerid, Chott el 87 E2 var. Shaṭṭ al Jarīd. *Salt lake* SW Tunisia
Jersey *89 D8 UK dependent territory* NW Europe
Jerusalem *103 H4 Ar.* El Quds, *Heb.* Yerushalayim; *anc.* Hierosolyma. *Country capital* (Israel) Jerusalem, NE Israel
Jerusalem *112 A4* Admin. region *district* E Israel
Jesenice *95 D7 Ger.* Assling. NW Slovenia
Jessore *135 G4* Khulna, W Bangladesh
Jesús María *64 C3* Córdoba, C Argentina
Jhānsi *134 D3* Uttar Pradesh, N India
Jhārkand *135 F4* Admin. region *state* N India
Jhelum *134 C2* Punjab, NE Pakistan
Ji *see* Hebei
Ji *see* Jilin
Jiangmen *128 C6* Guangdong, S China
Jiangsu *128 D4 var.* Chiang-su, Jiangsu Sheng, Kiangsu, Su. Admin. region *province* E China
Jiangsu Sheng *see* Jiangsu
Jiangxi *128 C6 var.* Chiang-hsi, Gan, Jiangxi Sheng, Kiangsi. Admin. region *province* S China
Jiangxi Sheng *see* Jiangxi
Jiaxing *128 D5* Zhejiang, SE China
Jiayi *see* Chiai
Jibuti *see* Djibouti
Jiddah *121 A5 Eng.* Jedda. *Country capital* (Saudi Arabia) Makkah, W Saudi Arabia
Jih-k'a-tse *see* Xigazê
Jihlava *99 B5 Ger.* Iglau, *Pol.* Igława. Jihlavský Kraj, C Czech Republic
Jilib *73 D6 It.* Gelib. Jubbada Dhexe, S Somalia
Jilin *128 D3 var.* Chi-lin, Girin, Ji, Jilin Sheng, Kirin. Admin. region *province* NE China
Jilin *129 E3 var.* Chi-lin, Girin, Kirin; *prev.* Yungki, Yunki. Jilin, NE China
Jilin Sheng *see* Jilin
Jīma *73 C5 var.* Jimma, *It.* Gimma. C Ethiopia
Jimbolia *108 A4 Ger.* Hatzfeld, *Hung.* Zsombolya. Timiș, W Romania
Jiménez *50 D2* Chihuahua, N Mexico
Jimma *see* Jīma
Jimsar *126 C3* Xinjiang Uygur Zizhiqu, NW China
Jin *see* Shanxi
Jin *see* Tianjin Shi
Jinan *128 C4 var.* Chinan, Chi-nan, Tsinan. Shandong, E China
Jingdezhen *128 C5* Jiangxi, S China
Jinghong *128 A6 var.* Yunjinghong. Yunnan, SW China
Jinhua *128 D5* Zhejiang, SE China
Jinīn *see* Jenīn
Jining *127 F3* Shandong, E China
Jinja *73 C6* S Uganda
Jinotega *52 D3* Jinotega, NW Nicaragua
Jinotepe *52 D3* Carazo, SW Nicaragua
Jinsha Jiang *128 A5 river* SW China
Jinzhong *128 C4 var.* Yuci. Shanxi, C China
Jinzhou *128 D3 var.* Chin-chou, Chinchow; *prev.* Chinhsien. Liaoning, NE China
Jisr ash Shadadi *see* Ash Shadādah
Jiu *108 B5 Ger.* Schil, Schyl, *Hung.* Zsil, Zsily. *River* S Romania
Jiujiang *128 C5* Jiangxi, S China
Jixi *129 E2* Heilongjiang, NE China
Jīzān *121 B6 var.* Qīzān. Jīzān, SW Saudi Arabia
Jizzakh *123 E2 Rus.* Dzhizak. Jizzakh Wiloyati, C Uzbekistan
Jizzax *see* Jizzax
João Pessoa *63 G2 prev.* Paraíba. *State capital* Paraíba, E Brazil
Jo'burg *see* Johannesburg
Jo-ch'iang *see* Ruoqiang
Jodhpur *134 C3* Rājasthān, NW India
Joensuu *85 E5* Itä-Suomi, E Finland
Jōetsu *131 C5 var.* Zyôetu. Niigata, Honshū, C Japan
Johanna Island *see* Anjouan
Johannesburg *78 D4 var.* Egoli, Erautini, Gauteng, *abbrev.* Jo'burg. Gauteng, NE South Africa
John Day River *46 C3 river* Oregon, NW USA
John o'Groats *88 C2* N Scotland, UK
Johnston Atoll *143 E1 US unincorporated territory* C Pacific Ocean
Johor Baharu *see* Johor Bahru
Johor Bahru *138 B3 var.* Johor Baharu, Johore Bahru. Johor, Peninsular Malaysia
Johore Bahru *see* Johor Bahru
Johore Strait *138 A1 Mal.* Selat Johor. *Strait* Malaysia/Singapore
Joinvile *see* Joinville
Joinville *63 E4 var.* Joinvile. Santa Catarina, S Brazil
Jokkmokk *84 C3* Norrbotten, N Sweden
Joliet *40 B3* Illinois, N USA
Jonava *106 B4 Ger.* Janow, *Pol.* Janów. Jonava, C Lithuania
Jonesboro *42 B1* Arkansas, C USA
Joniškis *106 C3 Ger.* Janischken. Joniškis, N Lithuania
Jönköping *85 B7* Jönköping, S Sweden
Jonquière *39 E4* Québec, SE Canada
Joplin *45 F5* Missouri, C USA
Jordan *119 B5 Ar.* Urdunn, *Heb.* HaYarden. *River* SW Asia
Jordan *119 B6 Ar.* Al Mamlakah al Urdunīyah al Hāshimīyah, Al Urdunn; *prev.* Transjordan. *Country* SW Asia

Jordan 119

Official name Hashemite Kingdom of Jordan
Formation 1946
Capital Amman
Population 5.5 million / 160 people per sq mile (62 people per sq km)
Total area 35,637 sq. miles (92,300 sq. km)
Languages Arabic
Religions Muslim (mainly Sunni) 92%, Other (mostly Christian) 8%
Ethnic mix Arab 98%, Armenian 1%, Circassian 1%

Jordan (continued)

Government Monarchy
Currency Jordanian dinar = 1000 fils
Literacy rate 91%
Calorie consumption 2769 calories

Jorhāt *135 H3* Assam, NE India
Jos *75 G4* Plateau, C Nigeria
Joseph Bonaparte Gulf *146 D2 gulf* N Australia
Jos Plateau *75 G4 plateau* C Nigeria
Jotunheimen *85 A5 mountain range* S Norway
Joûnié *118 A4 var.* Junīyah. W Lebanon
Joure *86 D2 Fris.* De Jouwer. Friesland, N Netherlands
Joutseno *85 E5* Etelä-Suomi, S Finland
Jowhar *see* Jawhar
JStorm Thurmond Reservoir *see* Clark Hill Lake
Juan Aldama *50 D3* Zacatecas, C Mexico
Juan de Fuca, Strait of *46 A1 strait* Canada/USA
Juan Fernández, Islas *57 A6 Eng.* Juan Fernandez Islands. *Island group* W Chile
Juazeiro *63 G2 prev.* Joazeiro. Bahia, E Brazil
Juazeiro do Norte *63 G2* Ceará, E Brazil
Juba *73 D6 Amh.* Genalē Wenz, *It.* Guiba, *Som.* Ganaane, Webi Jubba. *River* Ethiopia/Somalia
Juba *73 B5 var.* Jūbā. Bahr el Gabel, S Sudan
Júcar *93 E3 var.* Jucar. *River* C Spain
Juchitán *51 F5 var.* Juchitán de Zaragosa. Oaxaca, SE Mexico
Juchitán de Zaragosa *see* Juchitán
Judayyidat Hāmir *120 B3* S Iraq
Judenburg *95 D7* Steiermark, C Austria
Juigalpa *52 D3* Chontales, S Nicaragua
Juiz de Fora *63 F4* Minas Gerais, SE Brazil
Jujuy *see* San Salvador de Jujuy
Jūlā *see* Jālū
Juliaca *61 E4* Puno, SE Peru
Juliana Top *59 G3 mountain* C Suriname
Jumilla *93 E4* Murcia, SE Spain
Jumporn *see* Chumphon
Junction City *45 F4* Kansas, C USA
Juneau *36 D4 state capital* Alaska, USA
Junín *64 C4* Buenos Aires, E Argentina
Junīyah *see* Joûnié
Junkseylon *see* Phuket
Jur *73 B5 river* C Sudan
Jura *88 B4 island* SW Scotland, UK
Jura *95 A7 canton* NW Switzerland
Jura *90 D4 department* E France
Jurbarkas *106 B4 Ger.* Georgenburg, Jurburg. Jurbarkas, W Lithuania
Jūrmala *106 C3* Rīga, C Latvia
Juruá, Rio *62 C2 var.* Río Yuruá. *River* Brazil/Peru
Juruena, Rio *62 D3 river* W Brazil
Jutiapa *52 B2* Jutiapa, S Guatemala
Juticalpa *52 D2* Olancho, C Honduras
Juventud, Isla de la *54 A2 var.* Isla de Pinos, *Eng.* Isle of Youth; *prev.* The Isle of the Pines. *Island* W Cuba
Južna Morava *101 E5 Ger.* Südliche Morava. *River* SE Serbia and Montenegro (Yugo.)
Juzur Qarqannah *see* Kerkenah, Îles de
Jwaneng *78 C4* Southern, SE Botswana
Jylland *85 A7 Eng.* Jutland. *Peninsula* W Denmark
Jyväskylä *85 D5* Länsi-Suomi, W Finland

K

K2 *126 A4 Chin.* Qogir Feng, *Eng.* Mount Godwin Austen. *Mountain* China/Pakistan
Kaafu Atoll *see* Male' Atoll
Kaaimanston *59 G3* Sipaliwini, N Suriname
Kaakhka *see* Kaka
Kaala *see* Caála
Kaamanen *84 D2 Lapp.* Gámas. Lappi, N Finland
Kaapstad *see* Cape Town
Kaaresuvanto *84 C3 Lapp.* Gárassavon. Lappi, N Finland
Kabale *73 B6* SW Uganda
Kabinda *see* Cabinda
Kabinda *77 D7* Kasai Oriental, SE Dem. Rep. Congo
Kābol *see* Kābul
Kabompo *78 C2 river* W Zambia
Kābul *123 E4 var.* Kabul, *Per.* Kābol. *Country capital* (Afghanistan) Kābul, E Afghanistan
Kabul *see* Kābul
Kabwe *78 D2* Central, C Zambia
Kachchh, Gulf of *134 B4 var.* Gulf of Cutch, Gulf of Kutch. *Gulf* W India
Kachchh, Rann of *134 B4 var.* Rann of Kachh, Rann of Kutch. *Salt marsh* India/Pakistan
Kachh, Rann of *see* Kachchh, Rann of
Kadan Kyun *137 B5 prev.* King Island. *Island* Mergui Archipelago, S Myanmar
Kadavu *145 E4 prev.* Kandavu. *Island* S Fiji
Kadoma *78 D3 prev.* Gatooma. Mashonaland West, C Zimbabwe
Kadugli *72 B4* Southern Kordofan, S Sudan
Kaduna *75 G4* Kaduna, C Nigeria
Kadzhi-Say *123 G2 Kir.* Kajisay. Issyk-Kul'skaya Oblast', NE Kyrgyzstan
Kaédi *74 C3* Gorgol, S Mauritania
Kaffa *see* Feodosiya
Kafue *78 C2 river* C Zambia
Kafue *78 D2* Lusaka, SE Zambia
Kaga Bandoro *76 C4 prev.* Fort-Crampel. Nana-Grébizi, C Central African Republic
Kâgheț *74 D1 var.* Karet. *Physical region* N Mauritania
Kagi *see* Chiai
Kagoshima *131 B8 var.* Kagosima. Kagoshima, Kyūshū, SW Japan
Kagoshima-wan *131 A8 bay* SW Japan
Kagosima *see* Kagoshima
Kahmard, Daryā-ye *123 E4 prev.* Darya-i-Surkhab. *River* NE Afghanistan
Kahraman Maraş *see* Kahramanmaraş
Kahramanmaraş *116 D4 var.* Kahraman Maraş, Maraş, Marash. Kahramanmaraş, S Turkey
Kaiapoi *151 C6* Canterbury, South Island, NZ
Kaifeng *128 C4* Henan, C China
Kai, Kepulauan *139 F4 prev.* Kei Islands. *Island group* Maluku, SE Indonesia
Kaikohe *150 C2* Northland, North Island, NZ
Kaikoura *151 C5* Canterbury, South Island, NZ
Kaikoura Peninsula *151 C5 peninsula* South Island, NZ
Kainji Lake *see* Kainji Reservoir
Kainji Reservoir *75 F4 var.* Kainji Lake. *Reservoir* W Nigeria
Kaipara Harbour *150 C2 harbour* North Island, NZ
Kairouan *71 E2 var.* Al Qayrawān. E Tunisia
Kaisaria *see* Kayseri
Kaiserslautern *95 A5* Rheinland-Pfalz, SW Germany

Kaišiadorys *107 B5* Kaišiadorys, S Lithuania
Kaitaia *150 C2* Northland, North Island, NZ
Kajaani *84 E4 Swe.* Kajana. Oulu, C Finland
Kaka *122 C2 var.* Kaakhka. Dashkhovuzskiy Velayat, N Turkmenistan
Kake *36 D4* Kupreanof Island, Alaska, USA
Kakhovka *109 F4* Khersons'ka Oblast', S Ukraine
Kakhovs'ka Vodoskhovyshche *109 F4 Rus.* Kakhovskoye Vodokhranilishche. *Reservoir* SE Ukraine
Kākināda *132 D1 prev.* Cocanada. Andhra Pradesh, E India
Kaktovik *36 D2* Alaska, USA
Kalahari Desert *78 B4 desert* Southern Africa
Kalamariá *104 B4* Kentrikí Makedonía, N Greece
Kalámata *105 B6 prev.* Kalámai. Pelopónnisos, S Greece
Kalamazoo *40 C3* Michigan, N USA
Kalambaka *see* Kalampáka
Kálamos *105 C5* Attikí, C Greece
Kalampáka *104 B4 var.* Kalambaka. Thessalía, C Greece
Kalanchak *109 F4* Khersons'ka Oblast', S Ukraine
Kalarash *see* Călărași
Kalasin *136 D4 var.* Muang Kalasin. Kalasin, E Thailand
Kalāt *123 E5 Per.* Qalāt. Zābul, S Afghanistan
Kālat *134 B2 var.* Kelat, Khelat. Baluchistān, SW Pakistan
Kalbarri *147 A5* Western Australia
Kalecik *116 C3* Ankara, N Turkey
Kalemie *77 E6 prev.* Albertville. Shaba, SE Dem. Rep. Congo
Kale Sultanie *see* Çanakkale
Kalgan *see* Zhangjiakou
Kalgoorlie *147 B6* Western Australia
Kalima *77 D6* Maniema, E Dem. Rep. Congo
Kalimantan *138 D4 Eng.* Indonesian Borneo. *Geopolitical region* Borneo, C Indonesia
Kálimnos *see* Kálymnos
Kaliningrad *see* Kaliningradskaya Oblast'
Kaliningrad *106 A4* Kaliningradskaya Oblast', W Russian Federation
Kaliningradskaya Oblast' *106 B4 var.* Kaliningrad. Admin. region *province and enclave* W Russian Federation
Kalinkavichy *107 C7 Rus.* Kalinkovichi. Homyel'skaya Voblasts', SE Belarus
Kalispell *44 B1* Montana, NW USA
Kalisz *98 C4 Ger.* Kalisch, *Rus.* Kalish; *anc.* Calisia. Wielkopolskie, C Poland
Kalix *84 D4* Norrbotten, N Sweden
Kalixälven *84 D3 river* N Sweden
Kallaste *106 E3 Ger.* Krasnogor. Tartumaa, SE Estonia
Kallavesi *85 E5 lake* SE Finland
Kalloní *105 D5* Lésvos, E Greece
Kalmar *85 C7 var.* Calmar. Kalmar, S Sweden
Kalmthout *87 C5* Antwerpen, N Belgium
Kalpáki *104 A4* Ípeiros, W Greece
Kalpeni Island *132 B3 island* Lakshadweep, India, N Indian Ocean
Kaluga *111 B5* Kaluzhskaya Oblast', W Russian Federation
Kalush *108 C2 Pol.* Kałusz. Ivano-Frankivs'ka Oblast', W Ukraine
Kalutara *132 D4* Western Province, SW Sri Lanka
Kalvarija *107 B5 Pol.* Kalwaria. Marijampolė, S Lithuania
Kalyān *134 C5* Mahārāshtra, W India
Kálymnos *105 D6 var.* Kálimnos. *Island* Dodekánisos, Greece, Aegean Sea
Kama *110 D4 river* NW Russian Federation
Kamarang *59 F3* W Guyana
Kamchatka *see* Kamchatka, Poluostrov
Kamchatka, Poluostrov *115 G3 Eng.* Kamchatka. *Peninsula* E Russian Federation
Kamensk-Shakhtinskiy *111 B6* Rostovskaya Oblast', SW Russian Federation
Kamina *77 D7* Shaba, S Dem. Rep. Congo
Kamishli *see* Al Qāmishlī
Kamloops *37 E5* British Columbia, SW Canada
Kammu Seamount *152 C2 undersea feature* N Pacific Ocean
Kampala *73 B6 country capital* (Uganda) S Uganda
Kâmpóng Cham *137 D6 prev.* Kompong Cham. Kâmpóng Cham, C Cambodia
Kâmpóng Chhnăng *137 D6 prev.* Kompong. Kâmpóng Chhnăng, C Cambodia
Kâmpóng Saôm *137 D6 prev.* Kompong Som, Sihanoukville. Kâmpóng Saôm, SW Cambodia
Kâmpóng Spoe *137 D6 prev.* Kompong Speu. Kâmpóng Spœ, S Cambodia
Kâmpôt *137 D6* Kâmpôt, SW Cambodia
Kam"yanets'-Podil's'kyy *108 C3 Rus.* Kamenets-Podol'skiy. Khmel'nyts'ka Oblast', W Ukraine
Kam"yanka-Dniprovs'ka *109 F3 Rus.* Kamenka Dneprovskaya. Zaporiz'ka Oblast', SE Ukraine
Kamyshin *111 B6* Volgogradskaya Oblast', SW Russian Federation
Kanaky *see* New Caledonia
Kananga *77 D6 prev.* Luluabourg. Kasai Occidental, S Dem. Rep. Congo
Kananur *see* Cannanore
Kanara *see* Karnātaka
Kanash *111 C5* Chuvashskaya Respublika, W Russian Federation
Kanazawa *131 C5* Ishikawa, Honshū, SW Japan
Kanbe *136 B4* Yangon, SW Myanmar
Kānchīpuram *132 C2 prev.* Conjeeveram. Tamil Nādu, SE India
Kandahār *123 E5 Per.* Qandahār. Kandahār, S Afghanistan
Kandalakša *see* Kandalaksha
Kandalaksha *110 B2 var.* Kandalakša, *Fin.* Kantalahti. Murmanskaya Oblast', NW Russian Federation
Kandangan *138 D4* Borneo, C Indonesia
Kandava *106 C3 Ger.* Kandau. Tukums, W Latvia
Kandi *75 F4* N Benin
Kandy *132 D3* Central Province, C Sri Lanka
Kane Fracture Zone *66 B4 tectonic feature* NW Atlantic Ocean
Kāne'ohe *47 A8 var.* Kaneohe. O'ahu, Hawai'i, USA, C Pacific Ocean
Kangān *120 D4* Būshehr, S Iran
Kangaroo Island *149 A7 island* South Australia
Kangertittivaq *83 E4 Dan.* Scoresby Sund. *Fjord* E Greenland
Kangikajik *83 E4 var.* Kap Brewster. *Headland* E Greenland
Kaniv *109 E2 Rus.* Kanëv. Cherkas'ka Oblast', C Ukraine
Kanivs'ke Vodoskhovyshche *109 E2 Rus.* Kanevskoye Vodokhranilishche. *Reservoir* C Ukraine
Kanjiža *100 D2 Ger.* Altkanischa, *Hung.* Magyarkanizsa, Ókanizsa; *prev.* Stara Kanjiža. Serbia, N Serbia and Montenegro (Yugo.)
Kankaanpää *85 D5* Länsi-Suomi, W Finland
Kankakee *40 B3* Illinois, N USA
Kankan *74 D4* Haute-Guinée, E Guinea
Kannur *see* Cannanore
Kano *75 G4* Kano, N Nigeria
Kānpur *135 E3 Eng.* Cawnpore. Uttar Pradesh, N India
Kansas *49 F1 off.* State of Kansas; also known as Jayhawker State, Sunflower State. *State* C USA
Kansas *45 F5* Kansas, C USA
Kansas City *45 F4* Kansas, C USA
Kansas City *45 F4* Missouri, C USA
Kansas River *45 F5 river* Kansas, C USA
Kansk *115 E4* Krasnoyarskiy Kray, S Russian Federation
Kansu *see* Gansu
Kantalahti *see* Kandalaksha
Kántanos *105 C7* Kríti, Greece, E Mediterranean Sea
Kantemirovka *111 B6* Voronezhskaya Oblast', W Russian Federation
Kanton *145 F3 var.* Abariringa, Canton Island; *prev.* Mary Island. *Atoll* Phoenix Islands, C Kiribati
Kanye *78 C4* Southern, SE Botswana
Kaohsiung *128 D6 var.* Gaoxiong, *Jap.* Takao, Takow. S Taiwan
Kaolack *74 B3 var.* Kaolak. W Senegal
Kaolak *see* Kaolack
Kaolan *see* Lanzhou
Kaoma *78 C2* Western, W Zambia
Kap Brewster *see* Kangikajik
Kapelle *87 B5* Zeeland, SW Netherlands
Kapellen *87 C5* Antwerpen, N Belgium
Kap Farvel *see* Uummannarsuaq
Kapka, Massif du *76 C2 mountain range* E Chad
Kaplangky, Plato *see* Gaplaňgyr Platosy
Kapoeta *73 C5* Eastern Equatoria, SE Sudan
Kaposvár *99 C7* Somogy, SW Hungary
Kappeln *94 B2* Schleswig-Holstein, N Germany
Kapstad *see* Cape Town
Kaptsevichy *107 C7 Rus.* Koptsevichi. Homyel'skaya Voblasts', SE Belarus
Kapuas, Sungai *138 C4 prev.* Kapoeas. *River* Borneo, C Indonesia
Kapuskasing *38 C4* Ontario, S Canada
Kapyl' *107 C6 Rus.* Kopyl'. Minskaya Voblasts', C Belarus
Kap York *see* Innaanganeq
Kara-Balta *123 F2* Chuyskaya Oblast', N Kyrgyzstan
Karabil', Vozvyshennost' *see Garabil Belentligi*
Kara-Bogaz-Gol, Zaliv *see* Garabogaz Aylagy
Karabük *116 C2* Karabük, NW Turkey
Karāchi *134 B3* Sind, SE Pakistan
Karadeniz *see* Black Sea
Karadeniz Boğazı *see* İstanbul Boğazı
Karaferiye *see* Véroia
Karaganda *114 C4 Kaz.* Qaraghandy. Karaganda, C Kazakhstan
Karaginskiy, Ostrov *115 H2 island* E Russian Federation
Karak *see* Al Karak
Kara-Kala *see* Garrygala
Karakax *see* Moyu
Karakılısse *see* Ağrı
Karakol *123 G2 prev.* Przheval'sk. Issyk-Kul'skaya Oblast', NE Kyrgyzstan
Karakol *123 G2 var.* Karakolka. Issyk-Kul'skaya Oblast', NE Kyrgyzstan
Karakolka *see* Karakol
Karakoram Range *134 D1 mountain range* C Asia
Karaköse *see* Ağrı
Kara Kum *see* Garagum
Kara Kum Canal *see* Garagum Kanaly
Karakumskiy Kanal *see* Garagum Kanaly
Karakumy, Peski *see* Garagum
Karamai *see* Karamay
Karaman *116 C4* Karaman, S Turkey
Karamay *126 B2 var.* Karamai, Kelamayi, *prev. Chin.* K'o-la-ma-i. Xinjiang Uygur Zizhiqu, NW China
Karamea Bight *151 B5 gulf* South Island, NZ
Karapelit *104 E1 Rom.* Stejarul. Dobrich, NE Bulgaria
Kara-Say *123 G2* Issyk-Kul'skaya Oblast', NE Kyrgyzstan
Karasburg *78 B4* Karas, S Namibia
Kara Sea *see* Karskoye More
Karatau *114 C5 Kaz.* Qarataū. Zhambyl, S Kazakhstan
Karavás *105 B7* Kýthira, S Greece
Karbalā' *120 B3 var.* Kerbala, Kerbela. S Iraq
Kardhítsa *see* Kardítsa
Kardítsa *105 B5 var.* Kardhítsa. Thessalía, C Greece
Kärdla *106 C2 Ger.* Kertel. Hiiumaa, W Estonia
Karet *see* Kâgheț
Kargı *116 C2* Çorum, N Turkey
Kargilik *see* Yecheng
Kariba *78 D2* Mashonaland West, N Zimbabwe
Kariba, Lake *78 D3 reservoir* Zambia/Zimbabwe
Karibib *78 B3* Erongo, C Namibia
Karies *see* Karyés
Karigasniemi *84 D2 Lapp.* Garegegasnjárga. Lappi, N Finland
Karimata, Selat *138 C4 strait* W Indonesia
Karīmnagar *134 D5* Andhra Pradesh, C India
Karin *72 D4* Woqooyi Galbeed, N Somalia
Kariot *see* Ikaría
Káristos *see* Kárystos
Karkinits'ka Zatoka *109 E4 Rus.* Karkinitskiy Zaliv. *Gulf* S Ukraine
Karkūk *see* Kirkūk
Karlovac *100 B3 Ger.* Karlstadt, *Hung.* Károlyváros. Karlovac, C Croatia
Karlovy Vary *99 A5 Ger.* Karlsbad; prev. *Eng.* Carlsbad. Karlovarský Kraj, W Czech Republic
Karlskrona *85 C7* Blekinge, S Sweden
Karlsruhe *95 B6 var.* Carlsruhe. Baden-Württemberg, SW Germany
Karlstad *85 B6* Värmland, C Sweden
Karnāl *134 D2* Haryāna, N India
Karnātaka *132 C1 var.* Kanara; *prev.* Maisur, Mysore. Admin. region *state* W India
Karnobat *104 D2* Burgas, E Bulgaria
Karnul *see* Kurnool
Karpaten *see* Carpathian Mountains
Kárpathos *105 E7 It.* Scarpanto; *anc.* Carpathos, Carpathus. *Island* SE Greece
Kárpathos *105 E7* Kárpathos, SE Greece
Karpaty *see* Carpathian Mountains
Karpenísi *105 B5 prev.* Karpenísion. Intereá Ellás, C Greece
Kars *117 F2 var.* Qars. Kars, NE Turkey
Kārsava *106 D4 Ger.* Karsau; *prev.* Rus. Korsovka. Ludza, E Latvia
Karskiye Vorota, Proliv *110 E2 Eng.* Kara Strait. *Strait* N Russian Federation
Karskoye More *114 D2 Eng.* Kara Sea. *Sea* Arctic Ocean
Karyés *104 C4 var.* Karies. Ágion Óros, N Greece
Kárystos *105 C6 var.* Káristos. Évvoia, C Greece

Kasai *77 C6 var.* Cassai, Kassai. *River* Angola/Dem. Rep. Congo
Kasaji *77 D7* Shaba, S Dem. Rep. Congo
Kasama *78 D1* Northern, N Zambia
Kāsargod *132 B2* Kerala, SW India
Kāshān *120 C3* Eşfahān, C Iran
Kashi *126 A3 Chin.* Kaxgar, K'o-shih, *Uigh.* Kashgar. Xinjiang Uygur Zizhiqu, NW China
Kasongo *77 D6* Maniema, E Dem. Rep. Congo
Kasongo-Lunda *77 C7* Bandundu, SW Dem. Rep. Congo
Kásos *105 D7 island* S Greece
Kaspiysk *111 B8* Respublika Dagestan, SW Russian Federation
Kassai *see* Kasai
Kassala *72 C4* Kassala, E Sudan
Kassel *94 B4 prev.* Cassel. Hessen, C Germany
Kasserine *71 E2 var.* Al Qaşrayn. W Tunisia
Kastamonu *116 C2 var.* Castamoni, Kastamuni. Kastamonu, N Turkey
Kastamuni *see* Kastamonu
Kastaneá *104 B4* Kentrikí Makedonía, N Greece
Kastélli *105 C7* Kríti, Greece, E Mediterranean Sea
Kastoría *104 B4* Dytikí Makedonía, N Greece
Kástro *105 C6* Sífnos, Kykládes, Greece, Aegean Sea
Kastsyukovichy *107 E7 Rus.* Kostyukovichi. Mahilyowskaya Voblasts', E Belarus
Kastsyukowka *107 D7 Rus.* Kostyukovka. Homyel'skaya Voblasts', SE Belarus
Kasulu *73 B7* Kigoma, W Tanzania
Kasumiga-ura *131 D5 lake* Honshū, S Japan
Katahdin, Mount *41 G1mountain* Maine, NE USA
Katalla *36 C3* Alaska, USA
Katana *see* Qaṭanā
Katanning *147 B7* Western Australia
Katawaz *see* Zarghūn Shahr
Katchall Island *133 F3 island* Nicobar Islands, India, NE Indian Ocean
Kateríni *104 B4* Kentrikí Makedonía, N Greece
Katha *136 B2* Sagaing, N Myanmar
Katherine *148 A2* Northern Territory, N Australia
Kathmandu *124 C3 prev.* Kantipur. *Country capital* (Nepal) Central, C Nepal
Katikati *150 D3* Bay of Plenty, North Island, NZ
Katima Mulilo *78 C3* Caprivi, NE Namibia
Katiola *74 D4* C Côte d'Ivoire
Káto Achaïa *105 B5 var.* Kato Ahaia, Káto Akhaía. Dytikí Ellás, S Greece
Kato Ahaia *see* Káto Achaïa
Káto Akhaía *see* Káto Achaïa
Katoúna *105 A5* Dytikí Ellás, C Greece
Katowice *99 C5 Ger.* Kattowitz. Śląskie, S Poland
Katsina *75 G3* Katsina, N Nigeria
Kattaqo'rg'on *123 E2 var.* Kattaqŭrghon, *Rus.* Kattakurgan. Samarqand Wiloyati, C Uzbekistan
Kattaqŭrghon *see* Kattaqo'rg'on
Kattavía *105 E7* Ródos, Dodekánisos, Greece, Aegean Sea
Kattegat *85 B7 Dan.* Kattegatt. *Strait* N Europe
Kaua'i *47 A7 var.* Kauai. *Island* Hawaiian Islands, Hawai'i, USA, C Pacific Ocean
Kaufbeuren *95 C6* Bayern, S Germany
Kaunas *106 B4 Ger.* Kauen, *Pol.* Kowno; *prev.* Rus. Kovno. Kaunas, C Lithuania
Kavadarci *101 E6 Turk.* Kavadar. C FYR Macedonia
Kavajë *101 C6 It.* Cavaia, Kavaja. Tiranë, W Albania
Kavála *104 C3 prev.* Kaválla. Anatolikí Makedonía kai Thráki, NE Greece
Kāvali *132 D2* Andhra Pradesh, E India
Kavango *see* Cubango
Kavaratti Island *132 A3 island* Lakshadweep, India, N Indian Ocean
Kavarna *104 E2* Dobrich, NE Bulgaria
Kavengo *see* Cubango
Kavīr, Dasht-e *120 D3 var.* Great Salt Desert. *Salt pan* N Iran
Kavīr-e Lūt *see* Lūt, Dasht-e
Kawagoe *131 D5* Saitama, Honshū, S Japan
Kawasaki *130 A2* Kanagawa, Honshū, S Japan
Kawerau *150 E3* Bay of Plenty, North Island, NZ
Kaya *75 E3* C Burkina faso
Kayan *136 B4* Yangon, SW Myanmar
Kayan, Sungai *138 D3 prev.* Kajan. *River* Borneo, C Indonesia
Kayes *74 C3* Kayes, W Mali
Kayseri *116 D3 var.* Kaisaria; *anc.* Caesarea Mazaca, Mazaca. Kayseri, C Turkey
Kazach'ye *115 F2* Respublika Sakha (Yakutiya), NE Russian Federation
Kazakhskiy Melkosopochnik *114 C4 Eng.* Kazakh Uplands, Kirghiz Steppe, *Kaz.* Saryarqa. *Uplands* C Kazakhstan
Kazakhstan *114 B4 var.* Kazakstan, *Kaz.* Qazaqstan, Qazaqstan Respublikasy; *prev.* Kazakh Soviet Socialist Republic, *Rus.* Kazakhskaya SSR. *Country* C Asia

Kazakhstan 114

Official name Republic of Kazakhstan
Formation 1991
Capital Astana
Population 15.4 million / 15 people per sq mile (6 people per sq km)
Total area 1,049,150 sq. miles (2,717,300 sq. km)
Languages Kazakh, Russian, Ukrainian, Tatar, German, Uzbek, Uighur
Religions Muslim (mainly Sunni) 47%, Orthodox Christian 44%, other 9%
Ethnic mix Kazakh 53%, Russian 30%, other 9%, Ukrainian 4%, Tatar 2%, German 2%
Government Presidential system
Currency Tenge = 100 tiyn
Literacy rate 99%
Calorie consumption 2477 calories

Kazakh Uplands *see* Kazakhskiy Melkosopochnik
Kazan' *111 C5* Respublika Tatarstan, W Russian Federation
Kazanlŭk *104 D2 prev.* Kazanlik. Stara Zagora, C Bulgaria
Kazbegi *see* Kazbek
Kazbek *117 F1 var.* Kazbegi, *Geor.* Mqinvartsveri. *Mountain* N Georgia
Kāzerūn *120 D4* Fārs, S Iran
Kazvin *see* Qazvīn
Kéa *105 C6 prev.* Kéos, *anc.* Ceos. *Island* Kykládes, Greece, Aegean Sea
Kéa *105 C6* Kéa, Kykládes, Greece, Aegean Sea
Kea, Mauna *47 B8 mountain* Hawai'i, USA, C Pacific Ocean
Kéamu *see* Aneityum
Kearney *45 E4* Nebraska, C USA
Keban Barajı *117 E3 reservoir* C Turkey
Kebkabiya *72 A4* Northern Darfur, W Sudan
Kebnekaise *84 C3 mountain* N Sweden
Kecskemét *99 D7* Bács-Kiskun, C Hungary
Kediri *138 D5* Jawa, C Indonesia
Kędzierzyn-Kole *99 C5 Ger.* Heydebrech. Opolskie, S Poland
Keelung *see* Chilung
Keetmanshoop *78 B4* Karas, S Namibia
Kefallinía *105 A5 var.* Kefallonía. *Island* Iónioi Nísoi, Greece, C Mediterranean Sea
Kefallonía *see* Kefallinía
Kefe *see* Feodosiya
Kehl *95 A6* Baden-Württemberg, SW Germany
Keila *106 D2 Ger.* Kegel. Harjumaa, NW Estonia
Keïta *75 F3* Tahoua, C Niger
Keitele *84 D4 lake* C Finland
Keith *149 B7* South Australia
Këk-Art *123 G2 prev.* Alaykel', Alay-Kuu. Oshskaya Oblast', SW Kyrgyzstan
Kékes *99 C6 mountain* N Hungary
Kelamayi *see* Karamay
Kelang *see* Klang
Kelat *see* Kālat
Kelifskiy Uzboy *see* Kelif Uzboýy
Kelif Uzboýy *122 D3 var.* Kelifskiy Uzboy. *Salt marsh* E Turkmenistan
Kelkit Çayı *117 E3 river* N Turkey
Kelmė *106 B4* Kelmė, C Lithuania
Kélo *76 B4* Tandjilé, SW Chad
Kelowna *37 E5* British Columbia, SW Canada
Kelso *46 B2* Washington, NW USA
Keluang *138 B3 var.* Kluang. Johor, Peninsular Malaysia
Kem' *110 B3* Respublika Kareliya, NW Russian Federation
Kemah *117 E3* Erzincan, E Turkey
Kemaman *see* Cukai
Kemerovo *114 D4 prev.* Shcheglovsk. Kemerovskaya Oblast', C Russian Federation
Kemi *84 D4* Lappi, NW Finland
Kemijärvi *84 D3 Swe.* Kemiträsk. Lappi, N Finland
Kemijoki *84 D3 river* NW Finland
Kemin *123 G2 prev.* Bystrovka. Chuyskaya Oblast', N Kyrgyzstan
Kempele *84 D4* Oulu, C Finland
Kempten *95 B7* Bayern, S Germany
Kendal *89 D5* NW England, UK
Kendari *139 E4* Sulawesi, C Indonesia
Kenedy *49 G4* Texas, SW USA
Kenema *74 C4* SE Sierra Leone
Këneurgench *see* Köneürgenç
Kenge *77 C6* Bandundu, SW Dem. Rep. Congo
Keng Tung *136 C3 var.* Kentung. Shan State, E Myanmar
Kénitra *70 C2 prev.* Port-Lyautey. NW Morocco
Kennett *45 H5* Missouri, C USA
Kennewick *46 C2* Washington, NW USA
Kenora *38 A3* Ontario, S Canada
Kenosha *40 B3* Wisconsin, N USA
Kentau *114 B5* Yuzhnyy Kazakhstan, S Kazakhstan
Kentucky *40 C5 off.* Commonwealth of Kentucky; also known as The Bluegrass State. *State* C USA
Kentucky Lake *40 B5 reservoir* Kentucky/Tennessee, S USA
Kentung *see* Keng Tung
Kenya *73 C6 Country* E Africa

Kenya 73

Official name Republic of Kenya
Formation 1963
Capital Nairobi
Population 32 million / 146 people per sq mile (56 people per sq km)
Total area 224,961 sq. miles (582,650 sq. km)
Languages Kiswahili, English, Kikuyu, Luo, Kalenjin, Kamba
Religions Christian 60%, Traditional beliefs 25%, other 9%, Muslim 6%
Ethnic mix Other 30%, Kikuyu 21%, Luhya 14%, Luo 13%, Kalenjin 11%, Kamba 11%
Government Presidential system

Kenya (continued)

Currency Kenya shilling = 100 cents
Literacy rate 84%
Calorie consumption 2058 calories

Keokuk *45 G4* Iowa, C USA
Kępno *98 C4* Wielkopolskie, C Poland
Keppel Island *see* Niuatoputapu
Kepulauan Sangihe *see* Sangir, Kepulauan
Kerak *see* Al Karak
Kerala *132 C2 state* S India
Kerasunt *see* Giresun
Keratea *see* Keratéa
Keratéa *105 C6 var.* Keratea. Attikí, C Greece
Kerbala *see* Karbalā'
Kerbela *see* Karbalā'
Kerch *109 G5 Rus.* Kerch'. Respublika Krym, SE Ukraine
Kerchens'ka Protska *see* Kerch Strait
Kerchenskiy Proliv *see* Kerch Strait
Kerch Strait *109 G4 var.* Bosporus Cimmerius, Enikale Strait, *Rus.* Kerchenskiy Proliv, *Ukr.* Kerchens'ka Protska. *Strait* Black Sea/Sea of Azov
Kerguelen *141 C7 island* C French Southern and Antarctic Territories
Kerguelen Plateau *141 C7 undersea feature* S Indian Ocean
Kerí *105 A6* Zákynthos, Iónioi Nísoi, Greece, C Mediterranean Sea
Kerikeri *150 D2* Northland, North Island, NZ
Kerkenah, Îles de *102 D4 var.* Kerkenna Islands, *Ar.* Juzur Qarqannah. *Island group* E Tunisia
Kerkenna Islands *see* Kerkenah, Îles de
Kérkira *see* Kérkyra
Kerkrade *87 D6* Limburg, SE Netherlands
Kerkuk *see* Kirkūk
Kérkyra *104 A4 var.* Kérkira, *Eng.* Corfu. *Island* Iónioi Nísoi, Greece, C Mediterranean Sea
Kermadec Islands *152 C4 island group* NZ, SW Pacific Ocean
Kermadec Trench *143 E4 undersea feature* SW Pacific Ocean
Kermān *120 D3 var.* Kirman; *anc.* Carmana. Kermān, C Iran
Kermānshāh *120 C3 var.* Qahremānshahr; *prev.* Bākhtarān. Kermānshāh, W Iran
Kerrville *49 F4* Texas, SW USA
Kerulen *127 E2 Chin.* Herlen He, *Mong.* Herlen Gol. *River* China/Mongolia
Kerýneia *102 C5 var.* Girne, Kyrenia. N Cyprus
Kesennuma *130 D4* Miyagi, Honshū, C Japan
Keszthely *99 C7* Zala, SW Hungary
Ketchikan *36 D4* Revillagigedo Island, Alaska, USA
Kętrzyn *98 D2 Ger.* Rastenburg. Warmiusko-Mazurskie, NE Poland
Kettering *89 D6* C England, UK
Kettering *40 C4* Ohio, N USA
Keuruu *85 D5* Länsi-Suomi, W Finland
Keweenaw Peninsula *40 B1 peninsula* Michigan, N USA
Key Largo *43 F5* Key Largo, Florida, SE USA
Key West *43 E5* Florida Keys, Florida, SE USA
Khabarovsk *115 G4* Khabarovskiy Kray, SE Russian Federation
Khadera *see* Hadera
Khairpur *134 B3* Sind, SE Pakistan
Khalīj al 'Aqabah *see* Aqaba, Gulf of
Khalīj al 'Arabī *see* Gulf, The
Khalīj-e Fars *see* Gulf, The
Khalkidhikí *see* Chalkidikí
Khalkís *see* Chalkída

Khambhāt, Gulf of *134 C4 Eng.* Gulf of Cambay. *Gulf* W India
Khamīs Mushayt *121 B6 var.* Hamīs Musait. 'Asīr, SW Saudi Arabia
Khānābād *123 E3* Kunduz, NE Afghanistan
Khān al Baghdādī *see* Al Baghdādī
Khandwa *134 D4* Madhya Pradesh, C India
Khanh *see* Soc Trăng
Khaniá *see* Chaniá
Khanka, Lake *129 E2 var.* Hsing-k'ai Hu, Lake Hanka, *Chin.* Xingkai Hu, *Rus.* Ozero Khanka. *Lake* China/Russian Federation
Khanthabouli *136 D4 prev.* Savannakhét. Savannakhét, S Laos
Khanty-Mansiysk *114 C3 prev.* Ostyako-Voguls'k. Khanty-Mansiyskiy Avtonomnyy Okrug, C Russian Federation
Khān Yūnis *119 A7 var.* Khān Yūnus. S Gaza Strip
Khān Yūnus *see* Khān Yūnis
Khanzi *see* Ghanzi
Kharagpur *135 F4* West Bengal, NE India
Kharbin *see* Harbin
Kharkiv *109 G2 Rus.* Khar'kov. Kharkivs'ka Oblast', NE Ukraine
Kharmanli *104 D3* Khaskovo, S Bulgaria
Khartoum *72 B4 var.* El Khartûm, Khartum. *Country capital* (Sudan) Khartoum, C Sudan
Khartum *see* Khartoum
Khasavyurt *111 B8* Respublika Dagestan, SW Russian Federation
Khāsh, Dasht-e *122 D5 Eng.* Khash Desert. *Desert* SW Afghanistan
Khashim Al Qirba *see* Khashm el Girba
Khashm al Qirbah *see* Khashm el Girba
Khashm el Girba *72 C4 var.* Khashim Al Qirba, Khashm al Qirbah. Kassala, E Sudan
Khaskovo *104 D3* Khaskovo, S Bulgaria
Khaydarkan *123 F2 var.* Khaydarken. Oshskaya Oblast', SW Kyrgyzstan
Khaydarken *see* Khaydarkan
Khelat *see* Kālat
Kherson *109 E4* Khersons'ka Oblast', S Ukraine
Kheta *115 E2 river* N Russian Federation
Khíos *see* Chíos
Khirbet el 'Aujā et Tahtā *119 E7 var.* 'Aujā et Tahtā. E West Bank
Khiva see Xiva
Khiwa see Xiva
Khmel'nyts'kyy *108 C2 Rus.* Khmel'nitskiy; *prev.* Proskurov. Khmel'nyts'ka Oblast', W Ukraine
Khodasy *107 E6 Rus.* Khodosy. Mahilyowskaya Voblasts', E Belarus
Khodoriv *108 C2 Pol.* Chodorów, *Rus.* Khodorov. L'vivs'ka Oblast', NW Ukraine
Khodzhent *see* Khŭjand
Khoi *see* Khvoy
Khojend *see* Khŭjand
Khokand *see* Qo'qon
Kholm *123 E3 var.* Tashqurghan, *Pash.* Khulm. Balkh, N Afghanistan
Kholon *see* Holon
Khoms *see* Al Khums
Khong Sedone *see* Muang Khôngxédôn
Khon Kaen *136 D4 var.* Muang Khon Kaen. Khon Kaen, E Thailand
Khor *115 G4* Khabarovskiy Kray, SE Russian Federation
Khorat *see* Nakhon Ratchasima
Khorugh *123 F3 Rus.* Khorog. S Tajikistan
Khotan *see* Hotan
Khouribga *70 B2* C Morocco
Khovd *see* Hovd
Khowst *123 F4* Paktīā, E Afghanistan
Khoy *see* Khvoy
Khoyniki *107 D8 Rus.* Khoyniki. Homyel'skaya Voblasts', SE Belarus
Khrebet Kolymskiy *see* Kolyma Range
Khrebet Kopetdag *see* Koppeh Dāgh
Khrebet Lomonsova *see* Lomonosov Ridge
Khudzhand *see* Khŭjand
Khŭjand *123 E2 var.* Khodzhent, Khojend, *Rus.* Khudzhand; *prev.* Leninabad, *Taj.* Leninobod. N Tajikistan
Khulm *see* Kholm
Khulna *135 G4* Khulna, SW Bangladesh
Khums *see* Al Khums
Khust *108 B3 Cz.* Chust, Husté, *Hung.* Huszt. Zakarpats'ka Oblast', W Ukraine
Khvoy *120 C2 var.* Khoi, Khoy. Āzarbāyjān-e Bākhtarī, NW Iran
Khyber Pass *134 C1 var.* Kowtal-e Khaybar. *Pass* Afghanistan/Pakistan
Kiangmai *see* Chiang Mai
Kiang-ning *see* Nanjing
Kiangsi *see* Jiangxi
Kiangsu *see* Jiangsu
Kiáto *105 B6 prev.* Kiáton. Pelopónnisos, S Greece
Kiayi *see* Chiai
Kibangou *77 B6* Le Niari, SW Congo
Kibombo *77 D6* Maniema, E Dem. Rep. Congo
Kičevo *101 D6* SW FYR Macedonia
Kidderminster *89 D6* C England, UK
Kiel *94 B2* Schleswig-Holstein, N Germany
Kielce *98 D4 Rus.* Keltsy. Świętokrzyskie, C Poland
Kieler Bucht *94 B2 bay* N Germany
Kiev *see* Kyyiv
Kiffa *74 C3* Assaba, S Mauritania
Kigali *73 B6 country capital* (Rwanda) C Rwanda
Kigoma *73 B7* Kigoma, W Tanzania
Kihnu *106 C2 var.* Kihnu Saar, *Ger.* Kühnö. *Island* SW Estonia
Kihnu Saar *see* Kihnu
Kii-suidō *131 C7 strait* S Japan
Kikinda *100 D3 Ger.* Grosskikinda, *Hung.* Nagykikinda; *prev.* Velika Kikinda. Serbia, N Serbia and Montenegro (Yugo.)
Kikládhes *see* Kykládes
Kikwit *77 C6* Bandundu, W Dem. Rep. Congo
Kilien Mountains *see* Qilian Shan
Kilimane *see* Quelimane
Kilimanjaro *73 C7 var.* Uhuru Peak. *Mountain* NE Tanzania
Kilimanjaro *69 E5 region* E Tanzania
Kilingi-Nõmme *106 D3 Ger.* Kurkund. Pärnumaa, SW Estonia
Kilis *116 D4* Kilis S Turkey
Kiliya *108 D4 Rom.* Chilia-Nouă. Odes'ka Oblast', SW Ukraine
Kilkenny *89 B6 Ir.* Cill Chainnigh. S Ireland
Kilkís *104 B3* Kentrikí Makedonía, N Greece
Killarney *89 A6 Ir.* Cill Airne. SW Ireland
Killeen *49 G3* Texas, SW USA
Kilmain *see* Quelimane
Kilmarnock *88 C4* W Scotland, UK
Kilwa *see* Kilwa Kivinje
Kilwa Kivinje *73 C7 var.* Kilwa. Lindi, SE Tanzania
Kimberley *78 C4* Northern Cape, C South Africa
Kimberley Plateau *146 C3 plateau* Western Australia
Kimch'aek *129 E3 prev.* Sŏngjin. E North Korea
Kinabalu, Gunung *138 D3 mountain* East Malaysia
Kindersley *37 F5* Saskatchewan, S Canada
Kindia *74 C4* Guinée-Maritime, SW Guinea
Kindley Field *42 A4 air base* E Bermuda
Kindu *77 D6 prev.* Kindu-Port-Empain. Maniema, C Dem. Rep. Congo
Kineshma *111 C5* Ivanovskaya Oblast', W Russian Federation
King Island *149 B8 island* Tasmania, SE Australia
Kingman *48 A1* Arizona, SW USA
Kingman Reef *145 E2 US territory* C Pacific Ocean
Kingsford Smith *148 E2 international airport* (Sydney) New South Wales, SE Australia
King's Lynn *89 E6 var.* Bishop's Lynn, Kings Lynn, Lynn, Lynn Regis. E England, UK
King Sound *146 B3 sound* Western Australia
Kingsport *43 E1* Tennessee, S USA
Kingston *54 B5 country capital* (Jamaica) E Jamaica
Kingston *41 F3* New York, NE USA
Kingston *38 D5* Ontario, SE Canada
Kingston upon Hull *89 D5 var.* Hull. E England, UK
Kingston upon Thames *89 A8* SE England, UK
Kingstown *55 H4 country capital* (Saint Vincent and the Grenadines) Saint Vincent, Saint Vincent and the Grenadines
Kingsville *49 G5* Texas, SW USA
King William Island *37 F3 island* Nunavut, N Canada Arctic Ocean
Kinrooi *87 D5* Limburg, NE Belgium
Kinshasa *77 B6 prev.* Léopoldville. *Country capital* (Congo (Zaire)) Kinshasa, W Dem. Rep. Congo
Kintyre *88 B4 peninsula* W Scotland, UK
Kinyeti *73 B5 mountain* S Sudan
Kiparissía *see* Kyparissía
Kipili *73 B7* Rukwa, W Tanzania
Kipushi *77 D8* Shaba, SE Dem. Rep. Congo
Kirdzhali *see* Kŭrdzhali
Kirghiz Range *123 F2 Rus.* Kirgizskiy Khrebet; *prev.* Alexander Range. *Mountain range* Kazakhstan/Kyrgyzstan
Kirghiz Steppe *see* Kazakhskiy Melkosopochnik
Kiriath-Arba *see* Hebron
Kiribati *145 F2 Country* C Pacific Ocean

Kiribati 145

Official name Republic of Kiribati
Formation 1979
Capital Bairiki (Tarawa Atoll)
Population 98,549 / 360 people per sq mile (139 people per sq km)
Total area 277 sq. miles (717 sq. km)
Languages English, Kiribati
Religions Roman Catholic 53%, Kiribati Protestant Church 39%, other 8%
Ethnic mix Micronesian 96%, other 4%
Government Nonparty system
Currency Australian dollar = 100 cents
Literacy rate 99%
Calorie consumption 2922 calories

Kırıkhan *116 D4* Hatay, S Turkey
Kırıkkale *116 C3* Kırıkkale, C Turkey
Kirin *see* Jilin
Kirinyaga *73 C6 prev.* Mount Kenya. *Volcano* C Kenya
Kirishi *110 B4 var.* Kirisi. Leningradskaya Oblast', NW Russian Federation
Kirisi *see* Kirishi
Kiritimati *145 G2 prev.* Christmas Island. *Atoll* Line Islands, E Kiribati
Kirkenes *84 E2 var.* Kirkkoniemi. Finnmark, N Norway
Kirkkoniemi *see* Kirkenes
Kirkland Lake *38 D4* Ontario, S Canada
Kırklareli *116 A2 prev.* Kirk-Kilissa. Kırklareli, NW Turkey
Kirkpatrick, Mount *154 B3 mountain* Antarctica
Kirksville *45 G4* Missouri, C USA
Kirkūk *120 B3 var.* Karkūk, Kerkuk. N Iraq
Kirkwall *88 C2* NE Scotland, UK
Kirkwood *45 G4* Missouri, C USA
Kirman *see* Kermān
Kir Moab *see* Al Karak
Kirov *111 C5 prev.* Vyatka. Kirovskaya Oblast', NW Russian Federation
Kirovo-Chepetsk *111 D5* Kirovskaya Oblast', NW Russian Federation
Kirovohrad *109 E3 Rus.* Kirovograd; *prev.* Kirovo, Yelizavetgrad, Zinov'yevsk. Kirovohrads'ka Oblast', C Ukraine
Kīrthar Range *134 B3 mountain range* S Pakistan
Kirun' *see* Chilung
Kiruna *84 C3* Norrbotten, N Sweden
Kisangani *77 D5 prev.* Stanleyville. Orientale, NE Dem. Rep. Congo
Kislovodsk *111 B7* Stavropol'skiy Kray, SW Russian Federation
Kismaayo *73 D6 var.* Chisimayu, Kismayu, *It.* Chisimaio. Jubbada Hoose, S Somalia
Kismayu *see* Kismaayo
Kissidougou *74 C4* Guinée-Forestière, S Guinea
Kissimmee, Lake *43 E4 lake* Florida, SE USA
Kisumu *73 C6 prev.* Port Florence. Nyanza, W Kenya
Kisvárda *99 E6 Ger.* Kleinwardein. Szabolcs-Szatmár-Bereg, E Hungary
Kita *74 D3* Kayes, W Mali
Kitakyūshū *131 A7 var.* Kitakyûsyû. Fukuoka, Kyūshū, SW Japan
Kitakyûsyû *see* Kitakyūshū
Kitami *130 D2* Hokkaidō, NE Japan
Kitchener *38 C5* Ontario, S Canada
Kíthira *see* Kýthira
Kíthnos *see* Kýthnos
Kitimat *36 D4* British Columbia, SW Canada
Kitinen *84 D3 river* N Finland
Kitob *123 E3 Rus.* Kitab. Qashqadaryo Wiloyati, S Uzbekistan
Kitwe *78 D2 var.* Kitwe-Nkana. Copperbelt, C Zambia
Kitwe-Nkana *see* Kitwe
Kitzbühler Alpen *95 C7 mountain range* W Austria
Kivalina *36 C2* Alaska, USA
Kivalo *84 D3 ridge* C Finland
Kivertsi *108 C1 Pol.* Kiwerce, *Rus.* Kivertsy. Volyns'ka Oblast', NW Ukraine
Kivu, Lake *77 E6 Fr.* Lac Kivu. *Lake* Rwanda/Dem. Rep. Congo
Kızıl Irmak *116 C3 river* C Turkey
Kizil Kum *see* Kyzyl Kum
Kladno *99 A5* Středočesky Kraj, NW Czech Republic
Klagenfurt *95 D7 Slvn.* Celovec. Kärnten, S Austria
Klaipėda *106 B3 Ger.* Memel. Klaipėda, NW Lithuania
Klamath Falls *46 B4* Oregon, NW USA
Klamath Mountains *46 A4 mountain range* California/Oregon, W USA
Klang *138 B3 var.* Kelang; *prev.* Port Swettenham. Selangor, Peninsular Malaysia
Klarälven *85 B6 river* Norway/Sweden
Klatovy *99 A5 Ger.* Klattau. Plzeňský Kraj, W Czech Republic
Klazienaveen *86 E2* Drenthe, NE Netherlands
Klein Karas *78 B4* Karas, S Namibia
Kleisoúra *105 A5* Ípeiros, W Greece
Klerksdorp *78 D4* North-West, N South Africa
Klimavichy *107 E7 Rus.* Klimovichi. Mahilyowskaya Voblasts', E Belarus

Klintsy *111 A5* Bryanskaya Oblast', W Russian Federation
Klisura *104 C2* Plovdiv, C Bulgaria
Ključ *100 B3* Federacija Bosna I Hercegovina, NW Bosnia and Herzegovina
Kłobuck *98 C4* Śląskie, S Poland
Klosters *95 B7* Graubünden, SE Switzerland
Kluang *see* Keluang
Kluczbork *98 C4 Ger.* Kreuzburg, Kreuzburg in Oberschlesien. Opolskie, S Poland
Klyuchevskaya Sopka, Vulkan *115 H3 volcano* E Russian Federation
Knin *100 B4* Šibenik-Knin, S Croatia
Knjaževac *100 E4* Serbia, E Serbia and Montenegro (Yugo.)
Knokke-Heist *87 A5* West-Vlaanderen, NW Belgium
Knoxville *42 D1* Tennessee, S USA
Knud Rasmussen Land *82 D1 physical region* N Greenland
Kōbe *131 C6* Hyōgo, Honshū, SW Japan
København *85 B7 Eng.* Copenhagen; *anc.* Hafnia. *Country capital* (Denmark) Sjælland, København, E Denmark
Kobenni *74 D3* Hodh el Gharbi, S Mauritania
Koblenz *95 A5 prev.* Coblenz, *Fr.* Coblence, *anc.* Confluentes. Rheinland-Pfalz, W Germany
Kobryn *107 A6 Pol.* Kobryn, *Rus.* Kobrin. Brestskaya Voblasts', SW Belarus
K'obulet'i *117 F2* W Georgia
Kočani *101 E6* NE FYR Macedonia
Kočevje *95 D8 Ger.* Gottschee. S Slovenia
Koch Bihār *135 G3* West Bengal, NE India
Kōchi *131 B7 var.* Kôti. Kōchi, Shikoku, SW Japan
Kochi *see* Cochin
Kochiu *see* Gejiu
Kodiak *36 C3* Kodiak Island, Alaska, USA
Kodiak Island *36 C3 island* Alaska, USA
Koeln *see* Köln
Ko-erh-mu *see* Golmud
Koetai *see* Mahakam, Sungai
Koetaradja *see* Bandaaceh
Kōfu *131 D5 var.* Kôhu. Yamanashi, Honshū, S Japan
Kogarah *148 E2* New South Wales, SE Australia
Kogon *122 D2 Rus.* Kagan. Bukhoro Wiloyati, C Uzbekistan
Kohīma *135 H3* Nāgāland, E India
Koh I Noh *see* Büyükağrı Dağı
Kohtla-Järve *106 E2* Ida-Virumaa, NE Estonia
Kôhu *see* Kōfu
Kokand *see* Qo'qon
Kokkola *84 D4 Swe.* Karleby; *prev. Swe.* Gamlakarleby. Länsi-Suomi, W Finland
Koko *see* Qinghai Hu
Koko *75 F4* Kebbi, W Nigeria
Kokomo *40 C4* Indiana, N USA
Koko Nor *see* Qinghai
Kokrines *36 C2* Alaska, USA
Kokshaal-Tau *123 G2 Rus.* Khrebet Kakshaal-Too. *Mountain range* China/Kyrgyzstan
Kokshetau *114 C4 Kaz.* Kökshetaū; *prev.* Kokchetav. Severnyy Kazakhstan, N Kazakhstan
Koksijde *87 A5* West-Vlaanderen, W Belgium
Koksoak *38 D2 river* Québec, E Canada
Kokstad *78 D5* KwaZulu/Natal, E South Africa
Kola *see* Kol'skiy Poluostrov
Kolaka *139 E4* Sulawesi, C Indonesia
Kolam *see* Quilon
K'o-la-ma-i *see* Karamay
Kola Peninsula *see* Kol'skiy Poluostrov
Kolari *84 D3* Lappi, NW Finland
Kolárovo *99 C6 Ger.* Gutta; *prev.* Guta, *Hung.* Gúta. Nitriansky Kraj, SW Slovakia
Kolda *74 C3* S Senegal
Kolding *85 A7* Vejle, C Denmark
Kölen *81 E1 Nor.* Kjølen. *Mountain range* Norway/Sweden
Kolguyev, Ostrov *110 C2 island* NW Russian Federation
Kolhāpur *132 B1* Mahārāshtra, SW India
Kolhumadulu Atoll *132 A5 var.* Kolumadulu Atoll, Thaa Atoll. *Atoll* S Maldives
Kolín *99 B5 Ger.* Kolin. Středočesky Kraj, C Czech Republic
Kolka *106 C2* Talsi, NW Latvia
Kolkasrags *106 C2 prev. Eng.* Cape Domesnes. *Headland* NW Latvia
Kolkata *see* Calcutta
Kollam *see* Quilon
Köln *94 A4 var.* Koeln, *Eng./Fr.* Cologne; *prev.* Cöln, *anc.* Colonia Agrippina, Oppidum Ubiorum. Nordrhein-Westfalen, W Germany
Koło *98 C3* Wielkopolskie, C Poland
Kołobrzeg *98 B2 Ger.* Kolberg. Zachodniopomorskie, NW Poland
Kolokani *74 D3* Koulikoro, W Mali
Kolomna *111 B5* Moskovskaya Oblast', W Russian Federation
Kolomyya *108 C3 Ger.* Kolomea. Ivano-Frankivs'ka Oblast', W Ukraine
Kolpa *100 A2 Ger.* Kulpa, *SCr.* Kupa. *River* Croatia/Slovenia
Kolpino *110 B4* Leningradskaya Oblast', NW Russian Federation
Kólpos Ammóchostos *102 C5 var.* Famagusta Bay, *bay* E Cyprus
Kol'skiy Poluostrov *110 C2 Eng.* Kola Peninsula. *Peninsula* NW Russian Federation
Kolumadulu Atoll *see* Kolhumadulu Atoll
Kolwezi *77 D7* Shaba, S Dem. Rep. Congo
Kolyma *115 G2 river* NE Russian Federation
Kolyma Range *113 G2 var.* Khrebet Kolymskiy, *Eng.* Kolyma Range. *Mountain range* E Russian Federation
Komatsu *131 C5 var.* Komatu. Ishikawa, Honshū, SW Japan
Komatu *see* Komatsu
Kommunizma Pik *see* Kommunizm, Qullai
Kommunizm, Qullai *123 F3 var.* Qullai Garmo, *Eng.* Communism Peak, *Rus.* Kommunizma Pik; *prev.* Stalin Peak. *Mountain* E Tajikistan
Komoé *75 E4 var.* Komoé Fleuve. *River* E Côte d'Ivoire
Komoé Fleuve *see* Komoé
Komotiní *104 D3 var.* Gümüljina, *Turk.* Gümülcine. Anatolikí Makedonía kai Thráki, NE Greece
Komsomolets, Ostrov *115 E1 island* Severnaya Zemlya, N Russian Federation
Komsomol'sk-na-Amure *115 G4* Khabarovskiy Kray, SE Russian Federation
Kondolovo *104 E3* Burgas, E Bulgaria
Kondopoga *110 B3* Respublika Kareliya, NW Russian Federation
Kondoz *see* Kunduz
Kondūz *see* Kunduz
Köneürgenç *122 C2 Rus.* Këneurgench; *prev.* Kunya-Urgench. Dashkhovuzskiy Velayat, N Turkmenistan
Kong Christian IX Land *82 D4 Eng.* King Christian IX Land. *Physical region* SE Greenland
Kong Frederik IX Land *82 C3 Eng.* King Frederik IX Land. *Physical region* SW Greenland
Kong Frederik VIII Land *83 E2 Eng.* King Frederik VIII Land. *Physical region* NE Greenland
Kong Frederik VI Kyst *82 C4 Eng.* King Frederik VI Coast. *Physical region* SE Greenland
Kong Karls Land *83 G2 Eng.* King Charles Islands. *Island group* SE Svalbard
Kongo *see* Congo
Kongolo *77 D6* Shaba, E Dem. Rep. Congo
Kongor *73 B5* Jonglei, SE Sudan
Kong Oscar Fjord *83 E3 fjord* E Greenland
Kongsberg *85 B6* Buskerud, S Norway
Kông, Tônle *137 E5 Lao.* Xê Kong. *River* Cambodia/Laos
Konia *see* Konya
Konieh *see* Konya
Konin *98 C3 Ger.* Kuhnau. Wielkopolskie, C Poland
Konispol *101 C7 var.* Konispoli. Vlorë, S Albania
Konispoli *see* Konispol
Kónitsa *104 A4* Ípeiros, W Greece
Konitz *see* Chojnice
Konjic *100 C4* Federacija Bosna I Hercegovina, S Bosnia and Herzegovina
Konosha *110 C4* Arkhangel'skaya Oblast', NW Russian Federation
Konotop *109 F1* Sums'ka Oblast', NE Ukraine
Konstanz *95 B7 var.* Constanz, *Eng.* Constance; *hist.* Kostnitz, *anc.* Constantia. Baden-Württemberg, S Germany
Konstanza *see* Constanța
Konya *116 C4 var.* Konieh; *prev.* Konia, *anc.* Iconium. Konya, C Turkey
Kopaonik *101 D5 mountain range* S Serbia and Montenegro (Yugo.)
Koper *95 D8 It.* Capodistria; *prev.* Kopar. SW Slovenia
Köpetdag Gershi *122 C3 mountain range* Iran/Turkmenistan
Koppeh Dāgh *120 D2 var.* Khrebet Kopetdag. *Mountain range* Iran/Turkmenistan
Koprivnica *100 B2 Ger.* Kopreinitz, *Hung.* Kaproncza. Koprivnica-Križevci, N Croatia
Korat *see* Nakhon Ratchasima
Korat Plateau *136 D4 plateau* E Thailand
Korba *135 E4* Madhya Pradesh, C India
Korça *see* Korçë
Korçë *101 D6 var.* Korça, *Gk.* Korytsa, *It.* Corriza; *prev.* Koritsa. Korçë, SE Albania
Korčula *100 B4 It.* Curzola; *anc.* Corcyra Nigra. *Island* S Croatia
Korea Bay *127 G3 bay* China/North Korea
Korea Strait *131 A7 Jap.* Chōsen-kaikyō, *Kor.* Taehan-haehyŏp. *Channel* Japan/South Korea
Korhogo *74 D4* N Côte d'Ivoire
Korinthiakós Kólpos *105 B5 Eng.* Gulf of Corinth; *anc.* Corinthiacus Sinus. *Gulf* C Greece
Kórinthos *105 B6 Eng.* Corinth; *anc.* Corinthus. Pelopónnisos, S Greece
Koritsa *see* Korçë
Kōriyama *131 D5* Fukushima, Honshū, C Japan
Korla *126 C3 Chin.* K'u-erh-lo. Xinjiang Uygur Zizhiqu, NW China
Körmend *99 B7* Vas, W Hungary
Koróni *105 B6* Pelopónnisos, S Greece
Koror *144 A2 var.* Oreor. *Country capital* (Palau) Oreor, N Palau
Korosten' *108 D1* Zhytomyrs'ka Oblast', NW Ukraine
Koro Toro *76 C2* Borkou-Ennedi-Tibesti, N Chad
Kortrijk *87 A6 Fr.* Courtrai. West-Vlaanderen, W Belgium
Koryak Range *see* Koryakskoye Nagor'ye
Koryakskiy Khrebet *see* Koryakskoye Nagor'ye
Koryakskoye Nagor'ye *115 H2 var.* Koryakskiy Khrebet, *Eng.* Koryak Range. *Mountain range* NE Russian Federation
Koryazhma *110 C4* Arkhangel'skaya Oblast', NW Russian Federation
Korytsa *see* Korçë
Kos *105 E6 It.* Coo; *anc.* Cos. *Island* Dodekánisos, Greece, Aegean Sea
Kos *105 E6* Kos, Dodekánisos, Greece, Aegean Sea
Kō-saki *131 A7 headland* Nagasaki, Tsushima, SW Japan
Kościan *98 B4 Ger.* Kosten. Wielkopolskie, C Poland
Koscian *see* Lubań
Kościerzyna *98 C2* Pomorskie, NW Poland
Kosciusko, Mount *see* Kosciuszko, Mount
Kosciuszko, Mount *149 C7 prev.* Mount Kosciusko. *Mountain* New South Wales, SE Australia
Koshikijima-rettō *131 A8 var.* Kosikizima Rettô. *Island group* SW Japan
Košice *99 D6 Ger.* Kaschau, *Hung.* Kassa. Košický Kraj, E Slovakia
Kosikizima Rettô *see* Koshikijima-rettō
Koson *123 E3 Rus.* Kasan. Qashqadaryo Wiloyati, S Uzbekistan
Kosovo *101 D5 prev.* Autonomous Province of Kosovo and Metohija. *Region* S Serbia and Montenegro (Yugo.)
Kosovo Polje *101 D5* Serbia, S Serbia and Montenegro (Yugo.)
Kosovska Mitrovica *101 D5 Alb.* Mitrovicë; *prev.* Mitrovica, Titova Mitrovica. Serbia, S Serbia and Montenegro (Yugo.)
Kosrae *144 C2 prev.* Kusaie. *Island* Caroline Islands, E Micronesia
Kossou, Lac de *74 D5 lake* C Côte d'Ivoire
Kostanay *130 C4 var.* Kustanay, *Kaz.* Qostanay. Kostanay, N Kazakhstan
Kosten *see* Lubań
Kostenets *104 C2 prev.* Georgi Dimitrov. Sofiya, W Bulgaria
Kostnitz *see* Konstanz
Kostroma *110 B4* Kostromskaya Oblast', NW Russian Federation
Kostyantynivka *109 G3 Rus.* Konstantinovka. Donets'ka Oblast', SE Ukraine
Koszalin *98 B2 Ger.* Köslin. Zachodniopomorskie, NW Poland
Kota *134 D3 prev.* Kotah. Rājasthān, N India
Kota Baharu *see* Kota Bharu
Kota Bahru *see* Kota Bharu
Kotabaru *see* Jayapura
Kota Bharu *138 B3 var.* Kota Baharu, Kota Bahru. Kelantan, Peninsular Malaysia
Kotabumi *138 B4 prev.* Kotaboemi. Sumatera, W Indonesia
Kota Kinabalu *138 D3 prev.* Jesselton. Sabah, East Malaysia
Kotel'nyy, Ostrov *115 E2 island* Novosibirskiye Ostrova, N Russian Federation
Kôti *see* Kōchi
Kotka *85 E5* Kymi, S Finland
Kotlas *110 C4* Arkhangel'skaya Oblast', NW Russian Federation
Kotonu *see* Cotonou
Kotor *101 C5 It.* Cattaro. Montenegro, SW Serbia and Montenegro (Yugo.)
Kotovs'k *108 D3 Rus.* Kotovsk. Odes'ka Oblast', SW Ukraine
Kotovsk *see* Hîncești
Kotte *see* Sri Jayawardanapura
Kotto *76 D4 river* Central African Republic/Dem. Rep. Congo
Kotuy *115 E2 river* N Russian Federation
Koudougou *75 E4* C Burkina faso
Koulamoutou *77 B6* Ogooué-Lolo, C Gabon
Koulikoro *74 D3* Koulikoro, SW Mali
Koumra *76 C4* Moyen-Chari, S Chad
Kourou *59 H3* N French Guiana

Kousseir *see* Al Quşayr
Kousséri *76 B3 prev.* Fort-Foureau. Extrême-Nord, NE Cameroon
Koutiala *74 D4* Sikasso, S Mali
Kouvola *85 E5* Kymi, S Finland
Kovel' *108 C1 Pol.* Kowel. Volyns'ka Oblast', NW Ukraine
Kowloon *128 A2 Chin.* Jiulong. Hong Kong, S China
Kowtal-e Barowghīl *see* Baroghil Pass
Kowtal-e Khaybar *see* Khyber Pass
Kozáni *104 B4* Dytikí Makedonía, N Greece
Kozara *100 B3 mountain range* NW Bosnia and Herzegovina
Kozarska Dubica *see* Bosanska Dubica
Kozhikode *see* Calicut
Kōzu-shima *131 D6 island* E Japan
Kozyatyn *108 D2 Rus.* Kazatin. Vinnyts'ka Oblast', C Ukraine
Kpalimé *75 E5 var.* Palimé. SW Togo
Krâchéh *137 D6 prev.* Kratie. Krâchéh, E Cambodia
Kragujevac *100 D4* Serbia, C Serbia and Montenegro (Yugo.)
Kra, Isthmus of *137 B6 isthmus* Malaysia/Thailand
Kraków *99 D5 Eng.* Cracow, *Ger.* Krakau; *anc.* Cracovia. Małopolskie, S Poland
Krâlănh *137 D5* Siĕmréab, NW Cambodia
Kraljevo *100 D4 prev.* Rankovićevo. Serbia, C Serbia and Montenegro (Yugo.)
Kramators'k *109 G3 Rus.* Kramatorsk. Donets'ka Oblast', SE Ukraine
Kramfors *85 C5* Västernorrland, C Sweden
Kranéa *104 B4* Dytikí Makedonía, N Greece
Kranj *95 D7 Ger.* Krainburg. NW Slovenia
Krāslava *106 D4* Krāslava, SE Latvia
Krasnaye *107 C5 Rus.* Krasnoye. Minskaya Voblasts', C Belarus
Krasnoarmeysk *111 C6* Saratovskaya Oblast', W Russian Federation
Krasnodar *111 A7 prev.* Ekaterinodar, Yekaterinodar. Krasnodarskiy Kray, SW Russian Federation
Krasnodon *109 H3* Luhans'ka Oblast', E Ukraine
Krasnohvardiys'ke *109 F4 Rus.* Krasnogvardeyskoye. Respublika Krym, S Ukraine
Krasnokamensk *115 F4* Chitinskaya Oblast', S Russian Federation
Krasnokamsk *111 D5* Permskaya Oblast', W Russian Federation
Krasnoperekops'k *109 F4 Rus.* Krasnoperekopsk. Respublika Krym, S Ukraine
Krasnoyarsk *114 D4* Krasnoyarskiy Kray, S Russian Federation
Krasnystaw *98 E4 Rus.* Krasnostav. Lubelskie, E Poland
Krasnyy Kut *111 C6* Saratovskaya Oblast', W Russian Federation
Krasnyy Luch *109 H3 prev.* Krindachevka. Luhans'ka Oblast', E Ukraine
Krâvanh, Chuŏr Phnum *137 C6 Eng.* Cardamom Mountains, *Fr.* Chaîne des Cardamomes. *Mountain range* W Cambodia
Krefeld *94 A4* Nordrhein-Westfalen, W Germany
Kremenchuk *109 F2 Rus.* Kremenchug. Poltavs'ka Oblast', NE Ukraine
Kremenchuts'ke Vodoskhovyshche *109 F2 Eng.* Kremenchuk Reservoir, *Rus.* Kremenchugskoye Vodokhranilishche. *Reservoir* C Ukraine
Kremenets' *108 C2 Pol.* Krzemieniec, *Rus.* Kremenets. Ternopil's'ka Oblast', W Ukraine
Kreminna *109 G2 Rus.* Kremennaya. Luhans'ka Oblast', E Ukraine
Kresena *see* Kresna
Kresna *104 C3 var.* Kresena. Blagoevgrad, SW Bulgaria
Kretikon Delagos *see* Kritikó Pélagos
Kretinga *106 B3 Ger.* Krottingen. Kretinga, NW Lithuania
Krishna *132 C1 prev.* Kistna. *River* C India
Krishnagiri *132 C2* Tamil Nādu, SE India
Kristiansand *85 A6 var.* Christiansand. Vest-Agder, S Norway
Kristianstad *85 B7* Skåne, S Sweden
Kristiansund *84 A4 var.* Christiansund. Møre og Romsdal, S Norway
Kríti *105 C7 Eng.* Crete. *Island* Greece, Aegean Sea
Kritikó Pélagos *105 D7 var.* Kretikon Delagos, *Eng.* Sea of Crete; *anc.* Mare Creticum. *Sea* Greece, Aegean Sea
Križevci *100 B2 Ger.* Kreuz, *Hung.* Kőrös. Varaždin, NE Croatia
Krk *100 A3 It.* Veglia; *anc.* Curieta. *Island* NW Croatia
Krolevets' *109 F1 Rus.* Krolevets. Sums'ka Oblast', NE Ukraine
Kronach *95 C5* Bayern, E Germany
Kroonstad *78 D4* Free State, C South Africa
Kropotkin *111 A7* Krasnodarskiy Kray, SW Russian Federation
Krosno *99 D5 Ger.* Krossen. Podkarpackie, SE Poland
Krosno Odrzańskie *98 B3 Ger.* Crossen, Kreisstadt. Lubuskie, W Poland
Krško *95 E8 Ger.* Gurkfeld; *prev.* Videm-Krško. E Slovenia
Kruhlaye *107 D6 Rus.* Krugloye. Mahilyowskaya Voblasts', E Belarus
Kruja *see* Krujë
Krujë *101 C6 var.* Kruja, *It.* Croia. Durrës, C Albania
Krummau *see* Český Krumlov
Krung Thep *137 C5 var.* Krung Thep Mahanakhon, *Eng.* Bangkok. *Country capital* (Thailand) Bangkok, C Thailand
Krung Thep, Ao *137 C5 var.* Bight of Bangkok. *Bay* S Thailand
Krung Thep Mahanakhon *see* Krung Thep
Krupki *107 D6 Rus.* Krupki. Minskaya Voblasts', C Belarus
Krychaw *107 E7 Rus.* Krichëv. Mahilyowskaya Voblasts', E Belarus
Krym *see* Crimea
Krymskaya Oblast' *see* Crimea
Kryms'ki Hory *109 F5 mountain range* S Ukraine
Kryms'kyy Pivostriv *109 F5 peninsula* S Ukraine
Krynica *99 D5 Ger.* Tannenhof. Małopolskie, S Poland
Kryve Ozero *109 E3* Odes'ka Oblast', SW Ukraine
Kryvyy Rih *109 F3 Rus.* Krivoy Rog. Dnipropetrovs'ka Oblast', SE Ukraine
Ksar al Kabir *see* Ksar-el-Kebir
Ksar al Soule *see* Er-Rachidia
Ksar-el-Kebir *70 C2 var.* Alcázar, Ksar al Kabir, Ksar-el-Kébir, *Ar.* Al-Kasr al-Kebir, Al-Qsar al-Kbir, *Sp.* Alcazarquivir. NW Morocco
Ksar-el-Kébir *see* Ksar-el-Kebir
Kuala Dungun *see* Dungun
Kuala Lumpur *138 B3 country capital* (Malaysia) Kuala Lumpur, Peninsular Malaysia
Kuala Terengganu *138 B3 var.* Kuala Trengganu. Terengganu, Peninsular Malaysia
Kuala Trengganu *see* Kuala Terengganu
Kualatungkal *138 B4* Sumatera, W Indonesia
Kuang-chou *see* Guangzhou
Kuang-hsi *see* Guangxi Zhuangzu Zizhiqu
Kuang-tung *see* Guangdong
Kuang-yuan *see* Guangyuan
Kuantan *138 B3* Pahang, Peninsular Malaysia
Kuban' *109 G5 var.* Hypanis. *River* SW Russian Federation
Kubango *see* Cubango
Kuching *138 C3 prev.* Sarawak. Sarawak, East Malaysia
Kūchnay Darweyshān *122 D5* Helmand, S Afghanistan
Kuçova *see* Kuçovë
Kuçovë *101 C6 var.* Kuçova; *prev.* Qyteti Stalin. Berat, C Albania
Kudara *see* Ghŭdara
Kudus *138 C5 prev.* Koedoes. Jawa, C Indonesia
Kuei-chou *see* Guizhou
Kuei-lin *see* Guilin
Kuei-Yang *see* Guiyang
Kueyang *see* Guiyang
Kugluktuk 53 E3 *var.* Qurlurtuuq *prev.* Coppermine. Nunavut, NW Canada
Kuhmo *84 E4* Oulu, E Finland
Kühnö *see* Kihnu
Kuibyshev *see* Kuybyshevskoye Vodokhranilishche
Kuito *78 B2 Port.* Silva Porto. Bié, C Angola
Kuji *130 D3 var.* Kuzi. Iwate, Honshū, C Japan
Kukës *101 D5 var.* Kukësi. Kukës, NE Albania
Kukësi *see* Kukës
Kukong *see* Shaoguan
Kukukhoto *see* Hohhot
Kula Kangri *135 G3 var.* Kulhakangri. *Mountain* Bhutan/China
Kuldīga *106 B3 Ger.* Goldingen. Kuldīga, W Latvia
Kuldja *see* Yining
Kulhakangri *see* Kula Kangri
Kullorsuaq *82 D2 var.* Kuvdlorssuak. C Greenland
Kulmsee *see* Chełmża
Kŭlob *123 F3 Rus.* Kulyab. SW Tajikistan
Kulu *116 C3* Konya, W Turkey
Kulunda Steppe *114 C4 Kaz.* Qulyndy Zhazyghy, *Rus.* Kulundinskaya Ravnina. *Grassland* Kazakhstan/Russian Federation
Kum *see* Qom
Kuma *111 B7 river* SW Russian Federation
Kumamoto *131 A7* Kumamoto, Kyūshū, SW Japan
Kumanovo *101 E5 Turk.* Kumanova. N FYR Macedonia
Kumasi *75 E5 prev.* Coomassie. C Ghana
Kumayri *see* Gyumri
Kumba *77 A5* Sud-Ouest, W Cameroon
Kumertau *111 D6* Respublika Bashkortostan, W Russian Federation
Kumo *75 G4* Gombe, E Nigeria
Kumon Range *136 B2 mountain range* N Myanmar
Kumul *see* Hami
Kunashiri *see* Kunashir, Ostrov
Kunashir, Ostrov *130 E1 var.* Kunashiri. *Island* Kuril'skiye Ostrova, SE Russian Federation
Kunda *106 E2* Lääne-Virumaa, NE Estonia
Kunduz *123 E3 var.* Kondoz, Kundūz, Qondūz, *Per.* Kondūz. Kunduz, NE Afghanistan
Kuneitra *see* Al Qunayţirah
Kunene *see* Cunene
Kungsbacka *85 B7* Halland, S Sweden
Kungur *111 D5* Permskaya Oblast', NW Russian Federation
Kunlun Mountains *see* Kunlun Shan
Kunlun Shan *126 B4 Eng.* Kunlun Mountains. *Mountain range* NW China
Kunming *128 B6 var.* K'un-ming; *prev.* Yunnan. Yunnan, SW China
K'un-ming *see* Kunming
Kununurra *146 D3* Western Australia
Kuopio *85 E5* Itä-Suomi, C Finland
Kupang *139 E5 prev.* Koepang. Timor, C Indonesia
Kup"yans'k *109 G2 Rus.* Kupyansk. Kharkivs'ka Oblast', E Ukraine
Kura *117 H3 Az.* Kür, *Geor.* Mtkvari, *Turk.* Kura Nehri. *River* SW Asia
Kurashiki *131 B6 var.* Kurasiki. Okayama, Honshū, SW Japan
Kurasiki *see* Kurashiki
Kurdistan *117 F4 cultural region* SW Asia
Kŭrdzhali *104 D3 var.* Kirdzhali. Kŭrdzhali, S Bulgaria
Kure *131 B7* Hiroshima, Honshū, SW Japan
Küre Dağları *116 C2 mountain range* N Turkey
Kuressaare *106 C2 Ger.* Arensburg; *prev.* Kingissepp. Saaremaa, W Estonia
Kureyka *112 D2 river* N Russian Federation
Kuria Muria Islands *see* Ḩalāniyāt, Juzur al
Kurile Islands *see* Kuril'skiye Ostrova
Kurile-Kamchatka Depression *see* Kurile Trench
Kurile Trench *113 F3 var.* Kurile-Kamchatka Depression. *Undersea feature* NW Pacific Ocean
Kuril'sk *130 E1* Kuril'skiye Ostrova, Sakhalinskaya Oblats', SE Russian Federation
Kuril'skiye Ostrova *115 H4 Eng.* Kurile Islands. *Island group* SE Russian Federation
Ku-ring-gai *148 E1* New South Wales, SE Australia
Kurnool *132 C1 var.* Karnul. Andhra Pradesh, S India
Kursk *111 A6* Kurskaya Oblast', W Russian Federation
Kuršumlija *101 D5* Serbia, S Serbia and Montenegro (Yugo.)
Kuruktag *126 C3 mountain range* NW China
Kurume *131 A7* Fukuoka, Kyūshū, SW Japan
Kurupukari *59 F3* C Guyana
Kurzeme *106 B3 Eng.* Courland, *Ger.* Kurland. *Former province* W Latvia
Kushiro *130 D2 var.* Kusiro. Hokkaidō, NE Japan
Kusiro *see* Kushiro
Kuskokwim Mountains *36 C3 mountain range* Alaska, USA
Kuźnica *98 E2* Podlaskie, NE Poland
Kustanay *see* Kostanay
Küstence *see* Constanţa
Küstendje *see* Constanţa
Kütahya *116 B3 prev.* Kutaia. Kütahya, W Turkey
Kutai *see* Mahakam, Sungai
K'ut'aisi *117 F2* W Georgia
Kūt al 'Amārah *see* Al Kūt
Kut al Imara *see* Al Kūt
Kutaradja *see* Bandaaceh
Kutaraja *see* Bandaaceh
Kutch, Gulf of *see* Kachchh, Gulf of
Kutch, Rann of *see* Kachchh, Rann of
Kutina *100 B3* Sisak-Moslavina, NE Croatia
Kutno *98 C3* Łódzkie, C Poland
Kuujjuaq *39 E2 prev.* Fort-Chimo. Québec, E Canada
Kuusamo *84 E3* Oulu, Finland
Kuvango *see* Cubango
Kuvdlorssuak *see* Kullorsuaq
Kuwait *120 C4 var.* Dawlat al Kuwait, Koweit, Kuweit. *Country* SW Asia

Kuwait 120

Official name State of Kuwait
Formation 1961
Capital Kuwait City
Population 2.5 million / 363 people per sq mile (140 people per sq km)
Total area 6880 sq. miles (17,820 sq. km)
Languages Arabic, English
Religions Sunni Muslim 45%, Shi'a Muslim 40%, Christian, Hindu, and other 15%
Ethnic mix Kuwaiti 45%, Other Arab 35%, South Asian 9%, other 7%, Iranian 4%
Government Monarchy
Currency Kuwaiti dinar = 1000 fils
Literacy rate 83%
Calorie consumption 3170 calories

Kuwait *see* Al Kuwayt
Kuwait City *see* Al Kuwayt
Kuwajleen *see* Kwajalein Atoll
Kuwayt *120 C3* E Iraq
Kuybyshev Reservoir *see* Kuybyshevskoye Vodokhranilishche
Kuybyshevskoye Vodokhranilishche *111 C5 var.* Kuibyshev, *Eng.* Kuybyshev Reservoir. *Reservoir* W Russian Federation
Kuytun *126 B2* Xinjiang Uygur Zizhiqu, NW China
Kuzi *see* Kuji
Kuznetsk *111 B6* Penzenskaya Oblast', W Russian Federation
Kvaløya *84 C2 island* N Norway
Kvarnbergsvattnet *84 B4 var.* Frostviken. *Lake* N Sweden
Kvarner *100 A3 var.* Carnaro, *It.* Quarnero. *Gulf* W Croatia
Kvitøya *83 G1 island* NE Svalbard
Kwajalein Atoll *144 C1 var.* Kuwajleen. *Atoll* Ralik Chain, C Marshall Islands
Kwando *see* Cuando
Kwangchow *see* Guangzhou
Kwangju *129 E4 off.* Kwangju-gwangyŏksi, *var.* Guangju, Kwangchu, *Jap.* Kōshū. SW South Korea
Kwango *77 C7 Port.* Cuango. *River* Angola/Dem. Rep. Congo *see also* Cuango
Kwango *see* Cuango
Kwangsi *see* Guangxi Zhuangzu Zizhiqu
Kwangsi Chuang Autonomous Region *see* Guangxi Zhuangzu Zizhiqu
Kwangtung *see* Guangdong
Kwangyuan *see* Guangyuan
Kwanza *see* Cuanza
Kweichow *see* Guizhou
Kweilin *see* Guilin
Kweisui *see* Hohhot
Kweiyang *see* Guiyang
Kwekwe *78 D3 prev.* Que Que. Midlands, C Zimbabwe
Kwesui *see* Hohhot
Kwidzyń *98 C2 Ger.* Marienwerder. Pomorskie, N Poland
Kwigillingok *36 C3* Alaska, USA
Kwilu *77 C6 river* W Dem. Rep. Congo
Kwito *see* Cuito
Kyabé *76 C4* Moyen-Chari, S Chad
Kyaikkami *137 B5 prev.* Amherst. Mon State, S Myanmar
Kyaiklat *136 B4* Irrawaddy, SW Myanmar
Kyaikto *136 B4* Mon State, S Myanmar
Kyakhta *115 E5* Respublika Buryatiya, S Russian Federation
Kyaukse *136 B3* Mandalay, C Myanmar
Kyjov *99 C5 Ger.* Gaya. Brněnský Kraj, SE Czech Republic
Kykládes *105 D6 var.* Kikládhes, *Eng.* Cyclades. *Island group* SE Greece
Kými *105 C5 prev.* Kími. Évvoia, C Greece
Kyōto *131 C6* Kyōto, Honshū, SW Japan
Kyparissía *105 B6 var.* Kiparissía. Pelopónnisos, S Greece
Kyrá Panagía *105 C5 island* Vóreioi Sporádes, Greece, Aegean Sea
Kyrenia *see* Kerýneia
Kyrgyzstan *123 F2 var.* Kirghizia; *prev.* Kirgizskaya SSR, Kirghiz SSR, Republic of Kyrgyzstan. *Country* C Asia

Kyrgyzstan 123

Official name Kyrgyz Republic
Formation 1991
Capital Bishkek
Population 5.1 million / 67 people per sq mile (26 people per sq km)
Total area 76,641 sq. miles (198,500 sq. km)
Languages Kyrgyz, Russian, Uzbek, Tatar, Ukrainian
Religions Muslim (mainly Sunni) 70%, Orthodox Christian 30%**Ethnic mix** Kyrgyz 57%, Russian 19%, Uzbek 13%, other 7%, Tatar 2%, Ukrainian 2%
Government Presidential system
Currency Som = 100 tyyn
Literacy rate 97%
Calorie consumption 2882 calories

Kýthira *105 C7 var.* Kíthira, *It.* Cerigo; *Lat.* Cythera. *Island* S Greece
Kýthnos *105 C6 var.* Kíthnos, Thermiá, *It.* Termia; *anc.* Cythnos. *Island* Kykládes, Greece, Aegean Sea
Kýthnos *105 C6* Kýthnos, Kykládes, Greece, Aegean Sea
Kythréa *102 C5* N Cyprus
Kyūshū *131 B7 var.* Kyûsyû. *Island* SW Japan
Kyushu-Palau Ridge *125 F3 var.* Kyusyu-Palau Ridge. *Undersea feature* W Pacific Ocean
Kyustendil *104 B2 anc.* Pautalia. Kyustendil, W Bulgaria
Kyûsyû *see* Kyūshū
Kyusyu-Palau Ridge *see* Kyushu-Palau Ridge
Kyyiv *109 E2 Eng.* Kiev, *Rus.* Kiyev. *Country capital* (Ukraine) Kyyivs'ka Oblast', N Ukraine
Kyyivs'ke Vodoskhovyshche *109 E1 Eng.* Kiev Reservoir, *Rus.* Kiyevskoye Vodokhranilishche. *Reservoir* N Ukraine
Kyzyl *114 D4* Respublika Tyva, C Russian Federation
Kyzyl Kum *122 D2 var.* Kizil Kum, Qizil Qum, Qizilqum. *Desert* Kazakhstan/Uzbekistan
Kyzylorda *114 B5 var.* Kzyl-orda, Qizil Orda, *Kaz.* Qyzylorda; *prev.* Perovsk. Kyzylorda, S Kazakhstan
Kyzyl-Suu *123 G2 prev.* Pokrovka. Issyk-Kul'skaya Oblast', NE Kyrgyzstan
Kyzyl-orda *see* Kyzylorda

L

La Algaba *92 C4* Andalucía, S Spain
Laamu Atoll *see* Hadhdhunmathi Atoll
Laarne *87 B5* Oost-Vlaanderen, NW Belgium
La Asunción *59 E1* Nueva Esparta, NE Venezuela
Laâyoune *70 B3 var.* Aaiún. *Dependent territory capital* (Western Sahara) NW Western Sahara
la Baule-Escoublac *90 A4* Loire-Atlantique, NW France
Labé *74 C4* Moyenne-Guinée, NW Guinea
La Blanquilla *see* Blanquilla, Isla
Laborec *99 E5 Hung.* Laborca. *River* E Slovakia
Labrador *39 F2 cultural region* Newfoundland and Labrador, SW Canada
Labrador Basin *34 E3 var.* Labrador Sea Basin. *Undersea feature* Labrador Sea
Labrador Sea *82 A4 sea* NW Atlantic Ocean
Labrador Sea Basin *see* Labrador Basin
Labutta *137 A5* Irrawaddy, SW Myanmar
Laç *101 C6 var.* Laci. Lezhë, C Albania
La Calera *64 B4* Valparaíso, C Chile
La Carolina *92 D4* Andalucía, S Spain
Laccadive Islands *see* Lakshadweep
La Ceiba *52 D2* Atlántida, N Honduras
Lachanás *104 B3* Kentrikí Makedonía, N Greece
La Chaux-de-Fonds *95 A7* Neuchâtel, W Switzerland
Lachlan River *149 C6 river* New South Wales, SE Australia
Laci *see* Laç
la Ciotat *91 D6 anc.* Citharista. Bouches-du-Rhône, SE France
La Concepción *58 C1* Zulia, NW Venezuela
La Concepción *53 E5 var.* Concepción. Chiriquí, W Panama
La Condamine *91 C8* NW Andorra
Laconia *41 G2* New Hampshire, NE USA
La Crosse *40 A2* Wisconsin, N USA
La Cruz *52 D4* Guanacaste, NW Costa Rica
Lacus Asphaltites *see* Dead Sea
Ladoga, Lake *see* Ladozhskoye Ozero
Ladozhskoye Ozero *110 B3 Eng.* Lake Ladoga, *Fin.* Laatokka. *Lake* NW Russian Federation
Ladysmith *40 B2* Wisconsin, N USA
Lae *144 B3* Morobe, W PNG
La Esperanza *52 C2* Intibucá, SW Honduras
Lafayette *40 C4* Indiana, N USA
Lafayette *42 B3* Louisiana, S USA
La Fé *54 A2* Pinar del Río, W Cuba
Lafia *75 G4* Nassarawa, C Nigeria
la Flèche *90 B4* Sarthe, NW France
Lagdo, Lac de *76 B4 lake* N Cameroon
Laghouat *70 D2* N Algeria
Lago dos Gansos *see* Goose Lake
Lago General Carrera *see* Buenos Aires, Lago
Lago Nyassa *see* Nyasa, Lake
Lago Pampa Aullagas *see* Poopó, Lago
Lagos *92 B5 anc.* Lacobriga. Faro, S Portugal
Lagos *75 F5* Lagos, SW Nigeria
Lagos de Moreno *51 E4* Jalisco, SW Mexico
Lagouira *70 A4* SW Western Sahara
La Grande *46 C3* Oregon, NW USA
La Guaira *66 B4* Distrito Federal, N Venezuela
Laguna Merín *see* Mirim Lagoon
Lagunas *64 B1* Tarapacá, N Chile
Lagunillas *61 G4* Santa Cruz, SE Bolivia
La Habana *54 B2 var.* Havana. *Country capital* (Cuba) Ciudad de La Habana, W Cuba
Lahat *138 B4* Sumatera, W Indonesia
La Haye *see* 's-Gravenhage
Laholm *85 B7* Halland, S Sweden
Lahore *134 D2* Punjab, NE Pakistan
Lahr *95 A6* Baden-Württemberg, S Germany
Lahti *85 D5 Swe.* Lahtis. Etelä-Suomi, S Finland
Laï *76 B4 prev.* Behagle, De Behagle. Tandjilé, S Chad
Lai Châu *136 D3* Lai Châu, N Vietnam
Laila *see* Laylá
La Junta *44 D5* Colorado, C USA
Lake Charles *42 A3* Louisiana, S USA
Lake City *43 E3* Florida, SE USA
Lake District *89 C5 physical region* NW England, UK
Lake Havasu City *48 A2* Arizona, SW USA
Lake Jackson *49 H4* Texas, SW USA
Lakeland *43 E4* Florida, SE USA
Lakeside *47 C8* California, W USA
Lakewood *44 D4* Colorado, C USA
Lakhnau *see* Lucknow
Lakonikós Kólpos *105 B7 gulf* S Greece
Lakselv *84 D2* Finnmark, N Norway
Lakshadweep *132 A3 Eng.* Laccadive Islands. *Island group* India, N Indian Ocean
la Laon *see* Laon
Lalibela *72 C4* N Ethiopia
La Libertad *52 B1* Petén, N Guatemala
La Ligua *64 B4* Valparaíso, C Chile
Lalín *92 C1* Galicia, NW Spain
Lalitpur *135 F3* Central, C Nepal
La Louvière *87 B6* Hainaut, S Belgium
La Maçana *see* La Massana
La Maddalena *96 A4* Sardegna, Italy, C Mediterranean Sea
la Manche *see* English Channel
Lamar *44 D5* Colorado, C USA
La Marmora, Punta *97 A5 mountain* Sardegna, Italy, C Mediterranean Sea
La Massana *91 A8 var.* La Maçana. W Andorra
Lambaréné *77 A6* Moyen-Ogooué, W Gabon
Lamego *92 C2* Viseu, N Portugal
Lamesa *49 E3* Texas, SW USA
Lamezia Terme *97 D6* Calabria, SE Italy
Lamía *105 B5* Stereá Ellás, C Greece
Lamoni *45 F4* Iowa, C USA
Lampang *136 C4 var.* Muang Lampang. Lampang, NW Thailand
Lámpeia *105 B6* Dytikí Ellás, S Greece
Lanbi Kyun *137 B6 prev.* Sullivan Island. *Island* Mergui Archipelago, S Myanmar
Lancang Jiang *see* Mekong
Lancaster *47 C7* California, W USA
Lancaster *89 D5* NW England, UK
Lancaster *41 F4* Pennsylvania, NE USA
Lancaster Sound *37 F2 sound* Nunavut, N Canada
Lan-chou *see* Lanzhou
Lan-chow *see* Lanzhou
Landen *87 C6* Vlaams Brabant, C Belgium
Lander *44 C3* Wyoming, C USA
Landerneau *90 A3* Finistère, NW France
Landes *91 B5 department* SW France
Land's End *89 B8 headland* SW England, UK
Landshut *95 C6* Bayern, SE Germany
Langar *123 E2 Rus.* Lyangar. Nawoiy Wiloyati, C Uzbekistan
Langfang *128 D4* Hebei, E China
Langkawi, Pulau *137 B7 island* Peninsular Malaysia
Langres *90 D4* Haute-Marne, N France
Langsa *138 A3* Sumatera, W Indonesia
Lang Shan *127 E3 mountain range* N China
Lang Sơn *136 D3 var.* Langson. Lang Sơn, N Vietnam
Langson *see* Lang Sơn
Lang Suan *137 B6* Chumphon, SW Thailand
Languedoc *91 C6 cultural region* S France
Länkäran *117 H3 Rus.* Lenkoran'. S Azerbaijan
Lansing *40 C3 state capital* Michigan, N USA
Lanta, Ko *137 B7 island* S Thailand
Lantau Island *128 A2 Cant.* Tai Yue Shan, *Chin.* Landao. *Island* Hong Kong, S China

Lan-ts'ang Chiang *see* Mekong
Lanzarote *70 B3 island* Islas Canarias, Spain, NE Atlantic Ocean
Lanzhou *128 B4 var.* Lan-chou, Lanchow, Lan-chow; *prev.* Kaolan. Gansu, C China
Lao Cai *136 D3* Lao Cai, N Vietnam
Laojunmiao *see* Yumen
Laon *90 D3 var.* la Laon; *anc.* Laudunum. Aisne, N France
La Orchila, Isla *58 D1 island* N Venezuela
La Oroya *60 C3* Junín, C Peru
Laos *136 D4 Country* SE Asia

Laos 136

Official name Lao People's Democratic Republic
Formation 1953
Capital Vientiane
Population 5.7 million / 64 people per sq mile (25 people per sq km)**Total area** 91,428 sq. miles (236,800 sq. km)
Languages Lao, Mon-Khmer, Yao, Vietnamese, Chinese, French
Religions Buddhist 85%, Other (including animist) 15%
Ethnic mix Lao Loum 66%, Lao Theung 30%, other 2%, Lao Soung 2%
Government One-party state
Currency New kip = 100 at
Literacy rate 66%
Calorie consumption 2309 calories

La Palma *70 A3 island* Islas Canarias, Spain, NE Atlantic Ocean
La Palma *53 G5* Darién, SE Panama
La Paz *61 F4 var.* La Paz de Ayacucho. *Country capital* (Bolivia-legislative and administrative capital) La Paz, W Bolivia
La Paz *50 B3* Baja California Sur, NW Mexico
La Paz, Bahía de *50 B3 bay* W Mexico
La Paz de Ayacucho *see* La Paz
La Perouse Strait *130 D1 Jap.* Sōya-kaikyō, *Rus.* Proliv Laperuza. *Strait* Japan/Russian Federation
Lápithos *102 C5* NW Cyprus
Lapland *84 D3 Fin.* Lappi, *Swe.* Lappland. *Cultural region* N Europe
La Plata *64 D4* Buenos Aires, E Argentina
Lappeenranta *85 E5 Swe.* Villmanstrand. Etelä-Suomi, S Finland
Lappi *see* Lapland
Lappland *see* Lapland
Lapta *see* Lápithos
Laptev Sea *see* Laptevykh, More
Laptevykh, More *115 E2 Eng.* Laptev Sea. *Sea* Arctic Ocean
Lapua *85 D5 Swe.* Lappo. Länsi-Suomi, W Finland
La Puebla *see* Sa Pobla
Łapy *98 E3* Podlaskie
La Quiaca *64 C2* Jujuy, N Argentina
L'Aquila *96 C4 var.* Aquila, Aquila degli Abruzzo. Abruzzo, C Italy
Laracha *92 B1* Galicia, NW Spain
Laramie *44 C4* Wyoming, C USA
Laramie Mountains *44 C3 mountain range* Wyoming, C USA
Laredo *93 E1* Cantabria, N Spain
Laredo *49 F5* Texas, SW USA
Largo *43 E4* Florida, SE USA
Largo, Cayo *54 B2 island* W Cuba
Lario *see* Como, Lago di
La Rioja *93 E2* La Rioja, NW Argentina
Lárisa *104 B4 var.* Larissa. Thessalía, C Greece
Larissa *see* Lárisa
Lārkāna *134 B3 var.* Larkhana. Sind, SE Pakistan
Larkhana *see* Lārkāna
Larnaca *see* Lárnaka
Lárnaka *102 C5 var.* Larnaca, Larnax. SE Cyprus
Larnax *see* Lárnaka
la Rochelle *90 B4 anc.* Rupella. Charente-Maritime, W France
la Roche-sur-Yon *90 B4 prev.* Bourbon Vendée, Napoléon-Vendée. Vendée, NW France
La Roda *93 E3* Castilla-La Mancha, C Spain
La Romana *55 E3* E Dominican Republic
Larvotto *91 C8* N Monaco
La-sa *see* Lhasa
Las Cabezas de San Juan *92 C5* Andalucía, S Spain
Las Cruces *48 D3* New Mexico, SW USA
La See d'Urgel *93 G1 var.* La Seu d'Urgell, Seo de Urgel. Cataluña, NE Spain
La Serena *64 B3* Coquimbo, C Chile
La Seu d'Urgell *see* La See d'Urgel
la Seyne-sur-Mer *91 D6* Var, SE France
Lashio *136 B3* Shan State, E Myanmar
Lashkar Gāh *122 D5 var.* Lash-Kar-Gar'. Helmand, S Afghanistan
Lash-Kar-Gar' *see* Lashkar Gāh
La Sila *97 D6 mountain range* SW Italy
La Sirena *52 D3* Región Autónoma Atlántico Sur, E Nicaragua
Łask *98 C4* Łódzkie, C Poland
Las Lomitas *64 D2* Formosa, N Argentina
La Solana *93 E4* Castilla-La Mancha, C Spain
Las Palmas de Gran Canaria *70 A3* Gran Canaria, Islas Canarias, Spain, NE Atlantic Ocean
La Spezia *96 B3* Liguria, NW Italy
Lassa *see* Lhasa
Las Tablas *53 F5* Los Santos, S Panama
Las Tunas *54 C2 var.* Victoria de las Tunas. Las Tunas, E Cuba
Las Vegas *47 D7* Nevada, W USA
Latacunga *60 B1* Cotopaxi, C Ecuador
la Teste *91 B5* Gironde, SW France
Latina *97 C5 prev.* Littoria. Lazio, C Italy
La Tortuga, Isla *59 E1 var.* Isla Tortuga. *Island* N Venezuela
La Tuque *39 E4* Québec, SE Canada
Latvia *106 C3 Ger.* Lettland, *Latv.* Latvija,Latvijas Republika; *prev.* Latvian SSR, *Rus.* Latviyskaya SSR. *Country* NE Europe

Latvia 106

Official name Republic of Latvia
Formation 1991
Capital Riga
Population 2.3 million / 92 people per sq mile (36 people per sq km)
Total area 24,938 sq. miles (64,589 sq. km)
Languages Latvian, Russian
Religions Lutheran 55%, Roman Catholic 24%, other 12%, Orthodox Christian 9%
Ethnic mix Latvian 57%, Russian 32%, Belarussian 4%, Ukrainian 3%, Polish 2%, other 2%
Government Parliamentary system
Currency Lats = 100 santims
Literacy rate 99%
Calorie consumption 2809 calories

Laudunum *see* Laon
Lauenburg *see* Lębork
Lauenburg in Pommern *see* Lębork
Lau Group *145 E4 island group* E Fiji
Launceston *149 C8* Tasmania, SE Australia
La Unión *93 F4* Murcia, SE Spain
La Unión *52 C2* Olancho, C Honduras
Laurel *42 C3* Mississippi, S USA
Laurel *44 C2* Montana, NW USA
Laurentian Highlands *see* Laurentian Mountains
Laurentian Mountains *39 E3 var.* Laurentian Highlands, *Fr.* Les Laurentides. *Plateau* Newfoundland and Labrador/Québec, Canada
Lauria *97 D6* Basilicata, S Italy
Laurinburg *43 F1* North Carolina, SE USA
Lauru *see* Choiseul
Lausanne *95 A7 It.* Losanna. Vaud, SW Switzerland
Laut Banda *see* Banda Sea
Laut, Pulau *138 D4 prev.* Laoet. *Island* Borneo, C Indonesia
Laval *90 B3* Mayenne, NW France
Laval *38 D4* Québec, SE Canada
La Vega *55 E3 var.* Concepción de la Vega. C Dominican Republic
La Vila Jojosa *see* Villajoyosa
Lávrio *105 C6 prev.* Lávrion. Attikí, C Greece
Lawrence *41 G3* Massachusetts, NE USA
Lawrenceburg *42 C1* Tennessee, S USA
Lawton *49 F2* Oklahoma, C USA
La Yarada *61 E4* Tacna, SW Peru
Laylá *121 C5 var.* Laila. Ar Riyāḍ, C Saudi Arabia
Lazarev Sea *154 B1 sea* Antarctica
Lázaro Cárdenas *51 E5* Michoacán de Ocampo, SW Mexico
Læsø *85 B7 island* N Denmark
Leamhcán *see* Lucan
Leamington *38 C5* Ontario, S Canada
Lebak *139 E3* Mindanao, S Philippines
Lebanon *118 A4 Ar.* Al Lubnān, *Fr.* Liban. *Country* SW Asia

Lebanon 118

Official name Republic of Lebanon
Formation 1941
Capital Beirut
Population 3.7 million / 937 people per sq mile (362 people per sq km)
Total area 4015 sq. miles (10,400 sq. km)
Languages Arabic, French, Armenian, Assyrian
Religions Muslim 70%, Christian 30%
Ethnic mix Arab 94%, Armenian 4%, other 2%
Government Parliamentary system
Currency Lebanese pound = 100 piastres
Literacy rate 87%
Calorie consumption 3184 calories

Lebanon *45 G5* Missouri, C USA
Lebanon *41 G2* New Hampshire, NE USA
Lebanon *46 B3* Oregon, NW USA
Lebap *122 D2* Lebapskiy Velayat, NE Turkmenistan
Lebedyn *109 F2 Rus.* Lebedin. Sums'ka Oblast', NE Ukraine
Lębork *98 C2 var.* Lębórk, *Ger.* Lauenburg, Lauenburg in Pommern. Pomorskie, N Poland
Lebrija *92 C5* Andalucía, S Spain
Lebu *65 A5* Bío Bío, C Chile
le Cannet *91 D6* Alpes-Maritimes, SE France
Le Cap *see* Cap-Haïtien
Lecce *97 E6* Puglia, SE Italy
Lechainá *105 B6 var.* Lehena, Lekhainá. Dytikí Ellás, S Greece
Leduc *37 E5* Alberta, SW Canada
Leech Lake *45 F2 lake* Minnesota, N USA
Leeds *89 D5* N England, UK
Leek *86 E2* Groningen, NE Netherlands
Leer *94 A3* Niedersachsen, NW Germany
Leeuwarden *86 D1 Fris.* Ljouwert. Friesland, N Netherlands
Leeuwin, Cape *142 A5 headland* Western Australia
Leeward Islands *55 G3 island group* E West Indies
Leeward Islands *see* Sotavento, Ilhas de
Lefkáda *105 A5 It.* Santa Maura; *prev.* Levkás, *anc.* Leucas. *Island* Iónioi Nísoi, Greece, C Mediterranean Sea
Lefkáda *105 A5 prev.* Levkás. Lefkáda, Iónioi Nísoi, Greece, C Mediterranean Sea
Lefká Óri *105 C7 mountain range* Kríti, Greece, E Mediterranean Sea
Lefkímmi *105 A5 var.* Levkímmi. Kérkyra, Iónioi Nísoi, Greece, C Mediterranean Sea
Legaspi *139 E2 off.* Legaspi City. Luzon, N Philippines
Legnica *98 B4 Ger.* Liegnitz. Dolnośląskie
le Havre *90 B3 Eng.* Havre; *prev.* le Havre-de-Grâce. Seine-Maritime, N France
Lehena *see* Lechainá
Leicester *89 D6 Lat.* Batae Coritanorum. C England, UK
Leiden *86 B3 prev.* Leyden, *anc.* Lugdunum Batavorum. Zuid-Holland, W Netherlands
Leie *90 D2 Fr.* Lys. *River* Belgium/France
Leinster *89 B6 Ir.* Cúige Laighean. *Cultural region* E Ireland
Leipsoí *105 E6 island* Dodekánisos, Greece, Aegean Sea
Leipzig *94 C4 Pol.* Lipsk; *hist.* Leipsic, *anc.* Lipsia. Sachsen, E Germany
Leiria *92 B3 anc.* Collipo. Leiria, C Portugal
Leirvik *85 A6* Hordaland, S Norway
Lek *86 C4 river* SW Netherlands
Lekhainá *see* Lechainá
Lekhchevo *104 C2* Montana, NW Bulgaria
Leksand *85 C5* Kopparberg, C Sweden
Lelystad *86 D3* Flevoland, C Netherlands
le Mans *90 B3* Sarthe, NW France
Lemesós *102 C5 var.* Limassol. SW Cyprus
Lena *115 F3 river* NE Russian Federation
Lena Tablemount *141 B7 undersea feature* S Indian Ocean
Len Dao *128 C8 island* S Spratly Islands
Lengshuitan *128 C6* Hunan, S China
Leninabad *see* Khŭjand
Leninakan *see* Gyumri
Lenine *109 G5 Rus.* Lenino. Respublika Krym, S Ukraine
Leningorsk *114 D4 Kaz.* Leninogor. Vostochnyy Kazakhstan, E Kazakhstan
Leningrad *see* Sankt-Peterburg
Leningradskaya *154 B4 Russian research station* Antarctica
Leninobod *see* Khŭjand
Leninpol' *123 F2* Talasskaya Oblast', NW Kyrgyzstan
Lenti *99 B7* Zala, SW Hungary
Leoben *95 E7* Steiermark, C Austria
León *51 E4 var.* León de los Aldamas. Guanajuato, C Mexico
León *92 D1* Castilla-León, NW Spain
León *52 C3* León, NW Nicaragua
León de los Aldamas *see* León
Leonídi *105 B6* Pelopónnisos, S Greece
Lepe *92 C4* Andalucía, S Spain
le Portel *90 C2* Pas-de-Calais, N France
le Puy *91 C5 prev.* le Puy-en-Velay, *hist.* Anicium, Podium Anicensis. Haute-Loire, C France
Léré *76 B4* Mayo-Kébbi, SW Chad
Lerma *92 D2* Castilla-León, N Spain
Léros *105 D6 island* Dodekánisos, Greece, Aegean Sea
Lerrnayin Gharabakh *see* Nagorno-Karabakh
Lerwick *88 D1* NE Scotland, UK

Lesbos *see* Lésvos
Les Cayes *see* Cayes
Les Gonaïves *see* Gonaïves
Lesh *see* Lezhë
Leshan *128 B5* Sichuan, C China
les Herbiers *90 B4* Vendée, NW France
Leshi *see* Lezhë
Leskovac *101 E5* Serbia, SE Serbia and Montenegro (Yugo.)
Les Laurentides *see* Laurentian Highlands
Lesnoy *114 C3* Sverdlovskaya Oblast', C Russian Federation
Lesotho *78 D4 prev.* Basutoland. *Country* S Africa

Lesotho 78

Official name Kingdom of Lesotho
Formation 1966
Capital Maseru
Population 1.8 million / 154 people per sq mile (59 people per sq km)
Total area 11,720 sq. miles (30,355 sq. km)
Languages English, Sesotho, isiZulu
Religions Christian 90%, Traditional beliefs 10%
Ethnic mix Sotho 97%, European and Asian 3%
Government Parliamentary system
Currency Loti = 100 lisente
Literacy rate 81%
Calorie consumption 2320 calories

les Sables-d'Olonne *90 B4* Vendée, NW France
Lesser Antarctica *154 A3 var.* West Antarctica. *Physical region* Antarctica
Lesser Antilles *55 G4 island group* E West Indies
Lesser Caucasus *117 F2 Rus.* Malyy Kavkaz. *Mountain range* SW Asia
Lesser Sunda Islands *see* Nusa Tenggara
Lésvos *116 A3 anc.* Lesbos. *Island* E Greece
Leszno *98 B4 Ger.* Lissa. Wielkopolskie, C Poland
Lethbridge *37 E5* Alberta, SW Canada
Lethem *59 F3* S Guyana
Leti, Kepulauan *139 F5 island group* E Indonesia
Letpadan *136 B4* Pegu, SW Myanmar
Letsôk-aw Kyun *137 B6 var.* Letsutan Island; *prev.* Domel Island. *Island* Mergui Archipelago, S Myanmar
Letsutan Island *see* Letsôk-aw Kyun
Leuven *87 C6 Fr.* Louvain, *Ger.* Löwen. Vlaams Brabant, C Belgium
Leuze *see* Leuze-en-Hainaut
Leuze-en-Hainaut *87 B6 var.* Leuze. Hainaut, SW Belgium
Levanger *84 B4* Nord-Trøndelag, C Norway
Levelland *49 E2* Texas, SW USA
Leverkusen *94 A4* Nordrhein-Westfalen, W Germany
Levice *99 C6 Ger.* Lewentz, Lewenz, *Hung.* Léva. Nitriansky Kraj, SW Slovakia
Levin *150 D4* Manawatu-Wanganui, North Island, NZ
Levkímmi *see* Lefkímmi
Lewis, Isle of *88 B2 island* NW Scotland, UK
Lewis Range *44 B1 mountain range* Montana, NW USA
Lewiston *46 C2* Idaho, NW USA
Lewiston *41 G2* Maine, NE USA
Lewistown *44 C1* Montana, NW USA
Lexington *40 C5* Kentucky, S USA
Lexington *45 E4* Nebraska, C USA
Leyte *139 F2 island* C Philippines
Leżajsk *99 E5* Podkarpackie, SE Poland
Lezha *see* Lezhë
Lezhë *101 C6 var.* Lezha; *prev.* Lesh, Leshi. Lezhë, NW Albania
Lhasa *126 C5 var.* La-sa, Lassa. Xizang Zizhiqu, W China
Lhaviyani Atoll *see* Faadhippolhu Atoll
Lhazê *126 C5* Xizang Zizhiqu, W China
L'Hospitalet de Llobregat *93 G2 var.* Hospitalet. Cataluña, NE Spain
Liancourt Rocks *131 A5 Jap.* Takeshima, *Kor.* Tok-Do. *Island group* Japan/South Korea
Lianyungang *128 D4 var.* Xinpu. Jiangsu, E China
Liao *see* Liaoning
Liaodong Wan *127 G3 Eng.* Gulf of Lantung, Gulf of Liaotung. *Gulf* NE China
Liao He *125 E1 river* NE China
Liaoning *128 D3 var.* Liao, Liaoning Sheng, Shengking; *hist.* Fengtien, Shenking. Admin. region *province* NE China
Liaoyuan *129 E3 var.* Dongliao, Shuang-liao, *Jap.* Chengchiatun. Jilin, NE China
Liard *see* Fort Liard
Liban, Jebel *118 B4 Ar.* Jabal al Gharbt, Jabal Lubnān, *Eng.* Mount Lebanon. *Mountain range* C Lebanon
Libby *44 A1* Montana, NW USA
Liberal *45 E5* Kansas, C USA
Liberec *98 B4 Ger.* Reichenberg. Liberecký Kraj, N Czech Republic
Liberia *74 C5 Country* W Africa

Liberia 74

Official name Republic of Liberia
Formation 1847
Capital Monrovia
Population 3.4 million / 91 people per sq mile (35 people per sq km)
Total area 43,000 sq. miles (111,370 sq. km)
Languages Kpelle, Vai, Bassa, Kru, Grebo, Kissi, Gola, Loma, English
Religions Christian 68%, Traditional beliefs 18%, Muslim 14%
Ethnic mix Indigenous tribes (16 main groups) 95%, Americo-Liberians 5%
Government Transitional regime
Currency Liberian dollar = 100 cents
Literacy rate 56%
Calorie consumption 1946 calories

Liberia *52 D4* Guanacaste, NW Costa Rica
Libian Desert *see* Libyan Desert
Libourne *91 B5* Gironde, SW France
Libreville *77 A5 country capital* (Gabon) Estuaire, NW Gabon
Libya *71 F3 Ar.* Al Jamāhīrīyah al 'Arabīyah al Lībīyah ash Sha'bīyah al Ishtirākīyah; *prev.* Libyan Arab Republic. *Country* N Africa

Libya 71

Official name Great Socialist People's Libyan Arab Jamahariyah
Formation 1951
Capital Tripoli
Population 5.6 million / 8 people per sq mile (3 people per sq km)
Total area 679,358 sq. miles (1,759,540 sq. km)
Languages Arabic, Tuareg
Religions Muslim (mainly Sunni) 97%, other 3%
Ethnic mix Arab and Berber 95%, other 5%
Government One-party state
Currency Libyan dinar = 1000 dirhams
Literacy rate 82%
Calorie consumption 3333 calories

Libyan Desert *71 H4 var.* Libian Desert, *Ar.* Aş Şaḩrā' al Lībīyah. *Desert* N Africa
Libyan Plateau *103 F4 var.* Aḍ Ḍiffah. *Plateau* Egypt/Libya
Lichtenfels *95 C5* Bayern, SE Germany
Lichtenvoorde *86 E4* Gelderland, E Netherlands
Lichuan *128 C5* Hubei, C China
Lida *107 B5 Rus.* Lida. Hrodzyenskaya Voblasts', W Belarus
Lidköping *85 B6* Västra Götaland, S Sweden
Lidoríki *105 B5 prev.* Lidhorikíon, Lidokhorikion. Stereá Ellás, C Greece
Lidzbark Warmiński *98 D2 Ger.* Heilsberg. Warmińsko-Mazurskie, NE Poland
Liechtenstein *94 D1 Country* C Europe

Liechtenstein 94

Official name Principality of Liechtenstein
Formation 1719
Capital Vaduz
Population 33,145 / 535 people per sq mile (207 people per sq km)
Total area 62 sq. miles (160 sq. km)
Languages German, Italian, Alemannish dialect
Religions Roman Catholic 81%, other 12%, Protestant 7%
Ethnic mix Liechtensteiner 62%, Foreign residents 38%
Government Parliamentary system
Currency Swiss franc = 100 rappen/centimes
Literacy rate 99%
Calorie consumption Not available

Liège *87 D6 Dut.* Luik, *Ger.* Lüttich. Liège, E Belgium
Lienz *95 D7* Tirol, W Austria
Liepāja *106 B3 Ger.* Libau. Liepāja, W Latvia
Liezen *95 D7* Steiermark, C Austria
Liffey *89 B6 river* E Ireland
Lifou *144 D5 island* Îles Loyauté, E New Caledonia
Liger *see* Loire
Ligure, Appennino *96 A2 Eng.* Ligurian Mountains. *Mountain range* NW Italy
Ligurian Sea *96 A3 Fr.* Mer Ligurienne, *It.* Mar Ligure. *Sea* N Mediterranean Sea
Līhu'e *47 A7 var.* Lihue. Kaua'i, Hawai'i, USA, C Pacific Ocean
Lihula *106 D2 Ger.* Leal. Läänemaa, W Estonia
Likasi *77 D7 prev.* Jadotville. Shaba, SE Dem. Rep. Congo
Liknes *85 A6* Vest-Agder, S Norway
Lille *90 C2 var.* l'Isle, *Dut.* Rijssel, *Flem.* Ryssel; *prev.* Lisle, *anc.* Insula. Nord, N France
Lillehammer *85 B5* Oppland, S Norway
Lillestrøm *85 B6* Akershus, S Norway
Lilongwe *79 E2 country capital* (Malawi) Central, W Malawi
Lima *60 C4 country capital* (Peru) Lima, W Peru
Limanowa *99 D5* Małopolskie, S Poland
Limassol *see* Lemesós
Limerick *89 A6 Ir.* Luimneach. SW Ireland
Límnos *103 F3 anc.* Lemnos. *Island* E Greece
Limoges *91 C5 anc.* Augustoritum Lemovicensium, Lemovices. Haute-Vienne, C France
Limón *53 E4 var.* Puerto Limón. Limón, E Costa Rica
Limón *52 D2* Colón, NE Honduras
Limousin *91 C5 cultural region* C France
Limoux *91 C6* Aude, S France
Limpopo *78 D3 var.* Crocodile. *River* S Africa
Linares *92 D4* Andalucía, S Spain
Linares *64 B4* Maule, C Chile
Linares *51 E3* Nuevo León, NE Mexico
Lincoln *89 D5 anc.* Lindum, Lindum Colonia. E England, UK
Lincoln *45 F4 state capital* Nebraska, C USA
Lincoln *41 H2* Maine, NE USA
Lincoln Sea *34 D2 sea* Arctic Ocean
Linden *59 F3* E Guyana
Líndhos *see* Líndos
Lindi *73 D8* Lindi, SE Tanzania
Líndos *105 E7 var.* Líndhos. Ródos, Dodekánisos, Greece, Aegean Sea
Line Islands *145 G3 island group* E Kiribati
Lingeh *see* Bandar-e Langeh
Lingen *94 A3 var.* Lingen an der Ems. Niedersachsen, NW Germany
Lingen an der Ems *see* Lingen
Lingga, Kepulauan *138 B4 island group* W Indonesia
Linköping *85 C6* Östergötland, S Sweden
Linz *95 D6 anc.* Lentia. Oberösterreich, N Austria
Lion, Golfe du *91 C7 Eng.* Gulf of Lion, Gulf of Lions; *anc.* Sinus Gallicus. *Gulf* S France
Lipari Islands *see* Eolie, Isole
Lipari, Isola *97 D6 island* Isole Eolie, S Italy
Lipetsk *111 B5* Lipetskaya Oblast', W Russian Federation
Lipno *98 C3* Kujawsko-pomorskie, C Poland
Lipova *108 A4 Hung.* Lippa. Arad, W Romania
Liqeni i Ohrit *see* Ohrid, Lake
Lira *73 B6* N Uganda
Lisala *77 C5* Equateur, N Dem. Rep. Congo
Lisboa *92 B4 Eng.* Lisbon; *anc.* Felicitas Julia, Olisipo. *Country capital* (Portugal) Lisboa, W Portugal
Lisbon *see* Lisboa
Lisieux *90 B3 anc.* Noviomagus. Calvados, N France
Liski *111 B6 prev.* Georgiu-Dezh. Voronezhskaya Oblast', W Russian Federation
Lisle *see* Lille
l'Isle *see* Lille
Lismore *149 E5* Victoria, SE Australia
Lisse *86 C3* Zuid-Holland, W Netherlands
Litang *128 A5* Sichuan, C China
Līṭāni, Nahr el **135 B5 var.** Nahr al Litant. *River* C Lebanon
Lithgow *149 D6* New South Wales, SE Australia
Lithuania *106 B4 Ger.* Litauen, *Lith.* Lietuva, *Pol.* Litwa, *Rus.* Litva; *prev.* Lithuanian SSR, *Rus.* Litovskaya SSR. *Country* NE Europe

Lithuania 106

Official name Republic of Lithuania
Formation 1991
Capital Vilnius
Population 3.4 million / 135 people per sq mile (52 people per sq km)
Total area 25,174 sq. miles (65,200 sq. km)
Languages Lithuanian, Russian
Religions Roman Catholic 83%, other 12%, Protestant 5%
Ethnic mix Lithuanian 80%, Russian 9%, Polish 7%, other 2%, Belarussian 2%
Government Parliamentary system
Currency Litas (euro is also legal tender) = 100 centu
Literacy rate 99%
Calorie consumption 3384 calories

Litóchoro *104 B4 var.* Litohoro, Litókhoron. Kentrikí Makedonía, N Greece
Litohoro *see* Litóchoro
Litókhoron *see* Litóchoro
Little Alföld *99 C6 Ger.* Kleines Ungarisches Tiefland, *Hung.* Kisalföld, *Slvk.* Podunajská Rovina. *Plain* Hungary/Slovakia
Little Andaman *133 F2 island* Andaman Islands, India, NE Indian Ocean
Little Barrier Island *150 D2 island* N NZ
Little Bay *93 H5 bay* S Gibraltar
Little Cayman *54 B3 island* E Cayman Islands
Little Falls *45 F2* Minnesota, N USA
Littlefield *49 E2* Texas, SW USA
Little Inagua *54 D2 var.* Inagua Islands. *Island* S Bahamas
Little Minch, The *88 B3 strait* NW Scotland, UK
Little Missouri River *44 D2 river* NW USA
Little Nicobar *133 G3 island* Nicobar Islands, India, NE Indian Ocean
Little Rock *42 B1 state capital* Arkansas, C USA
Little Saint Bernard Pass *91 D5 Fr.* Col du Petit St-Bernard, *It.* Colle di Piccolo San Bernardo. *Pass* France/Italy
Little Sound *42 A5 bay* Bermuda, NW Atlantic Ocean
Littleton *44 D4* Colorado, C USA
Liu-chou *see* Liuzhou
Liuchow *see* Liuzhou
Liuzhou *128 C6 var.* Liu-chou, Liuchow. Guangxi Zhuangzu Zizhiqu, S China
Livanátes *105 B5 prev.* Livanátai. Stereá Ellás, C Greece
Līvāni *106 D4 Ger.* Lievenhof. Preiļi, SE Latvia
Liverpool *148 D2* New South Wales, SE Australia
Liverpool *39 F5* Nova Scotia, SE Canada
Liverpool *89 C5* NW England, UK
Livingston *44 B2* Montana, NW USA
Livingstone *78 C3 var.* Maramba. Southern, S Zambia
Livingstone *49 H3* Texas, SW USA
Livingstone Mountains *151 A7 mountain range* South Island, NZ
Livno *100 B4* Federacija Bosna I Hercegovina, SW Bosnia and Herzegovina
Livojoki *84 D4 river* C Finland
Livonia *40 D3* Michigan, N USA
Livorno *96 B3 Eng.* Leghorn. Toscana, C Italy
Lixoúri *105 A5 prev.* Lixoúrion. Kefallinía, Iónioi Nísoi, Greece, C Mediterranean Sea
Lizarra *see* Estella
Ljubljana *95 D7 Ger.* Laibach, *It.* Lubiana; *anc.* Aemona, Emona. *Country capital* (Slovenia) C Slovenia
Ljungby *85 B7* Kronoberg, S Sweden
Ljusdal *85 C5* Gävleborg, C Sweden
Ljusnan *85 C5 river* C Sweden
Llanelli *89 C6 prev.* Llanelly. SW Wales, UK
Llanes *92 D1* Asturias, N Spain
Llanos *58 D2 physical region* Colombia/Venezuela
Lleida *93 F2 Cast.* Lérida; *anc.* Ilerda. Cataluña, NE Spain
Lluchmayor *see* Llucmajor
Llucmajor *93 G3 var.* Lluchmayor. Mallorca, Spain, W Mediterranean Sea
Loaita Island *128 C8 island* W Spratly Islands
Loanda *see* Luanda
Lobatse *78 C4 var.* Lobatsi. Kgatleng, SE Botswana
Lobatsi *see* Lobatse
Löbau *94 D4* Sachsen, E Germany
Lobito *78 B2* Benguela, W Angola
Lob Nor *see* Lop Nur
Loburi *see* Lop Buri
Locarno *95 B8 Ger.* Luggarus. Ticino, S Switzerland
Lochem *86 E3* Gelderland, E Netherlands
Lockport *41 E3* New York, NE USA
Lodja *77 D6* Kasai Oriental, C Dem. Rep. Congo
Lodwar *73 C6* Rift Valley, NW Kenya
Łódź *98 D4 Rus.* Lodz. Łódzkie, C Poland
Loei *136 C4 var.* Loey, Muang Loei. Loei, C Thailand
Loey *see* Loei
Lofoten *84 B3 var.* Lofoten Islands. *Island group* C Norway
Lofoten Islands *see* Lofoten
Logan *44 B3* Utah, W USA
Logan, Mount *36 D3 mountain* Yukon Territory, W Canada
Logroño *93 E1 anc.* Vareia, *Lat.* Juliobriga. La Rioja, N Spain
Loibl Pass *95 D7 Ger.* Loiblpass, *Slvn.* Ljubelj. *Pass* Austria/Slovenia
Loi-Kaw *136 B4* Kayah State, C Myanmar
Loire *90 B4 var.* Liger. *River* C France
Loja *60 B2* Loja, S Ecuador
Lokitaung *73 C5* Rift Valley, NW Kenya
Lokoja *75 G4* Kogi, C Nigeria
Loksa *106 E2 Ger.* Loxa. Harjumaa, NW Estonia
Lolland *85 B8 prev.* Laaland. *Island* S Denmark
Lom *104 C1 prev.* Lom-Palanka. Montana, NW Bulgaria
Lomami *77 D6 river* C Dem. Rep. Congo
Lomas *60 D4* Arequipa, SW Peru
Lomas de Zamora *64 D4* Buenos Aires, E Argentina
Lombardia *96 B2 cultural region* N Italy
Lombok, Pulau *138 D5 island* Nusa Tenggara, C Indonesia
Lomé *75 F5 country capital* (Togo) S Togo
Lomela *77 D6* Kasai Oriental, C Dem. Rep. Congo
Lommel *87 C5* Limburg, N Belgium
Lomond, Loch *88 B4 lake* C Scotland, UK
Lomonosov Ridge *155 B3 var.* Harris Ridge, *Rus.* Khrebet Lomonsova. *Undersea feature* Arctic Ocean
Lompoc *47 B7* California, W USA
Lom Sak *136 C4 var.* Muang Lom Sak. Phetchabun, C Thailand
Łomża *98 D3 off.* Województwo Łomżyńskie, *Rus.* Lomzha. Podlaskie, NE Poland
Loncoche *65 B5* Araucanía, C Chile
London *89 A7 anc.* Augusta, *Lat.* Londinium. *Country capital* (UK) SE England, UK
London *40 C5* Kentucky, S USA
London *38 C5* Ontario, S Canada
Londonderry *88 B4 var.* Derry, *Ir.* Doire. NW Northern Ireland, UK
Londonderry, Cape *146 C2 headland* Western Australia
Londrina *63 E4* Paraná, S Brazil
Longa, Proliv *115 G1 Eng.* Long Strait. *Strait* NE Russian Federation
Long Bay *43 F2 bay* North Carolina/South Carolina, E USA
Long Beach *47 C7* California, W USA
Longford *89 B5 Ir.* An Longfort. C Ireland
Long Island *54 D2 island* C Bahamas
Long Island *41 G4 island* New York, NE USA
Long Island *see* Bermuda
Longlac *38 C3* Ontario, S Canada
Longmont *44 D4* Colorado, C USA
Longreach *148 C4* Queensland, E Australia
Long Strait *see* Longa, Proliv
Longview *49 H3* Texas, SW USA
Longview *46 B2* Washington, NW USA
Long Xuyên *137 D6 var.* Longxuyen. An Giang, S Vietnam
Longxuyen *see* Long Xuyên
Longyan *128 D6* Fujian, SE China
Longyearbyen *83 G2 dependent territory capital* (Svalbard) Spitsbergen, W Svalbard
Lons-le-Saunier *90 D4 anc.* Ledo Salinarius. Jura, E France
Lop Buri *137 C5 var.* Loburi. Lop Buri, C Thailand
Lop Nor *see* Lop Nur
Lop Nur *126 C3 var.* Lob Nor, Lop Nor, Lo-pu Po. *Seasonal lake* NW China
Loppersum *86 E1* Groningen, NE Netherlands
Lo-pu Po *see* Lop Nur
Lorca *93 E4 Ar.* Lurka; *anc.* Eliocroca, *Lat.* Illur co. Murcia, S Spain
Lord Howe Island *142 C4 island* E Australia
Lord Howe Rise *142 C4 undersea feature* SW Pacific Ocean
Loreto *50 B3* Baja California Sur, W Mexico
Lorient *90 A3 prev.* l'Orient. Morbihan, NW France
Lorn, Firth of *88 B4 inlet* W Scotland, UK
Loro Sae *see* East Timor
Lörrach *95 A7* Baden-Württemberg, S Germany
Lorraine *90 D3 cultural region* NE France
Los Alamos *48 C1* New Mexico, SW USA
Los Amates *52 B2* Izabal, E Guatemala
Los Angeles *47 C7* California, W USA
Los Ángeles *65 B5* Bío Bío, C Chile
Lošinj *100 A3 Ger.* Lussin, *It.* Lussino. *Island* W Croatia
Los Mochis *50 C3* Sinaloa, C Mexico
Los Roques, Islas *58 D1 island group* N Venezuela
Los Testigos, Isla *55 G5 island* NE Venezuela
Lost River Range *46 D3 mountain range* Idaho, C USA
Lot *91 B5 cultural region* C France
Lot *91 B5 river* S France
Lotagipi Swamp *73 C5 wetland* Kenya/Sudan
Louangnamtha *136 C3 var.* Luong Nam Tha. Louang Namtha, N Laos
Louangphabang *124 D3 var.* Louangphrabang, Luang Prabang. Louangphabang, N Laos
Louangphrabang *see* Louangphabang
Loudéac *90 A3* Côtes d'Armor, NW France
Loudi *128 C5* Hunan, S China
Louga *74 B3* NW Senegal
Louisiade Archipelago *144 B4 island group* SE PNG
Louisiana *42 A2 off.* State of Louisiana; also known as Creole State, Pelican State. *State* S USA
Louisville *40 C5* Kentucky, S USA
Louisville Ridge *143 E4 undersea feature* S Pacific Ocean
Loup River *45 E4 river* Nebraska, C USA
Lourdes *91 B6* Hautes-Pyrénées, S France
Louth *89 E5* E England, UK
Loutrá *104 C4* Kentrikí Makedonía, N Greece
Lóuva *78 C1* Lunda Norte, NE Angola
Louvain-la Neuve *87 C6* Wallon Brabant, C Belgium
Louviers *90 C3* Eure, N France
Lovech *104 C2* Lovech, N Bulgaria
Loveland *44 D4* Colorado, C USA
Lovosice *98 A4 Ger.* Lobositz. Ústecký Kraj, NW Czech Republic
Lowell *41 G3* Massachusetts, NE USA
Lower California *see* Baja California
Lower Hutt *151 D5* Wellington, North Island, NZ
Lower Lough Erne *89 A5 lake* SW Northern Ireland, UK
Lower Red Lake *45 F1 lake* Minnesota, N USA
Lower Tunguska *see* Nizhnyaya Tunguska
Lowestoft *89 E6* E England, UK
Lo-yang *see* Luoyang
Loyauté, Îles *144 D5 island group* S New Caledonia
Loyew *107 D8 Rus.* Loyev. Homyel'skaya Voblasts', SE Belarus
Loznica *100 C3* Serbia, W Serbia and Montenegro (Yugo.)
Lu *see* Shandong
Lualaba *77 D6 Fr.* Loualaba. *River* SE Dem. Rep. Congo
Luanda *78 A1 var.* Loanda, *Port.* São Paulo de Loanda. *Country capital* (Angola) Luanda, NW Angola
Luang Prabang *see* Louangphabang
Luang, Thale *137 C7 lagoon* S Thailand
Luangua, Rio *see* Luangwa
Luangwa *73 B8 var.* Aruângua, Rio Luangua. *River* Mozambique/Zambia
Luanshya *78 D2* Copperbelt, C Zambia
Luarca *92 C1* Asturias, N Spain
Lubaczów *99 E5 var.* Lúbaczów. Podkarpackie, SE Poland
Lubań *98 B4 var.* Koscian, *Ger.* Kosten. Dolnośląskie, SW Poland
Lubānas Ezers *see* Lubāns
Lubango *78 B2 Port.* Sá da Bandeira. Huíla, SW Angola
Lubāns *106 D4 var.* Lubānas Ezers. *Lake* E Latvia
Lubao *77 D6* Kasai Oriental, C Dem. Rep. Congo
Lübben *94 D4* Brandenburg, E Germany
Lübbenau *94 D4* Brandenburg, E Germany
Lubbock *49 E2* Texas, SW USA
Lübeck *94 C2* Schleswig-Holstein, N Germany
Lubelska, Wyżyna *98 E4 plateau* SE Poland
Lubin *98 B4 Ger.* Lüben. Dolnośląskie, W Poland
Lublin *98 E4 Rus.* Lyublin. Lubelskie, E Poland
Lubliniec *98 C4* Śląskie, S Poland
Lubny *109 F2* Poltavs'ka Oblast', NE Ukraine
Lubsko *98 B4 Ger.* Sommerfeld. Lubuskie, W Poland
Lubumbashi *77 E8 prev.* Élisabethville. Shaba, SE Dem. Rep. Congo
Lubutu *77 D6* Maniema, E Dem. Rep. Congo
Lucan *89 B5 Ir.* Leamhcán. E Ireland
Lucano, Appennino *97 D5 Eng.* Lucanian Mountains. *Mountain range* S Italy
Lucapa *78 C1 var.* Lukapa. Lunda Norte, NE Angola
Lucca *96 B3 anc.* Luca. Toscana, C Italy
Lucea *54 A4* W Jamaica
Lucena *139 E1 off.* Lucena City. Luzon, N Philippines
Lucena *92 D4* Andalucía, S Spain
Lučenec *99 D6 Ger.* Losontz, *Hung.* Losonc. Banskobystrický Kraj, C Slovakia
Luchow *see* Hefei
Lucknow *135 E3 var.* Lakhnau. Uttar Pradesh, N India
Lüda *see* Dalian
Luda Kamchiya *104 D2 river* E Bulgaria
Lüderitz *78 B4 prev.* Angra Pequena. Karas, SW Namibia

Ludhiāna *134 D2* Punjab, N India
Ludington *40 C2* Michigan, N USA
Luduş *108 B4 Ger.* Ludasch, *Hung.* Marosludas. Mureş, C Romania
Ludvika *85 C6* Kopparberg, C Sweden
Ludwiglust *94 C3* Mecklenburg-Vorpommern, N Germany
Ludwigsburg *95 B6* Baden-Württemberg, SW Germany
Ludwigsfelde *94 D3* Brandenburg, NE Germany
Ludwigshafen *95 B5 var.* Ludwigshafen am Rhein. Rheinland-Pfalz, W Germany
Ludwigshafen am Rhein *see* Ludwigshafen
Ludza *106 D4 Ger.* Ludsan. Ludza, E Latvia
Luebo *77 C6* Kasai Occidental, SW Dem. Rep. Congo
Luena *78 C2 var.* Lwena, *Port.* Luso. Moxico, E Angola
Lufira *77 E7 river* SE Dem. Rep. Congo
Lufkin *49 H3* Texas, SW USA
Luga *110 A4* Leningradskaya Oblast', NW Russian Federation
Lugano *95 B8 Ger.* Lauis. Ticino, S Switzerland
Lugenda, Rio *79 E2 river* N Mozambique
Lugo *92 C1 anc.* Lugus Augusti. Galicia, NW Spain
Lugoj *108 A4 Ger.* Lugosch, *Hung.* Lugos. Timiş, W Romania
Luhans'k *109 H3 Rus.* Lugansk; *prev.* Voroshilovgrad. Luhans'ka Oblast', E Ukraine
Luimneach *see* Limerick
Lukapa *see* Lucapa
Lukenie *77 C6 river* C Dem. Rep. Congo
Lukovit *104 C2* Lovech, NW Bulgaria
Łuków *98 E4 Ger.* Bogendorf. Lubelskie, E Poland
Lukuga *77 D7 river* SE Dem. Rep. Congo
Luleå *84 D4* Norrbotten, N Sweden
Luleälven *84 C3 river* N Sweden
Lulonga *77 C5 river* NW Dem. Rep. Congo
Lulua *77 D7 river* S Dem. Rep. Congo
Lumbo *79 F2* Nampula, NE Mozambique
Lumsden *151 A7* Southland, South Island, NZ
Lund *85 B7* Skåne, S Sweden
Lüneburg *94 C3* Niedersachsen, N Germany
Lungkiang *see* Qiqihar
Lungué-Bungo *78 C2 var.* Lungwebungu. *River* Angola/Zambia *see also* Lungwebungu
Lungwebungu *see* Lungué-Bungo
Luninyets *107 B7 Pol.* Łuniniec, *Rus.* Luninets. Brestskaya Voblasts', SW Belarus
Lunteren *86 D4* Gelderland, C Netherlands
Luong Nam Tha *see* Louangnamtha
Luoyang *128 C4 var.* Honan, Lo-yang. Henan, C China
Lúrio *79 F2* Nampula, NE Mozambique
Lúrio, Rio *79 E2 river* NE Mozambique
Lusaka *78 D2 country capital* (Zambia) Lusaka, SE Zambia
Lushnja *see* Lushnjë
Lushnjë *101 C6 var.* Lushnja. Fier, C Albania
Luso *see* Luena
Lūt, Dasht-e *120 D3 var.* Kavīr-e Lūt. *Desert* E Iran
Luton *89 D6* SE England, UK
Łutselk'e *37 F4 prev.* Snowdrift. Northwest Territories, W Canada
Luts'k *108 C1 Pol.* Łuck, *Rus.* Lutsk. Volyns'ka Oblast', NW Ukraine
Lutzow-Holm Bay *see* Lützow Holmbukta
Lützow Holmbukta *154 C2 var.* Lutzow-Holm Bay. *Bay* Antarctica
Luuq *73 D6 It.* Lugh Ganana. Gedo, SW Somalia
Luvua *77 D7 river* SE Dem. Rep. Congo
Luwego *73 C8 river* S Tanzania
Luxembourg *87 D8 var.* Lëtzebuerg, Luxemburg. *Country* NW Europe

Luxembourg 87

Official name Grand Duchy of Luxembourg
Formation 1867
Capital Luxembourg-Ville
Population 453,000 / 454 people per sq mile (175 people per sq km)
Total area 998 sq. miles (2586 sq. km)
Languages Luxembourgish, German, French
Religions Roman Catholic 97%, Protestant, Orthodox Christian, and Jewish 3%
Ethnic mix Luxembourger 73%, Foreign residents 27%
Government Parliamentary system
Currency Euro = 100 cents
Literacy rate 99%
Calorie consumption 3701 calories

Luxembourg *87 D8 country capital* (Luxembourg) Luxembourg, S Luxembourg
Luxor *72 B2 Ar.* Al Uqşur. E Egypt
Luza *110 C4* Kirovskaya Oblast', NW Russian Federation
Luz, Costa de la *92 C5 coastal region* SW Spain
Luzern *95 B7 Fr.* Lucerne, *It.* Lucerna. Luzern, C Switzerland
Luzon *139 E1 island* N Philippines
Luzon Strait *125 E3 strait* Philippines/Taiwan
L'viv *108 B2 Ger.* Lemberg, *Pol.* Lwów, *Rus.* L'vov. L'vivs'ka Oblast', W Ukraine
Lwena *see* Luena
Lyakhavichy *107 B6 Rus.* Lyakhovichi. Brestskaya Voblasts', SW Belarus
Lycksele *84 C4* Västerbotten, N Sweden
Lycopolis *see* Asyût
Lyel'chytsy *107 C7 Rus.* Lel'chitsy. Homyel'skaya Voblasts', SE Belarus
Lyepyel' *107 D5 Rus.* Lepel'. Vitsyebskaya Voblasts', N Belarus
Lyme Bay *89 C7 bay* S England, UK
Lynchburg *41 E5* Virginia, NE USA
Lynn Regis *see* King's Lynn
Lyon *91 D5 Eng.* Lyons; *anc.* Lugdunum. Rhône, E France
Lyozna *107 E6 Rus.* Liozno. Vitsyebskaya Voblasts', NE Belarus
Lypovets' *108 D2 Rus.* Lipovets. Vinnyts'ka Oblast', C Ukraine
Lysychans'k *109 H3 Rus.* Lisichansk. Luhans'ka Oblast', E Ukraine
Lyttelton *151 C6* Canterbury, South Island, NZ
Lyubotyn *109 G2 Rus.* Lyubotin. Kharkivs'ka Oblast', E Ukraine
Lyulyakovo *104 E2 prev.* Keremitlik. Burgas, E Bulgaria
Lyusina *107 B6 Rus.* Lyusino. Brestskaya Voblasts', SW Belarus

M

Ma'ān *119 B7* Ma'ān, SW Jordan
Maardu *106 D2 Ger.* Maart. Harjumaa, NW Estonia
Ma'aret-en-Nu'man *see* Ma'arrat an Nu'mān
Ma'arrat an Nu'mān *118 B3 var.* Ma'aret-en-Nu'man, *Fr.* Maarret enn Naamâne. Idlib, NW Syria
Maarret enn Naamâne *see* Ma'arrat an Nu'mān
Maaseik *87 D5 prev.* Maeseyck. Limburg, NE Belgium
Maastricht *87 D6 var.* Maestricht; *anc.* Traietum ad Mosam, Traiectum Tungorum. Limburg, SE Netherlands
Macao *129 C6 Chin.* Aomen, *Port.* Macao. S China
Macapá *63 E1 state capital* Amapá, N Brazil
Macassar *see* Ujungpandang
MacCluer Gulf *see* Berau, Teluk
Macdonnell Ranges *146 D4 mountain range* Northern Territory, C Australia
Macedonia, FYR *101 D6 var.* Macedonia, *Mac.* Makedonija, *abbrev.* FYR Macedonia, FYROM. *Country* SE Europe

Macedonia 101

Official name Republic of Macedonia
Formation 1991
Capital Skopje
Population 2.02 million / 204 people per sq mile (79 people per sq km)
Total area 9781 sq. miles (25,333 sq. km)
Languages Macedonian, Albanian, Serbo-Croat
Religions Orthodox Christian 59%, Muslim 26%, other 10%, Roman Catholic 4%, Protestant 1%
Ethnic mix Macedonian 64%, Albanian 25%, Turkish 4%, Roma 3%, other 2%, Serb 2%
Government Mixed presidential–parliamentary system
Currency Macedonian denar = 100 deni
Literacy rate 94%
Calorie consumption 2552 calories

Maceió *63 G3 state capital* Alagoas, E Brazil
Machachi *60 B1* Pichincha, C Ecuador
Machala *60 B2* El Oro, SW Ecuador
Machanga *79 E3* Sofala, E Mozambique
Machilīpatnam *132 D1 var.* Bandar Masulipatnam. Andhra Pradesh, E India
Machiques *58 C2* Zulia, NW Venezuela
Macías Nguema Biyogo *see* Bioco, Isla de
Măcin *108 D5* Tulcea, SE Romania
Macizo de las Guayanas *see* Guiana Highlands
Mackay *148 D4* Queensland, NE Australia
Mackay, Lake *146 C4 salt lake* Northern Territory/Western Australia
Mackenzie *37 E3 river* Northwest Territories, NW Canada
Mackenzie Bay *154 D3 bay* Antarctica
Mackenzie Mountains *36 D3 mountain range* Northwest Territories, NW Canada
Macleod, Lake *146 A4 lake* Western Australia
Macomb *40 A4* Illinois, N USA
Macomer *97 A5* Sardegna, Italy, C Mediterranean Sea
Macon *42 D2* Georgia, SE USA
Macon *45 G4* Missouri, C USA
Mâcon *91 D5 anc.* Matisco, Matisco Ædourum. Saône-et-Loire, C France
Macquarie Ridge *154 C5 undersea feature* SW Pacific Ocean
Macuspana *51 G4* Tabasco, SE Mexico
Ma'dabā *119 B6 var.* Mādabā, Madeba; *anc.* Medeba. 'Ammān, NW Jordan
Madagascar *79 F3 Malg.* Madagasikara; *prev.* Malagasy Republic. *Country* W Indian Ocean

Madagascar 79

Official name Republic of Madagascar
Formation 1960
Capital Antananarivo
Population 17.4 million / 77 people per sq mile (30 people per sq km)**Total area** 226,656 sq. miles (587,040 sq. km)
Languages Malagasy, French
Religions Traditional beliefs 52%, Christian (mainly Roman Catholic) 41%, Muslim 7%
Ethnic mix Other Malay 46%, Merina 26%, Betsimisaraka 15%, Betsileo 12%, other 1%
Government Presidential system
Currency Ariary = 5 iraimbilanja
Literacy rate 67%
Calorie consumption 2072 calories

Madagascar *79 F3 island* W Indian Ocean
Madagascar Basin *69 E7 undersea feature* W Indian Ocean
Madagascar Plateau *69 E7 var.* Madagascar Ridge, Madagascar Rise, *Rus.* Madagaskarskiy Khrebet. *Undersea feature* W Indian Ocean
Madagascar Ridge *see* Madagascar Plateau
Madagascar Rise *see* Madagascar Plateau
Madagaskarskiy Khrebet *see* Madagascar Plateau
Madang *144 B3* Madang, N PNG
Madanīyīn *see* Médenine
Made *86 C4* Noord-Brabant, S Netherlands
Madeba *see* Ma'dabā
Madeira *70 A2 var.* Ilha de Madeira. *Island* Portugal, NE Atlantic Ocean
Madeira *70 A2 var.* Madeira, *Port.* Arquipélago da Madeira. *Island group* Portugal, NE Atlantic Ocean
Madeira Plain *66 C3 undersea feature* E Atlantic Ocean
Madeira, Rio *62 D2 Sp.* Río Madera. *River* Bolivia/Brazil *see also* Madera, Río
Madeleine, Îles de la *39 F4 Eng.* Magdalen Islands. *Island group* Québec, E Canada
Madera *47 B6* California, W USA
Madhya Pradesh *135 E4 prev.* Central Provinces and Berar. Admin. region *state* C India
Madīnat ath Thawrah *118 C2 var.* Ath Thawrah. Ar Raqqah, N Syria Asia
Madison *40 B3 state capital* Wisconsin, N USA
Madison *45 F3* South Dakota, N USA
Madiun *138 D5 prev.* Madioen. Jawa, C Indonesia
Madona *106 D4 Ger.* Modohn. Madona, E Latvia
Madras *see* Tamil Nādu
Madras *see* Chennai
Madre de Dios *56 B4 off.* Departamento de Madre de Dios. *Department* E Peru
Madre de Dios, Río *61 E3 river* Bolivia/Peru
Madre del Sur, Sierra *51 E5 mountain range* S Mexico
Madre, Laguna *51 F3 lagoon* NE Mexico
Madre, Laguna *49 G5 lake* Texas, SW USA
Madre Occidental, Sierra *50 C3 var.* Western Sierra Madre. *Mountain range* C Mexico
Madre Oriental, Sierra *51 E3 var.* Eastern Sierra Madre. *Mountain range* C Mexico
Madrid *92 D3 country capital* (Spain) Madrid, C Spain
Madurai *132 C3 prev.* Madura, Mathurai. Tamil Nādu, S India
Madura, Pulau *138 D5 prev.* Madoera. *Island* C Indonesia

Maebashi *131 D5 var.* Maebasi, Mayebashi. Gunma, Honshū, S Japan
Maebasi *see* Maebashi
Mae Nam Khong *see* Mekong
Mae Nam Nan *136 C4 river* NW Thailand
Mae Nam Yom *136 C4 river* W Thailand
Maestricht *see* Maastricht
Maéwo *144 D4 prev.* Aurora. *Island* C Vanuatu
Mafia *73 D7 island* E Tanzania
Mafraq *see* Al Mafraq
Magadan *115 G3* Magadanskaya Oblast', E Russian Federation
Magangué *58 B2* Bolívar, N Colombia
Magdalena *56 A2 off.* Departamento del Magdalena. *Province* N Colombia
Magdalena *61 F3* Beni, N Bolivia
Magdalena *50 B1* Sonora, NW Mexico
Magdalena, Isla *50 B3 island* W Mexico
Magdalena, Río *58 B2 river* C Colombia
Magdeburg *94 C4* Sachsen-Anhalt, C Germany
Magelang *138 C5* Jawa, C Indonesia
Magellan, Strait of *65 B8 Sp.* Estrecho de Magallanes. *Strait* Argentina/Chile
Magerøy *see* Magerøya
Magerøya *84 D1 var.* Magerøy. *Island* N Norway
Maggiore, Lake *96 B1 It.* Lago Maggiore. *Lake* Italy/Switzerland
Maglaj *100 C3* Federacija Bosna I Hercegovina, N Bosnia and Herzegovina
Maglie *97 E6* Puglia, SE Italy
Magna *44 B4* Utah, W USA
Magnesia *see* Manisa
Magnitogorsk *114 B4* Chelyabinskaya Oblast', C Russian Federation
Magta' Laḥjar *74 C3 var.* Magta Lahjar, Magta' Lahjar, Magtá Lahjar. Brakna, SW Mauritania
Magway *see* Magwe
Magwe *136 A3 var.* Magway. Magwe, W Myanmar
Mahajanga *79 F2 var.* Majunga. Mahajanga, NW Madagascar
Mahakam, Sungai *138 D4 var.* Koetai, Kutai. *River* Borneo, C Indonesia
Mahalapye *78 D3 var.* Mahalatswe. Central, SE Botswana
Mahalatswe *see* Mahalapye
Mahān *120 D3* Kermān, E Iran
Mahānadi *135 F4 river* E India
Mahārāshtra *134 D5 state* W India
Mahbés *see* El Mahbas
Mahbūbnagar *134 D5* Andhra Pradesh, C India
Mahdia *71 F2 var.* Al Mahdīyah, Mehdia. NE Tunisia
Mahé *79 H1 island* Inner Islands, NE Seychelles
Mahia Peninsula *150 E4 peninsula* North Island, NZ
Mahilyow *107 D6 Rus.* Mogilëv. Mahilyowskaya Voblasts', E Belarus
Mahmūd-e 'Erāqī *see* Maḥmūd-e Rāqī
Maḥmūd-e Rāqī *123 E4 var.* Mahmūd-e 'Erāqī. Kāpīsā, NE Afghanistan
Mahón *93 H3 Cat.* Maó, *Eng.* Port Mahon; *anc.* Portus Magonis. Menorca, Spain, W Mediterranean Sea
Maicao *58 C1* La Guajira, N Colombia
Mai Ceu *see* Maych'ew
Mai Chio *see* Maych'ew
Maidstone *89 E7* SE England, UK
Maiduguri *75 H4* Borno, NE Nigeria
Maimāna *see* Meymaneh
Main *95 B5 river* C Germany
Mai-Ndombe, Lac *77 C6 prev.* Lac Léopold II. *Lake* W Dem. Rep. Congo
Maine *41 G2 off.* State of Maine; also known as Lumber State, Pine Tree State. *State* NE USA
Maine *90 B3 cultural region* NW France
Maine, Gulf of *41 H2 gulf* NE USA
Main Island *see* Bermuda
Mainland *88 C2 island* Orkney, N Scotland, UK
Mainland *88 D1 island* Shetland, NE Scotland, UK
Mainz *95 B5 Fr.* Mayence. Rheinland-Pfalz, SW Germany
Maio *74 A3 var.* Mayo. *Island* Ilhas de Sotavento, SE Cape Verde
Maisur *see* Karnātaka
Maisur *see* Mysore
Maizhokunggar *126 C5* Xizang Zizhiqu, W China
Maíz, Islas del *53 E3 var.* Corn Islands. *Island group* SE Nicaragua
Mājro *see* Majuro Atoll
Majunga *see* Mahajanga
Majuro Atoll *144 D2 var.* Mājro. *Atoll* Ratak Chain, SE Marshall Islands
Makale *see* Mek'elē
Makarov Basin *155 B3 undersea feature* Arctic Ocean
Makarska *100 B4 It.* Macarsca. Split-Dalmacija, SE Croatia
Makasar *see* Ujungpandang
Makassar *see* Ujungpandang
Makassar Strait *138 D4 Ind.* Selat Makasar. *Strait* C Indonesia
Makay *79 F3 var.* Massif du Makay. *Mountain range* SW Madagascar
Makeni *74 C4* C Sierra Leone
Makhachkala *114 A4 prev.* Petrovsk-Port. Respublika Dagestan, SW Russian Federation
Makin *144 D2 prev.* Pitt Island. *Atoll* Tungaru, W Kiribati
Makira *see* San Cristobal
Makiyivka *109 G3 Rus.* Makeyevka; *prev.* Dmitriyevsk. Donets'ka Oblast', E Ukraine
Makkah *121 A5 Eng.* Mecca. Makkah, W Saudi Arabia
Makkovik *39 F2* Newfoundland and Labrador, NE Canada
Makó *99 D7 Rom.* Macău. Csongrád, SE Hungary
Makoua *77 B5* Cuvette, C Congo
Makran Coast *120 E4 coastal region* SE Iran
Makrany *107 A6 Rus.* Mokrany. Brestskaya Voblasts', SW Belarus
Mākū *120 B2* Āzarbāyjān-e Bākhtarī, NW Iran
Makurdi *75 G4* Benue, C Nigeria
Mala *see* Malaita
Malabār Coast *132 B3 coast* SW India
Malabo *77 A5 prev.* Santa Isabel. *Country capital* (Equatorial Guinea) Isla de Bioco, NW Equatorial Guinea
Malacca *see* Melaka
Malacca, Strait of *138 B3 Ind.* Selat Malaka. *Strait* Indonesia/Malaysia
Malacky *99 C6 Hung.* Malacka. Bratislavský Kraj, W Slovakia
Maladzyechna *107 C5 Pol.* Molodeczno, *Rus.* Molodechno. Minskaya Voblasts', C Belarus
Málaga *92 D5 anc.* Malaca. Andalucía, S Spain
Malagarasi River *73 B7 river* W Tanzania
Malaita *144 C3 var.* Mala. *Island* N Solomon Islands
Malakal *73 B5* Upper Nile, S Sudan
Malakula *see* Malekula
Malang *138 D5* Jawa, C Indonesia
Malange *see* Malanje
Malanje *78 B1 var.* Malange. Malanje, NW Angola
Mälaren *85 C6 lake* C Sweden
Malatya *117 E4 anc.* Melitene. Malatya, SE Turkey
Mala Vyska *109 E3 Rus.* Malaya Viska. Kirovohrads'ka Oblast', S Ukraine
Malawi *79 E1 prev.* Nyasaland, Nyasaland Protectorate. *Country* S Africa

Malawi 79

Official name Republic of Malawi
Formation 1964
Capital Lilongwe
Population 12.1 million / 333 people per sq mile (129 people per sq km)
Total area 45,745 sq. miles (118,480 sq. km)
Languages Chewa, Lomwe, Yao, Ngoni, English
Religions Protestant 55%, Roman Catholic 20%, Muslim 20%, Traditional beliefs 5%
Ethnic mix Bantu 99%, other 1%
Government Presidential system
Currency Malawi kwacha = 100 tambala
Literacy rate 62%
Calorie consumption 2168 calories

Malawi, Lake *see* Nyasa, Lake
Malay Peninsula *124 D4 peninsula* Malaysia/Thailand
Malaysia *138 B3 var.* Federation of Malaysia; *prev.* the separate territories of Federation of Malaya, Sarawak and Sabah (North Borneo) and Singapore. *Country* SE Asia

Malaysia 138

Official name Federation of Malaysia
Formation 1963
Capital Kuala Lumpur; Putrajaya (administrative)
Population 24.4 million / 192 people per sq mile (74 people per sq km)
Total area 127,316 sq. miles (329,750 sq. km)
Languages Bahasa Malaysia, Malay, Chinese, Tamil, English
Religions Muslim (mainly Sunni) 53%, Buddhist 19%, Chinese faiths 12%, other 7%, Christian 7%, Traditional beliefs 2%
Ethnic mix Malay 48%, Chinese 29%, Indigenous tribes 12%, Indian 6%, other 5%
Government Parliamentary system
Currency Ringgit = 100 sen
Literacy rate 89%
Calorie consumption 2927 calories

Malaysia, Federation of *see* Malaysia
Malbork *98 C2 Ger.* Marienburg, Marienburg in Westpreussen. Pomorskie, N Poland
Malchin *94 C3* Mecklenburg-Vorpommern, N Germany
Malden *45 H5* Missouri, C USA
Malden Island *145 G3 prev.* Independence Island. *Atoll* E Kiribati
Maldives *132 A4 Country* N Indian Ocean

Maldives 132

Official name Republic of Maldives
Formation 1965
Capital Male'
Population 318,000 / 2741 people per sq mile (1060 people per sq km)
Total area 116 sq. miles (300 sq. km)
Languages Dhivehi (Maldivian), Sinhala, Tamil, Arabic
Religions Sunni Muslim 100%
Ethnic mix Arab–Sinhalese–Malay 100%
Government Nonparty system
Currency Rufiyaa = 100 lari
Literacy rate 97%
Calorie consumption 2587 calories

Male' *132 B4* Male' Atoll, C Maldives
Male' Atoll *132 B4 var.* Kaafu Atoll. *Atoll* C Maldives
Malekula *144 D4 var.* Malakula; *prev.* Mallicolo. *Island* W Vanuatu
Malesína *105 C5* Stereá Ellás, E Greece
Malheur Lake *46 C3 lake* Oregon, NW USA
Mali *75 E3 Fr.* République du Mali; *prev.* French Sudan, Sudanese Republic. *Country* W Africa

Mali 75

Official name Republic of Mali
Formation 1960
Capital Bamako
Population 13 million / 28 people per sq mile (11 people per sq km)
Total area 478,764 sq. miles (1,240,000 sq. km)
Languages Bambara, Fulani, Senufo, Soninke, French
Religions Muslim (mainly Sunni) 80%, Traditional beliefs 18%, Christian 1%, other 1%
Ethnic mix Bambara 32%, other 26%, Fulani 14%, Senufu 12%, Soninka 9%, Tuareg 7%
Government Presidential system
Currency CFA franc = 100 centimes
Literacy rate 26%
Calorie consumption 2376 calories

Malik, Wadi al see Milk, Wadi el
Mali Kyun *137 B5 var.* Tavoy Island. *Island* Mergui Archipelago, S Myanmar
Malindi *73 D7* Coast, SE Kenya
Malko Tŭrnovo *104 E3* Burgas, E Bulgaria
Mallaig *88 B3* N Scotland, UK
Mallawi *72 B2* C Egypt
Mallicolo *see* Malekula
Mallorca *93 G3 Eng.* Majorca; *anc.* Baleares Major. *Island* Islas Baleares, Spain, W Mediterranean Sea
Malmberget *84 C3* Norrbotten, N Sweden
Malmédy *87 D6* Liège, E Belgium
Malmö *85 B7* Skåne, S Sweden
Maloeḷap *see* Maloelap Atoll
Maloelap Atoll *144 D1 var.* Maloeḷap. *Atoll* E Marshall Islands
Małopolska *98 D4 plateau* S Poland
Malozemel'skaya Tundra *110 D3 physical region* NW Russian Federation
Malta *97 C8 Country* C Mediterranean Sea

Malta 97

Official name Republic of Malta
Formation 1964
Capital Valletta
Population 394,000 / 3177 people per sq mile (1231 people per sq km)
Total area 122 sq. miles (316 sq. km)
Languages Maltese, English
Religions Roman Catholic 98%, Other and nonreligious 2%
Ethnic mix Maltese 96%, other 4%
Government Parliamentary system
Currency Maltese lira = 100 cents
Literacy rate 93%
Calorie consumption 3496 calories

Malta *97 C8 island* Malta, C Mediterranean Sea
Malta *44 C1* Montana, NW USA
Malta *106 D4* Rēzekne, SE Latvia
Malta Channel *97 C8 It.* Canale di Malta. *Strait* Italy/Malta
Maluku *139 F4 Dut.* Molukken, *Eng.* Moluccas; *prev.* Spice Islands. *Island group* E Indonesia
Malung *85 B6* Kopparberg, C Sweden
Malyn *108 D2 Rus.* Malin. Zhytomyrs'ka Oblast', N Ukraine

Mamberamo, Sungai *139 H4 river* Papua, E Indonesia
Mambij *see* Manbij
Mamonovo *106 A4 Ger.* Heiligenbeil. Kaliningradskaya Oblast', W Russian Federation
Mamoré, Rio *61 F3 river* Bolivia/Brazil
Mamou *74 C4* Moyenne-Guinée, W Guinea
Mamoudzou *79 F2 dependent territory capital* (Mayotte) C Mayotte
Mamuno *78 C3* Ghanzi, W Botswana
Manacor *93 G3* Mallorca, Spain, W Mediterranean Sea
Manado *139 F3 prev.* Menado. Sulawesi, C Indonesia
Managua *52 D3 country capital* (Nicaragua) Managua, W Nicaragua
Managua, Lago de *52 C3 var.* Xolotlán. *Lake* W Nicaragua
Manakara *79 G4* Fianarantsoa, SE Madagascar
Manama *see* Al Manāmah
Mananjary *79 G3* Fianarantsoa, SE Madagascar
Manapouri, Lake *151 A7 lake* South Island, NZ
Manar *see* Mannar
Manas, Gora *123 E2 mountain* Kyrgyzstan/Uzbekistan
Manaus *62 D2 prev.* Manáos. *State capital* Amazonas, NW Brazil
Manavgat *116 B4* Antalya, SW Turkey
Manbij *118 C2 var.* Mambij, *Fr.* Membidj. Ḥalab, N Syria
Manchester *89 D5 Lat.* Mancunium. NW England, UK
Manchester *41 G3* New Hampshire, NE USA
Man-chou-li *see* Manzhouli
Manchuria *125 E1 cultural region* NE China
Máncio Lima *see* Japiim
Mand *see* Mand, Rūd-e
Mandalay *136 B3* Mandalay, C Myanmar
Mandan *45 E2* North Dakota, N USA
Mandeville *54 B5* C Jamaica
Mándra *105 C6* Attikí, C Greece
Mand, Rūd-e *120 D4 var.* Mand. *River* S Iran
Mandurah *147 A6* Western Australia
Manduria *97 E5* Puglia, SE Italy
Mandya *132 C2* Karnātaka, C India
Manfredonia *97 D5* Puglia, SE Italy
Mangai *77 C6* Bandundu, W Dem. Rep. Congo
Mangaia *145 G5 island group* S Cook Islands
Mangalia *108 D5 anc.* Callatis. Constanța, SE Romania
Mangalmé *76 C3* Guéra, SE Chad
Mangalore *132 B2* Karnātaka, W India
Mangaung *see* Bloemfontein
Mango *see* Sansanné-Mango
Mangoky *79 F3 river* W Madagascar
Manhattan *45 F4* Kansas, C USA
Manicouagan, Réservoir *38 D3 lake* Québec, E Canada
Manihiki *145 G4 atoll* N Cook Islands
Manihiki Plateau *143 E3 undersea feature* C Pacific Ocean
Maniitsoq *82 C3 var.* Manîtsoq, *Dan.* Sukkertoppen. S Greenland
Manila *139 E1 off.* City of Manila. *Country capital* (Philippines) Luzon, N Philippines
Manisa *116 A3 var.* Manissa; *prev.* Saruhan, *anc.* Magnesia. Manisa, W Turkey
Manissa *see* Manisa
Manitoba *37 F5 province* S Canada
Manitoba, Lake *37 F5 lake* Manitoba, S Canada
Manitoulin Island *38 C4 island* Ontario, S Canada
Manîtsoq *see* Maniitsoq
Manizales *58 B3* Caldas, W Colombia
Manjimup *147 A7* Western Australia
Mankato *45 F3* Minnesota, N USA
Manlleu *93 G2* Cataluña, NE Spain
Manly *148 E1* New South Wales, SE Australia
Manmād *134 C5* Mahārāshtra, W India
Mannar *132 C3 var.* Manar. Northern Province, NW Sri Lanka
Mannar, Gulf of *132 C3 gulf* India/Sri Lanka
Mannheim *95 B5* Baden-Württemberg, SW Germany
Manono *77 E7* Shabo, SE Dem. Rep. Congo
Manosque *91 D6* Alpes-de-Haute-Provence, SE France
Manra *145 F3 prev.* Sydney Island. *Atoll* Phoenix Islands, C Kiribati
Mansa *78 D2 prev.* Fort Rosebery. Luapula, N Zambia
Mansel Island *37 G3 island* Nunavut, NE Canada
Mansfield *40 D4* Ohio, N USA
Manta *60 A2* Manabí, W Ecuador
Manteca *47 B6* California, W USA
Mantova *96 B2 Eng.* Mantua, *Fr.* Mantoue. Lombardia, NW Italy
Manuae *145 G4 island* S Cook Islands
Manurewa *150 D3 var.* Manukau. Auckland, North Island, NZ
Manzanares *93 E3* Castilla-La Mancha, C Spain
Manzanillo *50 D4* Colima, SW Mexico
Manzanillo *54 C3* Granma, E Cuba
Manzhouli *127 F1 var.* Man-chou-li. Nei Mongol Zizhiqu, N China
Mao *76 B3* Kanem, W Chad
Maoke, Pegunungan *139 H4 Dut.* Sneeuw-gebergte, *Eng.* Snow Mountains. *Mountain range* Papua, E Indonesia
Maoming *128 C6* Guangdong, S China
Mapmaker Seamounts *125 H2 undersea feature* N Pacific Ocean
Maputo *78 D4 prev.* Lourenço Marques. *Country capital* (Mozambique) Maputo, S Mozambique
Marabá *63 F2* Pará, NE Brazil
Maracaibo *58 C1* Zulia, NW Venezuela
Maracaibo, Lago de *58 C2 var.* Lake Maracaibo. *Inlet* NW Venezuela
Maracaibo, Lake *see* Maracaibo, Lago de
Maracay *58 D2* Aragua, N Venezuela
Marada *see* Marādah
Marādah *71 G3 var.* Marada. N Libya
Maradi *75 G3* Maradi, S Niger
Maragha *see* Marāgheh
Marāgheh *120 C2 var.* Maragha. Āžarbāyjān-e Khāvarī, NW Iran
Marajó, Baía de *63 F1 bay* N Brazil
Marajó, Ilha de *63 E1 island* N Brazil
Marakesh *see* Marrakech
Maramba *see* Livingstone
Maranhão *63 F2 off.* Estado do Maranhão. *State* E Brazil
Marañón, Río *60 B2 river* N Peru
Maraş *see* Kahramanmaraş
Marash *see* Kahramanmaraş
Marathon *38 C4* Ontario, S Canada
Marathónas *105 C5 prev.* Marathón. Attikí, C Greece
Märäzä *117 H2 Rus.* Maraza. E Azerbaijan
Marbella *92 D5* Andalucía, S Spain
Marble Bar *146 B4* Western Australia
Marburg an der Lahn *94 B4 hist.* Marburg. Hessen, W Germany
March *see* Morava
Marche *91 C5 cultural region* C France
Marche *96 C3 cultural region* E Italy
Marche-en-Famenne *87 C7* Luxembourg, SE Belgium
Marchena, Isla *60 B5 var.* Bindloe Island. *Island* Galapagos Islands, Ecuador, E Pacific Ocean
Mar Chiquita, Laguna *64 C3 lake* C Argentina
Marcounda *see* Markounda
Mardān *134 C1* North-West Frontier Province, N Pakistan
Mar del Plata *65 D5* Buenos Aires, E Argentina
Mardin *117 E4* Mardin, SE Turkey
Maré *144 D5 island* Îles Loyauté, E New Caledonia
Marea Neagră *see* Black Sea
Mare Creticum *see* Kritikó Pélagos
Mareeba *148 D3* Queensland, NE Australia
Margarita, Isla de *59 E1 island* N Venezuela
Margate *89 E7 prev.* Mergate. SE England, UK
Marghita *108 B3 Hung.* Margitta. Bihor, NW Romania
Marhanets' *109 F3 Rus.* Marganets. Dnipropetrovs'ka Oblast', E Ukraine
María Cleofas, Isla *50 C4 island* C Mexico
Maria Island *149 C8 island* Tasmania, SE Australia
María Madre, Isla *50 C4 island* C Mexico
María Magdalena, Isla *50 C4 island* C Mexico
Mariana Trench *125 G4 undersea feature* W Pacific Ocean
Mariánské Lázně *99 A5 Ger.* Marienbad. Karlovarský Kraj, W Czech Republic
Marías, Islas *50 C4 island group* C Mexico
Maribor *95 E7 Ger.* Marburg. NE Slovenia
Marica *see* Maritsa
Maridi *73 B5* Western Equatoria, SW Sudan
Marie Byrd Land *154 A3 physical region* Antarctica
Marie-Galante *55 G4 var.* Ceyre to the Caribs. *Island* SE Guadeloupe
Mariental *78 B4* Hardap, SW Namibia
Mariestad *85 B6* Västra Götaland, S Sweden
Marietta *42 D2* Georgia, SE USA
Marijampolė *106 B4 prev.* Kapsukas. Marijampolė, S Lithuania
Marília *63 E4* São Paulo, S Brazil
Marín *92 B1* Galicia, NW Spain
Mar"ina Horka *107 C6 Rus.* Mar'ina Gorka. Minskaya Voblasts', C Belarus
Maringá *63 E4* Paraná, S Brazil
Marion *45 G3* Iowa, C USA
Marion *40 D4* Ohio, N USA
Marion, Lake *43 E2 reservoir* South Carolina, SE USA
Mariscal Estigarribia *64 D2* Boquerón, NW Paraguay
Maritsa *104 D3 var.* Marica, *Gk.* Évros, *Turk.* Meriç; *anc.* Hebrus. *River* SW Europe *see also* Évros/Meriç
Maritzburg *see* Pietermaritzburg
Mariupol' *109 G4 prev.* Zhdanov. Donets'ka Oblast', SE Ukraine
Marka *73 D6 var.* Merca. Shabeellaha Hoose, S Somalia
Markham, Mount *154 B4 mountain* Antarctica
Markounda *76 C4 var.* Marcounda. Ouham, NW Central African Republic
Marktredwitz *95 C5* Bayern, E Germany
Marlborough *148 D4* Queensland, E Australia
Marmande *91 B5 anc.* Marmanda. Lot-et-Garonne, SW France
Marmara Denizi *116 A2 Eng.* Sea of Marmara. *Sea* NW Turkey
Marmara, Sea of *see* Marmara Denizi
Marmaris *116 A4* Muğla, SW Turkey
Marne *90 C3 cultural region* N France
Marne *90 D3 river* N France
Maro *76 C4* Moyen-Chari, S Chad
Maroantsetra *79 G2* Toamasina, NE Madagascar
Maromokotro *79 G2 mountain* N Madagascar
Maroni River *59 G3 Dut.* Marowijne. *River* French Guiana/Suriname
Maros *see* Mureș
Marosch *see* Mureș
Marotiri *143 F4 var.* Îlots de Bass, Morotiri. *Island group* Îles Australes, SW French Polynesia
Maroua *76 B3* Extrême-Nord, N Cameroon
Marquesas Fracture Zone *153 E3 tectonic feature* E Pacific Ocean
Marquesas Islands *153 E3 island group* N French Polynesia
Marquette *40 B1* Michigan, N USA
Marrakech *70 C2 var.* Marakesh, *Eng.* Marrakesh; *prev.* Morocco. W Morocco
Marrakesh *see* Marrakech
Marrawah *149 C8* Tasmania, SE Australia
Marree *149 B5* South Australia
Marsá al Burayqah *71 G3 var.* Al Burayqah. N Libya
Marsabit *73 C6* Eastern, N Kenya
Marsala *97 B7 anc.* Lilybaeum. Sicilia, Italy, C Mediterranean Sea
Marsberg *94 B4* Nordrhein-Westfalen, W Germany
Marseille *91 D6 Eng.* Marseilles; *anc.* Massilia. Bouches-du-Rhône, SE France
Marshall *45 F2* Minnesota, N USA
Marshall *49 H2* Texas, SW USA
Marshall Islands *144 C1 Country* W Pacific Ocean

Marshall Islands 144

Official name Republic of the Marshall Islands
Formation 1986
Capital Majuro
Population 56,429 / 806 people per sq mile (312 people per sq km)
Total area 70 sq. miles (181 sq. km)
Languages Marshallese, English, Japanese, German
Religions Protestant 90%, Roman Catholic 8%, other 2%
Ethnic mix Micronesian 97%, other 3%
Government Presidential system
Currency US dollar = 100 cents
Literacy rate 91%
Calorie consumption Not available

Marshall Seamounts *125 H3 undersea feature* SW Pacific Ocean
Marsh Harbour *54 C1* Great Abaco, W Bahamas
Martaban *136 B4 var.* Moktama. Mon State, S Myanmar
Martha's Vineyard *41 G3 island* Massachusetts, NE USA
Martigues *91 D6* Bouches-du-Rhône, SE France
Martin *99 C5 Ger.* Sankt Martin, *Hung.* Turócszentmárton; *prev.* Turčianský Svätý Martin. Žilinský Kraj, N Slovakia
Martinique *55 G4 French overseas department* E West Indies
Martinique Channel *see* Martinique Passage
Martinique Passage *55 G4 var.* Dominica Channel, Martinique Channel. *Channel* Dominica/Martinique
Marton *150 D4* Manawatu-Wanganui, North Island, NZ
Martos *92 D4* Andalucía, S Spain
Marungu *77 E7 mountain range* SE Dem. Rep. Congo
Mary *122 D3 prev.* Merv. Maryyskiy Velayat, S Turkmenistan
Maryborough *see* Portlaoise
Maryborough *149 D4* Queensland, E Australia
Mary Island *see* Kanton

Maryland *41 E5 off.* State of Maryland; also known as America in Miniature, Cockade State, Free State, Old Line State. *State* NE USA
Maryland *42 D1* Tennessee, S USA
Maryville *45 F4* Missouri, C USA
Masai Steppe *73 C7 grassland* NW Tanzania
Masaka *73 B6* SW Uganda
Masallı *117 H3 Rus.* Masally. S Azerbaijan
Masasi *73 C8* Mtwara, SE Tanzania
Masawa *see* Massawa
Masaya *52 D3* Masaya, W Nicaragua
Mascarene Basin *141 B5 undersea feature* W Indian Ocean
Mascarene Islands *79 H4 island group* W Indian Ocean
Mascarene Plain *141 B5 undersea feature* W Indian Ocean
Mascarene Plateau *141 B5 undersea feature* W Indian Ocean
Maseru *78 D4 country capital* (Lesotho) W Lesotho
Mashhad *120 E2 var.* Meshed. Khorāsān, NE Iran
Mas-ha *119 D7* W Bank
Masindi *73 B6* W Uganda
Masīra *see* Maşīrah, Jazīrat
Masira, Gulf of *see* Maşīrah, Khalīj
Maşīrah, Jazīrat *121 E5 var.* Masīra. *Island* E Oman
Maşīrah, Khalīj *121 E5 var.* Gulf of Masira. *Bay* E Oman
Masis *see* Büyükağrı Dağı
Maskat *see* Masqaţ
Mason City *45 F3* Iowa, C USA
Masqaţ *121 E5 var.* Maskat, *Eng.* Muscat. *Country capital* (Oman) NE Oman
Massa *96 B3* Toscana, C Italy
Massachusetts *41 G3 off.* Commonwealth of Massachusetts; also known as Bay State, Old Bay State, Old Colony State. *State* NE USA
Massawa *72 C4 var.* Masawa, *Amh.* Mits'iwa. E Eritrea
Massenya *76 B3* Chari-Baguirmi, SW Chad
Massif Central *91 C5 plateau* C France
Massif du Makay *see* Makay
Massoukou *see* Franceville
Masterton *151 D5* Wellington, North Island, NZ
Masty *107 B5 Rus.* Mosty. Hrodzyenskaya Voblasts', W Belarus
Masuda *131 B6* Shimane, Honshū, SW Japan
Masuku *see* Franceville
Masvingo *78 D3 prev.* Fort Victoria, Nyanda, Victoria. Masvingo, SE Zimbabwe
Maşyāf *118 B3 Fr.* Misiaf. Ḩamāh, C Syria
Matadi *77 B6* Bas-Zaïre, W Dem. Rep. Congo
Matagalpa *52 D3* Matagalpa, C Nicaragua
Matale *132 D3* Central Province, C Sri Lanka
Matam *74 C3* NE Senegal
Matamata *150 D3* Waikato, North Island, NZ
Matamoros *50 D3* Coahuila de Zaragoza, NE Mexico
Matamoros *51 E2* Tamaulipas, C Mexico
Matane *39 E4* Québec, SE Canada
Matanzas *54 B2* Matanzas, NW Cuba
Matara *132 D4* Southern Province, S Sri Lanka
Mataram *138 D5* Pulau Lombok, C Indonesia
Mataró *93 G2 anc.* Illuro. Cataluña, E Spain
Mataura *151 B7 river* South Island, NZ
Mataura *151 B7* Southland, South Island, NZ
Mata Uta *see* Matā'utu
Matā'utu *145 E4 var.* Mata Uta. *Dependent territory capital* (Wallis and Futuna) Île Uvea, Wallis and Futuna
Matera *97 E5* Basilicata, S Italy
Matías Romero *51 F5* Oaxaca, SE Mexico
Mato Grosso *63 E4 prev.* Vila Bela da Santissima Trindade. Mato Grosso, W Brazil
Mato Grosso do Sul *63 E4 off.* Estado de Mato Grosso do Sul. *State* S Brazil
Mato Grosso, Planalto de *56 C4 plateau* C Brazil
Matosinhos *92 B2 prev.* Matozinhos. Porto, NW Portugal
Matsue *131 B6 var.* Matsuye, Matue. Shimane, Honshū, SW Japan
Matsumoto *131 C5 var.* Matumoto. Nagano, Honshū, S Japan
Matsuyama *131 B7 var.* Matuyama. Ehime, Shikoku, SW Japan
Matsuye *see* Matsue
Matterhorn *95 A8 It.* Monte Cervino. *Mountain* Italy/Switzerland *see also* Cervino, Monte
Matthews Ridge *59 F2* N Guyana
Matthew Town *54 D2* Great Inagua, S Bahamas
Matucana *60 C4* Lima, W Peru
Matue *see* Matsue
Matumoto *see* Matsumoto
Maturín *59 E2* Monagas, NE Venezuela
Matuyama *see* Matsuyama
Mau *135 E3 var.* Maunāth Bhanjan. Uttar Pradesh, N India
Maui *47 B8 island* Hawai'i, USA, C Pacific Ocean
Maulmain *see* Moulmein
Maun *78 C3* Ngamiland, C Botswana
Maunāth Bhanjan *see* Mau
Mauren *94 E1* NE Liechtenstein
Mauritania *74 C2 Ar.* Mūrītānīyah. *Country* W Africa

Mauritania 74

Official name	Islamic Republic of Mauritania
Formation	1960
Capital	Nouakchott
Population	2.9 million / 7 people per sq mile (3 people per sq km)
Total area	397,953 sq. miles (1,030,700 sq. km)
Languages	Hassaniyah Arabic, Wolof, French
Religions	Sunni Muslim 100%
Ethnic mix	Maure 81%, Wolof 7%, Tukolor 5%, other 4%, Soninka 3%
Government	Presidential system
Currency	Ouguiya = 5 khoums
Literacy rate	41%
Calorie consumption	2764 calories

Mauritius *79 H3 Fr.* Maurice. *Country* W Indian Ocean

Mauritius 79

Official name	Republic of Mauritius
Formation	1968
Capital	Port Louis
Population	1.2 million / 1671 people per sq mile (645 people per sq km)
Total area	718 sq. miles (1860 sq. km)
Languages	French Creole, Hindi, Urdu, Tamil, Chinese, English, French
Religions	Hindu 52%, Muslim 17%, Roman Catholic 26%, other 5%
Ethnic mix	Indo-Mauritian 68%, Creole 27%, Sino-Mauritian 3%, Franco-Mauritian 2%
Government	Parliamentary system
Currency	Mauritian rupee = 100 cents
Literacy rate	84%
Calorie consumption	2995 calories

Mauritius *141 B5 island* W Indian Ocean
Mawlamyine *see* Moulmein
Mawson *154 D2 Australian research station* Antarctica
Maya *52 B1 river* E Russian Federation
Mayadin *see* Al Mayādīn
Mayaguana *54 D2 island* SE Bahamas
Mayaguana Passage *54 D2 passage* SE Bahamas
Mayagüez *55 F3* W Puerto Rico
Mayamey *120 D2* Semnān, N Iran
Maya Mountains *52 B2 Sp.* Montañas Mayas. *Mountain range* Belize/Guatemala
Maych'ew *72 C4 var.* Mai Chio, *It.* Mai Ceu. N Ethiopia
Maydān Shahr *123 E4* Wardag, E Afghanistan
Mayebashi *see* Maebashi
Mayfield *151 B6* Canterbury, South Island, NZ
Maykop *111 A7* Respublika Adygeya, SW Russian Federation
Maymana *see* Meymaneh
Maymyo *136 B3* Mandalay, C Myanmar
Mayo *see* Maio
Mayor Island *150 D3 island* NE NZ
Mayor Pablo Lagerenza *see* Capitán Pablo Lagerenza
Mayotte *79 F2 French territorial collectivity* E Africa
May Pen *54 B5* C Jamaica
Mazabuka *78 D2* Southern, S Zambia
Mazaca *see* Kayseri
Mazār-e Sharīf *123 E3 var.* Mazār-i Sharif. Balkh, N Afghanistan
Mazār-i Sharif *see* Mazār-e Sharīf
Mazatlán *50 C3* Sinaloa, C Mexico
Mažeikiai *106 B3* Mažeikiai, NW Lithuania
Mazirbe *106 C2* Talsi, NW Latvia
Mazra'a *see* Al Mazra'ah
Mazury *98 D3 physical region* NE Poland
Mazyr *107 C7 Rus.* Mozyr'. Homyel'skaya Voblasts', SE Belarus
Mbabane *78 D4 country capital* (Swaziland) NW Swaziland
Mbacké *see* Mbaké
M'Baiki *see* Mbaïki
Mbaïki *77 C5 var.* M'Baiki. Lobaye, SW Central African Republic
Mbaké *74 B3 var.* Mbacké. W Senegal
Mbala *78 D1 prev.* Abercorn. Northern, NE Zambia
Mbale *73 C6* E Uganda
Mbandaka *77 C5 prev.* Coquilhatville. Equateur, NW Dem. Rep. Congo
M'Banza Congo *78 B1 var.* Mbanza Congo; *prev.* São Salvador, São Salvador do Congo. Zaire, NW Angola
Mbanza-Ngungu *77 B6* Bas-Zaïre, W Dem. Rep. Congo
Mbarara *73 B6* SW Uganda
Mbé *76 B4* Nord, N Cameroon
Mbeya *73 C7* Mbeya, SW Tanzania
Mbomou *see* Bomu
M'Bomu *see* Bomu
Mbour *74 B3* W Senegal
Mbuji-Mayi *77 D7 prev.* Bakwanga. Kasai Oriental, S Dem. Rep. Congo
McAlester *49 G2* Oklahoma, C USA
McAllen *49 G5* Texas, SW USA
McCamey *49 E3* Texas, SW USA
McClintock Channel *37 F2 channel* Nunavut, N Canada
McComb *42 B3* Mississippi, S USA
McCook *45 E4* Nebraska, C USA
McKean Island *145 E3 island* Phoenix Islands, C Kiribati
McKinley, Mount *36 C3 var.* Denali. *Mountain* Alaska, USA
McKinley Park *36 C3* Alaska, USA
McMinnville *46 B3* Oregon, NW USA
McMurdo Base *154 B4 US research station* Antarctica
McPherson *see* Fort McPherson
McPherson *45 E5* Kansas, C USA
Mdantsane *78 D5* Eastern Cape, SE South Africa
Mead, Lake *47 D6 reservoir* Arizona/Nevada, W USA
Meghālaya *113 G3 state*, NE India
Mecca *see* Makkah
Mechelen *87 C5 Eng.* Mechlin, *Fr.* Malines. Antwerpen, C Belgium
Mecklenburger Bucht *94 C2 bay* N Germany
Mecsek *99 C7 mountain range* SW Hungary
Medan *138 B3* Sumatera, E Indonesia
Medeba *see* Ma'dabā
Medellín *58 B3* Antioquia, NW Colombia
Médenine *71 F2 var.* Madanīyīn. SE Tunisia
Medford *46 B4* Oregon, NW USA
Medgidia *108 D5* Constanţa, SE Romania
Mediaş *108 B4 Ger.* Mediasch, *Hung.* Medgyes. Sibiu, C Romania
Medicine Hat *37 F5* Alberta, SW Canada
Medinaceli *93 E2* Castilla-León, N Spain
Medina del Campo *92 D2* Castilla-León, N Spain
Mediterranean Sea *102 D3 Fr.* Mer Méditerranée. *Sea* Africa/Asia/Europe
Médoc *91 B5 cultural region* SW France
Medvezh'yegorsk *110 B3* Respublika Kareliya, NW Russian Federation
Meekatharra *147 B5* Western Australia
Meemu Atoll *see* Mulaku Atoll
Meerssen *87 D6 var.* Mersen. Limburg, SE Netherlands
Meerut *134 D2* Uttar Pradesh, N India
Mehdia *see* Mahdia
Meheso *see* Mī'ēso
Me Hka *see* Nmai Hka
Mehrīz *120 D3* Yazd, C Iran
Mehtar Lām *see* Mehtarlām
Mehtarlām *123 F4 var.* Mehtar Lām, Meterlam, Methariam, Metharlam. Laghmān, E Afghanistan
Meiktila *136 B3* Mandalay, C Myanmar
Mejillones *64 B2* Antofagasta, N Chile
Mek'elē *72 C4 var.* Makale. N Ethiopia
Mékhé *74 B3* NW Senegal
Mekong *124 D3 var.* Lan-ts'ang Chiang, *Cam.* Mékôngk, *Chin.* Lancang Jiang, *Lao.* Mènam Khong, *Th.* Mae Nam Khong, *Tib.* Dza Chu, *Vtn.* Sông Tiên Giang. *River* SE Asia
Mékôngk *see* Mekong
Mekong, Mouths of the *137 E6 delta* S Vietnam
Melaka *138 B3 var.* Malacca. Melaka, Peninsular Malaysia
Melanesia *144 D3 island group* W Pacific Ocean
Melanesian Basin *142 C2 undersea feature* W Pacific Ocean
Melbourne *149 C7 state capital* Victoria, SE Australia
Melbourne *43 E4* Florida, SE USA
Melghir, Chott *71 E2 var.* Chott Melrhir. *Salt lake* E Algeria
Melilla *80 B5 anc.* Rusaddir, Russadir. Melilla, Spain, N Africa
Melilla *70 D2 enclave* Spain, N Africa
Melita *37 F5* Manitoba, S Canada
Melitopol' *109 F4* Zaporiz'ka Oblast', SE Ukraine
Melle *87 B5* Oost-Vlaanderen, NW Belgium
Mellerud *85 B6* Västra Götaland, S Sweden
Mellieha *102 B5* E Malta
Mellizo Sur, Cerro *65 A7 mountain* S Chile
Melo *64 E4* Cerro Largo, NE Uruguay

Melsungen *94 B4* Hessen, C Germany
Melun *90 C3 anc.* Melodunum. Seine-et-Marne, N France
Melville Island *146 D2 island* Northern Territory, N Australia
Melville Island *37 E2 island* Parry Islands, Northwest Territories/Nunavut, NW Canada
Melville, Lake *39 F2 lake* Newfoundland and Labrador, E Canada
Melville Peninsula *37 G3 peninsula* Northwest Territories, NE Canada
Membidj *see* Manbij
Memmingen *95 B6* Bayern, S Germany
Memphis *42 C1* Tennessee, S USA
Ménaka *75 F3* Goa, E Mali
Menaldum *86 D1 Fris.* Menaam. Friesland, N Netherlands
Mènam Khong *see* Mekong
Mendaña Fracture Zone *153 F4 tectonic feature* E Pacific Ocean
Mende *91 C5 anc.* Mimatum. Lozère, S France
Mendeleyev Ridge *155 B2 undersea feature* Arctic Ocean
Mendocino Fracture Zone *152 D2 tectonic feature* NE Pacific Ocean
Mendoza *64 B4* Mendoza, W Argentina
Menemen *116 A3* İzmir, W Turkey
Menengiyn Tal *127 F2 plain* E Mongolia
Menongue *78 B2 var.* Vila Serpa Pinto, *Port.* Serpa Pinto. Cuando Cubango, C Angola
Menorca *93 H3 Eng.* Minorca; *anc.* Balearis Minor. *Island* Islas Baleares, Spain, W Mediterranean Sea
Mentawai, Kepulauan *138 A4 island group* W Indonesia
Meppel *86 D2* Drenthe, NE Netherlands
Merano *96 C1 Ger.* Meran. Trentino-Alto Adige, N Italy
Merca *see* Marka
Mercedes *see* Villa Mercedes
Mercedes *64 D3* Corrientes, NE Argentina
Mercedes *64 D4* Soriano, SW Uruguay
Meredith, Lake *49 E1 reservoir* Texas, SW USA
Merefa *109 G2* Kharkivs'ka Oblast', E Ukraine
Mergui *137 B6* Tenasserim, S Myanmar
Mergui Archipelago *137 B6 island group* S Myanmar
Meriç *see* Maritsa
Mérida *92 C4 anc.* Augusta Emerita. Extremadura, W Spain
Mérida *58 C2* Mérida, W Venezuela
Mérida *51 H3* Yucatán, SW Mexico
Meridian *42 C2* Mississippi, S USA
Mérignac *91 B5* Gironde, SW France
Merkinė *107 B5* Varėna, S Lithuania
Merowe *72 B3 desert* W Sudan
Merredin *147 B6* Western Australia
Mersen *see* Meerssen
Mersey *89 D5 river* NW England, UK
Mersin *116 C4* İçel, S Turkey
Mērsrags *106 C3* Talsi, NW Latvia
Meru *73 C6* Eastern, C Kenya
Merzifon *116 D2* Amasya, N Turkey
Merzig *95 A5* Saarland, SW Germany
Mesa *48 B2* Arizona, SW USA
Meshed *see* Mashhad
Mesopotamia *57 C5 var.* Mesopotamia Argentina. *Physical region* NE Argentina
Mesopotamia Argentina *see* Mesopotamia
Messalo, Rio *79 E2 var.* Mualo. *River* NE Mozambique
Messana *see* Messina
Messene *see* Messina
Messina *97 D7 var.* Messana, Messene; *anc.* Zancle. Sicilia, Italy, C Mediterranean Sea
Messina *see* Musina
Messina, Stretto di *97 D7 Eng.* Strait of Messina. *Strait* SW Italy
Messíni *105 B6* Pelopónnisos, S Greece
Mestghanem *see* Mostaganem
Mestia *117 F1 var.* Mestiya. N Georgia
Mestiya *see* Mestia
Mestre *96 C2* Veneto, NE Italy
Meta *56 B2 off.* Departamento del Meta. *Province* C Colombia
Metairie *42 B3* Louisiana, S USA
Metán *64 C2* Salta, N Argentina
Metapán *52 B2* Santa Ana, NW El Salvador
Meta, Río *58 D3 river* Colombia/Venezuela
Meterlam *see* Mehtarlām
Methariam *see* Mehtarlām
Metharlam *see* Mehtarlām
Metković *100 B4* Dubrovnik-Neretva, SE Croatia
Métsovo *104 B4 prev.* Métsovon. Ípeiros, C Greece
Metz *90 D3 anc.* Divodurum Mediomatricum, Mediomatrica, Metis. Moselle, NE France
Meulaboh *138 A3* Sumatera, W Indonesia
Meuse *87 C6 Dut.* Maas. *River* W Europe *see also* Maas
Meuse *90 D3 department* NE France
Mexcala, Río *see* Balsas, Río
Mexicali *50 A1* Baja California, NW Mexico
Mexico *50 C3 var.* Méjico, México, *Sp.* Estados Unidos Mexicanos. *Country* N Central America

Mexico 50

Official name United Mexican States
Formation 1836
Capital Mexico City
Population 104 million / 140 people per sq mile (54 people per sq km)
Total area 761,602 sq. miles (1,972,550 sq. km)
Languages Spanish, Nahuatl, Mayan, Zapotec, Mixtec, Otomi, Totonac, Tzotzil, Tzeltal
Religions Roman Catholic 88%, other 7%, Protestant 5%
Ethnic mix Mestizo 60%, Amerindian 30%, European 9%, other 1%
Government Presidential system
Currency Mexican peso = 100 centavos
Literacy rate 91%
Calorie consumption 3160 calories

Mexico *45 G4* Missouri, C USA
México *51 E4 var.* Ciudad de México, *Eng.* Mexico City. *Country capital* (Mexico) México, C Mexico
Mexico City *see* México
Mexico, Gulf of *51 F2 Sp.* Golfo de México. *Gulf* W Atlantic Ocean
Meyadine *see* Al Mayādīn
Meymaneh *122 D3 var.* Maimāna, Maymana. Fāryāb, NW Afghanistan
Mezen' *110 D3 river* NW Russian Federation
Mezőtúr *99 D7* Jász-Nagykun-Szolnok, E Hungary
Mġarr *102 A5* Gozo, N Malta
Miahuatlán *51 F5 var.* Miahuatlán de Porfirio Díaz. Oaxaca, SE Mexico
Miahuatlán de Porfirio Díaz *see* Miahuatlán
Miami *43 F5* Florida, SE USA
Miami *49 G1* Oklahoma, C USA
Miami Beach *43 F5* Florida, SE USA
Mīāneh *120 C2 var.* Miyāneh. Āżarbāyjān-e Khāvarī, NW Iran
Mianyang *128 B5* Sichuan, C China
Miastko *98 C2 Ger.* Rummelsburg in Pommern. Pomorskie, N Poland
Mi Chai *see* Nong Khai
Michalovce *99 E5 Ger.* Grossmichel, *Hung.* Nagymihály. Košický Kraj, E Slovakia
Michigan *40 C1 off.* State of Michigan; also known as Great Lakes State, Lake State, Wolverine State. *State* N USA
Michigan, Lake *40 C2 lake* N USA
Michurinsk *111 B5* Tambovskaya Oblast', W Russian Federation
Micoud *55 F2* SE Saint Lucia
Micronesia *144 B1 Country* W Pacific Ocean
Micronesia *144 C1 island group* W Pacific Ocean

Micronesia 144

Official name Federated States of Micronesia
Formation 1986
Capital Palikir (Pohnpei Island)
Population 108,143 / 399 people per sq mile (154 people per sq km)
Total area 271 sq. miles (702 sq. km)
Languages Trukese, Pohnpeian, Mortlockese, Kosraean, English
Religions Roman Catholic 50%, Protestant 48%, other 2%
Ethnic mix Micronesian 100%
Government Nonparty system
Currency US dollar = 100 cents
Literacy rate 81%
Calorie consumption Not available

Mid-Atlantic Cordillera *see* Mid-Atlantic Ridge
Mid-Atlantic Ridge *66 C3 var.* Mid-Atlantic Cordillera, Mid-Atlantic Rise, Mid-Atlantic Swell. *Undersea feature* Atlantic Ocean
Mid-Atlantic Rise *see* Mid-Atlantic Ridge
Mid-Atlantic Swell *see* Mid-Atlantic Ridge
Middelburg *87 B5* Zeeland, SW Netherlands
Middelharnis *86 B4* Zuid-Holland, SW Netherlands
Middelkerke *87 A5* West-Vlaanderen, W Belgium
Middle America Trench *35 B7 undersea feature* E Pacific Ocean
Middle Andaman *133 F2 island* Andaman Islands, India, NE Indian Ocean
Middlesboro *40 C5* Kentucky, S USA
Middlesbrough *89 D5* N England, UK
Middletown *41 F4* New Jersey, NE USA
Middletown *41 F3* New York, NE USA
Mid-Indian Basin *141 C5 undersea feature* N Indian Ocean
Mid-Indian Ridge *141 C5 var.* Central Indian Ridge. *Undersea feature* C Indian Ocean
Midland *40 C3* Michigan, N USA
Midland *38 D5* Ontario, S Canada
Midland *49 E3* Texas, SW USA
Mid-Pacific Mountains *152 C2 var.* Mid-Pacific Seamounts. *Undersea feature* NW Pacific Ocean
Mid-Pacific Seamounts *see* Mid-Pacific Mountains
Midway Islands *152 D2 US territory* C Pacific Ocean
Miechów *99 D5* Małopolskie, S Poland
Międzyrzec Podlaski *98 E3* Lubelskie, E Poland
Międzyrzecz *98 B3 Ger.* Meseritz. Lubuskie, W Poland
Mielec *99 D5* Podkarpackie, SE Poland
Miercurea-Ciuc *108 C4 Ger.* Szeklerburg, *Hung.* Csíkszereda. Harghita, C Romania
Mieres del Camín *see* Mieres del Camino
Mieres del Camino *108 D1 var.* Mieres del Camín. Asturias, NW Spain
Mieresch *see* Mureș
Mī'ēso *73 D5 var.* Meheso, Miesso. C Ethiopia
Miesso *see* Mī'ēso
Miguel Asua *50 D3 var.* Miguel Auza. Zacatecas, C Mexico
Miguel Auza *see* Miguel Asua
Mijdrecht *86 C3* Utrecht, C Netherlands
Mikashevichy *107 C7 Pol.* Mikaszewicze, *Rus.* Mikashevichi. Brestskaya Voblasts', SW Belarus
Mikhaylovka *111 B6* Volgogradskaya Oblast', SW Russian Federation
Míkonos *see* Mýkonos
Mikre *104 C2* Lovech, N Bulgaria
Mikun' *110 D4* Respublika Komi, NW Russian Federation
Mikuni-sanmyaku *131 D5 mountain range* Honshū, N Japan
Mikura-jima *131 D6 island* E Japan
Milagro *60 B2* Guayas, SW Ecuador
Milan *see* Milano
Milange *79 E2* Zambézia, NE Mozambique
Milano *96 B2 Eng.* Milan, *Ger.* Mailand; *anc.* Mediolanum. Lombardia, N Italy
Milas *116 A4* Muğla, SW Turkey
Milashavichy *107 C7 Rus.* Milashevichi. Homyel'skaya Voblasts', SE Belarus
Mildura *149 C6* Victoria, SE Australia
Mile *see* Mili Atoll
Miles *149 D5* Queensland, E Australia
Miles City *44 C2* Montana, NW USA
Milford Haven *89 C6 prev.* Milford. SW Wales, UK
Milford Sound *151 A6 inlet* South Island, NZ
Milford Sound *151 A6* Southland, South Island, NZ
Mili Atoll *144 D2 var.* Mile. *Atoll* Ratak Chain, SE Marshall Islands
Mil'kovo *115 H3* Kamchatskaya Oblast', E Russian Federation
Milk River *44 C1 river* Montana, NW USA
Milk River *37 E5* Alberta, SW Canada
Milk, Wadi el *88 B4 var.* Wadi al Malik. *River* C Sudan
Milledgeville *43 E2* Georgia, SE USA
Mille Lacs Lake *45 F2 lake* Minnesota, N USA
Millennium Island *160 C8 prev.* Caroline Island, Thornton Island. *Atoll* Line Islands, E Kiribati
Millerovo *111 B6* Rostovskaya Oblast', SW Russian Federation
Mílos *105 C7 island* Kykládes, Greece, Aegean Sea
Mílos *105 C6* Mílos, Kykládes, Greece, Aegean Sea
Milton *151 B7* Otago, South Island, NZ
Milton Keynes *89 D6* SE England, UK
Milwaukee *40 B3* Wisconsin, N USA
Min *see* Fujian
Mīnā' Qābūs *140 B3* NE Oman
Minas Gerais *63 F3 off.* Estado de Minas Gerais. *State* E Brazil
Minatitlán *51 F4* Veracruz-Llave, E Mexico
Minbu *136 A3* Magwe, W Myanmar
Minch, The *88 B3 var.* North Minch. *Strait* NW Scotland, UK
Mindanao *139 F2 island* S Philippines
Mindanao Sea *see* Bohol Sea

Mindelheim *95 C6* Bayern, S Germany
Mindello *see* Mindelo
Mindelo *74 A2 var.* Mindello; *prev.* Porto Grande. São Vicente, N Cape Verde
Minden *94 B4 anc.* Minthun. Nordrhein-Westfalen, NW Germany
Mindoro *139 E2 island* N Philippines
Mindoro Strait *139 E2 strait* W Philippines
Mineral Wells *49 F2* Texas, SW USA
Mingäçevir *117 G2 Rus.* Mingechaur, Mingechevir. C Azerbaijan
Mingāora *134 C1 var.* Mingora, Mongora. North-West Frontier Province, N Pakistan
Mingora *see* Mingāora
Minho *92 B2 former province* N Portugal
Minho, Rio *92 B2 Sp.* Miño. *river* Portugal/Spain *see also* Miño
Minicoy Island *132 B3 island* SW India
Minius *see* Miño
Minna *75 G4* Niger, C Nigeria
Minneapolis *45 F2* Minnesota, N USA
Minnesota *45 F2 off.* State of Minnesota; also known as Gopher State, New England of the West, North Star State. *State* N USA
Miño *92 B2 var.* Mino, Minius, *Port.* Rio Minho. *River* Portugal/Spain *see also* Minho, Rio
Mino *see* Miño
Minot *45 E1* North Dakota, N USA
Minsk *107 C6 country capital* (Belarus) Minskaya Voblasts', C Belarus
Minskaya Wzvyshsha *107 C6 mountain range* C Belarus
Mińsk Mazowiecki *98 D3 var.* Nowo-Minsk. Mazowieckie, C Poland
Minto, Lac *38 D2 lake* Québec, C Canada
Minya *see* El Minya
Miraflores *50 C3* Baja California Sur, W Mexico
Miranda de Ebro *93 E1* La Rioja, N Spain
Miri *138 D3* Sarawak, East Malaysia
Mirim Lagoon *63 E5 var.* Lake Mirim, *Sp.* Laguna Merín. *Lagoon* Brazil/Uruguay
Mirim, Lake *see* Mirim Lagoon
Mírina *see* Mýrina
Mīrjāveh *120 E4* Sīstān va Balūchestān, SE Iran
Mirny *154 C3 Russian research station* Antarctica
Mirnyy *115 F3* Respublika Sakha (Yakutiya), NE Russian Federation
Mīrpur Khās *134 B3* Sind, SE Pakistan
Mirtóo Pélagos *105 C6 Eng.* Mirtoan Sea; *anc.* Myrtoum Mare. *Sea* S Greece
Miskito Coast *see* Mosquito Coast
Miskitos, Cayos *53 E2 island group* NE Nicaragua
Miskolc *99 D6* Borsod-Abaúj-Zemplén, NE Hungary
Misool, Pulau *139 F4 island* Maluku, E Indonesia
Mişrātah *71 F2 var.* Misurata. NW Libya
Mission *49 G5* Texas, SW USA
Mississippi *42 B2 off.* State of Mississippi; also known as Bayou State, Magnolia State. *State* SE USA
Mississippi Delta *42 B4 delta* Louisiana, S USA
Mississippi River *35 C6 river* C USA
Missoula *44 B1* Montana, NW USA
Missouri *45 F5 off.* State of Missouri; also known as Bullion State, Show Me State. *State* C USA
Missouri River *45 E3 river* C USA
Mistassini, Lac *38 D3 lake* Québec, SE Canada
Mistelbach an der Zaya *95 E6* Niederösterreich, NE Austria
Misti, Volcán *61 E4 mountain* S Peru
Misurata *see* Mişrātah
Mitchell *149 D5* Queensland, E Australia
Mitchell *45 E3* South Dakota, N USA
Mitchell, Mount *43 E1 mountain* North Carolina, SE USA
Mitchell River *148 C2 river* Queensland, NE Australia
Mi Tho *see* My Tho
Mitilíni *see* Mytilíni
Mito *131 D5* Ibaraki, Honshū, S Japan
Mits'iwa *see* Massawa
Mitspe Ramon *see* Mizpé Ramon
Mitú *58 C4* Vaupés, SE Colombia
Mitumba, Monts *77 E7 var.* Chaîne des Mitumba, Mitumba Range. *Mountain range* E Dem. Rep. Congo
Mitumba Range *see* Mitumba, Monts
Miyako *130 D4* Iwate, Honshū, C Japan
Miyako-jima *131 D6 island* Sakishima-shotō, SW Japan
Miyakonojō *131 B8 var.* Miyakonzyô. Miyazaki, Kyūshū, SW Japan
Miyakonzyô *see* Miyakonojō
Miyāneh *see* Mīāneh
Miyazaki *131 B8* Miyazaki, Kyūshū, SW Japan
Mizil *108 C5* Prahova, SE Romania
Miziya *104 C1* Vratsa, NW Bulgaria
Mizpé Ramon *119 A7 var.* Mitspe Ramon. Southern, S Israel
Mjøsa *85 B6 var.* Mjøsen. *Lake* S Norway
Mjøsen *see* Mjøsa
Mladenovac *100 D4* Serbia, C Serbia and Montenegro (Yugo.)
Mława *98 D3* Mazowieckie, C Poland
Mljet *101 B5 It.* Meleda; *anc.* Melita. *Island* S Croatia
Mmabatho *78 C4* North-West, N South Africa
Moab *44 B5* Utah, W USA
Moab, Kir of *see* Al Karak
Moa Island *148 C1 island* Queensland, NE Australia
Moanda *77 B6 var.* Mouanda. Haut-Ogooué, SE Gabon
Moba *77 E7* Shaba, E Dem. Rep. Congo
Mobay *see* Montego Bay
Mobaye *77 C5* Basse-Kotto, S Central African Republic
Moberly *45 G4* Missouri, C USA
Mobile *42 C3* Alabama, S USA
Mobutu Sese Seko, Lac *see* Albert, Lake
Mochudi *78 C4* Kgatleng, SE Botswana
Mocímboa da Praia *79 F2 var.* Vila de Mocímboa da Praia. Cabo Delgado, N Mozambique
Môco *78 B2 var.* Morro de Môco. *Mountain* W Angola
Mocoa *58 A4* Putumayo, SW Colombia
Mocuba *79 E3* Zambézia, NE Mozambique
Modena *96 B3 anc.* Mutina. Emilia-Romagna, N Italy
Modesto *47 B6* California, W USA
Modica *97 C7 anc.* Motyca. Sicilia, Italy, C Mediterranean Sea
Modimolle *78 D4 var.* Nylstroom, NE South Africa
Modriča *100 C3* Republika Srpska, N Bosnia and Herzegovina
Moe *149 C7* Victoria, SE Australia
Moero, Lac *see* Mweru, Lake
Mogadishu *see* Muqdisho
Mogilno *98 C3* Kujawski-pomorskie, C Poland
Mohammedia *70 C2 prev.* Fédala. NW Morocco
Mohave, Lake *47 D7 reservoir* Arizona/Nevada, W USA
Mohawk River *41 F3 river* New York, NE USA
Mohéli *79 F2 var.* Mwali, Mohilla, Mohila, *Fr.* Moili. *Island* S Comoros
Mohila *see* Mohéli
Mohilla *see* Mohéli
Mohns Ridge *83 F3 undersea feature* Greenland Sea/Norwegian Sea
Moho *61 E4* Puno, SW Peru
Mohoro *73 C7* Pwani, E Tanzania
Mohyliv-Podil's'kyy *108 D3 Rus.* Mogilev-Podol'skiy. Vinnyts'ka Oblast', C Ukraine
Moi *85 A6* Rogaland, S Norway
Moili *see* Mohéli
Mo i Rana *84 C3* Nordland, C Norway
Mõisaküla *106 D3 Ger.* Moisekűll. Viljandimaa, S Estonia
Moissac *91 B6* Tarn-et-Garonne, S France
Mojácar *93 E5* Andalucía, S Spain
Mojave Desert *47 D7 plain* California, W USA
Moktama *see* Martaban
Mol *87 C5 prev.* Moll. Antwerpen, N Belgium
Moldavia *see* Moldova
Moldavian SSR/Moldavskaya SSR *see* Moldova
Molde *85 A5* Møre og Romsdal, S Norway
Moldo-Too, Khrebet *123 G2 prev.* Khrebet Moldotau. *Mountain range* C Kyrgyzstan
Moldova *108 D3 var.* Moldavia; *prev.* Moldavian SSR, *Rus.* Moldavskaya SSR. *Country* SE Europe

Moldova 108

Official name Republic of Moldova
Formation 1991
Capital Chisinau
Population 4.3 million / 330 people per sq mile (128 people per sq km)
Total area 13,067 sq. miles (33,843 sq. km)
Languages Moldovan, Ukrainian, Russian
Religions Orthodox Christian 98%, Jewish 2%
Ethnic mix Moldovan 65%, Ukrainian 14%, Russian 13%, other 4%, Gagauz 4%
Government Parliamentary system
Currency Moldovan leu = 100 bani
Literacy rate 99%
Calorie consumption 2712 calories

Moldova Nouă *108 A4 Ger.* Neumoldowa, *Hung.* Újmoldova. Caraş-Severin, SW Romania
Moldoveanul *see* Vârful Moldoveanu
Molfetta *97 E5* Puglia, SE Italy
Mollendo *61 E4* Arequipa, SW Peru
Mölndal *85 B7* Västra Götaland, S Sweden
Molochans'k *109 G4 Rus.* Molochansk. Zaporiz'ka Oblast', SE Ukraine
Molodezhnaya *154 C2 Russian research station* Antarctica
Moloka'i *47 B8 var.* Molokai. *Island* Hawai'i, USA, C Pacific Ocean
Molokai Fracture Zone *153 E2 tectonic feature* NE Pacific Ocean
Molopo *78 C4 seasonal river* Botswana/South Africa
Mólos *105 B5* Stereá Ellás, C Greece
Moluccas *see* Maluku
Molucca Sea *139 F4 Ind.* Laut Maluku. *Sea* E Indonesia
Mombasa *73 D7 international airport* Coast, SE Kenya
Mombasa *73 D7* Coast, SE Kenya
Mombetsu *see* Monbetsu
Momchilgrad *104 D3 prev.* Mastanli. Kŭrdzhali, S Bulgaria
Møn *85 B8 prev.* Möen. *Island* SE Denmark
Monaco *91 E6 Country* W Europe

Monaco 91

Official name Principality of Monaco
Formation 1861
Capital Monaco-Ville
Population 32,130 / 42840 people per sq mile (16477 people per sq km)
Total area 0.75 sq. miles (1.95 sq. km)
Languages French, Italian, Monégasque, English
Religions Roman Catholic 89%, Protestant 6%, other 5%
Ethnic mix French 47%, other 20%, Monégasque 17%, Italian 16%
Government Monarchy
Currency Euro = 100 cents
Literacy rate 99%
Calorie consumption Not available

Monaco *91 C7 var.* Monaco-Ville; *anc.* Monoecus. *Country capital* (Monaco) S Monaco
Monaco, Port de *91 C8 bay* S Monaco
Monaco-Ville *see* Monaco
Monahans *49 E3* Texas, SW USA
Mona, Isla *55 E3 island* W Puerto Rico
Mona Passage *55 E3 Sp.* Canal de la Mona. *Channel* Dominican Republic/Puerto Rico
Monbetsu *130 D2 var.* Mombetsu, Monbetu. Hokkaidō, NE Japan
Monbetu *see* Monbetsu
Moncalieri *96 A2* Piemonte, NW Italy
Monchegorsk *110 C2* Murmanskaya Oblast', NW Russian Federation
Monclova *50 D2* Coahuila de Zaragoza, NE Mexico
Moncton *39 F4* New Brunswick, SE Canada
Mondovì *96 A2* Piemonte, NW Italy
Monfalcone *96 D2* Friuli-Venezia Giulia, NE Italy
Monforte *see* Monforte de Lemos
Monforte de Lemos *92 C1 var.* Monforte. Galicia, NW Spain
Mongo *76 C3* Guéra, C Chad
Mongolia *126 C2 Mong.* Mongol Uls. *Country* E Asia

Mongolia 126

Official name Mongolia
Formation 1924
Capital Ulan Bator
Population 2.6 million / 4 people per sq mile (2 people per sq km)
Total area 604,247 sq. miles (1,565,000 sq. km)
Languages Khalkha Mongolian, Kazakh, Chinese, Russian
Religions Tibetan Buddhist 96%, Muslim 4%
Ethnic mix Mongol 90%, Kazakh 4%, Chinese 2%, Russian 2%, other 2%
Government Mixed presidential–parliamentary system
Currency Tugrik (tögrög) = 100 möngö
Literacy rate 98%
Calorie consumption 1974 calories

Mongolia, Plateau of *124 D1 plateau* E Mongolia
Mongora *see* Mingāora
Mongu *78 C2* Western, W Zambia
Monkchester *see* Newcastle upon Tyne
Monkey Bay *79 E2* Southern, SE Malawi
Monkey River *see* Monkey River Town
Monkey River Town *52 C2 var.* Monkey River. Toledo, SE Belize
Monoecus *see* Monaco
Mono Lake *47 C6 lake* California, W USA

Monovar *93 F4 Cat.* Monover. País Valenciano, E Spain
Monover *see* Monovar
Monroe *42 B2* Louisiana, S USA
Monrovia *74 C5 country capital* (Liberia) W Liberia
Mons *87 B6 Dut.* Bergen. Hainaut, S Belgium
Monselice *96 C2* Veneto, NE Italy
Montagnes Rocheuses *see* Rocky Mountains
Montana *44 B1 off.* State of Montana; also known as Mountain State, Treasure State. *State* NW USA
Montana *104 C2 prev.* Ferdinand, Mikhaylovgrad. Montana, NW Bulgaria
Montargis *90 C4* Loiret, C France
Montauban *91 B6* Tarn-et-Garonne, S France
Montbéliard *90 D4* Doubs, E France
Mont Cenis, Col du *91 D5 pass* E France
Mont-de-Marsan *91 B6* Landes, SW France
Monteagudo *61 G4* Chuquisaca, S Bolivia
Monte-Carlo *91 C8* NE Monaco
Monte Caseros *64 D3* Corrientes, NE Argentina
Monte Cristi *54 D3 var.* San Fernando de Monte Cristi. NW Dominican Republic
Montegiardino *96 E2* SE San Marino
Montego Bay *54 A4 var.* Mobay. W Jamaica
Montélimar *91 D5 anc.* Acunum Acusio, Montilium Adhemari. Drôme, E France
Montemorelos *51 E3* Nuevo León, NE Mexico
Montenegro *101 C5 Serb.* Crna Gora. Admin. region *republic* SW Serbia and Montenegro (Yugo.)
Monte Patria *64 B3* Coquimbo, N Chile
Monterey *see* Monterrey
Monterey *47 B6* California, W USA
Monterey Bay *47 A6 bay* California, W USA
Montería *58 B2* Córdoba, NW Colombia
Montero *61 G4* Santa Cruz, C Bolivia
Monterrey *51 E3 var.* Monterey. Nuevo León, NE Mexico
Montes Claros *63 F3* Minas Gerais, SE Brazil
Montevideo *64 D4 country capital* (Uruguay) Montevideo, S Uruguay
Montevideo *45 F2* Minnesota, N USA
Montgenèvre, Col de *91 D5 pass* France/Italy
Montgomery *42 D2 state capital* Alabama, S USA
Monthey *95 A7* Valais, SW Switzerland
Montluçon *90 C4* Allier, C France
Montoro *92 D4* Andalucía, S Spain
Montpelier *41 G2 state capital* Vermont, NE USA
Montpellier *91 C6* Hérault, S France
Montréal *39 E4 Eng.* Montreal. Québec, SE Canada
Montrose *44 C5* Colorado, C USA
Montrose *88 D3* E Scotland, UK
Montserrat *55 G3 var.* Emerald Isle. *UK dependent territory* E West Indies
Monywa *136 B3* Sagaing, C Myanmar
Monza *96 B2* Lombardia, N Italy
Monze *78 D2* Southern, S Zambia
Monzón *93 F2* Aragón, NE Spain
Moonie *149 D5* Queensland, E Australia
Moora *147 A6* Western Australia
Moore *49 G1* Oklahoma, C USA
Moore, Lake *147 B6 lake* Western Australia
Moorhead *45 F2* Minnesota, N USA
Moose *38 C3 river* Ontario, S Canada
Moosehead Lake *41 G1 lake* Maine, NE USA
Moosonee *38 C3* Ontario, SE Canada
Mopti *75 E3* Mopti, C Mali
Moquegua *61 E4* Moquegua, SE Peru
Mora *85 C5* Kopparberg, C Sweden
Morales *52 C2* Izabal, E Guatemala
Morant Bay *54 B5* E Jamaica
Moratalla *93 E4* Murcia, SE Spain
Morava *99 C5 var.* March. *River* C Europe *see also* March
Morava *see* Velika Morava
Moravia *99 B5* Iowa, C USA
Moray Firth *88 C3 inlet* N Scotland, UK
Morea *see* Pelopónnisos
Moreau River *44 D2 river* South Dakota, N USA
Moree *149 D5* New South Wales, SE Australia
Morelia *51 E4* Michoacán de Ocampo, S Mexico
Morena, Sierra *92 C4 mountain range* S Spain
Moreni *108 C5* Dâmboviţa, S Romania
Mórfou *102 C5* W Cyprus
Morgan City *42 B3* Louisiana, S USA
Morghāb, Daryā-ye *122 D3 var.* Murgab, Murghab, *Turkm.* Murgap, Murgap Deryasy. *River* Afghanistan/Turkmenistan *see also* Murgap
Morioka *130 D4* Iwate, Honshū, C Japan
Morlaix *90 A3* Finistère, NW France
Mornington Abyssal Plain *67 A7 undersea feature* SE Pacific Ocean
Mornington Island *148 B2 island* Wellesley Islands, Queensland, N Australia
Morocco *70 B3 Ar.* Al Mamlakah. *Country* N Africa

Morocco 70

Official name Kingdom of Morocco
Formation 1956
Capital Rabat
Population 30.6 million / 178 people per sq mile (69 people per sq km)
Total area 172,316 sq. miles (446,300 sq. km)
Languages Arabic, Tamazight (Berber), French, Spanish
Religions Muslim (mainly Sunni) 99%, Other (mostly Christian) 1%
Ethnic mix Arab 70%, Berber 29%, European 1%
Government Monarchy
Currency Moroccan dirham = 100 centimes
Literacy rate 51%
Calorie consumption 3046 calories

Morocco *see* Marrakech
Morogoro *73 C7* Morogoro, E Tanzania
Moro Gulf *139 E3 gulf* S Philippines
Morón *54 C2* Ciego de Ávila, C Cuba
Mörön *126 D2* Hövsgöl, N Mongolia
Morondava *79 F3* Toliara, W Madagascar
Moroni *79 F2 country capital* (Comoros) Grande Comore, NW Comoros
Morotai, Pulau *139 F3 island* Maluku, E Indonesia
Morotiri *see* Marotiri
Morrinsville *150 D3* Waikato, North Island, NZ
Morris *45 F2* Minnesota, N USA
Morris Jesup, Kap *83 E1 headland* N Greenland
Morro de Môco *see* Môco
Morvan *90 D4 physical region* C France
Moscow *see* Moskva
Moscow *46 C2* Idaho, NW USA
Mosel *95 A5 Fr.* Moselle. *River* W Europe *see also* Moselle
Moselle *87 E8 Ger.* Mosel. *River* W Europe *see also* Mosel
Moselle *90 D3 department* NE France
Mosgiel *151 B7* Otago, South Island, NZ
Moshi *73 C7* Kilimanjaro, NE Tanzania
Mosjøen *84 B4* Nordland, C Norway
Moskva *111 B5 Eng.* Moscow. *Country capital* (Russian Federation) Gorod Moskva, W Russian Federation
Moskva *123 E3 Rus.* Moskovskiy; *prev.* Chubek. SW Tajikistan
Mosonmagyaróvár *99 C6 Ger.* Wieselburg-Ungarisch-Altenburg; *prev.* Moson and Magyaróvár, *Ger.* Wieselburg and Ungarisch-Altenburg. Győr-Moson-Sopron, NW Hungary
Mosquito Coast *53 E3 var.* Miskito Coast. *Coastal region* E Nicaragua
Mosquitos, Golfo de los *53 F4 Eng.* Mosquito Gulf. *Gulf* N Panama
Moss *85 B6* Østfold, S Norway
Mosselbaai *78 C5 var.* Mosselbai, *Eng.* Mossel Bay. Western Cape, SW South Africa
Mossendjo *77 B6* Le Niari, SW Congo
Mossoró *63 G2* Rio Grande do Norte, NE Brazil
Most *98 A4 Ger.* Brüx. Ústecký Kraj, NW Czech Republic
Mosta *102 B5 var.* Musta. C Malta
Mostaganem *70 D2 var.* Mestghanem. NW Algeria
Mostar *100 C4* Federacija Bosna I Hercegovina, S Bosnia and Herzegovina
Mosul see Al Mawşil
Mota del Cuervo *93 E3* Castilla-La Mancha, C Spain
Motagua, Río *52 B2 river* Guatemala/Honduras
Motril *92 D5* Andalucía, S Spain
Motru *108 B4* Gorj, SW Romania
Motueka *151 C5* Tasman, South Island, NZ
Motul *51 H3 var.* Motul de Felipe Carrillo Puerto. Yucatán, SE Mexico
Motul de Felipe Carrillo Puerto *see* Motul
Mouanda *see* Moanda
Mouhoun *see* Black Volta
Mouila *77 A6* Ngounié, C Gabon
Mould Bay *37 E2* Prince Patrick Island, Northwest Territories/Nunavut, N Canada
Moulins *90 C4* Allier, C France
Moulmein *136 B4 var.* Maulmain, Mawlamyine. Mon State, S Myanmar
Moundou *76 B4* Logone-Occidental, SW Chad
Moŭng Roessei *137 D5* Bătdâmbâng, W Cambodia
Moun Hou *see* Black Volta
Mountain Home *42 B1* Arkansas, C USA
Mount Ara *see* Büyükağrı Dağı
Mount Cook *151 B6* Canterbury, South Island, NZ
Mount Desert Island *41 H2 island* Maine, NE USA
Mount Fuji *see* Fuji-san
Mount Gambier *149 B7* South Australia
Mount Isa *148 B3* Queensland, C Australia
Mount Magnet *147 B5* Western Australia
Mount Pleasant *45 G4* Iowa, C USA
Mount Pleasant *40 C3* Michigan, N USA
Mount Vernon *40 B5* Illinois, N USA
Mount Vernon *46 B1* Washington, NW USA
Mourdi, Dépression du *76 C2 desert lowland* Chad/Sudan
Mouscron *87 A6 Dut.* Moeskroen. Hainaut, W Belgium
Mouse River *see* Souris River
Moussoro *76 B3* Kanem, W Chad
Moyen Atlas *70 C2 Eng.* Middle Atlas. *Mountain range* N Morocco
Mo'ynoq *122 C1 var.* Mŭynoq, *Rus.* Muynak. Qoraqalpoghiston Respublikasi, NW Uzbekistan
Moyobamba *60 B2* San Martín, NW Peru
Moyu *126 B3 var.* Karakax. Xinjiang Uygur Zizhiqu, NW China
Moyynkum, Peski *123 F1 Kaz.* Moyynqum. *Desert* S Kazakhstan
Mozambique *79 E3 prev.* People's Republic of Mozambique, Portuguese East Africa. *Country* S Africa

Mozambique 79

Official name Republic of Mozambique
Formation 1975
Capital Maputo
Population 18.9 million / 62 people per sq mile (24 people per sq km)
Total area 309,494 sq. miles (801,590 sq. km)
Languages Makua, Xitsonga, Sena, Lomwe, Portuguese
Religions Traditional beliefs 56%, Christian 30%, Muslim 14%
Ethnic mix Makua Lomwe 47%, Tsonga 23%, Malawi 12%, Shona 11%, Yao 4%, other 3%
Government Presidential system
Currency Metical = 100 centavos
Literacy rate 47%
Calorie consumption 1980 calories

Mozambique Basin *see* Natal Basin
Mozambique Channel *79 E3 Fr.* Canal de Mozambique, *Mal.* Lakandranon' i Mozambika. *Strait* W Indian Ocean
Mozambique Plateau *69 D7 var.* Mozambique Rise. *Undersea feature* SW Indian Ocean
Mozambique Rise *see* Mozambique Plateau
Mpama *77 B6 river* C Congo
Mpika *78 D2* Northern, NE Zambia
Mqinvartsveri *see* Kazbek
Mrągowo *98 D2 Ger.* Sensburg. Olsztyn, NE Poland
Mtwara *73 D8* Mtwara, SE Tanzania
Mualo *see* Messalo, Rio
Muang Chiang Rai *see* Chiang Rai
Muang Kalasin *see* Kalasin
Muang Không *137 D5* Champasak, S Laos
Muang Khôngxédôn *137 D5 var.* Khong Sedone. Salavan, S Laos
Muang Khon Kaen *see* Khon Kaen
Muang Lampang *see* Lampang
Muang Loei *see* Loei
Muang Lom Sak *see* Lom Sak
Muang Nakhon Sawan *see* Nakhon Sawan
Muang Namo *136 C3* Oudômxai, N Laos
Muang Nan *see* Nan
Muang Phalan *136 D4 var.* Muang Phalane. Savannakhét, S Laos
Muang Phalane *see* Muang Phalan
Muang Phayao *see* Phayao
Muang Phitsanulok *see* Phitsanulok
Muang Phrae *see* Phrae
Muang Roi Et *see* Roi Et
Muang Sakon Nakhon *see* Sakon Nakhon

Muang Samut Prakan *see* Samut Prakan
Muang Sing *136 C3* Louang Namtha, N Laos
Muang Ubon *see* Ubon Ratchathani
Muar *138 B3 var.* Bandar Maharani. Johor, Peninsular Malaysia
Mucojo *79 F2* Cabo Delgado, N Mozambique
Mudanjiang *129 E3 var.* Mu-tan-chiang. Heilongjiang, NE China
Mudon *137 B5* Mon State, S Myanmar
Muenchen *see* Munich
Muenster *see* Münster
Mufulira *78 D2* Copperbelt, C Zambia
Mughla *see* Muğla
Muğla *116 A4 var.* Mughla. Muğla, SW Turkey
Mūḩ, Sabkhat al *134 C3 lake* C Syria
Muir Éireann *see* Irish Sea
Muisne *60 A1* Esmeraldas, NW Ecuador
Mukacheve *108 B3 Hung.* Munkács, *Rus.* Mukachevo. Zakarpats'ka Oblast', W Ukraine
Mukalla *see* Al Mukallā
Mula *93 E4* Murcia, SE Spain
Mulaku Atoll *132 B4 var.* Meemu Atoll. *Atoll* C Maldives
Muleshoe *49 E2* Texas, SW USA
Mulhacén *93 E5 var.* Cerro de Mulhacén. *Mountain* S Spain
Mulhouse *90 E4 Ger.* Mülhausen. Haut-Rhin, NE France
Muller, Pegunungan *138 D4 Dut.* Müller-gerbergte. *Mountain range* Borneo, C Indonesia
Müllheim *95 A6* Baden-Württemberg, SW Germany
Mull, Isle of *88 B4 island* W Scotland, UK
Mulongo *77 D7* Shaba, SE Dem. Rep. Congo
Multān *134 C2* Punjab, E Pakistan
Mumbai *134 C5 prev.* Bombay. Mahārāshtra, W India
Munamägi *see* Suur Munamägi
Münchberg *95 C5* Bayern, E Germany
Muncie *40 C4* Indiana, N USA
Mungbere *77 E5* Orientale, NE Dem. Rep. Congo
Mu Nggava *see* Rennell
Munich *80 D4 var.* Muenchen, Bayern, SE Germany
Munkhafaḍ al Qaṭṭārah *see* Qaṭṭâra, Monkhafad el
Munster *89 A6 Ir.* Cúige Mumhan. *Cultural region* S Ireland
Münster *94 A4 var.* Muenster, Münster in Westfalen. Nordrhein-Westfalen, W Germany
Münster in Westfalen *see* Münster
Muong Xiang Ngeun *136 C4 var.* Xieng Ngeun. Louangphabang, N Laos
Muonio *84 D3* Lappi, N Finland
Muonioälv *84 D3 river* Finland/Sweden
Muqāṭ *119 C5* Al Mafraq, E Jordan
Muqdisho *73 D6 Eng.* Mogadishu, *It.* Mogadiscio. *Country capital* (Somalia) Banaadir, S Somalia
Mur *95 E7 SCr.* Mura. *River* C Europe
Muradiye *117 F3* Van, E Turkey
Murapara *see* Murupara
Murata *96 E2* S San Marino
Murchison River *147 A5 river* Western Australia
Murcia *93 E4 cultural region* SE Spain
Murcia *93 F4* Murcia, SE Spain
Mureş *108 A4 var.* Maros, Mureşul, *Ger.* Marosch, Mieresch. *River* Hungary/Romania *see also* Maros
Mureşul *see* Mureş
Murfreesboro *42 D1* Tennessee, S USA
Murgab *see* Murgap
Murgab *see* Morghāb, Daryā-ye/Murgap
Murgap *122 D3 var.* Murgab. Maryyskiy Velayat, S Turkmenistan
Murgap *122 D3 var.* Murgab, Murghab, *Pash.* Daryā-ye Morghāb, *Turkm.* Murgap Deryasy. *River* Afghanistan/Turkmenistan *see also* Morghāb, Daryā-ye
Murgap Deryasy *see* Morghāb, Daryā-ye/Murgap
Murghab *see* Morgháb, Daryá-ye/Murgap
Murghob *123 F3 Rus.* Murgab. SE Tajikistan
Murgon *149 E5* Queensland, E Australia
Müritz *94 C3 var.* Müritzee. *Lake* NE Germany
Müritzee *see* Müritz
Murmansk *110 C2* Murmanskaya Oblast', NW Russian Federation
Murmashi *110 C2* Murmanskaya Oblast', NW Russian Federation
Murom *111 B5* Vladimirskaya Oblast', W Russian Federation
Muroran *130 D3* Hokkaidō, NE Japan
Muros *92 B1* Galicia, NW Spain
Murray Fracture Zone *153 E2 tectonic feature* NE Pacific Ocean
Murray Range *see* Murray Ridge
Murray Ridge *112 C5 var.* Murray Range. *Undersea feature* N Arabian Sea
Murray River *149 B6 river* SE Australia
Murrumbidgee River *149 C6 river* New South Wales, SE Australia
Murska Sobota *95 E7 Ger.* Olsnitz. NE Slovenia
Murupara *150 E3 var.* Murapara. Bay of Plenty, North Island, NZ
Murviedro *see* Sagunto
Murwāra *135 E4* Madhya Pradesh, N India
Murwillumbah *149 E5* New South Wales, SE Australia
Murzuq, Idhān *71 F4 var.* Edeyin Murzuq. *Desert* SW Libya
Mürzzuschlag *95 E7* Steiermark, E Austria
Muş *117 F3 var.* Mush. Muş, E Turkey
Mûsa, Gebel *72 C2 mountain* NE Egypt
Musala *104 B3 mountain* W Bulgaria
Muscat *see* Masqaṭ
Muscatine *45 G3* Iowa, C USA
Musgrave Ranges *147 D5 mountain range* South Australia
Mush *see* Muş
Musina *78 D3 var.* Messina. Northern, NE South Africa
Muskegon *40 C3* Michigan, N USA
Muskogee *49 G1* Oklahoma, C USA
Musoma *73 C6* Mara, N Tanzania
Musta *see* Mosta
Musters, Lago *65 B6 lake* S Argentina
Muswellbrook *149 D6* New South Wales, SE Australia
Mut *116 C4* İçel, S Turkey
Mu-tan-chiang *see* Mudanjiang
Mutare *78 D3 var.* Mutari; *prev.* Umtali. Manicaland, E Zimbabwe
Mutari *see* Mutare
Mutsu-wan *130 D3 bay* N Japan
Muttonbird Islands *151 A8 island group* SW NZ
Mu Us Shamo *127 E3 var.* Ordos Desert. *Desert* N China
Muy Muy *52 D3* Matagalpa, C Nicaragua
Mŭynoq *see* Mo'ynoq
Mužlja *100 D3 Hung.* Felsőmuzslya; *prev.* Gornja Mužlja. Serbia, N Serbia and Montenegro (Yugo.)
Mwali *see* Mohéli
Mwanza *73 B6* Mwanza, NW Tanzania
Mweka *77 C6* Kasai Occidental, C Dem. Rep. Congo
Mwene-Ditu *77 D7* Kasai Oriental, S Dem. Rep. Congo
Mweru, Lake *77 D7 var.* Lac Moero. *Lake* Congo (Zaire)/Zambia
Mweru Wantipa, Lake *77 E7 lake* N Zambia
Myadzyel *107 C5 Pol.* Miadzioł Nowy, *Rus.* Myadel'. Minskaya Voblasts', N Belarus
Myanmar *136 A3 var.* Burma. *Country* SE Asia

Myanmar (Burma) 136

Official name Union of Myanmar
Formation 1948
Capital Rangoon (Yangon)
Population 49.5 million / 195 people per sq mile (75 people per sq km)
Total area 261,969 sq. miles (678,500 sq. km)
Languages Burmese, Shan, Karen, Rakhine, Chin, Yangbye, Kachin, Mon
Religions Buddhist 87%, Christian 6%, Muslim 4%, other 2%, Hindu 1%
Ethnic mix Burman (Bamah) 68%, other 13%, Shan 9%, Karen 6%, Rakhine 4%
Government Military-based regime
Currency Kyat = 100 pyas
Literacy rate 85%
Calorie consumption 2822 calories

Myanaung *136 B4* Irrawaddy, SW Myanmar
Myaungmya *136 A4* Irrawaddy, SW Myanmar
Myerkulavichy *107 D7 Rus.* Merkulovichi. Homyel'skaya Voblasts', SE Belarus
Myingyan *136 B3* Mandalay, C Myanmar
Myitkyina *136 B2* Kachin State, N Myanmar
Mykolayiv *109 E4 Rus.* Nikolayev. Mykolayivs'ka Oblast', S Ukraine
Mýkonos *105 D6 var.* Míkonos. *Island* Kykládes, Greece, Aegean Sea
Myrhorod *109 F2 Rus.* Mirgorod. Poltavs'ka Oblast', NE Ukraine
Mýrina *104 D4 var.* Mírina. Límnos, SE Greece
Myrtle Beach *43 F2* South Carolina, SE USA
Mýrtos *105 D8* Kríti, Greece, E Mediterranean Sea
Myślibórz *98 B3* Zachodniopomorskie, NW Poland
Mysore *132 C2 var.* Maisur. Karnātaka, W India
Mysore *see* Karnātaka
My Tho *137 E6 var.* Mi Tho. Tiên Giang, S Vietnam
Mytilene *see* Mytilíni
Mytilíni *105 D5 var.* Mitilíni; *anc.* Mytilene. Lésvos, E Greece
Mzuzu *79 E2* Northern, N Malawi

N

Naberezhnyye Chelny *111 D5 prev.* Brezhnev. Respublika Tatarstan, W Russian Federation
Nablus *119 A6 var.* Nābulus, *Heb.* Shekhem; *anc.* Neapolis, *Bibl.* Shechem. N West Bank
Nābulus *see* Nablus
Nacala *79 F2* Nampula, NE Mozambique
Nada *see* Danzhou
Nadi *145 E4 prev.* Nandi. Viti Levu, W Fiji
Nadur *102 A5* Gozo, N Malta
Nadvirna *108 C3 Pol.* Nadwórna, *Rus.* Nadvornaya. Ivano-Frankivs'ka Oblast', W Ukraine
Nadvoitsy *110 B3* Respublika Kareliya, NW Russian Federation
Nadym *114 C3* Yamalo-Nenetskiy Avtonomnyy Okrug, N Russian Federation
Náfpaktos *105 B5 var.* Návpaktos. Dytikí Ellás, C Greece
Náfplio *105 B6 prev.* Návplion. Pelopónnisos, S Greece
Naga *139 E2 off.* Naga City; *prev.* Nueva Caceres. Luzon, N Philippines
Nagano *131 C5* Nagano, Honshū, S Japan
Nagaoka *131 D5* Niigata, Honshū, C Japan
Nagara Pathom *see* Nakhon Pathom
Nagara Sridharmaraj *see* Nakhon Si Thammarat
Nagara Svarga *see* Nakhon Sawan
Nagasaki *131 A7* Nagasaki, Kyūshū, SW Japan
Nagato *131 A7* Yamaguchi, Honshū, SW Japan
Nāgercoil *132 C3* Tamil Nādu, SE India
Nagorno-Karabakh *117 G3 var.* Nagorno-Karabakhskaya Avtonomnaya Oblast , *Arm.* Lerrnayin Gharabakh, *Az.* Dağliq Qarabağ, *Rus.* Nagornyy Karabakh. *Former autonomous region* SW Azerbaijan
Nagorno-Karabakhskaya Avtonomnaya Oblast *see* Nagorno-Karabakh
Nagornyy Karabakh *see* Nagorno-Karabakh
Nagoya *131 C6* Aichi, Honshū, SW Japan
Nāgpur *134 D4* Mahārāshtra, C India
Nagqu *126 C5 Chin.* Na-ch'ii; *prev.* Hei-ho. Xizang Zizhiqu, W China
Nagykálló *99 E6* Szabolcs-Szatmár-Bereg, E Hungary
Nagykanizsa *99 C7 Ger.* Grosskanizsa. Zala, SW Hungary
Nagykőrös *99 D7* Pest, C Hungary
Nagyszentmiklós *see* Sânnicolau Mare
Naha *130 A3* Okinawa, Okinawa, SW Japan
Nahariya *see* Nahariyya
Nahariyya *119 A5 var.* Nahariya. Northern, N Israel
Nahr al 'Aṣī *see* Orantes
Nahr al Litant *see* Lītani, Nahr el
Nahr an Nīl *see* Nile
Nahr el Aassi *see* Orantes
Nahuel Huapi, Lago *65 B5 lake* W Argentina
Nā'īn *120 D3* Eşfahān, C Iran
Nain *39 F2* Newfoundland and Labrador, NE Canada
Nairobi *69 E5 country capital* (Kenya) Nairobi Area, S Kenya
Nairobi *73 C6 international airport* Nairobi Area, S Kenya
Najaf *see* An Najaf
Najima *see* Fukuoka
Najin *129 E3* NE North Korea
Najrān *121 B6 var.* Abā as Su'ūd. Najrān, S Saudi Arabia
Nakambé *see* White Volta
Nakamura *131 B7* Kōchi, Shikoku, SW Japan
Nakatsugawa *131 C6 var.* Nakatugawa. Gifu, Honshū, SW Japan
Nakatugawa *see* Nakatsugawa
Nakhodka *115 G5* Primorskiy Kray, SE Russian Federation
Nakhon Pathom *137 C5 var.* Nagara Pathom, Nakorn Pathom. Nakhon Pathom, W Thailand
Nakhon Ratchasima *137 C5 var.* Khorat, Korat. Nakhon Ratchasima, E Thailand
Nakhon Sawan *137 C5 var.* Muang Nakhon Sawan, Nagara Svarga. Nakhon Sawan, W Thailand
Nakhon Si Thammarat *137 C7 var.* Nagara Sridharmaraj, Nakhon Sithamnaraj. Nakhon Si Thammarat, SW Thailand
Nakhon Sithamnaraj *see* Nakhon Si Thammarat
Nakorn Pathom *see* Nakhon Pathom
Nakuru *73 C6* Rift Valley, SW Kenya
Nal'chik *111 B8* Kabardino-Balkarskaya Respublika, SW Russian Federation

Nālūt *71 F2* NW Libya
Namakan Lake *40 A1 lake* Canada/USA
Namangan *123 F2* Namangan Wiloyati, E Uzbekistan
Nambala *78 D2* Central, C Zambia
Nam Co *126 C5 lake* W China
Nam Đinh *136 D3* Nam Ha, N Vietnam
Namib Desert *78 B3 desert* W Namibia
Namibe *78 A2 Port.* Moçâmedes, Mossâmedes. Namibe, SW Angola
Namibia *78 B3 var.* South West Africa, *Afr.* Suidwes-Afrika, *Ger.* Deutsch-Südwestafrika; *prev.* German Southwest Africa, South-West Africa. *Country* S Africa

Namibia 78

Official name Republic of Namibia
Formation 1990
Capital Windhoek
Population 2 million / 6 people per sq mile (2 people per sq km)
Total area 318,694 sq. miles (825,418 sq. km)
Languages Ovambo, Kavango, English, Bergdama, German, Afrikaans
Religions Christian 90%, Traditional beliefs 10%
Ethnic mix Ovambo 50%, Other tribes 16%, Kavango 9%, other 9%, Damara 8%, Herero 8%
Government Presidential system
Currency Namibian dollar = 100 cents
Literacy rate 83%
Calorie consumption 2745 calories

Namo *see* Namu Atoll
Nam Ou *136 C3 river* N Laos
Nampa *46 D3* Idaho, NW USA
Nampula *79 E2* Nampula, NE Mozambique
Namsos *84 B4* Nord-Trøndelag, C Norway
Nam Tha *136 C4 river* N Laos
Namu Atoll *144 D2 var.* Namo. *Atoll* Ralik Chain, C Marshall Islands
Namur *87 C6 Dut.* Namen. Namur, SE Belgium
Namyit Island *128 C8 island* S Spratly Islands
Nan *136 C4 var.* Muang Nan. Nan, NW Thailand
Nanaimo *36 D5* Vancouver Island, British Columbia, SW Canada
Nanchang *128 C5 var.* Nan-ch'ang, Nanch'ang-hsien. Jiangxi, S China
Nanch'ang-hsien *see* Nanchang
Nan-ching *see* Nanjing
Nancy *90 D3* Meurthe-et-Moselle, NE France
Nandaime *52 D3* Granada, SW Nicaragua
Nānded *134 D5* Mahārāshtra, C India
Nandyāl *132 C1* Andhra Pradesh, E India
Nanjing *128 D5 var.* Nan-ching, Nanking; *prev.* Chianning, Chian-ning, Kiang-ning. Jiangsu, E China
Nanking *see* Nanjing
Nanning *128 B6 var.* Nan-ning; *prev.* Yung-ning. Guangxi Zhuangzu Zizhiqu, S China
Nan-ning *see* Nanning
Nanortalik *82 C5* S Greenland
Nanpan Jiang *136 D2 river* S China
Nanping *128 D6 var.* Nan-p'ing; *prev.* Yenping. Fujian, SE China
Nansei-Shotō *130 A2 var.* Ryukyu Islands. *Island group* SW Japan
Nansei Syotō Trench *see* Ryukyu Trench
Nansen Basin *155 C4 undersea feature* Arctic Ocean
Nansen Cordillera *155 B3 var.* Arctic-Mid Oceanic Ridge, Nansen Ridge. *Undersea feature* Arctic Ocean
Nansen Ridge *see* Nansen Cordillera
Nanterre *90 D1* Hauts-de-Seine, N France
Nantes *90 B4 Bret.* Naoned; *anc.* Condivincum, Namnetes. Loire-Atlantique, NW France
Nantucket Island *41 G3 island* Massachusetts, NE USA
Nanumaga *145 E3 var.* Nanumanga. *Atoll* NW Tuvalu
Nanumanga *see* Nanumaga
Nanumea Atoll *145 E3 atoll* NW Tuvalu
Nanyang *128 C5 var.* Nan-yang. Henan, C China
Napa *47 B6* California, W USA
Napier *150 E4* Hawke's Bay, North Island, NZ
Naples *80 D5 anc.* Neapolis. Campania, S Italy
Naples *43 E5* Florida, SE USA
Napo *56 A3 province* NE Ecuador
Napo, Río *60 C1 river* Ecuador/Peru
Naracoorte *149 B7* South Australia
Naradhivas *see* Narathiwat
Narathiwat *137 C7 var.* Naradhivas. Narathiwat, SW Thailand
Narbada *see* Narmada
Narbonne *91 C6 anc.* Narbo Martius. Aude, S France
Narborough Island *see* Fernandina, Isla
Nares Abyssal Plain *see* Nares Plain
Nares Plain *35 E6 var.* Nares Abyssal Plain. *Undersea feature* NW Atlantic Ocean
Nares Strait *82 D1 Dan.* Nares Stræde. *Strait* Canada/Greenland
Narew *98 E3 river* E Poland
Narmada *124 B3 var.* Narbada. *River* C India
Narowlya *107 C8 Rus.* Narovlya. Homyel'skaya Voblasts', SE Belarus
Närpes *85 D5 Fin.* Närpiö. Länsi-Suomi, W Finland
Narrabri *149 D6* New South Wales, SE Australia
Narrogin *147 B6* Western Australia
Narva *106 E2 prev.* Narova. *River* Estonia/Russian Federation
Narva *106 E2* Ida-Virumaa, NE Estonia
Narva Bay *106 E2 Est.* Narva Laht, *Ger.* Narwa-Bucht, *Rus.* Narvskiy Zaliv. *Bay* Estonia/Russian Federation
Narva Reservoir *106 E2 Est.* Narva Veehoidla, *Rus.* Narvskoye Vodokhranilishche. *Reservoir* Estonia/Russian Federation
Narvik *84 C3* Nordland, C Norway
Nar'yan-Mar *110 D3 prev.* Beloshchel'ye, Dzerzhinskiy. Nenetskiy Avtonomnyy Okrug, NW Russian Federation
Naryn *123 G2* Narynskaya Oblast', C Kyrgyzstan
Năsăud *108 B3 Ger.* Nussdorf, *Hung.* Naszód. Bistriţa-Năsăud, N Romania
Nase *see* Naze
Nāshik *134 C5 prev.* Nāsik. Mahārāshtra, W India
Nashua *41 G3* New Hampshire, NE USA
Nashville *42 C1 state capital* Tennessee, S USA
Näsijärvi *85 D5 lake* SW Finland
Nāsiri *see* Ahvāz
Nasiriya *see* An Nāşirīyah
Nassau *54 C1 country capital* (Bahamas) New Providence, N Bahamas
Nasser, Lake *72 B3 var.* Buhayrat Nasir, Buḩayrat Nāşir, Buḩeiret Nâşir. *Lake* Egypt/Sudan
Nata *78 C3* Central, NE Botswana
Natal *63 G2* Rio Grande do Norte, E Brazil
Natal Basin *141 A6 var.* Mozambique Basin. *Undersea feature* W Indian Ocean
Natanya *see* Netanya
Natchez *42 B3* Mississippi, S USA
Natchitoches *42 A2* Louisiana, S USA
Nathanya *see* Netanya
Natitingou *75 F4* NW Benin
Natsrat *see* Nazerat
Natuna Islands *124 D4 island group* W Indonesia
Naturaliste Plateau *141 E6 undersea feature* E Indian Ocean
Naugard *see* Nowogard
Naujamiestis *106 C4* Panevėžys, C Lithuania
Nauru *144 D2 prev.* Pleasant Island. *Country* W Pacific Ocean

Nauru 144

Official name Republic of Nauru
Formation 1968
Capital None
Population 12,570 / 1552 people per sq mile (599 people per sq km)
Total area 8.1 sq. miles (21 sq. km)
Languages Nauruan, Kiribati, Chinese, Tuvaluan, English
Religions Nauruan Congregational Church 60%, Roman Catholic 35%, other 5%
Ethnic mix Nauruan 62%, Other Pacific islanders 25%, Chinese and Vietnamese 8%, European 5%
Government Parliamentary system
Currency Australian dollar = 100 cents
Literacy rate 95%
Calorie consumption Not available

Nauta *60 C2* Loreto, N Peru
Navahrudak *107 C6 Pol.* Nowogródek, *Rus.* Novogrudok. Hrodzyenskaya Voblasts', W Belarus
Navapolatsk *107 D5 Rus.* Novopolotsk. Vitsyebskaya Voblasts', N Belarus
Navarra *93 E2 cultural region* N Spain
Navassa Island *54 C3 US unincorporated territory* C West Indies
Navoiy *123 E2 var.* Nawoiy, *Rus.* Navoi. Nawoiy Wiloyati, C Uzbekistan
Navojoa *50 C2* Sonora, NW Mexico
Navolat *see* Navolato
Navolato *66 C3 var.* Navolat. Sinaloa, C Mexico
Návpaktos *see* Náfpaktos
Nawabashah *see* Nawābshāh
Nawābshāh *134 B3 var.* Nawabashah. Sind, S Pakistan
Nawoiy *see* Navoiy
Naxçıvan *117 G3 Rus.* Nakhichevan'. SW Azerbaijan
Náxos *105 D6 var.* Naxos. Náxos, Kykládes, Greece, Aegean Sea
Náxos *105 D6 island* Kykládes, Greece, Aegean Sea
Nayoro *130 D2* Hokkaidō, NE Japan
Nazca *60 D4* Ica, S Peru
Nazca Ridge *57 A5 undersea feature* E Pacific Ocean
Naze *130 B3 var.* Nase. Kagoshima, Amami-ōshima, SW Japan
Nazerat *119 A5 var.* Natsrat, *Ar.* En Nazira, *Eng.* Nazareth. Northern, N Israel
Nazilli *116 A4* Aydın, SW Turkey
Nazrēt *73 C5 var.* Adama, Hadama. C Ethiopia
N'Dalatando *78 B1 Port.* Salazar, Vila Salazar. Cuanza Norte, NW Angola
Ndélé *76 C4* Bamingui-Bangoran, N Central African Republic
Ndendé *77 B6* Ngounié, S Gabon
Ndindi *77 A6* Nyanga, S Gabon
Ndjamena *76 B3 var.* N'Djamena; *prev.* Fort-Lamy. *Country capital* (Chad) Chari-Baguirmi, W Chad
Ndjolé *77 A5* Moyen-Ogooué, W Gabon
Ndola *78 D2* Copperbelt, C Zambia
Neagh, Lough *89 B5 lake* E Northern Ireland, UK
Néa Moudanía *104 C4 var.* Néa Moudhaniá. Kentrikí Makedonía, N Greece
Néa Moudhaniá *see* Néa Moudanía
Neápoli *104 B4 prev.* Neápolis. Dytikí Makedonía, N Greece
Neápoli *105 D8* Kríti, Greece, E Mediterranean Sea
Neápoli *105 C7* Pelopónnisos, S Greece
Neapolis *see* Nablus
Near Islands *36 A2 island group* Aleutian Islands, Alaska, USA
Néa Zíchni *104 C3 var.* Néa Zíkhni; *prev.* Néa Zíkhna. Kentrikí Makedonía, NE Greece
Néa Zíkhna *see* Néa Zíchni
Néa Zíkhni *see* Néa Zíchni
Nebaj *52 B2* Quiché, W Guatemala
Neblina, Pico da *62 C1 mountain* NW Brazil
Nebraska *44 D4 off.* State of Nebraska; also known as Blackwater State, Cornhusker State, Tree Planters State. *State* C USA
Nebraska City *45 F4* Nebraska, C USA
Neches River *49 H3 river* Texas, SW USA
Neckar *95 B6 river* SW Germany
Necochea *65 D5* Buenos Aires, E Argentina
Neder Rijn *86 D4 Eng.* Lower Rhine. *River* C Netherlands
Nederweert *87 D5* Limburg, SE Netherlands
Neede *86 E3* Gelderland, E Netherlands
Neerpelt *87 D5* Limburg, NE Belgium
Neftekamsk *111 D5* Respublika Bashkortostan, W Russian Federation
Negēlē *73 D5 var.* Negelli, *It.* Neghelli. C Ethiopia
Negelli *see* Negēlē
Neghelli *see* Negēlē
Negomane *79 E2 var.* Negomano. Cabo Delgado, N Mozambique
Negomano *see* Negomane
Negombo *132 C3* Western Province, SW Sri Lanka
Negotin *100 E4* Serbia, E Serbia and Montenegro (Yugo.)
Negra, Punta *60 A3 headland* NW Peru
Negreşti-Oaş *108 B3 Hung.* Avasfelsőfalu; *prev.* Negreşti. Satu Mare, NE Romania
Negro, Río *65 C5 river* E Argentina
Negro, Rio *62 D1 river* N South America
Negro, Río *64 D4 river* Brazil/Uruguay
Negros *139 E2 island* C Philippines
Nehbandān *120 E3* Khorāsān, E Iran
Neijiang *128 B5* Sichuan, C China
Nei Monggol Zizhiqu *see* Inner Mongolia
Nei Mongol *see* Inner Mongolia
Neiva *58 B3* Huila, S Colombia
Nellore *132 D2* Andhra Pradesh, E India
Nelson *37 G4 river* Manitoba, C Canada
Nelson *151 C5* Nelson, South Island, NZ
Néma *74 D3* Hodh ech Chargui, SE Mauritania
Neman *106 A4 Bel.* Nyoman, *Ger.* Memel, *Lith.* Nemunas, *Pol.* Niemen, *Rus.* Neman. *River* NE Europe
Neman *106 B4 Ger.* Ragnit. Kaliningradskaya Oblast', W Russian Federation
Neméa *105 B6* Pelopónnisos, S Greece
Nemours *90 C3* Seine-et-Marne, N France
Nemuro *130 E2* Hokkaidō, NE Japan
Neochóri *105 B5* Dytikí Ellás, C Greece
Nepal *135 E3 Country* S Asia

Nepal 135

Official name Kingdom of Nepal
Formation 1769
Capital Kathmandu
Population 25.2 million / 477 people per sq mile (184 people per sq km)
Total area 54,363 sq. miles (140,800 sq. km)
Languages Nepali, Maithili, Bhojpuri
Religions Hindu 90%, Buddhist 5%, Muslim 3%, Other (including Christian) 2%
Ethnic mix Nepalese 52%, Maithili 11%, Tibeto-Burmese 10%, Bhojpuri 8%, other 19%
Government Monarchy
Currency Nepalese rupee = 100 paise
Literacy rate 44%
Calorie consumption 2459 calories

Nereta *106 C4* Aizkraukle, S Latvia
Neretva *100 C4 river* Bosnia and Herzegovina/Croatia
Neringa *106 A3 var.* Nida, *Ger.* Nidden. Neringa, SW Lithuania
Neris *107 C5 Bel.* Viliya, *Pol.* Wilia; *prev. Pol.* Wilja. *River* Belarus/Lithuania
Nerva *92 C4* Andalucía, S Spain
Neryungri *115 F4* Respublika Sakha (Yakutiya), NE Russian Federation
Neskaupstadhur *83 E5* Austurland, E Iceland
Ness, Loch *88 C3 lake* N Scotland, UK
Néstos *104 C3 Bul.* Mesta, *Turk.* Kara Su. *River* Bulgaria/Greece *see also* Mesta
Netanya *119 A6 var.* Natanya, Nathanya. Central, C Israel
Netherlands *86 C3 var.* Holland, *Dut.* Koninkrijk der Nederlanden, Nederland. *Country* NW Europe

Netherlands 86

Official name Kingdom of the Netherlands
Formation 1648
Capital Amsterdam; The Hague (administrative)
Population 16.1 million / 1229 people per sq mile (475 people per sq km)
Total area 16,033 sq. miles (41,526 sq. km)
Languages Dutch, Frisian
Religions Roman Catholic 36%, other 34%, Protestant 27%, Muslim 3%
Ethnic mix Dutch 82%, Turkish 2%, Surinamese 2%, , Moroccan 2%, other 12%,
Government Parliamentary system
Currency Euro = 100 cents
Literacy rate 97%
Calorie consumption 3282 calories

Netherlands Antilles *55 E5 prev.* Dutch West Indies. *Dutch autonomous region* S Caribbean Sea
Netherlands New Guinea *see* Papua
Nettilling Lake *37 G3 lake* Baffin Island, Nunavut, N Canada
Neubrandenburg *94 D3* Mecklenburg-Vorpommern, NE Germany
Neuchâtel *95 A7 Ger.* Neuenburg. Neuchâtel, W Switzerland
Neuchâtel, Lac de *A7 Ger.* Neuenburger See. *Lake* W Switzerland
Neufchâteau *87 D8* Luxembourg, SE Belgium
Neumünster *94 B2* Schleswig-Holstein, N Germany
Neunkirchen *95 A5* Saarland, SW Germany
Neuquén *65 B5* Neuquén, SE Argentina
Neuruppin *94 C3* Brandenburg, NE Germany
Neusalz an der Oder *see* Nowa Sól
Neusiedler See *95 E6 Hung.* Fertő. *Lake* Austria/Hungary
Neustadt an der Weinstrasse *95 B5 prev.* Neustadt an der Haardt, *hist.* Niewenstat, *anc.* Nova Civitas. Rheinland-Pfalz, SW Germany
Neustrelitz *94 D3* Mecklenburg-Vorpommern, NE Germany
Neu-Ulm *95 B6* Bayern, S Germany
Neuwied *95 A5* Rheinland-Pfalz, W Germany
Neuzen *see* Terneuzen
Nevada *47 C5 off.* State of Nevada; also known as Battle Born State, Sagebrush State, Silver State. *State* W USA
Nevada, Sierra *92 D5 mountain range* S Spain
Nevers *90 C4 anc.* Noviodunum. Nièvre, C France
Neves *76 E2* São Tomé, S Sao Tome and Principe
Nevinnomyssk *111 B7* Stavropol'skiy Kray, SW Russian Federation
Nevşehir *116 C3 var.* Nevshehr. Nevşehir, C Turkey
Nevshehr *see* Nevşehir
Newala *73 C8* Mtwara, SE Tanzania
New Albany *40 C5* Indiana, N USA
New Amsterdam *59 G3* E Guyana
Newark *41 F4* New Jersey, NE USA
New Bedford *41 G3* Massachusetts, NE USA
Newberg *46 B3* Oregon, NW USA
New Bern *43 F1* North Carolina, SE USA
New Braunfels *49 G4* Texas, SW USA
Newbridge *89 B6 Ir.* An Droichead Nua. C Ireland
New Britain *144 B3 island* E PNG
New Brunswick *39 E4 Fr.* Nouveau-Brunswick. *Province* SE Canada
New Caledonia *144 D4 var.* Kanaky, *Fr.* Nouvelle-Calédonie. *French overseas territory* SW Pacific Ocean
New Caledonia *144 C5 island* SW Pacific Ocean
New Caledonia Basin *142 C4 undersea feature* W Pacific Ocean
Newcastle *see* Newcastle upon Tyne
Newcastle *149 D6* New South Wales, SE Australia
Newcastle upon Tyne *88 D4 var.* Newcastle; *hist.* Monkchester, *Lat.* Pons Aelii. NE England, UK
New Delhi *134 D3 country capital* (India) Delhi, N India
Newfoundland *39 G3 Fr.* Terre-Neuve. *Island* Newfoundland, SE Canada
Newfoundland *39 F2 Fr.* Terre Neuve. *Province* SE Canada
Newfoundland Basin *66 B3 undersea feature* NW Atlantic Ocean
New Georgia Islands *144 C3 island group* NW Solomon Islands
New Glasgow *39 F4* Nova Scotia, SE Canada
New Goa *see* Pānji
New Guinea *144 A3 Dut.* Nieuw Guinea, *Ind.* Irian. *Island* Indonesia/PNG
New Hampshire *41 F2 off.* State of New Hampshire; also known as The Granite State. *State* NE USA
New Haven *41 G3* Connecticut, NE USA
New Iberia *42 B3* Louisiana, S USA
New Ireland *144 C3 island* NE PNG
New Jersey *41 F4 off.* State of New Jersey; also known as The Garden State. *State* NE USA
Newman *146 B4* Western Australia
Newmarket *89 E6* E England, UK
New Mexico *48 C2 off.* State of New Mexico; also known as Land of Enchantment, Sunshine State. *State* SW USA
New Orleans *42 B3* Louisiana, S USA
New Plymouth *150 C4* Taranaki, North Island, NZ
Newport *40 C4* Kentucky, S USA
Newport *89 D7* S England, UK
Newport *89 C7* SE Wales, UK
Newport *41 G2* Vermont, NE USA
Newport News *41 F5* Virginia, NE USA
New Providence *54 C1 island* N Bahamas
Newquay *89 C7* SW England, UK
Newry *89 B5 Ir.* An tIúr. SE Northern Ireland, UK
New Sarum *see* Salisbury
New Siberian Islands *see* Novosibirskiye Ostrova
New South Wales *149 C6 state* SE Australia
Newton *45 G3* Iowa, C USA
Newtownabbey *89 B5 Ir.* Baile na Mainistreach. E Northern Ireland, UK
New Ulm *45 F2* Minnesota, N USA
New York *41 F4* New York, NE USA
New York *41 F3 state* NE USA
New Zealand *150 A4 abbrev.* NZ. *Country* SW Pacific Ocean

New Zealand 150

Official name New Zealand
Formation 1947
Capital Wellington
Population 3.9 million / 38 people per sq mile (15 people per sq km)
Total area 103,737 sq. miles (268,680 sq. km)
Languages English, Maori
Religions Anglican 24%, other 22%, Presbyterian 18%, Nonreligious 16%, Roman Catholic 15%, Methodist 5%
Ethnic mix European 77%, Maori 12%, Other immigrant 6%, Pacific islanders 5%
Government Parliamentary system
Currency New Zealand dollar = 100 cents
Literacy rate 99%
Calorie consumption 3235 calories

Neyveli *132 C2* Tamil Nādu, SE India
Ngangzê Co *126 B5 lake* W China
Ngaoundéré *76 B4 var.* N'Gaoundéré. Adamaoua, N Cameroon
N'Giva *78 B3 var.* Ondjiva, *Port.* Vila Pereira de Eça. Cunene, S Angola
Ngo *77 B6* Plateaux, SE Congo
Ngoko *77 B5 river* Cameroon/Congo
Ngourti *75 H3* Diffa, E Niger
Nguigmi *75 H3 var.* N'Guigmi. Diffa, SE Niger
Nguru *75 G3* Yobe, NE Nigeria
Nha Trang *137 E6* Khanh Hoa, S Vietnam
Niagara Falls *40 D3 waterfall* Canada/USA
Niagara Falls *41 E3* New York, NE USA
Niagara Falls *38 D5* Ontario, S Canada
Niamey *75 F3 country capital* (Niger) Niamey, SW Niger
Niangay, Lac *75 E3 lake* E Mali
Nia-Nia *77 E5* Orientale, NE Dem. Rep. Congo
Nias, Pulau *138 A3 island* W Indonesia
Nicaragua *52 D3 Country* Central America

Nicaragua 52

Official name Republic of Nicaragua
Formation 1838
Capital Managua
Population 5.5 million / 120 people per sq mile (46 people per sq km)
Total area 49,998 sq. miles (129,494 sq. km)
Languages Spanish, English Creole, Miskito
Religions Roman Catholic 80%, Protestant Evangelical 17%, other 3%
Ethnic mix Mestizo 69%, White 14%, Black 8%, Amerindian 5%, Zambo 4%
Government Presidential system
Currency Córdoba oro = 100 centavos
Literacy rate 77%
Calorie consumption 2256 calories

Nicaragua, Lago de *52 D4 var.* Cocibolca, Gran Lago, *Eng.* Lake Nicaragua. *Lake* S Nicaragua
Nicaragua, Lake *see* Nicaragua, Lago de
Nicaria *see* Ikaría
Nice *91 D6 It.* Nizza; *anc.* Nicaea. Alpes-Maritimes, SE France
Nicephorium *see* Ar Raqqah
Nicholas II Land *see* Severnaya Zemlya
Nicholls Town *54 C1* Andros Island, NW Bahamas
Nicobar Islands *124 B4 island group* India, E Indian Ocean
Nicosia *102 C5 Gk.* Lefkosía, *Turk.* Lefkoşa. *Country capital* (Cyprus) C Cyprus
Nicoya *52 D4* Guanacaste, W Costa Rica
Nicoya, Golfo de *52 D5 gulf* W Costa Rica
Nicoya, Península de *52 D4 peninsula* NW Costa Rica
Nida *see* Neringa
Nidden *see* Neringa
Nidzica *98 D3 Ger.* Niedenburg. Warmińsko-Mazurskie, NE Poland
Niedere Tauern *99 A6 mountain range* C Austria
Nieuw Amsterdam *59 G3* Commewijne, NE Suriname
Nieuw-Bergen *86 D4* Limburg, SE Netherlands
Nieuwegein *86 C4* Utrecht, C Netherlands
Nieuw Nickerie *59 G3* Nickerie, NW Suriname
Niğde *116 C4* Niğde, C Turkey
Niger *75 F3 Country* W Africa

Niger 75

Official name Republic of Niger
Formation 1960
Capital Niamey
Population 12 million / 25 people per sq mile (9 people per sq km)
Total area 489,188 sq. miles (1,267,000 sq. km)
Languages Hausa, Djerma, Fulani, Tuareg, Teda, French
Religions Muslim 85%, Traditional beliefs 14%, Other (including Christian) 1%
Ethnic mix Hausa 54%, Djerma and Songhai 21%, Fulani 10%, Tuareg 9%, other 6%
Government Presidential system
Currency CFA franc = 100 centimes
Literacy rate 17%
Calorie consumption 2118 calories

Niger *75 F4 river* W Africa

Nigeria *75 F4 Country* W Africa

Nigeria 75

Official name Federal Republic of Nigeria
Formation 1960
Capital Abuja
Population 124 million / 353 people per sq mile (136 people per sq km)
Total area 356,667 sq. miles (923,768 sq. km)
Languages Hausa, English, Yoruba, Ibo
Religions Muslim 50%, Christian 40%, Traditional beliefs 10%
Ethnic mix Other 29%, Hausa 21%, Yoruba 21%, Ibo 18%, Fulani 11%
Government Presidential system
Currency Naira = 100 kobo
Literacy rate 67%
Calorie consumption 2747 calories

Niger, Mouths of the *75 F5 delta* S Nigeria
Nihon *see* Japan
Niigata *131 D5* Niigata, Honshū, C Japan
Niihama *131 B7* Ehime, Shikoku, SW Japan
Ni'ihau *47 A7 var.* Niihau. *Island* Hawai'i, USA, C Pacific Ocean
Nii-jima *131 D6 island* E Japan
Nijkerk *86 D3* Gelderland, C Netherlands
Nijlen *87 C5* Antwerpen, N Belgium
Nijmegen *86 D4 Ger.* Nimwegen; *anc.* Noviomagus. Gelderland, SE Netherlands
Nikaria *see* Ikaría
Nikel' *110 C2* Murmanskaya Oblast', NW Russian Federation
Nikiniki *139 E5* Timor, S Indonesia
Nikopol' *109 F3* Pleven, N Bulgaria
Nikšić *101 C5* Montenegro, SW Serbia and Montenegro (Yugo.)
Nikumaroro *145 E3 prev.* Gardner Island, Kemins Island. *Atoll* Phoenix Islands, C Kiribati
Nikunau *145 E3 var.* Nukunau; *prev.* Byron Island. *Atoll* Tungaru, W Kiribati
Nile *68 D3 Ar.* Nahr an Nīl. *River* N Africa
Nile *72 B2 former province* NW Uganda
Nile Delta *72 B1 delta* N Egypt
Nîmes *91 C6 anc.* Nemausus, Nismes. Gard, S France
Nine Degree Channel *132 B3 channel* India/Maldives
Ninetyeast Ridge *141 D5 undersea feature* E Indian Ocean
Ninety Mile Beach *150 C1 beach* North Island, NZ
Ningbo *128 D5 var.* Ning-po, Yin-hsien; *prev.* Ninghsien. Zhejiang, SE China
Ninghsien *see* Ningbo
Ning-po *see* Ningbo
Ningxia *128 B4 off.* Ningxia Huizu Zizhiqu, *var.* Ning-hsia, Ningsia, *Eng.* Ningsia Hui, Ningsia Hui Autonomous Region. Admin. region *autonomous region* N China
Ningxia Huizu Zizhiqu *see* Ningxia
Nio *see* Íos
Niobrara River *45 E3 river* Nebraska/Wyoming, C USA
Nioro *74 D3 var.* Nioro du Sahel. Kayes, W Mali
Nioro du Sahel *see* Nioro
Niort *90 B4* Deux-Sèvres, W France
Nipigon *38 B4* Ontario, S Canada
Nipigon, Lake *38 B3 lake* Ontario, S Canada
Nippon *see* Japan
Niš *101 E5 Eng.* Nish, *Ger.* Nisch; *anc.* Naissus. Serbia, SE Serbia and Montenegro (Yugo.)
Nişab *120 B4* Al Ḩudūd ash Shamālīyah, N Saudi Arabia
Nisibin *see* Nusaybin
Nisiros *see* Nísyros
Nisko *98 E4* Podkarpackie, SE Poland
Nísyros *105 E7 var.* Nisiros. *Island* Dodekánisos, Greece, Aegean Sea
Nitra *99 C6 Ger.* Neutra, *Hung.* Nyitra. *River* W Slovakia
Nitra *99 C6 Ger.* Neutra, *Hung.* Nyitra. Nitriansky Kraj, SW Slovakia
Niuatobutabu *see* Niuatoputapu
Niuatoputapu *145 E4 var.* Niuatobutabu; *prev.* Keppel Island. *Island* N Tonga
Niue *145 F4 self-governing territory in free association with NZ* S Pacific Ocean
Niulakita *145 E3 var.* Nurakita. *Atoll* S Tuvalu
Niutao *145 E3 atoll* NW Tuvalu
Nivernais *90 C4 cultural region* C France
Nizāmābād *134 D5* Andhra Pradesh, C India
Nizhnekamsk *111 C5* Respublika Tatarstan, W Russian Federation
Nizhnevartovsk *114 D3* Khanty-Mansiyskiy Avtonomnyy Okrug, C Russian Federation
Nizhniy Novgorod *111 C5 prev.* Gor'kiy. Nizhegorodskaya Oblast', W Russian Federation
Nizhniy Odes *110 D4* Respublika Komi, NW Russian Federation
Nizhnyaya Tunguska *115 E3 Eng.* Lower Tunguska. *River* N Russian Federation
Nizhyn *109 E1 Rus.* Nezhin. Chernihivs'ka Oblast', NE Ukraine
Njazidja *see* Grande Comore
Njombe *73 C8* Iringa, S Tanzania
Nkayi *77 B6 prev.* Jacob. La Bouenza, S Congo
Nkongsamba *76 A4 var.* N'Kongsamba. Littoral, W Cameroon
Nmai Hka *136 B2 var.* Me Hka. *River* N Myanmar
Nobeoka *131 B7* Miyazaki, Kyūshū, SW Japan
Noboribetsu *130 D3 var.* Noboribetu. Hokkaidō, NE Japan
Noboribetu *see* Noboribetsu
Nogales *48 B3* Arizona, SW USA
Nogales *50 B1* Sonora, NW Mexico
Nogal Valley *see* Dooxo Nugaaleed
Nokia *85 D5* Länsi-Suomi, W Finland
Nokou *76 B3* Kanem, W Chad
Nola *77 B5* Sangha-Mbaéré, SW Central African Republic
Nolinsk *111 C5* Kirovskaya Oblast', NW Russian Federation
Nongkaya *see* Nong Khai
Nong Khai *136 C4 var.* Mi Chai, Nongkaya. Nong Khai, E Thailand
Nonouti *144 D2 prev.* Sydenham Island. *Atoll* Tungaru, W Kiribati
Noord-Beveland *86 B4 var.* North Beveland. *Island* SW Netherlands
Noordwijk aan Zee *86 C3* Zuid-Holland, W Netherlands
Nora *85 C6* Örebro, C Sweden
Norak *123 E3 Rus.* Nurek. W Tajikistan
Nord *83 F1* N Greenland
Nordaustlandet *83 G1 island* NE Svalbard
Norden *94 A3* Niedersachsen, NW Germany
Norderstedt *94 B3* Schleswig-Holstein, N Germany
Nordfriesische Inseln *see* North Frisian Islands
Nordhausen *94 C4* Thüringen, C Germany
Nordhorn *94 A3* Niedersachsen, NW Germany
Nordkapp *84 D1 Eng.* North Cape. *Headland* N Norway
Norfolk *45 E3* Nebraska, C USA
Norfolk *41 F5* Virginia, NE USA
Norfolk Island *142 D4 Australian external territory* SW Pacific Ocean
Norfolk Ridge *142 D4 undersea feature* W Pacific Ocean
Norias *49 G5* Texas, SW USA
Noril'sk *114 D3* Taymyrskiy (Dolgano-Nenetskiy) Avtonomnyy Okrug, N Russian Federation
Norman *49 G1* Oklahoma, USA
Normandie *90 B3 Eng.* Normandy. *Cultural region* N France
Normandy *see* Normandie
Normanton *148 C3* Queensland, NE Australia
Norrköping *85 C6* Östergötland, S Sweden
Norrtälje *85 C6* Stockholm, C Sweden
Norseman *147 B6* Western Australia
North Albanian Alps *101 C5 Alb.* Bjeshkët e Namuna, *SCr.* Prokletije. *Mountain range* Albania/Serbia and Montenegro (Yugo.)
Northallerton *89 D5* N England, UK
Northam *147 A6* Western Australia
North America *34 continent*
Northampton *89 D6* C England, UK
North Andaman *133 F2 island* Andaman Islands, India, NE Indian Ocean
North Australian Basin *141 E5 Fr.* Bassin Nord de l' Australie. *Undersea feature* E Indian Ocean
North Bay *38 D4* Ontario, S Canada
North Beveland *see* Noord-Beveland
North Cape *66 D1 headland* New Ireland, NE PNG
North Cape *150 C1 headland* North Island, NZ
North Cape *see* Nordkapp
North Carolina *43 E1 off.* State of North Carolina; also known as Old North State, Tar Heel State, Turpentine State. *State* SE USA
North Channel *40 D2 lake channel* Canada/USA
North Charleston *43 F2* South Carolina, SE USA
North Dakota *44 D2 off.* State of North Dakota; also known as Flickertail State, Peace Garden State, Sioux State. *State* N USA
Northeast Providence Channel *54 C1 channel* N Bahamas
Northeim *94 B4* Niedersachsen, C Germany
Northern Cook Islands *145 F4 island group* N Cook Islands
Northern Cyprus, Turkish Republic of *102 D5 disputed region* N Cyprus
Northern Dvina *see* Severnaya Dvina
Northern Ireland *88 B4 var.* The Six Counties. *Political division* UK
Northern Mariana Islands *142 B1 US commonwealth territory* W Pacific Ocean
Northern Sporades *see* Vóreioi Sporádes
Northern Territory *144 A5 territory* N Australia
North European Plain *81 E3 plain* N Europe
Northfield *45 F2* Minnesota, N USA
North Fiji Basin *142 D3 undersea feature* N Coral Sea
North Frisian Islands *94 B2 var.* Nordfriesische Inseln. *Island group* N Germany
North Huvadhu Atoll *132 B5 var.* Gaafu Alifu Atoll. *Atoll* S Maldives
North Island *150 B2 island* N NZ
North Korea *129 E3 Kor.* Chosŏn-minjujuŭi-inmin-kanghwaguk. *Country* E Asia

North Korea 129

Official name Democratic People's Republic of Korea
Formation 1948
Capital Pyongyang
Population 22.7 million / 488 people per sq mile (189 people per sq km)
Total area 46,540 sq. miles (120,540 sq. km)
Languages Korean, Chinese
Religions Atheist 100%
Ethnic mix Korean 100%
Government One-party state
Currency North Korean won = 100 chon
Literacy rate 99%
Calorie consumption 2201 calories

North Little Rock *42 B1* Arkansas, C USA
North Minch *see* Minch, The
North Mole *93 G4 harbour wall* NW Gibraltar
North Platte *45 E4* Nebraska, C USA
North Platte River *44 D4 river* C USA
North Pole *155 B3 pole* Arctic Ocean
North Saskatchewan *37 F5 river* Alberta/Saskatchewan, S Canada
North Sea *C3 Dan.* Nordsøen, *Dut.* Noordzee, *Fr.* Mer du Nord, *Ger.* Nordsee, *Nor.* Nordsjøen; *prev.* German Ocean, *Lat.* Mare Germanicum. *Sea* NW Europe
North Siberian Lowland *see* Severo-Sibirskaya Nizmennost'
North Siberian Plain *see* Severo-Sibirskaya Nizmennost'
North Taranaki Bight *150 C3 gulf* North Island, NZ
North Uist *88 B3 island* NW Scotland, UK
Northwest Atlantic Mid-Ocean Canyon *34 E4 undersea feature* N Atlantic Ocean
North West Highlands *88 C3 mountain range* N Scotland, UK
Northwest Pacific Basin *113 G4 undersea feature* NW Pacific Ocean
Northeast Providence Channel *54 C1 channel* N Bahamas
Northwest Territories *37 E3 Fr.* Territoires du Nord-Ouest. *Territory* NW Canada (the eastern part is now the territory of Nunavut)
Northwind Plain *155 B2 undersea feature* Arctic Ocean
Norton Sound *36 C2 inlet* Alaska, USA
Norway *85 A5 Nor.* Norge. *Country* N Europe

Norway 85

Official name Kingdom of Norway
Formation 1905
Capital Oslo
Population 4.5 million / 38 people per sq mile (15 people per sq km)
Total area 125,181 sq. miles (324,220 sq. km)
Languages Norwegian (*Bokmål* "book language" and *Nynorsk* "new Norsk"), Sámi
Religions Evangelical Lutheran 89%, Other and nonreligious 10%, Roman Catholic 1%
Ethnic mix Norwegian 93%, other 6%, Sámi 1%
Government Parliamentary system
Currency Norwegian krone = 100 øre
Literacy rate 99%
Calorie consumption 3382 calories

Norwegian Basin *83 F4 undersea feature* NW Norwegian Sea

Norwegian Sea *83 F4 Nor.* Norske Havet. *Sea* NE Atlantic Ocean
Norwich *89 E6* E England, UK
Noshiro *130 D4 var.* Nosiro; *prev.* Noshirominato. Akita, Honshū, C Japan
Noshirominato *see* Noshiro
Nosiro *see* Noshiro
Nosivka *109 E1 Rus.* Nosovka. Chernihivs'ka Oblast', NE Ukraine
Noşratābād *120 E3* Sīstān va Balūchestān, E Iran
Nossob *78 C4 river* E Namibia
Noteć *98 C3 Ger.* Netze. *River* NW Poland
Nóties Sporádes *see* Dodekánisos
Nottingham *89 D6* C England, UK
Nouâdhibou *74 B2 prev.* Port-Étienne. Dakhlet Nouâdhibou, W Mauritania
Nouakchott *74 B2 country capital* (Mauritania) Nouakchott District, SW Mauritania
Nouméa *144 C5 dependent territory capital* (New Caledonia) Province Sud, S New Caledonia
Nouvelle-Calédonie *see* New Caledonia
Nova Gorica *95 D8* W Slovenia
Nova Gradiška *100 C3 Ger.* Neugradisk, *Hung.* Újgradiska. Brod-Posavina, NE Croatia
Nova Iguaçu *63 F4* Rio de Janeiro, SE Brazil
Novara *96 B2 anc.* Novaria. Piemonte, NW Italy
Nova Scotia *39 F4 Fr.* Nouvelle Écosse. *Province* SE Canada
Nova Scotia *35 E5 physical region* SE Canada
Novaya Sibir', Ostrov *115 F1 island* Novosibirskiye Ostrova, NE Russian Federation
Novaya Zemlya *110 D1 island group* N Russian Federation
Novaya Zemlya Trench *see* East Novaya Zemlya Trench
Novgorod *see* Velikiy Novgorod
Novi Grad *see* Bosanski Novi
Novi Iskŭr *104 C2* Sofiya-Grad, W Bulgaria
Novi Pazar *101 D5 Turk.* Yenipazar. Shumen, NE Bulgaria
Novi Sad *100 D3 Ger.* Neusatz, *Hung.* Újvidék. Serbia, N Serbia and Montenegro (Yugo.)
Novoazovs'k *109 G4 Rus.* Novoazovsk. Donets'ka Oblast', E Ukraine
Novocheboksarsk *111 C5* Chuvashskaya Respublika, W Russian Federation
Novocherkassk *111 B7* Rostovskaya Oblast', SW Russian Federation
Novodvinsk *110 C3* Arkhangel'skaya Oblast', NW Russian Federation
Novohrad-Volyns'kyy *108 D2 Rus.* Novograd-Volynskiy. Zhytomyrs'ka Oblast', N Ukraine
Novokazalinsk *see* Ayteke Bi
Novokuznetsk *114 D4 prev.* Stalinsk. Kemerovskaya Oblast', S Russian Federation
Novolazarevskaya *154 C2 Russian research station* Antarctica
Novo mesto *95 E8 Ger.* Rudolfswert; prev. *Ger.* Neustadtl. SE Slovenia
Novomoskovs'k *109 F3 Rus.* Novomoskovsk. Dnipropetrovs'ka Oblast', E Ukraine
Novomoskovsk *111 B5* Tul'skaya Oblast', W Russian Federation
Novorossiysk *111 A7* Krasnodarskiy Kray, SW Russian Federation
Novoshakhtinsk *111 B6* Rostovskaya Oblast', SW Russian Federation
Novosibirsk *114 D4* Novosibirskaya Oblast', C Russian Federation
Novosibirskiye Ostrova *115 F1 Eng.* New Siberian Islands. *Island group* N Russian Federation
Novotroitsk *111 D6* Orenburgskaya Oblast', W Russian Federation
Novotroyits'ke *109 F4 Rus.* Novotroitskoye. Khersons'ka Oblast', S Ukraine
Novovolyns'k *108 C1 Rus.* Novovolynsk. Volyns'ka Oblast', NW Ukraine
Novy Dvor *107 B6 Rus.* Novyy Dvor. Hrodzyenskaya Voblasts', W Belarus
Novyy Buh *109 E3 Rus.* Novyy Bug. Mykolayivs'ka Oblast', S Ukraine
Novyy Uzen' *see* Zhanaözen
Nowa Sól *98 B4 var.* Nowasól, *Ger.* Neusalz an der Oder. Lubuskie, W Poland
Nowogard *98 B2 var.* Nowógard, *Ger.* Naugard. Zachodniopomorskie, NW Poland
Nowógard *see* Nowogard
Nowo-Minsk *see* Miusk Mazowiecki
Nowy Dwór Mazowiecki *98 D3* Mazowieckie, C Poland
Nowy Sącz *99 D5 Ger.* Neu Sandec. Małopolskie, S Poland
Nowy Tomyśl *98 B3 var.* Nowy Tomysl. Wielkopolskie, C Poland
Noyon *90 C3* Oise, N France
Nsanje *79 E3* Southern, S Malawi
Nsawam *75 E5* SE Ghana
Ntomba, Lac *77 C6 var.* Lac Tumba. *Lake* NW Dem. Rep. Congo
Nubian Desert *72 B3 desert* NE Sudan
Nu'eima *119 E7* E West Bank
Nueva Gerona *54 B2* Isla de la Juventud, S Cuba
Nueva Rosita *50 D2* Coahuila de Zaragoza, NE Mexico
Nuevitas *54 C2* Camagüey, E Cuba
Nuevo, Bajo *53 G1 island* NW Colombia
Nuevo Casas Grandes *50 C1* Chihuahua, N Mexico
Nuevo, Golfo *65 C6 gulf* S Argentina
Nuevo Laredo *51 E2* Tamaulipas, NE Mexico
Nui Atoll *145 E3 atoll* W Tuvalu
Nûk *see* Nuuk
Nuku'alofa *145 E5 country capital* (Tonga) Tongatapu, S Tonga
Nukufetau Atoll *145 E3 atoll* C Tuvalu
Nukulaelae Atoll *145 E3 var.* Nukulailai. *Atoll* E Tuvalu
Nukulailai *see* Nukulaelae Atoll
Nukunau *see* Nikunau
Nukunonu Atoll *145 E3 island* C Tokelau
Nukus *122 C2* Qoraqalpoghiston Respublikasi, W Uzbekistan
Nullarbor Plain *147 C6 plateau* South Australia/Western Australia
Nunap Isua *98 B5 var* Uummannarsuaq, *Dan.* Kap Farvel, *Eng.* Cape Farewell. *Headland* S Greenland
Nunavut *37 F3 territory* N Canada
Nuneaton *89 D6* C England, UK
Nunivak Island *36 B2 island* Alaska, USA
Nunspeet *86 D3* Gelderland, E Netherlands
Nuoro *97 A5* Sardegna, Italy, C Mediterranean Sea
Nuquí *58 A3* Chocó, W Colombia
Nurakita *see* Niulakita
Nuremberg *see* Nürnberg
Nurmes *84 E4* Itä-Suomi, E Finland
Nürnberg *95 C5 Eng.* Nuremberg. Bayern, S Germany
Nurota *123 E2 Rus.* Nurata. Nawoiy Wiloyati, C Uzbekistan
Nusa Tenggara *139 E5 Eng.* Lesser Sunda Islands. East Timor / C Indonesia
Nusaybin *117 F4 var.* Nisibin. Manisa, SE Turkey
Nuuk *82 C4 var.* Nûk, *Dan.* Godthaab, Godthåb. *Dependent territory capital* (Greenland) SW Greenland
Nyagan' *114 C3* Khanty-Mansiyskiy Avtonomnyy Okrug, N Russian Federation
Nyainqêntanglha Shan *126 C5 mountain range* W China
Nyala *72 A4* Southern Darfur, W Sudan
Nyamapanda *78 D3* Mashonaland East, NE Zimbabwe
Nyamtumbo *73 C8* Ruvuma, S Tanzania
Nyandoma *110 C4* Arkhangel'skaya Oblast', NW Russian Federation
Nyantakara *73 B7* Kagera, NW Tanzania
Nyasa, Lake *79 E2 var.* Lake Malawi; *prev.* Lago Nyassa. *Lake* E Africa
Nyasvizh *107 C6 Pol.* Nieśwież, *Rus.* Nesvizh. Minskaya Voblasts', C Belarus
Nyaunglebin *136 B4* Pegu, SW Myanmar
Nyeri *73 C6* Central, C Kenya
Nyima *126 C5* Xizang Zizhiqu, W China
Nyíregyháza *99 D6* Szabolcs-Szatmár-Bereg, NE Hungary
Nykøbing *85 B8* Storstrøm, SE Denmark
Nyköping *85 C6* Södermanland, S Sweden
Nylstroom *see* Modimolle
Nyngan *149 D6* New South Wales, SE Australia
Nyurba *115 F3* Respublika Sakha (Yakutiya), NE Russian Federation
Nyzhn'ohirs'kyy *109 F4 Rus.* Nizhnegorskiy. Respublika Krym, S Ukraine
Nzega *73 C7* Tabora, C Tanzania
Nzérékoré *74 D4* Guinée-Forestière, SE Guinea
Nzwani *see* Anjouan

O

O'ahu *47 A7 var.* Oahu. *Island* Hawai'i, USA, C Pacific Ocean
Oak Harbor *46 B1* Washington, NW USA
Oakland *47 B6* California, W USA
Oamaru *151 B7* Otago, South Island, NZ
Oaxaca *51 F5 var.* Oaxaca de Juárez; *prev.* Antequera. Oaxaca, SE Mexico
Oaxaca de Juárez *see* Oaxaca
Ob' *112 C2 river* C Russian Federation
Obal' *107 D5 Rus.* Obol'. Vitsyebskaya Voblasts', N Belarus
Oban *see* Halfmoon Bay
Oban *88 C4* W Scotland, UK
Obando *see* Puerto Inírida
Obeliai *106 C4* Rokiškis, NE Lithuania
Oberhollabrunn *see* Tulln
Ob, Gulf of *see* Obskaya Guba
Obihiro *130 D2* Hokkaidō, NE Japan
Obo *76 D4* Haut-Mbomou, E Central African Republic
Obock *72 D4* E Djibouti
Oborniki *98 C3* Wielkopolskie, C Poland
Obskaya Guba *114 D3 Eng.* Gulf of Ob'. *Gulf* N Russian Federation
Ob' Tablemount *141 B7 undersea feature* S Indian Ocean
Ocala *43 E4* Florida, SE USA
Ocaña *92 D3* Castilla-La Mancha, C Spain
Ocaña *58 B2* Norte de Santander, N Colombia
O Carballiño *108 C1 var* Carballiño. Gallicia, NW Spain
Occidental, Cordillera *61 E4 mountain range* W South America
Occidental, Cordillera *58 B2 mountain range* W Colombia
Occidental, Cordillera *60 D4 mountain range* W Peru
Ocean Falls *36 D5* British Columbia, SW Canada
Ocean Island *see* Banaba
Oceanside *47 C8* California, W USA
Ochakiv *109 E4 Rus.* Ochakov. Mykolayivs'ka Oblast', S Ukraine
Och'amch'ire *117 E2 Rus.* Ochamchira. W Georgia
Ocho Rios *54 B4* C Jamaica
Ochrida, Lake *see* Ohrid, Lake
Ocotal *52 D3* Nueva Segovia, NW Nicaragua
Ocozocuautla *51 G5* Chiapas, SE Mexico
Ocú *53 F5* Herrera, S Panama
Ōdate *130 D3* Akita, Honshū, C Japan
Oddur *see* Xuddur
Ödemiş *116 A4* İzmir, SW Turkey
Odense *85 B7* Fyn, C Denmark
Oder *98 B3 Cz./Pol.* Odra. *River* C Europe
Oderhaff *see* Szczeciński, Zalew
Odesa *109 E4 Rus.* Odessa. Odes'ka Oblast', SW Ukraine
Odessa *49 E3* Texas, SW USA
Odienné *74 D4* NW Côte d'Ivoire
Ôdôngk *137 D6* Kâmpóng Spoe, S Cambodia
Odoorn *86 E2* Drenthe, NE Netherlands
Of *117 E2* Trabzon, NE Turkey
Ofanto *97 D5 river* S Italy
Offenbach *95 B5 var.* Offenbach am Main. Hessen, W Germany
Offenbach am Main *see* Offenbach
Offenburg *95 B6* Baden-Württemberg, SW Germany
Ogaden *73 D5 Som.* Ogaadeen. *Plateau* Ethiopia/Somalia
Ōgaki *131 C6* Gifu, Honshū, SW Japan
Ogallala *44 D4* Nebraska, C USA
Ogbomosho *75 F4* Oyo, W Nigeria
Ogden *44 B4* Utah, W USA
Ogdensburg *41 F2* New York, NE USA
Ogulin *100 A3* Karlovac, NW Croatia
Ohio *40 C4 off.* State of Ohio; also known as The Buckeye State. *State* N USA
Ohio River *40 C4 river* N USA
Ohrid *101 D6 Turk.* Ochrida, Ohri. SW FYR Macedonia
Ohrid, Lake *101 D6 var.* Lake Ochrida, *Alb.* Liqeni i Ohrit, *Mac.* Ohridsko Ezero. *Lake* Albania/FYR Macedonia
Ohridsko Ezero *see* Ohrid, Lake
Ohura *150 D3* Manawatu-Wanganui, North Island, NZ
Oirschot *87 C5* Noord-Brabant, S Netherlands
Oise *90 C3 river* N France
Oistins *55 G2* S Barbados
Ōita *131 B7* Ōita, Kyūshū, SW Japan
Ojinaga *50 D2* Chihuahua, N Mexico
Ojos del Salado, Cerro *64 B3 mountain* W Argentina
Okaihau *150 C2* Northland, North Island, NZ
Okāra *134 C2* Punjab, E Pakistan
Okavanggo *see* Cubango
Okavango *see* Cubango
Okavango *78 C3 district* NW Namibia
Okavango Delta *78 C3 wetland* N Botswana
Okayama *131 B6* Okayama, Honshū, SW Japan
Okazaki *131 C6* Aichi, Honshū, C Japan
Okeechobee, Lake *43 E4 lake* Florida, SE USA
Okefenokee Swamp *43 E3 wetland* Georgia, SE USA
Okhotsk *115 G3* Khabarovskiy Kray, E Russian Federation
Okhotskoye More *115 G3 sea* NW Pacific Ocean
Okhotsk, Sea of *113 F3 sea* NW Pacific Ocean
Okhtyrka *109 F2 Rus.* Akhtyrka. Sums'ka Oblast', NE Ukraine
Oki-guntō *see* Oki-shotō
Okinawa *130 A3 island* SW Japan

Okinawa-shotō *130 A3 island group* SW Japan
Oki-shotō *131 B6 var.* Oki-guntō. *Island group* SW Japan
Oklahoma *49 F2 off.* State of Oklahoma; also known as The Sooner State. *State* C USA
Oklahoma City *49 G1 state capital* Oklahoma, C USA
Okmulgee *49 G1* Oklahoma, C USA
Oko, Wadi *72 C3 river* NE Sudan
Oktyabr'skiy *111 D6* Volgogradskaya Oblast', SW Russian Federation
Oktyabr'skoy Revolyutsii, Ostrov *115 E2 Eng.* October Revolution Island. *Island* Severnaya Zemlya, N Russian Federation
Okulovka *see* Uglovka
Okushiri-tō *130 C3 var.* Okusiri Tô. *Island* NE Japan
Okusiri Tô *see* Okushiri-tō
Öland *85 C7 island* S Sweden
Olavarría *65 D5* Buenos Aires, E Argentina
Oława *98 C4 Ger.* Ohlau. Dolnośląskie, SW Poland
Olbia *97 A5 prev.* Terranova Pausania. Sardegna, Italy, C Mediterranean Sea
Oldebroek *86 D3* Gelderland, E Netherlands
Oldenburg *94 B3* Niedersachsen, NW Germany
Oldenburg *94 C2* Schleswig-Holstein, N Germany
Oldenzaal *86 E3* Overijssel, E Netherlands
Old Harbour *54 B5* C Jamaica
Olëkma *115 F4 river* C Russian Federation
Olëkminsk *115 F3* Respublika Sakha (Yakutiya), NE Russian Federation
Oleksandrivka *109 E3 Rus.* Aleksandrovka. Kirovohrads'ka Oblast', C Ukraine
Oleksandriya *109 F3 Rus.* Aleksandriya. Kirovohrads'ka Oblast', C Ukraine
Olenegorsk *110 C2* Murmanskaya Oblast', NW Russian Federation
Olenëk *115 E3* Respublika Sakha (Yakutiya), NE Russian Federation
Olenëk *115 E3 river* NE Russian Federation
Oléron, Île d' *91 A5 island* W France
Olevs'k *108 D1 Rus.* Olevsk. Zhytomyrs'ka Oblast', N Ukraine
Ölgiy *126 C2* Bayan-Ölgiy, W Mongolia
Olhão *92 B5* Faro, S Portugal
Olifa *78 B3* Kunene, NW Namibia
Ólimbos *see* Ólympos
Olimpo *see* Fuerte Olimpo
Oliva *93 F4* País Valenciano, E Spain
Olivet *90 C4* Loiret, C France
Olmaliq *123 E2 Rus.* Almalyk. Toshkent Wiloyati, E Uzbekistan
Olomouc *99 C5 Ger.* Olmütz, *Pol.* Ołomuniec. Olomoucký Kraj, E Czech Republic
Olonets *110 B3* Respublika Kareliya, NW Russian Federation
Olovyannaya *115 F4* Chitinskaya Oblast', S Russian Federation
Olpe *94 B4* Nordrhein-Westfalen, W Germany
Olsztyn *98 D2 Ger.* Allenstein. Warmińsko-Mazurskie, NE Poland
Olt *108 B5 var.* Oltul, *Ger.* Alt. *River* S Romania
Oltenița *108 C5 prev. Eng.* Oltenitsa, *anc.* Constantiola. Călărași, SE Romania
Oltul *see* Olt
Olvera *92 D5* Andalucía, S Spain
Olympia *46 B2 state capital* Washington, NW USA
Olympic Mountains *46 A2 mountain range* Washington, NW USA
Ólympos *104 B4 var.* Ólimbos, *Eng.* Mount Olympus. *Mountain* N Greece
Olympus, Mount *see* Ólympos
Omagh *89 B5 Ir.* An Ómaigh. W Northern Ireland, UK
Omaha *45 F4* Nebraska, C USA
Oman *121 D6 Ar.* Salṭanat 'Umān; *prev.* Muscat and Oman. *Country* SW Asia

Oman 121

Official name Sultanate of Oman
Formation 1951
Capital Muscat
Population 2.9 million / 35 people per sq mile (14 people per sq km)
Total area 82,031 sq. miles (212,460 sq. km)
Languages Arabic, Baluchi, Farsi, Hindi, Punjabi
Religions Ibadi Muslim 75%, Other Muslim and Hindu 25%
Ethnic mix Arab 88%, Baluchi 4%, Persian 3%, Indian and Pakistani 3%, African 2%
Government Monarchy
Currency Omani rial = 1000 baizas
Literacy rate 74%
Calorie consumption Not available

Oman, Gulf of *120 E4 Ar.* Khalīj 'Umān. *Gulf* N Arabian Sea
Omboué *77 A6* Ogooué-Maritime, W Gabon
Omdurman *72 B4 var.* Umm Durmān. Khartoum, C Sudan
Ometepe, Isla de *52 D4 island* S Nicaragua
Ommen *86 E3* Overijssel, E Netherlands
Omsk *114 C4* Omskaya Oblast', C Russian Federation
Ōmuta *131 A7* Fukuoka, Kyūshū, SW Japan
Onda *93 F3* País Valenciano, E Spain
Ondjiva *see* N'Giva
Öndörhaan *127 E2* Hentiy, E Mongolia
Onega *110 B4 river* NW Russian Federation
Onega *110 C3* Arkhangel'skaya Oblast', NW Russian Federation
Onega, Lake *see* Onezhskoye Ozero
Onex *95 A7* Genève, SW Switzerland
Onezhskoye Ozero *110 B4 Eng.* Lake Onega. *Lake* NW Russian Federation
Ongole *132 D1* Andhra Pradesh, E India
Onitsha *75 G5* Anambra, S Nigeria
Onon Gol *127 E2 river* N Mongolia
Ononte *see* Orantes
Onslow *146 A4* Western Australia
Onslow Bay *43 F1 bay* North Carolina, E USA
Ontario *38 B3 province* S Canada
Ontario, Lake *41 E3 lake* Canada/USA
Onteniente *see* Ontinyent
Ontinyent *93 F4 var.* Onteniente. País Valenciano, E Spain
Ontong Java Rise *125 H4 undersea feature* W Pacific Ocean
Oostakker *87 B5* Oost-Vlaanderen, NW Belgium
Oostburg *87 B5* Zeeland, SW Netherlands
Oostende *87 A5 Eng.* Ostend, *Fr.* Ostende. West-Vlaanderen, NW Belgium
Oosterbeek *86 D4* Gelderland, SE Netherlands
Oosterhout *86 C4* Noord-Brabant, S Netherlands
Opatija *100 A2 It.* Abbazia. Primorje-Gorski Kotar, NW Croatia
Opava *99 C5 Ger.* Troppau. Ostravský Kraj, E Czech Republic
Opelika *42 D2* Alabama, S USA
Opelousas *42 B3* Louisiana, S USA
Opmeer *86 C2* Noord-Holland, NW Netherlands
Opochka *110 A4* Pskovskaya Oblast', W Russian Federation
Opole *98 C4 Ger.* Oppeln. Opolskie, S Poland
Opotiki *150 E3* Bay of Plenty, North Island, NZ
Oppidum Ubiorum *see* Köln
Oqtosh *123 E2 Rus.* Aktash. Samarqand Wiloyati, C Uzbekistan
Oradea *108 B3 prev.* Oradea Mare, *Ger.* Grosswardein, *Hung.* Nagyvárad. Bihor, NW Romania
Orahovac *101 D5 Alb.* Rahovec. Serbia, S Serbia and Montenegro (Yugo.)
Oran *70 D2 var.* Ouahran, Wahran. NW Algeria
Orange *91 D6 anc.* Arausio. Vaucluse, SE France
Orange *149 D6* New South Wales, SE Australia
Orangeburg *43 E2* South Carolina, SE USA
Orange Cone *see* Orange Fan
Orange Fan *69 C7 var.* Orange Cone. *Undersea feature* SW Indian Ocean
Orange Mouth *see* Oranjemund
Orangemund *see* Oranjemund
Orange River *78 B4 Afr.* Oranjerivier. *River* S Africa
Orange Walk *52 C1* Orange Walk, N Belize
Oranienburg *94 D3* Brandenburg, NE Germany
Oranjemund *78 B4 var.* Orangemund; *prev.* Orange Mouth. Karas, SW Namibia
Oranjestad *55 E5 dependent territory capital* (Aruba) W Aruba
Orantes *118 B3 var.* Ononte, *Ar.* Nahr el Aassi, Nahr al 'Aṣī. *River* SW Asia
Oravița *108 A4 Ger.* Orawitza, *Hung.* Oravicabánya. Caraș-Severin, SW Romania
Orbetello *96 B4* Toscana, C Italy
Orcadas *154 A1 Argentinian research station* South Orkney Islands, Antarctica
Orchard Homes *44 B1* Montana, NW USA
Ordino *91 A8* NW Andorra
Ordos Desert *see* Mu Us Shamo
Ordu *116 D2 anc.* Cotyora. Ordu, N Turkey
Ordzhonikidze *109 F3* Dnipropetrovs'ka Oblast', E Ukraine
Orealla *59 G3* E Guyana
Örebro *85 C6* Örebro, C Sweden
Oregon *46 B3 off.* State of Oregon; also known as Beaver State, Sunset State, Valentine State, Webfoot State. *State* NW USA
Oregon City *46 B3* Oregon, NW USA
Orël *111 B5* Orlovskaya Oblast', W Russian Federation
Orem *44 B4* Utah, W USA
Orenburg *111 D6 prev.* Chkalov. Orenburgskaya Oblast', W Russian Federation
Orense *see* Ourense
Oreor *see* Koror
Orestiáda *104 D3 prev.* Orestiás. Anatolikí Makedonía kai Thráki, NE Greece
Organ Peak *48 D3 mountain* New Mexico, SW USA
Orgeyev *see* Orhei
Orhei *108 D3 var.* Orheiu, *Rus.* Orgeyev. N Moldova
Orheiu *see* Orhei
Oriental, Cordillera *60 D3 mountain range* Bolivia/Peru
Oriental, Cordillera *61 F4 mountain range* C Bolivia
Oriental, Cordillera *58 B3 mountain range* C Colombia
Orihuela *93 F4* País Valenciano, E Spain
Orikhiv *109 G3 Rus.* Orekhov. Zaporiz'ka Oblast', SE Ukraine
Orinoco, Río *59 E2 river* Colombia/Venezuela
Orissa *135 F4 state* NE India
Orissaare *106 C2 Ger.* Orissaar. Saaremaa, W Estonia
Oristano *97 A5* Sardegna, Italy, C Mediterranean Sea
Orito *58 A4* Putumayo, SW Colombia
Orizaba, Volcán Pico de *35 C7 var.* Citlaltépetl. *Mountain* S Mexico
Orkney *see* Orkney Islands
Orkney Islands *88 C2 var.* Orkney, Orkneys. *Island group* N Scotland, UK
Orkneys *see* Orkney Islands
Orlando *43 E4* Florida, SE USA
Orléanais *90 C4 cultural region* C France
Orléans *90 C4 anc.* Aurelianum. Loiret, C France
Orléansville *see* Chlef
Orly *90 E2 international airport* (Paris) Essonne, N France
Orlya *107 B6 Rus.* Orlya. Hrodzyenskaya Voblasts', W Belarus
Ormuz, Strait of *see* Hormuz, Strait of
Örnsköldsvik *85 C5* Västernorrland, C Sweden
Oromocto *39 F4* New Brunswick, SE Canada
Orona *145 F3 prev.* Hull Island. *Atoll* Phoenix Islands, C Kiribati
Orosirá Rodhópis *see* Rhodope Mountains
Orpington *89 B8* SE England, UK
Orsha *107 E6 Rus.* Orsha. Vitsyebskaya Voblasts', NE Belarus
Orsk *114 B4* Orenburgskaya Oblast', W Russian Federation
Orșova *108 A4 Ger.* Orschowa, *Hung.* Orsova. Mehedinți, SW Romania
Orthez *91 B6* Pyrénées-Atlantiques, SW France
Ortona *96 D4* Abruzzo, C Italy
Oruba *see* Aruba
Oruro *61 F4* Oruro, W Bolivia
Ōsaka *131 C6 hist.* Naniwa. Ōsaka, Honshū, SW Japan
Osa, Península de *53 E5 peninsula* S Costa Rica
Osborn Plateau *141 D5 undersea feature* E Indian Ocean
Osh *123 F2* Oshskaya Oblast', SW Kyrgyzstan
Oshawa *38 D5* Ontario, SE Canada
Oshikango *78 B3* Ohangwena, N Namibia
Ō-shima *131 D6 island* S Japan
Oshkosh *40 B2* Wisconsin, N USA
Osijek *100 C3 prev.* Osiek, Osjek, *Ger.* Esseg, *Hung.* Eszék. Osijek-Baranja, E Croatia
Oskaloosa *45 G4* Iowa, C USA
Oskarshamn *85 C7* Kalmar, S Sweden
Oskil *109 G2 Rus.* Oskol. *River* Russian Federation/Ukraine
Oslo *85 B6 prev.* Christiania, Kristiania. *Country capital* (Norway) Oslo, S Norway
Osmaniye *116 D4* Osmaniye, admin. region *province* S Turkey
Osnabrück *94 A3* Niedersachsen, NW Germany
Osogov Mountains 120 B3 *var.* Osogovske Planine, Osogovski Planina, *Mac.* Osogovski Planini. *mountain range* Bulgaria/FYR, Macedonia
Osogovske Planine/Osogovski Planina/Osogovski Planini *see* Osogov Mountains
Osorno *65 B5* Los Lagos, C Chile
Oss *86 D4* Noord-Brabant, S Netherlands
Ossa, Serra d' *92 C4 mountain range* SE Portugal
Ossora *115 H2* Koryakskiy Avtonomnyy Okrug, E Russian Federation
Ostend *see* Oostende
Ostende *see* Oostende
Oster *109 E1* Chernihivs'ka Oblast', N Ukraine
Östersund *85 C5* Jämtland, C Sweden
Ostfriesische Inseln *94 A3 Eng.* East Frisian Islands. *Island group* NW Germany
Ostiglia *96 C2* Lombardia, N Italy

Ostrava *99 C5* Ostravský Kraj, E Czech Republic
Ostróda *98 D3 Ger.* Osterode, Osterode in Ostpreussen. Warmińsko-Mazurskie, NE Poland
Ostrołęka *98 D3 Ger.* Wiesenhof, *Rus.* Ostrolenka. Mazowieckie, C Poland
Ostrov *110 A4 Latv.* Austrava. Karlovarský Kraj, W Czech Republic
Ostrovets *see* Ostrowiec Świętokrzyski
Ostrovnoy *110 C2* Murmanskaya Oblast', NW Russian Federation
Ostrów *see* Ostrów Wielkopolski
Ostrowiec *see* Ostrowiec Świętokrzyski
Ostrowiec Świętokrzyski *98 D4 var.* Ostrowiec, *Rus.* Ostrovets. Świętokrzyskie, C Poland
Ostrów Mazowiecka *98 D3 var.* Ostrów Mazowiecki. Mazowieckie, C Poland
Ostrów Mazowiecki *see* Ostrów Mazowiecka
Ostrowo *see* Ostrów Wielkopolski
Ostrów Wielkopolski *98 C4 var.* Ostrów, *Ger.* Ostrowo. Wielkopolskie, C Poland
Osum *see* Osumit, Lumi i
Ōsumi-shotō *131 A8 island group* SW Japan
Osumit, Lumi i *101 D7 var.* Osum. *River* SE Albania
Osuna *92 D4* Andalucía, S Spain
Oswego *41 F2* New York, NE USA
Otago Peninsula *151 B7 peninsula* South Island, NZ
Otaki *150 D4* Wellington, North Island, NZ
Otaru *130 C2* Hokkaidō, NE Japan
Otavalo *60 B1* Imbabura, N Ecuador
Otavi *78 B3* Otjozondjupa, N Namibia
Oţelu Roşu *108 B4 Ger.* Ferdinandsberg, *Hung.* Nándorhgy. Caras-Severin, SW Romania
Otepää *106 D3 Ger.* Odenpäh. Valgamaa, SE Estonia
Oti *75 E4 river* W Africa
Otira *151 C6* West Coast, South Island, NZ
Otjiwarongo *78 B3* Otjozondjupa, N Namibia
Otorohanga *150 D3* Waikato, North Island, NZ
Otranto, Strait of *101 C6 It.* Canale d'Otranto. *Strait* Albania/Italy
Otrokovice *99 C5 Ger.* Otrokowitz. Zlínský Kraj, E Czech Republic
Ōtsu *131 C6 var.* Ōtu. Shiga, Honshū, SW Japan
Ottawa *41 E2 Fr.* Outaouais. Admin. region *river* Ontario/Quebec, SE Canada
Ottawa *38 D5 country capital* (Canada) Ontario, SE Canada
Ottawa *40 B3* Illinois, N USA
Ottawa *45 F5* Kansas, C USA
Ottawa Islands *38 C1 island group* Northwest Territories, C Canada
Ottignies *87 C6* Wallon Brabant, C Belgium
Ottumwa *45 G4* Iowa, C USA
Ōtu *see* Ōtsu
Ouachita Mountains *42 A1 mountain range* Arkansas/Oklahoma, C USA
Ouachita River *42 B2 river* Arkansas/Louisiana, C USA
Ouadi Howa *see* Howar, Wādi
Ouagadougou *75 E4 var.* Wagadugu. *Country capital* (Burkina Faso) C Burkina Faso
Ouahigouya *75 E3* NW Burkina faso
Ouahran *see* Oran
Oualata *see* Oualâta
Oualâta *74 D3 var.* Oualata. Hodh ech Chargui, SE Mauritania
Ouanary *59 H3* E French Guiana
Ouanda Djallé *76 D4* Vakaga, NE Central African Republic
Ouarâne *74 D2 desert* C Mauritania
Ouargla *71 E2 var.* Wargla. NE Algeria
Ouarzazate *70 C3* S Morocco
Oubangui *see* Ubangi
Oubangui-Chari *see* Central African Republic
Ouessant, Île d' *90 A3 Eng.* Ushant. *Island* NW France
Ouésso *77 B5* La Sangha, NW Congo
Oujda *70 D2 Ar.* Oudjda, Ujda. NE Morocco
Oujeft *74 C2* Adrar, C Mauritania
Oulu *84 D4 Swe.* Uleåborg. Oulu, C Finland
Oulujärvi *84 D4 Swe.* Uleträsk. *Lake* C Finland
Oulujoki *84 D4 Swe.* Uleälv. *River* C Finland
Ounasjoki *84 D3 river* N Finland
Ounianga Kébir *76 C2* Borkou-Ennedi-Tibesti, N Chad
Oup *see* Auob
Oupeye *87 D6* Liège, E Belgium
Our *87 D6 river* NW Europe
Ourense *92 C1 var. Cast.* Orense; *Lat.* Aurium. Galicia, NW Spain
Ourique *92 B4* Beja, S Portugal
Ourthe *87 D7 river* E Belgium
Ouse *89 D5 river* N England, UK
Outer Hebrides *88 B3 var.* Western Isles. *Island group* NW Scotland, UK
Outer Islands *79 G1 island group* SW Seychelles
Outes *92 B1* Galicia, NW Spain
Ouvéa *144 D5 island* Îles Loyauté, NE New Caledonia
Ouyen *149 C6* Victoria, SE Australia
Ovalle *64 B3* Coquimbo, N Chile
Ovar *92 B2* Aveiro, N Portugal
Overflakkee *86 B4 island* SW Netherlands
Overijse *87 C6* Vlaams Brabant, C Belgium
Oviedo *92 C1 anc.* Asturias. Asturias, NW Spain
Ovruch *108 D1* Zhytomyrs'ka Oblast', N Ukraine
Owando *77 B5 prev.* Fort-Rousset. Cuvette, C Congo
Owase *131 C6* Mie, Honshū, SW Japan
Owatonna *45 F3* Minnesota, N USA
Owen Fracture Zone *140 B4 tectonic feature* W Arabian Sea
Owen, Mount *151 C5 mountain* South Island, NZ
Owensboro *40 B5* Kentucky, S USA
Owen Stanley Range *144 B3 mountain range* S PNG
Owerri *75 G5* Imo, S Nigeria
Owo *75 F5* Ondo, SW Nigeria
Owyhee River *46 C4 river* Idaho/Oregon, NW USA
Oxford *89 D6 Lat.* Oxonia. S England, UK
Oxford *151 C6* Canterbury, South Island, NZ
Oxkutzcab *51 H4* Yucatán, SE Mexico
Oxnard *47 B7* California, W USA
Oyama *131 D5* Tochigi, Honshū, S Japan
Oyem *77 B5* Woleu-Ntem, N Gabon
Oyo *77 B6* Cuvette, C Congo
Oyo *75 F4* Oyo, W Nigeria
Ozark *42 D3* Alabama, S USA
Ozark Plateau *45 G5 plain* Arkansas/Missouri, C USA
Ozarks, Lake of the *45 F5 reservoir* Missouri, C USA
Ozbourn Seamount *152 D4 undersea feature* W Pacific Ocean
Ózd *99 D6* Borsod-Abaúj-Zemplén, NE Hungary
Ozero Khanka *see* Khanka, Lake
Ozero Ubsu-Nur *see* Uvs Nuur
Ozieri *97 A5* Sardegna, Italy, C Mediterranean Sea

P

Paamiut *82 B4 var.* Pâmiut, *Dan.* Frederikshåb. S Greenland
Pa-an *136 B4* Karen State, S Myanmar
Pabianice *98 C4* Łodz, C Poland
Pabna *135 G4* Rajshahi, W Bangladesh
Pachuca *51 E4 var.* Pachuca de Soto. Hidalgo, C Mexico
Pachuca de Soto *see* Pachuca
Pacific-Antarctic Ridge *154 B5 undersea feature* S Pacific Ocean
Pacific Ocean *152 D3 ocean*
Padalung *see* Phatthalung
Padang *138 B4* Sumatera, W Indonesia
Paderborn *94 B4* Nordrhein-Westfalen, NW Germany
Padma *see* Brahmaputra
Padova *96 C2 Eng.* Padua; *anc.* Patavium. Veneto, NE Italy
Padre Island *49 G5 island* Texas, SW USA
Padua *see* Padova
Paducah *40 B5* Kentucky, S USA
Paeroa *150 D3* Waikato, North Island, NZ
Páfos *102 C5 var.* Paphos. W Cyprus
Pag *100 A3 It.* Pago. *Island* Zadar SW Croatia
Page *48 B1* Arizona, SW USA
Pago Pago *145 F4 dependent territory capital* (American Samoa) Tutuila, W American Samoa
Pahiatua *150 D4* Manawatu-Wanganui, North Island, NZ
Pahsien *see* Chongqing
Paide *106 D2 Ger.* Weissenstein. Järvamaa, N Estonia
Paihia *150 D2* Northland, North Island, NZ
Päijänne *85 D5 lake* S Finland
Paine, Cerro *65 A7 mountain* S Chile
Painted Desert *48 B1 desert* Arizona, SW USA
Paisley *88 C4* W Scotland, UK
País Valenciano *93 F3 cultural region* NE Spain
País Vasco *93 E1 cultural region* N Spain
Paita *60 B3* Piura, NW Peru
Pakanbaru *see* Pekanbaru
Pakaraima Mountains *59 E3 var.* Serra Pacaraim, Sierra Pacaraima. *Mountain range* N South America
Pakistan *134 A2 var.* Islami Jamhuriya e Pakistan. *Country* S Asia

Pakistan 134

Official name Islamic Republic of Pakistan
Formation 1947
Capital Islamabad
Population 154 million / 516 people per sq mile (199 people per sq km)
Total area 310,401 sq. miles (803,940 sq. km)
Languages Punjabi, Sindhi, Pashtu, Urdu, Baluchi, Brahui
Religions Sunni Muslim 77%, Shi'a Muslim 20%, Hindu 2%, Christian 1%
Ethnic mix Punjabi 56%, Pathan (Pashtun) 15%, Sindhi 14%, Mohajir 7%, other 4%, Baluchi 4%
Government Presidential system
Currency Pakistani rupee = 100 paisa
Literacy rate 44%
Calorie consumption 2457 calories

Paknam *see* Samut Prakan
Pakokku *136 A3* Magwe, C Myanmar
Pak Phanang *137 C7 var.* Ban Pak Phanang. Nakhon Si Thammarat, SW Thailand
Pakruojis *106 C4* Pakruojis, N Lithuania
Paks *99 C7* Tolna, S Hungary
Paksé *see* Pakxé
Pakxé *137 D5 var.* Paksé. Champasak, S Laos
Palafrugell *93 G2* Cataluña, NE Spain
Palagruža *101 B5 It.* Pelagosa. *Island* SW Croatia
Palaiá Epídavros *105 C6* Pelopónnisos, S Greece
Palaiseau *90 D2* Essonne, N France
Palamós *93 G2* Cataluña, NE Spain
Palamuse *106 E2 Ger.* Sankt-Bartholomäi. Jõgevamaa, E Estonia
Pālanpur *134 C4* Gujarāt, W India
Palapye *78 D3* Central, SE Botswana
Palau *144 A2 var.* Belau. *Country* W Pacific Ocean

Palau 144

Official name Republic of Palau
Formation 1994
Capital Koror
Population 19,717 / 101 people per sq mile (39 people per sq km)
Total area 177 sq. miles (458 sq. km)
Languages Palauan, English, Japanese, Angaur, Tobi, Sonsorolese
Religions Christian 66%, Modekngei 34%
Ethnic mix Micronesian 87%, Filipino 8%, Asian 5%
Government Nonparty system
Currency US dollar = 100 cents
Literacy rate 98%
Calorie consumption Not available

Palawan *139 E2 island* W Philippines
Palawan Passage *138 D2 passage* W Philippines
Paldiski *106 D2 prev.* Baltiski, *Eng.* Baltic Port, *Ger.* Baltischport. Harjumaa, NW Estonia
Palembang *138 B4* Sumatera, W Indonesia
Palencia *92 D2 anc.* Palantia, Pallantia. Castilla-León, NW Spain
Palermo *97 C7 Fr.* Palerme; *anc.* Panhormus, Panormus. Sicilia, Italy, C Mediterranean Sea
Pāli *134 C3* Rājasthān, N India
Palikir *144 C2 country capital* (Micronesia) Pohnpei, E Micronesia
Palimé *see* Kpalimé
Palioúri, Akrotírio *104 C4 var.* Akra Kanestron. *Headland* N Greece
Palk Strait *132 C3 strait* India/Sri Lanka
Palliser, Cape *151 D5 headland* North Island, NZ
Palma *93 G3 var.* Palma de Mallorca. Mallorca, Spain, W Mediterranean Sea
Palma del Río *92 D4* Andalucía, S Spain
Palma de Mallorca *see* Palma
Palmar Sur *53 E5* Puntarenas, SE Costa Rica
Palma Soriano *54 C3* Santiago de Cuba, E Cuba
Palm Beach *148 E1* New South Wales, SE Australia
Palmer *154 A2 US research station* Antarctica
Palmer Land *154 A3 physical region* Antarctica
Palmerston *145 F4 island* S Cook Islands
Palmerston North *150 D4* Manawatu-Wanganui, North Island, NZ
Palmi *97 D7* Calabria, SW Italy
Palmira *58 B3* Valle del Cauca, W Colombia
Palm Springs *47 D7* California, W USA
Palmyra *see* Tudmur
Palmyra Atoll *145 G2 US privately owned unincorporated territory* C Pacific Ocean
Palo Alto *47 B6* California, W USA
Palu *139 E4 prev.* Paloe. Sulawesi, C Indonesia
Pamiers *91 B6* Ariège, S France
Pamir *var.* Daryā-ye Pāmīr, *Taj.* Dar"yoi Pomir. *River* Afghanistan/Tajikistan *see also* Pāmīr, Daryā-ye

Pamirs 123 F3 *Pash.* Daryā-ye Pāmīr, *Rus.* Pamir. *Mountain range* C Asia
Pâmiut *see* Paamiut
Pamlico Sound 43 G1 *sound* North Carolina, SE USA
Pampa 49 E1 Texas, SW USA
Pampas 64 C4 *plain* C Argentina
Pamplona 93 E1 *Basq.* Iruña; *prev.* Pampeluna, *anc.* Pompaelo. Navarra, N Spain
Pamplona 58 C2 Norte de Santander, N Colombia
Panaji *see* Pānji
Panama 53 G5 *Country* Central America

Panama 53

Official name Republic of Panama
Formation 1903
Capital Panama City
Population 3.1 million / 106 people per sq mile (41 people per sq km)
Total area 30,193 sq. miles (78,200 sq. km)
Languages English Creole, Spanish, Amerindian languages, Chibchan languages
Religions Roman Catholic 86%, other 8%, Protestant 6%
Ethnic mix Mestizo 60%, White 14%, Black 12%, Amerindian 8%, Asian 4%, other 2%
Government Presidential system
Currency Balboa = 100 centesimos
Literacy rate 92%
Calorie consumption 2386 calories

Panamá 53 G4 *var.* Ciudad de Panamá, *Eng.* Panama City. *Country capital* (Panama) Panamá, C Panama
Panama Basin 35 C8 *undersea feature* E Pacific Ocean
Panama Canal 53 F4 *canal* E Panama
Panama City *see* Panamá
Panama City 42 D3 Florida, SE USA
Panamá, Golfo de 53 G5 *var.* Gulf of Panama. *Gulf* S Panama
Panama, Gulf of *see* Panamá, Golfo de
Panamá, Isthmus of *see* Panamá, Istmo de
Panamá, Istmo de 53 G4 *Eng.* Isthmus of Panama; *prev.* Isthmus of Darien. *Isthmus* E Panama
Panay Island 139 E2 *island* C Philippines
Pančevo 100 D3 *Ger.* Pantschowa, *Hung.* Pancsova. Serbia, N Serbia and Montenegro (Yugo.)
Paneas *see* Bāniyās
Panevėžys 106 C4 Panevėžys, C Lithuania
Pangim *see* Pānji
Pangkalpinang 138 C4 Pulau Bangka, W Indonesia
Pang-Nga *see* Phang-Nga
Panjim *see* Pānji
Pānji 132 B1 *var.* Pangim, Panaji, Panjim, New Goa. Goa, W India
Pánormos 105 C7 Kríti, Greece, E Mediterranean Sea
Pantanal 63 E3 *var.* Pantanalmato-Grossense. *Swamp* SW Brazil
Pantanalmato-Grossense *see* Pantanal
Pantelleria, Isola di 97 B7 *island* SW Italy
Pánuco 51 E3 Veracruz-Llave, E Mexico
Pao-chi *see* Baoji
Paoki *see* Baoji
Paola 102 B5 E Malta
Pao-shan *see* Baoshan
Pao-t'ou *see* Baotou
Paotow *see* Baotou
Papagayo, Golfo de 52 C4 *gulf* NW Costa Rica
Papakura 150 D3 Auckland, North Island, NZ
Papantla 51 F4 *var.* Papantla de Olarte. Veracruz-Llave, E Mexico
Papantla de Olarte *see* Papantla
Papeete 145 H4 *dependent territory capital* (French Polynesia) Tahiti, W French Polynesia
Paphos *see* Páfos
Papilė 106 B3 Akmenė, NW Lithuania
Papillion 45 F4 Nebraska, C USA
Papua 139 H4 *var.* Irian Barat, Irian Jaya, West Irian, West New Guinea, West Papua; *prev.* Dutch New Guinea, Netherlands New Guinea. Admin. region *province* E Indonesia
Papua, Gulf of 144 B3 *gulf* S PNG
Papua New Guinea 144 B3 *prev.* Territory of Papua and New Guinea, *abbrev.* PNG. *Country* NW Melanesia

Papua New Guinea 144

Official name Independent State of Papua New Guinea
Formation 1975
Capital Port Moresby
Population 5.7 million / 33 people per sq mile (13 people per sq km)
Total area 178,703 sq. miles (462,840 sq. km)
Languages Pidgin English, Papuan, English, Motu, 750 (est.) native languages
Religions Protestant 60%, Roman Catholic 37%, other 3%
Ethnic mix Melanesian and mixed race 100%
Government Parliamentary system
Currency Kina = 100 toeas
Literacy rate 65%
Calorie consumption 2193 calories

Papuk 100 C3 *mountain range* NE Croatia
Pará 63 E2 *off.* Estado do Pará. *State* NE Brazil
Pará *see* Belém
Paracel Islands 125 E3 *disputed territory* SE Asia
Paraćin 100 D4 Serbia, C Serbia and Montenegro (Yugo.)
Paragua, Río 59 E3 *river* SE Venezuela
Paraguay 64 D2 *var.* Río Paraguay. *River* C South America
Paraguay 64 C2 *country* C South America

Paraguay 64

Official name Republic of Paraguay
Formation 1811
Capital Asunción
Population 5.9 million / 38 people per sq mile (15 people per sq km)
Total area 157,046 sq. miles (406,750 sq. km)
Languages Guaraní, Spanish, German
Religions Roman Catholic 96%, Protestant (including Mennonite) 4%
Ethnic mix Mestizo 90%, other 8%, Amerindian 2%
Government Presidential system
Currency Guaraní = 100 centimos
Literacy rate 92%
Calorie consumption 2576 calories

Paraguay, Río *see* Paraguay
Paraíba 63 G2 *off.* Estado da Paraíba; *prev.* Parahiba, Parahyba. *State* E Brazil
Parakou 75 F4 C Benin
Paramaribo 59 G3 *country capital* (Suriname) Paramaribo, N Suriname
Paramushir, Ostrov 115 H3 *island* SE Russian Federation
Paraná 63 E5 *off.* Estado do Paraná. *State* S Brazil
Paraná 57 C5 *var.* Alto Paraná. *River* C South America
Paraná 63 E4 Entre Ríos, E Argentina
Paranéstio 104 C3 Anatolikí Makedonía kai Thráki, NE Greece
Paraparaumu 151 D5 Wellington, North Island, NZ
Parchim 94 C3 Mecklenburg-Vorpommern, N Germany
Parczew 98 E4 Lubelskie, E Poland
Pardubice 99 B5 *Ger.* Pardubitz. Pardubický Kraj, C Czech Republic
Parechcha 107 B5 *Rus.* Porech'ye. Hrodzyenskaya Voblasts', NE Belarus
Parecis, Chapada dos 62 D3 *var.* Serra dos Parecis. *Mountain range* W Brazil
Parepare 139 E4 Sulawesi, C Indonesia
Párga 105 A5 Ípeiros, W Greece
Paria, Golfo de *see* Paria, Gulf of
Paria, Gulf of 59 E1 *var.* Golfo de Paria. *Gulf* Trinidad and Tobago/Venezuela
Parika 59 F2 NE Guyana
Paris 90 D1 *anc.* Lutetia, Lutetia Parisiorum, Parisii. *Country capital* (France) Paris, N France
Paris 49 G2 Texas, SW USA
Parkersburg 40 D4 West Virginia, NE USA
Parkes 149 D6 New South Wales, SE Australia
Parma 96 B2 Emilia-Romagna, N Italy
Parnahyba *see* Parnaíba
Parnaíba 63 F2 *var.* Parnahyba. Piauí, E Brazil
Pärnu 106 D2 *Ger.* Pernau, *Latv.* Pērnava; *prev.* Rus. Pernov. Pärnumaa, SW Estonia
Pärnu 106 D2 *var.* Parnu Jõgi, *Ger.* Pernau. *River* SW Estonia
Pärnu-Jaagupi 106 D2 *Ger.* Sankt-Jakobi. Pärnumaa, SW Estonia
Parnu Jõgi *see* Pärnu
Pärnu Laht 106 D2 *Ger.* Pernauer Bucht. *Bay* SW Estonia
Páros 105 C6 *island* Kykládes, Greece, Aegean Sea
Páros 105 D6 Páros, Kykládes, Greece, Aegean Sea
Parral *see* Hidalgo del Parral
Parral 64 B4 Maule, C Chile
Parramatta 148 D1 New South Wales, SE Australia
Parras 50 D3 *var.* Parras de la Fuente. Coahuila de Zaragoza, NE Mexico
Parras de la Fuente *see* Parras
Parsons 45 F5 Kansas, C USA
Pasadena 47 C7 California, W USA
Pasadena 49 H4 Texas, SW USA
Paşcani 108 C3 *Hung.* Páskán. Iaşi, NE Romania
Pasco 46 C2 Washington, NW USA
Pas de Calais *see* Dover, Strait of
Pasewalk 94 D3 Mecklenburg-Vorpommern, NE Germany
Pasinler 117 F3 Erzurum, NE Turkey
Pasłęk 98 D2 *Ger.* Preußisch Holland. Warmińsko-Mazurskie, NE Poland
Pasni 134 A3 Baluchistān, SW Pakistan
Paso de Indios 65 B6 Chubut, S Argentina
Passau 95 D6 Bayern, SE Germany
Passo del Brennero *see* Brenner Pass
Passo Fundo 63 E5 Rio Grande do Sul, S Brazil
Pastavy 107 C5 *Pol.* Postawy, *Rus.* Postavy. Vitsyebskaya Voblasts', NW Belarus
Pastaza, Río 60 B2 *river* Ecuador/Peru
Pasto 58 A4 Nariño, SW Colombia
Pasvalys 106 C4 Pasvalys, N Lithuania
Patagonia 57 B7 *physical region* Argentina/Chile
Patalung *see* Phatthalung
Patani *see* Pattani
Patavium *see* Padova
Patea 150 D4 Taranaki, North Island, NZ
Paterson 41 F3 New Jersey, NE USA
Pathein *see* Bassein
Pátmos 105 D6 *island* Dodekánisos, Greece, Aegean Sea
Patna 135 F3 *var.* Azimabad. Bihār, N India
Patnos 117 F3 Ağrı, E Turkey
Patos, Lagoa dos 63 E5 *lagoon* S Brazil
Pátra 105 B5 *Eng.* Patras; *prev.* Pátrai. Dytikí Ellás, S Greece
Pattani 137 C7 *var.* Patani. Pattani, SW Thailand
Pattaya 137 C5 Chon Buri, S Thailand
Patuca, Río 52 D2 *river* E Honduras
Pau 91 B6 Pyrénées-Atlantiques, SW France
Paulatuk 37 E3 Northwest Territories, NW Canada
Paungde 136 B4 Pegu, C Myanmar
Pavia 96 B2 *anc.* Ticinum. Lombardia, N Italy
Pāvilosta 106 B3 Liepāja, W Latvia
Pavlikeni 104 D2 Veliko Tŭrnovo, N Bulgaria
Pavlodar 114 C4 Pavlodar, NE Kazakhstan
Pavlohrad 109 G3 *Rus.* Pavlograd. Dnipropetrovs'ka Oblast', E Ukraine
Pawn 136 B3 *river* C Myanmar
Paxoí 105 A5 *island* Iónioi Nísoi, Greece, C Mediterranean Sea
Payo Obispo *see* Chetumal
Paysandú 64 D4 Paysandú, W Uruguay
Pazar 117 E2 Rize, NE Turkey
Pazardzhik 104 C3 *prev.* Tatar Pazardzhik. Pazardzhik, C Bulgaria
Pearl River 42 B3 *river* Louisiana/Mississippi, S USA
Pearsall 49 F4 Texas, SW USA
Peć 101 D5 *Alb.* Pejë, *Turk.* Ipek. Serbia, S Serbia and Montenegro (Yugo.)
Pechora 110 D3 *river* NW Russian Federation
Pechora 110 D3 Respublika Komi, NW Russian Federation
Pechorskoye More 110 D2 *Eng.* Pechora Sea. *Sea* NW Russian Federation
Pecos 49 E3 Texas, SW USA
Pecos River 49 E3 *river* New Mexico/Texas, SW USA
Pécs 99 C7 *Ger.* Fünfkirchen; *Lat.* Sopianae. Baranya, SW Hungary
Pedra Lume 74 A3 Sal, NE Cape Verde
Pedro Cays 54 C3 *island group* S Jamaica
Pedro Juan Caballero 64 D2 Amambay, E Paraguay
Peer 87 D5 Limburg, NE Belgium
Pegasus Bay 151 C6 *bay* South Island, NZ
Pegu 136 B4 *var.* Bago. Pegu, SW Myanmar
Pehuajó 64 C4 Buenos Aires, E Argentina
Pei-ching *see* Beijing
Peine 94 B3 Niedersachsen, C Germany
Pei-p'ing *see* Beijing
Peipus, Lake E3 *Est.* Peipsi Järv, *Ger.* Peipus-See, *Rus.* Chudskoye Ozero. *Lake* Estonia/Russian Federation
Peiraías 105 C6 *prev.* Piraiévs, *Eng.* Piraeus. Attikí, C Greece
Pèk 136 D4 *var.* Xieng Khouang; *prev.* Xiangkhoang. Xiangkhoang, N Laos
Pekalongan 138 C4 Jawa, C Indonesia
Pekanbaru 138 B3 *var.* Pakanbaru. Sumatera, W Indonesia
Pekin 40 B4 Illinois, N USA
Peking *see* Beijing

Pelagie, Isole *97 B8 island group* SW Italy
Pelly Bay *37 G3* Nunavut, N Canada
Peloponnese *see* Pelopónnisos
Peloponnesus *see* Pelopónnisos
Pelopónnisos *105 B6 var.* Morea, *Eng.* Peloponnese; *anc.* Peloponnesus. *Peninsula* S Greece
Pematangsiantar *138 B3* Sumatera, W Indonesia
Pemba *79 F2 prev.* Port Amelia, Porto Amélia. Cabo Delgado, NE Mozambique
Pemba *73 D7 island* E Tanzania
Pembroke *38 D4* Ontario, SE Canada
Penang *see* George Town
Penang *see* Pinang, Pulau
Penas, Golfo de *65 A7 gulf* S Chile
Penderma *see* Bandırma
Pendleton *46 C3* Oregon, NW USA
Pend Oreille, Lake *46 D2 lake* Idaho, NW USA
Peneius *see* Pineiós
Peng-pu *see* Bengbu
Peniche *92 B3* Leiria, W Portugal
Péninsule de la Gaspésie *see* Gaspé, Péninsule de
Pennine Alps *95 A8 Fr.* Alpes Pennines, *It.* Alpi Pennine; *Lat.* Alpes Penninae. *Mountain range* Italy/Switzerland
Pennine Chain *see* Pennines
Pennines *89 D5 var.* Pennine Chain. *Mountain range* N England, UK
Pennsylvania *40 D3 off.* Commonwealth of Pennsylvania; also known as The Keystone State. *State* NE USA
Penobscot River *41 G2 river* Maine, NE USA
Penong *149 A6* South Australia
Penonomé *53 F5* Coclé, C Panama
Penrhyn *145 G3 atoll* N Cook Islands
Penrhyn Basin *143 F3 undersea feature* C Pacific Ocean
Penrith *148 D1* New South Wales, SE Australia
Penrith *89 D5* NW England, UK
Pensacola *42 C3* Florida, SE USA
Pentecost *144 D4 Fr.* Pentecôte. *Island* C Vanuatu
Penza *111 C6* Penzenskaya Oblast', W Russian Federation
Penzance *89 C7* SW England, UK
Peoria *40 B4* Illinois, N USA
Perchtoldsdorf *95 E6* Niederösterreich, NE Austria
Percival Lakes *146 C4 lakes* Western Australia
Perdido, Monte *93 F1 mountain* NE Spain
Perece Vela Basin *see* West Mariana Basin
Pereira *58 B3* Risaralda, W Colombia
Pergamino *64 C4* Buenos Aires, E Argentina
Périgueux *91 C5 anc.* Vesuna. Dordogne, SW France
Perito Moreno *65 B6* Santa Cruz, S Argentina
Perlas, Archipiélago de las *53 G5 Eng.* Pearl Islands. *Island group* SE Panama
Perlas, Laguna de *53 E3 Eng.* Pearl Lagoon. *Lagoon* E Nicaragua
Perleberg *94 C3* Brandenburg, N Germany
Perm' *114 C3 prev.* Molotov. Permskaya Oblast', NW Russian Federation
Pernambuco *63 G2 off.* Estado de Pernambuco. *State* E Brazil
Pernambuco Abyssal Plain *see* Pernambuco Plain
Pernambuco Plain *67 C5 var.* Pernambuco Abyssal Plain. *Undersea feature* E Atlantic Ocean
Pernau *see* Pärnu
Pernik *104 B2 prev.* Dimitrovo. Pernik, W Bulgaria
Perote *51 F4* Veracruz-Llave, E Mexico
Perovsk *see* Kyzylorda
Perpignan *91 C6* Pyrénées-Orientales, S France
Perryton *49 F1* Texas, SW USA
Perryville *45 H5* Missouri, C USA
Persian Gulf *see* Gulf, The
Perth *147 A6 state capital* Western Australia
Perth *88 C4* C Scotland, UK
Perth Basin *141 E6 undersea feature* SE Indian Ocean
Peru *60 C3 Country* W South America

Peru 60

Official name Republic of Peru
Formation 1824
Capital Lima
Population 27.2 million / 55 people per sq mile (21 people per sq km)
Total area 496,223 sq. miles (1,285,200 sq. km)
Languages Spanish, Quechua, Aymara
Religions Roman Catholic 95%, other 5%
Ethnic mix Amerindian 50%, Mestizo 40%, White 7%, other 3%
Government Presidential system
Currency New sol = 100 centimos
Literacy rate 85%
Calorie consumption 2610 calories

Peru *see* Beru
Peru Basin *67 A5 undersea feature* E Pacific Ocean
Peru-Chile Trench *56 A4 undersea feature* E Pacific Ocean
Perugia *96 C4 Fr.* Pérouse; *anc.* Perusia. Umbria, C Italy
Péruwelz *87 B6* Hainaut, SW Belgium
Pervomays'k *109 E3 prev.* Ol'viopol'. Mykolayivs'ka Oblast', S Ukraine
Pervyy Kuril'skiy Proliv *115 H3 strait* E Russian Federation
Pesaro *96 C3 anc.* Pisaurum. Marche, C Italy
Pescara *96 D4 anc.* Aternum, Ostia Aterni. Abruzzo, C Italy
Peshāwar *134 C1* North-West Frontier Province, N Pakistan
Peshkopi *101 C6 var.* Peshkopia, Peshkopija. Dibër, NE Albania
Peshkopia *see* Peshkopi
Peshkopija *see* Peshkopi
Pessac *91 B5* Gironde, SW France
Petach-Tikva *see* Petah Tiqwa
Petah Tiqva *see* Petah Tiqwa
Petah Tiqwa *119 A6 var.* Petach-Tikva, Petah Tiqva, Petakh Tikva. Tel Aviv, C Israel
Petakh Tikva *see* Petah Tiqwa
Pétange *87 D8* Luxembourg, SW Luxembourg
Petchaburi *see* Phetchaburi
Peterborough *89 E6 prev.* Medeshamstede. E England, UK
Peterborough *38 D5* Ontario, SE Canada
Peterborough *149 B6* South Australia
Peterhead *88 D3* NE Scotland, UK
Peter I Island *154 A3 Norwegian dependency* Antarctica
Petermann Bjerg *83 E3 mountain* C Greenland
Petersburg *41 E5* Virginia, NE USA
Peters Mine *59 F3 var.* Peter's Mine. N Guyana
Peto *51 H4* Yucatán, SE Mexico
Petoskey *40 C2* Michigan, N USA
Petra *see* Wādī Mūsā
Petrich *104 C3* Blagoevgrad, SW Bulgaria
Petrinja *100 B3* Sisak-Moslavina, C Croatia
Petrodvorets *110 A4 Fin.* Pietarhovi. Leningradskaya Oblast', NW Russian Federation
Petrograd *see* Sankt-Peterburg
Petropavlovsk *114 C4 Kaz.* Petropavl. Severnyy Kazakhstan, N Kazakhstan
Petropavlovsk-Kamchatskiy *115 H3* Kamchatskaya Oblast', E Russian Federation
Petroşani *108 B4 var.* Petroşeni, *Ger.* Petroschen, *Hung.* Petrozsény. Hunedoara, W Romania
Petroschen *see* Petroşani
Petroşeni *see* Petroşani
Petrozavodsk *114 B2 Fin.* Petroskoi. Respublika Kareliya, NW Russian Federation
Petrozsény *see* Petroşani
Pevek *115 G1* Chukotskiy Avtonomnyy Okrug, NE Russian Federation
Pezinok *99 C6 Ger.* Bösing, *Hung.* Bazin. Bratislavský Kraj, W Slovakia
Pforzheim *95 B6* Baden-Württemberg, SW Germany
Pfungstadt *95 B5* Hessen, W Germany
Phangan, Ko *137 C6 island* SW Thailand
Phang-Nga *137 B7 var.* Pang-Nga, Phangnga. Phangnga, SW Thailand
Phangnga *see* Phang-Nga
Phanom Dang Raek *see* Dângrêk, Chuŏr Phnum
Phanom Dong Rak *see* Dângrêk, Chuŏr Phnum
Phan Rang *see* Phan Rang-Thap Cham
Phan Rang-Thap Cham *137 E6 var.* Phanrang, Phan Rang, Phan Rang Thap Cham. Ninh Thuân, S Vietnam
Phan Thiêt *137 E6* Binh Thuân, S Vietnam
Pharnacia *see* Giresun
Phatthalung *137 C7 var.* Padalung, Patalung. Phatthalung, SW Thailand
Phayao *136 C4 var.* Muang Phayao. Phayao, NW Thailand
Phenix City *42 D2* Alabama, S USA
Phet Buri *see* Phetchaburi
Phetchaburi *137 C5 var.* Bejraburi, Petchaburi, Phet Buri. Phetchaburi, SW Thailand
Philadelphia *see* 'Ammān
Philadelphia *41 F4* Pennsylvania, NE USA
Philippine Basin *125 F3 undersea feature* W Pacific Ocean
Philippines *139 E1 Country* SE Asia

Philippines 139

Official name Republic of the Philippines
Formation 1946
Capital Manila
Population 80 million / 695 people per sq mile (268 people per sq km)
Total area 115,830 sq. miles (300,000 sq. km)
Languages Filipino, Tagalog, Cebuano, Hiligaynon, Samaran, Ilocano, Bicolano, English
Religions Roman Catholic 83%, Protestant 9%, Muslim 5%, Other (including Buddhist) 3%
Ethnic mix Malay 95%, other 3%, Chinese 2%
Government Presidential system
Currency Philippine peso = 100 centavos
Literacy rate 93%
Calorie consumption 2372 calories

Philippines *139 E1 island group* W Pacific Ocean
Philippine Sea *125 F3 sea* W Pacific Ocean
Philippine Trench *142 A1 undersea feature* W Philippine Sea
Phitsanulok *136 C4 var.* Bisnulok, Muang Phitsanulok, Pitsanulok. Phitsanulok, C Thailand
Phlórina *see* Flórina
Phnom Penh *see* Phnum Penh
Phnum Penh *137 D6 var.* Phnom Penh. *Country capital* (Cambodia) Phnum Penh, S Cambodia
Phoenix *48 B2 state capital* Arizona, SW USA
Phoenix Islands *145 E3 island group* C Kiribati
Phôngsali *136 C3 var.* Phong Saly. Phôngsali, N Laos
Phong Saly *see* Phôngsali
Phrae *136 C4 var.* Muang Phrae, Prae. Phrae, NW Thailand
Phra Nakhon Si Ayutthaya *see* Ayutthaya
Phra Thong, Ko *137 B6 island* SW Thailand
Phuket *137 B7 var.* Bhuket, Puket, *Mal.* Ujung Salang; *prev.* Junkseylon, Salang. Phuket, SW Thailand
Phuket, Ko *137 B7 island* SW Thailand
Phumĭ Kâmpóng Trâbêk *137 D5* Kâmpóng Chhnăng, N Cambodia
Phumĭ Sâmraông *137 D5* Poŭthĭsăt, NW Cambodia
Phu Vinh *see* Tra Vinh
Piacenza *96 B2 Fr.* Paisance; *anc.* Placentia. Emilia-Romagna, N Italy
Piatra-Neamţ *108 C4 Hung.* Karácsonkő. Neamţ, NE Romania
Piauí *63 F2 off.* Estado do Piauí; *prev.* Piauhy. *State* E Brazil
Picardie *90 C3 Eng.* Picardy. *Cultural region* N France
Pichilemu *64 B4* Libertador, C Chile
Pico *92 A5 var.* Ilha do Pico. *Island* Azores, Portugal, NE Atlantic Ocean
Picos *63 F2* Piauí, E Brazil
Picton *151 C5* Marlborough, South Island, NZ
Piedras Negras *51 E2 var.* Ciudad Porfirio Díaz. Coahuila de Zaragoza, NE Mexico
Pielinen *84 E4 var.* Pielisjärvi. *Lake* E Finland
Pielisjärvi *see* Pielinen
Piemonte *96 A2 Eng.* Piedmont. *Cultural region* NW Italy
Pierre *45 E3 state capital* South Dakota, N USA
Piešťany *99 C6 Ger.* Pistyan, *Hung.* Pöstyén. Trnavský Kraj, W Slovakia
Pietermaritzburg *78 C5 var.* Maritzburg. KwaZulu/Natal, E South Africa
Pietersburg *see* Polokwane
Pigs, Bay of *see* Cochinos, Bahía de
Pijijiapán *51 G5* Chiapas, SE Mexico
Pikes Peak *44 C5 mountain* Colorado, C USA
Pikeville *40 D5* Kentucky, S USA
Pikinni *see* Bikini Atoll
Piła *98 B3 Ger.* Schneidemühl. Wielkopolskie, C Poland
Pilar *64 D3 var.* Villa del Pilar. Ñeembucú, S Paraguay
Pilcomayo *57 C5 river* C South America
Pilos *see* Pýlos
Pinang *see* George Town
Pinang, Pulau *138 B3 var.* Penang, Pinang; *prev.* Prince of Wales Island. *Island* Peninsular Malaysia
Pinar del Río *54 A2* Pinar del Río, W Cuba
Píndhos *see* Píndos
Píndhos Óros *see* Píndos
Píndos *104 A4 var.* Píndhos Óros, *Eng.* Pindus Mountains; *prev.* Píndhos. *Mountain range* C Greece
Pindus Mountains *see* Píndos
Pine Bluff *42 B2* Arkansas, C USA
Pine Creek *146 D2* Northern Territory, N Australia
Pinega *110 C3 river* NW Russian Federation
Pineiós *104 B4 var.* Piniós; *anc.* Peneius. *River* C Greece
Pineland *49 H3* Texas, SW USA

Pines, The Isle of the *see* Juventud, Isla de la
Pingdingshan *128 C4* Henan, C China
Pingkiang *see* Harbin
Ping, Mae Nam *136 B4 river* W Thailand
Piniós *see* Pineiós
Pinkiang *see* Harbin
Pínnes, Akrotírio *104 C4 headland* N Greece
Pinos, Isla de *see* Juventud, Isla de la
Pinotepa Nacional *51 F5 var.* Santiago Pinotepa Nacional. Oaxaca, SE Mexico
Pinsk *107 B7 Pol.* Pińsk. SW Belarus
Pinta, Isla *60 A5 var.* Abingdon. *Island* Galapagos Islands, Ecuador, E Pacific Ocean
Piombino *96 B3* Toscana, C Italy
Pioneer Mountains *46 D3 mountain range* Montana, N USA
Pionerskiy *106 A4 Ger.* Neukuhren. Kaliningradskaya Oblast', W Russian Federation
Piotrków Trybunalski *98 D4 Ger.* Petrikau, *Rus.* Petrokov. Łódzkie, C Poland
Piraeus *see* Peiraías
Pírgos *see* Pýrgos
Piripiri *63 F2* Piauí, E Brazil
Pirna *94 D4* Sachsen, E Germany
Pirot *101 E5* Serbia, SE Serbia and Montenegro (Yugo.)
Pisa *96 B3 var.* Pisae. Toscana, C Italy
Pisae *see* Pisa
Pisco *60 D4* Ica, SW Peru
Písek *99 A5* Budějovicky Kraj, S Czech Republic
Pishan *126 A3 var.* Guma. Xinjiang Uygur Zizhiqu, NW China
Pishpek *see* Bishkek
Pistoia *96 B3 anc.* Pistoria, Pistoriæ. Toscana, C Italy
Pisz *98 D3 Ger.* Johannisburg. Warminsko-Mazurskie, NE Poland
Pita *74 C4* Moyenne-Guinée, NW Guinea
Pitalito *58 B4* Huila, S Colombia
Pitcairn Island *143 G4 island* S Pitcairn Islands
Pitcairn Islands *143 G4 UK dependent territory* C Pacific Ocean
Piteå *84 D4* Norrbotten, N Sweden
Pitești *108 B5* Argeș, S Romania
Pitsanulok *see* Phitsanulok
Pittsburg *45 F5* Kansas, C USA
Pittsburgh *41 E4* Pennsylvania, NE USA
Pittsfield *41 F3* Massachusetts, NE USA
Piura *60 B2* Piura, NW Peru
Pivdennyy Buh *109 E3 Rus.* Yuzhnyy Bug. *River* S Ukraine
Placetas *54 B2* Villa Clara, C Cuba
Plainview *49 E2* Texas, SW USA
Planeta Rica *58 B2* Córdoba, NW Colombia
Planken *94 E1* C Liechtenstein
Plano *49 G2* Texas, SW USA
Plasencia *92 C3* Extremadura, W Spain
Plata, Río de la *64 D4 var.* River Plate. *Estuary* Argentina/Uruguay
Plateau du Bemaraha *see* Bemaraha
Platinum *36 C3* Alaska, USA
Plattensee *see* Balaton
Platte River *45 E4 river* Nebraska, C USA
Plattsburgh *41 F2* New York, NE USA
Plauen *95 C5 var.* Plauen im Vogtland. Sachsen, E Germany
Plauen im Vogtland *see* Plauen
Pļaviņas *106 D4 Ger.* Stockmannshof. Aizkraukle, S Latvia
Plây Cu *137 E5 var.* Pleiku. Gia Lai, C Vietnam
Pleiku *see* Plây Cu
Plenty, Bay of *150 E3 bay* North Island, NZ
Plérin *90 A3* Côtes d'Armor, NW France
Plesetsk *110 C3* Arkhangel'skaya Oblast', NW Russian Federation
Pleszew *98 C4* Wielkopolskie, C Poland
Pleven *104 C2 prev.* Plevna. Pleven, N Bulgaria
Pljevlja *100 C4 prev.* Plevlja, Plevlje. Montenegro, N Serbia and Montenegro (Yugo.)
Ploče *100 B4 It.* Plocce; *prev.* Kardeljevo. Dubrovnik-Neretva, SE Croatia
Płock *98 D3 Ger.* Plozk. Mazowieckie, C Poland
Plöcken Pass *95 C7 Ger.* Plöckenpass, *It.* Passo di Monte Croce Carnico. *Pass* SW Austria
Ploiești *108 C5 prev.* Ploești. Prahova, SE Romania
Plomári *105 D5 prev.* Plomárion. Lésvos, E Greece
Płońsk *98 D3* Mazowieckie, C Poland
Plovdiv *104 C3 prev.* Eumolpias, *anc.* Evmolpia, Philippopolis, *Lat.* Trimontium. Plovdiv, C Bulgaria
Plungė *106 B3* Plungė, W Lithuania
Plyeshchanitsy *107 D5 Rus.* Pleshchenitsy. Minskaya Voblasts', N Belarus
Plymouth *55 G3 dependent territory capital* (Montserrat) SW Montserrat
Plymouth *89 C7* SW England, UK
Plzeň *99 A5 Ger.* Pilsen, *Pol.* Pilzno. Plzeňský Kraj, W Czech Republic
Po *80 D4 river* N Italy
Pobeda Peak *see* Pobedy, Pik
Pobedy, Pik *126 B3 var.* Pobeda Peak, *Chin.* Tomur Feng. *Mountain* China/Kyrgyzstan *see also* Tomur Feng
Pocahontas *42 B1* Arkansas, C USA
Pocatello *46 E4* Idaho, NW USA
Pochinok *111 A5* Smolenskaya Oblast', W Russian Federation
Pocking *95 D6* Bayern, SE Germany
Poděbrady *99 B5 Ger.* Podiebrad. Středočesky Kraj, C Czech Republic
Podgorica *101 C5 prev.* Titograd. Montenegro, SW Serbia and Montenegro (Yugo.)
Podil's'ka Vysochina *108 D3 Rus.* Podol'skaya Vozvyshennost'. *Mountain range* SW Ukraine
Podkarpackie admin. region *province* SE Poland
Podol'sk *111 B5* Moskovskaya Oblast', W Russian Federation
Podravska Slatina *see* Slatina.
Podujevo *101 D5* Serbia, S Serbia and Montenegro (Yugo.)
Po, Foci del *96 C2 var.* Bocche del Po. *River* NE Italy
Pogradec *101 D6 var.* Pogradeci. Korçë, SE Albania
Pogradeci *see* Pogradec
Pohnpei *144 C2 prev.* Ponape Ascension Island. *Island* E Micronesia
Poinsett, Cape *154 D4 headland* Antarctica
Pointe-à-Pitre *55 G3* Grande Terre, C Guadeloupe
Pointe-Noire *77 B6* Le Kouilou, S Congo
Point Lay *36 C2* Alaska, USA
Poitiers *90 B4 prev.* Poictiers, *anc.* Limonum. Vienne, W France
Poitou *90 B4 cultural region* W France
Pokhara *135 E3* Western, C Nepal
Pokrovs'ke *109 G3 Rus.* Pokrovskoye. Dnipropetrovs'ka Oblast', E Ukraine
Pola de Lena *92 D1* Asturias, N Spain
Poland *98 B4 var.* Polish Republic, *Pol.* Polska, Rzeczpospolita Polska; *prev. Pol.* Polska Rzeczpospolita Ludowa, Polish People's Republic. *Country* C Europe

Poland 98

Official name Republic of Poland
Formation 1918
Capital Warsaw
Population 38.6 million / 328 people per sq mile (127 people per sq km)
Total area 120,728 sq. miles (312,685 sq. km)
Languages Polish
Religions Roman Catholic 93%, Other and nonreligious 5%, Orthodox Christian 2%
Ethnic mix Polish 97%, other 2%, Silesian 1%
Government Parliamentary system
Currency Zloty = 100 groszy
Literacy rate 99%
Calorie consumption 3397 calories

Poland *81 E3* Kiritimati, E Kiribati
Polatlı *116 C3* Ankara, C Turkey
Polatsk *107 D5 Rus.* Polotsk. Vitsyebskaya Voblasts', N Belarus
Pol-e Khomrī *123 E4 var.* Pul-i-Khumri. Baghlān, NE Afghanistan
Poli *see* Pólis
Polikastro *see* Polýkastro
Políkastron *see* Polýkastro
Polikrayshte *104 D2* Veliko Tŭrnovo, N Bulgaria
Pólis *102 C5 var.* Poli. W Cyprus
Polkowice *98 B4 Ger.* Heerwegen. Dolnośląskie, SW Poland
Pollença *93 G3 var.* Pollensa. Mallorca, Spain, W Mediterranean Sea
Pollensa *see* Pollença
Polohy *109 G3 Rus.* Pologi. Zaporiz'ka Oblast', SE Ukraine
Polokwane *78 D4 Var.* Pietersburg, NE South Africa
Polonne *108 D2 Rus.* Polonnoye. Khmel'nyts'ka Oblast', NW Ukraine
Polsko Kosovo *104 D2* Ruse, N Bulgaria
Poltava *109 F2* Poltavs'ka Oblast', NE Ukraine
Põlva *106 E3 Ger.* Pölwe. Põlvamaa, SE Estonia
Polyarnyy *110 C2* Murmanskaya Oblast', NW Russian Federation
Polýkastro *104 B3 var.* Polikastro; *prev.* Políkastron. Kentrikí Makedonía, N Greece
Polynesia *143 F4 island group* C Pacific Ocean
Pomeranian Bay *94 D2 Ger.* Pommersche Bucht, *Pol.* Zatoka Pomorska. *Bay* Germany/Poland
Pomorskiy Proliv *110 D2 strait* NW Russian Federation
Pompano Beach *43 F5* Florida, SE USA
Ponca City *49 G1* Oklahoma, C USA
Ponce *55 F3* C Puerto Rico
Pondicherry *132 C2 var.* Puduchcheri, *Fr.* Pondichéry. Pondicherry, SE India
Pondichéry *see* Pondicherry
Ponferrada *92 C1* Castilla-León, NW Spain
Poniatowa *98 E4* Lublin, E Poland
Pons Aelii *see* Newcastle upon Tyne
Ponta Delgada *92 B5* São Miguel, Azores, Portugal, NE Atlantic Ocean
Ponta Grossa *63 E4* Paraná, S Brazil
Pontarlier *90 D4* Doubs, E France
Ponteareas *92 B2* Galicia, NW Spain
Ponte da Barca *92 B2* Viana do Castelo, N Portugal
Pontevedra *92 B1 anc.* Pons Vetus. Galicia, NW Spain
Pontiac *40 D3* Michigan, N USA
Pontianak *138 C4* Borneo, C Indonesia
Pontivy *90 A3* Morbihan, NW France
Pontoise *90 C3 anc.* Briva Isarae, Cergy-Pontoise, Pontisarae. Val-d'Oise, N France
Ponziane, Isole *97 C5 island* C Italy
Poole *89 D7* S England, UK
Poopó, Lago *61 F4 var.* Lago Pampa Aullagas. *Lake* W Bolivia
Popayán *58 B4* Cauca, SW Colombia
Poperinge *87 A6* West-Vlaanderen, W Belgium
Poplar Bluff *45 G5* Missouri, C USA
Popocatépetl *51 E4 volcano* S Mexico
Poprad *99 D5 Ger.* Deutschendorf, *Hung.* Poprád. Prešovský Kraj, E Slovakia
Poprad *99 D5 Ger.* Popper, *Hung.* Poprád. *River* Poland/Slovakia
Porbandar *134 B4* Gujarāt, W India
Porcupine Plain *80 B3 undersea feature* E Atlantic Ocean
Pordenone *96 C2 anc.* Portenau. Friuli-Venezia Giulia, NE Italy
Poreč *100 A2 It.* Parenzo. Istra, NW Croatia
Pori *85 D5 Swe.* Björneborg. Länsi-Suomi, W Finland
Porirua *151 D5* Wellington, North Island, NZ
Porkhov *110 A4* Pskovskaya Oblast', W Russian Federation
Porlamar *59 E1* Nueva Esparta, NE Venezuela
Póros *105 A5* Kefallinía, Iónioi Nísoi, Greece, C Mediterranean Sea
Póros *105 C6* Póros, S Greece
Porsangerfjorden *84 D2 fjord* N Norway
Porsgrunn *85 B6* Telemark, S Norway
Portachuelo *61 G4* Santa Cruz, C Bolivia
Portadown *89 B5 Ir.* Port An Dúnáin. S Northern Ireland, UK
Portalegre *92 C3 anc.* Ammaia, Amoea. Portalegre, E Portugal
Port Alexander *36 D4* Baranof Island, Alaska, USA
Port Alfred *78 D5* Eastern Cape, S South Africa
Port An Dúnáin *see* Portadown
Port Angeles *46 B1* Washington, NW USA
Port Antonio *54 B5* NE Jamaica
Port Arthur *49 H4* Texas, SW USA
Port Augusta *149 B6* South Australia
Port-au-Prince *54 D3 country capital* (Haiti) C Haiti
Port-au-Prince *35 D7 international airport* E Haiti
Port Blair *133 F2* Andaman and Nicobar Islands, SE India
Port Charlotte *43 E4* Florida, SE USA
Port d'Envalira *91 B8* E Andorra
Port Douglas *148 D3* Queensland, NE Australia
Port Elizabeth *78 C5* Eastern Cape, S South Africa
Porterville *47 C7* California, W USA
Port-Gentil *77 A6* Ogooué-Maritime, W Gabon
Port Harcourt *75 G5* Rivers, S Nigeria
Port Hardy *36 D5* Vancouver Island, British Columbia, SW Canada
Port Harrison *see* Inukjuak
Port Hedland *146 B4* Western Australia
Port Huron *40 D3* Michigan, N USA
Portimão *92 B4 var.* Vila Nova de Portimão. Faro, S Portugal
Port Jackson *148 E1 harbour* New South Wales, SE Australia
Port Láirge *see* Waterford
Portland *41 G2* Maine, NE USA
Portland *46 B3* Oregon, NW USA
Portland *49 G4* Texas, SW USA
Portland *149 B7* Victoria, SE Australia
Portland Bight *54 B5 bay* S Jamaica

Portlaoighise *see* Portlaoise
Portlaoise *89 B6 Ir.* Portlaoighise; *prev.* Maryborough. C Ireland
Port Lavaca *49 G4* Texas, SW USA
Port Lincoln *149 A6* South Australia
Port Louis *79 H3 country capital* (Mauritius) NW Mauritius
Port Macquarie *149 E6* New South Wales, SE Australia
Portmore *54 B5* C Jamaica
Port Moresby *144 B3 country capital* (PNG) Central/National Capital District, SW PNG
Port Musgrave *149 B9 bay* Queensland, N Australia
Port Natal *see* Durban
Porto *92 B2 Eng.* Oporto; *anc.* Portus Cale. Porto, NW Portugal
Porto Alegre *63 E5 var.* Pôrto Alegre. *State capital* Rio Grande do Sul, S Brazil
Porto Alegre *76 E2* São Tomé, S Sao Tome and Principe
Porto Bello *see* Portobelo
Portobelo *53 G4 var.* Porto Bello, Puerto Bello. Colón, N Panama
Port O'Connor *49 G4* Texas, SW USA
Porto Edda *see* Sarandë
Portoferraio *96 B4* Toscana, C Italy
Port-of-Spain *55 H5 country capital* (Trinidad and Tobago) Trinidad, Trinidad and Tobago
Porto Grande *see* Mindelo
Portogruaro *96 C2* Veneto, NE Italy
Porto-Novo *75 F5 country capital* (Benin) S Benin
Porto Santo *70 A2 var.* Ilha do Porto Santo. *Island* Madeira, Portugal, NE Atlantic Ocean
Porto Torres *97 A5* Sardegna, Italy, C Mediterranean Sea
Porto Velho *62 D2 var.* Velho. *State capital* Rondônia, W Brazil
Portoviejo *60 A2 var.* Puertoviejo. Manabí, W Ecuador
Port Pirie *149 B6* South Australia
Port Said *72 B1 Ar.* Būr Sa'īd. N Egypt
Portsmouth *41 G3* New Hampshire, NE USA
Portsmouth *40 D4* Ohio, N USA
Portsmouth *89 D7* S England, UK
Portsmouth *41 F5* Virginia, NE USA
Port Stanley *see* Stanley
Port Sudan *72 C3* Red Sea, NE Sudan
Port Swettenham *see* Klang
Port Talbot *89 C7* S Wales, UK
Portugal *92 B3 Country* SW Europe

Portugal 92

Official name Republic of Portugal
Formation 1139
Capital Lisbon
Population 10.1 million / 284 people per sq mile (110 people per sq km)
Total area 35,672 sq. miles (92,391 sq. km)
Languages Portuguese
Religions Roman Catholic 97%, other 2%, Protestant 1%
Ethnic mix Portuguese 98%, African and other 2%
Government Parliamentary system
Currency Euro = 100 cents
Literacy rate 93%
Calorie consumption 3751 calories

Portuguese Timor *see* East Timor
Port-Vila *144 D4 var.* Vila. *Country capital* (Vanuatu) Éfaté, C Vanuatu
Porvenir *65 B8* Magallanes, S Chile
Porvenir *61 E3* Pando, NW Bolivia
Porvoo *85 E6 Swe.* Borgå. Etelä-Suomi, S Finland
Posadas *64 D3* Misiones, NE Argentina
Poschega *see* Požega
Posterholt *87 D5* Limburg, SE Netherlands
Postojna *95 D8 Ger.* Adelsberg, *It.* Postumia. SW Slovenia
Potamós *105 C7* Antikýthira, S Greece
Potenza *97 D5 anc.* Potentia. Basilicata, S Italy
P'ot'i *117 F2* W Georgia
Potiskum *75 G4* Yobe, NE Nigeria
Potomac River *41 E5 river* NE USA
Potosí *61 F4* Potosí, S Bolivia
Potsdam *94 D3* Brandenburg, NE Germany
Potwar Plateau *134 C2 plateau* NE Pakistan
Poŭthĭsăt *137 D6 prev.* Pursat. Poŭthĭsăt, W Cambodia
Po Valley *96 C2 It.* Valle del Po. *Valley* N Italy
Považská Bystrica *99 C5 Ger.* Waagbistritz, *Hung.* Vágbeszterce. Trenčiansky Kraj, W Slovakia
Poverty Bay *150 E4 inlet* North Island, NZ
Póvoa de Varzim *92 B2* Porto, NW Portugal
Powder River *44 D2 river* Montana/Wyoming, NW USA
Powell *44 C2* Wyoming, C USA
Powell, Lake *44 B5 lake* Utah, W USA
Požarevac *100 D4 Ger.* Passarowitz. Serbia, NE Serbia and Montenegro (Yugo.)
Poza Rica *51 F4 var.* Poza Rica de Hidalgo. Veracruz-Llave, E Mexico
Poza Rica de Hidalgo *see* Poza Rica
Požega *100 D4 prev.* Slavonska Požega. *Ger.* Poschega, *Hung.* Pozsega. Požega-Slavonija, NE Croatia
Pozsega *see* Požega
Poznań *98 C3 Ger.* Posen, Posnania. Wielkopolskie, C Poland
Pozoblanco *92 D4* Andalucía, S Spain
Pozzallo *97 C8* Sicilia, Italy, C Mediterranean Sea
Prachatice *99 A5 Ger.* Prachatitz. Budějovický Kraj, S Czech Republic
Prado del Ganso *see* Goose Green
Prae *see* Phrae
Prague *80 D3* Oklahoma, C USA
Praha *99 A5 Eng.* Prague, *Ger.* Prag, *Pol.* Praga. *Country capital* (Czech Republic) Středočesky Kraj, NW Czech Republic
Praia *74 A3 country capital* (Cape Verde) Santiago, S Cape Verde
Prato *96 B3* Toscana, C Italy
Pratt *45 E5* Kansas, C USA
Prattville *42 D2* Alabama, S USA
Pravda *104 D1 prev.* Dogrular. Silistra, NE Bulgaria
Pravia *92 C1* Asturias, N Spain
Prenzlau *94 D3* Brandenburg, NE Germany
Přerov *99 C5 Ger.* Prerau. Olomoucký Kraj, E Czech Republic
Presa de la Amistad *see* Amistad Reservoir
Preschau *see* Prešov
Prescott *48 B2* Arizona, SW USA
Preševo *101 D5* Serbia, SE Serbia and Montenegro (Yugo.)
Presidente Epitácio *63 E4* São Paulo, S Brazil
Prešov *99 D5 var.* Preschau, *Ger.* Eperies, *Hung.* Eperjes. Prešouský Kraj, E Slovakia
Prespa, Lake *101 D6 Alb.* Liqen i Prespës, *Gk.* Límni Megáli Préspa, Limni Prespa, *Mac.* Prespansko Ezero, *Serb.* Prespansko Jezero. *Lake* SE Europe
Presque Isle *41 H1* Maine, NE USA
Preston *89 D5* NW England, UK
Prestwick *88 C4* W Scotland, UK
Pretoria *78 D4 var.* Epitoli, Tshwane. *Country capital*(South Africa-administrative capital) Gauteng, NE South Africa
Préveza *105 A5* Ípeiros, W Greece
Pribilof Islands *36 A3 island group* Alaska, USA
Priboj *100 C4* Serbia, W Serbia and Montenegro (Yugo.)
Price *44 B4* Utah, W USA
Prichard *42 C3* Alabama, S USA
Priekulė *106 B3 Ger.* Prökuls. Gargždai, W Lithuania
Prienai *107 B5 Pol.* Preny. Prienai, S Lithuania
Prieska *78 C4* Northern Cape, C South Africa
Prijedor *100 B3* Republika Srpska, NW Bosnia and Herzegovina
Prijepolje *100 D4* Serbia, W Serbia and Montenegro (Yugo.)
Prilep *101 D6 Turk.* Perlepe. S FYR Macedonia
Primorsk *106 A4 Ger.* Fischhausen. Kaliningradskaya Oblast', W Russian Federation
Primorsko *104 E2 prev.* Keupriya. Burgas, E Bulgaria
Prince Albert *37 F5* Saskatchewan, S Canada
Prince Edward Island *39 F4 Fr.* Île-du Prince-Édouard. *Province* SE Canada
Prince Edward Islands *69 E8 island group* S South Africa
Prince George *37 E5* British Columbia, SW Canada
Prince of Wales Island *37 F2 island* Queen Elizabeth Islands, Nunavut, NW Canada
Prince of Wales Island *148 B1 island* Queensland, E Australia
Prince Patrick Island *37 E2 island* Parry Islands, Northwest Territories, NW Canada
Prince Rupert *36 D4* British Columbia, SW Canada
Prince's Island *see* Príncipe
Princess Charlotte Bay *148 C2 bay* Queensland, NE Australia
Princess Elizabeth Land *154 C3 physical region* Antarctica
Príncipe *77 A5 var.* Príncipe Island, *Eng.* Prince's Island. *Island* N Sao Tome and Principe
Príncipe Island *see* Príncipe
Prinzapolka *53 E3* Región Autónoma Atlántico Norte, NE Nicaragua
Pripet *107 C7 Bel.* Prypyats', *Ukr.* Pryp"yat'. *River* Belarus/Ukraine
Pripet Marshes *107 B7 wetland* Belarus/Ukraine
Priština *101 D5 Alb.* Prishtinë. Serbia, S Serbia and Montenegro (Yugo.)
Privas *91 D5* Ardèche, E France
Prizren *101 D5 Alb.* Prizreni. Serbia, S Serbia and Montenegro (Yugo.)
Probolinggo *138 D5* Jawa, C Indonesia
Progreso *51 H3* Yucatán, SE Mexico
Prokhladnyy *111 B8* Kabardino-Balkarskaya Respublika, SW Russian Federation
Prokuplje *101 D5* Serbia, SE Serbia and Montenegro (Yugo.)
Prome *136 B4 var.* Pyè. Pegu, C Myanmar
Promyshlennyy *110 E3* Respublika Komi, NW Russian Federation
Prostějov *99 C5 Ger.* Prossnitz, *Pol.* Prościejów. Olomoucký Kraj, E Czech Republic
Provence *91 D6 cultural region* SE France
Providence *see* Fort Providence
Providence *41 G3 state capital* Rhode Island, NE USA
Providencia, Isla de *53 F3 island* NW Colombia
Provideniya *172 B1* Chukotskiy Avtonomnyy Okrug, NE Russian Federation
Provo *44 B4* Utah, W USA
Prudhoe Bay *36 D2* Alaska, USA
Prusa *see* Bursa
Pruszków *98 D3 Ger.* Kaltdorf. Mazowieckie, C Poland
Prut *108 D4 Ger.* Pruth. *River* E Europe
Pruzhany *107 B6 Pol.* Prużana. Brestskaya Voblasts', SW Belarus
Prydz Bay *154 D3 bay* Antarctica
Pryluky *109 E2 Rus.* Priluki. Chernihivs'ka Oblast', NE Ukraine
Prymors'k *109 G4 Rus.* Primorsk; *prev.* Primorskoye. Zaporiz'ka Oblast', SE Ukraine
Przemysl *99 E5 Rus.* Peremyshl. Podkarpackie, SE Poland
Psará *105 D5 island* E Greece
Psël *109 F2 river* Russian Federation/Ukraine
Pskov *114 B2 Ger.* Pleskau, *Latv.* Pleskava. Pskovskaya Oblast', W Russian Federation
Pskov, Lake *E3 Est.* Pihkva Järv, *Ger.* Pleskauer See, *Rus.* Pskovskoye Ozero. *Lake* Estonia/Russian Federation
Ptsich *107 C7 Rus.* Ptich'. *River* SE Belarus
Ptsich *107 C7 Rus.* Ptich'. Homyel'skaya Voblasts', SE Belarus
Ptuj *95 E7 Ger.* Pettau; *anc.* Poetovio. NE Slovenia
Pucallpa *60 C3* Ucayali, C Peru
Puck *98 C2* Pomorskie, N Poland
Pudasjärvi *84 D4* Oulu, C Finland
Puduchcheri *see* Pondicherry
Puebla *51 F4 var.* Puebla de Zaragoza. Puebla, S Mexico
Puebla de Zaragoza *see* Puebla
Pueblo *44 D5* Colorado, C USA
Puerto Acosta *61 E4* La Paz, W Bolivia
Puerto Aisén *65 B6* Aisén, S Chile
Puerto Ángel *51 F5* Oaxaca, SE Mexico
Puerto Argentino *see* Stanley
Puerto Ayacucho *58 D3* Amazonas, SW Venezuela
Puerto Baquerizo Moreno *60 B5 var.* Baquerizo Moreno. Galapagos Islands, Ecuador, E Pacific Ocean
Puerto Barrios *52 C2* Izabal, E Guatemala
Puerto Bello *see* Portobelo
Puerto Berrío *58 B2* Antioquia, C Colombia
Puerto Cabello *58 D1* Carabobo, N Venezuela
Puerto Cabezas *53 E2 var.* Bilwi. Región Autónoma Atlántico Norte, NE Nicaragua
Puerto Carreño *58 D3* Vichada, E Colombia
Puerto Cortés *52 C2* Cortés, NW Honduras
Puerto Cumarebo *58 C1* Falcón, N Venezuela
Puerto Deseado *65 C7* Santa Cruz, SE Argentina
Puerto Escondido *51 F5* Oaxaca, SE Mexico
Puerto Francisco de Orellana *60 B1 var.* Coca. Napo, N Ecuador
Puerto Gallegos *see* Río Gallegos
Puerto Inírida *58 D3 var.* Obando. Guainía, E Colombia
Puerto La Cruz *59 E1* Anzoátegui, NE Venezuela
Puerto Lempira *53 E2* Gracias a Dios, E Honduras
Puerto Limón *see* Limón
Puertollano *92 D4* Castilla-La Mancha, C Spain
Puerto López *58 C1* La Guajira, N Colombia
Puerto Maldonado *61 E3* Madre de Dios, E Peru
Puerto México *see* Coatzacoalcos
Puerto Montt *65 B5* Los Lagos, C Chile
Puerto Natales *65 B7* Magallanes, S Chile
Puerto Obaldía *53 H5* San Blas, NE Panama
Puerto Plata *55 E3 var.* San Felipe de Puerto Plata. N Dominican Republic
Puerto Princesa *139 E2 off.* Puerto Princesa City. Palawan, W Philippines

Puerto Rico *55 F3 off.* Commonwealth of Puerto Rico; *prev.* Porto Rico. *US commonwealth territory* C West Indies
Puerto Rico *56 B1 island* C West Indies
Puerto Rico Trench *56 B1 undersea feature* NE Caribbean Sea
Puerto San José *see* San José
Puerto San Julián *65 B7 var.* San Julián. Santa Cruz, SE Argentina
Puerto Suárez *61 H4* Santa Cruz, E Bolivia
Puerto Vallarta *50 D4* Jalisco, SW Mexico
Puerto Varas *65 B5* Los Lagos, C Chile
Puerto Viejo *53 E4* Heredia, NE Costa Rica
Puertoviejo *see* Portoviejo
Puget Sound *46 B1 sound* Washington, NW USA
Puglia *97 E5 Eng.* Apulia. *Cultural region* SE Italy
Pukaki, Lake *151 B6 lake* South Island, NZ
Pukekohe *150 D3* Auckland, North Island, NZ
Puket *see* Phuket
Pukhavichy *107 C6 Rus.* Pukhovichi. Minskaya Voblasts', C Belarus
Pula *100 A3 It.* Pola; *prev.* Pulj. Istra, NW Croatia
Pulaski *40 D5* Virginia, NE USA
Pulau Butung *see* Buton, Pulau
Puławy *98 D4 Ger.* Neu Amerika. Lublin, E Poland
Pul-i-Khumri *see* Pol-e Khomrī
Pullman *46 C2* Washington, NW USA
Pułtusk *98 D3* Mazowieckie, C Poland
Puná, Isla *60 A2 island* SW Ecuador
Pune *134 C5 prev.* Poona. Mahārāshtra, W India
Punjab *134 C2 prev.* West Punjab, Western Punjab. *Province* E Pakistan
Puno *61 E4* Puno, SE Peru
Punta Alta *65 C5* Buenos Aires, E Argentina
Punta Arenas *65 B8 prev.* Magallanes. Magallanes, S Chile
Punta Gorda *53 E4* Región Autónoma Atlántico Sur, SE Nicaragua
Punta Gorda *52 C2* Toledo, SE Belize
Puntarenas *52 D4* Puntarenas, W Costa Rica
Punto Fijo *58 C1* Falcón, N Venezuela
Pupuya, Nevado *61 E4 mountain* W Bolivia
Puri *135 F5 var.* Jagannath. Orissa, E India
Puriramya *see* Buriram
Purmerend *86 C3* Noord-Holland, C Netherlands
Purus, Rio *62 C2 Sp.* Río Purús. *River* Brazil/Peru
Pusan *129 E4 off.* Pusan-gwangyŏksi, *var.* Busan, *Jap.* Fusan. SE South Korea
Püspökladány *99 D6* Hajdú-Bihar, E Hungary
Putorana Mountains *see* Putorana, Plato
Putorana, Plato *114 D3 var.* Gory Putorana, *Eng.* Putorana Mountains. *Mountain range* N Russian Federation
Putrajaya *138 B3 country capital* (Malaysia) Kuala Lumpur, Peninsular Malaysia
Puttalam *132 C3* North Western Province, W Sri Lanka
Puttgarden *94 C2* Schleswig-Holstein, N Germany
Putumayo, Río *58 B5 var.* Rio Içá. *River* NW South America *see also* Içá, Rio
Putumayo, Río *see* Içá, Rio
Puurmani *106 D2 Ger.* Talkhof. Jõgevamaa, E Estonia
Pyatigorsk *111 B7* Stavropol'skiy Kray, SW Russian Federation
P"yatykhatky *109 F3 Rus.* Pyatikhatki. Dnipropetrovs'ka Oblast', E Ukraine
Pyè *see* Prome
Pyetrykaw *107 C7 Rus.* Petrikov. Homyel'skaya Voblasts', SE Belarus
Pyinmana *136 B4* Mandalay, C Myanmar
Pýlos *105 B6 var.* Pilos. Pelopónnisos, S Greece
P'yŏngyang *129 E3 var.* P'yŏngyang-si, *Eng.* Pyongyang. *Country capital* (North Korea) SW North Korea
P'yŏngyang-si *see* P'yŏngyang
Pyramid Lake *47 C5 lake* Nevada, W USA
Pyrenees *102 B2 Fr.* Pyrénées, *Sp.* Pirineos; *anc.* Pyrenaei Montes. *Mountain range* SW Europe
Pýrgos *105 B6 var.* Pírgos. Dytikí Ellás, S Greece
Pyryatyn *109 E2 Rus.* Piryatin. Poltavs'ka Oblast', NE Ukraine
Pyrzyce *98 B3 Ger.* Pyritz. Zachodniopomorskie, NW Poland
Pyu *136 B4* Pegu, C Myanmar
Pyuntaza *136 B4* Pegu, SW Myanmar

Q

Qā' al Jafr *119 C7 lake* S Jordan
Qaanaaq *82 D1 var.* Qânâq, *Dan.* Thule. N Greenland
Qabātiya *119 E6* N West Bank
Qābis *see* Gabès
Qacentina *see* Constantine
Qafṣah *see* Gafsa
Qagan Us *see* Dulan
Qahremānshahr *see* Kermānshāh
Qaidam Pendi *126 C4 basin* C China
Qal'aikhum *123 F3 Rus.* Kalaikhum. S Tajikistan
Qal'at Bīshah *121 B5* 'Asīr, SW Saudi Arabia
Qalqīlya *119 D6* N West Bank
Qamdo *126 D5* Xizang Zizhiqu, W China
Qamishly *see* Al Qāmishlī
Qânâq *see* Qaanaaq
Qaqortoq *82 C4 Dan.* Julianehåb. S Greenland
Qara Qum *see* Garagum
Qarkilik *see* Ruoqiang
Qarokŭl *123 F3 Rus.* Karakul'. E Tajikistan
Qars *see* Kars
Qarshi *123 E3 Rus.* Karshi; *prev.* Bek-Budi. Qashqadaryo Wiloyati, S Uzbekistan
Qasigianguit *see* Qasigiannguit
Qasigiannguit *82 C3 var.* Qasigianguit, *Dan.* Christianshåb. C Greenland
Qasr Farâfra *72 B2* W Egypt
Qaṭanā *119 B5 var.* Katana. Dimashq, S Syria
Qatar *120 C4 Ar.* Dawlat Qaṭar. *Country* SW Asia

Qatar 120

Official name State of Qatar
Formation 1971
Capital Doha
Population 610,000 / 144 people per sq mile (55 people per sq km)
Total area 4416 sq. miles (11,437 sq. km)
Languages Arabic
Religions Muslim (mainly Sunni) 95%, other 5%
Ethnic mix Arab 40%, Indian 18%, Pakistani 18%, other 14%, Iranian 10%
Government Monarchy
Currency Qatar riyal = 100 dirhams
Literacy rate 82%
Calorie consumption Not available

Qattara Depression *see* Qaṭṭâra, Monkhafad el
Qaṭṭâra, Monkhafad el *88 A1 var.* Munkhafaḍ al Qaṭṭārah, *Eng.* Qattara Depression. *Desert* NW Egypt
Qazimämmäd *117 H3 Rus.* Kazi Magomed. SE Azerbaijan
Qazvīn *120 C2 var.* Kazvin. Qazvin, N Iran
Qena *72 B2 var.* Qinā; *anc.* Caene, Caenepolis. E Egypt
Qeqertarssuaq *see* Qeqertarsuaq
Qeqertarsuaq *82 C3 var.* Qeqertarssuaq, *Dan.* Godhavn. S Greenland
Qeqertarsuaq *82 C3 island* W Greenland
Qeqertarsuup Tunua *82 C3 Dan.* Disko Bugt. *Inlet* W Greenland
Qerveh *see* Qorveh
Qeshm *120 D4 var.* Jazīreh-ye Qeshm, Qeshm Island. *Island* S Iran
Qeshm Island *see* Qeshm
Qian *see* Guizhou
Qilian Shan *126 D3 var.* Kilien Mountains. *Mountain range* N China
Qimusseriarsuaq *82 C2 Dan.* Melville Bugt, *Eng.* Melville Bay. *Bay* NW Greenland
Qinā *see* Qena
Qing *see* Qinghai
Qingdao *128 D4 var.* Ching-Tao, Ch'ing-tao, Tsingtao, Tsintao, *Ger.* Tsingtau. Shandong, E China
Qinghai *126 C4 var.* Chinghai, Koko Nor, Qing, Qinghai Sheng, Tsinghai. Admin. region *province* C China
Qinghai Hu *126 D4 var.* Ch'ing Hai, Tsing Hai, *Mong.* Koko *Nor. lake* C China
Qinghai Sheng *see* Qinghai
Qingzang Gaoyuan *126 B4 var.* Xizang Gaoyuan, *Eng.* Plateau of Tibet. *Plateau* W China
Qinhuangdao *128 D3* Hebei, E China
Qinzhou *128 B6* Guangxi Zhuangzu Zizhiqu, S China
Qiong *see* Hainan
Qiqihar *128 D2 var.* Ch'i-ch'i-ha-erh, Tsitsihar; *prev.* Lungkiang. Heilongjiang, NE China
Qira *126 B4* Xinjiang Uygur Zizhiqu, NW China
Qitai *126 C3* Xinjiang Uygur Zizhiqu, NW China
Qīzān *see* Jīzān
Qizil Orda *see* Kyzylorda
Qizil Qum *see* Kyzyl Kum
Qizilrabot *123 G3 Rus.* Kyzylrabot. SE Tajikistan
Qom *120 C3 var.* Kum, Qum. Qom, N Iran
Qomul *see* Hami
Qondūz *see* Kunduz
Qo'qon *123 F2 var.* Khokand, Qŭqon, *Rus.* Kokand. Farghona Wiloyati, E Uzbekistan
Qorveh *120 C3 var.* Qerveh, Qurveh. Kordestān, W Iran
Qostanay *see* Kostanay
Qoubaïyât *118 B4 var.* Al Qubayyāt. N Lebanon
Qoussantîna *see* Constantine
Quang Ngai *137 E5 var.* Quangngai, Quang Nghia. Quang Ngai, C Vietnam
Quangngai *see* Quang Ngai
Quang Nghia *see* Quang Ngai
Quanzhou *128 D6 var.* Ch'uan-chou, Tsinkiang; *prev.* Chin-chiang. Fujian, SE China
Quanzhou *128 C6* Guangxi Zhuangzu Zizhiqu, S China
Qu'Appelle *37 F5 river* Saskatchewan, S Canada
Quarles, Pegunungan *139 E4 mountain range* Sulawesi, C Indonesia
Quarnero *see* Kvarner
Quartu Sant' Elena *97 A6* Sardegna, Italy, C Mediterranean Sea
Quba *117 H2 Rus.* Kuba. N Azerbaijan
Qubba *see* Ba'qūbah
Québec *39 E4 var.* Quebec. Québec, SE Canada
Quebec *38 D3 var.* Quebec. Admin. region *province* SE Canada
Queen Charlotte Islands *36 C5 Fr.* Îles de la Reine-Charlotte. *Island group* British Columbia, SW Canada
Queen Charlotte Sound *36 C5 sea area* British Columbia, W Canada
Queen Elizabeth Islands *37 E1 Fr.* Îles de la Reine-Élisabeth. *Island group* Northwest Territories/Nunavut, N Canada
Queensland *148 B4 state* N Australia
Queenstown *78 D5* Eastern Cape, S South Africa
Queenstown *151 B7* Otago, South Island, NZ
Quelimane *79 E3 var.* Kilimane, Kilmain, Quilimane. Zambézia, NE Mozambique
Quepos *53 E4* Puntarenas, S Costa Rica
Querétaro *51 E4* Querétaro de Arteaga, C Mexico
Quesada *53 E4 var.* Ciudad Quesada, San Carlos. Alajuela, N Costa Rica
Quetta *134 B2* Baluchistān, SW Pakistan
Quetzalcoalco *see* Coatzacoalcos
Quetzaltenango *see* Quezaltenango
Quezaltenango *52 A2 var.* Quetzaltenango. Quezaltenango, W Guatemala
Quibdó *58 A3* Chocó, W Colombia
Quilimane *see* Quelimane
Quillabamba *60 D3* Cusco, C Peru
Quilon *132 C3 var.* Kolam, Kollam. Kerala, SW India
Quimper *90 A3 anc.* Quimper Corentin. Finistère, NW France
Quimperlé *90 A3* Finistère, NW France
Quincy *40 A4* Illinois, N USA
Qui Nhon *see* Quy Nhơn
Quissico *79 E4* Inhambane, S Mozambique
Quito *60 B1 country capital* (Ecuador) Pichincha, N Ecuador
Qullai Garmo *see* Kommunizm, Qullai
Qum *see* Qom
Qunaytra *see* Al Qunayṭirah
Qŭqon *see* Qo'qon
Qurein *see* Al Kuwayt
Qŭrghonteppa *123 E3 Rus.* Kurgan-Tyube. SW Tajikistan
Qurlurtuuq *see* Kugluktuk
Qurveh *see* Qorveh
Quṣayr *see* Al Quṣayr
Quy Nhơn *137 E5 var.* Quinhon, Qui Nhon. Binh Đinh, C Vietnam
Qyteti Stalin *see* Kuçovë
Qyzylorda *see* Kyzylorda

R

Raab *100 B1 Hung.* Rába. *River* Austria/Hungary *see also* Rába
Raahe *84 D4 Swe.* Brahestad. Oulu, W Finland
Raalte *86 D3* Overijssel, E Netherlands
Raamsdonksveer *86 C4* Noord-Brabant, S Netherlands
Raasiku *106 D2 Ger.* Rasik. Harjumaa, NW Estonia
Rába *99 B7 Ger.* Raab. *River* Austria/Hungary *see also* Raab
Rabat *70 C2 var.* al Dar al Baida. *Country capital* (Morocco) NW Morocco
Rabat *see* Victoria
Rabat *102 B5* W Malta
Rabbah Ammon *see* 'Ammān
Rabbath Ammon *see* 'Ammān
Rabinal *52 B2* Baja Verapaz, C Guatemala
Rabka *99 D5* Małopolskie, S Poland
Râbniṭa *see* Rîbniṭa
Rabyanāh, Ramlat *71 G4 var.* Rebiana Sand Sea, ṣaḥrā' Rabyanāh. *Desert* SE Libya

Race, Cape *39 H3 headland* Newfoundland, Newfoundland and Labrador, E Canada
Rach Gia *137 D6* Kiên Giang, S Vietnam
Rach Gia, Vinh *137 D6 bay* S Vietnam
Racine *40 B3* Wisconsin, N USA
Rădăuţi *108 C3 Ger.* Radautz, *Hung.* Rádóc. Suceava, N Romania
Radom *98 D4* Mazowieckie, C Poland
Radomsko *98 D4 Rus.* Novoradomsk. Łódzkie, C Poland
Radomyshl' *108 D2* Zhytomyrs'ka Oblast', N Ukraine
Radoviš *101 E6 prev.* Radovište. E FYR Macedonia
Radviliškis *106 B4* Radviliškis, N Lithuania
Radzyń Podlaski *98 E4* Lubelskie, E Poland
Rae-Edzo *see* Edzo
Raetihi *150 D4* Manawatu-Wanganui, North Island, NZ
Rafa *see* Rafah
Rafaela *64 C3* Santa Fe, E Argentina
Rafah *119 A7 var.* Rafa, Rafaḥ, *Heb.* Rafiah, Raphiah. SW Gaza Strip
Rafaḥ *see* Rafah
Rafḥah *120 B4* Al Ḥudūd ash Shamālīyah, N Saudi Arabia
Rafiah *see* Rafah
Raga *73 A5* Western Bahr el Ghazal, SW Sudan
Ragged Island Range *54 C2 island group* S Bahamas
Ragusa *97 C7* Sicilia, Italy, C Mediterranean Sea
Rahachow *107 D7 Rus.* Rogachëv. Homyel'skaya Voblasts', SE Belarus
Rahaeng *see* Tak
Rahaţ, Ḩarrat *121 B5 lavaflow* W Saudi Arabia
Rahīmyār Khān *134 C3* Punjab, SE Pakistan
Raiatea *145 G4 island* Îles Sous le Vent, W French Polynesia
Rāichūr *132 C1* Karnātaka, C India
Rainier, Mount *34 A4 volcano* Washington, NW USA
Rainy Lake *38 A4 lake* Canada/USA
Raipur *135 E4* Madhya Pradesh, C India
Rājahmundry *135 E5* Andhra Pradesh, E India
Rajang *see* Rajang, Batang
Rajang, Batang *138 D3 var.* Rajang. *River* East Malaysia
Rājapālaiyam *132 C3* Tamil Nādu, SE India
Rājasthān *134 C3 state* NW India
Rājkot *134 C4* Gujarāt, W India
Rāj Nāndgaon *135 E4* Madhya Pradesh, C India
Rajshahi *135 G3 prev.* Rampur Boalia. Rajshahi, W Bangladesh
Rakahanga *145 F3 atoll* N Cook Islands
Rakaia *151 B6 river* South Island, NZ
Rakka *see* Ar Raqqah
Rakke *106 E2* Lääne-Virumaa, NE Estonia
Rakvere *106 E2 Ger.* Wesenberg. Lääne-Virumaa, N Estonia
Ralik Chain *144 D1 island group* Ralik Chain, W Marshall Islands
Ramadi *see* Ar Ramādī
Ramlat Ahl Wahībah *see* Wahībah, Ramlat Āl
Ramlat Al Wahaybah *see* Wahībah, Ramlat Āl
Râmnicu Sărat *108 C4 prev.* Râmnicul-Sărat, Rîmnicu-Sărat. Buzău, E Romania
Râmnicu Vâlcea *108 B4 prev.* Rîmnicu Vîlcea. Vâlcea, C Romania
Ramree Island *136 A4 island* W Myanmar
Ramtha *see* Ar Ramthā
Rancagua *64 B4* Libertador, C Chile
Rānchi *135 F4* Bihār, N India
Randers *85 B7* Århus, C Denmark
Rangiora *151 C6* Canterbury, South Island, NZ
Rangitikei *150 D4 river* North Island, NZ
Rangoon *see* Yangon
Rangpur *135 G3* Rajshahi, N Bangladesh
Rankin Inlet *37 G3* Nunavut, C Canada
Ranong *137 B6* Ranong, SW Thailand
Rapa Nui *see* Easter Island
Raphiah *see* Rafah
Rapid City *44 D3* South Dakota, N USA
Räpina *106 E3 Ger.* Rappin. Põlvamaa, SE Estonia
Rapla *106 D2 Ger.* Rappel. Raplamaa, NW Estonia
Rarotonga *145 G5 island* S Cook Islands, C Pacific Ocean
Ras al 'Ain *see* Ra's al 'Ayn
Ra's al 'Ayn *118 D1 var.* Ras al 'Ain. Al Ḩasakah, N Syria
Ra's an Naqb *119 B7* Ma'ān, S Jordan
Raseiniai *106 B4* Raseiniai, C Lithuania
Ras Hafun *see* Xaafuun, Raas
Rasht *120 C2 var.* Resht. Gīlān, NW Iran
Râşnov *108 C4 prev.* Rîşno, Rozsnyó, *Hung.* Barcarozsnyó. Braşov, C Romania
Ratak Chain *144 D1 island group* Ratak Chain, E Marshall Islands
Rätan *85 C5 var.* Ratan. Jämtland, C Sweden
Rat Buri *see* Ratchaburi
Ratchaburi *137 C5 var.* Rat Buri. Ratchaburi, W Thailand
Rastenburg *see* Kętrzyn
Rat Islands *36 A2 island group* Aleutian Islands, Alaska, USA
Ratlām *134 D4 prev.* Rutlam. Madhya Pradesh, C India
Ratnapura *132 D4* Sabaragamuwa Province, S Sri Lanka
Raton *48 D1* New Mexico, SW USA
Rättvik *85 C5* Kopparberg, C Sweden
Raudhatain *see* Ar Rawḍatayn
Raufarhöfn *83 E4* Nordhurland Eystra, NE Iceland
Raukawa *see* Cook Strait
Raukumara Range *150 E3 mountain range* North Island, NZ
Rāulakela 151 F4 *var* Rāurkela, *prev.* Rourkela. Orissa, E India
Rauma *85 D5 Swe.* Raumo. Länsi-Suomi, W Finland
Raurkela *see* Raulakela
Ravenna *96 C3* Emilia-Romagna, N Italy
Rāvi *134 C2 river* India/Pakistan
Rāwalpindi *134 C1* Punjab, NE Pakistan
Rawa Mazowiecka *98 D4* Łódzkie, C Poland
Rawicz *98 C4 Ger.* Rawitsch. Wielkopolskie, C Poland
Rawlins *44 C3* Wyoming, C USA
Rawson *65 C6* Chubut, SE Argentina
Rayak *118 B4 var.* Rayaq, Riyāq. E Lebanon
Rayaq *see* Rayak
Rayleigh *43 F1 state capital* North Carolina, SE USA
Rayong *137 C5* Rayong, S Thailand
Razāzah, Buḩayrat ar *120 B3 var.* Baḩr al Milḩ. *Lake* C Iraq
Razgrad *104 D2* Razgrad, N Bulgaria
Razim, Lacul *108 D5 prev.* Lacul Razelm. *Lagoon* NW Black Sea
Reading *41 F4* Pennsylvania, NE USA
Reading *89 D7* S England, UK
Realicó *64 C4* La Pampa, C Argentina
Reăng Kesei *137 D5* Bătdâmbâng, W Cambodia
Rebecca, Lake *147 C6 lake* Western Australia
Rebiana Sand Sea *see* Rabyanāh, Ramlat
Rebun-tō *130 C2 island* NE Japan
Rechytsa *107 D7 Rus.* Rechitsa. Brestskaya Voblasts', SW Belarus
Recife *63 G2 prev.* Pernambuco. *State capital* Pernambuco, E Brazil
Recklinghausen *94 A4* Nordrhein-Westfalen, W Germany
Recogne *87 C7* Luxembourg, SE Belgium
Reconquista *64 D3* Santa Fe, C Argentina
Red Deer *37 E5* Alberta, SW Canada
Redding *47 B5* California, W USA
Redon *90 B4* Ille-et-Vilaine, NW France
Red River *136 C2 var.* Yuan, *Chin.* Yuan Jiang, *Vtn.* Sông Hông Hà. *River* China/Vietnam
Red River *45 E1 river* Canada/USA
Red River *42 B3 river* Louisiana, S USA
Red River *35 C6 river* S USA
Red Sea *72 C3 anc.* Sinus Arabicus. *Sea* Africa/Asia
Red Wing *45 G2* Minnesota, N USA
Reefton *151 C5* West Coast, South Island, NZ
Reese River *47 C5 river* Nevada, W USA
Refahiye *117 E3* Erzincan, C Turkey
Regensburg *95 C6 Eng.* Ratisbon, *Fr.* Ratisbonne; *hist.* Ratisbona, *anc.* Castra Regina, Reginum. Bayern, SE Germany
Regenstauf *95 C6* Bayern, SE Germany
Reggane *70 D3* C Algeria
Reggio *see* Reggio nell' Emilia
Reggio Calabria *see* Reggio di Calabria
Reggio di Calabria *97 D7 var.* Reggio Calabria, *Gk.* Rhegion; *anc.* Regium, Rhegium. Calabria, SW Italy
Reggio Emilia *see* Reggio nell' Emilia
Reggio nell' Emilia *96 B2 var.* Reggio Emilia, *abbrev.* Reggio; *anc.* Regium Lepidum. Emilia-Romagna, N Italy
Reghin *108 C4 Ger.* Sächsisch-Reen, *Hung.* Szászrégen; *prev.* Reghinul Săsesc, *Ger.* Sächsisch-Regen. Mureş, C Romania
Regina *37 F5* Saskatchewan, S Canada
Registan *see* Rīgestān
Regium *see* Reggio di Calabria
Regium Lepidum *see* Reggio nell' Emilia
Rehoboth *see* Reḥovot
Rehoboth *78 B3* Hardap, C Namibia
Reḥovot *119 A6 var.* Rehoboth, Rehovoth, Rekhovot. Central, C Israel
Rehovoth *see* Reḥovot
Reid *147 D6* Western Australia
Reikjavik *see* Reykjavík
Ré, Île de *90 A4 island* W France
Reims *90 D3 Eng.* Rheims; *anc.* Durocortorum, Remi. Marne, N France
Reindeer Lake *37 F4 lake* Manitoba/Saskatchewan, C Canada
Reinga, Cape *150 C1 headland* North Island, NZ
Reinosa *92 D1* Cantabria, N Spain
Rekhovot *see* Reḥovot
Reliance *37 F4* Northwest Territories, C Canada
Rendina *see* Rentína
Rendsburg *94 B2* Schleswig-Holstein, N Germany
Rengat *138 B4* Sumatera, W Indonesia
Reni *108 D4* Odes'ka Oblast', SW Ukraine
Rennell *144 C4 var.* Mu Nggava. *Island* S Solomon Islands
Rennes *90 B3 Bret.* Roazon; *anc.* Condate. Ille-et-Vilaine, NW France
Reno *47 C5* Nevada, W USA
Renqiu *128 C4* Hebei, E China
Rentína *105 B5 var.* Rendina. Thessalía, C Greece
Republika Srpska Admin. region *republic* Bosnia and Herzegovina
République Centrafricaine *see* Central African Republic
Repulse Bay *37 G3* Nunavut, N Canada
Resht *see* Rasht
Resistencia *64 D3* Chaco, NE Argentina
Reşiţa *108 A4 Ger.* Reschitza, *Hung.* Resicabánya. Caraş-Severin, W Romania
Resolute *37 F2* Cornwallis Island, Nunavut, N Canada
Resolution Island *39 E1 island* Northwest Territories, NE Canada
Resolution Island *151 A7 island* SW NZ
Réunion *79 H4 off.* La Réunion. *French overseas department* W Indian Ocean
Réunion *141 B5 island* W Indian Ocean
Reus *93 F2* Cataluña, E Spain
Reutlingen *95 B6* Baden-Württemberg, S Germany
Reuver *87 D5* Limburg, SE Netherlands
Revillagigedo Islands *see* Revillagigedo, Islas
Revillagigedo, Islas *50 B5 Eng.* Revillagigedo Islands. *Island group* W Mexico
Rexburg *46 E3* Idaho, NW USA
Reyes *61 F3* Beni, NW Bolivia
Rey, Isla del *53 G5 island* Archipiélago de las Perlas, SE Panama
Reykjanes Basin *82 C5 var.* Irminger Basin. *Undersea feature* N Atlantic Ocean
Reykjanes Ridge *80 A1 undersea feature* N Atlantic Ocean
Reykjavík *83 E5 var.* Reikjavik. *Country capital* (Iceland) Höfudhborgarsvaedhi, W Iceland
Reynosa *51 E2* Tamaulipas, C Mexico
Rezé *90 A4* Loire-Atlantique, NW France
Rēzekne *106 D4 Ger.* Rositten; *prev.* Rus. Rezhitsa. Rēzekne, SE Latvia
Rezovo *104 E3 Turk.* Rezve. Burgas, E Bulgaria
Rhegion *see* Reggio di Calabria
Rhegium *see* Reggio di Calabria
Rhein *see* Rhine
Rheine *94 A3 var.* Rheine in Westfalen. Nordrhein-Westfalen, NW Germany
Rheine in Westfalen *see* Rheine
Rheinisches Schiefergebirge *95 A5 var.* Rhine State Uplands, *Eng.* Rhenish Slate Mountains. *Mountain range* W Germany
Rhenish Slate Mountains *see* Rheinisches Schiefergebirge
Rhine *80 D4 Dut.* Rijn, *Fr.* Rhin, *Ger.* Rhein. *River* W Europe
Rhinelander *40 B2* Wisconsin, N USA
Rhine State Uplands *see* Rheinisches Schiefergebirge
Rho *96 B2* Lombardia, N Italy
Rhode Island *41 G3 off.* State of Rhode Island and Providence Plantations; also known as Little Rhody, Ocean State. *State* NE USA
Rhodes *see* Ródos
Rhodope Mountains *104 C3 var.* Rodhópi Óri, *Bul.* Rhodope Planina, Rodopi, *Gk.* Orosirá Rodhópis, *Turk.* Dospad Dagh. *Mountain range* Bulgaria/Greece
Rhodope Planina *see* Rhodope Mountains
Rhodos *see* Ródos

Rhône *80 C4 river* France/Switzerland
Rhône *91 D6 department* E France
Rhum *88 B3 var.* Rum. *Island* W Scotland, UK
Ribble *89 D5 river* NW England, UK
Ribeira *92 B1* Galicia, NW Spain
Ribeirão Preto *63 F4* São Paulo, S Brazil
Riberalta *61 F2* Beni, N Bolivia
Rîbniţa *108 D3 var.* Râbniţa, *Rus.* Rybnitsa. NE Moldova
Rice Lake *40 A2* Wisconsin, N USA
Richard Toll *74 B3* N Senegal
Richfield *44 B4* Utah, W USA
Richland *46 C2* Washington, NW USA
Richmond *41 E5 state capital* Virginia, NE USA
Richmond *40 C5* Kentucky, S USA
Richmond *151 C5* Tasman, South Island, NZ
Richmond Range *151 C5 mountain range* South Island, NZ
Ricobayo, Embalse de *92 C2 reservoir* NW Spain
Ridgecrest *47 C7* California, W USA
Ried *see* Ried im Innkreis
Ried im Innkreis *95 D6 var.* Ried. Oberösterreich, NW Austria
Riemst *87 D6* Limburg, NE Belgium
Riesa *94 D4* Sachsen, E Germany
Rift Valley *see* Great Rift Valley
Rīga *106 C3 Eng.* Riga. *Country capital* (Latvia) Rīga, C Latvia
Riga, Gulf of *106 C3 Est.* Liivi Laht, *Ger.* Rigaer Bucht, *Latv.* Rīgas Jūras Līcis, *Rus.* Rizhskiy Zaliv; *prev. Est.* Riia Laht. *Gulf* Estonia/Latvia
Rīgān *120 E4* Kermān, SE Iran
Rīgestān *122 D5 var.* Registan. *Desert region* S Afghanistan
Riihimäki *85 D5* Etelä-Suomi, S Finland
Rijeka *100 A2 Ger.* Sankt Veit am Flaum, *It.* Fiume, *Slvn.* Reka; *anc.* Tarsatica. Primorje-Gorski Kotar, NW Croatia
Rijssel *see* Lille
Rijssen *86 E3* Overijssel, E Netherlands
Rimah, Wādī ar *120 B4 var.* Wādī ar Rummah. *Dry watercourse* C Saudi Arabia
Rimini *96 C3 anc.* Ariminum. Emilia-Romagna, N Italy
Rimouski *39 E4* Québec, SE Canada
Ringebu *85 B5* Oppland, S Norway
Ringkøbing Fjord *85 A7 fjord* W Denmark
Ringvassøya *84 C2 island* N Norway
Rio *see* Rio de Janeiro
Riobamba *60 B1* Chimborazo, C Ecuador
Rio Branco *56 B3 state capital* Acre, W Brazil
Río Bravo *51 E2* Tamaulipas, C Mexico
Río Cuarto *64 C4* Córdoba, C Argentina
Rio de Janeiro *63 F4 var.* Rio. *State capital* Rio de Janeiro, SE Brazil
Río Gallegos *65 B7 var.* Gallegos, Puerto Gallegos. Santa Cruz, S Argentina
Rio Grande *63 E5 var.* São Pedro do Rio Grande do Sul. Rio Grande do Sul, S Brazil
Río Grande *50 D3* Zacatecas, C Mexico
Rio Grande do Norte *63 G2 off.* Estado do Rio Grande do Norte. *State* E Brazil
Rio Grande do Sul *63 E5 off.* Estado do Rio Grande do Sul. *State* S Brazil
Rio Grande Plateau *see* Rio Grande Rise
Rio Grande Rise *57 E6 var.* Rio Grande Plateau. *Undersea feature* SW Atlantic Ocean
Ríohacha *58 B1* La Guajira, N Colombia
Río Lagartos *51 H3* Yucatán, SE Mexico
Riom *91 C5 anc.* Ricomagus. Puy-de-Dôme, C France
Río San Juan *53 E4 department* S Nicaragua
Rioverde *see* Río Verde
Río Verde *51 E4 var.* Rioverde. San Luis Potosí, C Mexico
Ripoll *93 G2* Cataluña, NE Spain
Rishiri-tō *130 C2 var.* Risiri Tô. *Island* NE Japan
Risiri Tô *see* Rishiri-tō
Risti *106 D2 Ger.* Kreuz. Läänemaa, W Estonia
Rivas *52 D4* Rivas, SW Nicaragua
Rivera *64 D3* Rivera, NE Uruguay
River Falls *40 A2* Wisconsin, N USA
River Plate *see* Plata, Río de la
Riverside *47 C7* California, W USA
Riverton *151 A7* Southland, South Island, NZ
Riverton *44 C3* Wyoming, C USA
Rivière-du-Loup *39 E4* Québec, SE Canada
Rivne *108 C2 Pol.* Równe, *Rus.* Rovno. Rivnens'ka Oblast', NW Ukraine
Rivoli *96 A2* Piemonte, NW Italy
Riyadh *see* Ar Riyāḍ
Riyāq *see* Rayak
Rize *117 E2* Rize, NE Turkey
Rizhao *128 D4* Shandong, E China
Rkîz *74 C3* Trarza, W Mauritania
Road Town *55 F3 dependent territory capital* (British Virgin Islands) Tortola, C British Virgin Islands
Roanne *91 C5 anc.* Rodunma. Loire, E France
Roanoke *41 E5* Virginia, NE USA
Roanoke River *43 F1 river* North Carolina/Virginia, SE USA
Roatán *52 C2 var.* Coxen Hole, Coxin Hole. Islas de la Bahía, N Honduras
Robbie Ridge *143 E3 undersea feature* W Pacific Ocean
Robert Williams *see* Caála
Robinson Range *147 B5 mountain range* Western Australia
Robson, Mount *37 E5 mountain* British Columbia, SW Canada
Robstown *49 G4* Texas, SW USA
Roca Partida, Isla *50 B5 island* W Mexico
Rocas, Atol das *63 G2 island* E Brazil
Rochefort *90 B4 var.* Rochefort sur Mer. Charente-Maritime, W France
Rochefort *87 C7* Namur, SE Belgium
Rochefort sur Mer *see* Rochefort
Rochester *45 G3* Minnesota, N USA
Rochester *41 G2* New Hampshire, NE USA
Rochester *41 E3* New York, NE USA
Rockall Bank *80 B2 undersea feature* N Atlantic Ocean
Rockall Trough *80 B2 undersea feature* N Atlantic Ocean
Rockdale *148 E2* New South Wales, SE Australia
Rockford *40 B3* Illinois, N USA
Rockhampton *148 D4* Queensland, E Australia
Rock Hill *43 E1* South Carolina, SE USA
Rockies *see* Rocky Mountains
Rockingham *147 A6* Western Australia
Rock Island *40 B3* Illinois, N USA
Rock Sound *54 C1* Eleuthera Island, C Bahamas
Rock Springs *44 C3* Wyoming, C USA
Rockstone *59 F3* C Guyana
Rocky Mount *43 F1* North Carolina, SE USA
Rocky Mountains *34 B4 var.* Rockies, *Fr.* Montagnes Rocheuses. *Mountain range* Canada/USA
Roden *86 E2* Drenthe, NE Netherlands
Rodez *91 C5 anc.* Segodunum. Aveyron, S France
Rodhópi Óri *see* Rhodope Mountains
Ródhos *see* Ródos
Rodi *see* Ródos
Rodopi *see* Rhodope Mountains
Ródos *105 E7 var.* Ródhos, *Eng.* Rhodes, *It.* Rodi; *anc.* Rhodos. *Island* Dodekánisos, Greece, Aegean Sea
Roermond *87 D5* Limburg, SE Netherlands
Roeselare *87 A6 Fr.* Roulers; *prev.* Rousselaere. West-Vlaanderen, W Belgium
Rogatica *100 C4* Republika Srpska, SE Bosnia and Herzegovina
Rogers *42 A1* Arkansas, C USA
Roger Simpson Island *see* Abemama
Roi Ed *see* Roi Et
Roi Et *137 D5 var.* Muang Roi Et, Roi Ed. Roi Et, E Thailand
Roja *106 C2* Talsi, NW Latvia
Rokiškis *106 C4* Rokiškis, NE Lithuania
Rokycany *99 A5 Ger.* Rokytzan. Plzeňský Kraj, W Czech Republic
Rokytzan *see* Rokycany
Rôlas, Ilha das *76 E2 island* S Sao Tome and Principe
Rolla *45 G5* Missouri, C USA
Roma *96 C4 Eng.* Rome. *Country capital* (Italy) Lazio, C Italy
Roma *149 D5* Queensland, E Australia
Roman *108 C4 Hung.* Románvásár. Neamţ, NE Romania
Roman *104 C2* Vratsa, NW Bulgaria
Romania *108 B4 Bul.* Rumŭniya, *Ger.* Rumänien, *Hung.* Románia, *Rom.* România, *SCr.* Rumunjska, *Ukr.* Rumuniya; *prev.* Republica Socialistă România, Roumania, Rumania, Socialist Republic of Romania, *Rom.* Romînia. *Country* SE Europe

Romania (continued)

Official name Romania
Formation 1878
Capital Bucharest
Population 22.3 million / 251 people per sq mile (97 people per sq km)
Total area 91,699 sq. miles (237,500 sq. km)
Languages Romanian, Hungarian (Magyar), Romani, German
Religions Romanian Orthodox 87%, Roman Catholic 5%, Protestant 4%, other 4%
Ethnic mix Romanian 89%, Magyar 7%, Roma 3%, other 1%
Government Presidential system
Currency Romanian leu = 100 bani
Literacy rate 97%
Calorie consumption 3407 calories

Rome *see* Roma
Rome *42 D2* Georgia, SE USA
Romny *109 F2* Sums'ka Oblast', NE Ukraine
Rømø *85 A7 Ger.* Röm. *Island* SW Denmark
Roncador, Serra do *56 D4 mountain range* C Brazil
Ronda *92 D5* Andalucía, S Spain
Rondônia *62 D3 off.* Estado de Rondônia; *prev.* Território de Rondônia. *State* W Brazil
Rondonópolis *63 E3* Mato Grosso, W Brazil
Rongelap Atoll *144 D1 var.* Rōnļap. *Atoll* Ralik Chain, NW Marshall Islands
Rõngu *106 D3 Ger.* Ringen. Tartumaa, SE Estonia
Rōnļap *see* Rongelap Atoll
Rønne *85 B8* Bornholm, E Denmark
Ronne Ice Shelf *154 A3 ice shelf* Antarctica
Roosendaal *87 C5* Noord-Brabant, S Netherlands
Roosevelt Island *154 B4 island* Antarctica
Roraima *62 D1 off.* Estado de Roraima; *prev.* Território de Rio Branco, Território de Roraima. *State* N Brazil
Roraima, Mount *59 E3 mountain* N South America
Røros *85 B5* Sør-Trøndelag, S Norway
Rosa, Lake *54 D2 lake* Great Inagua, S Bahamas
Rosario *64 D2* San Pedro, C Paraguay
Rosario *64 D4* Santa Fe, C Argentina
Rosarito *50 A1* Baja California, NW Mexico
Roscommon *40 C2* Michigan, N USA
Roseau *55 G4 prev.* Charlotte Town. *Country capital* (Dominica) SW Dominica
Roseburg *46 B4* Oregon, NW USA
Rosenberg *49 G4* Texas, SW USA
Rosengarten *94 B3* Niedersachsen, N Germany
Rosenheim *95 C6* Bayern, S Germany
Rosia *93 H5* W Gibraltar
Rosia Bay *93 H5 bay* SW Gibraltar
Roşiori de Vede *108 B5* Teleorman, S Romania
Roslavl' *111 A5* Smolenskaya Oblast', W Russian Federation
Rosmalen *86 C4* Noord-Brabant, S Netherlands
Ross *151 B6* West Coast, South Island, NZ
Rossano *97 E6 anc.* Roscianum. Calabria, SW Italy
Ross Ice Shelf *154 B4 ice shelf* Antarctica
Rosso *74 B3* Trarza, SW Mauritania
Rossosh' *111 B6* Voronezhskaya Oblast', W Russian Federation
Ross Sea *154 B4 sea* Antarctica
Rostak *see* Ar Rustāq
Rostock *94 C2* Mecklenburg-Vorpommern, NE Germany
Rostov *see* Rostov-na-Donu
Rostov-na-Donu *111 B7 var.* Rostov, *Eng.* Rostov-on-Don. Rostovskaya Oblast', SW Russian Federation
Rostov-on-Don *see* Rostov-na-Donu
Roswell *48 D2* New Mexico, SW USA
Rota *144 B1 island* S Northern Mariana Islands
Rothera *154 A2 UK research station* Antarctica
Rotorua *150 D3* Bay of Plenty, North Island, NZ
Rotorua, Lake *150 D3 lake* North Island, NZ
Rotterdam *86 C4* Zuid-Holland, SW Netherlands
Rottweil *95 B6* Baden-Württemberg, S Germany
Rotuma *145 E4 island* NW Fiji
Roubaix *90 C2* Nord, N France
Rouen *90 C3 anc.* Rotomagus. Seine-Maritime, N France
Round Rock *49 G3* Texas, SW USA
Rourkela *see* Rāulakela
Roussillon *91 C6 cultural region* S France
Rouyn-Noranda *38 D4* Québec, SE Canada
Rovaniemi *84 D3* Lappi, N Finland
Rovigo *96 C2* Veneto, NE Italy
Rovinj *100 A3 It.* Rovigno. Istra, NW Croatia
Rovuma, Rio *79 F2 var.* Ruvuma. *River* Mozambique/Tanzania *see also* Ruvuma
Rovuma, Rio *see* Ruvuma
Roxas City *139 E2* Panay Island, C Philippines
Royale, Isle *40 B1 island* Michigan, N USA
Royan *91 B5* Charente-Maritime, W France
Rozdol'ne *109 F4 Rus.* Razdolnoye. Respublika Krym, S Ukraine

Rožňava *99 D6 Ger.* Rosenau, *Hung.* Rozsnyó. Košický Kraj, E Slovakia
Ruapehu, Mount *150 D4 mountain* North Island, NZ
Ruapuke Island *151 B8 island* SW NZ
Ruatoria *150 E3* Gisborne, North Island, NZ
Ruawai *150 D2* Northland, North Island, NZ
Rubizhne *109 H3 Rus.* Rubezhnoye. Luhans'ka Oblast', E Ukraine
Ruby Mountains *47 D5 mountain range* Nevada, W USA
Rucava *106 B3* Liepāja, SW Latvia
Rūd-e Hīrmand *see* Helmand, Daryā-ye
Rūdiškės *107 B5* Trakai, S Lithuania
Rudnik *104 E2* Varna, E Bulgaria
Rudny *see* Rudnyy
Rudnyy *114 C4 var.* Rudny. Kostanay, N Kazakhstan
Rudolf, Lake *see* Turkana, Lake
Rudolfswert *see* Novo Mesto
Rudzyensk *107 C6 Rus.* Rudensk. Minskaya Voblasts', C Belarus
Rufiji *73 C7 river* E Tanzania
Rufino *64 C4* Santa Fe, C Argentina
Rugāji *106 D4* Balvi, E Latvia
Rügen *94 D2 headland* NE Germany
Ruggell *94 E1* N Liechtenstein
Ruhnu *106 C2 var.* Ruhnu Saar, *Swe.* Runö. *Island* SW Estonia
Ruhnu Saar *see* Ruhnu
Rūjiena *106 D3 Est.* Ruhja, *Ger.* Rujen. Valmiera, N Latvia
Rukwa, Lake *73 B7 lake* SE Tanzania
Rum *see* Rhum
Ruma *100 D3* Serbia, N Serbia and Montenegro (Yugo.)
Rumadiya *see* Ar Ramādī
Rumbek *73 B5* El Buhayrat, S Sudan
Rum Cay *54 D2 island* C Bahamas
Rumia *98 C2* Pomorskie, N Poland
Rummah, Wādī ar *see* Rimah, Wādī ar
Runanga *151 B5* West Coast, South Island, NZ
Runaway Bay *54 B4* C Jamaica
Rundu *78 C3 var.* Runtu. Okavango, NE Namibia
Runö *see* Ruhnu
Runtu *see* Rundu
Ruoqiang *126 C3 var.* Jo-ch'iang, *Uigh.* Charkhlik, Charkhliq, Qarkilik. Xinjiang Uygur Zizhiqu, NW China
Rupea *108 C4 Ger.* Reps, *Hung.* Kőhalom; *prev.* Cohalm. Braşov, C Romania
Rupel *87 B5 river* N Belgium
Rupert, Rivière de *38 D3 river* Québec, C Canada
Ruschuk *see* Ruse
Rusçuk *see* Ruse
Ruse *104 D1 var.* Ruschuk, Rustchuk, *Turk.* Rusçuk. Ruse, N Bulgaria
Rus Krymskaya ASSR *see* Crimea
Russellville *42 A1* Arkansas, C USA
Russian Federation *112 D2 var.* Russia, *Latv.* Krievija, *Rus.* Rossiyskaya Federatsiya. *Country* Asia/Europe

Russian Federation 112

Official name Russian Federation
Formation 1480
Capital Moscow
Population 143 million / 22 people per sq mile (8 people per sq km)
Total area 6,592,735 sq. miles (17,075,200 sq. km)
Languages Russian, Tatar, Ukrainian, Chavash, various other national languages
Religions Orthodox Christian 75%, other 15%, Muslim 10%

Russian Federation (continued)

Ethnic mix Russian 82%, Tatar 4%, Ukrainian 3%, Chavash 1%, other 10%
Government Presidential system
Currency Russian rouble = 100 kopeks
Literacy rate 99%
Calorie consumption 3014 calories

Rustaq *see* Ar Rustāq
Rust'avi *117 G2* SE Georgia
Rustchuk *see* Ruse
Ruston *42 B2* Louisiana, S USA
Rutanzige I M, Lake *see* Edward, Lake
Rutba *see* Ar Ruṭbah
Rutland *41 F2* Vermont, NE USA
Rutög *126 A4 var.* Rutog, Rutok. Xizang Zizhiqu, W China
Rutok *see* Rutog
Ruvuma *69 E5 var.* Rio Rovuma. *River* Mozambique/Tanzania *see also* Rovuma, Rio
Ruvuma *see* Rovuma, Rio
Ruwenzori *77 E5 mountain range* Uganda/Dem. Rep. Congo
Ruzhany *107 B6 Rus.* Ruzhany. Brestskaya Voblasts', SW Belarus
Ružomberok *99 C5 Ger.* Rosenberg, *Hung.* Rózsahegy. Žilinsky Kraj, N Slovakia
Rwanda *73 B6 prev.* Ruanda. *Country* C Africa

Rwanda 73

Official name Republic of Rwanda
Formation 1962
Capital Kigali
Population 8.4 million / 872 people per sq mile (337 people per sq km)
Total area 10,169 sq. miles (26,338 sq. km)
Languages Kinyarwanda, French, Kiswahili, English
Religions Roman Catholic 56%, Traditional beliefs 25%, Muslim 10%, Protestant 9%
Ethnic mix Hutu 90%, Tutsi 9%, Other (including Twa) 1%
Government Presidential system
Currency Rwanda franc = 100 centimes
Literacy rate 69%
Calorie consumption 2086 calories

Ryazan' *111 B5* Ryazanskaya Oblast', W Russian Federation
Rybinsk *110 B4 prev.* Andropov. Yaroslavskaya Oblast', W Russian Federation
Rybnik *99 C5* Śląskie, S Poland
Rybnitsa *see* Rîbniţa
Ryde *148 E1* New South Wales, SE Australia
Ryki *98 D4* Lublin, E Poland
Rypin *98 C3* Kujawsko-pomorskie, C Poland
Ryssel *see* Lille
Rysy *99 C5 mountain* S Poland
Ryukyu Islands *125 E3 island group* SW Japan
Ryukyu Trench *125 F3 var.* Nansei Syotō Trench. *Undersea feature* S East China Sea
Rzeszów *99 E5* Podkarpackie, SE Poland
Rzhev *110 B4* Tverskaya Oblast', W Russian Federation

S

Saale *94 C4 river* C Germany
Saalfeld *95 C5 var.* Saalfeld an der Saale. Thüringen, C Germany
Saalfeld an der Saale *see* Saalfeld
Saarbrücken *95 A6 Fr.* Sarrebruck. Saarland, SW Germany
Sääre *106 C2 var.* Sjar. Saaremaa, W Estonia
Saaremaa *106 C2 Ger.* Oesel, Ösel; *prev.* Saare. *Island* W Estonia
Saariselkä *84 D2 Lapp.* Suoločielgi. Lappi, N Finland
Sab' Ābār *118 C4 var.* Sab'a Biyar, Sa'b Bi'ār. Ḥimṣ, C Syria
Sab'a Biyar *see* Sab' Ābār
Šabac *100 D3* Serbia, W Serbia and Montenegro (Yugo.)
Sabadell *93 G2* Cataluña, E Spain
Sabah *138 D3 cultural region* Borneo, SE Asia
Sabanalarga *58 B1* Atlántico, N Colombia
Sabaneta *58 C1* Falcón, N Venezuela
Sab'atayn, Ramlat as *121 C6 desert* C Yemen
Sabaya *61 F4* Oruro, S Bolivia
Sa'b Bi'ār *see* Sab' Ābār
Şāberī, Hāmūn-e *var.* Daryācheh-ye Hāmūn, Daryācheh-ye Sīstān. *Lake* Afghanistan/Iran *see also* Sīstān, Daryācheh-ye
Sabhā *71 F3* C Libya
Sabi, Rio *see* Save, Rio
Sabinas *51 E2* Coahuila de Zaragoza, NE Mexico
Sabinas Hidalgo *51 E2* Nuevo León, NE Mexico
Sabine River *49 H3 river* Louisiana/Texas, SW USA
Sabkha *see* As Sabkhah
Sable, Cape *43 E5 headland* Florida, SE USA
Sable Island *39 G4 island* Nova Scotia, SE Canada
Şabyā *121 B6* Jīzān, SW Saudi Arabia
Sabzawar *see* Sabzevār
Sabzevār *120 D2 var.* Sabzawar. Khorāsān, NE Iran
Sachsen *94 D4 Eng.* Saxony, *Fr.* Saxe. *State* E Germany
Sachs Harbour *37 E2* Banks Island, Northwest Territories, N Canada
Sacramento *47 B5 state capital* California, W USA
Sacramento Mountains *48 D2 mountain range* New Mexico, SW USA
Sacramento River *47 B5 river* California, W USA
Sacramento Valley *47 B5 valley* California, W USA
Şa'dah *121 B6* NW Yemen
Sado *131 C5 var.* Sadoga-shima. *Island* C Japan
Sadoga-shima *see* Sado
Safad *see* Ẕefat
Safed *see* Ẕefat
Säffle *85 B6* Värmland, C Sweden
Safford *48 C3* Arizona, SW USA
Safi *70 B2* W Morocco
Safid Kūh, Selseleh-ye *122 D4 Eng.* Paropamisus Range. *Mountain range* W Afghanistan
Sagaing *136 B3* Sagaing, C Myanmar
Sagami-nada *131 D6 inlet* SW Japan
Sagan *see* Żagań
Sāgar *134 D4 prev.* Saugor. Madhya Pradesh, C India
Saghez *see* Saqqez
Saginaw *40 C3* Michigan, N USA
Saginaw Bay *40 D2 lake bay* Michigan, N USA
Sagua la Grande *54 B2* Villa Clara, C Cuba
Sagunt *see* Sagunto
Sagunto *93 F3 var.* Sagunt, *Ar.* Murviedro; *anc.* Saguntum. País Valenciano, E Spain
Saguntum *see* Sagunto
Sahara *68 B3 desert* Libya/Algeria
Sahara el Gharbîya *72 B2 var.* Aş Şaḩrā' al Gharbīyah, *Eng.* Western Desert. *Desert* C Egypt
Saharan Atlas *see* Atlas Saharien
Sahel *74 D3 physical region* C Africa
Sāḩilīyah, Jibāl as *118 B3 mountain range* NW Syria
Sāhīwāl *134 C2 prev.* Montgomery. Punjab, E Pakistan
şaḩrā' Rabyanāh *see* Rabyanāh, Ramlat
Saïda *119 A5 var.* Şaydā, Sayida; *anc.* Sidon. W Lebanon
Saidpur *135 G3 var.* Syedpur. Rajshahi, NW Bangladesh
Saigon *see* Hô Chi Minh
Sai Hun *see* Syr Darya
Saimaa *85 E5 lake* SE Finland
St Albans *89 E6 anc.* Verulamium. E England, UK
Saint Albans *40 D5* West Virginia, NE USA
St Andrews *88 C4* E Scotland, UK
Saint Anna Trough *see* Svyataya Anna Trough
St.Ann's Bay *54 B4* C Jamaica
St.Anthony *39 G3* Newfoundland, Newfoundland and Labrador, SE Canada
Saint Augustine *43 E3* Florida, SE USA
St Austell *89 C7* SW England, UK
St-Brieuc *90 A3* Côtes d'Armor, NW France
St. Catharines *38 D5* Ontario, S Canada
St-Chamond *91 D5* Loire, E France
St.Clair, Lake *40 D3 Fr.* Lac à L'Eau Claire. *Lake* Canada/USA
St-Claude *91 D5 anc.* Condate. Jura, E France
Saint Cloud *45 F2* Minnesota, N USA
St Croix *55 F3 island* S Virgin Islands (US)
Saint Croix River *40 A2 river* Minnesota/Wisconsin, N USA
St David's Island *42 B5 island* E Bermuda
St-Denis *79 G4 dependent territory capital* (Réunion) NW Réunion
St-Dié *90 E4* Vosges, NE France
St-Egrève *91 D5* Isère, E France
Saintes *91 B5 anc.* Mediolanum. Charente-Maritime, W France
St-Étienne *91 D5* Loire, E France
St-Flour *91 C5* Cantal, C France
Saint Gall *see* Sankt Gallen
St-Gall *see* Sankt Gallen
StGallen *see* Sankt Gallen
St-Gaudens *91 B6* Haute-Garonne, S France
St George *42 B4* N Bermuda
Saint George *149 D5* Queensland, E Australia
Saint George *44 A5* Utah, W USA
St.George's *55 G5 country capital* (Grenada) SW Grenada
St-Georges *59 H3* E French Guiana
St-Georges *39 E4* Québec, SE Canada
St George's Channel *89 B6 channel* Ireland/Wales, UK
St George's Island *42 B4 island* E Bermuda
Saint Helena *69 B6 UK dependent territory* C Atlantic Ocean
St.Helena Bay *78 B5 bay* SW South Africa
St Helier *89 D8 dependent territory capital* (Jersey) S Jersey, Channel Islands
Saint Ignace *40 C2* Michigan, N USA
St-Jean, Lac *39 E4 lake* Québec, SE Canada
Saint Joe River *46 D2 river* Idaho, NW USA
Saint John *41 H1 river* Canada/USA
Saint John *39 F4* New Brunswick, SE Canada
St John's *55 G3 country capital* (Antigua and Barbuda) Antigua, Antigua and Barbuda
St.John's *39 H3* Newfoundland, Newfoundland and Labrador, E Canada
Saint Joseph *45 F4* Missouri, C USA
St Julian's *102 B5* N Malta
St Kilda *88 A3 island* NW Scotland, UK
Saint Kitts and Nevis *55 F3 var.* Saint Christopher-Nevis. *Country* E West Indies

Saint Kitts & Nevis 55

Official name Federation of Saint Christopher and Nevis

Saint Kitts & Nevis (continued)

Formation 1983
Capital Basseterre**Population** 38,763 / 279 people per sq mile (108 people per sq km)
Total area 101 sq. miles (261 sq. km)
Languages English, English Creole
Religions Anglican 33%, Methodist 29%, other 22%, Moravian 9%, Roman Catholic 7%
Ethnic mix Black 94%, Mixed race 3%, Other and Amerindian 2%, White 1%
Government Parliamentary system
Currency Eastern Caribbean dollar = 100 cents
Literacy rate 98%
Calorie consumption 2997 calories

St-Laurent *see* St-Laurent-du-Maroni
St-Laurent-du-Maroni *59 H3 var.* St-Laurent. NW French Guiana
St. Lawrence *39 E4 Fr.* Fleuve St-Laurent. *River* Canada/USA
St. Lawrence, Gulf of *39 F3 gulf* NW Atlantic Ocean
Saint Lawrence Island *36 B2 island* Alaska, USA
St-Lô *90 B3 anc.* Briovera, Laudus. Manche, N France
St-Louis *90 E4* Haut-Rhin, NE France
Saint Louis *45 G4* Missouri, C USA
Saint Louis *74 B3* NW Senegal
Saint Lucia *55 E1 country* SE West Indies

Saint Lucia 55

Official name Saint Lucia
Formation 1979
Capital Castries
Population 162,157 / 687 people per sq mile (266 people per sq km)
Total area 239 sq. miles (620 sq. km)
Languages English, French Creole
Religions Roman Catholic 90%, other 10%
Ethnic mix Black 90%, Mulatto (mixed race) 6%, Asian 3%, White 1%
Government Parliamentary system
Currency Eastern Caribbean dollar = 100 cents
Literacy rate 95%
Calorie consumption 2849 calories

Saint Lucia Channel *55 H4 channel* Martinique/Saint Lucia
St-Malo *90 B3* Ille-et-Vilaine, NW France
St-Malo, Golfe de *90 A3 gulf* NW France
St Matthew's Island *see* Zadetkyi Kyun
St.Matthias Group *144 B3 island group* NE PNG
St-Maur-des-Fossés *90 E2* Val-de-Marne, N France
St.Moritz *95 B7 Ger.* Sankt Moritz, *Rmsch.* San Murezzan. Graubünden, SE Switzerland
St-Nazaire *90 A4* Loire-Atlantique, NW France
St-Omer *90 C2* Pas-de-Calais, N France
Saint Paul *45 F2 state capital* Minnesota, N USA
St-Paul, Île *141 C6 var.* St.Paul Island. *Island* NE French Southern and Antarctic Territories
St.Paul Island *see* St-Paul, Île
St Peter Port *89 D8 dependent territory capital* (Guernsey) C Guernsey, Channel Islands
Saint Petersburg *see* Sankt-Peterburg
Saint Petersburg *43 E4* Florida, SE USA
St-Pierre and Miquelon *39 G4 Fr.* Îles St-Pierre et Miquelon. *French territorial collectivity* NE North America
St-Quentin *90 C3* Aisne, N France
Saint Vincent *55 G4 island* N Saint Vincent and the Grenadines
Saint Vincent and the Grenadines *55 H4 country* SE West Indies

Saint Vincent & The Grenadines 55

Official name Saint Vincent and the Grenadines
Formation 1979
Capital Kingstown
Population 116,812 / 892 people per sq mile (344 people per sq km)
Total area 150 sq. miles (389 sq. km)
Languages English, English Creole
Religions Anglican 47%, Methodist 28%, Roman Catholic 13%, other 12%
Ethnic mix Black 66%, Mulatto (mixed race) 19%, Asian 6%, other 5%, White 4%
Government Parliamentary system
Currency Eastern Caribbean dollar = 100 cents
Literacy rate 83%
Calorie consumption 2609 calories

Saint Vincent Passage *55 H4 passage* Saint Lucia/Saint Vincent and the Grenadines
Saipan *142 B1 island country capital* (Northern Mariana Islands) S Northern Mariana Islands
Sajama, Nevado *61 F4 mountain* W Bolivia
Sajószentpéter *99 D6* Borsod-Abaúj-Zemplén, NE Hungary
Sakākah *120 B4* Al Jawf, NW Saudi Arabia
Sakakawea, Lake *44 D1 reservoir* North Dakota, N USA
Sakata *130 D4* Yamagata, Honshū, C Japan
Sakhalin *see* Sakhalin, Ostrov
Sakhalin, Ostrov *115 G4 var.* Sakhalin. *Island* SE Russian Federation
Sakhon Nakhon *see* Sakon Nakhon
Şäki *117 G2 Rus.* Sheki; *prev.* Nukha. NW Azerbaijan
Sakishima-shotō *130 A3 var.* Sakisima Syotô. *Island group* SW Japan
Sakisima Syotô *see* Sakishima-shotō
Sakiz *see* Saqqez
Sakiz-Adasi *see* Chíos
Sakon Nakhon *136 D4 var.* Muang Sakon Nakhon, Sakhon Nakhon. Sakon Nakhon, E Thailand
Saky *109 F5 Rus.* Saki. Respublika Krym, S Ukraine
Sal *74 A3 island* Ilhas de Barlavento, NE Cape Verde
Sala *85 C6* Västmanland, C Sweden
Salacgrīva *106 C3 Est.* Salatsi. Limbaži, N Latvia
Sala Consilina *97 D5* Campania, S Italy
Salado, Río *64 C3 river* C Argentina
Salado, Río *62 D5 river* E Argentina
Şalālah *121 D6* SW Oman
Salamá *52 B2* Baja Verapaz, C Guatemala
Salamanca *92 D2 anc.* Helmantica, Salmantica. Castilla-León, NW Spain
Salamanca *64 B4* Coquimbo, C Chile
Salamīyah *118 B3 var.* As Salamīyah. Ḩamāh, W Syria
Salang *see* Phuket
Salantai *106 B3* Kretinga, NW Lithuania
Salavan *137 D5 var.* Saravan, Saravane. Salavan, S Laos
Salavat *111 D6* Respublika Bashkortostan, W Russian Federation
Sala y Gomez *153 F4 island* Chile, E Pacific Ocean
Sala y Gomez Fracture Zone *see* Sala y Gomez Ridge
Sala y Gomez Ridge *153 G4 var.* Sala y Gomez Fracture Zone. *Tectonic feature* SE Pacific Ocean
Šalčininkai *107 C5* Šalčininkai, SE Lithuania
Saldus *106 B3 Ger.* Frauenburg. Saldus, W Latvia
Sale *149 C7* Victoria, SE Australia
Salé *70 C2* NW Morocco
Salekhard *114 D3 prev.* Obdorsk. Yamalo-Nenetskiy Avtonomnyy Okrug, N Russian Federation
Salem *46 B3 state capital* Oregon, NW USA
Salem *132 C2* Tamil Nādu, SE India
Salerno *97 D5 anc.* Salernum. Campania, S Italy
Salerno, Golfo di *97 C5 Eng.* Gulf of Salerno. *Gulf* S Italy
Salihorsk *107 C7 Rus.* Soligorsk. Minskaya Voblasts', S Belarus
Salima *79 E2* Central, C Malawi
Salina *45 E5* Kansas, C USA
Salina Cruz *51 F5* Oaxaca, SE Mexico
Salinas *47 B6* California, W USA
Salinas *60 A2* Guayas, W Ecuador
Salisbury *89 D7 var.* New Sarum. S England, UK
Sallyana *see* Salyan
Salmon River *46 D3 river* Idaho, NW USA
Salmon River Mountains *46 D3 mountain range* Idaho, NW USA
Salo *85 D6* Länsi-Suomi, W Finland
Salon-de-Provence *91 D6* Bouches-du-Rhône, SE France
Salonta *108 A3 Hung.* Nagyszalonta. Bihor, W Romania
Sal'sk *111 B7* Rostovskaya Oblast', SW Russian Federation
Salt *see* As Salţ
Salta *64 C2* Salta, NW Argentina
Saltash *89 C7* SW England, UK
Saltillo *51 E3* Coahuila de Zaragoza, NE Mexico
Salt Lake City *44 B4 state capital* Utah, W USA
Salto *64 D4* Salto, N Uruguay
Salton Sea *47 D8 lake* California, W USA
Salvador *63 G3 prev.* São Salvador. Bahia, E Brazil
Salween *124 C2 Bur.* Thanlwin, *Chin.* Nu Chiang, Nu Jiang. *River* SE Asia
Salyan *135 E3 var.* Sallyana. Mid Western, W Nepal
Salzburg *95 D6 anc.* Juvavum. Salzburg, N Austria
Salzgitter *94 C4 prev.* Watenstedt-Salzgitter. Niedersachsen, C Germany
Salzwedel *94 C3* Sachsen-Anhalt, N Germany
Šamac *see* Bosanski Šamac
Samakhixai *137 E5 var.* Attapu, Attopeu. Attapu, S Laos
Samalayuca *50 C1* Chihuahua, N Mexico
Samar *139 F2 island* C Philippines
Samara *114 B3 prev.* Kuybyshev. Samarskaya Oblast', W Russian Federation
Samarang *see* Semarang
Samarinda *138 D4* Borneo, C Indonesia
Samarqand *123 E2 Rus.* Samarkand. Samarqand Wiloyati, C Uzbekistan
Samawa *see* As Samāwah
Sambalpur *135 F4* Orissa, E India
Sambava *79 G2* Antsirañana, NE Madagascar
Sambir *108 B2 Rus.* Sambor. L'vivs'ka Oblast', NW Ukraine
Sambre *90 D2 river* Belgium/France
Samfya *78 D2* Luapula, N Zambia
Saminatal *94 E2 valley* Austria/Liechtenstein
Samnān *see* Semnān
Sam Neua *see* Xam Nua
Samoa *145 E4 var.* Sāmoa; *prev.* Western Samoa. *Country* W Polynesia

Samoa 145

Official name Independent State of Samoa
Formation 1962
Capital Apia
Population 178,000 / 163 people per sq mile (63 people per sq km)
Total area 1104 sq. miles (2860 sq. km)
Languages Samoan, English
Religions Christian 99%, other 1%
Ethnic mix Polynesian 90%, Euronesian 9%, other 1%
Government Parliamentary system
Currency Tala = 100 sene
Literacy rate 99%
Calorie consumption Not available

Samoa Basin *143 E3 undersea feature* W Pacific Ocean
Samobor *100 A2* Zagreb, N Croatia
Sámos *105 E6 prev.* Limín Vathéos. Sámos, Dodekánisos, Greece, Aegean Sea
Sámos *105 D6 island* Dodekánisos, Greece, Aegean Sea
Samosch *see* Someş
Samothráki *104 C4 anc.* Samothrace. *Island* NE Greece
Samothráki *104 D4* Samothráki, NE Greece
Sampit *138 C4* Borneo, C Indonesia
Samsun *116 D2 anc.* Amisus. Samsun, N Turkey
Samtredia *117 F2* W Georgia
Samui, Ko *137 C6 island* SW Thailand
Samut Prakan *137 C5 var.* Muang Samut Prakan, Paknam. Samut Prakan, C Thailand
San *99 E5 river* SE Poland
San *74 D3* Ségou, C Mali
Şan'ā' *121 B6 Eng.* Sana. *Country capital* (Yemen) W Yemen
Sana *100 B3 river* NW Bosnia and Herzegovina
Sana *see* Şan'ā'
Sanae *154 B2 South African research station* Antarctica
Sanaga *77 B5 river* C Cameroon
San Ambrosio, Isla *57 A5 Eng.* San Ambrosio Island. *Island* W Chile
Sanandaj *120 C3 prev.* Sinneh. Kordestān, W Iran
San Andrés, Isla de *53 F3 island* NW Colombia
San Andrés Tuxtla *51 F4 var.* Tuxtla. Veracruz-Llave, E Mexico
San Angelo *49 F3* Texas, SW USA
San Antonio *49 F4* Texas, SW USA
San Antonio *52 B2* Toledo, S Belize
San Antonio *64 B4* Valparaíso, C Chile
San Antonio Oeste *65 C5* Río Negro, E Argentina
San Antonio River *49 G4 river* Texas, SW USA
Sanāw *121 C6 var.* Sanaw. NE Yemen
San Benedicto, Isla *50 B4 island* W Mexico
San Benito *52 B1* Petén, N Guatemala
San Benito *49 G5* Texas, SW USA
San Bernardino *47 C7* California, W USA
San Blas *50 C3* Sinaloa, C Mexico
San Blas, Cape *42 D3 headland* Florida, SE USA
San Blas, Cordillera de *53 G4 mountain range* NE Panama
San Carlos *see* Quesada
San Carlos *48 B2* Arizona, SW USA

San Carlos *52 D4* Río San Juan, S Nicaragua
San Carlos de Bariloche *65 B5* Río Negro, SW Argentina
San Carlos del Zulia *58 C2* Zulia, W Venezuela
San Clemente Island *47 B8 island* Channel Islands, California, W USA
San Cristobal *144 C4 var.* Makira. *Island* SE Solomon Islands
San Cristóbal *see* San Cristóbal de Las Casas
San Cristóbal *58 C2* Táchira, W Venezuela
San Cristóbal de Las Casas *51 G5 var.* San Cristóbal. Chiapas, SE Mexico
San Cristóbal, Isla *60 B5 var.* Chatham Island. *Island* Galapagos Islands, Ecuador, E Pacific Ocean
Sancti Spíritus *54 B2* Sancti Spíritus, C Cuba
Sandakan *138 D3* Sabah, East Malaysia
Sandanski *104 C3 prev.* Sveti Vrach. Blagoevgrad, SW Bulgaria
Sanday *88 D2 island* NE Scotland, UK
Sanders *48 C2* Arizona, SW USA
Sand Hills *44 D3 mountain range* Nebraska, C USA
San Diego *47 C8* California, W USA
Sandnes *85 A6* Rogaland, S Norway
Sandomierz *98 D4 Rus.* Sandomir. Świętokrzyskie, C Poland
Sandoway *136 A4* Arakan State, W Myanmar
Sandpoint *46 C1* Idaho, NW USA
Sand Springs *49 G1* Oklahoma, C USA
Sandusky *40 D3* Ohio, N USA
Sandvika *85 A6* Akershus, S Norway
Sandviken *85 C6* Gävleborg, C Sweden
Sandy Bay *93 H5 bay* E Gibraltar
Sandy City *44 B4* Utah, W USA
Sandy Lake *38 B3 lake* Ontario, C Canada
San Esteban *52 D2* Olancho, C Honduras
San Felipe *58 D1* Yaracuy, NW Venezuela
San Felipe de Puerto Plata *see* Puerto Plata
San Félix, Isla *57 A5 Eng.* San Felix Island. *Island* W Chile
San Fernando *92 C5 prev.* Isla de León. Andalucía, S Spain
San Fernando *58 D2 var.* San Fernando de Apure. Apure, C Venezuela
San Fernando *46 D1* California, W USA
San Fernando *55 H5* Trinidad, Trinidad and Tobago
San Fernando de Apure *see* San Fernando
San Fernando del Valle de Catamarca *64 C3 var.* Catamarca. Catamarca, NW Argentina
San Fernando de Monte Cristi *see* Monte Cristi
San Francisco *47 B6* California, W USA
San Francisco del Oro *50 C2* Chihuahua, N Mexico
San Francisco de Macorís *55 E3* C Dominican Republic
San Gabriel *60 B1* Carchi, N Ecuador
San Gabriel Mountains *46 E1 mountain range* California, W USA
Sangir, Kepulauan *139 F3 var.* Kepulauan Sangihe. *Island group* N Indonesia
Sāngli *132 B1* Mahārāshtra, W India
Sangmélima *77 B5* Sud, S Cameroon
Sangre de Cristo Mountains *48 D1 mountain range* Colorado/New Mexico, C USA
San Ignacio *52 B1 prev.* Cayo, El Cayo. Cayo, W Belize
San Ignacio *50 B2* Baja California Sur, W Mexico
San Ignacio *61 F3* Beni, N Bolivia
San Joaquin Valley *47 B7 valley* California, W USA
San Jorge, Golfo *65 C6 var.* Gulf of San Jorge. *Gulf* S Argentina
San Jorge, Gulf of *see* San Jorge, Golfo
San José *see* San José del Guaviare
San Jose *47 B6* California, W USA
San José *52 B3 var.* Puerto San José. Escuintla, S Guatemala
San José *61 G3 var.* San José de Chiquitos. Santa Cruz, E Bolivia
San José *53 E4 country capital* (Costa Rica) San José, C Costa Rica
San José de Chiquitos *see* San José
San José de Cúcuta *see* Cúcuta
San José del Guaviare *58 C4 var.* San José. Guaviare, S Colombia
San Juan *55 F3 dependent territory capital* (Puerto Rico) NE Puerto Rico
San Juan *see* San Juan de los Morros
San Juan *64 B4* San Juan, W Argentina
San Juan Bautista *64 D3* Misiones, S Paraguay
San Juan Bautista Tuxtepec *see* Tuxtepec
San Juan de Alicante *93 F4* País Valenciano, E Spain
San Juan del Norte *53 E4 var.* Greytown. Río San Juan, SE Nicaragua
San Juan de los Morros *58 D2 var.* San Juan. Guárico, N Venezuela
San Juanito, Isla *50 C4 island* C Mexico
San Juan Mountains *48 D1 mountain range* Colorado, C USA
San Juan River *48 C1 river* Colorado/Utah, W USA
San Julián *see* Puerto San Julián
Sankt Gallen *95 B7 var.* St.Gallen, *Eng.* Saint Gall, *Fr.* St-Gall. Sankt Gallen, NE Switzerland
Sankt-Peterburg *110 B4 prev.* Leningrad, Petrograd, *Eng.* Saint Petersburg, *Fin.* Pietari. Leningradskaya Oblast', NW Russian Federation
Sankt Pölten *95 E6* Niederösterreich, N Austria
Sankuru *77 D6 river* C Dem. Rep. Congo
Şanlıurfa *117 E4 prev.* Sanli Urfa, Urfa, *anc.* Edessa. Şanlıurfa, S Turkey
San Lorenzo *60 A1* Esmeraldas, N Ecuador
San Lorenzo *61 G5* Tarija, S Bolivia
San Lorenzo, Isla *60 C4 island* W Peru
Sanlúcar de Barrameda *92 C5* Andalucía, S Spain
San Luis *50 A1 var.* San Luis Río Colorado. Sonora, NW Mexico
San Luis *52 B2* Petén, NE Guatemala
San Luis *64 C4* San Luis, C Argentina
San Luis Obispo *47 B7* California, W USA
San Luis Potosí *51 E3* San Luis Potosí, C Mexico
San Luis Río Colorado *see* San Luis
San Marcos *52 A2* San Marcos, W Guatemala
San Marcos *49 G4* Texas, SW USA
San Marino *96 E1 country capital* (San Marino) C San Marino
San Marino *96 D1 Country* S Europe

San Marino 96

Official name Republic of San Marino
Formation 1631
Capital San Marino
Population 28,119 / 1172 people per sq mile (461 people per sq km)
Total area 23.6 sq. miles (61 sq. km)
Languages Italian
Religions Roman Catholic 93%, Other and nonreligious 7%
Ethnic mix Sammarinese 80%, Italian 19%, other 1%
Government Parliamentary system
Currency Euro = 100 cents
Literacy rate 99%
Calorie consumption Not available

San Martín *154 A2 Argentinian research station* Antarctica
San Mateo *59 E2* Anzoátegui, NE Venezuela
San Matías *61 H3* Santa Cruz, E Bolivia
San Matías, Golfo *65 C5 var.* Gulf of San Matías. *Gulf* E Argentina
San Matías, Gulf of *see* San Matías, Golfo
Sanmenxia *128 C4 var.* Shan Xian. Henan, C China
Sânmiclăuş Mare *see* Sânnicolau Mare
San Miguel *50 D2* Coahuila de Zaragoza, N Mexico
San Miguel *52 C3* San Miguel, SE El Salvador
San Miguel de Ibarra *see* Ibarra
San Miguel de Tucumán *64 C3 var.* Tucumán. Tucumán, N Argentina
San Miguelito *53 G4* Panamá, C Panama
San Miguel, Río *61 G3 river* E Bolivia
Sannār *see* Sennar
Sânnicolaul-Mare *see* Sânnicolau Mare
Sânnicolau Mare *108 A4 var.* Sânnicolaul-Mare, *Hung.* Nagyszentmiklós; *prev.* Sânmiclăuş Mare, Sînnicolau Mare. Timiş, W Romania
Sanok *99 E5* Podkarpackie, SE Poland
San Pablo *61 F5* Potosí, S Bolivia
San Pedro *50 D3 var.* San Pedro de las Colonias. Coahuila de Zaragoza, NE Mexico
San Pedro *52 C1* Corozal, NE Belize
San-Pédro *74 D5* S Côte d'Ivoire
San Pedro de la Cueva *50 C2* Sonora, NW Mexico
San Pedro de las Colonias *see* San Pedro
San Pedro de Lloc *60 B3* La Libertad, NW Peru
San Pedro Mártir, Sierra *50 A1 mountain range* NW Mexico
San Pedro Sula *52 C2* Cortés, NW Honduras
San Rafael *64 B4* Mendoza, W Argentina
San Rafael Mountains *47 C7 mountain range* California, W USA
San Ramón de la Nueva Orán *64 C2* Salta, N Argentina
San Remo *96 A3* Liguria, NW Italy
San Salvador *52 B3 country capital* (El Salvador) San Salvador, SW El Salvador
San Salvador de Jujuy *64 C2 var.* Jujuy. Jujuy, N Argentina
San Salvador, Isla *60 A4 prev.* Watlings Island. *Island* E Bahamas
Sansanné-Mango *75 E4 var.* Mango. N Togo
Sansepolcro *96 C3* Toscana, C Italy
San Severo *97 D5* Puglia, SE Italy
Santa Ana *61 F3* Beni, N Bolivia
Santa Ana *46 D2* California, W USA
Santa Ana *52 B3* Santa Ana, NW El Salvador
Santa Ana Mountains *46 E2 mountain range* California, W USA
Santa Barbara *47 C7* California, W USA
Santa Barbara *50 C2* Chihuahua, N Mexico
Santa Catalina Island *47 B8 island* Channel Islands, California, W USA
Santa Catarina *63 E5 off.* Estado de Santa Catarina. *State* S Brazil
Santa Clara *54 B2* Villa Clara, C Cuba
Santa Clarita *46 D1* California, W USA
Santa Comba *92 B1* Galicia, NW Spain
Santa Cruz *61 G4 var.* Santa Cruz de la Sierra. Santa Cruz, C Bolivia
Santa Cruz *47 B6* California, W USA
Santa Cruz *76 E2* São Tomé, C Sao Tome and Principe
Santa Cruz Barillas *see* Barillas
Santa Cruz de la Sierra *see* Santa Cruz
Santa Cruz del Quiché *52 B2* Quiché, W Guatemala
Santa Cruz de Tenerife *70 A3* Tenerife, Islas Canarias, Spain, NE Atlantic Ocean
Santa Cruz, Isla *60 B5 var.* Indefatigable Island, Isla Chávez. *Island* Galapagos Islands, Ecuador, E Pacific Ocean
Santa Cruz Islands *144 D3 island group* E Solomon Islands
Santa Cruz, Río *65 B7 river* S Argentina
Santa Elena *52 B1* Cayo, W Belize
Santa Fe *48 D1 state capital* New Mexico, SW USA
Santa Fe *64 C4* Santa Fe, C Argentina
Santa Genoveva *50 B3 mountain* W Mexico
Santa Isabel *144 C3 var.* Bughotu. *Island* N Solomon Islands
Santa Lucia Range *47 B7 mountain range* California, W USA
Santa Margarita, Isla *50 B3 island* W Mexico
Santa Maria *92 A5 island* Azores, Portugal, NE Atlantic Ocean
Santa Maria *47 B7* California, W USA
Santa Maria *63 E5* Rio Grande do Sul, S Brazil
Santa María, Isla *60 A5 var.* Isla Floreana, Charles Island. *Island* Galapagos Islands, Ecuador, E Pacific Ocean
Santa Marta *58 B1* Magdalena, N Colombia
Santa Monica *46 D1* California, W USA
Santana *76 E2* São Tomé, S Sao Tome and Principe
Santander *92 D1* Cantabria, N Spain
Santanilla, Islas *53 E1 Eng.* Swan Islands. *Island* NE Honduras
Santarém *92 B3 anc.* Scalabis. Santarém, W Portugal
Santarém *63 E2* Pará, N Brazil
Santa Rosa *see* Santa Rosa de Copán
s
Santa Rosa *64 C4* La Pampa, C Argentina
Santa Rosa de Copán *52 C2 var.* Santa Rosa. Copán, W Honduras
Santa Rosa Island *47 B8 island* California, W USA
Sant Carles de la Rápida *see* Sant Carles de la Ràpita
Sant Carles de la Ràpita *93 F3 var.* Sant Carles de la Rápida. Cataluña, NE Spain
Santiago *64 B4 var.* Gran Santiago. *Country capital* (Chile) Santiago, C Chile
Santiago *92 B1 var.* Santiago de Compostela, *Eng.* Compostella; *anc.* Campus Stellae. Galicia, NW Spain
Santiago *55 E3 var.* Santiago de los Caballeros. N Dominican Republic
Santiago *74 A3 var.* São Tiago. *Island* Ilhas de Sotavento, S Cape Verde
Santiago *see* Santiago de Cuba
Santiago *53 F5* Veraguas, S Panama

Santiago de Compostela *see* Santiago
Santiago de Cuba *54 C3 var.* Santiago. Santiago de Cuba, E Cuba
Santiago de Guayaquil *see* Guayaquil
Santiago del Estero *64 C3* Santiago del Estero, C Argentina
Santiago de los Caballeros *see* Santiago
Santiago Pinotepa Nacional *see* Pinotepa Nacional
Santiago, Río *60 B2 river* N Peru
Santi Quaranta *see* Sarandë
Santissima Trinidad *see* Chilung
Sant Julià de Lòria *91 A8* SW Andorra
Santo *see* Espiritu Santo
Santo Antão *74 A2 island* Ilhas de Barlavento, N Cape Verde
Santo António *76 E1* Príncipe, N Sao Tome and Principe
Santo Domingo *54 D3 prev.* Ciudad Trujillo. *Country capital* (Dominican Republic) SE Dominican Republic
Santo Domingo de los Colorados *60 B1* Pichincha, NW Ecuador
Santo Domingo Tehuantepec *see* Tehuantepec
Santos *63 F4* São Paulo, S Brazil
Santos Plateau *57 D5 undersea feature* SW Atlantic Ocean
Santo Tomé *64 D3* Corrientes, NE Argentina
San Valentín, Cerro *65 A6 mountain* S Chile
San Vicente *52 C3* San Vicente, C El Salvador
São Francisco, Rio *63 F3 river* E Brazil
Sao Hill *73 C7* Iringa, S Tanzania
São João da Madeira *92 B2* Aveiro, N Portugal
São Jorge *92 A5 island* Azores, Portugal, NE Atlantic Ocean
São Luís *63 F2 state capital* Maranhão, NE Brazil
São Mandol *see* São Manuel, Rio
São Manuel, Rio *63 E3 var.* São Mandol, Teles Pirés. *River* C Brazil
São Marcos, Baía de *63 F1 bay* N Brazil
São Miguel *92 A5 island* Azores, Portugal, NE Atlantic Ocean
Saona, Isla *55 E3 island* SE Dominican Republic
Saône *91 D5 river* E France
São Nicolau *74 A3 Eng.* Saint Nicholas. *Island* Ilhas de Barlavento, N Cape Verde
São Paulo *63 E4 off.* Estado de São Paulo. *State* S Brazil
São Paulo *63 E4 state capital* São Paulo, S Brazil
São Paulo de Loanda *see* Luanda
São Pedro do Rio Grande do Sul *see* Rio Grande
São Roque, Cabo de *63 G2 headland* E Brazil
São Salvador *see* M'Banza Congo
São Salvador do Congo *see* M'Banza Congo
São Tiago *see* Santiago
São Tomé *76 E2 Eng.* Saint Thomas. *Island* S Sao Tome and Principe
São Tomé *77 A5 country capital* (Sao Tome and Principe) São Tomé, S Sao Tome and Principe
Sao Tome and Principe *76 D1 Country* E Atlantic Ocean

Sao Tome & Principe 76

Official name Democratic Republic of São Tomé and Príncipe
Formation 1975
Capital São Tomé
Population 175,883 / 474 people per sq mile (183 people per sq km)
Total area 386 sq. miles (1001 sq. km)
Languages Portuguese Creole, Portuguese
Religions Roman Catholic 84%, other 16%

Sao Tome & Principe (continued)

Ethnic mix Black 90%, Portuguese and Creole 10%
Government Presidential system
Currency Dobra = 100 centimos
Literacy rate 83%
Calorie consumption 2567 calories

São Tomé, Pico de *76 D2 mountain* São Tomé, S Sao Tome and Principe
São Vicente, Cabo de *92 B5 Eng.* Cape Saint Vincent, *Port.* Cabo de São Vicente. *Headland* S Portugal
São Vincente *74 A3 Eng.* Saint Vincent. *Island* Ilhas de Barlavento, N Cape Verde
Sápai *see* Sápes
Sapele *75 F5* Delta, S Nigeria
Sápes *104 D3 var.* Sápai. Anatolikí Makedonía kai Thráki, NE Greece
Sapir *see* Sappir
Sa Pobla *93 G3 var.* La Puebla. Mallorca, Spain, W Mediterranean Sea
Sappir *119 B7 var.* Sapir. Southern, S Israel
Sapporo *130 D2* Hokkaidō, NE Japan
Sapri *97 D6* Campania, S Italy
Sapulpa *49 G1* Oklahoma, C USA
Saqqez *120 C2 var.* Saghez, Sakiz, Saqqiz. Kordestān, NW Iran
Saqqiz *see* Saqqez
Sara Buri *137 C5 var.* Saraburi. Saraburi, C Thailand
Saragt *see* Sarahs
Saraguro *60 B2* Loja, S Ecuador
Sarahs *122 D3 var.* Saragt, Serakhs. Akhalskiy Velayat, S Turkmenistan
Sarajevo *100 C4 country capital* (Bosnia and Herzegovina). Federacija Bosna I Hercegovina, SE Bosnia and Herzegovina
Sarakhs *120 E2* Khorāsān, NE Iran
Saraktash *111 D6* Orenburgskaya Oblast', W Russian Federation
Saran' *114 C4 Kaz.* Saran. Karaganda, C Kazakhstan
Saranda *see* Sarandë
Sarandë *101 C7 var.* Saranda, *It.* Porto Edda; *prev.* Santi Quaranta. Vlorë, S Albania
Saransk *111 C5* Respublika Mordoviya, W Russian Federation
Sarasota *43 E4* Florida, SE USA
Saratov *114 B3* Saratovskaya Oblast', W Russian Federation
Saravan *see* Salavan
Saravane *see* Salavan
Sarawak *138 D3 cultural region* Borneo, SE Asia
Sarawak and Sabah (North Borneo) and Singapore *see* Malaysia
Sarcelles *90 D1* Val-d'Oise, N France
Sardegna *97 A5 Eng.* Sardinia. *Island* Italy, C Mediterranean Sea
Sardinia *see* Sardegna
Sarera, Teluk *see* Cenderawasih, Teluk
Sargasso Sea *66 B4 sea* W Atlantic Ocean
Sargodha *134 C2* Punjab, NE Pakistan
Sarh *76 C4 prev.* Fort-Archambault. Moyen-Chari, S Chad
Sārī *120 D2 var.* Sari, Sāri. Māzandarān, N Iran
Saría *105 E7 island* SE Greece
Sarıkamış *117 F3* Kars, NE Turkey
Sarikol Range *123 G3 Rus.* Sarykol'skiy Khrebet. *Mountain range* China/Tajikistan
Sark *89 D8 Fr.* Sercq. *Island* Channel Islands
Şarkışla *116 D3* Sivas, C Turkey
Sarmiento *65 B6* Chubut, S Argentina
Sarnia *38 C5* Ontario, S Canada
Sarny *108 C1* Rivnens'ka Oblast', NW Ukraine
Sarochyna *107 D5 Rus.* Sorochino. Vitsyebskaya Voblasts', N Belarus
Sarov *111 C5 prev.* Sarova. Respublika Mordoviya, SW Russian Federation
Sarova *see* Sarov
Sarpsborg *85 B6* Østfold, S Norway
Sartène *91 E7* Corse, France, C Mediterranean Sea
Sarthe *90 B4 cultural region* N France
Sárti *104 C4* Kentrikí Makedonía, N Greece
Saruhan *see* Manisa
Saryesik-Atyrau, Peski *123 G1 desert* E Kazakhstan
Sary-Tash *123 F2* Oshskaya Oblast', SW Kyrgyzstan
Sasebo *131 A7* Nagasaki, Kyūshū, SW Japan
Saskatchewan *37 F5 river* Manitoba/Saskatchewan, C Canada
Saskatchewan *37 F5 province* SW Canada
Saskatoon *37 F5* Saskatchewan, S Canada
Sasovo *111 B5* Ryazanskaya Oblast', W Russian Federation
Sassandra *74 D5 var.* Ibo, Sassandra Fleuve. *River* S Côte d'Ivoire
Sassandra *74 D5* S Côte d'Ivoire
Sassandra Fleuve *see* Sassandra
Sassari *97 A5* Sardegna, Italy, C Mediterranean Sea
Sassenheim *86 C3* Zuid-Holland, W Netherlands
Sassnitz *94 D2* Mecklenburg-Vorpommern, NE Germany
Sátoraljaújhely *99 D6* Borsod-Abaúj-Zemplén, NE Hungary
Sātpura Range *134 D4 mountain range* C India
Satsunan-shotō *130 A3 var.* Satunan Syotô. *Island group* SW Japan
Sattanen *84 D3* Lappi, NE Finland
Satu Mare *108 B3 Ger.* Sathmar, *Hung.* Szatmárnémeti. Satu Mare, NW Romania
Satunan Syotô *see* Satsunan-shotō
Saudi Arabia *121 B5 Ar.* Al 'Arabīyah as Su'ūdīyah, Al Mamlakah al 'Arabīyah as Su'ūdīyah. *Country* SW Asia

Saudi Arabia 121

Official name Kingdom of Saudi Arabia
Formation 1932
Capital Riyadh; Jiddah (administrative)
Population 24.2 million / 30 people per sq mile (11 people per sq km)
Total area 756,981 sq. miles (1,960,582 sq. km)
Languages Arabic
Religions Sunni Muslim 85%, Shi'a Muslim 15%
Ethnic mix Arab 90%, Afro-Asian 10%
Government Monarchy
Currency Saudi riyal = 100 halalat
Literacy rate 78%
Calorie consumption 2841 calories

Sauer *see* Sûre
Saulkrasti *106 C3* Rīga, C Latvia
Sault Sainte Marie *40 C1* Michigan, N USA
Sault Ste.Marie *38 C4* Ontario, S Canada
Saumur *90 B4* Maine-et-Loire, NW France
Saurimo *78 C1 Port.* Henrique de Carvalho, Vila Henrique de Carvalho. Lunda Sul, NE Angola
Sava *100 B3 Eng.* Save, *Ger.* Sau, *Hung.* Száva. *River* SE Europe
Sava *107 E6 Rus.* Sava. Mahilyowskaya Voblasts', E Belarus
Savá *52 D2* Colón, N Honduras
Savai'i *145 E4 island* NW Samoa
Savannah *43 E2* Georgia, SE USA
Savannah River *43 E2 river* Georgia/South Carolina, SE USA
Savanna-La-Mar *54 A5* W Jamaica
Save, Rio *79 E3 var.* Rio Sabi. *River* Mozambique/Zimbabwe
Saverne *90 E3 var.* Zabern; *anc.* Tres Tabernae. Bas-Rhin, NE France
Savigliano *96 A2* Piemonte, NW Italy
Savigsivik *see* Savissivik
Savinski *see* Savinskiy
Savinskiy *110 C3 var.* Savinski. Arkhangel'skaya Oblast', NW Russian Federation
Savissivik *82 D1 var.* Savigsivik. N Greenland
Savoie *91 D5 cultural region* E France
Savona *96 A2* Liguria, NW Italy
Savu Sea *139 E5 Ind.* Laut Sawu. *Sea* S Indonesia
Sawakin *see* Suakin
Sawdirī *see* Sodiri
Sawhāj *see* Sohâg
Şawqirah *121 D6 var.* Suqrah. S Oman
Sayanskiy Khrebet *112 D3 mountain range* S Russian Federation
Saýat *122 D3 var.* Sayat. Lebapskiy Velayat, E Turkmenistan
Sayaxché *52 B2* Petén, N Guatemala
Şaydā *see* Saïda
Sayḩūt *121 D6* E Yemen
Sayida *see* Saïda
Saynshand *127 E2* Dornogovĭ, SE Mongolia
Sayre *41 E3* Pennsylvania, NE USA
Say'ūn *121 C6 var.* Saywūn. C Yemen
Saywūn *see* Say'ūn
Scandinavia *66 D2 geophysical region* NW Europe
Scarborough *89 D5* N England, UK
Schaan *94 E1* W Liechtenstein
Schaerbeek *87 C6* Brussels, C Belgium
Schaffhausen *95 B7 Fr.* Schaffhouse. Schaffhausen, N Switzerland
Schagen *86 C2* Noord-Holland, NW Netherlands
Schebschi Mountains *see* Shebshi Mountains
Scheessel *94 B3* Niedersachsen, NW Germany
Schefferville *39 E2* Québec, E Canada
Scheldt *87 B5 Dut.* Schelde, *Fr.* Escaut. *River* W Europe
Schell Creek Range *47 D5 mountain range* Nevada, W USA
Schenectady *41 F3* New York, NE USA
Schertz *49 G4* Texas, SW USA
Schiermonnikoog *86 D1 Fris.* Skiermûntseach. *Island* Waddeneilanden, N Netherlands
Schijndel *86 D4* Noord-Brabant, S Netherlands
Schiltigheim *90 E3* Bas-Rhin, NE France
Schleswig *94 B2* Schleswig-Holstein, N Germany
Schleswig-Holstein *94 B2 cultural region* N Germany
Schönebeck *94 C4* Sachsen-Anhalt, C Germany
Schooten *see* Schoten
Schoten *87 C5 var.* Schooten. Antwerpen, N Belgium
Schouwen *86 B4 island* SW Netherlands
Schwabenalb *see* Schwäbische Alb
Schwäbische Alb *95 B6 var.* Schwabenalb, *Eng.* Swabian Jura. *Mountain range* S Germany
Schwandorf *95 C5* Bayern, SE Germany
Schwarzwald *95 B6 Eng.* Black Forest. *Mountain range* SW Germany
Schwaz *95 C7* Tirol, W Austria
Schweinfurt *95 B5* Bayern, SE Germany
Schwerin *94 C3* Mecklenburg-Vorpommern, N Germany

Schwiz *see* Schwyz
Schwyz *95 B7 var.* Schwiz. Schwyz, C Switzerland
Scilly, Isles of *89 B8 island group* SW England, UK
Scio *see* Chíos
Scoresby Sound *see* Ittoqqortoormiit
Scoresbysund *see* Ittoqqortoormiit
Scotia Sea *57 C8 sea* SW Atlantic Ocean
Scotland *88 C3 national region* UK
Scott Base *154 B4 NZ research station* Antarctica
Scott Island *154 B5 island* Antarctica
Scottsbluff *44 D3* Nebraska, C USA
Scottsboro *42 D1* Alabama, S USA
Scottsdale *48 B2* Arizona, SW USA
Scranton *41 F3* Pennsylvania, NE USA
Scupi *see* Skopje
Scutari *see* Shkodër
Scutari, Lake *101 C5 Alb.* Liqeni i Shkodrës, *SCr.* Skadarsko Jezero. *Lake* Albania/Serbia and Montenegro (Yugo.)
Scyros *see* Skýros
Searcy *42 B1* Arkansas, C USA
Seattle *46 B2* Washington, NW USA
Sébaco *52 D3* Matagalpa, W Nicaragua
Sebastían Vizcaíno, Bahía *50 A2 bay* NW Mexico
Sechura, Bahía de *60 A3 bay* NW Peru
Secunderābād *134 D5 var.* Sikandarabad. Andhra Pradesh, C India
Sedan *90 D3* Ardennes, N France
Seddon *151 D5* Marlborough, South Island, NZ
Seddonville *151 C5* West Coast, South Island, NZ
Sédhiou *74 B3* SW Senegal
Sedona *48 B2* Arizona, SW USA
Seesen *94 B4* Niedersachsen, C Germany
Segestica *see* Sisak
Segezha *110 B3* Respublika Kareliya, NW Russian Federation
Ségou *74 D3 var.* Segu. Ségou, C Mali
Segovia *92 D2* Castilla-León, C Spain
Segoviao Wangkí *see* Coco, Río
Segu *see* Ségou
Séguédine *75 H2* Agadez, NE Niger
Seguin *49 G4* Texas, SW USA
Segura *93 E4 river* S Spain
Seinäjoki *85 D5 Swe.* Östermyra. Länsi-Suomi, W Finland
Seine *90 D1 river* N France
Seine, Baie de la *90 B3 bay* N France
Sekondi *see* Sekondi-Takoradi
Sekondi-Takoradi *75 E5 var.* Sekondi. S Ghana
Selat Balabac *see* Balabac Strait
Selenga *127 E1 Mong.* Selenge Mörön. *River* Mongolia/Russian Federation
Sélestat *90 E4 Ger.* Schlettstadt. Bas-Rhin, NE France
Selfoss *83 E5* Sudhurland, SW Iceland
Sélibabi *74 C3 var.* Sélibaby. Guidimaka, S Mauritania
Sélibaby *see* Sélibabi
Selma *47 C6* California, W USA
Selway River *46 D2 river* Idaho, NW USA
Selwyn Range *148 B3 mountain range* Queensland, C Australia
Selzaete *see* Zelzate
Semarang *138 C5 var.* Samarang. Jawa, C Indonesia
Sembé *77 B5* La Sangha, NW Congo
Semey *see* Semipalatinsk
Seminole *49 E3* Texas, SW USA
Seminole, Lake *42 D3 reservoir* Florida/Georgia, SE USA
Semipalatinsk *114 D4 Kaz.* Semey. Vostochnyy kazakhstan, E Kazakhstan
Semnān *120 D3 var.* Samnān. Semnān, N Iran
Semois *87 C8 river* SE Belgium
Sendai *131 A8* Kagoshima, Kyūshū, SW Japan
Sendai *130 D4* Miyagi, Honshū, C Japan
Sendai-wan *130 D4 bay* E Japan
Senec *99 C6 Ger.* Wartberg, *Hung.* Szenc; *prev.* Szempcz. Bratislavský Kraj, W Slovakia
Senegal *74 C3 Fr.* Sénégal. *River* W Africa
Senegal *74 B3 Fr.* Sénégal. *Country* W Africa

Senegal 74

Official name Republic of Senegal
Formation 1960
Capital Dakar
Population 10.1 million / 136 people per sq mile (52 people per sq km)
Total area 75,749 sq. miles (196,190 sq. km)
Languages Wolof, Pulaar, Serer, Diola, Mandinka, Malinke, Soninke, French
Religions Sunni Muslim 90%, Traditional beliefs 5%, Christian (mainly Roman Catholic) 5%
Ethnic mix Wolof 43%, Toucouleur 24%, Serer 15%, other 11%, Diola 4%, Malinke 3%
Government Presidential system
Currency CFA franc = 100 centimes
Literacy rate 39%
Calorie consumption 2277 calories

Senftenberg *94 D4* Brandenburg, E Germany
Senica *99 C6 Ger.* Senitz, *Hung.* Szenice. Trnavský Kraj, W Slovakia
Senj *100 A3 Ger.* Zengg, *It.* Segna; *anc.* Senia. Lika-Senj, NW Croatia
Senja *84 C2 prev.* Senjen. *Island* N Norway
Senkaku-shotō *130 A3 island group* SW Japan
Senlis *90 C3* Oise, N France
Sennar *72 C4 var.* Sannār. Sinnar, C Sudan
Sens *90 C3 anc.* Agendicum, Senones. Yonne, C France
Sên, Stœng *137 D5 river* C Cambodia
Senta *100 D3 Hung.* Zenta. Serbia, N Serbia and Montenegro (Yugo.)
Seo de Urgel *see* La See d'Urgel
Seoul *see* Sŏul
Sept-Îles *39 E3* Québec, SE Canada
Seraing *87 D6* Liège, E Belgium
Serakhs *see* Sarahs
Seram, Pulau *139 F4 var.* Serang, *Eng.* Ceram. *Island* Maluku, E Indonesia
Serang *see* Seram, Pulau
Serang *138 C5* Jawa, C Indonesia
Serasan, Selat *138 C3 strait* Indonesia/Malaysia
Serbia *100 D4 Ger.* Serbien, *Serb.* Srbija. Admin. region *republic* Serbia and Montenegro (Yugo.)
Serbia and Montenegro (Yugo.) *100 D4 SCr.* Jugoslavija, Savezna Republika Jugoslavija. *Country* SE Europe

Serbia and Montenegro (Yugo.) 100

Official name Serbia and Montenegro
Formation 1992
Capital Belgrade
Population 10.5 million / 266 people per sq mile (103 people per sq km)
Total area 39,517 sq. miles (102,350 sq. km)
Languages Serbo-Croat, Albanian, Hungarian (Magyar)
Religions Orthodox Christian 65%, Muslim 19%, other 11%, Roman Catholic 4%, Protestant 1%

Serbia and Montenegro (Yugo.) (continued)

Ethnic mix Serb 62%, Albanian 17%, other 10%, Montenegrin 5%, Magyar 3%, Bosniak 3%
Government Parliamentary system
Currency Dinar (Serbia); euro (Montenegro) = 100 para (dinar); 100 cents (euro)
Literacy rate 98%
Calorie consumption 2778 calories

Serdar *122 C2 prev.* Gyzylarbat, Kizyl-Arvat. Balkanskiy Velayat, W Turkmenistan
Serdica *see* Sofiya
Serenje *78 D2* Central, E Zambia
Seres *see* Sérres
Seret *see* Siret
Sereth *see* Siret
Serhetabat *122 D4 prev.* Gushgy, Kushka. Maryyskiy Velayat, S Turkmenistan
Sérifos *105 C6 anc.* Seriphos. *Island* Kykládes, Greece, Aegean Sea
Serov *114 C3* Sverdlovskaya Oblast', C Russian Federation
Serowe *78 D3* Central, SE Botswana
Serpa Pinto *see* Menongue
Serpent's Mouth, The *59 F2 Sp.* Boca de la Serpiente. *Strait* Trinidad and Tobago/Venezuela
Serpukhov *111 B5* Moskovskaya Oblast', W Russian Federation
Serra dos Parecis *see* Parecis, Chapada dos
Sérrai *see* Sérres
Serrana, Cayo de *53 F2 island group* NW Colombia
Serranilla, Cayo de *53 F2 island group* NW Colombia
Serra Pacaraim *see* Pakaraima Mountains
Serra Tumucumaque *see* Tumuc Humac Mountains
Serravalle *96 E1* N San Marino
Sérres *104 C3 var.* Seres; *prev.* Sérrai. Kentrikí Makedonía, NE Greece
Sert *see* Siirt
Sesto San Giovanni *96 B2* Lombardia, N Italy
Sesvete *100 B2* Zagreb, N Croatia
Setabis *see* Xátiva
Sète *91 C6 prev.* Cette. Hérault, S France
Setesdal *85 A6 valley* S Norway
Sétif *71 E2 var.* Stif. N Algeria
Setté Cama *77 A6* Ogooué-Maritime, SW Gabon
Setúbal *92 B4 Eng.* Saint Ubes, Saint Yves. Setúbal, W Portugal
Setúbal, Baía de *92 B4 bay* W Portugal
Seul, Lac *38 B3 lake* Ontario, S Canada
Sevan *117 G2* C Armenia
Sevana Lich *117 G3 Eng.* Lake Sevan, *Rus.* Ozero Sevan. *Lake* E Armenia
Sevastopol' *109 F5 Eng.* Sebastopol. Respublika Krym, S Ukraine
Severn *89 D6 Wel.* Hafren. *River* England/Wales, UK
Severn *38 B2 river* Ontario, S Canada
Severnaya Dvina *110 C4 var.* Northern Dvina. *River* NW Russian Federation
Severnaya Zemlya *115 E2 var.* Nicholas II Land. *Island group* N Russian Federation
Severnyy *110 E3* Respublika Komi, NW Russian Federation
Severodvinsk *110 C3 prev.* Molotov, Sudostroy. Arkhangel'skaya Oblast', NW Russian Federation
Severomorsk *110 C2* Murmanskaya Oblast', NW Russian Federation
Severo-Sibirskaya Nizmennost' *115 E2 var.* North Siberian Plain, *Eng.* North Siberian Lowland. *Lowlands* N Russian Federation
Seversk *114 D4* Tomskaya Oblast', C Russian Federation
Severskiy Donets *see* Donets
Sevier Lake *44 A4 lake* Utah, W USA
Sevilla *92 C4 Eng.* Seville; *anc.* Hispalis. Andalucía, SW Spain
Seville *see* Sevilla
Sevlievo *104 D2* Gabrovo, N Bulgaria
Seychelles *79 G1 Country* W Indian Ocean

Seychelles 79

Official name Republic of Seychelles
Formation 1976
Capital Victoria
Population 80,469 / 774 people per sq mile (298 people per sq km)
Total area 176 sq. miles (455 sq. km)
Languages French Creole, English, French
Religions Roman Catholic 90%, Anglican 8%, Other 2%
Ethnic mix Creole 89%, Indian 5%, other 4%, Chinese 2%
Government Presidential system
Currency Seychelles rupee = 100 cents
Literacy rate 92%
Calorie consumption 2461 calories

Seydhisfjördhur *83 E5* Austurland, E Iceland
Seýdi *122 D2 var.* Seydi; *prev.* Neftezavodsk. Lebapskiy Velayat, E Turkmenistan
Seyhan *see* Adana
Sfákia *105 C8* Kríti, Greece, E Mediterranean Sea
Sfântu Gheorghe *108 C4 Ger.* Sankt-Georgen, *Hung.* Sepsiszentgyőrgy; *prev.* Şepşi-Sângeorz, Sfintu Gheorghe. Covasna, C Romania
Sfax *71 F2 Ar.* Şafāqis. E Tunisia
's-Gravenhage *86 B4 var.* Den Haag, *Eng.* The Hague, *Fr.* La Haye. *Country capital* (Netherlands-seat of government) Zuid-Holland, W Netherlands
's-Gravenzande *86 B4* Zuid-Holland, W Netherlands
Shaan *see* Shaanxi
Shaanxi *128 B5 var.* Shaan, Shaanxi Sheng, Shan-hsi, Shenshi, Shensi. Admin. region *province* C China
Shaanxi Sheng *see* Shaanxi
Shache *126 A3 var.* Yarkant. Xinjiang Uygur Zizhiqu, NW China
Shackleton Ice Shelf *154 D3 ice shelf* Antarctica
Shaddādī *see* Ash Shadādah
Shāhābād *see* Eslāmābād
Shahjahanabad *see* Delhi
Shahr-e Kord *120 C3 var.* Shahr Kord. Chahār Maḩall va Bakhtīārī, C Iran
Shahr Kord *see* Shahr-e Kord
Shāhrūd *120 D2 prev.* Emāmrūd, Emāmshahr. Semnān, N Iran
Shalkar *114 B4 var.* Chelkar. Aktyubinsk, W Kazakhstan
Shandī *see* Shendi
Shandong *128 D4 var.* Lu, Shandong Sheng, Shantung. Admin. region *province* E China
Shandong Sheng *see* Shandong
Shanghai *128 D5 var.* Shang-hai. Shanghai Shi, E China
Shang-hai *see* Shanghai
Shangrao *128 D5* Jiangxi, S China
Shan-hsi *see* Shaanxi
Shan-hsi *see* Shanxi
Shannon *89 A6 Ir.* An tSionainn. *River* W Ireland
Shan Plateau *136 B3 plateau* E Myanmar
Shansi *see* Shanxi
Shantarskiye Ostrova *115 G3 Eng.* Shantar Islands. *Island group* E Russian Federation
Shantou *128 D6 var.* Shan-t'ou, Swatow. Guangdong, S China
Shantung *see* Shandong
Shanxi *128 C4 var.* Jin, Shan-hsi, Shansi, Shanxi Sheng. Admin. region *province* C China

Shan Xian *see* Sanmenxia
Shanxi Sheng *see* Shanxi
Shaoguan *128 C6 var.* Shao-kuan, *Cant.* Kukong; *prev.* Ch'u-chiang. Guangdong, S China
Shao-kuan *see* Shaoguan
Shaqrā *see* Shuqrah
Shaqrā' *120 B4* Ar Riyāḍ, C Saudi Arabia
Shar *130 D5 var.* Charsk. Vostochnyy Kazakhstan, E Kazakhstan
Shari *see* Chari
Shari *130 D2* Hokkaidō, NE Japan
Shark Bay *147 A5 bay* Western Australia
Shashe *78 D3 var.* Shashi. *River* Botswana/Zimbabwe
Shashi *see* Shashe
Shatskiy Rise *125 G1 undersea feature* N Pacific Ocean
Shatt al-Hodna *see* Hodna, Chott El
Shaṭṭ al Jarīd *see* Jerid, Chott el
Shawnee *49 G1* Oklahoma, C USA
Shchadryn *107 D7 Rus.* Shchedrin. Homyel'skaya Voblasts', SE Belarus
Shchëkino *111 B5* Tul'skaya Oblast', W Russian Federation
Shchors *109 E1* Chernihivs'ka Oblast', N Ukraine
Shchuchinsk *114 C4 prev.* Shchuchye. Severnyy kazakhstan, N Kazakhstan
Shchuchyn *107 B5 Pol.* Szczuczyn Nowogródzki, *Rus.* Shchuchin. Hrodzyenskaya Voblasts', W Belarus
Shebekino *111 A6* Belgorodskaya Oblast', W Russian Federation
Shebeli *73 D5 Amh.* Wabē Shebelē Wenz, *It.* Scebeli, *Som.* Webi Shabeelle. *River* Ethiopia/Somalia
Sheberghān *123 E3 var.* Shibarghān, Shiberghan, Shiberghān. Jowzjān, N Afghanistan
Sheboygan *40 B2* Wisconsin, N USA
Shebshi Mountains *76 A4 var.* Schebschi Mountains. *Mountain range* E Nigeria
Shechem *see* Nablus
Shedadi *see* Ash Shadādah
Sheffield *89 D5* N England, UK
Shekhem *see* Nablus
Shelby *44 B1* Montana, NW USA
Sheldon *45 F3* Iowa, C USA
Shelekhov Gulf *see* Shelikhova, Zaliv
Shelikhova, Zaliv *115 G2 Eng.* Shelekhov Gulf. *Gulf* E Russian Federation
Shendi *72 C4 var.* Shandī. River Nile, NE Sudan
Shengking *see* Liaoning
Shenking *see* Liaoning
Shenshi *see* Shaanxi
Shensi *see* Shaanxi
Shenyang *128 D3 Chin.* Shen-yang, *Eng.* Moukden, Mukden; *prev.* Fengtien. Liaoning, NE China
Shepetivka *108 D2 Rus.* Shepetovka. Khmel'nyts'ka Oblast', NW Ukraine
Shepparton *149 C7* Victoria, SE Australia
Sherbrooke *39 E4* Québec, SE Canada
Shereik *72 C3* River Nile, N Sudan
Sheridan *44 C2* Wyoming, C USA
Sherman *49 G2* Texas, SW USA
's-Hertogenbosch *86 C4 Fr.* Bois-le-Duc, *Ger.* Herzogenbusch. Noord-Brabant, S Netherlands
Shetland Islands *88 D1 island group* NE Scotland, UK
Shibarghān *see* Sheberghān
Shiberghān *see* Sheberghān
Shibetsu *130 D2 var.* Sibetu. Hokkaidō, NE Japan
Shibh Jazīrat Sīnā' *see* Sinai
Shibushi-wan *131 B8 bay* SW Japan
Shigatse *see* Xigazê
Shih-chia-chuang *see* Shijiazhuang
Shihezi *126 C2* Xinjiang Uygur Zizhiqu, NW China
Shihmen *see* Shijiazhuang
Shijiazhuang *128 C4 var.* Shih-chia-chuang; *prev.* Shihmen. Hebei, E China
Shikarpur *134 B3* Sind, S Pakistan
Shikoku *131 C7 var.* Sikoku. *Island* SW Japan
Shikoku Basin *125 F2 var.* Sikoku Basin. *Undersea feature* N Philippine Sea
Shikotan, Ostrov *130 E2 Jap.* Shikotan-tō. *Island* NE Russian Federation
Shilabo *73 D5* E Ethiopia
Shiliguri *135 F3 prev.* Siliguri. West Bengal, NE India
Shilka *115 F4 river* S Russian Federation
Shillong *135 G3* E India
Shimbir Berris *see* Shimbiris
Shimbiris *72 E4 var.* Shimbir Berris. *Mountain* N Somalia
Shimoga *132 C2* Karnātaka, W India
Shimonoseki *131 A7 var.* Simonoseki; *hist.* Akamagaseki, Bakan. Yamaguchi, Honshū, SW Japan
Shinano-gawa *131 C5 var.* Sinano Gawa. *River* Honshū, C Japan
Shīndand *122 D4* Farāh, W Afghanistan
Shingū *131 C6 var.* Singû. Wakayama, Honshū, SW Japan
Shinjō *130 D4 var.* Sinzyô. Yamagata, Honshū, C Japan
Shinyanga *73 C7* Shinyanga, NW Tanzania
Shiprock *48 C1* New Mexico, SW USA
Shīrāz *120 D4 var.* Shīrāz. Fārs, S Iran
Shivpuri *134 D3* Madhya Pradesh, C India
Shizugawa *130 D4* Miyagi, Honshū, NE Japan
Shizuoka *131 D6 var.* Sizuoka. Shizuoka, Honshū, S Japan
Shklow *107 D6 Rus.* Shklov. Mahilyowskaya Voblasts', E Belarus
Shkodër *101 C5 var.* Shkodra, *It.* Scutari, *SCr.* Skadar. Shkodër, NW Albania
Shkodra *see* Shkodër
Shkubinit, Lumi i *101 C6 var.* Shkumbî, Shkumbin. *River* C Albania
Shkumbî *see* Shkubinit, Lumi i
Shkumbin *see* Shkubinit, Lumi i
Sholāpur *see* Solāpur
Shostka *109 F1* Sums'ka Oblast', NE Ukraine
Show Low *48 B2* Arizona, SW USA
Shpola *109 E3* Cherkas'ka Oblast', N Ukraine
Shreveport *42 A2* Louisiana, S USA
Shrewsbury *89 D6 hist.* Scrobesbyrig'. W England, UK
Shu *114 C5 Kaz.* Shū. Zhambyl, SE Kazakhstan
Shuang-liao *see* Liaoyuan
Shumagin Islands *36 B3 island group* Alaska, USA
Shumen *104 D2* Shumen, NE Bulgaria
Shumilina *107 E5 Rus.* Shumilino. Vitsyebskaya Voblasts', NE Belarus
Shuqrah *121 B7 var.* Shaqrā. SW Yemen
Shwebo *136 B3* Sagaing, C Myanmar
Shyichy *107 C7 Rus.* Shiichi. Homyel'skaya Voblasts', SE Belarus
Shymkent *114 B5 prev.* Chimkent. Yuzhnyy Kazakhstan, S Kazakhstan
Shyshchytsy *107 C6 Rus.* Shishchitsy. Minskaya Voblasts', C Belarus
Si *see* Syr Darya
Siam, Gulf of *see* Thailand, Gulf of
Sian *see* Xi'an
Siang *see* Brahmaputra
Siangtan *see* Xiangtan
Šiauliai *106 B4 Ger.* Schaulen. Šiauliai, N Lithuania
Sibay *111 D6* Respublika Bashkortostan, W Russian Federation
Šibenik *116 B4 It.* Sebenico. Šibenik-Knin, S Croatia
Siberia *see* Sibir'
Siberut, Pulau *138 A4 prev.* Siberoet. *Island* Kepulauan Mentawai, W Indonesia
Sibetu *see* Shibetsu
Sibi *134 B2* Baluchistān, SW Pakistan
Sibir' *115 E3 var.* Siberia. *Physical region* NE Russian Federation
Sibiti *77 B6* La Lékoumou, S Congo
Sibiu *108 B4 Ger.* Hermannstadt, *Hung.* Nagyszeben. Sibiu, C Romania
Sibolga *138 B3* Sumatera, W Indonesia
Sibu *138 D3* Sarawak, East Malaysia
Sibut *76 C4 prev.* Fort-Sibut. Kémo, S Central African Republic
Sibuyan Sea *139 E2 sea* C Philippines
Sichon *137 C6 var.* Ban Sichon, Si Chon. Nakhon Si Thammarat, SW Thailand
Sichuan *128 B5 var.* Chuan, Sichuan Sheng, Ssu-ch'uan, Szechuan, Szechwan. Admin. region *province* C China
Sichuan Pendi *128 B5 depression* C China
Sichuan Sheng *see* Sichuan
Sicilia *97 C7 Eng.* Sicily; *anc.* Trinacria. *Island* Italy, C Mediterranean Sea
Sicilian Channel *see* Sicily, Strait of
Sicily *see* Sicilia
Sicily, Strait of *97 B7 var.* Sicilian Channel. *Strait* C Mediterranean Sea
Sicuani *61 E4* Cusco, S Peru
Sidári *104 A4* Kérkyra, Iónioi Nísoi, Greece, C Mediterranean Sea
Sidas *138 C4* Borneo, C Indonesia
Siderno *97 D7* Calabria, SW Italy
Sîdi Barrâni *72 A1* NW Egypt
Sidi Bel Abbès *70 D2 var.* Sidi bel Abbès, Sidi-Bel-Abbès. NW Algeria
Sidirókastro *104 C3 prev.* Sidhirókastron. Kentrikí Makedonía, NE Greece
Sidley, Mount *154 B4 mountain* Antarctica
Sidney *44 D1* Montana, NW USA
Sidney *44 D4* Nebraska, C USA
Sidney *40 C4* Ohio, N USA
Sidon *see* Saïda
Sidra *see* Surt
Siedlce *98 E3 Ger.* Sedlez, *Rus.* Sesdlets. Mazowieckie, C Poland
Siegen *94 B4* Nordrhein-Westfalen, W Germany
Siemiatycze *98 E3* Podlaskie
Siena *96 B3 Fr.* Sienne; *anc.* Saena Julia. Toscana, C Italy
Sieradz *98 C4* Łódzkie, C Poland
Sierpc *98 D3* Mazowieckie, C Poland
Sierra de Soconusco *see* Sierra Madre
Sierra Leone *74 C4 Country* W Africa

Sierra Leone 74

Official name Republic of Sierra Leone
Formation 1961
Capital Freetown
Population 5 million / 181 people per sq mile (70 people per sq km)
Total area 27,698 sq. miles (71,740 sq. km)
Languages Mende, Temne, Krio, English
Religions Traditional beliefs 30%, Muslim 30%, Christian 10%, Other 30%
Ethnic mix Mende 35%, Temne 32%, Limba 8%, Kuranko 4%, other 21%
Government Presidential system
Currency Leone = 100 cents
Literacy rate 36%
Calorie consumption 1913 calories

Sierra Leone Basin *66 C4 undersea feature* E Atlantic Ocean
Sierra Leone Ridge *see* Sierra Leone Rise
Sierra Leone Rise *66 C4 var.* Sierra Leone Ridge, Sierra Leone Schwelle. *Undersea feature* E Atlantic Ocean
Sierra Leone Schwelle *see* Sierra Leone Rise
Sierra Madre *52 B2 var.* Sierra de Soconusco. *Mountain range* Guatemala/Mexico
Sierra Madre *see* Madre Occidental, Sierra
Sierra Nevada *47 C6 mountain range* W USA
Sierra Pacaraima *see* Pakaraima Mountains
Sierra Vieja *48 D3 mountain range* Texas, SW USA
Sierra Vista *48 B3* Arizona, SW USA
Sífnos *105 C6 anc.* Siphnos. *Island* Kykládes, Greece, Aegean Sea
Sigli *138 A3* Sumatera, W Indonesia
Siglufjördhur *83 E4* Nordhurland Vestra, N Iceland
Signal Peak *48 A2 mountain* Arizona, SW USA
Signan *see* Xi'an
Signy *154 A2 UK research station* South Orkney Islands, Antarctica
Siguatepeque *52 C2* Comayagua, W Honduras
Siguiri *74 D4* Haute-Guinée, NE Guinea
Siilinjärvi *84 E4* Itä-Suomi, C Finland
Siirt *117 F4 var.* Sert; *anc.* Tigranocerta. Siirt, SE Turkey
Sikandarabad *see* Secunderābād
Sikasso *74 D4* Sikasso, S Mali
Sikeston *45 H5* Missouri, C USA
Sikhote-Alin', Khrebet *115 G4 mountain range* SE Russian Federation
Siking *see* Xi'an
Siklós *99 C7* Baranya, SW Hungary
Sikoku *see* Shikoku
Sikoku Basin *see* Shikoku Basin
Šilalė *106 B4* Šilalė, W Lithuania
Silchar *135 G3* Assam, NE India
Silesia *98 B4 physical region* SW Poland
Silifke *116 C4 anc.* Seleucia. İçel, S Turkey
Siling Co *126 C5 lake* W China
Silinhot *see* Xilinhot
Silistra *104 E1 var.* Silistria; *anc.* Durostorum. Silistra, NE Bulgaria
Silistria *see* Silistra
Sillamäe *106 E2 Ger.* Sillamäggi. Ida-Virumaa, NE Estonia
Šilutė *106 B4 Ger.* Heydekrug. Šilutė, W Lithuania
Silvan *117 E4* Dıyarbakır, SE Turkey
Silverek *117 E4* Şanlıurfa, SE Turkey
Simanggang *see* Sri Aman
Simanichy *107 C7 Rus.* Simonichi. Homyel'skaya Voblasts', SE Belarus
Simav *116 B3* Kütahya, W Turkey
Simav Çayı *116 A3 river* NW Turkey
Simeto *97 C7 river* Sicilia, Italy, C Mediterranean Sea
Simeulue, Pulau *138 A3 island* NW Indonesia
Simferopol' *109 F5* Respublika Krym, S Ukraine
Simitli *104 C3* Blagoevgrad, SW Bulgaria
Şimleu Silvaniei *108 B3 Hung.* Szilágșomlyó; *prev.* Şimlăul Silvaniei, Şimleul Silvaniei. Sălaj, NW Romania
Simonoseki *see* Shimonoseki
Simpelveld *87 D6* Limburg, SE Netherlands
Simplon Pass *95 B8 pass* S Switzerland
Simpson *see* Fort Simpson
Simpson Desert *148 B4 desert* Northern Territory/South Australia

Sīnā' *see* Sinai
Sinai *72 C2 var.* Sinai Peninsula, *Ar.* Shibh Jazīrat Sīnā', Sīnā'. *Physical region* NE Egypt
Sinaia *108 C4* Prahova, SE Romania
Sinai Peninsula *see* Sinai
Sinano Gawa *see* Shinano-gawa
Sincelejo *58 B2* Sucre, NW Colombia
Sind *134 B3 var.* Sindh. Admin. region *province* SE Pakistan
Sindelfingen *95 B6* Baden-Württemberg, SW Germany
Sindh *see* Sind
Sindi *106 D2 Ger.* Zintenhof. Pärnumaa, SW Estonia
Sines *92 B4* Setúbal, S Portugal
Singan *see* Xi'an
Singapore *138 A1 Country* SE Asia

Singapore 138

Official name Republic of Singapore
Formation 1965
Capital Singapore
Population 4.3 million / 18220 people per sq mile (7049 people per sq km)
Total area 250 sq. miles (648 sq. km)
Languages Mandarin, Malay, Tamil, English
Religions Buddhist 55%, Taoist 22%, Muslim 16%, Hindu, Christian, and Sikh 7%
Ethnic mix Chinese 77%, Malay 14%, Indian 8%, other 1%
Government Parliamentary system
Currency Singapore dollar = 100 cents
Literacy rate 93%
Calorie consumption Not available

Singapore *138 B3 country capital* (Singapore) S Singapore
Singen *95 B6* Baden-Württemberg, S Germany
Singida *73 C7* Singida, C Tanzania
Singkang *139 E4* Sulawesi, C Indonesia
Singkawang *138 C3* Borneo, C Indonesia
Singora *see* Songkhla
Singû *see* Shingū
Sining *see* Xining
Siniscola *97 A5* Sardegna, Italy, C Mediterranean Sea
Sinj *100 B4* Split-Dalmacija, SE Croatia
Sinkiang *see* Xinjiang Uygur Zizhiqu
Sinkiang Uighur Autonomous Region *see* Xinjiang Uygur Zizhiqu
Sinnamarie *see* Sinnamary
Sinnamary *59 H3 var.* Sinnamarie. N French Guiana
Sînnicolau Mare *see* Sânnicolau Mare
Sinoie, Lacul *108 D5 prev.* Lacul Sinoe. *Lagoon* SE Romania
Sinop *116 D2 anc.* Sinope. Sinop, N Turkey
Sinsheim *95 B6* Baden-Württemberg, SW Germany
Sint Maarten *55 G3 Eng.* Saint Martin. *Island* N Netherlands Antilles
Sint-Michielsgestel *86 C4* Noord-Brabant, S Netherlands
Sint-Niklaas *87 B5 Fr.* Saint-Nicolas. Oost-Vlaanderen, N Belgium
Sint-Pieters-Leeuw *87 B6* Vlaams Brabant, C Belgium
Sintra *92 B3 prev.* Cintra. Lisboa, W Portugal
Sinujiif *73 E5* Nugaal, NE Somalia
Sinus Aelaniticus *see* Aqaba, Gulf of
Sinyang *see* Xinyang
Sinzyô *see* Shinjō
Sion *95 A7 Ger.* Sitten; *anc.* Sedunum. Valais, SW Switzerland
Sioux City *45 F3* Iowa, C USA
Sioux Falls *45 F3* South Dakota, N USA
Siping *128 D3 var.* Ssu-p'ing, Szeping; *prev.* Ssu-p'ing-chieh. Jilin, NE China
Siple, Mount *154 A4 mountain* Siple Island, Antarctica
Siquirres *53 E4* Limón, E Costa Rica
Siracusa *97 D7 Eng.* Syracuse. Sicilia, Italy, C Mediterranean Sea
Sir Darya *see* Syr Darya
Sir Edward Pellew Group *148 B2 island group* Northern Territory, NE Australia
Siret *108 C3 var.* Siretul, *Ger.* Sereth, *Rus.* Seret, *Ukr.* Siret. *River* Romania/Ukraine
Siret *see* Siret
Siretul *see* Siret
Sirikit Reservoir *136 C4 lake* N Thailand
Sīrjān *120 D4 prev.* Sa'īdābād. Kermān, S Iran
Sirna *see* Sýrna
Şırnak *117 F4* Şırnak, SE Turkey
Síros *see* Sýros
Sirte *see* Surt
Sirte, Gulf of *see* Surt, Khalīj
Sisak *100 B3 var.* Siscia, *Ger.* Sissek, *Hung.* Sziszek; *anc.* Segestica. Sisak-Moslavina, C Croatia
Siscia *see* Sisak
Sisimiut *82 C3 var.* Holsteinborg, Holsteinsborg, Holstenborg, Holstensborg. S Greenland
Sissek *see* Sisak
Sistema Penibético *see* Béticos, Sistemas
Siteía *105 D8 var.* Sitía. Kríti, Greece, E Mediterranean Sea
Sitges *93 G2* Cataluña, NE Spain
Sitía *see* Siteía
Sittang *136 B4 var.* Sittoung. *River* S Myanmar
Sittard *87 D5* Limburg, SE Netherlands
Sittoung *see* Sittang
Sittwe *136 A3 var.* Akyab. Arakan State, W Myanmar
Siuna *52 D3* Región Autónoma Atlántico Norte, NE Nicaragua
Siut *see* Asyût
Sivas *116 D3 anc.* Sebastia, Sebaste. Sivas, C Turkey
Sivers'kyy Donets' *see* Donets
Siwa *72 A2 var.* Sīwah. NW Egypt
Sīwah *see* Siwa
Six-Fours-les-Plages *91 D6* Var, SE France
Siyäzän *117 H2 Rus.* Siazan'. NE Azerbaijan
Sizuoka *see* Shizuoka
Sjar *see* Sääre
Sjælland *B8 Eng.* Zealand, *Ger.* Seeland. *Island* E Denmark
Sjenica *101 D5 Turk.* Seniça. Serbia, SW Serbia and Montenegro (Yugo.)
Skadar *see* Shkodër
Skagerak *see* Skagerrak
Skagerrak *85 A6 var.* Skagerak. *Channel* N Europe
Skagit River *46 B1 river* Washington, NW USA
Skalka *84 C3 lake* N Sweden
Skarżysko-Kamienna *98 D4* Świętokrzyskie, C Poland
Skaudvilė *106 B4* Tauragė, SW Lithuania
Skegness *89 E6* E England, UK
Skellefteå *84 D4* Västerbotten, N Sweden
Skellefteälven *84 C4 river* N Sweden
Ski *85 B6* Akershus, S Norway
Skíathos *105 C5* Skíathos, Vóreioi Sporádes, Greece, Aegean Sea
Skidal' *107 B5 Rus.* Skidel'. Hrodzyenskaya Voblasts', W Belarus
Skierniewice *98 D3* Lodzkie, C Poland
Skiftet *106 C1 Fin.* Kihti. *Strait* Gulf of Bothnia/Gulf of Finland
Skíros *see* Skýros
Skópelos *105 C5* Skópelos, Vóreioi Sporádes, Greece, Aegean Sea
Skopje *101 D6 var.* Üsküb, *Turk.* Üsküp; *prev.* Skoplje, *anc.* Scupi. *Country capital* (FYR Macedonia) N FYR Macedonia
Skoplje *see* Skopje
Skovorodino *115 F4* Amurskaya Oblast', SE Russian Federation
Skuodas *106 B3 Ger.* Schoden, *Pol.* Szkudy. Skuodas, NW Lithuania
Skye, Isle of *88 B3 island* NW Scotland, UK
Skýros *105 C5 var.* Skíros. Skýros, Vóreioi Sporádes, Greece, Aegean Sea
Skýros *105 C5 var.* Skíros; *anc.* Scyros. *Island* Vóreioi Sporádes, Greece, Aegean Sea
Slagelse *85 B7* Vestsjælland, E Denmark
Slatina *108 B5* Olt, S Romania
Slatina *100 C3 Hung.* Szlatina, *prev.* Podravska Slatina. Virovtica-Podravina, NE Croatia
Slavonska Požega *see* Požega
Slavonski Brod *100 C3 Ger.* Brod, *Hung.* Bród; *prev.* Brod, Brod na Savi. Brod-Posavina, NE Croatia
Slavuta *108 C2* Khmel'nyts'ka Oblast', NW Ukraine
Slawharad *107 E7 Rus.* Slavgorod. Mahilyowskaya Voblasts', E Belarus
Sławno *98 C2* Zachodniopomorskie, NW Poland
Sléibhte Chill Mhantáin *see* Wicklow Mountains
Slēmānī *see* As Sulaymānīyah
Sliema *102 B5* N Malta
Sligeach *see* Sligo
Sligo *89 A5 Ir.* Sligeach. NW Ireland
Sliven *104 D2 var.* Slivno. Sliven, C Bulgaria
Slivnitsa *104 B2* Sofiya, W Bulgaria
Slivno *see* Sliven
Slobozia *108 C5* Ialomiţa, SE Romania
Slonim *107 B6 Pol.* Słonim, *Rus.* Slonim. Hrodzyenskaya Voblasts', W Belarus
Slovakia *99 C6 Ger.* Slowakei, *Hung.* Szlovákia, *Slvk.* Slovensko. *Country* C Europe

Slovakia 99

Official name Slovak Republic
Formation 1993
Capital Bratislava
Population 5.4 million / 285 people per sq mile (110 people per sq km)
Total area 18,859 sq. miles (48,845 sq. km)
Languages Slovak, Hungarian (Magyar), Czech
Religions Roman Catholic 60%, other 18%, Atheist 10%, Protestant 8%, Orthodox Christian 4%
Ethnic mix Slovak 85%, Magyar 11%, other 2%, Roma 1%, Czech 1%
Government Parliamentary system
Currency Slovak koruna = 100 halierov
Literacy rate 99%
Calorie consumption 2894 calories

Slovak Ore Mountains *see* Slovenské rudohorie
Slovenia *95 D8 Ger.* Slowenien, *Slvn.* Slovenija. *Country* SE Europe

Slovenia 95

Official name Republic of Slovenia
Formation 1991
Capital Ljubljana
Population 2 million / 256 people per sq mile (99 people per sq km)
Total area 7820 sq. miles (20,253 sq. km)

Slovenia (continued)

Languages Slovene, Serbo-Croat
Religions Roman Catholic 96%, other 3%, Muslim 1%
Ethnic mix Slovene 83%, other 12%, Serb 2%, Croat 2%, Bosniak 1%
Government Parliamentary system
Currency Tolar = 100 stotinov
Literacy rate 99%
Calorie consumption 2935 calories

Slovenské rudohorie *99 D6 Eng.* Slovak Ore Mountains, *Ger.* Slowakisches Erzgebirge, Ungarisches Erzgebirge. *Mountain range* C Slovakia
Slov"yans'k *109 G3 Rus.* Slavyansk. Donets'ka Oblast', E Ukraine
Slowakisches Erzgebirge *see* Slovenské rudohorie
Słubice *98 B3 Ger.* Frankfurt. Lubuskie, W Poland
Sluch *108 D1 river* NW Ukraine
Słupsk *98 C2 Ger.* Stolp. Pomorskie, N Poland
Slutsk *107 C6 Rus.* Slutsk. Minskaya Voblasts', S Belarus
Smallwood Reservoir *39 F2 lake* Newfoundland and Labrador, S Canada
Smara *70 B3 var.* Es Semara. N Western Sahara
Smarhon' *107 C5 Pol.* Smorgonie, *Rus.* Smorgon'. Hrodzyenskaya Voblasts', W Belarus
Smederevo *100 D4 Ger.* Semendria. Serbia, N Serbia and Montenegro (Yugo.)
Smederevska Palanka *100 D4* Serbia, C Serbia and Montenegro (Yugo.)
Smila *109 E2 Rus.* Smela. Cherkas'ka Oblast', C Ukraine
Smiltene *106 D3 Ger.* Smilten. Valka, N Latvia
Smøla *84 A4 island* W Norway
Smolensk *111 A5* Smolenskaya Oblast', W Russian Federation
Snake *34 B4 river* Yukon Territory, NW Canada
Snake River *46 C3 river* NW USA
Snake River Plain *46 D4 plain* Idaho, NW USA
Sneek *86 D2* Friesland, N Netherlands
Sněžka *98 B4 Ger.* Schneekoppe. *Mountain* N Czech Republic
Śniardwy, Jezioro *114 D2 Ger.* Spirdingsee. *Lake* NE Poland
Snina *99 E5 Hung.* Szinna. Prešovský Kraj, E Slovakia
Snowdonia *89 C6 mountain range* NW Wales, UK
Snyder *49 F3* Texas, SW USA
Sobradinho, Represa de *63 F2 var.* Barragem de Sobradinho. *Reservoir* E Brazil
Sochi *111 A7* Krasnodarskiy Kray, SW Russian Federation
Société, Archipel de la *145 G4 var.* Archipel de Tahiti, Îles de la Société, *Eng.* Society Islands. *Island group* W French Polynesia
Society Islands *see* Société, Archipel de la
Socorro *48 D2* New Mexico, SW USA
Socorro, Isla *50 B5 island* W Mexico
Socotra *see* Suquṭrā
Soc Trăng *137 D6 var.* Khanh. Soc Trăng, S Vietnam
Socuéllamos *93 E3* Castilla-La Mancha, C Spain
Sodankylä *84 D3* Lappi, N Finland
Sodari *see* Sodiri
Söderhamn *85 C5* Gävleborg, C Sweden
Södertälje *85 C6* Stockholm, C Sweden
Sodiri *72 B4 var.* Sawdirī, Sodari. Northern Kordofan, C Sudan
Sofia *see* Sofiya
Sofiya *104 C2 var.* Sophia, *Eng.* Sofia; *Lat.* Serdica. *Country capital* (Bulgaria) Sofiya-Grad, W Bulgaria

Sogamoso *58 B3* Boyacá, C Colombia
Sognefjorden *85 A5 fjord* NE North Sea
Sohâg *72 B2 var.* Sawhāj, Suliag. C Egypt
Sohar *see* Şuḩār
Sohm Plain *66 B3 undersea feature* NW Atlantic Ocean
Sohrau *see* Żory
Sokal' *108 C2 Rus.* Sokal. L'vivs'ka Oblast', NW Ukraine
Söke *116 A4* Aydın, SW Turkey
Sokhumi *117 E1 Rus.* Sukhumi. NW Georgia
Sokodé *75 F4* C Togo
Sokol *110 C4* Vologodskaya Oblast', NW Russian Federation
Sokółka *98 E3* Białystok, NE Poland
Sokolov *99 A5 Ger.* Falkenau an der Eger; *prev.* Falknov nad Ohří. Karlovarský Kraj, W Czech Republic
Sokone *74 B3* W Senegal
Sokoto *75 F4 river* NW Nigeria
Sokoto *75 F3* Sokoto, NW Nigeria
Sokotra *see* Suquṭrā
Solāpur *124 B3 var.* Sholāpur. Mahārāshtra, W India
Solca *108 C3 Ger.* Solka. Suceava, N Romania
Sol, Costa del *92 D5 coastal region* S Spain
Soldeu *91 B7* NE Andorra
Solec Kujawski *98 C3* Kujawski-pomorskie, C Poland
Soledad, Isla *see* East Falkland
Soledad *58 B1* Anzoátegui, NE Venezuela
Solikamsk *114 C3* Permskaya Oblast', NW Russian Federation
Sol'-Iletsk *111 D6* Orenburgskaya Oblast', W Russian Federation
Solingen *94 A4* Nordrhein-Westfalen, W Germany
Sollentuna *85 C6* Stockholm, C Sweden
Solok *138 B4* Sumatera, W Indonesia
Solomon Islands *144 C3 prev.* British Solomon Islands Protectorate. *Country* W Pacific Ocean

Solomon Islands 144

Official name Solomon Islands
Formation 1978
Capital Honiara
Population 477,000 / 44 people per sq mile (17 people per sq km)
Total area 10,985 sq. miles (28,450 sq. km)
Languages English, Pidgin English, Melanesian Pidgin
Religions Church of Melanesia (Anglican) 34%, Roman Catholic 19%, South Seas Evangelical Church 17%, Methodist 11%, Seventh-day Adventist 10%, other 9%
Ethnic mix Melanesian 94%, Polynesian 4%, other 2%
Government Parliamentary system
Currency Solomon Islands dollar = 100 cents
Literacy rate 77%
Calorie consumption 2272 calories

Solomon Islands *144 C3 island group* PNG/Solomon Islands
Solomon Sea *144 B3 sea* W Pacific Ocean
Soltau *94 B3* Niedersachsen, NW Germany
Sol'tsy *110 A4* Novgorodskaya Oblast', W Russian Federation
Solwezi *78 D2* North Western, NW Zambia
Sōma *130 D4* Fukushima, Honshū, C Japan
Somalia *73 D5 Som.* Jamuuriyada Demuqraadiga Soomaaliyeed, Soomaaliya; *prev.* Italian Somaliland, Somaliland Protectorate. *Country* E Africa

Somalia 73

Official name Somalia
Formation 1960
Capital Mogadishu
Population 9.9 million / 41 people per sq mile (16 people per sq km)
Total area 246,199 sq. miles (637,657 sq. km)
Languages Somali, Arabic, English, Italian
Religions Sunni Muslim 98%, Christian 2%
Ethnic mix Somali 85%, other 15%
Government Transitional regime
Currency Somali shilling = 100 centesimi
Literacy rate 24%
Calorie consumption 1628 calories

Somali Basin *69 E5 undersea feature* W Indian Ocean
Sombor *100 C3 Hung.* Zombor. Serbia, NW Serbia and Montenegro (Yugo.)
Someren *87 D5* Noord-Brabant, SE Netherlands
Somerset *42 A5 var.* Somerset Village. W Bermuda
Somerset *40 C5* Kentucky, S USA
Somerset Island *37 F2 island* Queen Elizabeth Islands, Nunavut, NW Canada
Somerset Island *42 A5 island* W Bermuda
Somerset Village *see* Somerset
Somers Islands *see* Bermuda
Somerton *48 A2* Arizona, SW USA
Someş *108 B3 var.* Somesch, Someşul, Szamos, *Ger.* Samosch. *River* Hungary/Romania
Somesch *see* Someş
Someşul *see* Someş
Somme *90 C2 river* N France
Somotillo *52 C3* Chinandega, NW Nicaragua
Somoto *52 D3* Madriz, NW Nicaragua
Songea *73 C8* Ruvuma, S Tanzania
Sông Hông Hà *see* Red River
Songkhla *137 C7 var.* Songkla, *Mal.* Singora. Songkhla, SW Thailand
Songkla *see* Songkhla
Sông Srepok *see* Srêpôk, Tônle
Sông Tiên Giang *see* Mekong
Sonoran Desert *48 A3 var.* Desierto de Altar. *Desert* Mexico/USA *see also* Altar, Desierto de
Sonsonate *52 B3* Sonsonate, W El Salvador
Soochow *see* Suzhou
Sop Hao *136 D3* Houaphan, N Laos
Sophia *see* Sofiya
Sopot *98 C2 Ger.* Zoppot. Plovdiv, C Bulgaria
Sopron *99 B6 Ger.* Ödenburg. Győr-Moson-Sopron, NW Hungary
Sorgues *91 D6* Vaucluse, SE France
Sorgun *116 D3* Yozgat, C Turkey
Soria *93 E2* Castilla-León, N Spain
Soroca *108 D3 Rus.* Soroki. N Moldova
Sorong *139 F4* Papua, E Indonesia
Sørøy *see* Sørøya
Sørøya *84 C2 var.* Sørøy. *Island* N Norway
Sortavala *110 B3* Respublika Kareliya, NW Russian Federation
Sotavento, Ilhas de *74 A3 var.* Leeward Islands. *Island group* S Cape Verde
Sotkamo *84 E4* Oulu, C Finland
Souanké *77 B5* La Sangha, NW Congo
Soueida *see* As Suwaydā'
Souflí *104 D3 prev.* Souflíon. Anatolikí Makedonía kai Thráki, NE Greece
Soufrière *55 F2 volcano* S Dominica
Soukhné *see* As Sukhnah
Sŏul *129 E4 off.* Sŏul-t'ŭkpyŏlsi, *Eng.* Seoul, *Jap.* Keijō; *prev.* Kyŏngsŏng. *Country capital* (South Korea) NW South Korea
Soûr *119 A5 var.* Şūr; *anc.* Tyre. SW Lebanon
Souris River *45 E1 var.* Mouse River. *River* Canada/USA
Sourpi *105 B5* Thessalía, C Greece
Sousse *71 F2 var.* Sūsah. NE Tunisia
South Africa *78 C4 Afr.* Suid-Afrika. *Country* S Africa

South Africa 78

Official name Republic of South Africa
Formation 1934
Capital Pretoria; Cape Town; Bloemfontein
Population 45 million / 95 people per sq mile (37 people per sq km)
Total area 471,008 sq. miles (1,219,912 sq. km)
Languages English, isiZulu, isiXhosa, Afrikaans, Sepedi, Setswana, Sesotho, Xitsonga, siSwati, Tshivenda, isiNdebele
Religions Christian 68%, Traditional beliefs and animist 29%, Muslim 2%, Hindu 1%
Ethnic mix Black 79%, White 10%, Colored 9%, Asian 2%
Government Presidential system
Currency Rand = 100 cents
Literacy rate 86%
Calorie consumption 2921 calories

South America *56 continent*
Southampton *89 D7 hist.* Hamwih, *Lat.* Clausentum. S England, UK
Southampton Island *37 G3 island* Nunavut, NE Canada
South Andaman *133 F2 island* Andaman Islands, India, NE Indian Ocean
South Australia *149 A5 state* S Australia
South Australian Basin *142 B5 undersea feature* SW Indian Ocean
South Bend *40 C3* Indiana, N USA
South Beveland *see* Zuid-Beveland
South Bruny Island *149 C8 island* Tasmania, SE Australia
South Carolina *43 E2 off.* State of South Carolina; also known as The Palmetto State. *State* SE USA
South Carpathians *see* Carpaţii Meridionali
South China Basin *125 E4 undersea feature* SE South China Sea
South China Sea *124 D4 Chin.* Nan Hai, *Ind.* Laut Cina Selatan, *Vtn.* Biên Đông. *Sea* SE Asia
South Dakota *44 D2 off.* State of South Dakota; also known as The Coyote State, Sunshine State. *State* N USA
Southeast Indian Ridge *141 D7 undersea feature* Indian Ocean/Pacific Ocean
Southeast Pacific Basin *153 E5 var.* Belling Hausen Mulde. *Undersea feature* SE Pacific Ocean
South East Point *149 C7 headland* Victoria, S Australia
Southend-on-Sea *89 E6* E England, UK
Southern Alps *151 B6 mountain range* South Island, NZ
Southern Cook Islands *145 F4 island group* S Cook Islands
Southern Cross *147 B6* Western Australia
Southern Indian Lake *37 F4 lake* Manitoba, C Canada
Southern Ocean *67 B7 ocean*
Southern Uplands *88 C4 mountain range* S Scotland, UK
South Fiji Basin *142 D4 undersea feature* S Pacific Ocean
South Geomagnetic Pole *154 B3 pole* Antarctica
South Georgia *57 D8 island* South Georgia and the South Sandwich Islands, SW Atlantic Ocean
South Goulburn Island *146 E2 island* Northern Territory, N Australia
South Huvadhu Atoll *132 A5 var.* Gaafu Dhaalu Atoll. *Atoll* S Maldives
South Indian Basin *141 D7 undersea feature* Indian Ocean/Pacific Ocean
South Island *151 C6 island* S NZ
South Korea *129 E4 Kor.* Taehan Min'guk. *Country* E Asia

South Korea 129

Official name Republic of Korea
Formation 1948
Capital Seoul
Population 47.7 million / 1251 people per sq mile (483 people per sq km)
Total area 38,023 sq. miles (98,480 sq. km)
Languages Korean, Chinese
Religions Mahayana Buddhist 47%, Protestant 38%, Roman Catholic 11%, Confucianist 3%, other 1%
Ethnic mix Korean 100%
Government Presidential system
Currency South Korean won = 100 chon
Literacy rate 98%
Calorie consumption 3055 calories

South Lake Tahoe *47 C5* California, W USA
South Orkney Islands *154 A2 island group* Antarctica
South Ossetia *117 F2 former autonomous region* SW Georgia
South Pacific Basin *see* Southwest Pacific Basin
South Platte River *44 D4 river* Colorado/Nebraska, C USA
South Pole *154 B3 pole* Antarctica
South Sandwich Islands *57 D8 island group* SE South Georgia and South Sandwich Islands
South Sandwich Trench *57 E8 undersea feature* SW Atlantic Ocean
South Shetland Islands *154 A2 island group* Antarctica
South Shields *88 D4* NE England, UK
South Sioux City *45 F3* Nebraska, C USA
South Taranaki Bight *150 C4 bight* SE Tasman Sea
South Tasmania Plateau *see* Tasman Plateau
South Uist *88 B3 island* NW Scotland, UK
South West Cape *151 A8 headland* Stewart Island, NZ
Southwest Indian Ocean Ridge *see* Southwest Indian Ridge
Southwest Indian Ridge *141 B6 var.* Southwest Indian Ocean Ridge. *Undersea feature* SW Indian Ocean
Southwest Pacific Basin *143 E4 var.* South Pacific Basin. *Undersea feature* SE Pacific Ocean
Sovereign Base Area *102 C5 UK military installation* E Cyprus
Sovereign Base Area *102 C5 UK military installation* S Cyprus
Soweto *78 D4* Gauteng, NE South Africa
Spain *92 D3 Sp.* España; *anc.* Hispania, Iberia, *Lat.* Hispana. *Country* SW Europe

Spain 92

Official name Kingdom of Spain
Formation 1492
Capital Madrid
Population 41.1 million / 213 people per sq mile (82 people per sq km)
Total area 194,896 sq. miles (504,782 sq. km)
Languages Spanish, Catalan, Galician, Basque

Spain (continued)

Religions Roman Catholic 96%, other 4%
Ethnic mix Castilian Spanish 72%, Catalan 17%, Galician 6%, Basque 2%, other 2%, Roma 1%
Government Parliamentary system
Currency Euro = 100 cents
Literacy rate 98%
Calorie consumption 3422 calories

Spanish Town *54 B5 hist.* St.Iago de la Vega. C Jamaica
Sparks *47 C5* Nevada, W USA
Spartanburg *43 E1* South Carolina, SE USA
Spárti *105 B6 Eng.* Sparta. Pelopónnisos, S Greece
Spearfish *44 D2* South Dakota, N USA
Speightstown *55 G1* NW Barbados
Spencer *45 F3* Iowa, C USA
Spencer Gulf *149 B6 gulf* South Australia
Spey *88 C3 river* NE Scotland, UK
Spiess Seamount *67 C7 undersea feature* S Atlantic Ocean
Spijkenisse *86 B4* Zuid-Holland, SW Netherlands
Spíli *105 C8* Kríti, Greece, E Mediterranean Sea
Spīn Būldak *123 E5* Kandahār, S Afghanistan
Spirdingsee *see* Śniardwg, Jezioro
Spitsbergen *83 F2 island* NW Svalbard
Split *100 B4 It.* Spalato. Split-Dalmacija, S Croatia
Špoģi *106 D4* Daugvapils, SE Latvia
Spokane *46 C2* Washington, NW USA
Spratly Islands *138 B2 Chin.* Nansha Qundao. *Disputed territory* SE Asia
Spree *94 D4 river* E Germany
Springfield *40 B4 state capital* Illinois, N USA
Springfield *41 G3* Massachusetts, NE USA
Springfield *45 G5* Missouri, C USA
Springfield *40 C4* Ohio, N USA
Springfield *46 B3* Oregon, NW USA
Spring Garden *59 F2* NE Guyana
Spring Hill *43 E4* Florida, SE USA
Springs Junction *151 C5* West Coast, South Island, NZ
Springsure *148 D4* Queensland, E Australia
Spruce Knob *41 E4 mountain* West Virginia, NE USA
Srbinje *see* Foča
Srbobran *see* Donji Vakuf
Srebrenica *100 C4* Republika Srpska, E Bosnia and Herzegovina
Sredets *104 E2 prev.* Grudovo. Burgas, E Bulgaria
Sredets *104 D2 prev.* Sylemeshlii. Stara Zagora, C Bulgaria
Srednerusskaya Vozvyshennost' *109 G1 Eng.* Central Russian Upland. *Mountain range* W Russian Federation
Srednesibirskoye Ploskogor'ye *114 D3 var.* Central Siberian Uplands, *Eng.* Central Siberian Plateau. *Mountain range* N Russian Federation
Sremska Mitrovica *100 C3 prev.* Mitrovica, *Ger.* Mitrowitz. Serbia, NW Serbia and Montenegro(Yugo.)
Srêpôk, Tônle *137 E5 var.* Sông Srepok. *River* Cambodia/Vietnam
Sri Aman *138 C3 var.* Bandar Sri Aman, Simanggang. Borneo, East Malaysia
Sri Jayawardanapura *132 D3 var.* Sri Jayawardenepura; *prev.* Kotte. Western Province, W Sri Lanka
Sri Jayawardenepura *see* Sri Jayawardanapura
Srīkākulam *135 F5* Andhra Pradesh, E India
Sri Lanka *132 D3 prev.* Ceylon. *Country* S Asia

Sri Lanka 132

Official name Democratic Socialist Republic of Sri Lanka
Formation 1948
Capital Colombo
Population 19.1 million / 764 people per sq mile (295 people per sq km)
Total area 25,332 sq. miles (65,610 sq. km)
Languages Sinhala, Tamil, English, Sinhala-Tamil
Religions Buddhist 69%, Hindu 15%, Muslim 8%, Christian 8%
Ethnic mix Sinhalese 74%, Tamil 18%, Moor 7%, Burgher, Malay, and Veddha 1%
Government Mixed presidential–parliamentary system
Currency Sri Lanka rupee = 100 cents
Literacy rate 92%
Calorie consumption 2274 calories

Srpska, Republika *100 B3* Admin. region *republic* NE Bosnia and Herzegovina
Srinagarind Reservoir *137 C5 lake* W Thailand
Ssu-ch'uan *see* Sichuan
Ssu-p'ing *see* Siping
Ssu-p'ing-chieh *see* Siping
Stabroek *87 B5* Antwerpen, N Belgium
Stade *94 B3* Niedersachsen, NW Germany
Stadskanaal *86 E2* Groningen, NE Netherlands
Stafford *89 D6* C England, UK
Staicele *106 D3* Limbaži, N Latvia
Stakhanov *109 H3* Luhans'ka Oblast', E Ukraine
Stalinabad *see* Dushanbe
Stalingrad *see* Volgograd
Stalinobod *see* Dushanbe
Stalin Peak *see* Kommunizm, Qullai
Stalowa Wola *98 E4* Podkarpackie, SE Poland
Stamford *41 F3* Connecticut, NE USA
Stampalia *see* Astypálaia
Stanley *65 D7 var.* Port Stanley, Puerto Argentino. *Dependent territory capital* (Falkland Islands) East Falkland, Falkland Islands
Stanovoy Khrebet *113 E3 mountain range* SE Russian Federation
Stanthorpe *149 D5* Queensland, E Australia
Staphorst *86 D2* Overijssel, E Netherlands
Starachowice *98 D4* Świętokrzyskie, C Poland
Stara Pazova *100 D3 Ger.* Altpasua, *Hung.* Ópazova. Serbia, N Serbia and Montenegro (Yugo.)
Stara Zagora *104 D2 Lat.* Augusta Trajana. Stara Zagora, C Bulgaria
Starbuck Island *145 G3 prev.* Volunteer Island. *Island* E Kiribati
Stargard Szczeciński *98 B3 Ger.* Stargard in Pommern. Zachodniopomorskie, NW Poland
Starobil's'k *109 H2 Rus.* Starobel'sk. Luhans'ka Oblast', E Ukraine
Starobyn *107 C7 Rus.* Starobin. Minskaya Voblasts', S Belarus
Starogard Pomorskiei *98 C2 Ger.* Preussisch-Stargard. Pomorskie, N Poland
Starokostyantyniv *108 D2 Rus.* Starokonstantinov. Khmel'nyts'ka Oblast', NW Ukraine
Starominskaya *111 A7* Krasnodarskiy Kray, SW Russian Federation
Staryya Darohi *107 C6 Rus.* Staryye Dorogi. Minskaya Voblasts', S Belarus
Staryy Oskol *111 B6* Belgorodskaya Oblast', W Russian Federation
State College *41 E4* Pennsylvania, NE USA
Statesboro *43 E2* Georgia, SE USA
Staunton *41 E5* Virginia, NE USA
Stavanger *85 A6* Rogaland, S Norway
Stavers Island *see* Vostok Island
Stavropol' *111 B7 prev.* Voroshilovsk. Stavropol'skiy Kray, SW Russian Federation
Steamboat Springs *44 C4* Colorado, C USA
Steenwijk *86 D2* Overijssel, N Netherlands
Steier *see* Steyr
Steinkjer *84 B4* Nord-Trøndelag, C Norway
Stendal *94 C3* Sachsen-Anhalt, C Germany
Stephenville *49 F3* Texas, SW USA
Sterling *44 D4* Colorado, C USA
Sterling *40 B3* Illinois, N USA
Sterlitamak *114 B3* Respublika Bashkortostan, W Russian Federation
Stettiner Haff *see* Szczeciński, Zalew
Stevenage *89 E6* E England, UK
Stevens Point *40 B2* Wisconsin, N USA
Stewart Island *151 A8 island* S NZ
Steyr *95 D6 var.* Steier. Oberösterreich, N Austria
Stif *see* Sétif
Stillwater *49 G1* Oklahoma, C USA
Stirling *88 C4* C Scotland, UK
Stjørdalshalsen *84 B4* Nord-Trøndelag, C Norway
Stockach *95 B6* Baden-Württemberg, S Germany
Stockholm *85 C6 country capital* (Sweden) Stockholm, C Sweden
Stockton *47 B6* California, W USA
Stockton Plateau *49 E4 plain* Texas, SW USA
Stœng Trĕng *137 D5 prev.* Stung Treng. Stœng Trêng, NE Cambodia
Stoke *see* Stoke-on-Trent
Stoke-on-Trent *89 D6 var.* Stoke. C England, UK
Stómio *104 B4* Thessalía, C Greece
Stony Tunguska *112 D2 river* C Russian Federation
Store Bælt *see* Storebælt
Storebælt *85 B8 var.* Store Bælt, *Eng.* Great Belt, Storebelt. *Channel* Baltic Sea/Kattegat
Storebelt *see* Storebælt
Støren *85 B5* Sør-Trøndelag, S Norway
Storfjorden *83 G2 fjord* S Norway
Stornoway *88 B2* NW Scotland, UK
Storsjön *85 B5 lake* C Sweden
Storuman *84 C4 lake* N Sweden
Storuman *84 C4* Västerbotten, N Sweden
Stowbtsy *107 C6 Pol.* Stolbce, *Rus.* Stolbtsy. Minskaya Voblasts', C Belarus
Strabane *89 B5 Ir.* An Srath Bán. W Northern Ireland, UK
Strakonice *99 A5 Ger.* Strakonitz. Budějovický Kraj, S Czech Republic
Stralsund *94 D2* Mecklenburg-Vorpommern, NE Germany
Stranraer *89 C5* S Scotland, UK
Strasbourg *90 E3 Ger.* Strassburg; *anc.* Argentoratum. Bas-Rhin, NE France
Strășeni *108 D3 var.* Strasheny. C Moldova
Strasheny *see* Strășeni
Stratford *150 D4* Taranaki, North Island, NZ
Strathfield *148 E2* New South Wales, SE Australia
Straubing *95 C6* Bayern, SE Germany
Strehaia *108 B5* Mehedinți, SW Romania
Strelka *114 D4* Krasnoyarskiy Kray, C Russian Federation
Strofilia *see* Strofyliá
Strofyliá *105 C5 var.* Strofilia. Évvoia, C Greece
Stromboli, Isola *97 D6 island* Isole Eolie, S Italy
Stromeferry *88 C3* N Scotland, UK
Strömstad *85 B6* Västra Götaland, S Sweden
Strömsund *84 C4* Jämtland, C Sweden
Struga *101 D6* SW FYR Macedonia
Strumica *101 E6* E FYR Macedonia
Strumyani *104 C3* Blagoevgrad, SW Bulgaria
Strymónas *104 C3 Bul.* Struma. *River* Bulgaria/Greece *see also* Struma
Stryy *108 B2* L'vivs'ka Oblast', NW Ukraine
Studholme *151 B6* Canterbury, South Island, NZ
Sturgis *44 D3* South Dakota, N USA
Stuttgart *95 B6* Baden-Württemberg, SW Germany
Stykkishólmur *83 E4* Vesturland, W Iceland
Styr *108 C1 Rus.* Styr'. *River* Belarus/Ukraine
Su *see* Jiangsu
Suakin *72 C3 var.* Sawakin. Red Sea, NE Sudan
Subačius *106 C4* Kupiškis, NE Lithuania
Subaykhān *118 E3* Dayr az Zawr, E Syria
Subotica *100 D2 Ger.* Maria-Theresiopel, *Hung.* Szabadka. Serbia, N Serbia and Montenegro (Yugo.)
Suceava *108 C3 Ger.* Suczawa, *Hung.* Szucsava. Suceava, NE Romania
Su-chou *see* Suzhou
Suchow *see* Xuzhou
Sucre *61 F4 hist.* Chuquisaca, La Plata. *Country capital* (Bolivia-legal capital) Chuquisaca, S Bolivia
Sudan *72 A4 Ar.* Jumhuriyat as-Sudan; *prev.* Anglo-Egyptian *Sudan. country* N Africa

Sudan 72

Official name Republic of the Sudan
Formation 1956
Capital Khartoum
Population 33.6 million / 35 people per sq mile (13 people per sq km)
Total area 967,493 sq. miles (2,505,810 sq. km)
Languages Arabic, Dinka, Nuer, Nubian, Beja, Zande, Bari, Fur, Shilluk, Lotuko
Religions Muslim (mainly Sunni) 70%, Traditional beliefs 20%, Christian 9%, other 1%
Ethnic mix Other Black 52%, Arab 40%, Dinka and Beja 7%, other 1%
Government Presidential system
Currency Sudanese pound or dinar = 100 piastres
Literacy rate 60%
Calorie consumption 2288 calories

Sudbury *38 C4* Ontario, S Canada
Sudd *73 B5 swamp region* S Sudan
Sudeten *98 B4 var.* Sudetes, Sudetic Mountains, *Cz./Pol.* Sudety. *Mountain range* Czech Republic/Poland
Sudetes *see* Sudeten
Sudetic Mountains *see* Sudeten
Sudety *see* Sudeten
Südkarpaten *see* Carpații Meridionali
Sue *73 B5 river* S Sudan
Sueca *93 F3* País Valenciano, E Spain
Sue Wood Bay *42 B5 bay* W Bermuda
Suez *72 B1 Ar.* As Suways, El Suweis. NE Egypt
Suez Canal *72 B1 Ar.* Qanāt as Suways. *Canal* NE Egypt
Suez, Gulf of *72 B2 Ar.* Khalīj as Suways. *Gulf* NE Egypt
Suğla Gölü *116 C4 lake* SW Turkey
Şuḩār *121 D5 var.* Sohar. N Oman
Sühbaatar *127 E1* Selenge, N Mongolia
Suhl *95 C5* Thüringen, C Germany
Suixi *128 C6* Guangdong, S China
Sujāwal *134 B3* Sind, SE Pakistan
Sukabumi *138 C5 prev.* Soekaboemi. Jawa, C Indonesia
Sukagawa *131 D5* Fukushima, Honshū, C Japan
Sukarnapura *see* Jayapura
Sukhne *see* As Sukhnah
Sukhona *110 C4 var.* Tot'ma. *River* NW Russian Federation
Sukkertoppen *see* Maniitsoq
Sukkur *134 B3* Sind, SE Pakistan
Sukumo *131 B7* Kōchi, Shikoku, SW Japan
Sulaimaniya *see* As Sulaymānīyah
Sulaimān Range *134 C2 mountain range* C Pakistan
Sula, Kepulauan *139 E4 island group* C Indonesia
Sulawesi *139 E4 Eng.* Celebes. *Island* C Indonesia
Sulechów *98 B3 Ger.* Züllichau. Lubuskie, W Poland
Suliag *see* Sohâg
Sullana *60 B2* Piura, NW Peru
Sulphur Springs *49 G2* Texas, SW USA
Sulu Archipelago *139 E3 island group* SW Philippines
Sulu Sea *139 E2 Ind.* Laut Sulu. *Sea* SW Philippines
Sulyukta *123 E2 Kir.* Sülüktü. Oshskaya Oblast', SW Kyrgyzstan
Sumatera *137 B8 Eng.* Sumatra. *Island* W Indonesia
Sumatra *see* Sumatera
Sumba, Pulau *139 E5 Eng.* Sandalwood Island; *prev.* Soemba. *Island* Nusa Tenggara, C Indonesia
Sumba, Selat *139 E5 strait* Nusa Tenggara, S Indonesia
Sumbawanga *73 B7* Rukwa, W Tanzania
Sumbe *78 B2 prev.* N'Gunza, *Port.* Novo Redondo. Cuanza Sul, W Angola
Sumeih *73 B5* Southern Darfur, S Sudan
Summer Lake *46 B4 lake* Oregon, NW USA
Summit *93 H5 mountain* C Gibraltar
Sumqayıt *117 H2 Rus.* Sumgait. E Azerbaijan
Sumy *109 F2* Sums'ka Oblast', NE Ukraine
Sunbury *149 C7* Victoria, SE Australia
Sunda Islands *see* Greater Sunda Islands
Sunda, Selat *138 B5 strait* Jawa/Sumatera, SW Indonesia
Sunda Trench *see* Java Trench
Sunderland *88 D4 var.* Wearmouth. NE England, UK
Sundsvall *85 C5* Västernorrland, C Sweden
Sungaipenuh *138 B4 prev.* Soengaipenoeh. Sumatera, W Indonesia
Sunnyvale *47 A6* California, W USA
Suntar *115 F3* Respublika Sakha (Yakutiya), NE Russian Federation
Sunyani *75 E5* W Ghana
Suomussalmi *84 E4* Oulu, E Finland
Suŏng *137 D6* Kâmpóng Cham, C Cambodia
Suoyarvi *110 B3* Respublika Kareliya, NW Russian Federation
Supe *60 C3* Lima, W Peru
Superior *40 A1* Wisconsin, N USA
Superior, Lake *40 B1 Fr.* Lac Supérieur. *Lake* Canada/USA
Suqrah *see* Şawqirah
Suquṭrā *121 C7 var.* Sokotra, *Eng.* Socotra. *Island* SE Yemen
Şūr *see* Soûr
Şūr *121 E5* NE Oman
Surabaya *138 D5 prev.* Soerabaja, Surabaja. Jawa, C Indonesia
Surakarta *138 C5 Eng.* Solo; *prev.* Soerakarta. Jawa, S Indonesia
Šurany *99 C6 Hung.* Nagysurány. Nitriansky Kraj, SW Slovakia
Sūrat *134 C4* Gujarāt, W India
Suratdhani *see* Surat Thani
Surat Thani *137 C6 var.* Suratdhani. Surat Thani, SW Thailand
Surazh *107 E5 Rus.* Surazh. Vitsyebskaya Voblasts', NE Belarus
Surdulica *101 E5* Serbia, SE Serbia and Montenegro (Yugo.)
Sûre *87 D7 var.* Sauer. *River* W Europe *see also* Sauer
Surendranagar *134 C4* Gujarāt, W India
Surfers Paradise *149 E5* Queensland, E Australia
Surgut *114 D3* Khanty-Mansiyskiy Avtonomnyy Okrug, C Russian Federation
Surin *137 D5* Surin, E Thailand
Surinam *see* Suriname
Suriname *59 G3 var.* Surinam; *prev.* Dutch Guiana, Netherlands Guiana. *Country* N S America

Suriname 59

Official name Republic of Suriname
Formation 1975
Capital Paramaribo
Population 436,000 / 7 people per sq mile (3 people per sq km)
Total area 63,039 sq. miles (163,270 sq. km)
Languages Sranan (Creole), Dutch, Javanese, Sarnami Hindi, Saramaccan, Chinese, Carib
Religions Hindu 27%, Protestant 25%, Roman Catholic 23%, Muslim 20%, Traditional beliefs 5%
Ethnic mix Creole 34%, South Asian 34%, Javanese 18%, Black 9%, other 5%
Government Parliamentary system
Currency Suriname dollar (guilder until 2004) = 100 cents
Literacy rate 94%
Calorie consumption 2643 calories

Surkhob *123 F3 river* C Tajikistan
Surt *71 G2 var.* Sidra, Sirte. N Libya
Surt, Khalīj *71 F2 Eng.* Gulf of Sidra, Gulf of Sirti, Sidra. *Gulf* N Libya
Surtsey *83 E5 island* S Iceland
Suruga-wan *131 D6 bay* SE Japan
Susa *96 A2* Piemonte, NE Italy
Sūsah *see* Sousse
Susanville *47 B5* California, W USA
Susitna *36 C3* Alaska, USA
Susteren *87 D5* Limburg, SE Netherlands
Susuman *115 G3* Magadanskaya Oblast', E Russian Federation
Sutherland *148 E2* New South Wales, SE Australia
Sutlej *134 C2 river* India/Pakistan
Suur Munamägi *106 D3 var.* Munamägi, *Ger.* Eier-Berg. *Mountain* SE Estonia
Suur Väin *106 C2 Ger.* Grosser Sund. *Strait* W Estonia
Suva *145 E4 country capital* (Fiji) Viti Levu, W Fiji
Suwałki *98 E2 Lith.* Suvalkai, *Rus.* Suvalki. Podlaskie, NE Poland
Şuwār *see* Aş Şuwār
Suweida *see* As Suwaydā'
Suzhou *128 D5 var.* Soochow, Suchou, Suchow; *prev.* Wuhsien. Jiangsu, E China
Svalbard *83 E1 Norwegian dependency* Arctic Ocean
Svartisen *84 C3 glacier* C Norway
Svay Riĕng *137 D6* Svay Riĕng, S Cambodia
Sveg *85 B5* Jämtland, C Sweden
Svenstavik *85 C5* Jämtland, C Sweden
Svetlograd *111 B7* Stavropol'skiy Kray, SW Russian Federation
Svilengrad *104 D3 prev.* Mustafa-Pasha. Khaskovo, S Bulgaria
Svitlovods'k *109 F3 Rus.* Svetlovodsk. Kirovohrads'ka Oblast', C Ukraine
Svobodnyy *115 G4* Amurskaya Oblast', SE Russian Federation
Svyataya Anna Trough *172 C4 var.* Saint Anna Trough. *Undersea feature* N Kara Sea
Svyetlahorsk *107 D7 Rus.* Svetlogorsk. Homyel'skaya Voblasts', SE Belarus
Swabian Jura *see* Schwäbische Alb
Swakopmund *78 B3* Erongo, W Namibia
Swansea *89 C7 Wel.* Abertawe. S Wales, UK
Swarzędz *98 C3* Wielkopolskie, C Poland
Swatow *see* Shantou
Swaziland *78 D4 Country* S Africa

Swaziland 78

Official name Kingdom of Swaziland
Formation 1968
Capital Mbabane
Population 1.1 million / 166 people per sq mile (64 people per sq km)
Total area 6704 sq. miles (17,363 sq. km)
Languages English, siSwati, isiZulu, Xitsonga
Religions Christian 60%, Traditional beliefs 40%
Ethnic mix Swazi 97%, other 3%
Government Monarchy
Currency Lilangeni = 100 cents
Literacy rate 81%
Calorie consumption 2593 calories

Sweden *84 B4 Swe.* Sverige. *Country* N Europe

Sweden 84

Official name Kingdom of Sweden
Formation 1523

Sweden (continued)

Capital Stockholm
Population 8.9 million / 56 people per sq mile (22 people per sq km)
Total area 173,731 sq. miles (449,964 sq. km)
Languages Swedish, Finnish, Sámi
Religions Evangelical Lutheran 82%, other 13%, Roman Catholic 2%, Muslim 2%, Orthodox Christian 1%
Ethnic mix Swedish 88%, Foreign-born or first-generation immigrant 10%, Finnish and Sámi 2%
Government Parliamentary system
Currency Swedish krona = 100 öre
Literacy rate 99%
Calorie consumption 3164 calories

Swed Ormsö *see* Vormsi
Sweetwater *49 F3* Texas, SW USA
Świdnica *98 B4 Ger.* Schweidnitz. Wałbrzych, SW Poland
Świdwin *98 B2 Ger.* Schivelbein. Zachodniopomorskie, NW Poland
Świebodzice *98 B4 Ger.* Freiburg in Schlesien, Swiebodzice. Wałbrzych, SW Poland
Świebodzin *98 B3 Ger.* Schwiebus. Lubuskie, W Poland
Świecie *98 C3 Ger.* Schwertberg. Kujawski-pomorskie, C Poland
Swindon *89 D7* S England, UK
Świnoujście *98 B2 Ger.* Swinemünde. Zachodniopomorskie, NW Poland
Switzerland *95 A7 Fr.* La Suisse, *Ger.* Schweiz, *It.* Svizzera; *anc.* Helvetia. *Country* C Europe

Switzerland 95

Official name Swiss Confederation
Formation 1291
Capital Bern
Population 7.2 million / 469 people per sq mile (181 people per sq km)
Total area 15,942 sq. miles (41,290 sq. km)
Languages German, Swiss-German, French, Italian, Romansch
Religions Roman Catholic 46%, Protestant 40%, Other and nonreligious 12%, Muslim 2%
Ethnic mix German 65%, French 18%, Italian 10%, other 6%, Romansch 1%
Government Parliamentary system
Currency Swiss franc = 100 rappen/centimes
Literacy rate 99%
Calorie consumption 3440 calories

Sycaminum *see* Hefa
Sydney *148 D1 state capital* New South Wales, SE Australia
Sydney *39 G4* Cape Breton Island, Nova Scotia, SE Canada
Syedpur *see* Saidpur
Syemyezhava *107 C6 Rus.* Semezhevo. Minskaya Voblasts', C Belarus
Syene *see* Aswân
Syeverodonets'k *109 H3 Rus.* Severodonetsk. Luhans'ka Oblast', E Ukraine
Syktyvkar *110 D4 prev.* Ust'-Sysol'sk. Respublika Komi, NW Russian Federation
Sylhet *135 G3* Chittagong, NE Bangladesh
Synel'nykove *109 G3* Dnipropetrovs'ka Oblast', E Ukraine
Syowa *154 C2 Japanese research station* Antarctica
Syracuse *41 E3* New York, NE USA
Syrdariya *see* Syr Darya
Syr Darya *114 B4 var.* Sai Hun, Sir Darya, Syrdarya, *Kaz.* Syrdariya, *Rus.* Syrdar'ya, *Uzb.* Sirdaryo; *anc.* Jaxartes. *River* C Asia

Syria *118 B3 var.* Siria, Syrie, *Ar.* Al-Jumhūrīyah al-'Arabīyah as-Sūrīyah, Sūrīya. *Country* SW Asia

Syria 118

Official name Syrian Arab Republic
Formation 1941
Capital Damascus
Population 17.8 million / 250 people per sq mile (97 people per sq km)
Total area 71,498 sq. miles (184,180 sq. km)
Languages Arabic, French, Kurdish, Armenian, Circassian, Turkic languages, Assyrian, Aramaic
Religions Sunni Muslim 74%, Other Muslim 16%, Christian 10%
Ethnic mix Arab 89%, Kurdish 6%, other 3%, Armenian, Turkmen, and Circassian 2%
Government One-party state
Currency Syrian pound = 100 piasters
Literacy rate 83%
Calorie consumption 3038 calories

Syrian Desert *119 D5 Ar.* Al Hamad, Bādiyat ash Shām. *Desert* SW Asia
Sýrna *105 E7 var.* Sirna. *Island* Kykládes, Greece, Aegean Sea
Sýros *105 C6 var.* Síros. *Island* Kykládes, Greece, Aegean Sea
Syvash, Zatoka *109 F4 Rus.* Zaliv Syvash. *Inlet* S Ukraine
Syzran' *111 C6* Samarskaya Oblast', W Russian Federation
Szamos *see* Someş
Szamotuły *98 B3* Wielkopolskie, C Poland
Szczecin *98 B3 Eng./Ger.* Stettin. Zachodniopomorskie, NW Poland
Szczecinek *98 B2 Ger.* Neustettin. Zachodniopomorskie, NW Poland
Szczeciński, Zalew *98 A2 var.* Stettiner Haff, *Ger.* Oderhaff. *Bay* Germany/Poland
Szczytno *98 D3 Ger.* Ortelsburg. Olsztyn, NE Poland
Szechuan *see* Sichuan
Szechwan *see* Sichuan
Szeged *99 D7 Ger.* Szegedin, *Rom.* Seghedin. Csongrád, SE Hungary
Székesfehérvár *99 C6 Ger.* Stuhlweissenberg; *anc.* Alba Regia. Fejér, W Hungary
Szekszárd *99 C7* Tolna, S Hungary
Szenttamás *see* Srbobran
Szeping *see* Siping
Sziszek *see* Sisak
Szlatina *see* Slatina
Szolnok *99 D6* Jász-Nagykun-Szolnok, C Hungary
Szombathely *99 B6 Ger.* Steinamanger; *anc.* Sabaria, Savaria. Vas, W Hungary
Szprotawa *98 B4 Ger.* Sprottau. Lubuskie, W Poland

T

Table Rock Lake *49 G1 reservoir* Arkansas/Missouri, C USA
Tábor *99 B5* Budějovický Kraj, S Czech Republic
Tabora *73 B7* Tabora, W Tanzania
Tabrīz *120 C2 var.* Tebriz; *anc.* Tauris. Āžarbāyjān-e Khāvarī, NW Iran
Tabuaeran *145 G2 prev.* Fanning Island. *Atoll* Line Islands, E Kiribati
Tabūk *120 A4* Tabūk, NW Saudi Arabia
Täby *85 C6* Stockholm, C Sweden
Tachov *99 A5 Ger.* Tachau. Plzeňský Kraj, W Czech Republic
Tacloban *139 F2 off.* Tacloban City. Leyte, C Philippines
Tacna *61 E4* Tacna, SE Peru
Tacoma *46 B2* Washington, NW USA
Tacuarembó *64 D4 prev.* San Fructuoso. Tacuarembó, C Uruguay
Tademaït, Plateau du *70 D3 plateau* C Algeria
Tadmor *see* Tudmur
Tadmur *see* Tudmur
Tādpatri *132 C2* Andhra Pradesh, E India
Taegu *129 E4 off.* Taegu-gwangyŏksi, *var.* Daegu, *Jap.* Taikyū. SE South Korea
Taejŏn *129 E4 off.* Taejŏn-gwangyŏksi, *Jap.* Taiden. C South Korea
Tafassâsset, Ténéré du *75 G2 desert* N Niger
Tafila *see* Aṭ Ṭafīlah
Taganrog *111 A7* Rostovskaya Oblast', SW Russian Federation
Taganrog, Gulf of *109 G4 Rus.* Taganrogskiy Zaliv, *Ukr.* Tahanroz'ka Zatoka. *Gulf* Russian Federation/Ukraine
Taguatinga *63 F3* Tocantins, C Brazil
Tagus *92 C3 Port.* Rio Tejo, *Sp.* Río Tajo. *River* Portugal/Spain
Tagus Plain *80 A4 undersea feature* E Atlantic Ocean
Tahat *71 E4 mountain* SE Algeria
Tahiti *145 H4 island* Îles du Vent, W French Polynesia
Tahlequah *49 G1* Oklahoma, C USA
Tahoe, Lake *47 B5 lake* California/Nevada, W USA
Tahoua *75 F3* Tahoua, W Niger
T'aichung *128 D6 Jap.* Taichū; *prev.* Taiwan. C Taiwan
Taieri *151 B7 river* South Island, NZ
Taihape *150 D4* Manawatu-Wanganui, North Island, NZ
Tailem Bend *149 B7* South Australia
T'ainan *128 D6 Jap.* Tainan; *prev.* Dainan. S Taiwan
T'aipei *128 D6 Jap.* Taihoku; *prev.* Daihoku. *Country capital* (Taiwan) N Taiwan
Taiping *138 B3* Perak, Peninsular Malaysia
Taiwan *128 D6 var.* Formosa, Formo'sa. *Country* E Asia

Taiwan 128

Official name Republic of China (ROC)
Formation 1949
Capital Taipei
Population 22.6 million / 1815 people per sq mile (701 people per sq km)
Total area 13,892 sq. miles (35,980 sq. km)
Languages Amoy Chinese, Mandarin Chinese, Hakka Chinese
Religions Buddhist, Confucianist, and Taoist 93%, Christian 5%, other 2%
Ethnic mix Indigenous Chinese 84%, Mainland Chinese 14%, Aboriginal 2%
Government Presidential system
Currency Taiwan dollar = 100 cents
Literacy rate 96%
Calorie consumption Not available

T'aiwan Haihsia *see* Taiwan Strait
Taiwan Haixia *see* Taiwan Strait
Taiwan Strait *128 D6 var.* Formosa Strait, *Chin.* T'aiwan Haihsia, Taiwan Haixia. *Strait* China/Taiwan
Taiyuan *128 C4 prev.* T'ai-yuan, T'ai-yüan, Yangku. Shanxi, C China
Ta'izz *121 B7* SW Yemen
Tajikistan *123 E3 Rus.* Tadzhikistan, *Taj.* Jumhurii Tojikiston; *prev.* Tajik S.S.R. *Country* C Asia

Tajikistan 123

Official name Republic of Tajikistan
Formation 1991
Capital Dushanbe
Population 6.2 million / 112 people per sq mile (43 people per sq km)
Total area 55,251 sq. miles (143,100 sq. km)
Languages Tajik, Uzbek, Russian
Religions Sunni Muslim 80%, other 15%, Shi'a Muslim 5%
Ethnic mix Tajik 62%, Uzbek 24%, Russian 8%, other 4%, Tatar 1%, Kyrgyz 1%
Government Presidential system
Currency Somoni = 100 diram
Literacy rate 99%
Calorie consumption 1662 calories

Tak *136 C4 var.* Rahaeng. Tak, W Thailand
Takao *see* Kaohsiung
Takaoka *131 C5* Toyama, Honshū, SW Japan
Takapuna *150 D2* Auckland, North Island, NZ
Takhiatosh *see* Taxiatosh
Takhtakŭpir *see* Taxtako'pir
Takikawa *130 D2* Hokkaidō, NE Japan
Takla Makan Desert *see* Taklimakan Shamo
Taklimakan Shamo *126 B3 Eng.* Takla Makan Desert. *Desert* NW China
Takow *see* Kaohsiung
Takutea *145 G4 island* S Cook Islands
Talachyn *107 D6 Rus.* Tolochin. Vitsyebskaya Voblasts', NE Belarus
Talamanca, Cordillera de *53 E5 mountain range* S Costa Rica
Talara *60 B2* Piura, NW Peru
Talas *123 F2* Talasskaya Oblast', NW Kyrgyzstan
Talaud, Kepulauan *139 F3 island group* E Indonesia
Talavera de la Reina *92 D3 anc.* Caesarobriga, Talabriga. Castilla-La Mancha, C Spain
Talca *64 B4* Maule, C Chile
Talcahuano *65 B5* Bío Bío, C Chile
Taldykorgan *114 C5 Kaz.* Taldyqorghan; *prev.* Taldy-Kurgan. Almaty, SE Kazakhstan
Taldy-Kurgan/Taldyqorghan *see* Taldykorgan
Ta-lien *see* Dalian
Taliq-an *see* Tāloqān
Tal'ka *107 C6 Rus.* Tal'ka. Minskaya Voblasts', C Belarus
Tallahassee *42 D3 prev.* Muskogean. *State capital* Florida, SE USA
Tall al Abyaḍ *see* At Tall al Abyaḍ
Tallinn *106 D2 Ger.* Reval, *Rus.* Tallin; *prev.* Revel. *Country capital* (Estonia) Harjumaa, NW Estonia
Tall Kalakh *118 B4 var.* Tell Kalakh. Ḥimṣ, C Syria
Tallulah *42 B2* Louisiana, S USA
Talnakh *114 D3* Taymyrskiy (Dolgano-Nenetskiy) Avtonomnyy Okrug, N Russian Federation
Tal'ne *109 E3 Rus.* Tal'noye. Cherkas'ka Oblast', C Ukraine
Taloga *49 F1* Oklahoma, C USA
Tāloqān *123 E3 var.* Taliq-an. Takhār, NE Afghanistan
Talsi *106 C3 Ger.* Talsen. Talsi, NW Latvia
Taltal *64 B2* Antofagasta, N Chile
Talvik *84 D2* Finnmark, N Norway
Tamabo, Banjaran *138 D3 mountain range* East Malaysia
Tamale *75 E4* C Ghana
Tamana *145 E3 prev.* Rotcher Island. *Atoll* Tungaru, W Kiribati
Tamanrasset *71 E4 var.* Tamenghest. S Algeria
Tamar *89 C7 river* SW England, UK
Tamar *see* Tudmur
Tamatave *see* Toamasina
Tamazunchale *51 E4* San Luis Potosí, C Mexico
Tambacounda *74 C3* SE Senegal
Tambov *111 B6* Tambovskaya Oblast', W Russian Federation
Tambura *73 B5* Western Equatoria, SW Sudan
Tamchaket *see* Tâmchekkeṭ
Tâmchekkeṭ *74 C3 var.* Tamchaket. Hodh el Gharbi, S Mauritania
Tamenghest *see* Tamanrasset
Tamiahua, Laguna de *51 F4 lagoon* E Mexico
Tamil Nādu *132 C3 prev.* Madras. *State* SE India
Tam Ky *137 E5* Quang Nam-Đa Năng, C Vietnam
Tampa *43 E4* Florida, SE USA
Tampa Bay *43 E4 bay* Florida, SE USA
Tampere *85 D5 Swe.* Tammerfors. Länsi-Suomi, W Finland
Tampico *51 E3* Tamaulipas, C Mexico
Tamworth *149 D6* New South Wales, SE Australia
Tana *see* Deatnu/Tenojoki
Tanabe *131 C7* Wakayama, Honshū, SW Japan
Tana Bru *84 D2* Finnmark, N Norway
T'ana Hāyk' *72 C4 Eng.* Lake Tana. *Lake* NW Ethiopia
Tanais *see* Don
Tanami Desert *146 D3 desert* Northern Territory, N Australia
Ţăndărei *108 D5* Ialomiţa, SE Romania
Tandil *65 D5* Buenos Aires, E Argentina
Tanega-shima *131 B8 island* Nansei-shotō, SW Japan
Tane Range *136 B4 Bur.* Tanen Taunggyi. *Mountain range* W Thailand
Tanezrouft *70 D4 desert* Algeria/Mali
Ţanf, Jabal aţ *118 D4 mountain* SE Syria
Tanga *69 E5* Tanga, E Tanzania
Tanga *73 C7 region* E Tanzania
Tanganyika, Lake *73 B7 lake* E Africa
Tangeh-ye Hormoz *see* Hormuz, Strait of
Tanger *70 C2 var.* Tangiers, Tangier, *Fr./Ger.* Tangerk, *Sp.* Tánger; *anc.* Tingis. NW Morocco
Tangerk *see* Tanger
Tanggula Shan *126 C4 var.* Dangla, Tangla Range. *Mountain range* W China
Tangier *see* Tanger
Tangiers *see* Tanger
Tangla Range *see* Tanggula Shan
Tangra Yumco *126 B5 var.* Tangro Tso. *Lake* W China
Tangro Tso *see* Tangra Yumco
Tangshan *128 D3 var.* T'ang-shan. Hebei, E China
T'ang-shan *see* Tangshan
Tanimbar, Kepulauan *139 F5 island group* Maluku, E Indonesia
Tanna *144 D4 island* S Vanuatu
Tannenhof *see* Krynica
Tan-Tan *70 B3* SW Morocco
Tan-tung *see* Dandong
Tanzania *73 C7 Swa.* Jamhuri ya Muungano wa Tanzania; *prev.* German East Africa, Tanganyika and Zanzibar. *Country* E Africa

Tanzania 73

Official name United Republic of Tanzania
Formation 1964
Capital Dodoma

Tanzania (continued)

Population 37 million / 108 people per sq mile (42 people per sq km)
Total area 364,898 sq. miles (945,087 sq. km)
Languages Kiswahili, Sukuma, Chagga, Nyamwezi, Hehe, Makonde, Yao, Sandawe, English
Religions Muslim 33%, Christian 33%, Traditional beliefs 30%, other 4%
Ethnic mix Native African (over 120 tribes) 99%, European and Asian 1%
Government Presidential system
Currency Tanzanian shilling = 100 cents
Literacy rate 77%
Calorie consumption 1997 calories

Taoudenit *see* Taoudenni
Taoudenni *75 E2 var.* Taoudenit. Tombouctou, N Mali
Tapa *106 E2 Ger.* Taps. Lääne-Virumaa, NE Estonia
Tapachula *51 G5* Chiapas, SE Mexico
Tapajós, Rio *63 E2 var.* Tapajóz. *River* NW Brazil
Tapajóz *see* Tapajós, Rio
Ţarābulus *71 F2 var.* Ţarābulus al Gharb, *Eng.* Tripoli. *Country capital* (Libya) NW Libya
Tarābulus *see* Tripoli
Ţarābulus al Gharb *see* Ţarābulus
Ţarābulus ash Shām *see* Tripoli
Taraclia *108 D4 Rus.* Tarakilya. S Moldova
Taranaki, Mount *150 C4 var.* Egmont, Mount. *Mountain* North Island, NZ
Tarancón *93 E3* Castilla-La Mancha, C Spain
Taranto *97 E5 var.* Tarentum. Puglia, SE Italy
Taranto, Golfo di *97 E6 Eng.* Gulf of Taranto. *Gulf* S Italy
Tarapoto *60 C2* San Martín, N Peru
Tarare *91 D5* Rhône, E France
Tarascon *91 D6* Bouches-du-Rhône, SE France
Tarawa *144 D2 atoll* Tungaru, W Kiribati
Taraz *114 C5 prev.* Aulie Ata, Auliye-Ata, Dzhambul, Zhambyl. Zhambyl, S Kazakhstan
Tarazona *93 E2* Aragón, NE Spain
Tarbes *91 B6 anc.* Bigorra. Hautes-Pyrénées, S France
Tarcoola *149 A6* South Australia
Taree *149 D6* New South Wales, SE Australia
Tarentum *see* Taranto
Târgovişte *108 C5 prev.* Tîrgovişte. Dâmboviţa, S Romania
Târgu Jiu *108 B4 prev.* Tîrgu Jiu. Gorj, W Romania
Târgul-Neamţ *see* Târgu-Neamţ
Târgu Mureş *108 B4 prev.* Oşorhei, Tîrgu Mures, *Ger.* Neumarkt, *Hung.* Marosvásárhely. Mureş, C Romania
Târgu-Neamţ *108 C3 var.* Târgul-Neamţ; *prev.* Tîrgu-Neamţ. Neamţ, NE Romania
Târgu Ocna *108 C4 Hung.* Aknavásár; *prev.* Tîrgu Ocna. Bacău, E Romania
Târgu Secuiesc *108 C4 Ger.* Neumarkt, Szekler Neumarkt, *Hung.* Kezdivásárhely; *prev.* Chezdi-Oşorheiu, Târgul-Săcuiesc, Tîrgu Secuiesc. Covasna, E Romania
Tarija *61 G5* Tarija, S Bolivia
Tarīm *121 C6* C Yemen
Tarim Basin *124 C2 basin* NW China
Tarim He *126 B3 river* NW China
Tarma *60 C3* Junín, C Peru
Tarn *91 C6 cultural region* S France
Tarn *91 C6 river* S France
Tarnobrzeg *98 D4* Podkarpackie, SE Poland
Tarnów *99 D5* Małopolskie, S Poland
Tarragona *93 G2 anc.* Tarraco. Cataluña, E Spain
Tàrrega *93 F2 var.* Tarrega. Cataluña, NE Spain
Tarsus *116 C4* İçel, S Turkey
Tartu *106 D3 Ger.* Dorpat; *prev. Rus.* Yurev, Yur'yev. Tartumaa, SE Estonia
Ţarţūs *118 A3 Fr.* Tartouss; *anc.* Tortosa. Tarţūs, W Syria
Ta Ru Tao, Ko *137 B7 island* S Thailand
Tarvisio *96 D2* Friuli-Venezia Giulia, NE Italy
Tashi Chho Dzong *see* Thimphu
Tashkent *see* Toshkent
Tash-Kumyr *123 F2 Kir.* Tash-Kömür. Dzhalal-Abadskaya Oblast', W Kyrgyzstan
Tashqurghan *see* Kholm
Tasikmalaya *138 C5 prev.* Tasikmalaja. Jawa, C Indonesia
Tasman Basin *142 C5 var.* East Australian Basin. *Undersea feature* S Tasman Sea
Tasman Bay *151 C5 inlet* South Island, NZ
Tasmania *149 B8 prev.* Van Diemen's Land. *State* SE Australia
Tasmania *152 B4 island* SE Australia
Tasman Plateau *142 C5 var.* South Tasmania Plateau. *Undersea feature* SW Tasman Sea
Tasman Sea *142 C5 sea* SW Pacific Ocean
Tassili-n-Ajjer *71 E4 plateau* E Algeria
Tatabánya *99 C6* Komárom-Esztergom, NW Hungary
Tathlīth *121 B5* 'Asīr, S Saudi Arabia
Tatra Mountains *99 D5 Ger.* Tatra, *Hung.* Tátra, *Pol./Slvk.* Tatry. *Mountain range* Poland/Slovakia
Ta-t'ung *see* Datong
Tatvan *117 F3* Bitlis, SE Turkey
Ta'ū *145 F4 var.* Tau. *Island* Manua Islands, E American Samoa
Tau *see* Ta'ū
Taukum, Peski *123 G1 desert* SE Kazakhstan
Taumarunui *150 D4* Manawatu-Wanganui, North Island, NZ
Taungdwingyi *136 B3* Magwe, C Myanmar
Taunggyi *136 B3* Shan State, C Myanmar
Taunton *89 C7* SW England, UK
Taupo *150 D3* Waikato, North Island, NZ
Taupo, Lake *150 D3 lake* North Island, NZ
Tauragė *106 B4 Ger.* Tauroggen. Tauragė, SW Lithuania
Tauranga *150 D3* Bay of Plenty, North Island, NZ
Tauris *see* Tabrīz
Tavas *116 B4* Denizli, SW Turkey
Tavira *92 C5* Faro, S Portugal
Tavoy *137 B5 var.* Dawei. Tenasserim, S Myanmar
Tavoy Island *see* Mali Kyun
Tawakoni, Lake *49 G2 reservoir* Texas, SW USA
Tawau *138 D3* Sabah, East Malaysia
Ţawkar *see* Tokar
Tawzar *see* Tozeur
Taxco *51 E4 var.* Taxco de Alarcón. Guerrero, S Mexico
Taxco de Alarcón *see* Taxco
Taxiatosh *122 C2 var.* Takhiatosh, *Rus.* Takhiatash. Qoraqalpoghiston Respublikasi, W Uzbekistan
Taxtako'pir *122 D1 var.* Takhtakŭpir, *Rus.* Takhtakupyr. Qoraqalpoghiston Respublikasi, NW Uzbekistan
Tay *88 C3 river* C Scotland, UK
Taylor *49 G3* Texas, SW USA
Taymā' *120 A4* Tabūk, NW Saudi Arabia
Taymyr, Ozero *115 E2 lake* N Russian Federation
Taymyr, Poluostrov *115 E2 peninsula* N Russian Federation
Taz *114 D3 river* N Russian Federation
T'bilisi *117 G2 Eng.* Tiflis. *Country capital* (Georgia) SE Georgia
T'bilisi *112 B4 international airport* S Georgia
Tchien *see* Zwedru
Tchongking *see* Chongqing
Tczew *98 C2 Ger.* Dirschau. Pomorskie, N Poland
Te Anau *151 A7* Southland, South Island, NZ
Te Anau, Lake *151 A7 lake* South Island, NZ
Teapa *51 G4* Tabasco, SE Mexico
Teate *see* Chieti
Tebingtinggi *138 B3* Sumatera, N Indonesia
Tebriz *see* Tabrīz
Techirghiol *108 D5* Constanţa, SE Romania
Tecomán *50 D4* Colima, SW Mexico
Tecpan *51 E5 var.* Tecpan de Galeana. Guerrero, S Mexico
Tecpan de Galeana *see* Tecpan
Tecuci *108 C4* Galaţi, E Romania
Tedzhen *see* Tejen
Tedzhen *see* Harīrūd
Tees *89 D5 river* N England, UK
Tefé *62 D2* Amazonas, N Brazil
Tegal *138 C4* Jawa, C Indonesia
Tegelen *87 D5* Limburg, SE Netherlands
Tegucigalpa *52 C3 country capital* (Honduras) Francisco Morazán, SW Honduras
Teheran *see* Tehrān
Tehrān *120 C3 var.* Teheran. *Country capital* (Iran) Tehrān, N Iran
Tehuacán *51 F4* Puebla, S Mexico
Tehuantepec *51 F5 var.* Santo Domingo Tehuantepec. Oaxaca, SE Mexico
Tehuantepec, Golfo de *51 F5 var.* Gulf of Tehuantepec. *Gulf* S Mexico
Tehuantepec, Gulf of *see* Tehuantepec, Golfo de
Tehuantepec, Isthmus of *see* Tehuantepec, Istmo de
Tehuantepec, Istmo de *51 F5 var.* Isthmus of Tehuantepec. *Isthmus* SE Mexico
Tejen *122 C3 Rus.* Tedzhen. Akhalskiy Velayat, S Turkmenistan
Tejen *see* Harīrūd
Te Kao *150 C1* Northland, North Island, NZ
Tekax *51 H4 var.* Tekax de Álvaro Obregón. Yucatán, SE Mexico
Tekax de Álvaro Obregón *see* Tekax
Tekeli *114 C5* Almaty, SE Kazakhstan
Tekirdağ *116 A2 It.* Rodosto; *anc.* Bisanthe, Raidestos, Rhaedestus. Tekirdağ, NW Turkey
Te Kuiti *150 D3* Waikato, North Island, NZ
Tela *52 C2* Atlántida, NW Honduras
Telanaipura *see* Jambi
Tel Aviv-Jaffa *see* Tel Aviv-Yafo
Tel Aviv-Yafo *119 A6 var.* Tel Aviv-Jaffa. Tel Aviv, C Israel
Teles Pirés *see* São Manuel, Rio
Telish *104 C2 prev.* Azizie. Pleven, NW Bulgaria
Tell Abiad *see* At Tall al Abyaḑ
Tell Abyad *see* At Tall al Abyaḑ
Tell Kalakh *see* Tall Kalakh
Tell Shedadi *see* Ash Shadādah
Telšiai *106 B3 Ger.* Telschen. Telšiai, NW Lithuania
Teluk Irian *see* Cenderawasih, Teluk
Teluk Serera *see* Cenderawasih, Teluk
Temerin *100 D3* Serbia, N Serbia and Montenegro (Yugo.)
Temirtau *114 C4 prev.* Samarkandski, Samarkandskoye. Karaganda, C Kazakhstan
Tempio Pausania *97 A5* Sardegna, Italy, C Mediterranean Sea
Temple *49 G3* Texas, SW USA
Temuco *65 B5* Araucanía, C Chile
Temuka *151 B6* Canterbury, South Island, NZ
Tenasserim *137 B6* Tenasserim, S Myanmar
Ténenkou *74 D3* Mopti, C Mali
Ténéré *75 G3 physical region* C Niger
Tenerife *70 A3 island* Islas Canarias, Spain, NE Atlantic Ocean
Tengger Shamo *127 E3 desert* N China
Tengréla *74 D4 var.* Tingréla. N Côte d'Ivoire
Tenkodogo *75 E4* S Burkina faso
Tennant Creek *148 A3* Northern Territory, C Australia
Tennessee *42 C1 off.* State of Tennessee; also known as The Volunteer State. *State* SE USA
Tennessee River *42 C1 river* S USA
Tenojoki *see* Deatnu/Tana
Tepelena *see* Tepelenë
Tepelenë *101 C7 var.* Tepelena, *It.* Tepeleni. Gjirokastër, S Albania
Tepeleni *see* Tepelenë
Tepic *50 D4* Nayarit, C Mexico
Teplice *98 A4 Ger.* Teplitz; *prev.* Teplice-Šanov, Teplitz-Schönau. Ústecký Kraj, NW Czech Republic
Tequila *50 D4* Jalisco, SW Mexico
Teraina *145 G2 prev.* Washington Island. *Atoll* Line Islands, E Kiribati
Teramo *96 C4 anc.* Interamna. Abruzzo, C Italy
Tercan *117 E3* Erzincan, NE Turkey
Terceira *92 A5 var.* Ilha Terceira. *Island* Azores, Portugal, NE Atlantic Ocean
Teresina *63 F2 var.* Therezina. *State capital* Piauí, NE Brazil
Termia *see* Kýthnos
Términos, Laguna de *51 G4 lagoon* SE Mexico
Termiz *123 E3 Rus.* Termez. Surkhondaryo Wiloyati, S Uzbekistan
Termoli *96 D4* Molise, C Italy
Terneuzen *87 B5 var.* Neuzen. Zeeland, SW Netherlands
Terni *96 C4 anc.* Interamna Nahars. Umbria, C Italy
Ternopil' *108 C2 Pol.* Tarnopol, *Rus.* Ternopol'. Ternopil's'ka Oblast', W Ukraine
Terracina *97 C5* Lazio, C Italy
Terrassa *93 G2 Cast.* Tarrasa. Cataluña, E Spain
Terre Adélie *154 C4 disputed region* SE Antarctica
Terre Haute *40 B4* Indiana, N USA
Territoire du Yukon *see* Yukon Territory
Terschelling *86 C1 Fris.* Skylge. *Island* Waddeneilanden, N Netherlands
Teruel *93 F3 anc.* Turba. Aragón, E Spain
Tervel *104 E1 prev.* Kurtbunar, *Rom.* Curtbunar. Dobrich, NE Bulgaria
Tervueren *see* Tervuren
Tervuren *87 C6 var.* Tervueren. Vlaams Brabant, C Belgium
Teseney *72 C4 var.* Tessenei. W Eritrea
Tessalit *75 E2* Kidal, NE Mali
Tessaoua *75 G3* Maradi, S Niger
Tessenderlo *87 C5* Limburg, NE Belgium
Tessenei *see* Teseney

Testigos, Islas los *59 E1 island group* N Venezuela
Tete *79 E2* Tete, NW Mozambique
Teterow *94 C3* Mecklenburg-Vorpommern, NE Germany
Tétouan *70 C2 var.* Tetouan, Tetuán. N Morocco
Tetovo *101 D5 Alb.* Tetova, Tetovë, *Turk.* Kalkandelen. Razgrad, N Bulgaria
Tetuán *see* Tétouan
Tevere *96 C4 Eng.* Tiber. *River* C Italy
Teverya *119 B5 var.* Tiberias, Tverya. Northern, N Israel
Te Waewae Bay *151 A7 bay* South Island, NZ
Texarkana *42 A2* Arkansas, C USA
Texarkana *49 H2* Texas, SW USA
Texas *49 F3 off.* State of Texas; also known as The Lone Star State. *State* S USA
Texas City *49 H4* Texas, SW USA
Texel *86 C2 island* Waddeneilanden, NW Netherlands
Texoma, Lake *49 G2 reservoir* Oklahoma/Texas, C USA
Teziutlán *51 F4* Puebla, S Mexico
Thaa Atoll *see* Kolhumadulu Atoll
Thai Binh *136 D3* Thai Binh, N Vietnam
Thailand *137 C5 Th.* Prathet Thai; *prev.* Siam. *Country* SE Asia

Thailand 137

Official name Kingdom of Thailand
Formation 1238
Capital Bangkok
Population 62.8 million / 318 people per sq mile (123 people per sq km)
Total area 198,455 sq. miles (514,000 sq. km)
Languages Thai, Chinese, Malay, Khmer, Mon, Karen, Miao
Religions Buddhist 95%, Muslim 4%, Other (including Christian) 1%
Ethnic mix Thai 83%, Chinese 12%, Malay 3%, Khmer and Other 2%
Government Parliamentary system
Currency Baht = 100 stang
Literacy rate 93%
Calorie consumption 2486 calories

Thailand, Gulf of *137 C6 var.* Gulf of Siam, *Th.* Ao Thai, *Vtn.* Vinh Thai Lan. *Gulf* SE Asia
Thai Nguyên *136 D3* Băc Thai, N Vietnam
Thakhèk *136 D4 prev.* Muang Khammouan. Khammouan, C Laos
Thamarīd *see* Thamarīt
Thamarīt *121 D6 var.* Thamarīd, Thumrayt. SW Oman
Thames *89 B8 river* S England, UK
Thames *150 D3* Waikato, North Island, NZ
Thanh Hoa *136 D3* Vinh Phu, N Vietnam
Thanintari Taungdan *see* Bilauktaung Range
Thar Desert *134 C3 var.* Great Indian Desert, Indian Desert. *Desert* India/Pakistan
Tharthār, Buḩayrat ath *120 B3 lake* C Iraq
Thásos *104 C4 island* E Greece
Thásos *104 C4* Thásos, E Greece
Thaton *136 B4* Mon State, S Myanmar
Thayetmyo *136 A4* Magwe, C Myanmar
The Crane *55 H2 var.* Crane. S Barbados
The Dalles *46 B3* Oregon, NW USA
The Flatts Village *see* Flatts Village
The Hague *see* 's-Gravenhage
Theodosia *see* Feodosiya
The Pas *37 F5* Manitoba, C Canada
Therezina *see* Teresina
Thérma *105 D6* Ikaría, Dodekánisos, Greece, Aegean Sea
Thermaïkós Kólpos *104 B4 Eng.* Thermaic Gulf; *anc.* Thermaicus Sinus. *Gulf* N Greece
Thermiá *see* Kýthnos
Thérmo *105 B5* Dytikí Ellás, C Greece
The Rock *93 H4* E Gibraltar
The Six Counties *see* Northern Ireland
Thessaloníki *104 C3 Eng.* Salonica, Salonika, *SCr.* Solun, *Turk.* Selânik. Kentrikí Makedonía, N Greece
The Valley *55 G3 dependent territory capital* (Anguilla) E Anguilla
The Village *49 G1* Oklahoma, C USA
Thiamis *see* Thýamis
Thibet *see* Xizang Zizhiqu
Thief River Falls *45 F1* Minnesota, N USA
Thienen *see* Tienen
Thiers *91 C5* Puy-de-Dôme, C France
Thiès *74 B3* W Senegal
Thimbu *see* Thimphu
Thimphu *135 G3 var.* Thimbu; *prev.* Tashi Chho Dzong. *Country capital* (Bhutan) W Bhutan
Thionville *90 D3 Ger.* Diedenhofen. Moselle, NE France
Thíra *105 D7 prev.* Santorin, Santoríni, *anc.* Thera. *Island* Kykládes, Greece, Aegean Sea
Thíra *105 D7* Thíra, Kykládes, Greece, Aegean Sea
Thiruvanathapuram *see* Trivandrum
Thitu Island *128 C8 island* NW Spratly Islands
Tholen *86 B4 island* SW Netherlands
Thomasville *42 D3* Georgia, SE USA
Thompson *37 F4* Manitoba, C Canada
Thonon-les-Bains *91 D5* Haute-Savoie, E France
Thorlákshöfn *83 E5* Sudhurland, SW Iceland
Thornton Island *see* Millennium Island
Thouars *90 B4* Deux-Sèvres, W France
Thracian Sea *104 D4 Gk.* Thrakikó Pélagos; *anc.* Thracium Mare. *Sea* Greece/Turkey
Three Kings Islands *150 C1 island group* N NZ
Thrissur *see* Trichūr
Thuin *87 B7* Hainaut, S Belgium
Thule *see* Qaanaaq
Thumrayt *see* Thamarīt
Thun *95 A7 Fr.* Thoune. Bern, W Switzerland
Thunder Bay *38 B4* Ontario, S Canada
Thuner See *95 A7 lake* C Switzerland
Thung Song *137 C7 var.* Cha Mai. Nakhon Si Thammarat, SW Thailand
Thurso *88 C2* N Scotland, UK
Thýamis *104 A4 var.* Thiamis. *River* W Greece
Tianjin *128 D4 var.* Tientsin. Tianjin Shi, E China
Tianjin *see* Tianjin Shi
Tianjin Shi *128 D4 var.* Jin, Tianjin, T'ien-ching, Tientsin. *Admin. region municipality* E China
Tianshui *128 B4* Gansu, C China
Tiba *see* Chiba
Tiberias *see* Teverya
Tiberias, Lake *119 B5 var.* Chinnereth, Sea of Bahr Tabariya, Sea of Galilee, *Ar.* Bahrat Tabariya, *Heb.* Yam Kinneret. *Lake* N Israel
Tibesti *76 C2 var.* Tibesti Massif, *Ar.* Tībistī. *Mountain range* N Africa
Tibesti Massif *see* Tibesti
Tibet *see* Xizang Zizhiqu
Tibetan Autonomous Region *see* Xizang Zizhiqu
Tibet, Plateau of *see* Qingzang Gaoyuan
Tībistī *see* Tibesti
Tibnī *see* At Tibnī
Tiburón, Isla *50 B2 var.* Isla del Tiburón. *Island* NW Mexico
Tiburón, Isla del *see* Tiburón, Isla
Tîchît *74 D2 var.* Tichitt. Tagant, C Mauritania
Tichitt *see* Tîchît
Ticul *51 H3* Yucatán, SE Mexico
Tidjikdja *see* Tidjikja
Tidjikja *74 C2 var.* Tidjikdja; *prev.* Fort-Cappolani. Tagant, C Mauritania
T'ien-ching *see* Tianjin Shi
Tienen *87 C6 var.* Thienen, *Fr.* Tirlemont. Vlaams Brabant, C Belgium
Tien Shan *126 B3 Chin.* Thian Shan, Tian Shan, T'ien Shan, *Rus.* Tyan'-Shan'. *Mountain range* C Asia
Tientsin *see* Tianjin Shi
Tierp *85 C6* Uppsala, C Sweden
Tierra del Fuego *65 B8 off.* Provincia de la Tierra del Fuego. *Admin. region province* S Argentina
Tierra del Fuego *57 B8 island* Argentina/Chile
Tifton *42 D3* Georgia, SE USA
Tifu *139 F4* Pulau Buru, E Indonesia
Tighina *108 D4 Rus.* Bendery; *prev.* Bender. E Moldova
Tigranocerta *see* Siirt
Tigris *120 B2 Ar.* Dijlah, *Turk.* Dicle. *River* Iraq/Turkey
Tiguentourine *71 E3* E Algeria
Ti-hua *see* Ürümqi
Tihwa *see* Ürümqi
Tijuana *50 A1* Baja California, NW Mexico
Tikhoretsk *111 A7* Krasnodarskiy Kray, SW Russian Federation
Tikhvin *110 B4* Leningradskaya Oblast', NW Russian Federation
Tiki Basin *143 G3 undersea feature* S Pacific Ocean
Tiksi *115 F2* Respublika Sakha (Yakutiya), NE Russian Federation
Tilburg *86 C4* Noord-Brabant, S Netherlands
Tilimsen *see* Tlemcen
Tillabéri *75 F3 var.* Tillabéry. Tillabéri, W Niger
Tillabéry *see* Tillabéri
Tílos *105 E7 island* Dodekánisos, Greece, Aegean Sea
Timanskiy Kryazh *110 D3 Eng.* Timan Ridge. *Ridge* NW Russian Federation
Timaru *151 B6* Canterbury, South Island, NZ
Timbaki *see* Tympáki
Timbákion *see* Tympáki
Timbedgha *74 D3 var.* Timbédra. Hodh ech Chargui, SE Mauritania
Timbédra *see* Timbedgha
Timbuktu *see* Tombouctou
Timiș *108 A4 river* W Romania
Timișoara *108 A4 Ger.* Temeschwar, Temeswar, *Hung.* Temesvár; *prev.* Temeschburg. Timiș, W Romania
Timmins *38 C4* Ontario, S Canada
Timor *125 F5 island* Nusa Tenggara, East Timor/Indonesia
Timor Timur *see* East Timor
Timor Sea *125 F5 sea* E Indian Ocean
Timor Trench *see* Timor Trough
Timor Trough *125 F5 var.* Timor Trench. *Undersea feature* NE Timor Sea
Timrå *85 C5* Västernorrland, C Sweden
Tindouf *70 C3* W Algeria
Tineo *92 C1* Asturias, N Spain
Tingis | MM *see* Tanger
Tingo María *60 C3* Huánuco, C Peru
Tingréla *see* Tengréla
Tinhosa Grande *76 E2 island* N Sao Tome and Principe
Tinhosa Pequena *76 E1 island* N Sao Tome and Principe
Tinian *144 B1 island* S Northern Mariana Islands
Tínos *105 D6 anc.* Tenos. *Island* Kykládes, Greece, Aegean Sea
Tínos *105 D6* Tínos, Kykládes, Greece, Aegean Sea
Tip *101 E6* Papua, E Indonesia
Tipitapa *52 D3* Managua, W Nicaragua
Tip Top Mountain *38 C4 mountain* Ontario, S Canada
Tirana *see* Tiranë
Tiranë *101 C6 var.* Tirana. *Country capital* (Albania) Tiranë, C Albania
Tiraspol *108 D4 Rus.* Tiraspol'. E Moldova
Tiree *88 B3 island* W Scotland, UK
Tîrgu-Neamț *see* Târgu-Neamț
Tirlemont *see* Tienen
Tírnavos *see* Týrnavos
Tirol *95 C7 cultural region* Austria/Italy
Tiruchchirāppalli *132 C3 prev.* Trichinopoly. Tamil Nādu, SE India
Tiruppattūr *132 C2* Tamil Nādu, SE India
Tisza *103 F1 Ger.* Theiss, *Rom./Slvn./SCr.* Tisa, *Rus.* Tissa, *Ukr.* Tysa. *River* SE Europe *see also* Tisa
Tiszakécske *99 D7* Bács-Kiskun, C Hungary
Titano, Monte *96 E1 mountain* C San Marino
Titicaca, Lake *61 E4 lake* Bolivia/Peru
Titose *see* Chitose
Titu *108 C5* Dâmbovița, S Romania
Titule *77 D5* Orientale, N Dem. Rep. Congo
Tiverton *89 C7* SW England, UK
Tivoli *96 C4 anc.* Tiber. Lazio, C Italy
Tizimín *51 H3* Yucatán, SE Mexico
Tizi Ouzou *71 E1 var.* Tizi-Ouzou. N Algeria
Tiznit *70 B3* SW Morocco
Tlaquepaque *50 D4* Jalisco, C Mexico
Tlascala *see* Tlaxcala
Tlaxcala *51 F4 var.* Tlascala, Tlaxcala de Xicohténcatl. Tlaxcala, C Mexico
Tlaxcala de Xicohténcatl *see* Tlaxcala
Tlemcen *70 D2 var.* Tilimsen, Tlemsen. NW Algeria
Tlemsen *see* Tlemcen
Toamasina *79 G3 var.* Tamatave. Toamasina, E Madagascar
Toba, Danau *138 B3 lake* Sumatera, W Indonesia
Tobago *55 H5 island* NE Trinidad and Tobago
Tobol *114 C4 Kaz.* Tobyl. *River* Kazakhstan/Russian Federation
Tobol'sk *114 C3* Tyumenskaya Oblast', C Russian Federation
Tocantins *63 E3 off.* Estado do Tocantins. *State* C Brazil
Tocantins, Rio *63 F2 river* N Brazil
Tocoa *52 D2* Colón, N Honduras
Tocopilla *64 B2* Antofagasta, N Chile
Todi *96 C4* Umbria, C Italy
Todos os Santos, Baía de *63 G3 bay* E Brazil
Toetoes Bay *151 B8 bay* South Island, NZ
Tofua *145 E4 island* Ha'apai Group, C Tonga
Togo *75 E4* French Togoland. *Country* W Africa

Togo 75

Official name Republic of Togo
Formation 1960
Capital Lomé
Population 4.9 million / 233 people per sq mile (90 people per sq km)
Total area 21,924 sq. miles (56,785 sq. km)
Languages Ewe, Kabye, Gurma, French
Religions Traditional beliefs 50%, Christian 35%, Muslim 15%
Ethnic mix Ewe 46%, Kabye 27%, Other African 26%, European 1%
Government Presidential system
Currency CFA franc = 100 centimes
Literacy rate 60%
Calorie consumption 2287 calories

Tokanui *151 B7* Southland, South Island, NZ
Tokar *72 C3 var.* Ţawkar. Red Sea, NE Sudan
Tokat *116 D3* Tokat, N Turkey
Tokelau *145 E3 NZ overseas territory* W Polynesia
Tokio *see* Tōkyō
Tokmak *123 G2 Kir.* Tokmok. Chuyskaya Oblast', N Kyrgyzstan
Tokmak *109 G4 var.* Velykyy Tokmak. Zaporiz'ka Oblast', SE Ukraine
Tokoroa *150 D3* Waikato, North Island, NZ
Tokounou *74 C4* Haute-Guinée, C Guinea
Tokushima *131 C6 var.* Tokusima. Tokushima, Shikoku, SW Japan
Tokusima *see* Tokushima
Tōkyō *130 A1 var.* Tokio. *Country capital* (Japan) Tōkyō, Honshū, S Japan
Tōkyō Bay *130 A2 bay* SW Japan
Toledo *92 D3 anc.* Toletum. Castilla-La Mancha, C Spain
Toledo *40 D3* Ohio, N USA
Toledo Bend Reservoir *49 G3 reservoir* Louisiana/Texas, SW USA
Toliara *79 F4 var.* Toliary; *prev.* Tuléar. Toliara, SW Madagascar
Toliary *see* Toliara
Tolmin *95 D7 Ger.* Tolmein, *It.* Tolmino. W Slovenia
Tolna *99 C7 Ger.* Tolnau. Tolna, S Hungary
Tolosa *93 E1* País Vasco, N Spain
Toluca *51 E4 var.* Toluca de Lerdo. México, S Mexico
Toluca de Lerdo *see* Toluca
Tol'yatti *111 C6 prev.* Stavropol'. Samarskaya Oblast', W Russian Federation
Tomah *40 B2* Wisconsin, N USA
Tomakomai *130 D2* Hokkaidō, NE Japan
Tomar *92 B3* Santarém, W Portugal
Tomaschow *see* Tomaszów Mazowiecki
Tomaszów *see* Tomaszów Mazowiecki
Tomaszów Lubelski *98 E4 Ger.* Tomaschow. Lubelskie, E Poland
Tomaszów Mazowiecka *see* Tomaszów Mazowiecki
Tomaszów Mazowiecki *98 D4 var.* Tomaszów Mazowiecka; *prev.* Tomaszów, *Ger.* Tomaschow. Łódzkie, C Poland
Tombigbee River *42 C3 river* Alabama/Mississippi, S USA
Tombouctou *75 E3 Eng.* Timbuktu. Tombouctou, N Mali
Tombua *78 A2 Port.* Porto Alexandre. Namibe, SW Angola
Tomelloso *93 E3* Castilla-La Mancha, C Spain
Tomini, Gulf of *139 E4 var.* Teluk Tomini; *prev.* Teluk Gorontalo. *Bay* Sulawesi, C Indonesia
Tomini, Teluk *see* Tomini, Gulf of
Tomsk *114 D4* Tomskaya Oblast', C Russian Federation
Tomur Feng *see* Pobedy, Pik
Tonga *145 E4 var.* Friendly Islands. *Country* SW Pacific Ocean

Tonga 145

Official name Kingdom of Tonga
Formation 1970
Capital Nuku'alofa
Population 108,141 / 389 people per sq mile (150 people per sq km)
Total area 289 sq. miles (748 sq. km)
Languages English, Tongan
Religions Free Wesleyan 41%, other 17%, Roman Catholic 16%, Church of Jesus Christ of Latter-day Saints 14%, Free Church of Tonga 12%
Ethnic mix Polynesian 99%, other 1%
Government Monarchy
Currency Pa'anga (Tongan dollar) = 100 seniti
Literacy rate 99%
Calorie consumption Not available

Tongatapu *145 E5 island* Tongatapu Group, S Tonga
Tonga Trench *143 E3 undersea feature* S Pacific Ocean
Tongchuan *128 C4* Shaanxi, C China
Tongeren *87 D6 Fr.* Tongres. Limburg, NE Belgium
Tongking, Gulf of *128 B7 Chin.* Beibu Wan, *Vtn.* Vinh Bǎc Bô. *Gulf* China/Vietnam
Tongliao *127 G2* Nei Mongol Zizhiqu, N China
Tongshan *see* Xuzhou
Tongtian He *126 C4 river* C China
Tonj *73 B5* Warab, SW Sudan
Tônlé Sap *137 D5 Eng.* Great Lake. *Lake* W Cambodia
Tonopah *47 C6* Nevada, W USA
Tonyezh *107 C7 Rus.* Tonezh. Homyel'skaya Voblasts', SE Belarus
Tooele *44 B4* Utah, W USA
Toowoomba *149 E5* Queensland, E Australia
Topeka *45 F4 state capital* Kansas, C USA
Toplița *108 C3 Ger.* Töplitz, *Hung.* Maroshévíz; *prev.* Toplița Română, *Hung.* Oláh-Toplicza, Toplicza. Harghita, C Romania
Topoľčany *99 C6 Hung.* Nagytapolcsány. Nitriansky Kraj, SW Slovakia
Topolovgrad *104 D3 prev.* Kavakli. Khaskovo, S Bulgaria
Top Springs Roadhouse *146 D3* Northern Territory, N Australia
Torez *109 H3* Donets'ka Oblast', SE Ukraine
Torgau *94 D4* Sachsen, E Germany
Torhout *87 A5* West-Vlaanderen, W Belgium
Torino *96 A2 Eng.* Turin. Piemonte, NW Italy
Tornacum *see* Tournai
Torneälven *see* Tornionjoki
Torneträsk *84 C3 lake* N Sweden
Tornio *84 D4 Swe.* Torneå. Lappi, NW Finland
Torniojoki *see* Tornionjoki
Tornionjoki *84 D3 var.* Torniojoki, *Swe.* Torneälven. *River* Finland/Sweden
Toro *92 D2* Castilla-León, N Spain
Toronto *38 D5* Ontario, S Canada
Toros Dağları *116 C4 Eng.* Taurus Mountains. *Mountain range* S Turkey
Torquay *89 C7* SW England, UK
Torrance *46 D2* California, W USA
Torre, Alto da *92 B3 mountain* C Portugal
Torre del Greco *97 D5* Campania, S Italy
Torrejón de Ardoz *93 E3* Madrid, C Spain
Torrelavega *92 D1* Cantabria, N Spain
Torrens, Lake *149 A6 salt lake* South Australia
Torrent *93 F3 var.* Torrent de l'Horta, *Cas.* Torrente. País Valenciano, E Spain
Torrent de l'Horta *see* Torrent
Torrente *see* Torrent
Torreón *50 D3* Coahuila de Zaragoza, NE Mexico
Torres Strait *148 C1 strait* Australia/PNG
Torres Vedras *92 B3* Lisboa, C Portugal
Torrington *44 D3* Wyoming, C USA
Tórshavn *83 F5 Dan.* Thorshavn. *Dependent territory capital* (Faeroe Islands) N Faeroe Islands
To'rtko'l *122 D2 var.* Tŭrtkŭl, *Rus.* Turtkul'; *prev.* Petroaleksandrovsk. Qoraqalpoghiston Respublikasi, W Uzbekistan
Tortoise Islands *see* Galapagos Islands
Tortosa *93 F2 anc.* Dertosa. Cataluña, E Spain
Tortue, Montagne *59 H3 mountain range* C French Guiana
Tortuga, Isla *see* La Tortuga, Isla
Toruń *98 C3 Ger.* Thorn. Kujawskie-pomorskie, C Poland
Tõrva *106 D3 Ger.* Törwa. Valgamaa, S Estonia
Torzhok *110 B4* Tverskaya Oblast', W Russian Federation
Tosa-wan *131 B7 bay* SW Japan
Toscana *96 B3 Eng.* Tuscany. *Cultural region* C Italy
Toscano, Archipelago *96 B4 Eng.* Tuscan Archipelago. *Island group* C Italy
Toshkent *123 E2 Eng./Rus.* Tashkent. *Country capital* (Uzbekistan) Toshkent Wiloyati, E Uzbekistan
Totana *93 E4* Murcia, SE Spain
Tot'ma *see* Sukhona
Totness *59 G3* Coronie, N Suriname
Tottori *131 B6* Tottori, Honshū, SW Japan
Touâjîl *74 C2* Tiris Zemmour, N Mauritania
Touggourt *71 E2* NE Algeria
Toukoto *74 C3* Kayes, W Mali
Toul *90 D3* Meurthe-et-Moselle, NE France
Toulon *91 D6 anc.* Telo Martius, Tilio Martius. Var, SE France
Toulouse *91 B6 anc.* Tolosa. Haute-Garonne, S France
Toungoo *136 B4* Pegu, C Myanmar
Touraine *90 B4 cultural region* C France
Tourcoing *90 C2* Nord, N France
Tournai *87 A6 var.* Tournay, *Dut.* Doornik; *anc.* Tornacum. Hainaut, SW Belgium
Tournay *see* Tournai
Tours *90 B4 anc.* Caesarodunum, Turoni. Indre-et-Loire, C France
Tovarkovskiy *111 B5* Tul'skaya Oblast', W Russian Federation
Tower Island *see* Genovesa, Isla
Townsville *148 D3* Queensland, NE Australia
Towraghoudī *122 D4* Herāt, NW Afghanistan
Towson *41 F4* Maryland, NE USA
Towuti, Danau *139 E4 Dut.* Towoeti Meer. *Lake* Sulawesi, C Indonesia
Toyama *131 C5* Toyama, Honshū, SW Japan
Toyama-wan *131 B5 bay* W Japan
Toyota *131 C6* Aichi, Honshū, SW Japan
Tozeur *71 E2 var.* Tawzar. W Tunisia
Trâblous *see* Tripoli
Trabzon *117 E2 Eng.* Trebizond; *anc.* Trapezus. Trabzon, NE Turkey
Traiectum Tungorum *see* Maastricht
Traietum ad Mosam *see* Maastricht
Traiskirchen *95 E6* Niederösterreich, NE Austria
Trakai *107 C5 Ger.* Traken, *Pol.* Troki. Trakai, SE Lithuania
Tralee *89 A6 Ir.* Trá Lí. SW Ireland
Trá Lí *see* Tralee
Tralles *see* Aydın
Trang *137 C7* Trang, S Thailand
Transantarctic Mountains *154 B3 mountain range* Antarctica
Transsylvanische Alpen *see* Carpații Meridionali
Transylvania *108 B4 Eng.* Ardeal, Transilvania, *Ger.* Siebenbürgen, *Hung.* Erdély. *Cultural region* NW Romania
Transylvanian Alps *see* Carpații Meridionali
Trapani *97 B7 anc.* Drepanum. Sicilia, Italy, C Mediterranean Sea
Trâpeăng Vêng *137 D5* Kâmpóng Thum, C Cambodia
Traralgon *149 C7* Victoria, SE Australia
Trasimeno, Lago *C4 Eng.* Lake of Perugia, *Ger.* Trasimenischersee. *Lake* C Italy
Traverse City *40 C2* Michigan, N USA
Tra Vinh *137 D6 var.* Phu Vinh. Tra Vinh, S Vietnam
Travis, Lake *49 F3 reservoir* Texas, SW USA
Travnik *100 C4* Federacija Bosna I Hercegovina, C Bosnia and Herzegovina
Trbovlje *95 E7 Ger.* Trifail. C Slovenia
Třebíč *99 B5 Ger.* Trebitsch. Jihlavský Kraj, C Czech Republic
Trebinje *101 C5* Republika Srpska, S Bosnia and Herzegovina
Trebišov *99 D6 Hung.* Tőketerebes. Košický Kraj, E Slovakia
Trélazé *90 B4* Maine-et-Loire, NW France
Trelew *65 C6* Chubut, SE Argentina
Tremelo *87 C5* Vlaams Brabant, C Belgium
Trenčín *99 C5 Ger.* Trentschin, *Hung.* Trencsén. Trenčiansky Kraj, W Slovakia
Trenque Lauquen *64 C4* Buenos Aires, E Argentina
Trento *96 C2 Eng.* Trent, *Ger.* Trient; anc.Tridentum. Trentino-Alto Adige, N Italy
Trenton *41 F4 state capital* New Jersey, NE USA
Tres Arroyos *65 D5* Buenos Aires, E Argentina
Treskavica *100 C4 mountain range* SE Bosnia and Herzegovina
Tres Tabernae *see* Saverne
Treviso *96 C2 anc.* Tarvisium. Veneto, NE Italy
Trichūr *132 C3 var.* Thrissur. Kerala, SW India
Trier *95 A5 Eng.* Treves, *Fr.* Trèves; *anc.* Augusta Treverorum. Rheinland-Pfalz, SW Germany
Triesen *94 E2* SW Liechtenstein
Triesenberg *94 E2* SW Liechtenstein
Trieste *96 D2 Slvn.* Trst. Friuli-Venezia Giulia, NE Italy
Tríkala *104 B4 prev.* Trikkala. Thessalía, C Greece
Trincomalee *132 D3 var.* Trinkomali. Eastern Province, NE Sri Lanka
Trindade, Ilha da *67 C5 island* Brazil, W Atlantic Ocean
Trinidad *55 H5 island* C Trinidad and Tobago
Trinidad *61 F3* Beni, N Bolivia
Trinidad *44 D5* Colorado, C USA
Trinidad *64 D4* Flores, S Uruguay
Trinidad and Tobago *55 H5 Country* SE West Indies

Trinidad & Tobago 55

Official name Republic of Trinidad and Tobago
Formation 1962
Capital Port-of-Spain
Population 1.3 million / 656 people per sq mile (253 people per sq km)
Total area 1980 sq. miles (5128 sq. km)
Languages English Creole, English, Hindi, French, Spanish
Religions Roman Catholic 32%, Hindu 24%, Protestant 14%, Anglican 14%, Other and nonreligious 9%, Muslim 7%
Ethnic mix East Indian 40%, Black 40%, Mixed race 19%, White and Chinese 1%
Government Parliamentary system
Currency Trinidad and Tobago dollar = 100 cents
Literacy rate 99%
Calorie consumption 2756 calories

Trinité, Montagnes de la *59 H3 mountain range* C French Guiana
Trinity River *49 G3 river* Texas, SW USA
Trinkomali *see* Trincomalee
Tripoli *118 B4 var.* Tarābulus, Ţarābulus ash Shām, Trâblous; *anc.* Tripolis. N Lebanon
Tripoli *see* Ţarābulus
Trípoli *105 B6 prev.* Trípolis. Pelopónnisos, S Greece
Tripolis *see* Tripoli
Tristan da Cunha *69 B7 dependency of Saint Helena* SE Atlantic Ocean
Triton Island *128 B7 island* S Paracel Islands
Trivandrum *132 C3 var.* Thiruvanathapuram. Kerala, SW India
Trnava *99 C6 Ger.* Tyrnau, *Hung.* Nagyszombat. Trnavský Kraj, W Slovakia
Trogir *100 B4 It.* Traù. Split-Dalmacija, S Croatia
Troglav *100 B4 mountain* Bosnia and Herzegovina/Croatia
Trois-Rivières *39 E4* Québec, SE Canada
Trollhättan *85 B6* Västra Götaland, S Sweden
Tromsø *84 C2 Fin.* Tromssa. Troms, N Norway
Trondheim *84 B4 Ger.* Drontheim; *prev.* Nidaros, Trondhjem. Sør-Trøndelag, S Norway
Trondheimsfjorden *84 B4 fjord* S Norway
Troódos *102 C5 var.* Troodos Mountains. *Mountain range* C Cyprus
Troodos Mountains *see* Troódos
Troy *42 D3* Alabama, S USA
Troy *41 F3* New York, NE USA
Troyan *104 C2* Lovech, N Bulgaria
Troyes *90 D3 anc.* Augustobona Tricassium. Aube, N France
Trstenik *100 E4* Serbia, C Serbia and Montenegro (Yugo.)
Trujillo *52 D2* Colón, NE Honduras
Trujillo *92 C3* Extremadura, W Spain
Trujillo *60 B3* La Libertad, NW Peru
Truk Islands *see* Chuuk Islands
Trŭn *104 B2* Pernik, W Bulgaria
Truro *39 F4* Nova Scotia, SE Canada
Truro *89 C7* SW England, UK
Trzcianka *98 B3 Ger.* Schönlanke. Wielkopolskie, C Poland
Trzebnica *98 C4 Ger.* Trebnitz. Dolnośląskie, SW Poland
Tsalka *117 F2* S Georgia
Tsamkong *see* Zhanjiang
Tsangpo *see* Brahmaputra
Tsarevo *104 E2 prev.* Michurin. Burgas, E Bulgaria
Tsaritsyn *see* Volgograd
Tsefat *see* Zefat
Tsetserleg *126 D2* Arhangay, C Mongolia
Tsevat *see* Ẕefat
Tshela *77 B6* Bas-Zaïre, W Dem. Rep. Congo
Tshikapa *77 C7* Kasai Occidental, SW Dem. Rep. Congo
Tshuapa *77 D6 river* C Dem. Rep. Congo
Tshwane *see* Pretoria
Tsinan *see* Jinan
Tsing Hai *see* Qinghai Hu
Tsingtao *see* Qingdao
Tsingtau *see* Qingdao
Tsinkiang *see* Quanzhou
Tsintao *see* Qingdao
Tsitsihar *see* Qiqihar
Tsu *131 C6 var.* Tu. Mie, Honshū, SW Japan
Tsugaru-kaikyō *130 C3 strait* N Japan
Tsumeb *78 B3* Otjikoto, N Namibia
Tsuruga *131 C6 var.* Turuga. Fukui, Honshū, SW Japan
Tsuruoka *130 D4 var.* Turuoka. Yamagata, Honshū, C Japan
Tsushima *131 A7 var.* Tsushima-tō, Tusima. *Island group* SW Japan
Tsushima-tō *see* Tsushima
Tsyerakhowka *107 D8 Rus.* Terekhovka. Homyel'skaya Voblasts', SE Belarus
Tsyurupyns'k *109 E4 Rus.* Tsyurupinsk. Khersons'ka Oblast', S Ukraine
Tu *see* Tsu
Tuamotu Fracture Zone *143 H3 tectonic feature* E Pacific Ocean
Tuamotu, Îles *145 H4 var.* Archipel des Tuamotu, Dangerous Archipelago, Tuamotu Islands. *Island group* N French Polynesia
Tuamotu Islands *see* Tuamotu, Îles
Tuapi *53 E2* Región Autónoma Atlántico Norte, NE Nicaragua
Tuapse *111 A7* Krasnodarskiy Kray, SW Russian Federation
Tuba City *48 B1* Arizona, SW USA
Tubbergen *86 E3* Overijssel, E Netherlands
Tubize *87 B6 Dut.* Tubeke. Wallon Brabant, C Belgium
Tubmanburg *74 C5* NW Liberia
Ţubruq *71 H2 Eng.* Tobruk, *It.* Tobruch. NE Libya
Tubuai Islands *see* Australes, Îles
Tucker's Town *42 B5* E Bermuda
Tucson *48 B3* Arizona, SW USA
Tucumán *see* San Miguel de Tucumán
Tucumcari *49 E2* New Mexico, SW USA
Tucupita *59 E2* Delta Amacuro, NE Venezuela
Tucuruí, Represa de *63 F2 reservoir* NE Brazil
Tudela *93 E2 Basq.* Tutera; *anc.* Tutela. Navarra, N Spain
Tudmur *118 C3 var.* Tadmur, Tamar, *Gk.* Palmyra; *Bibl.* Tadmor. Ḩimş, C Syria
Tuguegarao *139 E1* Luzon, N Philippines
Tuktoyaktuk *37 E3* Northwest Territories, NW Canada
Tukums *106 C3 Ger.* Tuckum. Tukums, W Latvia
Tula *111 B5* Tul'skaya Oblast', W Russian Federation
Tulancingo *51 E4* Hidalgo, C Mexico
Tulare Lake Bed *47 C7 salt flat* California, W USA
Tulcán *60 B1* Carchi, N Ecuador
Tulcea *108 D5* Tulcea, E Romania
Tul'chyn *108 D3 Rus.* Tul'chin. Vinnyts'ka Oblast', C Ukraine
Tuléar *see* Toliara
Tulia *49 E2* Texas, SW USA
Tulle *91 C5 anc.* Tutela. Corrèze, C France
Tulln *95 E6 var.* Oberhollabrunn. Niederösterreich, NE Austria
Tully *148 D3* Queensland, NE Australia
Tulsa *49 G1* Oklahoma, C USA
Tuluá *58 B3* Valle del Cauca, W Colombia
Tulun *115 E4* Irkutskaya Oblast', S Russian Federation
Tumaco *58 A4* Nariño, SW Colombia
Tumba, Lac *see* Ntomba, Lac
Tumbes *60 A2* Tumbes, NW Peru
Tumkūr *132 C2* Karnātaka, W India
Tumuc Humac Mountains *63 E1 var.* Serra Tumucumaque. *Mountain range* N South America
Tunduru *73 C8* Ruvuma, S Tanzania
Tundzha *104 D3 Turk.* Tunca Nehri. *River* Bulgaria/Turkey *see also* Tunca Nehri
Tungabhadra Reservoir *132 C2 lake* S India
Tungaru *145 E2 prev.* Gilbert Islands. *Island group* W Kiribati
T'ung-shan *see* Xuzhou
Tungsten *36 D4* Northwest Territories, W Canada
Tung-t'ing Hu *see* Dongting Hu
Tunis *71 E1 var.* Tūnis. *Country capital* (Tunisia) NE Tunisia
Tūnis *see* Tunis
Tunis, Golfe de *102 D3 Ar.* Khalīj Tūnis. *Gulf* NE Tunisia
Tunisia *71 F2 Ar.* Al Jumhūrīyah at Tūnisīyah, *Fr.* République Tunisienne. *Country* N Africa

Tunisia 71

Official name Republic of Tunisia
Formation 1956
Capital Tunis
Population 9.8 million / 163 people per sq mile (63 people per sq km)
Total area 63,169 sq. miles (163,610 sq. km)
Languages Arabic, French
Religions Muslim (mainly Sunni) 98%, Christian 1%, Jewish 1%
Ethnic mix Arab and Berber 98%, Jewish 1%, European 1%
Government Presidential system
Currency Tunisian dinar = 1000 millimes
Literacy rate 73%
Calorie consumption 3293 calories

Tunja *58 B3* Boyacá, C Colombia
Tuong Buong *see* T,ơng Đ,ơng
Tupelo *42 C2* Mississippi, S USA
Tupiza *61 G5* Potosí, S Bolivia
Turabah *121 B5* Makkah, W Saudi Arabia
Turangi *150 D4* Waikato, North Island, NZ
Turan Lowland *122 C2 var.* Turan Plain, *Kaz.* Turan Oypaty, *Rus.* Turanskaya Nizmennost', *Turk.* Turan Pesligi, *Uzb.* Turon Pasttekisligi. *Plain* C Asia
Turan Oypaty *see* Turan Lowland
Turan Pesligi *see* Turan Lowland
Turan Plain *see* Turan Lowland
Turanskaya Nizmennost' *see* Turan Lowland
Ţurayf *120 A3* Al Ḩudūd ash Shamālīyah, NW Saudi Arabia
Turbat *134 A3* Baluchistān, SW Pakistan
Turda *108 B4 Ger.* Thorenburg, *Hung.* Torda. Cluj, NW Romania
Turek *98 C3* Wielkopolskie, C Poland
Turfan *see* Turpan
Turin *see* Torino
Turkana, Lake *89 C6 var.* Lake Rudolf. *Lake* N Kenya
Turkish Republic of Northern Cyprus *102 D5 Ger.* Dependent territory, *disputed territory.* Cyprus
Turkestan *114 B5 Kaz.* Türkistan. Yuzhnyy Kazakhstan, S Kazakhstan
Turkey *116 B3 Turk.* Türkiye Cumhuriyeti. *Country* SW Asia

Turkey 116

Official name Republic of Turkey
Formation 1923
Capital Ankara
Population 71.3 million / 240 people per sq mile (93 people per sq km)
Total area 301,382 sq. miles (780,580 sq. km)
Languages Turkish, Kurdish, Arabic, Circassian, Armenian, Greek, Georgian, Ladino
Religions Muslim (mainly Sunni) 99%, other 1%
Ethnic mix Turkish 70%, Kurdish 20%, other 8%, Arab 2%
Government Parliamentary system
Currency Turkish lira = 100 kurus
Literacy rate 87%
Calorie consumption 3343 calories

Türkmenabat *122 D3 prev.* Chardzhev, Chardzhou, Chardzhui, Leninsk-Turkmenski, *Turkm.* Chärjew. Lebapskiy Velayat, E Turkmenistan
Turkmen Aylagy *122 B2 Rus.* Turkmenskiy Zaliv. *Lake gulf* W Turkmenistan
Turkmenbashi *see* Türkmenbaşy
Türkmenbaşy *122 B2 var.* Turkmenbashi; *prev.* Krasnovodsk. Balkanskiy Velayat, W Turkmenistan
Türkmenbaşy Aylagy *122 A2 prev.* Krasnovodskiy Zaliv, Krasnowodsk Aylagy. *Lake gulf* W Turkmenistan
Turkmenistan *122 B2 prev.* Turkmenskaya Soviet Socialist Republic. *Country* C Asia

Turkmenistan 122

Official name Turkmenistan
Formation 1991
Capital Ashgabat
Population 4.9 million / 26 people per sq mile (10 people per sq km)
Total area 188,455 sq. miles (488,100 sq. km)
Languages Turkmen, Uzbek, Russian, Kazakh, Tatar
Religions Sunni Muslim 87%, Orthodox Christian 11%, other 2%
Ethnic mix Turkmen 77%, Uzbek 9%, Russian 7%, other 4%, Kazakh 2%, Tatar 1%
Government One-party state
Currency Manat = 100 tenga
Literacy rate 98%
Calorie consumption 2738 calories

Turkmenskiy Zaliv *see* Türkmen Aylagy
Turks and Caicos Islands *55 E2 UK dependent territory* N West Indies
Turlock *47 B6* California, W USA
Turnagain, Cape *150 D4 headland* North Island, NZ
Turnhout *87 C5* Antwerpen, N Belgium
Turnov *98 B4 Ger.* Turnau. Liberecký Kraj, N Czech Republic
Turnu Măgurele *108 B5 var.* Turnu-Măgurele. Teleorman, S Romania
Turon Pasttekisligi *see* Turan Lowland
Turpan *126 C3 var.* Turfan. Xinjiang Uygur Zizhiqu, NW China
Turpan Pendi *126 C3 Eng.* Turpan Depression. *Depression* NW China
Tŭrtkŭl *see* To'rtko'l

Turuga *see* Tsuruga
Turuoka *see* Tsuruoka
Tuscaloosa *42 C2* Alabama, S USA
Tusima *see* Tsushima
Tuticorin *132 C3* Tamil Nādu, SE India
Tutrakan *104 D1* Silistra, NE Bulgaria
Tutuila *145 F4 island* W American Samoa
Tuvalu *145 E3 prev.* Ellice Islands. *Country* SW Pacific Ocean

Tuvalu 145

Official name Tuvalu
Formation 1978
Capital Fongafale, on Funafuti Atoll
Population 11,305 / 1130 people per sq mile (435 people per sq km)
Total area 10 sq. miles (26 sq. km)
Languages Tuvaluan, Kiribati, English
Religions Church of Tuvalu 97%, other 1%, Baha'i 1%, Seventh-day Adventist 1%
Ethnic mix Polynesian 96%, other 4%
Government Nonparty system
Currency Australian dollar and Tuvaluan dollar = 100 cents
Literacy rate 98%
Calorie consumption Not available

Ṭuwayq, Jabal *121 C5 mountain range* C Saudi Arabia
Tuxpán *51 F4 var.* Tuxpán de Rodríguez Cano. Veracruz-Llave, E Mexico
Tuxpan *50 D4* Jalisco, C Mexico
Tuxpan *50 D4* Nayarit, C Mexico
Tuxpán de Rodríguez Cano *see* Tuxpán
Tuxtepec *51 F4 var.* San Juan Bautista Tuxtepec. Oaxaca, S Mexico
Tuxtla *51 G5 var.* Tuxtla Gutiérrez. Chiapas, SE Mexico
Tuxtla *see* San Andrés Tuxtla
Tuxtla Gutiérrez *see* Tuxtla
Tuy Hoa *137 E5* Phu Yên, S Vietnam
Tuz Gölü *116 C3 lake* C Turkey
Tuzla *100 C3* Federacija Bosna I Hercegovina, NE Bosnia and Herzegovina
Tver' *110 B4 prev.* Kalinin. Tverskaya Oblast', W Russian Federation
Tverya *see* Teverya
Twin Falls *46 D4* Idaho, NW USA
Tychy *99 D5 Ger.* Tichau. Śląskie, S Poland
Tyler *49 G3* Texas, SW USA
Tympáki *105 C8 var.* Timbaki; *prev.* Timbákion. Kríti, Greece, E Mediterranean Sea
Tynda *115 F4* Amurskaya Oblast', SE Russian Federation
Tyne *88 D4 river* N England, UK
Tyôsi *see* Chōshi
Tyre *see* Soûr
Týrnavos *104 B4 var.* Tírnavos. Thessalía, C Greece
Tyrrhenian Sea *97 B6 It.* Mare Tirreno. *Sea* N Mediterranean Sea
Tyumen' *114 C3* Tyumenskaya Oblast', C Russian Federation
Tyup *123 G2 Kir.* Tüp. Issyk-Kul'skaya Oblast', NE Kyrgyzstan
Tywyn *89 C6* W Wales, UK
Tzekung *see* Zigong
T,ơng Đ,ơng *136 D4 var.* Tuong Buong. Nghê An, N Vietnam

U

Uanle Uen *see* Wanlaweyn
Uaupés, Rio *see* Vaupés, Río
Ubangi *77 C5 Fr.* Oubangui. *River* C Africa
Ubangi-Shari *see* Central African Republic
Ube *131 B7* Yamaguchi, Honshū, SW Japan
Ubeda *93 E4* Andalucía, S Spain
Uberaba *63 F4* Minas Gerais, SE Brazil
Uberlândia *63 F4* Minas Gerais, SE Brazil
Ubol Rajadhani *see* Ubon Ratchathani
Ubol Ratchathani *see* Ubon Ratchathani
Ubon Ratchathani *137 D5 var.* Muang Ubon, Ubol Rajadhani, Ubol Ratchathani, Udon Ratchathani. Ubon Ratchathani, E Thailand
Ubrique *92 D5* Andalucía, S Spain
Ucayali, Río *60 D3 river* C Peru
Uchiura-wan *130 D3 bay* NW Pacific Ocean
Uchquduq *122 D2 Rus.* Uchkuduk. Nawoiy Wiloyati, N Uzbekistan
Uchtagan, Peski *see* Uçtagan Gumy
Uçtagan Gumy *122 C2 Rus.* Peski Uchtagan. *Desert* NW Turkmenistan
Udaipur *134 C3 prev.* Oodeypore. Rājasthān, N India
Uddevalla *85 B6* Västra Götaland, S Sweden
Udine *96 D2 anc.* Utina. Friuli-Venezia Giulia, NE Italy
Udintsev Fracture Zone *154 A5 tectonic feature* S Pacific Ocean
Udipi *see* Udupi
Udon Ratchathani *see* Ubon Ratchathani
Udon Thani *136 C4 var.* Ban Mak Khaeng, Udorndhani. Udon Thani, N Thailand
Udorndhani *see* Udon Thani
Udupi *132 B2 var.* Udipi. Karnātaka, SW India
Uele *77 D5 var.* Welle. *River* NE Dem. Rep. Congo
Uelzen *94 C3* Niedersachsen, N Germany
Ufa *111 D6* Respublika Bashkortostan, W Russian Federation
Ugāle *106 C2* Ventspils, NW Latvia
Uganda *73 B6 Country* E Africa

Uganda 73

Official name Republic of Uganda
Formation 1962
Capital Kampala
Population 25.8 million / 335 people per sq mile (129 people per sq km)
Total area 91,135 sq. miles (236,040 sq. km)
Languages Luganda, Nkole, Chiga, Lango, Acholi, Teso, Lugbara, English
Religions Roman Catholic 38%, Protestant 33%, Traditional beliefs 13%, Muslim (mainly Sunni) 8%, other 8%
Ethnic mix Bantu tribes 50%, other 45%, Sudanese 5%
Government Nonparty system
Currency New Uganda shilling = 100 cents
Literacy rate 69%
Calorie consumption 2398 calories

Uglovka *110 B4 var.* Okulovka. Novgorodskaya Oblast', W Russian Federation
Uhuru Peak *see* Kilimanjaro
Uíge *78 B1 Port.* Carmona, Vila Marechal Carmona. Uíge, NW Angola
Uinta Mountains *44 B4 mountain range* Utah, W USA
Uitenhage *78 C5* Eastern Cape, S South Africa
Uithoorn *86 C3* Noord-Holland, C Netherlands
Ujelang Atoll *144 C1 var.* Wujlān. *Atoll* Ralik Chain, W Marshall Islands
Ujungpandang *139 E4 var.* Macassar, Makassar; *prev.* Makasar. Sulawesi, C Indonesia
Ujung Salang *see* Phuket
Ukhta *114 C3* Respublika Komi, NW Russian Federation
Ukiah *47 B5* California, W USA
Ukmergė *106 C4 Pol.* Wiłkomierz. Ukmergė, C Lithuania
Ukraine *108 C2 Ukr.* Ukrayina; *prev.* Ukrainian Soviet Socialist Republic, Ukrainskaya S.S.R. *Country* SE Europe

Ukraine 108

Official name Ukraine
Formation 1991
Capital Kiev
Population 47.7 million / 205 people per sq mile (79 people per sq km)
Total area 223,089 sq. miles (603,700 sq. km)
Languages Ukrainian, Russian, Tatar
Religions Christian (mainly Orthodox) 95%, other 4%, Jewish 1%
Ethnic mix Ukrainian 73%, Russian 22%, other 4%, Jewish 1%
Government Presidential system
Currency Hryvna = 100 kopiykas
Literacy rate 99%
Calorie consumption 3008 calories

Ulaanbaatar *127 E2 Eng.* Ulan Bator. *Country capital* (Mongolia) Töv, C Mongolia
Ulaangom *126 C2* Uvs, NW Mongolia
Ulan Bator *see* Ulaanbaatar
Ulanhad *see* Chifeng
Ulan-Ude *115 E4 prev.* Verkhneudinsk. Respublika Buryatiya, S Russian Federation
Ulft *86 E4* Gelderland, E Netherlands
Ullapool *88 C3* N Scotland, UK
Ulm *95 B6* Baden-Württemberg, S Germany
Ulsan *129 E4 Jap.* Urusan. SE South Korea
Ulster *89 B5 cultural region* N Ireland
Ulungur Hu *126 B2 lake* NW China
Uluru *147 D5 var.* Ayers Rock. *Rocky outcrop* Northern Territory, C Australia
Ulyanivka *109 E3 Rus.* Ul'yanovka. Kirovohrads'ka Oblast', C Ukraine
Ul'yanovsk *111 C5 prev.* Simbirsk. Ul'yanovskaya Oblast', W Russian Federation
Uman' *109 E3 Rus.* Uman. Cherkas'ka Oblast', C Ukraine
Umán *51 H3* Yucatán, SE Mexico
Umanak *see* Uummannaq
Umanaq *see* Uummannaq
Umbro-Marchigiano, Appennino *96 C3 Eng.* Umbrian-Machigian Mountains. *Mountain range* C Italy
Umeå *84 C4* Västerbotten, N Sweden
Umeälven *84 C4 river* N Sweden
Umiat *36 D2* Alaska, USA
Umm Buru *72 A4* Western Darfur, W Sudan
Umm Durmān *see* Omdurman
Umm Ruwaba *72 C4 var.* Umm Ruwābah, Um Ruwāba. Northern Kordofan, C Sudan
Umm Ruwābah *see* Umm Ruwaba
Umnak Island *36 A3 island* Aleutian Islands, Alaska, USA
Um Ruwāba *see* Umm Ruwaba
Umtali *see* Mutare
Umtata *78 D5* Eastern Cape, SE South Africa
Una *100 B3 river* Bosnia and Herzegovina/Croatia
Unac *100 B3 river* W Bosnia and Herzegovina
Unalaska Island *36 A3 island* Aleutian Islands, Alaska, USA
'Unayzah *120 B4 var.* Anaiza. Al Qaşīm, C Saudi Arabia
Uncía *61 F4* Potosí, C Bolivia
Uncompahgre Peak *44 B5 mountain* Colorado, C USA
Ungarisches Erzgebirge *see* Slovenské rudohorie
Ungava Bay *39 E1 bay* Québec, E Canada
Ungava, Péninsule d' *38 D1 peninsula* Québec, SE Canada
Ungheni *108 D3 Rus.* Ungeny. W Moldova
Üngüz Angyrsyndaky Garagum *122 C2 Rus.* Zaunguzskiye Garagumy. *Desert* N Turkmenistan
Unimak Island *36 B3 island* Aleutian Islands, Alaska, USA
Union *43 E1* South Carolina, SE USA
Union City Tennessee, S USA
United Arab Emirates *121 C5 Ar.* Al Imārāt al 'Arabīyah al Muttaḩidah, *abbrev.* UAE; *prev.* Trucial States. *Country* SW Asia

United Arab Emirates 121

Official name United Arab Emirates
Formation 1971
Capital Abu Dhabi
Population 3 million / 93 people per sq mile (36 people per sq km)
Total area 32,000 sq. miles (82,880 sq. km)
Languages Arabic, Farsi, Indian and Pakistani languages, English
Religions Muslim (mainly Sunni) 96%, Christian, Hindu, and other 4%
Ethnic mix Asian 60%, Emirian 25%, Other Arab 12%, European 3%
Government Monarchy
Currency UAE dirham = 100 fils
Literacy rate 77%
Calorie consumption 3340 calories

United Kingdom *89 B5 abbrev.* UK. *Country* NW Europe

United Kingdom 89

Official name United Kingdom of Great Britain and Northern Ireland
Formation 1707
Capital London
Population 59.3 million / 636 people per sq mile (245 people per sq km)
Total area 94,525 sq. miles (244,820 sq. km)
Languages English, Welsh, Scottish Gaelic, Irish Gaelic
Religions Anglican 45%, Other and nonreligious 36%, Roman Catholic 9%, Presbyterian 4%, Muslim 3%, Methodist 2%, Hindu 1%
Ethnic mix English 80%, Scottish 9%, West Indian, Asian, and other 5%, Northern Irish 3%, Welsh 3%
Government Parliamentary system
Currency Pound sterling = 100 pence
Literacy rate 99%
Calorie consumption 3368 calories

United States of America *35 B5 var.* America, The States, *abbrev.* U.S., USA. *Country*

United States of America 35

Official name United States of America
Formation 1776
Capital Washington D.C.
Population 294 million / 83 people per sq mile (32 people per sq km)
Total area 3,717,792 sq. miles (9,626,091 sq. km)
Languages English, Spanish, Chinese, French, German, Tagalog, Vietnamese, Italian, Korean, Russian, Polish

United States of America (continued)

Religions Protestant 52%, Roman Catholic 25%, Other and nonreligious 19%, Muslim 2%, Jewish 2%
Ethnic mix White 69%, Hispanic 13%, Black American/African 13%, Asian 4%, Native American 1%
Government Presidential system
Currency US dollar = 100 cents
Literacy rate 99%
Calorie consumption 3766 calories

Unst *88 D1 island* NE Scotland, UK
Ünye *116 D2* Ordu, W Turkey
Upala *52 D4* Alajuela, NW Costa Rica
Upata *59 E2* Bolívar, E Venezuela
Upemba, Lac *77 D7 lake* SE Dem. Rep. Congo
Upernavik *82 C2 var.* Upernivik. C Greenland
Upernivik *see* Upernavik
Upington *78 C4* Northern Cape, W South Africa
Upolu *145 F4 island* SE Samoa
Upper Klamath Lake *46 A4 lake* Oregon, NW USA
Upper Lough Erne *89 A5 lake* SW Northern Ireland, UK
Upper Red Lake *45 F1 lake* Minnesota, N USA
Uppsala *85 C6* Uppsala, C Sweden
Ural *112 B3 Kaz.* Zayyq. *River* Kazakhstan/Russian Federation
Ural Mountains *see* Ural'skiye Gory
Ural'sk *114 B3 Kaz.* Oral. Zapadnyy Kazakhstan, NW Kazakhstan
Ural'skiye Gory *114 C3 var.* Ural'skiy Khrebet, *Eng.* Ural Mountains. *Mountain range* Kazakhstan/Russian Federation
Ural'skiy Khrebet *see* Ural'skiye Gory
Uraricoera *62 D1* Roraima, N Brazil
Urbandale *45 F3* Iowa, C USA
Uren' *111 C5* Nizhegorodskaya Oblast', W Russian Federation
Urganch *122 D2 Rus.* Urgench; *prev.* Novo-Urgench. Khorazm Wiloyati, W Uzbekistan
Urgut *123 E3* Samarqand Wiloyati, C Uzbekistan
Uroševac *101 D5 Alb.* Ferizaj. Serbia, S Serbia and Montenegro (Yugo.)
Ŭroteppa *123 E2 Rus.* Ura-Tyube. NW Tajikistan
Uruapan *51 E4 var.* Uruapan del Progreso. Michoacán de Ocampo, SW Mexico
Uruapan del Progreso *see* Uruapan
Uruguai, Rio *see* Uruguay
Uruguay *64 D4 prev.* La Banda Oriental. *Country* E South America

Uruguay 64

Official name Eastern Republic of Uruguay
Formation 1828
Capital Montevideo
Population 3.4 million / 50 people per sq mile (19 people per sq km)
Total area 68,039 sq. miles (176,220 sq. km)
Languages Spanish
Religions Roman Catholic 66%, Other and nonreligious 30%, Jewish 2%, Protestant 2%
Ethnic mix White 90%, Mestizo 6%, Black 4%
Government Presidential system
Currency Uruguayan peso = 100 centésimos

Uruguay (continued)

Literacy rate 98%
Calorie consumption 2848 calories

Uruguay *64 D3 var.* Rio Uruguai, Río Uruguay. *River* E South America
Uruguay, Río *see* Uruguay
Urumchi *see* Ürümqi
Urumqi *see* Ürümqi
Ürümqi *126 C3 var.* Tihwa, Urumchi, Urumqi, Urumtsi, Wu-lu-k'o-mu-shi, Wu-lu-mu-ch'i; *prev.* Ti-hua. *Autonomous region capital* Xinjiang Uygur Zizhiqu, NW China
Urumtsi *see* Ürümqi
Urup, Ostrov *115 H4 island* Kuril'skiye Ostrova, SE Russian Federation
Urziceni *108 C5* Ialomiţa, SE Romania
Usa *110 E3 river* NW Russian Federation
Uşak *116 B3 prev.* Ushak. Uşak, W Turkey
Ushuaia *65 B8* Tierra del Fuego, S Argentina
Usinsk *110 E3* Respublika Komi, NW Russian Federation
Üsküb *see* Skopje
Üsküp *see* Skopje
Usmas Ezers *106 B3 lake* NW Latvia
Usol'ye-Sibirskoye *115 E4* Irkutskaya Oblast', C Russian Federation
Ussel *91 C5* Corrèze, C France
Ussuriysk *115 G5 prev.* Nikol'sk, Nikol'sk-Ussuriyskiy, Voroshilov. Primorskiy Kray, SE
Ustica, Isola d' *97 B6 island* S Italy
Ust'-Ilimsk *115 E4* Irkutskaya Oblast', C Russian Federation
Ústí nad Labem *98 A4 Ger.* Aussig. Ústecký Kraj, NW Czech Republic
Ustka *98 C2 Ger.* Stolpmünde. Pomorskie, N Poland
Ust'-Kamchatsk *115 H2* Kamchatskaya Oblast', E Russian Federation
Ust'-Kamenogorsk *114 D5 Kaz.* Öskemen. Vostochnyy Kazakhstan, E Kazakhstan
Ust'-Kut *115 E4* Irkutskaya Oblast', C Russian Federation
Ust'-Olenëk *115 E3* Respublika Sakha (Yakutiya), NE Russian Federation
Ustrzyki Dolne *99 E5* Podkarpackie, SE Poland
Ust Urt *see* Ustyurt Plateau
Ustyurt Plateau *122 B1 var.* Ust Urt, *Uzb.* Ustyurt Platosi. *Plateau* Kazakhstan/Uzbekistan
Ustyurt Platosi *see* Ustyurt Plateau
Usulután *52 C3* Usulután, SE El Salvador
Usumacinta, Río *52 B1 river* Guatemala/Mexico
Utah *48 A1 off.* State of Utah; also known as Beehive State, Mormon State. *State* W USA
Utah Lake *44 B4 lake* Utah, W USA
Utena *106 C4* Utena, E Lithuania
Utica *41 F3* New York, NE USA
Utrecht *86 C4 Lat.* Trajectum ad Rhenum. Utrecht C Netherlands
Utsunomiya *131 D5 var.* Utunomiya. Tochigi, Honshū, S Japan
Uttaranchal *135 E2* Admin. region *state* N India
Uttar Pradesh *135 E3 prev.* United Provinces, United Provinces of Agra and Oudh. *State* N India
Utunomiya *see* Utsunomiya
Uulu *106 D2* Pärnumaa, SW Estonia
Uummannaq *82 C3 var.* Umanak, Umanaq. C Greenland
Uummannarsuaq *see* Nunap Isua
Uvalde *49 F4* Texas, SW USA
Uvaravichy *107 D7 Rus.* Uvarovichi. Homyel'skaya Voblasts', SE Belarus
Uvea, Île *145 E4 island* N Wallis and Futuna
Uvs Nuur *126 C1 var.* Ozero Ubsu-Nur. *Lake* Mongolia/Russian Federation
'Uwaynāt, Jabal al *88 A3 var.* Jebel Uweinat. *Mountain* Libya/Sudan
Uyo *75 G5* Akwa Ibom, S Nigeria
Uyuni *61 F5* Potosí, W Bolivia
Uzbekistan *122 D2 Country* C Asia

Uzbekistan 122

Official name Republic of Uzbekistan
Formation 1991
Capital Tashkent
Population 26.1 million / 151 people per sq mile (58 people per sq km)
Total area 172,741 sq. miles (447,400 sq. km)
Languages Uzbek, Russian, Tajik, Kazakh
Religions Sunni Muslim 88%, Orthodox Christian 9%, other 3%
Ethnic mix Uzbek 71%, other 12%, Russian 8%, Tajik 5%, Kazakh 4%
Government Presidential system
Currency Som = 100 tiyin
Literacy rate 99%
Calorie consumption 2197 calories

Uzhhorod *108 B2 Rus.* Uzhgorod; *prev.* Ungvár. Zakarpats'ka Oblast', W Ukraine
Užice *100 D4 prev.* Titovo Užice. Serbia, W Serbia and Montenegro (Yugo.)

V

Vaal *78 D4 river* C South Africa
Vaals *87 D6* Limburg, SE Netherlands
Vaasa *85 D5 Swe.* Vasa; *prev.* Nikolainkaupunki. Länsi-Suomi, W Finland
Vaassen *86 D3* Gelderland, E Netherlands
Vác *99 C6 Ger.* Waitzen. Pest, N Hungary
Vadodara *134 C4 prev.* Baroda. Gujarāt, W India
Vaduz *94 E2 country capital* (Liechtenstein) W Liechtenstein
Váh *99 C5 Ger.* Waag, *Hung.* Vág. *River* W Slovakia
Väinameri *106 C2 prev.* Muhu Väin, *Ger.* Moon-Sund. *Sea* E Baltic Sea
Valachia *see* Wallachia
Valday *110 B4* Novgorodskaya Oblast', W Russian Federation
Valdecañas, Embalse de *92 D3 reservoir* W Spain
Valdepeñas *93 E4* Castilla-La Mancha, C Spain
Valdés, Península *65 C6 peninsula* SE Argentina
Valdez *36 C3* Alaska, USA
Valdia *see* Weldiya
Valdivia *65 B5* Los Lagos, C Chile
Val-d'Or *38 D4* Québec, SE Canada
Valdosta *43 E3* Georgia, SE USA
Valence *91 D5 anc.* Valentia, Valentia Julia, Ventia. Drôme, E France
Valencia *46 D1* California, W USA
Valencia *58 D1* Carabobo, N Venezuela
Valencia *93 F3* País Valenciano, E Spain
Valencia, Golfo de *93 F3 var.* Gulf of Valencia. *Gulf* E Spain
Valencia, Gulf of *see* Valencia, Golfo de
Valenciennes *90 D2* Nord, N France
Valera *58 C2* Trujillo, NW Venezuela
Valga *106 D3 Ger.* Walk, *Latv.* Valka. Valgamaa, S Estonia
Valira *91 A8 river* Andorra/Spain
Valjevo *100 C4* Serbia, W Serbia and Montenegro (Yugo.)
Valjok *see* Válljohka
Valka *106 D3 Ger.* Walk. Valka, N Latvia
Valkenswaard *87 D5* Noord-Brabant, S Netherlands
Valladolid *92 D2* Castilla-León, NW Spain
Valladolid *51 H3* Yucatán, SE Mexico
Vall d'Uxó *93 F3* País Valenciano, E Spain
Valle de La Pascua *58 D2* Guárico, N Venezuela
Valledupar *58 B1* Cesar, N Colombia
Vallejo *47 B6* California, W USA
Vallenar *64 B3* Atacama, N Chile
Valletta *97 C8 prev.* Valetta. *Country capital* (Malta) E Malta
Valley City *45 E2* North Dakota, N USA
Válljohka *84 D2 var.* Valjok. Finnmark, N Norway
Valls *93 G2* Cataluña, NE Spain
Valmiera *106 D3 Est.* Volmari, *Ger.* Wolmar. Valmiera, N Latvia
Valozhyn *107 C5 Pol.* Wołożyn, *Rus.* Volozhin. Minskaya Voblasts', C Belarus
Valparaiso *40 C3* Indiana, N USA
Valparaíso *64 B4* Valparaíso, C Chile
Valverde del Camino *92 C4* Andalucía, S Spain
Van *117 F3* Van, E Turkey
Vanadzor *117 F2 prev.* Kirovakan. N Armenia
Vancouver *36 D5* British Columbia, SW Canada
Vancouver *46 B3* Washington, NW USA
Vancouver Island *36 D5 island* British Columbia, SW Canada
Van Diemen Gulf *146 D2 gulf* Northern Territory, N Australia
Vänern *85 B6 Eng.* Lake Vaner; *prev.* Lake Vener. *Lake* S Sweden
Vangaindrano *79 G4* Fianarantsoa, SE Madagascar
Van Gölü *117 F3 Eng.* Lake Van; *anc.* Thospitis. *Salt lake* E Turkey
Van Horn *48 D3* Texas, SW USA
Van, Lake *see* Van Gölü
Vannes *90 A3 anc.* Dariorigum. Morbihan, NW France
Vantaa *85 D6 Swe.* Vanda. Etelä-Suomi, S Finland
Vanua Levu *145 E4 island* N Fiji
Vanuatu *144 C4 prev.* New Hebrides. *Country* SW Pacific Ocean

Vanuatu 144

Official name Republic of Vanuatu
Formation 1980
Capital Port Vila
Population 212,000 / 45 people per sq mile (17 people per sq km)
Total area 4710 sq. miles (12,200 sq. km)
Languages Bislama (Melanesian pidgin), English, French, other indigenous languages
Religions Presbyterian 37%, other 19%, Anglican 15%, Roman Catholic 15%, Traditional beliefs 8%, Seventh-day Adventist 6%
Ethnic mix Melanesian 94%, other 3%, Polynesian 3%
Government Parliamentary system
Currency Vatu = 100 centimes
Literacy rate 34%
Calorie consumption 2565 calories

Van Wert *40 C4* Ohio, N USA
Varakļani *106 D4* Madona, C Latvia

Vārānasi *135 E3 prev.* Banaras, Benares, *hist.* Kasi. Uttar Pradesh, N India
Varangerfjorden *84 E2 fjord* N Norway
Varangerhalvøya *84 D2 peninsula* N Norway
Varannó *see* Vranov nad Topl'ou
Varaždin *100 B2 Ger.* Warasdin, *Hung.* Varasd. Varaždin, N Croatia
Varberg *85 B7* Halland, S Sweden
Vardar *101 E6 Gk.* Axiós. *River* FYR Macedonia/Greece *see also* Axiós
Varde *85 A7* Ribe, W Denmark
Varėna *107 B5 Pol.* Orany. Varėna, S Lithuania
Varese *96 B2* Lombardia, N Italy
Vârful Moldoveanu *108 B4 var.* Moldoveanul; *prev.* Vîrful Moldoveanu. *Mountain* C Romania
Varkaus *85 E5* Itä-Suomi, C Finland
Varna *104 E2 prev.* Stalin, *anc.* Odessus. Varna, E Bulgaria
Varnenski Zaliv *104 E2 prev.* Stalinski Zaliv. *Bay* E Bulgaria
Vasilikí *105 A5* Lefkáda, Iónioi Nísoi, Greece, C Mediterranean Sea
Vasilishki *107 B5 Pol.* Wasiliszki, *Rus.* Vasilishki. Hrodzyenskaya Voblasts', W Belarus
Vaslui *108 D4* Vaslui, C Romania
Västerås *85 C6* Västmanland, C Sweden
Vasyl'kiv *109 E2 Rus.* Vasil'kov. Kyyivs'ka Oblast', N Ukraine
Vaté *see* Efate
Vatican City *97 A7 Country* S Europe

Vatican City 97

Official name State of the Vatican City
Formation 1929
Capital Vatican City
Population 911 / 5359 people per sq mile (2070 people per sq km)
Total area 0.17 sq. miles (0.44 sq. km)
Languages Italian, Latin
Religions Roman Catholic 100%
Ethnic mix The current pope is Polish, ending nearly 500 years of Italian popes. Cardinals are from many nationalities, but Italians form the largest group. Most of the resident lay persons are Italian.
Government Papal state
Currency Euro = 100 cents
Literacy rate 99%
Calorie consumption Not available

Vatnajökull *83 E5 glacier* SE Iceland
Vättern *85 B6 Eng.* Lake Vatter; *prev.* Lake Vetter. *Lake* S Sweden
Vaughn *48 D2* New Mexico, SW USA
Vaupés, Río *58 C4 var.* Rio Uaupés. *River* Brazil/Colombia *see also* Uaupés, Rio
Vava'u Group *145 E4 island group* N Tonga
Vavuniya *132 D3* Northern Province, N Sri Lanka
Vawkavysk *107 B6 Pol.* Wołkowysk, *Rus.* Volkovysk. Hrodzyenskaya Voblasts', W Belarus
Växjö *85 C7 var.* Vexiö. Kronoberg, S Sweden
Vaygach, Ostrov *110 E2 island* NW Russian Federation
Veendam *86 E2* Groningen, NE Netherlands
Veenendaal *86 D4* Utrecht, C Netherlands
Vega *84 B4 island* C Norway
Veisiejai *107 B5* Lazdijai, S Lithuania
Vejer de la Frontera *92 C5* Andalucía, S Spain
Veldhoven *87 D5* Noord-Brabant, S Netherlands
Velebit *100 A3 mountain range* C Croatia
Velenje *95 E7 Ger.* Wöllan. N Slovenia
Veles *101 E6 Turk.* Köprülü. C FYR Macedonia
Velho *see* Porto Velho
Velika Morava *100 D4 var.* Glavn'a Morava, Morava, *Ger.* Grosse Morava. *River* C Serbia and Montenegro (Yugo.)
Velikaya *113 G2 river* NE Russian Federation
Velikiye Luki *110 A4* Pskovskaya Oblast', W Russian Federation
Velikiy Novgorod *110 B4 prev.* Novgorod. Novgorodskaya Oblast', W Russian Federation
Veliko Tŭrnovo *104 D2 prev.* Tirnovo, Trnovo, Tŭrnovo. Veliko Tŭrnovo, N Bulgaria
Velingrad *104 C3* Pazardzhik, C Bulgaria
Vel'ký Krtíš *99 D6* Banskobystrický Kraj, C Slovakia
Vellore *132 C2* Tamil Nādu, SE India
Velobriga *see* Viana do Castelo
Velsen *see* Velsen-Noord
Velsen-Noord *86 C3 var.* Velsen. Noord-Holland, W Netherlands
Vel'sk *110 C4 var.* Velsk. Arkhangel'skaya Oblast', NW Russian Federation
Velsk *see* Vel'sk
Velvendos *see* Velvendós
Velvendós *104 B4 var.* Velvendos. Dytikí Makedonía, N Greece
Velykyy Tokmak *see* Tokmak
Vendôme *90 C4* Loir-et-Cher, C France
Venezia *96 C2 Eng.* Venice, *Fr.* Venise, *Ger.* Venedig; anc. Venetia. Veneto, NE Italy
Venezuela *58 D2 prev.* Estados Unidos de Venezuela, United States of Venezuela. *Country* N South America

Venezuela 58

Official name Bolivarian Republic of Venezuela
Formation 1830
Capital Caracas
Population 25.7 million / 75 people per sq mile (29 people per sq km)
Total area 352,143 sq. miles (912,050 sq. km)
Languages Spanish, Amerindian languages
Religions Roman Catholic 89%, Protestant and other 11%
Ethnic mix Mestizo 69%, White 20%, Black 9%, Amerindian 2%
Government Presidential system
Currency Bolívar = 100 centimos
Literacy rate 93%
Calorie consumption 2376 calories

Venezuela, Golfo de *58 C1 Eng.* Gulf of Maracaibo, Gulf of Venezuela. *Gulf* NW Venezuela
Venezuelan Basin *56 B1 undersea feature* E Caribbean Sea
Venice *see* Venezia
Venice *42 C4* Louisiana, S USA
Venice, Gulf of *96 C2 It.* Golfo di Venezia, *Slvn.* Beneški Zaliv. *Gulf* N Adriatic Sea
Venlo *87 D5 prev.* Venloo. Limburg, SE Netherlands
Venta *106 B3 Ger.* Windau. *River* Latvia/Lithuania
Ventimiglia *96 A3* Liguria, NW Italy
Ventspils *106 B2 Ger.* Windau. Ventspils, NW Latvia
Vera *64 D3* Santa Fe, C Argentina
Veracruz *51 F4 var.* Veracruz Llave. Veracruz-Llave, E Mexico
Veracruz Llave *see* Veracruz
Vercelli *96 A2 anc.* Vercellae. Piemonte, NW Italy
Verdal *see* Verdalsøra
Verdalsøra *84 B4 var.* Verdal. Nord-Trøndelag, C Norway
Verde, Costa *92 D1 coastal region* N Spain
Verden *94 B3* Niedersachsen, NW Germany
Veria *see* Véroia
Verkhoyanskiy Khrebet *115 F3 mountain range* NE Russian Federation
Vermillion *45 F3* South Dakota, N USA
Vermont *41 F2 off.* State of Vermont; also known as The Green Mountain State. *State* NE USA
Vernal *44 B4* Utah, W USA
Vernon *49 F2* Texas, SW USA
Véroia *104 B4 var.* Veria, Vérroia, *Turk.* Karaferiye. Kentrikí Makedonía, N Greece
Verona *96 C2* Veneto, NE Italy
Vérroia *see* Véroia
Versailles *90 D1* Yvelines, N France
Verviers *87 D6* Liège, E Belgium
Vesdre *87 D6 river* E Belgium
Veselinovo *104 D2* Shumen, NE Bulgaria
Vesoul *90 D4 anc.* Vesulium, Vesulum. Haute-Saône, E France
Vesterålen *84 B2 island group* N Norway
Vestfjorden *84 C3 fjord* C Norway
Vestmannaeyjar *83 E5* Sudhurland, S Iceland
Vesuvio *97 D5 Eng.* Vesuvius. *Volcano* S Italy
Veszprém *99 C7 Ger.* Veszprim. Veszprém, W Hungary
Vetrino *104 E2* Varna, E Bulgaria
Veurne *87 A5 var.* Furnes. West-Vlaanderen, W Belgium
Vexiö *see* Växjö
Viacha *61 F4* La Paz, W Bolivia
Viana de Castelo *see* Viana do Castelo
Viana do Castelo *92 B2 var.* Viana de Castelo; *anc.* Velobriga. Viana do Castelo, NW Portugal
Vianen *86 C4* Zuid-Holland, C Netherlands
Viangchan *136 C4 Eng./Fr.* Vientiane. *Country capital* (Laos) C Laos
Viangphoukha *136 C3 var.* Vieng Pou Kha. Louang Namtha, N Laos
Viareggio *96 B3* Toscana, C Italy
Viborg *85 A7* Viborg, NW Denmark
Vic *93 G2 var.* Vich; *anc.* Ausa, Vicus Ausonensis. Cataluña, NE Spain
Vicenza *96 C2 anc.* Vicentia. Veneto, NE Italy
Vich *see* Vic
Vichy *91 C5* Allier, C France
Vicksburg *42 B2* Mississippi, S USA
Victoria *102 A5 var.* Rabat. Gozo, NW Malta
Victoria *79 H1 country capital* (Seychelles) Mahé, SW Seychelles
Victoria *49 G4* Texas, SW USA
Victoria *36 D5* Vancouver Island, British Columbia, SW Canada
Victoria *149 C7 state* SE Australia
Victoria Bank *see* Vitória Seamount
Victoria de Durango *see* Durango
Victoria de las Tunas *see* Las Tunas
Victoria Falls *78 C2 waterfall* Zambia/Zimbabwe
Victoria Falls *78 C3* Matabeleland North, W Zimbabwe
Victoria Island *37 F3 island* Northwest Territories/Nunavut, NW Canada
Victoria, Lake *73 B6 var.* Victoria Nyanza. *Lake* E Africa
Victoria Land *154 C4 physical region* Antarctica
Victoria Nyanza *see* Victoria, Lake
Victoria River *146 D3 river* Northern Territory, N Australia
Victorville *47 C7* California, W USA
Vicus Ausonensis *see* Vic
Vidalia *43 E2* Georgia, SE USA
Vidin *104 B1 anc.* Bononia. Vidin, NW Bulgaria
Vidzy *107 C5 Rus.* Vidzy. Vitsyebskaya Voblasts', NW Belarus
Viedma *65 C5* Río Negro, E Argentina
Vieng Pou Kha *see* Viangphoukha
Vienna *see* Wien
Vienne *91 D5 anc.* Vienna. Isère, E France
Vienne *90 B4 river* W France
Vientiane *see* Viangchan
Vierzon *90 C4* Cher, C France
Viesīte *106 C4 Ger.* Eckengraf. Jēkabpils, S Latvia
Vietnam *136 D4 Vtn.* Công Hoa Xa Hôi Chu Nghia Viêt Nam. *Country* SE Asia

Vietnam 136

Official name Socialist Republic of Vietnam
Formation 1976
Capital Hanoi
Population 81.4 million / 648 people per sq mile (250 people per sq km)
Total area 127,243 sq. miles (329,560 sq. km)
Languages Vietnamese, Chinese, Thai, Khmer, Muong, Nung, Miao, Yao, Jarai
Religions Buddhist 55%, Other and nonreligious 38%, Christian (mainly Roman Catholic) 7%
Ethnic mix Vietnamese 88%, other 6%, Chinese 4%, Thai 2%
Government One-party state
Currency Dông = 10 hao = 100 xu
Literacy rate 93%
Calorie consumption 2533 calories

Vietri *see* Viêt Tri
Viêt Tri *136 D3 var.* Vietri. Vinh Phu, N Vietnam
Vieux Fort *55 F2* S Saint Lucia
Vigo *92 B2* Galicia, NW Spain
Vijayawāda *132 D1 prev.* Bezwada. Andhra Pradesh, SE India
Vijosa *see* Vjosës, Lumi i
Vijosë *see* Vjosës, Lumi i
Vila *see* Port-Vila
Vila Artur de Paiva *see* Cubango
Vila da Ponte *see* Cubango
Vila de Mocímboa da Praia *see* Mocímboa da Praia
Vila do Conde *92 B2* Porto, NW Portugal
Vila do Zumbo *78 D2 prev.* Vila do Zumbu, Zumbo. Tete, NW Mozambique
Vilafranca del Penedès *93 G2 var.* Villafranca del Panadés. Cataluña, NE Spain
Vila General Machado *see* Camacupa
Viļaka *106 D4 Ger.* Marienhausen. Balvi, NE Latvia
Vilalba *92 C1* Galicia, NW Spain
Vila Nova de Gaia *92 B2* Porto, NW Portugal
Vila Nova de Portimão *see* Portimão
Vila Pereira de Eça *see* N'Giva
Vila Real *92 C2 var.* Vila Rial. Vila Real, N Portugal
Vila Rial *see* Vila Real
Vila Robert Williams *see* Caála
Vila Serpa Pinto *see* Menongue
Vilhelmina *84 C4* Västerbotten, N Sweden

Vilhena *62 D3* Rondônia, W Brazil
Vília *105 C5* Attikí, C Greece
Viliya *107 C5 Lith.* Neris, *Rus.* Viliya. *River* W Belarus
Viljandi *106 D2 Ger.* Fellin. Viljandimaa, S Estonia
Vilkaviškis *106 B4 Pol.* Wyłkowyszki. Vilkaviškis, SW Lithuania
Villa Acuña *50 D2 var.* Cuidad Acuña. Coahuila de Zaragoza, NE Mexico
Villa Bella *61 F2* Beni, N Bolivia
Villacarrillo *93 E4* Andalucía, S Spain
Villa Cecilia *see* Ciudad Madero
Villach *95 D7 Slvn.* Beljak. Kärnten, S Austria
Villacidro *97 A5* Sardegna, Italy, C Mediterranean Sea
Villa Concepción *see* Concepción
Villa del Pilar *see* Pilar
Villafranca de los Barros *92 C4* Extremadura, W Spain
Villafranca del Panadés *see* Vilafranca del Penedès
Villahermosa *51 G4 prev.* San Juan Bautista. Tabasco, SE Mexico
Villajoyosa *93 F4 var.* La Vila Jojosa. País Valenciano, E Spain
Villa María *64 C4* Córdoba, C Argentina
Villa Martín *61 F5* Potosí, SW Bolivia
Villa Mercedes *64 C4 prev.* Mercedes. San Luis, C Argentina
Villanueva *50 D3* Zacatecas, C Mexico
Villanueva de la Serena *92 C3* Extremadura, W Spain
Villanueva de los Infantes *93 E4* Castilla-La Mancha, C Spain
Villarrica *64 D2* Guairá, SE Paraguay
Villavicencio *58 B3* Meta, C Colombia
Villaviciosa *92 D1* Asturias, N Spain
Villazón *61 G5* Potosí, S Bolivia
Villena *93 F4* País Valenciano, E Spain
Villeurbanne *91 D5* Rhône, E France
Villingen-Schwenningen *95 B6* Baden-Württemberg, S Germany
Vilnius *107 C5 Pol.* Wilno, *Ger.* Wilna; *prev. Rus.* Vilna. *Country capital* (Lithuania) Vilnius, SE Lithuania
Vil'shanka *109 E3 Rus.* Olshanka. Kirovohrads'ka Oblast', C Ukraine
Vilvoorde *87 C6 Fr.* Vilvorde. Vlaams Brabant, C Belgium
Vilyeyka *107 C5 Pol.* Wilejka, *Rus.* Vileyka. Minskaya Voblasts', NW Belarus
Vilyuy *115 F3 river* NE Russian Federation
Viña del Mar *64 B4* Valparaíso, C Chile
Vinaròs *93 F3* País Valenciano, E Spain
Vincennes *40 B4* Indiana, N USA
Vindhya Mountains *see* Vindhya Range
Vindhya Range *134 D4 var.* Vindhya Mountains. *Mountain range* N India
Vineland *41 F4* New Jersey, NE USA
Vinh *136 D4* Nghê An, N Vietnam
Vinh Loi *see* Bac Liêu
Vinh Thai Lan *see* Thailand, Gulf of
Vinishte *104 C2* Montana, NW Bulgaria
Vinita *49 G1* Oklahoma, C USA
Vinkovci *100 C3 Ger.* Winkowitz, *Hung.* Vinkovcze. Vukovar-Srijem, E Croatia
Vinnytsya *108 D2 Rus.* Vinnitsa. Vinnyts'ka Oblast', C Ukraine
Vinson Massif *154 A3 mountain* Antarctica
Viranşehir *117 E4* Şanlıurfa, SE Turkey
Vîrful Moldoveanu *see* Vârful Moldoveanu
Virginia *41 E5 off.* Commonwealth of Virginia; also known as Mother of Presidents, Mother of States, Old Dominion. *State* NE USA
Virginia *45 G1* Minnesota, N USA
Virginia Beach *41 F5* Virginia, NE USA
Virgin Islands *see* British Virgin Islands
Virgin Islands (US) *55 F3 var.* Virgin Islands of the United States; *prev.* Danish West Indies. *US unincorporated territory* E West Indies
Virgin Islands of the United States *see* Virgin Islands (US)
Virôchey *137 E5* Rôtânôkiri, NE Cambodia
Virovitica *100 C2 Ger.* Virovititz, *Hung.* Verőcze; *prev. Ger.* Werowitz. Virovitica-Podravina, NE Croatia
Virton *87 D8* Luxembourg, SE Belgium
Virtsu *106 D2 Ger.* Werder. Läänemaa, W Estonia
Vis *100 B4 It.* Lissa; *anc.* Issa. *Island* S Croatia
Vis *see* Fish
Visaginas *106 C4 prev.* Sniečkus. Ignalina, E Lithuania
Visākhapatnam *135 E5* Andhra Pradesh, SE India
Visalia *47 C6* California, W USA
Visby *85 C7 Ger.* Wisby. Gotland, SE Sweden
Viscount Melville Sound *37 F2 prev.* Melville Sound. *Sound* Northwest Territories/Nunavut, N Canada
Visé *87 D6* Liège, E Belgium
Viseu *92 C2 prev.* Vizeu. Viseu, N Portugal
Visoko *100 C4* Federacija Bosna I Hercegovina, C Bosnia and Herzegovina
Visttasjohka *84 D3 Swe.* Kalixälven. *River* N Sweden
Vistula *see* Wisła
Vistula Lagoon *98 C2 Ger.* Frisches Haff, *Pol.* Zalew Wiślany, *Rus.* Vislinskiy Zaliv. *Lagoon* Poland/Russian Federation
Viterbo *96 C4 anc.* Vicus Elbii. Lazio, C Italy
Viti Levu *145 E4 island* W Fiji
Vitim *115 F4 river* C Russian Federation
Vitoria *see* Vitoria-Gasteiz
Vitória *63 F4* Espírito Santo, SE Brazil
Vitoria Bank *see* Vitória Seamount
Vitória da Conquista *63 F3* Bahia, E Brazil
Vitoria-Gasteiz *93 E1 var.* Vitoria, *Eng.* Vittoria. País Vasco, N Spain
Vitória Seamount *67 B5 var.* Victoria Bank, Vitoria Bank. *Undersea feature* C Atlantic Ocean
Vitré *90 B3* Ille-et-Vilaine, NW France
Vitsyebsk *107 E5 Rus.* Vitebsk. Vitsyebskaya Voblasts', NE Belarus
Vittoria *see* Vitoria-Gasteiz
Vittoria *97 C7* Sicilia, Italy, C Mediterranean Sea
Vizianagaram *135 E5 var.* Vizianagram. Andhra Pradesh, E India
Vizianagram *see* Vizianagaram
Vjosës, Lumi i *101 C7 var.* Vijosa, Vijosë, *Gk.* Aóos. *River* Albania/Greece *see also* Aóos
Vlaardingen *86 B4* Zuid-Holland, SW Netherlands
Vladikavkaz *111 B8 prev.* Dzaudzhikau, Ordzhonikidze. Severnaya Osetiya-Alaniya, SW Russian Federation
Vladimir *111 B5* Vladimirskaya Oblast', W Russian Federation
Vladivostok *115 G5* Primorskiy Kray, SE Russian Federation
Vlagtwedde *86 E2* Groningen, NE Netherlands
Vlasotince *101 E5* Serbia, SE Serbia and Montenegro (Yugo.)
Vlieland *86 C1 Fris.* Flylân. *Island* Waddeneilanden, N Netherlands
Vlijmen *86 C4* Noord-Brabant, S Netherlands
Vlissingen *87 B5 Eng.* Flushing, *Fr.* Flessingue. Zeeland, SW Netherlands
Vlorë *101 C7 prev.* Vlonë, *It.* Valona, Vlora. Vlorë, SW Albania
Vöcklabruck *95 D6* Oberösterreich, NW Austria
Vohimena, Tanjona *79 F4 Fr.* Cap Sainte Marie. *Headland* S Madagascar
Voiron *91 D5* Isère, E France
Vojvodina *100 D3 Ger.* Wojwodina. *Region* N Serbia and Montenegro (Yugo.)
Volcán de Chiriquí *see* Barú, Volcán
Volga *111 B7 river* NW Russian Federation
Volga Delta *81 G4 delta* Astrakhanskaya Oblast', SW Russian Federation
Volga Uplands *81 G3 Russ.* Privolzhskaya Vozvyshennost' *mountain range* W Russian Federation
Volgodonsk *111 B7* Rostovskaya Oblast', SW Russian Federation
Volgograd *111 B7 prev.* Stalingrad, Tsaritsyn. Volgogradskaya Oblast', SW Russian Federation
Volkhov *110 B4* Leningradskaya Oblast', NW Russian Federation
Volnovakha *109 G3* Donets'ka Oblast', SE Ukraine
Volodymyr-Volyns'kyy *108 C1 Pol.* Włodzimierz, *Rus.* Vladimir-Volynskiy. Volyns'ka Oblast', NW Ukraine
Vologda *110 B4* Vologodskaya Oblast', W Russian Federation
Vólos *105 B5* Thessalía, C Greece
Vol'sk *111 C6* Saratovskaya Oblast', W Russian Federation
Volta *75 E5 river* SE Ghana
Volta Blanche *see* White Volta
Volta, Lake *75 E5 reservoir* SE Ghana
Volta Noire *see* Black Volta
Volturno *97 D5 river* S Italy
Volzhskiy *111 B6* Volgogradskaya Oblast', SW Russian Federation
Võnnu *106 E3 Ger.* Wendau. Tartumaa, SE Estonia
Voorst *86 D3* Gelderland, E Netherlands
Voranava *107 C5 Pol.* Werenów, *Rus.* Voronovo. Hrodzyenskaya Voblasts', W Belarus
Vorderrhein *95 B7 river* SE Switzerland
Vóreioi Sporádes *105 C5 var.* Vórioi Sporádhes, *Eng.* Northern Sporades. *Island group* E Greece
Vórioi Sporádhes *see* Vóreioi Sporádes
Vorkuta *114 C2* Respublika Komi, NW Russian Federation
Vormsi *106 C2 var.* Vormsi Saar, *Ger.* Worms, Swed. Ormsö. *Island* W Estonia
Vormsi Saar *see* Vormsi
Voronezh *111 B6* Voronezhskaya Oblast', W Russian Federation
Võru *106 D3 Ger.* Werro. Võrumaa, SE Estonia
Vosges *90 E4 mountain range* NE France
Vostochno-Sibirskoye More *115 F1 Eng.* East Siberian Sea. *Sea* Arctic Ocean
Vostock Island *see* Vostok Island
Vostok *154 C3 Russian research station* Antarctica
Vostok Island *145 G3 var.* Vostock Island; *prev.* Stavers Island. *Island* Line Islands, SE Kiribati
Voznesens'k *109 E3 Rus.* Voznesensk. Mykolayivs'ka Oblast', S Ukraine
Vrangelya, Ostrov *115 F1 Eng.* Wrangel Island. *Island* NE Russian Federation
Vranje *101 E5* Serbia, SE Serbia and Montenegro (Yugo.)
Vranov *see* Vranov nad Topl'ou
Vranov nad Topl'ou *99 D5 var.* Vranov, *Hung.* Varannó. Prešovský Kraj, E Slovakia
Vratsa *104 C2* Vratsa, NW Bulgaria
Vrbas *100 C3 river* N Bosnia and Herzegovina
Vrbas *100 C3* Serbia, NW Serbia and Montenegro (Yugo.)
Vsetín *99 C5 Ger.* Wsetin. Zlínský Kraj, E Czech Republic
Vučitrn *101 D5* Serbia, S Serbia and Montenegro (Yugo.)
Vukovar *100 C3 Hung.* Vukovár. Vukovar-Srijem, E Croatia
Vulcano, Isola *97 C7 island* Isole Eolie, S Italy
Vung Tau *137 E6 prev. Fr.* Cape Saint Jacques, Cap Saint-Jacques. Ba Ria-Vung Tau, S Vietnam
Vyatka *111 C5 river* NW Russian Federation
Vyborg *110 B3 Fin.* Viipuri. Leningradskaya Oblast', NW Russian Federation
Vyerkhnyadzvinsk *107 D5 Rus.* Verkhnedvinsk. Vitsyebskaya Voblasts', N Belarus
Vyetryna *107 D5 Rus.* Vetrino. Vitsyebskaya Voblasts', N Belarus
Vynohradiv *108 B3 Cz.* Sevluš, *Hung.* Nagyszöllös, *Rus.* Vinogradov; *prev.* Sevlyush. Zakarpats'ka Oblast', W Ukraine

W

Wa *75 E4* NW Ghana
Waal *86 C4 river* S Netherlands
Wabash *40 C4* Indiana, N USA
Wabash River *40 B5 river* N USA
Waco *49 G3* Texas, SW USA
Waddān *71 F3* NW Libya
Waddeneilanden *86 C1 Eng.* West Frisian Islands. *Island group* N Netherlands
Waddenzee *86 C1 var.* Wadden Zee. *Sea* SE North Sea
Waddington, Mount *36 D5 mountain* British Columbia, SW Canada
Wādī as Sīr *119 B6 var.* Wadi es Sir. 'Ammān, NW Jordan
Wadi es Sir *see* Wādī as Sīr
Wadi Halfa *72 B3 var.* Wādī Ḩalfā'. Northern, N Sudan
Wādī Mūsā *119 B7 var.* Petra. Ma'ān, S Jordan
Wad Madanī *see* Wad Medani
Wad Medani *72 C4 var.* Wad Madanī. Gezira, C Sudan
Waflia *139 F4* Pulau Buru, E Indonesia
Wagadugu *see* Ouagadougou
Wagga Wagga *149 C7* New South Wales, SE Australia
Wagin *147 B7* Western Australia
Wāh *134 C1* Punjab, NE Pakistan
Wahai *139 F4* Pulau Seram, E Indonesia

Wahiawā *47 A8 var.* Wahiawa. O'ahu, Hawai'i, USA, C Pacific Ocean
Wahībah, Ramlat Āl *121 E5 var.* Ramlat Ahl Wahībah, Ramlat Al Wahaybah, *Eng.* Wahibah Sands. *Desert* N Oman
Wahibah Sands *see* Wahībah, Ramlat Āl
Wahpeton *45 F2* North Dakota, N USA
Wahran *see* Oran
Waiau *151 A7 river* South Island, NZ
Waigeo, Pulau *139 G4 island* Maluku, E Indonesia
Waikaremoana, Lake *150 E4 lake* North Island, NZ
Wailuku *47 B8* Maui, Hawai'i, USA, C Pacific Ocean
Waimate *151 B6* Canterbury, South Island, NZ
Waiouru *150 D4* Manawatu-Wanganui, North Island, NZ
Waipara *151 C6* Canterbury, South Island, NZ
Waipawa *150 E4* Hawke's Bay, North Island, NZ
Waipukurau *150 D4* Hawke's Bay, North Island, NZ
Wairau *151 C5 river* South Island, NZ
Wairoa *150 D2 river* North Island, NZ
Wairoa *150 E4* Hawke's Bay, North Island, NZ
Waitaki *151 B6 river* South Island, NZ
Waitara *150 D4* Taranaki, North Island, NZ
Waiuku *150 D3* Auckland, North Island, NZ
Wakasa-wan *131 C6 bay* C Japan
Wakatipu, Lake *151 A7 lake* South Island, NZ
Wakayama *131 C6* Wakayama, Honshū, SW Japan
Wake Island *142 D1 atoll* NW Pacific Ocean
Wake Island *152 C2 US unincorporated territory* NW Pacific Ocean
Wakkanai *130 C1* Hokkaidō, NE Japan
Walachei *see* Wallachia
Walachia *see* Wallachia
Wałbrzych *98 B4 Ger.* Waldenburg, Waldenburg in Schlesien. Dolnośląskie, SW Poland
Walcourt *87 C7* Namur, S Belgium
Wałcz *98 B3 Ger.* Deutsch Krone. Zachodniopomorskie, NW Poland
Waldia *see* Weldiya
Wales *89 C6 Wel.* Cymru. *National region* UK
Wales *36 C2* Alaska, USA
Wales Island, Prince of *see* Pinang, Pulau
Walgett *149 D5* New South Wales, SE Australia
Walker Lake *47 C5 lake* Nevada, W USA
Wallachia *108 B5 var.* Walachia, *Ger.* Walachei, *Rom.* Valachia. *Cultural region* S Romania
Walla Walla *46 C2* Washington, NW USA
Wallis and Futuna *145 E4 Fr.* Territoire de Wallis et Futuna. *French overseas territory* C Pacific Ocean
Walnut Ridge *42 B1* Arkansas, C USA
Walthamstow *89 B7* SE England, UK
Walvis Bay *78 A4 Afr.* Walvisbaai. Erongo, NW Namibia
Walvish Ridge *see* Walvis Ridge
Walvis Ridge *69 B7 var.* Walvish Ridge. *Undersea feature* E Atlantic Ocean
Wan *see* Anhui
Wanaka *151 B6* Otago, South Island, NZ
Wanaka, Lake *151 A6 lake* South Island, NZ
Wanchuan *see* Zhangjiakou
Wandel Sea *83 E1 sea* Arctic Ocean
Wandsworth *89 A8* SE England, UK
Wanganui *150 D4* Manawatu-Wanganui, North Island, NZ
Wangaratta *149 C7* Victoria, SE Australia
Wanki, Río *see* Coco, Río
Wanlaweyn *73 D6 var.* Wanle Weyn, *It.* Uanle Uen. Shabeellaha Hoose, SW Somalia
Wanle Weyn *see* Wanlaweyn
Wanxian *128 B5* Chongqing, C China
Warangal *135 E5* Andhra Pradesh, C India
Warburg *94 B4* Nordrhein-Westfalen, W Germany
Ware *37 E4* British Columbia, W Canada
Waremme *87 C6* Liège, E Belgium
Waren *94 C3* Mecklenburg-Vorpommern, NE Germany
Wargla *see* Ouargla
Warkworth *150 D2* Auckland, North Island, NZ
Warnemünde *94 C2* Mecklenburg-Vorpommern, NE Germany
Warner *49 G1* Oklahoma, C USA
Warnes *61 G4* Santa Cruz, C Bolivia
Warrego River *149 C5 seasonal river* New South Wales/Queensland, E Australia
Warren *40 D3* Michigan, N USA
Warren *40 D3* Ohio, N USA
Warren *41 E3* Pennsylvania, NE USA
Warri *75 F5* Delta, S Nigeria
Warrnambool *149 B7* Victoria, SE Australia
Warsaw *see* Mazowieckie
Warszawa *98 D3 Eng.* Warsaw, *Ger.* Warschau, *Rus.* Varshava. *Country capital* (Poland) Mazowieckie, C Poland
Warta *98 B3 Ger.* Warthe. *River* W Poland
Warwick *149 E5* Queensland, E Australia
Washington *44 A2 off.* State of Washington; also known as Chinook State, Evergreen State. *State* NW USA
Washington D. C. *41 E4 country capital* (USA) District of Columbia, NE USA
Washington, Mount *41 G2 mountain* New Hampshire, NE USA
Wash, The *89 E6 inlet* E England, UK
Waspam *53 E2 var.* Waspán. Región Autónoma Atlántico Norte, NE Nicaragua
Waspán *see* Waspam
Watampone *139 E4 var.* Bone. Sulawesi, C Indonesia
Waterbury *41 F3* Connecticut, NE USA
Waterford *89 B6 Ir.* Port Láirge. S Ireland
Waterloo *45 G3* Iowa, C USA
Watertown *41 F2* New York, NE USA
Watertown *45 F2* South Dakota, N USA
Waterville *41 G2* Maine, NE USA
Watford *89 A7* SE England, UK
Watsa *77 E5* Orientale, NE Dem. Rep. Congo
Watts Bar Lake *reservoir* Tennessee, S USA
Wau *73 B5 var.* Wāw. Western Bahr el Ghazal, S Sudan
Waukegan *40 B3* Illinois, N USA
Waukesha *40 B3* Wisconsin, N USA
Wausau *40 B2* Wisconsin, N USA
Waverly *45 G3* Iowa, C USA
Wavre *87 C6* Wallon Brabant, C Belgium
Wāw *see* Wau
Wawa *38 C4* Ontario, S Canada
Waycross *43 E3* Georgia, SE USA
Wearmouth *see* Sunderland
Webster City *45 F3* Iowa, C USA
Weddell Plain *154 A2 undersea feature* SW Atlantic Ocean
Weddell Sea *154 A2 sea* SW Atlantic Ocean
Weener *94 A3* Niedersachsen, NW Germany
Weert *87 D5* Limburg, SE Netherlands
Weesp *86 C3* Noord-Holland, C Netherlands
Węgorzewo *98 D2 Ger.* Angerburg. Warmińsko-Mazurskie, NE Poland
Weimar *94 C4* Thüringen, C Germany
Weissenburg *see* Weissenburg in Bayern
Weissenburg in Bayern *95 C6 var.* Weissenburg. Bayern, SE Germany
Weiswampach *87 D7* Diekirch, N Luxembourg
Wejherowo *98 C2* Pomorskie, NW Poland
Welchman Hall *55 G1* C Barbados
Weldiya *72 C4 var.* Waldia, *It.* Valdia. N Ethiopia
Welkom *78 D4* Free State, C South Africa
Welle *see* Uele
Wellesley Islands *148 B2 island group* Queensland, N Australia
Wellington *151 D5 country capital* (NZ) Wellington, North Island, NZ
Wellington *see* Wellington, Isla
Wellington *45 F5* Kansas, C USA
Wellington, Isla *65 A7 var.* Wellington. *Island* S Chile
Wells *46 D4* Nevada, W USA
Wellsford *150 D2* Auckland, North Island, NZ
Wells, Lake *147 C5 lake* Western Australia
Wels *95 D6 anc.* Ovilava. Oberösterreich, N Austria
Wembley *89 A8* SE England, UK
Wemmel *87 B6* Vlaams Brabant, C Belgium
Wenatchee *46 B2* Washington, NW USA
Wenchi *75 E4* W Ghana
Wen-chou *see* Wenzhou
Wenchow *see* Wenzhou
Wenmen Island *see* Wolf, Isla
Wenzhou *128 D5 var.* Wen-chou, Wenchow. Zhejiang, SE China
Werda *78 C4* Kgalagadi, S Botswana
Werkendam *86 C4* Noord-Brabant, S Netherlands
Weser *94 B3 river* NW Germany
Wessel Islands *148 B1 island group* Northern Territory, N Australia
West Antarctica *see* Lesser Antarctica
West Bank *119 A6 disputed region* SW Asia
West Bend *40 B3* Wisconsin, N USA
West Bengal *135 F4 state* NE India
West Cape *151 A7 headland* South Island, NZ
West Des Moines *45 F3* Iowa, C USA
Westerland *94 B2* Schleswig-Holstein, N Germany
Western Australia *146 B4 state* W Australia
Western Desert *see* Sahara el Gharbîya
Western Dvina *85 E7 Bel.* Dzvina, *Ger.* Düna, *Latv.* Daugava, *Rus.* Zapadnaya Dvina. *River* W Europe
Western Ghats *134 C5 mountain range* SW India
Western Isles *see* Outer Hebrides
Western Sahara *70 B3 UK disputed territory* N Africa
Western Samoa *see* Samoa
Westerschelde *87 B5 Eng.* Western Scheldt; *prev.* Honte. *Inlet* S North Sea
West Falkland *65 C7 var.* Isla Gran Malvina. *Island* W Falkland Islands
West Fargo *45 F2* North Dakota, N USA
West Irian *see* Papua
West Mariana Basin *142 B1 var.* Perece Vela Basin. *Undersea feature* W Pacific Ocean
West Memphis *42 B1* Arkansas, C USA
West New Guinea *see* Papua
West Papua *see* Papua
Weston-super-Mare *89 D7* SW England, UK
West Palm Beach *43 F4* Florida, SE USA
Westport *151 C5* West Coast, South Island, NZ
West River *see* Xi Jiang
West Siberian Plain *see* Zapadno-Sibirskaya Ravnina
West Virginia *40 D4 off.* State of West Virginia; also known as The Mountain State. *State* NE USA
Wetar, Pulau *139 F5 island* Kepulauan Damar, E Indonesia
Wetzlar *95 B5* Hessen, W Germany
Wevok *36 C2 var.* Wewuk. Alaska, USA
Wewuk *see* Wevok
Wexford *89 B6 Ir.* Loch Garman. SE Ireland
Weyburn *37 F5* Saskatchewan, S Canada
Weymouth *89 D7* S England, UK
Wezep *86 D3* Gelderland, E Netherlands
Whakatane *150 E3* Bay of Plenty, North Island, NZ
Whale Cove *37 G3* Nunavut, C Canada
Whangarei *150 D2* Northland, North Island, NZ
Wharton Basin *141 D5 var.* West Australian Basin. *Undersea feature* E Indian Ocean
Whataroa *151 B6* West Coast, South Island, NZ
Wheatland *44 D3* Wyoming, C USA
Wheeler Peak *48 D1 mountain* New Mexico, SW USA
Wheeling *40 D4* West Virginia, NE USA
Whitby *89 D5* N England, UK
Whitefish *44 B1* Montana, NW USA
Whitehaven *89 C5* NW England, UK
Whitehorse *36 D4 territory capital* Yukon Territory, W Canada
White Nile *72 B4 Ar.* Al Baḩr al Abyaḑ, An Nīl al Abyaḑ, Bahr el Jebel. *River* SE Sudan
White Nile *72 B4 var.* Bahr el Jebel. *River* S Sudan
White River *44 D3 river* South Dakota, N USA
White Sea *see* Beloye More
White Volta *75 E4 var.* Nakambé, *Fr.* Volta Blanche. *River* Burkina faso/Ghana
Whitianga *150 D2* Waikato, North Island, NZ
Whitney, Mount *47 C6 mountain* California, W USA
Whitsunday Group *148 D3 island group* Queensland, E Australia
Whyalla *149 B6* South Australia
Wichita *45 F5* Kansas, C USA
Wichita Falls *49 F2* Texas, SW USA
Wichita River *49 F2 river* Texas, SW USA

Wickenburg *48 B2* Arizona, SW USA
Wicklow *89 B6 Ir.* Cill Mhantáin. *Cultural region* E Ireland
Wicklow Mountains *89 B6 Ir.* Sléibhte Chill Mhantáin. *Mountain range* E Ireland
Wieliczka *99 D5* Małopolskie, S Poland
Wieluń *98 C4* Łódzkie, C Poland
Wien *95 E6 Eng.* Vienna, *Hung.* Bécs, *Slvk.* Vídeň, *Slvn.* Dunaj; *anc.* Vindobona. *Country capital* (Austria) Wien, NE Austria
Wiener Neustadt *95 E6* Niederösterreich, E Austria
Wierden *86 E3* Overijssel, E Netherlands
Wiesbaden *95 B5* Hessen, W Germany
Wight, Isle of *89 D7 island* S England, UK
Wijchen *86 D4* Gelderland, SE Netherlands
Wijk bij Duurstede *86 D4* Utrecht, C Netherlands
Wilcannia *149 C6* New South Wales, SE Australia
Wilhelm, Mount *144 B3 mountain* C PNG
Wilhelm-Pieck-Stadt *see* Guben
Wilhelmshaven *94 B3* Niedersachsen, NW Germany
Wilkes Barre *41 F3* Pennsylvania, NE USA
Wilkes Land *154 C4 physical region* Antarctica
Willard *48 D2* New Mexico, SW USA
Willcox *48 C3* Arizona, SW USA
Willebroek *87 B5* Antwerpen, C Belgium
Willemstad *55 E5 dependent territory capital* (Netherlands Antilles) Curaçao, Netherlands Antilles
Williston *44 D1* North Dakota, N USA
Wilmington *41 F4* Delaware, NE USA
Wilmington *43 F2* North Carolina, SE USA
Wilmington *40 C4* Ohio, N USA
Wilrijk *87 C5* Antwerpen, N Belgium
Winchester *89 D7 hist.* Wintanceaster, *Lat.* Venta Belgarum. S England, UK
Winchester *41 E4* Virginia, NE USA
Windhoek *78 B3 Ger.* Windhuk. *Country capital* (Namibia) Khomas, C Namibia
Windorah *148 C4* Queensland, C Australia
Windsor *41 G3* Connecticut, NE USA
Windsor *148 D1* New South Wales, SE Australia
Windsor *38 C5* Ontario, S Canada
Windsor *89 D7* S England, UK
Windward Islands *55 H4 island group* E West Indies
Windward Islands *see* Barlavento, Ilhas de
Windward Passage *54 D3 Sp.* Paso de los Vientos. *Channel* Cuba/Haiti
Winisk *38 C2 river* Ontario, S Canada
Winisk *38 C2* Ontario, C Canada
Winnebago, Lake *40 B2 lake* Wisconsin, N USA
Winnemucca *47 C5* Nevada, W USA
Winnipeg *37 G5* Manitoba, S Canada
Winnipeg, Lake *37 G5 lake* Manitoba, C Canada
Winnipegosis, Lake *38 A3 lake* Manitoba, C Canada
Winona *45 G3* Minnesota, N USA
Winschoten *86 E2* Groningen, NE Netherlands
Winsen *94 B3* Niedersachsen, N Germany
Winston Salem *43 E1* North Carolina, SE USA
Winsum *86 D1* Groningen, NE Netherlands
Winterswijk *86 E4* Gelderland, E Netherlands
Winterthur *95 B7* Zürich, NE Switzerland
Winton *148 C4* Queensland, E Australia
Winton *151 A7* Southland, South Island, NZ
Wisconsin *40 A2 off.* State of Wisconsin; also known as The Badger State. *State* N USA
Wisconsin Rapids *40 B2* Wisconsin, N USA
Wisconsin River *40 B3 river* Wisconsin, N USA
Wisła *98 C2 Eng.* Vistula, *Ger.* Weichsel. *River* Śląskie, S Poland
Wismar *94 C2* Mecklenburg-Vorpommern, N Germany
Wittenberge *94 C3* Brandenburg, N Germany
Wittlich *95 A5* Rheinland-Pfalz, SW Germany
Wittstock *94 C3* Brandenburg, NE Germany
W.J. van Blommesteinmeer *59 G3 reservoir* E Suriname
Władysławowo *98 C2* Pomorskie, N Poland
Włocławek *98 C3 Ger./Rus.* Vlotslavsk. Kujawsko-pomorskie, C Poland
Włodawa *98 E4 Rus.* Vlodava. Lubelskie, E Poland
Wlotzkasbaken *78 B3* Erongo, W Namibia
Wodonga *149 C7* Victoria, SE Australia
Wodzisław Śląski *99 C5 Ger.* Loslau. Śląskie, S Poland
Wōjjā *see* Wotje Atoll
Woking *89 D7* SE England, UK
Wolf, Isla *60 A4 var.* Wenmen Island. *Island* W Ecuador
Wolfsberg *95 D7* Kärnten, SE Austria
Wolfsburg *94 C3* Niedersachsen, N Germany
Wolgast *94 D2* Mecklenburg-Vorpommern, NE Germany
Wollaston Lake *37 F4* Saskatchewan, C Canada
Wollongong *149 D6* New South Wales, SE Australia
Wolvega *86 D2 Fris.* Wolvegea. Friesland, N Netherlands
Wolverhampton *89 D6* C England, UK
Wŏnsan *129 E3* SE North Korea
Woodburn *46 B3* Oregon, NW USA
Woodland *47 B5* California, W USA
Woodruff *40 B2* Wisconsin, N USA
Woods, Lake of the *38 A3 Fr.* Lac des Bois. *Lake* Canada/USA
Woodville *150 D4* Manawatu-Wanganui, North Island, NZ
Woodward *49 F1* Oklahoma, C USA
Worcester *89 D6 hist.* Wigorna Ceaster. W England, UK
Worcester *41 G3* Massachusetts, NE USA
Worcester *78 C5* Western Cape, SW South Africa
Workington *89 C5* NW England, UK
Worland *44 C3* Wyoming, C USA
Worms *95 B5 anc.* Augusta Vangionum, Borbetomagus, Wormatia. Rheinland-Pfalz, SW Germany
Worms *see* Vormsi
Worthington *45 F3* Minnesota, N USA
Wotje Atoll *144 D1 var.* Wōjjā. *Atoll* Ratak Chain, E Marshall Islands
Woudrichem *86 C4* Noord-Brabant, S Netherlands
Wrangel Island *see* Vrangelya, Ostrov
Wrangel Plain *155 B2 undersea feature* Arctic Ocean
Wrocław *98 C4 Eng./Ger.* Breslau. Dolnośląskie, SW Poland
Września *98 C3* Wielkopolskie, C Poland
Wuchang *see* Wuhan
Wuday 'ah *121 C6* Najrān, S Saudi Arabia
Wuhai *127 E3* Nei Mongol Zizhiqu, N China
Wuhan *128 C5 var.* Han-kou, Han-k'ou, Hanyang, Wuchang, Wu-han; *prev.* Hankow. Hubei, C China
Wuhsi *see* Wuxi
Wuhsien *see* Suzhou
Wuhu *128 D5 var.* Wu-na-mu. Anhui, E China
Wujlān *see* Ujelang Atoll
Wukari *75 G4* Taraba, E Nigeria
Wuliang Shan *128 A6 mountain range* SW China
Wu-lu-k'o-mu-shi *see* Ürümqi
Wu-lu-mu-ch'i *see* Ürümqi
Wu-na-mu *see* Wuhu
Wuppertal *94 A4 prev.* Barmen-Elberfeld. Nordrhein-Westfalen, W Germany
Würzburg *95 B5* Bayern, SW Germany
Wusih *see* Wuxi
Wuxi *128 D5 var.* Wuhsi, Wu-hsi, Wusih. Jiangsu, E China
Wuyi Shan *125 E3 mountain range* SE China
Wye *89 C6 Wel.* Gwy. *River* England/Wales, UK
Wyndham *146 D3* Western Australia
Wyoming *44 B3 off.* State of Wyoming; also known as The Equality State. *State* C USA
Wyoming *40 C3* Michigan, N USA
Wyszków *98 D3 Ger.* Probstberg. Mazowieckie, C Poland

X

Xaafuun, Raas *72 E4 var.* Ras Hafun. *Headland* NE Somalia
Xaçmaz *117 H2 Rus.* Khachmas. N Azerbaijan
Xaignabouli *136 C4 prev.* Muang Xaignabouri, *Fr.* Sayaboury. Xaignabouli, N Laos
Xai-Xai *79 E4 prev.* João Belo, Vila de João *Bel.* Gaza, S Mozambique
Xalapa *51 F4 var.* Jalapa, Jalapa Enríquez. Veracruz-Llave, SE Mexico
Xam Nua *136 D3 var.* Sam Neua. Houaphan, N Laos
Xankändi *117 G3 Rus.* Khankendi; *prev.* Stepanakert. SW Azerbaijan
Xánthi *104 C3* Anatolikí Makedonía kai Thráki, NE Greece
Xátiva *93 F3 var.* Jativa;*anc.* Setabis. País Valenciano, E Spain
Xauen *see* Chefchaouen
Xeres *see* Jeréz de la Frontera
Xiaguan *see* Dali
Xiamen *128 D6 var.* Hsia-men; *prev.* Amoy. Fujian, SE China
Xi'an *128 C4 var.* Changan, Sian, Signan, Siking, Singan, Xian. Shaanxi, C China
Xian *see* Xi'an
Xiangkhoang *see* Pèk
Xiangtan *128 C5 var.* Hsiang-t'an, Siangtan. Hunan, S China
Xiao Hinggan Ling *128 D2 Eng.* Lesser Khingan Range. *Mountain range* NE China
Xichang *128 B5* Sichuan, C China
Xieng Khouang *see* Pèk
Xieng Ngeun *see* Muong Xiang Ngeun
Xigaze *see* Xigazê
Xigazê *126 C5 var.* Jih-k'a-tse, Shigatse, Xigaze. Xizang Zizhiqu, W China
Xi Jiang *124 D3 var.* Hsi Chiang, *Eng.* West River. *River* S China
Xilinhot *127 F2 var.* Silinhot. Nei Mongol Zizhiqu, N China
Xilokastro *see* Xylókastro
Xin *see* Xinjiang Uygur Zizhiqu
Xingkai Hu *see* Khanka, Lake
Xingu, Rio *63 E2 river* C Brazil
Xingxingxia *126 D3* Xinjiang Uygur Zizhiqu, NW China
Xining *127 E4 var.* Hsining, Hsi-ning, Sining. *Province capital* Qinghai, C China
Xinjiang *see* Xinjiang Uygur Zizhiqu
Xinjiang Uygur Zizhiqu *126 B3 var.* Sinkiang, Sinkiang Uighur Autonomous Region, Xin, Xinjiang. Admin. region *autonomous region* NW China
Xinpu *see* Lianyungang
Xinxiang *128 C4* Henan, C China
Xinyang *128 C5 var.* Hsin-yang, Sinyang. Henan, C China
Xinzo de Limia *92 C2* Galicia, NW Spain
Xiqing Shan *124 D2 mountain range* C China
Xiva *122 D2 var.* Khiwa, *Rus.* Khiva. Khorazm Wiloyati, W Uzbekistan
Xixón *see* Gijón
Xizang *see* Xizang Zizhiqu
Xizang Gaoyuan *see* Qingzang Gaoyuan
Xizang Zizhiqu *126 B4 var.* Thibet, Tibetan Autonomous Region, Xizang, *Eng.* Tibet. Admin. region *autonomous region* W China
Xolotlán *see* Managua, Lago de
Xuddur *73 D5 var.* Hudur, *It.* Oddur. Bakool, SW Somalia
Xuwen *128 C7* Guangdong, S China
Xuzhou *128 D4 var.* Hsu-chou, Suchow, Tongshan; *prev.* T'ung-shan. Jiangsu, E China
Xylókastro *105 B5 var.* Xilokastro. Pelopónnisos, S Greece

Y

Ya'an *128 B5 var.* Yaan. Sichuan, C China
Yabēlo *73 C5* C Ethiopia
Yablis *53 E2* Región Autónoma Atlántico Norte, NE Nicaragua
Yablonovyy Khrebet *115 F4 mountain range* S Russian Federation
Yabrai Shan *127 E3 mountain range* NE China
Yafran *71 F2* NW Libya
Yaghan Basin *67 B7 undersea feature* SE Pacific Ocean
Yahotyn *109 E2 Rus.* Yagotin. Kyyivs'ka Oblast', N Ukraine
Yahualica *50 D4* Jalisco, SW Mexico
Yakima *46 B2* Washington, NW USA
Yakima River *46 B2 river* Washington, NW USA
Yakoruda *104 C3* Blagoevgrad, SW Bulgaria
Yaku-shima *131 B8 island* Nansei-shotō, SW Japan
Yakutat *36 D4* Alaska, USA
Yakutsk *115 F3* Respublika Sakha (Yakutiya), NE Russian Federation
Yala *137 C7* Yala, SW Thailand
Yalizava *107 D6 Rus.* Yelizovo. Mahilyowskaya Voblasts', E Belarus
Yalong Jiang *128 A5 river* C China
Yalova *116 B3* Yalova, NW Turkey
Yalpuh, Ozero *108 D4 Rus.* Ozero Yalpug. *Lake* SW Ukraine
Yalta *109 F5* Respublika Krym, S Ukraine

Yalu 125 E2 *Chin.* Yalu Jiang, *Jap.* Oryokko, *Kor.* Amnok-kang. *River* China/North Korea

Yamaguchi 131 B7 *var.* Yamagutı. Yamaguchi, Honshū, SW Japan

Yamaguti *see* Yamaguchi

Yamal, Poluostrov 114 D2 *peninsula* N Russian Federation

Yambio 73 B5 *var.* Yambiyo. Western Equatoria, S Sudan

Yambiyo *see* Yambio

Yambol 104 D2 *Turk.* Yanboli. Yambol, E Bulgaria

Yamdena, Pulau 139 G5 *prev.* Jamdena. *Island* Kepulauan Tanimbar, E Indonesia

Yam HaMelah *see* Dead Sea

Yam Kinneret *see* Tiberias, Lake

Yamoussoukro 74 D5 *country capital* (Côte d'Ivoire) C Côte d'Ivoire

Yamuna 134 D3 *prev.* Jumna. *River* N India

Yana 115 F2 *river* NE Russian Federation

Yanbu 'al Baḩr 121 A5 Al Madīnah, W Saudi Arabia

Yangambi 77 D5 Orientale, N Dem. Rep. Congo

Yangchow *see* Yangzhou

Yangiyo'l 123 E2 *var.* Yangiyûl, *Rus.* Yangiyul'. Toshkent Wiloyati, E Uzbekistan

Yangiyûl *see* Yangiyo'l

Yangon 136 B4 *Eng.* Rangoon. *Country capital* (Myanmar) Yangon, S Myanmar

Yangtze *see* Chang Jiang

Yangtze Kiang *see* Chang Jiang

Yangzhou 128 D5 *var.* Yangchow. Jiangsu, E China

Yankton 45 E3 South Dakota, N USA

Yannina *see* Ioánnina

Yanskiy Zaliv 113 F2 *bay* N Russian Federation

Yantai 128 D4 *var.* Yan-t'ai; *prev.* Chefoo, Chih-fu. Shandong, E China

Yan-t'ai *see* Yantai

Yaoundé 77 B5 *var.* Yaunde. *Country capital* (Cameroon) Centre, S Cameroon

Yap 144 A1 *island* Caroline Islands, W Micronesia

Yapanskoye More *see* East Sea/Japan, Sea of

Yapen, Pulau 139 G4 *prev.* Japen. *Island* E Indonesia

Yap Trench 142 B2 *var.* Yap Trough. *Undersea feature* SE Philippine Sea

Yap Trough *see* Yap Trench

Yapurá *see* Caquetá, Río

Yapurá *see* Japurá, Rio

Yaqui, Río 50 C2 *river* NW Mexico

Yaransk 111 C5 Kirovskaya Oblast', NW Russian Federation

Yarega 110 D4 Respublika Komi, NW Russian Federation

Yarkant *see* Shache

Yarlung Zangbo Jiang *see* Brahmaputra

Yarmouth *see* Great Yarmouth

Yarmouth 39 F5 Nova Scotia, SE Canada

Yaroslavl' 110 B4 Yaroslavskaya Oblast', W Russian Federation

Yarumal 58 B2 Antioquia, NW Colombia

Yasyel'da 107 B7 *river* SW Belarus

Yatsushiro 131 A7 *var.* Yatusiro. Kumamoto, Kyūshū, SW Japan

Yatusiro *see* Yatsushiro

Yaunde *see* Yaoundé

Yavarí *see* Javari, Rio

Yaviza 53 H5 Darién, SE Panama

Yavoriv 108 B2 *Pol.* Jaworów, *Rus.* Yavorov. L'vivs'ka Oblast', NW Ukraine

Yazd 120 D3 *var.* Yezd. Yazd, C Iran

Yazoo City 42 B2 Mississippi, S USA

Yding Skovhøj 85 A7 *hill* C Denmark

Ýdra 105 C6 *var.* Ídhra. *Island* S Greece

Ye 137 B5 Mon State, S Myanmar

Yecheng 126 A3 *var.* Kargilik. Xinjiang Uygur Zizhiqu, NW China

Yefremov 111 B5 Tul'skaya Oblast', W Russian Federation

Yekaterinburg 114 C3 *prev.* Sverdlovsk. Sverdlovskaya Oblast', C Russian Federation

Yelets 111 B5 Lipetskaya Oblast', W Russian Federation

Yell 88 D1 *island* NE Scotland, UK

Yellowknife 37 E4 *territory capital* Northwest Territories, W Canada

Yellow River *see* Huang He

Yellow Sea 128 D4 *Chin.* Huang Hai, *Kor.* Hwang-Hae. *Sea* E Asia

Yellowstone River 44 C2 *river* Montana/Wyoming, NW USA

Yel'sk 107 C7 *Rus.* Yel'sk. Homyel'skaya Voblasts', SE Belarus

Yelwa 75 F4 Kebbi, W Nigeria

Yemen 121 C7 *Ar.* Al Jumhūrīyah al Yamanīyah, Al Yaman. *Country* SW Asia

Yemen 121

Official name Republic of Yemen
Formation 1990
Capital Sana
Population 20 million / 92 people per sq mile (36 people per sq km)
Total area 203,849 sq. miles (527,970 sq. km)
Languages Arabic
Religions Sunni Muslim 55%, Shi'a Muslim 42%, Christian, Hindu, and Jewish 3%
Ethnic mix Arab 95%, Afro-Arab 3%, Indian, Somali, and European 2%
Government Presidential system
Currency Yemeni rial = 100 sene
Literacy rate 49%
Calorie consumption 2050 calories

Yemva 110 D4 *prev.* Zheleznodorozhnyy. Respublika Komi, NW Russian Federation

Yenakiyeve 109 G3 *Rus.* Yenakiyevo; *prev.* Ordzhonikidze, Rykovo. Donets'ka Oblast', E Ukraine

Yenangyaung 136 A3 Magwe, W Myanmar

Yendi 75 E4 NE Ghana

Yengisar 126 A3 Xinjiang Uygur Zizhiqu, NW China

Yenierenköy *see* Agialoúsa

Yenisey 114 D3 *river* Mongolia/Russian Federation

Yenping *see* Nanping

Yeovil 89 D7 SW England, UK

Yeppoon 148 D4 Queensland, E Australia

Yerevan 117 F3 *var.* Erevan, *Eng.* Erivan. *Country capital* (Armenia) C Armenia

Yeriho *see* Jericho

Yerushalayim *see* Jerusalem

Yeu, Île d' 90 A4 *island* NW France

Yevlax 117 G2 *Rus.* Yevlakh. C Azerbaijan

Yevpatoriya 109 F5 Respublika Krym, S Ukraine

Yeya 109 H4 *river* SW Russian Federation

Yezd *see* Yazd

Yezyaryshcha 107 E5 *Rus.* Yezerishche. Vitsyebskaya Voblasts', NE Belarus

Yiannitsá *see* Giannitsá

Yichang 128 C5 Hubei, C China

Yıldızeli 116 D3 Sivas, N Turkey

Yinchuan 128 B4 *var.* Yinch'uan, Yin-ch'uan, Yinchwan. Ningxia, N China

Yinchwan *see* Yinchuan

Yin-hsien *see* Ningbo

Yining 126 B2 *var.* I-ning, *Uigh.* Gulja, Kuldja. Xinjiang Uygur Zizhiqu, NW China

Yíthion *see* Gýtheio

Yogyakarta 138 C5 *prev.* Djokjakarta, Jogjakarta, Jokyakarta. Jawa, C Indonesia

Yokohama 131 D5 Aomori, Honshū, C Japan

Yokohama 130 A2 Kanagawa, Honshū, S Japan

Yokote 130 D4 Akita, Honshū, C Japan

Yola 75 H4 Adamawa, E Nigeria

Yonago 131 B6 Tottori, Honshū, SW Japan

Yong'an 128 D6 *var.* Yongan. Fujian, SE China

Yonkers 41 F3 New York, NE USA

Yonne 90 C4 *river* C France

Yopal 58 C3 *var.* El Yopal. Casanare, C Colombia

York 89 D5 *anc.* Eboracum, Eburacum. N England, UK

York 45 E4 Nebraska, C USA

York, Cape 148 C1 *headland* Queensland, NE Australia

Yorkton 37 F5 Saskatchewan, S Canada

Yoro 52 C2 Yoro, C Honduras

Yoshkar-Ola 111 C5 Respublika Mariy El, W Russian Federation

Youngstown 40 D4 Ohio, N USA

Youth, Isle of *see* Juventud, Isla de la

Yreka 46 B4 California, W USA

Yssel *see* IJssel

Ysyk-Köl *see* Issyk-Kul', Ozero

Yu *see* Henan

Yuan *see* Red River

Yuan Jiang *see* Red River

Yuba City 47 B5 California, W USA

Yucatan Channel 51 H3 *Sp.* Canal de Yucatán. *Channel* Cuba/Mexico

Yucatan Peninsula 35 C7 *peninsula* Guatemala/Mexico

Yuci *see* Jinzhong

Yue *see* Guangdong

Yueyang 128 C5 Hunan, S China

Yukhavichy 107 D5 *Rus.* Yukhovichi. Vitsyebskaya Voblasts', N Belarus

Yukon 36 C2 *river* Canada/USA

Yukon *see* Yukon Territory

Yukon Territory 36 D3 *var.* Yukon, *Fr.* Territoire du Yukon. Admin. region *territory* NW Canada

Yulin 128 C6 Guangxi Zhuangzu Zizhiqu, S China

Yuma 48 A2 Arizona, SW USA

Yumen 128 A3 *var.* Laojunmiao, Yümen. Gansu, N China

Yun *see* Yunnan

Yungki *see* Jilin

Yung-ning *see* Nanning

Yunjinghong *see* Jinghong

Yunki *see* Jilin

Yunnan 128 A6 *var.* Yun, Yunnan Sheng, Yünnan, Yun-nan. Admin. region *province* SW China

Yunnan *see* Kunming

Yunnan Sheng *see* Yunnan

Yuruá, Río *see* Juruá, Rio

Yushu 126 D4 Qinghai, C China

Yuty 64 D3 Caazapá, S Paraguay

Yuzhno-Sakhalinsk 115 H4 *Jap.* Toyohara; *prev.* Vladimirovka. Ostrov Sakhalin, Sakhalinskaya Oblast', SE Russian Federation

Yuzhou *see* Chongqing

Ýylanly 122 C2 *var.* Il'yaly. Dashkhovuzskiy Velayat, N Turkmenistan

Z

Zaanstad 86 C3 *prev.* Zaandam. Noord-Holland, C Netherlands

Zabaykal'sk 115 F5 Chitinskaya Oblast', S Russian Federation

Zabern *see* Saverne

Zabīd 121 B7 W Yemen

Ząbkowice *see* Ząbkowice Śląskie

Ząbkowice Śląskie 98 B4 *var.* Ząbkowice, *Ger.* Frankenstein, Frankenstein in Schlesien. Wałbrzych, SW Poland

Zábřeh 99 C5 *Ger.* Hohenstadt. Olomoucký Kraj, E Czech Republic

Zacapa 52 B2 Zacapa, E Guatemala

Zacatecas 50 D3 Zacatecas, C Mexico

Zacatepec 51 E4 Morelos, S Mexico

Zacháro 105 B6 *var.* Zaharo, Zakháro. Dytikí Ellás, S Greece

Zadar 100 A3 *It.* Zara; *anc.* Iader. Zadar, SW Croatia

Zadetkyi Kyun 137 B6 *var.* St. Matthew's Island. *Island* Mergui Archipelago, S Myanmar

Zafra 92 C4 Extremadura, W Spain

Żagań 98 B4 *var.* Zagań, Żegań; *Ger.* Sagan. Lubuskie, W Poland

Zagazig 72 B1 *var.* Az Zaqāzīq. N Egypt

Zágráb *see* Zagreb

Zagreb 100 B2 *Ger.* Agram, *Hung.* Zágráb. *Country capital* (Croatia) Zagreb, N Croatia

Zāgros, Kūhhā-ye 120 C3 *Eng.* Zagros Mountains. *Mountain range* W Iran

Zāgros Mountains *see* Zāgros, Kūhhā-ye

Zaharo *see* Zacháro

Zāhedān 120 E4 *var.* Zahidan; *prev.* Duzdab. Sīstān va Balūchestān, SE Iran

Zahidan *see* Zāhedān

Zaḩlah *see* Zahlé

Zahlé 118 B4 *var.* Zaḩlah. C Lebanon

Záhony 99 E6 Szabolcs-Szatmár-Bereg, NE Hungary

Zaire *see* Congo

Zaječar 100 E4 Serbia, E Serbia and Montenegro (Yugo.)

Zakháro *see* Zacháro

Zākhō 120 B2 *var.* Zākhū. N Iraq

Zākhū *see* Zākhō

Zákinthos *see* Zákynthos

Zakopane 99 D5 Małopolskie, S Poland

Zakota Pomorskiea *see* Danzig, Gulf of

Zákynthos 105 A6 *var.* Zákinthos, *It.* Zante. *Island* Iónioi Nísoi, Greece, C Mediterranean Sea

Zalaegerszeg 99 B7 Zala, W Hungary

Zalău 108 B3 *Ger.* Waltenberg, *Hung.* Zilah; *prev. Ger.* Zillenmarkt. Sălaj, NW Romania

Ẕalim 121 B5 Makkah, W Saudi Arabia

Zambesi *see* Zambezi

Zambeze *see* Zambezi

Zambezi 78 D2 *var.* Zambesi, *Port.* Zambeze. *River* S Africa

Zambezi 78 C2 North Western, W Zambia

Zambia 78 C2 *off.* Republic of Zambia; *prev.* Northern Rhodesia. *Country* S Africa

Zambia 78

Official name Republic of Zambia
Formation 1964
Capital Lusaka
Population 10.8 million / 38 people per sq mile (15 people per sq km)
Total area 290,584 sq. miles (752,614 sq. km)
Languages Bemba, Tonga, Nyanja, Lozi, Lala-Bisa, Nsenga, English
Religions Christian 63%, Traditional beliefs 36%, Muslim and Hindu 1%
Ethnic mix Bemba 34%, Other African 26%, Tonga 16%, Nyanja 14%, Lozi 9%, European 1%
Government Presidential system
Currency Zambian kwacha = 100 ngwee
Literacy rate 80%
Calorie consumption 1885 calories

Zamboanga *139 E3 off.* Zamboanga City. Mindanao, S Philippines
Zambrów *98 E3* Podlaskie, E Poland
Zamora *92 D2* Castilla-León, NW Spain
Zamora de Hidalgo *50 D4* Michoacán de Ocampo, SW Mexico
Zamość *98 E4 Rus.* Zamoste. Lubelskie, E Poland
Zancle *see* Messina
Zanda *126 A4* Xizang Zizhiqu, W China
Zanesville *40 D4* Ohio, N USA
Zanjān *120 C2 var.* Zenjan, Zinjan. Zanjān, NW Iran
Zante *see* Zákynthos
Zanthus *147 C6* Western Australia
Zanzibar *73 C7 Swa.* Unguja. *Island* E Tanzania
Zanzibar *73 D7* Zanzibar, E Tanzania
Zaozhuang *128 D4* Shandong, E China
Zapadna Morava *100 D4 Ger.* Westliche Morava. *River* C Serbia and Montenegro (Yugo.)
Zapadnaya Dvina *110 A4* Tverskaya Oblast', W Russian Federation
Zapadno-Sibirskaya Ravnina *114 C3 Eng.* West Siberian Plain. *Plain* C Russian Federation
Zapadnyy Sayan *114 D4 Eng.* Western Sayans. *Mountain range* S Russian Federation
Zapala *65 B5* Neuquén, W Argentina
Zapiola Ridge *67 B6 undersea feature* SW Atlantic Ocean
Zapolyarnyy *110 C2* Murmanskaya Oblast', NW Russian Federation
Zaporizhzhya *109 F3 Rus.* Zaporozh'ye; *prev.* Aleksandrovsk. Zaporiz'ka Oblast', SE Ukraine
Zapotiltic *50 D4* Jalisco, SW Mexico
Zaqatala *117 G2 Rus.* Zakataly. NW Azerbaijan
Zara *116 D3* Sivas, C Turkey
Zarafshon *122 D2 Rus.* Zarafshan. Nawoiy Wiloyati, N Uzbekistan
Zaragoza *93 F2 Eng.* Saragossa; *anc.* Caesaraugusta, Salduba. Aragón, NE Spain
Zarand *120 D3* Kermān, C Iran
Zaranj *122 D5* Nīmrūz, SW Afghanistan
Zarasai *106 C4* Zarasai, E Lithuania
Zárate *64 D4 prev.* General José F.Uriburu. Buenos Aires, E Argentina
Zarautz *93 E1 var.* Zarauz. País Vasco, N Spain
Zarauz *see* Zarautz
Zaraza *59 E2* Guárico, N Venezuela
Zarghūn Shahr *123 E4 var.* Katawaz. Paktīkā, SE Afghanistan
Zaria *75 G4* Kaduna, C Nigeria
Zarós *105 D8* Kríti, Greece, E Mediterranean Sea
Zarqa *see* Az Zarqā'
Żary *98 B4 Ger.* Sorau, Sorau in der Niederlausitz. Lubulskie, W Poland
Zaunguzskiye Garagumy *see* Üngüz Angyrsyndaky Garagum
Zavet *104 D1* Razgrad, N Bulgaria
Zavidovići *100 C3* Federacija Bosna I Hercegovina, N Bosnia and Herzegovina
Zawia *see* Az Zāwiyah
Zawiercie *98 D4 Rus.* Zavertse. Śląskie, S Poland
Zawīlah *71 F3 var.* Zuwaylah, *It.* Zueila. C Libya
Zaysan, Ozero *114 D5 Kaz.* Zaysan Köl. *Lake* E Kazakhstan
Zbarazh *108 C2* Ternopil's'ka Oblast', W Ukraine
Zduńska Wola *98 C4* Łódzkie, C Poland
Zeebrugge *87 A5* West-Vlaanderen, NW Belgium
Zeewolde *86 D3* Flevoland, C Netherlands
Żegań *see* Żagań
Zefat *119 B5 var.* Safed, Tsefat, *Ar.* Safad. Northern, N Israel
Zeist *86 C4* Utrecht, C Netherlands
Zele *87 B5* Oost-Vlaanderen, NW Belgium
Zelenoborskiy *110 B2* Murmanskaya Oblast', NW Russian Federation
Zelenograd *111 B5* Moskovskaya Oblast', W Russian Federation
Zelenogradsk *106 A4 Ger.* Cranz, Kranz. Kaliningradskaya Oblast', W Russian Federation
Zelle *see* Celle
Zel'va *107 B6 Pol.* Zelwa. Hrodzyenskaya Voblasts', W Belarus
Zelzate *87 B5 var.* Selzaete. Oost-Vlaanderen, NW Belgium
Žemaičių Aukštumas *106 B4 physical region* W Lithuania
Zemst *87 C5* Vlaams Brabant, C Belgium
Zemun *100 D3* Serbia, N Serbia and Montenegro (Yugo.)
Zenica *100 C4* Federacija Bosna I Herzegovina, C Bosnia and Herzegovina
Zenjan *see* Zanjān
Zeravshan *123 E3 Taj./Uzb.* Zarafshon. *River* Tajikistan/Uzbekistan
Zevenaar *86 D4* Gelderland, SE Netherlands
Zevenbergen *86 C4* Noord-Brabant, S Netherlands
Zeya *113 E3 river* SE Russian Federation
Zgierz *98 C4 Ger.* Neuhof, *Rus.* Zgerzh. Łódź, C Poland
Zgorzelec *98 B4 Ger.* Görlitz. Dolnośląskie, SW Poland
Zhabinka *107 A6 Pol.* Żabinka, *Rus.* Zhabinka. Brestskaya Voblasts', SW Belarus
Zhambyl *see* Taraz
Zhanaozen *114 A4 Kaz.* Zhangaözen, *prev.* Novyy Uzen'. Mangistau, W Kazakhstan
Zhangaözen *see* Zhanaozen
Zhangaqazaly *see* Ayteke Bi
Zhang-chia-k'ou *see* Zhangjiakou
Zhangdian *see* Zibo
Zhangjiakou *128 C3 var.* Changkiakow, Zhang-chia-k'ou, *Eng.* Kalgan; *prev.* Wanchuan. Hebei, E China
Zhangzhou *128 D6* Fujian, SE China
Zhanjiang *128 C7 var.* Chanchiang, Chan-chiang, *Cant.* Tsamkong, *Fr.* Fort-Bayard. Guangdong, S China
Zhaoqing *128 C6* Guangdong, S China
Zhe *see* Zhejiang
Zhejiang *128 D5 var.* Che-chiang, Chekiang, Zhe, Zhejiang Sheng. Admin. region *province* SE China
Zhejiang Sheng *see* Zhejiang
Zheleznodoroznyy *106 A4 Ger.* Gerdauen. Kaliningradskaya Oblast', W Russian Federation
Zheleznogorsk *111 A5* Kurskaya Oblast', W Russian Federation
Zhengzhou *128 C4 var.* Ch'eng-chou, Chengchow; *prev.* Chenghsien. Henan, C China
Zhezkazgan *114 C4 Kaz.* Zhezqazghan; *prev.* Dkaraganda. Karaganda, C Kazakhstan
Zhlobin *107 D7* Homyel'skaya Voblasts', SE Belarus
Zhmerynka *108 D2 Rus.* Zhmerinka. Vinnyts'ka Oblast', C Ukraine
Zhodzina *107 D6 Rus.* Zhodino. Minskaya Voblasts', C Belarus
Zhovkva *108 B2 Pol.* Żółkiew, *Rus.* Zholkev, Zholkva; *prev.* Nesterov. L'vivs'ka Oblast', NW Ukraine
Zhovti Vody *109 F3 Rus.* Zhëltyye Vody. Dnipropetrovs'ka Oblast', E Ukraine
Zhovtneve *109 E4 Rus.* Zhovtnevoye. Mykolayivs'ka Oblast', S Ukraine
Zhydachiv *108 B2 Pol.* Żydaczów, *Rus.* Zhidachov. L'vivs'ka Oblast', NW Ukraine
Zhytkavichy *107 C7 Rus.* Zhitkovichi. Homyel'skaya Voblasts', SE Belarus
Zhytomyr *108 D2 Rus.* Zhitomir. Zhytomyrs'ka Oblast', NW Ukraine
Zibo *128 D4 var.* Zhangdian. Shandong, E China
Zielona Góra *98 B4 Ger.* Grünberg, Grünberg in Schlesien, Grüneberg. Lubuskie, W Poland
Zierikzee *86 B4* Zeeland, SW Netherlands
Zigong *128 B5 var.* Tzekung. Sichuan, C China
Ziguinchor *74 B3* SW Senegal
Žilina *99 C5 Ger.* Sillein, *Hung.* Zsolna. Žilinský Kraj, N Slovakia
Zimbabwe *78 D3 prev.* Rhodesia. *Country* S Africa

Zimbabwe 78

Official name Republic of Zimbabwe
Formation 1980
Capital Harare
Population 12.9 million / 86 people per sq mile (33 people per sq km)
Total area 150,803 sq. miles (390,580 sq. km)
Languages Shona, isiNdebele, English
Religions Syncretic (Christian/traditional beliefs) 50%, Christian 25%, Traditional beliefs 24%, Other (including Muslim) 1%
Ethnic mix Shona 71%, Ndebele 16%, Other African 11%, White 1%, Asian 1%
Government Presidential system
Currency Zimbabwe dollar = 100 cents
Literacy rate 90%
Calorie consumption 2133 calories

Zimnicea *108 C5* Teleorman, S Romania
Zimovniki *111 B7* Rostovskaya Oblast', SW Russian Federation
Zinder *75 G3* Zinder, S Niger
Zinjan *see* Zanjān
Zipaquirá *58 B3* Cundinamarca, C Colombia
Zittau *94 D4* Sachsen, E Germany
Zlatni Pyasŭtsi *104 E2* Dobrich, NE Bulgaria
Zlín *99 C5 prev.* Gottwaldov. Zlinský Kraj, E Czech Republic
Złotów *98 C3* Wielkopolskie, C Poland
Znam"yanka *109 F3 Rus.* Znamenka. Kirovohrads'ka Oblast', C Ukraine
Żnin *98 C3* Kujawski-pomorskie, C Poland
Znojmo *99 B5 Ger.* Znaim. Brněnský Kraj, SE Czech Republic
Zoetermeer *86 C4* Zuid-Holland, W Netherlands
Zolochiv *108 C2 Pol.* Złoczów, *Rus.* Zolochev. L'vivs'ka Oblast', W Ukraine
Zolochiv *109 G2 Rus.* Zolochev. Kharkivs'ka Oblast', E Ukraine
Zolote *109 H3 Rus.* Zolotoye. Luhans'ka Oblast', E Ukraine
Zolotonosha *109 E2* Cherkas'ka Oblast', C Ukraine
Zomba *79 E2* Southern, S Malawi
Zongo *77 C5* Equateur, N Dem. Rep. Congo
Zonguldak *116 C2* Zonguldak, NW Turkey
Zonhoven *87 D6* Limburg, NE Belgium
Żory *99 C5 var.* Zory, *Ger.* Sohrau. Śląskie, S Poland
Zouar *76 C2* Borkou-Ennedi-Tibesti, N Chad
Zouérat *74 C2 var.* Zouérate, Zouîrât. Tiris Zemmour, N Mauritania
Zouérate *see* Zouérat
Zouîrât *see* Zouérat
Zrenjanin *100 D3 prev.* Petrovgrad, Veliki Bečkerek, *Ger.* Grossbetschkerek, *Hung.* Nagybecskerek. Serbia, N Serbia and Montenegro (Yugo.)
Zubov Seamount *67 D5 undersea feature* E Atlantic Ocean
Zueila *see* Zawīlah
Zug *95 B7 Fr.* Zoug. Zug, C Switzerland
Zugspitze *95 C7 mountain* S Germany
Zuid-Beveland *87 B5 var.* South Beveland. *Island* SW Netherlands
Zuidhorn *86 E1* Groningen, NE Netherlands
Zuidlaren *86 E2* Drenthe, NE Netherlands
Zula *72 C4* E Eritrea
Züllichau *see* Sulechów
Zundert *87 C5* Noord-Brabant, S Netherlands
Zunyi *128 B5* Guizhou, S China
Županja *100 C3 Hung.* Zsupanya. Vukovar-Srijem, E Croatia
Zürich *95 B7 Eng./Fr.* Zurich, *It.* Zurigo. Zürich, N Switzerland
Zürichsee *95 B7 Eng.* Lake Zurich. *Lake* NE Switzerland
Zutphen *86 D3* Gelderland, E Netherlands
Zuwārah *71 F2* NW Libya
Zuwaylah *see* Zawīlah
Zuyevka *111 D5* Kirovskaya Oblast', NW Russian Federation
Zvenyhorodka *109 E2 Rus.* Zvenigorodka. Cherkas'ka Oblast', C Ukraine
Zvishavane *78 D3 prev.* Shabani. Matabeleland South, S Zimbabwe
Zvolen *99 C6 Ger.* Altsohl, *Hung.* Zólyom. Banskobystricky Kraj, C Slovakia
Zvornik *100 C4* E Bosnia and Herzegovina
Zwedru *74 D5 var.* Tchien. E Liberia
Zwettl *95 E6* Wien, NE Austria
Zwevegem *87 A6* West-Vlaanderen, W Belgium
Zwickau *95 C5* Sachsen, E Germany
Zwolle *86 D3* Overijssel, E Netherlan
Zyôetu *see* Jōetsu
Żyardów *98 D3* Mazowieckie, C Poland
Zyryanovsk *114 D5* Vostochnyy Kazakhstan, E Kazakhstan